MW01493854

Final Destiny

Final Destiny

The Future Reign of the Servant Kings

Fourth Revised Edition

Joseph C. Dillow, Th.D.

Final Destiny: The Future Reign of the Servant Kings

Fourth Revised Edition 2018

Published by Grace Theology Presss.

Fourth Printing Revised Edition 2018
Third Printing Revised Edition 2015
Second Printing, Revised Edition 2014
First Printing 2013

ISBN-13: 978-0-9916588-4-8
ISBN-10: 991658841

eISBN 10: 991658833
eISBN 13: 978-0-9916588-3-1

All emphases in quoted material are the writer's unless otherwise noted.

Please send notices of errors including page # and a phrase containing the error to:
jodydillow@mindspring.com

Special Sales: Most Grace Theology Press titles are available in special quantity discounts. Custom imprinting or excerpting can also be done to fit special needs. Contact Grace Theology Press at info@gracetheology.org.

Dedication

WHEN THE Wise Man said, "*An excellent wife, who can find? For her worth is far above jewels,*" I am confident that he had in mind someone like my wonderful wife, Linda. For forty-eight years she has been my greatest encourager, my lover, and my best friend. "*Her children rise up and bless her; Her husband also, and he praises her, saying: 'Many daughters have done nobly, But you excel them all.' Charm is deceitful and beauty is vain, But a woman who fears the* L*ORD*, *she shall be praised.*" One of the greatest joys of my life has been knowing and being loved by Linda Dillow. Thank you, my love, for marrying me!

Acknowledgments

A WORK OF this size would have been impossible without the help of many friends. At the risk of omitting someone, let me begin to express my appreciation. First of all, Dr. Roy Zuck, former professor of Dallas Theological Seminary and editor of the Seminary journal *Bibliotheca Sacra*, who has worked faithfully editing this manuscript, chapter by chapter, for many months. His incredible "eagle eye" not only noted many of my errors, but greatly improved the readability. Without his encouragement and expertise, I would never have been able to complete this. Dr. Zuck went to be with the Lord in March of 2013.

Mike Comtois, the pastor of Faith Bible Church in Winkler, Manitoba, Canada has been a wonderful encouragement. Thank you, Mike, for reading every chapter, making many wise exegetical and theological observations and picking up even more of my mistakes. Mike pressed me for several years to get this revision done, and without his help, I doubt I could have finished it before the *Parousia*!

I owe a tremendous debt of gratitude to Dr. Glen Riddle. Glen is an outstanding Greek and Hebrew scholar, a colleague, and longtime friend. With meticulous care he corrected my Greek transliteration, grammatical, and lexical errors. His numerous suggestions and challenges to my interpretations on a number of occasions resulted in my revising several sections.

Mary Nees contributed her eagle eye to finding many errors that others overlooked. In addition she made many helpful suggestions.

One of the finest biblical scholars I know, Dr. Paul Tanner, who formerly taught Hebrew at the International School of Theology in Singapore and then at the Jordan Evangelical Theological Seminary in Amman, has been of inestimable help in guiding my thinking about many difficult passages. Paul's assistance is especially appreciated because even though he came to different conclusions on some of these passages, he willingly and graciously entered into very insightful discussion with me and sharpened my thinking. Thank you, Paul, for your friendship in Christ over the years.

A longtime friend and seminary classmate, Wendall Hollis, who received his PhD from Trinity Evangelical Divinity School in New Testament, has had a great impact on original version of this book, *The Reign of the Servant Kings*, but also upon this update and revision as well.

It is not often that one finds a critical exegetical thinker who can force you to keep to the text and the context as well as my good friend Dr. Ken Mitchell. On numerous occasions I sent chapters that I was thinking through to Ken, and he often showed me errors in my thinking. On a number of difficult passages, Ken's insights gave me the answers I had been struggling to find for months. What a blessing to have a pastor like Ken who has so graciously blessed me with his encouragement.

For those who read footnotes, you will note a number of references to the *Journal of the Grace Evangelical Society.* I would like to especially thank Bob Wilkin, President of GES for his helpful input, his many books and for publishing this excellent journal. Time and again when I was stumped on the meaning of various passages, I would turn to this journal and find insightful perspectives from scholars who had gone before me.

Dr. Fred Chay, Professor of Theology at Phoenix Theological Seminary has become a good friend, helpful interlocutor, and helped me think critically as I attempted this reconstruction of a coherent new paradigm for understanding New Testament soteriology.

Dr. Dave Anderson (President of the Grace School of Theology) has always been readily available and on a number of occasions has given me insights that never occurred to me. As a pastor who founded ten churches, a Greek professor for ten years at Dallas Theological Seminary, Dave has brought unique insights to many who are thinking through the grace alone paradigm for understanding New Testament soteriology.

Professor Nate Moyer graciously read through the final version and identified additional errors. I especially want to thank Dr. Lewis Schoettle who published the first version of this book called *The Reign of the Servant Kings*. Lewis has invested much of his life in promoting the doctrines of the Kingdom of Heaven. Through the Shoettle Publishing Company in Miami Springs, FL., he published many excellent books on this wonderful theme. With painstaking care, he went through every page of *Final Destiny* and found numerous errors. Thank you, Lewis, for making me look better than I am!

Among those who helped on editing the manuscript, I wish to thank Marty Cauley who gave many hours of his time and identified numerous errors which I had missed. Marty frequently gave me very thoughtful objections to some of my interpretations and worked with me to suggest solutions. His book, *The Outer Darkness*, deserves broad reading.

Thanks also to Dr. Charles Bing, Sam Riney, Berry Fiess, and Paul Carpenter for reading various sections and giving very helpful input.

The library at Tyndale House in Cambridge England has been a source of invaluable help. The exhaustive research facilities, and time for reflection with other scholars from around the world, provided an excellent atmosphere for study and writing. David Instone-Brewer, an expert in Second Temple Jewish literature was of considerable help and read several chapters and gave valuable input.

Besides Tyndale House, my main research source is Logos Bible Software. With over 2,500 books and 20 journals on my laptop, all fully searchable, I was able to locate many articles and book sections that would have been impossible otherwise. If you don't own it, buy it! (www.logos.com).

My friend and colleague Nici Barrett, who works in the BEE World office (www.beeworld.org) with me, worked faithfully with Dr. Zuck in making all the many corrections. Nici is a course publisher for our ministry and has worked on making the twenty BEE World courses available through our Internet Biblical Seminary (www.internetseminary.org).

I would like to thank my friend and son-in-law, Stephen DuPuis, Founder and CEO of the DuPuis group (http://www.dupuisgroup.com) who conceptualized the initial design for the cover. Many thanks to Adam McIver, a designer with the DuPuis Group who developed the final version of the outstanding cover for this book.

Abbreviations

AD. Anno Domini (After Christ)

ALGNT. Timothy Friburg, Barbara Friberg, and Neva F. Miller. *Analytical Lexicon of the Greek New Testament.* Baker's New Testament Greek Library. Grand Rapids: Baker Books, 2000.

Abbott-Smith. Abbott-Smith, G. *A Manual Greek Lexicon of the New Testament.* Edinburgh: T. & T. Clark, 1937.

BC. Before Christ

BAGD. Arndt, William F., and Gingrich, F. Wilbur. *A Greek-English Lexicon of the New Testament and Other Early Christian Literature.* Chicago: University of Chicago Press, 1957.

BDAG. Arndt, W.; Danker, F. W. and Bauer W. *A Greek English Lexicon of the New Testament and Other Early Christian Literature,* 3rd ed. Chicago: University of Chicago Press, 2000.

BDB. Francis Brown, S. R Driver, and Charles A. Briggs. *A Hebrew and English Lexicon of the Old Testament.* London: Oxford University Press, 1966.

BibSac. Bibliotheca Sacra

BKC. *The Bible Knowledge Commentary.* Edited by John F. Walvoord and Roy B. Zuck. 2 vols. Wheaton, IL: Victor, 1983, 1995. Reprint, Colorado Springs, CO: Cook, 1996.

ca.. circa (around)

CBQ. Catholic Biblical Quarterly

cf.. Compare

DBLH. *Dictionary of Biblical Languages with Semantic Domains: (Hebrew) Old Testament.* Oak Harbor, WA. Logos Research Systems Inc., 1997.

DBLGNT. *Dictionary of Biblical Languages with Semantic Domains: Greek (New Testament).* Oak Harbor, WA. Logos Research Systems, Inc., 1997.

DM. H. E. Dana and Julius R. Mantey. *A Manual Grammar of the Greek New Testament.* New York: Macmillan Co., 1955.

e.g.. for example

EDNT. Exegetical Dictionary of the New Testament

EGT. *Expositor's Greek Testament.* Edited by W. Robertson Nicoll. 5 vols. Reprint ed., Grand Rapids: Wm. B. Eerdmans Publishing Co., 1967.

EVQ. Evangelical Quarterly

ff. Following

GGBB. Wallace, Daniel, *Greek Grammar Beyond the Basics: An Exegetical Syntax of the New Testament.* Grand Rapids: Zondervan Publishing House, 1996.

Gr. Greek

GTJ. Grace Theological Journal

HAL. Ludwig Koehler and Walter Baumgartner. *The Hebrew and Aramaic Lexicon of the Old Testament.* Leiden: J. J. Brill, 1994.

Heb. Hebrew

Ibid.. Same work referred to previously

IDB. *Interpreter's Dictionary of the Bible.* Ed. by George Arthur Butrick. New York: Abingdon Press, 1962.

Idem.. Same author as in previous work cited

ISBE. *International Standard Bible Encyclopedia.* Edited by James Orr. 5 vols. Grand Rapids: Wm. B. Eerdmans Publishing Co., 1929.

NISBE. *International Standard Bible Encyclopedia.* Revised ed. Edited by Geoffrey W. Bromiley. 4 vols. Grand Rapids: Wm. B. Eerdmans Publishing Co., 1980-88.

JBL. Journal of Biblical Literature

JETS. Journal of the Evangelical Theological Society

JOTGES. Journal of the Grace Evangelical Society

JSNT. Journal for the Study of the New Testament

JSOT. Journal for the Study of the Old Testament

Lange's. Lange, John Peter. *Lange's Commentary on the Holy Scriptures.* Ed. and trans. by Philip Schaff. 12 vols. 1868-70. Reprint ed., Grand Rapids: Zondervan Publishing House, 1960.

LEH LXX J. Lust, et. Al., A Greek-English Lexicon of the Septuagint. Stuttgart: Deutsche Biblegesellshaft, 1992

LexAL LXX The Lexham Analytical Lexicon of the Septuagint. Bellingham, WA: Lexham Press, 2012

Louw-Nida. *Greek-English Lexicon of the New Testament Based upon Semantic Domains.* Edited by J. P. Louw and E. Nida. New York: United Bible Societies, 1988.

LSJ. Henry George Liddell and Robert Scott. *A Greek-English Lexicon.* 1907; reprint ed., rev. and augmented by Henry Stuart Jones and Robert McKenzie. Oxford: Clarendon Press, 1968.

LXX. *The Septuagint Version, With Apocrypha—Greek and English.* Reprint ed., Grand Rapids: Zondervan Publishing House, 1978.

m. The Mishnah

MM. James Hope Moulton and George Milligan. *The Vocabulary of the Greek Testament.* One-vol. ed., 1930; reprint ed., Grand Rapids: Wm. B. Eerdmans Publishing Co., 1974.

NASB. *New American Standard Bible.* La Habra, Calif.: Lockman Foundation, 1971.

NCV. *New Century Version.* Nashville: Nelson, 1982.

NICNT. *The New International Commentary on the New Testament.* Edited by F. B. Bruce. Grand Rapids: Wm. B. Eerdmans Publishing Company, 1959.

NIDNTT. *New International Dictionary of New Testament Theology.* Edited by Colin Brown. 3 vols. Grand Rapids: Zondervan Publishing House, 1975-1978.

NIDOTTE. *New International Dictionary of Old Testament Theology and Exegesis.* Edited by Willem A. VanGemeren. 5 vols. Grand Rapids: Zondervan Publishing House, 1997.

NISBE. *International Standard Bible Encyclopedia.* Revelation ed. Edited by Geoffrey W. Bromiley. 4 vols. Grand Rapids: Wm. B. Eerdmans Publishing Co., 1980-1988.

NIV. *New International Version.* Grand Rapids: Zondervan Publishing House, 1978.

NKJV. *New King James Version.* Nashville: Thomas Nelson, 1982.

NRSV. *New Revised Standard Version.* Nashville: Thomas Nelson, 1989.

SBJT. Southern Baptist Journal of Theology

Schaff. *The Creeds of Christendom.* 6th ed. Edited by Philip Schaff. 3 vols. Reprint ed. Grand Rapids: Baker Book House, 1985.

TDNT. *Theological Dictionary of the New Testament.* Edited by Gerhard Kittel and Gerhard Friedrich. Edited and trans. by Geoffrey W. Bromiley. 10 vols. Grand Rapids: Zondervan Publishing House, 1964-1976.

TDNTA. *Theological Dictionary of the New Testament.* Ed. by Gerhard Kittel and Gerhard Friedrich. Trans. and abridged in one volume by Geoffrey W. Bromiley. Grand Rapids: Wm. B. Eerdmans Publishing Co., 1985.

TJ. Trinity Journal

TNTC. *The Tyndale New Testament Commentaries.* Edited by R. V. G Tasker. 20 vols. London: Tyndale Publishing House, 1957-1965.

TRENT. David Instone-Brewer. *Traditions of the Rabbis from the Era of the New Testament. Vol:1 Prayer and Agriculture.* Grand Rapids: Wm. B. Eerdmans Publishing Co., 2004.

TWOT. *Theological Wordbook of the Old Testament.* Ed. by R. Laird Harris, Gleason L. Archer Jr., and Bruce K. Waltke. 2 vols. Chicago: Moody Press, 1980.

VCED Vine, W.E., Unger, Merril F., and White, William, *Vines Complete Expository Dictionary of the New and Old Testament Words.* Nashville, TN: Thomas Nelson, 1996.

Vine. Vine, W. & Bruce, F. (1981). *Vine's Expository Dictionary of Old and New Testament Words.* Old Tappan, NJ: Revell Co., 1981.

WPNT. Robertson, A. T. *Word Pictures in the New Testament.* Oak Harbor: Logos Research Systems, 1997.

WTJ. Westminster Theological Journal

Zodhiates. Zodhiates, S. *The Complete Word Study Dictionary of the New Testament.* Chattanooga: AMG Publishers, 2000.

ZPED. *Zondervan Pictorial Encyclopedia of the Bible.* Edited by Merrill C. Tenney. 5 vols. Grand Rapids: Zondervan Publishing House, 1976.

Table of Contents

VOLUME 2. ASSURANCE

Foreword

IT HAS been over twenty years since the publication of Joseph Dillow's groundbreaking book, *The Reign of the Servant Kings* (1991). In that work he contributed significantly to a new paradigm for understanding faith, works, assurance, eternal security and rewards. We are pleased to see this comprehensive update and revision called *Final Destiny: The Future Reign of the Servant Kings*. As the title indicates the final destiny of man is the reign of His servants, who serve, honor, and glorify God for all eternity.

When I first read *The Reign of the Servant Kings*, it really captured my belief that there needs to be something that will cause people who have received Christ as their Saviour to realize that there is much more for believers to receive in the future than anyone can imagine today.

In the fourth church that he was pastoring, Bud Strauss, a dear friend of mine, became aware of the fact that he had terminal cancer. His church in Escondido, California, had grown to several thousand during his ministry. They had to have three services on Sunday morning and two on Saturday night. In order to have enough strength, after preaching he would go immediately to his office to rest for a few minutes. Then he would come back and preach the next time. And the same for the third time.

His wife wrote me a note saying, "When my husband found out he had terminal cancer, he told the people, 'I have been trying for many years to teach you how to live for Christ. Now I would like to teach you how to die for Christ.'"

At the close of the one meeting, I said to him, "Bud, have you ever thought about the Biblical doctrine of reward?" He gave me a sick look and said, "No. I think that is rather self-serving." I replied, "Well, self-serving is sort of like selfishness, isn't it? And selfishness is sin. And if Jesus is encouraging us to sin, then he is a sinner, and we don't have a Saviour. I'll tell you what. I have a book here, *The Reign of the Servant Kings*, that I recently paid $23 for, but I would like to give it to you asking you to read it. If you promise me that you will read it, I will give it to you." He did read it, and it marvelously re-vamped his thinking, to the point that he preached fourteen messages straight from week to week on the Biblical doctrine of reward. This was even put into a tape series.

Ever since the Council of Trent (1545) and the Westminster Assembly (1643) the relationship between faith, works, and rewards has been in the forefront of theological discussion. The issue of eternal security in particular has been polarized between two options, the Arminian view that salvation can be lost and the Westminster view that God will preserve the elect in a life of good works to the final hour and bring them safely to heaven when they die. Calvin's cliché "faith alone saves, but the faith that saves is not alone" has been accepted by many as gospel.

For many, the Reformed view has caused serious doubts about whether or not assurance of personal salvation is really possible. Furthermore, how would their teaching that all "true" Christians always persevere in a life of good works square with Scripture and experience? In the minds of many, it does not. For years the church has wondered if there is another option between these two extremes. There is. *Final Destiny* beautifully presents, and thoroughly documents, the conclusion that salvation cannot be lost and additional rewards await the faithful Christian. However, along with the wonderful promise of treasures in heaven, Dillow discusses the possibility of a negative consequence facing the unfaithful Christian as well. This introduces the final accountability much needed in the Christian church today.

During the past decades, there has been an explosion of books, articles, and conferences discussing these issues which are so critical to the historical faith alone gospel of the Reformers. While the viewpoint Dr. Dillow calls, "the Partners" has received enormous praise and has demonstrated its explanatory power, opponents, particularly among those in the Reformed faith, have not been silent.

Web sites, blogs, journal articles, and books have proliferated indicating that a grenade has been lobbed into the house of Calvin. Unfortunately the vast majority of critiques of the Free Grace viewpoint evidence a shallow acquaintance with much of the relevant literature. From this time on, anyone interested in the doctrines of grace and the viewpoints of those who embrace this revolutionary Partner paradigm, must seriously interact with this seminal work or they are likely to be uninformed.

More importantly, Dr. Dillow has identified a disturbing movement among evangelical scholars who merge works into faith and claim they are a condition for final arrival into heaven. This goes beyond the traditional Reformed position of Lordship salvation and introduces a convergence with Catholic theology into historical evangelicalism. *Final Destiny* does a brilliant job of addressing this new trend.

The scope of this work is breathtaking. Virtually every passage related to these critical issues is discussed. Many difficult-to-explain verses of the New Testament have been capably clarified. For example, if faith alone is the requirement for entering heaven when we die, why is entrance into the Kingdom limited to those who "do the will of the Father" and who have surpassing righteousness? How are these sayings which have been understood by some to teach that works are a necessary condition of kingdom entrance to be harmonized with the faith alone requirement of Jesus in the Gospel of John and the books of Romans and Galatians?

Recently, there has been a tidal wave of books advocating evangelical universalism and the abandonment of the doctrine of final damnation. With a thorough acquaintance with the relevant extra-biblical literature, Dr. Dillow brings new light on both the certainty of final separation from God and the application of the warnings regarding *Gehenna* to the life of Christians.

The thousands who appreciated *Reign of the Servant Kings* have long awaited the publication of a more complete discussion of the critical issues involved. This updated and thoroughly revised version has more than met our expectations. With outstanding scholarship and thorough attention to exegetical and theological detail, Joseph Dillow has given us a magnificent vision of the final destiny of man.

I heartily commend this work to the Christian community.

Dr. Earl Radmacher
President Emeritus, Western Theological Seminary
August 15, 2012

Volume 1

Salvation

Introduction to Volume 1

EVERYONE HAS a story about how they came to know Christ. Here is mine. I became a Christian on September 5, at 10:30 PM at a college student conference at the Mount Herman Christian Conference Center, near my home in Sunnyvale, California, in 1963. My life as a college student was wild and immature. In my freshman year I fell in love with a young woman named Mikie Thomas. We dated for three or four months. One night about 3:00 AM the highway patrol called my fraternity house to tell me that Mikie has been killed in an automobile accident. I was devastated.

For the next year I went down to her home to spend one weekend a month with her parents, Jane and Lloyd Thomas. Both Mikie and now her parents talked to me about a personal relationship with Jesus Christ. "Mom" and "Papa" reached out to me and loved me into the kingdom.

It occurred a year later at Mount Herman. I was the only non-Christian at this conference and was loaded with unanswered questions. Somehow, during those days, the Holy Spirit brought clarity to my mind. The pieces began to fit together, and I was ready to believe in Christ for salvation. That night, I did. In the following weeks and months, my entire life was transformed. The Lord Jesus gripped me and changed me.

Early on I got involved with Campus Crusade for Christ and they trained me to share my faith. I was on fire, talking to any student on campus who would listen.

Linda (whom I met at the conference) and I were married a year later. For three months I worked in a lumber mill as we both finished our degrees at the University of Oregon in Eugene.

In the summer before our marriage, I worked for another three months on the swing shift. Every day at 4:00 I headed to the lumber mill to glue laminated beams together until midnight. The foreman at this plant had recently become a member of a well-known non-Christian cult and was quite excited about his faith. He was a fine man and really helped me learn how to work.

Needless to say, I was anxious to convert him to biblical Christianity and one night, while on a 30 minute break, I waded in. As I enthusiastically spoke to him of the wonders of salvation by faith alone in Christ alone and apart from works, he pulled out his Bible and read a passage in Romans 2 which says that God,

> *WILL RENDER TO EVERY MAN ACCORDING TO HIS DEEDS: to those who by perseverance in doing good seek for glory and honor and immortality, eternal life. (Romans 2:6–10)*

My boss looked at me and said, "Jody, my Bible says you are wrong."

There it was. I stared blankly at Paul's statement, not knowing what to say. In the clearest possible words, Paul declares that eternal life is awarded for "doing good works," not because of faith alone.

I discovered that this was not the only passage which seemed to teach salvation by works alone. Often Jesus predicated entrance into the kingdom on good works. He told the rich young ruler that inheriting eternal life could only be his by obeying the Mosaic Law. When the charismatic prophets pled for entrance into the kingdom of heaven in Matthew 7:21, He told them that "*only he who does the will of my Father in heaven will enter.*" The "will of the Father" seemed to be obedience to what He had been teaching in the preceding chapters of the Sermon on the Mount.

What goes on here, I wondered? With these questions rattling around in my mind, I went off to Dallas Seminary right after graduating in science. For the next four years I majored in Greek. Five years later, I returned to pursue my doctor's degree in Systematic Theology.

As might be expected, the passages which seemed to teach a works salvation had been given considerable attention by Protestant theologians for centuries. While in seminary I embraced plausible solutions which were based upon a mildly Reformed perspective. They were reasonable, but, for me, not adequate. It was not until I began research on my previous book, *The Reign of the Servant Kings* that I settled on a very compelling and eminently more satisfying solution to all these works passages. Therefore, it was fifteen years after my conversation with my boss at the lumber mill that I finally understood what Paul meant in Romans 2:6-7. We will discuss this in some detail in Chapter 17.

These three volumes which I have called *Final Destiny* are the result of twenty years of research. It became evident as this exploration was pursued, that each passage led to other passages which in turn led to other passages. A web of connected links all over the New Testament had to be addressed. It soon became obvious that the typical two to three hundred page book would not be adequate and would leave too many "Yes, but …" questions lingering in the readers' minds.

So … I wrote three volumes!

Volume 1 of this series deals with the doctrine of salvation. However, the approach will not cover the usual categories found in the standard systematic theologies. Instead, the problem passages related to faith and works will receive emphasis. The goal is a comprehensive, coherent, and consistent paradigm for understanding New Testament salvation. I have called this new paradigm, the Partner Paradigm, which I will explain in Chapter 1.

Volume 2 will focus our attention on many issues related to assurance of salvation and eternal security. Warning passages in the New Testament (such as Hebrews 6) have troubled many hearts. "Am I truly saved?" they ask. "Can my salvation be lost?"

Volume 3 takes us to the goal of the project. How does one integrate the biblical emphasis on rewards into the teaching of salvation in the New Testament? Are there "degrees of glory," or, are all rewarded equally? What is the final significance of my life? How will God evaluate how I have lived? One day we will all be held accountable for our lives and will be rewarded for both the good and the bad we have done. This is a much neglected theme in contemporary church life.

There are many questions which commentators and theologians often pass over or which they do not answer well. It is to many of these issues we will now turn our attention. Readers of volume one will find suggested answers to the following questions and many others.

- What is the Partner paradigm and how does it differ from the Reformed and Arminian perspectives?
- Is repentance a requirement for personal salvation? If so, how does this differ from a salvation by works?
- Must I give up everything and turn from all known sin if I want to receive the free gift of eternal life?
- What is the inheritance which we will one day receive? Is it "heaven when we die?" If so, how do we explain that it is usually received on the basis of works.
- If "flesh and blood cannot inherit the kingdom" how can there be any mortal beings present to populate the millennial earth?
- What does it mean to "enter into rest" in the book of Hebrews? We are told that we must "strive" to enter. Does this suggest that salvation is by works after all?
- When Paul said that we must confess with our mouth that Jesus is Lord and believe with our heart if we want to be saved, does this not clearly say that salvation is not by faith alone but must also include submission to the Lordship of Christ with a public confession?
- Jesus tells us that we must deny ourselves and take up our cross and follow Him if we desire to "save our souls." Are these conditions for final entrance into heaven?
- What does it mean to enter the kingdom? Since in many passages this entrance is based upon works, how is it possible to maintain the Protestant doctrine that salvation is by faith alone apart from works?
- Jesus told his followers that if they want to enter the kingdom, they must do so by the "narrow gate" and pursue the "narrow way." What is this gate and way?
- Jesus told the rich young ruler that if he wanted to inherit eternal life, obtain eternal life, or inherit the kingdom, that he must obey the Mosaic Law. Is this not a clear statement of a works salvation?
- Are salvation and works always and inevitably linked? If so how do we explain the biblical examples of people, like Solomon, who were born again but who did not persevere in works to the end of life?
- What did Jesus mean when He said "by their fruits you will know them?" How should we understand James' teaching that "faith without works is dead" and that kind of faith alone cannot save?

These questions and many others will consume our thoughts as we explore the Partner paradigm for salvation in this volume.

Joseph Dillow
Monument, CO
September, 2012

Prologue

SOMETIME IN the limitless expanse of eternity past, a universal tragedy had occurred. The Morning Star, known as Lucifer,[1] God's perfect one, full of wisdom and beauty,[2] the angelic being whom God had appointed as ruler over the ancient cosmos[3] . . . had fallen. It was before . . . the Beginning. The prophet Ezekiel paints a picture of divine grief in his woeful description of this betrayal (Ezekiel 28:11-19). Lucifer had been given everything. Yet, he became proud.[4] He concluded that God's gifts were more important than the giver, that dependence on God and obedience to His revealed will were not necessary. He became the Satan, God's adversary.[5]

The Lord of hosts could have destroyed this rebel immediately. But instead, Yahweh brought into existence a plan that would forever answer this satanic alternative, a plan that would involve God personally in a moral demonstration of His love and grace. The King Himself would one day demonstrate the superiority of His ways—dependence and servanthood.

To achieve His eternal purpose, the manifestation of His Glory, He created the known universe out of nothing.[6]

Yet, for an unspecified period of time, mournful silence and darkness reigned because of Satan's rebellion. Had God forgotten? Had He decided to ignore this challenge to His sovereignty? Had He decided to look the other way? The silence of God was deafening. The angelic sons of God yearned for the universe to be cleansed from Satan's' moral darkness and the silence to be broken. [7]

Suddenly—it was!

> *And God said, "Let there be light," and there was light. God saw that the light was good, and he separated the light from the darkness. God called the light "day," and the darkness he called "night." And there was evening, and there was morning—the first day (Genesis 1:3-5).*

---

1 Isaiah 14:12-17.

2 Ezekiel 28:12.

3 Ezekiel 28:14.

4 Ezekiel 28:17; 1 Timothy 3:6.

5 The word "Satan" means "adversary."

6 This is not the Pre-creation chaos view which the present writer formerly held in earlier editions of this book. Nor is it the gap theory which suggests a gap between Genesis 1:1 and 1:2. This is a fairly traditional view of the fall of Satan in eternity past and the creation of the current universe ex-nihilo many years after that.

7 And when the silence was broken they shouted for joy (Job 38:7)!

"At last!" thought Michael, God's archangel. "Our Lord will now establish his rule and vindicate the superiority of His ways!"

He placed a man and his wife, beings inferior to the Satan, in a garden on a planet called Earth. He then cast the Satan to the ground in that Garden and a battle between Man and Satan was initiated. To the winner of this conflict, rulership of the planet would be granted. God's righteousness would once again reign on earth and through this He would be glorified.

Then God said, "Let us make man in our image, in our likeness, and let them rule over the fish of the sea and the birds of the air, over the livestock, over all the earth, and over all the creatures that move along the ground (Genesis 1:26).

As the angels looked on, in the words of Donald Barnhouse, it is as if the Lord declared:

We shall give this rebellion a thorough trial. We shall permit it to run full course. The universe shall see what a creature, even the greatest can do apart from God. We shall set up an experiment, and permit the universe of creatures to watch it, during this brief interlude between eternity past and eternity future called "time." In it the spirit of independence shall be allowed to expand to the utmost. And the wreck and the ruin which shall result will demonstrate to the universe, and forever, that there is no life, no joy, no peace, apart from a complete dependence upon the Most High God, possessor of heaven and earth. [8]

"But," said Michael, "what is this? A man? This creature is so weak, so inferior to the Satan. Why has the King placed **HIM** on the earth and told **HIM** to rule there?[9] How can such an insignificant creature, much lower than the angels,[10] possibly accomplish the divine purpose? Surely a great mistake has been made!"

What is the significance of man? That question has been on the lips of both poet and philosopher since man first began to think about these things. Thousands of years later as the shepherd David gazed upward into the brilliantly star-covered sky, he was crushed to the ground with a sense of his own insignificance, and he exclaimed,

When I consider your heavens,
the work of your fingers,
the moon and the stars,
which you have set in place,
what is man that you are mindful of him? (Psalm 8:3-4).

David's mind, apparently reflecting on the divine commission in Genesis, received a flash of illumination:

You made him a little lower than
the heavenly beings
and crowned him with glory and honor.
You made him ruler over the works
of your hands;
you put everything under his feet

---

8 Barnhouse, *The Invisible War*, 60.

9 Genesis 1:26-27

10 Psalms 8:5; Hebrews 2:7.

Oh Lord, *our Lord,*
how majestic is your name in
all the earth! (Psalm 8:6-9).

Man was to rule! The lesser creature, would be crowned with glory and honor; the inferior creature, would be placed in rulership over the Satan's world! The glory, honor, and sovereignty that the Satan had stolen in independence and unbelief would be regained by the inferior creature living in servanthood and faith! In this way pride is rebuked. God's ultimate purpose was to manifest His glory. That glory would be uniquely demonstrated when the Creator himself would adopt the path of humility and dependence. Years later the Savior would say, "He who is least among you all—he is the greatest" (Luke 9:48).

God decides to humble the proud and independent in a unique way. He intends that the lower creature, man (created lower than the angels and hence lower than the Satan), should achieve the highest position ("all things in subjection under His feet," Hebrews 2:8). Thus the lower creature would achieve by dependence on God a higher position than the higher creature, Satan, achieved through independence. For "*it is not to angels that He has subjected the world to come, about which we are speaking*" (Hebrews 2:5). Out of the least, God will bring the greatest. As MAN the Savior defeated the enemy. As MAN He silenced the principalities and powers. And as MAN He will reign over the future kingdom of God on this earth.

This future kingdom is the subject of hundreds of passages in the Old Testament. It will be a glorious reign of servant kings that will extend to "*all the works of His hands.*" (This may suggest that one day mankind will rule the galaxies!) The lion will lie down with the lamb, universal righteousness will reign, there will be no war. Disease will be abolished, and the world of the Satan will be placed under the rule of the Servant King and His companions (Hebrews 1:9).

Consistent with His divine purpose, God chose to establish His kingdom through the elevation of a seemingly obscure and insignificant Semitic tribe, Israel. Greece, Rome, Egypt, Babylon, France, Germany, Russia, United States or any other powerful nation on earth. That future glory falls to those followers of Christ both within Israel and within His church, who, like their Master, live in dependence and obedience.

Later the prophets, the psalmists, and the apostle Paul call this magnificent rescue mission "the righteousness of God." God's righteousness is His faithfulness to His word.[11] God made promises to Abraham that through him all the nations would be blessed.[12] What were those promises? Through this inconsequential Semitic tribe, Israel, specifically through Abraham and his "Seed," the divine plan to liberate the fallen planet and reveal his glory would be implemented.

The controlling principle of the biblical philosophy of history rests in the precept of the second before the first. "*God has chosen the foolish things of the world to shame the wise, and God has chosen the weak things of the world to shame the things which are strong*" (1 Corinthians 1:27). Only in this way is the self-praise of man destroyed. A pervading characteristic of the whole course of redemption is that God chooses the younger before the elder, sets the smaller in priority over the greater, and chooses the second before the first. Not Cain but Abel and his substitute Seth; not Japheth but Shem; not Ishmael but

---

11 Romans 3:3-4.

12 Genesis 12:1-3.

Isaac; not Esau but Jacob; not Manasseh but Ephraim;[13] not Aaron but Moses;[14] not Eliab but David;[15] not the Old Covenant but the New;[16] not the first Adam but the last Adam.[17] The first becomes last and the last becomes first.[18] The great nations are set aside,[19] and God elects to establish His purposes through two insignificant mediums, the Israel of God (the believing remnant of the last days) and the body of Christ (the invisible church).

But the first Adam, deceived by the serpent, chose the path of the father of lies, and acting independently, contrary to His design, fell into sin. As a result, the newly created universe was subjected to the universal bondage of decay,[20] and the sons of men were born in need of a redeemer; and Satan instead of Man, became the ruler of this world.[21]

Here the beauty and symmetry of the divine plan became evident. Not only did God purpose to elevate the role of a servant and the disposition of trust, but He gave His Son, the Second Man and the Last Adam,[22] as a savior. He who is of the essence of God became a servant. He "made Himself nothing, taking the very nature of a servant" (Philippians 2:7). He obeyed finally and completely; "*He humbled Himself and became obedient to death, even death on a cross*" (2:8). And in this way, living by exactly the opposite set of principles from the Satan, He achieved higher glory:

> *Therefore God exalted him to the highest place and gave him the name that is above every name, that at the name of Jesus every knee should bow, in heaven and on earth and under the earth and every tongue confess that Jesus Christ is Lord, to the glory of God the Father (Philippians 2:9-11).*

Those who would rule with Him must find their lives in the same way: "*Your attitude should be the same as that of Christ Jesus*" (Philippians 2:5). The future rulers of God's creation must, like their King, be servants now. There will be no room for pride nor hubris, only a heartfelt desire to extend the blessing and glory of God throughout the created order. Unlike the Satan and his modern-day followers, they will have no desire to be lord over their subjects. Instead, like their Lord, they will desire only to serve those over whom they rule:

> *Jesus called them together and said, "You know that the rulers of the Gentiles lord it over them, and their high officials exercise authority over them.* ***Not so with you.*** *Instead, whoever wants to become great among you must be your servant, and whoever wants to be first must be your slave, just as the Son of Man did not come to be served, but to serve, and to give his life as a ransom for many" (Matthew 20:25-28).*

They will be greatly loved and valued by their subjects. Instead of disobedience there

---

13 Genesis 48:14.

14 Exodus 7:1.

15 1 Samuel 16:6-13.

16 Hebrews 8:13.

17 1 Corinthians 15:45.

18 Matthew 19:30.

19 Daniel 2:7 ff; Romans 1:24, 26, 28.

20 Romans 8:20-22.

21 See Luke 4:6-7; John 16:11; 12:31; 2 Corinthians 4:4; Ephesians 2:2.

22 1 Corinthians 15:45. There are only two "Adams," i.e., two federally representative heads of humanity. Jesus is the last Adam but only the second man; there will be many other men as God intended men to be.

will be servanthood, to God and to others. The second Adam put it this way, "*Blessed are the poor in spirit, for* **theirs** *is the kingdom of heaven. . . . Blessed are the meek, for* **they** *will inherit the earth*" (Matthew 5:3-5).

We are to become the servant kings. That is our destiny. This destiny was often called "salvation" by the prophets.[23] This does not refer to salvation from eternal damnation, but to the glorious privilege of reigning with the Messiah in the final destiny of man, the messianic salvation. In the eternal plan only those who strive to be servants now can qualify for this great future privilege then. In order to be "great" in the kingdom of heaven, to rule there, we must first become humble like a little child.[24] "*The greatest among you will be your servant. For whoever exalts himself will be humbled, and whoever humbles himself will be exalted*" (Matthew 23:11-12).

If God's eternal plan revolves around demonstrating the moral superiority of humility and servanthood, it is of the utmost importance that we learn this lesson now. All Christians are not servants, and only those who are will be great in the kingdom. Only those sons of God who are "sons indeed" will be co-heirs with their coming King in the final destiny of man.

Many who have been saved by the King are not presently living for Him. Many who have begun lives of discipleship have not persevered. They risk forfeiture of this great future. But we are "Partners (Gr *Metochoi*) of Christ, [only] if we hold our confidence firmly to the end" (Hebrews 3:14). However, those who are obedient and dependent servants now and who persevere in discipleship to the final hour will be among Christ's *Metochoi*, the servant kings, in the thousand-year kingdom of the Son of Man. All Christians will be in the kingdom, but tragically not all will be co-heirs there.

By losing their lives believers find their ultimate significance.[25] Each act of service is not only an expression of God's eternal purpose but is preparation and training for our final destiny. When we "have the same mind which is in Christ Jesus" (Philippians 2:5), we become "sons of God," people who are like Him. In so doing, we manifest Him, that is, we display who He is—a God of love and humility. To express this in the manner the Scriptures do, "We glorify Him" (Psalm 86:12; John 16:4; 21:19). Yes, the final answer to the Satan's rebellion, and the ultimate meaning of human existence, is to be found in the future reign of the servant kings. But who are they, and how do we join their company? Let us begin.

---

23 A discussion of the various meanings of "salvation" will be undertaken in later chapters. See Chapters 12 and 13.

24 Matthew 18:4.

25 Mark 8:35.

1

The Partner Paradigm

ROMANIA IN the 1980's was not the most desirable place to be. The people were brutally oppressed by one of the most despotic dictators in Eastern Europe, Nicolai Ceacescu. In this ruthless police state, all the phones were bugged, many of the people were on the payroll of the Securitate (secret police). Believers were routinely harassed, denied good jobs, interrogated, refused admission to the universities, and sometimes imprisoned because of their stand for Christ.

Yet in the midst of this communist control, there was a thriving church of Baptists, Brethren, Pentecostals, Reformed, Lutheran, and Romanian Orthodox. The highlight of my ministry life was working with these wonderful people for fourteen years while we lived and traveled from Vienna, Austria.

For many years the Bible delivery ministries (a.k.a "Bible smugglers") had been delivering Bibles across these barbed wire and machine gun guarded borders to thousands of believers hungry to know the Scriptures. Then in 1979 a historic meeting took place in Vienna in which a number of these missions gathered to explore the possibility of a joint co-operative project to launch a covert extension biblical training program behind the Iron Curtain. God met all of us in an amazing way and together these missions formed an entity which came to be known as Biblical Education by Extension or BEE. These missions had concluded that the real need was no longer for more Bibles, but for trained people who could teach the Bible, and BEE was born.

On one of my first trips into this country, I met with a wonderful group of Baptist pastors in Bucharest, a twenty-seven hour train ride from Vienna. After leaving the train station we carefully made our way through the winding streets of the city, making every effort to avoid being followed by the secret police. Our destination was a humble Baptist church on Popa Rusu 22. Upon entering the church we were met with the usual warmth and joy of the Romanian people. The twelve pastors gathered around a table in a room warmed by a coal-heated stove, sipped very sweet Romanian coffee and settled in for forty hours of study of Hebrews chapters one to six.

You might be asking, "What does this have to do with this book?" Read on!

Although I had been teaching the Bible for many years in the United States, I had never met a group so thirsty to know and teach their Bibles. It was a joy to be with them. As we journeyed through the first six chapters of the Epistle to the Hebrews, the teaching was periodically interrupted with shouts of "Fantastic! Fantastic!" They would raise their hands begging me to slow down so they could record every word, a missionary's dream group.

Things went well until we came to Hebrews chapter six. When they discovered that I believed in eternal security, they were astonished. "How," they wondered, "could anyone believe this?" Of course Hebrews six was a central passage for them. They were not argumentative and the discussion that followed was energetic and warm. One of them, Valsile Talosh, who became a close friend, was a trained lawyer and he led the cross-examination.

Following in the footsteps of their Berean forebears, they asked me to return a few months later so they could study further to see "if these things were so."[26] For several days we went through many passages of the New Testament which seemed to them to show that salvation could be lost. For the most part, they seemed to accept my explanations as plausible.

However, there was a problem. As I walked home each night and prayed and reflected on the conversation of the preceding hours, I realized that I was very inconsistent in how I interpreted many of the relevant scriptures. I had dealt with the warning passages in the book of Hebrews in one way, and the warnings in the rest of the New Testament in another. To explain Hebrews chapter six I suggested that this warning was addressed to "true" believers who were being warned about a loss of reward/inheritance not loss of salvation. But in the rest of the New Testament when we interacted on John 15, or Colossians 1:22-23, for example, I said these warnings were addressed to people who had only professed faith in Christ, and they were being warned that if they did not make their profession real by reexamining their foundations, repenting, and believing in Christ from the heart, they were in danger of eternal separation from God. In other words, they were not in danger of losing salvation because they never had it to begin with.

This inconsistency troubled me, and I began to doubt my approach. It seemed to me that a careful reading of all these passages indicated that in fact they were addressed to believers, as my Romanian interlocutors insisted, and not to mere professors in Christ. But there was danger of loss. I came to realize that in Hebrews I was answering from a "free grace" perspective but in the rest of the New Testament I was answering from my (formerly) Reformed perspective. This inconsistency led me into eight years of research on this subject which resulted in my previous book, *The Reign of the Servant Kings: A Study of Eternal Security and the Final Significance of Man.*

In the years since the publication of that book, there has been considerable development and further reflection on the paradigm presented there. Numerous books and journal articles, pro and con, have been published from which I have learned much and which have sharpened my thinking. I am flattered, amazed, and humbled that so many have asked me to publish a book in which I would present my responses to the critics, explain any modifications to my thinking, and cover other exegetical and theological issues which I passed over in *The Reign of the Servant Kings.* The volumes to follow are my attempt to answer these requests.

My good friend, Dave Anderson, president of Grace School of Theology, has made a poignant point about paradigms. He correctly notes that all comprehensive attempts to explain the mind of God as revealed in Scripture must face certain passages which are not easily incorporated into the broader pattern. This side of heaven all we can hope

[26] Acts 17:11.

to achieve is a paradigm which has the fewest difficulties. The magnificent Reformed confessions have contributed richly to the Christian church for hundreds of years. I emerged from graduate school believing much of it. It worked. It gave me a framework of understanding that helped me interpret and apply the New Testament to my life. Yet, I always felt there were many problems with it and that numerous passages simply did not "fit." I have come to believe, and hope these volumes will demonstrate, that the viewpoint which I now label "the Partners" is the most satisfactory understanding of New Testament soteriology with the fewest problems and provides us with a compelling and highly motivational perspective on the issues of salvation, assurance, and rewards.

We begin by asking, "What is the Partner paradigm and how does it differ from the other understandings of these issues which permeate church history and contemporary Christian thinking?"

The Eternal Security of the Saints

Obviously the question of eternal security is inextricably involved with the question of free grace. If eternal life is truly offered "without cost" and salvation once received can never be lost, it might seem that some would take the grace of God for granted and live unfaithful lives. All motivation is lost, it is feared, to persevere in the life of faith. For the person who claims he is a Christian and who lives a sinful life, the Arminian warns him that he is in danger of losing his salvation. The English Puritans, on the other hand, simply said he never had salvation to begin with and he should reexamine his commitment because he is in danger of eternal separation from God. Only the man who perseveres in a life of good works to the final hour, they said, is truly saved.

The Reformed doctrine of the perseverance of the saints was in response to the accusations that the Reformation would logically result in moral laxity. The doctrine of perseverance was also a means of refuting the Arminian teaching of conditional security. The intent of this book is to demonstrate that the doctrine of perseverance of the saints is absent from Scripture, and, if not carefully stated, it could compromise the freeness of the grace of God. This is a book about the eternal security of the saints, a doctrine that the writer feels has good scriptural support. Yet this doctrine has labored under amazing exegetical contortions at the hands of its advocates. The history of interpretation must, of course, render the final verdict, but if one had to choose between Arminian and Calvinist interpretations of the relevant passages, the writer's opinion is that the Arminian view is closer to the text. Fortunately one need not choose between either of those interpretations, and the purpose of this book is to chart a third and mediating path.

This investigation will lead us into many related doctrines, such as the relationship between justification and sanctification, the assurance of salvation, and the relevance of the warning passages in the New Testament. Can a Christian commit apostasy? Does the New Testament teach the existence of carnal Christians? In addition, we will examine all of the passages commonly brought to bear on the question of eternal security and consider both Calvinist and Arminian interpretation.

THE EXPERIMENTAL PREDESTINARIAN

At the outset of our discussion it is important to define our terms carefully. Some, for example, maintain that historically the doctrine of perseverance meant only that no true Christian would ever commit apostasy. While some may have limited the doctrine to this mere continuation of belief, the vast majority of the Reformed confessions and theological works definitely viewed perseverance as a perseverance in good works.

ACCORDING TO THE PROTESTANT CREEDS. From the earliest post-Reformation creeds, perseverance was always associated with a life of practical victory against sin as well as continuation in faith.[27]

The specific occasion of the discussion of perseverance in the Canons of Dort (1619) was the controversy with the Remonstrants, who denied this doctrine. The Canons make it explicitly clear that, even though a believer may lapse into carnality for a time, he will always return to repentance:

> *By such enormous sins, however, they very highly offend God, incur a deadly guilt, grieve the Holy Spirit, interrupt the exercise of faith, very grievously wound their consciences, and sometimes lose the sense of God's favor, **for a time, until on their returning into the right way by serious repentance**, the light of God's fatherly countenance again shines upon them.*[28]

A lapse is only an "interruption" and lasts only "for a time until." The doctrine of perseverance guarantees, not just that believers will not apostatize, but that, when they backslide,

> *[God] preserves in them the incorruptible seed of regeneration from perishing or being totally lost; and again, by his Word and Spirit, **he certainly and effectually renews them to repentance**, to a sincere and godly sorrow for their sins, that they may seek and obtain remission in the blood of the Mediator, may again experience the favor of a reconciled God, through faith adore his mercies, and henceforward more diligently work out their own salvation with fear and trembling.*[29]

When a believer falls, God "certainly and effectually" renews him to repentance so that he will more diligently work out his own salvation with fear and trembling. The assurance that God will always enable believers to persevere in good works by providing a way of escape when they fall (5.11) stimulates believers to persevere in piety, patience, prayer, and in suffering (5.12) and makes them more careful to continue in the ways of the Lord (5.11).[30]

---

27 The Heidelberg Catechism (1563), for example, says (Q. 127): "Since we are so weak in ourselves that we cannot stand a moment while our deadly enemies, the devil, the world, and our own flesh assail us without ceasing, be pleased to preserve and strengthen us by the power of the Holy Spirit, that we may make a firm stand against them, and not sink in this spiritual war, until we come off at last with complete victory." See Philip Schaff, "The Heidelberg Catechism," in *The Creeds of Christendom: The Evangelical Protestant Creed* (Grand Rapids: Baker, 1985), 3:335. Perseverance is a complete victory in the spiritual war against sin and not just a refusal to commit apostasy. Furthermore, this perseverance is ultimately God's work, not ours. It is God who will "preserve and strengthen" us.

28 Philip Schaff, "The Canons of the Synod of Dort," ibid., 3:593 (5.5).

29 Ibid., 3:593-94 (5.7).

30 The French Confession of Faith states, "We believe also that faith is not given to the elect not only to introduce

The Westminster Confession refers to the fact of perseverance in the following manner: French Confession of Faith

They whom God hath accepted in His Beloved, effectually called and sanctified by His Spirit, can neither totally nor finally fall away from the state of grace; but shall certainly persevere therein to the end, and be eternally saved.[31]

What did the Westminster divines mean by "fall away from the state of grace"? What did it mean to persevere in the state of grace? They did not limit it to a mere continuation of believing but to a perseverance in good works.

Nevertheless they may, through the temptations of Satan and of the world, the prevalence of corruption remaining in them, and the neglect of the means of their preservation, fall into grievous sins; and for a time continue therein: whereby they incur God's displeasure, and grieve his Holy Spirit; come to be deprived of some measure of their graces and comforts; have their hearts hardened; and their consciences wounded; hurt and scandalize others, and bring temporal judgments upon themselves.[32]

What the Holy Spirit prevents is "final" falling, and falling is clearly a falling into grievous sins, not just apostasy. Furthermore, perseverance guarantees that such falling is only temporary and, as stated in the Canons of Dort, can only last "for a time."

In agreement with the above, the Belgic confession declares,

We believe that this true faith, being wrought in man by the hearing of the Word of God and the operation of the Holy Spirit, sanctifies him and makes him a new man, ***causing him to live a new life****, and freeing him from the bondage of sin.*[33]

If one is truly born again, the Holy Spirit will "cause" him to live a new life.

ACCORDING TO THE REFORMED THEOLOGIANS. In the writings of Reformed theologians it is likewise clear that they referred to a perseverance in fruit-bearing, and not just a perseverance in faith.[34] For example Calvin in his discussion of perseverance and the good

---

them into the right way, but also to make them continue in it to the end. For as it is God who hath begun the work, He will also perfect it." See Schaff, "The French Confession of Faith," 3:371.

31 "The Westminster Confession of Faith," in Schaff, *History of the Christian Church*, 3:636 (17.1).

32 Ibid., 3:637 (17.3).

33 The Belgic Confession, in *Historic Creeds and Confessions*. electronic ed. (Oak Harbor, WA: Logos Research Systems, 1997), Article 24, "Man's Sanctification and Good Works."

34 Reformed Baptist theologian Augustus Hopkins Strong says that the saints' perseverance is "the human side or aspect of that spiritual process which, as viewed from the divine side, we call sanctification." He speaks of it as "the voluntary continuance, on the part of the Christian, in faith and well-doing" (Augustus Hopkins Strong, *Systematic Theology* (Philadelphia: Judson Press, 1907), 881. In this he is correct. The Reformed doctrine of perseverance is simply another way of saying that justification and sanctification are united and that perseverance is the gradual growth in grace that occurs in the life of all those who are truly regenerate. Gerstner defines the doctrine of the saints' perseverance in this way: "Theologically speaking, it refers to the fifth point of the Calvinistic doctrinal system that true Christians will continue in faith and holiness forever. Thus Jonathan Edwards finds the very definition of a Christian to be, according to John 8:31, one who continues in the Word of Christ" (John Gerstner, "Perseverance," in *Baker's Dictionary of Theology*, ed. Everett F. Harrison (Grand Rapids: Baker Book House, 1960), 403-4.

works that God works in us (Philippians 2:13), says that God "supplies the persevering effort until the effect is obtained." The effect is the willing and the working of His good pleasure. In fact, he says, in our perseverance in good works "we go on without interruption, and persevere even to the end."[35] For Calvin the perseverance of the saints was much more than preventing their apostasy from faith; it was a positive sanctification in good works.

In his chapter on perseverance in *Redemption Accomplished and Applied*, Reformed theologian John Murray insists that the doctrine of the saints' perseverance is a doctrine of perseverance in good works. "The crucial test of true faith," says Murray, "is endurance to the end, abiding in Christ, and continuance in his Word."[36] For Murray the doctrine of perseverance is not just a teaching that the true Christian cannot commit apostasy but that he cannot "abandon himself to sin; he cannot come under the dominion of sin; he cannot be guilty of certain kinds of unfaithfulness." His whole chapter is a sustained argument that perseverance cannot be separated from a life of works. He says, "Let us appreciate the doctrine of the perseverance of the saints and recognize that we may entertain the faith of our security in Christ only as *we persevere in faith and holiness to the end*."[37] "The perseverance of the saints reminds us very forcefully that only those who persevere to the end are truly saints."[38] For Murray as in all the Calvinist creeds that preceded him, the doctrine of the saints' perseverance is the doctrine that those who are truly saints will persevere in faith and holiness to the final hour.

Murray also argues against the Arminians that such a doctrine cannot lead to antinomianism "because, by definition, it means persevering *in holiness and not in unholiness*. It not only promotes but *consists in strenuous and persevering efforts after conformity to Christ*."[39]

Charles Hodge, outstanding Reformed theologian of the nineteenth century, clearly asserts the doctrine of perseverance.

> *It must be remembered that what the Apostle argues to prove is not merely the certainty of the salvation of those that believe; but* ***their certain perseverance in holiness****. Salvation in sin, according to Paul's system, is a contradiction in terms. This* ***perseverance in holiness*** *is secured partly by the inward secret influence of the Spirit, and partly by all the means adapted to secure that end—instructions, admonitions, exhortations, warnings, the means of grace, and the dispensations of his providence.*[40]

The various instructions, warnings, and exhortations in the New Testament have as their object continuance in good works and holy living, not just the prevention of apostasy.

Robert Dabney, well-known Reformed Presbyterian theologian who lectured at Union Theological Seminary in Virginia in the nineteenth century, was equally insistent that the Reformed doctrine of the saints' perseverance was not just a teaching that true

---

35 John Calvin, "Prefatory Address to Francis, King of France," in *Institutes of the Christian Religion* (Grand Rapids: Wm. B. Eerdmans Publishing Co., 1964), 2.3.9.

36 John Murray, *Redemption--Accomplished and Applied* (Grand Rapids: Wm. B. Eerdmans Pub. Co., 1955), 152.

37 Ibid., 155.

38 Ibid., 155.

39 Gerstner, "Perseverance," 404.

40 Charles Hodge, *Systematic Theology*, 3 vols. (Grand Rapids: Wm. B. Eerdmans Publishing Co., 1977), 3:112-13.

saints will not commit apostasy but that they will persevere in a life of good works. He begins his discussion with Philippians 1:6 and observes, "We have here the Apostle's plain expression of his belief in the perseverance of the truly regenerate, in a state of repentance, unto the end."[41] For Dabney the perseverance of the saints is perseverance in holiness.[42]

Similarly, Louis Berkhof defines perseverance as "that continuous operation of the Holy Spirit in the believer, by which the work of divine grace that is begun in the heart, is continued and brought to completion."[43] This, of course, closely approximates the Reformed definition of sanctification. It is not just the prevention of apostasy but the growth in holiness Berkhof intends to convey in his doctrine of the saints' perseverance. Like Hodge, he argues against the Arminians' charge of antinomianism by saying:

> *It is hard to see how a doctrine which assures the believer of a* ***perseverance in holiness*** *can be an incentive for sin. It would seem that* ***the certainty of success in the active striving for sanctification*** *would be the best possible stimulus to ever greater exertion.*[44]

As in the historic creeds, Berkhof is careful to emphasize that perseverance is God's work, not that of the believers. "It is, strictly speaking, not man but God who perseveres." He gives a formal definition of perseverance as follows: "That continuous operation of the Holy Spirit in the believer, by which the work of divine grace that is begun in the heart, is continued and brought to completion."[45]

So the doctrine of the saints' perseverance is a guarantee of success in the active striving for sanctification. That is why William Shedd discusses perseverance under the topic of sanctification in his *Dogmatic Theology*.[46] In the final analysis it is a perseverance in holiness and not just a preventer of apostasy.

CONCLUSION. This brief survey of the various confessions and theologies of the Reformed faith leads to five points in the Reformed doctrine of perseverance:

1. All who have been justified by God's grace will never lose their justification.
2. Instead, they will persevere in a life of good works and holiness to the final hour.
3. This perseverance is the work of God in which man cooperates.
4. The amount of good works will vary, but the thrust and direction of the life will always be toward holiness.
5. When believers fall into sin, their fall will be only temporary, and they will always (if they are truly regenerate) come to repentance. As Thiessen put it, they will not "fail to return from their backsliding in the end."[47]

---

41 Robert L. Dabney, *Lectures in Systematic Theology*, reprint ed. (Grand Rapids: Zondervan Publishing House, 1972), 688.

42 Ibid., 692.

43 Louis Berkhof, *Systematic Theology* (Grand Rapids: Wm. B. Eerdmans Publishing Co., 1996), 546.

44 Ibid., 548.

45 Ibid., 546.

46 William G. T. Shedd, *Dogmatic Theology*, Classic reprint ed. (Minneapolis: Klock & Klock, 1979), 557.

47 Henry Clarence Thiessen and Vernon D. Doerksen, *Lectures in Systematic Theology*, rev. ed. (Grand Rapids: Wm. B. Eerdmans Publishing Co., 1979), 294.

Historically, this doctrine began in the Puritan tradition, and the Puritans called themselves "experimentalists." This is because they felt that Christ must be experienced, and that in order to ascertain whether one is a Christian, one must perform an experiment. He must ask, "Have I believed?" and "Are there evidences of works in my life?" If the answer to these questions is yes, he is justified in claiming that he is probably saved. Of course the final verdict can be rendered only at the end of one's life when the evidence of final perseverance is demonstrated. They commonly employed this syllogism:

MAJOR PREMISE: Those who have believed and give evidence of sanctification are probably saved.

MINOR PREMISE: I have believed and have some evidences of sanctification in my life.

CONCLUSION: Therefore, I am probably saved.

This approach to assurance is "experimental" in that the hypothesis "I am saved" is being tested by an experiment.

A second distinguishing mark of those in this tradition has been a strong emphasis on eternal predestination. In addition, these Puritan divines placed unusual emphasis on the doctrines of particular grace and limited (or "definite") atonement, a logical (but not exegetical!) extension of predestination. A helpful label then would include the words "experimental" and "predestination." R. T. Kendall has suggested the label "Experimental Predestinarians," which will be used throughout this book.[48]

THE NEONOMIAN

More recently others have openly abandoned the conclusions of the Reformation and boldly assert that salvation is by works after all. In this, they are following Reformed theology to its logical conclusion. After revisiting passages such as Romans 2:13, the story of the rich young ruler, and references to "entering the kingdom" by means of works, these writers have concluded that Rome is partially correct. Justification has initial and final aspects and both are soteriological. The former depends on faith alone and the latter on supposedly non-meritorious works that God produces in the believer. Salvation in this system is a process, not an event, and works are a "constituent" and a "condition" for final salvation.[49] In this system the gospel is "back-loaded" not just by demanding that works are the necessary evidence of salvation but also making works the means, condition, and constituent part of final justification. Good works are not just a necessary *result* of justification as the Experimental Predestinarian maintains; they are necessary as the *way* of justification.

---

48 R. T. Kendall, *Calvin and English Calvinism to 1649* (Oxford: Oxford University Press, 1979).

49 These viewpoints will be addressed throughout the book. Some of its more recent advocates are Thomas R. Schreiner and Ardel B. Caneday, *The Race Set Before Us: A Biblical Theology of Perseverance and Assurance* (Downers Grove, IL: InterVarsity Press, 2001). Thomas R. Schreiner, "Perseverance and Assurance: A Survey and a Proposal," *SBJT* 2(1998). Paul A. Rainbow, *The Way of Salvation: The Role of Christian Obedience in Justification* (Waynesboro, GA: Paternoster, 2005). Alan P. Stanley, *Did Jesus Teach Salvation by Works? The Role of Works in Salvation in the Synoptic Gospels* (Eugene, OR: Pickwick Publishers, 2006).

Early on this was seen as a threat to the Reformation. W. R. Godfrey notes, "The much greater danger [than antinomianism] historically facing the Reformation balance of law and gospel has been moralism and legalism. Moralists or neonomians so stress Christian responsibility, that obedience becomes more than the fruit or evidence of faith. *Rather obedience comes to be seen as a constituent element of justifying faith.* Legalism inevitably undermines Christian assurance and joy and tends to create a self-centered, excessively introspective piety—remarkably like medieval piety."[50] Modern-day Neonomians such as John MacArthur, John Piper, Paul Rainbow, Alan Stanley, and Thomas Schreiner share the belief that obedience is a constituent element of justifying faith.

MacArthur, a Neonomian advocate, expresses his theology this way: "Salvation isn't the result of an intellectual exercise. It comes from a life lived in obedience and service to Christ as revealed in the Scripture; it's the fruit of actions, not intentions. There's no room for passive spectators: words without actions are empty and futile. . .. The life we live, not the words we speak, determines our eternal destiny."[51] Salvation, he says, "comes from" and is the "fruit of actions." *Obviously, this is salvation by faith plus works.*

THE PARTNER

This book will discuss four basic theological approaches to the questions of security and perseverance. While labels often import connotations not shared by those designated, they are nevertheless helpful in distinguishing between positions. In this book the term "Arminian" refers to those followers of Jacobus Arminius who have held that it is possible for a Christian to lose his salvation. For them, the warning passages (e.g., Hebrews 6) refer to regenerate people.

The term "Calvinist" refers to those who feel that one who is born again cannot lose his salvation and will necessarily and inevitably continue in good works until the end of life (the "Experimental Predestinarian"). The warning passages, according to Experimental Predestinarians, are addressed to unregenerate people who have professed faith in Christ but who do not possess Christ in the heart.

The designation for the third position is Neonomian. These interpreters have taken the Experimentalist paradigm to its logical conclusion, that is, final justification is based upon God produced, non-meritorious works. We will argue that in spite of their denials, they, in fact, teach salvation plus works in contradiction to the New Testament doctrine of salvation by Christ alone through faith alone.

The fourth theological approach I have termed the Partner paradigm.

> *For we have become partakers [lit.,* ***Partners, Gr Metochoi]*** *of Christ, if we hold fast the beginning of our assurance firm until the end (Hebrews 3:14).*

The word "Partner" designates the theological approach to be presented in this book. The Partner is one who, like the Calvinist, holds to the eternal security of the Christian but who, like the Arminian, believes the warning passages in the New Testament apply to Christians. The Partner perseveres in good works to the end of life. He is the faithful

---

50 W. R. Godfrey, "Law and Gospel," in *New Dictionary of Theology*, ed. Sinclair B. Ferguson and J. I. Packer (Downers Grove, IL: InterVarsity Press, 2000).

51 John MacArthur, *Hard to Believe: The High Cost and Infinite Value of Following Jesus* (Nashville: Thomas Nelson, 2003), 93.

Christian who will reign with Christ in the coming messianic kingdom. He will be one of the servant kings. The danger the Partner faces is not loss of salvation but spiritual impoverishment, severe discipline in time, and a forfeiture of reward, namely, disinheritance in the future millennial kingdom and throughout the eternal state. For the Partner, the existence of the carnal Christian is not only a lamentable fact of Christian experience but is explicitly taught in the Bible as well.

A comparison and contrast between these four theological positions (the Arminian, the Experimental Predestinarian, the Neonomian, and the Partner) constitute a major portion of this book. The distinctives of the Partner doctrine are these:

1. Those who have been born again will normally give some evidence of growth in grace and spiritual interest and commitment.[52] John Hart says it well, "It is not denied that genuine faith will result in some change in the believer. Those holding to the Free Grace teaching do not assert that faith can exist without any change whatsoever. Most, if not all Free Grace proponents, believe that good works will inevitably result from faith, but not necessarily as visibly as we desire them to appear and not necessarily as consistently as the Lord would desire them to appear."[53] The key words are "visibly" and "consistently."[54]
2. Justification is by faith alone. Faith involves three things: believing assent, personal persuasion, and confident trust in the finished work of Christ for the free gift of forgiveness of sins. Repentance (defined as admitting personal guilt), discipleship, or submission to Christ as Lord are not conditions for salvation. Salvation is a free gift of undeserved favor received by faith and is available without cost (Rev 21:6), whereas discipleship costs one's entire life (Matthew 16:25). Because salvation involves trusting Christ for the forgiveness of sin, it is psychologically impossible to come to Christ for salvation and yet not admit personal guilt and need for a savior. One does not go to a physician unless he is sick and wants to be healed.
3. The assurance of salvation is found by looking outwardly to Christ. As the gospel promise and the beauty of the Redeemer are held before the believer's gaze, assurance is the result of such contemplation. Spiritual "fruit" is helpful as a secondary confirmation of one's regenerate state, but its absence does not necessarily invalidate one's salvation. If a believer is looking biblically and dependently to Christ, a lifestyle of sin will be psychologically, spiritually, and biblically impossible (Romans 6:1, 11; 8:35-39; Hebrews 11:1-2).

---

52 This is true because: (1) at conversion a person has believed and thus changed his perspective about sin and Christ. He knows who Christ is and what He has done for him and is therefore predisposed to allow Christ to change him. And (2) he has been flooded with new motivations toward godliness accompanied by the indwelling of the Holy Spirit. According to (3) the parable of the soils the second man experienced some growth, a kind of fruit (see discussion of this parable on pp. 532 ff. But he may soon after conversion quench the Spirit, walk by means of the flesh, and thus fail to give visible evidence of these initial inner workings. A life of sanctification will not inevitably and necessarily follow justification.

53 John F. Hart, "The Faith of Demons," *JOTGES* 8, no. 2 (1995): 40.

54 Zane Hodges agrees. "We must add that there is no need to quarrel with the Reformers' view that where there is justifying faith, works will undoubtedly exist too. This is a reasonable assumption for any Christian unless he has been converted on his death bed! But it is quite wrong to claim that a life of dedicated obedience is guaranteed by regeneration, or even that such works as there are must be visible to a human observer" (Zane C. Hodges, *Absolutely Free! A Biblical Reply to Lordship Salvation* (Dallas: Redención Viva, 1989), 215.

4. Christians may fail to persevere in faith, and in some cases they may even deny the faith altogether (Hebrews 3:12).[55] While continuous growth in Christ is commanded in the New Testament, it is possible for a Christian to lapse into carnality and finish his course walking like an unsaved person. The automatic and necessary lifelong unity between justification and sanctification imagined by the Experimental Predestinarians is not taught in Scripture.
5. The warning passages in the New Testament address regenerate people, not merely professing people, and they express real dangers to the regenerate. The danger, however, is not loss of salvation but severe temporal divine discipline (possibly, even physical death) as well as shame and loss of reward at the Judgment Seat of Christ (1 John 2:28; 2 John 8; 2 Corinthians 5:10).
6. A life of good works is the intended and commanded outcome of justification but is not inevitable (Romans 8:12).
7. Those who have believed on Christ and have been regenerated by His Holy Spirit can never fall away from salvation. They shall be preserved in a state of salvation to the final hour and be eternally saved. This preservation is guaranteed regardless of the amount of works or lack thereof in the believer's life (John 6:38-40).
8. The motive for godly living is not to be found in either fear of losing salvation (Arminian) or wondering if one is saved (Experimental Predestinarian). Rather, it is to be found negatively in the fear of disapproval, and positively in gratitude for a salvation already assured, anticipating the Master saying, "Well done!" The doctrine of eternal rewards usually has a more prominent place in encouraging a life of good works in the Partner view than in Arminian or Experimental Predestinarian views (1 Corinthians 9:24-27; 2 Corinthians 5:10; 2 John 8).[56]

Conclusion

A conversation recently held with an articulate exponent of the Experimental Predestinarian position revealed once again how difficult communication can sometimes be. Listening to this well-known theologian describe what he thought to be the position of those called Partners, it was evident how thoroughly our theological backgrounds can hinder our abilities to understand one another. We were discussing saving faith. In this scholar's frame of reference there were only two possibilities regarding faith. It was either mere intellectual assent or personal commitment. That there was a third possibility, reliance and inner conviction, did not seem to occur to him. Furthermore, if you did not hold to his view that faith is commitment then you must believe that all that was necessary for salvation was praying a prayer and giving intellectual assent to some facts about Christ. In addition he said the Partner viewpoint leads to the conclusion that there are two classes of Christians, carnal and spiritual, and that it is acceptable to be either one!

In another example D. A. Carson laments that those espousing the Partner viewpoint are "happy to speak of Christians ceasing to name the name of Christ and denying the faith

---

55 See discussion of this point in chapter 33.

56 John MacArthur, for example, has only one sentence devoted to this subject in his entire book on discipleship. MacArthur, *Hard to Believe: The High Cost and Infinite Value of Following Jesus*, 145.

completely."[57] Happy!? To suggest that the viewpoint represented in the pages to follow yields a theology that is indifferent to the pursuit of personal holiness is not only insulting, but it is logically, theologically, and exegetically false.

Carson misunderstands the Partner viewpoint. The charge of "easy-believism" has become a kind of "cuss" word for Experimental Predestinarians for all who disagree with their doctrines of saving faith and perseverance. The objects of Carson's jibe are those who "feel no pull toward holiness." It is not clear how Carson has perceived the inner feelings and motivations of those he condemns or how he would know their saved status if he had ever met such people. But for those like Carson who may assume that moral laxity is either the direct teaching or the logical implication of the Partner position, please withhold judgment until you have finished these pages! Like our Experimental Predestinarian friends, we would have serious doubts about the salvation of a person who claims he is a Christian and gives little or no evidence of it in his life. Such an individual could hardly be said to have assurance of salvation. We too are concerned about those who seem to think they can pray a prayer and live indifferently to Christ's claims and yet believe they will go to heaven anyway.

True, a general lack of spiritual vitality seems lacking in many parts of the Western church today. Whether many who profess Christ are truly regenerate, none can say with certainty. However, we can all agree that the problem of spiritual lethargy, lukewarm Christians, and even carnality is widespread and must be addressed. Possibly a major cause of this difficulty is that we have not challenged our congregations with the sobering realities of our glorious future. God has said mankind's destiny is to "rule and have dominion," and that destiny has yet to be fulfilled. However, if the Partner view of perseverance is right, only those Christians who persevere in a life of good works will have a share in this future glory. For unfaithful Christians there will be shame and profound regret when they stand before the Lord at the Judgment Seat of Christ.

In the Experimental Predestinarian view all who are Christians will be rewarded, and some more than others. All that can be lost is a higher degree of blessedness, but all will be blessed. Could it be that this happy ending has lulled many into thinking they can continue their lukewarmness with no eternal consequences to pay?

To answer this question, we must consider some foundational thoughts. Some basic interpretive principles are at the root of much of the controversy between Calvinists, Neonomians, Arminians and Partners.

---

57 D. A. Carson, "Reflections on Christian Assurance," *WTJ* 54(Spring 1992): 275.

2

Interpretation and Perseverance

IN RECENT years it has become quite fashionable to speak of the power of paradigms. Originally a Greek scientific term, today the word "paradigm" more commonly refers to a perception, a model, or a frame of reference. This refers to the way we "see" the world. The reason paradigms are said to have "power" is that they determine how we perceive things. They are lurking in the background of virtually every conclusion we make. We seldom question their accuracy, and we are usually unaware that we even have them. We commonly *assume* that the way we see things is the way they really are. Our attitudes, behaviors, and even our theology often grow out of these assumptions. The way we see things unconsciously affects our conclusions. This is why two theologians can look at the same data and come to radically opposite conclusions. Not that the facts are different. Instead the paradigms they bring to the facts strongly influence their interpretations.

The late Stephen Covey illustrates this phenomenon with an experience that happened to him one Sunday morning on a subway in New York. People were sitting quietly. Some were reading newspapers, some were lost in thought, and some were resting, their eyes closed. It was apparently a calm, peaceful scene. Then suddenly a man and his children entered the subway. The children were so loud and rambunctious that the whole climate changed instantly. People in the subway were distracted and upset.

The man sat down next to him and closed his eyes, apparently oblivious to the situation. The children were yelling and throwing things, even grabbing people's papers. It was quite disturbing. And yet, while all this was going on, the man sitting next to him did nothing. It was difficult not to feel irritated. Covey could not believe that this man could be so insensitive as to let his children run wild like that and do nothing about it, taking no responsibility at all. It was easy to see that everyone else on the subway felt irritated too. So finally Covey, with what he felt was unusual patience and restraint, turned to him and said, "Sir, your children are really disturbing a lot of people. I wonder if you couldn't control them a little more?"

The man lifted his gaze as if to come to a consciousness of the noise for the first time and said softly, "Oh, you're right. I guess I should do something about it. We just came from the hospital where their mother died about an hour ago. I don't know what to think, and I guess they don't know how to handle it either."

Covey continues: "Can you imagine what I felt at that moment? My paradigm shifted. Suddenly I *saw* things differently, and because I *saw* differently, I *thought* differently, I *felt* differently, I *behaved* differently. My irritation vanished. I didn't have to worry about controlling my attitude or my behavior; my heart was filled with the man's pain. Feelings of sympathy and compassion flowed freely. 'Your wife just died? Oh, I'm so sorry! Can you tell me about it? What can I do to help?' Everything changed in an instant."[58]

In order for some readers of this book to share the author's conclusions, they will need to undergo a paradigm shift. Such a shift often happens after we have reflected on things and sincerely tried to see them from a different point of view. This is that "Aha!" experience we feel when things fall into place for the first time. Our perceptions change and with them how we interpret the data of our sensory experience.

All interpreters of Scripture, including the present writer, bring certain paradigms to their reading of the Bible. These paradigms are "givens." They are things we do not need to think about. They are "obviously" true. Often we are unaware we have them until data that challenge them are presented. At that point we can either reinterpret that data within the framework of our old paradigm or begin to do some fundamental thinking. Perhaps our paradigm is wrong.

About forty years ago the writer underwent such a paradigm shift which resulted in a different way of understanding numerous difficult and often perplexing passages in the New Testament. He concluded that his theological traditions sometimes hindered rather than illuminated his understanding of the Bible. In a similar way, the reader is invited on a journey of discovery, a journey which will take him to familiar passages. Yet, as he travels he will be asked to consider the data from a different point of view.

Such a request is difficult to make because of the very nature of this book. It is a book of polemical theology. From beginning to end the author is attempting to persuade the reader of a particular point of view. Having been exposed to these kinds of books himself, the writer knows full well that his own initial reaction to such presentations is to continue to interpret the data from the perspective of his own settled paradigms. We all naturally do this.

As the reader journeys to various sections of Scripture and is asked to see the same data from a different paradigm, he will often have the thought, "Yes, but what about this other passage?" Those desiring to get the most out of this book will need to hold their opinions until the last page. A complete index to every Scripture reference is included. Hopefully, passages that seem to contradict certain interpretations will be found in this index.

We now commence our journey with a discussion of two exegetical issues that must first be cleared away if we are to correctly understand how the New Testament writers viewed the perseverance of the saints. The paradigm shift begins.

Theological Exegesis

Scholars widely recognize that differing principles of interpretation play a determinative role in theological discussion. The basic difference between the premillennialist and amillennialist views of Old Testament prophecy, for example, is basically a difference in interpretive approach. The amillennialist feels he has New Testament justification for spiritualizing the Old Testament predictions and applying them to the church. He believes the New Testament authors did this. The premillennialist feels that no New Testament author would have spiritualized a prophetic utterance so that its meaning differs from the intended meaning of the original author.

---

[58] Stephen R. Covey, *The Seven Habits of Highly Effective People* (New York: Schuster, 1989), 30-31.

What is not widely recognized, however, is that this same hermeneutical difference underlies much of the dispute on the doctrine of perseverance. What is the ultimate determinant of the meaning of a particular text: the intent of the original author, or a comparison of that text with other texts (selected by the interpreter)?

Possibly Charles Hodge was aware that strict attention to the intended meaning of texts could yield theological conclusions at variance with his. So he vigorously protested, "They [Arminians] seem to regard it as a proof of independence to make each passage mean simply what its grammatical structure and logical connection indicate, without the least regard to the analogy of Scripture."[59] No doubt his Arminian opponents would view this as a faulty characterization. For they are interested in the analogy of Scripture also.

Should the single intent of the original author be the primary determinant in our theological constructs? The answer to that question is obvious. Yes! If the intent of the original author does not determine meaning, then someone else's intent, that of the interpreter, takes over, and all controls are lost. The biblical theology movement has tended to agree with premillennialists that the Old Testament teaches the future existence of a literal earthly kingdom.

The Protestant doctrine of the analogy of faith has in practice sometimes become what might be called "theological exegesis." What started as a valid attempt to allow other Scriptures to help interpret the meaning of obscure passages has sometimes been abused in that obviously clear passages are interpreted in a way that will harmonize with a particular theological tradition. Instead of permitting each text to speak for itself, the theological system determines the meaning. For example, consider a common interpretation of Romans 2:6-7:

> *Who will render to every man according to his deeds: to those who by perseverance in doing good seek for glory and honor and immortality, eternal life; but to those who are selfishly ambitious and do not obey the truth, but obey unrighteousness, wrath and indignation.*

Nothing about this passage is obscure. It says that those who persevere in doing good will obtain eternal life. However, because that seems to involve a contradiction with the doctrine of justification by faith alone, our theological system is brought in to save the day:

> *A person's habitual conduct, whether good or evil, reveals the condition of his heart. Eternal life is not rewarded for good living; that would contradict many other Scriptures which clearly state that salvation is not by works, but is all of God's grace to those who believe (e.g., Romans 6:23; 10:9-10; 11:6; Ephesians 2:8-9; Titus 3:5). A person's doing good* ***shows*** *that his heart is regenerate. Such a person, redeemed by God, has eternal life.*[60]

It may be true that a person's "habitual conduct" reveals the condition of his heart, but the text is not addressing that issue. According to Paul, eternal life **is** "rewarded for good living." How else could he say it: "God will render to every man *according to his deeds*"? Shouldn't we let this stand?[61]

---

59 Hodge, *Systematic Theology*, 3:167.

60 John A. Witmer, "Romans," in *BKC: New Testament*, ed. John F. Walvoord and Roy B. Zuck (Colorado Springs: Cook, 1996), 445.

61 How this can be reconciled with Paul's doctrine of justification by faith alone will be considered below, pp. 225 ff.

Although Turretin demanded that "an empty head must be brought to Scripture,"[62] it is, of course, impossible to remove the analogy of faith from our exegesis; indeed, it would not be proper to do so. As Bildad said to Job, *"Can the papyrus grow up without a marsh? Can the rushes grow without water?"* (Job 8:11). There is always something prior to any viewpoint.

Each of us approaches the Bible with certain theological pre-understandings, certain paradigms. Even when we are conscious of them, it is still difficult to negate their controlling influence. Johnson is correct when he observes:

> *It seems reasonable that the agenda we set for ourselves, the problems for which we seek exegetical solutions, reflect our understanding of tension and harmony with what the rest of Scripture clearly teaches. And is not the exegetical question that we ask just as important as the exegetical means we use to answer that question?*[63]

The teachers of the Reformed faith are not the only ones practicing "theological exegesis." The present writer candidly admits that many of the interpretations found in the pages to follow were strongly influenced by a theological pre-understanding that has been brought to the texts in question.

The analogy of faith should be viewed as an important and proper element of the exegetical process, but not the most important one. It should not dictate our exegesis, substitute for exegesis, or simply be subsequent to exegesis. Rather, it is part of valid exegetical procedure, but it is impossible in the real world to postpone it to the end of the interpretive process.

We all begin with certain assumptions, an "initial guess," about what the Scriptures teach on certain subjects. E. D Hirsch in his wonderful book, *Validity in Interpretation*,[64] teaches that it is proper and inevitable that we begin with such initial guesses. He proposes that we state this initial guess as a proposition. Then, he says, we should descend into the details to see if the relevant passages (or details of a particular passage) are explained by and cohere with the initial guess. When we observe certain things that do not fit, we need to go back, modify our initial proposition, and then study the details again. This iterative procedure is repeated until there is a good correspondence between the initial guess as to what is being taught in a passage or topic and the details of the many passages relevant to it. When that correspondence criterion is satisfied we have arrived at "validity in interpretation."

This is the procedure that the writer has tried to follow in the remainder of this book. Obviously the writer does not claim for himself theological neutrality. Arminians, Experimental Predestinarians, Neonomians, and Partners all utilize theological exegesis, but all should try to avoid making our theological preunderstanding determine the outcomes of our interpretive process.

---

62 Frances Turretin, cited by H. Wayne Johnson, 'The "Analogy of Faith' and Exegetical Methodology: A Preliminary Discussion on Relationships," *JETS* 31, no. 1 (1988): 76.

63 Ibid., 76-77.

64 E. D. Hirsch, *Validity in Interpretation* (New Haven, CT: Yale University Press, 1967).

Illegitimate Totality Transfer

An exegetical error that has tended to obfuscate the clarity of vision of the disputants over the doctrine of perseverance is what James Barr calls illegitimate totality transfer, "The error that arises, when the 'meaning' of a word (understood as the total series of relations in which it is used in the literature) is read into a particular case as its sense and implication there, may be called 'illegitimate totality transfer.'"[65]

Kittel's famous *Theological Dictionary of the New Testament* has been severely criticized from this vantage point by Barr. Kittel's work, contrary to popular perception, is not just a dictionary. He states in the introduction that external lexicography (i.e., meanings derived from dictionaries and concordance usage) is not his purpose. Rather, his burden is what he calls "internal lexicography."[66] By this he means "concept history." His burden is to present the "theological idea" behind a word. The result is that we do not always get from Kittel only the meaning of the word but also the theology of it as perceived by the writer of the particular article. Users of this dictionary often make the mistake of citing Kittel as a lexical rather than a theological authority. While this is sometimes justified, these volumes need to be read with discrimination.

Experimental Predestinarian commentators frequently commit this error in regard to terms like "inheritance" and "eternal life." Because inheritance sometimes means heaven, and "eternal life" sometimes means regeneration or final entrance into heaven, these meanings are lumped into the word and this new expanded definition of the terms is imported into other contexts.[67]

A classic illustration of this faulty procedure will be discussed in the next chapter on repentance. Beginning with the assumption that the "theological idea" of repentance involves personal turning from sin, escape from eternal condemnation, and is a condition for obtaining eternal life, Behm's article in *The Theological Dictionary of the New Testament* proceeds to read this idea into faith.[68]

Words Have Meaning Only in Context

This practice of going through the concordance, noting associations in various contexts, adding up all the related usages, reading them into the semantic value of the word, and carrying that freighted new meaning into other contexts is an illegitimate totality transfer.[69] It is quite common to hear in theological discussion, "The usage is predominantly this, so it is likely that this is the sense in this particular passage." One must be careful when using such a statistical approach. As Louw has pointed out, "A word does not have a meaning without a context; it only has possibilities of meaning."[70]

Frequency of use only suggests a probable meaning which would be suggested to a reader before considering any contextual indicators as to what is meant. "Open the trunk" would probably be understood by most Americans as "Open the rear end of the car," unless

[65] James Barr, *The Semantics of Biblical Languages* (London: Oxford University Press, 1961).

[66] Gerhard Kittel, "Preface," TDNT, 1:vii

[67] See chapters 4-11 for discussion of inheritance.

[68] Johannes Behm, "*metanoeō*," TDNT, 4:1000-1006.

[69] Barr, *The Semantics of Biblical Languages*, 206-62.

[70] J. P. Louw, *Semantics of New Testament Greek* (Philadelphia: Fortress Press, 1982), 40.

the context had placed them in the attic of the house. Those from England, however, would probably understand the sentence to mean, "Open the box."

Suppose, for example, an "exegete" had been reading a mystery novel which involved many chapters of discussion regarding the contents of the trunk in the attic. The size of the trunk, the color of the trunk, and, most important, clues to its contents were the subject of pages of intrigue. Then a bit unexpectedly he reads, "He went to the driveway and opened the trunk." Our exegete "knows" that "trunks" refer to boxes in the attic. From usage, therefore, he assumes that it must have been temporarily moved to the driveway. It is statistically more probable that a colored box of a certain size is meant. So theological exegesis is brought in to force the word "trunk" to mean "box," and the illegitimate totality transfer is made to speculate on its color, size, and other characteristics. After the required footnotes, which establish that the author has read and interacted with the "literature," and discussion of the use of the word "trunk" by "this particular author in all prior examples," we are told that apparently the box was moved to the driveway even though there is no mention of this in the text. The absurdity of this is at once apparent. The meanings of words are primarily determined by the usage in a particular context and that has more force than a hundred usages elsewhere. Trunks in driveways are the posteriors of automobiles! The context determines the meaning. The study of usages helps determine the range of known meanings but not the meaning in a particular context. A good exegete of the above story would know that usage establishes that the word "trunk," when connected in context with an automobile, regularly signifies a storage area in an auto, not in an attic.

Illegitimate Identity Transfer

The example above about a "trunk" is an example of a related error that Barr calls the illegitimate identity transfer. This occurs when a meaning in one context is said to be the meaning in all contexts. The discussion of "trunk" above illustrates this. But perhaps a biblical illustration will be helpful. James Rosscup appears to commit the error of the illegitimate identity transfer in his attempt to define the meaning of the "overcomer" in Revelation 2-3.[71] First John 5:4 states that the overcomer is a Christian and that all who are Christians are, in a particular sense, overcomers. Those who know the Lord have, according to John, overcome by virtue of the fact that they have believed and for no other reason. In Revelation, however, the overcomer is one who has "kept the word of My perseverance" (Revelation 3:10) and who "keeps My deeds until the end" (Revelation 2:26). As a result of this faithful behavior, the overcomer receives various rewards. Rosscup, in the interests of the Reformed doctrine of perseverance, wants the overcomer in 1 John (all Christians) to mean the same thing as the overcomer in Revelation. He misunderstands the context of 1 John and feels it refers to tests of whether one is a Christian. In fact, as will be discussed later; it refers to tests of our walk and fellowship with God, as the opening verses indicate.[72] All who are overcomers in 1 John, therefore, may or may not be walking in fellowship; but all who are overcomers in Revelation are. An overcomer in 1 John is simply a Christian; an overcomer in Revelation is a persevering Christian.

---

[71] James E. Rosscup, "The Overcomers of the Apocalypse," *Grace Theological Journal* 3(Fall 1982): 261-86.

[72] I will establish this view later in vol. 2, chapter 31.

Rosscup reasons that, since the overcomer in 1 John is a Christian, it must be the same in Revelation. This, however, is importing a contextually derived usage, "justified saint," into the semantic value of the word and then taking this new meaning to another context. An overcomer is simply a "victor," and the word itself does not even imply that the victor is a Christian; he could be a victor in the athletic games.

In summary, meanings are to be derived from context. To use the analogy of the elephant's nose, when the context includes such references as Africa, one understands that to pull on the trunk clearly refers to pulling on an elephant's nose and not opening the rear end of a car. Now in 1 John, the context is one of overcoming the world by faith and, as a result, becoming regenerate. In Revelation, however, the context involves overcoming by deeds of obedience, and the result is merited rewards. All Christians are overcomers in the former sense, but not all are overcomers in the latter. To import the meaning of "become a Christian by faith" from 1 John into the sense of the word in Revelation would be about as accurate as insisting that the man in Dallas who was pulling on the trunk of his car was yanking on an elephant's nose! It is an illegitimate identity transfer.

Theological Science

Calvin gave us our first systematic theology. He insisted that interpretations had to have a scientific justification. The allegorizing of the Middle Ages was rejected, and sound canons of hermeneutics were embraced for the first time since Augustine. By scientific justification we mean, first, that in order for an interpretation to be true, it must be grounded in the objective data of history, lexicography, culture, grammar, and context.

Five things characterize a scientific hypothesis.[73] First, the data collected must be relevant. Applied to the interpretation of Scripture, this means that passages used in support of a hypothesis must be relevant and not pulled out of contexts.

Second, data must submit to a "falsifiability criterion." If contrary data invalidate it, it must be abandoned. Karl Popper has made the falsifiability criterion a principal pillar of modern scientific investigation. In order for a theory to have any scientific value, it must be capable of being proved wrong. When dealing with an induction, we cannot always be sure that we have collected all the data, so the possibility of invalidation must always be part of a theory, or it is not a scientific theory. Similarly, a theological "theory" which is incapable of falsification is questionable in terms of its explanatory value.

The doctrine of the perseverance of the saints certainly qualifies as a valid scientific theory. It has been argued by capable men on the basis of a particular interpretation of many biblical passages. It qualifies as a scientific theory because it is capable of falsification. If there is one example in the Bible of a person who was born again, fell away from the Lord, and persisted in his disobedience up to the point of physical death, then the theory of the saints' perseverance has been disproved and must be abandoned. As will be argued later, the Reformed doctrine of perseverance fails completely on this test alone.[74]

Third, one's view should usually be consistent with prior established interpretations. We must always heed the teaching ministry of the Holy Spirit in response to the prayerful

---

73 The following discussion is adapted to the science of theology from John F. Hawley and Katherine A. Holcomb, *Foundations of Modern Cosmology*, 2nd. ed. (Oxford: University Press, 2005), 18-21.

74 See vol. 2, chapter 32.

and diligent study of Bible students throughout history. Only with reluctance should one abandon these conclusions. On this score the Reformed doctrine of perseverance does well, better in fact, than the interpretive paradigm set forth in the pages to follow. I will respond to this legitimate concern later.[75]

Fourth, the best hypothesis is the simplest. In about AD 1300 William of Ockham introduced the scientific principle that whatever explanation involves the fewest assumptions is to be preferred. Called Ockham's Razor, this view says that when one is confronted with contrary evidence which requires many secondary explanations in order to justify its existence, it is a bad theory. The continued introduction of secondary assumptions in order to explain the theory in the light of seemingly contradictory evidence results in a crumbling house of cards. The efficiency (explanatory value) of any theory is simply the number of facts correlated divided by the number of assumptions made.

In theology, when a particular theological position must be maintained by secondary assumptions, it is worthless. This is preeminently the case in the Experimental Predestinarians' doctrine of the saints' perseverance. When confronted with apparently contradictory evidence that a true saint in the Bible has persisted in disobedience, they will often offer the secondary assumption, based on their system, that he was not a true saint at all. Or when warnings are addressed to "little children," "brethren," "saints," and those "sanctified forever," a secondary assumption, not supported by the text, is brought in to say that these terms refer to "wheat and tares" and the specific descriptions are only the language of courtesy, not of fact. This continual addition of *ad hoc* explanations which are either not alluded to in the texts in question, or are specifically refuted by them, renders the theory useless. It becomes incapable of falsification because any data contrary to it is simply negated by additional assumptions. Text after text is often ignored in this way until the whole edifice verges on collapse like the proverbial house of cards.

Fifth, a good criterion for an interpretive paradigm is explanatory power. This "is a quantification of the facts the hypothesis can encompass and explain."[76] The efficiency of an interpretive paradigm is simply the number of biblical facts correlated divided by the number of assumptions made. All theories begin with certain initial assumptions but when many assumptions must be made in order to justify the theory, its explanatory power is useless. As will be argued in the pages to follow, the Experimental Predestinarian paradigm for understanding the theology of the New Testament fails dramatically on this score. Hawley says, "In order to be accepted, any new hypothesis must represent an improvement. It must explain more facts, or provide better explanations of existing knowledge, than does the older theory."[77] In this regard the Partner paradigm succeeds admirably.

Theology is a science; in fact, it was once known as "the queen of the sciences." Every science is composed of two things, facts and the interpretation of those facts. The facts of astronomy do not constitute astronomy, and the facts of chemistry or history do not constitute chemistry or history. Science is the facts *plus* their correlation and interpretation. The Bible is no more a system of theology than nature is a system of chemistry or physics.

The task of a theologian is to collect, authenticate, arrange, and explain the facts of revelation. The natural scientist does the same with the facts of nature. When he does

---

[75] See pp. 1046-1052

[76] Hawley and Holcomb, *Foundations of Modern Cosmology*, 20.

[77] Ibid.

this, however, he must not modify one experimental fact in order to accommodate it with another apparently contradictory one. Instead, he searches for a higher synthesis, larger than each fact, which will explain both. The Protestant doctrine of the analogy of faith has sometimes been extended to justify the modification of the obvious meaning of a text, the "experimental fact," in view of other facts.

The theologian must show how facts in one part of Scripture correlate and explain facts in another part, but he must not modify the facts in order to do so. The chemist does not manufacture facts; the theologian should not either. He must take them as they are. He will systematically gather all the data from revelation on a certain subject and then draw general conclusions. The Bible is to a theologian what nature is to a scientist. Our duty is to collect the facts of revelation, arrange them, and apply them to the hearts of our students. False theories in science and false doctrines in theology are often due to errors of fact. Furthermore the collection of facts must be comprehensive. An incomplete induction led men to believe that the sun moved around the earth.

If we come across biblical data that seem to contradict our system, we must reassess our system and not reinterpret those facts in light of the system. This is a lifelong work. Our goal is not to defend the viewpoint of any denomination but to know the mind of God. This means that the doctrines of the Bible, like the principles and laws of natural science, are not imposed on the facts but are derived from them.

But after forty years of reading the writings of the Experimental Predestinarians, studying their passages in the Greek New Testament, and interacting personally with their advocates, this writer is convinced that they tend to allow their theological system to determine and not just influence the meaning of many passages. An interpretive framework has so dominated their minds that their method of exegesis cannot always be called exegesis. It sometimes seems to be an honest attempt to explain away passage after passage in order to sustain a theory of the saints' perseverance in good works at all costs. No doubt they would accuse the present writer of the same faulty procedure; and I, of course, would respectfully disagree. Their motivation for this is pure, if unconscious. It lies in the nagging fear that, if their doctrine is abandoned, there is no answer to the Arminians with their denial of eternal security, and even more important, there is no answer to the charge of being antinomian. Indeed, to give up the doctrine of perseverance is, according to Experimental Predestinarians, to turn the grace of God into lasciviousness.

Of course that does not necessarily follow, but there is no question that in some cases carnal believers will do just that. This is why Paul was charged with antinomianism (Romans 3:8; 6:1). But the Partner's position satisfactorily answers the Arminian objections to eternal security by allowing the texts to speak plainly. The charge of antinomianism is also easily answered in that there is no greater inducement to godliness than the love of Christ, the unconditional acceptance of the Father, the hope of hearing Him say, "Well done!", and the fear of millennial disinheritance at the Judgment Seat of Christ.

We must derive our doctrines from the Bible and not make the Bible teach what we think is necessary. If a man denies that an innocent man can die for the sins of the guilty, he must deny that Christ bore our sins. If a man denies that the merit of one man can be imputed to another, then he must deny the scriptural doctrine of justification. If he believes that a just God would never allow anyone to go to the lake of fire, then he must do so contrary to the doctrine of Scripture. Obviously our whole system of revealed truth is useless unless we are committed to derive our theology from it and not impose our theology on it. If the Bible teaches that a Christian may be carnal, then our system of theology must be adjusted to accommodate this fact. "It is the fundamental principle of all sciences, and of theology among the rest, that theory is to be determined by facts, and not facts by theory. As natural science was a chaos until the principle of induction was admitted and faithfully carried out, so theology is a jumble of human speculations, not worth a straw, when men refuse to apply the same principle to the study of the Word of God."[78]

Summary

Every interpreter assumes a certain paradigm that influences his understanding of many passages. While it is sometimes necessary to give our paradigms more sway than we like, in the final analysis we must strive to allow the text to determine our paradigm.

In the process of interpreting what the original writers of Scripture meant, we have sometimes fallen into the error called illegitimate totality transfer. This occurs when a theological idea arrived at from a number or scriptures (or even a tradition) is read into a phrase or a word, and then that understanding of the word is carried throughout the Bible. A related error is the illegitimate identity transfer. This occurs when the meaning of a word in one context is transferred to its meaning in another context, whether it fits the differing context or not. One can illustrate this with the word "trunk" (a box in the attic or the circumference of a tree) in secular literature or the word "overcomer" in the Bible. In 1 John it means any Christian, but in the book of Revelation, the context demands that it refers to persevering Christians.

Finally, theology is a science and as such our interpretations must be the simplest ones consistent with the context and must be able to be refuted if contrary data are presented. The advocates of the Reformed doctrine of perseverance exempt their doctrine from falsification by assuming that warning passages addressed to "brothers," "little children," "beloved," those who "have tasted the heavenly gift," or "saints" must refer to those who profess Christ but whose professions may not be real.

In the next chapter we will turn to a subject which is surrounded by considerable controversy. What is repentance? Did not Jesus say, "*Repent for the kingdom of heaven is at hand*"?

---

[78] Hodge, *Systematic Theology*, 1:14-15.

3
Repentance

I REMEMBER ONE day sitting in a theology class and as soon as the bell rang, the professor gave us a sixty-second assignment. He then described a fictional scenario. A man has been hit by an automobile and you, being near the scene, rush to his aid. He has only a minute or so to live. As he fades away, he looks you in the eye and asks, "How can I know if I will go to heaven?" Because the time is limited, you have exactly sixty seconds to answer. The professor asked us to write out our answer, and then we all passed our answers up to the front. He then proceeded to read them. It was amusing to hear the variety of gospel presentations written by those graduate students in systematic theology.

One of the conditions for entering heaven that was commonly expressed in these sixty-second "masterpieces" was that the man must repent of his sins. One even suggested that a search for a cup of water was necessary so the man could at least be baptized by sprinkling before passing on. Others said he should pray, asking Jesus to come into his heart. Others felt that believing on Christ for the remission of sins was the only requirement.

In the book of Acts another man was facing death, not by automobile but by execution. The Philippian jailer, who was on guard when an earthquake hit the prison holding Paul the apostle, knew the game was up. When a prisoner escaped, no matter the cause, the normal procedure in the Roman Empire was that the guard on duty was to be executed. We know nothing of the jailer's religious convictions before the earthquake, but whatever they were he began to reevaluate them when he saw Paul on his way out of the jail. Since he thought he had better make amends with his Maker, he asked Paul, "What must I do to be saved?" No doubt, Paul had much more than sixty seconds to give an answer. However, unlike the graduate students in the theology class, Paul needed only five seconds. He simply said, "*Believe on the Lord Jesus Christ and you will be saved*" (NKJV).

Paul said nothing about baptism or promising God to turn from all known sin and change his life. Did Paul give this man an incomplete gospel? Should he have mentioned the need for repentance? Experimental Predestinarians say "Yes." I will suggest in the following discussion that the answer to this question depends upon what one means by "repentance." If it means "turn from sin," that is not a requirement. What did John the Baptist mean when he called upon the nation to repent for the forgiveness of sins and to "repent for the kingdom of heaven is at hand" (Matthew 3:2)?

MacArthur forcefully insists, "No evangelism that omits the message of repentance can properly be called the gospel, for sinners cannot come to Jesus Christ apart from a radical change of heart, mind, and will."[79] If repentance (defined as surrender to the Lordship of Christ) is necessary for salvation, the gospel of John did not achieve its intended aim (John 20:31) because submission to the Lordship of Christ is never mentioned in John's gospel as a condition for receiving eternal life.

The Westminster Confession says, "Although repentance is not to be relied on as any payment of the penalty for sin, or any cause of the pardon of sin (which is God's act of free grace in Christ); yet repentance is so necessary for all sinners, that no one may expect pardon without it."[80] By "repentance" the Confession means that one must turn from all sin and submit to the Lordship of Christ. Larry Nees suggests this illustration of what the Confession is really saying. "I'll freely give you $100. But first you must pull all the weeds out of your garden. Your weed-pulling is not work. I am not paying you to pull weeds. Your weed-pulling is not required as a way to pay me back. This $100 is a free gift. However, unless you pull all the weeds, I will not give you the $100."[81]

Many of our Experimental Predestinarian friends believe that saving faith necessarily implies a lifelong turning from sin.[82] Yet when a life of turning from sin is incorporated into the concept of faith, then faith becomes a life of works, and salvation is reduced to a kind of "faith/works." Is this the correct understanding of faith and repentance in the New Testament?

The Meaning of Repentance

Many would agree that a basic meaning of *metanoeō* is simply to "change the mind" or feel remorse or regret.[83] It is an "afterthought" or "second opinion." Charles Ryrie, for example, says, "Repentance means a genuine change of mind that affects the life in some way. Like other significant theological terms it must be defined specifically by asking a further question, namely, change the mind about what? Christians can repent of specific sins and stop doing them (Revelation 2:5; 2 Corinthians 7:9)." Do non-Christians have to repent? Ryrie says yes if one defines repentance correctly. "Saving repentance," he says, "has to involve a change of mind about Jesus Christ so that whatever a person thought of Him before, he changes his mind and trusts Him to be his Savior."[84] This approach seems quite plausible to me and works in the majority of the passages where repentance is mentioned in the New Testament.

However, Reformed writers stress the specific idea of changing one's mind about sin, that is, turning from sin in order to obtain eternal life. The standard Greek lexicons support the Reformed view.[85] For example, appeal is often made to Behm's article on *metanoia* in the *Theological Dictionary of the New Testament*. Behm notes that in many of the prophetic

---

79 John MacArthur, *The Gospel According to Jesus* (Grand Rapids: Zondervan Publishing House, 1988), 81.

80 Westminster Confession of Faith, chap. 15.

81 Larry Nees, Personal Communication, May 10, 2011.

82 See for example Curtis I. Crenshaw, *Lordship Salvation: The Only Kind There Is - An Evaluation of Jody Dillow's The Reign of the Servant Kings and Other Antinomian Arguments* (Memphis: Footstool Publications, 1994), 8.

83 BDAG, 640. This lexicon adds, "be converted" but that is a theological idea read into the word. It refers to a change in one's "way of thinking" (Wisdom of Solomon 12:10).

84 Charles Ryrie, *Basic Theology* (Chicago: Moody Press, 1999), 390.

85 For example, the lexicon of Louw-Nida says that repentance is "the total change, both in thought and behavior, with respect to how one should both think and act," Louw-Nida, 1:509.

utterances the call is "to return to an earlier good relation between Israel and Yahweh."[86] He then incorrectly relates the Gr word *metanoeō* with the Hebrew word *shuv*,[87] which means "to return" or "to turn." The problem is that in the Septuagint there is no instance where shuv ("to turn") is translated by *metanoeō* ("to repent")! No matter, Behm defines *metanoia* by means of a study of the word *shuv* anyway. By associating *shuv* with *metaneo*, he develops a theological idea of metanoia and commits the totality transfer. Well then, what does *metanoeō* mean? Three things are involved in this *metanoia/shuv* according to Behm: (1) Obedience to God's will; (2) trust in Yahweh; and (3) turning from everything ungodly.[88] In the message of Jesus and John the Baptist, Behm claims that *metanoia* is required to give one "a place in the coming salvation."[89] He confusedly adds that, "God grants conversion through baptism," apparently believing in baptismal regeneration[90]

He states that this repentance involves "final and unconditional decision," a "*definitive* turning from evil," "*radical* conversion," "*total* surrender," "*total* commitment to the will of God," and "*total* obedience" to God.[91] There must be "turning from *all* that is against God."[92] The "unmitigated severity" of the demand for repentance requires that one's "conduct at *all times and in all situations*" must illustrate its effect on the whole man. Furthermore there can be no going back. If one does go back, he forfeits his salvation and "faces eschatological judgment."[93]

Behm began with the theological idea that repentance involves individual submission to the Lordship of Christ to become a Christian and he then associated it with faith.[94] Behm writes, "John avoids the loaded terms *metonoeō* and *metanoia*, but he, too, has the matter itself no less definitely than Paul." How so? "For him [John], too, faith includes conversion."[95] Really? Behm never gives any proof. This is part of his theological idea (illegitimate totality transfer) about how one becomes a Christian in a process in which faith and repentance are essential parts..[96]

Are these the conditions for obtaining the free gift of eternal life through believing, which is taught throughout the New Testament? If they are, we can be assured that Behm himself (and others who teach this works-salvation doctrine) are not in the kingdom of God, nor is anyone else in the history of Christianity. Behm appeals to the power of the

---

86 Behm, "*metanoia*," TDNT, 4:985.

87 This should be transliterated *shub*, however, it is pronounced *shuv* and we will transliterate that way from this point on.

88 Ibid., 4:986.

89 Ibid., 4:1001.

90 Ibid.

91 Ibid., 4:1002.

92 Ibid., 4:1001.

93 Ibid., 4:1005 (italics added). He cites Hebrews 6:6 and 10:26.

94 This writer is not the only one who has noted this faulty methodology in Behm's article. Sauer, a very articulate Experimental Predestinarian, in an excellent doctoral dissertation observes, "Behm commits a lexical faux pas that has far reaching consequences in his article on repentance." R. C. Sauer, "A Critical and Exegetical Examination of Hebrews 5:11-6:8" (PhD diss., University of Manchester, 1981), 305.

95 Behm "*metanoia*," 4:1005.

96 Some readers may sense the writer is being too harsh with Behm. However, the definition of the gospel and the eternal destiny of thousands who read his book are at stake; Paul would have been harsher, "let him be accursed!" (Galatians 1:9).

Spirit to affect these total absolutes of character change. "This unconditional requirement," he says, "is not met by man's own achievement."[97] It is a gift.[98] We agree that the Spirit's enablement is a gift, but human effort is also involved (Philippians 2:12-13; 4:13). While divine enablement is certainly part of the new covenant, it is pure fantasy to teach that the Holy Spirit produces these absolutes in the life of a nonbeliever as a condition of his receiving the gift of eternal life. Equally fallacious is the idea that the Holy Spirit produces such total conversion in the life of one who is already regenerate, which, according to Behm and other Experimental Predestinarians is apparently required for entrance into the kingdom. Without fear of contradiction, we can say that the Holy Spirit has never produced that degree of absolute, total, and final obedience in the lives of any of them, or anyone else, including this writer. If one doubts this, he has only to interview our wives! Yet they continually use this kind of unguarded language, leaving their readers in confusion, promulgating a preposterous view of the conditions of obtaining eternal life and the characteristics of those who possess it. This jargon of the pulpit (and many commentaries) has left millions of genuine Christians "turning in the wind" with concerns about their eternal destiny. In fact it is "another gospel!"[99]

A careful study of all uses of *metanoeō* and *metanoia* in the Septuagint and comparing them with the related Hebrew words reveals two things: (1) the consistency with which *metanoeō* translates *nāḥam* [Heb "be sorry, repent, regret," "change one's mind" (Exodus 32:14; Jeremiah 26:19; Psalm 110:4][100] and *epistrephō* translates *shuv*; and (2) *metanoeō* has different translations: relent, repent, and change the mind. Why then do scholars consistently say that *metanoeō* means to turn or return?[101] The best interpretation of *metanoeō* in the New Testament is to acknowledge, to change one's mind about something, to admit, to feel sorry for. A good Old Testament illustration of this usage would be Jeremiah 8:6.

---

97 Behm, "*metanoia*," 4:1003.

98 Calvin rejected this kind of Roman Catholic reasoning, "The Sophists, who delight in sporting with Scripture and in empty cavils, think they have a subtle evasion when they expound works to mean, such as unregenerate men do literally, and by the effect of free will, without the grace of Christ, and deny that these have any reference to spiritual works. Thus according to them, man is justified by faith as well as by works, provided these are not his own works, but gifts of Christ and fruits of regeneration; Paul's only object in so expressing himself being to convince the Jews, that in trusting to their own strength they foolishly arrogated righteousness to themselves, whereas it is bestowed upon us by the Spirit of Christ alone, and not by studied efforts of our own nature. But they observe not that in the antithesis between legal and gospel righteousness, which Paul elsewhere introduces, all kinds of works, with whatever name adorned, are excluded (Galatians 3:11, 12). For he says that the righteousness of the Law consists in obtaining salvation by doing what the Law requires, but that the righteousness of faith consists in believing that Christ died and rose again (Romans 10:5–9). Moreover, we shall afterwards see, at the proper place, that the blessings of sanctification and justification, which we derive from Christ, are different. Hence it follows, that not even spiritual works are taken into account when the power of justifying is ascribed to faith." Calvin, "Institutes," 3, 11, 14.

99 This is a problem with adding repentance (defined as turning from sin) as a condition for salvation. No one can define how much repentance is enough. Furthermore each culture has its own ideas of what is to be included, from crying in remorse for three days by the "criers" in China to some groups in Eastern Europe who felt a woman must repent of wearing lipstick before she could become a Christian. Must the tribal chief in Africa divest himself of 19 of his 20 wives before he can exercise "genuine" faith in Christ?

100 Leonard J. Coppes, "*nāḥam*," in TWOT, 2:570. "Hence, *metanoeō* is equivalent to the Heb. *niḥam* (niph.), to be sorry about something," NIDNTT, 1:357.

101 This seems to be based on tradition and a prior theological idea.

I have listened and heard, they have spoken what is not right; No man ***repented*** *of his wickedness, saying, "****What have I done?****" Everyone turned to his course, like a horse charging into the battle.*

Note that "repented" is described as saying "What have I done?" It is an admission of guilt. As a result, they manifested the fruit of repentance and "turned their course."

Even though the word means to admit one is wrong and to regret it in the majority of contexts, in some contexts *metanoeō* has incorrectly been understood to mean to turn from sin.[102] Looking at their recognition of guilt, Jesus said the Ninevites "repented" (Gr *metanoeō*, Matthew 12:41) but Jonah, looking at the result of their conviction, said they "turned" (Heb *shuv*, LXX *epistrephō*). They first admitted they were wrong (repented) and then they manifested the fruit of repentance, they turned from sin. One does not turn from sin unless he first believes it is wrong, that is, unless he repents. At any rate, the subject is not the individual salvation of Ninevites but the national salvation of the city. The Ninevites did repent but it did not save them from damnation, only faith in the coming Messiah of Isaiah 53 could do that. Nations are not saved from damnation, only individuals are. The city of Nineveh was saved from a temporal catastrophe.

The Gr word *metanoeō* occurs 14 times in the Septuagint. In each case it is the chosen translation for the Hebrew word *nāḥam,*[103] to change the mind or to feel sorry for. There are 108 usages of *nāḥam* in the Hebrew Bible and not one of them means "to turn."

Thus, we should look to *nāḥam*, "to regret," rather than to *shuv*, "to return," as the probable background to the New Testament usage of the *metanoia* word group. Frequently it communicates an emotion such as "to regret, to become remorseful."[104] It often means "to comfort."[105] The only places where it is translated "to relent" in the sense of desisting from an action is when Yahweh promised "to relent" if the nation or individuals met certain conditions.[106] But even there the idea of "change of mind" or "regret" are perfectly acceptable translations.[107] Often it is translated "to change the mind"[108] or "to be sorry."[109]

This suggests that *metanoeō* refers to regret or admission of guilt rather than turning from sin. Turning from sin would have been indicated by *shuv*, which the Septuagint

---

102 Luke 13:5; Matthew 3:2; 4:17; Revelation 9:21. Bob Wilkin, notes that Jonah 3:10 uses the Hebrew word *shuv* which the LXX translated ἀποστρέφω, "turn away," BDAG 122 (not *metanoeō*). Robert N. Wilkin, "Does Your Mind Need Changing? Repentance Reconsidered," *JOTGES* 11, no. 1 (Spring 1998).

103 1 Samuel 15:29; Jeremiah 4:28; 8:6; 18:10; 31:19; Joel 2:13, 14; Amos 7:3, 6; Jonah 3:9, 10; 4:2; Zechariah 8:14; once (in Proverbs 20:25) it's translated *baqar* ("to seek, inquire"). Where the Qal for Hebrew verbs and first person singular indicative forms for Greek verbs are normally cited in this book, the Niphal is given for *nāḥam* because the Qal is not found.

104 James Swanson, *Dictionary of Biblical Languages: Hebrew Old Testament*, 2nd ed. (Seattle: Logos Research Systems, 2001), 688.

105 Genesis 37:35; Ruth 2:13; 1 Chronicles 7:22, etc.

106 Isaiah 57:6; Jeremiah 15:6; 42:10; Jonah 3:10; 4:2; Joel 2:13, 14.

107 In Genesis 6:6, for example, God "is sorry (Heb *nāḥam*) that he made man;" "The Lord changed his mind about the harm which he said he would do" (Exodus 32:14); "The Glory of Israel will not lie or change His mind (*nāḥam*)" (1 Samuel 15:29); "The Lord relented (*nāḥam*) from the calamity" (2 Samuel 24:16); "The Lord saw and was sorry (*nāḥam*) over the calamity" (1 Chronicles 21:15); "The Lord has sworn and will not change his mind (*nāḥam*), 'You are a priest forever after the order of Melchizedek'" (Psalm 110:4). LSJ says, "μετάνοια, ἡ, *change of mind or heart, repentance, regret,*" *1115.*

108 Exodus 32:14; 23:19; Psalm 110:4.

109 Judges 21:6, 15; 1 Chronicles 21:15; Psalms 90:13.

translated by *epistrephō*, "to turn." The notion of admission of guilt and regret fits well with the usages of *metanoeō* in the New Testament where believers also are asked to repent (see discussion below). Therefore, there should be no objection to understanding it to mean the same thing when it is applied to unbelievers.

Do all nonbelievers need to repent in order to be saved? This depends upon two prior assumptions. The first involves what one believes is the intent of the atonement and as a result, the content of the gospel offer. The second concerns what one means by "repent."

Regarding the intent of the atonement, some believe that the universal propitiation mentioned in 1 John 2:2 was intended to actually remove sin as an issue for all unbelievers. The penalty has been paid for all and there can be no additional payment by the sinner. Thus, it might be argued that an admission of guilt, that is, "repentance," is not necessary as a condition for final entrance to heaven because the penalty for sin has already been paid, and guilt is no longer an issue.[110]

The interpretation of the universal atonement passages has been a subject of discussion for centuries and honorable men have come to different conclusions. Consider Paul's statement,

> *So then as through one transgression there resulted condemnation to all men, even so through one act of righteousness there resulted justification of life to all men (Romans 5:18).*

In his discussion of this verse, Augustine argued that while the atonement is available for all, it is applicable only to those who are justified by faith in Christ. In other words, it is sufficient for all but efficient only for those who believe,[111] which is the present writer's view. In regard to 2 Corinthians 5:19 where Paul says, "*God was in Christ reconciling the world to himself*," Charles Ryrie says,

> *God's provision of reconciliation is universal. Because of the death of Christ the position of the world was changed—people were now able to be saved. But that alone saves no one, for the ministry of reconciliation must be faithfully discharged by proclaiming the Gospel message. When an individual believes, then he receives the reconciliation God provided in Christ's death (2 Cor. 5:18–21). The world has been reconciled, but people need to be reconciled. The universal reconciliation changes the position of the world from an unsalvable condition to a salvable one. Individual reconciliation through faith actually brings that reconciliation in the individual's life and changes the position of the individual from unsaved to saved.* ***Then, and only then, are his sins forgiven, though they were paid for on the cross.***[112]

If Augustine and Ryrie are correct in their belief that the intent of the atonement was to render men salvable but did not procure forgiveness until they individually accepted the reconciliation, a different situation exists regarding what must be believed in order to

---

110 I will discuss these issues in more detail in chapter 59 below.

111 He says, "The term '*all*' is therefore used in a way which shows that no one can be supposed able to be saved by any other means than through Christ Himself. For if in a city there be appointed but one instructor, we are most correct in saying: That man teaches all in that place; not meaning, indeed, that all who live in the city take lessons of him, but that no one is instructed unless taught by him. In like manner no one is justified unless Christ has justified him." Augustine, "A Treatise on Nature and Grace: Chapter 48 - How the Term 'All' Is to Be Understood," in *Nicene and Post Nicene Fathers First Series Volume V: Saint Agustin: Anti-Pelagian Writings*, ed. Philip Schaff (New York: Christian Literature Company, 1887), 138.

112 Ryrie, *Basic Theology*, 338. (emphasis mine)

be saved. If the nonbeliever is unforgiven and still in his sins, he must therefore come to Christ believing he needs a savior from the penalty of sin. If so, then one must *admit* that he needs a savior from sin, that is, repent as a precursor to saving faith. Thus, the intent and extent of the atonement is a critical prior assumption.

Secondly, if by "repent" one means "to turn from all known sin, desist from it, and submit to the Lordship of Christ," this has little basis in how the words *metanoia* and *metanoeō* are used in the Old or New Testaments. But if one understands these words as an admission of guilt and regret for sin, then of course repentance is a necessary preparatory condition of personal salvation (for clarification see discussion below under "A Preparatory Stage Leading to Saving Faith"). However, this is far different from Behm's concept of repentance, which he says means to turn from all known sins.

There are 56 references to repent and repentance in the New Testament (34 to *metanoeō*, "to repent"; and 22 occurrences of *metanoia*, "repentance"). A study of these references yields three ways in which repentance was used in the New Testament, and none of them refers to faith in Christ for individual salvation.

Repentance of the Nation

The older commentaries and Bible dictionaries are almost unanimous in saying that repentance is part of conversion, understanding Jesus' primary message to be how a person can be converted and go to heaven when he dies.[113] We must ask, "What was new about that?" Personal forgiveness was available through the Mosaic sacrificial system in that it pointed them in faith to the Messiah of Isaiah 53. What is wrong with asking sinners to mend their ways? If that is all that Jesus meant, it seems that the leaders (who were preoccupied with sin and purity) would have heralded Him as a national hero. To start asking *the nation* to repent (to admit they were wrong and want to do something about it), however, is another matter and was bound to raise the ire of the religious leaders. While repentance in the Gospels certainly has a personal moral aspect, N. T. Wright has noted that the primary focus of Jesus' calls to repentance is addressed to the nation, not individuals. That repentance was followed by bringing forth the fruit of repentance is what the nation was to do if they were to escape national catastrophe. Such occurred in AD 70 because they refused to do either.[114] If they would respond properly, the diaspora would end and the kingdom would be restored to Israel.[115]

These calls to the nation to admit their error and bring forth fruit are frequent. Solomon warned the nation against falling away from Yahweh but assured them that if they say, "*We have sinned and have committed iniquity, we have acted wickedly, if they return (Heb shuv, LXX epistrephō) to Thee with all their heart and with all their soul in the land of their enemies who have taken them captive* ..." (1 Kings 8:47–48). In other words, if they admit they are wrong (repent) and then bring forth the fruit of repentance, then God would hear their prayer and they will be forgiven (1 Kings 8:47-50). To admit wrongdoing is to repent, and to turn from it is to "bring forth the fruit of repentance." Solomon had in view a national repentance and a national forgiveness of sins. If the nation heeded these

113 Johannes Behm, "*metanoia*," in TDNT, 4:975.

114 N. T. Wright, *Jesus and the Victory of God* (Minneapolis: Fortress Press, 1996), 246-58.

115 See Matthew 3:2, 8, 11; 4:17; 11:20, 21; 12:41; Mark 1:4, 15; 6:12; Luke 3:3; 5:32; 10:13; 11:32; 13:3, 5; 16:30; Acts 2:38; 3:19; 5:31; 13:24; Romans 2:4; 2 Peter 3:9.

calls, they would escape temporal judgment and would be gathered to the land and receive national forgiveness and cleansing.

Another example of national repentance is the repentance of Nineveh, recorded in Jonah 3:4-10. Jonah arrived and warned the Ninevites of certain judgment if they did not repent. The Ninevites "believed God," and "turned [Heb *shuv*] from their evil ways" (Jonah 3:10). As a result, God "relented" (Heb *nāḥam,* "changed His mind") and "did not bring upon them the destruction he had threatened." Here was a national repentance in which the nation admitted they were wrong and then brought forth the fruits of repentance. As a result they were saved from a national calamity. The citizens of Nineveh did not escape the judgment of eternal separation from God, but the nation escaped temporal devastation.[116]

These prophetic calls echo those of John the Baptist to the nation and do not refer to individual conversion in order to go to heaven when one dies. Repentance, according to N. T. Wright, is what Israel must do if her exile is to come to an end.[117] Deuteronomy spoke of Israel returning to Yahweh with her whole heart, and that this would be a condition for forgiveness and a return from exile (Deuteronomy 30:2, 8). Thus when Jesus said, "*Repent, for the kingdom of heaven is at hand*" (Matthew 3:2), He was calling the nation to repent and receive national forgiveness. "*The axe,*" said John, "*is already laid to the root of the tree*" (Matthew 3:10). If the nation repented (admitted they were wrong) and then brought forth the fruits of repentance (changed the behavior), they could avoid the "wrath to come." If repentance led to a change of national behavior, bearing good fruit, they would not "be cut down and thrown in the fire" (Matthew 3:10).[118] Luke connects this "wrath" with the temporal wrath that the Roman armies would bring on the nation unless they changed their ways (Luke 21:23). Israel must cease from seeking revenge on Rome and instead by humility it must have a spirit of reconciliation and become a spiritual and moral guide to the Gentile world.[119]

THE EXILE HAD NOT YET ENDED

N. T. Wright has made it abundantly clear that repentance as a condition of personal salvation is probably the last thing they would have associated with John's and Jesus'

---

116 When we come to the New Testament, we would propose that Jesus and John were echoing the calls of Isaiah for a national repentance if they were to be "saved from temporal devastation," "For thus the Lord GOD, the Holy One of Israel, has said, 'In repentance and rest you will be saved, in quietness and trust is your strength' But you were not willing" (Isaiah 30:15). If Judah would repent, they would be saved from the coming Assyrian invasion. Similarly in Jesus' time, if the nation would repent they would be saved from the Roman invasion looming ominously on the horizon. Montefiore calls this "prophetic" repentance. C. G. Montefiore, "Rabbinic Conceptions of Repentance," *Jewish Quarterly Review* 16, no. 2 (January 1904): 209-57.

117 Wright, *Jesus and the Victory of God*, 248. (Deuteronomy 30:2,8). The prophets repeatedly spoke of this return from exile: Isaiah 44:22; 45:22; 55:7; Jeremiah 3:10, 12, 14, 22; 4:1, 5:3; 15:19; 18; Ezekiel 14:6; Hosea 3:5, 6; 6:1; 7:10; Joel 2:12; Haggai 2:17; Zechariah 1:3-6; 10:9-10. See also N. T. Wright, *The New Testament and the People of God: Christian Origins and the Question of God*, reprint, SPCK ed. (London: Society for Promoting Christian Knowledge, 1992), 272-78.

118 The judgment of "unquenchable fire" (Matthew 3:12) need not be equated with eternal damnation. Fire is a common symbol in the Bible for God's wrath in time, not eternity. For example it is used this way in Amos 1:4, 7, 10, 12, 14; 2:2, 5. See also Isaiah 9:10; Jeremiah 21:12-14; 22:6-7; 48:45; Ezekiel 15:1-8; Hosea 8:14; Nahum 1:6; Zephaniah 1:18. An unquenchable fire is a metaphor for a "terrible" fire. The forgiveness of sins was a virtual equivalent for "return from exile."

119 Cecil John Cadoux, *The Historic Mission of Jesus: A Constructive Re-examination of the Eschatological Teaching in the Synoptic Gospels* (New York: Harper, 1943), 163.

invitations.[120] Even though they were back in the land, they believed that the exile had not ended. The high priest, Caiaphas, acknowledged that even though many Jews still lived in the land, the people were not united as one people. "*The children of God*," He said, "*are scattered abroad* [*diaskorpizō*][121]" (John 11:52). The verb *diaskorpizō* was commonly used in the Septuagint for the scattering of Israel.[122] "This perception of Israel's present condition was shared by writers across the board in second-temple Judaism."[123]

Instone-Brewer cites numerous examples confirming Wright's thesis from Jewish literature in the era of the New Testament. For example, Blessing #5 of the so-called "Eighteen Benedictions" reads, "*Cause us to repent, Lord, to you, and we will repent. Renew our days as at the start. Blessed are you Lord, who desires repentance*."[124] This is a prayer for a renewal of the nation to former glory conditioned on national repentance.[125] Benediction #6 says, "*Forgive us our Father, for we have sinned against you. Blot out and remove our transgressions*." Individuals were expected to pray these prayers three times a day, and possibly Jesus prayed the "Eighteen" following this pattern. These citations substantiate that even though the Jews lived in the land, they still viewed themselves as in exile. They understood that to end this exile they had to repent as a nation and receive national forgiveness.

An early pseudepigraphical work dated AD 7-30 speaks of consummation at the end of the age as a day of national repentance.[126] Charles summarizes this commonly held belief, "A great national repentance was to usher in the new kingdom of God, and was a necessary condition of its coming."[127] In fact the New Testament presents the coming of

---

120 Wright, *The New Testament and the People of God: Christian Origins and the Question of God*, 268-69.

121 Louw-Nida, 1:199, This verb means to "cause a group or gathering to disperse or scatter, with possible emphasis on the distributive nature of the scattering (that is to say, each going in a different direction)."

122 Deuteronomy 30:3; Jeremiah 9:15; 10:21; 24:9; Ezekiel 5:10; 6:8; 22:15; 28:25; Zechariah 11:6.

123 Wright, *The New Testament and the People of God: Christian Origins and the Question of God*, 269. Tobit 14:5-7, for example, describes the nation as still in exile long after the return under Ezra and Nehemiah and looks for a time when "they all will return from their exile." Similarly, Baruch 3:6-8 says, "For you have put the fear of you in our hearts so that we would call upon your name; and we will praise you in our exile, for we have put away from our hearts all the iniquity of our ancestors who sinned against you. See, we are today in our exile where you have scattered us, to be reproached and cursed and punished for all the iniquities of our ancestors, who forsook the Lord our God."

124 Tractate: Berakhot: Blessings, quoted by David Instone-Brewer, *Traditions of the Rabbis from the Era of the New Testament: Vol. 1, Prayer and Agriculture* (Grand Rapids: Wm. B. Eerdmans Publishing Co., 2004), 1:98. These "tractates" are part of the Mishnah, which was compiled around AD 200. They contain, however, some citations that are believed to be pre-AD 70.

125 The prayers continue in Blessing #10 for "the gathering of the redeemed [exiles]. Blessed are you Lord who gathers the expelled of the people of Israel" (ibid., 1:99; ibid.) And then in Blessing #11 they pray, "Restore our judges as in former times, and our counselors as in the beginning; and reign over us" (ibid). The eschatology in these prayers, according to Instone-Brewer, dates from before the destruction of the temple in AD 70. It is concerned with the continuing ingathering of Israel (Blessing #10), and the restoration of Jewish self-rule (Blessing #11).

126 *The Assumption of Moses*, 1.18.

127 Robert Henry Charles, *Commentary on the Pseudepigrapha of the Old Testament*, 2 vols. (Bellingham, WA: Logos Research Systems, 1913, 2004), 2:415. Charles quotes a number of sources from Jewish literature. "'If Israel practices repentance, it will be redeemed; if not, it will not be redeemed,' Sanh. 97b. 'Israel will not fulfill the great repentance before Elijah comes,' Pirke R. Eliezer, 43; cf. Malachi 4:6, and Luke 1:16, 17; Matt. 17:10–12. 'If all Israel together repented for a single day, redemption through the Messiah would follow,' Pesikta 163b." See also Jubilees 1:15, "And after this they will turn to Me from amongst the Gentiles with all their heart and with all their soul and with all their strength, and I will gather them from amongst all the Gentiles." Daniel 9:4-19 presents the idea of a national repentance as a condition of restoration.

the kingdom, the restoration from exile, the restoration of the Davidic theocracy, and the millennium as contingent on Israel's national repentance.[128]

FORGIVENESS OF SINS EQUALS RESTORATION FROM EXILE

What concerned the people of Israel was how and when God would move to reverse this state of national exile. "If Israel's God was to deliver his people from exile, it could only be because he had somehow dealt with the problem which has caused her to go there in the first place, namely, her sin."[129] Exile could end only when the nation's sin was forgiven (see 1 Kings 8:34). "If sin has caused her exile, her forgiveness will mean her national re-establishment." Wright continues, "This needs to be emphasized in the strongest possible terms, *the most natural meaning of the phrase 'the forgiveness of sins' to a first-century Jew is not in the first instance the remission of individual sins, but the putting away of the whole nation's sins.* This is the major, national context within which all individual dealing-with-sin must be understood."[130] Their minds were filled with the words of the Old Testament prophets announcing the future day when the nation would return to the land and their exile would be reversed.

For example in 520 BC the prophet Zechariah delivered this word from Yahweh to the exiled people of God,

> *Therefore say to them, "Thus says the LORD of hosts, 'Return [Heb shuv] to Me,' declares the LORD of hosts, 'that I may return to you,' says the LORD of hosts" (Zechariah 1:3).*

He was calling on the nation to admit their sin and turn from it. Turning from sin does not equal repentance; instead it is the fruit of repentance. If they would admit their wrongdoing and turn from it, God would return to them and the exile would end. When John and Jesus said, "*Repent, the kingdom of heaven is at hand,*" they were echoing these thoughts from the Old Testament prophets. However, in order for the nation's exile to end and the Davidic theocracy to be restored, something more than repentance, admission of guilt, was needed, they must also "*bring forth fruit in keeping with repentance*" (Matthew 3:8). They must "bear good fruit," not just repent (3:10). Acknowledging that they were wrong and regretting it (repentance) it is one thing, but bringing forth the fruit of repentance (turning from sin) is another. Repentance and "turning from sin" are two different things. Throughout the New Testament, fruit is the only observable test of true admission of guilt and regret (Matthew 7:16; Luke 6:43; Ephesians 5:9). Merely admitting one's need and guilt is not enough. It must be followed by faith in Christ. Their failure to do this and produce fruit indicating they had done it resulted in the removal of the kingdom of God from that generation. "*Therefore I say to you, the kingdom of God will be taken away from you and given to a people, producing the fruit of it*" (Matthew 21:43).

The calls to bring forth the fruit of repentance in the Old Testament are the same as the exhortations "to turn" (Heb *shuv*). They were calls to the nation to return to covenant loyalty, not calls to individuals to obtain eternal salvation. The touchstone of all the prophetic calls is found in Moses' warning to the nation as they prepared to enter the promised land. In Deuteronomy 4 he warned them that if they slipped into idolatry they needed to know

---

128 For an excellent development of this theme see Stanley D. Toussaint and Jay A. Quine, "No, Not Yet: The Contingency of God's Promised Kingdom," *BibSac* 164, no. 654 (April-June 2007): 131-47.

129 Wright, *The New Testament and the People of God: Christian Origins and the Question of God*, 273.

130 Ibid., 273.

that God is a "consuming fire" and that He will bring temporal punishment on the nation. Nevertheless, He would not "forget the covenant ... which He swore to" their fathers (Deuteronomy 4:15, 23, 26-27). The punishment for national sin was national exile.

Hosea called to the nation, "*Return* [Heb *shuv*], *O Israel, to the LORD your God. Your sins have been your downfall!*" (Hosea 14:1). A national forgiveness of sins, to "take away all iniquity," is associated with this prophetic call to turn from their sinful ways.[131] It was sin that sent them into exile. Only the forgiveness of sins can reverse it. Similarly, Jeremiah cried to the fallen nation,

> ***And I will restore the fortunes of Judah and the fortunes of Israel*** *and will rebuild them as they were at first. I will cleanse them from all their iniquity by which they have sinned against Me, and* ***I will pardon all their iniquities*** *by which they have sinned against Me and by which they have transgressed against Me (Jeremiah 33:7-8).*

Restoration and national forgiveness are closely linked.

> *The punishment of your iniquity has been completed, O daughter of Zion;* ***He will exile you no longer****. But He will punish your iniquity, O daughter of Edom; He will expose your sins! (Lamentations 4:22).*

Isaiah also cried out,

> *This is what the Sovereign LORD, the Holy One of Israel, says: "In repentance* [Heb *shuv;* LXX, *apostrephō*] *and rest is your salvation, in quietness and trust is your strength, but you would have none of it" (Isaiah 30:15).*[132]

For Isaiah, "salvation" was deliverance from the Assyrians, for John the Baptist it was from Roman wrath. The NIV should have translated "in turning" and not "in repentance"; the word in Hebrew is *shuv* ("to turn"), not *nāḥam* ("to repent"). They must not only admit their guilt (repent); they must also act on it by turning from it! The calls for national turning from sin are frequent. Hear Malachi and Ezekiel:

> *"From the days of your fathers you have turned aside from My statutes and have not kept them. Return* [Heb *shuv*, "to turn"] *to Me, and I will return to you," says the LORD of hosts. "But you say, 'How shall we return?'" (Malachi 3:7).*
> *For I will take you from the nations, gather you from all the lands and bring you into your own land. Then I will sprinkle clean water on you, and you will be clean; I will cleanse you from all your filthiness and from all your idols. Moreover, I will give you a new heart and put a new spirit within you; and I will remove the heart of stone from your flesh and give you a heart of flesh.... Thus says the Lord GOD, "On the day that I cleanse you from all your iniquities, I will cause the cities to be inhabited, and the waste places will be rebuilt" (Ezekiel 36:24-26, 33).*

These verses present the close connection between returning from exile and cleansing from sin.

131 "It should be noted that in a number of places *shuv* means 'to return from exile'" (see "*shuv*" in TWOT, 909). "In the Qal: naturally in Ezr and Neh (Ezr 2:1; Neh 7:6); also Isa 10:22; Jer 22:10; Zech 10:9), *inter alia*; in the Hiphil: I Kgs 8:34; Jer 12:15, *inter alia*. The association between the ideas of a return from exile and a return to the covenant should be obvious. A return from exile was reclamation as much as a return from any form of sin. That God should permit either return is corroborative of his covenantal faithfulness" (ibid).

132 The NASB translated *apostrephō*, "to turn away," by the word "repentance," but the word *nāḥam* is not in the Hebrew.

Consider in this regard Luke 3:3, "*And he came into all the district around the Jordan, preaching a baptism of repentance for* [Gr *eis*, "toward"] the forgiveness of sins." With this statement, Jesus echoes the "prophetic forgiveness" promised to the nation if they would repent, that is, if they would admit their error, desire to change their behavior (Gr *metanoeō*), and then make plans to rectify the situation (Gr *epistrephō*). Such repentance would lead to a return from exile and escape from temporal national catastrophe. Certainly, a personal dimension was involved. As individuals repented they joined the believing remnant, which Jesus was calling out.[133]

After saying that John came offering a baptism of repentance for the forgiveness of sins (Luke 3:4-6), John cites Isaiah 40:3-5. That passage speaks of Israel's return from captivity to see the salvation of God, that is, the restored Davidic theocracy. He announced a national repentance and a national return from exile.[134] This return is what is meant by "forgiveness of sins."

When Peter addressed the Sanhedrin, he made the same point. "*He is the one whom God exalted to His right hand as a Prince and a Savior, to grant repentance to Israel, and forgiveness of sins*" (Acts 5:31). The call to repentance is addressed to the nation and the outcome is "forgiveness of sins," return from exile, and the reestablishment of the Davidic theocracy (Acts 1:6; 3:19-21). The application to individuals of this national call to repentance demanded by John and Jesus was one of individual preparation which could lead to faith in Christ and thus baptism by the Holy Spirit. However, it was directly a call to the nation, an offer of the kingdom.[135]

Consider Luke 24:47: "*that repentance and remission of sins should be preached in His name to all nations, beginning at Jerusalem*" (NKJV).

As Luke demonstrated in the book of Acts, the kingdom embraces the Gentiles as well as Israel, and this announcement to the Gentiles of the eschatological coming of the kingdom, that is, "the forgiveness of sins," serves as a precursor to Acts (volume 2 of Luke's two-volume work).[136] "Repentance for forgiveness of sins" refers to the "true and final"[137] forgiveness of sins, future establishment of the kingdom of God, the messianic salvation, and the ultimate return from exile (cf. Romans 11:26-27). Paul wrote,

---

133 For good discussion of national repentance see David R. Anderson, "The National Repentance of Israel," *JOTGES* 11, no. 2 (Autumn 1998): 24-25.

134 The references to clearing the way are "usually taken in Isaiah to refer to God's going before his exiles and allowing them to return to the land following the Babylonian captivity" (Darrell L. Bock, *Luke 9:51-24:53*, Baker Exegetical Commentary on the New Testament (Grand Rapids: Baker Book House, 1996), 291.

135 National forgiveness would come to the nation when the nation repented, that is, by admitting their guilt and accepting the offer of the kingdom. (Personal forgiveness comes to any individual who believes on Christ.) This national forgiveness is called "redemption" (Luke 1:68), "salvation from our enemies and... all who hate us" (v. 71) and deliverance from the hand of our enemies (v. 74). All these terms speak of national salvation, redemption, deliverance and forgiveness, i. e., messianic salvation.

136 That this message of the future establishment of the kingdom to Israel should be preached to "all nations" represents the broadening of the promise as originally anticipated in the Abrahamic covenant (Genesis 12:1-3) that the world would be blessed through him. This promise is repeated by Luke saying God would "remember His holy covenant" (Luke 1:72); bring "salvation" (deliverance from Israel's enemies, v. 74); restoration to the land and establishment of the Davidic theocracy, by the "forgiveness of sins" (v. 77) (the national forgiveness granted to the believing remnant), and that the Gentiles would be included in these blessings (v. 32). This version of the Great Commission therefore announces the fulfillment of human destiny when the rule of God is finally implemented through Christ at His second coming.

137 See Wright, *Jesus and the Victory of God*, 272-73.

> *And so all Israel will be saved; just as it is written, "The deliverer will come from Zion, he will remove ungodliness from Jacob. And this is my covenant with them,* ***when I take away their sins."***

Here Paul wrote of the sins of the nation being removed, as predicted in scores of Old Testament prophecies.

Luke picked up this theme in Acts 1:6:

> *So when they had come together, they were asking Him, saying, "Lord, is it at this time You are* ***restoring the kingdom to Israel?"***

And again in Acts 3:19-21:

> *Therefore* ***repent*** *and return,* ***that your sins may be wiped away****, in order that* ***times of refreshing may come*** *from the presence of the Lord; and that He may send Jesus, the Christ appointed for you, whom heaven must receive until* ***the period of restoration of all things*** *about which God spoke by the mouth of His holy prophets from ancient time.*

The "times of refreshing" and "the restoration of all things" refer to the prophetic promises of the restoration of the Davidic theocracy as in Acts 1:6.[138] This ultimate return from exile will not be achieved unless a generation of Israel repents so that *their sins may be wiped away* and their final restoration secured. This is the message John the Baptist announced when he came preaching "a baptism of repentance for the forgiveness of sins" (Luke 3:3).

Judgment in this sense was temporal and national as well as individual, but neither eternal nor soteriological. This is evident from passages like Luke 13:5[139] and Matthew 12:41.

Many New Testament passages fall into this category.[140] When Jesus said, "*I have not come to call the righteous but sinners to repentance*" (Luke 5:32), He was speaking of His invitation to all to participate in the great national repentance and restoration from exile.

REPENTANCE IN ACTS 2:38

One New Testament reference to repentance deserves more discussion. In response to his sermon about Christ and how the nation had crucified their Messiah, they said, "What shall we do?" Peter told the nation to repent and acknowledge Jesus as the Christ.

---

138 Although some have interpreted the "times of refreshing" as being fulfilled in the present age as spiritual blessings, Toussaint and Quine convincingly argue that this refers to the establishment of the future kingdom, the final return from exile. "Peter is saying that if Israel repented, the Messiah would come and the kingdom would arrive." (Toussaint and Quine, "No, Not Yet: The Contingency of God's Promised Kingdom," 141-45.

139 Jesus stressed that those who do not repent will be killed by Roman soldiers and crushed by falling stones (Luke 13:5). Repentance, Wright says, "is not, then, simply the individual moral turning from private sin" (Wright, *Jesus and the Victory of God*, 253). Jesus was saying that violent rebel activity against Rome must be repented of, and He was thus connecting this kind of repentance of the nation with the hope of their escaping the judgment of AD 70. He was telling the nation to give up their way of responding to Rome and pursuing national and political aims and to trust Him instead. This repentance will result in the nation being brought back from exile and the remnant being established. See Wright, *Jesus and the Victory of God*, 254.

140 Matthew 3:2, 8, 11; 4:17; 11:20-21; 12:41; Mark 1:4, 5; Luke 3:3; 10:13; 11:32; 13:3; 16:30; 24:47; Acts 2:38 (see Wright, *Jesus and the Victory of God*, 273, for discussion); 3:19 ("times of refreshing" means the restoration of the kingdom as in 1:6); Acts 5:31; 13:24.

Repent, and each of you be baptized in the name of Jesus Christ for the forgiveness of your sins; and you will receive the gift of the Holy Spirit (Acts 2:38).

Peter gave two conditions, repent, that is, admit their guilt (which they were prepared to do, v. 37) and be baptized, which in turn would secure two results, the forgiveness of sins and the gift of the Holy Spirit. This is a repetition of John's call to the nation to repent which would lead to forgiveness of sins, that is, restoration from exile and messianic salvation (Acts 3:19). When followed by baptism, they would receive the gift of the Holy Spirit, the outpouring of which Joel spoke (see discussion below). Thus, if the nation repented, they would experience national forgiveness and return from exile.[141]

But what about the promise that they would receive the gift of the Holy Spirit on the condition of baptism? While this is likely a reference to the outpouring of the Spirit on the nation it applies to the regeneration of individuals as well. Neither Peter nor any first-century Jew would have separated baptism from faith. Baptism was not necessary for salvation; faith alone was. But if you were to ask a first-century Jew who had trusted in Christ as Messiah, "Are you a believer in Christ," he would say, "Oh, yes, I have been baptized." We know, however, that he would not have understood baptism to be the saving condition. He would have thought that baptism and faith were two ways of saying the same thing. But if you pressed him and asked, "If you were not baptized in water does that mean you did not receive the gift of the Holy Spirit?," he would say, "Well, no, it was faith alone in Christ alone that resulted in my receiving the gift of the Holy Spirit." How do we know that he would have said (or thought) like this? We know it because Peter said in Acts 10:47, "*Surely no one can refuse the water for these to be baptized who have received the Holy Spirit just as we did, can he*?" The house of Cornelius *had already received* the Holy Spirit and *then* they were baptized. Furthermore, when the Philippian jailer asked, "*What must I do to be saved?*" Paul did not mention baptism. He said, "*Believe in the Lord Jesus, and you will be saved*" (Acts 16:31). Then, later on, he and his household were baptized (v. 33).

Personal and national forgiveness were related.[142] For centuries it has been customary to think of "forgiveness of sins" is mainly a gift to individual sinners. While that is certainly true, and is clearly involved in Acts 2:38, for "men of Israel" (Acts 2:14, 22), as discussed above, the "forgiveness of sins" was another way of saying, "return from exile" (cf. Lamentations 4:22). Furthermore, it is clear from Peter's address to his brethren in Acts 3:19 that is precisely what he had in mind in Acts 2:38. National repentance would lead to national restoration and the "times of refreshing." This longing for deliverance from the rule of Rome, restoration of the Temple, and the final national forgiveness of sins, that is, return from exile, was the broader context of Peter's message. This was a call for national repentance in order to escape national catastrophe (Luke 19:41-44; Matthew 3:10-12; 24:1-2).

A Call to Restoration to Fellowship

A second meaning for repentance is applied to believers who need to confess their

141 This interpretation is confirmed in Acts 3:19-20 when Peter made a final offer of national forgiveness and promised that if they repented, "the times of refreshing" and the "restoration of all things about which God spoke by the mouth of His holy prophets" would occur (Acts 3:19-21).

142 Karl Ludwig Schmidt, "*basileus*," TDNT, 1:586, "It is the community which stands under the promise; the individual attains to salvation as its member."

sins or are challenged to follow Christ as His disciples. Many occurrences of *metanoia* and *metanoeō* fit in this category.[143] When we sin and desire to be restored to fellowship, we must confess our sins (1 John 1:9). Repentance in first-century Judaism likewise involved restoration of fellowship with God within the covenant for the person who was already saved.[144]

This was also the thrust of Paul's call to repentance in 2 Corinthians 7:10. "*Godly sorrow brings repentance that leads to salvation.*" The "salvation" in view is not salvation leading to heaven, because he is addressing those who are already saved. Instead it is a deliverance from suffering loss, and positively a restoration of fellowship with God. This godly sorrow was a discipline in time intended by God to lead to salvation from spiritual ruin and to fruitfulness.

> *All discipline for the moment seems not to be joyful, but* ***sorrowful****; yet to those who have been trained by it, afterwards it yields the* ***peaceful fruit of righteousness*** *(Hebrews 12:11).*

This salvation refers to the "peaceful fruit of righteousness," not final entrance into heaven. Many verses speak of the repentance of believers (2 Corinthians 7:9-10; 2 Corinthians 12:21; Revelation 2:5; 3:3).

When Paul said, "*with gentleness correcting those who are in opposition, if perhaps God may grant them repentance leading to the knowledge of the truth*" (2 Timothy 2:25), he was addressing true believers in the congregation who had embraced false teachings about the resurrection. Timothy was to restore them to "the truth" with gentleness. The "truth" in this context was not the gospel (as in 1 Timothy 2:4), but a correct understanding of the doctrine of the resurrection. The noun *metanoia* is best understood here as an admission of guilt, that is, confession (Gr *homologeō*, 1 John 1:9). These genuine believers were to admit they were wrong and were to change their minds about their false understanding of the resurrection.

Clement of Rome applied repentance to Christians. "Desiring, therefore, that *all His beloved* should be partakers of repentance, He has, by His almighty will, established these declarations."[145] While granting the central idea of the passage can "be validly extended, beyond the reference to Christians which it has in Peter," Bauckham nevertheless insists that the theme of the passage is "the idea of the present respite *before the Parousia* as granted for Christians to repent."[146]

Possibly Peter had a similar idea in mind when he wrote, "*The Lord is not slow about His promise, as some count slowness, but is patient toward you, not wishing for any to* ***perish*** *but for all to come to repentance*" (2 Peter 3:9). The only other place where the words "perish" and "repentance" occur together is Luke 13:3, where "perish" refers to physical death and not eternal separation from God.

What does "perish" (Gr *apollumi*) mean? While it is often assumed that the word refers to final damnation, that is not at all clear from the context. Even the reference to

---

143 Luke 15:7, 10; 17:3, 4; Acts 8:22; 2 Corinthians 7:9, 10; 12:21; 2 Tim 2:25; Hebrews 6:1, 6; 12:27; Revelation 2:5, 16, 21, 22; 3:3, 19. For discussion of individual passages see the scripture index.

144 E. P. Sanders, *Paul and Palestinian Judaism* (Minneapolis: Fortress Press, 1977), 178, 79.

145 1 Clement 8:41.

146 Richard Bauckham, *Jude, 2 Peter*, Word Biblical Themes (Dallas: Word Publishers, 1990), 50:314.

perishing in the days of Noah (2 Peter 3:6) says only that they died physically, drowning in the flood. The word often refers to the spiritual ruin of Christians,[147] or of physical death.[148] In some cases it apparently parallels a common Jewish expression which means "to trifle away one's life."[149] In 2 John 8 it means "to lose [Gr *apollumi*] what you have worked for" (i.e., reward).

Peter was saying that it is not God's "wish" (NASB, ESV) that any *of the believers* die before they had opportunity to repent and return to fellowship with God.[150] They needed to admit they were wrong to accept the false teaching they have accepted (i.e., the promise of "freedom" 2 Peter 2:19) and their involvement in the lusts of the world (vv. 18-22).

The unbelieving mockers who were tempting them into false teaching were not being addressed or warned; Peter's believing readers were being warned. These mockers are designated "they" (3:3-7) in contrast to the readers, "you" (vv. 8-9). That believers are being addressed, and not the mockers, is evident from the fact that he called them "beloved" (v. 8). He was warning them that the "day of the Lord" may come unexpectedly ("like a thief," v. 10), and that his readers need to repent before it happens.[151] This unexpected arrival of the day of the Lord correlates well with the pretribulational rapture. This heightens the urgency of Peter's exhortation; the rapture could occur at any moment. The context of 2 Peter 2 and 3 is a warning addressed to Christians who have become entangled and overcome by the lusts of the world so that their last state is worse than their former one, that is, before they were justified (2 Peter 2:20). God's delay in judgment is evidence of His patience, grace, and love. He was giving them time to reconsider their wasted lives. Repentance is best understood as an exhortation to Christians to admit their guilt (change their minds about sin), and agree with God (i.e., confess) about them, thus reestablishing fellowship with God through forgiveness (1 John 1:9).

This concept of repentance leading to a restoration of fellowship with God comes close to the common Reformed notion that repentance is virtually a synonym for sanctification, and that the entire life of the believer is to be one of repentance.[152] Hodge

---

147 Matthew 10:42; 1 Corinthians 8:11.

148 Matthew 2:13; 8:25; 12:14; 22:7; 2 Corinthians 2:9.

149 For example, Matthew 10:39 (see Oepke, "ἀπόλλυμι, ἀπώλεια, ἀπολλύων," in TDNT, 1:394).

150 The Greek word *boulomai* sometimes means "to wish, want, desire."

151 Premillennialists understand the "day of the Lord" to encompass the period beginning with the tribulation and continuing through the millennium to the new heavens and the new earth. During this time (at the end of the millennium) the present earth and heavens will pass away. What relevance then is this to the believers in the first century who would never see that event even if Christ did return in AD 100? Peter's answer is that the reason they should change their ways is because what they are investing their lives in is fleeting; it is temporal and not eternal. He wrote, "*Since all these things are to be destroyed in this way, what sort of people ought you to be in holy conduct and godliness*" (2 Peter 3:11). The issue is not when it occurs, but the fact that what they were investing their lives in is insignificant, transitory, and destined to be burned up. They might die physically or experience total spiritual ruin (i.e., perish) before the judgment comes and they would therefore miss the opportunity to be properly prepared to meet their Master. Like the foolish virgins (Matthew 25:10), it would be too late. As Peter said, "*You therefore, beloved, knowing this beforehand, be on your guard so that you are not carried away by the error of unprincipled men and fall from your own steadfastness*" (2 Peter 3:17).

152 Luther said, "A definite corollary follows from what has been said. If a person's whole life is one of repentance and a cross of Christ, not only in voluntary afflictions but also in temptations of the devil, the world, and the flesh, and more especially also in persecutions and sufferings, as is clear from what has been said previously, and from the whole of Scripture and from examples of the Saint of saints himself and all the martyrs, then

says, "Repentance is a daily experience of the Christian as long as the struggle with sin continues in his heart and life (Psalms 19:12, 13; Luke 9:23; Galatians 6:14; 5:24)."[153] Both Calvin[154] and Luther[155] noted that the entire life of the believer is to be one of repentance.

The parable of the prodigal son illustrates this usage. Here a son is being restored to fellowship with his Father (Luke 15:11-32). He did not become a son after he repented. And in Luke 15, the woman did not gain ownership of the coin after she found it (it was always hers), and the shepherd did not gain a lamb after he found it. The lamb belonged to the shepherd before it was "lost." All three of these parables, as demonstrated elsewhere, refer to believers who were lost and then found.[156] Many other examples could be cited.[157]

When Jesus spoke of the joy in heaven over one "sinner" who repents, He was not speaking of salvation from eternal separation from God, but of restoration to fellowship (Luke 15:7, 10).[158] "Sinner" was the Pharisaic definition of the believing followers (the crowds) of Christ.[159] It was Christ's willingness to have dinner with the "people of the land," the *'am ha'arets*, which resulted in the rebuke from the Pharisees which was the occasion of the parable of the prodigal son.[160]

---

it is evident that the cross continues until death and thereby to entrance into the kingdom" ("Career of the Reformer" in Martin Luther, *Luther's Works*, ed. J. J. Pelikan, H. C. Oswald, and H. T. Lehmann (Philadelphia: Fortress Press, 1968), 31:89.

153 Archibald Alexander Hodge, *A Commentary on the Confession of Faith: with Questions for Theological Students and Bible Classes* (Philadelphia: Presbyterian Board of Publication, 1992; reprint), 15,2.

154 For Calvin, repentance continued throughout the life of the Christian, but it is the fruit of faith, as noted previously. And faith cannot come in Calvin's thinking without regeneration. So after the regenerating work of the Spirit, the gift of faith is implanted in the elect, and out of this faith comes repentance, which was defined as the mortification of the old nature (the flesh) and the quickening of the new nature (the spirit) unto holiness. (Calvin, "Institutes," 3,2,9.)

155 "Explanation of the Ninety-five Theses or Explanation of the Disputation Concerning the Value of Indulgences," in Luther, *Luther's Works*, 31:83.

156 For proof see elsewhere pp. 705. Also, note that Jesus came to seek and to save that which was lost (Lk 19:10-11). While one cannot exclude the possibility that the lost in this passage refer to the eternally damned, in this particular context, blind Bartimaeus is called a "son of Abraham" (v. 10), that is, a true spiritual son of Abraham who was lost in the sense of wandering from his relationship with God. To a large extent, his lostness was a result of the false shepherds (the Pharisees) who had led the sheep astray. There is no evidence here that "lost" means damned. "Lost" (Gr *apollumi*) most often (though not always) refers to what one might call a carnal Christian or one who is "out of fellowship." For discussion of this point see pp. 293 ff.

157 Luke 3:8; 5:32; 15:7; 17:3-4 (between believers), Acts 8:22; 2 Corinthians 7:9,10; 12:21; Revelation 2:5, 16, 21; 3:3, 19.

158 This view of "sinners" of course is not shared by all. E. P. Sanders rejects it, E. P. Sanders, *Jesus and Judaism* (Philadelphia: Fortress Press, 1985), 175-211; Sanders, *Paul and Palestinian Judaism*. Karl Heinrich Rengstdorf, TDNT, 1:327 notes that the word "sinners" can refer to the wicked, that is, nonbelievers (the view he prefers in Luke 15:1), or to one who does not subject himself to Pharisaic ordinances. We prefer the latter in this context because the parables are specifically against the Pharisees (15:2). See Wright, *Jesus and the Victory of God*, 264-68. "'Sinners' may carry the more technical sense of those whose lack of observance of legal regulations placed them outside the 'pure' company which Pharisees kept (Mann here translates 'nonobservant Jews'), but the term is probably used in a more general sense, with the focus at least as much on moral as on ritual offence." See R. T. France, *The Gospel of Mark: A Commentary on the Greek Text* (Grand Rapids: Wm. B. Eerdmans Publishing Co., 2002), 132.

159 The crowds in the synoptics are, for the most part, believing followers of Christ. Most of Christ's disciples came from the *am ha'arets*, "the people of the land." See pp. 271 ff. for discussion of the believing nature of the crowds.

160 A "sinner" was not a non-Christian but rather one of the *am ha'arets*. They were sinners in the Pharisaic sense of those who did not keep the legalistic minutiae of Pharisaic regulations. Moore says that the *am ha'arets*

John addressed the church at Ephesus with these words:

*Therefore remember from where you have fallen, and repent and do the deeds you did at first; or else I am coming to you and will remove your lampstand out of its place—**unless you repent** (Revelation 2:5).*

These were true believers who had had good works and had persevered under trial (Revelation 2:2-5). However, they had fallen from their initial love for Christ and had become carnal (v. 4). They were called on to "repent," that is, to confess their sin and do the deeds they did when they were initially born again. Repentance here manifestly would result in a restoration of the believer to his personal walk with Christ, not escape from eternal separation from God.

A Preparatory Stage Leading to Saving Faith

A third usage of "repentance" is to admit that one has sinned and to have a sense of regret about it as a necessary precursor to saving faith. This preparatory stage prior to saving faith involves an admission of guilt and one's need for a savior (Matthew 12:41).[161] When Jesus and John challenged the nation to repent, this may have involved a preparatory stage toward accepting Jesus as the Messiah. But a person or a nation can repent forever and never be saved. Only faith in Christ can save an individual from damnation or a nation from temporal catastrophe.

REPENTANCE IS A NECESSARY PRECURSOR TO SAVING FAITH

John Wesley used to say that repentance was the porch of religion, faith was the door, and holiness was the religion itself.[162] We agree, repentance can lead to it; it is the "porch." Acts 11:18, for example, states that a repentance "*leads to* life." But as the rest of the New Testament proclaims, only faith alone gets one through the door.

When they heard this, they quieted down and glorified God, saying, "Well then, God has granted to the Gentiles also the repentance **that leads to** [Gr, *eis*, "to, toward"] *life" (Acts 11:18).*[163]

were the "common people." The term was often used to describe the masses in contrast to the scholars. The common man was one who was ignorant of the duties of his religion. The educated class looked down on them, viewing them as rude, ill-bred, and dirty. An educated man would never marry a woman of this class. Those in view in the parable of the prodigal son are the Pharisees and the *am ha'arets*. A Pharisee would not travel with one of these "sinners" nor would he ever have dinner at his table. George F. Moore, "The Am-ha-arets (the people of the land) and the Haberim (Associates)," in F. J. Foakes-Jackson et al., *The Beginnings of Christianity : The Acts of the Apostles*, 5 vols. (Grand Rapids: Baker Book House, 1979), 1:440 ff. Everything related to the *am ha'arets* was considered ceremonially unclean, and the term "sinners" meant people who were ceremonially unclean and not the "unsaved."

161 Some Scriptures fitting this category are Acts 11:18; 19:4; 17:30; 20:21; 26:20.

162 Letter to Thomas Church, "Principles of a Methodist Farther Explained VI" in John Wesley, *The Works of John Wesley: Addresses, Essays, and Letters* (Albany, OR: Ages Software, 2000). Wesley, however, believes that the porch, the door, and holiness itself must all be always present, or the faith is not genuine. By repentance Wesley means a conviction of sin and fear of damnation.

163 Like the Law, repentance is a tutor which "leads us to (*eis*, 'toward') Christ" (Galatians 3:24).

This grant of repentance may refer to the realization that Gentiles could be saved apart from the Mosaic Law and the necessity of first becoming Jews. While "life" may refer to abundant life, I see no problem with the common conclusion that it refers to regeneration. Repentance, admission of guilt, "leads" to eternal life.

Paul told the sneering philosophers that God is calling all men to "repent" (Acts 17:30). By "repent" he meant admit they are wrong about their false ideas of God, their guilt before Him, and need for forgiveness. We are then told that "some believed" (v. 34), indicating that faith can follow repentance, but that faith and repentance are separate things. The concept of repentance as leading to salvation, but not causing it, is found in numerous passages of the New Testament.[164]

If one defines repentance as an admission of guilt, repentance is clearly necessary for salvation. If one defines repentance as turning from every known sin and submitting to the Lordship of Christ, it is not. The former reflects an attitude associated with the recognition of one's need for a savior from sin. The latter is an action, a work. The former is a result of the fact that God convicts the world of sin and individuals in particular (John 16:8-11). If a purpose of the Law is to reveal our sin (Romans 3:19-20), is it not necessary that we admit what God has revealed?! If one of the ministries of the Holy Spirit is to convict us of our sin, is it not necessary to admit that of which the Holy Spirit has convicted us, that is, repent?

Another illustration of this usage is the case of Cornelius. He was a God-fearer, that is, one who was aware that sin was wrong and that he needed God (Acts 10:2). However, he was not "saved" until later (11:14). Repentance moved him in the direction of salvation but did not save him.[165] One might argue that genuine repentance *always* leads to faith, but I know of no biblical evidence that substantiates this.

In his speech to the Ephesian elders, Paul summed up his ministry by saying, "*solemnly testifying to both Jews and Greeks of repentance toward God and faith in our Lord Jesus Christ*" (Acts 20:21). The word "toward" indicates that repentance can lead one to God, and it may (or may not) be followed by faith in Christ. This echoes the sequence in Hebrews 6:1: first, repentance from dead works, then faith toward God, then instruction.

Repentance and faith are different things. Repentance can lead to faith, but it does not always do so. Conversely, a refusal to acknowledge one's sin and having no desire to turn from it (regret), blocks the path toward faith and acceptance of God's free offer by faith.

In cases where the call to repentance is addressed to unbelievers we must ask, "What does it mean?" and "What is the effect of this repentance?" It is commonly asserted that the meaning of the term when addressed to unbelievers is to turn from all known sin and submit to the Lordship of Christ; it is the "flip side of faith."[166] Yet turning from sin, according to John the Baptist, is the "fruit in keeping with repentance" and does not

---

164 For a good discussion of repentance by one who holds views similar to this writer's see Dave Anderson, "Repentance is for all Men," *Journal of the Grace Evangelical Theological Society* 11, no. 1 (Spring 98): 11-12. Or as Zane Hodges put it, "it is a call to the people of all nations to find harmony with God through Jesus Christ" (Zane C. Hodges, *Harmony with God: A Fresh Look at Repentance* (Dallas, TX: Redención Viva, 2001), 78. In Acts 20:21 repentance and faith are clearly separate issues.

165 See Hodges, *Harmony*, 81.

166 Millard Erickson, for example, assumes without discussion that this verse proves that repentance (in the sense of turning from sin) is part of the gospel message. Millard J. Erickson, *Christian Theology* (Grand Rapids: Baker Book House, 1985), 937.

equal it. However, if the above discussion is valid, there are no illustrations of repentance meaning "turning" in the Old or New Testaments. Instead, when addressed to individuals, it is a call to admit they are wrong, acknowledge their need for a savior from sin, and change their minds about who Christ is (if it needs changing). However, if one stops there and never exercises faith in Christ, he will not be saved.[167]

A missionary friend in Romania recently sent me this note,

> *I would probably say that a person* ***must****, at some level, recognize his sinfulness (see his need for a Savior to save him from his sin, etc.) when he comes to Christ by faith. Otherwise why would he come? And to me, anyway, this recognition would have to include some sort of desire, again at some level, for moral change. It's hard for me to understand how someone can recognize his sinfulness before God (and that God is offended by his sin), come to Him by faith asking for forgiveness, and not at the same time have a desire for moral change. For me, it would be like a non-Christian saying to God, "God, I see that I have really blown it and upset you, and I'm genuinely asking you to forgive me, but at this point I have no desire whatsoever to live any differently. Just forgive me now, and we'll see if the desire comes later or not."*[168]

Of course when one says, "Why else would he come?" many other reasons than forgiveness of sin come to mind. Certainly, as the writer above says, "at some level" there must be an acknowledgment of sin and a desire to be different, but that may or may not be *foremost* in his mind. The nonbeliever may be seeking a new life, purpose in life, or he may be thinking, "This is the right thing to do if Jesus is who He claimed to be." However, there should be no objection to the requirement that at some level (known only to God) there is a desire to acknowledge one's guilt before God and to want a new way of life which includes moral change. So conceived, repentance is not a promise to God that one will change or submit to His Lordship. It is an expression of a desire for a new way of life, an admission of one's need for a Savior. The African chief does not have to promise God he will get rid of 19 of his 20 wives as a condition for receiving personal salvation; a prostitute does not have to promise God she will never turn another trick; and the heroin addict does not have to commit never again to shoot up. Jesus accepts their admission of wrongdoing and their desire to change and He says, in essence,

> *These things are not the issue right now. We need to get to these things later and we will. Right now, I love you and I want to give you a new life and grant to you forgiveness without cost.*[169]

REPENTANCE IN ACTS 20:21

At the risk of losing the reader in more technical discussion, a comment is in order

---

[167] While there are legitimate differences of opinion about the content of such faith, personally I believe that such faith in Christ involves belief that He is the Messiah (that is, Lamb of God), He is the Son of God (that is, He is of the same essence as God, He is deity), and that one can have eternal life by believing on His name (John 20:31, John 3:16; John 8:58). I therefore have no problem with Charles Ryrie's statement that in order to be saved "I need to believe that He died for my sins and rose triumphant over sin and death." For a similar view see Charles Ryrie, *So Great Salvation: What It Means to Believe in Jesus Christ* (Wheaton, IL: Victor Books, 1989), 40.

[168] Al Ginter, personal communication, August 11, 2011.

[169] Revelation 21:6 and 22:17.

regarding the Greek construction in Acts 20:21, "*repentance toward God and faith in our Lord Jesus Christ*." The Greek text unites "repentance" and "faith" under the same article, "the," and it would literally be translated "*the* repentance toward God and faith toward our Lord Jesus." Because both terms are united under one article, it is not uncommon for writers to claim they are equal or always belong together in some way, or more commonly, that they are "two sides of the same coin." But this rule of Greek grammar applies "*only* with personal, singular, and non-proper nouns," and thus it has only marginal relevance to Acts 20:21.

For example when Matthew referred to "the elders and the chief priests and the scribes" (Matthew 16:21), all of which are united under the article (in the Greek text there is no "the" before "chief priests" or "scribes"), he did not mean they were identical or that they always belonged together. When Americans refer to "the congress and people of the United States" they are not equating them or saying that when you have one you always have the other. In fact, many would say they are often unrelated! Similarly, like repentance and faith, we know that elders, chief priests, and scribes are different and that it is not always the case that when you find repentance, you always find faith.

Greek grammarian Daniel Wallace argues that the construction suggests a "unity of some sort." He cites Acts 20:21 as an illustration of this unity where the first noun (repentance) is a subset of the second (faith). He says, "The evidence suggests that, in Luke's usage, saving faith includes repentance. In those texts which speak simply of faith a 'theological shorthand' seems to be employed: Luke envisions repentance as the inceptive act of which the entirety may be called πίστις."[170] I would say that the unity is that repentance is a necessary precursor to faith but is not included within it. Salvation is a two-step process. The first is an admission of guilt and the second is trust in Christ alone by faith alone for forgiveness. According to (John 16:8-11), the Holy Spirit convicts the world of sin. While "world" (Gr *kosmos*) does not always mean every man in the world, it probably does here. Are we to believe He only selectively convicts? Scripture indicates *all* are convicted (cf. John 1:9 where world = every man; Romans 1:18, 20 "without excuse"; 2:14-16). That conviction proves to the conscience that one is a sinner. In the face of such irresistible proof, the sinner must agree, that is, admit he is wrong or "repent." Therefore to say that repentance is not a necessary precursor to faith implies that the Holy Spirit cannot really prove to our conscience that we are guilty!

What then does "*repentance toward God and faith in our Lord Jesus Christ*" mean? The preceding discussion leads us to conclude that to have "repentance toward God" is to change one's mind about sin and admit that one is a sinner needing a Savior (repent). This, then, prepares the way for "faith in our Lord Jesus Christ."

Summary

The New Testament contains many calls to individuals and to the nation Israel to repent. Although repentance is defined in the many lexicons and Bible dictionaries as a call to turn from sin,[171] it has been shown that there is no lexical evidence for this. The repentance word group is not grounded on the Heb word *shuv* ("to turn") but on the Heb

---

170 Daniel Wallace, *Greek Grammar Beyond the Basics* (Grand Rapids: Zondervan Publishing House, 1996), 289.

171 For example, the lexicon of Louw-Nida says, the emphasis in μετανοέω and μετάνοια seems to be more specifically the total change, both in thought and behavior, with respect to how one should both think and act." Louw-Nida, 1:509.

word *nāḥam* ("to regret, to admit wrongdoing, to feel sorry about"). Even though the Gr word *metanoeō* is frequently translated "to turn from sin" the Heb word, *shuv*, is never translated by *metanoeō* in the Septuagint. In fact, *metanoeō* in the Septuagint always translates *nāḥam*.

In the New Testament the *metanoia* word group is used in three ways. First, the major use in the Gospels is a call to the nation to admit their departure from God and the Law and to receive a national forgiveness. First-century Jews would have understood a national forgiveness of sins to be a reversal of exile and the re-establishment of the Davidic theocracy, not individual salvation. This is evident from the way John the Baptist's hearers responded to John's message. They said, "*Then what shall we do?*" (Luke 3:10, 12, 14). If the subject was personal soteriology, surely the one who came to prepare the way for the Lamb of God, would not have said, "*bear fruits in keeping with repentance*" (v. 8), that is, "do good works." He would have said, "Believe in the One who comes after me." One can admit guilt (repent) and do good works for years, and, in addition, be baptized, and yet not be saved (e.g. Cornelius). It happens frequently in our churches today. Only faith in the Messiah can save. If, as some maintain, he was exhorting them to turn from sin (their definition of repent) and then prove that they were saved by doing good works, that means that John believed turning from sin and being baptized were the conditions for personal salvation or, alternatively, that this "*brood of vipers*" (i.e. sons of the devil) were already saved and needed to demonstrate it! Clearly John's message was not about personal salvation. It was about national repentance and forgiveness resulting in a return from exile and escape from the coming wrath of 70 AD. Either way, these interpretations leave John's listeners dangling over precipice of hell with no explanation of the Gospel which John's Lord would teach (John 3:16).

Second, in many other passages the call to repent is addressed to those who are already believers. In those cases the call to repent is a call for them to confess their sins and admit they are wrong, and thus to be restored to fellowship with God.

Third, when nonbelievers are called on to repent, it is in the most general sense, a call to acknowledge guilt before God and their need for forgiveness. As such, repentance is a necessary precursor to saving faith. It means that a nonbeliever must admit his sin to God, acknowledge he is wrong, and be willing to seek a new way of life. That necessary precursor must then be followed by faith in the Lord Jesus Christ for personal salvation.

Is repentance necessary for personal salvation? It depends upon what one means by "repentance." If it means turn from sin and submit to the Lordship of Christ, it is not necessary. But, as argued in this chapter, if repentance means to admit that one is guilty and needs a Savior from sin, of course repentance is necessary. This is clearly taught in the Gospel of John (John 16:8-9) where we are told that the Holy Spirit convicts the world of sin. That means He brings them to a sense that they are wrong, they are guilty, and they need a Savior. That is repentance. No one comes to the Lamb of God who takes away sin (John 1:36), if he is not convinced that he is guilty and needs a Savior to take away his sin.

4

Two Kinds of Inheritance

THE READER may be surprised that a discussion of the saints' perseverance should begin with a study of the inheritance in the Old Testament. It is therefore appropriate at the outset of this discussion to explain what the inheritance of the saints means and its relevance to the doctrine of perseverance. These conclusions may be set forth in the following propositions:

1. There is a difference between inheriting the land of Canaan and living there. The former refers to ownership and the latter to mere residence.
2. While Israel was promised the inheritance as a nation, the condition for maintaining their inheritance-right to the land of Canaan was faith, obedience, and completion of their divine calling. The promise, while national, was applied only to the believing and obedient remnant.
3. The inheritance is not to be equated with heaven but with something in addition to heaven, promised to those believers who faithfully obey the Lord.
4. Just as Old Testament believers forfeited their earthly inheritance through disobedience, we can also forfeit our future reward (inheritance) by a similar failure. Loss of inheritance, however, does not mean loss of salvation.
5. Two kinds of inheritance were enjoyed in the Old Testament. All Israelites who had believed and were therefore regenerate had God as their inheritance, but not all inherited the land. This paves the way for the concept that the New Testament may also teach two inheritances. We are all heirs of God, but we are not all joint-heirs with Christ, unless we persevere to the end of life. The former refers to our salvation and the latter to our reward.
6. A child of Israel was both an heir of God and an heir of Canaan by virtue of faith in God. Yet only those believers in Israel who lived faithful lives would maintain their status as firstborn sons. These were the ones who would actually receive what had been promised to them as an inheritance.

The relevance of these conclusions to the doctrine of the saints' perseverance is obvious. First, if this is in fact the Old Testament view, this surely must have informed the thinking of the New Testament writers. If that is so, then many passages that have been considered as descriptions of the elect (as opposed to the nonelect) are in fact descriptions of believers who will obtain an inheritance in heaven, as opposed to believers who will not.

For example, Paul warns the Corinthians, "*Do you not know that the wicked will not inherit the kingdom of God*?"[172] If "inheriting the kingdom" means "going to heaven," then Paul is saying no wicked person can go to heaven. Such an interpretation would be consistent with any system of theology that says that the permanently carnal Christian is a fiction. If, on the other hand, "to inherit the kingdom" refers not to entering heaven but to something in addition to regeneration, then an entirely different interpretation of the passage emerges. Instead of warning merely professing Christians that they may not be Christians at all, he is telling true Christians that if they do not change their behavior, even though they will be in the kingdom, they will not inherit it; in fact they will be "least" in the kingdom (Matthew 5:19).

In numerous New Testament passages believers are called heirs. We are told that we will "inherit the kingdom," "inherit eternal life," and that the Spirit is the "earnest of our inheritance." Commonly, these passages have been taken to refer to our final deliverance from eternal damnation and ultimate arrival in heaven. A severe problem develops, however, when one carefully examines the usage of the term "inheritance" in the Old and New Testaments. When used of Israel's acquisition of Canaan, it refers, almost without exception, to something that is obtained, in part, by their faithful obedience. In view of the many Reformed commentaries that suggest that inheriting Canaan is a type of entering heaven, this creates an obvious problem for their teaching that entrance into heaven comes by faith alone apart from works.

Because of this contradiction to the doctrine of justification by faith alone, no lack of exegetical ingenuity has been exercised in reinterpreting the obvious meaning of certain New Testament passages.

The New Testament writers frequently refer to the inheritance of the saints by quoting passages referring to the land of Canaan in the Old Testament. How was the inheritance in the Old Testament obtained? Was it viewed as a reward for faithful service, something earned, or was it a free gift? Of what did it consist? Was it a type of heaven, as Experimental Predestinarians teach, or was it a type for additional blessing for those who were already saved? Certainly, the view of the inheritance in the New Testament was directly informed by the Old Testament world of thought.

In the book of Daniel, the Lord calls Daniel "esteemed one." What a privilege to have God address that faithful believer in that manner. As a result of the life he lived, Gabriel promised that at the end of the age, Daniel would receive his "*allotted portion*."

> *But as for you, go your way to the end; then you will enter into rest and rise again for your allotted portion at the end of the age (Daniel 12:13).*

His "portion" refers to reward in the age to come. The Hebrew word refers to his allotted inheritance.

The Old Testament presents two inheritances (possessions) the people of God will enjoy. All will have God as an inheritance, but only some will "possess the land." All who know the Lord have Him as "their God," but only those who obey the Lord wholeheartedly, as Caleb did, will have an inheritance in the land of Canaan.

---

172 1 Corinthians 6:9.

God Is Our Inheritance

First, the inheritance is God Himself. The Levites, in contrast to the rest of the nation, were to have no inheritance in the land (Deuteronomy 14:27).

> *The priests, who are Levites--indeed the whole tribe of Levi--are to have no allotment or inheritance with Israel. They shall live on the offerings made to the* Lord *by fire, for that is their inheritance. They shall have no inheritance among their brothers; the* Lord *is their inheritance, as he promised them (Deuteronomy 18:1-2).*[173]

Here is an inheritance received directly from God on the basis of promise only with no works involved. There is no territory involved.[174] This foreshadows one type of inheritance mentioned in the New Testament: believers are "heirs of God," through birth and for no other reason.

The prerogative of having God as their inheritance went not just to the Levites but also to all who know the Lord. The psalmist viewed God as his *klēros* ("lot, portion, inheritance," LXX)[175]: "*The* Lord *is the portion of* **my inheritance** *and my cup; thou dost support my lot*" (Psalm 16:5). In other places David says:

> *My flesh and my heart may fail*
> *But God is the strength of my heart*
> *And my portion* [*klēros*, LXX] *forever (Psalm 73:26).*

> *The* Lord *is my portion* [*klēros*];
> *I promised to keep thy words (Psalm 119:57).*

> *I cried out to Thee, O* Lord*;*
> *I said, "Thou art my refuge,*
> *My portion* [*klēros*] *in the land of the living" (Psalm 142:5).*

God is the people's portion now, and He will be their inheritance in the future as well:

> *"This is the covenant I will make with the house of Israel after that time," declares the* Lord*. "I will put my law in their minds and write it on their hearts.* ***I will be their God, and they will be my people****" (Jeremiah 31:33).*

Not only will God own His people, but also they will possess Him. The references to "I am the God of Abraham, Isaac, and Jacob" convey a similar thought. Not only do the people have an inheritance in the land, but God Himself is theirs. This applies only to those within Israel who are regenerate.

---

173 See also Joshua 7:14; 14:1-5; 18:7.

174 Eaton correctly observes, "The institution of the Levites thus prepared the way for an 'inheritance' conferred directly by God himself rather than mediated through the legislative arrangements concerning Israelite territory." Michael A. Eaton, *No Condemnation: A New Theology of Assurance* (Downers Grove, IL: InterVarsity Press, 1995), 177.

175 Johannes Herrmann, "klēronomos, et. al." in TDNT, 3:774.

The Inheritance Granted by Works to Those Already Saved

AN INHERITANCE WAS A "POSSESSION"

Nothing is more fundamental to the meaning of the Heb word *nachala* than the idea of "possession."[176] The land of Canaan was Israel's promised possession.[177] The notions of permanence and succession are found in some contexts,[178] but they are absent in others and are therefore not part of the basic significance of the word.[179] Craston avoids this error when he summarizes:

> *The Old Testament terms for heir, inheritance, do not necessarily bear the special sense of hereditary succession and possession, although they are found in laws concerning succession to the headship of the family, with consequent control of the family property (Genesis 15:3-5; Numbers 27:1-11; Numbers 36:1-13; Deuteronomy 21:15-17).*[180]

When the psalmist says, "*Rise up, O God, for all the nations are your inheritance*" (Psalm 82:8), he does not mean that God receives the nations on the death of His parent!

Zane Hodges is certainly correct when he says,

> *In fact, a survey of the Biblical use of the word to inherit shows that it is most frequently a synonym for to possess or to own. Equally, the word inheritance usually indicates property of some sort which a person owns. One can find numerous passages where this is true (for example, Genesis 15:7–8; Exodus 34:9; Leviticus 20:24; 25:46; Numbers 16:14; 18:21; 26:52–55; Deuteronomy 12:12; Joshua 17:14; Judges 2:6; Ruth 4:5; 1 Kings 21:2, 3; Job 42:15; Mark 12:7; Acts 7:5; and many more). If we keep the idea of ownership in mind, obviously the kingdom is not owned by those who are only citizens there. Citizens are subjects of a kingdom, not its owners. Instead, it is the king to whom a kingdom really belongs.*[181]

Leon Morris correctly insists that, even though the word properly denotes property received as a result of death, the Old Testament concept of inheritance has no implication of hereditary succession, as it does in classical Greek. Rather, he says, the term refers only to sanctioned and settled possession.[182] The fact that a son became an heir in no way guaranteed that he would obtain the inheritance. The father had the right to insist that the son meet the conditions of the inheritance or give it to another. An obvious illustration of this is that the Exodus generation was promised an inheritance, the land of Canaan.

---

176 AS, 248. The Greek words cited here have the same sense of "possession."

177 1 Chronicles 16:18; Joshua 18:20; Numbers 26:53; Deuteronomy 4:38; Psalm 105:11.

178 E.g., Leviticus 25:46.

179 Contra Leonard J. Coppes who, like many others, asserts that an inheritance is a "permanent possession as a result of succession," ("*mahal*," in TWOT, 2:569). Coppes himself admits this when he refers to "those many passages where the idea of possession was conceived of as permanent and not entailing the idea of succession (I Sam. 26:19)" (Ibid.). See also Genesis 15:7-8; Deuteronomy 16:20; Leviticus 20:24; Isaiah 57:13; 54:3. Jeremiah says, "Therefore I will give their wives to other men, and their fields to new owners [Heb., their fields to those who will inherit them]" (Jeremiah 8:10). Those who inherit are simply "owners."

180 R. C. Craston, "Inheritance," in *Evangelical Dictionary of Theology* (Grand Rapids: Baker Book House, 1984), 561. ibid.

181 Zane C. Hodges, "Romans 8: Who are the Heirs?," *Chafer Theological Journal* 9, no. 2 (Fall 2003): 10.

182 Leon Morris, *The Epistle to the Romans*, Pillar New Testament Commentary (Grand Rapids: Wm. B. Eerdmans Publishing Co., 1988), 317. He cites, in part, comments from F. J. A. Hort, *The First Epistle of St. Peter* (London, 1898), 35.

However, they were also warned about the possibility of losing it and the need to obey God, fight the battle, and live by faith if they were to obtain the inheritance they were promised.

This fact will have relevance in subsequent chapters when discussing the inheritance granted to Christians. There we will argue that both the Old and New Testaments present two kinds of inheritance, one of which is an inheritance that comes to us as sons of God by faith and through no other means. In the Old Testament this was equivalent to having God as one's inheritance. However, both testaments present an additional inheritance that can come to sons and is not guaranteed to them just because they are sons. It is awarded to faithful sons only.

AN INHERITANCE COULD BE GAINED OR LOST

Nothing could be plainer from the Old Testament presentation of the inheritance than that it was often obtained through faithful obedience to Yahweh. "In many instances of Biblical usage, the theological meaning of the word goes beyond the legalistic. Apart from any legal processes, it may characterize the bestowal of a gift or possession upon his people by a merciful God, in fulfillment of a promise or as a reward for obedience."[183]

During the Mosaic period, the Israelites' enjoyment of the inheritance depended on their obeying the Torah.

> *Hear now, O Israel, the decrees and laws I am about to teach you.* ***Follow them*** *so that you may live and may go in and* ***take possession*** [Heb *yarash*, "inherit"] *of the land that the Lord, the God of your fathers, is giving you (Deuteronomy 4:1).*
>
> ***Do what is right and good in the Lord's sight****, so that it may go well with you and you may go in and* ***take over*** [Heb *yarash*, "inherit"] *the good land that the Lord promised on oath to your forefathers (Deuteronomy 6:18).*

Israelites were told that they could lose their inheritance through disobedience: *you shall be torn from the land where you are entering to possess it* [Heb *yarash*, "to inherit"] (Deuteronomy 28:63). An inheritance could be won through battle and struggle as in Joshua and Caleb, or it could be lost through disobedience. Either way works were involved.[184]

Many figurative terms refer to inheritance that have the meaning "to acquire" (e.g., the wise man shall inherit glory [Proverbs 3:35]; the troubler shall inherit wind [Proverbs 11:29]; the simple shall inherit folly [Proverbs 14:18]. William Brown has noted that "in these usages the 'inheritance' is acquired as a natural consequence or reward for one's character or actions,"[185] a meaning we will find often in the New Testament.

---

183 O. J. Babb, "Inheritance," in IDB, 701.

184 One critic in an effort to substantiate his thesis that the Jews always possess the land and that works have nothing to do with the inheritance says, "Numbers 32:29, 30. If the men of Gad and Reuben rebelled by not crossing the Jordan to fight, then they would be forced to take their inheritance on the west side of the Jordan. It appears that God was willing to give an inheritance to rebellious people!" This Experimental Predestinarian believes that the inheritance is heaven and that all true Christians persevere in a life of holiness to the final hour. Thus in order to sustain the fiction of the inheritance being all of grace and not of works, he ends up arguing against his own position that one who inherits always works!

185 William E. Brown, "The New Testament Concept of the Believer's Inheritance" (ThD diss., Dallas Theological

The idea of merit related to the inheritance is seen in its earliest Old Testament references. Abraham is told that failure to obey the work of circumcision will result in forfeiture of the inheritance (Genesis 17:14). Caleb will inherit the land because he followed God "wholeheartedly" (Numbers 14:24).

> *But because my servant Caleb has a different spirit, and follows me wholeheartedly, I will bring him into the land he went to, and his descendants will inherit it.*
>
> *I, however, followed the* Lord *my God wholeheartedly. So on that day Moses swore to me, "The land on which your feet have walked will be your inheritance and that of your children forever* ***because you have followed the*** **Lord** ***my God wholeheartedly****" (Joshua 14:8-9, cf. v. 14).*

In contrast to those Israelites who disobeyed, Caleb was rewarded with an inheritance, the land of Canaan. Caleb and Joshua, only two out of two million, inherited the land. But surely the two million were composed mainly of those who were justified![186] Yet only those who "had a different spirit" and who "followed the Lord wholeheartedly" inherited the land. Numerous passages in the Old Testament demonstrate that the inheritance (the land of Canaan)[187] was granted only to those who faithfully obeyed the Law.[188]

For example, they will have success in their battle to inherit the land only on the condition that they are "strong and courageous" and that they "obey all the law" that Moses gave them.[189] Furthermore, they are promised "rest" (victory after the conquest of the land of Canaan), but it will be theirs only as they fight and "take possession" (Joshua 1:13-15). So the inheritance of Canaan was rewarded on obedience. Also, David's reign was predicated on his obedience and character.[190] We are therefore amazed to read in B. F. Westcott's commentary on Hebrews:

> *From these examples it will appear that the dominant Biblical sense of "inheritance" is the enjoyment by a rightful title of that which is not the fruit of personal exertion.*[191]

Seminary, 1984), 30. Brown also lists many places in the Apocrypha where inheritance means to acquire as a "natural consequence of one's character" (ibid., 30. The Mishnah has much discussion on what was necessary for one to have a share in the world to come (m. San. 10). To have a share, or inherit, the world to come, seems to be the same as "go to heaven when one dies." To ensure this inheritance, one must do good works and not be evil. One can see the works salvation clearly emerging in a systematic form in post-70 AD Judaism. Personal character was required to inherit the world to come. One must honor his parents (m. Peah 1.1) and demonstrate piety (m. R. Num 19:1). It appears that by this time inheritance was an expression for salvation and must be obtained by works. E. P. Sanders has nuanced this idea. In his understanding, one enters the covenant (salvation) by grace, but one maintains his position in the covenant by works. This Arminian viewpoint may be what is behind the rabbinic emphasis on works. They do works not to acquire the inheritance, but to maintain it.

186 The Exodus generation "believed in the Lord," and therefore were saved (Exodus 14:31). They believed His promises and sang praises to Him (Psalms 106:12).

187 The land of Canaan is often equated with inheritance in the Old Testament. See, for example, Deuteronomy 15:4; 19:14; 25:19; 26:1.

188 See Exodus 23:30; Deuteronomy 2:31; 11:11-24; 16:20; 19:8-9; Joshua 11:23; 1:6-7.

189 Joshua 1:6-7.

190 Psalms 37:9-11. "Hope" does not refer to saving faith. David was already a saved man. Hope refers to the attitude of a saved man who continues to trust and does not give up, a man who perseveres in faith.

191 B. F. Westcott, *The Epistle to the Hebrews*, reprint ed. (Grand Rapids: Wm. B. Eerdmans Publishing Co., 1965).

Clearly, "the fruit of personal exertion" is found in scores of passages. Israel would only be successful in their conquest and acquisition of the land of Canaan if they trusted God and obeyed completely. Joshua would be surprised to learn that obtaining the inheritance of Canaan required no work on his part; that it came solely on the basis of promise. The Jordan was to be crossed, battles were to be fought and victories were to be won before the inheritance that was allocated to Israel by divine promise could come into their possession.

This is not to deny that Israel conquered the land by God's grace. God led the way and fought for her. He sent fear and confusion among her enemies, worked miracles, and inspired her people to obey. Had God not done these things, Israel would not have succeeded. Yet, like the Christian life, there is a synergism between God's part and ours (Philippians 2:12-13) and we do have a part. As Paul said, "*I can do all things through Christ who strengthens me*" (Philippians 4:13). We do it, God strengthens. It is not "all of God." Israel conquered the land because of her righteousness and because God went before them and encouraged them to obey.

A poignant example from American history illustrates this point. During the Revolutionary War, the British General Howe had inflicted heavy casualties on George Washington's troops on Long Island, NY. The British then prepared to capture and destroy the remaining 8,000 troops on Brooklyn Heights. Washington, greatly outnumbered, realized to fight would mean defeat and the likely end of the war. Surrender was unthinkable! To retreat was the only thing to do. But how?

The British completely blocked any route on land which left only the wide East River. The American Army could have easily been surrounded by the British but Providential adverse weather conditions kept British ships from sailing up the East River.

According to the Cambridge Theological Seminary account,

> *As a result the American Army was able to make an attempt to escape. To make sure the British did not discover their retreat, Washington set out to evacuate his army in great secrecy. He set orders for every rowboat, sailboat and seagoing vessel to be collected in the area. At 8:00 pm on the night of August 29, 1776 the evacuation of the troops commenced. Heavy rain was falling as the evacuation began and the adverse winds which hindered the British ships continued. In this weather, the sailboats were of little use and only few rowboats were employed in the retreat. At this rate, evacuation seemed impossible. But at 11:00 pm the Northeast wind which had raged for three days amazingly stopped and the water became so calm that the boats could be loaded with extra weight. A gentle breeze arose from the South and Southwest which favored their travel across the river to New York.*
>
> *The retreat continued throughout the darkness of the pre-dawn. But as the sun began to rise, many troops were yet to be evacuated. Their death seemed apparent. But again, an astonishing thing occurred.*
>
> *Major Benjamin Talmage was still on the island and he recorded what happened in his memoirs: "After dawn of the next day approached, those of us who remained in the trenches became very anxious for our own safety and when the dawn appeared there were several regiments here on duty.*
>
> *At this time, a very dense fog began to rise out of the ground and off the river. It seemed to settle in a peculiar manner over both encampments. I recollect this peculiar Providential occurrence perfectly well. And so very dense was the atmosphere that I could scarcely discern*

a man six yards distance. We tarried until the sun had risen but the fog remained as dense as ever.”

The fog remained until the last boats left Long Island.[192]

This event was so astonishing that surely the explanation given by many of the Colonists was true: *“That God was defending the cause of liberty.”*[193]

The point is that God provided the fog, but Washington developed and executed the plan. Yet in the end, they would all say, “God delivered us!” Like the believer’s good works, it was a Divine deliverance in which man cooperated. To express it like Solomon did, we would say, “*The horse is prepared for the day of battle, But victory belongs to the* Lord” (Proverbs 21:31). Or, as David said, “*He trains my hands for battle, So that my arms can bend a bow of bronze*” (Psalm 18:34). David bent the bow, but God (through years of practice) trained David how to do it.

The inheritance could be obtained by faith plus obedience, but it could also be lost by disobedience. Even Moses was excluded from the land of Canaan (i.e., the inheritance) because of his disobedience (Deuteronomy 4:21-22). Clearly Moses will be in heaven, but he forfeited his earthly inheritance. Failure to enter Canaan did not necessarily equate with failure to have eternal life; if so, Canaan provides a poor type of heaven.

Even though Israel had become God’s firstborn son (Exodus 4:22-23), the entire wilderness generation, with the exception of Caleb and Joshua, forfeited the inheritance due to the firstborn. God disinherited them, and they wandered in the wilderness for forty years, and most of them died there.

Another generation of Israelites similarly forfeited their inheritance rights and was sold as slaves into Babylon (586 BC). Jeremiah laments:

*Our **inheritance** has been turned over to aliens,*
Our homes to foreigners (Lamentations 5:2).

For that generation of Jews, Israel’s disobedience had resulted in the loss of their inheritance, the land of Canaan.[194]

A classic example of the forfeiture of one’s inheritance rights was the case of Reuben, Jacob’s firstborn, who lost his inheritance rights.[195] The possibility of the forfeiture of the land of Canaan is presented in David’s challenge to the nation and to his son Solomon.[196] Clearly, an inheritance is both given and taken, “*You shall take their land, and I will give it to you to possess it* [Heb *yarash*, ‘to take by force’].”

The Old Testament distinguishes between inhabiting the land and inheriting it, or to put it in other words, between merely living in the land and possessing it. Abraham, for example, inhabited the land and lived there, but he never inherited it (Hebrews 11:13). He

---

192 http://www.ministers-best-friend.com/George-Washington-Prays-God-sends-Supernatural-Fog-to-Allow-Escape.html

193 Ibid.

194 Westcott, *The Epistle to the Hebrews*. Of course the Abrahamic promise guarantees the ultimate possession of the land by the final generation of Jews who will return to the Lord in faith just prior to Jesus’ second coming. However, the generation of the Babylonian captivity forever lost their inheritance. An inheritance can be lost.

195 2 Chronicles 5:1-2.

196 2 Chronicles 28:8.

lived there, but he never owned it (Genesis 21:33; 35:27).[197] As we shall see later, the New Testament also acknowledges that there is a difference between living in the kingdom and having an inheritance there.

In the Old Testament the "alien" was someone who "did not enjoy the rights usually possessed by a resident."[198] The *gēr* had "no inherited rights."[199] Moses named his son Gershom in memory of his stay in Midian (Exodus 18:3) where he lived as an alien without inheritance rights. Abraham, Isaac, and Jacob lived as strangers in Canaan (Exodus 6:4), meaning that they had no property rights there.

The Levites, in particular, were told that they would have no inheritance rights in the land:

> *The LORD said to Aaron, "You will have no inheritance in their land, nor will you have any share*[200] *among them. I am your share and your inheritance among the Israelites" (Numbers 18:20).*[201]

Therefore it is perfectly proper to think of living in a land where one had no inheritance or property. In fact inheriting the land is far more than merely living there.[202] Even though

---

197 There is a difference between living in the land and inheriting or owning the land. "May he give you and your descendants the blessing given to Abraham, so that you may take possession [Heb *yarash*, 'to inherit'] of the land where you now live as an alien" (Genesis 28:4). Jacob did not own the land, that is, he had not inherited it, but he lived there.

198 Harold Steigers, "*gēr*," in TWOT, 1:155-56.

199 BDB, 158.

200 The parallelism equates "share" with "inheritance."

201 See also Numbers 18:23-24.

202 Wright, *The New Testament and the People of God: Christian Origins and the Question of God*, 269. Experimental Predestinarians are troubled by the idea that a believer can obtain anything through their own devotion to God. Thus all of these passages that seem to suggest that the inheritance is conditioned on the believers' works are countered by saying that even though the Israelites were disobedient, they still lived in the land of Canaan. Living there is then equated with inheriting it! However, there is more to inheritance than living in the land. Someone may live in my house (perhaps as a guest or because I rented it to them), but I can assure you they will not inherit it. Inheritance implies ownership. And ownership, while unconditionally guaranteed to the Israel of faith in the last days, will come only to any particular generation of Jews who are obedient. The unconditional nature of the Abrahamic covenant will be finally fulfilled at the second coming "when I take away their sins" and when "the Deliverer will come from Zion" (Romans 11:26-27). Whether a particular generation of Jews inherited the land depended on God's promises and their faithfulness to meet the requirement of the covenant. No generation of Jews has ever met the conditions and no generation of Jews has ever inherited *all* the land for an *everlasting possession* as the promise specified. Nehemiah would be surprised to learn that on their return from Babylon, the nation had inherited the land. He said, "Behold, we are slaves today, And as to the land which You gave to our fathers to eat of its fruit and its bounty, behold, we are slaves in it" (Nehemiah 9:36). To be a "slave" in the land in no sense fulfills the biblical promises of existing at rest and under the full blessing of God. When Jesus says, "I wanted to gather you ... but you were unwilling" (Matthew 23:37) and "the kingdom of God will be taken away from you and given to a people, producing the fruit of it" (Matthew 21:43), are we to imagine that the corrupt generation of Jews who rejected their Messiah were heirs of the unconditional Abrahamic promise? If so, why were they destroyed? They lost the inheritance because of disobedience. When Paul said that Israel has been "cut off" from the Abrahamic promise until the final generation of faith is grafted back in, are we to understand that the generation that was "cut off because of their disobedience" (Romans 11:26-27) was an heir to the land? That generation, though living in the land, was disinherited and still in exile. N. T. Wright observes, "They believed that, in all the senses which mattered, Israel's exile was still in progress. ...The exile is not yet really over. This perception of Israel's present condition was shared by writers across the board in second temple Judaism," ibid., 269.

Israel was disobedient they still lived in the land, they never inherited the land; they never possessed it fully because they were disobedient.[203]

The New Testament parallel may be found in the well-known distinction between the believer's legal standing as the heir of all things, and his state, that is, between his position and his experience. Just because all the blessings in heavenly places are ours (Ephesians 1:3), the believer must "trust and obey" in order to *experience* what is his. This is the same with every generation of Jews. The nation may be the legal heir of the land, but any generation can forfeit that inheritance and never experience it.

This point is made abundantly clear by the writer of 1 and 2 Chronicles. Acts of obedience and piety were rewarded with building programs,[204] victory in war,[205] progeny,[206] popular support,[207] and large armies.[208] On the other hand, disobedience brought military defeat,[209] disaffection of the population,[210] illness,[211] and judgment.[212] A people living in the land and in unbelief suffering retribution from God is not the kind of inheritance the Old Testament speaks of in reference to the unconditional promise to the nation.[213] The inheritance is not merely living on a piece of real estate, ruled over and taxed by foreign kings (Nehemiah 9:36-37). Certainly the promise to the nation is unconditional. This inheritance ultimately depends on God's promise. However, for any particular generation of Jews to experience the inheritance, obedience to the covenant was required. The repeated pattern of Israel's history was sin and rebellion; yet they remained in (possessed) the land for hundreds of years, mounting up sin and ungodliness! This was because of God's longsuffering. Finally when the cup of their abominations was full and the Lord's patience was exhausted, He exiled them to Babylon.

Israel's disobedience resulted in their being uprooted from the land and in not enjoying the inheritance (2 Chronicles 7:19-20). God never promised anything to a generation of rebels. Instead, it will be to the "Israel of God" (Galatians 6:16), the believing remnant of the last days,[214] that the promises will finally be fulfilled.

---

203 Robert B. Chisholm, "Does God Change His Mind?," *BibSac* 152, no. 2 (October-December 1995): 152. Thus, the fact that Israel inhabited the land during the time of the judges and the carnal kings of the northern and southern kingdoms in no way invalidates the fact that the inheritance was granted only to a particular generation based on their obedience to Yahweh. The fact that God continued to allow them to remain in the land until the Assyrian invasion in 722 B.C. and the Babylonian exile in 586 B.C. is a manifestation of His longsuffering and grace. His delay was because of His great mercy and grace (Nehemiah 9:1). But during those times of unbelief and rebellion they were not inheriting the land in the Old Testament sense that involved the blessing of God and not mere residence. They did not in the words of Obadiah, "possess their possessions" (Obadiah 17).

204 2 Chronicles 11:5; 14:6–7; 16:6; 17:12; 24:13; 26:2, 6, 9–10; 27:3–4; 32:3–5, 29–30; 33:14; 34:10–13.

205 2 Chronicles 13:13–18; 14:8–15 ; 20:2–30; 25:14; 26:11–15; 27:5–7; 32:20–22.

206 2 Chronicles 3:1–9; 11:18–22; 13:21; 14:2–7; 21:1–3; 25:5; 26:4–5.

207 2 Chronicles 11:13–17; 15:10–15 ; 17:5; 19:4–11; 20:27–30; 23:1–17; 30:1–26; 34:29–32 ; 35:24–25.

208 2 Chronicles 11:1; 14:8; 17:12–19; 25:5; 26:10.

209 2 Chronicles 12:1–9; 16:1–9; 21:8–11, 16–17; 24:23–24; 25:15–24; 28:4–8, 16–25; 33:10; 35:20–24; 36:15–20.

210 2 Chronicles 16:10; 21:19; 24:25–26; 25:27–28; 28:27; 33:24–25.

211 2 Chronicles 16:12; 21:16–20; 26:16–23.

212 2 Chronicles 16:2–9; 19:1–3; 20:35–37; 22:3–9; 25:7–13; 28:16–21; 32:31.

213 For discussion of "retribution theology" in Chronicles see Raymond B. Dillard, "Reward and Punishment in Chronicles: The Theology of Immediate Retribution," *WSJ* 46, no. 1 (Spring 1984): 164-71.

214 Most modern scholars believe that Paul's "Israel of God" is not the church, but refers to the believing Jewish

INHERITANCE OFFERED TO THE BELIEVING ABRAHAM

This second kind of inheritance discussed above, the inheritance of Canaan, was promised to Abraham and his descendants on the basis of a divine oath.[215] But a tension was apparent. They were told that if they "*do what is good and right in the* LORD*'s sight*" (Deuteronomy 6:18), they would have victory over the Canaanites and possess the land (Deuteronomy 11:22-25). The promises to Abraham provide a significant illustration of an inheritance being granted on the basis of works to one who has already been saved. Abraham was a saved man when the Abrahamic covenant was made. Then the inheritance promise made to him was an addition to personal salvation (Genesis 12:1-3). God told Abraham,

> *I am the* LORD, *who brought you out of Ur of the Chaldeans to give you this land to take possession of it (Genesis 15:7).*

This promise of the land is followed by a covenant in verses 8-17 and is repeated in verse 18.

> *On that day the* LORD *made a covenant with Abram and said, "To your descendants I give this land, from the river of Egypt to the great river, the Euphrates" (Genesis 15:18).*

Yet with this unconditional guarantee, conditions were attached. If the inheritance was to be Abram's, then, God said, (1) "go from your country … and I will bless" (Genesis 12:1-2); (2) "walk blameless" before the Lord (Genesis 17:2); (3) circumcise all your children (Genesis 17:11-14);[216] and (4) offer your son Isaac (Genesis 22:16). Abraham was told,

> *Walk before Me, and be blameless. "[So that] I will establish My covenant between Me and you, And I will multiply you exceedingly" (Genesis 17:1-2).*[217]

In his comment on this verse Bruce Waltke says, "Total obedience is the necessary condition to experience the covenant promises. This significant command is later repeated

---

remnant of the last days. See S. Lewis Johnson, "Paul and the 'Israel of God': An Exegetical and Eschatological Case-Study," in *Essays in Honor of J. Dwight Pentecost*, ed. Stanley D. Toussaint and Charles H. Dyer (Chicago: Moody Press, 1968), 183. Surprisingly, some have contended that the absence of a fully developed Old Testament doctrine of heaven is proof that Canaan should be interpreted as a type of heaven. But what kind of argument is this? Are we to say that the absence of something is evidence that it exists? Just because Old Testament saints did not know about something, does not mean that their statements should not be taken at face value. Is absence of knowledge justification for spiritualizing the text, that is, reading the word "heaven" into the word "Canaan"?

215 Genesis 12:7; 15:18-21; 26:3; 28:13; Exodus 6:8.

216 Possibly circumcision was a "sign" and not a condition.

217 The Hebrew text is best translated, "So that I will establish" (Francis Foulkes, "Philippians," in *The New Bible Dictionary: 21st Century Edition*, ed. D. A. Carson, et al. (Downers Grove, IL: InterVarsity Press, 1994, 15). Cf. Genesis 19:5; 23:4; 9:7, 9. Chisholm concurs saying, "Genesis 17:1–2 should be translated: 'Walk [imperative] before Me and be [waw + imperative] blameless in order that I might ratify [waw + cohortative] My covenant between Me and you and greatly multiply [waw + cohortative] your numbers. Again the blessing is contingent on Abram's obedience to the divine imperatives," Chisholm, "Does God Change His Mind?," 390.

to the Israelite Kings (Solomon in 1 Kings 9:4-5; Hezekiah in 2 Kings 20:3). Such a high standard is appropriate for Abraham[218] who will become the father of kings (cf. Gen 24:40; 48:15)."[219]

Although the promise to his descendants was guaranteed (Genesis 15:18), it appears that if Abraham personally was to experience the blessings of the covenant, he must persevere in faith, obeying the Lord. This also applies to his seed, the children of Israel.[220]

This conditionality is expressed right from the beginning:

> *I swear by myself, declares the* Lord, *that* **because you have done this** *and have not withheld your son, your only son, I will surely bless you and make your descendants as numerous as the stars in the sky and as the sand on the seashore. Your descendants will* **take possession** *[Heb "yarash"]* ***of the cities of their enemies*** *(Genesis 22:16-17).*

The actual possession of the land ("the cities of their enemies") was obtained by obedience even though it was guaranteed by an oath! But if the inheritance was guaranteed, how could it be conditional?

Walter Kaiser explains, "The conditionality was not attached to the promise but only to the participants who would benefit from the abiding promises. If the condition of faith was not evident, then the patriarch would become a mere transmitter of the blessing without personally inheriting any of its gifts directly."[221]

If Abraham had disobeyed, Kaiser maintains, then God would still have transmitted the promise through Isaac, but Abraham himself would not have experienced any of the blessings. The promises of the nation, and the seed, and the land were unconditional and everlasting, but God would no longer have been "with him" (Genesis 21:22), and he would no longer be a "friend of God" (James 2:23).

Regardless of Israel's obedience or disobedience, God will ultimately raise up a believing remnant, the "Israel of God," who will believe. At that time all Israel will be saved (Romans 11:26-27), and their sins will be taken away. God will put his law within them (Jeremiah 31:33), He will "*cause spirit to enter*" them (Ezek 37:5, literal translation); and

---

[218] Abraham was already a "saved man" when an inheritance, something in addition to personal salvation was promised to him on the grounds of his obedience. In Genesis 15:1-6 Abraham is promised an heir and in Genesis 15:18 an inheritance, the land of Canaan. Yet in 15:6 we are told, "Abram believed the Lord, and he credited it to him as righteousness." Ross points out that this verse refers to Abram's conversion which occurred years earlier when he left Ur. The form of the verb "believed" shows that his faith did not begin after the events recorded in Genesis 15:1-5. "Abraham's faith is recorded here because it is foundational for making the covenant. The Abrahamic Covenant did not give Abraham redemption; it was a covenant made with Abram, who had already believed and to whom righteousness had already been imputed" (Allen P. Ross, "Genesis," in BKC, 1:55).

[219] Bruce K. Waltke, *Genesis: A Commentary* (Grand Rapids: Zondervan Publishing House, 2001), 259.

[220] David R. Anderson explains, "Here is the point. Once Abraham or David was given his grant [inheritance], it could not be taken away. But since these grants included promises regarding future generations (seed), and since these grants were rewards based on the faithfulness of the initial recipient, how can the blessings (rewards) of the grant accrue to future generations if they are unfaithful? The answer is that they cannot. Isaac illustrates this principle in Genesis 26. Abraham has died. Now God appears to Isaac and challenges him to future obedience: "Do not go to Egypt." God promises Isaac that He will confirm or establish the oath He swore to his father Abraham if only Isaac will be obedient to stay in the land. Isaac was faithful, so the promises of the grant continued to flow through him." Anderson, "The National Repentance of Israel," 17-18.

[221] Walter Kaiser, *Toward an Old Testament Theology* (Grand Rapids: Zondervan Publishing House, 1978), 94.

He will pour out "*the Spirit of grace and of supplication, so that they will look on Me whom they have pierced*" (Zechariah 12:10). The ultimate fulfillment of the Abrahamic covenant is guaranteed by the promises of God. This is made clear by the fact that when the covenant was made in Genesis 15:9-21, it was God alone who walked between the parts of the animal, sealing the covenant while Abraham slept! Furthermore this covenant includes the promise that the land will be his for an "everlasting" possession. But for any generation of Jews or Abraham himself to experience the blessings of the covenant, they must obey the covenant stipulations.

Similarly, Jesus told His disciples that they would be His "friends" only if they obeyed him (John 15:14). Walvoord puts it this way, "All agree that the individual enjoyment of blessing under the covenant is to a large degree dependent upon the individual's faith and obedience. That is quite different than stating that the fulfillment of the covenant as a whole is conditioned upon obedience of the nation as a whole."[222] "An individual could deprive himself of the immediate blessings of the covenant through gross disobedience. The point is that in spite of such individual actions, the covenant would have its complete fulfillment."[223]

God's unilateral unconditional commitment to provide the inheritance makes it potentially available to every generation of Israelites. However, for any generation to "possess their possessions" is conditioned on their obedience. Only then will they literally "inherit their inheritance" (Obadiah 17).[224] "Those who enter into covenant with God receive an inheritance, but they must act to take possession of it and must live uprightly to maintain their inheritance. This idea is no doubt the background for the beatitude, and '*blessed are the meek, for they shall inherit the earth*' (Matthew 5:5)."[225] Moses says the same thing. "*We will not return to our homes until every one of the sons of Israel has possessed his inheritance* [lit., 'Inherited his inheritance']" (Numbers 32:18).[226]

In a similar vein Eaton notes,

> *Actual possession of the inheritance remains in the future. Confirmed by oath, it will be given to him by a reward for the obedience of Genesis 22. Even at this early state, inheritance is reward for obedience given by oath.*[227]

These conclusions are fully compatible with what the writer to the Hebrews said when he called the covenant/inheritance "rest." Notice these clear passages.

---

222 John F. Walvoord, *The Millennial Kingdom* (Findlay, OH: Dunham Publishing Co., 1959), 155.

223 Ibid., 153. Similarly Charles Ryrie says, "Fulfillment of the Abrahamic Covenant is not equivalent to enjoyment of that covenant. Simply because the children of Israel did not enjoy the promises and provisions of the covenant does not mean that these promises will not be fulfilled" Charles C. Ryrie, *The Basis of the Premillennial Faith* (New York: Loizeaux Brothers, 1953), 59.

224 This is what the prophet Obadiah said when he spoke of Israel's future restoration saying, "The house of Jacob will possess [Heb ārash] their possessions [Heb. *morash*]" (Obadiah 17). The phrases could be translated, "inherit their inheritance" and both the verb and the noun are often related to the inheritance of the land.

225 John E. Hartley, in *TWOT*, 1:410.

226 See also Numbers 34:15. It is one thing to have a legal claim to an inheritance; it is another thing to actually receive it (Num 34:14-15). In Israel's case the latter was conditioned on persevering faith in the conquest of their enemies. Jeremiah refers to this same concept in reverse saying that one day Israel will "disinherit" those who "disinherited" Israel (Jeremiah 49:2).

227 Eaton, *No Condemnation: A New Theology of Assurance*, 176.

Therefore, let us fear if, while a promise remains of entering His rest, any one of you may seem to have come short of it (Hebrews 4:1).

The inheritance/rest can be lost.

Next we learn that obtaining this inheritance/rest requires work, and does not come by faith alone.

Therefore let us be diligent to enter that rest, so that no one will fall, through following the same example of disobedience (Hebrews 4:11).

Finally we are told that this inheritance/rest is a reward for obedience.

Therefore, do not throw away your confidence, which has a great reward. For you have need of endurance, so that when you have done the will of God, you may receive what was promised (Hebrews 10:35–36).

What was "promised" is the fulfillment of the Abrahamic covenant, an inheriting of the inheritance, a possessing of what was guaranteed if the conditions of faith plus obedience are met.

INHERITANCE OFFERED TO THE BELIEVING EXODUS GENERATION

A second illustration of the fact that in the Old Testament the inheritance was offered only to those who have already believed is the Exodus generation. In passage after passage the inheritance is offered to these believers as something in addition to having God as their inheritance. But were they saved? Or were they merely under the covenant and not regenerated as Experimental Predestinarians maintain?

The writer to the Hebrews teaches that the Exodus generation as a whole was saved. He tells us that "*by faith they crossed the dead sea,*" and "*by faith the walls of Jericho fell*" (Hebrews 11:29-30). The nation, as a whole, exercised faith.

Paul teaches the same:

[They] drank the same spiritual drink, for they drank from the spiritual rock that accompanied them, and that rock was Christ. Nevertheless God was not pleased with most of them; their bodies were scattered over the desert (1 Corinthians 10:4-5).

The Israelites, as a nation, revealed their regenerate condition when they promised, "We will do everything the LORD has said" (Exodus 19:8). They "*believed in the Lord*" and that they "bowed and worshiped" (Exodus 4:31). Furthermore, they not only believed, but they also "feared the Lord" (Ex 14:31).[228] The latter term can roughly be equated with what Experimental Predestinarians refer to as submission to the Lordship of Christ. They had "bowed down and worshiped" and trusted in the blood of the Passover Lamb (Exodus 12:27-28). By faith they drank (1 Corinthians 10:4-5), that is, they "trusted in" (John 4:13-14; 6:53-56) that spiritual rock, which was Christ. Regarding the people of the Exodus, Jeremiah wrote, "*I remember the devotion of your youth, how as a bride you loved me and*

[228] The Hiphil form of the word "believe" (Heb āmen) is the way the Old Testament expresses genuine saving faith. See Jack B. Scott, "āman," in TWOT, 51.

followed me through the desert, through a land not sown. Israel was holy to the Lord, the first fruits of his harvest; ... declares the Lord" (Jeremiah 2:1-3, NIV).

On Experimental Predestinarian grounds, here is a group of people who believed in Yahweh, who were devoted to Him, and who followed Him. In other words, they were saved people. Yet in spite of all this, they never obtained Canaan, their inheritance, because of their unbelief and disobedience. If they were not saved, then the Experimentalist paradigm is fiction, and if they were saved, then the argument of this book is substantiated, true believers can fall away.

R. T. Kendall, pastor of Westminster Chapel in London, has observed:

> *It would be a serious mistake to dismiss the children of Israel in the wilderness by writing them off as unregenerate from the start. To say that such people were never saved is to fly in the face of the memorable fact that they kept the Passover. They obeyed Moses, who gave an unprecedented, if not strange command to sprinkle blood on either side and over the doors (Exodus 12:7). But they did it ... If obeying Moses' command to sprinkle blood on the night of the Passover was not a type of saving faith, I do not know what is. These people were saved. We shall see them in Heaven, even if it turns out they were "saved so as by fire" (1 Corinthians 3:15).*[229]

Here two categories of Old Testament regenerate saints are presented: those who inherited the land and those who did not. The inheritance (possession) was dependent on their obedience. After many years a new generation arose. This generation not only believed in Yahweh; they trusted Him and obeyed Him. This generation did inherit the land. Not all who entered were obedient, just as not all who left Egypt were regenerate, but the nation as a whole was obedient. The Old Testament writers, as is well established, thought in corporate terms.

Not surprisingly the New Testament writers similarly viewed the inheritance of the saints from a twofold perspective. All regenerate people have God as their inheritance, or as Paul puts it, are "heirs of God" (Romans 8:17a; Galatians 4:7). That heirship is received on the basis of faith alone. But there is another inheritance in the New Testament, an inheritance which, like that of the Israelites, is rewarded for faithfulness. That inheritance is being heirs of the kingdom and joint-heirs with the Messiah (2 Timothy 2:12; Romans 8:17b).[230]

Conditional Inheritance in the New Testament

"YOU WILL HAVE NO PART WITH ME" (JOHN 13:10)

In our Lord's interaction with the Eleven in the upper room, He kneels and washes the Apostles' feet. When He begins to cleanse Peter's feet, the astonished and humiliated Apostle says, "*Never shall you wash my feet.*" Jesus replies, "*If I do not wash you, you have no part (*Gr *meros) with me*" (John 13:8). Peter then asks that the Lord to wash not only his hands and feet but to wash his entire body.

229 R. T. Kendall, *Once Saved, Always Saved*, reprint, Waynesboro, GA: Authentic Media, 2005 ed. (London: Hodder and Straughton, 1984), 115.

230 These passages will be developed in the section on inheritance in the New Testament (see p. 734 and scripture index).

Jesus said to him, "He who has bathed (Gr *louō) needs only to wash* (Gr *niptō) his feet, but is completely clean; and you are clean, but not all of you* [referring to Judas]*" (John 13:10).*

The perfect participle of *louō* ("bathe") points to the result of a completed action, a current state. Peter was fully washed in the past with the result that he remains in that state now. Although this is not universally accepted, there is probably "a distinction between *louō* (*to bathe*, to apply water to the whole body), and *niptō* (*to wash* a part of the body.")[231] *Louō* is commonly understood as a reference to regeneration (Titus 3:5), and foot washing (*niptō*) is a metaphor for cleansing the daily sins.[232] In view of the fact that Peter has been "bathed" and only needs to wash his feet, two different relationships with Christ are signified. The "bath" is for regeneration, and the foot washing is for fellowship. One finds the concept in 1 John 1:9 of a cleansing related to post-salvation sins via confession and resulting in restoration of fellowship. As Calvin said long ago, "What is here spoken of is not the forgiveness of sins, but the renewal, by which Christ, by gradual and uninterrupted succession, delivers his followers entirely from the sinful desires of the flesh."[233]

Note especially that if Peter fails to deal with the daily sins, if he fails to persevere in his walk with Christ, he will have no "part" (*meros*) with Him. The word is commonly associated with the inheritance. It is a part in contrast to the whole.[234] Paul reflected this idea when he said, "*giving thanks to the Father, who has qualified us to share* (Gr *meris*) 'in' the inheritance of the saints in light" (Colossians 1:12). *Meris* "which is basically synonymous with *meros*,"[235] refers to "a portion of the whole which has been divided up."[236] One finds this word often used of an Israelite's portion of the inheritance of the land of Canaan. Each tribe (except that of Levi) was to have its "share" (*meris*) in the promised land (Numbers 18:20; Deuteronomy 12:12; 14:27).

Carson notes, that the notion of "'having a 'part' (*meros*) 'in' something is regularly used with respect to inheritance (*e.g*, and, in Jewish thought, can refer to participation in eschatological blessing."[237] Luke 15:12 is instructive, "*And the younger of them said to his father, 'Father, give me the share* (Gr *meros*) *of the estate that falls to me.' And he divided his wealth between them.*"

This term refers to the portion or share of the inheritance which was granted to the heir, a portion which was granted conditionally. In John 13:10, Jesus informs Peter that his involvement in future service for Christ could be nullified, and that he could also lose his inheritance portion in the Messianic Kingdom. At stake here is the conditional aspect of the inheritance. That aspect, that "portion," is based upon a faithful, cleansed life.

---

231 Vincent, 2:227.

232 (But even they who have been thoroughly cleansed (bathed) by Christ and incur defilement in their daily walk (feet), do not need to be radically cleansed (radical renewal), but need only to wash or rinse their feet (daily cleansing from sin)." Joseph Kickasola, "Leviticus and Triune Communion," *Ashland Theological Journal* 10(1977): 36.

233 John Calvin, *John*, Calvin's Commentaries (Albany, OR: Ages Software., 1998), s.v. "John 13:10"; Calvin, "Institutes," s.v. John 13:10.

234 BDAG 633.

235 EDNT, 2:209.

236 BDAG 632.

237 D. A. Carson, *The Gospel According to John* (Downers Grove, IL: InterVarsity, 1991), 464.

It is the daily cleansing which is needed for sanctification. While the bath secures eternal life and final entrance into heaven, one's portion or inheritance in the world to come is dependent upon his daily faithful walk with Christ. The inheritance is conditional, based upon faith working through love (Galatians 5:6).

"TO OBTAIN AN INHERITANCE" (1 PETER 1:3-5)

The conditional aspect of our inheritance is also taught by Peter. It is "*kept through faith*" and obtained only "*if we share in His sufferings.*" All Christians are heirs of God, but not all will inherit the kingdom.

In 1 Peter 1:3-5 the apostle exclaims:

> *Blessed be the God and Father of our Lord Jesus Christ, who according to His great mercy has caused us to be born again to a living hope through the resurrection of Jesus Christ from the dead,* ***to obtain an inheritance which is imperishable and undefiled and will not fade away, reserved in heaven for you,*** *who are protected by the power of God through faith* [better, "faithfulness"] *for a salvation ready to be revealed in the last time.*

We have been born again "to" this inheritance. The prepositional phrase "to obtain" (Gr *eis*, "to") may be rendered "in order to obtain" as the NASB translation above suggests.[238]

The New Century Version translates 1 Peter 1:4, "*God has something stored up for you in heaven, where it will never decay or be ruined or disappear*," making clear the distinction intended between heaven and something stored up for us there, our inheritance-reward.

The inheritance is "kept *in* heaven" and is not the same thing as the sphere in which it is kept, that is, heaven. That reward *in* heaven and not heaven itself is meant is clarified by the fact that persistent faith is the means God uses to secure it for us. This inheritance/reward is called "salvation" in the next verse. And we "are protected by the power of God through faith for a salvation ready to be revealed in the last time."[239]

Experimental Predestinarians Caneday and Schreiner simply assume that this salvation is final entrance into heaven and that the inheritance which is kept in heaven for us is equal to heaven.[240] We disagree. This salvation comes to us via persistent faith. Justification-salvation comes in an instant of time via faith alone. But this salvation is future and refers to the intended completion of our salvation: reward, inheritance, and joint participation with Christ in the fulfillment of human destiny. This goal, toward which all history has been moving, will be "*revealed in the last time*" (1 Peter 1:5). Only Christ's *Metochoi* (Partners) will share in this salvation.

While it is true that this "keeping" is achieved by God the Father through Jesus Christ (Jude 1),[241] we are also to "keep" ourselves (Jude 21), something we ourselves must do.[242]

---

238 A parallel construction may be found in Luke 5:4, "*And when He had finished speaking, He said to Simon, 'Put out into the deep water and let down your nets for* (Gr *eis) a catch*,'" that is, "in order that you might obtain a catch." See also Mark 1:44; Romans 3:25; Ephesians 4:12; 2 Thessalonians 1:5; Matthew 8:4; John 18:37; Luke 2:32

239 See full discussion of this passage on pp. 213 ff.

240 Schreiner and Caneday, *The Race Set Before Us*, 246.

241 Note the perfect passive participle in v. 1. Compare vv. 24-25 where we learn that God does this keeping through Christ.

242 "Keep" is aorist imperative.

The inheritance kept in heaven for us is a common rewards theme found in the Sermon on the Mount (Matthew 6:19-20),

> *Do not lay up for yourselves treasures upon earth, where moth and rust destroy, and where thieves break in and steal. But lay up for yourselves treasures in heaven, where neither moth nor rust destroys, and where thieves do not break in or steal.*[243]

Like the inheritance in 1 Peter 1:4, the "treasures in heaven" are similarly resistant to decay and do not refer to heaven but to rewards there. Elsewhere, the word "imperishable" is associated with rewards awaiting the righteous (1 Corinthians 9:25) where they refer to an imperishable crown; and the word translated "not fade away" is associated with the reward of "the unfading crown of glory" (1 Peter 5:4).

OBTAINING AN INHERITANCE (ACTS 20:32)

Similarly we read in Acts 20:32,

> *Now I commit you to God and to the word of his grace, which can build you up and give you an inheritance among all those who are sanctified.*

The inheritance comes as a result of being built up (i.e., brought to maturity, strengthened, edified)[244] by "the word of his grace." Being "built up" is the common term for edification, strengthening, and spiritual growth.[245] The agency God uses for this maturing process is "*the word of his grace*." A similar thought is expressed in 1 Peter 2:2, "*Like newborn babies, crave pure spiritual milk, so that by it you may grow up in your salvation*." Salvation from damnation is one thing, being built up in it, matured, and edified is another. It is only to those built up and who are mature that the inheritance is granted. The inheritance is a reward; it is conditioned upon works; it is not going to heaven when one dies.

The Inheritance and Heaven—New Testament Parallels?

Many outstanding commentaries and theological works have taught that entrance into the land of Canaan in the Old Testament was a type foreshadowing the believer's arrival into heaven. Arthur Pink, for example, in his commentary on Hebrews discusses the inheritance/rest of the believer and parallels the Hebrews' journey from Egypt to Canaan with the Christians' journey from spiritual death to heaven.[246] In a similar vein A. B. Davidson says that the writer identifies the Old Testament rest (the land of Canaan) with the Christian's salvation.[247]

Amillennialists have often drawn the parallel between Canaan and heaven. Hoekema,

---

[243] See also Luke 12:33.

[244] Cf. Acts 9:31; 1 Thessalonians 5:11.

[245] ALGNT, 278. Cf. 1 Corinthians 14:4; 2 Corinthians 10:8. See EDNT, 2:496.

[246] Arthur Pink, *An Exposition of Hebrews* (Grand Rapids: Baker, 1968), 196.

[247] A. B. Davidson, *The Epistle to the Hebrews* (Edinburgh: T. & T. Clark, 1959), 91-92. By the term "salvation" Davidson means the Christian's final deliverance from final damnation, a meaning far removed from the Old Testament world in which the writer to the Hebrews moved.

for example, explains, "Canaan, therefore, was not an end in itself; it pointed forward to the new earth ... of which Canaan was only a type."[248] Or as Patrick Fairbairn put it:

> *The occupation of the earthly Canaan by the natural seed of Abraham, in its grand and ultimate design, was a type of the occupation by the redeemed church of her destined inheritance of glory.*[249]

A more singularly inappropriate parallel could hardly be found. An inheritance that could be merited by obedience and forfeited through disobedience is hardly a good "type" of heaven. Both aspects are an embarrassment to those of the Reformed persuasion. On the one hand, the forfeiture of the inheritance through disobedience contradicts their doctrine of the eternal security of the believer. On the other hand, the works required to obtain the inheritance in the Old Testament contradicts their doctrine of justification by faith alone. Pink explains the works problem by viewing Israel's struggle to cross the desert and enter the land as a parable of perseverance in holiness. In this way the problem of works as a condition for entering Canaan is solved by saying that all true believers work. The problem is that this would mean there were only two believers, Caleb and Joshua, among the entire two million in Israel who persevered and therefore proved their regenerate status. However, this fails to fit the biblical data which shows most of the Exodus generation were saved.[250] If the inheritance is heaven, then all two million Israelites, except Joshua and Caleb, perished in the lake of fire. This is extremely difficult to believe. As Farrar put it:

> *If ... the **rest** meant **heaven**, it would be against all Scripture analogy to assume that **all** the Israelites who died in the wilderness were excluded from future happiness. And there are many other difficulties which will at once suggest themselves.*[251]

Those from the Arminian tradition could immediately point out that the failure to enter the land anticipates their belief in conditional security. They too, however, must struggle with the problem of the works involved in obtaining it.

Only by allowing inheritance to mean "possession" and acknowledging that it will be awarded for faithful perseverance, can the parallel drawn out by the New Testament authors be explained. The inheritance is not salvation in the sense of final deliverance from eternal damnation but the reward that comes to the faithful in Israel as a result of wholehearted obedience. Similarly, in the New Testament the inheritance is a reward. Canaan does not parallel heaven or the new earth; instead it suggests the rewards the saints will enjoy in heaven. These are earned by faithful obedience and may, like the inheritance of the Old Testament, be forfeited through disobedience or a failure to persevere.

---

248 Anthony A. Hoekema, *The Bible and the Future* (Grand Rapids: Wm. B. Eerdmans Publishing Co., 1979), 279. Hoekema gives no evidence substantiating this assertion.

249 Patrick Fairbairn, *Typology of Scripture*, reprint ed., vol. 2 (New York: Funk and Wagnalls, 1900), 2:3-4.

250 See discussion on pp. 70 ff.

251 F. W. Farrar, *The Epistle of Paul the Apostle to the Hebrews*, Cambridge Greek Testament for Schools and Colleges (Cambridge: Cambridge University Press, 1984), 67.

Summary

The Old Testament teaches that there are two kinds of inheritance. The first, God is their inheritance. No conditions are attached to belief in Him, and it may be safely assumed that this corresponds with what one might call personal salvation. In the remainder of this book, we will refer to this inheritance as our birth-inheritance.

However, there is another kind of inheritance, an inheritance granted to those who are already saved and is in addition to personal, soteriological salvation. This inheritance was illustrated from the beginning with the guarantee made to Abraham that he would have a seed, a land, a great name, and that through him all the Gentiles would be blessed (Genesis 12:13). Yet whether Abraham would personally experience that blessing would be contingent on his obedience. Similarly, his seed, the Exodus generation, who were heirs of the promise, nevertheless needed to cross the Jordan, engage the enemy, and obey the Lord wholeheartedly (Numbers 14:9) if they were to conquer the land and obtain the inheritance that had been given to the seed of Abraham by divine promise. In the following chapters this kind of inheritance will be called our reward-inheritance.

The inheritance, while given to the descendants in general by promise, was obtained by individuals or groups only by persevering faith. This was seen in the life of Abraham and is forcefully illustrated in the experience of the Israelites and their attempted initial entrance into Canaan. In Numbers 14:14 ff. several things should be noted: (1) they were forgiven for their unbelief and grumbling (Numbers 14:20); (2) they disobeyed and tested the Lord ten times (Numbers 14:22); (3) those who disobeyed and who were "men" (accountable), who saw the miracles, would never enter the land of Canaan (vv. 22-23); (4) possessing Canaan is the same as inheriting the land (14:24); and (5) *only those believers who have "a different spirit" and who follow the Lord "wholeheartedly" would obtain the inheritance* (14:24; cf. Joshua 14:9).

These people as a group are saved people, the people of God. According to Paul, they "all drank the same spiritual drink, for they were drinking from a spiritual rock which followed them; and the rock was Christ" (1 Corinthians 10:4). While some may not have been saved, only two of them inherited the land because only two out of two million met the conditions. Thus, all the rest will go to heaven (positional inheritance by faith) but forfeited their reward-inheritance. This thought is in the mind of the writer to the Hebrews in Hebrews 3:7 ff where obtaining the inheritance is equated with "entering rest."[252] The instant they accepted the Passover, were circumcised, and by faith moved out of Egypt, the inheritance was potentially theirs as children of God. But God has never promised anything to rebels who do not trust Him. That generation did not continue to walk in faith and their corpses were strewn in the wilderness (1 Corinthians 10:5).

If the Old Testament presented two kinds of inheritance, heirs of God by faith alone and heirs of the land by faith plus obedience, it is not surprising that the New Testament writers understood the inheritance promises in the same way. The following chapters will demonstrate that this is indeed the case.

---

[252] The "inheritance-rest" of the book of Hebrews will be discussed on pp. 141 ff.

5

Becoming an Heir of the World

THE PRECEDING chapter established that the Old Testament mentions two different inheritances: (1) all believers have God as their inheritance, and (2) faithful believers inherit the land. Also, the New Testament refers to two kinds of inheritance. This is illustrated in the life of Abraham in Romans 4 and then is stated explicitly in Romans 8:17, which refers to all believers as "heirs of God" and mentions that those who suffer together with Christ will in addition be co-heirs with Christ.

Becoming an Heir of the World (Romans 4)

Experimental Predestinarians often cite Romans 4 to prove their idea that the inheritance and justification are the same. However, precisely the opposite conclusion could be drawn. Justification before God, Paul says, comes through faith alone as it did to Abraham (Romans 4:1-5), David (Romans 4:6-8), and throughout the Old Testament (Rom 4:9-12). Abraham's faith was "reckoned" to him as righteousness (4:3). The word "reckon" and the context means "to account to him a righteousness that does not inherently belong to him."[253] But in verse 12 Paul moved beyond Abraham's initial justification to walking in faith throughout one's life.

> *And he received the sign of circumcision, a seal of the righteousness of the faith which he had while uncircumcised, that he might be the father of all who believe without being circumcised, that righteousness might be reckoned to them, and the father of circumcision to those who not only are of the circumcision, but who also follow in the steps of the faith of our father Abraham which he had while uncircumcised. (Romans 4:11-12)*

Verses 11-12 state the purposes for which Abraham received the sign and seal of circumcision: that (1) he might be the father of all who believe without being circumcised, and (2) that he might be the father of circumcision (i.e., of the people to whom the covenant was made, the Jews) not only to believing Jews but also to all those who "*follow in the steps of faith of our father Abraham*." Thus he is not only the father of those who believe for justification, but he is also the father of those who persist in believing, who follow in Abraham's steps.

---

[253] For a helpful exposition of this text see O. Palmer Robertson, "Genesis 15:6 : New covenant expositions of an old covenant text," *WTJ* 42, no. 2 (1980): 265. Another good discussion that includes comment on the New Perspective on Paul is Michael F. Bird, "Incorporated Righteousness A Response To Recent Evangelical Discussion Concerning The Imputation Of Christ's Righteousness in Justification," *JETS* 47, no. 2 (June 2004): 253-75. Bird argues that believers should speak of their being righteous as a result of their being in Christ rather than by a direct imputation from Christ.

What were those steps? The book of Hebrews mentions three; two are mentioned in Romans 4. First, "he left Ur, obeying by faith and going to Canaan, not knowing where he was going (Hebrews 11:8; Acts 7:4); second, by faith he lived as an alien in Canaan. He was willing to by-pass the security and status symbols of life with an eye toward God's promise of provision (Hebrews 11:9–10). These occurred while he was still uncircumcised. But there is a third step for which he was again counted righteous many years later: by faith he committed to offer up Isaac during the major test of his life (Hebrews 11:17–18)."[254]

This kind of obedience is not what saved him, but it qualified him to become the heir of the world: numberless progeny, possession of the land of Canaan, and that all the nations of the earth shall be blessed through his seed (Cranfield, *Romans*, 239).

"If Abraham is our father or prototype *in practice*—in personal experience—we too will:

- Obey God's Word once we grasp its meaning, even if we have unanswered questions.
- Believe God when He says that He will provide for all our needs in Christ Jesus, and thus not become anxious over the material things of life.
- Move forward to trust and obey Him to the best of our ability regardless of dangers, trials, and opposition."[255]

From eternity past God purposed that Abraham would be a special kind of father. He was to be an example of what it means to believe. But he is not only the father of those who believe and become sons of God through one act of faith. He is also the father in a special sense of a certain category of Christians,[256] those who "follow in his steps." Initial belief is an act, but following in his steps is a lifetime of choices. The word "follow" is the Gr word which often means "behave." It means "to live in accordance with" (e.g. Galatians 5:25),[257] and in some contexts had the connotation of going in a line or marching in battle order.[258]

Beginning in verse 13, Paul discusses the second sense in which Abraham is a father. Paul has just said that Abraham was not only justified by faith (4:3) but that he also became an heir of the world by faith. This latter point must now be proved, and Paul begins his proof with the word "for."

Some have argued that to be an heir of the world is a functional equivalent to being an "heir of God" (a birth-inheritance) because the preceding context is about justification by faith. Like beauty, however, "context" is often in the eye of the beholder. It is true that the preceding context is about justification by faith, but beginning in verse 12, the following context is about justification by works (see discussion below). The initial justification before God was granted to Abraham by the single act of faith alone; but the inheritance of the world (the reward-inheritance) came because of life well-lived, that is, by his walk of faith.

---

254 George Meisinger, "Salvation by Faith Alone Part 1 of 2," *Chafer Theological Journal* 5, no. 2 (April 1999): 26.

255 Ibid.

256 Abraham, of course, did not cease to be the father of unfaithful Christians, but he was not their progenitor because they do not follow his example. Most of the commentators miss this crucial point. See the excellent article by Meisinger, "Salvation by Faith Alone Part 1 of 2," 2-27. for development of this theme.

257 Louw-Nida 1:504; and BDAG, 946.

258 LSJ, 747.

Paul now speaks of an inheritance (becoming an "heir of the world"), as something we receive after justification by means of the "righteousness of faith" (Romans 4:13).

> *For the promise to Abraham or to his descendants that he would be heir of the world was not through the Law, but through the righteousness of faith (Romans 4:13).*

The "*righteousness of faith*" embraces both justification and sanctification. For discussion of the "*righteousness of faith*" in Romans 9:30 see p. 173 and 10:6 on pp. 178-80. In justification God accepts faith in Christ as a fully adequate substitute for the works which God requires. God reckons our faith as the righteousness we lack. But the "*righteousness of faith*" also includes right behavior which flows from faith. Because the following context defines it as persistence in faith ("*he did not waver in unbelief but grew strong in faith,*" v. 20, cf. 18, 19), and because of this "*he was able also to perform,*" (v. 21), it may be that the sanctification aspect of the "*righteousness of faith*" is in view in vv. 13-22). Because of his persevering faith, Abraham was able to become an heir of the world. But justification and inheritance (being an heir of the world) are not the same thing. This is clear from the following considerations.

First, Abraham's justification is confirmed in Genesis 15:6, but the inheritance is first mentioned in verses 7-8. God tells Abraham, "*I brought you out ... to give you this land to inherit it.*" Abraham was probably justified when, by faith, he left Ur (Hebrews 11:8; Acts 7:4). Now God promises him the land-inheritance.[259] Abraham did not begin to inherit until Genesis 22:17, more than thirty years later.

Second, justification and inheritance are obtained in different ways. Justification comes through initial faith (Romans 3:22-28; 4:3, 5), but the inheritance comes through persistent faith (Romans 4:20). Being justified, we have peace with God (Romans 5:1-2); becoming and heir of the world is an added blessing.

Third, Genesis 15:13 makes it clear that inheriting the world is not the same as justification. While some have argued that "*heir of the world* means nothing more than becoming 'heirs of God' by faith alone,"[260] this is logically contradictory. "If A comes through B, then A and B are different."[261] In other words if "inheriting the world" comes through the righteousness of faith (justification), then inheriting the world does not equal justification (the righteousness of faith).

To what, then, does "the promise" of becoming an "heir of the world" refer? There is no doubt that this refers to the promises of the Abrahamic covenant (Genesis 12:1-3).[262] Expressing it in the language used in this book, it is the reward-inheritance. Abraham was promised a seed, a land, a great nation, a great name, and that he would be a blessing to the entire world and the father of many nations.[263] Paul states clearly that the inheritance

---

[259] These points are made by Michael Eaton, *Return to Glory: Preaching Through Romans* (Carlisle, UK: Paternoster Press, 1999), 84-87.

[260] René A. López, "Romans," in *The Grace New Testament Commentary*, ed. Robert N. Wilkin (Denton, TX: Grace Evangelical Society, 2010), 644.

[261] See Eaton, *No Condemnation: A New Theology of Assurance*, 181-82.

[262] See Psalms 37:9, 11, 27, 29, 34; cf. Matthew 5:5. "Paul's use of the word [heir] usually has the promise(s) to the patriarchs explicitly in view (so also 9:4, 8–9; 15:8; Galatians 3:14–29; 4:23, 28; also Ephesians 2:12; 3:6; so too Acts 7:17; 13:32; 26:6; Hebrews 4:1; 6:12–17; etc.)" James D. G. Dunn, *Romans 9-16*, The Word Biblical Commentary (Dallas: Word, 2002), 212.

[263] It is not true that Galatians 3:8-9 reduced Genesis 12:1-4 to one thing, justification by faith. Galatians 3

and promise he has in view in vv. 13-25 are ownership of the earth and a multitude of descendants. "*In hope against hope he believed, in order that he might become a father of many nations, according to that which had been spoken, "So SHALL YOUR DESCENDANTS BE*" (Romans 4:18).

Moo summarizes nicely,

> *This language does not exactly match any promise to Abraham found in the Old Testament but succinctly summarizes the three key provisions of the promise as it unfolds in Genesis: that Abraham would have an immense number of descendants, embracing "many nations" (Genesis 12:2; 13:16; 15:5; 17:4–6, 16–20; 22:17), that he would possess "the land" (Genesis 13:15–17; 15:12–21; 17:8), and that he would be the medium of blessing to "all the peoples of the earth" (Genesis 12:3; 18:18; 22:18). Particularly noteworthy is the promise in Genesis 22:17b that Abraham's seed would "possess the gate of their enemies." Later in the Old Testament, there are indications that the promise of the land had come to embrace the entire world (cf. Isaiah 55:3–5), and many Jewish texts speak of Israel's inheritance in similar terms. Against this background—to which we can add Jesus' beatitude, "Blessed are the gentle, for they shall inherit the earth"—Paul probably refers generally to all that God promised his people.*[264]

But possessing the world and being saved are not the same thing. The Jews contended that this second promise also came by obedience to the Mosaic Law, and they were, in part, correct. There was nothing wrong with pursuing the Mosaic Law. In fact, it was commanded!

However, the promise was not "through Law." I understand this to mean that the promise of the inheritance did not come through the Mosaic Covenant but was granted hundreds of years earlier through the Abrahamic Covenant. However, when the Law entered, Israel's means of obtaining the inheritance certainly did involve obedience to the Law by faith. If they did not obey, they were disinherited. The final outcome of their disobedience was the exile. If the Law was pursued by persistent faith, heirship of the world would be obtained. The problem was that "*they did not pursue it by faith, but as though it were by works. They stumbled over the stumbling stone*" (Romans 9:32).

Paul's point is that obedience to Torah "by faith" was a condition of obtaining the inheritance for those under the Law, that is, those living during the dispensation of Law. But it was faith that was always the central principle. This is proven by the fact that the promise was granted to Abraham before the Torah was given.

There is nothing controversial about this viewpoint. Believers today walk by faith, and the Old Testament believers obeyed by faith (Hebrews 11).

Israel had reduced the Law to a series of manmade regulations, legalisms, and had lost the inner spirit and trust in Yahweh that the Law commanded. Furthermore, even though it was God's plan to bless the world through Israel (i.e., God's righteousness), Israel had set aside the righteousness of God (God's faithfulness to His promise) and assumed that God's righteousness was to bless Israel only.[265]

---

extracts the blessing to the world and equates that aspect of the Abrahamic promise to justification by faith. But the promises of a great name, the land, a seed, and many nations encompass more than final entrance into heaven.

264 Douglas J. Moo, *The Epistle to the Romans*, The New International Commentary on the New Testament (Grand Rapids: Wm. B. Eerdmans Publishing Co., 1996), 274.

265 We will discuss the meaning of "the righteousness of God" in Chapter 13 where we will show that it refers

Paul continues,

> *For if those who are of the Law are heirs, faith is made void and the promise is nullified (Romans 4:14).*

The phrase "those who are of the Law" refers to the Jews, but more specifically those who believe that the inheritance can be obtained by obedience to the Mosaic Law apart from faith (Romans 9:32). But how does their viewpoint make faith "void" and nullify the promise?" Moo asks, "Why are faith and the promise rendered futile if Jews apart from faith are the heirs?"[266] Paul gives two reasons.

First, the Law, as law, apart from faith (Romans 9:32) simply brought about judgment, verse 15.

> *For the Law brings about wrath, but where there is no law, there also is no violation (Romans 4:15)*

Faith preceded the Law, and even under the Law dispensation, Jews must obey the law by faith, otherwise, the Law only brings wrath. Law brought about the knowledge of sin (Romans 3:20). Simply obeying the commands of Torah apart from faith does not enable one to obtain the reward-inheritance, that is, to become an heir of the world.

Secondly, if only Jews can become heirs (they were the only ones who had Law), then the promise that God intended to bless the world through the Jews is nullified. It becomes an empty promise if only a small ethnic group is the focus.

> *For this reason it is by faith, that it might be in accordance with grace, in order that the promise may be certain to all the descendants, not only to those who are of the Law, but also to those who are of the faith of Abraham, who is the father of us all (Romans 4:16).*

The reason that the reward-inheritance ("the promise") is obtained by faith is that if it was by Law, then only those under the Law, the Jews, could be heirs and yet the promise is explicitly stated in Genesis to be for the whole world through the Jews.[267]

Paul now develops the theme that "righteousness of faith" (justification) not only involved the initial act by which faith is accepted for righteousness, but *this same faith, when exercised through the daily experience of life* secured for Abraham approval before God and also a son (Isaac) through whom he became an heir of the world. His point in verses 13ff. is that the same kind of faith that brought justification, that is, sheer trust in the promise of God, *when persisted in,* becomes inheriting faith without any recourse to the Mosaic Law.[268] Obedience to the Law, even by faith, was not part of Abraham's journey at all. The Mosaic Law had not even been revealed to him.

---

to God's character, not His gift. Specifically, it refers to His faithfulness to His promises to bless the world through Israel.

266 Moo, *The Epistle to the Romans*, 275.

267 There is no need to go for the "hidden premise" solution as Moo does. He says, "If it is the case that the inheritance is to be based on adherence to the law, then there will be no heirs, because no fallen human being can adequately adhere to the law—and that means that faith is exercised in vain and the promise will never be fulfilled." Ibid. The error of this hypothetical offer of salvation will be discussed in Chapter 13, pp. 186 ff.

268 Ibid., 273.

What then is this faith? It is clearly a faith beyond that which is required for initial salvation.

In hope against hope he believed, so that he might become a father of many nations according to that which had been spoken, "So SHALL YOUR DESCENDANTS BE" (Romans 4:18).

One does not need to persist in faith and "in hope against hope" believe for forensic justification. No! A walk of faith persevered in is what Paul has in view. That faith is what is necessary to become the father of many nations, that is, become an heir of the world.

Yet, with respect to the promise of God, he did not waver in unbelief but grew strong in faith, giving glory to God (Romans 4:20).

The faith in view is not for salvation but trust in the promise of God that he would have a son. He did not waver in unbelief. Saving faith is an event and not a life of not wavering!

Paul explains what he means by faith in verse 21. He says, faith is,

Being fully assured that what God had promised, He was able also to perform.

Faith is believing the promises of God.

Was it in "*hope against hope that he believed*" for justification? No! He was already justified. His persevering faith was in regard to the birth of Isaac (vv. 17-19). This faith required trusting God over a period of time and not wavering. This faith was independent of the Mosaic Law which was instituted 430 years later. The end product of this faith is not justification before God,[269] but a reward-inheritance obtained by persistent faith.[270] By such lifelong trust, Abraham, who had already become an heir of God (justified before God, birth-inheritance), but could also become a co-heir with Christ (reward-inheritance), a partner in the fulfillment of human destiny (Romans 8:17).

This faith apart from the Law which Paul has just illustrated is the same kind of faith that justified Abraham in the first place. "Therefore also IT WAS RECKONED TO HIM AS RIGHTEOUSNESS" (Romans 4:22). But we might ask, "Since he was already reckoned righteous more than thirty years earlier (Hebrews 11:8; Genesis 15:6), was he being reckoned righteous again?" Read on.

This statement may be understood in several ways. Neonomian commentator, Thomas Schreiner, says, "Genuine faith adheres to God's promise despite the whirlwind of external circumstances that imperil it."[271] Like James Dunn, he correctly notes that verse 3 and verse 22 form an *inclusio*,[272] bracketing the discussion of the faith that is reckoned as

---

[269] That kind of inheritance was obtained by the initial act of faith.

[270] C. E. B. Cranfield has warned against the danger of interpreting the inheritance by its parallel usage in Galatians 4:7. He points out that while there are parallels, there are such significant differences that to ignore them would be to seriously obscure the transcendent significance of what is being said in Romans 8. C. E. B. Cranfield, *A Critical and Exegetical Commentary on the Epistle to the Romans* (New York: T. & T. Clark International, 2004), 405. Cranfield's own view of the passage differs from the writer's, but his warning is appropriate for all.

[271] Thomas R. Schreiner, *Romans* (Grand Rapids: Baker Book House, 1998), 239.

[272] James D. G. Dunn, *Romans 1-8*, Word Biblical Commentary (Dallas: Word, 2002), 221.

righteousness. He sees the intervening verses showing what a genuine faith is in contrast to one that is spurious. In other words, the faith that justifies is the faith that perseveres. In the exposition above, however, we have argued that the subject is not genuine faith versus false faith but initial faith versus persevering faith. The former secures justification, and the latter secures a reward-inheritance.

Another possible interpretation is that Paul is referring back to Abraham's original justification. If that is the case then he is saying that this kind of faith, believing in what God promises, is what saved Abraham in the first place. Furthermore, believing in what God promised is what characterized his entire life.

But why, one might ask, should subsequent acts of faith result in his being reckoned as righteous? Calvin viewed justification as the imputation of righteousness of Christ to the believer. He says this must repeatedly go on all through life, "since after such great progress, he [Abraham] is still said to be justified by faith, it thence easily appears that the saints are justified freely even unto death."[273] This is necessary because all the good works of the justified person are still polluted Therefore, he says, "*in order that their good works may please God, it is necessary that these works themselves should be justified by gratuitous imputation; but some evil is always inherent in them.*"[274] As suggested above, however, it may be best to say that our subsequent acts of faith are reckoned as righteousness. Justification is the gracious act of God who "knows that we are dust" (Psalm 103:14) whereby he accepts our faith as a fully adequate substitute for perfect behavior. This applies not only to our entrance into heaven, but also to our daily walk of faith.

If our good works are done in faith, that is, if they are gold, silver, or precious stones, then God reckons that faith as equivalent to meeting his moral demands. The Catholics ridicule this as a "legal fiction"; Protestants call it grace. If our works are not done in faith, they are wood, hay, and stubble (1 Corinthians 3:12-15). An encouraging thrust of this message to the Christian is that even though he knows that the best of his works are sullied, when exercised in faith, God justifies him and he is deemed acceptable to God and will one day be rewarded. This continual justification of our works flows from persistent faith and walking in the steps of Abraham.

The best interpretation is that Paul quotes Genesis 15:6 a second time to show that not only did believing at a point in time result in faith being reckoned to Abraham as righteousness (Romans 4:3, 5, 9), but persevering and unwavering faith over a period of time is a fulfillment of the original declaration of his faith being reckoned to him as righteousness. Which is it: initial faith or persevering faith? The answer of James 2:20-23

---

[273] ibid., 409. In his Institutes he says, "God does not (as many foolishly imagine) impute that forgiveness of sins once for all, as righteousness; so that having obtained the pardon of our past life we may afterwards seek righteousness in the Law. This were only to mock and delude us by the entertainment of false hopes. For since perfection is altogether unattainable by us, so long as we are clothed with flesh, and the Law denounces death and judgment against all who have not yielded a perfect righteousness, there will always be ground to accuse and convict us unless the mercy of God interpose, and ever and anon absolve us by the constant remission of sins" (Calvin, "Institutes," 3.14.10. The Westminster Confession notes, "God does from all eternity decree to justify all the elect; nevertheless, they are not [consciously] justified, until the Holy Spirit does in due time actually apply Christ unto them" (11.4)

[274] Elsewhere he says, "As we ourselves, when we have been engrafted in Christ, are righteous in God's sight because our iniquities are covered by Christ's sinlessness, so our works are righteous and are thus regarded because whatever fault is otherwise in them is buried in Christ's purity, and is not charged to our account," see Calvin, *Romans*, 345.

is "both." According to James, when Abraham offered up his son Isaac more than seventy years after departing from Ur (the exact number of years is uncertain), this was another fulfillment of the declaration in Genesis 15:6 that "*ABRAHAM BELIEVED GOD, AND IT WAS RECKONED TO HIM AS RIGHTEOUSNESS.*"

James tells us that there are two different kinds of justification: justification for initial salvation before God and justification before God in the sense of vindication of a life well-lived. Thus the declaration of righteousness in Romans 4:22 is a continuing fulfillment (James' term, James 2:23) of the same kind of confident trust in Yahweh manifested in Genesis 15:6. By means of this unwavering persistence in trusting God (in spite of impossible circumstances) then, to use James' words, his "faith was perfected," that is, "matured" (James 2:22), and he received vindication-justification before God.

He had already been justified (acquitted and forgiven of sins) by faith when he was called out of Ur (Hebrews 11:8). In Genesis 22:17, he won God's approval (vindication-justification) by his persevering faith. Through this persevering faith, his faith matured (James 2:22); and the declaration of Genesis 15:6 received another fulfillment (James 2:23). He secured the promises and became an heir of the world. If we follow in his steps, we too will rule with Christ in the coming kingdom.

Eaton summarizes,

> *As I understand it, 4:13-21 shows that saving faith, when persisted in, becomes inheriting faith, without any use of the Mosaic Law. The same point appears conversely in 4:22-25. The faith that inherits without any use of the Mosaic Law is not other than the faith that saved us in the first place. The difference between the two is simply a matter of persistence!*[275]

To which, we might add, the latter is another fulfillment of the former as James has stated (James 2:23).

Co-Heirs with Christ (Romans 8:17)

> *The Spirit Himself bears witness with our spirit that we are children of God; and if children, heirs also, heirs of God, and fellow-heirs with Christ if indeed we suffer with Him in order that we may also be glorified with Him (Romans 8:16-17).*

This passage, in agreement with Galatians 4:7, says we are all heirs of God by virtue of the fact that we are His children. But it says something else. It says we are also co-heirs with Christ "if indeed we share in His sufferings." To be a "co-heir" with Christ means "inheriting together with"[276] Christ. "We are God's heirs, and we are, in addition, Christ's fellow-heirs if we share His sufferings now in order to share His splendor hereafter." The second heirship mentioned in this verse is conditional upon our joining with Him in His sufferings. Being an heir of God is conditioned on being born into His family through faith alone, but being a joint-heir of the kingdom (reward-inheritance) is conditioned upon our spiritual perseverance.[277]

---

275 Eaton, *No Condemnation: A New Theology of Assurance*, 183.

276 BDAG, 952

277 The translation above has been slightly changed from the rendering in the NIV. In the Greek text punctuation marks were added by later editors, and the writer has placed the comma after "heirs of God" rather than after "co-heirs of Christ," thus implying that two heirships, not one, are taught. This punctuation fits better with

The fact that this second heirship is conditional is acknowledged by Sanday[278] and Denney.[279] However, since both these commentators equate these two heirships as one, they labor under the difficulty of explaining how all of a sudden Paul is teaching that salvation from eternal damnation is conditioned upon the believer persevering in suffering. In fact Sanday specifically connects verse 17 with a "current Christian saying" (2 Timothy 2:11), which makes rulership in the kingdom the issue and not salvation from eternal separation from God. Their difficulty would be resolved and the obvious harmony with 2 Timothy 2:11 explained on the simple assumption taught elsewhere of two heirships.

Schreiner and Caneday maintain that all true Christians will receive the inheritance, but then they confusedly say, "the inheritance will be ours as God's children, but only if we suffer with Christ."[280] Exactly! As long as the 'inheritance' is distinct from the inheritance gained by birth this is a correct statement. Some Christians will persevere in suffering, and some will not; those who do not, will not inherit. The cause, suffering (this assumes *perseverance* in suffering) with Him, secures the effects, a share in His reward-inheritance and glory. They continue the confusion by saying, "So the cause-effect relationship does not concern the ground of our inheritance, but the means by which God gives the inheritance."[281] This corresponds precisely with the Partner viewpoint that they think they are refuting: the means by which we obtain the reward-inheritance is by perseverance with Christ, even in suffering. The "ground" of both the reward-inheritance and the birth-inheritance is the death of Christ. However, the inheritance is not heaven, as Schreiner and Caneday assume, but the believer's reward in Christ's kingdom (many references relate the coming "glory" of Christ with His future kingdom).

The conditional particle *eiper* regularly takes the meaning "if indeed"[282] as translated in the NIV, and not necessarily "if as is the fact." Dunn strongly rejects the translation "if as is the fact," saying, "Here again a distinction between εἰ and εἴπερ is evident: in v 17a εἰ denotes a necessary and sufficient condition fulfilled = 'since'; but εἴπερ denotes a condition not yet fulfilled and therefore a consequence dependent on the fulfillment of the condition."[283] It is, according to the lexicon of Louw-Nida, "an emphatic marker of condition."[284] The difference is significant. If we translate "if as is the fact" (i.e., "since"), then Paul is saying that all Christians are joint-heirs. If we translate "if indeed," then the conditional nature of joint-heirship is emphasized. In favor of the translation "if indeed" and the placement of the comma after "heirs of God" is the fact that "The final sentence

---

the flow of the context. A literal translation from the Greek: "Now if we are children, we are also heirs—on the one hand, heirs of God. But, on the other hand, we are joint-heirs with Christ, if indeed we suffer together (with Him) such that we also should be glorified together (with Him)."

278 William Sanday and Arthur C. Headlam, *A Critical and Exegetical Commentary on the Epistle of the Romans* (New York: Scribner's Sons, 1897), 204.

279 James Denney, "Paul's Epistle to the Romans," in *The Expositor's Greek Testament*, ed. W. Robertson Nicoll (Grand Rapids: Wm. B. Eerdmans Publishing Co.), 2:648.

280 Of course, we know what they mean. All true children of God will suffer with Christ.

281 Schreiner and Caneday, *The Race Set Before Us*, 177.

282 BAGD, 219; Abbott-Smith, 130; 1 Corinthians 8:5; 15:15. See also 2 Thessalonians 1:6. Even in Romans 3:30, where it can be rendered "since," that meaning is suggested by the context. In Romans, since it is in an exhortation, the basic meaning should be accepted.

283 Dunn, *Romans 1-8*, 456.

284 LN, 1:785.

which follows and the sharp break in thought more naturally suggests a hortatory and conditional understanding. Only those who resist the flesh with suffering can overcome."[285] Both Godet[286] and some Experimental Predestinarians like Denney[287] acknowledge that there is a condition to obtaining the co-heirship with Christ.

Moo notes, "Paul makes clear that this suffering is the condition for the inheritance."[288] He argues that *eiper* implies a real condition but to translate "since we are suffering with him" is probably an over-interpretation of the word. How then does he resolve the obvious problem that this reduces the text to a passage advocating works salvation? He believes that all true Christians will "suffer during this present time *in order to* join Christ in glory.[289] In other words, perseverance is the means which God uses to bring us to heaven. In spite of his denials, this is a faith plus works salvation by means of God-produced non-meritorious works characteristic of all "true" Christians. He is a Neonomian.

William Brown, who understands *eiper* to refer to reality, takes the classical Experimentalist approach. He denies that suffering is a condition of salvation (this would contradict his belief in *sola fide*) but an inevitable and necessary characteristic of those who are "truly" saved.[290]

But it is not necessary to adopt either of these extremes. Rather, verse 17 introduces two inheritances. If we are sons of God, that is, His children, then we are heirs of God (birth-inheritance), and we will also be joint-heirs with Christ (reward-inheritance) if we share in the sufferings of Christ. The child of God who puts to death the misdeeds of the body will be a co-heir with Christ.[291] The fact that we share deliverance from eternal damnation is not based upon sharing in His sufferings. Otherwise, as will be demonstrated later,[292] salvation is earned by and based on works. Paul specifically says that we are heirs of God by virtue of the fact that we are sons and for no other reason in Galatians 4:7. Yet in Romans 8:17 he says that this heirship is conditioned upon works, perseverance in suffering. Contextual considerations suggest that two kinds of thus two kinds of inheritances in view.[293]

---

285 Ernst Käiseman, *Commentary on Romans* (Grand Rapids: Wm. B. Eerdmans Publishing Co., 1980), 229.

286 Frédéric Louis Godet, *Commentary on Romans*, reprint ed. (Grand Rapids: Kregel Publications, 1977), 311. "To reach the possession of the inheritance, there is yet one condition to be satisfied: if we suffer with Him." Godet may be an Arminian, though his position is a bit unclear.

287 James Denney stresses, "The inheritance attached to Divine sonship is attained only on the condition expressed in the clause *eiper*" (Denny, "Paul's Epistle to the Romans," 2:648).

288 Moo, *The Epistle to the Romans*, 506.

289 Ibid., 506.

290 Brown, "The New Testament Concept of the Believer's Inheritance", 100.

291 Wilber Smith similarly views the co-heirship with Christ in this passage as conditional and graduated the same way and relates the joint-heirship with Christ to Psalms 2:8, "Ask of Me, and I will give you the nations for thine inheritance, and the uttermost parts of the earth for thy possession" (Eric Sauer, *The Biblical Doctrine of Heaven* [Chicago: Moody Press, 1968], 193.) The inheritance refers not to heaven but to our reward in the kingdom, reigning with Christ. Also, this view may be found in G. H. Lang, *Firstborn Sons: Their Rights and Risks*, reprint ed. (Miami Springs, FL: Schoettle Publishing Co., 1984), 123.

292 See extensive discussion of this point in chapters 37 and 38.

293 Others have noted this possible interpretation. William R. Newell, for example, says, "Here two schools of interpretation part company, one boldly saying that all the saints are designated, and all shall reign with Christ; the other, that reigning with Christ depends upon voluntary choosing of a path of suffering with Him" (William R. Newell, *Romans: Verse by Verse* [Chicago: Moody Press, 1938], 318).

The footnote in the NET Bible on Romans 8:17 argues against the Partner viewpoint. They say, "The difficulty of this view, however, is that it ignores the correlative conjunctions *men . . . de* (*men . . . de*, 'on the one hand . . . on the other hand'): the construction strongly suggests that the inheritances cannot be separated since both explain 'then heirs.' For this reason, the preferred translation puts this explanation in parentheses."

Au contraire! Paul's use of the correlative Greek particles *men ... de*[294] *substantiates* the Partner view. Not readily translatable in English, the sense is something like this: "On the one hand (*men ...*) heirs of God, and on the other hand (*de*) joint heirs of Christ." These particles, when coupling two phrases together, are normally disjunctive and imply a contrast, not equality, between the items compared. In fact in every usage of these particles in this way in Romans, they are always contrastive and never conjunctive.[295] This suggests that the disjunction comes after the word "God" and not after the word "Christ." In other words, all believers are heirs of God, and they will be joint-heirs with Christ only *if* they suffer with Him. Of course, Paul does not mean that suffering alone qualifies us to be joint-heirs; it is *perseverance* in suffering, faithfulness, that is necessary.

In addition to the immediate context and the normal meaning of *eiper*, the broader context of the New Testament supports the dual heirship view of Romans 8:17. The inheritance is usually conditioned on obedience, and salvation from eternal separation from God is always by faith alone. To become a joint-heir with Christ, one of His *Metochoi*, even if one fails often, the sum of his life must be characterized by perseverance:

> *Here is a trustworthy saying:*
> *If we died with Him,*
> *we will also live with Him;*
> ***if we endure,***
> ***we will also reign with Him.***
> *If we disown Him,*
> *He will disown us;*
> *If we are faithless,*
> *but He will remain faithful,*
> *for He cannot disown Himself (2 Timothy 2:11-13).*

Virtually all commentators understand 2 Timothy 2:12 as explaining or being parallel to Romans 8:17. It seems that this connection is evident because of the parallel construction and similar theme. If there is something contingent in the believer's future in the former, then this would suggest that there is something contingent in the latter as well. As in Romans 8:17 reigning with Christ seems to be conditioned on endurance. The converse, to disown Him, will result in His disowning us when He rewards His church according to the things done in the body, whether "good or bad" (2 Corinthians 5:10). The possibility of being " disowned" does not refer to loss of salvation, because the apostle clarifies that, even when we are "faithless," He will remain faithful to us. But it does mean that believers may be "disqualified for the prize" (1 Corinthians 9:27), stand ashamed at His coming (1 John 2:28), and lose the reward for which they worked (2 John 8).

---

[294] Wendell Hollis, personal communication, June 21, 1989.

[295] See Romans 2:7-8, 25; 5:16; 6:11; 7:25; 8:10, 17; 9:21; 11:22, 28; 14:2, 5; 16:19.

One must also remember that a reader of the New Testament would not have approached Romans 8:17 with the theological pre-understanding of post-reformation Experimentalist theology. Perhaps the fact that we have been influenced by those Reformed traditions has led many to equate the inheritance with heaven and co-heirship with going to heaven with Christ. That seems "natural" to many because the biblical concept of inheritance and heirship has been obscured from view by the widely disseminated creedal definitions of Westminster Calvinism.

The purpose for which we suffer is "in order that we may be glorified with Him." With this statement, William Pass notes that Paul echoes a common New Testament theme regarding the "glory unique to those who will be co-heirs with Christ because of having suffered with him in obedience."[296] This is the glory that will be revealed to us (Romans 8:18). But it is not certain that we will be so glorified, because a purpose clause describes intent and not necessarily certainty. The presence of the phrase further suggests that *eiper* should be translated "if indeed" rather than "seeing that." Even rendering it "seeing that" necessarily implies something contingent in view of the purpose clause. If they do not suffer with Him, and it is evident from the New Testament that many Christians do not, then they will not achieve the purpose that such co-suffering was intended to achieve.

What does it mean to be glorified with Him? Some have made the mistake of equating being glorified with Him, which happens only to the faithful Christian, with the glorification referred to in Romans 8:30 which occurs to all Christians. In verse 17, however, the glory of the Messiah is in view and the possibility that we might share in it. In verse 30 our own glorification is in view. That glorification seems to refer to the perfect conformity to the image of Christ referred to in verse 29.[297]

To be glorified with Him is to be awarded a share in His glory. This glory is what Jesus referred to as being "great in the kingdom of heaven" (Matthew 5:19).[298] The passage is speaking in messianic terms. He has mentioned that we can "suffer with," "inherit with," and "be honored with" the Messiah. "To glorify" is commonly understood as "to honor."[299] The lexicon notes that "glory" commonly refers to "honor as enhancement or recognition of status or performance, *fame, recognition, renown, honor, prestige*."[300] Believers may possibly share in the Messiah's sufferings, inheritance, and honor.[301] Meyer seems to agree: "The inheritance, which God ... transfers to His children as their property, is the salvation and glory of the messianic kingdom."[302]

---

[296] See the interesting recent article on Romans 8:17 from the Partner viewpoint by William N. W. Pass III, "A Reexamination of Calvin's Approach to Romans 8:17," *BibSac* 170, no. 677 (January-March 2013): 78. Cf Hebrews 10:32-36. See also Colossians 1:22-23; Jude 24; and Ephesians 1:4. This glory embraces the New Testament doctrine of rewards, see Chapters 61-63.

[297] F. F. Bruce, *Romans: An Introduction and Commentary*, Tyndale New Testament Commentaries (Downers Grove, IL: Intervarsity Press, 2008), 178.

[298] See discussion on pp. 279 ff.

[299] See any Greek lexicon.

[300] BDAG, 257.

[301] Sanday and Headlam point out that the inheritance referred to was commonly the secure and permanent possession of the land of Canaan won by the Messiah and that it ultimately became a symbol for all the messianic blessings. See Sanday and Headlam, *A Critical and Exegetical Commentary on the Epistle of the Romans*, 203.

[302] Heinrich August Meyer, *A Critical and Exegetical Handbook to the Epistle to the Romans* (Winnona Lake, IN: Alpha Publications, 1979), 317.

This future glory of the messianic reign was often referred to in the Old Testament. The "glory of God" in this sense, according to Von Rad, was not so much His intrinsic nature "but the final actualization of His claim to rule the world."[303] Indeed, the equation of the glory of Messiah with His messianic reign and of the need for believers to persevere in order to obtain a share in it is common in the New Testament.[304]

And they said to Him, "Grant that we may sit in Your glory, one on Your right, and one on Your left" (Mark 10:37).

When the Son of Man comes in his glory, and all the angels with him, he will sit on his throne in heavenly glory (Matthew 25:31).

The need to persevere in doing good as a necessary precondition for sharing in that glory is elsewhere taught in Romans and 2 Corinthians.

To those who by persistence in doing good seek glory, honor and immortality, He will give eternal life ... but glory, honor and peace for everyone who does good: first for the Jew, then for the Gentile (Romans 2:7, 10).

The contingent nature of sharing in the future glory of Christ is implied in several of Paul's epistles:

For our light and momentary troubles are achieving for us an eternal glory that far outweighs them all (2 Corinthians 4:17).

He called you to this through our gospel, that you might share in the glory of our Lord Jesus Christ (2 Thessalonians 2:14).

Summary

Being familiar with the Old Testament, the apostle Paul naturally assumed that believers have two kinds of inheritance. He illustrates this from the life of Abraham. Abraham was already justified when he received the promise that he would be an heir of the world. God became his birth-inheritance through the righteousness of faith, and he was born again. But subsequently Yahweh promised him that he would one day obtain a second kind of inheritance, a reward-inheritance, that is, he would become an "heir of the world." Paul explains that this second inheritance was awarded not because of the initial act of faith but because of a faith that perseveres to the end of life. Abraham did persevere. He hoped against hope that he would receive a son.

Experimental Predestinarians actually agree that in order to become an heir of the world, persistence in the same kind of faith that granted justification to begin with must characterize the believer's life. The difference is that they understand that becoming an heir of the world means something like going to heaven when one dies, and all true Christians,

303 Gerhard von Rad, "k^e^bōd" in TDNT, 2:242. For example, the whole earth is full of the glory of the Lord (Isaiah 6:3), His glory is above the earth (Psalms 57:5, 11), and all the nations will see His glory (i.e., dominion) and declare it to the Gentiles (Isaiah 66:18-19).

304 See Matthew 19:28; 24:30; 25:31; Mark 8:38; 13:26; Luke 9:26; Colossians 3:4; Hebrews 2:10; 1 Peter 4:13.

they say, will evidence perseverance in faith, not as a condition, they say, of final entrance into heaven, but as a manifestation of genuine faith. The Partners, on the other hand, understand heirship of the world to be a reward beyond initial salvation, being a co-heir with Christ in the final destiny of man. Becoming a co-heir with Christ is grounded on perseverance in faith to the end of life.

In Romans 8:17, Paul tells us there are two kinds of inheritance: all believers are heirs of God (birth-inheritance), and for those who set their life goal to be perseverance in suffering with Christ (even if they sometimes fail), they can become co-heirs with Christ (reward-inheritance).

To be a co-heir with Christ is what Paul elsewhere calls "inheriting the kingdom." This is the theme of the next five chapters.

6

Inheriting the Kingdom in Corinthians and Galatians

SEVERAL YEARS ago a popular Hollywood movie told the story of a wealthy man who was passing on his inheritance to a rather irresponsible son. Soon after his death, his lawyer called the son into his office to show him his father's will which he had recorded in a video. In the video he told his son that he intended to pass on his inheritance to him, but before he could access it, he must do twelve things. Failure to complete these tasks would result in disinheritance.

Disinheritance! Even to suggest that such a thing could happen to a true believer in Christ draws gasps of surprise, even though such a fact is mentioned in many places in the New Testament. Two such passages are the subject of this chapter.

> *Do you not know that the wicked will not inherit* [Gr *klēronomeō*] *the kingdom of God? Do not be deceived: Neither the sexually immoral nor idolaters nor adulterers nor male prostitutes nor homosexual offenders nor thieves nor slanderers nor swindlers will inherit* [*klēronomeō*] *the kingdom of God (1 Corinthians 6:9-10).*

> *Envying, drunkenness, carousing, and things like these, of which I forewarn you, just as I have forewarned you, that those who practice such things will not* **inherit the kingdom of God** *(Galatians 5:21).*

The heirs of the kingdom of God, in either its millennial or eternal phase, are its owners and rulers and not just its residents. Inheriting the kingdom is not exactly the same thing as entering it. Kendall has taught us, "In other words, salvation is unchangeable but our inheritance in the kingdom of God is not unchangeable. Once saved, always saved, but our *inheritance* in God's kingdom may change considerably."[305] This changeable inheritance is our reward-inheritance. Even some Experimental Predestinarians acknowledge this distinction. Lenski, for example, observes that "shall inherit" should not be reduced to mean only "shall participate in." That latter may be done without ownership.[306] The loss of one's inheritance is not the same as loss of salvation.

But according to Paul it is possible for a Christian to be disinherited! We read in 1 Corinthians 6:10 that unrighteous Christians will lose their reward-inheritance in the kingdom of God.

---

305 Kendall, *Once Saved, Always Saved*, 92.

306 R. C. H. Lenski, *The Interpretation of I and II Corinthians* (Minneapolis: Augsburg Publishing Co., 1963), 247.

Or do you not know that the ***unrighteous will not inherit the kingdom of God?*** *Do not be deceived; neither fornicators, nor idolaters, nor adulterers, nor effeminate, nor homosexuals, nor thieves, nor the covetous, nor drunkards, nor revilers, nor swindlers, will inherit the kingdom of God (1 Corinthians 6:9–10).*

The Inheritance in 1 Corinthians

What does it mean to "inherit the kingdom of God," and who are the "unrighteous"? In Jewish literature the term included the idea of entering into salvation in the "world to come" and also to obtain "treasure" there.[307] However, in spite of current fascination with all things pseudepigraphal and mishnaic, considerable caution should be exercised in using Second Temple literature for interpretation of the New Testament.[308] To base conclusions on these sources and assume they reflected Paul's perspective on terms like "inherit the kingdom" is at best speculative.[309] It is preferable to interpret the phrase from the New Testament documents and possible Old Testament allusions.

But does the passage refer to unrighteous Christians, or does it refer to non-Christians who may have been loosely associated with the church and whose lack of perseverance in holiness has demonstrated that they were not Christians at all? Or does it imply, as Arminians suggest, that true believers can be disinherited in the sense of losing salvation?[310]

René López believes that those who will not inherit the kingdom are nonbelievers, and that "inherit the kingdom" means "go to heaven when you die." He argues, "Rather than saying, 'You do wrong; wrongdoers will not inherit the kingdom; thus, you will not inherit,' he concludes, 'You do wrong; wrongdoers will not inherit; but you are not wrongdoers.'"[311] However, Paul does not say, "You *are* not wrongdoers." He says they *were* wrongdoers before they were washed and sanctified, and he argues in the context and the whole book (see below) that they *still are* wrongdoers in their behavior. The subject is behavior, not

[307] One example from the Mishnah says, "The disciples of Abraham our father enjoy the benefit [of their learning] in this world and yet inherit the world to come, as it is said, That I may cause those who love me to inherit substance, and so that I may fill their treasures (Proverbs 8:21)." Apparently, to "inherit the world to come" means to obtain "substance" and many treasures. This inheritance is granted on the basis of works, to "those who love me." The phrase is ambiguous. It could be understood to mean that inheriting the world to come means finding substance and full treasure there, that is, reward.

[308] I have discussed this problem in detail elsewhere, see pp. 857 ff.

[309] René López, for example, is overly dependent on the bearing of extra-biblical literature on the meaning of the phrase "inherit the kingdom." René A. López, "The Pauline Vice List and Inheriting the Kingdom" (PhD diss., Dallas Theological Seminary, 2010), 218-20. See discussion on pp. 857 ff.,"Gehenna in the Pseudepigrapha which questions his confidence in the relevance of this literature to New Testament Interpretation. In fact, according to Marty Cauley, López apparently overlooked the fact that even in Enoch the inheritance is sometimes a reward for a faithful life (2 Enoch 9:1). See Marty Cauley, *The Outer Darkness*, 2 vols. (Sylva, NC: Misthological Press, 1231 Monteith Branch Road, 2012), 475-76.

[310] For example, Wesley said, "He that through the power of faith endureth to the end in humble, gentle, patient love; he, and he alone, shall, through the merits of Christ, "inherit the kingdom prepared from the foundation of the world" See "On Charity," Wesley, *The Works of John Wesley: Addresses, Essays, and Letters*, 91.3.13. Robertson and Plummer also see this as an indication that true believers can lose their salvation, that is, be disinherited. They say that Paul, "reminds the Corinthians that, although all Christians are heirs, yet heirs may be disinherited. They may disqualify themselves," Archibald Robertson and Alfred Plummer, *A Critical and Exegetical Commentary on the First Epistle of Paul to the Corinthians*, The International Criticial Commentry (New York: C. Scribner's Sons, 1911), 118.

[311] López, "The Pauline Vice List and Inheriting the Kingdom", 224-25.

identity! He says that wrongdoers will not inherit, and he argues throughout the book that they are wrongdoers. If one merely assumes that the wrongdoers (Gr *adikoi*, "wicked") are not Christians, well then, they are not. But that is the point in question. Who are the *adikoi*?

One might argue that the term "unrighteous" (Gr *adikos*) refers to those who are unregenerate in 1 Corinthians 6:1.[312] However, the near antecedent in verse 8, "*you yourselves do wrong* [Gr *adikeō*]," should be determinative for the meaning of "unrighteous" (i.e., "those who do wrong") in verse 9, and not the more remote use of the noun form of this verb (Gr *adikos*) in verse 1. Elsewhere, however, adikos does not refer to soteriological status, but to character (Romans 3:5). Even though they are unsaved, verse 1 probably refers to their character; they are "unjust" judges.

The related noun *adikia* ("unrighteousness, wrongdoing")[313] is used many times in the New Testament of those who are believers. For example, Paul says, "Do not go on presenting the members of your body to *adikia*," and "let everyone who names the name of the Lord abstain from *adikia*" (2 Timothy 2:19).[314]

We are told in verse 9 that the "wicked" (Gr *adikoi*) will not inherit this kingdom, and in verse 1 the same word is used of non-Christians (cf. 6:6). In fact, the contrast between the righteous, *dikaioi*, and the unrighteous, *adikoi*, is common in the New Testament,[315] and those whose lives are characterized by *adikia* are in some contexts eternally condemned.[316] But this kind of argument assumes that *adikoi* is a kind of technical term for those lacking the imputed righteousness of Christ. The illegitimate identity transfer is committed to import the contextually derived suggestion of one kind of consequence of being *adikos* into the semantic value of the word. However, it is a general term for those (Christian or non-Christian) who lack godly character.[317] Both Christians and non-Christians can be *adikoi*. In fact, in 6:8 the apostle declares that the Corinthians are acting like *adikoi* (he uses the verbal form, *adikeō*) just like the non-Christians of verse 1. Robertson and Plummer are correct when they say, "The word ['wicked' in v. 9] is suggested by the previous, *adikeō* ['you cheat and do wrong,' v. 8], and not with the *adikoi*, ['the wicked,' of v. 1]."[318]

Exegetically, this seems better for several reasons. First, the verbal form of *adikoi* in verse 8 (Gr *adikeō*) is the near antecedent, and one normally looks there first. Paul is speaking of the behavior of these Christians in verse 8. Wicked people, whether they are believers (vv. 8-9) or nonbelievers (v. 1), do not inherit God's kingdom. *The New Century Version* captures the close connection between the verses by translating this way:

> *But you yourselves* ***do wrong*** *and cheat, and you do this to other believers! Surely you know that the* ***people who do wrong*** *will not inherit God's kingdom (1 Corinthians 6:8-9, NCV).*

---

312 However, it is also used elsewhere of true believers in Luke 16:10.

313 BDAG, 20.

314 See the promise of forgiveness and cleansing for believers from *adikia* (1 John 1:9).

315 See Matthew 5:45; Acts 24:15; 1 Peter 3:18.

316 Cf. Romans 1:18, 29; 2:8; 2 Thessalonians 2:10-12; 2 Peter 2:13-15.

317 See usage in Luke 16:10-11; 18:11; Hebrews 6:10.

318 Robertson and Plummer, *A Critical and Exegetical Commentary on the First Epistle of Paul to the Corinthians*, 118.

As Paul put it elsewhere, they walk as "mere men" (1 Corinthians 3:4).

But second, it is highly unlikely that the wicked of verse 9 could be non-Christians because Paul says, "Do not be deceived," the wicked will not inherit the kingdom. Why would Christians think that non-Christians would inherit God's kingdom?[319]

> *Instead, you yourselves cheat and do wrong [adikeō], and you do this to your brothers (1 Corinthians 6:8).*

Here Paul uses the verb form, *adikeō*, of the adjective *adikos*. He says in verse 8 that they "cheat and do wrong," and then in verse 9 he warns them concerning the eternal consequences of their behavior. He is not warning non-Christians that they will not inherit the kingdom; he is warning Christians, those who do wrong and do it to their brothers. It is pointless to argue that true Christians could never be characterized by the things in this list when Paul connects the true Christians of verse 8 with the individuals in verse 9.

The strong contrast between their past conversion ("and such were some of you") and the strong adversative "but" (Gr *alla*), used three times to stress the contrast between the old life and the new, has led some to conclude that since this describes the behavior of the Corinthians before they were converted the term must refer to unconverted people.[320] However, the term refers to *unconverted behavior* and not *unconverted people!* Paul is clear elsewhere that they walk as "mere men," that is, the Corinthian believers behave like unconverted people (1 Corinthians 3:3). The very strong contrast is not between being saved and unsaved but between the fact that though they were washed, sanctified, and justified, they are still acting as if nothing happened. They are still acting unrighteously.

Also, it is wrong to argue that only nonbelievers are the objects of the warning because of their bad behavior, when the entire context of 1 Corinthians describes activities of Christians which parallel nearly every item in verses 9-10. They were involved in sexual immorality (5:1; 6:15); idolatry (5:11), covetousness (probable motive in lawsuits, 6:1); drunkenness (5:11; 11:21); dishonoring the Lord's Table (11:30--for this reason some of them experienced the sin unto death); adultery and incest (5:1); and they were arrogant (4:18; 5:6). Yet these people who are acting unrighteously, *adikeō, and* are guilty of all these things, have been washed, sanctified, and justified in the name of the Lord Jesus Christ (6:11)! They were washed and saved from all those things, and yet they are still doing them.[321] That is the terrible inconsistency that grieves the apostle through all sixteen chapters of this book. His burden in 6:9-10 is not to call into question their salvation (he specifically says they are saved in v. 11)[322] but to warn them that, if they do not change their

---

319 Some have argued that this is an encouragement not to be like non-Christians. Why would anyone want to be like people who will not go to heaven?

320 See Brown, "The New Testament Concept of the Believer's Inheritance", 121.

321 As Christian F. Kling puts it, "He goes on to remind the Corinthians that for them these trials belonged to the past, and that indulgence in such vices was for them a backsliding into their old heathenish state, which utterly contradicted their high Christian experience," Christian Friedrich Kling, "1 Corinthians" in Christian Friedrich Kling, *The First Epistle of Paul to the Corinthians*, ed. J. P. Lange, et al., 12 vols., A Commentary on the Holy Scriptures (Grand Rapids: Zondervan Publishing House, 1960), 126.

322 He has said they were "sanctified in Christ Jesus, called to be saints" (1 Corinthians 1:2) but that they were carnal (1 Corinthians 3:1, 3).

behavior, they, like Esau, will forfeit their reward-inheritance.[323] As Kendall put it, "It was not salvation, then, but their inheritance in the kingdom of God these Christians were in danger of forfeiting."[324] Obviously, he was not warning believers that nonbelievers will not go to heaven.[325]

This warning, of course, does not mean that a person who commits one of these sins will not enter heaven. It does mean that, if he commits such a sin and persists in it without confessing and receiving cleansing (1 John 1:9), he will lose his right to rule with Christ in the eternal phase of the Kingdom of God in the new heavens and new earth (1 Corinthians 15:50).[326] That is, he will lose his reward-inheritance even though he will maintain his birth-inheritance. Those walking in such a state (without their sin confessed) face eternal consequences if their Lord should suddenly appear and find them unprepared. They will truly be ashamed "before Him at His coming" (1 John 2:28, cf. Revelation 3:11) and lose what they have worked for (2 John 8, Mark 4:25). For this reason, Jesus exhorted the church in Philadelphia, "I am coming quickly; hold fast what you have, so that no one will take your crown" (Revelation 3:11).

The Inheritance in Galatians

Galatians 3:18 and 29 introduces the subject of an inheritance that comes to believers simply because they "belong to Christ" through faith alone; this is their birth-inheritance.

---

323 For excellent development along the lines of the interpretation presented here see Robert Wilkin, "Christians Who Lose Their Legacy: Gal 5:21," *JOTGES* 4, no. 2 (Autumn 91): 23-27.

324 Kendall, *Once Saved, Always Saved*, 96.

325 But, possibly, this is not a warning at all; instead, it is an exhortation. This has been capably argued by René López. See René A. López, "Does the Vice List in 1 Corinthians 6:9-10 Describe Believers or Unbelievers," *BibSac* 164, no. 653 (January-March 2007): 59-73. López suggests that Paul is exhorting the Corinthians to live like who they really are, justified, sanctified, and cleansed saints. However, it is difficult to see that this exhortation would have any telling force. López counters, "That Paul exhorts believers instead of warning them here should not be undermined as lacking a punch to motivate believers to change. Many times the element of embarrassment by reprimand before a group of peers could perhaps carry more weight than having a fear of discipline, since exposing a person's error in public may have a deeper conviction than being disciplined by the Lord in private" (López, "The Pauline Vice List and Inheriting the Kingdom", 258). Perhaps, but exhortations without some consequence attached too often fall on deaf ears. Nothing in the context suggests that Paul's intent is to embarrass them before other believers. Furthermore, the seriousness of their sin and Paul's threats elsewhere that their wrongdoing could lead to temporal judgment, physical death, or full loss of reward in the future (1 Corinthians 3:15; 10:7-12; 11:32; 16:22; 2 Corinthians 3:5; 5:10-11), surely point the readers in the direction of a warning, and not a mere exhortation to be good because they are good positionally. In 2 Corinthians 5:10-11 he warns, "*For we must all appear before the Judgment Seat of Christ, so that each one may be recompensed for his deeds in the body, according to what he has done, whether good or bad. Therefore,* ***knowing the fear of the Lord****, we persuade men* …." Warnings are typical of Paul's motivational scheme in the Corinthian correspondence. López himself admits that in the parallel passage in Ephesians 5:2-7 "Paul warned the Christians … 'to live obediently and 'not be partakers' in the sins of the 'children of disobedience,' because this logically brings God's wrath upon them." Ibid., 269. He also equates reward at the Judgment Seat of Christ with the inheritance in 1 Corinthians 3:12-15, "Paul, like Jewish law, places conditions of obedience on believers in order for them to inherit further privileges that required more than membership in the spiritual family (1 Corinthians 3:12-15; 4:8; 5:5; Galatians 4:1-7; 6:1-8; Romans 8:17b-18; 14:11-12; 2 Timothy 2:12-14; cf. Matthew 10:33; Luke 12:9; 19:11-27; Revelation 2:26-27; 3:21; 5:10; 22:12)." Ibid., 86.

326 In view of this verse it is likely that when Paul uses the term "inherit the kingdom of God" the millennium is not in the forefront, although, of course, they will not inherit there either. For full discussion of this see the following two chapters.

In previous chapters we have discussed another kind of inheritance, one that comes to the believer in Christ as a result of his works, a reward for a life well-lived. As we shall see in the book of Galatians, like the Old Testament, there are two kinds of inheritance: one that comes to us by faith alone, and, for no other reason, one that comes to us as a reward for persevering in faith plus works.

AN INHERITANCE BASED ON PROMISE

> *For if the inheritance is based on law, it is no longer based on a promise; but God has granted it to Abraham by means of a promise (Galatians 3:18).*

The first kind of inheritance mentioned in the Epistle to the Galatians is the inheritance based on promise. As in the Old Testament, all believers have God as their inheritance (their birth-inheritance). For Paul this is expressed by the saying that we are all "heirs of God" (Rom 8:17; Galatians 3:29; 4:7); "sons of God" (Galatians 3:26); and "sons of Abraham" (Galatians 3:7).[327] The promise referred to in Galatians 3:18 is also in 3:8 and 16 and recalls the promise to Abraham that "all the nations will be blessed through you" (Galatians 3:8).[328]

The inheritance in this verse is not linked to the land promise but with that aspect of the Abrahamic promise that referred to the gift of justification to the Gentiles, "*in you all the families of the earth will be blessed*" (Genesis 12:3). The land promise in the Old Testament was associated with works, but having God as one's inheritance was not. The heirs of 3:29 become heirs by virtue of being sons, and through no other means; they are heirs of God, that is, possessors of eternal life. The word "heir" is used again in 4:7:

> *So you are no longer a slave, but a son; and since you are a son, God has made you also an heir [klēronomos].*

All Christians are heirs of God by faith alone. Paul's use of *klēronomia* in 4:30 is another example of the inheritance of "heaven when one dies" which is granted by faith alone, our birth-inheritance.[329]

In summary, the inheritance of Galatians 3:18 and 4:30 is parallel not with the land promises of Canaan, but with the gift of justification to the Gentiles, and refers to their birth-inheritance. This passage is often incorrectly used to equate the inheritance of

---

327 Paul does not say, as the NASB translates, that the inheritance was not "based on" the Law (3:18). He says it was not "from" the Law, that is, it does not come from the Mosaic Covenant, the dispensation of Law; instead it was granted by means of promise. Thus the Mosaic covenant, coming 430 years later, cannot abrogate the Abrahamic covenant that had been ratified (3:15) by God and therefore could not be annulled. The fact that it is not from the dispensation of the Law, does not mean that one need not obey God from a faithful heart to experience its benefits. It is clear from the Old Testament that the temporal aspects of the inheritance do not come by faith alone. These aspects refer to possession of the land and living in safety under God's blessing there; and this was obtained by faithful obedience.

328 Genesis 12:3; 22:18; 26:4; 28:14.

329 It should be noted that this usage is found in an illustration from the Old Testament (Galatians 4:24-31). He is using the illustration of Hagar and Sarah to refute the notion that law and grace can be mixed. He says he speaks "figuratively." He is using the term "heir" in the general sense of "possessor" to figuratively illustrate that this kind of heirship is never appropriated by a mixture of Sinai and the Jerusalem above, Ishmael and Isaac, law and grace; neither is the inheritance of heaven.

the land of Canaan with heaven, but the land of Canaan is not even the subject of the passage!

AN INHERITANCE BASED ON WORKS

A second kind of inheritance mentioned in Galatians is an inheritance that is obtained only by progressive sanctification. In contrast to the inheritance granted to faith alone (mentioned in 3:18, 29; 4:7, 30), Paul describes another kind of inheritance, a reward-inheritance that is awarded for persevering faith, a lifestyle reflecting Christlikeness:

> *envying, drunkenness, carousing, and things like these, of which I forewarn you, just as I have forewarned you, that those who practice such things will not* ***inherit the kingdom of God*** *(Galatians 5:21).*

To obtain the soteriological aspects of the inheritance granted to all "sons" (Galatians 4:6), one must believe and nothing more (Galatians 3:6); to obtain an inheritance in the kingdom of God, one must persevere in belief and obey God from the heart (Galatians 5:16, 21). As Paul put it later, all that matters is "*faith working through love*" (Galatians 5:6).

Galatians 5:21 is addressed to believers who have been told beforehand ("forewarned") that their behavior, if persisted in, will result in a forfeiture of their reward-inheritance in the kingdom of God even though they retain their birth-inheritance.[330] The contrast is not between those who will not inherit ("those who practice such things," 5:21) and those who belong to Christ (5:24). Rather the contrast is between believers who will inherit and those who will not. The term "forewarn" (Gr *prolegō*) means to "tell beforehand." In many passages it includes an implied warning (e.g. 1 Thessalonians 4:6; Galatians 1:9).[331] That meaning fits this context well.

If inheriting the kingdom in these texts refers to going to heaven, then the apostle's sublime exhortation to these believers is reduced to the banal observation: "Remember, non-Christians do not go to heaven," an exhortation which would have little relevance to these Galatian Christians who "belong to Christ Jesus" (Galatians 5:24).[332] Surely R. T. Kendall is correct when he says:

> *Are we to say that anybody who* ***does*** *any of these things (e.g. envying, strife) is not going to heaven? Not at all. But such things as "covetousness," "foolish talking," as well as sexual immorality forfeit one's inheritance in God's kingdom.*[333]

According to Paul, this second kind of inheritance is NOT unconditional to all

---

[330] Contra Brown who attempts to mute the force of the verb *prolegō* ("tell beforehand", warn) to mean only "tell beforehand." He then says, "Thus, Paul is not threatening the Galatians but rather restating a principle." See Brown, "The New Testament Concept of the Believer's Inheritance."

[331] BDAG, 868.

[332] The fact that these believers "have crucified the sinful nature" can hardly refer to the idea that all Christians have sacrificially negated the impulses of the flesh. The unexpected occurrence of the active voice may be paralleled with 1 Corinthians 9:22, "I have become all things to all men in order that by all means I might save some." The passage echoes a Romans 6:1-11 (written later), our joint crucifixion with Christ at initial salvation, which must be put into experience by reckoning and yielding.

[333] Kendall, *Once Saved, Always Saved*, 96.

believers. He says, we must "walk by the Spirit" if we are to obtain this inheritance (Galatians 5:25). If we do not, we will not inherit, because "*envying, drunkenness, carousing, and things like these, of which I forewarn you, just as I have forewarned you, that those who practice such things will not inherit the kingdom of God*" (Galatians 5:21). So in 3:18 Paul says the inheritance is granted by means of promise, that is, by faith alone (the birth-inheritance). Yet in 5:21, he says that those already saved,[334] who have received the birth-inheritance by faith alone, may possibly *not* obtain the reward-inheritance because of their bad behavior. The inheritance granted to all "sons" (Gal 4:7) cannot be lost, but the privilege of inheriting the kingdom can! This difference is because in 3:18 and 4:7 Paul speaks of the soteriological aspect of the blessing to Abraham and in 5:21, he is speaking of reward aspect granted for obedience.

It is significant that whenever the verb "to inherit" is used in the future tense in the New Testament *it always refers to obtaining the inheritance by means of doing, not faith alone.*[335] In those cases it refers to that aspect of our inheritance which is conditioned upon faithful endurance.

In Galatians 6 he says further, "*Do not be deceived, God is not mocked; for whatever a man sows this he will also reap. For the one who sows to his own flesh will from the flesh reap corruption, but the one who sows to the Spirit will from the Spirit reap eternal life*" (Galatians 6:7–8). The outcomes resulting from "reaping" are either "corruption" or "eternal life," that is, spiritual failure or a rich experience of eternal life. In this instance eternal life is granted for works, that is, for "sowing" and not for faith alone. This aspect of eternal life refers to an enhanced experience of eternal life rewarded for faithfulness. It refers to the results of living life, not to gaining life. When eternal life is presented as an acquisition in the present, faith alone is the only condition mentioned.[336]

What about "corruption"? Does this refer to separation from God? Nowhere in the New Testament is "corruption" linked with damnation; it is always associated with the corruption that exists in this world.[337] Furthermore, a "man thus reaps the fruit of what he has done."[338] Reaping comes as a result of doing, not only by believing; it comes by works, not by faith alone. "Sowing and reaping are the beginning and end of a growth process."[339] Justification before God is an event, not a process. Corruption and eternal life in this passage are not soteriological contrasts, they are temporal life contrasts.

Many commentators, when they see the phrase "eternal life" in Galatians 6:8 ("reap eternal life") automatically assume without discussion that this refers to "heaven when one dies." Because they "know" this, they struggle with the meaning of corruption, which they know does not mean eternal separation from God. Ronald Y. K. Fung, for example, while admitting that corruption refers to "physical and moral deterioration together,"

---

334 One does not exhort non-Christians to "walk by the Spirit."

335 Matthew 5:5; 19:16, 29; 25:46, cf. v. 35; Mark 10:17, 30; Luke 10:25, 18, 30; John 4:36; 12:25; Galatians 6:8; 1 Corinthians 6:9, 10; Galatians 4:30; 5:21; Jude 21; Revelation 21:7. See full discussion on pp. 222 ff.

336 John 3:15, 16; 4:14, drink=believe; 4:30; 5:24, 39-40; 6:27-29, 40, 47, 54, 68-69; 10:27-28, follow=believe; 17:2; Acts 13:46-48, worthy=believe; Romans 2:7; 5:21; 1 Timothy 1:16; Titus 3:5-7; 1 John 5:11,13. See "Earned as a Reward," 222 ff.

337 See 1 Corinthians 15:50; Colossians 2:22; 2 Peter 1:4; 2:12, 19.

338 Hauck, "θερίζω, θερισμός, in TDNT 3:132.

339 EDNT, 2:145.

nevertheless, incorrectly assumes that eternal life must refer to heaven. In order to make this interpretation fit, he says, "Corruption refers to physical death and disintegration, from which, for those who sow to the flesh, there is no rising to eternal life."[340] The statement is not just confusing; it is wrong. Sinful believers do rise to eternal life (e.g. Matthew 5:19; 1 Corinthians 3:15; 15:50 ff.) with resurrection bodies. After telling us that reaping eternal life is a result of a lifelong process of sowing and that the "eschatological yield is determined by present sowing," he confusedly states that "eternal life is a gift which comes from the Spirit."[341] Such are the bafflements resulting from Experimental Predestinarian exegesis.[342]

This passage is directed at believers, not those who have insincerely or falsely professed faith in Christ. They are exhorted to "do good" to all men and especially to those of the household of faith (6:10) and not to "lose heart in doing good" (v. 9). If believers do not walk by the Spirit, even though they will "go to heaven when they die," they will not "inherit the kingdom"; they will not experience the blessing of Abraham to its fullest.

It is a tragedy of immense proportions that Experimental Predestinarians, equating the inheritance only with heaven, have removed these much-needed warnings addressed to carnal Christians. Instead they apply them only to those who have professed but not really possessed faith in Christ. Carnal Christians dismiss the warnings because they "know" they are Christians and hence lapse into a lukewarm, uncommitted Christianity, unaware of the terrible consequences they face at the Judgment Seat of Christ.

Summary

In 1 Corinthians, Paul introduces the theme of inheriting the kingdom. To inherit the kingdom of God is to reign with Christ in the new heavens and the new earth; it refers to obtaining the reward-inheritance. Paul is clear that those whose lives are characterized by unrighteousness will not inherit this kingdom, that is, they will not be co-heirs with Christ there. The warning is addressed to true Christians who, like the carnal Corinthians, are walking as "mere men" and who "do wrong."

Consistent with the Old Testament, the book of Galatians presents two kinds of inheritance. The first is equivalent to the Old Testament blessing of having God as one's

---

340 Ronald Y. K. Fung, *The Epistle to the Galatians*, The New International Commentary on the New Testament (Grand Rapids: Wm. B. Eerdmans Publishing Co., 1988), 295.

341 Ibid., 295.

342 Some avoid the discussion by ambiguously saying that "destruction" is the final end of those who sow to the flesh. Thus, destruction is destruction! But this is not very helpful. For example see Richard N. Longnecker, *Galatians*, Word Biblical Commentary (Dallas: Word, 2002), 280. Timothy George simply asserts that "eternal life" refers to heaven and that corruption refers to eternal damnation, and then he never bothers to explain how one obtains this eternal life by means of sowing, that is, works, thus leaving readers of his commentary confused, Timothy George, *Galatians*, The New American Commentary (Nashville: Broadman & Holman Publishers, 1994), 423. Indifferent to the theological issue of a works salvation, Betz also ignores the issue, and gratuitously asserts, without proof, that "corruption" refers to damnation. Calvin says, "Though eternal life is a reward, it does not follow either that we are justified by works, or that works are meritorious of salvation. The undeserved kindness of God appears in the very act of honouring the works which his grace has enabled us to perform, by promising to them a reward to which they are not entitled." His admission that eternal life is here a "reward" certainly would demand that justification is by works. Calvin falls back on the fact that because God enables us to perform these works we obtain the reward of heaven to which we have no claim. However, salvation is by faith alone apart from works, whether enabled by God or self. Calvin, *Galatians*, 179.

inheritance. For Paul this was being an "heir through God" (Galatians 4:7). This inheritance came through promise and not works (Galatians 3:29). Yet he describes another kind of inheritance, one that is granted to those who sow to the Spirit (6:7-8), walk in the Spirit (Galatians 5:16), and who manifest a Christlike lifestyle (Galatians 5:21). This second kind of inheritance will not be available to those who practice unrighteousness (Galatians 5:21). The warning is parallel to that in 1 Corinthians 6:9-10.

In another passage (Ephesians 5:5) the apostle speaks of losing one's inheritance because of bad ethical behavior. However, we will delay our examination of the inheritance in Ephesians until a later chapter. We first must complete our discussion of the references to inheritance in 1 Corinthians. In the following chapter we will consider the meaning of "inherit the kingdom of God" in 1 Corinthians 15:50.

7 Inheriting the New Heavens and New Earth

IN THE preceding chapters we discussed what it means to inherit something. Our conclusion was that in the New Testament and the Old, the inheritance is often presented as something worked for, a reward for faithfulness (Colossians 3:24; Matthew 25:34 ff.), and initially consists in being a co-heir with Christ in the millennium (Romans 8:17; 2 Timothy 2:12).

In this chapter and the next, we will continue our exploration of the meaning of the phrase "inherit the kingdom of God" in 1 Corinthians. According to 1 Corinthians 15:50, flesh and blood cannot inherit the kingdom of God.

> *Now I say this, brethren, that* ***flesh and blood cannot inherit the kingdom of God;*** *nor does the perishable inherit the imperishable. Behold, I tell you a mystery; we will not all sleep, but we will all be changed, in a moment, in the twinkling of an eye, at the last trumpet; for the trumpet will sound, and the dead will be raised imperishable, and we will be changed (1 Corinthians 15:50–52).*

If this event occurs before the millennium and if "inherit" means to "get in," there must be a transformation of the living before the kingdom of God begins.

Elsewhere, Paul describes the rapture of the church using similar language.

> *For the Lord Himself will descend from heaven with a shout, with the voice of the archangel and with the trumpet of God, and the dead in Christ will rise first. Then we who are alive and remain will be caught up together with them in the clouds to meet the Lord in the air, and so we shall always be with the Lord (1 Thessalonians 4:16–17).*

The similarity of language between these verses has led many to accept the view that both passages refer to the rapture. Also, many wrongly assume that the rapture occurs at the end of the tribulation.

For those who believe in a literal millennium and who also believe that *inheriting* the kingdom and *entering* the kingdom (in the sense of personal salvation) mean the same thing, some difficulties arise. If flesh and blood cannot *inherit/enter* the kingdom, then there must be a transformation of all living believers at the second coming. If all living believers are transformed at the second coming, and if nonbelievers cannot enter the kingdom (understood as final salvation from damnation) because they are not born again, an obvious difficulty emerges. Where are the mortal believers which Isaiah (Isaiah 65:10) says will populate the millennium?[343]

[343] See discussion below.

If we assume for the moment that *entering* the kingdom refers to soteriological admittance into the millennium or eternal state, then there must be a distinction between *inheriting* the millennial kingdom and *entrance* into it. If *inheriting* the kingdom means the same thing as *entering* the kingdom, then only those in resurrected bodies can get into the millennium and no mortals will populate the millennial earth.

Given the above assumptions, there is no escape from this conclusion. This substantiates the argument in the preceding chapters that an inheritance is something in addition to initial entrance into eternal life. Robert Wilkin is correct when he says, "For those of us who believe that there will be people with un-resurrected bodies who take part in the kingdom, Paul must be talking about something other than soteriological kingdom entrance. First Corinthians 15:50 refutes any view which understands inheriting the kingdom as merely getting in."[344]

This problem confounds post-tribulationalism, which assumes that this transformation of the living referred to in 1 Thessalonians 4:18 and 1 Corinthians 15:50 occurs at the second advent. If that is so, then, all are transformed (1 Corinthians 15:51, "*all* will be changed") and no unbelievers can enter the kingdom because one must be born again in order to enter the kingdom (John 3:3-5). This is confirmed by Rev 19:19-21 and Matthew 25:46 which say all unbelievers will be cast into the lake of fire at the beginning of the millennium. Thus, there would be no mortals left to populate the millennial earth in contradiction to many passages in the Old Testament (see discussion below). A pretribulation rapture helps solve this problem by saying that the "*Parousia*" mentioned in 1 Corinthians 15:23 as well as the rapture and transformation of the living in 1 Thessalonians 4:17 occur seven years prior to the second advent. During the following seven years of tribulation, millions will come to Christ and will populate the millennial kingdom in mortal bodies.

However, the pretribulation view also presents a problem for those who draw distinctions between *inheriting* and *entering* (in the sense of "getting in") the kingdom. Why? Pretribulation advocates commonly argue that the problem of populating the millennium is solved by the fact that the mortal believers who survive the tribulation will enter the millennium.[345] However, since they also argue that "inherit" is a soteriological term (and not a reward term), and since Paul says that flesh and blood cannot inherit the kingdom, this would require that all those mortal survivors of the tribulation must be given resurrection bodies or they cannot enter/inherit the kingdom at all. Even if one grants that "inherit" means to "rule with Christ," Paul says that flesh and blood cannot inherit. This means either that: (1) only resurrected and transformed saints will inherit the kingdom and no mortals will,[346] or (2) that *inheriting* the kingdom in 1 Corinthians 15:50 does not refer to either the rapture or the second coming. Instead, it refers to *inheriting the eternal phase* of the kingdom, the new heavens and the new earth.

---

[344] Wilkin, "Christians Who Lose Their Legacy: Gal 5:21," 31.

[345] For example, Walvoord says, "If the church is translated before the tribulation period, there is ample time for a new generation of believers to come into being from Jew and Gentile background to qualify for entrance into the millennial kingdom at the second coming of Christ. The problem of populating the millennium is thereby quickly solved and many related Scriptures are given a natural and literal interpretation." John F. Walvoord, "Premillennialism and the Tribulation Part IV: Pretribulationism (continued)," *BibSac* 112, no. 446 (April 1955): 100. See also, Walvoord, *The Millennial Kingdom*, 253.

[346] This was the view of George N. H. Peters, George N. H. Peters, *The Theocratic Kingdom of Our Lord Jesus, the Christ, as Covenanted in the Old Testament and Presented in the New Testament*, reprint ed. (Grand Rapids: Kregel Publications, 1972), 2:573.

That mortals will have no inheritance in the millennium and only faithful resurrected saints will have that privilege contradicts the entire thrust of the inheritance promises in the New Testament, and thus option 1 is highly improbable. Surely the many promises of obtaining an inheritance mentioned in the preceding chapters must also apply to these faithful and persevering mortal saints who enter the millennial phase of the eternal kingdom of God. And they do. Those tribulation saints who "overcome" are greatly rewarded for their faithfulness in the tribulation (Revelation 2:7; 3:5, 12) and will reign with Christ (Revelation 3:21).[347] Jesus tells the faithful unresurrected saints who have persevered through the tribulation horrors to "inherit the kingdom" (Matthew 25:34). There is no mention of them being translated at a posttribulational rapture or changed into glorified bodies. If they were transformed, there would be no mortals available to populate the millennial earth. Or one might say, "the faithful tribulation saints who persevered will be given resurrection bodies at this time and only carnal unfaithful tribulation saints in mortal bodies will enter the kingdom." This has to be inserted to fit a posttribulational system of thought. The discussion descends into absurdity and speculation!

Therefore, option 2 is the most plausible view. However, this means that 1 Corinthians 15:50-53 cannot refer to the rapture of the church (either pre or post tribulation) as is commonly assumed.[348] And it does not. In the following discussion I will show that these verses refer to the transformation of the living and resurrection of the dead at the end of the millennium.

Flesh and Blood Cannot Inherit the Kingdom of God

The central passage related to this issue is 1 Corinthians 15:50-52.

I declare to you, brothers, that flesh and blood cannot inherit the kingdom of God, nor does the perishable inherit the imperishable.

Controversy centers on when this event occurs. Some equate this event with the rapture of the church in 1 Thessalonians 4:14-17. Others believe that it refers to inheriting the eternal state. Those holding the latter view are generally amillennialists and view the *Parousia* and the beginning of the eternal state as co-terminus.

In the interests of clarity, before diving into the rather complicated discussion to follow, it is best to set forth the conclusions at the beginning.

I will argue that the rapture occurs before the tribulation when all believers then living are transformed and receive their glorified bodies (1 Thessalonians 4:14-17). During the tribulation, the 144,000 Jewish missionaries mentioned in Revelation 7:1-10 evangelize the world and millions come to Christ. Those who survive the tribulation will then appear at

---

[347] They will also "inherit all things" in the eternal state (Revelation 21:7).

[348] Assuming all believing survivors of the tribulation are transformed, who then is left to populate the millennial kingdom? *Ad hoc* arguments must then be brought in. One such argument is that while all believers are transformed at the second coming, those who have survived the horrors of the tribulation but not yet reached the age of accountability are not transformed. They will enter the kingdom in mortal bodies and find salvation, but none of them will rule or inherit there; only glorified saints will. This writer used this rather strained argument in a previous edition of this book. See Joseph C. Dillow, *The Reign of the Servant Kings: A Study of Eternal Security and the Final Significance of Man* (Miami Springs, FL: Schoettle Publishing Co., 1992), 78-79.

the judgment of the sheep and the goats (Matthew 25:31-46). Those who have been faithful will inherit vassal kingships within Christ's kingdom (Matthew 25:34) based on their acts of charity to the needy.[349]

There is no transformation of the living at the second coming of Christ. Saved men and women in their mortal bodies will *enter* the kingdom, and the faithful sheep among them will *inherit* it as their reward for living faithfully during the horrors of the tribulation era. Even though there will be no transformation of the living at the second coming, there will be resurrection of the believing dead. Those who died during the tribulation along with the Old Testament saints will be physically resurrected. The faithful among them, along with the church, and the future "Israel of God" will also inherit the kingdom in their resurrected bodies. They *will reign* with Christ.

Then, at the end of the millennium, those who have reigned with Christ in mortal bodies during the millennial phase of the kingdom of God and who died will be resurrected so that their earthly inheritance can extend into the eternal state. Furthermore, those believers who remain alive and have not "fallen asleep" will be transformed in the twinkling of an eye (1 Corinthians 15:50-52) and enter the new heavens and new earth in resurrection bodies. Thus, 1 Corinthians 15:50-52 does not refer to the rapture at all, but to the transformation of the living at the beginning of the eternal phrase of the kingdom of God, the new heavens and the new earth. The objections to this interpretation will be the subject of the remainder of this chapter.

But first, we must establish that there will in fact be mortals in the millennium. What is the scriptural basis for this?

Mortals in the Millennium

Knowing his Old Testament, it must have been quite clear to the apostle Paul that believing men and women in mortal bodies will be in the millennial kingdom. During this kingdom the rejoicing of the bride and the bridegroom will be heard (Jeremiah 33:11) and children will play in the streets of Zion and people will age (Zechariah 8:4-5; cf. Isaiah 60:22). *"Thus says the Lord of hosts, 'Old men and old women will again sit in the streets of Jerusalem, each man with his staff in his hand because of age. And the streets of the city will be filled with boys and girls playing in its streets'"* (Zechariah 8:4–5).

If there are children, there will be marriage and physical procreation which according to Jesus cannot occur with people in resurrection bodies (Matthew 22:30). According to the prophets, there will be physical death (Isaiah 65:20; Ezekiel 36:11; 44:25), and longevity will be restored (Isaiah 65:20). Due to sin (which is inconsistent with the eternal state) a multitude of unregenerate men in mortal bodies will rebel at the end of the thousand-year kingdom and will be "devoured," hardly an experience of resurrected and immortal saints (1 John 3:2; Revelation 20:7-10). We are told that Jesus will reign over His enemies in the millennium (Psalms 110:2; 1 Corinthians 15:25). There will be no enemies or sin in the eternal state among those with resurrection bodies (1 John 3:2), but sin will still exist in the millennium. Also, we are told that things will "wear out" (Isaiah 65:20). The millennium is not a perfect state.[350]

---

[349] When Jesus said to the faithful sheep in Matthew 25:34, "inherit the kingdom," this is best rendered, "inherit the kingship." The reference is to subordinate (i.e., vassal) kingships within the restored Davidic theocracy (five cities, ten cites, etc.).

[350] Jeffrey Townsend, "Is the Present Age the Millennium?," *Bib Sac* 140, no. 559 (July 1983): 207-12.

Objections to Placing 1 Corinthians 15:51 at the End of the Millennium

Four objections have been raised against this interpretation.

SIMILARITIES TO THE RAPTURE IN 1 THESSALONIANS 4:15-18

First, the similarities between 1 Corinthians 15:50-52 and 1 Thessalonians 4:14-17 have convinced many that they must refer to the same event, the rapture of the church, which according to premillennialists occurs before the millennium.

> *For this we say to you by the word of the Lord, that we who are alive, and remain until the coming of the Lord, shall not precede those who have fallen asleep. For the Lord Himself will descend from heaven with a shout, with the voice of the archangel, and with the trumpet of God; and the dead in Christ shall rise first. Then we who are alive and remain shall be caught up together with them in the clouds to meet the Lord in the air, and thus we shall always be with the Lord. Therefore comfort one another with these words (1 Thessalonians 4:15–18).*

> *Now I say this, brethren, that flesh and blood cannot inherit the kingdom of God; nor does the perishable inherit the imperishable. Behold, I tell you a mystery; we shall not all sleep, but we shall all be changed, in a moment, in the twinkling of an eye, at the last trumpet; for the trumpet will sound, and the dead will be raised imperishable, and we shall be changed (1 Corinthians 15:50–52).*

Those who equate these passages place them either at the pretribulation rapture or at a posttribulation rapture at the second coming. Posttribulationists do this even though they have no explanation for how their view allows mortal believers into the kingdom.

If these two passages both refer to the same event, the transformation of the living at the rapture (whenever the rapture occurs), there is no solution to the premillennial conundrum that mortal believers must be in the millennium, since all have been transformed at the Second Coming. That is why it is impossible to believe they refer to the same aspect of Christ's *Parousia*.[351]

But are the similarities sufficient to prove that these two passages refer to the same event? I suggest that they are not. The differences appear more significant than the similarities. What are the similarities and differences?

Since we know that there will be a transformation and resurrection of those who sleep (i.e., die), at the end of the millennium, it is no argument to say that these two passages *must* refer to the same event when we know that the major aspects of these two passages (sleep, transformation, resurrection) will also occur at both the end of the millennium and at the rapture (whenever it is).

Because all of the similarities between these passages would also be characteristic of a resurrection and transformation at the gateway to the new heavens and the new earth, the similarities are not decisive, and the differences are more significant. Furthermore, if they

351 As argued above, the *Parousia* is not a single event; it refers to the arrival and ensuing presence of Christ beginning at the rapture and continuing to the end of the millennium. A number of resurrections will occur during this *Parousia*. To confine them all to the second coming results in the impossibilities mentioned above. Furthermore, there is no exegetical or contextual need to confine them all to one single aspect of the *Parousia*. It may be the disbelief in a pretribulation rapture that has led many commentators to force this unnatural meaning (single event, the second coming) on the word.

refer to the same event, then no passage of Scripture speaks of the resurrection of the dead and the transformation of the living at the end of the millennium. It has to be theologically inferred. If 1 Corinthians 15:50 refers to that final resurrection and change of the living, we have explicit scriptural basis for this important doctrine.

SIMILARITIES	DIFFERENCES
We will not all sleep...refers to those still alive.	The kingdom (not mentioned in 1 Thessalonians 4).
Being changed...speaks of resurrection.	Occurs at the "end" (when Christ turns the millennium over to the Father).
Trumpet of God.	Occurs when death is destroyed (it is not destroyed at the time of the rapture or at the second coming).
Shout of the archangel.	
Death continues after the rapture in the millennium.	The saints inherit the imperishable—(the millennium is not imperishable, only the eternal state is).
A "snatching away" in a rapture.	No mention of a *Parousia*.
	No mention of Christ descending (this is because He is already on earth and has been for a thousand years).
	No mention of saints being taken up into the air.
	No mention of the shout of the archangel.
	Last trumpet, not the trumpet call of God.
	This is the last trumpet in 1 Corinthians 15:50, but there are many trumpets after the rapture (Revelation 11:15-18; Mt. 24:30, etc.).
	Death is permanently abolished.

There is no rapture in 1 Corinthians 15:50-52; no ascent into heaven and no descent of Christ to earth (because He is already on the earth and has been for a thousand years). Rather there is a transformation of the living and a resurrection of all the dead who died during the millennium, believers and nonbelievers (Revelation 20:5).

SIMILARITIES TO 1 CORINTHIANS 15:23

But another objection must be addressed if the view that "inherit the kingdom" in verse 50 refers to inheriting the eternal state and the resurrection in verses 51-52 occurs at the end of the millennium. Not only does this passage have similarities to 1 Thessalonians 4:17 and following which refers to the rapture, it also has similarities to 1 Corinthians 15:23 which clearly refers to the rapture.

> *For as in Adam all die, so also in Christ all will be made alive. But each in his own order: Christ the first fruits, after that those who are Christ's* ***at His coming****, then comes the end, when He hands over the kingdom to the God and Father, when He has abolished all rule and all authority and power (1 Corinthians 15:22–24).*

Doesn't this clearly say that those who belong to Christ will be brought to life, resurrected, at His coming? (Gr *Parousia*). (Note: This is not the *transformation* of the *living*). It is argued that this passage is parallel to the resurrection in 1 Corinthians 15:50 and thus identifies that resurrection in verse 50 as occurring at the *Parousia* and not at the end of the millennium. This seems very unlikely because this would imply that the transformation of the living mentioned in verse 50 happens here as well. If that were so, then there would be no mortal believers left to inherit the kingdom.

A POSTMILLENNIAL RESURRECTION WOULD BE IRRELEVANT

A third objection to placing the transformation mentioned in 1 Corinthians 15:50 ff. at the beginning of the eternal state is that if this is so, we have no detailed account of the translation and resurrection of the living *in this chapter* that occurs at the *Parousia*. Since the resurrection most relevant to these Corinthian believers is the resurrection at the *Parousia* in verse 23, this is the one about which we would expect Paul to give more detail.

When Paul describes the resurrection in verses 50 and following, he presents it as something of which he/they expect to be a part, and by application, believers who follow them in time. Some feel that this is the expectation of the church. This is made emphatic by the repeated use of "we" three times in verses 51-52. It is something that they hoped, and we hope to experience. Some think it is totally foreign to the context to suddenly discuss a topic that does not affect them/us at all, a resurrection at the end of the millennium. Why? The reason is that as believers, we will have already been resurrected one thousand years earlier.[352]

However, the fact that Paul uses "we" three times in verses 51-52 no more suggests that Paul necessarily expects them to experience this resurrection than when Jesus said to His disciples "when *you* see the abomination of desolation spoken of by the prophet Daniel" (Matthew 24:15), proves that Jesus expected them to witness an event that would occur in the middle of the tribulation at least two thousand years later. When Paul says "*we will not all sleep*," this is a "prophetic we" where a local group by metonymy stands for whatever group in the future will experience the fulfillment of the prophecy. There are scores of examples of this in the Bible's prophetic literature.

Are we to say all passages motivating believers toward godliness based on their future life in the eternal phase of the kingdom are irrelevant because that life occurs one thousand years after they have already been resurrected and rewarded at the rapture? One only needs to consider the parallel situation in 2 Peter 3:10-13 to see this cannot be true. In this passage believers in the church age are urged to live lives of "holiness and godliness" on the basis of a future event (the dissolution of the heavens and the earth) which occurs at the end of the millennium, an event which similarly occurs over one thousand years after they have already been resurrected. He says, "*Since all these things are to be destroyed in this way, what sort of people ought you to be in holy conduct and godliness*" (2 Peter 3:11). The issue is not when it occurs, but the fact that what they are investing their lives in is insignificant, transitory, and destined to be burned up.

After John describes the new heavens and the new earth, the eternal phase of the kingdom, God gives encouragement to His people saying, *"He who overcomes shall inherit these things, and I will be his God and he will be My son"* (Revelation 21:7). But these "overcomers" have already been rewarded and judged a thousand years earlier. In Revelation 22:12 the Lord Jesus encourages His believers that He is coming quickly and will reward the overcomers. The reward is that: (1) they will enter by the gates (the way of honor) into the city in the eternal phase, and (2) they will have a right to the tree of life, that is, special communion with God.

---

[352] Thanks to Dr. Ken Mitchell for pointing out this difficulty, personal communication, January 10, 2010.

Apparently events occurring at the end of the millennium can have a profound motivational effect on believers now and in Peter's and John's minds are not at all irrelevant to their readers. This is consistent with numerous prophecies in which the eschatological re-gathering of Israel is promised.[353] In Ezekiel 11:16, for example, the exiles in Babylon in 586 BC are told, "*Thus says the Lord GOD, 'I will gather you from the peoples and assemble you out of the countries among which you have been scattered, and I will give you the land of Israel'*" (Ezekiel 11:17).[354] When He said, "I will gather you," He was using "you" to refer to a future generation of Jews over twenty-five hundred years later. Was the prophecy irrelevant to the exiles in Babylon because of this?

The relevant issue for the Corinthians is the *fact* of the future resurrection, not when it occurs. As Gordon Fee puts it, "Paul's concern is singular: to demonstrate on the basis of Christ's resurrection the necessity of the resurrection of the dead by tying that event to the final events of the End, particularly the defeat of death" (cf. vv. 54–55).[355] It is just as relevant a refutation of the false teachers if it occurs at the end of the millennium as it is if it occurs at the second coming. The relevance to the Corinthians is that the false teachers are refuted, and that one day the believers will have resurrection bodies in the eternal state. That is relevant![356] The main idea of the chapter is not the timing of the resurrection but the reality of it. Thus this writer fully agrees with Wretlind's conclusion that by using "we" three times Paul has in mind all persons who will share the image of the heavenly man (v. 49). [357] Therefore the mystery of verse 51, which speaks of a transformation, refers to the transformation of any believer living at the time of the last trumpet. "The 'we' refers to any member of the first Adam's race who becomes a member of the second Adam's race."[358] This conclusion is decisively confirmed by the fact that Paul cites Isaiah 25:8 and Hosea 13:14. If Paul meant that "we" included only church saints, he would not have cited these verses that include the "we" saints in the millennium, specifically believing Israelites.

PAUL EXPLICITLY REFERS TO ONLY ONE RESURRECTION AT THE *PAROUSIA*

Also, it is argued that the resurrection at the *Parousia* is supposedly the only one to which Paul explicitly refers, and that it seems to be the main thing Paul has in mind in chapter 15.[359] In response, it needs to be stressed that the resurrection at the *Parousia* is not the only resurrection mentioned in the chapter. It is likely that the phrase "then comes the end" (v. 23) refers to the end of the resurrection process and *refers to the third resurrection at the end of the millennium.* Why? The subject matter in this verse is the order of resurrections,

---

353 See Deuteronomy 30:6; Jeremiah 31:31-34; Ezekiel 36:26-27; Joel 2:28-29.

354 See also Ezekiel 16:60-63.

355 Gordon D. Fee, *The First Epistle to the Corinthians* (Grand Rapids: Wm. B. Eerdmans Publishing Co., 1987), 243.

356 Furthermore, what is inherited in 1 Corinthians 15:50 is imperishable; and occurs when death is finally destroyed, when God is made all in all. The resurrection at the *Parousia* (v. 23) cannot be the same as the resurrection and transformation at 1 Corinthians 15:50. It makes no difference what the parallels are with 1 Thessalonians 4:14-17. They are most likely separate events, regardless of the fact that there are some similarities.

357 Dennis O. Wretlind, "The Last Trumpet: A Demarcation Event between the Present Temporal World and the Eternal World to Come" (PhD diss., Dallas Theological Seminary, 1997), 234.

358 Ibid., 234.

359 Thanks to Dr. Paul Tanner for pointing out this difficulty, personal communication, December 26, 2009.

and therefore the "end" likely refers to the end of this sequence of resurrections. We are told that what occurs at "the end" is the destruction of death (v. 26). When is death finally destroyed? It is not destroyed at the beginning of the millennium. It will be destroyed by the resurrection. We will discuss this in more detail in the following chapter.

Summary

We have considered all the arguments that suggest that 1 Corinthians 15:50 ff. refers to the rapture. All of them are found wanting. The similarities of this event to the rapture described in 1 Thessalonians 4:17 are noted but are irrelevant. Because the things similar in each of these passages would occur at both the rapture and the necessary transformation at the beginning of the eternal state, the differences are more important than the similarities. Furthermore, there is no parallel in 1 Corinthians 15:51 to the resurrection at Christ's *Parousia*. If they were the same event, then there would be no mortals in the kingdom in contradiction to the rest of the Bible. The verses in 1 Corinthians 15:50 follow chronologically after verse 24 and explain what happens at "the end" of the millennium. It is no argument at all to say that a postmillennial transformation and inheritance has no relevance to the Corinthians because they will not experience it. Scripture commonly uses future events that the hearers will not directly experience as motivational influences. That they will one day inherit the eternal state if they are faithful is just as motivational as inheriting the millennial phase of the kingdom. In fact, it is more so, because the inheritance in view lasts for all eternity.

Having dealt with the objections to viewing the inheritance in 1 Corinthians 15:50 as occurring at the beginning of the new heavens and the new earth, it now remains to demonstrate the positive evidence that this passage relates to the inception of the eternal state. We now turn to this discussion in the next chapter.

8
The End

IN THE previous chapter we argued that three resurrections are mentioned in 1 Corinthians 15, Christ's resurrection, those who are Christ's at His pretribulational *Parousia*, and a resurrection and transformation at "the end" of the millennial kingdom when death is swallowed up. These may be diagramed as follows.

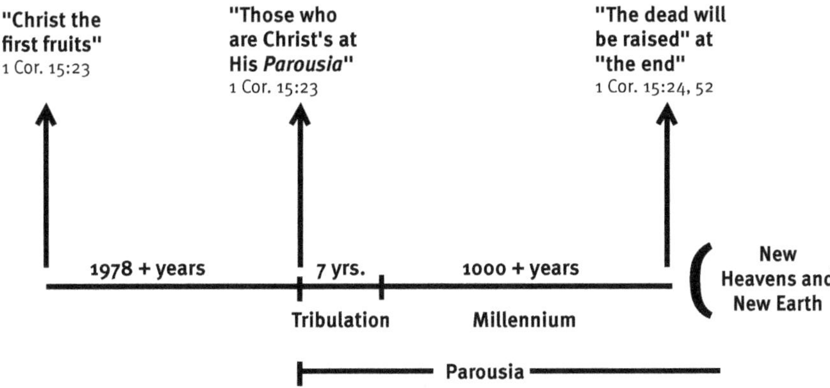

In that chapter we presented the major objections to placing the resurrection mentioned in 1 Corinthians 15:50 ff. at the beginning of the eternal state. We now must present the positive evidence, only hinted at in the previous chapter, which establishes the time of this final transformation that Paul says will occur "*in a moment, in the twinkling of an eye, at the last trumpet; for the trumpet will sound, and the dead will be raised imperishable, and we will be changed*" (1 Corinthians 15:52). When does this "last trumpet" sound its final summons?

Regarding the timing of the trumpet blast, pretribulationists have a problem. They associate the last trumpet of 1 Corinthians 15:52 with the pretribulational rapture, but that "last" trumpet is clearly not the "last" trumpet in the Bible. Various explanations are given. For example, some say that the trumpet in 1 Corinthians 15:52 is the "last" for the church but that the "last" trumpets mentioned in Revelation 11:15 and Matthew 24:30 are the last trumpets for Israel.[360] These ad hoc arguments are needed to counter objections from posttribulationists. These teachers reasonably point out that the trumpet in Matthew 24:30

[360] J. Dwight Pentecost, *Things to Come: A Study in Biblical Eschatology*, reprint ed. (Grand Rapids: Zondervan Publishing House, 1964), 189.

occurs at the second coming and surely comes after the supposedly "last" trumpet of those holding to a pretribulation rapture.

Understandably, amillennialist theologian Vern Poythress objects to pretribulationalism saying, "After all, the one in 1 Corinthians 51:52 is the 'last.'"[361] Robert Gundry argues that it makes good sense to understand the last trumpet of 1 Corinthians 15:52 with the "trumpet of God" in 1 Thessalonians 4:16, the great trumpet at the posttribulational advent of Christ in Matthew 24:31, and the seventh trumpet of Revelation 11:15-18.[362] We agree with Poythress and Gundry that "last" does indeed mean "last." There are no more trumpets after the last trumpet.

To equate all these trumpets and place them at the second advent would place the transformation mentioned in 1 Corinthians 15:51 at the second advent, and this would contradict the conclusions of the preceding chapter. In response we first consider the flow of the argument in 1 Corinthians 15 as outlined by Wretlind:[363]

1. Verses 1-11—affirmation of the gospel message with a special emphasis on the resurrection.
2. Verses 12-19—an argument against the idea there is no such thing as resurrection from the dead.
3. Verses 20-28—an examination of the eschatological consequences for believers based on the fact that Christ did rise.
4. Verses 29-34—a sermon exposing the practical ramifications involved if believers were to accept the false notion that there is no resurrection from the dead.
5. Verses 35-58—an explanation of what form the resurrection body will take, a form adapted to the conditions of the future state.

Wretlind concludes that verses 50-58 function as a summary and conclusion of the preceding discussion and an introduction to what follows. As a conclusion, verse 50 states that the earthly body is not equipped for its future heavenly (not millennial) habitation. This is suggested by the earthly/heavenly contrast in the preceding verses and the future "image of the heavenly" in verse 49. Thus, in agreement with this writer's conclusion, he concludes that the millennium is not in view; instead, Paul is discussing the future heavenly state. "As an introduction the verse speaks of the future habitation of man in an incorruptible kingdom of God."[364]

The argument of 1 Corinthians 15 draws a straight line between verses 24-28 to verses 50-58. The latter verses explain what happens at "the end" (v. 24), when Christ will have turned over the millennial kingdom to the God and Father and the final phase of the kingdom of God begins, that is, the eternal state. We agree with Wretlind that "the arguments set forth for tying verses 50 and following to 'the end' in verses 24-28 appear incontrovertible."[365] What are those arguments? It will be demonstrated that "the end" that occurs in 1 Corinthians 15:23 is the same event described in verses 50-53.

---

[361] Vern S. Poythress, *Understanding Dispensationalists* (Grand Rapids: Zondervan Publishing House, 1987), 76.

[362] Robert Gundry, *The Church and the Tribulation* (Grand Rapids: Zondervan Publishing House, 1973), 148.

[363] Wretlind, "The Last Trumpet: A Demarcation Event between the Present Temporal World and the Eternal World to Come", 106-15.

[364] Ibid., 114-15.

[365] Ibid., 164. "Verses 50 ff. are logically and theologically tied to verses 24-28, that Christ must subjugate all enemies including death before He delivers over His rulership to the Father." Ibid., 201.

When Does "the End" Occur?

Amillennialists, of course, deny that "the end" in verse 24 refers to the end of the millennium.[366] For them, this is the end of the current age which occurs at the *Parousia*. There is no intermediate kingdom between "those who are Christ's at His coming" (1 Corinthians 15:24) and "then comes the end" (v. 24). The difficulty of the presence of mortals in the kingdom is a non-issue for them because they do not believe in an earthly kingdom. The difficulty, however (for them), would be that the Old Testament prophecies describe an era that is decidedly not perfect and involves death and sin. As a result they have to deal with scores of Old Testament predictions that contradict their system.[367]

Because they deny the existence of a millennium, many amillennialists approach 1 Corinthians 15 with a presupposition that since there is no millennium, no intermediate kingdom could be taught in 1 Corinthians 15.

Note verses 22-26.

1. Christ the first fruits (v. 23),
2. after that those who are Christ's at His coming (v. 23),
3. then comes the end (v. 24):
    a. when He hands over the kingdom to the God and Father (v. 24),
    b. when He has abolished all rule and all authority and power (v. 24).
    c. For He must reign until He has put all His enemies under His feet. The last enemy that will be abolished is death (vv. 25-26).

Notice there is an interval of over 1900+ years between "Christ the first fruits," and "those who are Christ's at his coming." Is there also an interval between the *Parousia* and "the end"? Gerhardus Vos says, "No." A key factor in this discussion is the meaning of "then" (Gr *eita*) in verse 24. In order to interpret this passage in compliance with his amillennial system, Vos needs this word to mean "next" with no implied "*protracted* interval" prior to "the end." He says that *eita* "can be used to express *momentary* sequence of events."[368] In other words, a *momentary* or perhaps "immediate" interval can be permitted but not a *protracted* one. Basically, he is attempting to assign the meaning "at the same time" to the Gr word *eita*. However, the Gr word *eita* is used 15 times in the New Testament and in every instance it implies an interval.[369] In many cases it is not momentary or immediate. Earlier in this very chapter Paul says, "*and that He appeared to Cephas, then [eita] to the twelve. After that [epeita] He appeared to more than five hundred brethren at one time,... then [epeita] He appeared to James, then [eita] to all the apostles; and last of all, as to one untimely born, He appeared to me also*" (1 Corinthians 15:5–8). Obviously, more than a

---

[366] E.g., Herman Ridderbos, *The Coming of the Kingdom* (Grand Rapids: Presbyterian and Reformed Publishing Co., 1962), 556-62. Also Gerhardus Vos, *The Pauline Eschatology* (Grand Rapids: Wm. B. Eerdmans Publishing Co., 1972), 235-46.

[367] One friend who rejected his former amillennial belief in favor of premillennialism commented that his conversion occurred because he had to "throw out half of the Old Testament" [obviously hyperbole], because as an amillennialist he was unable to understand its wonderful prophecies of an earthly kingdom as they would have been understood by the prophets and their listeners.

[368] Vos, *The Pauline Eschatology*, 243.

[369] Cf. Mark 4:17, 28(2x); 8:25; Luke 8:12; John 13:5; 19:27; 20:27; 1 Corinthians 15:5, 7, 24; 1 Timothy 2:13; 3:10; James 1:15; Hebrews 12:9.

"momentary" period of time elapsed between these resurrection appearances.[370] This usage is common in the New Testament. For example, in describing the gradual growth of the kingdom in the present age, Mark 4:28 says, "*The soil produces crops by itself; first the blade, then* [*eita*] *the head, then* [*eita*] *the mature grain in the head.*"

Since amillennialists say that this parable teaches the gradual growth and development of Christ's kingdom over the past two thousand years, it is clear that they understand *eita* as implying a *protracted* interval in passages which would not contradict their system if they were understood as "momentary"! But there is nothing in the semantic value of the word that requires a "momentary" sense. It simply means "a point of time following another point."[371] Had Paul intended to indicate that "the end" occurred almost at the same time as the resurrection of the saints "at His coming," he would most likely have used the Gr word *tote*. This word can suggest "at the same time"[372] or "immediately following,"[373] but *eita* never does. Whether the interval involved is momentary or protracted depends on the context.

In this context the interval is protracted. He must reign *until* He has put all His enemies under His feet. And the end will occur when death is abolished (v. 26). This does not occur at the *Parousia* but only at the end of the millennium. Amillennialists argue that His reign begins with "Christ the first fruits" (we are now in the imperfect time of His reign), but to the contrary, the New Testament says His conquest of His enemies begins with the *Parousia*. This is when He "sits on his glorious throne," and His disciples will "sit on thrones judging the twelve tribes of Israel" (Matthew 19:28). This is when He begins to rule the nations "with a rod of iron" (Revelation 2:27). None of that happened when He ascended to His Father's throne at His ascension to reign at the right hand of God in heaven.

When amillennialists object that it should not take Christ one thousand years to "bring his enemies into subjection" and such would be "wholly out of character for the omnipotent God,"[374] they forget that in their system the omnipotent Christ is now reigning from the right hand of the Father, and yet His enemies reign supreme on the earth. If the kingdom handed over to the Father in verse 24 is the current interadvent age (as amillennialists maintain), it is a rather anemic kingdom, and "wholly out of character for the omnipotent God"! Millard Erickson candidly admits, "For as we look about us at the present time, we do not see him ruling very actively."[375] Furthermore, during this current "kingdom," Christ never overcomes His enemies. Is it not "wholly out of character" for the sovereign God of Reformed amillennialism to take 1979[376] years plus to overcome His enemies and never achieve it within history? The kingdom in verse 24 involves a period of time during which He reigns and begins after the *Parousia* (v. 23). Only that kingdom on earth fits the descriptions of the glorious kingdom predicted in the Old Testament prophets. Then at the

---

370 See Robert D. Culver, "A Neglected Millennial Passage from Saint Paul," *BibSac* 113, no. 450 (April-June 1956): 148.

371 Louw-Nida, 1:644.

372 James Swanson, *A Dictionary of Biblical Languages: Greek New Testament*, 2nd ed. (Seattle: Logos Research Systems, 2001), s.v. "tote". BDAG, 1012.

373 EDNT, 3:367.

374 See Gary D. Long, *Context! Evangelical Views of the Millennium Examined* (Charleston, SC: Sovereign Grace Ministries, 2002), 98.

375 Erickson, *Christian Theology*, 786.

376 From AD 33 (time of Christ's death) to 2013 (year in which this book was published) = 1979 years.

end of that kingdom, that is, at the end of the millennium, death is swallowed up in victory and is destroyed in an instant.

"The end" occurs when death is finally destroyed by the resurrection of the dead and the transformation of the living. First Corinthians 15:24-26 is similar to verses 53-56. If verses 24-26 refer to the victory over death at the end of the millennium, then it is probable that the references to death being swallowed up in victory in verses 51-56 also refer to the end, and not the beginning of the millennium.

And it is clear, is it not, that Jesus' victory over death described in verses 24-26 occurs at the end of the millennium and not at the *Parousia*? In those verses we are told that the "end" will come "when he hands over the kingdom to God the Father after he has destroyed all dominion, authority, and power" (v. 24). This is the time when Christ has turned the millennium over to God the Father and all the rebels within the kingdom are destroyed. At that time Paul says, "*the last enemy to be destroyed is death*" (v. 26). This establishes the fact that the time of kingdom inheritance in verse 50 is at the end of the millennium (the beginning of the eternal state), as verses 54-55 imply.

In an expanded explanation of what happens at "the end" (v. 24), Paul tells us that "*we shall not all sleep, but we will be changed*" (v. 51). The "end" is the time when the third resurrection occurs, the third phase of "each in his own order" (v. 23). Furthermore, as confirmed in verse 51, those resurrected at the end are those who are "in Christ" who are "made alive." The reference is to the dead and living saints at the end of the millennium.[377]

When Does the Transformation in 1 Corinthians 15:51 Occur?

Paul explicitly assigns this third resurrection to the time when death is swallowed up (v. 54) and when the "imperishable" phase of the kingdom of God begins, the new heavens and the new earth (v. 53). The abolition of death in verse 26 obviously equates with the time when "*death is swallowed up in victory*" in verse 54, thus equating "the end" with the transformation in verse 51.

This destruction of death must occur before God becomes "all in all" (v. 28), thus linking verses 22-24 with verses 50-55.[378] God becoming "all in all" does not occur at the

---

[377] This does not refer to a resurrection of unbelievers as Conzelmann thinks. He says, "Then τέλος would have to mean 'the rest,' namely, all the rest of the dead." However, this does not refer to the "rest of the dead." Instead it refers to the transformation and resurrection of the believing dead referred to in 1 Corinthians 15:51-52. Paul only has those "who are Christ's" in view (v. 22). See Hans Conzelmann, *1 Corinthians: A Commentary on the First Epistle to the Corinthians*, Hermeneia (Philadelphia: Fortress Press, 1975), 270. Conzelmann's conclusion is necessary because of his prior exegesis in which he concludes that the "end" is coterminous with the second advent and that there is no "intermediate kingdom" between.

[378] Thiselton notes that "Paul has already designated the end time or the last day as that in which God will be All in all." Anthony C. Thiselton, *The First Epistle to the Corinthians: A Commentary on the Greek Text* (Grand Rapids: Wm. B. Eerdmans Publishing Co., 2000), 1290. If verses 24-26 refer to the victory over death at the end of the millennium, then it is probable that the references to death being swallowed up in victory in verses 51-56 also refer to the end, and not the beginning of the millennium. And, it is clear, is it not, that the victory over death described in verses 24-26 occurs at the end of the millennium and not at the Parousia? In those verses we are told that the "end" will come "when he hands over the kingdom to God the Father after he has destroyed all dominion, authority, and power" (v. 24). This is the time when Christ has turned the millennium over to God the Father and all the rebels within the kingdom are destroyed. At that time, Paul says, "the last enemy to be destroyed is death" (v. 26). This seems to establish that the time of kingdom inheritance in verse 50 is at the end of the millennium (the beginning of the eternal state) as verses 54-55 imply.

beginning of the millennium but at the end, "when he has put all things in subjection under his feet" (v. 27), and when death is finally abolished (verses 54-44) and "swallowed up" in the eternal state (v. 54).

In the new heavens and the new earth, "*there will no longer be any death*" (Revelation 21:4), thus linking 1 Corinthians 15:54-55 with the eternal state and not the rapture. Kistemaker is correct in writing, "The phrase [inherit the kingdom in v. 50] relates to the final stage in which God's kingdom is set free from powers that now reign. These powers must all submit to Jesus Christ, who at the time of the consummation delivers the kingdom to God the Father (v. 24)."[379]

This conclusion is definitively established by the fact that Paul cites Isaiah 25:8 in 1 Corinthians 15:54 to pinpoint the time when death is finally destroyed. Isaiah says,

> *He will swallow up death for all time, and the Lord GOD will wipe tears away from all faces, and He will remove the reproach of His people from all the earth; for the LORD has spoken (Isaiah 25:8).*

By quoting Isaiah in 1 Corinthians 15:54, Paul identifies the time of the transformation of the living in verse 51 as the time when death is swallowed up "*for all time.*" That did not occur at the *Parousia*/second coming or *Parousia*/rapture. Death continued after that time and into the millennium. The destruction of death occurs at the time of the transformation of the living in 1 Corinthians 15:51-54, when God will "*wipe tears away from faces.*" John cites this very passage from Isaiah, locating this event at the end of the millennium and the beginning of the eternal state (Revelation 21:1-4). At this time, John says, that "*there shall no longer be any death*" (Revelation 21:4). Therefore the transformation of the living in 1 Corinthians 15:50-52 cannot refer to the rapture! Instead, it refers to the third resurrection mentioned in the chapter which occurs at "the end" of the millennium.[380]

---

379 Simon J. Kistemaker, *Exposition of the First Epistle to the Corinthians* (Grand Rapids: Baker Book House, 1993), 581.

380 The time period involved extends from the celebratory banquet which inaugurates the millennium (v. 6), to the extension of His rule over all the nations (v. 7) during the restored Davidic theocracy (Acts 1:6), and then on into the eternal state when death is "swallowed up for all time" and when "*the Lord GOD* ***will wipe tears away*** *from all faces, And He will remove the reproach of His people from all the earth; For the LORD has spoken*" (Isaiah 25:8). We know that death is not swallowed up in the millennium (Isaiah 65:20), so unless Isaiah is contradicting himself in 25:8, he must see the new heavens and the new earth as having an initial phase where death is not yet swallowed up, that is, the millennial phase. Furthermore, the wiping away of all tears referred to in this verse occurs at the end of the millennium according to John (Revelation 21:4). Since God's future kingdom includes both the Messiah's millennial reign and the eternal state, Isaiah telescoped them together (cf. Isaiah 65:17-25). It is possible that in Isaiah 25:6-12 we have an example of prophetic foreshortening where events separated in time are telescoped closely together in the prophetic vision with no mention of the time periods in between. See discussion of this concept in John F. Walvoord, *The Revelation of Jesus Christ* (Chicago: Moody Press, 1966), 311; and John Martin, "Isaiah," in *BKC: Old Testament*, ed. John F. Walvoord and Roy B. Zuck (Colorado Springs: Cook, 1996), 1074. Paul then cites Hos 13:14 in 1 Corinthians 15:55. "*O death, where is your victory? O death, where is your sting?*" (NASB). Hosea makes this statement in the middle of a passage that refers to judgment on the northern kingdom in 722 BC. "*Shall I ransom them from the power of Sheol? Shall I redeem them from death? O Death, where are your thorns? O Sheol, where is your sting? Compassion will be hidden from My sight*" (Hosea 13:14). Paul then quotes phrases from this passage and applies them in verse 55 to the time of the resurrection in 1 Corinthians 15:50. However, since the Hosea passage is not speaking of the millennium (that comes in Hosea 14), this citation creates no particular problem for the timing of the resurrection in 1 Corinthians 15:50. Rather, these statements in the midst of an announcement of judgment, promise that in the future God will erase the sting of death. That future time

What Is Inherited in 1 Corinthians 15:50?

Beginning in 1 Corinthians 15:50, Paul concludes his resurrection discourse. He has just completed his answer to the first question raised in verse 35, "what kind of body" will we have in the resurrection. Now he addresses the second question, "How are the dead raised?" Several events are involved in this answer: (1) the kingdom of God will be inherited; (2) there will a transformation of the living into glorified bodies; (3) there will be a resurrection of the dead; and (4) the last trumpet will close out human history with a final summons. Inheriting the kingdom of God is the final goal of history. When that is achieved, victory is complete and the new heavens and new earth begin.

The sequence of events described in verses 50-57 sounds similar to verses 23-28. In verses 22-28 there are two kingdoms mentioned: first Christ rules, and then He turns over His rule to the God and Father at "the end." In the former Christ is the focal point and in the latter, God the Father. This suggests that there are two phases of the eschatological kingdom, millennial and eternal.

For those who accept the interpretation of an intermediate kingdom in 1 Corinthians 15:22-26,[381] there must be a distinction between the kingdom of God in the eternal state and that preliminary phase of the kingdom of God, when the saints inherit the earth and fulfill the Abrahamic promise. And there is. The latter is perishable and the former is imperishable. The idea that the kingdom of God is implemented in successive phases is common[382] and may be suggested by Ephesians 5:5. For some amillennialists, the kingdom of Christ is the present form of the kingdom, and the kingdom of God is the eternal state.[383] For premillennialists, the kingdom of Christ is either a present form of the kingdom,[384] or it is the millennial phase of the kingdom of God, which merges into the final phase of the kingdom of God in the eternal state.[385]

---

is unspecified in Hosea, but Paul tells us it is at a time when death is finally swallowed up, that is, the eternal state.

381 For full discussion of the intermediate kingdom in 1 Corinthians 15 see Wilber B. Wallis, "The Problem of an Intermediate Kingdom in 1 Corinthians 15:20-28," *JETS* 18, no. 4 (Fall 1975): 229-42. Also note the excellent article by Culver, "A Neglected Millennial Passage from Saint Paul."

382 R. B. Gaffin explains his amillennial construction by saying, "These present and future aspects [of the kingdom] cohere not as two or more kingdoms but as the one eschatological kingdom arriving in successive stages or installments. Concretely, these stages are distinguished by the critical junctures in the work of Christ, resulting in a basic three-stage structure: a. the period of Jesus' earthly ministry, b. the period from his exaltation to his return (the time of the church), and c. the period beyond his return." R. B. Gaffin, "Kingdom of God" in Godfrey, "Law and Gospel," 368. The present writer, a premillennialist, would identify these stages as a present mystery form of the kingdom, followed by the millennial kingdom (the kingdom of Christ), and the future kingdom of God (the eternal state).

383 E.g., Peter Thomas O'Brien, *The Letter to the Ephesians*, The Pillar New Testament Commentary (Grand Rapids: Wm. B. Eerdmans Publishing Co., 1999), 361. Also Fee, *The First Epistle to the Corinthians*, 356-57.

384 For a progressive dispensationalist perspective see Darrell L. Bock, "Current Messianic Activity and OT Davidic Promise: Dispensationalism, Hermeneutics, and NT Fulfillment," *TJ* 15, no. 1 (Spring 1994): 60. See also Craig A. Blaising and Darrell L. Bock, *Progressive Dispensationalism* (Wheaton, IL: Bridgeport - Victor Books, 1993), 232-83; Robert L. Saucy, *The Case for Progressive Dispensationalism: The Interface between Dispensational & Non-dispensational Theology* (Grand Rapids: Zondervan Publishing House, 1993). Mark Saucy argues that the future kingdom is present in a hidden form, Mark Saucy, "The Kingdom-of-God Sayings in Matthew," *BibSac* 151, no. 602 (April 1994): 232-83.

385 Harold W. Hoehner, *Ephesians: An Exegetical Commentary* (Grand Rapids: Baker Academic, 2002), 662. Richard R. Melick notes, "He did seem to distinguish between them. The kingdom of Christ is an intermediate

There "must be a kingdom which flesh and blood can inherit."[386] Flesh and blood cannot inherit the eternal phase of the kingdom of God because it is imperishable; but flesh and blood *can* inherit the millennial phase of the kingdom of God because it is not imperishable.[387] The subject matter of 1 Corinthians 15, then, is not a translation at the rapture, but a transformation at the beginning of the new heavens and the new earth.

Christ's kingdom is mentioned ten times in the New Testament, and in each instance it refers to the future millennium.[388] The present writer understands all references to the kingdom of God in the New Testament to refer to the future kingdom which will be implemented in two phases: the kingdom of Christ (the millennium), and then finally the eternal state, the final phase of the kingdom of God. Ralph Alexander neatly summarizes the relationship between the millennial and eternal phases of the kingdom of God, "In light of the whole Scripture, it appears that the millennium is like a 'first-fruits' of the eternal state. The millennium will be like a preview of the eternal messianic kingdom that will be revealed fully in the eternal state. Therefore, because the two are alike in nature, they share distinct similarities. Yet because they are both different revealed time periods, they would likewise reflect some dissimilarities."[389]

Who Inherits at "the End"?

All will be changed, according to 1 Corinthians 15:50. Does this mean that all will also inherit? No. When the apostle declares that only those in resurrection bodies will inherit the kingdom (i.e., the eternal state, and not the millennium),[390] he does not say (or imply) that *all* resurrected saints will inherit the kingdom. He says that *only* resurrected saints *can* inherit.[391] Earlier, Paul connects inheriting the kingdom with an obedient lifestyle and not with personal salvation (1 Corinthians 6:9-10). Those resurrected believers who have been faithful will be Christ's co-heirs. The resurrected believers who have not been faithful will not be among His partners in the fulfillment of human destiny. The fact that

kingdom which will someday be handed over to the Father. This is taught directly in 1 Corinthians 15:24. The ultimate state of existence for the believer is the kingdom of God, but God planned for Christ and his kingdom to be the focus in the interval between the cross and the return of Christ." Richard R. Melick, *Philippians, Colossians, Philemon*, New American Commentary (Nashville: Broadman and Holman, 1991), 207.

386 Hodge, *Systematic Theology*, 2:609.

387 This assumes that "inherit" refers to reward and not soteriological entrance into the kingdom.

388 See Matthew 16:28; Luke 1:33; 22:29-30; 23:42; John 18:36; Colossians 1:13; 2 Timothy 4:1, 18; 2 Peter 1:11. Even in the one instance, Colossians 1:13, where it could be argued that the kingdom of Christ is present now, it can be understood with F. F. Bruce, that "In the affirmation that believers have already been brought into the kingdom of God's beloved Son we have an example of truly realized eschatology. That which in its fullness lies ahead of them has already become effective in them. 'Those whom he justified he also glorified'" (Romans 8:30). F. F. Bruce, *The Epistles to the Colossians, to Philemon, and to the Ephesians* (Grand Rapids: Wm. B. Eerdmans Publishing Co., 1984), 52.

389 Ralph Alexander, "Ezekiel," in *The Expositor's Bible Commentary: Isaiah, Jeremiah, Lamentations, Ezekiel*, ed. Frank E. Gaebelein (Grand Rapids: Zondervan Publishing House, 1986), 945. Wretlind discusses in some detail the common distinction between the kingdom of Christ and the kingdom of God, Wretlind, "The Last Trumpet: A Demarcation Event between the Present Temporal World and the Eternal World to Come", 156-64.

390 Only resurrected and/or glorified saints in Israel united with a glorified saints church will rule in the eternal phase of kingdom.

391 See Peters, *The Theocratic Kingdom of Our Lord Jesus, the Christ, as Covenanted in the Old Testament and Presented in the New Testament*, 1:602. Peters equates inheriting the kingdom with becoming a ruler in it.

"all" will be changed before they can enter the eternal state (v. 51) in no way requires that "all" will inherit. Getting a resurrection body is not the same as obtaining an inheritance. As Paul has made abundantly clear earlier in the same epistle, not all believers will inherit (1 Corinthians 6: 9-11).[392]

Who then inherits in the millennium? While all believers will enter the kingdom in the sense of being saved, only three groups will inherit/rule there. First, all the Old Testament saints will be raised from the dead at the second coming (Daniel 12:1-2); the faithful among them (like David) will rule with Christ, but the unfaithful (like Saul and Solomon) will enter but not rule there.

Second, those who have been faithful servants in this age and who will be resurrected (if dead) or transformed (if still living) at the rapture will inherit the kingdom God in its millennial phase, becoming co-heirs with the king (Romans 8:17b; 2 Timothy 2:12). Because they have been transformed at the rapture, they can inherit both the millennial and eternal phases of the kingdom. *Believers in "flesh and blood" can inherit the millennial phase when they enter the kingdom but can only inherit the eternal phase of the kingdom after they are transformed at the beginning of the eternal state (1 Corinthians 15:50-52).*

Third, those who have been faithful to the King and rendered charity to the poor during the tribulation will, as mortals, inherit the perishable millennial phase of the kingdom of God ("vassal kingships" in the kingdom of God, Matthew 25:34 ff.).[393] Having "endured to the end," they "will be saved" (Matthew 24:13). Salvation in this instance is not personal deliverance from eternal condemnation. Rather it refers to participation in the messianic salvation of the Old Testament, inheriting the kingdom as a co-heir with Christ and reigning with Him (Romans 8:17; 2 Timothy 2:12), a reward for their faithful endurance.

Summary

Some among the believers in Corinth were teaching there would be no resurrection of the dead. The primary concern of 1 Corinthians 15 was to refute this error and expand in more detail the doctrine of the future resurrection. The mere fact that there would be a resurrection was sufficient to refute the false teachers and affirm the believers. When it would occur was not particularly relevant.

In 1 Corinthians 15:50, Paul declares that "flesh and blood" cannot inherit the kingdom of God. As shown above, Paul has the eternal phase of the kingdom of God in view. Because of this, the transformation and resurrection of the living saints at this time (vv. 51-52) cannot be the same as the resurrection of those who are Christ's at the *Parousia*. Instead, they refer to the third resurrection, the resurrection which occurs at "the end" of the millennium when death is abolished by resurrection.

The interpretation suggested in this and the preceding chapter, and this interpretation alone, satisfies the biblical requirements that must be met if there are to be mortal believers living in and inheriting the earth in the millennium. What are those requirements? There are three:

---

392 See pp. 91–94 above. Also Wilkin, "Christians Who Lose Their Legacy: Gal 5:21," 31.

393 For full discussion of Matthew 25:34 and the receiving of vassal kingships see elsewhere in this book, pp. 840 ff.

1. There must be an interval between the rapture and the second coming or there would be no mortals to enter the millennium and inherit it.
2. There can be no transformation of the living from the perishable to the imperishable at the second coming.
3. Inheriting the kingdom cannot mean the same thing as getting into the kingdom.

Why must these requirements be met?

THE NECESSITY OF AN INTERVAL. Regarding the first point above, if all are changed at the rapture, and if the rapture occurs at the same time as the second coming, then no mortals would be left to populate the millennial kingdom. The pretribulation rapture allows for the fact that millions will come to Christ after the rapture during the tribulation through the efforts of the 144,000 from every tribe of Israel.

The logic is simple:

MAJOR PREMISE: There cannot be a transformation of the living at the second coming aspect of the *Parousia.*

MINOR PREMISE: There is a transformation of the living at the rapture aspect of the *Parousia.*

CONCLUSION: The second coming-*Parousia* and rapture-*Parousia* cannot be the same event.

Ryrie has clearly set forth this problem for those who hold to a postribulational rapture.[394]

NO TRANSFORMATION OF THE LIVING AT THE SECOND COMING. Second, there can be no transformation of the living at the second coming. Otherwise, there would be no mortals to populate the millennium. However, if inheriting the kingdom in 1 Corinthians 15:50, which mentions the transformation of the living, occurs at the gateway to the new heavens and the new earth one thousand years later, then this difficulty is removed. There is no mention of the transformation of the living in 15:21-23 because it does not happen at the *Parousia.* Christ's servant kings who were transformed at the rapture will inherit the kingdom of God in both its millennial and the eternal phases.

It is true that flesh and blood cannot inherit the *eternal phase* of the kingdom of heaven, because the perishable cannot inherit the imperishable. But the perishable *can* inherit the millennial phase of the kingdom of God because that phase of the kingdom is *not* imperishable. In fact, it will be destroyed (2 Peter 3:10-11). What will be inherited in 1 Corinthians 15:50, therefore, cannot be the millennium; it must be the eternal state. Only the eternal state is imperishable.

Furthermore, the timing of this inheritance is not at either the rapture or the second advent, but when "He has put all enemies under His feet" (1 Corinthians 15:25), and only then "*God may be all in all*" (15:28). God is not "all in all" in the millennium; there

---

394 Charles Ryrie, *What You Should Know about the Rapture* (Chicago: Moody Press, 1981), 73-89.

are still enemies (Revelation 20:7-11).[395] God becoming "all in all" does not occur at the beginning of the millennium but at the end "*when he has put all things in subjection under his feet*" (1 Corinthians 15:27); when death is finally abolished (15:54-55). Death will not be abolished in the millennium (Isaiah 65:20), but it will be "swallowed up" in the eternal state (1 Corinthians 15:54). John states that it is in the new heavens and the new earth "*there will no longer be any death*" (Revelation 21:4), thus linking 1 Corinthians 15:54-55 with the eternal state rather than the rapture. Kistemaker is correct in writing, "The phrase ['inherit the kingdom' in v. 50] relates to the final stage in which God's kingdom is set free from powers that now reign. These powers must all submit to Jesus Christ, who at the time of the consummation delivers the kingdom to God the Father (v. 24)."[396]

It is possible that what Paul has in mind here is the liberation of creation from the bondage of decay and the glorious freedom of the children of God as they enter the eternal state when their bodies are redeemed (Romans 8:20-23). The transformation predicted in 1 Corinthians 15:50-56 best fits the description John gives in Revelation 21:1-5 of the eternal state.

INHERITING THE MILLENNIUM IS NOT THE SAME AS GETTING INTO THE KINGDOM. If, as many commentators assume, inheriting the kingdom means getting into the millennium, and if flesh and blood cannot inherit, then flesh and blood cannot get in and there will be no mortals in the kingdom. But if inheriting the kingdom is related to ruling with Christ and rewards (i.e., high status in the kingdom), then believers in mortal bodies can not only enter the kingdom, but they also can be co-heirs with Christ there.[397] Therefore, the third requirement is that to "inherit the kingdom of God" in the millennium is not the same as physically entering it.[398] All believers will enter the millennium, but only the faithful will rule/inherit there.[399] That inheriting the kingdom is not necessarily the same as getting

395 Anthony Thiselton notes that "Paul has already designated the end time or the last day as that in which God will be all in all." Thiselton, *The First Epistle to the Corinthians: A Commentary on the Greek Text*, 1290.

396 Kistemaker, *Exposition of the First Epistle to the Corinthians*, 581.

397 In subsequent chapters in this book, I will argue that to "enter the kingdom" does not refer to soteriological or geographical entrance into the kingdom. Instead it refers to entering into a kingdom way of living now (discipleship) leading to "greatness" in the future reign.

398 This is true in spite of the statement in Revelation 22:2 that in the new heavens and the new earth the leaves of the tree of life provide "healing for the nations." This "healing" refers retrospectively to the healing that has already occurred through the cross of Christ. This includes physical as well as spiritual healing. Another possibility is that the word "healing" (Gr *therapeia*) refers not to medicinal healing but to "the complete absence of physical and spiritual want. The life to come will be a life of abundance and perfection." Robert H. Mounce, *The Book of Revelation*, The New International Commentary on the New Testament (Grand Rapids: Wm. B. Eerdmans Publishing Co., 1997), 400. There is no room here for two kinds of bodies in the eternal state, enhanced mortal bodies which do not need healing but can have broken bones and the glorified resurrection bodies mentioned elsewhere. These bodies are "imperishable." They are like Jesus' body in His resurrection (Philippians 3:21), physical but glorified and indestructible. There can be no physical wounds because this would involve deterioration and death of flesh or bone cells which must then be replaced. Death has been forever removed at the beginning of the eternal state.

399 One might argue that unfaithful believing mortals may enter the kingdom and yet not inherit. This, however, leads to the ridiculous conclusion that the millennium is populated by carnal Christians because all the faithful ones will receive resurrection bodies.

into the kingdom is further proven by the fact that the priests in the millennium will enter the kingdom, but they will not inherit it. God is their inheritance. Clearly, entering the kingdom of God cannot be the same as inheriting the kingdom of God, or the priests would not enter (Ezekiel 44:28).

9 Inheriting the Kingdom in Ephesians

EPHESIANS INCLUDES three references to inheriting the kingdom: Ephesians 1:11, 14; 5:5.

God's Inheritance in the Saints

The first reference to an inheritance in Ephesians is in 1:11,

> *Also we have obtained an inheritance, having been predestined according to His purpose who works all things after the counsel of His will.*

This translation is incorrect. The words "obtained an inheritance" should be translated "were made a heritage,"[400] as translated in the ASV.[401] Thus the predestination here is not to obtain an inheritance but *to be a heritage.* It is God's inheritance "in the saints" (Ephesians 1:18) that Paul has in mind, not the believer's inheritance in heaven. It should be noted that God's inheritance of the saints involved His effort, His work. Jesus said that He came to do the Father's work. When He had completed it, He screamed, "*Tetelestai*" ("it is finished"). The church was allocated to Him in eternity past, but it became His in experience when He completed thirty-three years of high priestly work. Even God's inheritance in the saints was conditioned on the work of the Son of God.

The Earnest of Our Inheritance

In Ephesians 1:14, however, Paul speaks of another inheritance, one that is granted to the saints:

> *who is given as a pledge of our inheritance, with a view to the redemption of God's own possession, to the praise of His glory.*

Believers are God's inheritance, and also believers have an inheritance in heaven. This text raises two questions: What is meant by "inheritance"? And what is a "pledge"? First, we will consider the meaning of "pledge." Along with being our seal, the Holy Spirit is our pledge (Gr *arrabōn*).

---

400 See Hoehner, *Ephesians: An Exegetical Commentary*, 225. The verb is an aorist passive.

401 Also the NET Bible has, "we too have been claimed as God's own possession."

Scholars differ on how this word should be translated. The NASB, RSV, and NCB render it "pledge," a view followed by many Reformed interpreters.[402] The NIV, NAB, ASV, HCSB, KJV, Message, and NET Bible on the other hand opt for "deposit" or "earnest." In that case *arrabōn* refers to a "first installment, down payment, deposit, pledge.[403] This "obligates the contracting party to make further payments"[404] if the buyer provides what is purchased. Westcott says, "Ἀρραβών is properly a deposit paid as security for the rest of the purchase money; and then, by a natural transference, the first installment of a treasure given as a pledge for the delivery of the remainder."[405] God, so to speak, has legally bound Himself to provide our inheritance.

Thus the inheritance in this verse refers to our birth-inheritance which is our incredible positional treasure that we have because we are "in Him." The *arrabōn* is also mentioned in the context of 2 Corinthians 5:1-8. There it is a pledge of the eternal, heavenly habitation we have waiting for us—100% guaranteed by God.

An Inheritance in the Kingdom of God

The final passage relating to inheritance in Ephesians is 5:5.

> *For this you know with certainty, that no immoral or impure person or covetous man, who is an idolater, has an inheritance in the kingdom of Christ and God* (Ephesians 5:5).

While the inheritance in Ephesians 1:14 refers to our birth-inheritance which comes to us by faith alone, in Ephesians 5:5 Paul addresses our reward-inheritance which can be lost or enhanced.

In what appears to be a violation of the immediate context, Hoehner states, "The contrast in this passage is between those who inherit and those who receive the wrath of God, not between faithful and unfaithful disciples." "It is a contrast," he says, "between heaven and hell and not a comparison of degree."[406] Lincoln agrees, "The writer assumes that his readers are not among such people."[407]

On the other hand, it seems obvious that the context is specifically speaking of filthy behavior "among saints" (v. 3) and *not* only among nonbelievers, except by means of bad example. If this context was not describing activity by the saints, why is Paul warning them not to do it in verses 3-4? In Hoehner's view, the warning is then reduced down to the banality of "remember, that nonbelievers do not go to heaven." This thought, however, would have little impact on sinning believers. This view would have the Ephesian believers

---

[402] For example Murray Harris, "Review of A. M. Hunter, Probing the New Testament," *JETS* 15, no. 4 (Fall 1972): 247. "When Paul uses this term (2 Corinthians 1:22; 5:5; Ephesians 1:14) he is probably not conceiving of the Spirit as God's 'down-payment' on the believer's inheritance, an initial and provisional installment differing from the full payment not in kind but in degree, but rather as the God-given pledge of the believer's acquisition of immortality through a resurrection transformation, as God's guarantee of the fulfillment of his promises, and as the divine assurance of the realization of the Christian's hope."

[403] O. Becker, "*arrabōn*," in NIDNTT, 2:39.

[404] BDAG, 134.

[405] B. F. Westcott, *Saint Paul's Epistle to the Ephesians: The Greek Text with Notes and Addenda*, Classic Commentaries on the Greek New Testament (New York: The MacMillian Company, 1909), 17.

[406] Hoehner, *Ephesians: An Exegetical Commentary*, 661.

[407] Andrew T. Lincoln, *Ephesians* (Dallas: Word Books, 1990), 325.

thinking, "Well, I am a believer, and I am going to heaven, so this warning does not apply to me."

One might argue that a believer should be gripped by the intensity of God's hatred against sin and that is the point of the warning. God hates sin, so one should not sin. But that hardly compares with the threat of being disinherited (forfeiting one's lot in the kingdom). This view emasculates the passage of a warning. What is the warning to the believer?

The believer is warned that he might forfeit his reward-inheritance.[408]

A plausible view is that this passage is both a warning and an exhortation to live like children of light. They were "formerly" in darkness (v. 8) but they are now children of light. Therefore, Paul is exhorting them to live like who they really are.[409] The reference to the Kingdom is a reference to their *reward-inheritance*. The element of warning is not that these believers will fail to obtain their *birth-inheritance*, but that they will fail to obtain their *reward-inheritance*. Furthermore, they may also experience God's temporal wrath that Paul described in Romans 1:18-32.[410]

Usually, Reformed writers say a warning like this is God's means of guaranteeing by His irresistible grace that a true believer would never become immoral or covetous, or an idolater, and so forth. He is warned against this lifestyle because if he falls into it, that will prove that he was never a believer in the first place. This is ridiculous. First, this means that if he is a believer, then God warns the believer regarding a fate that He knows will never befall him, namely, eternal separation from God. Thus God is lying to the believer in order to motivate him to persevere. Second, if all "true" believers always obey then, as Fuller explains, "A command that everyone keeps is superfluous, and a reward that everyone receives for a virtue that everyone has is nonsense."[411] And, third, if the person addressed is only a professing believer but not a "true" believer, this means he is being told to correct his behavior if he wants to obtain eternal life. In other words, salvation is by works and not by faith alone apart from works. Or, alternatively, if he changes his life, he can prove to himself and to others that he is truly regenerate. However, he must persevere in that change of life to the end of life to validate that this change is really evidence of regeneration. Of course he cannot know if he will persevere until he has, thus, assurance now is impossible. This contradicts to the glorious promises of eternal life conditioned upon faith alone (and not perseverance) all over the New Testament.

Another common Reformed response is to say that since the inheritance in Ephesians 1:14 is heaven and is guaranteed by the pledge, it must be heaven in 5:5. Since believers

---

408 Hoehner avoids discussing the nature of the warning for Christians saying only that "Christians should not be deceived into thinking that this warning is merely empty words [Ephesians 5:6] (*kenois*, trans. 'empty')." "Empty" here means "void of God's wrath" (cf. Colossians 3:6). God's view of sin should be taken seriously. Believers should be imitators of God, not evildoers. Hoehner never tells what the consequences are for Christians who do not heed the warning. See Harold Hoehner, "Ephesians" in *The Bible Knowledge Commentary: New Testament*, ed. John F. Walvoord and Roy B. Zuck, reprint, Colorado Springs: Cook, 1996 ed. (Wheaton, IL: Victor Books, 1983), 2:368.

409 "As Christians their behavior should now display the virtues which come from their new nature as saints." López, "The Pauline Vice List and Inheriting the Kingdom", 270; ibid.

410 López says, "Ephesians 5:6-7 also shows that believers who behave like unbelievers incur temporal discipline like unbelievers" (ibid., 270).

411 J. William Fuller, "I Will Not Erase His Name from the Book of Life (Revelation 3:5)," *JETS* 26, no. 3 (1983): 255.

are guaranteed heaven (the doctrine of eternal security), the warning in Ephesians 5:5 must be addressed to nonbelievers. Such argumentation is persuasive only to those who "know" that the inheritance promised to believers is heaven itself and not our reward-inheritance there. In agreement with Experimental Predestinarians, Peter O'Brien assures his readers that the warning "speaks with certainty of exclusion from the kingdom of Christ and of God."[412] But the text does not say that. It says that they will be excluded from an inheritance in the kingdom of God. Furthermore, one could just as easily argue that since the inheritance in Ephesians 5:5 is based on works and refers (as it does elsewhere) to a reward-inheritance for work done (e.g, Matthew 25:34-36), it could mean this in Ephesians 1:14 as well.

The immoral or impure person to whom he refers in Ephesians 1:5 describes the saints in verse 4. Hoehner himself acknowledges that "the deeds of darkness" which need to be "exposed" in verse 11 are the deeds of believers, not unbelievers.[413] F. F. Bruce agrees: "When Paul tells the believing Ephesians in Ephesians 5:11, 'And do not participate in the unfruitful deeds of darkness, but instead even expose them' (Ephesians 5:11), he is telling other believers in the community to rebuke the sinning believer in a spirit of humility."[414]

The fact that wrath comes "upon the sons of disobedience" in Ephesians 5:6 reminds them that non-Christians (2:2) experience the wrath of God for the very behavior some of the Ephesian Christians are manifesting. Paul is saying, "Do not do the same things for which unbelievers are condemned." Such behavior is logically inconsistent and morally repugnant to grace. "*Shall we continue in sin that grace may abound? God forbid!*" (Romans 6:1-2). As Paul says, "*Do not be partners with them*" (v. 7). It is surely possible that the Ephesians could be partners with them, indeed some of them were (vv. 3-4), but the consequence for believers is not the wrath of eternal separation from God, but disinheritance.

Paul often warns believing Christians of this fate. The Corinthians, for example, as explained in the previous chapter, are warned that "the unrighteous will not inherit the kingdom of God" and then reminded them, "And such were some of you" (1 Corinthians 6:9-11). The problem at Corinth was that they had begun to act like they had before they became Christians. They "were" like that and now some are like that once more! This is clear

---

412 O'Brien, *The Letter to the Ephesians*, 362. Hermann Olshausen agrees but, like O'Brien, he feels the need to qualify, "But of course the doctrine that carnal living excludes from the kingdom of God is not to be understood as implying that no one whoever committed a carnal sin can enter into the kingdom of God; the very readers of Paul's epistle had previously lived as heathens (verse 8). It is rather meant to declare that without thorough conversion and purification from such things, no one can be in the Holy Kingdom of God." See Hermann Olshausen, *Ephesians*, trans. A. C. Kendrick, reprint ed., 6 vols., vol. 5 (Bowling Green, KY: reprint by Guardian of Truth Foundation, 2005), 125. Similarly, O'Brien begins his qualifications by saying, "The apostle is not asserting that the believer who ever falls into these sins is automatically excluded from God's kingdom. Rather, what is envisaged here is the person who has given himself or herself up without shame or repentance to this way of life." O'Brien, *The Letter to the Ephesians*, 363. For O'Brien, such a person is a believer who loses his salvation.

413 "Whose deeds are to be exposed?" It is all too easy to conclude that it is the deeds of those in darkness. Nevertheless, it is more likely that it refers to believers who are participating in the unfruitful works of darkness. Ibid., 679.

414 Bruce, *The Epistles to the Colossians, to Philemon, and to the Ephesians*, 375. Like Hoehner, Bruce is inconsistent. On the one hand, he says the immoral people of 5:5 are nonbelievers because they have no inheritance, but then in verse 11 he says that those who participate in the deeds of darkness are believers and fellow believers need to confront them.

throughout the book where divisions, lawsuits, fornication, selfishness, and drunkenness are a constant problem.[415] Because they know that true Christians do commit some of the very deeds Paul condemns, those holding the view that the inheritance refers to heaven begin to qualify the Scriptural statements. They state, for example, that only "persistent sinners are excluded from God's kingdom."[416] How much is persistent? Would the latter portion of Solomon's life in which he was fornicating with over one thousand women and worshipping Baal qualify as persistent? If so, will the inspired author of three books of the Bible who manifested godly piety for many years be excluded from heaven? Unless one wants to assert that Solomon and a host of others in the Bible who were in fact "persistent" sinners were not actually born again, this argument lacks conviction.[417]

The warning against losing one's inheritance in Ephesians 5:5 is addressed to true believers and the danger is loss of reward. As Jesus explained, the inheritance can involve ten cities, five cities, or no cities, that is, no reward-inheritance (Luke 19:11-27). And Paul says, there are degrees of glory (1 Corinthians 15:41), and some can lose it all (1 Corinthians 3:15). John agrees, saying that rewards can be lost (2 John 8). Of the eighteen instances in the New Testament where the verb *klēronomeō* ("to inherit") is used, thirteen of them suggest that a work is involved in order to obtain the inheritance.[418] Contrary to popular opinion, "There is no thought here of 'inheritance' from someone who has died."[419] The writer to Hebrews, for example, exhorts believers: "that you be not sluggish, but imitators of those who *through faith and patience inherit the promises*" (Hebrews 6:12). John adds, "*He who overcomes* shall inherit these things, and I will be his God and he will be My son" (Revelation 21:7). Jesus explains, "Inherit the kingdom prepared for you from the foundation of the world. '*For I was hungry, and you gave Me something to eat*'" (Matthew 25:34-35). Inheriting the kingdom is based on faith plus works. This, in turn, requires that the inheritance is not always the same as heaven itself.

If these passages are allowed to speak plainly, only three options are open:

1. Experimental Predestinarian: The inheritance is heaven and the passages referring to loss of inheritance must be addressed to those who only profess faith in Christ.
2. Arminian: The inheritance is heaven and can be lost by a failure to persevere.
3. The Partners: The inheritance is a future reward-inheritance to be enjoyed in the kingdom, is conditioned on works, and the inheritance is not heaven itself. It is our share in the glory of Christ's kingdom and heaven which varies in degree depending on our faithfulness now.

The Experimental Predestinarian view dies the death of a thousand qualifications. Suggested alternative "explanations" must be manufactured to explain away the works-salvation inference which is obvious to all. A sound hermeneutical principle is that the

---

415 See discussion above, pp. 94 ff.

416 O'Brien, *The Letter to the Ephesians*, 362.

417 For extensive discussion of the "carnal" Christians, see vol. 2, chapter 32.

418 Matthew 5:5; 19:29; 25:34; Hebrews 6:12; 12:17; Mark 10:17; Luke 10:25; 18:18; 1 Peter 3:9; 1 Corinthians 6:9-10; Galatians 5:21; Revelation 21:7.

419 Paul Ellingworth and Howard A. Hatton, *A Handbook on Paul's First Letter to the Corinthians*, UBS Handbook Series (New York: United Bible Societies, 1995), 130.

simplest explanation is best. The efficiency of any theory is simply the amount of data correlated divided by the number of assumptions made. On those criteria, the simplest and most efficient explanation of Ephesians 5:5 is to acknowledge that our inheritance in that context is rewards and not heaven.

10

The Inheritance in Hebrews

The Inheritance

THE VERB *klēronomeō* occurs four times in the book of Hebrews.[420] Its usage there is not inconsistent with its usage elsewhere, a reward for a life of faithfulness. The inheritance can be forfeited because of disobedience, as in the case of Esau (Hebrews 12:17), and it is only obtained by persevering, that is, by "faith and patience" (Hebrews 6:12). Jesus has inherited a superior name to that of the angels (Hebrews 1:4). He achieved this inheritance by perseverance in suffering (Hebrews 2:10; Philippians 2:9-11).[421] Similarly, His companions (Hebrews 1:9, Gr *Metochoi*) will "inherit salvation" (Hebrews 1:14) in the same way. Thus he says, "*Do not throw away your confidence; it will be richly rewarded. You need to persevere so that when you have done the will of God, you will receive what he has promised*" (Hebrews 10:35-36).

Perseverance to the end and faithfully doing the will of God are the conditions for obtaining the inheritance-salvation in this epistle, conditions that are absent from the Pauline teaching of obtaining salvation (in the sense of final deliverance from eternal damnation) on the basis of faith alone. As will be discussed below, a different salvation is in view: co-rulership with Christ in the coming kingdom.

The noun *klēronomia* occurs twice in Hebrews (9:15; 11:8). In 11:8 it refers to Abraham's acquisition of the land of Canaan. Whereas that land was guaranteed on oath, it was obtained by spiritual obedience. What is stressed in Hebrews 11 is that Abraham "obeyed and went." Had he not obeyed, he would not have inherited.

The other use of the noun is in 9:15:

> *And for this reason He is the mediator of a new covenant,* ***in order that*** *since a death has taken place for the redemption of the transgressions that were committed under the first covenant, those who have been called may receive the promise of the eternal inheritance.*

The reason we have received an eternal redemption and cleansing from sin is "*in order that*" we might "*receive the promise of an eternal inheritance.*"

Paul Tanner notes,

---

[420] Hebrews 1:4; 1:14; 6:12; 12:17.

[421] Christ's obedience as the condition for obtaining His new name, LORD JESUS CHRIST (Philippians 2:9-11, "therefore"), seems to be similar to His receiving His inheritance.

> *The purpose of His obtaining eternal redemption for us is that we might ultimately receive an inheritance that we can eternally enjoy and from which we can benefit. The text does not say, however, that all believers will automatically receive this. The "eternal redemption" is absolutely free, but not necessarily the eternal inheritance. The latter appears to be conditional for at least two reasons.*[422]

The first reason we know that this inheritance is not free is that the author has just said that our cleansing was so that we might "serve the living God" (v. 14). Service for God is required if one is to obtain this reward-inheritance.

Second, throughout the letter the writer specifies how the promise of a reward-inheritance is to be obtained. It is by "*faith and patience*" (Hebrews 6:12) and "*holding firm to the* end" (3:14) that we might "*inherit what has been promised*." The writer echoes this theme once again in 10:36, saying, "*For you have need of endurance, so that when you have done the will of God, you may receive what was promised.*"[423]

To what does the promise of an eternal inheritance in Hebrews 9:5 refer? Kaiser insists that the inheritance in Hebrews 9:15 is "the firm possession of the land as Hebrews 11:9 most assuredly asserts."[424] Christ's mediatorial work has as its aim that His sons should enter into that partnership with Him. Their achievement of that destiny, however, as explained here and elsewhere in the book, is conditioned upon obedience from the heart. George N. H. Peters (citing Col. 3:24) agrees that what I have called the "reward-inheritance" is based upon works and actions.[425]

No doubt Peters has Hebrews 4:1 in mind, the promise of the remaining rest. To inherit the rest is to inherit the land; metaphorically it means more. We will discuss this "rest" in the next chapter, but anticipating our conclusion there, we may say that the promise of rest refers to the completion of our task and subsequent entrance into our reward. It appears to have similar meaning in Hebrews 11:9, 13 when it is used of the land promises to the patriarchs. They too were to remain faithful to the end of life, and, in so doing, they entered into rest and will one day possess the land. The inheritance should take the meaning it takes elsewhere in Hebrews—ownership of the millennial land of Canaan, the future reign of the servant kings, joint rulership with Messiah in the heavenly country, the millennial land of Palestine.[426]

Esau Lost His Inheritance

One of the sternest warnings of the New Testament is in Hebrews 12:12-29. The writer of the epistle to the Hebrews challenges them to pursue sanctification and cautions that without it no one will "see the Lord." Some have held that this refers to a "beatific vision"

---

[422] Paul Tanner, "Hebrews," in *The Grace New Testament Commentary* (Denton, TX: Grace Evangelical Society, 2010), 1067.

[423] Similarly, Jesus obtained an inheritance through His cross-work and a faithful life (Hebrews 1:2-4); Noah obtained an inheritance because he "prepared an ark"; Abraham received an inheritance because he "obeyed by going out" (11:8); and Esau lost his inheritance because of evil works (12:17).

[424] Kaiser, *Toward an Old Testament Theology*, 69.

[425] Peters, *The Theocratic Kingdom of Our Lord Jesus, the Christ, as Covenanted in the Old Testament and Presented in the New Testament*, 2:387.

[426] Peters is correct in saying, "This promise, let the reader notice, of inheriting the land forever, is found in the Abrahamic covenant," ibid., 1:322.

which some Christians will enjoy in heaven and some will not.[427] However, in view of the other references in Scripture to seeing the Lord, it may be best to understand the phrase as referring to a deeper Christian experience.[428] Then he warns them regarding the loss of their inheritance rights:

> *See that no one is sexually immoral or is godless like Esau, who for a single meal sold his inheritance rights as the oldest son. Afterward, as you know, when he wanted to inherit [klēronomeō] this blessing, he was rejected. He could bring about no change of mind, though he sought the blessing with tears (Hebrews 12:16-17).*

The cultural background behind the Esau incident is relevant. Esau was the firstborn son, and therefore by birth he had the rights and privileges described as belonging to the firstborn.

When his father died, he received a double share of the inheritance (Deuteronomy 21:17). During his life he was preeminent among his brothers (Genesis 43:33). God had originally intended to make the firstborn of the sons of Israel His priests. However, because of the disobedience in the wilderness, He took that blessing from the firstborn and gave it to the Levites instead (Numbers 8:14-18).

God often violated His own rule regarding the firstborn blessing. Sometimes this was based on grace. Isaac was selected ahead of Ishmael, the firstborn; and Jacob was chosen instead of Esau for the blessing of the firstborn. Sometimes the reversal of the firstborn right to the inheritance was based on merit. To the end of his life it was the father's prerogative to determine the disposal of his property.[429] If the eldest son was not qualified, then the father could give it to the son who was. The Scripture only requires that, if the firstborn right is denied to the eldest, that it not be a matter of favoritism (Deuteronomy 21:15-17). Even though Reuben was Jacob's firstborn, the inheritance rights passed to the sons of Joseph (1 Chronicles 5:1-2; Genesis 49:3-4), and ultimately to Judah, the fourth in line, because he prevailed over his brothers (Genesis 49:8-10).

The rights and privileges of the firstborn were given, provisionally, at birth. The right to the inheritance was his, but he could lose it. It was necessary that the firstborn son maintain these rights. He must be worthy of the elevated status and honor. All the sons are heirs, but only those who met the conditions of the firstborn achieved the elevated status and authority and retained their inheritance. The many New Testament references to something conditional in the future life of the believer may reflect this Old Testament distinction between the firstborn son who retained his privilege and those like Esau who did not. Those Christians who suffer with Him (Romans 8:17), who endure (2 Timothy 2:15), and who are the overcomers in the book of Revelation are the faithful firstborn sons.

Esau, although heir to the rights of the firstborn, counted them of little value. Like some true believers in every generation, he lacked interest in the inheritance (Hebrews 12:17), "*What profit shall the birthright do to me*?" According the Law, he was first in line

---

427 For example Lang, *Firstborn Sons: Their Rights and Risks*, 98.

428 Enoch did not "see death," that is, he did not "experience" it (Hebrews 11:5). Moses "endured as seeing Him," (Hebrews 11:27), that is, he experienced God richly and therefore was enabled to endure. In Matthew 5:8 the peacemakers will "see God," that is, they will really know Him and walk with Him. In Job 42:5, Job came to "see" God as a result of his trial. The meaning is that he came to know Him more deeply and intimately.

429 1 Chronicles 26:10: "Shimri the first (for though he was not the firstborn, his father made him the first)."

for the inheritance (Deuteronomy 21:17). In order to satisfy his passing appetite, he sold his inheritance for a meal. His lack of interest was confirmed by a divine oath (Genesis 25:31-33). Later in life he changed his mind and regretted his rash decision. Yet he was unable to change his father's mind. G. H. Lang makes this poignant observation:

> *Of Esau himself the history gives, as a final picture, a man who has risen above his earlier hatred of his brother (Genesis 32-33), and who at last joins him at the graveside of his father. Thus he is the type of one of the family of God who lapses into carnality and bitterness, but years after is restored in soul, yet who nevertheless cannot regain the full position. He is the first that shall be last though still in the family.*[430]

Like Esau, true Christians[431] are children of God; we are firstborn sons. Because of that we possess the rights of the firstborn, we do not have to earn these rights. They are given to us through the grace of God. However, we must value and keep these rights and are warned by Esau's example regarding the possibility of not doing so.

But even though we cannot forfeit eternal life, we can forfeit our inheritance rights.[432] This should not come as a surprise because the inheritance in the Old Testament could be forfeited through disobedience. In the words of John, a believer can "*lose what he has worked for*" (2 John 8). This fact surely informed the viewpoint of the New Testament writers! While this is not the same as losing one's justification, the consequences for eternity are serious. At the Judgment Seat of Christ our works will be revealed by "fire" (1 Corinthians 3:13): "*It will be revealed with fire, and the fire will test the quality of each man's work.*" It is possible for a Christian's life work to be burned up because the building materials were wood, hay, and stubble. Only those works done in obedience to the Lord, out of proper motivation and in dependence on Him (gold, silver, and precious stones), will survive the searing heat! Some will survive with very little to carry with them into eternity. As Paul put it:

> *If it is burned up, he will suffer loss;* ***he himself will be saved****, but only as one escaping through the flames (1 Corinthians 3:15).*

Sauer summarizes:

> *The position of being a child of God is, indeed, not forfeitable, but not the total fullness of the heavenly birthright [inheritance]. In this sense there is urgent need to give diligence to make our calling and election sure. "For thus shall be richly supplied unto you the entrance into the eternal kingdom of our Lord and Savior Jesus Christ" (2 Peter 1:10-11).*[433]

---

430 G. H. Lang, *The Epistle to the Hebrews* (Hayesville, NC: Schoettle Publishing Co., 1985), 254.

431 Whether or not Esau was saved is not relevant to this discussion. The writer uses him as an illustration of the fact that the saved can lose their firstborn inheritance rights. His example is applied to those who have come to the church of the firstborn ones (Hebrews 12:23). The Gr word translated "firstborn" is plural, and therefore the firstborn ones are referred to and not Christ as the firstborn. To come to the "church of the firstborn" means to be called to the privilege of being a firstborn son. All Christians are called to be part of that assembly and by birth have a right to be there. However, they may forfeit that right and never achieve their calling. That is the thrust of all the warnings of the book of Hebrews. See chapters 20 and 21.

432 This interpretation assumes that the readers of this epistle are genuine Christians and not merely professing ones. This point will be established in chapters 20 and 21.

433 Eric Sauer, *In the Arena of Faith: A Call to a Consecrated Life* (Grand Rapids: Wm. B. Eerdmans Publishing Co., 1956), 154.

The sobering fact here is that our decisions have eternal consequences that cannot be reversed. Even though one can repent and be restored to fellowship with God, believers will one day face the consequences of their sins at the Judgment Seat of Christ.

"To take a very simple example—if a young man loses his purity or a girl her virginity, nothing can ever bring it back. The choice was made and the choice stands. God can and will forgive, but God Himself cannot turn back the clock and unmake the choice or undo the consequences."[434]

Christ's Inheritance: A More Excellent Name (Hebrews 1:4)

Lest there be any doubt as to whether an inheritance is reward for a faithful life, consider the example of the "author of our salvation" (Hebrews 2:10).

> *When He had made purification of sins, He sat down at the right hand of the Majesty on high;* ***having become*** [Gr *ginomai*] *as much better than the angels, as He has inherited a more excellent name than they (Hebrews 1:3–4).*

The Son of God "became" (Gr *ginomai*) something He was not before. Had the writer wanted to say that Jesus "was" what He always had been, he would have used a form of the verb "to be" (Gr *eimi*). But one of the meanings of *ginomai* is "to come to acquire or experience a state."[435] He had finished His life work, making purification for sins, and, as a result, He became something through experience. What did He become? The text says that He became better than the angels and inherited a better name, the name, "Son." But wasn't the eternal Son of God always better than the angels, always a Son? Attridge and Koester state the problem precisely, "The language used of the Son's superiority, 'become' and 'inherited,' appears somewhat odd, given the preceding remarks about the Son's primordial relationship with the Father. The tension, already noted in vs. 2, between what Christ is from all eternity and what he is at his exaltation, again surfaces."[436]

Having stated the difficulty, unfortunately, they give us no help toward a solution. In a manner somewhat typical of "biblical" theologians, they pass over the issue saying, "Yet the implication that Christ became the son at some point should not be pressed."[437] But Athanasius pressed it and saved the church from the Arian heresy.[438] The implication is there, and one must explain how it is that He "became better than the angels."

Westcott gives us the answer. In agreement with the church fathers, he argues that the word "become" (Gr *ginōmai*) "is used of the Lord's human nature and not of His divine Personality."[439] Thus He became better than the angels in His human nature. While living in

---

[434] William Barclay, *The Gospel of Matthew*, rev. ed., 2 vols. (Philadelphia: Westminster Press, 1975), 210.

[435] Louw-Nida, 1:153.

[436] Harold W. Attridge and Helmut Koester, *Hebrews: A Commentary on the Epistle to the Hebrews*, Hermeneia (Philadelphia: Fortress Press, 1989), 47.

[437] Ibid., 47.

[438] E.g., Athanasius says, "This being so understood, it is parallel also respecting the Son, that whatever, and however often, is said, such as, 'He became' and 'become,' should ever have the same sense: so that as, when we see the words in question, 'become better than the angels' and 'He became,' we should not conceive any original becoming of the Word, nor in any way fancy from such terms that He is originate; but should understand Paul's words of His ministry and economy when He became man." See Athanasius, *Four Discourses Against the Arians*, Discourse 1, Chapter 10, 64.

[439] Westcott, *The Epistle to the Hebrews*, 17.

flesh as the God-man, He was inferior. In fact He was a mere servant (Philippians 2:7). But because of His faithfulness, He was highly exalted.

Two questions remain: (1) What did Jesus inherit? (2) What were the conditions He met to become better and to obtain this inheritance?

WHAT DID CHRIST INHERIT?: THE TITLE OF "SON"

In regard to the first question, we are told that He inherited a better name, that of "Son." This seems obvious from the context where the writer cites Psalm 2:7, "*For to which of the angels did He ever say, 'Thou art My Son, Today I have begotten Thee?' And again, 'I will be a Father to Him And He shall be a Son to Me'?*" (Hebrews 1:5).

But the Lord Jesus was always a Son in the Trinitarian sense. However, He became a son in a unique sense. Upon His resurrection He was "*declared to be the Son of God*" (Romans 1:4). Even though He does not yet rule from David's throne, at that time He was begotten as the messianic King of Israel. All the kings of Israel were called sons of God and the Lord Jesus is THE Son of God. By citing 2 Samuel 7:14 in Hebrews 1:5 (cf. Romans 1:4), which was addressed to David ("*I will be his Father, and he shall be my son*"), the author of Hebrews made this specific link. The inherited title of "Son" refers to His messianic investiture, not His eternal essence.

The prophets anticipated a day when David's "Greater Son" would come as the peaceful ruler (Micah 5:2-4; cf. Psalms 89:27) who had four names (Isaiah 9:6). Gabriel announced this to Mary saying, "*The Holy Spirit will come upon you, and the power of the Most High will overshadow you; and for that reason the holy offspring shall be called the Son of God*" (Luke 1:35; cf. Luke 1:68 ff.).

Paul Tanner summarizes, "In Ancient Near Eastern thought, when a god elevated a person to kingship, the king assumed the status of being the deity's 'first-born.'"[440] This analogy is applied to the Messiah in Psalms 89:3-4, 26-27. Hence this has nothing to do with physical birth or origin, but rather with the time of coronation. The time of this begetting is "Today," that unique occasion when the Messiah is elevated to the status of Davidic king. Acts 13:33 connects Psalms 2:7 with the resurrection of Jesus. One day He will sit on David's throne. He has been coronated but will not rule from that throne until His Parousia. There is no way that the present era can in any sense be described as the Davidic Kingdom of peace, harmony, prosperity, and justice described in the Old Testament prophecies. In the meantime, He sits at the right hand of the Father. By His resurrection and ascension to the Father's right hand, Jesus has been declared "the Son of God" (cf. Romans 1:3-4), though He must await the second coming for the formal inauguration of His kingdom.

Also, Psalm 2 speaks of the Messiah's inheritance, "*You have only to ask me, and I will give you the nations as your inheritance*" (Psalms 2:8). This is the basis by which the author can say that the Son has been "appointed heir of all things" (Hebrews 1:2). Clearly no angel ever attained the honor that this Davidic Son has."[441]

---

[440] Tanner, "Hebrews," 1035.

[441] According to F. F. Bruce, "The eternity of Christ's divine Sonship is not brought into question by this view; the suggestion rather is that he who was the Son of God from everlasting entered into the full exercise of all the prerogatives implied by his Sonship when, after his suffering had proved the completeness of his obedience, he was raised to the Father's right hand." F. F. Bruce, *The Epistle to the Hebrews*, rev. ed., The New International Commentary on the New Testament (Grand Rapids: Wm. B. Eerdmans Publishing Co., 1990), 54.

WHY DID HE INHERIT IT? - BECAUSE OF HIS FAITHFUL LIFE

But the answer to the second question leads us into the subject of this chapter. What were the conditions Jesus met in order to obtain this inheritance, this title of Son? Since it was because He became better than the angels that He obtained the inheritance, how and in what sense did He become better? Hebrews gives the answer. It was "*because of the suffering of death crowned with glory and honor, that by the grace of God He might taste death for everyone*" (Hebrews 2:9). It was "*by becoming obedient to the point of death, even death on a cross ... God highly exalted him*" (Philippians 2:8). He was "*made perfect*" through *sufferings* (Hebrews 2:10).

During His sojourn on earth the eternal Son of God "*made himself nothing, taking the form of a servant, being born in the likeness of men*" (Philippians 2:7, ESV). For the first time in all eternity, the second person of the Trinity acquired a human nature and for thirty-three years He lived life as God intended man to live it. "*For a little while was made lower than the angels,*" and then, having faithfully completed His life work, He was "*crowned with glory and honor because of the suffering of death, so that by the grace of God he might taste death for everyone* (Hebrews 2:9, ESV). For a "little while" He was lower than the angels but because of His perseverance in suffering and the fact that He was crowned with glory, He became a Son "indeed." The crown He received is the victor's crown (Gr *stephanos*), awarded to the victor in an athletic contest.[442]

Apparently, in some sense, the second person of the Trinity was not always "perfect," and *in a specific sense*, was not always a "Son."[443] Therefore, "*He had to be made like His brethren in all things, that He might become a merciful and faithful high priest in things pertaining to God, to make propitiation for the sins of the people*" (Hebrews 2:17). By suffering and experiencing life in the same manner His brethren did, He became a merciful priest who can experientially identify with our plight. "*For since He Himself was tempted in that which He has suffered, He is able to come to the aid of those who are tempted*" (Hebrews 2:18), and "*he can deal gently with the ignorant and misguided, since he himself also is beset with weakness*" (Hebrews 5:2).

Furthermore, only by living without sin could He qualify to make propitiation for the sins of the people. A sinless sacrifice was needed. When He became a Son, He became not only the messianic King, but He also became a priest! He is indeed superior to the angels! The writer makes this clear later when he associates Psalm 2:7-8 with Psalms 110:4, implying he was begotten as a Son on His resurrection and ascension. At that time the Father says of Him, "*THOU ART A PRIEST FOREVER ACCORDING TO THE ORDER OF MELCHIZEDEK*" (Hebrews 5:6).

But how did He qualify for these high honors: messianic King, High Priest, and an inheritance? The answer is that He "LOVED *RIGHTEOUSNESS AND HATED LAWLESSNESS; THEREFORE GOD, THY GOD, HATH ANOINTED THEE WITH THE OIL OF GLADNESS ABOVE THY COMPANIONS*" (Hebrews 1:9). His anointing to receive His inheritance ("*heir of all things,*" v. 2) came to Him because of His good works and His character. If the inheritance granted to the Son of God was obtained because of His faithful life, how can it come to

---

442 BDAG, 944.

443 He was, of course, always a Son in terms of His essence, but He became a Son in the sense of messianic investiture on His bodily resurrection and ascension.

believers apart from the same? An inheritance based on faithfulness is a reward; it is not initial salvation. Christ did not enter into salvation because of His faithful obedience as a servant to the point of death. Instead, He entered into His kingship and future messianic rule of the restored Davidic theocracy (Acts 1:6). "*He was appointed heir of all things*" (Hebrews 1:2).

Like the Captain of our salvation, who though He was a Son, became a Son in a different sense at the time of His messianic investiture, we too, even though we are sons of God (John 1:12-13; Gal 3:26; Luke 20:36) by faith alone, can become sons in a fuller sense. "*Blessed are the peacemakers, for they shall be called sons of God*" (Matthew 5:9). When Christians are led by the Spirit, they are truly sons of God: "*For all who are being led by the Spirit of God, these are sons of God*" (Romans 8:14). Also, like our Captain, we too, will one day be crowned with glory and honor and the entire creation will be subjected to Christ's servant kings as they (Hebrews 2:7) rule with Him. We also will be "better than the angels" (1 Corinthians 6:2-3).

Noah Became an Heir

Hebrews 11 has often been called the "faith hall of fame." This designation refers to how Old Testament heroes of faith illustrated the walk of faith and thus became a cloud of witnesses whose examples we are exhorted to follow (Hebrews 12:1). Note, it was their "walk" of faith which is in view and not the initial act of faith whereby they became just before God. This fact has a bearing on our understanding of the faith of Noah.

> *By faith Noah, being warned by God about things not yet seen, in reverence prepared an ark for the salvation of his household, by which he condemned the world, and became an heir of the righteousness which is according to faith (Hebrews 11:7).*

We are told that Noah "became an heir of the righteousness which is according to" (Gr *kata*) faith." But, we must ask, "Does 'faith' refer to the initial act of faith through which we are saved, or does it refer to a 'walk' of faith which is to characterize the life of those who are already justified? Clearly, the context of Hebrews 11 is not discussing how these believers were saved, but how they walked by faith throughout their lives. For example, we read, "*By faith Noah prepared an ark;*" "*by faith*" *when Abraham was called, he obeyed*"; "*by faith*" Abraham offered up Isaac; "*by faith*" Moses' parents hid him; and "*by faith*" Moses left Egypt, etc. Their walk of faith is in view.

Furthermore, while it is common to understand "righteousness" in verse 7 as right standing before God through faith alone, Paul Tanner has shown that this meaning is highly unlikely in the Epistle to the Hebrews.[444] He points out that the word "righteousness" is never used in Hebrews in a forensic sense. It is always used (6x) of moral righteousness and not legal justification.[445] For example, "the word of righteousness" in 5:13 is a word about a quality of discernment which characterizes the mature in contrast to the baby Christian. The Old Testament saints performed "acts of righteousness" (Hebrews 11:33), and our Father trains us through disciplines so that we may know "the peaceful fruit of

---

444 Paul Tanner, personal communication, May 8, 2012.

445 See 1:9; 5:13; 7:2; 11:7, 33; 12:11.

righteousness" (Hebrews 12:11). These training sessions are designed to produce ethical righteousness in our lives.

Tanner says, "Since 'faith' in Hebrews 10—11 is not 'saving faith,' and since 'righteousness' in Hebrews is not 'forensic imputed righteousness,' this verse is probably talking about something else. Noah was a man of faith, and as Genesis 6:8 teaches us, he was a 'righteous and blameless man.'"

The writer of our Epistle tells us that Noah "*became an heir (Gr klēronomos) of the righteousness which is according (Gr kata) to faith.*" A *klēronomos* is "one who receives something as a possession."[446] What Noah came to possess is a righteous quality of life. Attridge concurs saying, "What Noah's story exemplifies is the reverent reliance upon God's promises and consequent faithful action that enables one—in a quite un-Pauline fashion—to do what is righteous."[447]

This righteous quality was "according to faith." The Greek preposition, *kata*, is best rendered as "corresponds"[448] or, "according to the standard of his walk by faith." In other words, his righteous quality of life corresponds with how he walked by faith.[449]

One might paraphrase,

He possessed a moral quality of life which corresponded to his walk of faith.[450]

Summary

Throughout the book of Hebrews the writer speaks of an inheritance that may come to believers in Christ on the basis of faithfulness. Those faithful followers are called "Partners of Christ," Christ's *Metochoi*. Abraham illustrates this well. The writer states that "*he obeyed and went,*" and as a result he obtained an inheritance. This inheritance/reward for obedience is called an "*eternal inheritance*" later on in the book (9:15). This "eternal inheritance" comes to the believers because of their service for Christ (9:14) and because of their faith and patience (6:12). In other words, this eternal inheritance is only awarded to Christ's *Metochoi*, His partners who hold firm to the end of life (3:14).

That the inheritance is not heaven but something in addition to heaven, which can be obtained by faithfulness or lost because of disobedience, is illustrated in the life of Esau. Even though he was the firstborn son and had the right to a double portion of the inheritance, he lost his inheritance because of his disobedience. And he could not get it back (12:16-17). Once again, as in the rest of the New Testament, we see that the inheritance is something linked to works, and not faith alone.

Finally, the writer states that Christ obtained the inheritance of a "more excellent name," the name "Son" (1:4). This did not come to Him automatically because He was already the Son in essence. What conditions did the Son of God have in order to obtain the title of "Son" and be "better than the angels"? We are told that it was "*because of the suffering of death*" (2:9) and the fact that He "loved righteousness and hated lawlessness" (1:9). To

---

[446] BDAG, 548.

[447] Attridge and Koester, *Hebrews: A Commentary on the Epistle to the Hebrews*, 320.

[448] NIDNTT, 3:1200.

[449] See Romans 8:5 where to be "according to the Spirit" means to walk according to the Spirit.

[450] Or, possibly, he possessed a moral quality of life which was directed by his walk of faith. In Galatians 5:17 he speaks of "those whose lives are directed by (Gr *kata*) the Spirit" (NIDNTT, 3:1200).

obtain these high honors, it was necessary that He become like us and live as we must live. Because of His character and His faithful completion of His life work (to make purification for sins), He qualified for the inheritance of a better name. If the "Captain of our salvation" obtained His inheritance because of the faithful life that He lived and the character He possessed, certainly His brothers must follow a similar path. An inheritance is something beyond initial salvation. It is a reward granted to those who finish their life work, who love righteousness and hate lawlessness, who hold fast to the end. Some Christians will, and some like Esau will not.

11

The Inheritance—The Rest of Hebrews

ONE CAN safely say that the greatest known evangelist in the history of the church since the apostle Paul was an Anglican clergyman from England named George Whitefield. He was the one who launched the Wesleyan revivals and who first preached in the fields of England to thousands of coal miners and working folk.

God led him to America where he sparked what came to be known as the Great Awakening, the first great revival in the New World. For many years he preached tirelessly, traveling thousands of miles on horseback, spreading the gospel throughout the colonies.

According to John Pollock, on September 29, 1770, George Whitefield gave his last sermon. Upon arrival, the organizers of the event urged him not to preach. Why? He was weak and frail from years of faithful service throughout the colonies. As a result of his ministry, a mighty revival swept through the early American frontier.[451]

"Sir," they said, "you are more fit to go to bed than to preach."

Whitefield had a heart ailment, and he knew the end was near.

"True, sir," George replied. Then he clasped his hand and looked up to heaven and said. "Lord Jesus, I am weary in thy work but not of it. If I have not finished my course, let me go and speak for thee once more in the fields, and seal thy truth, and come home and die!"

Mounting the pulpit, the words of his last sermon came slowly at first. But after a while, it seemed his foggy brain cleared and looking upward to heaven he said, "Works? Works? A man get to heaven by works? I would as soon think of climbing to the moon on a rope of sand."

For the next two hours, no one would have known that he was suffering from debilitating weakness and exhaustion. He proclaimed a magnificent sermon about the glories of the Christ. At the end of the second hour he cried out, "I go! I go to rest prepared. My sun has arisen, and by the aid of heaven has given light to many. It is now about to set—No! It is about to rise to the zenith of immortal glory. I have outlived many on earth, but they cannot outlive me in heaven. O thought divine! I should soon be in a world where time, age, pain and sorrow are unknown. My body fails, my spirit expands. How willingly would I live forever to preach Christ! But I die to be with Him."

He looked forward to entering into "rest."

Then, tottering from the platform, they took him immediately to bed. He awoke at two in the morning and wanted something to drink, a little cider.

---

451 Most of the following wording and all of the illustration is adapted from John Pollock, *George Whitefield and the Great Awakening* (Garden City, NY: Doubleday, 1972), 267-72.

"My asthma is coming on again," he wheezed. "I must have two or three days' rest. Two or three days' riding, without preaching, will set me up again."

They opened the window and the thought of going without preaching caused him to say, "I hope I shall be better by and by. A good pulpit sweat today may give me relief. I shall be better after preaching."

The local churches had expected him to preach in a few hours.

Pollock then concludes his description of the last words of this remarkable evangelist and servant of Christ.

"His servant Richard said, 'I wish you would not preach so often, sir.'"

"I had rather wear out than rust out," panted George.

He had apparently caught a cold preaching the previous day.

Then he sat up in bed, eyes closed and began to pray. He commended his friends to God. He prayed for England and his preaching colleagues laboring there, one by one bringing them before the throne of grace. Then he crossed the Atlantic to Georgia, then to Pennsylvania, and New England. Those present said he seemed completely oblivious to his surroundings and his pain. He knew only that he talked with his faithful unchangeable Friend.

Heaven was only a hair's breath away. For Richard Smith, it was awe inspiring.

"My asthma, my asthma" he croaked. Actually his heart was giving way.

"I am almost suffocated. I can scarcely breathe. My asthma quite chokes me."

He got out of bed and stumbled to the open window. Outside, Newbury Port lay asleep. For five minutes he stood there, gasping. He fought for breath as the first glimmer of a new dawn caught the waters of the estuary and would soon break over New England.

He turned to Richard and Parsons: "I am dying," he said.

Then he mounted the waiting chariot.[452]

George Whitefield had finished his course. When the chariot entered, as he put it, "he entered into rest."

Perhaps no other writer of the New Testament reflected as deeply and profoundly upon the theme of the inheritance and final entrance into "rest" as did the author of the epistle to the Hebrews. In this chapter we discover one of his favorite expressions for the inheritance—he called it "rest." But, as we will see, "rest" for him was much more than going to heaven when one dies. It was what one entered into when he has finished his work; it was that sense of satisfaction that one like Whitefield feels when he knows that he has come to the end of a life well lived. It is the reward that comes to the faithful, persevering Christian who has lived with the end in view.

God's Rest

Addressing believers undergoing persecution and considering a return to Judaism, the writer of the epistle to the Hebrews presses on them the failure of the Exodus generation and warns them of a similar fate. With unusual insight he notes that their failure to enter into rest was a failure to finish their work, precisely the danger facing the Hebrews who were considering an abandonment of their confession.

452 Ibid., 272.

The readers of this epistle were in danger of "falling away" (Hebrews 6:6) and "ignoring a great salvation" (Hebrews 2:3). All five of the warning passages in the book are directed against this peril. To encourage their perseverance in the midst of persecutions, he sets before them the example of Israelites in the wilderness who fell away and did not enter into Canaan. Because they failed to finish their work, God said,

So I declared on oath in my anger,
They shall never enter my rest (Hebrews 3:11).

THE REST IS THE LAND OF CANAAN

In the Old Testament this "rest" was equated with the land God swore they would not enter into (Psalm 95:11; Numbers 14:21-23).[453] On this basis, A. B. Davidson concludes, "What appears to be spoken of is simply possession of the land of Canaan."[454]

Also, the terms "rest" and " Canaan" seem to be used interchangeably in many places:

*You are not to do as we do here today, everyone as he sees fit, since you have not yet reached the **resting place** and the **inheritance** the LORD your God is giving you (Deuteronomy 12:8-9).*

Sun sees in this passage a "theological equation of 'rest' with the secured settlement of the Promised Land."[455]

*But you will cross the Jordan and settle in the **land** the LORD your God is giving you as an **inheritance**, and he will give you **rest** from all your enemies around you so that you will live in safety (Deuteronomy 12:10).*

In the future, Zion, the capital of Palestine, will be God's resting place:
For the LORD has chosen Zion, he has desired it for his dwelling: This is my resting place for ever and ever (Psalm 132:13-14).

F. F. Bruce comments that "Canaan [is] the 'rest' or home which God had prepared for them." He argues that in the above passage "Canaan is called 'the rest and the inheritance, which Jehovah thy God giveth thee.'"[456] Similarly, Walter Kaiser insists that the land of Canaan is the rest of Deuteronomy 12:9 and that the word is used of a "place," "geographical, material, and spatial" as well as of a "condition."[457]

THE REST IS OUR FINISHED WORK

The book of Joshua enriches the concept of "rest" beyond mere possession of the land; it also refers to successful conquest, the completion of their work.

---

453 See also Deuteronomy 1:34-36; Numbers 32:10-12; cf. Deuteronomy 12:9.

454 Davidson, *The Epistle to the Hebrews*, 99. Davidson, however, while acknowledging that this is the meaning of the Old Testament texts, wants to spiritualize them to mean heaven.

455 H. T. C. Sun, "Rest, Resting Place," in *NISBE* (1979), 4:143.

456 Bruce, *The Epistle to the Hebrews*, 99.

457 Walter Kaiser, *The Uses of the Old Testament in the New* (Chicago: Moody Press, 1985), 157. The interchangeability between the terms "rest" and "land" is suggested by the following passages as well (Deuteronomy 3:18-20; Joshua 1:13).

> *The* LORD *gave them* **rest** *on every side, just as he had sworn to their forefathers. Not one of their enemies withstood them; the* LORD *handed all their enemies over to them. Not one of all the* LORD*'s good promises to the house of Israel failed; every one of them was fulfilled (Joshua 21:44-45).*

Coppes concludes from this and similar passages[458] that rest included the notion of "to defeat Israel's enemies and give them rest (victory and security) in the land."[459] A definite relationship between land and rest exists because "possession of the land brings 'rest' (Deuteronomy 12:9; 25:19; Josh 1:13; 21:44), that is, both freedom from foreign domination and the end of wandering."[460] Rest is the inheritance, but it is also a condition or state of finished work and victory over enemies which the Israelites entered into when they obtained the inheritance.

But when did the Israelites enter into rest? It was not when they entered into Canaan, for that is when their battle to obtain the inheritance began. Nor did their rest occur when they crossed the river Jordan to attack Jericho (Joshua 3-4). The rest came after the victory had been won and the inheritance was distributed (Joshua 12-22). Between initial entry into the land and the final conquest there were victories to be wrought and battles to win, a task to complete. They entered into rest in Joshua 12 when they received the inheritance.[461] At that point they enjoyed freedom from enemies and had completed their work, just as God had completed His work in creation.

Nothing is particularly new about this approach. Indeed, it has been articulated in numerous books on the spiritual life. In these books the journey of Israel from Egypt to Canaan is compared with the Christian life. As it is commonly taught,[462] Israel's time in Egypt pictures the unregenerate man, the wandering in the wilderness is the carnal Christian, and the crossing of the Jordan into Canaan is the spiritual Christian. The victories over the Canaanites are illustrative of the victorious Christian. No longer wandering in the wilderness of unbelief but clothed in the full armor of God, the believer is fighting the "principalities and powers." And as a reward, he obtains the inheritance in Joshua 12-22 when the land is distributed. Books on the spiritual life often connect this with the distribution of crowns at the Judgment Seat of Christ.

However, many writers persist in the view that the land of Canaan is somehow typical of the future millennial kingdom.[463] We will argue that it is typical of our inheritance in the kingdom, participation with Christ as one of His *Metochoi* in the messianic partnership.

Is entering the land a type of entering the kingdom? And, if it is, are not all who enter heirs of that kingdom? To state the question is to answer it. Obviously not! The book of Joshua supplies at least one illustration of an Israelite who in fact entered the land but who

---

[458] E.g., Deuteronomy 12:10; 2 Samuel 7:1; 1 Kings 5:4; 1 Chronicles 22:9.

[459] Leonard J. Coppes, "*nuah*," in TWOT, 2:562.

[460] B. L. Bandstra, "Land," in NISBE, 3:71.

[461] The writer to the Hebrews states that this was not a complete fulfillment of the promised rest (Hebrews 3-4).

[462] See Ian Thomas, *The Saving Life of Christ* (Grand Rapids: Zondervan Publishing House, 1955); Alan Redpath, *Victorious Christian Living* (Old Tappan, NJ: Revell Co., 1955).

[463] Indeed, the Old Testament promises that one day Israel will return to the land (Ezekiel 37:21-22), be established as an independent state (Ezekiel 37:22), be in possession of the old city of Jerusalem, and become a focal point of global concern (Zechariah 12:1-4). Thus such a parallel can be drawn. These land promises are all fulfilled in the future kingdom.

never finished his task. As a result, he never obtained the inheritance and never entered into rest. His name was Achan. After the successful conquest of Jericho, this regenerate "son" of God (Joshua 7:19) stole some of the plunder for himself and then lied about it (vv. 10-11). Such impurity among the people of God made them impotent against their enemies (v. 12).

The same situation existed in the early church when Ananias and Sapphira lied to the Holy Spirit. They claimed some material things had been given to the church, but they had in fact held back some for themselves (Acts 5:3). The result for Achan was capital punishment (Joshua 7:24-26). The same happened to Ananias and Sapphira (Acts 5:5).

It is therefore evident that a man can enter into the land but not obtain the inheritance there and never enter into rest. The former was available to all Israelites on the basis of a promise, but the latter came only to those who obeyed and won the victory.

In Hebrews 4 the writer to the Hebrews explains that Christians enter into rest when they complete the lifelong work of committed discipleship. But like the exodus generation (and later Achan), not all Christians finish their work. A proper illustration of the relationship between the journeys of the children of Israel and the Christian life is suggested by the diagram below.

From Egypt to Canaan

Natural Man	Carnal Christian	Spiritual Christian	Rewarded Christian
In Egypt	In the Wilderness	Crossing the Jordan	Entering Rest
Ex. 1 Ex. 11	Ex. 12 Ex. 34	Josh. 1 Josh. 11	Josh. 12 Josh. 22
Slave Generation	Exodus Generation	Second Generation	
Lost	Redeemed	Discipleship	Rewarded
1 Cor. 2:14	1 Cor. 3:1-3	Rom. 12:1-2	2 Cor. 5:10

Those Israelites who crossed the Jordan and entered the land were saved people. They are now aligning themselves with God's purpose. He brought their fathers out of Egypt to bring them into the promised land (Deuteronomy 4:37-38). The Exodus generation never finished the work God gave them to do. However, the second generation committed themselves to accomplish God's purpose; they crossed the Jordan, entered into battle, and conquered the land. As a result, they finished the work God gave them to do. They "entered into rest." Typologically, this is portrayed in Joshua 12 where, after the battles have been won and their work accomplished, they are rewarded by the distribution of the land. It is then that they entered into rest.[464]

---

[464] Paul writes that "these things occurred as examples" (1 Corinthians 10:6), so there is some justification for such interpretations. The journey of the Exodus generation and their sons to possess Canaan in a striking way portrays the theology of entering into rest.

The readers of this epistle who similarly finish their work are called *Metochoi*, members of the messianic partnership (Hebrews 3:14).

Christ's Metochoi: The Partners

This magnificent concept of entering into rest was uniquely appropriate to apply to the readers of the epistle to the Hebrews who were in danger, like the Exodus generation, of failing to complete their life work by doing the will of God to the end (Hebrews 10:36). So He warns them saying,

> *For we have become partakers* [Gr *Metochoi*, plural] *of Christ, if we hold fast the beginning of our assurance firm until the end (Hebrews 3:14).*

What does it mean to be one of Christ's "partners"? Paul uses the synonym in 1 Corinthians 9:23, "*I do all things for the sake of the gospel, so that I may become a fellow partaker* [Gr *synkoinōnos*] *of it*." Piper misunderstands and thinks that to become a *metochos* means "to obtain what the Gospel promises," that is, heaven when we die. He argues that Paul "becomes all things to all men" (1 Corinthians 9:22) so that Paul can save not only himself from damnation, but also others.[465] We disagree. To become a "fellow partaker of the gospel" does not mean "to be saved" at the end, but rather to become a partner in the spreading of the gospel ministry as the preceding context of 1 Corinthians 9:23 makes clear.

The phrase "for we have come to share in Christ" (ESV, NIV) is best translated "for we are partners [*metochoi*] of Christ (NASB)" (Gr *Metochoi gar tou Christou gegonamen*). The perfect tense "have come" (*gegonamen*) takes the most basic sense of the perfect, the intensive perfect. "It is a strong way of saying that a thing is. Usually its closest approximation is the English present."[466] The genitive "of Christ" is the simple genitive of possession. We may therefore translate, "We are partners of Christ" or "we are Christ's partners."

The Gr *metochos* means "partner or companion."[467] The word is found in classical Gr for a wife, a member of a board of officials, a partner in business, or the joint owner of a house.[468] Men may or may not be joined together as thieves, destroyers, or robbers, but they are all still men; only their partnership in a particular enterprise is in question. Similarly, Christians may or may not be joined together with Christ in the coming "messianic partnership," but they are still Christians.

How is one a partner "in" another person? The NASB translation above is preferable.. Someone could certainly "share with" a person but not "in." Perhaps some of the difficulty is that the translators are attempting to read the Pauline concept of "in Christ" into this Gr word. If the word *metochos* means to be "in Christ" or be "part of Christ," then the verse is suggesting that we are Christians if and only if we persevere to the end. This, of course, is a translation favored by many Experimental Predestinarians. If, on the other hand, the word *metochos* suggests something like "companion" with Christ, then an entirely different kind

---

465 John Piper, *Beyond the Gold* (Desiring God Radio, May 14, 2006).

466 DM, 202.

467 BAGD, 516. In the LXX it often means "companions," see Hermann Hanse, "*echō*," in TDNTA, p. 289.

468 LSJ, 1122.

of relationship is in view. In fact it is highly unlikely that *metochos* implies the Pauline idea of being "in Christ." Montefiore comments:

> *Most commentators take the phrase to mean that we are* **Partners of Christ** *or that* **we share in Christ**. *This Pauline concept, however, is entirely alien to our author who regards Christ not as the new humanity into whom believers are incorporated by faith union, but as head of the Christian family, the son among brothers.*[469]

Similarly Hughes writes:

> *There is, indeed, a certain ambiguity associated with the Greek noun used here since it may mean either "Partners with" someone in a particular activity or relationship, in which case it denotes "companions" or "partners," as in 1:9 and Luke 5:7 (the only occurrence of the noun outside the Epistle to the Hebrews in the New Testament), or "Partners of."*[470]

Hughes argues that the former interpretation should be favored here. He notes that the Israelites were *partners with* Moses in the wilderness parallel (and not *partners of*) and that the same sense is found in Hebrews 1:9, where it is implied that the Christians are the companions of the royal Son. Farrar has adopted the same view:

> *But the meaning may rather be "Partners* **with** *Christ;" for the thought of mystical union with Christ extending into the spiritual unity and identity, which makes the words "in Christ" the monogram of St. Paul, is scarcely alluded to by the writer. His thoughts are rather of "Christ for us" than of "Christ in us."*[471]

Finally, Martyn Lloyd-Jones explains it this way, "It means 'participant' or 'sharer.'[472] It is sometimes used for 'associate', 'partner'. A partner is a man who goes along with another man in a business or whatever it may chance to be."[473]

But being Christ's partner is not the same as being God's son. Only sons are partners, but not all sons are partners—only those who "*hold firmly to the end the confidence*" they had at first. The word *metochos* was used in the papyri for a partner or associate in a business enterprise. One manuscript contains a portion of a sentence which reads, "We Dionysius, son of Socrates and the associate [*Metochoi*] collectors of public clothing."[474] Apparently Dionysius and his associates were partners in a tax-collecting business. A man named Sotas was also writing receipts for tax bills paid and collected through his company:

---

469 Hugh Montefiore, *A Commentary on the Epistle to the Hebrews* (Peabody, MA: Hendrickson Publishers, 1987), 78.

470 Philip Edgcumbe Hughes, *A Commentary on the Epistle to the Hebrews* (Grand Rapids: Wm. B. Eerdmans Publishing Co., 1977), 149.

471 Farrar, *The Epistle of Paul the Apostle to the Hebrews*, 63.

472 To use Wallace's categories, it is an attributive genitive which "specifies an *attribute* or innate quality." It also adds a bit of emphasis – partners *of Christ*. Wallace, *Greek Grammar Beyond the Basics*, s.v. "The Genitive Case".

473 Martyn Lloyd-Jones, *Romans Chapter 8:17-39: The Final Perseverance of the Saints* (Grand Rapids: Zondervan Publishing House, 1976), 322.

474 MM, 406.

"... paid to Sotas and associates [*Metochoi*], collectors of money-taxes."[475] A similar usage is found in the New Testament in reference to Simon Peter's fishing business. He was a partner with James and John (Luke 5:10):

> *When they had done so, they caught such a large number of fish that their nets began to break. So they signaled their partners [Metochoi] in the other boat to come and help them (Luke 5:6-7).*

It was perfectly normal for a king to surround himself with certain associates with whom he maintained a more intimate relationship than he did with all other citizens of his kingdom. In the Old Testament one might think of David's mighty men (2 Samuel 23:8-39) or perhaps of David's invitation to the crippled Mephibosheth to eat at his table like one of the king's sons (2 Samuel 9:7, 11, 13). Certainly, the disastrous counsel which Rehoboam received from "the young men who had grown up with him and [who] were serving him" (1 Kings 12:8) could be said to have come from his partners, his *Metochoi*.

In the Roman world it was a great privilege to be known as a "friend of Caesar." At Jesus' trial when the Jews questioned whether Pilate was a "friend of Caesar" (John 19:12), Pilate reversed himself in trying to release Jesus. Suetonius, in his *The Deified Julius*, says of these "friends of Caesar":

> *Moreover when he came to power he advanced some of his* ***friends to the highest position, even though they were of the humblest origin*** *and when taken to task for it flatly declared that if he had been helped in defending his honor by brigands and cutthroats he would have requited such men in the same way.*[476]

Perhaps, in a similar vein, we might think of the honor of being a member of Caesar's household (Philippians 4:22). The term "Caesar's household" was commonly applied to the imperial civil service throughout the empire. Philo says, "If Agrippa had not been a king, but instead one of Caesar's household, would he not have had some privilege or honor?"[477]

God's King-Son in the epistle to the Hebrews has likewise surrounded Himself with companions (Hebrews 1:9, Gr *Metochoi*). In the case of David there were many citizens living in his kingdom other than those who ate at his table and his mighty men. Many lived under Rehoboam's sovereignty who were not among those with whom he grew up. There were many in Caesar's kingdom who did not have the official title "friend of Caesar" or "member of Caesar's household," and probably there were many in the businesses of Sotas, Dionysius, and Peter who were not "associates."

Jesus made it clear that only those Christians who "*do the will of My Father in heaven*" are His "friends" (Matthew 12:48-50). He told them that friendship with Him was conditional: "*You are My friends if you do what I command*" (John 15:14). He even spoke of Christians who could in no way be considered His friends because He "would not entrust Himself to them, for He knew all men" (John 2:24). Yet these from whom He drew back had "believed in His name" and were, therefore, born again.[478]

---

475 Ibid.

476 Suetonius, "The Deified Augustus," in *The Lives of the Caesars* (Available at www.books.google.com), LXXII, p. 35.

477 A. Rupprecht, "Caesar's Household," in ZPED, 1:683.

478 Many people saw the miraculous signs and *episteusan eis to onoma autou* ("believed on His name"). Yet Jesus

The *Metochoi* of King Jesus, then, are His co-heirs in the rule of the messianic kingdom. They are those friends, partners, and companions who have endured the trials of life and were faithful to the end, and who will therefore obtain the inheritance-rest. As early as the fourth century, Origen held this view of the Partners. In his letter to Gregory he concludes with a blessing that he may not only be a saved man, but in addition, "May you also be a Partner [Gr *Metochoi*], and be *ever increasing your inheritance*, that you may say not only, 'We are become Partners of Christ,' but also Partners of God."[479] A Partner, says Origen, is one who is "ever increasing his inheritance," so that he may become the Father's partner as well as Christ's.

The danger in Hebrews 3:14 is not that his readers would lose their justification but that they might lose their inheritance by forfeiting their position as one of Christ's *Metochoi* in the coming kingdom. To help them avoid this danger, the writer applies to them the lesson of the failure of the Exodus generation to enter rest. His readers are also in danger of not entering into rest.

Entering into Rest (Hebrews 4:1-11)

Having set before their eyes the failure of the Exodus generation, he now warns them against the possibility of failure in their Christian lives as well.

THE WARNING (4:1-2)

> *Therefore, since the promise of entering his rest still stands, let us be careful that none of you be found to have fallen short of it (Hebrews 4:1).*

There is no reason for assuming that the rest (Gr *katapausis*) in Hebrews 4 is any different from the inheritance of Canaan obtained by obedience as described in Hebrews 3. The transition between the chapters is smooth, the application is precise and without any qualification, and the same word, *katapausis,* is used. It involved a spiritual victory over all opposing enemies which was achieved by spiritual faith-obedience to the King. As pointed out earlier, Moses clearly links the "rest" with the inheritance of Canaan.

> *for you have not as yet come to the resting place and the inheritance which the LORD your God is giving you (Deuteronomy 12:9; cf. 3:18-20).*

Later the writer refers to this again, saying, "*He who is coming will not delay*," and in light of that he urges his readers to persevere, and not turn back to Judaism, so that they might "*receive what he has promised*" (Hebrews 10:36-37). Because Christ could return at any moment (the pretribulation rapture), there is a special urgency, exhorting them to complete what they have begun. He continues,

---

would not *episteuen auton autois* ("entrust Himself to them") because He "knew all men." The phrase "believe on His name" is used throughout John for saving faith. Note especially John 3:18 where the same phrase is used. The phrase *pisteuō eis* is John's standard expression for saving faith. One believes "on Him" or "in His name," 6:40; 7:39; 8:30; 10:42; 11:25; 11:26; 12:11. Therefore, Calvin's claim in *Institutes* (3.2.12), that they did not have true faith but were only borne along "by some impulse of zeal which prevented them from carefully examining their hearts," is fallacious.

479 "Letter from Origin to Gregory" in Alexander Roberts, James Donaldson, J. A. Cleveland, The Ante-Nicene Fathers 4, *Translations of the Writings of the Fathers Down to AD 325.* (Grand Rapids: William B. Eerdmans Publishing Co., 1973), 3, p. 393.

For we also have had the gospel preached to us, just as they did; but the message they heard was of no value to them because those who heard did not combine it with faith (Hebrews 4:2).

What "gospel" was preached to them? It probably was not the good news of forgiveness of sins. There is no reference to such a gospel in the context of this warning passage. The word "gospel" simply means "good news." Our Reformation heritage has perhaps caused us to limit this expression to only one kind of good news, deliverance from eternal damnation. But the good news they received was the promise of entering into God's rest. The writer will define this more clearly in the verses to follow.

THE PRESENT EXISTENCE OF THE REST (4:3-7)

Now we who have believed enter that rest, just as God has said, "So I declared on oath in my anger, 'They shall never enter my rest.'" And yet his work has been finished since the creation of the world (Hebrews 4:3).

Here the writer to the Hebrews makes it explicit that only those who believe enter into rest. The phrase "we who have believed" should be translated "we who believe."[480] His interest is not in those who have believed at a point in time but in those who continue to believe to the end of life (3:6, 14). Perseverance in faith, not a one-time exercise of it, guarantees that believers enter into rest.

He quotes Psalms 95:11 again, which is a Davidic commentary on the failure of the Exodus generation. This rest, this experience of finished work that comes through meritorious acquisition of the land of Canaan, is God's rest. The significance of the statement, "*And yet His work has been finished since the creation of the world*" is difficult to interpret precisely. Why is it included? Our author probably means that God completed His work of creation and has offered the experience of completed work to every believer since then.

In the discussion above it was argued that the meaning of entering into rest included not only the obtaining of the inheritance of Canaan but also signified the completion of one's labor. This possible meaning of the term in the Old Testament is now made explicit by the writer to the Hebrews in the words to follow:

For somewhere he has spoken about the seventh day in these words: "And on the seventh day God rested from all his work." And again in the passage above he says, "They shall never enter my rest" (Hebrews 4:4-5).

The precise connection between God having finished His work and their not finishing theirs by entering the land seems to be as follows. Since God has completed His work, the experience of completed work, rest, has been available to all since the creation of the world. The fact that God "rested" does not mean that He was tired, but that His task was finished. Believers enter into that experience the same way God did, by finishing the task. Possession of Canaan was the task the wilderness generation was to complete. The concept of rest is thus enriched to mean finished work. For the readers of this epistle, to enter into rest meant to finish well, to persevere to the end.

---

[480] The aorist participle indicates that no one will enter unless they have believed. While it says nothing about the absolute time or specific time or length of time, it does say the believing has preceded the entering.

NO FINAL REST UNDER JOSHUA (4:6-9)

It still remains that some will enter that rest, and those who formerly had the gospel preached to them did not go in, because of their disobedience. Therefore God again set a certain day, calling it Today, when a long time later he spoke through David, as was said before: "Today, if you hear his voice, do not harden your hearts" (Hebrews 4:6-7).

The Exodus generation failed to enter the land. They never finished their task, and that task still remains to be completed! But someone might argue that the entire promise of the land of Canaan was fulfilled under Joshua. Did not the Old Testament say that the conquest of the land was the fulfillment of the promised rest (Joshua 22:4; 23:1)? This view is answered by the following words:

For if Joshua had given them rest, God would not have spoken later about another day. There remains, then, a Sabbath-rest for the people of God (Hebrews 4:8-9).

If the experience of Sabbath rest had been fulfilled in Joshua's conquest of the land, then David, four hundred years later, would not still be offering the same promise in Psalms 95:11 and saying it is available "today." The writer is evidently setting before his Christian readers the hope of an inheritance, the land of Canaan, which metaphorically also speaks of finished work. This future inheritance is still to be obtained; the experience of finished work is still to be achieved!

HOW THE REST IS OBTAINED (4:10-11)

He now explains how the rest is to be obtained:

For anyone who enters God's rest also rests from his own work, just as God did from his. Let us, therefore, make every effort to enter that rest, so that no one will fall by following their example of disobedience (4:10-11).

As Christian believers they will have an inheritance in the land of Canaan in the future millennial kingdom, if they make every effort to finish their course. They are to enter rest the same way the Exodus generation should have, by finishing their work. This was how God entered into the experience of rest.

To apply "every effort" (Gr *spoudazō*) is a strong term and hardly appropriate for the means for obtaining heaven by faith alone, without cost, and apart from works. Peter exhorted his readers, "*Be more diligent* [Gr *spoudazō*] *to make certain about His calling and choosing you; for as long as you practice these things, you will never stumble*" (2 Peter 1:10). As demonstrated elsewhere, this means that the believer is to apply virtues to his Christian life in order to establish a strong foundation so that he will not fall into sin.[481] The psalmist echoes this idea when he says that failing to apply the virtue of humility almost caused his feet to stumble (Psalm 73:2-3).[482] Peter also says that in regard to their eternal future they should "*be diligent to* [Gr *spoudazō*] *be found by Him in peace, without spot and blameless*" (2 Peter 3:14, NKJV). Timothy was commanded to "*be diligent* [Gr *spoudazō*] *to present*

[481] See discussion in vol. 2, chapter 30, p. 458.

[482] Cf. 1 Kings 11:2-4, 9. Solomon "turned away" from God.

yourself approved to God, a worker who does not need to be ashamed, rightly dividing the word of truth" (2 Timothy 2:15, NKJV). None of these exhortations has anything to do with proving that one is saved by persevering in good works, as Experimentalists maintain.

Entering rest is, therefore, more than obtaining the land of Canaan, although it is also that. It is the fulfillment of man's destiny to "rule and have dominion" (Genesis 1:26-28). It is the finishing of our work: "*for anyone who enters God's rest also rests* (Gr *katapauō*, "to bring to an end"[483]) *from his own work, just as God did from His*" (Hebrews 4:10). The concept of "rest" is clearly associated with successful completion. Or as the writer expressed it in Hebrews 10:36:

> *You need to persevere so that when you* ***have done the will of God****, you will receive what he has promised.*

In a similar way Jesus said, "*My food is to do the will of him who sent me and to finish his work*" (John 4:34).

The conclusion is that the content of the inheritance in Hebrews 3 and 4 is the messianic partnership of Hebrews 3:14. By being faithful to Christ to the final hour, we finish our course and obtain this inheritance. While this involves ownership of the land of Canaan, the capital of the millennial earth (Isaiah 2:1-4), it includes more than that. It signifies completion of our life work by faithful perseverance to the final hour. It means living there in the heavenly country, ruling from the heavenly city with the King. Only Christ's *Metochoi* will reign with Him in the kingdom. To be invited to rule with Christ on earth in the coming kingdom is synonymous with hearing Him say:

> *Well done, good and faithful servant! You have been faithful with a few things; I will put you in charge of many things. Come and share your master's happiness! (Matthew 25:21).*

There are many in the kingdom today, but only some will inherit the land in the consummation. That is why the rest must be worked for:

> *Let us, therefore, make every effort to enter that rest, so that no one will fall by following their example of disobedience (Hebrews 4:11).*

Consistent with its usage throughout the New Testament, the inheritance (rest) must be earned. Unlike heaven, it is not a free gift, nor is there anything in this passage about perseverance in holiness as proof of the presence of saving faith. Not all Christians will make that effort or will make equal effort, and those distinctions will be acknowledged by Christ in the coming reign of the *Metochoi* during the millennial kingdom.

Summary

A major theme of the book of Hebrews is the inheritance-rest which is still available to believers. The writer of this epistle draws on the Old Testament background to warn the Hebrews that they are in danger of a failure similar to that of the Exodus generation.

---

[483] BDAG, 524.

Because they are considering a return to Judaism, they may never finish their work. He reminds them that God swore to the Israelites of old that they would never enter the land of Canaan and never obtain the inheritance they sought.

Believers enter into that rest only when they persevere in faith to the end of life. When they do this, they will obtain a share in the inheritance, the millennial land of Canaan, and will rule with Christ as one of His *Metochoi* there. Rest is not just the land itself; it also includes the state or condition of "finished work," of final perseverance, into which the faithful Christian will enter. God has not set aside His promises to Israel. The promise of the inheritance, the land, is eternally valid, and those Christians who remain faithful to their Lord to the end of life will share in that inheritance along with the Old Testament saints and the great company of the *Metochoi* in the future reign of the servant kings.

12

Our Great Salvation

IT WOULD be difficult to find a concept that is richer and more varied in meaning than the biblical concept of salvation. The breadth of salvation is so sweeping and its intended aim so magnificent that in many contexts the words used defy precise definition. Yet these difficulties have not thwarted numerous interpreters from assuming, often without any contextual justification, that the words used invariably mean "deliverance from eternal damnation" or "to go to heaven when you die." Many may be surprised to learn that this meaning of "salvation" (Gr *sōtēria*) would have been the least likely meaning to come to the mind of a reader of the Bible in the first century. Indeed, in 812 usages of the various Hebrew words translated "to save" or "salvation" in the Old Testament, none of them clearly relate to personal salvation from eternal separation from God or final entrance into heaven.

As will be seen in the following discussion, the tendency to assume that salvation always refers to final deliverance from eternal separation from God has led many to interpret certain passages incorrectly. When James, for example, says, "*Can that faith save him?*" (James 2:14), implying a negative answer, the Experimental Predestinarians understandably are perplexed about the apparent conflict with Paul. However, if salvation means something other than "to go to heaven when you die," the apparent conflict evaporates.

Usage of the Greek words for salvation in extra-biblical literature clearly shows a broad range of meaning. In those documents it is never associated with salvation from final separation from God; instead it means health, prosperity, rescue, survival, well-being, or happiness.[484]

Usage in the Old Testament

The principal Old Testament word, *yasha*, which is translated *sōtēria* in the LXX, is used 353 times in the Masoretic text. Apparently, the original meaning may have been something like "to make wide or sufficient,"[485] and originally the noun meant "width, spaciousness, freedom from restraint."[486] Salvation could be from the misery of slavery

484 MM, 622. A similar usage is found in Acts 27:34, where food is needed for "survival."

485 John E. Hartley, "yasha," in TWOT, 1:414.

486 R. E. O. White, "Salvation," in *Evangelical Dictionary of Theology*, ed. Walter Elwell (Grand Rapids: Baker Book House, 1984), 967.

in Egypt,[487] from adversaries,[488] or from oppression.[489] "It evidently includes divinely bestowed deliverance from every class of spiritual and temporal evil to which mortal man is subjected."[490]

In a study of the concept of salvation in the Old Testament, René López has identified seven kinds of salvation:[491] salvation from external evils in general,[492] complete restoration from enemies or in battle,[493] salvation from moral troubles,[494] salvation from dominion by other nations,[495] individual salvation from enemies,[496] salvation to prosperity,[497] and a national and spiritual salvation involving Israel's possession of the nations and future restoration from exile.[498] None of these refers to individual salvation from eternal damnation.

By far the most common usage in the Old Testament is of God's deliverance of His people from their struggles or enemies (Exodus 14:30).[499] Scores of passages could be cited.[500] In Psalm 118:13-14 the psalmist says that when the Lord "helped" him, this was his "salvation." This meaning has been considerably enriched by the New Testament writers when they point out that the salvation of Christ also saves us from our enemies--the world, the flesh, and the Satan. Spiritual victory in life is salvation!

Often, the word means blessing, health, or happiness,[501] restoration to fellowship,[502] or the future blessings of the messianic kingdom.[503] Regarding the latter, God says to Jeremiah (Jeremiah 30:10) that one day He will "*save*" the nation "*from afar*" and that the result will be "*quiet and ease*," and they will never be afraid. Salvation in this passage is the final restoration from exile. "'*O Lord, save Your people, the remnant of Israel.' Behold, I am bringing them from the north country, and I will gather them from the remote parts of the earth*" (Jeremiah 31:7-8). This is the messianic salvation.

In the last days Yahweh will bring full messianic salvation for His people (e.g., Isaiah 43:5 ff.; Jeremiah 31:7; 46:27; Zechariah 8:7)."[504] At that time, in the future earthly kingdom, Israel "*will draw water from the wells of salvation*" (Isaiah 12:3), and the entire world will participate in the messianic salvation (Isaiah 45:22; 49:6). In that day Israel will say,

---

[487] Exodus 14:13; 15:2.

[488] Psalm 106:10.

[489] Judges 3:31.

[490] Robert Baker Girdlestone, *Synonyms of the Old Testament: Their Bearing on Christian Doctrine* (Grand Rapids: Wm. B. Eerdmans Publishing Co., 1948), 125.

[491] René A. López, "Old Testament Salvation - From What?," *JOTGES* 16, no. 2 (Autumn 2003): 50-57.

[492] 2 Chronicles 20:9; 6:28-30.

[493] Psalm 33:16.

[494] Proverbs 18:10; 28:18.

[495] Judges 13:5.

[496] Job 13:16; Psalm 86:2.

[497] 2 Samuel 23:5.

[498] Isaiah 45:17; 52:8.

[499] See 1 Samuel 22:4.

[500] E.g., Numbers 10:9; Psalm 18:3; Isaiah 30:15; 45:17; Jeremiah 30:17.

[501] See Psalms 7:10; 28:8, 9; 86:16; Jeremiah 17:14.

[502] See Psalms 51:12; 6:3-6; Ezekiel 37:23.

[503] Psalms 132:16; Isaiah 25:9; 43:3, 5, 8, 19; 44:3, 20; Jeremiah 31:7.

[504] J. Schneider, "Redemption," in NIDNT, 3:208.

"Behold, this is our God for whom we have waited that He might save us. This is the LORD for whom we have waited; Let us rejoice and be glad in His salvation" (Isaiah 25:9). The enemies of Israel will be put to shame in that future day, *"but Israel will be saved by the LORD with an everlasting salvation"* (Isaiah 45:17). The messianic salvation is called the "everlasting salvation" because the kingdom of the Messiah will last forever. The phrase is strikingly similar to the phrase "eternal salvation" in Hebrews 5:9. Isaiah 52:10 states that *"all the ends of the world will see the salvation of our God."* In that glorious future era His people will know His name, and the feet of those who proclaim salvation will be called beautiful (Isaiah 52:7). The psalmist also anticipated salvation in this sense, *"Oh, that the salvation of Israel would come out of Zion! When the LORD restores His captive people, Jacob will rejoice, Israel will be glad"* (Psalm 14:7).

Usage in the New Testament

The enriched meaning of the word for salvation is seen in the New Testament. The verb *sōzō* occurs 106 times and the noun *sōtēria* 46 times. The meaning "deliver from eternal damnation," while nonexistent in the Old Testament, is common in the New. Statistically *sōzō* is used 40 percent of the time in this way[505] and *sōtēria* 35 percent.[506] Like the Old Testament it sometimes simply means healing or recovery of health. When this happens, the notion of "deliver" means to deliver from disease, or, simply, "to heal." For example, in response to the faith and resultant healing of the woman who had been bleeding for twelve years, Jesus said, "Your faith has healed [Gr *sōzō*] you" (Matthew 9:21-22). This meaning is quite common (19 percent).[507]

Consistent with its most frequent usage in the Old Testament (LXX), *sōzō* often means to deliver from some danger (19 percent). For example, when Jesus was in the garden, He prayed, *"Save* [Gr *sōzō*] *me from this hour"* (John 12:27).[508]

SALVATION OF THE TROUBLED

Similar to the idea of deliverance from danger, but with a distinctively positive emphasis, are the references in which salvation is viewed as victorious endurance and not just escape. Paul's concern over the *sōtēria* of the believers at Corinth may reflect this thought:

> *If we are distressed, it is for your comfort and salvation* [Gr *sōtēria*]; *if we are comforted, it is for your comfort, which produces in you patient endurance of the same sufferings we suffer (2 Corinthians 1:6).*

Their "salvation" is not their deliverance from trouble, it is patient endurance through it, that is, an aspect of sanctification.

505 E.g., Acts 4:12; 11:14; Romans 8:24; 9:27; 1 Corinthians 5:5; Jude 23.

506 Acts 4:12; 13:26; Romans 1:16; 10:1; 2 Corinthians 6:2; Ephesians 1:13.

507 See Mark 3:4; 5:23, 28, 34; Luke 6:9; 8:36, 48, 50; John 11:12; James 5:15. No instance of sōtēria in this sense occurs.

508 See Matthew 8:25; 14:30; 24:22; Luke 1:71; 23:35, 37, 39; John 12:27; Acts 7:52; 27:20, 31, 34; 1 Thessalonians 5:9.

The thought of deliverance from danger (possibly either getting out of jail or, perhaps, better, delivered from failure) fits the meaning of salvation here in Philippians.

> *Yes, and I will continue to rejoice, for I know that through your prayers and the help given by the Spirit of Jesus Christ, what has happened to me will turn out for my deliverance* [*sōtēria*]. *I eagerly expect and hope that I will in no way be ashamed, but will have sufficient courage so that now as always Christ will be exalted in my body, whether by life or by death.*

SALVATION OF A WIFE

Another passage that has exercised much exegetical ingenuity is 1 Timothy 2:15:

> *But women will be saved [sōzō] through childbearing--if they continue in faith, love and holiness with propriety.*

This is certainly a novel approach for obtaining deliverance from future wrath! The meaning of *sōzō* in this passage is once again something like "spiritual health," a full and meaningful life. This thought fits the context quite well. Paul has just excluded women from positions of teaching authority in the church (1 Timothy 2:9-14). What then is their primary destiny? They will find life through fulfilling their role as a mother *if* they continue in faith, love, and holiness with propriety. A salvation that comes only to mothers who persist in faithful service is not the same as the faith-alone salvation taught elsewhere in Scripture. For this reason many interpreters agree with Litfin and understand "saved" as being "preserved from insignificance by means of her role in the family."[509] A woman will normally find her fulfillment and meaning in life not by pursuing the male role but by being a wife and mother. But she must follow this vocation with faith and love.

SALVATION OF A CHRISTIAN LEADER

Similarly, in the same book Paul exhorts Timothy:

> *Watch your life and doctrine closely. Persevere in them, because if you do, you will* ***save*** *[sōzō] both* ***yourself*** *and your hearers (1 Timothy 4:16).*

Many writers are perplexed by this injunction. How can a person who is already saved and justified by faith alone still need to persevere and watch his life in order to be saved and enter heaven? One Experimentalist writer puts it this way, "This call to perseverance again emphasizes human involvement in the salvation process. Ultimately it is the Lord who keeps and saves, but the continued perseverance of the believer is also required. The question of how these two doctrines can be balanced has bedeviled many centuries of church history."[510] The reason it has "bedeviled" many is that for some strange reason they assumed that "saved" must mean "saved from eternal damnation." It does not always mean that, even in 1 Timothy.[511]

---

[509] A. Duane Litfin, "1 Timothy," in *BKC New Testament*, ed. John F. Walvoord and Roy B. Zuck (Colorado Sprngs: Cook, 1985), 736.

[510] W. D. Mounce; *Pastorals*, Word Biblical Commentary (Grand Rapids: Wm. B. Eerdmans Publishing Co., 2002), 266.

[511] Strangely this misunderstanding is found in many commentaries. This is a classic illustration of theological

Salvation in this passage is conditioned on watching one's life and doctrine and persevering in this attitude. In Piper's Neonomian understanding of this exhortation[512], by means of perseverance Timothy is to ensure that he will finally be saved. However, salvation in this verse does not refer to final entrance into heaven. Rather it refers to progressive deliverance from sin. Timothy cannot save others by being good! He can, however, teach and model progress in the life of faith and thus encourage many of them to follow his example.[513]

God exhorted Ezekiel along the same lines:

> *But if you warn the wicked man to turn from his ways, and he does not do so, he will die for his sin, but you will have **saved yourself** (Ezekiel 33:9).*

Both Timothy and Ezekiel are regenerate and justified saints who are still in need of being saved, of finding spiritual wholeness, or possibly, as one writer suggested, of "continuous preservation from surrounding evil,"[514] or perhaps, saved from the doctrine of demons (1 Timothy 4:1).[515] Timothy is not to neglect his gift (4:14), and the mothers are not to neglect their calling of motherhood (1 Timothy 2:15). If both heed this injunction, they will find a rich and rewarding experience of fellowship with Jesus Christ in this life and a great reward in the future. He will "save himself from failure and a wasted life."[516] He will truly "save his life" and the lives of many of this flock who observe his progress and follow his example (1 Timothy 4:15). Also, this passage may be understood as referring to Christ's exhortation that one can save his life by means of losing it. That is, one can find true meaning and fulfillment only by giving one's life up for full discipleship.[517] The context makes it clear that Paul is exhorting believers to "work out" their own deliverance/salvation rather than "work for" it (Philippians 2:12-13).

---

exegesis where the interpreter is so enmeshed in his incorrect view that the true Christian always perseveres in godliness to the final hour, that he explains every text in a way that will be consistent with his Experimental Predestinarian assumptions. This also illustrates the illegitimate totality transfer in which many writers include in the word "saved" the meaning of "saved from eternal damnation."

512 As mentioned above, Paul referred to how a woman can be saved through the bearing of children (1 Timothy 2:15). The word "saved" obviously does not mean "saved from eternal damnation," as some Neonomians, such as John Piper, have argued. Piper, *Beyond the Gold.*

513 It is probable that Paul refers to the salvation of the soul (see chapters 15 and 16 below).

514 Girdlestone, *Synonyms of the Old Testament: Their Bearing on Christian Doctrine*, 74. He believes Hebrews 5:9 refers to the same kind of salvation.

515 Kenneth Wuest says, "The salvation spoken of here cannot be the salvation of the sinner nor the preservation of the saint in salvation, for the reason that both of these are a work of God for man. The salvation referred to here is understood by a study of the context (vv. 1–3), namely, being saved from the teachings of demon-influenced men. That is, by the reading of the Word, by exhortation from it, and by a clear explanation of its meaning, Timothy and his hearers will be saved from becoming entangled in these heresies." Kenneth Wuest, *Wuest's Word Studies from the Greek New Testament* (Grand Rapids: Wm. B. Eerdmans Publishing Co., 1984), First Timothy, p. 76.

516 Tom Constable, *Tom Constable's Expository Notes on the Bible* (Garland, TX: Galaxie Software, 2003), s.v. "1 Timothy 4:6". Guy King suggests that the salvation in view is salvation from being "put on the shelf" and being "cast aside," not "cast out." See Guy H. King, *A Leader Led* (Edinburgh: Marshall, Morgan, & Scott, 1951), 86.

517 See elsewhere in this book, pp. 205 ff.

REIGNING WITH CHRIST IN THE KINGDOM

Often in the Old Testament, salvation has messianic overtones. Old Testament salvation refers to the future regathering of the nation Israel and their establishment as rulers in a universal kingdom under the kingship of David's Greater Son, the messianic salvation. It is not surprising then to find that both *sōzō* and *sōtēria* often have similar connotations in the New Testament: joint participation with Christ in the coming kingdom rule.

This may be the thought behind our Lord's famous saying, "*But he who stands firm to the end will be saved* [*sōzō*]" (Matthew 24:13). The context refers to the terrors of the future tribulation. While the meaning may simply be, "He who endures to the end will be physically delivered at the second coming," that seems a bit banal, lacks encouragement, and is redundant. If the content of the salvation here is positive reward or honor, then a great motive for endurance has been provided. The salvation here may well be receiving a vassal kingship in the kingdom and the right to rule there. The condition of salvation in this passage is steadfast endurance, which does not yield under persecution but perseveres to the final hour, that is, either the end of the tribulation or the end of life. Marshall argues, "It probably indicates not so much endurance to the very end of the period of tribulation but, rather, endurance to the very limit, even to the point of death."[518]

The key word is "endure." It is not mere survival which secures this salvation but endurance. It refers to steadfast faith in God. The one who denies himself, picks up his cross and follows Christ faithfully to the end will be saved in a positive sense. Lane suggests that salvation here means "vindication." In contrast to the world's condemnation and rejection during the horrors of the tribulation, if they endure faithfully, they will be shown to be right and will be honored by Christ, they will be vindicated for holding fast.[519]

A few chapters later, Jesus refers to salvation as saving their souls. As we will demonstrate later, this means to find a rich life now by self-denial, taking up our cross and following Christ, so that we will be favorably recompensed at the Judgment Seat of Christ.

In another passage we are told that at the judgment of the sheep and the goats, the King will say to those on his right, "Come, you who are blessed by my Father; take your inheritance, the kingdom [Gr *basileian*, a kingship, – five cities, ten cities, etc.] prepared for you since the creation of the world" (Matthew 25:34). This is indeed the messianic salvation.

In another reference to salvation the apostle says:

> *Therefore I endure everything for the sake of the elect, that they too may obtain the salvation* [*sōtēria*] *that is in Christ Jesus, with eternal glory (2 Timothy 2:10).*

While the majority of the commentators understand the "elect" to refer to the unregenerate who have not yet believed (but certainly will), there is good reason to understand the term in this context as a synonym for a regenerate saint. In every New Testament usage of the term applied to people it *always* refers to a justified saint. Conversely, it *never* refers to someone who was elect in eternity past but who has not yet entered into

---

518 I. Howard Marshall, *Kept by the Power of God: A Study of Perseverance and Falling Away*, 2nd ed. (Minneapolis: Bethany Fellowship, 1974), 74.

519 William Lane, *Commentary on the Gospel of Mark* (Grand Rapids: Wm. B. Eerdmans Publishing Co., 1974), 464.

the purpose of their election, justification.[520] Cremer is emphatic on this point. He says that the "view decisively appearing in the N.T, viz. that the *eklektoi* are persons who not only are *in thesi* the objects of the divine election, but who are so in fact, *i.e.,* those who have entered upon the state of reconciliation. ... Thus *hoi eklektoi* denote those in whom God's saving purpose ... of free love is realized."[521] There appear to be no particular contextual indicators against applying this consistent usage of the term to 2 Timothy 2:10.[522] It is best to understand by "the elect," Paul has in mind Timothy and the faithful men of verse 2. Timothy is being exhorted to suffer in his ministry, just as Paul has been imprisoned for his ministry to the "elect." The idea of Paul suffering for the sanctification and growth of the churches is a common New Testament theme[523] and is easily seen in this passage as well.

Here, then, are saved people in need of salvation! The salvation in view is necessarily sanctification, or perhaps, more precisely, victorious perseverance through trials (1:8; 2:3, 9). Elsewhere in the Pastorals, "salvation" has referred to aspects of sanctification, and the present context certainly supports such a meaning. (e.g., 1 Timothy 2:15; 4:16). The setting is the dismal situation of apostasy (in 1:15, shortly to be identified, 2:17-18). Paul reminds Timothy that loyalty to the profession of faith (v. 11) does not go unrewarded (Romans 8:17; 2 Timothy 2:12). If they persevere, they will obtain not only victory but also eternal honor (2 Timothy 2:10), reward at the Judgment Seat of Christ.

Salvation in the Book of Hebrews

With his emphasis on the Old Testament, it is to be expected that the writer of Hebrews would use the word *sōtēria* in a sense akin to its Hebrew background. For him salvation is participation with Christ in the future kingdom rule. This is the promised messianic salvation in which God would one day bless the world through Israel and the church.

The word "salvation" (Gr *sōtēria*) occurs seven times in Hebrews[524] and the verb "save" (*sōzō*) occurs twice,[525] and these words never refer to salvation from eternal damnation. The concept of salvation in Hebrews falls into two categories: physical salvation from death (Hebrews 5:7), and the messianic Salvation (Hebrews 1:14; 2:3, 10; 5:9; 6:9; 7:25; 9:28).

The phrase "saved to the "uttermost" (Gr *pantelēs*, "completely"[526]) in 7:25 cannot refer to salvation from the penalty for sin. Paul Tanner's discussion is worth quoting in full:

---

520 The word *eklektos* is used twenty-two times in the New Testament. Jesus says that for the sake of the "elect" the days of the tribulation will be shortened (Matthew 24:22; Mark 13:21). Even the "elect," He says, can be led astray (Mark 13:22). Paul states the "elect" are the justified (Romans 8:33) and that they are Christians, "chosen of God" (Colossians 3:12). The Christian lady to whom John writes is the "chosen lady" (2 John 13) and the "chosen" of Revelation 17:14 are faithful Christians. In some places the word *eklektos* begins to take the meaning commonly found in secular Greek: "choice one," as in Romans 16:13. See MM, 196.

521 Hermann Cremer, *Biblico-theologial Lexicon of New Testament Greek* (New York: T. & T. Clark, 1954), 405.

522 Indeed, some of the commentators, perhaps struck by this usage, have misunderstood the term to apply to "those chosen for Christianity, both those already Christians and those not yet converted." George A. Denzer, "The Pastoral Letters," in *Jerome Biblical Commentary*, ed. Raymond E. Brown, Joseph A. Fitzmeyer, and Roland E. Murphy (Englewood Cliffs, NJ: Prentice Hall, 1968), 2:358. This would then require different meanings of the word "salvation," that is, deliverance from eternal damnation for the unsaved, and sanctification for the saved.

523 Cf. Colossians 1:24; 2 Corinthians 1:5-6; 4:12.

524 Hebrews 1:14; 2:3, 10; 5:9; 6:9; 9:28; 11:7.

525 Hebrews 5:7; 7:25.

526 BDAG, 754.

> *It would be quite theologically inaccurate to say that a Christian's personal salvation from the penalty of sin depends on Christ's ongoing intercession for him. That depends solely on the work of Christ on the Cross! That is why Jesus cried out from the Cross, "It is finished," and why Paul in Col 2:13–14 could proclaim that God has forgiven us all our trespasses and wiped out the handwriting of requirements that was against us, "having nailed it to the Cross." That kind of salvation is not dependent on the Cross plus ongoing intercession!*[527]

Paul Tanner also notes that this salvation is available to those who "*draw near to God through Him*," that is, to those who are already saved in a soteriological sense. He notes that the word used for 'come to' is *proserchomenous*. This verb is used seven times in the epistle (4:16; 7:25; 10:1; 10:22; 11:6; 12:18, 22), and "it always speaks of a post-conversion activity."[528]

"Messianic salvation" refers to the future restoration of the Davidic theocracy. Believers, who are "saved" in this sense, are those who will obtain a share in this great future. They are those who will be rewarded with an inheritance which involves ruling with Christ. They have truly "saved" their souls.

In Hebrews 1 the writer says it is possible that believers can inherit this salvation.

> *Are not all angels ministering spirits sent to serve those who will inherit salvation* [*sōtēria*]*? (1:14).*

Only those believers who persevere in faith to the end will "inherit salvation." The writer is thinking in Old Testament terms, quoting the Psalms, and anticipating this salvation as future ("will inherit"). He is thinking of the messianic salvation proclaimed by the prophets mentioned above; he is not referring to personal salvation from eternal separation from God. In 1:8-9, for example, he quotes the messianic Psalm 45:1, which describes the kingdom of the Messiah and His companions (Gr *Metochoi*). In Hebrews 1:13 he cites Psalm 110:1, another messianic psalm, where David says, "*Sit at my right hand until I make your enemies a footstool for your feet.*" This psalm was quite appropriate because it anticipates the day when the enemies of Messiah and His people will be defeated. One day the enemies of the readers, those who were persecuting them and therefore tempting them to cast aside their confession of faith, will likewise be destroyed. Then in the next verse he mentions the great salvation.

Surely, the immediate associations with the quotations from the Psalms would lead us to think of the future messianic salvation and not redemption from eternal separation from God. Hodges is correct,

> *And it is particularly in the Psalms, from which he chiefly quoted in this chapter, that the term "salvation" has a well-defined sense. In the Psalms this term occurs repeatedly to describe the deliverance of God's people from the oppression of their* **enemies** *and their consequent enjoyment of God's blessings. In the Septuagint, the Greek Bible so familiar to the writer, the word "salvation (sōtēria) was used in this sense in Psalm 3:2, 8; 18:2, 35, 46, 50; 35:3; 37:39; 71:15; 118:14-15, 21; 132:16; and elsewhere. This meaning is uniquely suitable here where the Son's own triumph over enemies has just been mentioned.*[529]

---

527 Paul Tanner, "Hebrews," in *The Grace New Testament Commentary* (Denton, TX: Grace Evangelical Society, 2010), 1060.

528 Ibid..

529 Zane C. Hodges, "Hebrews," in *BKC: New Testament*, ed. John F. Walvoord and Roy B. Zuck (Colorado Springs: Cook, 1996), 782-83.

Furthermore, as argued in earlier chapters in this book, the verb "to inherit," when used in the future tense, in the New Testament often has the sense of "to obtain by works." That this messianic salvation is a salvation that can be obtained by works is taught in Hebrews 5:9.

> *And having been made perfect, He became* ***to all those who obey Him*** *the source of eternal salvation (Hebrews 5:9).*

We are therefore justified in being skeptical of an interpretation that says that salvation here is deliverance from eternal damnation.

The writer continues to speak of this messianic salvation in Hebrews 2:3 saying,

> *How will we escape if we neglect* ***so great a salvation****? After it was at the first spoken through the Lord, it was confirmed to us by those who heard (Hebrews 2:3).*

The salvation to which he refers in Hebrews 2:3 is the subject of Hebrews 2:5-18, the future reign of David's Greater Son, the Messiah, and of our participation with Him in the final destiny of man, to rule over the works of God's hand (2:7-8).

Because this salvation is so "great," the readers are in great danger if they choose to neglect it. Many of them are considering a return to Judaism and to abandoning their faith in Christ.

Commentators commonly recognize that the warnings in Hebrews are parentheses in his argument. From 1:4 to 2:18 the writer presents the superiority of Christ to the angels. The rulership over God's works has been commissioned not to angels but to God's Son and His companions (1:9; 2:10). In the middle of the argument he inserts a warning, Hebrews 2:1-4, in which he exhorts them not to neglect this great future, this great *sōtēria*. Then in verse 5 he picks up the argument from which he momentarily departed at the end of 1:14. The "for" (*gar*) refers back to 1:14:

> *For [gar] unto the angels hath He not put in subjection the world to come,* ***whereof we speak*** *(2:5, KJV).*

The subjection of the world to come is the *sōtēria* "*of which we are speaking*" in Hebrews 1:14 and 2:3. This salvation is not final entrance into heaven or deliverance from eternal separation from God. It is being a co-heir with Christ in the world to come. He then gives an exposition of Psalm 8:1-9 which in turn is David's exposition of the final destiny of man set forth in Genesis 1:26-28. To "inherit" that salvation is simply to have a share with Christ in ruling in that kingdom. This is the "great salvation" which they are not to neglect.[530] The neglected salvation is not our final deliverance from eternal separation from God. That is not the salvation "about which we are speaking."[531]

Entering into this salvation is conditional. He has just mentioned this salvation in 1:14. He states there is a danger from which we cannot escape if we neglect it. For the writer of

[530] See Thomas Kem Oberholtzer, "The Eschatological Salvation of Hebrews 1:5-2:5," *BibSac* 145 (January-March 1988): 83-87.

[531] George N. H. Peters, commenting on Hebrews 1:14, puts it this way, "Salvation includes far more than moral and bodily regeneration, for it embraces the covenanted kingdom of God, the inheritance of David's Son, the joint-heirship and reign with Christ." Peters, *The Theocratic Kingdom of Our Lord Jesus, the Christ, as Covenanted in the Old Testament and Presented in the New Testament*, 3:451.

the epistle, the danger to which he refers is not loss of justification, "*because by one sacrifice he has made perfect forever those who are being made holy*" (Hebrews 10:14). Our eternal destiny is secure. What is contingent is whether or not we will be "richly rewarded" and "receive what He has promised" (Hebrews 10:36), which is achieved only "through faith and patience" (Hebrews 6:12) and obedience (Hebrews 5:9).

Paul Tanner summarizes,

> *Thus to neglect "so great a salvation" does not mean a rejection of the gospel, but rather a failure to properly care about the future aspect of our salvation associated with Christ's Second Coming and kingdom. Believers can do this by failing to endure in their Christian walk, by abandoning their confession of the Lord Jesus, and by not living by faith. For the Jewish believing audience, this might be accompanied by a retreat into some form of Judaism and its system of animal sacrifices.*[532]

The writer says that this salvation "*was at the first spoken through the Lord*" (Hebrews 2:3). But where did the Lord speak of this salvation? While one could think of the Lord's teaching to Nicodemus regarding salvation from eternal damnation, the context of Hebrews 2:5-10 suggests another salvation, the offer of the messianic kingdom.

> *And I confer on you a kingdom, just as my Father conferred one on me, so that you may eat and drink at my table in my kingdom and sit on the throne, judging the twelve tribes of Israel (Luke 22:29-30).*

> *Jesus said to them, "I tell you the truth, at the renewal of all things, when the Son of Man sits on his glorious throne, you who have followed me will also sit on twelve thrones judging the twelve tribes of Israel" (Matthew 19:28).*

> *Repent, for the kingdom of heaven is near (Matthew 4:17).*

The coming kingdom of heaven announced here by Jesus is none other than the predicted kingdom-salvation of the Old Testament, the restoration of the kingdom to Israel (Acts 1:6).[533] The miracles that confirmed it (Hebrews 2:4) are powers of the coming age (Hebrews 6:5).

Such a salvation, joint participation with Christ in the coming kingdom rule, is contingent on the believer's faithful perseverance and obedience. That is why he says:

> *Although he was a son, he learned obedience from what he suffered and, once made perfect, he became the source of eternal salvation* [sōtēria] *for* **all who obey** *him (Hebrews 5:8-9).*

Here, in no uncertain terms, he declares that this salvation is based on works of obedience and not just faith alone. Therefore, personal salvation from sin is not in view. Furthermore, nothing here suggests the common Experimental Predestinarian teaching that all who are born again will obey Him. Nothing in the book of Hebrews suggests that this is a description of all true Christians.

This entire unit of the book (4:14-5:10) is not about the Experimentalist's "professing" believer's need for deliverance from damnation. The unit begins with "*let us hold fast our*

---

[532] Tanner, "Hebrews," 1037-38.

[533] Because of Israel's rejection, the final form of that kingdom, the millennium, was postponed until the second advent but was inaugurated in a mystery form in the present age.

confession" (Hebrews 4:14) and ends with "*He became to all those who obey Him the source of eternal salvation*" (Hebrews 5:9). To "hold fast" and to "obey Him" are clearly the same ideas.

Finally, this obedience is clearly parallel with Christ's obedience in the preceding verse, "*he learned obedience from the things which he suffered.*" His obedience was educational, not soteriological. The writer applies the same concept to his readers in Hebrews 12:11.

This salvation is "eternal" because it is final, complete, and lasts for all eternity and can never be taken away. The phrase "everlasting salvation" is evidently borrowed from Isaiah 45:17. In both places the reference is not to deliverance from eternal damnation but to the unending nature of the messianic kingdom.

Of this salvation in Hebrews 2:3, Christ became the "source" (Gr *aitia*, "the cause, and author").[534] In what sense is He the "cause" of the great future? It seems that His death and resurrection made it possible, and His priestly ministry of comfort and intercession makes it available to those who obey Him. Christ as priestly helper, and not as offered sacrifice, is in the forefront in this section of the epistle (5:2; but esp. 4:14-16; 2:17-18). That kind of priestly ministry is necessary to assist the heirs of salvation along the path their Captain has gone (2:10). The priestly ministry of sacrifice for sins does not come into focus until the next major section of the epistle, where the writer demonstrates that Jesus is superior to Aaron (7:1-10:39).

The next reference to *sōtēria* as messianic salvation in Hebrews is Hebrews 6:9:

> *Even though we speak like this, dear friends, we are confident of better things in your case-- things that accompany salvation [sōtēria].*

The "things" to which he refers are defined in the following verses (6:10-12): work and love, diligence to the end, and faith and patience. Salvation is the victorious participation with Christ in the coming kingdom (Hebrews 1:14), which only those who persevere as companions of the King will inherit.[535] Paul Tanner says it well: "The author thinks of the time when man will be crowned with glory and honor, ruling jointly with Christ in his resurrected state. This is the glorious destiny of believers who are faithful to Christ in this life (cf. Revelation 02:26–27)."[536] This salvation is the inheritance-rest mentioned in Hebrews 4. The writer obviously expects that his readers will persevere to the end, enter into rest, and obtain these blessings.

Finally, the writer states that this messianic salvation is something that believers should eagerly wait for.

> *So Christ was sacrificed once to take away the sins of many people; and he will appear a second time, not to bear sin* [Gr *chōris*, "apart from sin"], *but to bring salvation* [*sōtēria*] *to those who are waiting* [*apekdechomai*] *for him (Hebrews 9:28).*

In His first advent Christ came with reference to sin: He died for it. But in His second advent, He comes "apart from," without reference to sin. Christ came to bear the sins of

534 Abbott-Smith, 15.

535 Hodges says, "The 'salvation' referred to should be understood in congruity with its meaning in 1:14. It is that experience of victory and glory which the persevering companions of the King inherit." Hodges, "Hebrews," 796.

536 Tanner, "Hebrews," 1054.

"many," but He will only bring this messianic salvation "*to those who are waiting for him.*" The verb *apekdechomai* commonly means to "wait eagerly" or "wait patiently."[537] Zane Hodges notes, "those who are waiting for Him" constitute "a smaller circle than those whom His death has benefited. They are, as all his previous exhortations reveal, the ones who '*hold firmly till the end the confidence we had at first*' (3:14). The 'salvation' He will bring them at His second coming will be the 'eternal inheritance' of which they are heirs (cf. 9:15; 1:14)."[538] It is a share in the dominion of the Son of Man over the millennial earth (Hebrews 2:5-8).

The verse is precisely parallel to Paul's anticipation of receiving the crown of righteousness which goes to those who "love His appearing" (2 Timothy 4:8, KJV). For the writer to the Hebrews, they "wait eagerly for it;" for Paul they "love" it. The readers of the epistle would understand that to which he was referring to. Indeed, the major theme of the book is to exhort them to continue to wait patiently, to endure faithfully in the midst of their trials:

> *So do not throw away your confidence; it will be richly rewarded. You need to persevere*[539] *so that when you have done the will of God, you will receive what he has promised (Hebrews 10:35-36).*

Some of the readers were considering throwing away their confidence, returning to Judaism. They would not be the ones found waiting eagerly, who have "labored to enter into rest" (Hebrews 4:11), and who have "done the will of God" (10:36), that is, finished their work.

Summary

Salvation is a broad term. However, only with difficulty can the common meaning of "deliver from eternal damnation" be made to fit into numerous passages. The word commonly means "to make whole," "to sanctify," "to endure victoriously," or "to be delivered from some general trouble or difficulty." Without question, the common impulsive reaction, that assumes that "salvation" always has eternal deliverance in view, has seriously compromised the ability of many to objectively discern what the New Testament writers intended to teach. As a result, Experimental Predestinarian views have gained wider acceptance than they should have.

Of particular interest are the nine times the writer to the Hebrews uses the words *sōzō* (2x) or *sōtēria* (7x). Predominately, he refers to the future messianic rule when all things will be brought into subjection to the King and His companions, His *Metochoi* (Hebrews 1:9, 14; 2:5-8). Those who wait eagerly for this salvation (Hebrews 9:28) and who obey Him (Hebrews 5:9) will have a share with Him in His future reign.

---

537 See Philippians 3:20; 1 Peter 3:20; 1 Corinthians 1:7.

538 Hodges, "Hebrews," 796.

539 Note Hebrews 12:1-3.

13 Messianic Salvation

AS THE previous chapter has shown, the words for salvation present a multifaceted theme. In some cases the word refers to the "salvation" of a person who is troubled in some way, and in others it refers to the present growth of the believer in Christ's way of life. He is "being saved" now. Sometimes it simply means to be healed of some physical ailment. In one place we are told that a wife can be "saved" through childbearing.

In this chapter we will discuss what I have chosen to call "messianic salvation." This theme was a constant vision of the prophets. One day God's covenant faithfulness to Israel would be demonstrated. One day the Abrahamic covenant, in which God promised He would bless the world through Abraham's descendants and give them the Land forever, will be fulfilled.[540] Messianic salvation involves the fulfillment of these promises, a national repentance and forgiveness of sin, reversal of exile, re-possession of the land, and the restoration of the Davidic theocracy (Acts 1:6). This salvation is equivalent to what Jesus and John preached when they proclaimed, "The kingdom of heaven is at hand." Paul says,

Brethren, my heart's desire and my prayer to God for them is for their salvation (Romans 10:1).

What kind of salvation does Paul have in mind? It is likely that Paul has messianic and not personal salvation in view in Romans 10 because of the references to salvation in the preceding context. In Romans 9:29 Paul quotes Isaiah 1:9, directing attention to the Assyrian invasion of Northern Israel around 722 BC. Unless the Lord leaves some survivors, the nation will end up being completely destroyed like Sodom and Gomorrah. But a remnant did survive the Assyrian invasion, and this remnant was a fulfillment of the promise that a remnant would one day return to the Lord.

Similarly, Paul refers to the remnant doctrine in Romans 9:27-28. There, he quotes Isaiah 10:22-23, which speaks of the remnant that will be saved (Romans 9:27). The salvation in view is a national salvation from sin; it is not salvation from the lake of fire. Instead, it is the fulfillment of the promise to Israel that she would one day experience a national salvation, a deliverance from God's strong temporal displeasure (Gr *orgē*) with sin, a national forgiveness of sins, and the restoration of the Davidic theocracy (cf. Acts 1:6; Rom 11:26-27).

Jeremiah pleads for the salvation of the remnant that will finally be fulfilled in Romans 11:26-27.

---

[540] Genesis 12:1-3; 15:18-21; 17:2-9; 22:15-18.

Jeremiah says,

> *O Lord, save Thy people, The remnant of Israel.*

God answers,

> *Behold, I am bringing them from the north country, and I will gather them from the remote parts of the earth (Jeremiah 31:7-8).*

This salvation is the promised restoration from exile and ultimate deliverance from enemies. Amos echoed this theme saying, "*I will bring back my people, Israel; they will rebuild the cities lying in rubble and settle down*" (Amos 9:13-15, NET). When enemies attacked the nation, David prayed, "*Oh, that salvation for Israel would come out of Zion! When God restores the fortunes of his people, let Jacob rejoice and Israel be glad*!" (Psalm 53:6).

In the first century, Israel once again faced temporal destruction because of God's present wrath. If they had repented, they would "live" (see Acts 3:19-20). Elsewhere, Paul warned the Jewish nation that if they refused to turn to the Stone they had rejected, they faced a national catastrophe.

> *Take heed therefore, so that the thing spoken of in the Prophets may not come upon you: "Behold, you scoffers, and marvel, and perish; For I am accomplishing a work in your days, A work which you will never believe, though someone should describe it to you" (Acts 13:40–41).*

In the last days, Yahweh will bring full salvation for His people (e.g., Isaiah 43:5 ff.; Jeremiah 31:7; 46:27; Zechariah 8:7).[541] At that time, in the future earthly kingdom Israel "*will draw water from the wells of salvation*" (Isaiah 12:3), and the entire world will participate in the messianic salvation (Isaiah 45:22; 49:6). In that day, Israel will say, *"Behold, this is our God for whom we have waited that He might save us. This is the Lord for whom we have waited; Let us rejoice and be glad in His salvation*" (Isaiah 25:9).

The enemies of Israel will be put to shame in that future day, "*but Israel will be saved by the Lord with an everlasting salvation*" (Isaiah 45:17). The messianic salvation is called the "everlasting salvation" because the kingdom of the Messiah will last forever, beyond the millennium and into the new heavens and the new earth.[542]

Turning to the Gospels we read that while filled with the Spirit, Zacharias announced that the time was near, the culmination of Israel's story was about to be (potentially) fulfilled; God's righteousness, His covenant faithfulness, was about to be demonstrated. He announced, "*Salvation* FROM OUR ENEMIES, *And* FROM THE HAND OF ALL WHO HATE US … *to remember His holy covenant, The oath which He swore to Abraham our father*" (Luke 1:68–79).

---

541 J. Schneider, "Redemption," in NIDNT, 3:208.

542 The phrase is strikingly similar to the phrase "eternal salvation" in Hebrews 5:9. Isaiah 52:10 states that "all the ends of the world will see the salvation of our God." In that glorious future era, His people will know His name, and the feet of those who proclaim salvation will be called beautiful (Isaiah 52:7). The psalmist also anticipated salvation in this sense, "Oh, that the **salvation of Israel** would come out of Zion! When the Lord restores His captive people, Jacob will rejoice, Israel will be glad" (Psalms 14:7).

However, Israel rejected this salvation. They "*stumbled over their stumbling stone*" (Romans 9:32), Jesus their Messiah. As a result, both Jesus and John announced terrible temporal consequences. "*The axe,*" said John, "*is already laid at the foot of the trees*" (Matthew 3:10). While weeping, Jesus pronounced judgment on the nation, "*Behold, your house is being left to you desolate!*" (Matthew 23:37–39).

Furthermore, He said the temple itself would be destroyed (Matthew 24:1-2). This shattering prediction would be fulfilled in the generation of those then living (Matthew 24:34).

As Paul writes the Epistle to the Romans in AD 58, Israel stands under God's wrath. The predictions of John and Jesus of a coming national catastrophe are about to come true. Within twelve years of John's writing, the Roman armies under Titus will destroy the city and the temple in one of the worst holocausts in Jewish history. Israel was much in need of messianic salvation!

Paul quotes Scripture related to Israel's temporal destruction in the immediately preceding context of Romans 10:1 (see 9:25-29; 10:11), and then concludes this section of Romans with the same theme of future messianic national salvation from the attacking armies (Romans 11:26-27; cf. Zechariah 14). This surely suggests that when he says he desires Israel's "salvation," he refers to the line of cumulative fulfillment of the remnant doctrine, the ultimate messianic salvation under David's Greater Son. If that salvation had come as a result of Israel's national repentance and the personal salvation of many individual Jews, the terrible devastation that threatened the nation (AD 70) could be avoided. *The "messianic salvation" involves a return from exile and national rescue from the coming national catastrophe!* Of course, for individual Jews who chose to embrace it, it also entails *personal rescue from damnation.* Israel was seeking this salvation but failed to obtain it (Romans 11:7, 11).[543]

In Romans 10:1 Paul expresses his strong desire that God would stay His hand and that this terrible temporal destruction and dispersion might be avoided. He prays for the messianic salvation which would save Israel from this coming temporal national devastation. Peter himself made a final offer to the nation in Acts chapter 3,

> *Repent therefore and return, that your sins may be wiped away, in order that* ***times of refreshing*** *may come from the presence of the Lord; and that He may send Jesus, the Christ appointed for you, whom heaven must receive until* ***the period of restoration of all things*** *about which God spoke by the mouth of His holy prophets from ancient time (Acts 3:19–21).*

The wiping away of their sins certainly included the forgiveness of personal sins, but this phrase, as shown in chapter 3, refers to a national forgiveness and the return from exile, the messianic salvation. Peter says that it is not too late, "*the times of refreshing*" and "*the restoration of all things*" (the restoration of the Davidic theocracy, Acts 1:6), can still come about if the nation will repent of their sins and turn to their Messiah. In Romans 10:1, Paul prays that Peter's offer will be accepted.

But Israel did not accept Peter's offer. In Romans 10:2-4, Paul explains why.

---

543 Some within Israel and the many Gentiles did obtain it. Gentiles were grafted into Israel's promises and also were individually saved when they believed in Christ (Romans 11:11). The "salvation" they received in Romans 11:11 was not only individual, they had that in the Old Testament (Romans 2:14-15). What was added was co-heirship with Israel in the Abrahamic promises (cf. Ephesians 2:12-16; Romans 11:17).

Israel's Distortion of God's Plan (Romans 10:2-4)

For I testify about them that they have a zeal for God, but not in accordance with knowledge. For disregarding (Gr agnoeō, BDAG, 13, option 2) God's righteousness and seeking to establish their own, they did not subject themselves to the righteousness of God. For Christ is the end of the law for righteousness to everyone who believes (Romans 10:2–4).

Romans 10:1-14 raises a number of interesting questions about salvation, the righteousness of God, calling upon the name of the Lord, the conflicts between Paul's Judaizing opponents, and the gospel of grace which Paul proclaimed. Paul says that Israel was ignorant of "God's righteousness." What is meant by "God's righteousness?"

Calvin understood God's righteousness to mean God's gift of the imputed righteousness of Christ and that is a fair understanding based on one common interpretation of 2 Corinthians 5:21.

However, the debate over the meaning of the "righteousness of God" is not so easily settled by quoting passages from Calvin or other Reformed theological works. Does the phrase refer to God's character or His gift? Those following Luther and Protestant theology have usually assumed the latter. The "righteousness of God," they say, "is the gift of righteousness imputed to the believer."

A study of the phrases "righteousness of God" or "Your righteousness" indicates that the term is used in three ways. For full discussion, see the "Excursus on the Righteousness of God" at the end of this chapter. In the discussion to follow, we adopt the view suggested by N. T. Wright.

N. T. Wright notes that often the righteousness of God refers to His faithfulness to His promises to Abraham in the Abrahamic covenant (Genesis 15:1-4). Many times the expression "for your sake" refers to God's promises to be faithful to His covenant.[544] The righteousness of God in Romans 10:3 is His faithfulness to His covenantal promises to Abraham to bless the world through Abraham and his descendants, to make his name great, and to grant to his descendants the land of Israel forever. In other words, it refers to God's plan to establish His Lordship over the earth through the descendants of Abraham.[545] This righteousness is not the imputed righteousness of Christ imputed to the believer in Romans 4:3, 5, 6, 9, 11, 13, 22; 5:17. Instead it refers to that other kind of righteousness mentioned in Romans, ethical character. It is "His" righteousness and speaks of His faithfulness and justice (Romans 3:5, 21, 25, 26). Righteousness in Romans is not always forensic justification. For example, it often refers to ethical behavior (Romans 6:13, 16, 18, 19, 20; 10:5; 14:17).

Isaiah specifically calls God's righteousness "his salvation," saying, "*I bring near My righteousness, it is not far off; And My salvation will not delay. And I will grant salvation in Zion, And My glory for Israel*" (Isaiah 46:13). God's righteousness is the messianic

---

[544] Daniel 9:17; Ezekiel 26:32; Psalms 31:3; 106:7.

[545] For further discussion see the "Excursus on the Righteousness of God" at the end of this chapter. "Righteousness of God" is found eight times in the New Testament (Romans 1:17; 3:5, 21, 22; 10:3; 2 Corinthians 5:21; James 1:20; 2 Peter 1:1). If one substitutes "plan" for "righteousness of God" in each of these passages, it is plain that, with the exception of 2 Corinthians 5:21, the substitution makes perfect sense. Even 2 Corinthians 5:21 could refer to God's plan in the sense the Apostles themselves are the current expression of that plan in that they are bearers of the Gospel message. Thus, "we, the Apostles, have become the expression of God's faithfulness to His plan to bless the world through Israel."

salvation.[546] This understanding of God's righteousness fits the preceding context of Romans 10:1 perfectly. It also means that Paul continues his discussion of the messianic salvation which the Jewish nation had distorted. Israel had turned the righteousness of God, the messianic salvation, into a plan to bless Israel only instead of a plan to bless Gentiles as well as Jews through Israel (Romans 1:16; 10:19-20).

This is what Paul means when he says that the Jews "*were seeking to establish their own [righteousness]*" (Romans 10:3), that is, their own way of interpreting and obeying the covenant. While some have understood "*their own righteousness*" as Israel's attempt to establish right standing before God by means of law-righteousness,[547] that does not provide a suitable contrast to "the righteousness of God." If the righteousness of God does not refer to God's gift, but to His faithfulness to His plan to bless the world through Israel, then one must understand Israel's quest "*to establish their own*" righteousness as *their plan* to fulfill the Abrahamic promise their way instead of God's way. Israel had reduced the righteousness of God, the messianic salvation, to a promise to Israel alone, excluding the Gentiles. That is, they willfully ignored it. As a result, they rejected their own Messiah, the one to whom their Law pointed (v. 4), stumbling over "the stumbling stone" (Romans 9:32).[548] Therefore, they must incur the national consequences.

The word "establish" (Gr *histēmi*) is commonly translated "to uphold, maintain, validate."[549] It is possible that Paul had in mind the Lord's teaching when He said, "*You nicely set aside the commandment of God in order to keep* (Gr *histēmi*) *your tradition*" (Mark 7:9). Those traditions involved, among other things, the belief that Israel alone was the object of the Abrahamic promise and Gentiles must become Jews if they wanted to share its benefits.

As Paul explains, "*For disregarding* [Gr *agnoeō*] *God's righteousness and seeking to establish their own, they did not subject themselves to the righteousness of God.*" Israel certainly knew about God's plan to bless the world through Israel, but they *willfully* ignored it, making themselves the center of blessing and not God's universal plan.[550] Numerous Scriptures tell us that their problem was not lack of knowledge, it was hardness of heart.[551] In 2 Corinthians 3:14 Paul says, "Their minds were hardened" [Gr *pōroō*, "to harden, petrify"[552]]. Garland is correct, "Israel's fundamental problem is not a failure to comprehend the law but a failure to obey it (Rom 2:17–29; Gal 6:13). They do not suffer from an intellectual deficiency but from

---

546 See also Isaiah 56:1. Earlier, he says again, "I will bring near my deliverance [Heb ṣedeq, 'righteousness'] swiftly, my salvation has gone out and my arms will rule the peoples; the coastlands wait for me, and for my arm they hope" (Isaiah 51:5, NRSV). Notice how the NRSV translates the Hebrew ṣedeq, "righteousness" as "deliverance" in the sense of salvation from the invading armies. Paul relates it not only to the coming national catastrophe, but to the final deliverance from the armies arrayed against the people of God—God's righteousness is the messianic salvation (Rom 11:26-27).

547 Moo, for example, says, "As Paul shows in v. 3, the Jews have not recognized the manifestation of God's righteousness in Christ and have sought rather to establish their own, based on the doing of the law (cf. 9:32 and 10:5), Douglas J. Moo, "Romans," in *New Dictionary of Biblical Theology*, ed. T. D. Alexander and B. S. Rosner (Downers Grove, IL: Intervarsity Press, 2001), 631.

548 For Israel to "submit to the righteousness of God" does not refer to a commitment to submit to the Lordship of Christ, but rather to believe on Christ. "That Israel's 'not submitting,'" says Moo, "is equivalent to their not having faith is evident from the parallel texts in this passage (9:32a; cf. v. 33b; 10:5-6)." Moo, *The Epistle to the Romans*, 634.

549 BDAG, 482.

550 BDAG, 13.

551 Isaiah 6:9–10; 29:10–12; Jeremiah 5:21–24; Ezekiel 12:2; Mark 4:10–12; John 12:39–40; Acts 28:25–27.

552 BDAG, 900.

a moral one that prevents them from seeing and believing, hearing and understanding."[553] They had set aside the commandments of God in order to maintain their traditions.

The problem of Jewish exclusiveness is found elsewhere in the New Testament. It became a major issue at the Jerusalem counsel in Acts 15. At that counsel the notion that one must first become a Jew in order to be saved was soundly rejected. God's covenant faithfulness, that is, His righteousness, extended beyond Israel to the entire world. God's plan to bless the world through Abraham's descendants was clear in the Old Testament. In Christ, He made it fully manifest saying, "*The mystery which has been hidden from the past ages and generations; but has now been manifested to His saints, to whom God willed to make known what is the riches of the glory of this mystery among the Gentiles, which is Christ in you, the hope of glory.*" (Colossians 1:26–27). Issues relating to Jewish ritual cleansings, holy days, baptisms, and circumcision were no longer relevant.[554]

Christ Is the End of the Law for Righteousness

In Christ, the messianic salvation has arrived and the distortion of God's covenant faithfulness as applying to Israel only must be abandoned. Paul says that the reason for their rejection was that they (willfully) failed to grasp that "*Christ is the end of the law for righteousnesss* [i.e., for living life not gaining life, see below] *to everyone who believes*" (Romans 10:4). This new way of living was available "to everyone," not just Jews, and it was available to the one "*who believes*" in Christ; therefore, there was no need for works of Torah.

END OF THE LAW AS A WAY OF LIVING (ROMANS 10:4)

What does it mean that "*Christ is the end* (Gr *telos*) *of the Law*?"[555] The word *telos* has legitimately been understood as either "end"[556] or "goal."[557] Some combine them to mean Christ is both the termination and the goal.[558] Either way, the system of Law ended with Christ, and the time for the fulfillment of God's cosmic plan had arrived.[559] Thus, Christ

---

553 D. E. Garland, *2 Corinthians*, New American Commentary (Nashville: Broadman & Holman Publishers, 1999), 191.

554 See Mark 7:3-5; Romans 14:2-4; Jewish ancestral traditions have been done away, Galatians 1:14; Colossians 2:16-23.

555 The word "Law" also has been variously understood; however, most scholars today agree that the Mosaic Law is in view. Moo, "Romans," 636.

556 Brice L. Martin, *Christ and the Law in Paul* (Eugene, OR: Wipf and Stock Publishers, 1989), 129-38.

557 See George E. Howard, "Christ The End of the Law: The Meaning of Romans 10:4 ff.," *Journal of Biblical Literature* 88, no. 3 (September 1969): 332. Walter C. Kaiser, "Leviticus 18:5 and Paul: Do This And You Will Live (Eternally?)," *JETS* 14, no. 1 (Winter 1971).

558 Douglas Moo understands it to mean "culmination" in a temporal sense. With the coming of Christ, the authority of the law of Moses is in some sense at an end. Thus, a salvation-historical meaning is implied. "As Christ consummates one era of salvation history, so he inaugurates a new one." Moo, *The Epistle to the Romans*, 641. Frédéric Louis Godet and A. Cousin, *Commentary on St. Paul's Epistle to the Romans*, 2 vols. (Bellingham, WA: Logos, 2009), 2:196. Both of these scholars see "goal" or "aim" as involved as well. Godet says, "This latter meaning that of end, no doubt implies the notion of aim; for if the law terminates with Christ, it is only because in Him it has reached its aim. Nevertheless it is true that the contrast established in the following development between the righteousness of the law and that of faith requires, as an explanation properly so called, the meaning of end, and not aim." Moo, *The Epistle to the Romans*, 640.

559 Paul wrote in Galatians 3:24 that "the Law has become our tutor to lead us to Christ, so that we may be justified by faith." A "tutor" was one who had responsibility for someone who needed guidance. He was a

fulfilled the goal of the Law "with respect to righteousness."[560] What relationship did the law have to righteousness? One thing is evident, it never had any connection with *forensic* righteousness.

Paul makes this clear when he said earlier in Romans, "*For we maintain that a man is justified by faith apart from works of the Law*" (Romans 3:28).

How then, were people justified before God in the Old Testament? "*For it is impossible for the blood of bulls and goats to take away sins*" (Hebrews 10:4). Again Paul answers, "*For what does the Scripture say? 'ABRAHAM BELIEVED GOD, AND IT WAS CREDITED TO HIM AS RIGHTEOUSNESS'*" (Romans 4:3).

Justification was always by faith and never by law. "*This is the only thing I want to find out from you: did you receive the Spirit by the works of the Law, or by hearing with faith?*" (Galatians 3:2). Paul taught that only those of faith in both the Old and the New Testaments are sons of Abraham, "*Therefore, be sure that it is those who are of faith who are sons of Abraham* (Galatians 3:6–7).

He then told the Galatians that the Law was unrelated to forensic righteousness (justification).

> *Now that no one is justified by the Law before God is evident; for, "THE RIGHTEOUS MAN SHALL LIVE BY FAITH" (Galatians 3:11).*
>
> *For if a law had been given which was able to impart life, then righteousness would indeed have been based on law (Galatians 3:21).*
>
> *I do not nullify the grace of God, for if righteousness comes through the Law, then Christ died needlessly (Galatians 2:21).*

It is not possible for Paul to make it clearer that he believed the Law and forensic justification were completely unrelated to each other.

Why then do commentators consistently read Romans 10:4 as if the "righteousness" refers to forensic righteousness? When Paul says, "*For Christ is the end of the law for righteousness to everyone who believes,*" he could not have intended that Christ was the end of the Law *in relationship to forensic righteousness* because Paul never believed that forensic

---

guardian, leader, guide (BDAG, 748). These guardians were assigned to a child from ages 6 to 16 to constrain and discipline him. But the book of Hebrews consistently argues that the Law had not only a constraining function, but also a teaching function. The writer argues forcefully that the Old Testament taught the people about a superior priest and a superior sacrifice to come. He showed that the promise of the Melchizedekian priesthood proved that the Levitical priesthood was temporary and would one day be superseded. God told Moses that the Tabernacle was made according to a "pattern," and thus Israel knew from the Law that the "reality" had yet to be fulfilled (Hebrews 8:5-6). The Old Testament pointed Israel to a new covenant (Jeremiah 31; Hebrews 8:7-13). Then in Hebrews 9 the writer explains that the old covenant anticipated the new: "The Holy Spirit is signifying this, that the way into the holy place has not yet been disclosed while the outer tabernacle is still standing, which is a symbol for the present time. Accordingly both gifts and sacrifices are offered which cannot make the worshiper perfect in conscience" (Hebrews 9:8-9). He then explains, "For the Law, since it has only a shadow of the good things to come and not the very form of things, can never, by the same sacrifices which they offer continually year by year, make perfect those who draw near" (Hebrews 10:1). The Law was a "shadow" of things to come, that is, the Law only pointed to the things to come and was not their reality. This was a teaching function of the Law and in this way it pointed to something better. Christ, according to Hebrews, was indeed the "goal of the Law." See Calvin, "Institutes," 2.7.2.

560 The Gr preposition *eis* is here understood to mean "marker of a specific point of reference, for, to, with respect to, with reference to" (BDAG, 288).

righteousness had anything to do with the Law! How could Paul say something had ended which never began in the first place!

As we shall argue below, the Law's only direct connection with righteousness was with *ethical*, not forensic righteousness, with sanctification and not justification, with living life, not gaining it. What ended with Christ was not the Law in relationship to forensic righteousness (it never had one); rather, the Law's connection with ethical righteousness ended with Christ with the inauguration of the New Covenant way of living. In the verses to follow, Paul proves this from Deuteronomy arguing that the time of fulfillment which Moses predicted in that passage had finally arrived.

This understanding, that Christ was the end of the Law system for living life (not gaining it), for ethical righteousness (not forensic righteousness) harmonizes nicely with Paul's statements in Romans 11, which say that Israel was cut off from being the centerpiece of God's plan to bless the world and the Gentiles were grafted in.[561] It also is consistent with the verses to follow, which speak of the ethical and sanctifying righteousness based upon the Law.

DIKAIOSUNĒ IN ROMANS

There is a tendency among interpreters to understand "righteousness" (Gr *dikaiosunē)* in Romans as always referring to forensic rather than ethical righteousness. It is true that it often refers to forensic righteousness. It is found 92 times in the New Testament, and its meaning varies depending on the context. It can mean "quality or state of juridical correctness with focus on redemptive action, righteousness,"[562] that is, forensic justification. In many instances it means, "the quality or characteristic of upright behavior, uprightness, righteousness,"[563] that is, ethical righteousness.

This same variation in meaning is found in the book of Romans where *dikaiosunē* occurs frequently. In 14 instances it refers to forensic righteousness,[564] and in 16 places it refers to ethical righteousness.[565] Some of the categorizations in the preceding two footnotes are, of course, debatable, and will be established in the discussion to follow. The point is that one cannot automatically interpret righteousness in Romans as forensic justification just because that is a major theme of the book. The book is also very concerned with practical righteousness. Indeed, Paul devotes seven chapters to practical, ethical righteousness (Romans 6-8 and 13-16) but only five to forensic justification (Romans 1-5).

As an example of ethical righteousness, one might cite Romans 14:17, "*for the kingdom of God is not eating and drinking, but **righteousness and peace and joy** in the Holy Spirit.*" Of course, it occurs most frequently in the sanctification section of Romans. For example, "*For just as you presented your members as slaves to impurity and to lawlessness, resulting in further lawlessness, so now present your members as **slaves to righteousness, resulting in sanctification***" (Romans 6:19). We shall argue in this section below and in the next section that Romans 10 is focused more on sanctification than justification and that righteousness

---

561 See discussion of this passage on pp. 627 ff.

562 BDAG, 247.

563 BDAG, 248.

564 Romans 1:17; 3:21, 22, 35, 26; 4:3, 5, 6, 9, 11, 13, 22; 5:17; 10:10.

565 Romans 3:5; 5:21; 6:13, 16, 18, 19, 20; 8:10; 9:30; 31; 10:3; 4, 5, 6; 14:17.

in that chapter (with the exception of Romans 10:10) is specifically related to ethical behavior and not justification.

I see no reason why the remaining references in Romans 9:30, 31 cannot also be understood as ethical and not forensic righteousness. In v. 30 Paul states,

> *What shall we say then? That Gentiles, who did not pursue righteousness, attained righteousness, even the righteousness which is by faith (Romans 9:30).*

What is it that the Gentiles "*did not pursue*"? Certainly, they did not pursue forensic justification. But Paul's complaint about the Gentiles in Romans 1:18-32 was that they suppressed ethical righteousness and lived degenerate lives. The focus of his concern was that they did not pursue ethical righteousness! But then, after finding Christ, they found the sanctifying righteousness by faith, and began to do what the law required. They showed that they had entered into the New Covenant by faith alone because "*the works of the Law were written on their hearts*" (Romans 2:15).[566] As demonstrated elsewhere, in the case of Noah,[567] the "*righteousness which is by faith*" refers to ethical righteousness by "faithfulness" (Gr *pistis*, BDAG, 818). This was how Noah obtained the "righteousness which is according to faith" (Hebrew 11:6-7). He *worked for it* for 120 years! He did not work for forensic justification!

The Jews, in contrast to the Gentiles, pursued a "law of righteousness." The word "pursued" (Gr *diōkō*) means "run after," and is quite strong (BDAG, 254). It is normally associated with the ethical righteousness that believers should pursue such as hospitality (Romans 12:13), mutual peace (Romans 14:19; 1 Peter 3:11; Hebrews 12:14), holiness, love (1 Corinthians 14:1), doing good (1 Thessalonians 5:15), and righteousness (1 Timothy 6:11; 2 Timothy 2:22). The "law of righteousness" is the law of ethical behavior. That is what the Law was all about, and there was nothing wrong with pursing that. They were commanded to do so. The problem was that, even though they pursued a "law of righteousness," they did not arrive at it because they pursued it by works and not by faith, that is, they pursued by means of externalisms and self-effort. One does not "pursue" forensic righteousness. One receives it in an instant by faith alone apart from pursuit. The entire Pharisaic system, of which Paul had been a part, was consumed with ethical righteousness. They had reduced Torah to a set of rules regarding purity, cleansing, ritual feasts, and Sabbath regulations. Their purpose in this pursuit was not forensic justification. They assumed that as the people of God and members of the Covenant, they already were saved. Why did they pursue ethical righteousness? According to their Old Testament, it was *not* to get into the Covenant (be saved) but to stay in (but that is a different discussion for a whole other book!).

THE ETHICAL RIGHTEOUSNESS OF "MY PEOPLE"

A possible objection to understanding the Jews' pursuit of righteousness as ethical righteousness instead of forensic, is that earlier Paul describes the remnant in soteriological, not ethical terms. In Romans 9:25-26, Paul quotes Hosea, "*And I will say to those who were not My people, 'You are My people!' And they will say, 'You are my God!'*" (Hosea 2:23). The

---

[566] See discussion of this passage on pp. 227 ff.

[567] See discussion on pp. 585 ff.

designation, "My people," is thought to be a soteriological designation, indicating those who have been saved from damnation. Paul follows with a quotation from Hosea 1:10, which says, "*It will be said to them, 'You are the sons of the living God.'*" Apart from the difficulty that this passage is directed to Israel in Hosea and Paul applies it to Gentiles in Romans,[568] the meaning of the passage teaches Gentiles will also be called "My People." In Romans Paul has described "sons of God" in ethical terms (Romans 8:14). They are full grown sons who are "led by the Spirit" (see full discussion on pp. 728 ff., 797, 677).

The phrase "My people" linked with "your God," occurs nine times in the Old Testament.[569] While the phrase includes the notion of regeneration and individual salvation in the Millennium (Ezekiel 36:26), the characteristic which the prophets emphasize is not their regeneration but their obedience. The condition for becoming one of God's people is to obey Him. Jeremiah says,

> ***Obey My voice, and I will be your God, and you will be My people****; and you will walk in all the way which I command you, that it may be well with you (Jeremiah 7:23).*

> *Listen to My voice, and do according to all which I command you;* ***so you shall be My people****, and I will be your God (Jeremiah 11:4).*

Being God's people and having God as their God was based upon obedience and not faith alone for salvation. Therefore, even though the designations assume personal salvation, their significance is that they *describe ethical and not forensic righteousness*. In the Ezekiel prophecy of the final fulfillment of the New Covenant in the Millennium, we read, "*I will put My Spirit within you and* ***cause you to walk in My statutes, and you will be careful to observe My ordinances.*** *You will live in the land that I gave to your forefathers; so you will be* ***My people, and I will be your God***" (Ezekiel 36:27-28). While one must first have personal salvation (regeneration), nevertheless, the outstanding characteristic of "My people" in v. 28 is not their saved status, but their ethical righteousness: they will "*walk in My statutes*" and will be "*careful to observe My ordinances*" (cf. Deuteronomy 32:5).

Thus, when Paul quotes Hosea to prove that the Gentiles will one day become "My people," even though he assumes personal salvation, his point is that they will be obedient and possess the ethical righteousness which Israel did not possess.

The Sanctifying Righteousness Based on the Law (Romans 10:5)

> *For Moses writes that the man who practices the righteousness which is based on law shall live by that righteousness (Romans 10:5).*

The word "for" in verse 5 signifies a logical relationship between verse 5 and what went before. What is that logical relationship? He has just said that the reason Israel needs "salvation" is that they have rejected God's plan for saving the world through Israel in Jesus the Messiah and reduced it to a plan to save Jews only. For Gentiles to share in the Messianic Salvation they had to obey Torah. Paul counters that since Christ is the "end of the law for

568 For discussion on this issue see the article by J. Paul Tanner, "The New Covenant and Paul's Quotations from Hosea," *BibSac* 162, no. 645 (January 2005): 95-110.

569 Leviticus 26:12; Isaiah 49:1; Jeremiah 7:23; 11:4; 30:22; Hosea 1:9; Joel 2:26; 27; Ezekiel 36:26.

ethical righteousness as a tutor (Galatians 3:24) for guiding one toward an ethical way of life (the "law of righteousness, Romans 9:31-32), Gentiles do not need to obey Torah and they do not need to become Jews.

According to Romans 2:20-30, ethical righteousness under the Law system only "imparted life to responsive hearers."[570] It avails only to those who believe (10:4). They did not believe in the Stone, and thus they could not receive the messianic salvation.

Paul's citation of Leviticus 18:5 in Romans 10:5,[571] regarding the righteousness based on Law, is notoriously difficult to interpret. It has been understood in two ways.[572] Some have argued that Moses teaches in Leviticus 18:5 that justification could be obtained by works of the Law, and that Paul cites Moses' incorrect perspective in Romans 10:5-6 in order to correct it with another citation from Moses (Romans 10:6-8; Deuteronomy 30:12-14).[573] This solution is unsatisfactory because it pits Moses against Moses and cannot be taken seriously by anyone who believes in the inspiration of the Old Testament. Furthermore, Romans 9-11 is about Israel and her national salvation. Paul completed his discussion of personal soteriology in Romans 5.

The most common view is that Paul speaks hypothetically. If one could hypothetically obey the Law, he could obtain eternal life by this means. But since no one can do this, there must be another way to obtain eternal life. And there is, by faith alone, which Paul turns to in Romans 10:6-8.

This view must be decisively rejected because it understands "life" in a manner differently from how Moses uses the term and because it involves God in a deception, promising heaven on the basis of works when he knows that this is impossible. For full discussion of the hypothetical view, see the "Excursus on the Hypothetical View" at the end of this chapter.

Is there a better solution? Yes there is. But first, one must ask, "To what does 'the righteousness which is based upon the Law' in Romans 10:5 refer?"

The purpose of the Law of Moses in the Old Testament was to give guidance on how to live life to the fullest under the covenant.[574] According to Leviticus 18:5, which Paul quotes in Romans 10:5, the law leads to "life" when pursued by faith. The Law, Kaiser correctly says, "deals with Israel's sanctification."[575] Sprinkle concurs, "'Life' is a common term used in Deuteronomistic literature to refer to a covenantal blessing, a blessing that is contingent upon obedience (e.g. Deuteronomy 4:1; 5:32-33; 8:1; 16:20; 30:6, 15-20)."[576]

570 Ralph P. Martin, *2 Corinthians*, Word Biblical Commentary (Dallas: Word, 1998), 54.

571 See also Deuteronomy 4:39-40.

572 Cranfield suggests a third alternative, but it has not gained much consensus. He suggests that the "Man" who obeys the Law perfectly is Christ, and He does it on our behalf. See Cranfield, *A Critical and Exegetical Commentary on the Epistle to the Romans*, 521.

573 Sanders, *Paul and Palestinian Judaism*, 483, n37.

574 The Torah was not given for purely legal purposes. It was given for "instruction" and sanctification (Exodus 24:12; Deuteronomy 17:11; 24:8). Kaiser notes, "The meaning of Torah, then, is directional guidance for walking on the path of life." Walter Kaiser, "The Law as Guidance for the Promotion of Holiness," in *Five Views on Law and Gospel*, ed. Wayne G. Strickland (Grand Rapids: Zondervan Publishing House, 1996), 193.

575 Ibid., 185.

576 Preston M. Sprinkle, *Law and Life*, Wissenschaftliche Untersuchungen zum Neuen Testament - 2 Reihe (Tubingen: Mohr Siebeck, 2008), 33. Karlberg correctly observes, "Under the Sinaitic arrangement obedience to the law (i.e., works) was the means of inheriting temporal reward: prosperity in the land of Canaan." Mark W. Karlberg, "The Search for an Evangelical Consensus on Paul and the Law," *JETS* 40, no. 4 (December 1997): 568.

Paul defines the righteousness based on Law in precisely this manner in the next phrase in Romans 10:5b. It is the righteousness by which a justified person may "live."

Ethical righteousness based on the Law led to an abundant life and reward. It was obtained by "doing" as well as believing. This righteousness enabled one to live well in the land. It refers to sanctification, not justification, living life rather than just gaining life, behavior in this life and not final salvation.[577] This righteousness is achieved by faith (Genesis 15:6) plus "doing" (Leviticus 18:5; Ezekiel 20:11). Thus when Schreiner objects that "the notion that righteousness 'comes from' the law is contrary to the heart of Pauline theology,"[578] he missed the point.[579] There is nothing in Pauline theology that suggests that sanctifying righteousness ("abundant life") was incompatible with the Law. What Paul did object to was the concept of a forensic righteousness ("regenerate life") based upon law. No one can find justification before God by means of the Law, but the one who practiced the Law by faith could flourish in life by means of such faith-obedience, that is, he "lives."[580]

Once one understands that the righteousness based on the Law refers to ethical righteousness, the problems that have consumed many commentary pages disappear. There is no longer any conflict between Moses and Paul or between Moses and Moses. As John Hart summarizes, "Moses spoke of keeping the law for sanctifying righteousness by 'doing' (i.e., by works produced through faith). While the Law cannot impart 'regenerate life' (Galatians 3:21) it can impart 'abundant life.' Moses (and the Lord) never intended that the law could be kept without faith. The Old Testament is replete with suggestions that faith is the key element in one's relationship to God."[581]

Why, then, did Paul cite Leviticus 18:5 to show that Christ is the goal toward whom the Law pointed? We suggest that he may have had in mind earlier references in Romans and other epistles.

> *But now we have been released from the Law, having died to that by which we were bound, so that we serve in newness of the Spirit and not in oldness of the letter (Romans 7:6).*

---

577 In Ezekiel 20:11-12; Leviticus 18:5 is cited again in reference to abundant life.

578 Schreiner, *Romans*, 553.

579 Schreiner understands that Paul interprets Leviticus 18:5 to mean that one might "hypothetically" become regenerate (i.e., "live") if he obeyed the Law perfectly. But because no one can live it perfectly, the Law condemns us.

580 That this is Paul's meaning is clear from the oft-repeated NT citation of Habakkuk 2:4, "the just shall live by faith" (cf. Romans 1:17). It is true that, grammatically, the phrase "by faith" can qualify either "the just" or "shall live." If it qualifies the former, the text means, "the one who is just by faith" therefore "lives." In other words, the person who is justified is also regenerated, has eternal life, and will go to heaven when he dies. But Habakkuk is calling upon Israel to live by faith and to continue to trust God in the face of a terrible vision (Habakkuk 2:1-3) regarding a future invasion by Babylon (Habakkuk 1:5-11). Therefore, it is illegitimate to understand "live by faith" as adjectivally modifying "the just." It must be understood adverbially modifying "shall live." Contra Thomas L. Stegall, *The Gospel of the Christ: A Biblical Response to the Crossless Gospel Regarding the Contents of Saving Faith* (Milwaukee: Grace Gospel Press, 2009). The righteous man who has been forensically justified (the "just") lives life by "faith," that is, by his faithful endurance in the midst of trials. The writer to the Hebrews clearly uses the Habakkuk citation in the same manner, exhorting his fellow Christians not to fall away, but to endure. *"For you have need of endurance, so that when you have done the will of God, you may receive what was promised. For yet in a very little while, He who is coming will come, and will not delay.* ***But My righteous one shall live by faith****; And if he shrinks back, My soul has no pleasure in him"* (Hebrews 10:36–38). It is true that one gains eternal life by faith, but it is also true that for the writer to the Hebrews, for Habakkuk, and for Paul that the Christian *lives* life by faith as well.

581 John F. Hart, "Why Confess Christ: The Use and Abuse of Romans 10:9-10," *JOTGES* 12, no. 2 (1999).

On the one hand, Paul believed with Moses that the law was for sanctification, but, on the other hand, he knew that only those who responded to it could be sanctified. Furthermore, for all its beauty and glory, it was a burdensome system involving daily sacrifices and 643 minor commandments to clarify the application of the Ten and other external Levitical regulations. While some found "life indeed" under the Law (see Hebrews 11, the Psalms, and the Prophets) it was still a burdensome way to pursue sanctification. In fact, it even caused rebellion (Romans 7:8). As such, it pointed to a better way, and Israel was specifically told that one day there would be a better way under the New Covenant.

Why then did God give the Law? This is too much to discuss here, but Paul says it was a "tutor" (Galatians 3:24) and was intended to be only a temporary guardian (Galatians 3:23). I suggest that when Paul spoke of the righteousness based upon the Law in Romans 10:5, all of these associations would come to the Galatians' minds as well. They desired release from this burden, and Paul says release had come. Specifically, they would remember the promise of Deuteronomy 30:6. Paul, therefore, turns to that fulfillment in Romans 10:6-8.

Yet, even under that covenant, if one wanted to obey, God would help. That is evident from the spirituality of Hebrews 11 and the Psalms. Certainly, God would not mock Israelites with a command they could not perform.[582] David asked of God, "*Create in me a pure heart, O God, and renew a steadfast spirit within me, and grant me a willing spirit to sustain me*" (Psalms 51:10-12). Isaiah said, "*He gives strength to the weary, And to him who lacks might He increases power those who wait for the LORD will gain new strength; They will mount up with wings like eagles, They will run and not get tired, They will walk and not become weary*" (Isaiah 40:29-31).

Waltke says, "In other words, the provisions of the New Covenant were always available to the true Israel, but it was not God's mode of administering old Israel as a nation."[583]

The prophets anticipated a time in which God's Spirit would be poured out and circumcision of the flesh would be replaced by circumcision of the heart. I suggest that Romans 10:5 must be read in light of Romans 7:8; 8:3-4 and Romans 8:13. Paul has explained earlier in Romans that this time of fulfillment has come. He says,

> *For what the Law could not do, weak as it was through the flesh, God did: sending His own Son in the likeness of sinful flesh and as an offering for sin, He condemned sin in the flesh, in order that the requirement of the Law might be fulfilled in us, who do not walk according to the flesh,* ***but according to the Spirit*** *(Romans 8:3–4).*

In the time of fulfillment, the experience of "life," anticipated in the Law and predicted by the prophets, is now fulfilled in Christ.

582 We therefore strongly disagree with Paul Barnett who, in his commentary on 2 Corinthians 3:7, teaches that the Law was a ministry of death and condemnation because of "the spiritual incapacity of the people to fulfill its just requirements." See Paul Barnett, *The Second Epistle to the Corinthians*, The New International Commentary on the New Testament (Grand Rapids: Wm. B. Eerdmans Publishing Co., 1997), 180. It was not beyond the spiritual incapacity of the people to fulfill if they responded and did what David did and ask for help (Deuteronomy 30:11)! The problem was that mere external commandments could not enable anyone to obey, as Paul said, "for what the Law could not do, weak as it was through of the flesh" (Romans 8:3). There was some enablement in the Old Testament, the Spirit was "with them," but nothing in comparison with the New Covenant when the Spirit is "in you."

583 Bruce K. Waltke and Charles Yu, *An Old Testament Theology: An Exegetical, Canonical, and Thematic Approach*, 1st ed. (Grand Rapids: Zondervan Publishing House, 2007), 440.

> *For if you are living according to the flesh, you must die; but if by the Spirit you are putting to death the deeds of the body,* ***you will live*** *(Romans 8:13).*

Under the Old Covenant, one found "life" by means of faith-obedience to the Torah; under the New Covenant, one finds "life" by walking according to the Spirit. Although the method is the same (faith-obedience), Torah is no longer the guide, and the Holy Spirit has come to indwell and not just be "with" the believer.

The essence of Paul's response might be summarized this way, "Yes, it is true that Moses says one can obtain life (blessing in the land, sanctification) under the law; however, that goal was never fully achieved by Old Testament Israel." It awaited the outpouring of the Holy Spirit in the New Covenant for its fulfillment. That outpouring has happened at Pentecost. The Holy Spirit was "with" them in the Old Testament, enabling a partial fulfillment of the law, but the ultimate fulfillment of the Law awaited the time in which the Holy Spirit would be "in" them (John 14:16-17; Romans 8:3-4). As Paul explained earlier in Romans, "*If by the Spirit you are putting to death the deeds of the body, you will live*" (Romans 8:13).

As proof that this new way of living was prophetically anticipated and has finally arrived, Paul cites Deuteronomy 30:11-14 in Romans 10:6-8.

The Sanctifying Righteousness Based on Faith (Romans 10:6-8)

> *And* [Gr *de*] *the righteousness based on faith speaks as follows: "Do not say in your heart, 'Who will ascend into heaven?' (that is, to bring Christ down), or 'Who will descend into the abyss?' (that is, to bring Christ up from the dead)." But what does it say? "The word is near you, in your mouth and in your heart"—that is, the word of faith which we are preaching (Romans 10:6-8).*

But these verses (Romans 10:6-8) raise interpretive difficulties as well.[584] It will be helpful to note the context of Deuteronomy 30 as a key to unraveling some of the confusion. Moses began by predicting *when* Deuteronomy 30 will be fulfilled. He says that it will happen after the time of judgment: when they were banished to all nations (Deuteronomy 30:1-3); when you "*return to the Lord your God and obey him with all your heart and soul*" (v. 2); and "***then*** *the Lord will restore you from captivity and have compassion upon you and will gather you again from all the peoples where the Lord your God has scattered you*" (v. 3).[585]

---

584 According to Preston Sprinkle's reasoning, Paul has Moses saying one thing in Leviticus 18:5 and then contradicting himself in Deuteronomy 30:12-14. In the former, supposedly, Moses taught justification by works, but in the latter, he taught justification by faith alone, Sprinkle, *Law and Life*, 169-82.

585 Schreiner correctly observes that Paul begins his discussion of this passage by noting the future fulfillment of Deuteronomy 30:6: Israel will return to the Lord following exile, after He has circumcised their hearts and removed the hardness that has prevented them from keeping the Torah (30:6). It is likely that Paul would have seen this prophecy fulfilled with the coming of Christ. Yet, that generation of Jews rejected this fulfillment, and only those who believe in Christ now have their hearts circumcised so that they now keep the law (cf. Romans 2:26–29; Philippians 3:3; Colossians 2:11–12). Yet one day, "all Israel will saved," at the time when the "Deliverer will come from Zion" (Romans 11:26). Since Deuteronomy 29–30 itself locates the experience of God's blessing in the future, Paul's application of this text to the coming of Christ is defensible, see Schreiner, *Romans*, 557-58. Schreiner argues that the day of Israel's exile is over, and the fulfillment of Deuteronomy 30:6 is found in the first coming of Christ. Admittedly, one could draw that conclusion were it not for the fact that both Jesus and Paul declare the exile was not yet over and that complete fulfillment of these predictions had not yet occurred (e.g., Acts 1:6). Paul makes it plain in Romans 11:25-29 that he does not intend this citation of Deuteronomy 30:12-14 to mean what Schreiner says it means. Paul says there that

In this section Paul moves from a discussion of the nation in general to "you," individual believers. What applies to the nation applies to individuals within the nation as well. This is a dual reference: nation and individuals.

In Deuteronomy 30:6, Moses explains what kind of righteousness will occur to Israel in that future day.

> *The LORD your God will circumcise your hearts and the hearts of your descendants, so that you may love him with all your heart and with all your soul, and live (Deuteronomy 30:6, NIV84).*

In the clearest possible terms, *Moses speaks not only of regeneration, but of ethical behavior.* Of course, forensic righteousness is assumed in the passage he quotes, but Moses' focus is on ethical righteousness which emerges from it. This was Moses' predication of the New Covenant which is further elaborated in Jeremiah 31.

> *"The time is coming," declares the LORD, "when I* ***will make a new covenant*** *with the house of Israel and with the house of Judah. It will not be like the covenant I made with their forefathers when I took them by the hand to lead them out of Egypt, because they broke my covenant, though I was a husband to them," declares the LORD. "This is the covenant I will make with the house of Israel after that time," declares the LORD.* ***"I will put my law in their minds and write it on their hearts.*** *I will be their God, and they will be my people" (Jeremiah 31:31–33, NIV84).*

Similarly Ezekiel spoke of the future day when he prophesied,

> *I will give you a new heart and put a new spirit in you; I will remove from you your heart of stone and give you a heart of flesh. And I will put my Spirit in you and* ***move you to follow my decrees and be careful to keep my laws*** *(Ezekiel 36:26–27, NIV84).*

> *My servant David will be king over them, and they will all have one shepherd.* ***They will follow my laws and be careful to keep my decrees*** *(Ezekiel 37:24, NIV84).*

In these passages it is clear that a major focus of the New Covenant was behavior, and not only atonement. That being so, when we see the word "righteousness" (Gr *dikaiosunē*) in Romans 10:1-6, we should consider that Paul may have ethical character qualities in mind, as well as forensic justification. As argued above, the righteousness of God similarly refers to His character, not His gift.

Jesus announced the inauguration of this New Covenant in the Lord's Supper (Luke 22:20), and the anonymous homily to the Hebrews speaks of the New Covenant as already in force (Hebrews 8:8; 12:24).

What is the "righteousness based upon faith?" [Gr *hē ek pisteōs dikaiosunē, "the from faith righteousness"*]. The passage Paul quotes (Deuteronomy 30:11-14) clearly refers to ethical and not forensic righteousness. A similar phrase is found in only one other place in the New Testament (Hebrews 11:7) where we are told that *because of his good works*, Noah "*inherited the righteousness which is according to faith* [Gr *tēs kata pistin dikaiosunēs,*

---

the return from exile has not yet occurred; Israel has not yet been saved. Indeed, his prayer in 10:1 for their salvation/return from exile shows that he does not understand that the final fulfillment of Deuteronomy 30 has occurred. In order to square this citation by Paul with what he says elsewhere, one must assume that a partial fulfillment has occurred.

'the according to faith righteousness']." In the context of Hebrews, "righteousness" is ethical righteousness (not forensic justification) and faith is the walk of faith and not the initial transaction by which we are born again.[586] This suggests that like Romans 4:13, the righteousness based upon faith includes both justification, and also (if persevered in) sanctifying righteousness (see pp. 79 ff.). However, in contrast to the Law being the guide for sanctification which involved obedience to external rituals and laws, under the righteousness based on faith, the old way has ended and the believers now walk by the Spirit.

In accordance with the New Covenant he describes a time in which ethical righteousness would be based on faith alone and enabled by the Spirit, and not by pursuing an external standard.

Thus, when Paul continues in verse 6, "*But the righteousness based on faith,*" he is carrying the statement of Romans 10:5 one step further and speaking of the predicted future time in which the end of the Law system for sanctification would arrive. He is not setting Moses against Moses. He is not saying that Moses taught salvation by Law according to Romans 10:5 and then changed to salvation by faith in v. 6. Nor is he contrasting Moses in v. 5 with Paul in v. 6. He is contrasting the old way of sanctification (by Law) with the new way Moses predicted would one day be inaugurated.

In accordance with the New Covenant, he describes a time in which ethical righteousness would be based on faith alone and enabled by the Spirit, and not by pursuing an external standard.

With this background in mind, let us now read Romans 10:6-8 with new eyes.

> *But the righteousness based on faith speaks as follows: "Do not say in your heart, 'Who will ascend into heaven?' (that is, to bring Christ down), or 'Who will descend into the abyss?' (that is, to bring Christ up from the dead)." But what does it say? "The word is near you, in your mouth and in your heart"—that is,* ***the word of faith*** *which we are preaching (Romans 10:6–8).*

The "word of faith" which Paul was preaching was in some way consistent with what Moses taught. But what does saying in one's heart, "*Who will go up to heaven*?" have to do with this? Probably, ascending to heaven to bring Christ down reflects Jewish belief that Christ has not yet come. According to the "righteousness which is by faith," however, Christ has already come down from heaven. The ethical "righteousness which is by faith" is like the "*word of faith which we are preaching*" in regard to its accessibility.

The "word of faith" which Paul preaches is the whole way of faith, "from faith to faith: (Romans 1:17). It was from faith for justification (3:24) to faith for sanctification (10:6-8). But why would Paul cite a passage from Deuteronomy 30:11-14, which all interpreters agree speaks of ethical and not forensic righteousness, to prove that the "word of faith" he is preaching is consistent with what Moses taught?

All interpreters struggle with this problem. It is commonly recognized that the ethical righteousness to which Moses refers is not the "word of faith which" Paul preaches. In the context of Deuteronomy, the former refers to ethical righteousness but the "word of faith" which Paul preaches refers to the preaching of forensic righteousness.

---

[586] For discussion of Hebrews 11:7 see pp. 585 ff.

Perhaps Moo has the best solution when he says, "What is this point? That the message about the righteousness of faith, preached by Paul and the other apostles, is, *like the law of God, accessible and understandable*: 'the word is near you, in your mouth and in your heart.'"[587] Thus Paul is not saying that Deuteronomy 30 is teaching justification by faith, but it is teaching that just as sanctifying righteousness of the Old and New Covenant is readily assessable, so is Paul's doctrine of faith alone in Christ alone. One does not have to search through all the earth and heaven to obtain access to it. In other words, in respect to its easy accessibility, the "word of faith which we are preaching" is, as Moo says, ***like*** the ethical righteousness based on faith of Deuteronomy 30. It ***does not equal*** that righteousness, but it is ***like*** it in that both are "near." Citing Deuteronomy 30:14, Paul concludes,

> *But what does it say? "The word is near you, in your mouth and in your heart"—that is, the word of faith which we are preaching (Romans 10:8).*

The Old Testament Law was not near and was not in their heart. A future day was predicted when it would be near, written on the heart. The old way of sanctification would be replaced, and the old system *was* replaced! Baptism replaced circumcision (Galatians 2:3-5; 6:12-14); the Lord's Supper replaced the Passover (Matthew 26:26-29; 1 Corinthians 11:23-26). The annual Jewish festal calendar was no longer in force (Galatians 4:10; Colossians 2:16). All of the purity rules regarding ceremonial defilement, intended to enforce awareness that sin cuts one off from fellowship with God no longer applied (Mark 7:19; 1 Timothy 4:3-4). The Sabbath was no longer observed on Saturday but was moved to the Lord's Day, Sunday (Revelation 1:10). Christ is the end of the law in respect to righteousness! The new covenant, as prophesied by Jeremiah, will replace the outward imposition of the Law on a people of rebellious heart. Rather, under this new covenant, the Law of God will be in the hearts and minds of a forgiven people who, from least to greatest, will "know the Lord" (Jeremiah 31:33–34).[588]

The "word of faith" (v. 8) which Paul is preaching, refers to the phrase "from faith to faith," (Romans 1:17), faith for forensic righteousness and faith for sanctification and salvation from temporal judgment and trial. The predicted future day, in which ethical righteousness would be readily assessable to all by faith apart from Torah has arrived. Neither ethical righteousness (which Moses predicted) nor forensic justification (which Paul preached) required difficult searching or mediation through a priesthood and system involving external legalisms to obtain. Both were then and are now appropriated simply by faith. Under the new covenant one does not look externally to laws, commands, rituals, and liturgy to live for God, now that God's Spirit is readily available in our hearts. The old has been done away. Christ is the end of the law with respect to ethical righteousness.

The gospel that Paul preaches, like the sanctifying righteousness which is by faith ("*the righteousness which is by faith*") is a "word of faith," and it is near and in our hearts. Therefore, both ethical righteousness (which is by faith, v. 4) and forensic justification (by faith, v. 8) are now readily available, even though Jewish unbelief said they were not. The new covenant has been inaugurated.

---

[587] Moo, "Romans," 656.

[588] Barnett, *The Second Epistle to the Corinthians*, 176-77.

Summary

Salvation from the temporal consequences of sin is a common theme in both the Old and New Testaments. Paul prays for Israel's salvation in Romans 10:1. In view of the passages he cites in Romans 9 about this salvation, it is clear that he has national Israel's salvation from a temporal catastrophe in view, that is, the coming Roman invasion of AD 70.

The reason they need this messianic salvation is because they have rejected the Stone, their Messiah, and pursued their own plan for experientially obtaining God's promises to Abraham. Instead of submitting to God's plan to bless the world through Israel ("the righteousness of God"), they turned the plan inward and changed it to a plan to bless Israel only. They rejected the Stone. As a result, they did not obtain the ethical righteousness based on faithfulness; they did not repent, and they faced a national catastrophe.

Because his opponents denied that Christ was the end of the law (v. 4), Paul cites two passages from the Law to show that the word of faith which he was preaching was consistent with and anticipated by the teaching of Moses in the Torah. First, Leviticus 18:5 prescribed the Old Testament means of obtaining sanctification. This passage is alluded to in Deuteronomy 30:6, where Moses anticipates a future day in which God will circumcise the hearts of his people "so that you may live." However, this system was external and burdensome and was only a guardian and tutor until the new way, the sanctifying righteousness by faith promised in the New Covenant, should arrive.[589]

Paul then cites a second passage (Deuteronomy 30:11-14) against his opponents. These verses make two points. First, they show that sanctification would one day be by faith alone enabled by the Spirit and apart from Law. Secondly, they show that the "word of faith" Paul is preaching (forensic justification) is likewise based upon faith and not Law and is readily available by faith alone. Since Christ has already come down from above, has died, and has been raised from the dead, nothing remains for anyone to do to obtain the justifying righteousness based on faith. Indeed, like the sanctifying righteousness of the New Covenant it is near and readily available, "in your heart and in your mouth" so that "you may observe it."

Excursus on the Righteousness of God

The term "the righteousness of God" is used by the biblical writers in three different ways.[590] First, it refers to God's character in general. The word righteousness (Gr *dikaiosunē*) means "conformity with a norm." For example, in Acts 17:31, we are told

[589] According to Ball, "The Mosaic Law is a guardian appointed to protect the infancy of the nation, and to train it for the period when, in the fullness of time, it should enter upon the inheritance." For a good discussion of the background of the "tutor" in Roman households, see W. E. Ball, *St. Paul and Roman Law and Other Studies on the Origin and Form of Doctrine* (Edinburgh: T&T Clark, 1901), 31-32.

[590] It seems to me that both John Piper and N. T. Wright miss this obvious point. They both want the phrase "the righteousness of God" to mean the same thing in every instance in the New Testament. For Piper it always means the imputed righteousness of Christ (2 Corinthians 5:21), and for Wright it always means "God's faithfulness to his promise to Abraham to bless the world through Abraham and his descendants." Why? It is obvious that the phrase can mean different things depending upon the context in which it is used. See John Piper, *The Future of Justification: A Response to N. T. Wright* (Wheaton, IL: Crossway Books, 2007), 62-63. See also Wright's rather strained attempt to make 2 Corinthians 5:21 (an obvious reference to imputed righteousness) fit into his covenant faithfulness theory, N. T. Wright, *Justification: God's Plan and Paul's Vision* (Downers Grove, IL: InterVarsity, 2009), 158-67.

that when He returns, Jesus will "judge the world in righteousness," that is, in conformity to the norm of divine standards. At that time the King will wage war "in righteousness" (Revelation 19:11), in conformity to the divine standards or norms. Throughout the Gospels, "righteousness" frequently refers to conformity to a norm, the ethical standards of the kingdom teaching.[591] Often the Bible refers to God's righteousness in the sense of His conformity to the norms of virtue, justice, integrity, love, and faithfulness.

Secondly, it can refer to a righteousness from (source) God (Philippians 3:9), a righteousness received by the believer. This is what theologians often call forensic justification. When this concept dawned upon him, Luther's burdens were lifted and he testifies that he was born again.[592] This is what Paul refers to when he says, "*He made Him who knew no sin to be sin on our behalf, so that we might become the righteousness of God in Him*" (2 Corinthians 5:21). The righteousness of God is imputed to the believer, granting him a perfect standing before the throne of justice.[593]

Thirdly, God's righteousness is commonly understood as His faithfulness to His covenant promises to Abraham. What the prophets anticipated has taken place in Christ: God has intervened in human history to establish His salvation.[594] Taylor refers to the righteousness of God as "his saving faithfulness promised through the law and prophets."[595]

The idea that the righteousness of God refers to His faithfulness to His plan and His promise to bless the world through Israel based upon His covenant with Abraham is found in a number of passages.

For example, in Psalm 31:1, we read, "*In You, O Lord, I have taken refuge; let me never be ashamed; in Your righteousness deliver me*" (Psalm 31:1). David pleads for deliverance

---

591 See Matthew 3:15; 5:6, 20; 6:33; Luke 1:75; John 16:8; 1 Peter 2:24; Hebrews 1:9. In James 1:20, it clearly means "right conduct" in conformity to the norms of God's righteousness.

592 Luther says, "The words 'righteous' and 'righteousness of God' struck my conscience like lightning. When I heard them I was exceedingly terrified. If God is righteous [I thought], he must punish. But when by God's grace I pondered, in the tower and heated room of this building, over the words, 'He who through faith is righteous shall live' [Romans 1:17] and 'the righteousness of God' [Romans 3:21], I soon came to the conclusion that if we, as righteous men, ought to live from faith and if the righteousness of God contributes to the salvation of all who believe, then salvation won't be our merit but God's mercy. My spirit was thereby cheered. For it's by the righteousness of God that we're justified and saved through Christ. These words [which had before terrified me] now became more pleasing to me. The Holy Spirit unveiled the Scriptures for me in this tower." Martin Luther, "Table Talk: No. 3232c: Description of Luther's 'Tower Experience' Between June 9 and July 21, 1532," in *Luther's Works*, ed. J. J. Pelikan, H. C. Oswald, and H. T. Lehman (Philadelphia: Fortress Press, 1999), 54:193. He says, "At last, by the mercy of God, meditating day and night, I gave heed to the context of the words, namely, 'In it the righteousness of God is revealed, as it is written, 'He who through faith is righteous shall live.' There I began to understand that the righteousness of God is that by which the righteous lives by a gift of God, namely by faith. And this is the meaning: the righteousness of God is revealed by the gospel, namely, the passive righteousness with which merciful God justifies us by faith, as it is written, 'He who through faith is righteous will enter paradise itself through open gates.'" Martin Luther, "Career of the Reformer IV," in *Luther's Works*, ed. H. C. Pelikan (Philadelphia: Fortresss Press, 1999), 34:337.

593 N. T. Wright argues that it is doubtful that "the righteousness of God" in Romans 1:17, the verse which God used to cause Luther to be born again, refers to God's gift. He says, "Luther's alternative, however fruitful in opening new worlds of theology to him, was in some ways equally misleading, for it directed attention away from the biblical notion of God's covenant faithfulness and instead placed greater emphasis upon the status of the human being." N. T. Wright, "Righteousness," in *New Dictionary of Theology*, ed. Sinclair B. Ferguson and J. I. Packer (Downers Grove, IL: InterVarsity Press, 2000), 592.

594 Moo, "Romans," s.v. "Justification".

595 S. S. Taylor, "Faith, Faithfulness," ibid. (InterVarsity), s.v. "The Faithfulness of Christ".

on the basis of God's righteousness, His faithfulness to His promises to sustain and bless the descendants of Abraham. Craigie says that the phrase "recalls God's character as one committed to his people in covenant. And the covenant commitment included a commitment to deliver from distress,"[596] and because of God's faithfulness to His covenant, God "has promised to take care of him."[597]

For another example, consider Daniel's prayer.[598]

> *Alas, O Lord, the great and awesome God, who keeps His covenant and loving kindness for those who love Him and keep His commandments (Daniel 9:4).*

God is a God who "keeps his covenant." A few verses later Daniel prays,

> *Righteousness belongs to You, O Lord, but to us open shame, as it is this day (Daniel 9:7).*

God's righteousness is His faithfulness to keep His covenant.

Because Yahweh is faithful to His covenant promises, that is, He is righteous to keep His word, Daniel pleads,

> *O Lord, in accordance with all Your righteous acts, let now Your anger and Your wrath turn away from Your city Jerusalem (Daniel 9:16).*

The nation was under a curse, occupied by Babylonian armies and enslaved in Babylon. The prophet pleads that in accordance with His righteousness, His covenant faithfulness, God will lift the curse and deliver the nation. He was asking God to act in fulfillment of His promises to the nation that were first made to Abraham.

Recall Yahweh's assurances to David,

> *My covenant I will not violate, nor will I alter the utterance of My lips. Once I have sworn by My holiness; I will not lie to David. His descendants shall endure forever, and his throne as the sun before Me. It shall be established forever like the moon, And the witness in the sky is faithful [Selah] (Psalm 89:34–37).*

The throne of David will one day be the center of God's rule over the earth. It was through Israel that God's faithfulness to His promises will be fulfilled. God's plan since the call of Abraham has been to bless the world through Israel.

In the midst of the current national crisis David pleads,

> *Where are Thy former **lovingkindnesses**, O Lord, Which Thou didst swear to David in Thy **faithfulness**? (Psalm 89:49).*

The psalmist equated God's faithfulness with His righteousness and the messianic salvation,

> *I have not hidden Thy **righteousness** within my heart; I have spoken of Thy **faithfulness** and Thy **salvation** (Psalm 40:10).*

---

596 P. C. Craigie, *Psalms 1-50*, Word Biblical Commentary (Dallas: Word, 2002), 260.

597 Willem VanGemeren, *New International Dictionary of Old Testament Theology and Exegesis*, 5 vols. (Grand Rapids: Zondervan Publishing House, 1997), 263. See also, Wright, *The New Testament and the People of God*, 271-72.

598 The following discussion of God's righteousness follows Wright, *Justification: God's Plan and Paul's Vision*, 62-71.

God's righteousness in this passage is equated with His faithfulness. The ideas are closely related in Old Testament thinking.

Traditionally, Protestantism has incorrectly argued (in my view) that the "righteousness of God" often refers only to forensic imputation, God's gift. However, we have shown above that in some places it can refer to His faithfulness to His covenant promises to bless the world through Israel in faithfulness to His promises to Abraham. Whether it refers to substitution of faith for obedience (God's gift), that is, justification, or to God's character, must always be determined by the context in which the phrase is used.

In Philippians 3:9, Paul speaks of a righteousness which "comes from God." This is the gift of forensic justification. However, Romans 10:3 speaks of the righteousness "of God" which refers to His character, specifically His covenant faithfulness.

There are two contextual factors in Romans 9-11 which point to the fact that the righteousness of God in Romans 10:3 refers to His character—specifically, God's fidelity to divine standards which He set up, His promises to Abraham to bless the world through Israel (Genesis 15:1-4).

What are those factors? First, the context of Romans 9-11 is about Israel's failure to accomplish God's plan through them and God's faithfulness to achieve His purposes in spite of their failure. As a nation they are in need of salvation by God (Romans 10:1). It was God's plan to bless the nations and save the world through them. To them, belonged the adoption, the glory, the covenants, the Law and the giving of the temple service (Romans 9:3); yet they rejected the Stone, their Messiah. Paul asks, "Does this mean that God's plan to bless the world through this nation failed?" Not at all! "*But it is not as though the word of God has failed. For they are not all Israel who are descended from Israel*" (Romans 9:6). Because of this, the nation has been temporarily cut off from the "vine" of the Abrahamic promise into which the church has been grafted (Romans 11:17). Yet one day, God's righteousness, that is, His faithfulness to His covenant promises, guarantees that the Abrahamic covenant will be fulfilled (Romans 11:26-27).

In other words, God's righteousness in this context refers to faithfulness to His plan to bless the world through Israel and her Messiah.[599] God's faithfulness will not fail. One day, God will fulfill His plan to bless the entire world through Israel (Romans 11:24-31) because "*from the standpoint of God's choice they are beloved for the sake of the fathers; for the gifts and the calling of God are irrevocable*" (Romans 11:28–29).

The Old Testament contexts from which Paul cites passages to prove his thesis are a second contextual factor establishing that the righteousness of God refers to God's irrevocable faithfulness to His covenant promises to bless the world through Israel. Romans 10:1-13 has repeated allusions to the Abrahamic Covenant in Genesis 15 and references to the covenantal focus in Deuteronomy 27-30.[600]

---

599 If, as some believe, the citation from Habakkuk 2:4 in Romans 1:17 is best rendered, "the righteous shall live by God's faithfulness," the phrase "the righteousness of God" in the same verse would most likely refer to God's faithfulness. For example, Beale says, "The 'faithfulness' of which Habakkuk writes is the faithfulness of the Lord to fulfill the promise of salvation given in the 'vision' (3:1–15)." G. K. Beale and D. A. Carson, *Commentary on the New Testament Use of the Old Testament* (Grand Rapids: Baker Academic, 2007), 610.

600 See discussion below on Genesis 15:6; Leviticus 18:5; Deuteronomy 30:6, 11-20.

Excursus on the Hypothetical View

The most common view of Romans 10:5 is that Paul speaks hypothetically. "Life" (i.e., heaven when one dies, forensic justification), according to the hypothetical view, could hypothetically be obtained by works if one could perform them perfectly. This interpretation of Romans 10:5 suggests that Paul cites Leviticus 18:5 to show that, hypothetically, if one could obey the Law perfectly, he could obtain eternal life.[601] This, as Paul declares elsewhere, is impossible (Romans 3:10). According to the hypothetical interpretation, Paul makes it clear in Galatians 3:21 that "*if a law had been given that could impart life, then righteousness would certainly have come by the law*" (NIV). Since Romans 10:5 says life *can* be obtained by the Law, some argue that Romans 10:5 must be speaking hypothetically,[602] or else it contradicts Galatians 3:21.[603] Admittedly, this is plausible and fits well with Paul's arguments.[604] This is the traditional Reformed view.

A problem with this is that it implies that Moses and Paul are using "life" in two different senses. As an Apostle, he *can* do that. There are other places in the New Testament where an Old Testament phrase or word is indeed used in a different sense by a New Testament writer. My view is that one should not entertain that a different sense is intended unless the New Testament context requires it. Romans 10 does not. For Moses, "life" refers to abundant life in the land. How then Paul could cite this verse to show that heaven (i.e., "life") could hypothetically be obtained by perfect obedience. His Jewish opponents would laugh at such exegesis!

---

601 For example, Robert H. Mounce says, "The problem lies in the fact that no one is able to live up to the requirements of the law. Although law points us in the right direction, it provides no power to achieve its demands." R. H. Mounce, *Romans*, The New American Commentary (Nashville: Broadman & Holman, 1995), 208. Moo says that this means that the one who attempts to establish a relationship with God by the Law is seeking relationship by "doing," but he is unable to keep the Law adequately as Paul has shown in Romans 1:18-3:20. Moo, *The Epistle to the Romans*, 649. However, Romans 1:18-3:20 is speaking about entering into a relationship with God (gaining life), but the Law refers to maintaining a relationship (living life). Apparently Moo is confusing justification and sanctification. Jamieson agrees, "This is the one way of justification and life—by 'the righteousness which is of (or, by our own obedience to) the law.'" Robert Jamieson, A. R. Fausset, and David Brown, *A Bible Commentary: Critical, Practical and Explanatory* (Oak Harbor, WA: Logos Research Systems), s.v. "Romans 10:5". See also Calvin; Hodge; Haldane; Alford; and Stephen Westerholm, *Israel's Law and the Church's Faith* (Grand Rapids: Wm. B. Eerdmans Publishing Co., 1988), 134-35.

602 Schreiner explains the hypothetical offer this way: "The one who keeps the commands of the Mosaic Law will experience eternal life (v. 5). This is the righteousness demanded by the law. But the verse implies that no one keeps the law, and thus righteousness cannot be attained via the law."Schreiner, *Romans*, 549. See also Robert Haldane, *Exposition of the Epistle to the Romans* (Marshallton, DL: The National Foundation for Christian Education, 1970), 512. Haldane expresses it this way, "To live by the law requires, as Moses had declared, that the law be perfectly obeyed. But this tó fallen man is impossible," ibid., 504.

603 For example, Timothy George says, "In connection with v. 10 [Galatians 3:10] this statement can be understood as a hypothetical contrary-to-fact condition: if someone really were to fulfill the entire corpus of Pentateuchal law, with its 242 positive commands and 365 prohibitions (according to one rabbinic reckoning), then indeed such a person could stand before God at the bar of judgment and demand admittance to heaven on the basis of his or her performance. Yet, where on earth can such a flawless person be found?" George, *Galatians*, 235.

604 This interpretation is advocated by Haldane, "To live by the law requires, as Moses had declared, that the law be perfectly obeyed. But this to fallen man is impossible. The law knows no mercy; it knows no mitigation; it overlooks not even the smallest breach, or the smallest deficiency. One guilty thought or desire would condemn forever. Whoever, then, looks for life by the law, must keep the whole law in thought, word, and deed, and not be chargeable with the smallest transgression." Haldane, *Exposition of the Epistle to the Romans*, s.v. "Romans 10:5".

Moo concurs with the hypothetical view, but with a more nuanced interpretation. He agrees that Paul is speaking hypothetically, but he insists that Paul could not be quoting Moses to mean something other than what Moses meant in Leviticus 18:5. Life for Israel, he correctly says, means a "prolonging her enjoyment of the blessings of God in the promised land," not regeneration or heaven.[605] He suggests, however, that Paul is quoting Leviticus 18:5 to "summarize what for him is the essence of law: blessing is contingent on obedience."[606] So, according to Moo, there is no contradiction between Paul and Moses, or Moses and Moses (in Deuteronomy 30:12-14). Paul is simply extracting the concept of "doing" from Moses' words to stress the essence of Law and is not suggesting that the verse applies to obtaining eternal life.[607]

However, Moses would be surprised to learn that the essence of the Law was that blessing was contingent *only* on obedience and that basically the Law was a matter of doing. For Moses the essence of the Law was obedience *by faith*, just as it is today under grace. "*By faith Moses ... refused to be called the son of Pharaoh's daughter*" (Hebrews 11:24), and "*by faith he left Egypt*" (v. 27). The essence of the Law for Moses was not obedience abstracted from reliance on God in order to secure blessing. Instead, it was faith-obedience to secure blessing and that, according to Hebrews 11, is the way it has always been. Obviously, Moo sees no difficulty with the notion that one can extract a phrase out of Moses' words and then use that phrase to teach something with which Moses would disagree.

The hypothetical interpretation involves a hidden premise.

MAJOR PREMISE: If you obey the commandments, you will go to heaven ("live").
MINOR (HIDDEN) PREMISE: You must obey them perfectly, and no one can.
CONCLUSION: No one will go to heaven by obeying commandments.

However, there are decisive reasons for rejecting this view.[608] First, "life" in Leviticus, 18:5, as mentioned above, refers to a blessed life in the land which comes from the pursuit of the Law by faith. Virtually all commentators agree on this.[609] This passage raises the

---

605 Moo, *The Epistle to the Romans*, 647.

606 Ibid., 648.

607 Calvin seems to have adopted a similar view: "But because he had to dispute with perverse teachers, who pretended that men merited justification by the works of the Law, he was sometimes obliged, in refuting their error, to speak of the Law in a more restricted sense, merely as law, though, in other respects, the covenant of free adoption is comprehended under it." Calvin, "Institutes," 2.7.2.

608 Wakefield objects that it interprets the Old Testament in a way that places Leviticus 18:5 in direct contradiction to Deuteronomy 30:12-14. Paul is then quoting Deuteronomy to counter the meaning of Leviticus. Andrew H. Wakefield asks, "Is it possible that Paul might consider one portion of Scripture to be valid, while another is not?" Andrew H. Wakefield, *Where to Live: The Hermeneutical Significance of Paul's Citations from Scripture in Galatians 3:1-14* (Atlanta: Society of Biblical Literature, 2003), 83. Second, it interprets Leviticus 18:5 in a way that differs from its meaning in its original context. The difficulty is that in the context of Leviticus 18, the promise of "life" relates not to eternal life in the sense of regeneration or "heaven when I die." Instead, it refers to a rich life now, life within the covenant. The promise of life refers to behavior, not soteriology; to living life, not gaining it. There seems to be little dispute about this. Moo says, "In its context, Leviticus 18:5 summons Israel to obedience to the commandments of the Lord as a means of prolonging her enjoyment of the blessings of God in the promised Land."

609 John Murray acknowledges, "In the original setting it [Leviticus 18:5], does not appear to have any reference to legal righteousness." John Murray, *The Epistle to the Romans* (Grand Rapids: Wm. B. Eerdmans Publishing Co., 1965), 51. As expected, advocates of the New Perspective also agree that "life" in Lev 18:5 refers to life

problem regarding how the New Testament writers made use of Old Testament citations. Experimental Predestinarians take a much more lenient view of the requirement that the starting point should be the intended meaning of the Old Testament writer. Viewing these texts, like Leviticus 18:5, in this manner allows Tremper Longman to say the intended meaning is not the "complete" meaning.[610] In our view, however, this criterion allows Experimentalists to regard the intended meaning rather loosely, and it often amounts to saying the New Testament writers changed the meaning of the Old Testament writer and not just "completed" it.[611] We believe that Howard is correct when he says, "No modern interpretation of Paul should be used as evidence that he understood it in a way other than the original context implied."[612]

Second, it is difficult to see anything in the contexts of Romans 10 or Leviticus 18:5 that suggest this hypothetical offer. There is no inference that the Jews were unable to do this. In fact Moses says precisely the opposite. According to him, the Old Testament believer *can* do it.

> *See, I have taught you statutes and judgments just as the Lord my God commanded me,* ***that you should do*** *... For this commandment which I command you today* ***is not too difficult for you****, nor is it out of reach (Deuteronomy 4:5; 30:11, NASB95).*

---

within the covenant and not eschatological life. See Dunn, *Romans 9-16*, 601. See also Don Garlington, *An Exposition of Galatians: A New Perspective/Reformational Reading*, 2nd ed. (Eugene, OR: Wipf and Stock Publishers, 2004), 163. "Life," according to F. Duane Lindsay, signifies that "obedience to God's laws produces in His people happy and fulfilled lives (cf. 26:3-13; Deut. 28:1-14)." F. Duane Lindsay, "Leviticus," in *BKC*, ed. John F. Walvoord and Roy B. Zuck (Colorado Springs: Cook, 1996), 1:200. The *New Bible Commentary* says, "To live in the fullest sense meant the full enjoyment of the blessings and well-being of the covenant relationship with God which was already established by his redeeming action. Such life came through obedience to the law of the God, which was the response to salvation; it did not achieve or earn it," *The New American Bible Commentary: 21st Century Edition*, ed. D. A. Carson, 3rd ed. (Downers Grove, IL: InterVarsity Press, 1994), s.v. "Lev 18:5". M. F. Rooker says, "Proper response to these laws and the other legislations handed down to the Israelites holds the promise of providing an abundant life (18:5) ... The phrase 'the man who obeys them will live by them' should thus be viewed as promising a meaningful, secure life for those who are faithful to God and who exhibit their faithfulness by obedience to the Law." M. F. Rooker, *Leviticus*, The New American Commentary (Nashville: Broadman and Holman, 2000), 240. Wenham is correct, "What is envisaged is a happy life in which a man enjoys God's bounty of health, children, friends, and prosperity. Keeping the law is the path to divine blessing, to a happy and fulfilled life in the present (Leviticus 26:3–13; Deuteronomy 28:1–14)." Gordon J. Wenham, *The Book of Leviticus*, New International Commentary on the Old Testament (Grand Rapids: Wm. B. Eerdmans Publishing Co., 1979), 253. Even Moo, who adopts a hypothetical view admits, "The verse [Leviticus 18:5] is not speaking about the attainment of eternal life; and Paul clearly does not believe that the Old Testament teaches that righteousness is based upon the law (see Romans 5)." Moo, *The Epistle to the Romans*, 648.

610 Tremper Longman III, "What I Mean by Historical-Grammatical Exegesis—Why I Am Not a Literalist," *Grace Theological Journal Volume* 11, no. 2 (Fall 1990). Longman gives a capable defense of this Reformed amillennial method of handling his issue.

611 For a compelling defense of the premillennial understanding of this issue see S. Lewis Johnson, *The Old Testament in the New* (Grand Rapids: Zondervan Publishing House, 1980). See also, Elliott E. Johnson, "What I Mean by Historical-Grammatical Interpretation and How That Differs from Spiritual Interpretation," *Grace Theological Journal Volume* 11, no. 2 (Fall 1990).

612 Howard, "Christ The End of the Law: The Meaning of Romans 10:4 ff.," 334. Calvin agrees, "We must always have a regard to the end for which they quote passages, for they are very careful as to the main object, ***so as not to turn Scripture to another meaning***; but as to words and other things, which bear not on the subject in hand, they use great freedom." John Calvin, Calvin's Commentaries: Hebrews (Albany, OR: Ages Software, 1998), s.v. "Hebrews 10:6" (emphasis added).

Third, the hypothetical view incorrectly assumes that righteousness by the Law is possible only if one lives without sin. However, there are reasons to believe that Paul did not understand Leviticus 18:5 in this manner. To keep the Law or to "do it" involved doing all of it. This included the sacrifices whereby one could offer atonement for sin. Law-keeping obviously, then, did not mean perfection of life.

Fourth, the hypothetical view of Leviticus 18:5 pits Moses against Moses with Leviticus 18:5 promising eternal life in return for works, and Deuteronomy 30:11-14 and Genesis 15:6 promising eternal life in return for faith. Paul then would be pitting the Old Testament against itself by citing Deuteronomy 30:12–14 to counter the meaning of Leviticus 18:5. This would mean that Moses, and consequently God (who revealed the Law to Moses), contradicted himself. According to this view, in Romans 10:5 God promises eternal life for "doing," but in verses 6-8 He says that eternal life comes on the basis of faith alone.

Fifth, and more seriously, the hypothetical view involves God in a deception. "Would God lead the Jews to believe that hypothetically they could obtain life in the sense of going to heaven, knowing they could not?" This, many have argued, is an indefensible position for it suggests that Paul here "gets involved in the cynicism that God explicitly provides men with a law 'unto life' while knowing from the start that this instrument will not work."[613]

Wakefield objects, "According to this view, God essentially holds out what amounts to a false promise. Even if Leviticus 18:5 is true in theory [i.e., if one could obey the Law one could become regenerate] it is false in practice—and worse yet, that precise combination, the fact that God offers a promise which He must certainly know can never be actualized, makes the promise seem not just false, but deceptive, the perpetration of a divine fraud."[614]

613 H. Raisanen, *Paul and the Law* (Philadelphia: Fortress Press, 1986), 265. Quoted by Westerholm, *Israel's Law and the Church's Faith*, 101.

614 Wakefield, *Where to Live: The Hermeneutical Significance of Paul's Citations from Scripture in Galatians 3:1-14*, 81.

14

Confessing Jesus as Lord

DURING THE Roman persecution of the Christian church in the early centuries, the Romans attempted to force believing Christians to confess Caesar, not Jesus, as Lord. A common method of doing this was to bring a person before the magistrate. The magistrate would then say,

"In order to secure the unity and peace of the empire it is necessary that all Roman citizens confess Caesar as Lord."

"You understand this?"

The Christian would then respond,

"Yes."

"You claim to be a Christian and you therefore refuse to confess Caesar as Lord. Is that correct?"

Once again, "Yes."

Then the magistrate would bring the man's wife and children into the court and stand them in front of him.

"Is this your wife and are these your children?"

With great fear and emotion, the Christian husband would say, "Yes."

Then the magistrate would continue.

"If you are not willing to confess Caesar as Lord and deny Christ, we will slay your wife and children right now before your eyes."

"Let me ask you again, will you confess Caesar as Lord?"

This scene was frequently repeated throughout the Roman Empire. For those who believe that it is necessary to publicly confess Christ as Lord if one wants to go to heaven when one dies, I would ask, "If you were confronted with this very real situation, what would you do?"

I hope I could say that if it was only my life alone that was on the line, I would deny Caesar and publicly confess Christ. However, to be brutally honest, I am not so sure what I would say if confronted with this situation which faced believing people in the early centuries. Are we seriously going to say that a man who hesitates and then cannot confess Christ publicly in this situation is consigned to an eternity of eternal separation from God?

Evangelistic campaigns have often used Romans 10:9-10 as a basis for calling people down front in response to several refrains of "Just as I Am" or "Amazing Grace," and asking them to make a public confession of Christ. Why? The verse clearly says that unless one makes a verbal confession of Christ, he will not be saved, that is, in their view, go to heaven when he dies. The problem this creates is that it requires that in order to secure final entrance into heaven an additional work must be added to the Reformation credo, *Sola Fide*, "faith alone."

Confessing Jesus as Lord (Romans 10:9-10)

> *If you confess with your mouth Jesus as Lord, and believe in your heart that God raised Him from the dead, you will be saved; for with the heart a person believes, resulting in righteousness, and with the mouth he confesses, resulting in salvation (Romans 10:9–10).*

A striking thing about these verses is that two things are necessary for "salvation:" (1) confessing the Lord Jesus, and (2) believing in one's heart that God has raised Him from the dead (v. 9). Yet only one thing is necessary for justifying righteousness (which guarantees our entrance into heaven), believing with the heart (v. 10a). The former is external, public, and physical, and the latter is internal, private, and spiritual.

Since salvation in the immediately preceding context refers to deliverance from sin's *temporal* consequences, this should be one's starting point in understanding "*that if you confess with your mouth Jesus as Lord, and believe in your heart that God raised Him from the dead, you will be saved* [delivered from God's temporal wrath]."

In verses 5-15, Paul is discussing the salvation of individuals, not the nation. In fact, verse 4 is directly continued in verse 16 and following. The intervening verses are an aside in which he deals with Israel's distortion of the Law into a system of works righteousness for individuals.

Even though he now speaks of how to find justification before God, it is clear that he draws a distinction between justification and salvation! Confession with the mouth, Paul says, leads to deliverance (salvation), but believing in the heart leads to justification. Thus, deliverance and justification in this context appear to be different things.

If confession of Jesus as Lord means to acknowledge Christ's Lordship publicly as a condition for escaping final separation from God, as some maintain,[615] then it is the only place in the New Testament where any condition in addition to faith is added for personal salvation (escape from the lake of fire).

To confess Jesus as Lord with the "mouth" means to publicly call upon Him as Lord and ask Him for divine assistance. Since there is no "the" or "as" in the Greek text, one might translate, "*Confess, Lord Jesus*," that is, it is a call for help! While one might assume that this call for divine assistance includes a "profession of allegiance"[616] (Gr *homologeō*) and a public admission of Jesus "as" (NASB) God, fundamentally, it is a cry for help in time of need (see v. 13 and discussion below). This was very significant in the first century because the Romans required one to acknowledge that Nero was Lord/God. If one was to be saved, he must be willing to publicly identify with Jesus, not Caesar. Only in this way can a believer find "salvation," but salvation from what?[617]

---

615 A typical example is James R. Edwards' statement, "The righteousness of faith consists of belief and confession. Belief means active trust in God's goodness to us in Jesus Christ, as opposed to mere intellectual assent to a propositional truth. And confession means a deliberate and public witness to that belief." James R. Edwards, *Romans*, New International Biblical Commentary (Peabody, MA: Hendrickson Publishers, 1992), 255.

616 BDAG, 708.

617 For a thorough discussion of this passage which considers all of the various Reformed options, see Fred Chay and John P. Correia, *The Faith That Saves: The Nature of Faith in the New Testament* (Haysville, NC: Schoettle

Paul makes it plain that belief in Christ results in righteousness (i.e., justification). However, confession with the mouth results in "salvation." While Canfield states that "it is clear that no substantial distinction is intended between *dikaiosunē* [righteousness] and *sōtēria* [salvation], both referring to eschatological salvation,[618] Alford does not think this is "clear." He says, "Clearly the words [righteousness] and [salvation] are not used here for the same thing."[619] Godet agrees, "There is in his [Paul's] eyes a real distinction to be made between *being justified* and *being saved*."[620]

Just as individuals can be saved from temporal expressions of God's wrath by believing and confessing Christ, so can the Jewish nation. Paul is establishing the point that for the nation to be saved from coming temporal judgment, they must do what individuals must do, believe and confess and then call upon the name of the Lord for help. While the context of these verses refer to the salvation of individuals, the primary focus of chapters 9-11 is not about the salvation of individual Jews, rather it is about the *salvation of the nation from God's temporal judgment*. That the nation is very central in his thinking is evident from the following context and is the subject of all of Romans 11.[621]

If Israel is to escape national catastrophe and experience national salvation they must first repent and be saved as individuals and possess forensic righteousness. However, they must possess ethical righteousness as well. John the Baptist addressed the nation saying,

> *Repent, for the kingdom of heaven is at hand (Matthew 3:2).*

And, then he exhorted the Pharisees and Sadducees,

> *Bear fruit in keeping with repentance (Matthew 3:8).*

Only by repenting and then believing in Christ for personal salvation and bearing fruit (ethical righteousness) can Israel escape the looming Roman invasion of AD 70.

Publishing Co., 2008), 101-10. See also Hart, "Why Confess Christ: The Use and Abuse of Romans 10:9-10," 3-35.

618 Cranfield, *A Critical and Exegetical Commentary on the Epistle to the Romans*, 531.

619 Henry Alford and Everett Falconer Harrison, "Matthew," in *The Greek Testament: with a Critically Revised Text, a Digest of Various Readings, Marginal References to Verbal and Idiomatic Usage, Prolegomena, and a Critical and Exegetical Commentary* (Chicago: Moody Press, 1958), 2:240.

620 Godet adds, "Salvation includes ... sanctification and glory. Hence it is that while the former depends only on faith, the latter implies persevering fidelity in the profession of the faith, even to death and to glory." Godet, *Commentary on Romans*, 209. In other words contrary to the thesis of this book, one must persevere in good works to the end of life in order to be saved.

621 What about the possibility that the one who believes in Christ will necessarily confess Him as Lord? Reformed doctrine argues that salvation refers to deliverance from eternal damnation and because all who truly believe, also confess, it is perfectly proper in their view to view confession as a "condition" of salvation in the sense that this is a *necessary evidence* that always follows from genuine faith. For example, Leon Morris says, "But Paul does not contemplate an inner state that is not reflected in outward conduct. If anyone really believes he will confess Christ, so it is natural to link the two." Morris, *The Epistle to the Romans*, 384. However, this is an insertion of one's theological bias into the text. It is not inevitable that a man who believes in Christ will also confess Him as Lord. John illustrates this in John 12:42-43. "Nevertheless many even of the rulers believed in Him, but because of the Pharisees they were not confessing Him, for fear that they would be put out of the synagogue; for they loved the approval of men rather than the approval of God." On the authority of Christ who declared that anyone who believes on Him will have eternal life (John 3:14-16), we can say that these particular Pharisees were born again. However, they will not be "saved" from any temporal difficulties; they will obtain no divine aid in time of trial.

Calling on the Name of the Lord (Romans 10:11-13)

> *For the Scripture says, "Whoever believes in Him SHALL not be ASHAMED." For there is no distinction between Jew and Greek; for the same Lord is Lord of all, abounding in riches for all who call on Him; for "Whoever will call* (Gr *epikaleō*) *on the name of the Lord will be saved" (Romans 10:11–13, author's translation).*

The phrases "call upon the name of the Lord" (v. 13) and "confess" Lord Jesus (v. 9) complement each other. Both are required for "salvation."

What does it mean to "call on the name of the *Lord*" (Romans 10:13)? Is this an exercise of faith for personal salvation, as some contend? Probably not. Throughout the Old Testament in general and certainly in Joel 2:32 in particular, to call "on the name of the Lord" meant to ask Him for assistance, to depend on Him,[622] or to worship Him.

For example, when the believing Abraham built an altar to the Lord, we are told that "*he called upon the name of the Lord*" (Genesis 12:8). That is, he worshiped. He did not call upon Him to receive personal salvation. Later, his son Isaac did the same (Genesis 26:5).

When Moses ascended Sinai, he "called upon the name of the Lord" (Exodus 34:5). He was not calling upon Him for personal salvation from damnation. Moses was already saved in that sense. He was calling upon Him in worship.

Those who trust in Yahweh, who are saved, are described in Scripture as those who "call upon the Lord." It was not their initial act of believing in Yahweh for personal salvation that identified them, but the fact that they are characterized as people who depend upon the Lord for assistance in times of trouble and who worship Yahweh only (Psalm 14:4; 53:4; 79:6; Jeremiah 10:25).

Calling upon the name of the Lord was a call made by those already saved to seek help from Yahweh. For example, after Yahweh delivered David from the hand of Saul, he said, "*I call upon the Lord, who is worthy to be praised, And I am saved from my enemies*" (Psalm 18:3). This "call" was not to save him from damnation, but from his enemies. Again, he says, "*In my distress I called upon the Lord, and cried to my God for help; He heard my voice out of His temple, And my cry for help before Him came into His ears*" (Psalm 18:6). To call upon the name of the Lord is not a call for personal salvation but it is a call for "help."

- Believers in Psalm 80:18 call upon the name of the Lord that He may revive them.
- In Psalm 99:6 the people called upon the Lord and He answered them.
- Believers are instructed to call upon the name of the Lord, that is, to trust Him and worship Him (Psalm 105:1).
- To offer a sacrifice of thanksgiving is related to calling upon the name of the Lord (Psalm 116, 17).

Wenham notes that "To call on the name of the Lord" is used elsewhere in Genesis (Genesis 12:8; 13:4; 21:33; 26:25), and it seems to be an umbrella phrase for worship, most obviously prayer and sacrifice.[623] Only those already born again can worship.

---

[622] Cf. Genesis 4:26; 12:8; 13:4; 21:33; Deuteronomy 4:7; Judges 6:21; 8:17; 9:4; 16:2; 1 Samuel 12:17–18; 2 Samuel 22:4, 7; Psalms 4:1; 14:4; 18:3, 6; Isaiah 55:6; 64:17; Jeremiah 10:25; Lamentations 3:55, 57; 2 Maccabees 3:22, 31; 4:37; 7:37; 8:2; 12:6; Joel 2:32 [LXX 3:5]; Zephaniah 3:9; 13:9.

[623] Gordon J. Wenham, *Genesis 1-15* (Dallas: Word, 1987), 116.

The believing David "called on the Lord" numerous times in the Psalms.[624] God commands believers to call on Him "in the day of trouble," not for salvation from sin, but for salvation ("rescue") from trouble. The Lord instructed David saying, "*Call upon me in the day of trouble; I will deliver you, and you will honor me*" (Psalm 50:15, NIV). In the LXX it means "to call on the Lord in prayer."[625]

In a parallel to Romans 10:13 David says, "*I shall call upon God and the Lord will save me*" (Psalm 55:16, cf. Psalms 86:7; 91:15). In fact, when David "calls on the name of the Lord," he asserts that God will "*save my life*" (lit., "save my soul," Psalm 116:2, 13, 17). The psalmist is already saved in the sense of personal salvation, but he calls on the Lord to "save his soul" from a temporal calamity. In another parallel to the salvation in Romans 10:13, David says, "*I call upon the Lord, who is worthy to be praised, and I am saved from my enemies*" (Psalm 18:3). Dunn notes that "A typical assumption in these passages is that this is an activity which marks off the devout of Israel."[626] In other words, only those who are already saved, regenerated, and justified can call on the name of the Lord.

An Old Testament parallel which explains Romans 10:13 is the contest between Elijah and the prophets of Baal on Mount Carmel. It was there that Elijah, a prophet who was already justified, called upon the name of the Lord asking that He would manifest His power (1 Kings 18:24) and affirm to the false prophets that Elijah alone was the true prophet of God (v. 22). He was certainly not calling upon the name of the Lord in order to be saved from damnation.

Also in the New Testament "calling on the name of the Lord" is something only those who are already justified can do.[627] In 1 Corinthians 1:12 the phrase "call upon (Gr *proskaleō*) the name of the Lord" "describes those whom we call Christians."[628] Therefore the parallel phrase, "confess Lord Jesus" is something only a justified saint can do (cf. 1 Corinthians 12:3). A non-Christian cannot call on the name of the Lord in worship or for assistance (with any justified claim to expect it) because he is not yet born again.[629] Paul wrote to the Corinthians: "*To the church of God which is at Corinth, to those who have been sanctified in Christ Jesus, saints by calling, with all who in every place call upon the name of our Lord Jesus Christ*" (1 Corinthians 1:2).[630]

---

624 Cf. Psalms 31:17; 80:18; 86:5; 116:17; 141:1.

625 Wenham, *Genesis 1-15*, 116.

626 Dunn, *Romans 9-16*, 610-11.

627 Calling on the name of the Lord is standard Old Testament terminology for what believers do to ask for God's aid in regard to some temporal difficulty, publicly identifying with Him (Genesis 4:26; 26:25; 1 Kings 18:24-27; Psalms 14:4; 18:3; 31:17; 50:15; 53:4; 79:6; 80:18; 116:2; Isaiah 55:6; 64:7; Jeremiah 29:12). See López, René, "Romans Unlocked: Power to Deliver (Springfield, Missouri: 21st Century Press, 2005), 214 for discussion. In Acts 7:59; 9:14; 21:1; 1 Corinthians 1:2; and 2 Timothy 2:22 this phrase seems to identify the Christian community as those who worship Him and confess Him publicly.

628 Karl Ludwig Schmidt, "*proskaleō*" in TDNT 3:500.

629 The following discussion follows Hodges, *Absolutely Free! A Biblical Reply to Lordship Salvation*, 193-94.

630 Wherever Christians met in worship, they would appeal to the Lord Jesus for assistance by calling on His name. Christians were known by this description; they were simply those who called on the Lord (Acts 9:14, 21). Paul similarly urged Timothy to flee youthful lusts and to "pursue righteousness, faith, love and peace, with those who call upon the name of the Lord" (2 Timothy 2:22). Peter exhorted the believers, "*And if you call upon the Father, ... conduct yourselves throughout the time of your sojourning here in fear*" (1 Peter 1:17, NKJV). Stephen, as he was being stoned to death, "called on the Lord" and asked Him to receive his spirit (Acts 7:59). Pagans called on their various gods for assistance. But the early Christians called on the name

Paul makes this explicitly clear in Romans 10:14.

How then will they call on Him in whom they have not believed? How shall they believe in Him whom they have not heard? And how shall they hear without a preacher?

A chronological sequence is intended here. An Israelite cannot hear unless first there is a preacher. He cannot believe unless first he has heard. And he cannot call on the name of the Lord unless he has first believed. Thus, only those who have *already believed* and are therefore *already justified* can call on the name of the Lord. Because to "confess Jesus as Lord" and to "call on the name of the Lord" are parallel, and since the latter is something that only those who have already believed can do, it follows that confessing Jesus as Lord is not the same thing as believing on Him for salvation. Instead, it is something those already saved must do in order to be delivered from calamity.

There is no example that I can find anywhere in Scripture where calling upon the name of the Lord has anything to do with calling upon Him for personal salvation in a soteriological sense. In every instance it is an act of worship, a request for assistance, or a description of those who already possess soteriological-justification,[631] and who trust, worship, and obey Yahweh only. The fact that Paul uses this extremely common, well-defined expression from the Old Testament, when he speaks of calling on the name of the Lord, should be decisive in determining the meaning of salvation in Romans 10:13 and therefore in verse 1.

The interpretation suggested above is confirmed by the citation from Joel in Romans 10:13. Those who call on the name of the Lord are those who confess Jesus as Lord, and the result is salvation. *Yet this "salvation" in Joel has nothing to do with deliverance from eternal separation from God.*[632] Rather, it is deliverance from the temporal consequences of sin.

The kind of salvation in view must be determined by the immediate context in Romans and the Old Testament citations. This verse (Romans 10:13) is a quotation from Joel 2:32 and once again it refers to *the physical deliverance from the future day of temporal wrath on the earth and the restoration of the Jews to Palestine,* and not deliverance from eternal damnation. Salvation in verse 13 means exactly what it meant in verses 1, 9, and 10. It is the messianic salvation of the nation that would include their deliverance from temporal (not eternal) destruction.

When the people of God call on Christ for assistance, confessing Him as Lord, they will be "saved." Paul says that one day, Israel will call on the name of the Lord and all Israel (the nation) will be saved from the surrounding armies that will be attacking them (Romans

---

of the Lord for divine help in time of need. Romans would call on Caesar for assistance by invoking that formula, a Roman citizen would make legal appeal to the highest authority. Paul himself used this phrase when he said: "I stand at Caesar's judgment seat, where I ought to be judged. To the Jews I have done no wrong, as you very well know … I appeal (Gr *epikaleō*) to Caesar" (Acts 25:10-11). The word "appeal" is the same Greek word for "call on" used in Romans 10:13. The point is that to call on the name of the Lord was a distinctively Christian privilege. Non-Christians cannot call on Him. Also, to call on Him is not a condition of salvation from eternal damnation but of deliverance in time from the enemies of God's people.

631 As in Psalms 14:4; 53:4; 79:6; Jeremiah 10:25.

632 Contra Dunn who says, "Paul evidently felt justified in giving the text a more universal scope because of the eschatological significance of Christ" Dunn, *Romans 9-16*, 610. Dunn's comment reveals the root of the matter. Does Paul or any other New Testament apostle have authority to change the intended meaning of the Old Testament text?

11:26). In that day Israel will "call on my name" (Zechariah 13:9) and God will "answer them," that is, save them from the surrounding armies (Zechariah 14:3). But for the nation to obtain this kind of salvation either from the Romans in AD 70 or from the armies of the world in the last day (Zechariah 14:1-2), they must not be ashamed of the one "whom they have pierced" (Zechariah 12:10). The theme of calling upon the name of the name of the Lord is a common theme found all over the Old Testament. However, one must not be ashamed of if he expects Him to respond.

Paul continues,

For the Scripture says, "Whoever believes in Him will not be disappointed [Gr kataischunō]" (Romans 10:11).

This verse can be understood in two ways. The traditional translation renders the Gr word *kataischunō* as "will not be disappointed" (future passive). This is perfectly plausible and fits the context well. If this is the meaning, then Paul is promising that if they call upon the Lord, confessing Him publicly, they will not be disappointed. He will help them in their distress. Applied to Israel, his meaning is that if they do this, they will be spared the coming national catastrophe. The passage is not speaking of soteriology but of a promise of help in time of national distress.

There is another possibility. The passage could be translated:

For the Scripture says, "Whoever believes in Him SHALL not be ASHAMED (Gr kataischunō)" (Romans 10:11, author's translation).

In the author's translation above, note that it was translated "shall not be ashamed." If that is correct, then the verse is an exhortation not to be ashamed of Christ, but to be willing to publicly confess Him. Even though the nation has been offended by the "rock of offense" (Romans 9:33, Jesus the Christ), no Jewish believer, nor the nation as a whole, should refuse to confess Christ publicly if they want deliverance.

It is very understandable that Jews in particular would be hesitant to publicly acknowledge Jesus as their Lord and Messiah (cf. John 12:42-43). Paul now addresses their timidity and tells them that they must not be ashamed (Gr *kataischunō*) of believing in Christ as their Messiah and King.

While the NASB translated *kataischunō* as "disappoint," it can mean "to dishonor, disgrace" or to "put to shame."[633] If that is the meaning, then Paul is saying that believers must not allow themselves to be dishonored.[634]

Paul quotes Isaiah 28:16 to establish that they must not be ashamed. However, that verse in English is translated this way:

Therefore thus says the Lord God, "Behold, I am laying in Zion a stone, a tested stone, A costly cornerstone for the foundation, firmly placed. He who believes in it will not be disturbed [Heb ḥûš]" (Isaiah 28:16).

---

633 BDAG, 517.

634 This approach was suggested to me by Zane Hodges in his commentary on *Romans*. See Zane C. Hodges, *Romans* Deliverance from Wrath (Corinth, TX: Grace Evangelical Theological Society, 2012), 301-303.

The LXX translated the Hebrew word "*ḥûš*," which means "hurry, make haste, hasten"[635] or "to hurry off"[636] by *kataischunō* which means either "to dishonor, disgrace" or "be disappointed."[637] Paul is quoting the LXX translation. But how does one get from "to hurry off" to "be not disappointed" in Romans 10:11?

The context of Isaiah 28:16 concerns the threat of a coming invasion of the Northern Kingdom by Senacherib, King of Assyria, in 722 B.C. The Southern Kingdom, Judah, is being warned that they too face danger. The LXX translators apparently understood "*ḥûš*" which means "to hurry" or "to run away" as being ashamed (Gr *kataischunō, LXX).* Instead of running in shame and doing things like making covenants of death with Egypt (Isaiah 28:18), Judah was to trust in the Temple ("*a tested stone*," "*firmly placed*") as God's sure foundation and evidence of His presence with the nation in the face of this threat to their existence.[638] To trust in the Temple is obviously a metaphor for trusting in Yahweh's protection. Instead of being ashamed and running away, they are to remain steadfast and trusting in God's promises to protect His people. Grogan says, "A literal rendering [that is, 'hasten away'] makes good sense because ... it can suggest a contrast with waiting on God (cf. 8:17; 25:9; 26:8; 30:18; 33:2 et al.)."[639] Instead of waiting on Yahweh, they made alliances with Egypt;[640] they were ashamed[641] and ran away.[642]

In this second translation, Paul is telling the nation that if they believe in Jesus then they "*shall not be ashamed of Christ,*" if they want to be "saved from a national catastrophe."[643] Having just crucified and rejected Him, they would naturally be ashamed to do this,[644] therefore they must confess Him publicly (v. 9).

Paul is picking up a theme that launched the argument of his epistle.

---

635 BDB, 301.

636 HAL, 300.

637 BDAG, 517.

638 Grogan says, "As the altar of God in the temple was treated as a place of refuge (Exod 21:14; 1 Kings 1:50), so God himself would be a holy place of refuge for them (cf. Ezek 11:16). If, however, they refused belief, he would be a stone of stumbling they would fall over." See Geoffrey W. Grogan, "Isaiah," in *Expositor's Bible Commentary*, ed. Frank E. Gabelein (Grand Rapids: Zondervan, 1986), 181.

639 Ibid., 182.

640 Isaiah 28:15, "a covenant with death."

641 Isaiah 28:16, LXX, *kataischunō.*

642 NIDOTTE renders *ḥûš* "hurry, hasten," 2:54.

643 Earlier Paul cited Isaiah 28:16, "*Therefore thus says the Lord God, 'Behold, I am laying in Zion a stone, a tested stone, a costly cornerstone for the foundation, firmly placed. He who believes in it will not be disturbed*" (Isaiah 28:16). As Cranfield points out, this translation is "either an incorrect translation of the Hebrew, or based on a different reading. The RV translation of Isaiah reads '*shall not make haste*.'" See Cranfield, *A Critical and Exegetical Commentary on the Epistle to the Romans*, 281. By translating the phrase "will not be disappointed" (Romans 9:33, 10:11) as an exhortation, "shall not be disappointed," the Old Testament quotation makes sense. In Isaiah's time the faithful are not to run away in haste, bringing shame on themselves when confronted with the Assyrian invasion. In the New Testament Paul applies this concept to the believer who may be ashamed to openly confess Christ; he runs away from this confession. This would explain why the LXX translated the Hebrew word *ḥûš*, "go quickly" by *kataischunō*, "put to shame." They are "put to shame" because they are "dismayed" in the sense of hurrying (J. A. Motyer, *The Prophecy of Isaiah: An Introduction and Commentary* (Downers Grove, IL: InterVarsity Press, 1993), s.v. "Isa. 28:16". They are full of fear because they do not trust Yahweh.

644 See Zane Hodges, *Romans: Deliverance from Wrath*, ed.. Robert N. Wilkin and John H. Niemelä (Corinth, TX: Grace Evangelical Society, 2013), 302.

For I am not ashamed of the gospel, for it is the power of God for salvation to everyone who believes, to the Jew first and also to the Greek (Romans 1:16).

Leon Morris notes, "It is perhaps a little curious that Paul writes *I am not ashamed of the gospel.* Why should he feel it necessary to utter this disclaimer?"[645] The answer is that *because Paul has made a decision not to be ashamed and a decision to publicly confess Christ,* he experiences deliverance ("salvation") from the various forms of God's temporal displeasure with sin. He is exhorting the Romans not to shrink away from a public identification with Christ, no matter what the consequences. If those who are already justified desire to be saved from the temporal consequences of sin, they must not shame themselves by being secret Christians and refusing to confess Christ openly.[646]

Jesus also taught that the believing disciples must never shrink from publicly confessing Christ; they must never be ashamed of Him.

For whoever is ashamed [Gr *epaischunomai*[647]] *of Me and My words in this adulterous and sinful generation, the Son of Man will also be ashamed of him when He comes in the glory of His Father with the holy angels (Mark 8:38).*

Similarly Paul exhorted Timothy,

Therefore do not be ashamed (Gr *epaischunomai*) *of the testimony of our Lord, or of me His prisoner; but join with me in suffering for the gospel according to the power of God (2 Timothy 1:8).*

However, Romans 10:11 is translated ("will not be disappointed," or "shall not be ashamed"), there is no need to accept the common view found in many commentaries that a public confession of Christ or submission to Him as the Lord on one's life is a requirement for going to heaven when one dies.

These verses state a common New Testament teaching. Two things (beyond justification) are necessary for sanctification and deliverance from the temporal consequences of sin: public identification with Christ in which one acknowledges Him as God (no secret Christians allowed); and calling on Him in prayer, asking for His help. However, only *one* thing is necessary for justification, i.e., believing.

Summary

Let us review briefly what Paul has taught us as discussed in this and the preceding chapter.

Brethren, my heart's desire and my prayer to God for them is for their salvation (Romans 10:1).

---

645 Morris, *The Epistle to the Romans*, 66.

646 Elsewhere Paul rebuked the Corinthians because they "brought to shame [Gr *kataiskunō*]" (1 Corinthians 11:22) the poor in the community, furthermore a man can "disgrace" his head by having a hat on while praying (1 Corinthians 11:4).

647 "To experience a painful feeling or sense of loss of status because of some particular event or activity, be ashamed," BDAG, 357.

Paul continues his theme of the messianic salvation promised to Israel to which he has been alluding in the latter verses of Romans 9. His prayer is for the salvation of the nation from the looming national catastrophe. If Israel repents, then the Lord will bring His promised messianic salvation. The messianic salvation is the national forgiveness of sin, the reversal of exile, and the restoration of the Davidic theocracy. But why do they face national danger? Paul explains,

For I testify about them that they have a zeal for God, but not in accordance with knowledge. For not knowing about God's righteousness and seeking to establish their own, they did not subject themselves to the righteousness of God (Romans 10:2–3).

Israel willfully rejected God's righteousness, that is, God's covenant faithfulness; His promise to grant messianic salvation to the world through Israel. Israel turned it inward into a plan to bless Israel only, that is, they established their own righteousness.

For Christ is the end of the law for righteousness to everyone who believes (Romans 10:4).

With the arrival of the Messiah, God has announced that the old system of obtaining personal righteousness through the rituals and regulations of the Law has come to an end.

For Moses writes that the man who practices the righteousness which is based on law shall live by that righteousness (Romans 10:5).

Yes, it is true, Paul says, that the Old Testament taught a righteousness which was based upon the Law. However, this righteousness was sanctifying righteousness. Even though God always met the need for anyone under the Old Covenant who wanted assistance in obeying Torah's commands, it was an external, burdensome system which often prompted rebellion.

The Law could only take the believing Israelite so far. If obeyed by faith, he could have a rich life in the land. But Moses anticipated a better way of living life under the New Covenant. That new way of living life has arrived.

But the righteousness based on faith speaks as follows: "DO NOT SAY IN YOUR HEART, 'WHO WILL ASCEND INTO HEAVEN?' (that is, to bring Christ down), or 'WHO WILL DESCEND INTO THE ABYSS?' (that is, to bring Christ up from the dead)." But what does it say? "THE WORD IS NEAR YOU, IN YOUR MOUTH AND IN YOUR HEART"—that is, the word of faith which we are preaching (Romans 10:6–8).

According to the passages in Deuteronomy 30:6 and 11-14, the righteousness based on faith which Moses predicted would replace the old system of righteousness. According to Moses, this was also sanctifying righteousness. The difference between the righteousness based on the law and the righteousness based on faith was that the latter involved the new way of living life under the New Covenant. The new way was internal, spiritual and readily available to all, Jew and Gentile. The new way of living life, and hence escaping the national catastrophe, had arrived. One does not need to go to heaven or down into the abyss to obtain it. This easy availability is like the word of faith for forensic justification which Paul has been preaching. The word of faith, the gospel, which Paul preached taught that like sanctification under the New Covenant, justification also was readily available by faith alone.

So then, how can Israel appropriate this messianic salvation and be rescued from the catastrophe facing the nation which was predicted by Jesus and John? Paul answers,

> *If you confess with your mouth Jesus as Lord, and believe in your heart that God raised Him from the dead, you will be saved; for with the heart a person believes, resulting in righteousness, and with the mouth he confesses, resulting in salvation (Romans 10:9–10).*

From this it is clear that justification and salvation are two different things. Two things are necessary for "salvation" – believing that God raised Christ from the dead and publicly confessing Him as God, asking Him for Divine help. If Israel will do this, the messianic salvation will occur as Peter promised in Acts 3, and they will be delivered from the Roman invasion.

However, only one thing is necessary for justification, believing from the heart. To obtain the messianic salvation of Romans 10:1, Israel must not only believe on Christ for justification but they must be willing to publicly confess Him.

> *For the Scripture says, "WHOEVER BELIEVES IN HIM SHALL NOT BE ASHAMED" (Romans 10:11, author's translation).*

But to publicly confess Him was not only dangerous, it was also humiliating. The nation had crucified their Messiah. Therefore, they must not refuse to publicly confess their sin and acknowledge Him as God. They *shall* not be ashamed to do this!

> *For there is no distinction between Jew and Greek; for the same Lord is Lord of all, abounding in riches for all who call on Him; for "WHOEVER WILL CALL ON THE NAME OF THE LORD WILL BE SAVED" (Romans 10:12–13).*

God's covenant faithfulness to Israel, "the righteousness of God," was intended to be a plan for the world through Israel and not Israel only. Both Jew and Greek may equally share in this personal and messianic salvation. To call upon the name of the Lord is to ask the Lord for assistance in the midst of trials as the context of this Old Testament citation proves. If Israel will call upon Him, they can be spared the coming catastrophe and enjoy the restoration of the Davidic theocracy.

However, calling upon the divine Lord for assistance in the face of trials is something only those who are already justified and born again can do.

> *How then will they call on Him in whom they have not believed? How will they believe in Him whom they have not heard? And how will they hear without a preacher? How will they preach unless they are sent? Just as it is written, "HOW BEAUTIFUL ARE THE FEET OF THOSE WHO BRING GOOD NEWS OF GOOD THINGS!" (Romans 10:14–15).*

Unless Israel first believes on Christ, they cannot call upon Him for assistance. To call upon the name of the Lord does not mean to believe on Christ for initial salvation. This plea for divine assistance is something those who have already believed on Christ must do if they want help to face the trials of life.

Romans 10 continues the story of Israel which Paul began in Romans 9:6. Yet, the principles of calling upon the name of the Lord for help and publicly confessing Him apply to individual believers as well. We must not shrink back in shame from publicly confessing him – no secret Christians allowed. Furthermore, He is always ready to assist us in our trials when we call upon Him.

> *No temptation has overtaken you but such as is common to man; and God is faithful, who will not allow you to be tempted beyond what you are able, but with the temptation will* ***provide the way of escape*** *also, so that you will be able to endure it (1 Corinthians 10:13).*

15

How to Save Your Soul

AS I write this chapter (October 5, 2011), the television news is saturated with one story. Steve Jobs, legendary founder of Apple, Inc., died today, having lost his final battle with pancreatic cancer.

Jobs has been part of all of our lives since he invented the first personal computer, the Apple II in 1977. From the Apple II, to the MacIntosh in 1984, to the iMac in 1998, and on to the iPod in 2001, Jobs has been the most innovative chief executive officer and visionary technology leader of this generation. The introduction of the iPhone in 2007 and then the iPad in 2010 solidified his global impact as over 120 million people have purchased and used his products daily. Singlehandedly, he has introduced innovation after innovation and taught the world how to interact with media and technology using devices that consumers love.

He also revolutionized the movie business by founding Pixar, which produced "Toy Story" and "Finding Nemo." He was a pop culture icon. Time magazine listed him as one of the world's 100 most influential people. His death marks the passing of a history in which many in our generation have participated.

In 2003 he was diagnosed with pancreatic cancer. Five years later he appeared on stage, noticeably thinner, and he said he had been pronounced cancer-free. Then in early 2011 he announced he was taking a leave of absence, and in August he appointed a new chief executive officer.

I have always been interested in the last words of great men. Several years before his death, while speaking at Stanford University in 2005, Jobs said,

> *This is the closest I have been to facing death. And I hope it is the closest I get for a few more decades. Having lived through it, I can now say this to you with a bit more certainty than when death was a useful but purely intellectual concept. No one wants to die.*
>
> *Remembering that I will be dead soon is the most important tool I have ever encountered to help me make the big choices in life. That's because almost everything, all external expectations, all pride, all fear of embarrassment or failure – these things just fall away in the face of death leaving only what's truly important.*

For Steve Jobs, the things that were most important to him were his wife and his family. As the shadows lengthened, he chose more and more to live life with the end in view.

But his words remind all of us to ask the important questions, "What is the final meaning of our lives?" In moments of silent reflection, this momentous question has no doubt loomed large in the minds of many. In the next two chapters we will consider Jesus' answer. Our final significance, He says, is in obtaining the salvation of our souls. What does this mean?

Saving Our Soul

Immediately after Jesus announced to His astonished disciples that He must go to Jerusalem and face execution, "*Peter took Him aside and began to rebuke Him, saying, 'God forbid it, Lord! This shall never happen to You.*'" Immediately the Lord rebuked His impulsive follower. "*He turned and said to Peter, 'Get behind Me, Satan! You are a stumbling block to Me; for you are not setting your mind on God's interests, but man's*'" (Matthew 16:22-23).

Our Lord is saying to the Father of lies, "Satan, I have already fought and won that battle with you. At the beginning of my ministry you offered Me the kingdom without the cross. I have rejected your plan. Get behind Me!"

Then, turning to His disciples, He exhorted them with these words: "Whoever wishes to save his life will lose it and whoever loses his life for my sake will save it."

Satan has just tempted Him a second time to "save his life" by placing His own concerns above the will of God. Jesus knows that His disciples will be tempted in the same way He was. So He exhorts them saying, "*If anyone wishes to come after me, he must deny himself, and take up his cross and follow me*" (Matthew 16:24).

"You must be willing to do what I am about to do, if you want to be My disciple."

He then pronounces what has often been called the great paradox. It is a paradox that speaks to the heart of Christian discipleship.[648]

> *For whoever wishes to save his life will lose it; but whoever loses his life for My sake will find it. For what will it profit a man if he gains the whole world and forfeits his soul? Or what will a man give in exchange for his soul? For the Son of Man is going to come in the glory of His Father with His angels, and* WILL THEN REPAY EVERY MAN ACCORDING TO HIS DEEDS *(Matthew 16:24–27).*

The fact that this saying is addressed to His disciples (see v. 20, 21, 24)[649] immediately raises doubts about the traditional view that the expression "save your soul" is related to soteriology.[650]

---

648 This paradox is expressed in various ways in other passages in the Gospels. See Matthew 10:33; 39; Mark 8:35; Luke 9:24; 17:33; John 12:25.

649 It is clear from the passages parallel to Matthew 16:24-26 that believing disciples are in view. Luke 17:33 is addressed to the disciples alone as they are with Him privately on the Mount of Olives (17:21). The exhortation in Luke 9:24 is also addressed privately to the disciples (9:18). In 9:23 He specifies that it is to "them" that He speaks. Of course there is no one else to whom He could speak as He is alone with them. See Matthew 16:5, 6, 13, 17, 20, 21, 24.

650 Mark alone adds that He called "the crowd" as well (Mark 8:34). While this could signify that the message is evangelistic in tone and is a call to personal salvation, this is unlikely for several reasons. First, in the other instances it is specified that the message was directed at the disciples, suggesting that He was targeting believers, regardless of who else may be listening. Second, self-denial is nowhere else in the New Testament a condition of obtaining final entrance into heaven. Also, just because the "crowd" is called, this in no way implies they were nonbelievers. We can just as easily assume they are a "believing" crowd and that Mark included this reference because he wanted to stress that the conditions of following Christ as a committed disciple apply to all believers and not just the Twelve. "By calling the crowd Jesus indicates that the conditions for following him are relevant to all believers, and not for the disciples alone. This had important implications for Christians at Rome and elsewhere. It indicated that the stringent demand of self-renunciation and

Jesus says that if anyone wants to "come after" Him, they must meet certain conditions. To "come after" means to "follow as a committed disciple." This describes a process and not an event,[651] such as entrance into salvation. Luke says this must be done "daily" (Luke 9:23). Obviously this cannot be a requirement for personal salvation, because that comes from exercising faith as a single event. Because the passage is addressed to those who are already regenerate, and because a process of following Christ is in view rather than initial entrance into eternal life, the context strongly suggests that this passage has nothing to do with final entrance into heaven (being saved) or postmortem condemnation (being lost).

A structural issue bears strongly on the meaning of this saying. First, Matthew presents the saying in verse 24. Then he follows with three verses (25, 26, 27) each beginning with the word "for" (Gr *gar*), thus tightly connecting these verses and giving further explanation of what it means to "save" one's "soul." Verse 27 states that it involves rewards (or the lack thereof) to disciples, "*For the Son of Man is going to come in the glory of His Father with His angels, and* WILL THEN REPAY EVERY MAN ACCORDING TO HIS DEEDS" (Matthew 16:27).

CLAUSE 1: SAVING THE SOUL

"For whoever desires to save his life (Gr *psychē*, *'soul' will lose it"* (Matthew 16:25). In this saying Christ warns His disciples of the great danger of placing the salvation of one's soul above a life of discipleship. Notice the introductory "for" in v. 25, Gr *gar*. If saving one's life means "go to heaven," and losing it means "damnation," then Jesus is illogically saying that everyone who attempts to find salvation will be damned. This verse explains His statement in verse 24 where He says, "*If anyone would come after me, he must deny himself and take up his cross and follow me.*" The person who wants to "save his life" is the person who does not want to deny himself, pick up his cross daily and follow Christ. He wants to save his life from these hardships. Jesus is announcing a profound principle of life: the one who seeks to avoid the hardships that God's will might entail (in Christ's case, crucifixion) will lose his life, that is, "lose the true significance of his life." To "save one's life" in this first clause, means to attempt to keep it from hardship and possible martyrdom.

The parallel passage in Luke 17:33, confirms this understanding of "save a soul" (preservation of one's physical life and avoidance of hardship). Jesus says, "*Remember Lot's wife. Whoever seeks to keep his life* [Gr *sōsai tēn psychēn*] *shall lose it, and whoever loses his life shall preserve it*" (Luke 17:32-33). Obviously Jesus is not saying that everyone who tries to avoid persecution will be killed and everyone who dies will live! Rather, He is using the situation of Lot and his wife as a metaphor for a deeper spiritual reality. Lot's wife illustrates the negative consequences of placing this world and its possessions ahead of the will of God. (See p. 405, FN 1372).

Earlier, Jesus warned believers about the danger of looking back, "*No one, after putting his hand to the plow and looking back, is fit for the kingdom of God*" (Luke 9:62). Being "fit"

---

cross-bearing extends not only to Church leaders but to all who confess that Jesus is the Messiah." Lane, *Commentary on the Gospel of Mark*, 306. Furthermore Watson has persuasively argued that the crowd is a believing crowd. For discussion of the regenerate nature of the "crowds" in Matthew and Mark see pp. 271 ff. in this volume and D. F. Watson, "People, Crowd," in *Dictionary of Jesus and the Gospels*, ed. Joel B. Green, Scott McKnight, and I. Howard Marshall (Downers Grove, IL: InterVarsity, 1992), 608.

[651] Neonomians, of course, view salvation as a process and not an event. This unorthodox view is similar to that of Roman Catholicism.

for the kingdom of God and personal salvation are not the same thing.[652] It is one thing to enter the kingdom, it is another to be worthy of it. No one can ever be worthy of personal salvation, but by the kind of life a person leads one can be worthy of the kingdom. As the New Testament makes clear, all believers will be in the kingdom, but some will be saved only through fire, and only those who are faithful will reign there. In Matthew 16 and Luke 9, Jesus is addressing those who are already saved. It can be dangerous to follow Christ. In fact, a believer must take up his cross and deny himself, even to the point of a willingness to suffer persecution and possible death or martyrdom.

In the Garden of Gethsemane, Jesus addressed His Father saying, "*Now My soul has become troubled; and what shall I say, 'Father, save Me from this hour'? But for this purpose I came to this hour*" (John 12:27). The Messiah was tempted to seek to save His life, that is, His soul. But He knows that is not the Father's will. Rather, He must literally lose His life if He is to fulfill His life's purpose.

These phrases, in Clause 1, describe a man who loves his life more than following Christ. What is the result? Clause 2 tells us that he will lose it.

CLAUSE 2: LOSING ONE'S LIFE

"Will lose it" (Matthew 16:25). What does it mean to "lose one's soul?" Many commentators understand that the saying "to lose one's life/soul" means final separation from God. In this understanding a person who is unwilling to submit to the Lordship of Christ (i.e., deny himself and take up his cross daily) will be consigned to the lake of fire. But does "loss" refer to the lake of fire or some other kind of loss? The Gr word used by Matthew in verse 25 for "will lose" is *apollumi,* but the word for "lose" in verse 27 is *zēmioō.* Unless the context dictates otherwise, *apollumi* should normally be translated "ruin, destroy, lose,"[653] with no necessary suggestion of final separation from God. Similarily *zēmioō* means to "suffer damage/loss."[654]

In the next phrase Jesus says, "*Whoever loses his life for My sake.*" If losing one's life means "going to the lake of fire," then we have the absurdity "he who loses his life (goes to the lake of fire), will find his life (goes to heaven)." Obviously Jesus is speaking of losing and finding life as metaphors for something else.[655]

This expression "to lose one's life" presupposes the familiar Jewish expression "*abad nephesh,*" which has the sense of "to trifle away one's life,"[656] or "to go astray" (Psalm

[652] Bock notes, "Double-minded discipleship is worthless. Given this term, 'getting saved' is not the only point. Rather, the issue is how one serves and follows Jesus effectively. These categories come after an initial commitment, though the two processes are closely related." Darrell L. Bock, *Luke*, 2 vols. (Grand Rapids: Baker Books, 1994), 2:984.

[653] BDAG, 115. For discussion of this word see infra. 286.

[654] BDAG, 428.

[655] Charles Bing summarizes this nicely, "The paradox Jesus used has great meaning. What He appears to be saying is this: "Whoever desires to preserve himself from the hardships of God's will of self-denial and cross-bearing will in fact forfeit the essential quality (= true spiritual value) of the present life he is trying to preserve. On the other hand, whoever forfeits himself to God's will of self-denial and hardships will discover the greater essential quality (spiritual value) of the present life he was willing to forfeit." This interpretation, therefore, does not describe eternal salvation, but rather a higher quality of experience with God in this life, with implications for the eschatological life, as the next section will show. Charles C. Bing, "Coming to Terms with Discipleship," *JOTGES* (Spring 1992): 42.

[656] Albrecht Oepke, "*apollumi*," in TDNT 1:394.

119:176).[657] Attempting to save one's life by avoidance of danger and seeking after the pleasures of this world is not true life. "The man is deluded."[658] A person who sets his sights on this life will lose true life and exchange it for a cheap imitation.[659]

Anyone who invests his life in trying to save it from difficulty and avoiding the call of discipleship might possibly find what he has been looking for: security, material well-being, and escape from hardship. However, he is deceived if he thinks he will "save his life." The Christian who does this will have wandered astray, "trifled away" his life. He will actually lose the true significance of his life.[660] Like the man who invests his entire life in the pursuit of money and climbing the corporate ladder only to lose his family and integrity, he will find at the end that the ladder he has been climbing was leaning against the wrong wall.[661]

In another passage Paul says of those who love money that "*those who want to get rich fall into temptation and a snare and many foolish and harmful desires which plunge men into ruin and destruction. For the love of money is a root of all sorts of evil, and some by longing for it have wandered away from the faith and pierced themselves with many griefs*" (1 Timothy 6:9–10). Paul is speaking here of believers in the church who have "wandered away from the faith" (one does not wander away from a faith he never possessed). Like the prodigal son (who was a son of his father!),[662] they were plunged into ruin and "destruction" (Gr *apōleia*), that is, they were pierced through with many griefs. In attempting to save their lives by pursuit of material happiness, they lost their lives.

CLAUSE 3: FOR MY SAKE

"He who has lost his life [soul] for my sake."

The great paradox is that the one who is willing to lose his life in the sense of self-denying discipleship and obedience to Christ even to the point of physical death will find the true life he always wanted. To lose one's life is evidently an explanation of what Jesus has just said, regarding committed discipleship, "*If anyone wishes to come after Me, he must*

---

657 HAL, 4:1767.

658 See Luke 9:24; cf. Matthew 10:39; 16:25; Mark 8:35. John Nolland says that this person will lose his life "possibly in terms of deprivation and constriction of life." John Nolland, The Gospel of Matthew: A Commentary on the Greek Text (Grand Rapids: Wm. B. Eerdmans Publishing Co., 2005), 692.

659 All regenerate believers have "life," but only when they heed the call to discipleship and follow Christ faithfully will they experience the abundant life that Christ promised and enjoy an "abundant" entrance into the kingdom of heaven (2 Peter 1:11). An abundant entrance is supplied to Christians who consistently add to their faith the qualities of 2 Peter 1:5-7 and thus become fruitful and are secured against stumbling (2 Peter 1:10). To lose one's soul does not mean to go to the lake of fire when one dies. Rather, it means to "trifle away one's life," resulting in loss of significance and a negative recompense at the final judgment (Matthew 16:27).

660 Bing, "Coming to Terms with Discipleship," 43.

661 In the Apocalypse of Moses 25:2 "lose your life" refers to the "possibility of death in childbearing as a result of agony and trembling during the birthing process." James H. Charlesworth, ed. *The Old Testament Pseudepigrapha*, 1st ed. (Garden City, NY: Doubleday,1983), 2:174. Josephus uses the same phrase for the loss of physical life as a result of being taken captive in war, "Wars of the Jews" in F. Josephus and W. Whiston, *The Works of Josephus: Complete and Unabridged* (Peabody, MA: Hendrickson Publishers, 1987), IV, 2, 107. Elsewhere, he uses it of David's fear of losing his physical life, "Antiquities of the Jews" in ibid., v,1,1, 5. In one place he speaks of "lose one's life" as losing physical life as preferable to hearing such reproachful words," "Antiquities of the Jews" in ibid., xvi, 11, 2, 364.

662 For discussion of the parable of the prodigal son, see pp. 707 below.

deny himself, and take up his cross and follow Me" (Mark 8:34). Some see this as a verse announcing the "way of salvation," but there is nothing here about believing in Christ for eternal life. Jesus is not presenting this as a gospel call, but rather a call to self-denial which is a call to discipleship. The way to salvation is not by self-denial; it is by faith in Christ.

CLAUSE 4: SAVING ONE'S LIFE

In the first clause above, the "salvation of a soul" meant preservation from the danger, hardship, and the life of self-denial involved in following Christ as a fully committed disciple. Now, Jesus talks about the true "salvation of a soul."

> *...but whoever loses his life for My sake* ***will find it*** *(Matthew 16:25).*

Mark renders the saying this way,

> *...but whoever loses his life for My sake and the gospel's* ***will save it****" (Mark 8:35).*

It is clear that "will find it" in Matthew equals "will save it" in Mark.[663]

But what does it mean to save or find one's soul (life)? Does it refer to entrance into heaven or to an abundant life with reward?

The traditional view is that saving one's soul in Mark 8:35 or finding life Matthew 16:25 is a statement about how one can go to heaven when he dies.[664] But the concept of the "salvation of a soul" is never linked to the idea of going to heaven.[665] The condition for saving one's soul is to lose one's life, that is, self-denial and taking up one's cross and following Christ. This is far different from the gospel offer of salvation from damnation without cost. The single condition for entering heaven when one dies, according to Jesus, is to believe on Him.[666]

Obviously this means that the believer who gives up all to follow Christ finds true life, abundant life.[667] Everything he thought he had before he made the decision to deny himself

---

663 Mark 8:35; Luke 9:2.

664 Contra Harder who says, "If he is willing to 'lose his soul,' that is give up the self-life and deny himself and follow Christ, he will find 'life.' He will find a rich and meaningful life and will save his soul for eternity. The meaning is evident from the example of Jesus himself and his death and resurrection: true life is ever only won through self-denial." G. Harder, "Soul," in NIDNTT, 682. For Harder "life" refers to a rich life now, with which we would agree, but he wrongly says it also involves final entrance into heaven. Had he said that "save his soul for eternity" means "have a richer experience in eternity," this would have been consistent with the faith-alone gospel taught throughout the New Testament.

665 The word "soul" (Gr *psychē*) occurs 102 times in the New Testament. While many times it refers to one's physical life, it also means "the self," in the sense of one's own person. The rich man, for example says, he "will say to my soul" (Luke 12:19). Jesus may have that meaning in mind when He says, "He who loves his life loses it" (John 12:25). He says, "My soul has now become troubled" (John 12:27).

666 Earlier Matthew wrote, "*He who* ***has found*** *his life will lose it, and he who has lost his life for My sake will find it*" (Matthew 10:37-39). Finding one's soul in verse 37 is the same as saving one's soul in 16:25. Matthew takes us to a later point in this man's life and describes what he "has found" (aorist participle), Mark says, "Whoever wishes to save (aorist infinitive) his life", that is, the present life in this world. Life for this man was "found" by avoiding hardship and persecution and pursuing the opposite (security, material well-being, and personal happiness). Instead of "find" or "save" Luke uses "preserve" (Luke 17:33) and John uses "love" (John 12:25) thus saving, finding, preserving, and loving one's life are related ideas. They all suggest the danger of the negative consequences of a believer's uncommitted life, of his loving his personal life more than God's will.

667 Leon Morris says, "Full and abundant life is the life of service, the life in Christ, the life that takes anyone out

daily and to take up his cross and follow Christ was nothing compared to the life he now knows as a disciple. Clearly the issue is not gaining life, but living it. Fred Chay is correct, "It is far easier to see that this is how a person is to live daily as a Christian. The issue then is not how to become a Christian, but how to live life as a Christian once an individual has been born again. This is again the difference between being born and growing."[668]

John adds an additional statement, he who "*hates his life in this world will keep it to life eternal*" (John 12:25). By losing one's life here through making God's will one's priority a believer develops a quality of life that will be *preserved into eternity*. There is a correlation between the life in Christ one develops now by growth in discipleship and the degree to which he will experience eternal life in heaven. What is developed now will be preserved in the new heavens and the new earth. Our capacity to experience Christ now correlates with that capacity in the afterlife; there are degrees of glory. As Billy Graham once put it, everyone's cup will be full, but they will be of different sizes.

Forfeiting Our Soul

In the next verse Jesus explains to His regenerate disciples what it means for one of them to lose his soul.

> *For what will it profit a man if he gains the whole world and forfeits his soul? Or what will a man give in exchange for his soul? (Matthew 16:26).*

The word "for" (Gr *gar*) connects this verse immediately with what precedes it and explains it. Losing one's soul is the opposite of saving one's soul. Therefore it means to lose the final significance of one's life, to be "ruined."

What does it mean to "gain the whole world?" In Clause 1 above, Jesus spoke of the man who seeks to "save his life." He now expands on this by explaining that the one who seeks this not only wants to avoid the hardship of following Christ, but he also wants to "gain the whole world." Like Lot's wife, he desired to enjoy all the pleasures and joys of this world instead of the supreme pleasure of self-denying discipleship to Christ.

The believer who follows this course will "forfeit his soul." Luke replaces the word "soul" with the word "himself." It is the loss of one's true self, loss of that for which God has designed him. When Mark speaks of losing (*apollumi*) one's life, Luke and Matthew substitute the word *zēmioō*, which means loss in the sense of "to suffer damage."[669] This man has "damaged" his spiritual life with negative consequences at the Judgment Seat of Christ. *Zēmioō* is the same word used in 1 Corinthians 3:15 for the loss suffered at the Judgment Seat of Christ.

Our Final Significance

The ultimate salvation of the soul comes when it is positively "repaid according to its deeds," that is, recompensed for following Christ. That saving a soul includes a reward is clarified by the third "for" (Gr *gar*), which explains what is meant in verse 26.

---

of concentration on merely selfish concerns and puts ultimate meaning into life," Leon Morris, *The Gospel According to Matthew*, The Pillar New Testament Commentary (Grand Rapids: Wm. B. Eerdmans Publishing Co., 1992), 432-33.

[668] Fred Chay, "A Textual and Theological Exposition of the Logion: The Salvation of the Soul" (ThD diss., Trinity Theological Seminary, 2003), 186.

[669] BDAG 428. Cf. 1 Corinthians 3:15; 2 Corinthians 7:9; Philippians 3:8.

For the Son of Man is going to come in the glory of His Father with His angels, and WILL THEN REPAY EVERY MAN ACCORDING TO HIS DEEDS *(Matthew 16:27).*

The subject matter is rewards for service (Matthew 10:40-42); not final entrance into heaven. What is too frequently overlooked is that this verse is directed to believing disciples and is speaking of the reward or punishment that will come to believers at the Judgment Seat of Christ. The word rendered "repay" is *apodidōmi* and means "reward, pay back, recompense, whether positive or not."[670] This hardly refers to final salvation which is not a payment for work done but is a gift of grace granted through faith alone.

All men, believers and unbelievers, will be judged according to their deeds. The believer will be judged at the Judgment Seat of Christ (2 Corinthians 5:10). There the issue will be reward or its loss. The unbeliever will be judged at the Great White Throne, where it will be shown that his deeds were inadequate (Revelation 20:11-15).

Based upon the discussion above, we suggest this definition for the saying, "save your soul."

To save our soul means to find a rich life now by self-denial, taking up our cross and following Christ, so that we will be favorably recompensed at the Judgment Seat of Christ.

Ultimate Loss

Every believer will be recompensed, either positively or negatively. Jesus concludes His warning in a passage added to this dialogue by Mark.

For whoever is ashamed (Gr *epaischunomai*) *of Me and My words in this adulterous and sinful generation, the Son of Man will also be ashamed* (Gr *epaischunomai*) *of him when He comes in the glory of His Father with the holy angels (Mark 8:38).*

That believers can experience shame at the Judgment Seat of Christ is taught elsewhere. "*Now, little children, abide in Him, so that when He appears, we may have confidence and not shrink away from Him in shame at His coming*" (1 John 2:28; cf. Mark 4:25).[671] Paul exhorted Timothy using the same word Jesus used for shame, "*Therefore do not be ashamed (Gr epaischunomai) of the testimony of our Lord, or of me His prisoner; but join with me in suffering for the gospel according to the power of God*" (2 Timothy 1:8, NASB). Probably, both verses (2 Timothy 1:8 and Matthew 8:38) refer to being ashamed in the sense of "fear of human ridicule,"[672] leading to an unwillingness to confess Him before men. Jesus may have in mind the rulers mentioned in John 12:42 who believed in Him but would not confess Him publicly because of the fear of man. As discussed in chapter 14, Romans 10:13 echoes a similar theme and should be translated "*whoever believes in Him shall not be ashamed*" (Gr *kataischunō*, "to be ashamed"[673]), or possibly, "shall not be disappointed" (by Christ at the judgment).

While the outcome of a believer's life could be positive reward at the judgment seat, it could also be negative rebuke. This negative assessment of one's life can result in two

---

670 LN 2,167.

671 We will discuss this concept extensively in other chapters 48-49.

672 NIDNTT, 3:563.

673 The passive can be rendered "be put to shame" or simply "be ashamed." BDAG, 517.

things: (1) shame and (2) Jesus denying that person before the Father in heaven.[674]

> *Therefore everyone who confesses Me before men, I will also confess him before My Father who is in heaven. But whoever denies Me before men, I will also deny him before My Father who is in heaven (Matthew 10:32-33).*

What could it mean for Christ to "deny" someone at the final judgment? Could this possibly happen to a believer? Does such a denial imply final condemnation to the lake of fire? Matthew 16:27 helps explain what denial by Christ will mean. It relates to a recompense for works done. This would exclude any notion that final entrance to heaven or exclusion from such entrance could be in view. Entrance into heaven is via faith alone apart from works (Ephesians 2:8-9). Paul makes it clear that the denial is not soteriological because even when we are unfaithful he says, "*It is a trustworthy statement: If we endure, we will also reign with Him; If we deny Him, He also will deny us; If we are faithless, He remains faithful, for He cannot deny Himself*" (2 Timothy 2:13).

The denial, then, is a denial of those rewards, and the shame is the experience a believer can feel, knowing that Christ is ashamed of his life. To experience Christ being ashamed of them and denying them rewards will cause an excruciating experience of profound regret, a "wailing and gnashing of teeth" (Matthew 24:51).[675]

Summary

As a summary of what has been said, let us look once again at the exchange between Peter and Christ which precipitated Christ's challenge to the Twelve which we call the "great paradox" ("*whoever wishes to save his life, will lose it*").

For the first time, Jesus has explained to His disciples that He must go to Jerusalem and face execution. Peter rebukes Christ (Mk 8:35). Rather than accept Peter's statement as an expression of genuine concern and love, Christ calls it what it is, a temptation from Satan! He then added, "*For whoever wishes to save his life will lose it, but whoever loses his life for My sake and the gospel's will save it.*"

In effect He is saying to Peter and the Twelve,

> *At the beginning of My ministry I already faced and turned away from this temptation. The Satan had offered Me the kingdoms of this world if I would decide to abandon God's will. Had I done so, I could have gained the whole world. But had I chosen the easy way, a kingdom without a cross, I would have forfeited My life purpose on earth. I would be denied the honor and approval of My Father, for whom I live.*

---

[674] Many commentators often assume, without proof, that this must refer to postmortem condemnation to the lake of fire. This is assumed because of a prior (incorrect) theological commitment that declares that believers always manifest a life of good works, and therefore those in view could not be believers. Christ could never be ashamed of a believer, they say, because all believers pursue holiness to the final hour. Also it is assumed, incorrectly we believe, that because there is no condemnation for those in Christ Jesus (there could be no punishment meted out to believers). After all, they argue, has not Jesus "paid it all"? We will discuss this concern elsewhere. Suffice it to say here, all believers experience the punishment of physical death (Rom 5:12), so there is no argument that God cannot or will not punish His people either in time (1 Corinthians 11:29-32; Acts 5:4-5) or at the Judgment Seat of Christ.

[675] See discussion of "wailing and gnashing of teeth" in vol. 3, chapter 49.

If I were to listen to Peter's rebuke, I would be giving up the final significance of My life. The Father's will for My life is that I provide salvation for the world. Nothing is more important than that I fulfill the very reason for My coming.

Likewise, there is nothing more important for you, than that you place God's will above any of your earthly desires, just as I am doing. This paradox is something all My brothers need to grasp.

If anyone should choose to save his life, he will lose it. If I were to make that choice, to save My life, to avoid execution, I could certainly do it. I could call ten thousand angels. However, if I did make that choice, I would be setting My desires above My Father's call and would never accomplish My life work. I would lose the final meaning of My life.

Only when a person is willing to abandon his life to the will of God, as I am about to do, will he be able to achieve his final significance. Only then will he be able to look back and say, 'It is finished, it is complete.' Only by making this choice to go to Jerusalem and face death, can I truly save My life, even though it will appear to many that I have lost it.

Brothers, it must be the same with you. Make it your life purpose to place the Father's will above your own no matter what temporal loss or hardship this might entail. Then and only then will you truly save your life. Then and only then will you be My co-heir in the future reign of My servant kings.

What does it mean to "save a soul?" As stated earlier in this chapter,

To save our soul means to find a rich life now by self-denial, taking up our cross and following Christ, so that we will be favorably recompensed at the Judgment Seat of Christ.

And though you have not seen Him, you love Him, and though you do not see Him now, but believe in Him, you greatly rejoice with joy inexpressible and full of glory, obtaining as the outcome of your faith the salvation of your souls (1 Peter 1:8–9).

16

Receiving the Salvation of Our Souls Now

JESUS SPOKE often of the salvation of the soul. It would be surprising if His brother James and His leading apostle, Peter, did not share the same concept of saving the soul which was taught to them by their Master. In a later chapter we will consider how James uses this logion to exhort his believing readers to break the shackles of a dead faith, and to revitalize it.[676] In this chapter, however, Peter's sublime exhortation to persevere in faithfulness in the midst of many trails is the subject.

In the preceding chapter we concluded that to "save one's soul" means to find a rich life now by self-denial, taking up one's cross, and following Christ, so that we will be favorably recompensed at the Judgment Seat of Christ. To save a soul in the present is what theologians call sanctification or Christian growth.

As we will see, Peter learned his Master's teaching well and he applies this profound principle of life to his readers who needed encouragement to press on in faithfulness in the midst of their trials. He tells them, like Jesus told him, that if they do, they can obtain the salvation of their souls both now and in the life to come.

Persevering to Obtain the Inheritance

He begins by setting their hearts aglow with a vision of the great future.

> *Blessed be the God and Father of our Lord Jesus Christ, who according to His great mercy has caused us to be born again to a living hope through the resurrection of Jesus Christ from the dead, to obtain an inheritance which is imperishable and undefiled and will not fade away, reserved in heaven for you ... protected by faith (1 Peter 1:3–5).*

Born again to a living hope. What a wonderful thought! We suggest that this "living hope" includes eternal life, final salvation, and the inheritance. This is the same as the hope that Moo, in his Colossians commentary, calls, "the totality of blessing that awaits the Christian in the life to come."[677] However, the particular aspect of this hope, specified in 1 Peter 1:4, is the inheritance.

This rebirth is "*to obtain an inheritance which is imperishable and undefiled and will not fade away, reserved in heaven for you*" (1 Peter 1:4). All earthly rewards rust and fade away. Right at the beginning of this exhortation, the meaning of "inheritance" must be

[676] See chapter 28.

[677] Douglas J. Moo, *Colossians and Philemon*, The Pillar New Testament Commentary (Grand Rapids: Wm. B. Eerdmans Publishing Co., 2008), 85.

determined. Experimental Predestinarians understand the inheritance to refer to Moo's "totality of blessing" and not just one aspect of it. In previous chapters we have shown that this is not true.

This inheritance is not heaven; it is an inheritance "in" heaven. An inheritance which is a reward "in" heaven is not the same as an inheritance "which is" heaven. We are reminded of our Lord's exhortation, "*But store up for yourselves treasures in heaven, where neither moth nor rust destroys, and where thieves do not break in or steal*" (Matthew 6:20). Like the reward-inheritance, these treasures are "in" heaven and are not heaven itself. The rich young ruler was told to lay up treasure "in" heaven by doing good works (Matthew 19:21). Paul agrees, calling the inheritance an inheritance "in" the kingdom, not an inheritance "which is" the kingdom (Ephesians 5:5).

Peter equates this inheritance with "salvation."

> *Who are protected by the power of God through faith for a salvation ready to be revealed in the last time (1 Peter 1:5).*

What is this "salvation?" In verse 9, Peter will say that it is the "*salvation of your souls.*" We will discuss this below.

How is this salvation/inheritance to be procured? God *and* the believer are both involved in obtaining it. Peter gently reminds them in verse 5 that they "*are protected by the power of God through faith for a salvation ready to be revealed in the last time.*" The phrase "*are protected*" refers to present protection that the life of faithfulness to God provides. It is a military metaphor for a city being surrounded by its army, protecting it from all attack.[678] As Peter wrote, "*His divine power has granted to us everything pertaining to life and godliness, through the true knowledge of Him who called us by His own glory and excellence*" (2 Peter 1:3).

However, the believer has a part as well. This protection is obtained "through faith" (1 Peter 1:5, 7). The Gr word for "faith" [*pistis*] could refer to "faith" as an initial act of faith whereby we are saved. It can also mean "faithfulness," which speaks of a lifelong endurance in faith.

Does this protection by God guard us from sin and unbelief? Absolutely, but only if we appropriate it.[679] Here again the two sides of sanctification must be kept in mind.[680] Schreiner and Caneday completely misrepresent the position taken by this writer when they imply that the Partners' view "assumes his power has no role in our faith."[681] To the contrary, God's power, in the Partner's view, has everything to do with our faith. The

---

[678] BDAG, 1066.

[679] This does not thwart God's sovereignty as Experimental Predestinarians maintain. God has arranged sanctification so that both God and man are involved in the maturation process. If God wanted to cause sanctification regardless of man's response of faith (which is a choice and not an inevitable action), He could have. But as the New Testament abundantly testifies He has not done things the way they imagine.

[680] In our opinion, Schreiner and Caneday forget this synergistic aspect of sanctification when they assert, "If God's power does not protect us from unbelief, it is hard to see what it does." The answer is, that God's power plus our choices to appropriate it are mutually involved. Schreiner and Caneday effectively throw their argument away when they say on the next page, "Faith, of course, is a human choice. Thus, we can legitimately say that Peter must choose to exercise faith to obtain the final inheritance" (p. 248).

[681] Schreiner and Caneday, *The Race Set Before Us*, 247.

Partner's view teaches that apart from God's power and other operations in the heart of thebeliever, no believer would persevere to obtain the inheritance-reward. God's part is to strengthen (Philippians 4:13), motivate (Philippians 2:13), warn (e.g. Hebrews 2:3; 1 Peter 1:17), command (1 Peter 1:13-16), and give us hope and encouragement (Romans 15:13). Our part is to "keep ourselves," walk in the Spirit, work out our salvation, etc. God has provided all we need for life and godliness (2 Peter 1:3-4) and yet we must add to our faith "moral excellence," and to moral excellence, knowledge, and to knowledge we must add self-control and to self-control we must add perseverance and to perseverance godliness, and to godliness we must add brotherly kindness and to our brotherly kindness we must add love (1 Peter 1:5-7). And "*if these qualities are yours and are increasing, they render you neither useless nor unfruitful in the true knowledge of our Lord Jesus Christ*" (1 Peter 1:8).

In Peter's writings faith is an enduring thing, that is, faithfulness, not an event.[682] To be protected "through faith" is, as Davids suggests, to be protected "through committing themselves in trust and obedience to God."[683] The initial act of faith is one thing, but perseverance in faith is another. We therefore agree with Michaels that "*pistis* here does not refer primarily to a person's conversion or initial acceptance of the Christian gospel. It is faith understood as continuing trust or faithfulness."[684] In view of the present context's emphasis on trials, faithfulness fits the context better. Peter wants them to endure and persevere.

Assuming that enduring faithfulness is the definition, we are alerted to the fact that by "inheritance" and "salvation" Peter is not referring to final entrance into heaven which is secured immediately by a single act of faith. Instead he speaks of something in addition to personal salvation; something that is obtained by perseverance in faith; this is the "reward of the inheritance" of which Paul spoke (Colossians 3:24).

Peter continues,

> *so that the proof of your faith, being more precious than gold which is perishable, even though tested by fire, may be found to result in praise and glory and honor at the revelation of Jesus Christ (1 Peter 1:7).*

Successful perseverance in trials (the proof of your faith having been "tested by fire") will result in praise and glory and honor at the revelation of Christ, the Judgment Seat of Christ. The phrase "proof of your faith" speaks of a faith that endures, in contrast to a faith that does not. For the Christian the outcome of enduring faith will be praise and honor from Christ when "*each man's praise will come to him from God*" (1 Corinthians 4:5). As Davids says regarding this verse, "In the final judgment God gives his 'well done,' a form of praise, to humans (Matt. 25:14–30; Romans 2:29; 1 Corinthians 4:5)."[685]

---

682 See 1 Peter 1:9, 21; 5:9; 2 Peter 1:5.

683 Peter H. Davids, *The First Epistle of Peter*, New International Commentary on the New Testament (Grand Rapids: Wm. B. Eerdmans Publishing Co., 1990), 53. Wayne Grudem agrees, "Faith is regularly a personal activity of individual believers" Wayne Grudem, *1 Peter*, Tyndale New Testament Commentaries (Grand Rapids: Wm. B. Eerdmans Publishing Co., 1988), 58.

684 J. Ramsey Michaels, *1 Peter*, Word Biblical Commentary (Dallas: Word, 2002), 23. Joseph Fitzmeyer refers to faith in this passage as "constancy" or "fidelity," Joseph A. Fitzmeyer, "First Peter," in *The Jerome Biblical Commentary*, ed. Raymond E. Brown, Roland E. Murphy, and Joseph A. Fitzmeyer (Englewood Cliffs, NJ: Prentice-Hall, 1968), 2:364. Jobes calls it "continuing trust." Karen H. Jobes, *Peter*, Baker Exegetical Commentary on the New Testament (Grand Rapids: Baker Academic, 2005), 87.

685 Davids, *The First Epistle of Peter*, 58.

EARNED AS A RECOMPENSE

At this point (skipping over v. 8), Peter introduces the goal of our faith: the salvation of our souls,

> *obtaining [Gr komizō] as the outcome of your faith the salvation of your souls (1 Peter 1:9).*

Two things demand further explanation. (1) What does "*obtain*" mean and (2) What is the meaning of the salvation of your souls?

In this verse Peter's readers learn that the "outcome" (Gr *telos*, "goal") of their faith is the "salvation of their souls." We are told (v. 9) that this salvation of our souls is "*obtained*" (Gr *komizō*) as the goal of our faithful endurance. The word *komizō* most likely refers to obtaining a recompense (a return for something one has done, payment, receiving something one deserves).

Komizō would be a strange word to use for a salvation that comes to us by faith alone apart from works. While this word can mean "receive" with no necessary inference of receiving as a wage, in eschatological contexts it means "to get back something that is one's own or owed to one, get back, recover."[686] It is always found in the middle voice (as it is in 1 Peter 1:9), "obtain for oneself" with one exception (Luke 7:37), and it frequently means "a recompense."[687]

For example, the writer to the Hebrews says, "*For you have need of endurance, so that when you have done the will of God, you may receive* [Gr *komizō*] *what was promised*" (Hebrews 10:36). Receiving what was promised is contingent on works, doing the will of God. Paul tells us, "*For we must all appear before the Judgment Seat of Christ, so that each one may be recompensed* [Gr *komizō*] *for his deeds in the body, according to what he has done, whether good or bad*" (2 Corinthians 5:10). *Komizō* in this passage refers to a reward for "deeds done in the body." As indicated in 2 Corinthians 5:10, these "rewards" can be negative as well. Paul reminds the Colossians, "*For he who does wrong will receive* [Gr *komizō*] *the consequences of the wrong which he has done, and that without partiality*" (Colossians 3:25). Here the recompense (payment for what one has done) is a result of doing wrong, not good.[688] Peter himself uses *komizō* one other time with its object being "*the crown of glory,*" a special reward granted to pastors who faithfully shepherd their flock (1 Peter 5:4).

---

686 BDAG, 557.

687 "*komizō*," in EDNT, 2:307.

688 Davids notes, "The verb for 'receiving' [Gr *komizō*] is frequently used for obtaining a prize or reward (2 Corinthians 5:10; Ephesians 6:8; Hebrews 11:13; cf. 1 Peter 5:4)." Davids, *The First Epistle of Peter*, 59. Michaels says, "Peter has in mind explicitly the praise, glory, and honor that God bestows on his servants, and only implicitly the praise, glory, and honor that is his in the act of giving. These three terms inevitably suggest the notion of reward, specifically as an eschatological reward, for they are all part of the 'salvation' for which the Christian community waits (cf. vv 5, 9, 10)." But then his Reformed theology creeps in and he hastily says, "They are not 'prizes' awarded on the basis of merit but simply the eschatological equivalent of 'genuine faith' itself." We ask, "How one can avoid the obvious intent that these honors are indeed 'prizes'? How one can say this passage teaches that "praise, honor, and glory" always result from initial faith, is a mystery that only those steeped in Reformed theology can understand (Michaels, *1 Peter*, 31).

THE SALVATION OF OUR SOULS IN THE PRESENT

The second question that must be answered in 1 Peter 1:9 is "What is the meaning of the salvation of your souls?" Experimental Predestinarians understand "salvation of your souls" as a reference to final entrance into heaven. However, this phrase is never used that way in the Old Testament and does not fit well in the immediate context. As shown above, according to Peter, this recompense, this payment for work done is "the outcome" of their enduring faith."[689] Enduring faith is not what saves us, it is what rewards us.

We concluded in chapter 15, that the idiomatic phrase "save your soul" in Matthew means "to find a rich life now by self-denial, taking up one's cross and following Christ, so that we will be favorably recompensed at the Judgment Seat of Christ"[690] (Matthew 16:24–25).

Peter teaches the same thing when he says that because of their faithful perseverance, believers are receiving this salvation in the present but it will result in their receiving honor, praise, and participation with Christ in the future. The great future is being experienced now. In the future, according to verse 10, they will receive the final outcome of the salvation of their souls now, deliverance from all their difficulties and enemies. Also, they will, if they remain faithful, receive the blessing of the inheritance in heaven as well.

But that future salvation of their souls can be experienced in the present as well. How so? As they are steadfast and faithful, they experience the benefits of the future salvation in the present. In Christ's words, they find "life," that is, true life now (Matthew 16:25) and they will save their lives for eternity. Dave Anderson explains,

> *Saving our lives for eternity is the goal (1:9) of the Christian life. The salvation the angels were so curious about was one that included suffering before glory. They had never suffered and were somewhat mystified by Christ's own condescension to suffer before glory.*[691]

In other words, 1 Peter 1:9 has sanctification and reward, rather than sanctification only in view. We therefore fully agree with Fred Howe when he says, "The process described in verse 9 is the entire process of growth in the Christian life, the process of appropriating in one's own life more and more of the blessings of salvation."[692]

This way of viewing the passage is widely held. Edwin Blum, for example, says:

> *For you are receiving [komizomenoi, a present causal participle], giving the reason for the paradoxical joy while stressing that the anticipated salvation is even* ***now in the process of realization****. The "goal" [telos] or consummation of faith is "the salvation of your souls." ... The "soul" is used in the Semitic biblical sense of "self" or "person." Therefore the thought of this section closes with the believer's enjoyment of the future salvation in this present age.*[693]

---

689 Michaels, *1 Peter*, 35.

690 Fred Chay nicely summarizes the meaning of saving a soul this way: "As a Christian chooses to give his or her life for the service of Jesus, although it may look as though he is losing his life, he is in fact preserving it. That which is preserved is the ability to enjoy eternity by being rewarded by Jesus for faithful service. The result for a life of faithfulness on earth is reward experienced in heaven," Chay, "A Textual and Theological Exposition of the Logion: The Salvation of the Soul", 162.

691 Dave Anderson, personal communication, September 29, 2011.

692 Fred Howe, "God's Grace in Peter's Theology," *BibSac* 157, no. 628 (October-December 2000): 434.

693 Edward Blum, "1 Peter," in *The Expositor's Bible Commentary*, ed. Frank E. Gaebelein (Grand Rapids:

Selwyn, while also seeing an eschatological element in 1:9, nevertheless observes that the salvation here is present as well: "The doctrine of faith issuing in a salvation realized in part here and now is not uncommon in N.T."[694] Hart insists, "*komizomenoi* implies that already they are receiving what is due to them."[695]

What is the present expression of future salvation which they are receiving? In what way does steadfast faith bring salvation to their souls now? What is the salvation of a life (soul) in the present? It is not deliverance from eternal separation from God or entrance into heaven! The battle in which their souls were engaged and from which they needed deliverance was the battle against fleshly lusts (2:11), the battle for purity (1:22), and the battle for survival in the midst of trials (1:6). These are the enemies these readers face. As they trust God and set their gaze on the great future and remain faithful to Him now, they experience the salvation that consists in victorious perseverance in trials and triumph over the pollutions of the age, a salvation which will one day reach its ultimate goal: praise, honor, and glory at the Judgment Seat of Christ.

Many Experimental Predestinarians also understand the passage the same way. For Wayne Grudem, the salvation of the soul in the present is "Christian growth."

> *The process described in v. 9 is the entire process of growth in the Christian life, the process of appropriating in one's own life more and more of the blessings of salvation. This process happens, Peter says, as Christians continually believe in Christ and continually rejoice because of that personal trust in him. Such day by day faith and joy produces an unexpected benefit: continual growth toward Christian maturity.*[696]

Peter speaks again about the present salvation of the soul when he says in the next chapter, "*Like newborn babies, long for the pure milk of the word, so that by it you may grow in respect to salvation*" (1 Peter 2:2).

A PART IN THE MESSIANIC SALVATION IN THE FUTURE

Some have objected that this cannot be true because the next verse begins, "*As to this salvation, the prophets inquired*" (1 Peter 1:10). They say the salvation referred to in this verse is the future salvation of the soul and not its present salvation, and therefore believe it refers to entrance into heaven. Since the salvation in verse 10 refers back to the salvation in verse 9, they conclude that the salvation in verse 9 must be future as well. In this way some notion of "entrance into heaven" is read into the words.

Does this not prove that "salvation" means final entrance into heaven? If not, of what, then, does this *future* salvation consist? Examine verse 10 more carefully.

> *As to this salvation, the prophets who prophesied of the grace that would come to you made careful searches and inquiries (1 Peter 1:10).*

Zondervan Publishing House, 1976), 221.

694 Edward Gordon Selwyn, *The First Epistle of Peter* (London: Macmillan & Co., 1947), 133. He cites Acts 14:9; 15:11; 2 Thessalonians 2:13; 2 Timothy 3:15; Hebrews 10:39.

695 J. H. A. Hart, "The First Epistle General of Peter," in *The Expositor's Greek Testament*, ed. W. Robertson Nicoll (Grand Rapids: Wm. B. Eerdmans Publishing Co., 1967), 45.

696 Grudem, *1 Peter*, 67.

The salvation into which the prophets inquired had nothing to do with final deliverance from eternal separation from God or final entrance into heaven. Rather it is "the grace to come." While there is an understandable impulse to equate this with heaven when one dies, despite that impulse, we must understand this "grace to come" to be something into which the prophets inquired. Peter is the only one to use this expression, and it is found only in this chapter in the New Testament. Therefore we must rely on this context alone to understand it and not depend on a theological pre-understanding that "grace" must mean heaven when one dies.

This "grace to come" *into which the prophets inquired* was the final deliverance from all of Israel's enemies, the future messianic salvation of which Isaiah spoke (Isaiah 45:17) which we discussed in an earlier chapter.[697] When one receives this future salvation in the present (sanctification), he will also, "inherit it" as a reward in the future. He will "save his soul" in the present and at the Judgment Seat of Christ.

This understanding of the text is consistent with the Old Testament anticipation of a future messianic salvation when Israel will be finally delivered from her enemies; the Holy Spirit will be poured out; and the Davidic theocracy will be restored. This was a subject of much first century Jewish speculation. When the future salvation is experienced in the present, it is sanctification, protection, and growth for the people of God. When experienced in the future, it is the final and permanent deliverance from all enemies. If the believers are faithful to the end, they will not only experience this salvation now, but they will also obtain it in the future as a reward.

Therefore this national, future "grace" has a temporal, individual aspect as well. The ultimate outcome of it will be "praise, glory, and honor" (v. 7). Because of a life well-lived, they would hear the Master's "well done" and be invited to inherit kingships prepared for them before the foundation of the world (Matthew 25:34).[698] They would become co-heirs with Christ. That is the individual aspect of the "grace to come." Not all believers will have a share in this future messianic salvation. Some will reign with Him and some will not. This is a "grace" because God was not under any obligation to reward us for our faithfulness, and because any reward we receive from Him is vastly over-generous wages. That God chose to obligate Himself to reward us is pure grace.[699]

How to Receive Soul Salvation Now

To obtain the benefits of this salvation in the present Peter says that we must live with the end in view.

> *Therefore, prepare your minds for action, keep sober in spirit,* ***fix your hope completely on the grace to be brought to you at the revelation of Jesus Christ*** *(1 Peter 1:13).*

The remaining verses in the chapter explain what he means by receiving the salvation of one's soul in the present. To obtain it we are not to be "conformed to their former lusts"

---

697 See pp. 165 ff.

698 For an extensive discussion of this passage see pp. 839 ff.

699 See discussion of this issue on pp. 587 ff.

(v. 14) and are to be holy in all our behavior (v. 15). We are to be aware that one day their Father will *"impartially judge according to each one's work,"* and therefore we are told, *"conduct yourselves in fear during the time of your stay on earth"* (1 Peter 1:17).

Summary

It is not at all surprising that for Peter, the salvation of a soul has both present and future dimensions. It is recompense both in time and eternity for a life well-lived. His Lord taught him the same thing in different words. On the Mount of Transfiguration Jesus told him that to save one's soul means to find a rich life now by self-denial, taking up our cross, and following Christ, so that we will be favorably recompensed at the Judgment Seat of Christ.

In different words, the apostle explains that the "salvation of a soul" in the present is to grow in the Christian life. Such a life, when continued to the end results in receiving a share in the future messianic salvation. The key to obtaining this future inheritance is to fix one's attention on the glories of this future age and live one's life in the present in hopes of hearing the Master's "Well done!" One day the divine Judge will issue a verdict *according to each one's work*. With this magnificent vision Peter exhorts his readers to persevere in trials, avoid being conformed to this world, and to live holy lives. If we do this, we will grow in respect to salvation.

This chapter is not about how to get to heaven when one dies; it is about discipleship, growth, and reward. To save one's soul means for Peter the same thing his Master taught. To save one's soul means to find a rich life now by self-denial, taking up one's cross, and following Christ, so that we will be favorably recompensed at the Judgment Seat of Christ, that is, at the grace to come.

Jews and Gentiles who persevere in faith will have a share in this salvation. We will earn it as recompense, a reward (v. 9). We will be co-heirs with the Messiah in His kingdom reign (Romans 8:17; 2 Timothy 2:12).

17

Inheriting Eternal Life

WHEN JESUS met the rich young ruler, His final journey to Jerusalem was well under way. Seeing Jesus from afar, this wealthy, young man ran excitedly toward Him wanting to know how to be complete in his faith. After falling at Jesus' feet and calling Him "Good teacher," he posed a question which is the subject of this chapter. "*What shall I do to inherit eternal life?*" (Luke 18:18). Here was a man who spoke of eternal issues; he certainly wanted to save his soul.[700]

However, it is evident from the way Jesus answers his question, that Jesus did not understand the young man's query the way many modern interpreters do. If by "inherit eternal life" this young ruler was asking about how to go to heaven when he died, surely Jesus would have answered him the same way He answered the unsaved Nicodemus, "*Whoever believes on Him will not perish, but have eternal life.*" But Jesus did not answer that way because Jesus knew that this young man already had eternal life through faith alone. Now he wanted to inherit it! He wanted to know how to lay up treasure in heaven.

Receiving eternal life as a gift was granted to all without cost. The conditions for inheriting it, however, would cost this initially enthusiastic young man everything.

Jesus answered,

You know the commandments.

Commandments!? What do they have to do with receiving the free gift of eternal life? Nothing! But they have everything to do with inheriting eternal life as a reward, and that is what was on the young man's mind.

That eternal life as a reward was in view is clear from our Lord's response to Peter about being "saved." He said,

> *And everyone who has left houses or brothers or sisters or father or mother or children or farms for My name's sake, will receive many times as much, and will inherit eternal life (Matthew 19:29).*

Receiving eternal life by grace alone is one thing, but to enjoy its richness and ultimately receive it as a reward is entirely another. It involves denying one's self, taking up one's cross daily, and following Christ. To inherit eternal life is another way of saying, "save your soul." But as we will see, for the rich young ruler, the price was too high; he went away sorrowful.

---

[700] For full discussion of this encounter see Chapter 24.

The apostle Paul agrees with his master. In a famous passage in the Epistle to the Romans he explains that God

> *WILL RENDER TO EACH PERSON ACCORDING TO HIS DEEDS: to those who by perseverance in doing good seek for glory and honor and immortality, eternal life (Romans 2:6–7).*

Eternal life will be awarded to a person "according to his deeds."

Given Freely as a Gift

All readers of the New Testament are familiar with the wonderful gospel promise of the free gift of eternal life. That our final eschatological entrance into eternal life is ours by faith alone apart from any works was one of the key emphases of the Reformation.

> *For God so loved the world that he gave his one and only Son, that whoever believes in him shall not perish but have eternal life [zōē aiōnios] (John 3:16).*

> *I tell you the truth, whoever hears my word and believes him who sent me has eternal life [zōē aiōnios] and will not be condemned; he has crossed over from death to life (John 5:24).*

> *For my Father's will is that everyone who looks to the Son and believes in him shall have eternal life [zōē aiōnios], and I will raise him up at the last day (John 6:40).*

Eternal life can be ours, now, on the condition that we believe in Him, and for no other condition. Yes, eternal life is ours on the basis of faith alone.

Earned as a Reward

The phrase "eternal life" (Gr *zōē aiōnios*) occurs 41 times in 43 verses in the Greek New Testament. Its common meaning of the free gift of regeneration resulting in final entrance into heaven on the basis of faith alone is well documented. However, a careful reading of the New Testament data indicates that eternal life is viewed from two different perspectives. Every time eternal life is presented as an *acquisition in the future* (15 times, 35%), it is always based on works.[701] When eternal life is presented as an *acquisition in the present* (19 times, 44%), faith alone is the only condition mentioned.[702] The fact that one third of the time (35%) the acquisition of eternal life conditioned on works surely signifies that the two different aspects of eternal life are in view: its initial acquisition by faith alone, and an enhanced experience of eternal life subsequent to its initial acquisition conditioned on faith plus obedience. The former relates to gaining life and the latter living it, leading to an abundant inheritance in the future. For example:

> *To those who by persistence in doing good seek glory, honor and immortality, he will give eternal life [zōē aiōnios] (Romans 2:7).*

---

[701] Matthew 19:16, 29; 25:46 (cf. v. 35); Mark 10:17, 30; Luke 10:25, 18, 30; John 4:36; 6:27; 12:25; Romans 2:7; 6:22; Galatians 6:8; Jude 21.

[702] John 3:15, 16; 4:14, drink=believe; 4:30; 5:24, 39-40; 6:27-29, 40, 47, 54; 68-69; 10:27-28, follow=believe; 17:2; Acts 13:46-48, worthy=believe; Romans 2:7; 5:21; 1 Timothy 1:16; Titus 3:5-7; 1 John 5:11,13.

The one who sows to please his sinful nature, from that nature will reap destruction; the one who sows to please the Spirit, from the Spirit will reap eternal life [zōē aiōnios] (Galatians 6:8).

The man who loves his life will lose it, while the man who hates his life in this world will keep it for eternal life [zōē aiōnios]. Whoever serves me must follow me; and where I am my servant also will be. My Father will honor the one who serves me (John 12:25-26).

And everyone who has left houses or brothers or sisters or father or mother or children or fields for my sake will receive a hundred times as much and will inherit eternal life [zōē aiōnios] (Matthew 19:29).

Because the addition of works as a condition for receiving eternal life seems to contradict the clear teaching elsewhere that eternal life is ours by faith alone, various theological bypasses have been constructed. Since Experimental Predestinarians "know" that "genuine" faith always and inevitably results in a lifetime pursuit of holiness, they explain the conundrum by saying that the works associated with eternal life are not *conditions* of final entrance into heaven but instead are the *characteristics* of those who do.

A better solution is simply to acknowledge that just as there are two kinds of inheritance, two dimensions to salvation, so there are two sides to eternal life. It is commonly recognized that *aiōnios* (eternal) when associated with "life" includes more than unending existence. The lexicon of Louw-Nida, for example, says, "In combination with ζωή there is evidently not only a temporal element, but also a qualitative distinction."[703] In those cases they suggest that the idea of "real life" be included in the translations. Under the article on the related Gr noun *aiōn*, Guhrt comments, "The word 'eternal' here indicates a definite quality: it is a different life from the old existence typified by hate, lack of love, sin, pain and death."[704] We must remember that eternal life in the Bible is not a static entity; it is more than the initial gift of regeneration.[705] It is a dynamic relationship with Christ Himself which grows and increases in richness as we take up our cross daily, deny ourselves, and follow Him. Jesus taught us about this dynamic relationship when He said:

Now this is eternal life [zōē aiōnios]: that they may know you, the only true God, and Jesus Christ, whom you have sent (John 17:3).

Advancing in this dynamic dimension of eternal life is what Jesus referred to as saving one's soul. He explained elsewhere that this life was intended to grow and become more abundant: "*I have come that they may have life, and have it to the full*" (John 10:10). But growth is not automatic; it is conditioned on our responses. Only by the exercise of spiritual disciplines, such as prayer, community with other believers, personal worship, obedience, faith, study of the Scriptures, and proper responses to trials, does our intimacy with Christ increase.

---

703 Louw-Nida, 1:641.

704 J. Guhrt, "*aiōn*," in NIDNTT, 832.

705 John 3:36; 20:31; 1 John 3:14, 15; 5:12.

This is what the apostle Paul referred to when he challenged Timothy to "take hold of eternal life":

> *Fight the good fight of the faith. Take hold of the eternal life to which you were called when you made your good confession in the presence of many witnesses (1 Timothy 6:12).*

Possessing eternal life is one thing in the sense of initial entrance, but "taking hold" of it is another. The former is static; the latter is dynamic. The former depends on God; the latter depends on us. The former comes through faith alone; "taking hold" requires faith plus "keeping commandments" (1 Timothy 6:14). Those who are rich in this world and who give generously "*will lay up treasure for themselves as a firm foundation for the coming age, so that they may take hold of the life that is truly life*" (1 Timothy 6:19). Eternal life is not only the gift of regeneration; it is also "true life" that is cultivated by faith and acts of obedience.

This should not surprise us. On page after page of the Bible, the richness of our spiritual life is conditioned on our spiritual obedience. Israel was instructed in this manner:

> *Hear now, O Israel, the decrees and the laws I am about to teach you. Follow them so that **you may live** and may go in and take possession of the land that the* Lord*, the God of your father, is giving you (Deuteronomy 4:1).*

A similar thought is expressed in Leviticus 18:5 where the Israelites are told:

> *Keep my decrees and laws, for the man who obeys them will live by them. I am the* Lord.

As long as we remember that eternal life is fundamentally a quality of life in relationship to God, this should not cause us any difficulty with the numerous passages that stress that justification is by faith alone.

In Galatians 6:8-9, for example, eternal life is something earned by the sower.

> *The one who sows to his own flesh will from the flesh reap corruption, but the one who sows to the Spirit will from the Spirit reap eternal life. Let us not lose heart in doing good, for in due time we will reap if we do not grow weary (Galatians 6:8–9).*

If this passage is speaking of final salvation from eternal damnation, then salvation is based on works. If we sow to please the Spirit, we will reap (future tense) eternal life. Paul calls it a harvest "*if we do not lose heart in doing good.*" Eternal life is earned by sowing to the Spirit and persevering "in doing good."[706]

Eternal life has some parallels with physical life. Physical life is received as a gift, but then it must be developed. Children often develop to their full physical and mental ability under the auspices of their parents. In order for eternal life to flourish, we must also be obedient to our Divine Parent.

[706] When Paul says that we can reap eternal life by doing good, there is no inference at all that this life of love is a characteristic of all who are saved as Neonomians claim. For example Don Garlington asserts, "The validity of our claims to be admitted into the eschatological kingdom will be weighed in the balances not of our talk, our 'verbal orthodoxy', but of our love." Garlington, *An Exposition of Galatians: A New Perspective/Reformational Reading*, 300. Rather, like the faithful sheep in Matthew 25:31-46, who inherit a kingship in the future kingdom because of their acts of love, those believers in Galatia will reap an enhanced experience of eternal life if they do likewise. See discussion of the sheep and goats judgment on pp. 839 below.

Final Justification in Romans 2:5-13

In light of the preceding discussion, we have the key for understanding the interpretive difficulties raised in Romans 2:5-13. Whenever eternal life is viewed as a reward in the New Testament, it is presented as something to be acquired in the future. But when it is presented as a gift, it is something acquired in the present. No one can receive it as a reward, that is, experience it to a more abundant degree, until he has first received eternal life freely as a gift.

Bearing this in mind, note that Romans 2:5-13 speaks of eternal life being conditioned on works.

God will give to each person according to what he has done (2:6).

To those who by persistence in doing good seek glory, honor and immortality, He will give eternal life (2:7).

> *But for those who are self-seeking and who reject the truth and follow evil, there will be wrath and anger (2:8).*
>
> *There will be trouble and distress for every human being who does evil: first for the Jew, then for the Gentile (2:9).*

But glory, honor and peace for everyone who does good; first for the Jew, then for the Gentile (2:10).

Paul introduces this section with a general principle: God will reward, that is, "pay back, recompense" (Gr *apodidōmi*)[707] each man according to his works (v. 6). *Apodidōmi* means "to meet a contractual or other obligation, *pay, pay out, fulfill.*"[708]

Paul then applies this general principle to the regenerate in 2:7 and 2:10 and to the unregenerate in 2:8-9. The literary structure of the passage makes 2:8-9 parallel and 2:7 and 2:10 parallel.

The main problem in the passage is that verses 7 and 10 promise eternal life on the basis of works, which is in complete contradiction to what Paul says in Romans 3:19-22, ***if*** *eternal life means go to heaven when you die.*

This difficulty has been keenly felt by all interpreters of the epistle. In general, four solutions have been suggested. Arminians, such as the great French scholar, Frédéric Godet, say that initial entrance into salvation is by faith alone, but in order to obtain final entrance, "God demands from him, as the recipient of grace, the fruits of grace."[709] If those fruits fail, salvation can be lost.

Experimentalists like Hodge and Haldane propose that Paul is speaking hypothetically. In other words, if anyone by persistence in doing good sought eternal life, and performed these works perfectly, God would reward him with heaven for his efforts. However, Paul has stated elsewhere that no one seeks God and no one "does good" (Romans 3:12). Therefore, these commentators conclude that this is a hypothetical offer of heaven.

---

[707] Louw-Nida, 2:28. Note Jesus said to the scribes and chief priests, "Render [*apodidōmi*] to Caesar the things that are Caesar's" (Luke 20:25).

[708] BDAG, 109.

[709] Godet and Cousin, *Commentary on St. Paul's Epistle to the Romans*, 1:196.

John Murray objects to the hypothetical view by pointing out that the principle of being rewarded for doing good is found in many other passages of Scripture as well. "If the [hypothetical] solution proposed by the interpreters quoted above were to be applied to Romans 2:6-16, then not only this passage but these other passages would have to be interpreted after this pattern. But examination of these other passages will show the impossibility of this procedure."[710] Furthermore, Paul does not seem to be speaking hypothetically. He is making a specific assertion. N. T. Wright objects, "When Paul appears to be laying down first principles about God's future judgment, he is laying down first principles about God's future judgment."[711]

Paul is not talking about what God would do if we perfectly obeyed, but what He actually will do if we obey.

Murray's own solution is a third option that is widely held. He correctly observes that the general principle of verse 6 is applied to the saved in verses 7 and 10 and to the unsaved in verses 8 and 9. But then his theological system intrudes, and he says, regarding verse 7, "The just are characterized first of all as those who 'seek for glory and honor and incorruption.'"[712] However, the passage does not say that the just are characterized by those things. No one would argue that the just *should be* characterized by those things, but Murray has plainly read his doctrine of perseverance in holiness into the text. Witmer takes the same approach:

> *A person's habitual conduct, whether good or evil, reveals the condition of his heart. Eternal life is not rewarded for good living; that would contradict many other Scriptures which clearly state that salvation is not by works, but is all of God's grace to those who believe (e.g., Romans 6:23; 10:9-10; 11:6; Ephesians 2:8-9; Titus 3:5). A person's doing good* ***shows*** *that his heart is regenerate. Such a person, redeemed by God, has eternal life.*[713]

It may be true that a person's "habitual conduct" reveals the condition of his heart, but the text is not addressing that issue. According to Paul, eternal life is "rewarded for good living." How else could he say it? "God will render to every man according to [Gr *kata*, 'according to the standard of'] his deeds" or "because of"[714] his deeds.

What about the Neonomians? How do they understand this perplexing passage? They simply admit that final entrance into heaven is, in part, based on the good that a person does. Wright provides a good example. Aware that he has been criticized for saying that there is a final soteriological justification by works, he responds that Paul taught the same thing: "I am frequently challenged on this point in public and lectures and seminars, and my normal reply is that I did not write Romans 2; Paul did."[715] Of course one must assume that Wright's understanding of what Paul wrote is correct!

---

[710] Murray, *The Epistle to the Romans*, 63. He cites Matthew 16:27; 25:31-46; John 5:29; 1 Corinthians 3:11-15; 2 Corinthians 5:10; Galatians 6:7-10; Ephesians 6:8; Colossians 3:23-24.

[711] Wright, *Justification: God's Plan and Paul's Vision*, 183.

[712] Murray, *The Epistle to the Romans*, 63. See also Schreiner and Caneday, *The Race Set Before Us*, 166. They say that Paul "speaks of the kind of person whom God will justify in the Day of Judgment. It is the obedient, not the disobedient, person." Apparently, in their view, Solomon, who finished his life worshiping Baals and fornicating with one thousand wives and concubines will not be in heaven.

[713] Witmer, "Romans," 2:445.

[714] ALGNT, 216.

[715] Wright, *Justification: God's Plan and Paul's Vision*, 184.

A final option is that eternal life in this passage does not refer to soteriological entrance into the kingdom, but to a rich experience that begins now and issues in reward in the future when it will be granted to the believer because of his good works. Once the frequent use of eternal life in the future as a reward to works is accepted, this simple solution is evident. It is true that in Pauline thought no *unjustified* person can obtain eternal life on the basis of works. But it is also true that the *justified* person can!

In this future time, the time of "*the day of God's wrath when His righteous judgment will be revealed*" (2:5), God will judge everyone, Christians and non-Christians, on the basis of their works. The general principle in verse 6 is that each person, saved and unsaved, will be rewarded according to his works in this future day.

Paul refers in this passage to a well-known Old Testament truth.

> *He who pursues righteousness and loyalty finds life, righteousness and honor (Proverbs 21:21).*

> *The reward of humility and the fear of the LORD are riches, honor and life (Proverbs 22:4).*

The Old Testament taught that believers who pursue righteousness and humility will receive abundant life and honor. We need look no further than this to explain Paul's words, nor do we need to impose the Experimental Predestinarian theology on the passage to unpack its meaning.

This principle is frequently taught in the New Testament as well; Christians and non-Christians will have their lives examined. The Christian will stand before the Judgment Seat of Christ where he will be judged according to his works:[716]

> *For we must all appear before the Judgment Seat of Christ, that each one* ***may receive what is due him for the things done while in the body****, whether good or bad (2 Corinthians 5:10).*

The non-Christian will stand before the Great White Throne where he will be judged according to his works:

> *I saw a great white throne and him who was seated on it. . . . And I saw the dead, great and small, standing before the throne, and books were opened. Another book was opened, which is the book of life. The dead were* ***judged according to what they had done*** *as recorded in the books (Revelation 20:11-12).*

The outcome of the Christian's judgment is either rewards or the loss of rewards. The outcome of the non-Christian's judgment is always the lake of fire because his works are not adequate to redeem.

Judgment on Gentile Christians

Paul then launches into an expansion of the theme that Gentile Christians will be judged according to their works in Romans 2:12-16. His point in this section is that God is impartial. All will be judged according to their works, Christian and non-Christian, Jew and Gentile.

Paul begins by saying,

> *For all who have sinned without the Law will also perish without the Law, and all who have sinned under the Law will be judged [Gr krinō, "evaluated"] by the Law (Romans 2:12).*

---

[716] Romans 14:12; 2 Corinthians 5:10; Galatians 6:6. And Jesus spoke of this in Matthew 12:36-37; John 5:28, 29, etc.

Those who have not been exposed to divine revelation will perish (Gr *apollumi*), a reference in this context to eternal separation from God.[717] But those who have received divine revelation will have their lives evaluated by it, that is, they will be "judged" (Gr *krinō* "evaluated"), not necessarily "condemned," by it. The word means "evaluate" in verse 3, and again in verse 16 where God does not condemn the hidden things, He evaluates them. Some hidden things will be condemned, and some will be honored. All our secrets will one day be exposed.[718]

Romans 2:13 is the problematic statement that has resulted in thousands of pages of discussion.[719]

> *For it is not the hearers of the Law who are just before God, but the doers of the Law will be justified.*

From this the Council of Trent concluded that there is a final justification by works, a justification which secures entrance into heaven, a view now being accepted by some evangelicals as well.[720] Some from a Reformed persuasion have great difficulty with the verse because they, like the Catholics, assume that justification here refers to forensic justification, a declaration of righteousness. This creates a contradiction with Romans 3:28 and Galatians 2:16,

> *For we maintain that a man is justified by faith apart from works of the Law (Romans 3:28).*

> *Nevertheless knowing that a man is not justified by the works of the Law but through faith in Christ Jesus, even we have believed in Christ Jesus, so that we may be justified by faith in Christ and not by the works of the Law; since by the works of the Law no flesh will be justified (Galatians 2:16).*

In one place Paul says that by works of Law a man is "justified" and in another place he says, that by works of Law no man can be justified. This is obviously a contradiction *if justification means the same thing in both places.* But it does not. In Romans 3:4 Paul illustrates a different meaning of justification, one that is similar to that of James.

> *May it never be! Rather, let God be found true, though every man be found a liar, as it is written, "THAT YOU MAY BE JUSTIFIED IN YOUR WORDS, AND PREVAIL WHEN YOU ARE JUDGED" (Romans 3:4).*

---

717 In other contexts it can refer to temporal, psychological and spiritual ruin (e.g. 1 Corinthians 8:11).

718 BDAG, 567 defines this category of usage as to make a judgment based on taking various factors into account, judge, think, consider, look upon (1 Corinthians 10:15, 11:13). Apparently the common meaning was "to divide" and hence the idea of discrimination emerged. ALGNT, 238 suggests it means "making a personal evaluation *think of as better, prefer* (Rom 14.5); ... forming a personal opinion *evaluate, think, judge* (Acts 13:46)."

719 For good discussions of the options see Moo, *The Epistle to the Romans*, 139-48. See also Cranfield, *A Critical and Exegetical Commentary on the Epistle to the Romans*, 1:150-51.

720 "Some texts indicate that righteousness is a future gift believers do not yet have. ...There are indications, therefore, that righteousness should be included in the already-but-not-yet tension that informs New Testament soteriology." Schreiner and Caneday, *The Race Set Before Us*, 79. See also Stanley, *Did Jesus Teach Salvation by Works*, 333. "It is my opinion that the troublesome James 2:14-26 passage teaches judgment on the basis of works." By works, Stanley means works of the Christian man produced in him by God. In regard to Romans 2:13, Stanley feels that practical righteousness is a condition for obtaining final glorification (ibid., 196-197).

Here Paul uses "justified" in the sense of "being vindicated," "demonstrated to be morally right, *prove to be right*."[721] This is the justification James spoke of (James 2:14 ff.). According to James there are two kinds of justification.[722]

You see that a man is justified by works and not by faith alone (James 2:24).

They have already been justified in the forensic sense, acquitted once-and-for-all by God's declaration (Romans 5:1), and they will never experience eternal separation from God. But it is clear that there is a justification by works in the New Testament which means "to be vindicated as morally right," approved by God for a life well-lived.

The more common justification is that which is by faith alone and is a judicial act (Romans 5:1) whereby Christ's righteousness is imputed to us (2 Corinthians 5:21). Since one is by works and the other is by faith, the context must determine which is meant. If works are the condition of justification in Romans 2:13, obviously it cannot refer to a forensic declaration which is obtained by faith alone apart from works.

Paul does not say that the result of justification in Romans 2:13 is personal salvation. Later he will refer to it as "praise from God," a phrase Paul links with reward (1 Corinthians 4:5). Surprisingly Neonomian writers Schreiner and Caneday, who espouse the Reformed view, candidly admit that justification in 2:13 refers to the fact that a person will "receive praise from God."[723] Exactly! Romans 2:29, which speaks of receiving praise, defines the kind of justification mentioned in 2:13 – it is a vindication and praise, not soteriological entrance into heaven. However, these writers never follow up on their insight, and as a result they confusedly interpret "praise" as referring to soteriological entrance into heaven rather than reward.[724] But receiving praise is not the same thing as obtaining final justification and entrance into heaven. Instead it speaks of the affirmation of a life well-lived. The justification referred to here is clearly different from the justification in Romans 3:28. Why would God praise a person for entering heaven? They did nothing to deserve it. That kind of entrance is received freely by believing apart from any work.

We therefore paraphrase Romans 2:13 in this manner,

For it is not the hearers of the Law who are ethically righteous[725] *before God, but the doers of the Law will be declared to be morally upright.*[726]

Paul continues, exploring the inner reflections believers entertain as they stand before the Judgment Seat of Christ.

For when Gentiles who do not have the Law do instinctively the things of the Law, these, not having the Law, are a law to themselves, their conscience bearing witness and their thoughts alternately accusing or else defending them (Romans 2:14-15).

---

[721] BDAG, 249. This is a common meaning of the verb in the New Testament (Matthew 11:19, 12:37; Luke 7:35, 10:29, 16:15; 1 Corinthians 4:4; 1 Timothy 3:16).

[722] We will discuss this passage in detail later, see chapter 28.

[723] Schreiner and Caneday, *The Race Set Before Us*, 166.

[724] They even admit that *epainos* denotes eschatological reward from God (1 Corinthians 4:5; 1 Peter 1:7). But they miss the point and equate reward with salvation instead of something in addition to salvation. "The reward," they say, "should not be construed as something given above and beyond eternal life" (p. 166).

[725] *Dikaios* here means "one who does right" (BDAG, 246) as in Romans 5:7 and 3:10. The immediate context is about the one who "does evil" (v. 9) and the one who "does good" (10).

[726] "Will be justified," that is, "will be vindicated as ethically good people."

While it often said that these Gentiles are moral pagans, it should be obvious that Paul has Christian Gentiles in mind in verses 12-15. He says that those in view have the Law "*written on their hearts*" (v. 15), indicating regeneration by the Holy Spirit. Similarly Paul says to the Corinthians, "*You are a letter of Christ, cared for by us, written not with ink but with the Spirit of the living God, not on tablets of stone but on tablets of human hearts*" (2 Corinthians 3:3). He describes them in Romans 2:26-29 as those "*who keep the requirements of the law*" and hence are to be "*regarded as circumcision.*"

They are ones like the true Jew "who is one inwardly; and circumcision is that which is of the heart, by the Spirit, not by the letter; and his praise is not from men, but from God" (Romans 2:29). Do nonbelievers "do instinctively the things of the Law"? Is that their natural bent? Probably the phrase "do instinctively" (Gr "*phusis*") should not be connected with "works of the law" but rather with the preceding phrase "do not have the law." Thus we translate, "Gentiles which do not possess the law by nature, that is, by virtue of their birth."[727] The NIV renders the following phrase "a law for themselves," as something like "a law for their benefit."[728]

In view of these considerations above, we agree with N. T. Wright, "These people are Christians, on whose hearts the Spirit has written the law, and whose secrets, when revealed, will display the previously hidden works of God."[729]

Paul continues,

> *their conscience bearing witness and their thoughts alternately accusing or else defending them (Romans 2:15).*

This internal reflection will occur in the heart of every believing Gentile as he stands before the Judgment Seat of Christ and recalls how he has lived his life.

The presence of such activity shows that those in view have the Law written on their hearts; they are saved people. When their conscience brings to mind their failings, as a result of this internal debate, Cranfield and Sanday argue that "these Gentile Christians will know that their lives fell far short of the perfect fulfillment of the Law's requirement (cf. 7:14ff)—at the same time, in the midst of their painful awareness of their sinfulness, their *thoughts will also be able to remind them that they truly believed and had begun to have their lives turned in the direction of obedience. Through this mêlée of accusing and defending thoughts the reality of their commitment will be attested.*"[730]

---

727 William Sanday, *A Critical and Exegetical Commentary on the Epistle to the Romans*, 6th ed. (Edinburgh: T. & T. Clark, 1975), 156. Cranfield points to other passages in Paul where φύσις is connected to the preceding words, not the following words: 1:26; 2:27; 11:21, 24 (three times); 1 Corinthians 11:14; Galatians 2:15; 4:8; Ephesians 2:3. The word occurs elsewhere in the New Testament only in James 3:7 and 2 Peter 1:4. The one Pauline occurrence which might seem to point in the opposite direction is 1 Corinthians 11:14.

728 Contra John Piper who incorrectly translates "a law to themselves." Piper, *Future of Justification*, 107. Rather, the Gentiles "have" a law for their benefit, wrought internally in them by the New Covenant operation of the Holy Spirit.

729 Wright, *Justification: God's Plan and Paul's Vision*, 191. Wright points to Romans 2:26-29 and 1 Corinthians 3 as proof.

730 Cranfield, *A Critical and Exegetical Commentary on the Epistle to the Romans*, 1:162. This verse is a problem for Thomas Schreiner. He thinks it would be "strange" if this referred to a believer who is a "doer of the law" Schreiner, *Romans*, 124. Why not? At the Judgment Seat of Christ some will draw back in shame (1 John 2:28), and all will have their secret thoughts examined. It seems natural that even the most godly of saints will have mixed feelings about their faithfulness as they await the Lord's verdict.

Summary

The Christian who perseveres in doing good works can obtain the reward of eternal life, that is, an enriched experience of that life given to him freely at justification through faith alone. It is true that no unjustified man can obtain rewards in heaven by works, but the regenerate saint can. The unjustified can never earn honor, glory, and peace, but the justified can if he shows "*persistence in doing good*" (Romans 2:7).

The Reformed doctrine of perseverance in holiness has often based its scriptural appeal on many of the passages discussed in the preceding chapters. "The perseverance of the saints," John Murray says, "reminds us very forcefully that only those who preserve to the end are truly saints." Romans 2 is often used to support their view. We suggest, however, that the aspect of eternal life in that chapter is not final entrance into heaven as the Experimentalist maintains. Instead, it refers to that enriched experience of life gained by faithful perseverance in doing good and which final results in hearing the Master say, "Well done!"

No doubt Paul learned this truth from his Master who similarly said that believers who have "*done good*" will attain to "*a resurrection of life*," and unbelievers who "*committed the evil deeds to a resurrection of judgment*" (John 5:29). This passage has troubled interpreters because it could be understood to teach a works salvation. However, if one understands the "resurrection of life" as the "*better resurrection*," a resurrection to special honor, of which Hebrews spoke (Hebrews 11:35, see discussion below on pp. 1021 ff.) instead of the general resurrection to be experienced by all believers, these passages harmonize well. It also eliminates the perplexing problem of a works salvation which is totally foreign to John's gospel. This understanding of the resurrection of life also is consistent with the Partner view of Paul's desire that he might "*attain to the resurrection from the dead*" (Philippians. 3:11, see discussion on pp. 1027 ff.). Furthermore, a resurrection to special honor based upon doing good deeds provides a more suitable contrast to a resurrection to judgment based upon evil deeds than a general resurrection to life granted to all believers on the basis of faith alone apart from doing good.

Perhaps, a simpler solution is to acknowledge that generally speaking Christians as a whole are viewed as good people who are expected to do good works and who do good works. However calling them "good" doesn't tell us much. It doesn't say anything about persevering in good to the end of one's life. It doesn't say how much good. It doesn't tell us how consistent the doing of good was. David Anderson suggests, "So we would have to conclude that the two verbs (doing and practicing) are gnomic aorist participles making a general statement of what characterizes the justified and the condemned." In other words, the normal Christian life would be characterized by doing good. If this is the sense, then Jesus is using a figure of speech called synecdoche where the part is used for the whole. In this case, the part, the majority of Christians who do good works, is used by synecdoche for the whole, all Christians, including those who are lawless. (See discussion of synecdoche on pp. 844 ff.).

Experimentalists believe that entrance into salvation, eternal life, and inheritance usually refers to final deliverance from eternal damnation. Their problem is that in many passages, entrance is conditioned up works. In order to maintain their Reformation confession that salvation is by faith alone apart from works, they are forced to argue in a circle. How so? They appeal to these same verses to support the very system used to give these "works passages" their meaning.

18

Entering the Kingdom

PERHAPS YOU have heard the story of Bill Miller. Bill was a farmer and reflected the values so commonly associated with the hardworking folk of the rural Midwest. "Ethical," "faithful husband," "loving father," and "devoutly religious" were all terms his friends and neighbors used to describe him at his funeral. One day while plowing the fields, this seventy-two-year-old man of character had a heart attack and "bought the farm."

As the story goes, Bill ascended to the gates of heaven and was met there by Saint Peter. Standing before the awesome entry way, Bill's gaze was fixed on a magnificent arched sign above the massive oak doors which read, "Entrance to The Kingdom of Heaven – 1,000 Points." (By now you know this story is pure fiction, but there is a point to be made – read on!)

Peter greeted Bill, saying, "Welcome, Bill. I am here to evaluate your life and to determine whether you will be allowed to enter the kingdom of heaven. Let's get started."

"Bill," said St. Peter, "What have you done? Why should you be permitted to enter?"

"Well," Bill replied, "I have been a loving husband to my wonderful wife for 50 years. I served her and loved her selflessly."

"Wonderful," said Peter. "That will be one point!"

Looking at the 1,000-point requirement on the sign over the door, Bill said, "One point! Is that all I get?"

Peter was quite pleased with this man and marked down his score on the yellow pad he brought with him.

"What else, Bill?"

"Hmmm…." Bill thought for a moment. "I have raised four wonderful children. They all believe in God; are involved in serving their communities, and have reputations as men and women of character."

"Very impressive!" exclaimed Peter. "This is outstanding. Rarely have I seen a man like you appear before me. That will be one point," and he made another mark on his yellow pad. "What else?"

Realizing that his whole life had so far amounted to only two points toward the 1,000-point goal, Bill confidently announced what he thought would surely cause the gates to swing wide open.

He said, "I have been faithful in church attendance and believed in God. What's more, I have been heavily involved in the work of my church and I have given substantially of my material goods to charity."

Peter gazed with amazement at this God-fearing man. Bill could tell he had made an impact.

"Rarely have I seen such an incredible demonstration of doing good, loving others, and serving one's family as I see you have done. Well done, Bill. That will be one point," Peter said.

Looking again at the 1,000-point marker over the entry way and realizing that his whole life amounted to only 3 points toward this goal, Bill exclaimed, "One point!! Well, Peter, it is only by the grace of God that I will get in here!"

Immediately Peter responded, "That will be 997 points, welcome to the kingdom of heaven. I gave you three points to keep you talking, but in reality you got no points. Salvation is by grace alone."

This story emerges from the lore of folk theology and raises some questions which this chapter will address.

What is the kingdom of heaven? Does it refer to heaven when we die as the story assumes? If so, why is this kingdom presented in the Gospels as something we can enter and experience now and not just after we too have "bought the farm"?

If entrance into heaven is based on grace alone, why did Jesus say that only those who do the will of the Father will enter? Why did He say that in order to enter the kingdom of heaven, we must be better people than the scribes and Pharisees?

Based on these statements and a number of others that we will consider, Bill's theology was mistakenly grounded on a misunderstanding of the teaching of Christ in several passages, or was it?

Are Works a Condition for Entering the Kingdom?

The New Testament includes 23 references to entering the kingdom, entering into "life," seeking "life," or seeking the kingdom.[731] These passages, commonly called the "entry sayings," are usually understood to refer to entrance into personal salvation either now or in the eschatological future. However, in many of these passages, entry into the kingdom or into "life" appears to be predicated on works.[732] If the traditional idea that "the kingdom" always refers to individual salvation and that "entrance into the kingdom" always refers to "getting saved" or going to heaven when one dies is accepted, as Bill did, then there emerges an apparent conflict with the faith-alone gospel of the New Testament.

For example to "enter the kingdom"[733] requires a righteousness that is greater than that of the scribes and Pharisees (Matthew 5:20).[734] Those who enter the kingdom must do so through the path of discipleship, the narrow gate (Matthew 7:13, 14). In order to enter

[731] The "entry sayings" refer to these phrases: (1) "enter the kingdom of heaven" (Matthew 5:20; 7:21; 18:3; 19:23, 24; 23:13; Mark 9:47; 10:15, 25; Luke 18:17, 24, 25; John 3:5; Acts 14:22); (2) "entering into life" (Matthew 18:8, 9; 19:17; Mark 9:43; (3) "seeking life" (Luke 17:33; Romans 2:7); (4) "seeking the kingdom" (Matthew 6:33; 13:45; Luke 12:31). These seem to be parallel and explain one another.

[732] See G. Todd Wilson, "Conditions for Entering the Kingdom," *Perspectives in Religious Studies* 5(Spring 1978): 40.

[733] Equivalent expressions to "enter the kingdom" are "enter into life" and "enter into joy" and in some cases "inherit the kingdom" (see Schneider, "*eiserchomai*," TDNT, 2.677).

[734] Some understand this "greater righteousness" to refer to either forensic justification or a characteristic of all who are saved. However, as will be demonstrated later, both these options are inconsistent with the context. See pp. 235 ff.

the kingdom, one must do the "will of the Father," that is, obey the precepts taught in the Sermon on the Mount (Matthew 7:21).[735] To "enter into life," which is an equivalent phrase, one must deal radically with sin, reject it, and remove it from one's lifestyle (Matthew 18:3, 9).[736] To enter the kingdom, one must be "converted" (Matthew 18:3, 9). Jesus tells the rich young ruler that to "enter into life" (which he equates with entering the kingdom, v. 23) one must "keep the commandments" (Matthew 19:17).[737] Strenuous moral effort is required if one is to enter the kingdom (Mark 10:24, "how hard").

It should be obvious to any unbiased reader that the calls to enter the kingdom are conditioned upon works. Neonomian writers, believing that entering the kingdom means "going to heaven," simply call a spade a spade and in agreement with the Catholics boldly assert that salvation is secured by non-meritorious, God-produced works in the believer. It is disappointing that the Evangelical Theological Society is now publishing books and articles advocating this viewpoint. A recent example from the pen of Edmund Neufeld says, "Each [beatitude] is an aspect of the condition by which the follower of Christ receives salvation from God."[738]

In the following discussion I will argue that in the Gospel of Matthew the calls to enter the kingdom are addressed to those who are already born again. They are challenges to live out one's faith, *not* invitations to personal salvation, entrance into heaven, or entrance into the Millennial Kingdom. The next three chapters will be devoted to establishing this understanding of the "entry" sayings.

The Greater Righteousness

A passage to which we will frequently return in the following chapters is Matthew 5:20.

For I say to you that unless your righteousness surpasses that of the scribes and Pharisees, you will not enter the kingdom of heaven (Matthew 5:20).

With this simple statement, our Lord set in motion debates that would consume a sea of ink and a forest of paper. This statement raises two interesting questions. What is this superior righteousness that is necessary for entrance? What is meant by the phrase "enter the kingdom"? This chapter discusses the first question and some of the implications for New Testament soteriology emerging from the answer. In the following chapter we will discuss what it means to enter the kingdom.

In the history of interpretation, two basic answers have been given to the first question. The surpassing righteousness is either the imputed righteousness of Christ or it is ethical behavior as specified in the Sermon on the Mount.

---

735 To obey the will of the Father seems to refer to good works in Matthew 12:50. And it is highly unlikely that the "will of the Father" in the context of the Sermon on the Mount is to believe on Christ for salvation as it is in John 6:40. For discussion of this phrase, see pp. 311 ff.

736 "This unconditional orientation to the coming kingdom demands sacrifice, namely, a clean break with everything that would hinder or prejudice the newly established existence of man before God (cf. the sayings about offences in Matthew 18:8 ff.)," ibid., 2.677.

737 True, the disciples ask, "Who then can be saved?" As already demonstrated, "saved" does not have to refer to soteriological entrance into heaven. As has been shown earlier, the salvation in view is the deliverance of the soul by self-denying discipleship to Christ, leading to high honor and reward in the kingdom, see pp. 205 ff.

738 Edmund K. Neufeld, "The Gospel in the Gospels: Answering the Question 'What must I do to be saved?' From the Synoptics," *JETS* 51, no. 2 (June 2008): 273.

THE IMPUTED RIGHTEOUSNESS OF CHRIST

Some believe that the only righteousness that enables one to enter the kingdom is the perfect righteousness of Christ that is imputed to the believer at the moment he believes (2 Corinthians 5:21). That this is the kind of righteousness in view is supposedly proven by Matthew 5:48, where Jesus says we are to be as perfect as God is.

In this view the Sermon is designed to convince men who are seeking salvation by works that they are wretched and cannot possibly live up to the perfect righteousness necessary to obtain salvation by works. In Dwight Pentecost's words, "The Lord seeks to convict the multitude of their need of Messiah by setting forth the true interpretation of what constitutes righteousness. In Matthew 5:21—7:6 the Lord's ministry is one of conviction."[739] In other words, Jesus is using the "Law" to convict His hearers of their total inability to do anything to obtain heaven when they die. Once convinced that their own righteousness is inadequate, they will be open for the gospel solution, being reckoned righteous in Christ. But if this is the intent of the Sermon, one must ask, "Why does Jesus never explain the escape route?" He who came to seek and to save the lost leaves the lost in a helpless situation.

This viewpoint emerges from the assumption that entering the kingdom refers to final entrance into eternal life. If that is true, James Boice then argues, "righteousness" *cannot* mean ethical righteousness because that would mean one obtains heaven by works as maintained by Roman Catholics and Neonomians. He claims that Jesus is not saying that to get to heaven one must have slightly higher degree of the same kind of righteousness. Jesus is saying that if a person is to get to heaven, he must have a better and different kind of righteousness, the imputed righteousness of Christ. He suggests as proof that Philippians 3:4-9 is analogous to Matthew 5:48.

> *I count all things to be loss in view of the surpassing value of knowing Christ Jesus my Lord, for whom I have suffered the loss of all things, and count them but rubbish so that I may gain Christ, and may be found in Him, not having a righteousness of my own derived from the Law, but that which is through faith in Christ, the righteousness which comes from God on the basis of faith (Philippians 3:4–9).*[740]

Matthew 5:48 qualifies the quality of the righteousness needed as being as "*perfect as your heavenly Father is perfect.*" The only righteousness that meets that requirement is the justifying righteousness of Jesus Christ.[741] The problem is that nothing in the sermon or in Matthew's gospel speaks of righteousness this way. Therefore, there is little reason to bring Pauline concerns about imputed, legal righteousness into the passage as many do.[742] It is far

---

[739] J. Dwight Pentecost, "The Purpose of the Sermon on the Mount: Part 3," *BibSac* 115, no. 460 (October-December 1958): 314.

[740] James Montgomery Boice, *The Sermon on the Mount* (Grand Rapids: Zondervan Publishing House, 1972), 102-03.

[741] Hal M. Haller, "Matthew," in *The Grace New Testament Commentary*, ed. Robert N. Wilkin (Denton, TX: Grace Evangelical Society, 2010), 25.

[742] Nor is an appeal to Genesis 15:6 satisfactory ("Abraham believed the Lord, and he credited it to him as righteousness"). The immediate context takes priority. Joachim Jeremias and others have stressed that there is certainly validity to the idea that the Law can be a preparation for Christ, "But what does the actual text of the sermon say? Where in the sermon does one find even a hint on which such an interpretation could

more likely that the standard of being "perfect" is a goal toward which all should strive. It is not a requirement to be "as perfect as God is" in order to enter final salvation.

The factor causing most scholars to reject this view is that Matthew himself defines what he means by "righteousness." The word "righteousness" in Matthew's gospel never means "imputed righteousness."[743] In this sermon righteousness refers to ethical kingdom behavior as will be demonstrated in the following discussion.

ETHICAL INWARD RIGHTEOUSNESS

The view that most closely fits the immediate context is that the greater righteousness is the ethical behavior described in the Sermon on the Mount. This behavior is achieved by daily dependence upon Christ and reflects an inner attitude that complies with the spirit of the Law. When the Law is obeyed with this spirit, it leads to a kingdom way of living. The Pharisees had reduced Torah to external legalisms and specific acts of obedience.

Matthew is writing to a Jewish audience, an audience steeped in the Old Testament. Therefore, a starting place to understanding righteousness is their Scripture which speaks of righteousness in two ways.[744] First, and fundamentally, they knew that their faith could be counted as righteousness, as the encounter with Abraham clearly explained (Genesis 15:6). That kind of righteousness led to personal salvation. But the Old Testament also spoke of righteousness as ethical behavior, just like Matthew does. It involved worshiping God only,[745] faithfully loving God,[746] serving the Lord, speaking truth, not doing any evil to one's neighbor,[747] not saying anything that is twisted or crooked,[748] defending the cause of the poor and the needy,[749] avoiding partiality, making decisions with equity,[750] and being generous.[751]

---

be based? The commands in many places do not appear to be an impossible ideal but things that have the possibility of fulfillment (e.g., Matthew 5:29-30; 7:4-5; 7:13-27)." Joachim Jeremias, *The Sermon on the Mount* (Philadelphia: Fortress Press, 1963), 7-8. R. T. France also argues that "righteousness" in Matthew "is the conduct required of God's people rather than the Pauline sense of a gift bestowed by God," R. T. France, *The Gospel of Matthew*, New International Critical Commentary (Grand Rapids: Wm. B. Eerdmans Publishing Co., 2007), 119, 89. See also W. D. Davies and Dale C. Allison, *A Critical and Exegetical Commentary on the Gospel According to Saint Matthew* (Edinburgh: T. & T. Clark, 1988), 1:449. They correctly say, "The meaning of 'righteousness' in 5:20 is determined by the paragraphs that follow. 'Righteousness' is therefore Christian character and conduct in accordance with the demands of Jesus—right intention, right word, right deed. Hence 'righteousness' does not refer, even implicitly, to God's gift. The Pauline (forensic, eschatological) connotation is absent" (p. 449). And one may also compare 5:47: "And if you greet only your brothers, what are you doing more than others?" "The greater righteousness is a doing more. It is therefore a quantitative advance" (ibid. 500).

743 Cf. R. C. H. Lenski, *The Interpretation of St. Matthew's Gospel*, reprint ed. (Minneapolis: Augsburg Publishing Co., 1943), 215-16.

744 For good discussion and substantiation that righteousness in the Sermon refers to ethical behavior and not forensic justification, see Charles H. Talbert, *Reading the Sermon on the Mount: Character Formation and Ethical Decision Making in Matthew 5-7* (Grand Rapids: Baker Academic, 2004).

745 Psalms 106:3.

746 Psalms 15:2-3.

747 Joshua 24:14.

748 Proverbs 3:8.

749 Psalms 72:1-4.

750 Leviticus 19:15.

751 Psalms 37:21.

Matthew echoes these Old Testament themes. He never mentions or even hints at the righteousness granted to Abraham through faith alone. For Matthew, righteousness involves poverty of spirit, meekness, mercifulness, and purity of heart (Matt 5:3-12). His subject is sanctification, not personal justification.

Matthew 5:20 begins with, "For I tell you." In customary rabbinic fashion, which Jesus followed throughout the gospels, this phrase is a title for what follows, the antitheses in verses 22-44.[752] The surpassing righteousness is defined by these antitheses. It far exceeds the righteousness of the scribes and Pharisees in six particulars: murder (5:21-25), adultery (5:27-30), divorce (5:31-32), oaths (5:33-37), retaliation (5:38-42), and loving one's enemies (5:43-48).

In each case Christ takes His hearers far beyond outward acts and penetrates to inner attitudes and motivations.[753] One may compare 5:47, "*And if you greet only your brothers, what are you doing more than others*?" It is clear that "the greater righteousness is *doing more*. Jesus states that the righteousness of which He speaks is a matter of works. "*Beware of practicing* [Gr *poieō*, "what is done"[754]] *your righteousness before men to be noticed by them; otherwise you have no reward with your Father who is in heaven*" (Matthew 6:1).

In the verses that follow Matthew 6:1, Jesus continues to define what He means by righteousness. If one is to enter the kingdom, his life must be characterized by almsgiving (6:1-4), prayer (6:5-15), and fasting (6:16-18). These acts of righteousness must not be done for the praise of men. It manifests itself in trusting our heavenly Father for our needs (6:25-34) and in removing our own faults before judging others (7:15). The one exercising this righteousness obeys the Golden Rule (7:12). The *higher* righteousness involves entering the kingdom through the narrow gate rather than the broad gate. This higher righteousness is inward as well as outward obedience to the will of God as found in the Sermon on the Mount.[755]

If "entering the kingdom" means "go to heaven when you die," and the surpassing righteousness is ethical behavior, Jesus would be contradicting Himself, because elsewhere

---

752 Ulrich Luz and Helmut Koester, *Matthew 1-7: A Commentary*, rev ed., Hermeneia (Minneapolis: Fortress Press, 2007), 221.

753 Neonomian writer Edmund Neufeld is correct in saying "the five antitheses that complete Matthew 5, and the sections on almsgiving, prayer, and fasting give our reader more information about Jesus' kind of righteousness." Neufeld, "The Gospel in the Gospels: Answering the Question 'What must I do to be saved?' From the Synoptics," 273. Davies and Allison agree, "The meaning of 'righteousness' in 5:20 is determined by the paragraphs that follow. 'Righteousness' is therefore Christian character and conduct in accordance with the demands of Jesus—right intention, right word, right deed. Hence 'righteousness' does not refer, even implicitly, to God's gift. The Pauline [forensic, eschatological] connotation is absent." Davies and Allison, *A Critical and Exegetical Commentary on the Gospel According to Saint Matthew*, 499.

754 BDAG, 839.

755 In what way does this righteousness "surpass" that of the scribes and Pharisees? Based on Matthew 23:3-4, it may be that it is a difference between belief and practice. Their doctrine of ethical behavior may be correct, but they failed to practice it. The Sermon marks three distinctives of kingdom-entry righteousness in contrast to that of the Pharisees. First, the antitheses of 5:21-48 state that mere external compliance with the law is not good enough. The spirit of the law must be obeyed, and the internal attitudes are more important than mere external observance. Second, this obedience is not to be understood through the grid of human tradition as demonstrated by the repeated phrase, "you have heard it said, but I say unto you." Third, reliance on external performance of religious practices counts for nothing (Matt 6:1-18). When you give alms, do it in secret, and when you pray, go into your closet and do not do it in order to be seen of others. Hans Dieter Betz and Adela Yarbro Collins, *The Sermon on the Mount: A Commentary on the Sermon on the Mount, Including the Sermon on the Plain (Matthew 5:3-7:27 and Luke 6:20-49)*, Hermeneia (Minneapolis: Fortress Press, 1995), 193.

He said entrance into heaven is based on faith (e.g., John 3:16).[756] Betz and Collins assert that Jesus does, in fact, teach salvation by works, "Ethical demands should shape this way of life; but the purpose of such demands is primarily eschatological in that their *goal is to qualify the disciple for entering into the kingdom of the heavens.*"[757] In other words, final entrance into the eschatological kingdom is obtained through a "righteousness achieved by human action."[758] How is this to be harmonized with the claims of Jesus in the gospel of John that salvation comes by faith in His name, not by human action? Betz weakly replies that "*In some way* God provides this righteousness through Jesus Christ for those who believe in him."[759] He never tells us what this way is or where it is mentioned in the Sermon on the Mount.

While many other commentators do not hesitate to assert "that moral effort is necessary in order to enter the kingdom,"[760] they often give no clear explanation as to how this can be harmonized with the New Testament teaching that salvation is by faith alone.[761] Elsewhere Jesus, Paul, and John make it absolutely clear that faith alone is all that is needed for salvation from sin (John 3:16); it is apart from works (Ephesians 2:8-9); and is "without cost" (Revelation 21:6). How is this apparent conflict to be harmonized?

Harmonizing Matthew and Paul

There have been at least five attempts to explain the apparent discrepancy between the *sola fide, sola gratia* gospel of Paul and Jesus and the faith-plus-works requirement for kingdom entrance presented in Matthew's gospel.[762]

SALVATION IS BY WORKS

Some, like Betz and Collins quoted above, indifferent to inspiration and the biblically-based conclusions of the Reformation simply state that this is a contradiction and assume

756 R. T. France also argues that "righteousness" in Matthew "is the conduct required of God's people rather than the Pauline sense of a gift bestowed by God," (*The Gospel of Matthew*, 89, 119). John Nolland agrees, "The close integration of v. 20 into the thought sequence of vv. 17–20 makes clear that the faithful practice of the requirements of the Law is in view," Nolland, *The Gospel of Matthew: A Commentary on the Greek Text*, 224.

757 Betz and Collins, *The Sermon on the Mount: A Commentary on the Sermon on the Mount, Including the Sermon on the Plain (Matthew 5:3-7:27 and Luke 6:20-49)*, 189.

758 Ibid., 190.

759 Ibid.

760 I. Howard Marshall, *The Gospel of Luke: A Commentary on the Greek Text* (Grand Rapids: Wm. B. Eerdmans Publishing Co., 1978), 565.

761 Stephen Westerholm, for example, says in reference to Matthew 5:20; 7:13-14, 21 that "Jesus declares how people must live if they are to enter the kingdom of God," Stephen Westerholm, *Understanding Matthew: The Early Christian Worldview of the First Gospel* (Grand Rapids: Baker Book House, 2006), 112. True, but if "entering the kingdom" means "go to heaven," then this is achieved by living well, not simple faith, and the gospel is negated. Steven D. Fraade, "Juda (Place) - Judaism," in *The Yale Anchor Bible Dictionary*, ed. David Noel Freedman (New York: Doubleday, 1966), 112. Or consider this statement, "Entry 'into the *basileia*' is promised as a reward to those who do a better righteousness (5:20), to the one who does the will of the Father (7:21)," Richard Bauckham, *The Fate of the Dead: Studies on the Jewish and Christian Apocalypses*, Supplements to Novum Testamentum (Boston: Brill, 1998), 84. In other words, according to Bauckham, entry into heaven is obtained by good works. Surprisingly, he feels no need to give help to busy pastors reading his book on how to resolve this difficulty.

762 See Petri Luomanen, *Entering the Kingdom of Heaven: A Study on the Structure of Matthew's View of Salvation* (Tübingen: Mohr Siebeck, 1998), 7-44.

that Matthew taught salvation by works and Paul by faith alone. The Sermon on the Mount contains the requirements for entering the kingdom of heaven, and entering the kingdom, they say, refers to eschatological admission to heaven. In order to enter the land in the Old Testament, commandments had to be obeyed (Deuteronomy 30), and Jesus is the new lawgiver requiring obedience to the surpassing righteousness of the Sermon.[763] Entering the land and entering the kingdom are similar in this view. Kümmel links Jesus to the Rabbis, "according to which a man must fulfill certain conditions to partake of the eschatological glory."[764]

SALVATION IS BY GRACE

Consistent with the conclusions of the Reformation, many others stress that Matthew also stresses salvation by grace just like Paul does. No doubt Matthew is in full agreement with the apostle Paul, but the poverty of clear statements about *sola fide* and *sola gratia* coupled with the many statements about works suggest that Matthew's "gospel of the kingdom" was not primarily about soteriology. I will argue in the next chapter that entering the kingdom often refers to entering into a way of living, the kingdom way of living specified in the Sermon on the Mount. The Sermon is instruction for Christians on what it means to be a Christ-follower.

It is difficult to find references in Matthew to grace alone. Typically interpreters find the gospel of grace by stretching the meaning of various passages to the breaking point. Some, for example, discover the gospel buried in Matthew 9:13 ("*I desire compassion*"). Others see the gospel in the fact that the exhortation to follow Jesus (Matthew 16:24 ff.) occurs after, not before, the prediction of the passion (16:21 ff.). Others find the Pauline doctrine of "in Christ" in the references to a connection between Christ and the believers in such passages as Matthew 10:24, 40; 18:5; 25:31-37; 28:16-20.[765] Some find the gospel in Jesus' statement, "*Blessed are the poor in spirit, for theirs is the kingdom of heaven*" (Matthew 5:3).[766]

And, of course, outside of Matthew, Luke 12:31-32 is cited, "*Do not be afraid, little flock, for your Father has chosen gladly to give you the kingdom.*" However, elsewhere this supposed "gift" comes to them because they performed good works, acts of charity (Matthew 25:35-36). In fact the preceding verse explains that the condition for obtaining the kingdom is to "seek" it (Luke 12:31). Also, since those whom Jesus addresses in the

---

[763] See Hans Windisch, *Der sinn der Bergpredigt, ein Beitrag zum geschichtlichen verständnis der Evangelien und zum Problem der Richtigen Exegese*, 2., stark umgearb., erweiterte und verbe aufl. ed. (Leipzig: J. C. Hinrichs, 1937).

[764] W. G. Kümmel, *Promise and Fulfillment* (London: SCM Press, 1957), 53.

[765] See W. D. Davies, *The Setting of the Sermon on the Mount* (Cambridge: University Press, 1964), 92-99.

[766] Of course Matthew's Jewish audience knew that the Old Testament predicted that Messiah would die for their sins (Isaiah 53). That hardly justifies the claim that Matthew's intended purpose was to present the gospel of grace. By all accounts, Matthew's "gospel" is not about soteriology, it is about discipleship. It is directed at those who are already saved to instruct them how to live. Those who want to see the Gospel of Matthew as loaded with comments, inferences, or assumption about free grace, salvation by faith alone, etc. must simply read those inferences into passages which plainly are not addressing that issue. As far as I know, they cannot point to one passage in Matthew that clearly stresses salvation by grace or even assumes it. Certainly, Matthew believed in salvation by grace alone in Christ alone, but that is not the purpose of his gospel and there are not passages in it which clearly teach it. That is not to say that Matthew would deny it! If the gospel of salvation by faith alone is to be inferred from many passages in Matthew, why is it that the majority of evangelical and liberal scholars for centuries have viewed Matthew and Paul to be in "apparent" conflict?

Sermon are already saved, Bock says the "kingdom" here does not refer to salvation. Instead it refers to the "kingdom blessings that are the product of pursuing the kingdom."[767]

SALVATION IS ALWAYS EVIDENCED BY WORKS

Most Experimentalists turn the Sermon on the Mount into a test of salvation. Lloyd-Jones, for example, argues that being as perfect as God is (Matthew 5:48) is "the essential definition of Christian." Then, of course, he begins backtracking. He explains that being as perfect as God is only a matter of having something unique about our lives that non-Christians do not have. "The question we must ask ourselves, then, if we want to know for certain whether we are truly Christian or not, is this, 'Is there something special and unique about me and my life which is never to be found in the non-Christian.'"[768] This characteristic of the Christian life, he says, is never to be found in a non-Christian and it is "special and unique" to the Christian. Many others hold this same view.[769]

This is the classic Experimental Predestinarian solution. When Jesus says one must have surpassing righteousness in order to enter the kingdom, this is not, they say, a *condition* of entrance, but the *characteristic* of the truly saved. Or when He says that only those who "do the will of the Father" will enter the kingdom, He is referring to those who are regenerate. All who are regenerate will do the will of the Father, that is, obey the Sermon, and therefore, once again, this is only a description of those who have "genuinely" believed.

Because Hagner admits that those called on to enter the kingdom are regenerate saints, he has a theological problem on his hands. He says, "The verse is addressed, it must be

---

767 Bock, *Luke*, 2:1165.

768 Martyn Lloyd-Jones, *Studies in the Sermon on the Mount* (Grand Rapids: Wm. B. Eerdmans Publishing Co., 1971), 314. He then devotes several pages to identify the special and unique qualities which all Christians have; he is concerned about the spirit of the Law and not the letter; his attitude toward morality is positive and not negative like the natural man; he does not view himself as worthy of heaven; he sees non-Christians as sinners, as dupes of Satan; he sees God as someone who is to be obeyed and feared; his great motivation is love, and he gives without counting the cost; he rejoices in tribulation because he sees hidden meaning in them. For each quality Lloyd-Jones draws a contrast with some imagined quality of the natural man. No one would deny that all Christians should have these qualities, but the plain facts of experience are that they do not! Furthermore, this is no test of certainty at all. How can one tell if there is something special and unique about himself? How does he know that this or that quality is special and unique enough to be certain it is evidence of being a Christian, especially when Lloyd-Jones acknowledges that non-Christians can have many Christian characteristics? He admits that people who do not believe in God can have a "high" ethical standard and be very moral.

769 D. A. Carson says, "The verb 'surpasses' [in v. 20] suggests that the new righteousness outstrips the old both qualitatively and quantitatively. Anything less does not enter the kingdom." In quality and quantity! To outstrip it in quality is to say it is another kind of righteousness altogether. Forensic justification? Carson does not say. To outstrip it in quantity means there is more of it. But then, as is typical of many commentators, he leaves his readers hanging on the precipice of a works salvation and gives no explanation. He says, "And that teaching, far from being more lenient, is nothing less than perfection (see on 5:48)." As an illustration from Matthew of the meaning of "righteousness," he refers to Matthew 25:31-34, the righteous behavior of the faithful sheep who ministered to the poor. Thus the inference is that Carson believes that in order to enter the Kingdom, we must do good works, and possibly, they must be as good as God's. Obviously, Carson, a solid evangelical, does not believe that. D. A. Carson, "Matthew," in The Expositor's Bible Commentary, Matthew, Mark, Luke (Grand Rapids: Zondervan, 1984), 146. Alford says that it is not altogether imperative in meaning but includes the imperative sense "such shall be the state, the aim of Christians." Alford and Harrison, "Matthew," 1:55. See also Gordon Lewis and Bruce Demarest, *Integrative Theology* (Grand Rapids, MI: Zondervan Publishing House, 1987), 2:240. Cf also Charles H. Spurgeon, *Spurgeon's Sermons* (Albany, OR: Ages Software, 1998), vol. 53.

remembered, to those who are the recipients of the kingdom."[770] If that is true, then how can those who are already "recipients of the kingdom," that is, are saved, be called on to enter it? Haven't saved people already entered it? With an egregious example of theological exegesis, Hagner's Experimental Predestinarian system comes into play. He says, "To belong to the kingdom means to follow Jesus' teaching. Hence, the kingdom and the righteousness of the kingdom go together; they cannot be separated."[771]

But, in Matthew 5:19 Jesus says they *can* be separated. The one who disobeys even the least of the commandments and teaches others to do the same "will be least *in* the kingdom." That is, to use Hagner's term, he is a "recipient of the kingdom." The righteousness of the kingdom and belonging to the kingdom can indeed, contrary to Hagner, be separated.[772]

GETTING SAVED IS BY FAITH BUT STAYING SAVED IS BY WORKS

A view that is much more believable is the Arminian view, more recently referred to by E. P. Sanders as covenantal nomism. Sanders suggests that the gospel writers have been too hard on the Pharisees. True religion of the Jews involved their walking with God by faith in response to the covenant. However, to stay in the covenant, one must obey the commandments.[773] But in reality this is another version of faith plus works.

SALVATION BY FAITH PLUS WORKS

A final attempt to harmonize the apparent discrepancy between a "faith alone" view of salvation and the seemingly contradictory statements made by Jesus regarding the conditions for entering the kingdom is what may be called a Neonomian view of salvation.[774] Stanley boldly asserts that ethical righteousness is necessary to make one "eligible" to enter the kingdom. This ethical behavior, he says, is not just *evidence* that one is saved, but is a *condition* for obtaining final entrance into heaven. As an initially justified sinner progresses along his "pilgrimage" (which Stanley says is the process of being saved and eventually entering heaven),[775] "Somewhere along the way," he says, "converted sinners become righteous and therefore eligible to enter the kingdom."[776]

"It is important," he says, "that we treat salvation in the Gospels as a way of life rather than a one-time conversion experience."[777] This view is reminiscent of the Roman

---

770 Donald A. Hagner, *Matthew 14-28*, Word Biblical Commentary (Dallas: Word Books, 2002), 109.

771 Ibid., 109.

772 Hagner weakly asserts that those who are "least" have kept the Law "for the most part"! Betz and Collins disagree. "His violation consists of the setting aside of the commandments altogether, either in their entirety or by selection. He is presented as a teacher who not only sets aside the commandments but also teaches the people to do the same. In sum, he is an apostate teaching apostasy." Betz and Collins, *The Sermon on the Mount: A Commentary on the Sermon on the Mount, Including the Sermon on the Plain (Matthew 5:3-7:27 and Luke 6:20-49)*, 185.

773 Sanders, *Paul and Palestinian Judaism*, 422-23.

774 For discussion, see pp. 20 above.

775 He says that "salvation is a pilgrimage," Stanley, *Did Jesus Teach Salvation by Works*, 326. Evangelical orthodoxy has normally understood salvation as a single "event" in time, which then ensues in a pilgrimage, thereby distinguishing justification and sanctification.

776 Ibid., 175.

777 Ibid., 167.

Catholic Council of Trent.[778] He believes that becoming righteous enough to enter is a condition[779] for entrance, and that in the life of a true believer, he will always be made righteous enough.[780] Since salvation is by faith and salvation is a process and not an event, it follows that the faith that saves is a persistent faith[781] and that final salvation is achieved by fulfillment of the process of justification and sanctification. The Council decrees that "faith co-operating with good works increases in that justice [i.e., believers will become more and more righteous in daily life] which they have received through the grace of Christ, and are still further justified."[782] Obviously, Stanley's views differ from those of orthodox evangelicals. He believes that "becoming righteous enough to enter" is a condition[783] for entrance, and that in the life of a true believer, he will always be made righteous enough.[784]

A major difficulty with Stanley's view is that justification in the New Testament is presented as something that has already happened to the believer and is complete at the point he believed.

As Shedd points out, "It is a single act of God which sets the believer in a justified state or condition."; 'who shall lay anything to the charge of God's elect? who is he that condemns?' (8:33–34); 'he that hears my word and believes on him that sent me has everlasting life and shall not come into condemnation' (John 5:24)."[785] In Stanley's soteriology there may still be a charge that could be brought against God's elect; a "believer" may still suffer condemnation (presumably, because he is not a "true" believer). He rejects the Reformation view of justification by faith alone. According to Stanley final justification depends on whether God works enough righteousness in him to make him eligible to avoid damnation. When Stanley claims that his views of justification are a legitimate expression of the historic evangelical faith, one is reminded of Calvin's retort to the Catholics, "It is like killing a man in the public square and then claiming he is not dead."

---

778 Although the phraseology is different, this concept could have been lifted directly from the Council of Trent. The Council decrees, "If anyone says that justifying faith is nothing else than confidence in divine mercy, which remits sins for Christ's sake, or that it is this confidence alone that justifies us, let him be anathema." *Canon and Decrees of the Council of Trent*, trans. H. J. Schroeder (Rockford, IL: Tan, 1978), 43 - end. The canons continue, "If anyone says that a man who is justified and, however perfect, is not bound to observe the commandments of God and the Church, but only to believe, as if the Gospel were a bare and absolute promise of eternal life without the condition of observing the commandments, let him be anathema," ibid., 44. The Council believes that works are a condition for obtaining final salvation. It is difficult to distinguish their views from those of Stanley.

779 Stanley, *Did Jesus Teach Salvation by Works*, 335.

780 This, of course, negates the teaching of forensic imputation which forever settles the believers account with God regardless of his subsequent behavior. In his book Stanley never mentions imputation in connection with justification. In agreement with Stanley, Paul A. Rainbow writes, "An arrow's eventual resting place is fixed the moment it leaves the bowstring, but it will reach the target provided only that it traverses the arc between the two points, impelled by the force that set it in motion. Imputation puts believers on a sure course to final justification and eternal life, provided that the very God whose will it was to find in sinners' favor at the cross also wills to refashion them after the image of his Son," For a similar view see Rainbow, *Way of Salvation*, 211.

781 Ibid., 251.

782 *Canon and Decrees of the Council of Trent*, 36.

783 Stanley, *Did Jesus Teach Salvation by Works*, 335.

784 Rainbow, *Way of Salvation*, 211.

785 Shedd, *Dogmatic Theology*, 797.

According to the New Testament, I am already eligible for heaven because I have already been acquitted, justified. "*He who knew no sin was made to be sin for us that we might be made the righteousness of God in him*" (2 Corinthians 5:21). At the point in time I believed, I was made eligible! "*Therefore, having been justified by faith, we have peace with God through our Lord Jesus Christ*" (Romans 5:1). I have already been declared righteous and, as a result, I currently have peace with God. I am not left in doubt. I have an objective promise I rely on. And this justification secures freedom from condemnation from all sin, past, present, and future, "*For by one offering He has perfected for all time those who are sanctified*" (Hebrews 10:14).

Summary

In this chapter we have raised an issue that has engaged the minds of interpreters of the New Testament for centuries. The Synoptic gospels often seem to teach that salvation is by works or faith plus works, as the Roman Catholic Church has long maintained.

Because Protestants believe in *sola fide,* they have made many attempts to bring Paul and Matthew into harmony on this matter. The problem is particularly pronounced in regard to the entry sayings that many have understood to teach that entrance into the kingdom of heaven is conditioned on works. To resolve this dilemma, some have suggested that salvation by grace alone is found in Matthew, but that it is not so explicitly stated as it is in Paul's epistles.

The traditional Experimental Predestinarian approach suggests that works are not conditions at all. Instead, when Jesus says that only those who do the will of the Father will enter the kingdom, He is describing the *characteristics* of all who are saved, not the *conditions* of final entrance.

The Arminians, of course, are somewhat bemused by all this. Believing as they do that salvation can be lost, they have a simple solution: one is saved by faith alone, but he must persevere in a life of works or he will lose his justification. So the believer who does not do the will of the Father is one who has committed apostasy; he has lost the salvation he initially possessed.

Neonomians like Alan Stanley, Paul Rainbow, Thomas Schreiner, and Ardel Caneday simply assert that salvation is by faith plus works. Of course, they nuance it in such a way as to avoid saying what this seems to say. According to these writers, these works are the God-produced, non-meritorious works that are always and inevitably produced in the life of those who have "truly" believed and who have "genuine" faith. This view will be addressed in considerable detail in later chapters. At this point in our discussion, it is sufficient to say that in my opinion this is the most unlikely of all the above interpretations. It conflicts with the clear statements of Scripture that a person is already justified at the moment he believes in Christ. There is no soteriological justification in the future, as they maintain. Instead there will be a vindication-justification in the sense of a declaration of a life well-lived.

In this chapter, in agreement with the majority of commentators, we have concluded that the "surpassing righteousness" is an inward disposition that penetrates to the true meaning of the law. It surpasses the righteousness of the scribes and Pharisees in that they focused on external legalisms and lost the true inner significance of Torah.

What then is the solution to the apparent contradiction between Matthew and Paul? In my opinion, all of the current options are exercises in theological exegesis that have led to a dead end.

To find a credible, contextually valid approach to this difficulty, we must focus our attention on the true meaning of the phrase "enter the kingdom." Conventional conservative theology has always assumed that this refers to entrance into personal salvation or one's final entrance into the millennium or the eternal state. While that is sometimes true, in the following chapters we will suggest that the phrase often refers to entrance into that aspect of the kingdom which may be called "the kingdom way of life leading to higher honor."

19

Entering into Life and Discipleship

WHAT DOES it mean to "enter the kingdom"? Jesus spoke frequently of the need for His *believing followers* to enter the kingdom of heaven. For example, He said,

> *For I say to you that unless your righteousness surpasses that of the scribes and Pharisees, you will not enter the kingdom of heaven (Matthew 5:20).*

The word "your" indicates that He is speaking *particularly* to His saved disciples, and not an unbelieving group. As shown in the preceding chapter, Jesus seems to say that "righteousness" (that is, a righteous lifestyle) is a necessary condition for entrance into the kingdom of heaven. However, if a life of good works is necessary for kingdom entrance, an apparent contradiction appears between the faith-alone criterion for final salvation taught elsewhere and Matthew 5:20. On the one hand, Jesus and Paul maintain that salvation is by faith alone, but here Jesus seems to say that salvation requires works. Jesus has made it clear in Matthew 5:19 that a life of good works is *not* necessary to be in the kingdom. The five explanations of this tension outlined in the preceding chapter are all inadequate.[786] In order to resolve this difficulty, we first need to explore the answer to the question, "What is the meaning of the phrase 'enter the kingdom'?"

To answer this we must consider a number of interrelated issues and parallel passages. The more one descends into the details, the more it becomes evident that the issues are rather complex. To whom, for example is Jesus speaking? Some argue that it is to the disciples; others believe those addressed are a mixed crowd including those who have not yet put their faith in Him. An equally important question is, "What does Jesus mean by the 'kingdom of heaven'?" Is this a reference to the future kingdom or is He referring to a present reality of some sort? This may have importance in what it means to enter it. Whatever we conclude about His statements in Matthew 5:19-20, it must be in harmony with the conclusion of the Sermon in Matthew 7:13 ff. This requires that we must decide on the meaning of the broad and narrow ways. We must also explain how the contrast between "life" in 7:14 and "destruction" in 7:13 relate to entering or not entering the kingdom. What about those who say "Lord, Lord" to Him in 7:21, but who do not enter the kingdom because they have not "done the will of the Father"? It seems obvious to many that whatever "enter the kingdom" means, it likely means the same thing in 7:21 that it does in 5:20. If the entrants in 7:21 cannot enter because they have not "done the will of the Father," does this mean they cannot

[786] A recent example is Roger Mohrlang, *Matthew and Paul: A Comparison of Ethical Perspectives*, Monograph series / Society for New Testament Studies (New York: Cambridge University Press, 1984).

enter because they have not lived out the ethics of the preceding chapters of the Sermon, or does the "will of the Father" possibly mean "believing on Him" as it does in John 6:40? How is it possible that those who have done miracles in His name are not allowed entrance? In fact Jesus says to them, "Depart from me." Does this refer to eternal separation from God thus helping us interpret the *destruction* of those who chose the broad way (7:13)? What about parallel passages elsewhere in Matthew such as the encounter with the rich young ruler where entering the kingdom, inheriting the kingdom, inheriting eternal life, treasure in heaven, and obtaining life all seem to be similar or closely related ideas?

A number of "entry sayings" in the New Testament must be considered together if one is to arrive at the meaning of "enter the kingdom" and to have a satisfactory explanation of the apparent contradiction between the faith-alone condition for obtaining final salvation and the seeming requirement of works as an addition to it found in a number of passages in the New Testament. What are these entry sayings?

Entry Sayings

The term "entry sayings" refers to these phrases: (1) "enter the kingdom of heaven" (Matthew 5:20; 7:21; 18:3; 19:23, 24; 23:13; Mark 9:47; 10:15, 25; Luke 18:17, 24, 25; John 3:5; Acts 14:22); (2) "entering into life" (Matthew 18:8, 9; 19:17; Mark 9:43); (3) "seeking life" (Luke 17:33; Romans 2:7); and (4) "seeking the kingdom" (Matthew 6:33; 13:45; Luke 12:31). These seem to be parallel and explain each other.

What did Jesus mean when He spoke of entering the kingdom of heaven?

Old Testament Background

The Old Testament includes no specific statements about entering the kingdom.[787] However, the allusions, such as they are, all indicate that this entrance is something those *already saved* can do and is based on works.[788]

The closest analogies to entering the kingdom in the Old Testament are of three kinds: entering the land, entering the temple precincts, and the renewal ceremony at Shechem.

ENTERING THE LAND

God's commandments regarding the fact that entering the kingdom requires obedience[789] have been noted by many, and are commonly associated with entering into

---

787 Actually there is one. In Daniel 11:9 we read, "Then the latter will enter the realm of the king of the South, but will return to his own land" (NASB). To enter the "realm" (Hebrews *malkūt*) can be understood as entering the "geographical sphere of the kingdom." In fact it is translated "kingdom" more than forty times in the NASB.

788 For a good discussion of possible Old Testament antecedents to the phrase "the kingdom of God" see C. C. Caragounis, "Kingdom of God/Kingdom of Heaven," in *Dictionary of Jesus and the Gospels*, ed. Joel B. Green, Scot McKnight, and I. Howard Marshall (Downers Grove, IL: InterVarsity Press, 1992), 417-18. He notes, "Yet though the term is absent, the idea is present throughout the Old Testament. In a number of instances Yahweh is presented as king (Deut 9:26 [LXX]; 1 Samuel 12:12; Psalms 24:10 [LXX, 23:10]; 29:10 [LXX, 28:10]; Isaiah 6:5; 33:22; Zeph 3:15; Zech 14:16, 17). At other places he is ascribed a royal throne (Ps 9:4 [LXX 9:5]; 45:6 [LXX, 44:7]; 47:8 [LXX, 46:9]; Isaiah 6:1; 66:1; Ezekiel 1:26; Sir 1:8) while occasionally his continuous or future reign is affirmed (Psalms 10:16 [LXX, 9:37]; 146:10 [LXX, 145:10]; Isaiah 24:23; Wis. 3:8). In fact Psalms 22:28 (MT, 22:29; LXX, 21:29) says 'The kingdom belongs to the Lord.'"

789 Deuteronomy 4:1; 6:17-18; 16:20; 28, 20, etc. "The background for the expression is to be found in the Old

one's inheritance, the promised land, or entering into rest.[790] In these passages the people are challenged to embrace the conditions necessary to enter the land of Canaan.

> *Now, O Israel, listen to the statutes and the judgments which* ***I am teaching you to perform****, so that you may live and go in and take possession of the land which the LORD, the God of your fathers, is giving you (Deuteronomy 4:1).*

> ***You shall do what is right and good*** *in the sight of the LORD, that it may be well with you and that you may go in and possess the good land which the LORD swore to give your fathers (Deuteronomy 6:18).*

They must listen to the Lord's regulations and obey them; if they were to do so, they would "live" and "go in and possess the land."

ENTERING THE TEMPLE

The passages in the Psalms that list prerequisites for entrance into the temple gates are understood by many[791] as background to the notion of entering the kingdom in the New Testament.

> *O LORD, who may abide in Your tent? Who may dwell on Your holy hill?* ***He who walks with integrity, and works righteousness****, And speaks truth in his heart (Psalm 15:1–2).*

> *Who may ascend into the hill of the LORD? And who may stand in His holy place?* ***He who has clean hands and a pure heart****, Who has not lifted up his soul to falsehood And has not sworn deceitfully (Psalm 24:3).*

> ***Enter His gates with thanksgiving****, and His courts with praise. Give thanks to Him, bless His name (Psalm 100:3).*

To "ascend the hill of the Lord" (Psalm 24:3), that is, to enter the sanctuary area, is for believers to "enter into fellowship" with God.

David said,

> *Open to me the gates of righteousness; I shall enter through them, I shall give thanks to the LORD. This is the gate of the LORD; the righteous will enter through it (Psalm 118:19–20).*

Only those who are ethically righteous before God were to enter and offer sacrifices of righteousness in the temple. Thus the gates were called "the gates of righteousness."

Isaiah says that in the future millennium, God will "*open the gates*" of the city so that "*the righteous nation may enter.*" This "righteous nation" is the faithful remnant, "*the one*

Testament, in the idea of entering the promised land (Numbers 20:24; Judges 18:9; As. Mos. 2:1)." Davies and Allison, *A Critical and Exegetical Commentary on the Gospel According to Saint Matthew*, 1:499. That entrance was conditioned on obedience, that is, works. There were battles to be fought and victories to be won.

790 "Particularly important in relation to the preaching of Jesus, which speaks of entry into the kingdom of God, is the similar expression concerning the entry of the people of Israel into the promised land (εἰσέρχεσθαι εἰς τὴν γῆν, Exodus, Leviticus, Numbers, Deuteronomy), often together with κληρονομεῖν (εἰσελθεῖν καὶ κληρονομεῖν, e.g., Deuteronomy 6:18). The same concept underlies the phrase εἰσέρχεσθαι εἰς τὴν κατάπαυσιν, 'into the rest of God,' in Psalms 94:11," Schneider, "*eiserchomai*," in TDNT, 2:684.

791 E.g., Psalms 15, 24; 118:19-21. See John P. Meier, *Law and History in Matthew's Gospel: A Redactional Study of Mt. 5:17-48* (Rome: Biblical Institute Press, 1976), 113. We are to "enter His gates with thanksgiving" (Psalms 104:4).

that remains faithful" (Isaiah 26:2). Those who have been faithful will enter into higher status ("*through the gates*," Revelation 22:14), the entrance of honor reserved for those who have persevered faithfully to the end.[792] This is the "*rich, welcome into the eternal kingdom of our Lord and Savior Jesus Christ*" (2 Peter 1:11, NIV) anticipated by the apostle Peter.

In all instances the calls to enter the temple or the land are addressed to those who who seem to be viewed as saved (Exodus 14:31).[793] This suggests that in the New Testament the calls to enter the kingdom may be addressed to believers, challenging them to a higher level of commitment. This understanding is confirmed by the renewal ceremony at Shechem.

THE RENEWAL CEREMONY AT SHECHEM

Every seven years the Israelites held a renewal ceremony in which they were to decide whether they would continue to live according to the demands of the covenant (Deuteronomy 31:10-13).[794] If they said "yes," they were to manifest this by a commitment to obey the commandments. This renewal and recommitment did not save them. Instead "the purpose ... was to further the relationship with God which his salvation activity on their behalf made possible."[795] The result of this obedience was not justification before God but a dynamic relationship with the God who had redeemed them. This dynamic relationship is called "life" (Deuteronomy 30:15, 19).

Later in His Sermon on the Mount, Jesus defined entering the kingdom as entering through the narrow way (Matthew 7:13-14), and He speaks of it as *entering into life,* that is, a rich life with God now.[796]

In summary, these Old Testament parallels may suggest that entering the kingdom is something that those already justified can do. If the renewal ceremony at Shechem is a valid parallel to entering the kingdom in the New Testament, it may refer to a renewal of one's commitment to be a disciple.

The entry sayings ("enter the kingdom," "enter into life," "seek life," and "seek His kingdom") are all related. These phrases are pregnant with rich implications that include (1) entry into a rich experience of life, (2) entry into discipleship, and (3) a fuller, abundant entry involving high status (being a co-heir with Christ) granted to disciples in the coming kingdom. The phrase "to enter into life" may refer to any, or all, of these. Only the specific context can determine whether any particular one is being emphasized over the others.

Entering the Sanctuary and Entering the Kingdom

The parallel mentioned above between entering the sanctuary in the Old Testament and entering the kingdom in the New is compelling and deserves further exploration. Christ's calls to enter the kingdom, seek the kingdom, and enter in to life echo the calls to worship at the sanctuary. He told the Samaritan woman,

---

792 See discussion on pp. 951 ff.

793 We assume that it is probable that the nation led by Joshua was, as a group, born again.

794 See discussion in Gerhard von Rad, *Old Testament Theology*, 2 vols. (New York: Harper, 1962), 1:192-203.

795 Norman Perrin, *The Kingdom of God in the Teaching of Jesus* (Philadelphia: Westminster Press, 1963), 204.

796 To "enter into life" is to embrace a rich way of life, both now *and* in the future kingdom as a result of entering a kingdom way of living now. One cannot have one without the other (Matthew 18:8). In his conversation with the rich young ruler Jesus seems to equate entering into life as equivalent to "treasure in heaven," inheriting the kingdom, and a rich experience of life both now and in the future (Matthew 19:16, 17, 23).

But an hour is coming, and now is, when the true worshipers will worship the Father in spirit and truth; for such people the Father seeks to be His worshipers. "God is spirit, and those who worship Him must worship in spirit and truth" (John 4:23–24).

Because the Temple is gone, how does one express this call to worship under the New Covenant? Worship in the Old Testament and the New was an entire lifestyle that included specific acts of praise." It involved sacrifices of praise, a life of holiness, prayer, seeking God, and generosity to the poor. When Jesus explained what He meant by "kingdom of heaven," and called His born again followers to enter it,[797] the new order was being announced. No longer were they required to go through an intermediary priest or go to a specific place.

The qualifications for kingdom entrance under the New Covenant are strikingly similar to the qualifications to worship in the sanctuary under the Old Covenant. This similarity is evident in many ways. First, note that a qualification for sanctuary and kingdom entrance was that one must already be one of the people of God.[798] Worshipers must have confessed that God was their God (Psalm 22;1, 10; 63:1) and proclaim the Shema (Deuteronomy 6:4). They were the sheep of His pasture (Psalm 95:6-7) and they declared that it was by grace that they had access to His courts. Similarly, Jesus referred to His followers as His sheep, His little ones, and addressed the call to enter the kingdom to His born again disciples (Matthew 5:1-2).

Also, Old Testament believers who desired to enter the sanctuary must first demonstrate their faith by means of their works. Psalm 15:1-5 lists twelve qualifications for sanctuary entrance: walk blamelessly, do what is right, speak truth from the heart, do not take up a reproach against one's friend, do not slander others, do not do evil to one's neighbor, despise vile persons, honor and fear the Lord, honor those who fear Yahweh, do not take a bribe, do not lend money at interest, and be willing to stick to one's word even if it causes himself personal hurt. Jesus also required obedience to the Sermon on the Mount as a condition for kingdom entrance (Matthew 7:21).

Those under the Old Covenant who desired to enter the sanctuary in worship must be characterized by humility (1 Chronicles 29:14), devotion to the Lord (Psalm 63:1-5; 66:8-20), and a generous spirit (Leviticus 7:15-16; Psalms 42:1-4; 63:1-8). Kingdom entrance, according to Jesus also required humility (Matthew 18:3) and seeking the Kingdom (Matthew 6:33; Luke 12:31). In fact, the kingdom was to be prized as something of great value, a pearl (Matthew 13:45).

They certainly needed to possess an ethical righteousness that surpassed the righteousness of the scribes and the Pharisees in the first century if they were to enter into the sanctuary. Believers in Christ similarly must possess a surpassing righteousness if they are to enter into the kingdom-way-of-life leading to higher status in the future millennium.

Old Testament worshipers approached the sanctuary for many reasons. One was that they desired blessing from God (Numbers 6:22-27). Jesus promised an inheritance to those believers who chose to enter the kingdom, and He promised "life" to those who chose the narrow way (Matthew 7:13-14).

---

[797] In the next chapter I will show that the calls to enter the kingdom are addressed to those who have already entered it in a soteriological sense.

[798] For wonderful exposition of the reasons why they came to the sanctuary and the qualifications for entrance see Allen P. Ross, *Recalling the Hope of Glory* (Grand Rapids: Kregel Publications, 2006), 271-89 and 97-307.

Of course, worshipers entered the sanctuary for the purpose of prayer (1 Kings 8:22-61). In the Sermon on the Mount Jesus stressed the importance of prayer for those who would enter the kingdom (Matthew 6:5-15).

Old Testament believers came to the sanctuary for the purpose of seeing God. The psalmist said, "*I have seen you in the sanctuary and beheld your power and your glory*" (Psalm 63:2, NIV84). Elsewhere he declared that his life's main desire was to gaze upon the Lord, "*One thing I ask of the LORD, this is what I seek: that I may dwell in the house of the LORD all the days of my life, to gaze upon the beauty of the LORD and to seek him in his temple*" (Psalm 27:4, NIV84). Jesus also stressed this in the entry sayings. He told Nicodemus that unless he was first born again, he could not "*see the kingdom*" and in the Discourse on Discipleship told His followers, "*Blessed are the pure in heart, for they will see God*" (Matthew 5:8, NIV84).

Finally, a major purpose of entering the sanctuary area in the Old Testament was to renew the covenant. After hearing instruction from the priests, they made faithful commitments (Exodus 24:3, 7). David said, "*Here I am, I have come ... To do your will, O my God, is my desire, your law is within my heart* (Psalm 40:7-8). Formal occasions such as the annual feasts and the renewal ceremony at Shechem were organized for this very purpose. Jesus also called upon His believing disciples to renew and heighten their commitments when He told them, "*Seek ye first his kingdom and his righteousness, and all these things will be given to you*" and to "*enter by the narrow way*." The same theme is evident in His challenge to "*Take my yoke upon you and learn from me, for I am gentle and humble in heart, and you will find rest for your souls*" (Matthew 11:29, NIV84). The call to New Covenant commitment is likewise evident when He told them, "*No one who puts his hand to the plow and looks back is fit for service in the kingdom of God*" (Luke 9:62, NIV84). These thoughts are found in many passages.[799] They suggest that the calls to enter the kingdom in the New Testament may have evoked recollections in the hearts of the thirsty hearers of concerning the Old Testament requirements for sanctuary entrance announced through Moses; One Greater than Moses is now here.

The Tabernacle in the Old Testament was a sanctuary which anticipated this future kingdom. In his wonderful book, *Recalling the Hope of Glory*, Allen P. Ross says, "This kingdom of God on earth was a place where the people of God could come to find refuge from the world outside, to find peace, security, and wholeness."[800] Even though the future millennial kingdom was not a reality in the wilderness, aspects of it could be experienced there through the worship in the wilderness sanctuary.

These parallels between the requirements for entering the sanctuary and entering the kingdom are striking and suggest that to enter the kingdom was to enter into a *lifestyle* of worshipping God, a kingdom way of living, and not only personal salvation from damnation. Only those already born again could enter the sanctuary, and they did so on the condition of having lived righteous lives.

What Is the Kingdom of God?

What is the kingdom? Before we can know what it means to enter the kingdom, we must first know what the kingdom is.

One would think that a simple answer would be the forthcoming, since this was the central focus of Jesus' teaching ministry. But, it is not. Thousands of books, journal articles,

799 Matthew 5:20; 7:21; 18:3; 19:23, 24; 23:13; Mark 9:47; 10:15, 25; Luke 18:17, 24, 25.

800 Ross, *Recalling the Hope of Glory*, 250.

and sermons have been produced with varying understandings of this important concept. After pondering this question for many years and researching the biblical evidence, this writer would like to propose an answer to this question which, while new (in some respects), is in fact an eclectic summary of the insights of many thinkers throughout the history of the church.

The problem which has confounded Bible students regarding the meaning of this theme is that the phrase "kingdom of God" seems to mean different things in different contexts. In some places the kingdom means the restored Davidic theocracy predicted in the Old Testament (Acts 1:6), but in others it is described as "near"[801] or "in your midst."[802] Certainly the restored Davidic theocracy was not in their midst in any literal sense. Bock's suggestion is best, "The emphasis here would be that the Pharisees confront the kingdom in Jesus. They do not need to look all around for it because its central figure is in front of their eyes."[803]

Sometimes the kingdom of heaven seems to refer to the power of God. For example, Jesus says, "*If I cast out demons by the Spirit of God, the kingdom of God has come upon you*" (Matthew 12:28). In some places the kingdom of God is a righteous way of life (the "narrow gate" and the "narrow way"), and in others it is an experience of kingdom life that one can enjoy now, "*The kingdom of God is ....righteousness, peace and joy in the Holy Spirit*" (Romans 14:17).[804] When does the kingdom come? This too has generated thousands of pages of discussion. In some contexts some aspects of the kingdom seem to be a present reality, and in others it is the future reign of Christ on earth or, in amillennialism it is the new heavens and the new earth. Is it present, or future, or both?

With respect for those who differ, I would like to make this simple suggestion: *the kingdom of God is the future establishment of God's rule over the earth which begins in the millennium and extends into eternity future and into the new heavens and the new earth.* Bruce Waltke says, "The two testaments are united by the ideology that God is establishing his kingship over a hostile world to establish his glory. The bond that unites the testaments is the sense of God's divine activity in revelatory history in progressively establishing his rule in heaven on earth from creation of the cosmos (Genesis 1) to his creation of the new cosmos (Revelation 21-22)."[805] It is God's response to the Satan's challenge that independence and unbelief are acceptable in God's creation. Through the Last Adam, the Second Man, the mandate given to the couple in the garden to rule and have dominion will be finally fulfilled in the kingdom of heaven. However, this needs to be unpacked.

---

801 This could, of course, mean "near" in the sense of contingency. Then the announcement means that if national Israel repents, the Davidic kingdom will be restored to Israel.

802 Some hold that this means that the Davidic theocracy is in their midst in the person of the King. This seems rather forced to me. I prefer the interpretation which says that the divine manifestation of power and the wonderful teachings of the kingdom (like the Sermon on the Mount) are in their midst. Louw-Nida note that while some scholars say that the phrase "can be interpreted as a potentiality for participation and hence be translated 'within your grasp,' ... it is more likely that one should understand the phrase ἐντὸς ὑμῶν in Lk 17:21 as a spacial relationship, for example, 'in your midst' or 'among you.'" (See 83.9), Louw-Nida, 1:320. This view is based upon papyri manuscripts and has been questioned by some. Bock objects to this understanding of the phrase, "Also against this view is that it could be regarded as a non-answer. On this view, Jesus has said it is not by signs that the kingdom comes, but it is within your grasp. The essential question still remains, 'Where is it so that I can obtain it?' Thus, this option does not really supply a sufficient answer to deal with the question." See Bock, *Luke 9:51-24:53*, 1416.

803 Ibid., 1416.

804 Alternatively, this phrase could mean "the kingdom which we will one day enter is ....."

805 Waltke and Yu, *An Old Testament Theology: An Exegetical, Canonical, and Thematic Approach*, 45.

It is beyond controversy that the kingdom of heaven involves more than the restoration of the Davidic rule to the nation of Israel in the millennium. In fact the reduction of the kingdom to this concept alone has greatly impoverished the church, reducing it to personal salvation or final entrance into heaven or the millennium. Yet as presented in the Bible the kingdom is more than personal salvation or even the Davidic rule. It is the rule of Christ's servant kings throughout eternity future. It is a new way of living and to "enter" it is a call to discipleship, not always an invitation to enter heaven when one dies. The kingdom is a way of a life, divine power, a permeating influence for good, and the new heavens and the new earth. Passages that seem to define the kingdom in different ways are in fact different aspects or dimensions of the single future kingdom of God. Which aspect is in the forefront is usually made clear by the context. When one is "born again" (John 3:3-5), he is transferred into the New Covenant, the foundation for the future millennium (Colossians 1:13). He enters the kingdom in the sense of personal salvation.

We do not believe that the kingdom of heaven has been inaugurated as progressive dispensationalists teach. Jesus is not on David's throne today. But there is no reason to deny that certain aspects of this future kingdom are being experienced today. The writer to the Hebrews spoke of his readers as those who had "tasted" (Gr *geuomai*, "to experience") of the "*powers of the age to come*" (Hebrews 6:5). Clearly, believers today experience a foretaste of what it will be like when Christ returns. This in no way implies that the "age to come" began in the life of Christ.

When the entry sayings seem to speak of entering into the kingdom in the present, we understand them to mean entry *now* into salvation or into the kingdom-way of life. That way of life can be entered and (to a degree) experienced today!

If one looked at Acts 1:6 alone, he would be justified in concluding that the kingdom of God was only the restored Davidic theocracy. But that is only one aspect of the message of the kingdom. The kingdom of God predicted in the Old Testament was more than the Davidic kingdom. That aspect of the kingdom was offered to Israel, rejected, and has been postponed. It is not in force today, but will be when Christ returns. However, other aspects of the Old Testament hope are clearly in force today. When we read that Jesus "preached the kingdom of God,"[806] or "proclaimed the gospel of the kingdom,"[807] it is best to assume, unless the immediate context dictates otherwise, that more than the restoration of the kingdom to Israel is meant (see Luke 9:60, 62; Acts 1:3; 8:12; Hebrews 1:8).

Certainly, a major aspect of the kingdom of heaven predicted in the Old Testament was an outpouring of the Holy Spirit in a new and distinctive way. Joel announced that the kingdom would be a time of the pouring out of the Spirit on all flesh (Joel 2:28-29). Peter said that this aspect of the kingdom was fulfilled (at least in part) at Pentecost (Acts 2:17). Through Ezekiel God promised that in the millennial kingdom that He would put His Spirit in them and cause them to "walk in my statutes" (Ezekiel 36:27). While this is ultimately fulfilled through Israel in the future, Jesus made it clear that the promise of the indwelling of the Spirit, a distinctive of the kingdom of heaven, is available in this age to all who believe (John 14:17).

Dispensationalists have correctly noted that the fact that certain aspects of the future millennial kingdom are being experienced today in no way justifies the teaching that the kingdom reign of David's Greater Son has been inaugurated and we are in it now. When

---

[806] Luke 4:43; 8:1; Acts 28:31.

[807] Matthew 4:23; 9:35; 24:14; Luke 16:16.

contemporary evangelical scholars use phrases such as "already" and "not yet," it is confusing and incorrect. It is true that some of the blessings of the future millennium are already available. But that is not all that these scholars mean. They also believe that the future reign of the Messiah has already begun as well, making the preposterous claim that the kingdom has been inaugurated. How one can accept this in view of the Nazi holocaust and the terrible wars and degeneration of culture in the twentieth century is simply unexplainable. And there are such clear passages as Hebrews 1:13 and 2:8 which tell us that when He returns and establishes the predicted kingdom, all things will be in subjection to Him. That is not the case now. Although there will still be enemies of the King, death, and a final war against Messiah and His rule, the idea that the world we see today is the beginning of the golden day of King Jesus sitting on the Davidic Throne is indefensible. This view makes a mockery of God's sovereign rule. Yet they define the kingdom as God's rule and play down the idea that it refers to a place, a realm! No! To suggest that His future reign has begun means that God's glorious kingdom is a trivial and thwarted influence in the current world which is sliding toward catastrophe. This view of "already" also makes a mockery of the Old Testament promises.

How is it possible that we are in the kingdom now in view of the fact that Jesus and John the Baptist told us that global judgment would precede the arrival of the kingdom? Jesus said that prior to the kingdom, "*There will be a great tribulation, such as has not occurred since the beginning of the world until now, nor ever will*" (Matthew 24:21). The Olivet Discourse details the events of this global catastrophe that will precede the coming of the Son of Man and the establishment of His Kingdom (Matthew 24:15-28). He says that "*after the tribulation of those days*" the Son of Man will come and then He will establish His Kingdom and "*sit upon His glorious throne*" (Matthew 25:31).

When we turn to the book of Acts, the kingdom has still not been inaugurated, it is still not "already." After forty days of post-resurrection teaching on the subject of the kingdom of God, the apostles ask Jesus, "*Lord, is it at this time you are restoring the kingdom to Israel?*" (Acts 1:6). He responds, "*It is not for you to know the times or epochs*" (v. 7). Then in Acts 3 Peter re-offers the kingdom to Israel saying, "*Therefore repent and return, so that your sins may be wiped away, in order that times of refreshing may come from the presence of the Lord*" (Acts 3:19). There was a condition that must be fulfilled if the kingdom was to come, the nation must repent.

Peter echoes the teaching of his Lord who similarly gave that condition saying, "*Repent, for the kingdom of heaven is near*" (Matthew 4:17). The word "near" does not mean "here!" It was "near" in the sense of contingency. If Israel repented and embraced Jesus as her messiah, the kingdom that was "near" would have become "here." Since the kingdom will not come until Israel repents and since Israel has not repented, the kingdom has not come and we are not in an "already" form of a future kingdom now. One day, the Israel of God, that is, the believing remnant of the last days,[808] will repent and the kingdom will be established (Romans 11:25-28). In the meantime, the kingdom has been "*taken away*" from that evil and adulterous generation (Matthew 21:43). In a future era the kingdom will be given to a "nation" (the believing remnant of the last days) producing the "fruit of it." The context requires that the believing *Jewish* nation of the last days, not the Gentiles or the church, is in view. Israel is often referred to as a "nation" (cf. Acts Acts 10:22; John 11:48).

---

[808] For proof that the Israel of God is not the church but is the believing remnant of Israel of the last days see Johnson, "Paul and the 'Israel of God': An Exegetical and Eschatological Case-Study."

Clayton Sullivan has challenged this settled consensus of evangelical scholarship arguing that when scholars use this "already – not yet" language, it is a bait and switch. They are using the term kingdom, in the same phrase, as meaning two different things, the language error called a *shift in referents.*[809] The "not yet" referent refers to the kingdom as the Golden Age. The "already" referent refers to the kingdom as curative power (or we might say healings, demon exorcisms, or new life available in Christ). Obviously, new life in Christ is not the same as the Golden Age! Sullivan says,

> *On the one hand they look us in the eye and declare, "the kingdom was present in Jesus' exorcisms." While still looking us in the eye and mesmerizing us with discussions about how basileia [kingdom] is to be understood in terms of malkuth [Aramaic for "reign"], they go one step further and affirm, "And by the way, this kingdom we have told you was present, is also future." But in this future claim they abandon their bait's reference to the kingdom (a curative power) and switch to an entirely different referent (the Golden Age)."*[810]

A study of all places in the New Testament where the kingdom is mentioned reveals seven aspects of the single kingdom of God: (a) the power of God,[811] (b) a permeating influence throughout the world,[812] (c) the messianic kingdom predicted in the Old Testament,[813] (d) a kingdom way of living or the experience of kingdom life,[814] (e) the new heavens and the

---

809 Clayton Sullivan, *Rethinking Realized Eschatology* (Macon, GA: Mercer University Press, 1988), 46-48.

810 Ibid., 47.

811 Matthew 12:28; 13:11; Luke 10:9, 11; 11:20. "But if I cast out demons by the Spirit of God, then the kingdom of God has come upon you" (Matthew 12:28). In this instance the rule of God has broken in over the demons. Also the kingdom is presented as a source of healing power. "Heal the sick who are there and tell them, 'The kingdom of God is near you'" (Luke 10:9). L. D. Hurst expresses it this way: "The Kingdom Is Present As a Divine Power Breaking in upon the Kingdom of Satan and Overthrowing the Power of Satan in the World." See L. D. Hurst, "Ethics of Jesus," in *Dictionary of Jesus and the Gospels*, ed. Joel B. Green, Scott McKnight, and I. Howard Marshall (Downers Grove, IL: InterVarsity Press, 1992), 212.

812 Matthew 11:12; 13:24, 31, 33, 38, 47; Mark 4:11, 26-29; 8:10; Luke 13:18, 20; Colossians 4:11. See ibid., 212. The parables of the mustard seed (Matthew 13:31-32) and the leaven (Matthew 13:33) have often been understood to suggest that the kingdom of heaven is a permeating influence that lifts and elevates human existence. Kingdom work can involve healing (Luke 10:9). This global impact resulting from individual Christians experiencing this kingdom way of life and being salt and light in the world is well documented in the social, political, and scientific advancement of mankind. See Nancy Pearcey and Charles B. Thaxton, *The Soul of Science: Christian Faith and Natural Philosophy* (Wheaton, IL: Crossway Books, 1994). When Jesus said "No one who puts his hand to the plow and looks back is fit for service in the kingdom of God" (Luke 9:62), He was no doubt referring to the kingdom as a present reality for which one could be useful in doing kingdom work. For an excellent discussion of Christianity's positive impact on the world see Alvin J. Schmidt, *Under the Influence: How Christianity Transformed Civilization* (Grand Rapids: Zondervan Publishing House, 2001).

813 Matthew 3:2; 4:17; 5:19; 7:21; 8:11,12; 10:7; 13:41; 16:28; 18:1, 4;:23; 20:1, 21; 21:43; 22:2; 25:1, 34; 26:29; Mark 1:15; 3:24; 9:1; 11:10; 14:25; 15:43; Luke 1:33; 4:43; 8:1; 11:2, 17, 18; 13:28, 29; 14:15; 19:11, 12, 15; 21:31; 22:18, 29, 30; 23:42, 51; John 18:36; Acts 1:6; 19:8(?); 20:25; 28:23(?); 1 Corinthians 6:9, 10(?); 15:24; Ephesians 5:5; 2 Thessalonians 1:5; 2 Timothy 4:1; Hebrews 12:28; James 2:5; Revelation 11:15; 12:10.

814 Hurst says, "Following Jesus and entering the kingdom are equated. In Luke 9:57–62 (par. Mt 8:18–22) the three claimants to discipleship each want to be included among Jesus' disciples. Again, when Jesus says that the last one is not fit for the kingdom, the natural implication is that being a disciple of Jesus and entering the kingdom are different ways of describing the same thing" Hurst, "Ethics of Jesus," 212. Matthew 5:3; 5:10; 5:20; 6:33; 11:11; 13:44, 45, 52; 16:19; 19:12, 14, 23; 21:31; 23:13; Mark 9:47; 10:14, 15; 23, 24, 25; 12:34; Luke 6:20; 7:28; 9:2, 11; 12:31, 32; 16:16; 17:20, 21; 18:16, 17; 18; 24-25, 29?; John 3:3, 5; Acts 14:22(?); 28:23(?); 31; Romans 14:17; 1 Corinthians 4:20; 1 Thessalonians 2:12(?); Revelation 1:9.

new earth,[815] (f) the Messianic Banquet,[816] and finally, (g) the sphere of personal salvation.[817] Graphically, one can illustrate this concept by the diagram below.

Several important observations may be made about this list and diagram.[818] First, kingdom entrance is sometimes spoken of as entrance into the sphere of personal salvation or into the future millennium. One must be born again if one is to enter the millennium (John 3:2-5). Jesus tells the Pharisees that "*some shall not taste death till they see the Son of Man coming in His kingdom*" (Matthew 16:28). When the Apostle Paul tells us in Colossians 1:13 that we have been transferred into "the kingdom of His dear Son," he means we are currently in the sphere of personal salvation.

But second, it makes no difference whether the reader agrees with how this writer has categorized the various references in the footnotes. It is probable that the seven categories encompass all the kingdom references, but which verses fit in which category is certainly debatable and is irrelevant to the general conclusion of this chapter.

Third, even though in a particular passage one aspect of the kingdom may be prominent, it is still acceptable and also probable that several other aspects may lurk in the background.

---

815 1 Corinthians 15:50; 1 Corinthians 6:10(?); Galatians 5:20(?); 2 Timothy 4:18(?); 1 Peter 1:11(?). This seems to be the force of Jesus' exhortation to His regenerate disciples when He said to them, "But seek first His kingdom and His righteousness, and all these things will be added to you" (Matthew 6:33). It is to this aspect of the kingdom of God that Paul referred when he said, "*The kingdom of God is not eating and drinking, but righteousness and peace and joy in the Holy Spirit*" (Romans 14:17). In many of the references to entering the kingdom one might translate "come to enjoy" the kingdom. See BDAG, 294, Matthew 5:20, 7:21; Mark 9:43, 10:15, 23ff., Luke 18:17,25; and even John 3:5 as possible illustrations.

816 Isaiah 25:6; Matthew 8:10-13; Mark 14:25; Luke 13:22-30; 14:16-24; 22:29-30.

817 John 3:5; Matthew 13:19, 24 (a "field" of evangelistic effort), 47; Mark 9:47; Colossians 1:13

818 In this diagram the arrows on the rim indicate that all aspects of the kingdom of God are interrelated and flow into one another. The kingdom of God is in the center, the sovereign rule of God over all. His creation is the focus. From that kingdom various manifestations and experiential aspects emerge. This is the proclamation of "the gospel of the kingdom" (Matthew 9:35). That phrase embraces all seven aspects of the kingdom of heaven.

Fourth, attempts to force uniformity on a meaning of the kingdom based on one of these aspects are doomed to fail. Yet there is a consistency. The broader category—the kingdom of God defined as the establishment of God's rule over the earth which extends into eternity future in the new heavens and the new earth is involved in every mention of the kingdom in the New Testament. When one attempts to elevate one aspect of His rule, (e.g., the Davidic kingdom or the benevolent and uplifting spread of kingdom influences throughout the world) above other aspects and raise that aspect to a definition, it is impossible to make the definition fit with many passages.

Fifth, and most important, in each place where entering the kingdom of God is mentioned, the call is always (except John 3:5) to those who have already entered it in the sense of personal salvation.

What then do the entry sayings mean? When Jesus invites His believing followers to enter the kingdom of heaven, He is obviously not inviting them to accept the gospel and be saved. They are already saved. Instead, this invitation to enter the kingdom involves a call to enter a rich experience of life; to enter a kingdom way of living (discipleship) by seeking the kingdom way of life; and to enter in to higher status in the future reign of His Servant Kings.

The remainder of this chapter discusses the first two aspects of the kingdom, and the next chapter will discuss the third meaning, including a more detailed explanation of Matthew 5:20.

Entering into a Rich Experience of Life

The entry sayings have been understood to mean that one enters the kingdom of heaven in the present (the so-called "already" part). If the Kingdom of God is future, and it is, then how is it possible that one can enter the kingdom of God now? In the discussion to follow, I will suggest that one does not enter the future kingdom of God now, but the entry sayings are to be understood as entering into certain aspects of the future kingdom which can be experienced now through the New Covenant.

In His discussion with the rich young ruler, Jesus equates "entering the kingdom" with the phrase "enter life" (Gr *eiserchomai tēn zōēn, Matthew* 19:17, 23). The Gr word, *eiserchomai*, can mean "to move into a space"[819] in which case it would signify physical entrance into the realm of the millennial reign. However, what is often not appreciated, is that this word, like its English counterpart, often means "to experience"[820] or "to enter into an event or state, to come to enjoy something." For example "to enter life crippled" (Mark 9:43) is best understood "to experience life crippled."[821] Or when the Lord says, "Pray that you may not enter into temptation," He means, "Pray that you will not experience temptation," or simply, "Pray that you will not be tempted" (Matthew 26:41; Luke 22:40). When the writer to the Hebrews speaks of entering into rest, as demonstrated in an earlier chapter, he means that a believer can enter into the experience of finished work, that is, he can faithfully

---

819 BDAG, 293..

820 Ibid. 293.

821 Louw-Nida translates this verse, "It is better for you to come to experience (true) life with one hand than to keep two hands and end up in *Gehenna*," Louw-Nida, 90.70. However, I understand "true life" to refer to a rich experience of eternal life obtained by faith, works of love, and commitment to do the will of God. Furthermore, as will be shown later, Gehenna does not refer to damnation (see chapters 54-56).

complete his life work (Hebrews 4:1, 3, 5, 10).[822] When Jesus tells the disciples that "others have labored, and you have entered into their labor," He means that the disciples will enter into the labor in the harvest fields as well (John 4:38).[823] To "enter" in this instance means to enter into the action of laboring. When the nobles "entered into a curse" on themselves if they ever did not obey God's law in Nehemiah 10:29 (LXX, 10:30), this means that they assumed responsibility to obey it by taking an oath.

Entering the kingdom now involves entering into an aspect of the future kingdom available under the New Covenant, a new way of life now, a rich way of living before God by means of the Spirit.

The perplexing saying of Jesus in Matthew 5:30 begins to make good sense when "enter" is understood this way. "*And if your right hand makes you stumble, cut it off, and throw it from you; for it is better for you that one of the parts of your body perish, than for your whole body to go into hell* [Gr *Gehenna*, 'the valley of Hinnom']." This passage is being addressed to His "disciples" (Matthew 5:1-2). Those being invited to "enter into life" are already born again.[824] Similarly in Matthew 18:8 where this saying is repeated, it is clearly stated that those addressed are disciples, "*at that time his disciples came to him*" (Matthew 18:1). Since no one will enter eternal life in heaven with a hand cut off, it may be best to translate as the lexicon of Louw-Nida does, it is better for you to come to experience (true) life [enter the kingdom] with one hand than to keep two hands and end up in *Gehenna* [The Valley of

---

822 See pp. 141-144 and pp. 147 ff.

823 BDAG, 293.

824 Experimental Predestinarians and Neonomians believe that this verse refers to regeneration and eventually to entering into life in heaven or the millennium. Often, appeal is made to extra-biblical Jewish sources to support this. For example, Alan Stanley appeals to Targum Pseudo-Johnathan which was written in AD 700 (it contains the names of Mohammed's wives!, [NISBE, 4:728]) and to the notoriously unreliable Tosefta Hullin, both of which understand Deuteronomy 22:7 as "life in the world to come." He also appeals to the Babylonian Talmud, AD 600 and the Jerusalem Talmud, AD 400, Stanley 95. But why appeal to these works? I will reserve discussion for this point for a later chapter (see chapter 54). Their relevance to understanding Jesus or Judaism in AD 30 is remote. It is far more likely that Jesus would have understood the term as it was used in the Hebrew Scriptures. Another phrase found frequently in the Pseudepigrapha and the Mishna is "enter into the life of the world to come" (Pirke Aboth, *Sayings of the Fathers*, 6.4; m. Aboth 2:7–8; m. Baba Mesia 2:11E). These citations are often used to prove that "enter into life" in the Gospels means "enter into life in the world to come." However, apart from the fact that these are questionable sources of the gospel references (see discussion in the Pseudepigrapha, 857 ff.), the Gospels never refer to "life in the world to come." They use one term, "life," to embrace both (a) entering into life, life now, abundant life by being a disciple of Christ and (b) an enhanced experience of life in the future kingdom. Jesus called it "treasure in heaven." Neither do the Pseudepigrapha nor the Mishna ever use the phrase "enter into life." Similarity does not equal equality! The equation of "enter life" exclusively with "enter life in the world to come" seems to be an example of Samuel Sandmel's warning against parallelomania. "Two passages [enter into the world to come" in Pirke Aboth and "enter into life" in the Gospels] may sound the same in splendid isolation from their context, but when seen in context, [they] reflect difference rather than similarity." See Samuel Sandmel, "Parallelomania," *JBL* 81, no. 1 (1962): 3. Furthermore, the meaning of the phrase "world to come" (in the Tannaitic literature cited) is different from that of the New Testament. Philip S. Alexander says, "The concept of 'the world to come' seems to have weakened in the Mishah to denote little more than the state of affairs which will result from the successful implementation of its religious and political program. And that program will be achieved by the obedience and piety of the individual Jew, not through some dramatic divine intervention in history, or through the agency of a messianic redeemer." Philip S. Alexander, "Torah and Salvation in Tannaitic Literature," in *Justification and Variegated Nomism: The Complexities of Second Temple Judaism*, ed. D. A. Carson, Peter Thomas O'Brien, and Mark A. Seifrid (Grand Rapids: Baker Academic, 2001), 1:275.

Hinnom]."[825] These born-again people are being called to a kingdom way of living by means of committed discipleship.[826] After all, the Kingdom is an experience (Romans 14:17).

The idea that kingdom entrance is not just entrance into the restored Davidic theocracy, but is also a rich experience of God, is found in many places in the New Testament.[827] It is clear that Jesus invests the term "life" in Leviticus 18:5 with more than a rich life now. In His discussion with the rich young ruler, Jesus equates it with "treasure in heaven" (Matthew 19:21) and the reward of ruling with Him in the future kingdom (Matthew 19:28).

Because works are associated with life in these passages in Matthew, there should be no objection to accepting the latter sense of the term there. When a believer who already possesses eternal life in the sense of personal salvation is asked to enter into life (as in Matthew 7:14; 18:9; 19:29) on the basis of works, what objection can there be to understanding this as entering into a fuller experience of life with God in his present experience resulting in an enhanced experience of life coming world?[828] Jesus taught this when He instated the New Covenant (Matthew 26:28) as the foundational aspect of the kingdom of God. The writer to the Hebrews tells us that this covenant is now in operation (Hebrews 8:13; 9:15; 12:24).[829]

---

825 Louw-Nida, 807. As will be demonstrated later, "*Gehenna*" should be rendered "Valley of Hinnom." It probably does not refer to damnation, but to the shame of a wasted life which is of no more value than a corpse tossed into the unquenchable (i.e., "terrible") fire of the burning garbage dump outside the city. See discussion of *Gehenna,* pp. 911, 854, 873. The other phrases in this verse, "worm dieth not" and "unquenchable fire" do not refer to damnation, but to shame and the terrible nature of being rebuked and disinherited by Christ ("I will deny him") at the Judgment Seat of Christ. See pp. 903 ff.

826 The only other place the phrase occurs in the New Testament is in the conversation with the rich young ruler. For a full discussion of Jesus' encounter with the rich young ruler and how that passage is harmonized with my understanding of "enter the kingdom" in Matthew 5:20 see pp. 342 ff.

827 The parables of the hidden treasure (Matthew 13:44) and the hidden pearl show the response necessary to "possess" (i.e., experience now) the kingdom. The parables describe a man who "finds" the kingdom. In the former, the motivation for the response was the great joy in discovering the treasure, though obviously the value of the treasure stimulated the joy. No price was too high for a treasure that brought such joy, even if one had to sell all he had to raise the cash. In the latter parable, the response grew out of the great value of the pearl, although doubtless its discovery brought the merchants great joy. Finding or entering the kingdom is an experience of joy in God now, not a prediction of entrance in the millennium or new earth. These seekers did not find the restored Davidic theocracy; they found a rich experience with God. Jesus tells His believing disciples, who have already entered the kingdom in a saving sense, "*But seek first his kingdom and* [Gr *kai,* "which is" or "namely"] *his righteousness, and these things will be given to you as well*" (Matthew 6:33, NIV). This suggests that seeking the kingdom is something beyond initial entrance. To seek the kingdom is to seek an ethical righteousness, a kingdom lifestyle. Granted, to seek does not necessarily mean "to enter," but the focus in the passage is the kingdom as a way of life, not as initial salvation (for it is addressed to those who are already regenerate). At any rate, one who does not seek the kingdom now will not enter into greatness in that kingdom in the future. Paul tells us that the kingdom of God is more than a geographical sphere; it is "righteousness and peace and joy in the Holy Spirit" (Romans 14:17), and that it consists not just in words but in power (1 Corinthians 1:17).

828 Against the interpretation being suggested here, one could cite Jesus' dramatic warning against lust and adultery, "*If your eye causes you to stumble, pluck it out and throw it from you. It is better for you* ***to enter life*** *with one eye, than to have two eyes and be cast into the fiery hell*" (Matthew 18:9). Entering life healthy without one part of the body missing is contrasted with entering "fiery hell" (Gr *Gehenna*). Later, I will argue that to enter "fiery hell," means to enter into shame at the judgment seat of Christ. From this it has been plausibly argued that entering life, being the opposite of final damnation, must refer to final entrance into heaven or soteriological entrance into the millennium. It may be that Jesus is using hyperbole here. See discussion in chapter 56; esp. pp. 879 ff.

829 Paul Tanner says, "The New Testament is clear that this New Covenant was inaugurated by the blood of Christ shed at Calvary and has been operative since that time (Luke 22:20; 1 Cor 11:25; 2 Cor 3:6). At the

Entry into a Kingdom Way of Living

Closely related to the idea of entering into life, as mentioned above, is the concept of entering into a kingdom way of living, that is, discipleship. In the teaching of Christ, this specifically means to live life according to the principles of the Sermon on the Mount.

We are on Old Testament ground here. As discussed above, entering the kingdom in the New Testament mirrors the calls to worship the Lord in the Old. Those Old Testament invitations to enter the sanctuary and regularly renew one's commitment to Yahweh in the annual renewal ceremony are mirrored in Christ's call to His believing disciples to enter the kingdom of heaven in the New Testament.

Like faith and works in the Experimental Predestinarian system, "life," a "kingdom way of living," and rich life in the future kingdom are necessarily united. One cannot have one without the other.

If a person in the Gospels is called a disciple or follower of Christ, this means he is a fully committed believer. Yet obviously not everyone who followed Jesus could be considered a disciple in the full sense of the word as Jesus intended it. New followers need to be continually challenged to greater degrees of commitment (Matthew 8:18-23).

The call to enter the kingdom in the sense of entering into a kingdom way of living is expressed in three ways in the Gospels.

- A call to fully committed discipleship
- A call to seek the kingdom way of life
- A call to enter the narrow gate and the narrow way

ENTERING THE KINGDOM AND ENTERING INTO DISCIPLESHIP

The chart on the next page shows the similarities between entering the kingdom and being a disciple.

The demands Jesus makes on those who would enter the kingdom and those who would become disciples are practically identical.[830]

Hurst says,

> *Following Jesus and entering the kingdom are equated. In Luke 9:57–62 (par. Mt 8:18–22) the three claimants to discipleship each want to be included among Jesus' disciples. Again, when Jesus says that the last one is not fit for the kingdom, the natural implication is that being a disciple of Jesus and entering the kingdom are different ways of describing the same thing.*[831]

Cross the Old Covenant was replaced by the New Covenant, and all believers since then are participants in the New Covenant and are no longer under the Mosaic Law (Rom 7:4–7; 1 Cor 9:19–21; Heb 7:18). Though inaugurated at the Cross, it would be best to think of the New Covenant as being progressively fulfilled, since there is still an aspect of it that awaits fulfillment with Israel as a nation (cf. Rom 11:25–27)." Tanner, "Hebrews," 1063.

[830] T. W. Manson, *The Teaching of Jesus: Studies of Its Form and Content* (Cambridge: University Press, 1963), 205. Manson concludes, "The inference to be drawn from this comparison would seem to be that, in the mind of Jesus, to become a genuine disciple of his and enter into the Kingdom of God amounted to much the same thing" (Ibid. 120). Of course Manson is assuming that becoming a "genuine disciple" is what evangelicals would call "getting saved" and involves submission to the Lordship of Christ. His confusion is manifest because earlier he argued strongly that the entry sayings were addressed to those who were already "saved" (Ibid. 120).

[831] Hurst, "Ethics of Jesus," 212.

If works are required to "enter the kingdom" and the same works are required to become a disciple, then entering the kingdom seems to be the same thing as becoming a disciple. This results in the difficulty mentioned above. How can this be harmonized with the faith-alone gospel Jesus taught in the Gospel of John?[832]

Perhaps the most common explanation of this difficulty is to assume that since all true Christians work (the Reformed doctrine of perseverance), these passages describe the *characteristics* of those who enter and not the *conditions for* entrance. For example, one writer says,

> *But while Matthew views final judgment in terms of "what one has done" (Matt 16:27), these "works" do not serve as "proofs of accomplishment" but rather as "means of recognition" which "show where the person is rooted." Judgment is therefore not so much a matter of reward for actions as it is an acknowledgment of the stance which human beings have already taken toward Jesus, the Son of Man who comes to judge.*[833]

While this is very clever, it presupposes that the Experimental Predestinarian paradigm for understanding the connection between saving faith and a life of works is true. But more importantly, it directly contradicts what Jesus said in Matthew 5:19 where He speaks of those who do not have a "means of recognition" but who are nevertheless "in" the kingdom.

ENTRANCE INTO THE KINGDOM	DISCIPLESHIP
A childlike spirit (Mark 10:15)[836]	
Readiness to sacrifice (1) material goods (Mark 10:23),[837] (2) physical well-being (Mark 9:47),[838] (3) family ties (Luke 9:61).[839]	Complete self-sacrifice (Mark 8:34; Luke 14:28-33) involving family ties (Matthew 10:37; Luke 14:26) and even life itself (Matthew 10:39; Mark 8:35; Luke 17:33)
Absolute obedience to God's will (Matthew 5:20; 7:21)	Obedience to Jesus (Matthew 10:38; Mark 8:34; Luke 14:27)
	Persevering loyalty to Jesus in all circumstances (Matthew 10:32-33; Mark 8:38; Luke 12:8 ff.).

832 Ibid., 212.

833 J. I. Packer, Merrill Chapin Tenny, and William White, *Illustrated Manners and Customs of the Bible* (Nashville: Thomas Nelson, 1997), 146.

834 As I will show later, to receive the kingdom like a little child has nothing to do with childlike trust in the person of Christ for salvation. Rather, it refers to the action that one who is already a Christian takes by adopting the lowest and most insignificant status. The first will be last. The conversion of a believer, not a nonbeliever, is in view.

835 For full discussion of Christ's encounter with the rich young ruler see chapter 24.

836 Entering the kingdom in this passage is contrasted with being cast into *Gehenna*. This suggests to many that entering the kingdom, which is the opposite of *Gehenna*, must therefore refer to soteriological entrance into eternal life. However, the Greek word *Gehenna*, translated "hell" is literally, the Valley of Hinnom. It refers to a garbage dump outside of Jerusalem. To be cast into the Valley of Hinnom is to have one's life assessed as to its effectiveness for the cause of Christ and finding it has no more value than a pile of garbage. When the salt loses its saltiness, Jesus says it is no longer fit for the "manure" pile (Luke 14:34-35). This is discussed extensively on pp. 518 ff. and chapter 57.

837 Most commentators understand that being worthy ("fit for") the kingdom and "entering the kingdom" are the same thing. We agree. However, as the discussion to follow will demonstrate, entering the kingdom refers to entering into a kingdom-way-of-living now, leading to higher honor and worthiness in the future reign of Christ. It is not about gaining life; it is about living it.

Similarly, John Stott argues that the greater righteousness is an inner heart righteousness, which the Pharisees lack and is necessary for kingdom entrance.

> *So Christian righteousness is heart-righteousness. It includes those deep and secret places of the human personality which nobody sees but God, and which are usually the last fortress[es] to surrender to his authority. Yet without heart-righteousness we cannot enter the Kingdom, for heart-righteousness is impossible without a new heart, a new heart depends on a new birth, and new birth is indispensable to Kingdom citizenship.*[838]

But it is clear from the immediately preceding verse (Matthew 5:19) that a "heart righteousness" is not necessary for kingdom entrance in the sense of entering into final salvation. But according to verse 19, it *is* necessary for "greatness," higher status, in the kingdom.

The best and simplest explanation for the works conditions for the "entry sayings" is to draw a distinction between becoming a Christian and being a disciple. If works are required to "enter the kingdom" and the same works are required to become a disciple, then entering the kingdom seems to be the same thing as becoming a disciple. All disciples are Christians, but not all Christians are disciples. God does not rule in the hearts of all Christians.[839] That is why (in the Gospel of Matthew) Jesus is continually calling on those who have already believed on Him to take the next step, to become His disciples. Or, as He said to the rich young ruler, "*if you want to be complete*," obey the commandments.[840]

To "enter the kingdom" in this sense is to enter into the kingdom's rule over one's life, which leads to ruling with Christ in the future, or to put it in contemporary terms, to make a "lordship decision," or as Jesus taught, to pursue a life that will lead to the salvation of your soul. Most of the entry sayings are addressed to disciples, who are already saved and relate to sanctification and/or status, not soteriology. Regarding the Sermon on the Mount, Baxter is correct, "This 'insider's discourse [teaching for those who are saved], then, while being delivered in the full hearing of the masses, is anything but entrance-focused [in the sense of personal salvation] in its content. These parallels and the narrative setting would argue against understanding 'enter' in an 'evangelistic' way."[841]

This is the critical decision facing all who name Christ as their Savior. This is what Paul meant when he said, "*Therefore I urge you, brethren, by the mercies of God, to present your bodies a living and holy sacrifice, acceptable to God, which is your spiritual service of worship*" (Romans 12:1). As Jesus did in the parable of the narrow gate and the narrow way (Matthew 7:13-14),[842] so Paul is challenging true believers to come under the rule of God in their daily lives.[843]

---

838 Haller, "Matthew," 273.

839 See chapter 32 for extensive biblical documentation of this point.

840 As argued elsewhere, we believe that the rich young ruler was probably a new believer in Christ who wanted to know what the next step would be for him to obtain treasure in heaven. Unfortunately, he finds that it is too demanding. See discussion on pp. 344 ff.

841 Wayne Baxter, "The Narrative Setting of the Sermon on the Mount," *Trinity Journal* 25, no. 1 (Spring 2004): 36.

842 See discussion in Chapter 21.

843 France says, "To enter the kingdom of heaven does not mean to go to a place called heaven (though the eternal life of heaven will be its expected outcome, see on 18:8–9), but to come under God's rule, to become

To "enter the kingdom" in Matthew 5:20 means to "live by its standards," i.e., to enter into the way of life of the future kingdom in the present by submitting to the Lordship of Christ, which leads to greatness in the future reign of the servant kings. We are children of the coming king and heirs of the world to come. We must live like heirs of the future reign now, but that does not mean the future reign of the servant kings, the Golden Age of the kingdom, has been inaugurated. One cannot live like this unless he has an internal personal righteousness which surpasses the external legalistic righteousness of the Pharisees. The idea of "greatness" or higher status will be developed in the next chapter.

We agree with Baxter's conclusion that "Matthew 5:20 does not seem to raise the question of 'soteriology' as much as it raises the question of 'sanctification.' In other words, it is not so much how to get into the kingdom [in the sense of personal salvation] that is in view as much as it is how kingdom-dwellers ought to conduct their lives."[844]

SEEKING THE KINGDOM WAY OF LIFE (MATTHEW 6:33)

In Matthew 6:33, Jesus exhorts His saved followers to "seek the kingdom." This is another way of calling them to fully committed discipleship relationship, that is, entering into a kingdom way of living. When Jesus says, "*But seek first His kingdom and His righteousness, and all these things will be added to you,*" probably, as many have suggested,[845] the phrase "*and His righteousness*" explains the preceding words "His kingdom."[846] Luke says simply, "*Seek His kingdom*" which, according to Bock, is commonly understood to mean "to seek to live in a way that honors God's presence and rule."[847] Jesus explains what seeking the kingdom means, when He says to His disciples that one must be willing to sell his possessions (Luke 18:24) if he wants to "enter the kingdom." This act is equivalent to laying up treasure in heaven, seeking kingdom priorities, a theme Jesus spoke of elsewhere (Luke 12:31-34).

---

one of those who recognize his kingship and live by its standards, to be God's true people." France, *The Gospel of Matthew*, 190. Being an Experimentalist, France believes that all true believers will do this (ibid., 801).

844 Baxter, "The Narrative Setting of the Sermon on the Mount," 35.

845 "Righteousness" is apparently in apposition to "kingdom," explaining it further. The use of *kai* in this way is common. BDAG, 495 (cf. Matthew 21:5; Mark. 5:19; John. 1:16; Romans 1:5; 13:11; Philippians. 3:7; Ephesians 2:8. E.g., Matthew 8:33, "*they told everything,* ***namely,*** *what had happened to those who were possessed*"). Thus Donald A. Hagner suggests that "and his righteousness," is practically epexegetical of the preceding phrase. Hagner, *Matthew 14-28*, 166. William Hendriksen and Simon Kistemaker agree: "These two (kingdom and righteousness) go together. In fact, 'the kingdom of God is [means, implies] righteousness' (Romans 14:17), a righteousness both imputed to men and imparted to them, both of legal standing and of ethical conduct." William Hendriksen and Simon Kistemaker, *Exposition of the Gospel According to Matthew* (Grand Rapids: Baker Book House, 2001), 354. As Davies and Allison put it, "Thus to seek the kingdom is to seek righteousness and to seek righteousness is to seek the kingdom." Davies and Allison, *A Critical and Exegetical Commentary on the Gospel According to Saint Matthew*, 661. Luz and Koester state it this way: "The 'kingdom of the heavens' is righteousness.'" Luz and Koester, *Matthew 1-7: A Commentary*, 130.

846 Hagner, Matthew 1–13, 166. Luz agrees: "The concept is ethicized. Matthew adds to the traditional "seek first [God's] kingdom"—presumably epexegetically—'and his righteousness,' δικαιοσύνη in Matthew being a quality of activity required of people," U. Luz, "βασιλεία," in EDNT 1:203.

847 Bock, *Luke 9:51-24:53*, 1164. Klappert says, "This ethical understanding of the kingdom is also found in the Apocrapha. Thus the LXX can identify the *basileia* with the four cardinal virtues (4 Macc. 2:23), and in Wis. 6:20 we read, 'The desire for wisdom leads to a kingdom.' 'To the mind he gave the law; and one who lives subject to this will rule a kingdom that is temperate, just, good, and courageous'" (4 Macc. 2:23, NRSV). See Klappert, "King, Kingdom," in NIDNTT, 2:374. I am proposing that in the account of the rich young ruler the phrases "inherit the Kingdom," "enter into life", "enter the kingdom" and "treasure in heaven," while not precisely equal, nevertheless convey similar ideas. See elsewhere in this book, pp. 343 ff.

With some overstatement Herman Ridderbos comments,

> *The kingdom of God and righteousness are spoken of in the form of a hendiadys,*[848] *and the phrase 'for the sake of righteousness' in 5:10 is elsewhere replaced by that of 'for the sake of the kingdom' (Luke 18:29), or by 'for my sake and the gospel's' (Mark 10:29), or 'for my name's sake' (Matthew 19:29). It may be rightly said, therefore, that sometimes kingdom and ethical righteousness are synonymous concepts in Jesus' preaching.*[849] *The one is unthinkable without the other.*[850]

In other words believers are to seek His kingdom, *which* is His righteousness.[851] This defines the kingdom itself in this passage as a way of life. Elsewhere Jesus teaches that it involves forgiving others (cf. Matthew 18:22-35) and a lifetime of preparation for His return (25:1 ff.).

ENTERING THE NARROW WAY

Further evidence that "enter the kingdom" in the Sermon on the Mount does not refer to entering into salvation is seen in the famous saying about the narrow way.

> *Enter by the narrow gate; for the gate is wide, and the way is broad that leads to destruction, and many are those who enter by it. For the gate is small, and the way is narrow that leads to life, and few are those who find it (Matthew 7:13–14).*

We reserve full discussion of this parable for later (see Chapter 21), but it is evident that the "enter the narrow way" saying is parallel to the other entry saying, "enter the kingdom." The gate and the way are entered now and lead us onto a path of abundant entrance into the future kingdom. It is clear that, in the context of the Sermon on the Mount, the way entered is not equivalent to "Jesus as *"the way, the truth, and the life."* Rather, it refers to a way of life, the lifestyle Jesus has been advocating in the preceding chapters. The alternative destinies, destruction and life, are not eternal separation from God or heaven, but spiritual ruin in this life and the life to come, in contrast to a rich experience of "true" life, that is, the beatitudes which open Jesus' sermon.

"THOSE WHO ENTER" (MATTHEW 23:13)

Matthew's final reference to entering the kingdom is in 23:13.

> *Woe to you, teachers of the law and Pharisees, you hypocrites! You shut the kingdom of heaven in men's faces. You yourselves do not enter, nor will you let those enter* ***who are trying to*** *(Matthew 23:13).*

---

848 A hendiadys is a figure of speech where two words are employed, but only one thing or idea is meant. For example, "God created the heavens and the earth" means "God created the universe."

849 I would say that this is only sometimes true. For example, when the disciples query Jesus regarding the restoration of the kingdom to Israel (Acts 1:6), they refer to the restoration of the Davidic theocracy and not personal ethical righteousness.

850 Ridderbos, *The Coming of the Kingdom*, 286.

851 If the use of *kai* is explicative ("for the purpose of explaining what goes before it," BDAG, 495), then the text may mean that righteousness is the aspect of the kingdom in view here. Thus, the text predicates that the aspect of the kingdom in view is an internal spiritual righteousness which leads to the lifestyle of the Sermon on the Mount. Newman and Stine go even further suggesting these terms may be synonymous, "It is possible also to understand his kingdom and his righteousness to be essentially synonymous." Barclay Moon Newman and Philip C. Stine, *A Translator's Handbook on the Gospel of Matthew* (New York: United Bible Societies, 1992), 192.

This is commonly understood to mean that the Pharisees are keeping those who are trying to enter into salvation from being born again. This assumes that "enter" means enter into salvation. As suggested above and in the following chapter, to enter the kingdom is *not* necessarily about personal salvation or entrance into the millennium. Instead, it refers to entering into higher status in the future kingdom by entering into a kingdom way of living now. Many of those who had believed in Christ were seeking to enter into the kingdom way of living Christ outlined in the Sermon on the Mount. The Pharisees, however, were hindering them by insisting that they put "*new wine into old wineskins*," resulting in the destruction of both (Mark. 2:22).

What is it that the Pharisees do not enter into? And what are they hindering others from entering? The Pharisees "do not enter," that is, they do not enter into a kingdom way of living, preferring externalisms instead. But worse, because of their negative influence "*those who would enter*" (ESV) or "*who are trying* to" (NIV) are not allowed to "go in," that is, to enter the kingdom way of living which leads to treasure in heaven.

Jesus is telling His disciples to avoid the hypocrisy of the Pharisees. They are to "*do and observe, but do not do according to their deeds; for they say things and do not do them*" (Matthew 23:3). While it is certain that the Pharisees are hindering many from being saved, what this chapter speaks of is not the obstacles to personal salvation but the obstacles to the kingdom way of living. The issue is sanctification, not soteriology, about "*doing*" and not faith alone for justification. Jesus says, "*They tie up heavy burdens and lay them on men's shoulders, but they themselves are unwilling to move them with so much as a finger*" (Matthew 23:4). He says, "***Do not do** according to their deeds*" (v. 3).

After introducing their hypocrisy in Matthew 23:1-10, Jesus says, "*But the greatest among you shall be your servant*" (Matthew 23:11). Recalling Matthew 5:19-20 and Matthew 18:1-4, Jesus returns to the subject of greatness in the kingdom.[852] In contrast to the Pharisees who seek greatness now by calling attention to their titles and robes, Jesus' followers can only find greatness in the future by humbling themselves and becoming servants. Only then can they be "exalted" (Matthew 23:12). By their desire for both love and honor from men and respectful greetings in the marketplace (vv. 5-8), the Pharisees model a kind of life directly opposite to what a committed disciple must follow.

The passage echoes the warning of Matthew 7:14, "*watch out for false prophets.*" Like Matthew 23:13, true believers, who have just been challenged to a lifestyle of entering by the narrow gate and proceeding along the way (7:13), are alerted to the danger of those who would hinder their commitment.

The warning has particular relevance to all who have the task of calling believers to higher levels of commitment. We must be careful that neither our theology nor our lives, hinder those who want to enter into the grace way of life.

Entry into Initial Salvation

A central passage on entering the kingdom is in Jesus' interview with Nicodemus.

> *Jesus answered and said to him, "Truly, truly, I say to you, unless one is born again he cannot see the kingdom of God." Nicodemus said to Him, "How can a man be born when he is old? He cannot enter a second time into his mother's womb and be born, can he?" Jesus answered,*

[852] For discussion of entering into greatness in the kingdom, see pp. 279 ff.

"Truly, truly, I say to you, unless one is born of water and the Spirit he cannot enter into the kingdom of God" (John 3:3–5).

This aspect of the future kingdom, spiritual rebirth, is available now because of the installation of the New Covenant and the outpouring of the Holy Spirit.

Summary

The "entry sayings" in the Gospels have been fodder for much theological discussion. What does it mean to "enter the kingdom"? What did Jesus mean when He spoke about the kingdom of heaven? In this chapter we concluded that the background to the entry sayings is found in the Old Testament ideas about entering the land, entering the temple precincts, and the renewal ceremony at Shechem. In each case believers are the subject. This paves the way for the concept that many of the entry sayings in the New Testament are addressed to believers as well. This is substantiated by contextual indicators surrounding the various entry sayings.

The message about the kingdom of God, that believers are called on to enter, is a multifaceted thing. This kingdom is the sovereign rule of God over His creation, but it has seven different aspects: the restored Davidic theocracy, the Messianic Banquet, the power of God, the new heavens and the new earth, and experience of discipleship and kingdom life, spiritual rebirth and a permeating influence that has uplifted the plight of mankind for centuries. Which aspect, or aspects, is/are in view depends on the context. To enter (Gr *eiserchomai*) the kingdom signifies entrance into discipleship or entrance into a kingdom way of life. It means "to begin to experience" kingdom life (LN, 1:806). The subject is sanctification, not soteriology.

On several occasions in the above discussion, we have connected kingdom entrance with "greatness." The connection between becoming great in the kingdom and entering the kingdom needs more discussion. This is the subject of the next chapter.

Excursus on the Kingdom as the Sphere of Personal Salvation

The above discussion entails the idea that the kingdom, whatever it is, is a sphere of genuine spiritual reality. It is not a sphere of mere profession of faith in Christ. Yet, that conclusion is not shared by all. There is a persistent belief that the kingdom of heaven in this age is the sphere of profession and that both believers and nonbelievers are "in" the kingdom.[853] One passage that has been particularly influential in supporting this viewpoint is Jesus' Parable of the Wheat and the Tares in Matthew 13:24-31, 36-43.[854] In particular, 13:41 is often mentioned.

---

853 For example, McIver says, "According to the parable, the membership of this community is not co-terminus with the membership of the future kingdom. The present "kingdom" has a membership where the children of the kingdom and the children of the evil one are so inextricably intermingled that they will not be separated until the last judgment which will usher in the future kingdom." See Robert K. McIver, "The Parable of the Weeds Among the Wheat (Matt 13:24-30, 36-43) and the Relationship Between the Kingdom and the Church as Portrayed in the Gospel of Matthew," *JBL* 114, no. 4 (1995): 43-59.

854 Of course, since Luther and Augustine believed this, one must admit that the interpretation is possible. The difficulty is that Jesus clearly says, that unless one is born of the Spirit one cannot enter the kingdom. The bad fish, therefore, were not ever in the kingdom at all. This fact suggests that the comparison to the kingdom is that the message of the kingdom is cast broadly. All are invited from every nation, "The net is cast over a wide cross-section of people, and while the message saves some, it will leave others unconvinced; those who have failed to respond to it are presumably among the 'bad fish' of this parable."

The Son of Man will send forth His angels, and they will gather out of His kingdom all stumbling blocks, and those who commit lawlessness, and will cast them into the furnace of fire; in that place there shall be weeping and gnashing of teeth (Matthew 13:41-42).

The key phrase is "out of His kingdom." This might suggest that the kingdom of heaven consists of true and false believers and that when Christ comes there is a "cleansing of the kingdom."[855] A problem with this is that the kingdom is elsewhere entered only by being "born again" (John 3:2-5) and is equated with the sphere of genuine reality for the believing community. How then can tares be in this kingdom? Let us go back to the beginning of the parable and consider it carefully.

Jesus presented another parable to them, saying, "The kingdom of heaven may be compared to a man who sowed good seed in his field" (Matthew 13:24).

Davies notes a problem here, if the kingdom equals the true church, "One must hold that Matthew believed that the church was peopled with 'sons of the evil one' and also, at the same time, that the church could be fitly described as the Son of Man's kingdom. We deem this unlikely."[856] Jesus has just said in verse 38 that the location of the tares is the field and the field is the world, not the kingdom.[857] How then can the kingdom equal the world and at the same time be an umbrella for the tares? Obviously, it cannot.

I suggest that the kingdom in this passage refers to the future restored Davidic theocracy. The question is, "When does this aspect of the kingdom begin?" According to Matthew 16:27 and Matthew 25:31, it will begin when the Lord returns and sends out His angels. Toussaint is correct, "It would seem His earthly kingdom begins with His appearance and return. The judgment is the introduction to His kingdom; judgment marks the beginning of His reign. Since this is so, it would be natural to say angels will gather sinners out of His kingdom. Matthew 13:41 does not prove there is a present form of the kingdom"[858] consisting of believers and non-believers.

When Christ returns, the first order of business is to remove those who never entered the kingdom in a saving sense prior to His return. Allen says, "This must not be interpreted in such a way as to suggest that the kingdom is conceived of as a present condition of things within which tares and wheat grow together. When the Son of Man has come, then the kingdom also will have come. Hence at that future date the tares can be said to be

---

The bad fish are not in the kingdom. France, *The Gospel of Matthew*, p. 542. Saucy, commenting of the parable of the wheat and the weeds has a similar view, "The weeds are cast out of the kingdom, but this is only with its coming at the end of the age, with the return of Christ. They could not be said to be 'in the kingdom' today." See Saucy, *The Case for Progressive Dispensationalism: The Interface between Dispensational & Non-dispensational Theology*, p. 100.

855 Hendriksen and Kistemaker, *Exposition of the Gospel According to Matthew*, 572.

856 Davies and Allison, *A Critical and Exegetical Commentary on the Gospel According to Saint Matthew*, 430.

857 Calvin understood the "world" to be something like the "world of the church." He says, "It is an appropriate comparison, when the Lord calls the Church his field, for believers are the seed of it; and though Christ afterwards adds that the field is the world, yet he undoubtedly intended to apply this designation, in a peculiar manner, to the Church, about which he had commenced the discourse." Calvin, *The Harmony of the Gospels: Calvin's Commentary on Matthew, Mark, and Luke*, s.v. "Matthew 13:24-33".

858 Stanley D. Toussaint, "The Church and Israel," *Conservative Theological Journal* 2, no. 7 (Dec 1998): 362.

gathered out of His kingdom."[859] As Nolland put it, "It is probably best to see the rooting out of evil as part of what the Son of Man does to establish his rule, in which case 'his kingdom' should be equated neither with the field nor with the church."[860]

Excursus on the Parable of the Two Brothers (Matthew 21:28-32)

In this parable Jesus confronts the priests who were not entering the kingdom and yet scorned those who were. Two brothers were asked by their father to work in his vineyard. One told his Father he would not work, but later regretted it (Gr *metamelomai*) and then did go. The other said he would go, but then did not. Jesus asks, "Which of the two did the will of the Father?" Obviously, it was the one whose actions accorded with his words. The sinners "*go into the kingdom*" (ESV), because when John came in the "*way of righteousness*" they "believed" him. They believed his warning that the nation faced a national catastrophe, and if they did not repent and embrace the "way of righteousness" (which Luke defines as the kingdom way of living, Luke 3:10-14), God's wrath would be poured out on Israel. It does not say, "They believed in Christ for personal salvation." Rather, they believed his message, "*the way of righteousness.*" What was that message? While some suggest it was the message of salvation, it is more reasonable to conclude, with many scholars,[861] that this phrase refers to a life lived according to the will of God, the way of kingdom living specified in the Law and the Prophets (Proverbs 8:20; 12:28; 16:31; 2 Peter 2:21). If "go into the kingdom" refers to personal salvation, then soteriological entrance into the kingdom is based upon changing one's way of life and not simple faith in Christ alone. The context is not about soteriology. It is about repenting and embracing the kingdom way of living, the way of righteousness. To "go into the kingdom," therefore means to go into the "way of righteousness." The sinners did that, the priests did not. Thus the repentance of the tax-collectors and harlots is either (1) the repentance of a group of his believing followers or (2) repentance understood as a preparatory stage to saving faith which leads to personal salvation when they believe on Christ like the disciples of John the Baptist did in Acts 19:1-5, (see chapter 3, pp. 52 ff.)

This understanding of the parable is confirmed by Matthew 21:29. The second son "*regretted* it and went." In other words, he repented ("regretted" his initial decision) and then did the work the father commanded him to do. Thus, doing the will of father *in the context of the Parable of the Two Sons* meant going to work in the father's vineyard. The "will of the Father" is obeying His commands.

---

859 Willoughby C. Allen, *A Critical and Exegetical Commentary on the Gospel According to St. Matthew*, The International Critical Commentary (New York: C. Scribner's Sons, 1907), 153.

860 Nolland, *The Gospel of Matthew: A Commentary on the Greek Text*, 560.

861 See D. C. Arichea and H. Hatton, A Handbook on the Letter from Jude and the Second Letter from Peter (New York: United Bible Societies, 1993), 138; Richard Bauckham, Jude, 2 Peter, Word Biblical Themes (Dallas: Word Publishers, 1990), 278; Allen, A Critical and Exegetical Commentary on the Gospel According to St. Matthew, 277; W. D. Davies and Dale C. Allison, A Critical and Exegetical Commentary on the Gospel According to Saint Matthew (Edinburgh: T. & T. Clark, 1988), 170.

20

Entering into Greatness

IN THE preceding chapter we established that to "enter the kingdom" is a very pregnant phrase. It includes three concepts: (1) a call to enter into personal salvation or soteriological entrance into the millennium; (2) a call to enter a rich life now by following the principles of the Sermon on the Mount; and, (3) a call to greatness, that is, an abundant entrance into the kingdom.

To be great in God's kingdom one must cultivate the surpassing righteousness and move beyond the entry level of discipleship that characterizes many believers.

In this chapter we will discuss that aspect of the kingdom which we called the kingdom way of life. To "enter the kingdom" is used in the sense of an entrance into fully committed discipleship leading to higher status, an abundant entrance into the restored Davidic theocracy. The Apostle John referred to it as an entrance "by the gates" (Revelation 22:14). We will see that this insight is key to unraveling the apparent contradiction between Matthew 5:19 and 5:20 to be discussed below. It will also solve the apparent contradiction between Matthew and Paul regarding the faith-alone requirement for personal salvation taught throughout the New Testament.

However, before addressing this point, we must digress and explore an important issue. Who is being addressed in the sermon: believing disciples (Matthew 5:1-2), or a mixed crowd composed of believers and unbelievers? This is very important because if the sermon's *intended audience* is only believers, then Jesus is clearly telling believing disciples how they must behave, if they want to enter the kingdom.

The Intended Audience of the Sermon

While some argue on the basis of Matthew 7:28 that the Sermon on the Mount was directed to a mixed crowd of believers and unbelievers, Matthew specifically says that the sermon was addressed to believers, His disciples. One would think that His opening statement would settle the matter.

> *And when He saw the multitudes [Gr ochlos], He went up on the mountain; and after He sat down,* ***His disciples came to Him****. And opening His mouth He began* ***to teach them****, saying (Matthew 5:1-2).*

Yes, at the end of the sermon the crowds were amazed (Matthew 7:28). This shows that the crowds were listening in. Wayne Baxter challenges the assumption that the crowds were part of the *intended* audience on three grounds. "First, the crowds listen to the Sermon

(4:25–5:1a), but Jesus explicitly addresses 'his disciples' and not simply the 'crowds'" (5:1b–2). Second, as was probably the case here, Jesus was not adverse to teaching His disciples in the presence of an audience (Matthew 23:1; 21:45). Third, much of Jesus' teaching is not 'evangelistic' per se, but presupposes a 'beyond-entry-level' discipleship."[862]

There is an unfortunate tendency to view the "crowds" in the Gospels as disinterested bystanders, merely curious "hangers on" who have no saving relationship to Christ. Why?[863] Minear suggests, "One answer would point to the nondescript character of the words for *ochlos* which modern lexica have made standard. English readers tend to read into the Greek text the neutral or negative connotation in modern speech of crowd, people, throng, and multitude."[864]

However, the Gospels present a different picture. Often these crowds are followers who believed on Him. They were part of a larger group of disciples from whom the twelve were selected; they are *believing* crowds.[865] Regarding the multitude (*ochlos*) sitting around Him, Jesus says that they are "*my brother and sister and mother*" (Mark 3:32-35).[866]

One can also see that the intended audience of the Sermon was true believers by the way in which Jesus characterizes them as regenerate people.[867] He tells them, for example, that when they are persecuted they will be rewarded in heaven (5:12). He calls them "*salt of the earth*," and the "*light of the world*" (5:13-14).[868]

He says to them that "theirs is the kingdom of heaven," "they shall see God," and "Blessed[869] are you when people insult you, persecute you and falsely say all kinds of evil against you because of me" (Matthew 5:11). This is not the gospel to a mixed multitude. Furthermore, He speaks of their "reward in heaven." His disciples have been so impacted by Jesus' message that He exhorts them saying, "Let your light shine before men, that they may see your good deeds, and praise your Father in heaven" (v. 16).

---

862 Baxter, "The Narrative Setting of the Sermon on the Mount," 35.

863 Paul S. Minear, "Audience Criticism and Markan Ecclesiology," in *Neues Testament und Geschichte*, ed. Oscar Cullman and Bo Reicke (Tübingen: J. C. B. Mohn [Paul Siebeck], 1972), 79-89. He also says that commentators have been inclined, almost without exception, to assign to the term *mathētai* [disciples] the inclusive range of Luke-Acts, in which disciples are virtually equivalent to Christians (Acts 11:26). "By contrast, Mark limited the term to the Twelve who were appointed by Jesus and given quite special authority for accomplishing quite special tasks" ibid., 88.

864 Ibid., 88.

865 Ibid.

866 The word for "crowd" in Mark 3:32-35 is *ochlos*, as in Matthew 5:1-2.

867 This seems to refute Luz and Helmut's view that both disciples and crowds are equally part of the intended audience based on Matthew 7:29. Realizing that the ethical instruction is appropriate only for those who are already saved, they say the crowds are "proleptically ... already following Jesus"! Luz and Koester, *Matthew 1-7: A Commentary*, p. 182.

868 These are those who are called on to glorify their "Father who is in heaven" (5:16). He gives them instruction in avoiding adultery (5:27-29) and anger (5:21-22); he speaks of their being rewarded in heaven if they love their enemies (5:46); he commands his listeners to set their goal on being as perfect as God is (5:48). We are told that those addressed are not unbelieving Gentiles (5:47). His intended audience is warned not to practice their righteousness before men, or they will have no reward in heaven (6:1). They give to the poor and seek instruction on how to pray (6:9). Jesus specifically tells the intended audience that God is their Father (6:9), knowing that only regenerate sons of God have God as their Father (John 1:12-13).

869 "To be blessed is to receive God's approval, favor, endorsement, congratulations. It is much more than 'happy' since the word 'happiness' conveys only a subjective shallow notion of serendipity, not the conviction of being a recipient of God's grace." See David L. Turner, *Matthew*, Baker Exegetical Commentary on the New Testament (Grand Rapids: Baker Academic, 2008), 149.

Does one give nonbelievers instruction on prayer, rewards, almsgiving, and fasting (6:16-18), and then tell them these are conditions for personal salvation? Those addressed offer sacrifices at the altar (v. 24), "give to the poor" (6:3), and are told that God is their *"Father in heaven"* (Matthew 7:11).

Would this be true of a crowd of unbelievers? Those addressed are admonished to *"lay up treasure in heaven"* (6:20-21). The Sermon on the Mount is, as France calls it, "The Discourse on Discipleship," and not a presentation of the gospel. That is why in Luke's introduction to the Sermon, even though both a large "throng" (Gr *plēthos*, "number") of people and a large "crowd" (Gr *ochlos*) of disciples were present (Luke 6:17), we read that Jesus: *"Turning His gaze* ***toward His disciples*** *He began to say, 'Blessed are you who are poor, for yours is the kingdom of God'"* (Luke 6:20).[870]

If Jesus is addressing the unsaved, why is it that He never gives them the gospel? There is no reference anywhere in the sermon to believing on Christ or His death for sin. The unsaved would be left with the idea that salvation is by works if the sermon was intended for a mixed multitude of the saved and unsaved and if "enter the kingdom" meant "go to heaven when you die."

The Sermon on the Mount is not an evangelistic sermon.[871] It is an exhortation to believers to fully committed discipleship.[872] That is why Joachim Jeremias says that the sermon is "intended to show the young Christians, who have not only heard the message of Jesus but also opened their hearts to it, what manner of life they should lead in the future."[873]

---

870 R.T France correctly says, "The teaching is addressed, initially at least, not to the crowds, but rather to the narrower circle of his committed disciples, to whom we have been introduced in 4:18-22, and who are now taken apart from the crowds to be instructed on what their new commitment involves. The focus of these chapters is not then the wider proclamation of the 'good news' of the kingdom (4:23), but the instruction of those who have already responded to that proclamation and now need to learn what life in the 'kingdom of heaven' is really about." France, *The Gospel of Matthew*, 153. Craig Blomberg agrees: "Identifying the disciples as Jesus' audience is crucial for recognizing the ethics of the sermon as applying to those already committed to Jesus as a group of his followers trying to live together in community." Craig L. Blomberg, *Matthew*, New American Commentary (Nashville: Broadman and Holman Publishers, 2001), 97. R. T. France notes, "The audience is clearly specified as his disciples, as opposed to the crowds. The latter reappear as a wider audience in 7:28, but they are clearly not the main focus of the teaching." R. T. France, "Matthew," in *The New Bible Commentary*, ed. D. A. Carson, *21st Century* (Downers Grove, IL: InterVarsity Press, 1994), 911. Hagner agrees, "These introductory verses indicate that Jesus addresses primarily the disciples in the sermon." Hagner, *Matthew 14-28*, 84.

871 At least one scholar has pointed out that the sermon has all the characteristics of an ordination ceremony. Jesus spends the night before in prayer to God and at daybreak He calls a number of followers to Him and selects twelve whom He names apostles. He then descends to a level place on the slope of the mountain and gives a charge to those whom He has just appointed. Like many ordination services in the centuries to follow, the official retires in prayer and subsequently selects the elders or other officials early in the morning. This is commonly followed by a formal exhortation to the congregation. From this Kenneth E. Kirk concludes that "Luke regards the beatitudes as addressed directly to the apostles and their potential successors in the Christian ministry." Kenneth E. Kirk, *The Vision of God: The Christian Doctrine of the Summum Bonum*, The Bampton Lectures for 1928 (New York: Longmans, Green and Co., 1928), 43.

872 Turner notes, "Jesus evidently retires to the mountainside to teach his disciples more privately, but it is doubtful that the crowd is entirely absent from his discourse." Turner, *Matthew*, 141. Hagner is even more specific. "Jesus went to the mountain apparently in the hope of escaping the crowds who pressed upon him to be healed (cf. 4:23–25). But this was to be a special time of teaching for his disciples, who 'came to him.'" Hagner, *Matthew 14-28*, 86.

873 Jeremias, *The Sermon on the Mount*, 31.

He is calling on these believing people who have already entered the kingdom in the sense of personal salvation to "enter the kingdom." But why would those who have already entered the kingdom be called on to enter it?

The Apparent Contradiction between Matthew 5:19 and 20

Verse 19 reads, "*Whoever then annuls one of the least of these commandments, and teaches others to do the same, shall be called least in the kingdom of heaven.*" The future tense "shall be" focuses our attention on this person's status in the future reign of Christ on earth.[874] Jesus had been accused of abolishing the Law. To the contrary, He says, even the least important laws must be obeyed.

The individual in this verse will be "in" the kingdom; but he has not only disobeyed even the least of the commandments, but he has also actively taught others to do the same! He himself not only "disobeys" (Gr *luō*, "to do away with, destroy, bring to an end, abolish"[875]), he actually causes little ones to stumble (as in Matthew 18:6). He is a dangerous teacher for he is saying that God said things He did not say thus incurring the judgment of James 3:1. He is a saved person,[876] but will have the lowest status. As Allen puts it in reference to Matthew 5:19,

> *If any of His disciples taught men to disobey any of its commandments, he would be placed in an inferior position in the coming Kingdom. If he was a faithful servant of the law, and upheld its authority before men, he would receive high rank in the Kingdom.*[877]

Betz agrees,

> *One should note that a remarkable paradox results from this evaluation, for, contrary to what one would expect,* ***a place in the kingdom of God is not denied even to the disloyal teacher who seeks to set aside Jesus' teaching.*** *Thus, one may assume that in the honorific title "great" is promised to a loyal teacher in the heavenly kingdom.*[878]

---

874 What is meant by "the least of these commandments"? Does it mean least in importance? Does it refer to the rabbinic distinction between lesser and weightier Torah commandments? Because of the specific words Jesus used (Gr *nomos* "law" and *entolē* "commandment"), it is suggested by some that He has in view His interpretation of the Torah as given in the Sermon on the Mount, probably the teaching of Jesus from 5:21 onward. See Betz and Collins, *The Sermon on the Mount: A Commentary on the Sermon on the Mount, Including the Sermon on the Plain (Matthew 5:3-7:27 and Luke 6:20-49)*, p. 186. D. A. Carson, agrees saying that the commands refer "to the commands of the kingdom of heaven. They are the commands already given, and the commands still to come, in the Sermon on the Mount." See D. A. Carson, *Jesus' Sermon on the Mount and His Confrontation with the World* (Grand Rapids: Baker Book House, 1987), 40.

875 BDAG, 607.

876 There is a word play on the word "least." The one who disobeys the least of the commandments will be least in the kingdom. Yet these teachers will be "in" the kingdom. John Nolland is correct, "Being 'least in the kingdom of heaven' still leaves one in the kingdom and not outside it." Nolland, *The Gospel of Matthew: A Commentary on the Greek Text*, 222. Yet Nolland goes on to say in regard to the surpassing righteousness requirement for "entering the kingdom" in verse 20, "The threat of exclusion from the kingdom of heaven corresponds closely with the sentiment of verse 19, where, however, the discussion takes place in terms of rank in the kingdom" (ibid., 225). In other words, he admits that entering the kingdom in verse 20 "corresponds closely" with the idea of rank within the kingdom in verse 19, but then he denies that they "correspond closely." Certainly, the ideas of being in the kingdom and therefore saved do not "correspond closely" with the idea of being excluded from the kingdom altogether!

877 Allen, *A Critical and Exegetical Commentary on the Gospel According to St. Matthew*, 45.

878 Betz and Collins, *The Sermon on the Mount: A Commentary on the Sermon on the Mount, Including the Sermon on the Plain (Matthew 5:3-7:27 and Luke 6:20-49)*, 188.

The issue is status, not soteriology.

The traditional interpretation understands "enter the kingdom" in verse 20 to mean entering into heaven or soteriological entrance into the millennium. This sets Matthew 5:19 and 5:20 in contradiction to each other. *In verse 19 a man not having the surpassing righteousness is "in" the kingdom, but according to verse 20 he does not have the surpassing righteousness greater than that of the Scribes and Pharisees that is necessary to enter it!* However, if "enter the kingdom" refers to presently entering the way of living characteristic of the future kingdom, there is no contradiction. Living that way *now* leads to a higher status, an abundant entrance (2 Peter 1:11) (greatness) in that future kingdom. Both ("entering" and "greatness") refer to sanctification and status, not soteriology. The person in verse 19 is the regenerate saint who was "salt," but he had become one of the "saltless" ones mentioned in verse 13. His end, having taken the broad way and avoiding the narrow way of discipleship, is "destruction" (Matthew 7:13-14), that is, spiritual, psychological, and possibly physical ruin.[879] His life is of no more value, according to Jesus, than flavorless salt cast onto a manure pile (Lk. 14:35). Paradoxically, this man who is declared to be "in" the kingdom does not, according to Matthew 5:20, possess the righteousness necessary to "enter" it!

It is surprising that many commentators do not discuss this problem.[880] Carson, for example, in his thoughtful exposition of the Sermon on the Mount leaves careful readers perplexed. On the one hand he acknowledges that being least in the kingdom refers to "ranking *within* the kingdom" and notes that these rankings depend on obedience to Jesus. But on the other hand, he says that those without surpassing righteousness can have no admittance.[881] Does Carson believe that those who disobey even the least of the commandments and who teach others to do the same have the required surpassing righteousness necessary for kingdom entrance? He never explains.

How can a person be "in" the kingdom when he does not possess the surpassing inward righteousness necessary to enter it? There have been six possible ways of harmonizing these verses. First, one could say that the man in verse 19 who is "in" yet "least," is only in the kingdom in a professing sense. He is not really born again, because if he was, he would have submitted to the Lordship of Christ and would obey Him.[882] This was the view of

---

879 Thus, while we can agree that a carnal Christian without works is a monstrosity, Norman Shepherd's statement that "faith alone justifies but a justified person with faith alone would be a monstrosity which never exists in the kingdom of grace," contradicts the teaching of Christ. Clearly such monsters can exist "in" the kingdom of God. Norman Shepherd, "Justification by Faith Alone," *Reformation and Revival* 11, no. 2 (2002): 88. I will show in a later chapter that "destruction" does not refer to final damnation, see pp. 294 ff.

880 This is particularly surprising in Alan Stanley's well-researched and well-written book, which argues that salvation in the Gospels is by the good works of the regenerate man as well as by faith, Alan Stanley, *Did Jesus Teach Salvation by Works: The Role of Works in Salvation in the Synoptic Gospels* (Eugene, OR: Pickwick, 2006). This omission is also found in Hendriksen and Kistemaker, *Exposition of the Gospel According to Matthew*, 293. and Rainbow, *Way of Salvation*. Even R. T. France in his excellent commentary on Matthew passes over the problem. On the one hand, he admits that those least "in" the kingdom are truly regenerate people (p. 188), but on the other hand, he insists that in order to enter the kingdom a radical obedience to God and complete self-giving to one's neighbor is necessary (p. 190). In fact, he says that those who simply keep the rules, "however conscientiously, haven't even started as far as the kingdom of heaven is concerned." Yet those who are least in the kingdom not only do not keep the rules but disobey them and teach others to do the same and yet they are, according to France, saved people. See France, *The Gospel of Matthew*, 188-90.

881 Carson, *Jesus' Sermon on the Mount and His Confrontation with the World*, 41.

882 Everett F. Harrison, "Romans," in *The Expositor's Bible Commentary*, ed. Frank E. Gaebelein and Everett F. Harrison (Grand Rapids: Zondervan Publishing House, 1976), 246. "Jesus taught that when people repent,

Augustine,[883] Chrysostom,[884] and Martin Luther.[885] This requires that kingdom in verse 19 is only the sphere of profession, and in verse 20 it means "the sphere of reality." However, there is no hint in the context of such a change of meaning.[886] Are we to assume that the one who is "great in the kingdom" is likewise only a professing Christian? To be "in the kingdom" is to be saved.[887]

A second solution to this difficulty is to say that the man who is "least" is regenerate but that being "least" implies that he "had kept the law for the most part."[888] A more

---

believe the Gospel and acknowledge his Lordship by doing his will they 'enter the Kingdom' (Matthew 5:20; 7:21; etc.)." As John Stott, Ronald Sider, Rene Padilla, and others have shown, salvation in the New Testament is always a God-related term, and while it is not to be confused with changed ethical behavior and social justice, salvation cannot be isolated from ethical behavior. Only those who confess Christ as Lord enter the Kingdom." This of course directly contradicts what Jesus said in verse 19.

883 Augustine notes that there are two classes of people who are "in" the kingdom of heaven, law-breakers and those who do the law. The problem, of course, is that verse 20 states that one cannot be a law-breaker and "enter" the kingdom. Augustine's solution is to say the meaning of kingdom of heaven in verse 19 differs from that in verse 20, the former being the sphere of profession only and the latter the sphere of those who are born again. He argues that the visible church today is the kingdom of heaven in which there are wheat and tares, saved and unsaved. Augustine, *City of God*, 20:46-50.

884 Chrysostom shares a similar view and offers an additional insight. He quotes Matthew 5:22, "*Whoever says to his brother, 'You good-for-nothing,' shall be guilty before the supreme court; and whoever says, 'You fool,' shall be guilty enough to go into the fiery hell.*" Chrysostom asks, "And how could it be reasonable, that while he who called his brother fool (Matthew 5:22), and transgressed but one commandment, falls into hell; [but] the breaker of them all, and instigator of others to the same, [Matthew 5:19] should be within the kingdom?" Therefore, he concludes with Augustine that the man who is "in" the kingdom and is "least" is one who has only professed faith and is not really born again, and he will be cast into hell. However, this solution, like Augustine's flies flatly in the face of the clear statement that he is in fact "in" the kingdom, saved. Augustine defines the kingdom in verse 19 as the professing church. Yet there is not warrant in the text for this at all. It emerges from his theology. Surely, if "kingdom" meant something different in verse 20 from what it meant in verse 19, there would be some textual indicator. But there is none at all.

885 Luther says, "The phrase 'shall be called least in the kingdom of heaven' means simply that he shall not be in the kingdom of heaven." Martin Luther, "The Sermon on the Mount" in Luther, *Luther's Works*, 21:71.

886 Davies and Allison properly object to this interpretation saying, "Does 'least in the kingdom of heaven' entail utter exclusion from the final state of the blessed? Perhaps not. The idea of rank in heaven and of degrees of reward is found not only in rabbinic writings but also in the gospel of Matthew (5:12; 10:41–42; 20:23)." Davies and Allison, *A Critical and Exegetical Commentary on the Gospel According to Saint Matthew*, 497. Then in an attempt to harmonize this with the fact that a person who lacks surpassing righteousness cannot even enter the kingdom (v. 20), they curiously say, "Although the threat in 5:20 is the converse of the promise in 5:19, in both verses eschatology provides the motivation for proper behavior" ibid., 500. But there is nothing "converse" about this at all. It is flatly contradictory, a fact they seem to be hiding under a word which means "reversed in order," and completely obfuscates the intent of the passage. John P. Meier convincingly refutes the idea that to be "least" means to be "excluded" from the kingdom. He notes that there is no evidence in the New Testament that the word "least" (Gr *elachistos*) is ever associated with exclusion from the kingdom or damnation. Meier, *Law and History in Matthew's Gospel: A Redactional Study of Mt. 5:17-48*, 92-95. Contra G. Shrenk, "*entolē*," TDNT 2:548.

887 Jesus said, "*Truly, truly, I say to you, unless one is born of water and the Spirit he cannot enter into the kingdom of God*" (John 3:5). Since the man in verse 19 is declared to be "in" the kingdom, and thus has entered it, we can say on the authority of Christ that he is born again.

888 "It is unlikely," Hagner says, "that 'least' refers to those excluded from the Kingdom." Rather, "it is directly related to the idea of rewards as a motivation for conduct." Hagner, *Matthew 14-28*, 108. Craig Blomberg does not comment on the issue of the seeming contradiction but says that the man who is least is a saved man but ranks less in the present age not necessarily in the future kingdom (Blomberg, *Matthew*, 105). But again, we must ask, "How can he be a saved man if his righteousness does not exceed that of the scribes and Pharisees, which it clearly does not?" Also nothing in the context links this man's station to only the

nuanced version of this approach suggests levels of righteousness. The lowest level was the unbelieving Pharisee; the next level up is the man who is "least," and the highest level are those who do the greater righteousness. The idea here is that the person who is least is certainly better than the Pharisee who externalized everything and who never believed in Christ. Thus, there is no contradiction between verses 19 and 20. The person in this view does possess the greater righteousness necessary for entrance, because it is greater than that of the Pharisees.

But, one must ask, "How much greater righteousness did Jesus have in mind?" The problem with this interpretation is that it reduces the "greater righteousness" to something only minimally above that of the Pharisees. Jesus does not define the greater righteousness that way. He defines it all through the Sermon *as a fully committed kingdom lifestyle.* He gives this definition in particular in the verses immediately following where He delineates the six antitheses that mark out exactly what He means. We must ask, "How is it possible that a person who disobeys God and teaches others to dilute their commitment to Christ by teaching them things God did not say, has 'kept the law for the most part,' or, for that matter, has kept it at all?" "How is it possible that this level of greater righteousness is the kind of '*greater*' righteousness needed for kingdom entrance which Jesus had in mind?"

Neonomians do not offer a solution or even seem to be aware of the difficulty. Instead, they use Matthew 5:20 as proof that entrance into heaven is "conditioned" upon God produced non-meritorious works.[889] For example, Alan Stanley argues that he is not teaching a salvation conditioned on works, because he is not "arguing that the righteousness required for entering the kingdom originated with man himself." He never explains how the person of v. 19 could possibly have those works and yet be in the kingdom.[890]

A third option is to deny there is any tension between these verses at all. The Pharisees in verse 20 are actually regenerate carnal believers, and thus are in fact the "least" referred to in verse 19. This solution also fails. Since surpassing righteousness is required for entrance, and since the Pharisees do not have such righteousness, this solution would reduce the high standard of surpassing righteousness down to the level of a man who disobeys and who teaches others to do the same. Furthermore, Jesus' continual condemnation of the Pharisees suggests that many of them were not in the kingdom at all, and certainly not in it in the sense of a kingdom way of living. He calls them fools, blind guides, hypocrites, and whitewashed tombs (Matthew 23:37).

---

present age. Blomberg gratuitously throws in this unsupported comment because of his theological bias against the idea of rewards. Davies and Allison see "least" not as exclusion from the kingdom, but as referring to rankings within it, "Does 'least in the kingdom of heaven' entail utter exclusion from the final state of the blessed? Perhaps not (cf. As. Mos. 12:10–13)." Davies and Allison, *A Critical and Exegetical Commentary on the Gospel According to Saint Matthew*, 497. The idea of rank in heaven and of degrees of reward is found not only in rabbinic writings but also in the Gospel of Matthew (5:12; 10:41–42; 20:23). We will discuss Blomberg's denial of degrees of glory in a later chapter, pp. 991 ff.

889 This viewpoint is one of the tenants of the so-called "Federal Vision" or the "Auburn Avenue Theology." This unorthodox view has recently been the focus of a special report (and refutation) published by a commission of the PCA. See Report of the Ad Interim Study Committee on Federal Vision New Perspective, and Auburn Avenue theology." The burden of this report is to refute the claim made by those teaching these viewpoints that their views are consistent with the Westminster Confession. See http://www.pcaac.org/2007GeneralAssembly/. For a more detailed critique of this new development in Experimental Predestinarian circles, see Johnson and Waters, *By Faith Alone: Answering Challenges to the Doctrine of Justification.*

890 Stanley, *Did Jesus Teach Salvation by Works,* 318. I will discuss this option in more detail in vol. 2, chapter 37.

A fourth suggestion is that in verse 20 Jesus is telling His disciples that since Pharisees cannot get into the kingdom by following their version of righteousness, why would the disciples want to follow a way of life, as believers, which could never get them into the kingdom in the first place? In other words, they ought to be motivated to pursue a higher kind of righteousness as a way of Christian living, because the kind of righteousness pursued by the Pharisees leads only to separation from God. However, this vacates the challenge and warning of any consequence for failure to heed it.

A fifth interpretation argues that beginning in verse 20 there is a shift in the audience. Prior to verse 20 believers were addressed, but this verse and following are addressed to a mixed group who is being warned about not going to heaven when they die, that is, not entering the kingdom. This however does not square with the plain words of the text. Addressing the believing disciples, Jesus says, "*For I say to* ***you****, that unless* ***your righteousness*** *exceeds the righteousness of the Scribes and the Pharisees you will not enter the kingdom.*" He is clearly exhorting His believing disciples to live according to an inner righteousness. But, if they are believing (and therefore saved) disciples, how is it that they will not enter the kingdom, if "enter the kingdom" means personal salvation!?

Furthermore, there is no difference in the descriptions of those addressed in 5:17-7:29 in comparison to those addressed in 5:1-16. They are addressed as those who have God as their Father (6:1), a title available only to those who have already believed on Jesus' name (John 1:12-13); they can obtain reward in heaven (6:1, 3, 5); and they are given instruction on how to pray (6:9), etc.[891] Throughout the remainder of the sermon, there is instruction to those who have already believed and there is no evidence that a different audience has suddenly come to the forefront.[892]

All of these solutions fail because all of them begin with the assumption that to enter the kingdom refers to soteriology.

As argued above, the call to enter the kingdom is addressed to those who are already in the kingdom in the sense of personal salvation; it is a call to fully committed discipleship. The subject matter of the sermon is sanctification and status, not soteriology.

This leads to a final possibility for explaining the apparent contradiction between Matthew 5:19 and 5:20, and it resolves the apparent contradiction between the works salvation seemingly taught in Matthew and the rest of the New Testament.

Let me state the contradictions once again before we proceed.

1. In Matthew 5:19 Jesus speaks of a man who is "in" the kingdom but who clearly does not have the surpassing righteousness required by verse 20 which is necessary to enter it.

[891] In Luke's version of the Lord's Prayer he writes, "And it came about that while He was praying in a certain place, after He had finished, one of His disciples said to Him, 'Lord, teach us to pray just as John also taught his disciples.'" And He said to them, "When you pray, say: 'Father, hallowed be Thy name. Thy kingdom come.'" (Luke 11:1-2). It is probably on another occasion that this request from His disciples occurred. Bock suggests, "If two events are present, Jesus takes a public prayer and makes it a model for the disciples to follow. He offered the prayer to the disciples in the Sermon on the Mount and now makes it a model." Bock, *Luke 9:51-24:53*, 1046. While the placement of this prayer in the life of Christ is a problem, it is clear that "one of his disciples said to him," and He responded to the disciples saying, "When you pray."

[892] Appeals to the narrow door being Jesus Himself are gratuitous. The argument applies only if one "knows" that the narrow door applies to Christ. I have argued elsewhere that it does not. The narrow door is the decision a believing saint makes to accept the responsibilities of a fully committed disciple and enter into this way of life, enduring all trials that may come his way.

2. If entering the kingdom in Matthew 5:20 refers to final entrance into heaven or the millennium, and if the surpassing righteousness required is works, then entering the kingdom requires works and not faith alone. This would contradict what Jesus taught in the Gospel of John and what Paul taught in Romans and Galatians.

The preceding discussion has established three things.

1. The surpassing righteousness is an inward righteousness resulting in the character qualities described in the Sermon on the Mount.
2. The intended audience of the Sermon is those who are already saved.
3. The call to enter the kingdom is a call to those who are saved to become fully committed disciples by living out the Sermon on the Mount.

In Matthew 5:19-20 Jesus connects kingdom entrance now and in the future with the final outcome of a successful life, honor in the future reign. He is saying what He has said elsewhere but in a different way: by entering into the future kingdom's way of living now believers will save their souls for eternity, that is, find their life's ultimate meaning and significance and be honored with high status in the future reign of the servant kings.

That final entrance is described by Peter as an abundant entrance, "*For in this way the entrance into the eternal kingdom of our Lord and Savior Jesus Christ will be abundantly supplied to you*" (2 Peter 1:11). The apostle John described this final entrance as entering "*through the gates* [the way of victory and honor] *into the city*" (Revelation 22:14).

Let's explore this concept in more detail.

Becoming Great in the Kingdom

In substantiation of the interpretation that Matthew 5:20 refers to entering into higher honor in the future kingdom by entering the kingdom way of living now, it should be noted that in v. 20 Jesus points back to verse 19. Verse 20 begins with "for."[893] Questions that would naturally be raised by the distinction between least and great in verse 19 would be, "What is the definition of 'great'?" and "How can I become great?" The disciples often discussed these questions (Matthew 18:1; 23:11; Mark 9:34; Luke 9:46; 22:24-26). Verse 20 gives the answer. Greatness comes by living out the surpassing inward righteousness,

---

893 Those addressed are "salt." The danger is that they will lose their saltiness. It is true that the introductory "for" (Gr *gar*) does not necessarily indicate a strict cause-effect relationship. John P. Meier makes this point so that he can then assert a non-sequitur that its function is only to carry the thought onwards and that there is *no* tight connection with what precedes. Meier, *Law and History in Matthew's Gospel: A Redactional Study of Mt. 5:17-48*, 124. In logic this is called the fallacy of the false obversion. No one, to my knowledge, has ever asserted that the connection between verses 19 and 20 is one of cause-effect. This is like the sign in the window that says, "These eggs are guaranteed never to turn brown." The false obversion is that the eggs in other stores were once white and then turned brown. In Meier's case, the false obversion is that since *gar* does not always mean cause-effect, it therefore only means, "Ok, let's consider another point." But *gar* does normally indicate a close connection with what went on before. BDAG (p. 189) even gives "marker of cause" as its first translation. It can also mean "marker of clarification," or "marker of inference, certainly, by all means" etc. In no case that I am aware of in the New Testament is *gar* so loose that it has no close connection with what precedes. In point of fact, "Γάρ generally indicates a causal relation between two statements, whereby the second statement gives a reason for or explains the first," Karl Kertelge, "*dikaiosunē*," in EDNT 1:328. In classical Greek the first meaning is "introducing the reason or cause of what precedes," LSJ 338.

one higher than that of the scribes and Pharisees which was external and legalistic. In other words, high status results from living out the Sermon on the Mount.[894] While one cannot prove that Paul had this passage (Matthew 5:20) in mind, it has been noted that in Romans 2:7 and 2:10, he argues in a similar way.[895]

The only other time the phrase "enter the kingdom" is used in the Sermon on the Mount is in 7:21. There we are told that the condition for kingdom entrance is "*doing the will of the Father*." I will discuss this phrase in more detail later.[896] My conclusion will be consistent with the view of the majority of Matthean scholars that in the context of the Sermon on the Mount to do the "will of the Father" means to obey the teaching of the sermon.

The view that entering the kingdom refers to entering into a kingdom way of living leading to greatness in the kingdom is confirmed by the similar passage in Matthew 18. That chapter opens with this statement: "*At that time the disciples came to Jesus and said, 'Who then is greatest in the kingdom of heaven?'*" (Matthew 18:1). Once again, the subject matter is "greatness" in the kingdom; once again, the passage is addressed to His disciples, and once again, Jesus speaks of entrance.

> *And he said: "I tell you the truth, unless you change* [Gr *strephō*, : "inward change," BDAG, 948] *and become like little children, you will never enter the kingdom of heaven. Therefore, whoever humbles himself like this child is the* ***greatest in the kingdom of heaven*** (NIV).

---

894 It is interesting that one of the most frequently cited scholarly works on salvation in Matthew implicitly acknowledges that this is what Matthew teaches but dismisses it. Petri Luomanen says that in Matthew 5:20 "Matthew adopted and elaborated verse 19" only because it serves Matthew's purposes. Having embraced the distinction between what Jesus taught and what the words which the community needs to put in His mouth in order to "legitimize" themselves (p. 88-90), Luomanen assumes we do not know what Jesus really said and Luomanen is not concerned with whether these were Jesus' purposes. "The contrast between least and great helps Matthew in highlighting how important it is to teach people all the ordinances of the law without 'relaxing' any of them." The fact that the saying actually implies a distinction in the future kingdom of which Luomanen does not approve does not bother him in this connection. This ambiguity, too, is understandable in the light of Matthew's legitimating concerns (ibid., 91). Luomanen, *Entering the Kingdom*, 88-90. In other words, "entrance" and being "great" MUST be different things. To avoid the more obvious conclusion that they are the same thing, he resorts to saying that Matthew's contradiction can only be explained by the fact that Matthew did not really mean it; the juxtaposition of these terms are only to serve his purpose establishing the importance of the law. See ibid., 91. Could it be that "entrance" and becoming "great" *are* the same thing in this particular passage, and entrance does not always refer to soteriological entrance into the future kingdom?

895 "*God 'will give to each person according to what he has done.' To those who by persistence in doing good seek glory, honor and immortality, he will give eternal life. But for those who are self-seeking and who reject the truth and follow evil, there will be wrath and anger. There will be trouble and distress for every human being who does evil: first for the Jew, then for the Gentile; but glory, honor and peace for everyone who does good: first for the Jew, then for the Gentile. For God does not show favoritism*" (Romans 2:6-11). This passage is notoriously difficult to interpret. See discussion of this passage on pp. 225 ff. However, if one were to understand "eternal life" as a rich experience of life now, rather than heaven when one dies, the works versus faith alone tension in the passage evaporates. Both nonbelievers (vv. 7-8) and believers will be judged according to their works. For the faithful believer, the outcome is a rich experience of eternal life now and "glory, honor, and peace" in the future kingdom, a reward. The analogous parallel to "greatness in the kingdom" is probably not coincidental.

896 See pp. 312 ff.

Verse 4 begins with "whoever then" or "whoever therefore," linking it closely with the preceding. It appears that entering the kingdom and becoming great there are parallel phrases. Experimental Predestinarian writer Craig Blomberg agrees, "So the criterion for greatness is precisely the criterion for entrance."[897] Luomanen finds that "it is interesting to note how Matthew answers the question about greatness *in* the kingdom of heaven by introducing the requirements of *entrance*."[898] However, Jesus is not speaking of soteriology here because those addressed are His disciples who are already in the kingdom in the sense of being saved. To paraphrase our understanding of Jesus' words, we might say, "Unless you are willing to take a low status and become a servant of all, you will not enter the kingdom way of living and obtain greatness in the millennium." R. T. France is correct, "Usage so far in this gospel indicates that 'the kingdom of heaven' here refers to the new values which Jesus is inculcating."[899] Entrance into the kingdom refers to entrance into *that aspect of the kingdom* that I have called the *experience of the kingdom way of life*, that is, into "*discipleship*." Conversion (v. 3) and cutting off one's hand (vv. 8-9) are required, not faith alone (Revelation 21:6). This would lead to the status the disciples sought.

Let me expand on this a bit more. Jesus introduces a child as a model for how the disciples are to think about their desire for greatness. France explains, it is

> *about accepting for oneself a position in the social scale which is like that of children, that is as the lowest in the hierarchy of authority and decision-making, those subject to and dependent on adults.*[900]

The phrase "humbles (Gr *tapeinoō*, 'to lose status') himself"[901] or "take the lowly position" in verse 4 confirms this understanding of what the context already demands. Children are socially as well as physically "little ones" (v. 6). If the disciples' question about being "great" was prompted by a desire to exercise authority over others, they have started at the wrong end. Their "grown-up" sense of social position puts them out of sympathy with God's value-scale.[902]

All Christians enter the realm of the kingdom, but Jesus says that only those who change their lives ("be converted," NASB, Gr *strephō* "to turn, to change") and assume a servant status, living out the higher righteousness of the Sermon on the Mount, will enter their kingship (Matthew 25:34, five cites, ten cities, etc.), that is, will become great there.

The condition for obtaining greatness is that one must change his life. Does this establish that what is in view is initial salvation? Not at all! This need for change is addressed to those who are already saved, the disciples, "*at that time some of the disciples came to Jesus and said, 'Who then is greatest in the kingdom of heaven?'*" (Matthew 18:1). What is in view here is the conversion of those who are already saved! As some

---

[897] Craig L. Blomberg, "Degrees of Reward in the Kingdom of Heaven?," JETS 35, no. 2 (1992): 166. One can assume, however, that Blomberg believes all "true" believers will be great because he does not believe there are any distinctions or degrees of glory.

[898] Luomanen, *Entering the Kingdom*, 240.

[899] France, *The Gospel of Matthew*, 675.

[900] Ibid., 676-77.

[901] BDAG, 990.

[902] France, *The Gospel of Matthew*, 676-77.

have noted, "the Christian life is a life of conversion."[903] To "convert" means to turn from wanting to be the greatest to wanting to be the least, the servant of all. Or, as Davies and Allison explain, "to start one's spiritual life afresh," (Davies and Allison, Matthew, 2:758). The issue is sanctification, not soteriology.

Also the parallel phrase in Luke 18:17 clarifies the relationship between "entering the kingdom" and receiving the kingdom. "*Truly I say to you, whoever does not receive the kingdom of God like a child will not enter it [at all].*"[904] The phrase "*at all*" is not in the Greek text. To receive a kingdom does not mean "be saved. It means to "receive royal authority"[905] (Luke 19:15). Thus to "*not receive the kingdom*" may mean, "*will not receive authority*" in the kingdom.

For example, in the parable of the nobleman who went to a far country, Jesus says that the nobleman's purpose was to "*receive a kingdom for himself*" (Luke 19:12), that is, he was to receive ruling authority over a kingdom. Thus, Jesus equates entering the kingdom with receiving ruling authority there and not with initial salvation. The section begins and ends with questions about greatness and rewards (Luke 18:14; 19:17).[906] The meaning is that one must receive the right to rule by taking the lowest status, that of a child, or he will not enter into the kingship, that is, enter into greatness in the kingdom, that is, and abundant entrance (2 Peter 1:11) .

Jesus repeatedly stressed this theme (Matthew 23:11; Mark 9:35) and modeled it by His life (Philippians 2:5-11).

All Christians will go to heaven when they die, but not all will share in His rule. This abundant entry (ruling with Him) is granted only to those children of God who have persevered in a life of discipleship to the final hour. "*We have become Partners of Christ,*" says the writer to the Hebrews, only "*if we hold fast the beginning of our assurance firm to the end*" (Hebrews 3:14).[907] For this reason, Christians need "*endurance, so that when you have done the will of God, you may receive what was promised*" (Hebrews 10:36), which is called a "great reward" (Gr *misthapodosia,* "payment of wages,"[908] Hebrews 10:35).

---

903 George W. Peters, "The Meaning of Conversion," *BibSac* 120, no. 479 (July - September 1963): 237.

904 Paul also exhorts true believers to become children (1 Corinthians 14:20) as does Peter (1 Peter 2:2).

905 There are some parables from a Jewish Midrash (commentary, *Mekhilta*) on Exodus 20:2 which provide an interesting parallel to the phrase "receive the kingdom." "They said to him: Yes, yes. Rabbi (?) says it was to make known to the glory of Israel in that when they all stood at Mount Sinai to receive the Law, they were all of one heart to receive the kingdom of heaven with joy." Cited by T. W. Manson, *The Teaching of Jesus: Studies of Its Form and Content*, 2nd ed. (Cambridge: University Press, 1955), 132. In a second parable, "So the Omnipresent said to Israel: I am Jehovah thy God .... I am he whose Kingdom you received in Egypt. They said to him: It is so. God replied: As you received my Kingdom receive my decrees" (*Mekhilta*, cited by Manson, 132).

906 "I tell you, this man went to his house justified rather than the other; for everyone who exalts himself will be humbled, but he who humbles himself will be exalted" (Luke 18:14). "And he said to him, 'Well done, good slave, because you have been faithful in a very little thing, you are to be in authority over ten cities'" (Luke 19:17).

907 Partnership with Christ involves sharing with Him in kingdom work now. This could be the work of evangelism or it could be His work of compassion which today is manifested as the permeating influence of the kingdom mentioned in the parable of the mustard seed and the leaven. It is possible this is what Jesus had in mind when He said, "No one who puts his hand to the plow and looks back is fit for service in the kingdom of God" (Luke 9:62). He is being called to be useful, to enter the kingdom in the sense of entering into partnership with Christ.

908 BDAG, 653.

This interpretation of "enter the kingdom" not only explains the disparity between Matthew 5:19 and 20 but also solves the problem of kingdom entrance being conditioned on works. Those passages speak of sanctification and status, not soteriology.[909] Matthew is not looking at salvation from different perspectives, that is, beginning and end of a process as Neonomians assert; in fact, he is not looking at salvation at all! Instead he is looking at "entering the kingdom" and *not* "salvation." Writers often assume without proof that these two concepts are "obviously" always the same.

Applying the above discussion to Matthew 5:20, we might paraphrase this way:

> *For I say to you disciples that unless you possess and inward righteousness which surpasses the external legalism of the scribes and Pharisees, you will not enter into the kingdom way of living which leads to greatness in the future kingdom.*

Taken in this sense, the calls to entering the kingdom are calls to fully committed discipleship resulting in greater reward in the future restoration of the Davidic theocracy (Acts 1:6).

Entering the Kingdom (Life, Way of Life, Greatness)

If the above interpretation is correct, one might say that entering the kingdom encompasses three realities: abundant life, discipleship, and abundant entrance on the final day. All three dimensions of the kingdom are inextricably linked to each other. One cannot have one without the other. In a given context, one of the three may be in view, but all must be assumed because it is impossible to have any one of the three without the other two. So when Jesus says one must have an inner surpassing righteousness to enter a future kingdom way of living now and high honor in the millennial kingdom in the future, this necessarily includes the ideas of entering into discipleship now in order to qualify for this abundant entrance. As a result, one can enter into a rich experience of life in the present. That is why Jesus in His conversation with the rich young ruler and with the lawyer, equated life, entering the kingdom, inheriting the kingdom, treasure in heaven, life, and salvation as overlapping or equivalent terms.

In other words, entering the kingdom in the sense of entering the kingdom way of life is not only an event, but it is also a lifetime of choices. It certainly includes an event, abundant entrance into the restored Davidic theocracy, but it entails a process of living out the kingdom way of life now.

Experimental Predestinarians should not object to this. They do the same in their discussions of faith and works. They say that one entails the other. One cannot have faith without works; they are inextricably linked to each other. Thus, in their view, to say one enters the kingdom by works simply assumes prior faith and merely describes the character of the saved, not conditions for entrance. They should therefore not object when the Partners say that entering into greatness (an abundant entrance, 2 Peter 1:11) in the

---

909 It is correctly argued that Matthew 5:20 and 7:21 are parallel to each other. In Matthew 5:20 we learn that surpassing righteousness is necessary to enter the kingdom and in 7:21 we learn that doing the will of the Father is a requirement. Many incorrectly assume that in both cases "entering the kingdom" means go to heaven when you die. As argued above, however, that assumption is incorrect. Entering the kingdom in both passages refers to entering into greatness there by becoming the servant of all and living out the Sermon on the Mount.

kingdom in the future necessarily entails entering into a kingdom way of living now, a commitment to full discipleship in the present.

Do Some Miss the Kingdom?

In the discussion above we have shown that the warnings about not entering the kingdom refer to a failure to enter into a kingdom way of living. Only those who heed this call to discipleship will enter into honor and greatness in the future and hear the King say, "Well done!"

Yet, there are some who understand these entry passages to teach that those who disobey the least of His commandments and teach others to do the same will miss the kingdom altogether. They will either spend the millennium in the darkness outside the kingdom in a kind of Protestant purgatory, or they will spend that time in heaven with God. These views were held, for example, by Watchman Nee and some of the older Brethren writers (Govett, Pember, Panton) and more recently, Whipple, Finley, and Faust.

However, the only scriptural evidences for this view are the very passages which we have been discussing and which we understand to teach that failure to enter means failure to enter into a kingdom way of living leading to greatness, not to missing the kingdom.

Furthermore, there are decisive reasons for rejecting their viewpoint.

First, Jesus clearly says that these disobedient Christians *will be in the kingdom*. They will be in it but are called least there (Matthew 5:19). They clearly do not "miss" the kingdom; they will be "in" it and not in a "darkness outside" the kingdom.

Second, in our discussion of 1 Thessalonians 5:9-10, we showed that whether a believer is "awake or asleep" he will obtain salvation which is deliverance from the tribulation wrath. The terms "awake or asleep" refer to two kinds of Christians.[910] Some are awake, alert, and expectantly await and prepare for the Lord's coming. Others are "morally" asleep and not watchful. Yet both will "live together with Him." Earlier Paul said that when believers are snatched away from earth at the rapture, they "shall always be with the Lord" (1 Thessalonians 4:17). They will not be in heaven with the Father, or in the darkness outside the kingdom. Instead, they will be on earth "with the Lord." Of course, in eternity future, they will be with the Lord on the new earth.

Another passage that refutes the idea that some believers will be excluded from the kingdom of heaven is the Parable of the Minas (Luke 19:11-27). In this parable, the King, the Lord Jesus, gives a mina to three servants. The mina probably represents an opportunity for serving Him, for investing their lives. While two of them do invest their lives and receive ten cities or five cities (metaphors for opportunities for service and responsibility), one did nothing. When the King returns at the Judgment Seat of Christ (2 Corinthians 5:10), the servants will give an account of what they have done with their lives. It is important to note that each of the three servants, including the unfaithful, do get into the kingdom. The one who did not invest his life has what he was given taken from him. He is "saved through fire" (1 Corinthians 3:15). We know that he is in the kingdom, because he is contrasted with those who are not! J. B. Hixson notes, "Here's the key: ALL servants get into the Kingdom, though the one who did nothing with his mina

---

910 See discussion of this in vol. 2, chapter 32.

does not have any rewards (cf. 1 Cor 3:15). The ones who are *excluded* from the kingdom are the unbelieving citizens (i.e., unbelieving Jews) who rejected their Messiah."[911] As Jesus put it, "*These enemies of mine, who did not want Me to reign over them, bring them here and slay them in My presence*" (Luke 19:27).

Summary

Let us now summarize the various threads of discussion in the preceding chapters. We have shown that the phrase "enter the kingdom" always involves several concepts. First, it involves entering into a kingdom way of living, variously described as "entering into life," seeking the "kingdom and His righteousness," entering the narrow gate, receiving the kingdom as a little child, doing the will of the Father, pursuing the surpassing righteousness of the Sermon on the Mount, and being converted.

Second, the entry sayings involve entrance into royal authority in the kingdom, ruling with Christ, or, as Matthew states it, greatness. The idea that entering the kingdom involves entering into ruling is established on four grounds.

1. The only satisfactory way of explaining the apparent contradiction between Matthew 5:19 and 5:20 (and of harmonizing the many passages in the New Testament that teach that works are a condition for entering the kingdom of heaven) with the clear teaching of the New Testament, that faith is the only requirement for final salvation, is to reject the common notion that entering the kingdom always relates to soteriology. Instead, it often speaks of entering a kingdom way of living leading to ruling with Christ in the future.
2. Matthew 18:1-4 equates entering the kingdom with being great there.
3. Luke 18:17 equates entering the kingdom with "receiving the kingdom." Receiving the kingdom does not refer to becoming a Christian; rather it refers to receiving royal authority in the kingdom (Luke 19:12).
4. In his discussion with the rich young ruler, Jesus promises the disciples that "*they will sit on twelve thrones, judging the twelve tribes of Israel*" (Matthew 19:28), thus equating "entering the kingdom," treasure in heaven, entering life and inheriting eternal life with the action of judging/ruling in His kingdom.[912]

In science there is a common axiom applied to evaluate effectiveness or "explanatory power" of a theory: the number of data correlated divided by the number of assumptions made. The higher the ratio, the better the theory. Those holding to the theory that "enter the kingdom" refers to soteriological entrance have, on this basis, an extremely ineffective theory. They must assume that surpassing righteousness is something other than ethical behavior or that all "true" Christians possess it; they must assume that all true Christians are salt when the text says that one can become saltless; they must assume that one can be "in" the kingdom and yet not be saved; they must assume that the narrow door of endurance in persecution is a condition for entering the kingdom and that all believers will so endure; they must assume that the entry requirement is humility of a child and

911 Thanks to J. B. Hixson for this suggestion. Personal communication, March 10, 2011.

912 For full discussion of Christ's encounter with the rich young ruler see chapter 24 below.

not only believing on Christ; they must assume that to enter the kingdom one must sell all and give to the poor and that all who are truly Christians, when asked to do so, will do so; they must assume that the Sermon on the Mount is addressed to unbelievers as well as believers; they must assume that all true believers "do the will of the Father" even though the sermon in Matthew 5:19 says some do not; and most of all they must assume that even though the sermon never mentions the cross, faith in Christ, or His death for our sins, one obtains enough information by listening to it and obeying it that he can enter heaven when he dies.

Of course, they have explanations for all these passages which seem on the surface to contradict their theory. But when one has to explain away passage after passage in this manner and utilize a theological system to do so, we have to ask whether something is wrong with the traditional view of entering the kingdom. However, when utilizing *one* exegetically derived assumption interpreting "enter the kingdom" as a dynamic relationship with God which encompasses entering into life, entering into a kingdom way of living, and an abundant entrance into the restored Davidic theocracy, *all* this data is correlated and is consistent with Pauline theology. The so-called conflict between Matthew and Paul evaporates. The theory proposed in this chapter is highly effective and rich in explanatory power.

That being so, why not simply acknowledge that the phrase "enter the kingdom" always includes the New Testament concepts of life, discipleship, and rewards? To enter the kingdom is to save one's soul; to find the final significance of one's life, to save it for a reward-inheritance in eternity. When the phrase is associated with good works, there is no need to assume that entrance into heaven is meant. This call to discipleship, Jesus promises, will lead to greatness in the future millennium. All believers will enter the realm (no believer "misses" the kingdom), but, as the New Testament abundantly confirms, only the faithful believers who have persevered will be great there and have an inheritance there.

While the Partner viewpoint is a minority one, it is interesting that in the 13th century Thomas Aquinas (1224-1274) compiled from the works of the fathers a comment by Pseudo-Chrysostom (5th or 6th century AD) that proposed a similar interpretation of Matthew 5:19-20:

> *But seeing that to break the least commandments and not to keep them are one and the same,* ***why does He say above of him that breaks the commandments, that he shall be the least in the kingdom of heaven, and here of him who keeps them not, that he shall not enter into the kingdom of heaven?*** *... For a man to be in the kingdom is not to reign with Christ, but only to be numbered among Christ's people;* ***what He says then of him that breaks the commandments is, that he shall indeed be reckoned among Christians, yet the least of them****. But he who enters into the kingdom, becomes partaker of His kingdom with Christ.* ***Therefore he who does not enter into the kingdom of heaven, shall not indeed have a part of Christ's glory, yet shall he be in the kingdom of heaven.***[913] *(emphasis added).*

---

[913] Saint Thomas Aquinas and John Henry Newman, *St. Matthew* vol. 1, Catena Aurea: Commentary on the Four Gospels, Collected out of the Works of the Fathers (Oxford: John Henry Parker, 1874), 174.

21

Enter by the Narrow Gate

ONE OF the most frequently quoted sections of the Sermon on the Mount contains Jesus' famous teaching regarding entering by the broad gate or the narrow gate.

> *Enter by the narrow gate for the gate is wide, and the way is broad that leads to destruction, and many are those who enter by it. For the gate is small, and the way is narrow that leads to life, and few are those who find it (Matthew 7:13-14).*

This simple entry saying, when considered more carefully, raises a number of questions. Is this exhortation addressed to regenerate people or only those who are somewhat interested in Christ's teaching? What are they being exhorted to enter: personal salvation, heaven, or a kingdom way of life? When does this entrance occur, immediately or in the future? What is meant by "life" and "destruction"? Is the gate at the beginning or end of the disciple's journey?

Challenge to Accept the Gospel?

A popular view of this parable is that it is a warning to non-Christians that they must choose the narrow gate if they ever hope to enter the kingdom of heaven, that is, final salvation. In other words, entering the gate is conversion and acceptance of the gospel. Those holding this view have understood the means of obtaining personal salvation in two different ways.

BY MEANS OF SELF-DENIAL AND OBEDIENCE

Two writers describe it this way, "In order to enter by the narrow gate one must strip himself of many things, such as a consuming desire for earthly goods, the unforgiving spirit, selfishness, and especially self-righteousness. The narrow gate is therefore the gate of *self-denial* and obedience."[914] This is compared with the effort and struggle that Joshua engaged in to conquer the land.[915] Another insists, "We have to turn our back on the world and forsake our cherished sins." We cannot become Christians "without denying self, taking up our cross and following him."[916]

---

[914] Hendriksen and Kistemaker, *Exposition of the Gospel According to Matthew*, 369.

[915] Ibid., 369.

[916] Arthur Pink, *An Exposition of the Sermon on the Mount* (Grand Rapids: Baker Book House, 1974), 324-25.

One of the most beloved preachers of our era, Dr. Martyn Lloyd-Jones, a popular expositor of Experimental Predestinarian ideas, presents a confusing view of the gospel in his understanding of this passage.[917] His first problem is that he calls entering the narrow gate, "the gospel of Jesus Christ."[918] But there is no mention of the gospel here. Where is the teaching about Christ dying for our sins and rising from the dead? Where is the explanation found all throughout the New Testament that eternal life is obtained by faith apart from works?

The gospel according to Lloyd-Jones is a complicated affair involving many steps. He says that we have to leave behind all worldliness, breaking with the crowd and the "vast majority of people."[919] This is the "first step in becoming a Christian."[920] Also he says we must leave outside "the things that please the world."[921] Next we must leave *ourselves* "outside." Here he cites a passage that is addressed to Christians, and he applies it to the gospel, "*Put off the old man*" (Ephesians 4:22; Colossians 3:8).[922] It is extremely difficult to become a Christian, according to Lloyd-Jones. In fact, "It means living like Christ Himself."[923] Furthermore, to become a Christian one "must be ready for suffering and persecution."[924]

This may be the gospel according to Lloyd-Jones, but is this the gospel according to Jesus and Paul?[925] Becoming a Christian is not a matter of self-denial and obedience, for salvation costs us nothing. It is a gift. "*I will give to the one who thirsts from the spring of the water of life without cost*" (Revelation 21:6; 22:17). The route to salvation is by faith alone, apart from works (Ephesians 2:8-9; Titus 3:5). This is a serious problem for those who say that this parable tells how to find personal salvation. The condition of works for entrance strongly suggests that entrance in this parable is not entrance into heaven, but entrance into a way of life, the experience of kingdom life now, the kingdom way of living as explained in the sermon. One must enter the narrow gate and the narrow way every day, not just once!

BY MEANS OF FAITH IN JESUS AS THE WAY

Another Experimental Predestinarian writer, James Montgomery Boice, views this parable as a challenge to nonbelievers to accept Jesus as "the way, the truth, and the life." Entrance through the narrow gate, he says, is entrance through Christ for salvation.[926] Those entering by the broad gate are those who think there are many ways to God, a

---

917 Lloyd-Jones, *Studies in the Sermon on the Mount*, 227-28.

918 Ibid., 221.

919 Ibid.

920 Ibid., 222.

921 Ibid., 223.

922 Ibid., 225.

923 Ibid.

924 Ibid., 226.

925 Paul tells us some ingredients of a gospel message, "*I make known to you, brethren, the gospel which I preached to you, which also you received ... For I delivered to you as of first importance what I also received, that Christ died for our sins according to the Scriptures, and that He was buried, and that He was raised on the third day according to the Scriptures*" (1 Corinthians 15:3-4). Neither is Lloyd-Jones' gospel consistent with what Jesus taught, "*For God so loved the world, that He gave His only begotten Son, that whoever believes in Him shall not perish, but have eternal life.*" The parable of the broad and narrow way makes no mention of any of these things.

926 Boice, *The Sermon on the Mount*, 287.

viewpoint consistent with postmodern pluralism. There were many types of religions being promoted in first-century Palestine, and the person entering the broad gate is one who refuses to enter by the only way (John 14:6).

This solution is much clearer, and avoids the works salvation into which Lloyd-Jones is led. However, there is nothing in the text to suggest this interpretation. Furthermore, it begs the question, "What is meant by the word 'way'?" Is it a way of salvation or a way of life? We will address this question below.

A major objection, however, to understanding both of the above viewpoints (the narrow gate as the way of salvation) is the fact that the sermon is addressed to those who are already saved! As discussed in the previous chapter (Chapter 20), Matthew specifically says that the sermon was addressed to believers, His disciples.

The gospel is never presented in the Sermon; rather a way of living for the redeemed is outlined. When we come, therefore, to the warning about the narrow and broad gates, we should keep in mind that true believers are being warned. But what is the nature of this warning?

A Challenge to Be Sure You Are a Disciple

A second way of understanding the exhortation and warning in the parable is that it is not a challenge to *become* a Christian, but is a challenge *to be sure you are one*! As pointed out above, the salvation view of this passage leads to the conclusion that salvation is by means of works of obedience.

Martyn Lloyd-Jones faces the issue directly. "Does this teach that a man saves himself by his decision and action?"[927] Good question. In a radical modification of the text he offers a solution based on his Experimential Predestinarian theology. He says, "I do not save myself by entering in at the straight gate, but by doing so I announce the fact that I am saved."[928] He further clarifies the issue (or confuses it?) by saying that entering the gate does not refer to getting into heaven, instead, it refers to the fact that a person who will go to heaven is a person who has entered the gate and is currently pursuing the narrow way.

> *I do not save myself by entering in at the straight gate, but by doing so I announce the fact that I am saved.... It is only Christian people who are to be found along the narrow way, and you do not make yourself a Christian by entering in. You are entering in and walking upon it because you are saved.*[929]

In other words all true believers will choose the narrow way. It is clear, however, that Solomon,[930] Saul,[931] Amaziah,[932] the twelve sons of Jacob,[933] the carnal Christians in Corinth,[934] the Christians whose life works will be burned up at the Judgment Seat

---

927 Lloyd-Jones, *Studies in the Sermon on the Mount*, 237.

928 Ibid., 237.

929 Ibid., 237-38.

930 1 Kings 11:1-2.

931 1 Samuel 13:13-14.

932 2 Chronicles 25:2.

933 Genesis 37:20, 27, 34-35.

934 1 Corinthians 3:1-5.

of Christ,[935] the carnal Christian who committed incest with his mother-in-law,[936] the Christian who draws back in "shame" when the Lord returns,[937] the Pharisees who "believed on him" (a technical term in John for saving faith) and yet refused to confess their faith publicly,[938] the Christians at Corinth who refused to turn from their impurity,[939] Demas,[940] Phygelus and Hermogenes,[941] Hymenaeus and Alexander who made shipwreck of their faith,[942] and many others in the Bible did not.[943] None of these believers chose the narrow gate and entered on the narrow way.

Lloyd-Jones' ideas that entering the gate either announces one's commitment or proves it are not even remotely hinted at in the text. Also, this flatly contradicts what Lloyd-Jones himself has been saying in the preceding pages of his book as quoted above. Earlier he wrote that self-sacrifice was "the first step in becoming a Christian." This illustrates the labyrinth of qualifications and "clarifications" necessary for those who hold that this is a gospel passage.

Of course, another question necessarily follows, "How can I know for sure that I am in fact on the narrow way?" Lloyd-Jones, realizing the difficulty into which he has led his readers, asks, "Does a failure to live the Christian life fully prove that we are on the broad way [the way to eternal separation from God]?"[944] Notice the word "fully." Earlier he said that in order to determine whether a person is a Christian, the "ultimate test," is this: "Have I committed myself to this way of life? Is it the thing which controls my life? Is it the governing and controlling issue in our actual decisions and practice?" He says, "I must give myself to it, come what may … it is going to be my life."[945] Most would understand him to be saying that this is the test that would "fully" prove that one is a Christian.

Now in typical Experimental Predestinarian fashion, the qualifications begin. He begins to sandpaper the rough edges. "The picture," Lloyd-Jones says, "must not be pressed in detail."[946] We are told that failure does not "fully" prove we are on the highway to eternal separation from God, after all. Earlier it was the "ultimate test." In the final analysis, his pastoral heart retreats from the previous statements and reduces the "ultimate test" of actually doing the will of God to "hungering and thirsting." If one has hunger and thirst, he says, "I can assure you that you are in it."[947]

Of course, Lloyd-Jones is a thorough evangelical. As such, he holds strongly to justification by faith alone. Others of a more liberal persuasion sometimes embrace an Arminian view of this passage that salvation can be lost.[948]

---

935 1 Corinthians 3:15.

936 1 Corinthians 5:1.

937 1 John 2:28.

938 John 12:42-43.

939 1 Corinthians 12:21.

940 2 Timothy 4:10.

941 2 Timothy 1:15.

942 1 Timothy 1:18-20.

943 See full discussion of the carnal Christian in Chapter 32.

944 Ibid., 238.

945 Ibid., 230.

946 Ibid., 238.

947 Ibid., 238.

948 Luz and Koester, for example, tell their readers, "Salvation depends upon this way." They believe that the passage is addressed to believers in Jesus but that believers should not assume they have assurance of

Lloyd-Jones' difficulties arise from the fact that he knows this is addressed to disciples. Furthermore, he assumes that "life" means "go to heaven," "destruction" refers to final separation from God, and "entering" the narrow gate means entrance into the kingdom of God, that is, being saved. Given these premises, this text patently teaches that disciples must do good works in order to go to heaven.

Lloyd-Jones and other interpreters who share his view may believe what they want, but the text itself says nothing about one's choice proving that he is saved or lost, either before entering the gate (so Lloyd-Jones) or after it. That is a theological notion that would certainly perplex a first-century fisherman. He would take the words of Christ at face value and not interpret them theologically along the lines of post-Reformation polemics! Entrance secures the result of either life or destruction. It does not prove which result a person had obtained prior to entrance!

A Challenge to Live as a Disciple

The final option for understanding this parable is that both of the travelers are true believers. What is in view is a call to true believers to make a decision: a decision to follow Christ as a disciple and to live out the Sermon on the Mount in their own lives.

To correctly choose between these interpretive options one must come to a correct answer of three questions.

- What is being entered into, salvation or a way of life?
- What is meant by "destruction," final separation from God or spiritual/psychological ruin in this life?
- What is meant by "life," heaven when one dies or a rich life now?

WHAT IS ENTERED INTO?

What then is "entered"? Entrance refers to entrance into a "way," either "broad" or "narrow." Because they are disciples, they have already entered into personal salvation and are already guaranteed physical entrance into the millennium. What is at stake here is whether or not they enter into Christ's way of life as outlined in the Sermon on the Mount on their journey to this future kingdom.

"In the NT *hodós* ['way'] primarily refers to the way *of life*, the *manner of life* demanded by God (Acts 14:6; Romans 3:16f.; James 1:8; 5:20; 2 Peter 2:15, 21, etc.),"[949] a meaning usually found in Matthew.[950] This is parallel to "entering the kingdom" in Matthew 5:20: "*For I say to you that unless your righteousness surpasses that of the scribes and Pharisees, you will not enter the kingdom of heaven.*" Possession of an inward ethical and spiritual righteousness is necessary for entrance into the narrow way; the kingdom way of life leading to "life" and honor and avoiding "destruction." The parallelism between entering

salvation. They could fall away and only those believers who follow the narrow way will ultimately be saved. Luz and Koester, *Matthew 1-7: A Commentary*, 373. They attempt to insert the idea of grace into their works-salvation by claiming that salvation in Matthew is a synergism between works and grace and that grace is provided in that the Sermon gives "the impulse and direction for action."

[949] Martin Völkel, "*hodos*," in EDNT, 2:491.

[950] See Matthew 3:3; 5:20; 7:13-14, 24-27; 21:32; 22:16 where the way is a way of living, not "Jesus is the way" to personal salvation. (It is possible, however, that 22:16 refers to the way of salvation.)

the kingdom in 5:20 and entering onto "a way" in 7:13 suggests that, like "way," the aspect of the kingdom in view in the Sermon on the Mount is a way of life; a way of life which leads to an abundant entrance into the future millennium.

There is nothing here about entering into a way of salvation. Moral righteousness, not faith alone for salvation, is the condition for entering the kingdom way of living in Matthew. Thus, the traveler is not entering salvation when he enters the gate, he is entering into the kingdom way of life which if pursued will result in "life" and greatness both now and in eternity. Those described were already "in" the kingdom when they are being exhorted to enter it (Matthew 5:19-20).

One can certainly see parallel thoughts in Psalm 119. The psalmist spoke of this entrance into a way of life when he said, "*I have chosen the faithful way; I have placed Your ordinances before me*" (Psalm 119:30).[951]

While many commentaries understand "way" to mean the way of salvation, the text does not suggest this. A believer enters the narrow gate every time he chooses to follow the path of discipleship throughout his life;[952] entering is not a one-time thing. The two ways are presented to him daily. When he chooses the narrow gate in the various decisions of life, he proceeds along the narrow way of perseverance. When he shuns the call to discipleship, he proceeds along the broad way. Both gates and ways ultimately will lead

---

[951] He asked God to make him "walk in the path" of God's commandments; "revive me in your ways" (vv. 35, 37). He wanted God to grant him a rich "life" (v. 77), just as Jesus promised "life" to the man who entered the narrow gate and followed the narrow way. Additional parallels are found in the psalmist's statement, "*Before I was afflicted, I went astray*" (v. 67). The psalmist says that he will keep his feet from every "evil way" (similar to the broad way of Matthew 7:13) and hate every "false way" (Psalms 119:104). As Jesus put it, the broad way leads to "destruction." When God's compassion comes to the psalmist, he will "live," that is, live richly; he will flourish. The gate that is entered is the entry point into a path, a way of life. In what appears to be a particularly glaring example of importing one's theology into the text, Carson writes, "Jesus is not encouraging committed disciples, 'Christians,' to press on along the narrow way and be rewarded in the way marked by persecution and rewarded in the end. Jesus' 'disciples' are therefore not full-fledged Christians in the post-Pentecost sense." D. A. Carson, "Matthew," in *The Expositor's Bible Commentary, Volume 8: Matthew, Mark, Luke* (Grand Rapids: Zondervan Publishing House, 1984), 189. What is a "full-fledged Christian" in the "post-Pentecost sense"? Carson argues his case on bare assertion and circular reasoning about the nature of entering the kingdom and gives no proof for his tenuous view that only professing believers are being addressed.

[952] One of the earliest commentaries on this passage is the Didache (late first or early second century). Known as "The Teaching of the Twelve Apostles," this small document opens with a discussion of the "two ways." The way of life is not the way of obtaining justification but is defined as, "Now this is the way of life, 'you shall love God, who made you'; second, 'your neighbor as yourself'; and whatever you do not wish to happen to you, do not do to another" (Didache 1:1-2). Conversely, the way of death is not hell nor does it say it leads to the lake of fire. Rather, it is an ungodly manner of life. Such a way includes things like "You shall not covet your neighbor's possessions; you shall not commit perjury; you shall not give false testimony; you shall not speak evil; you shall not hold a grudge." The way of death is "evil and completely cursed" (Didache 5.1). The reason it is "cursed" is not because it sends one to damnation but because the justified saints are in danger of becoming ones "from whom gentleness and patience are far away, loving worthless things, pursuing [earthly] reward, having no mercy for the poor, not working on behalf of the oppressed, not knowing him who made them, murderers of children, corrupters of God's creation, turning away from someone in need, oppressing the afflicted, advocates of the wealthy, lawless judges of the poor, utterly sinful. May you be delivered, children, from all these things!" Throughout this document, the assumed readers are justified saints. They are referred to as "My Child" (Didache 4.1), and he warns those who already possess the fear of God that they might lose it (Didache 4.10). It is a way of life or a way of death that is set before the already believing and regenerate disciples (Didache 6.1-2). Michael W. Holmes, *The Apostolic Fathers: Greek Texts and English Translations* (Grand Rapids: Baker Book House, 1999), 249.

him to the millennial kingdom at the Second Advent, but the one who chooses the broad gate and way will find that his life is spiritually ruined in the interim and he will suffer loss at the Judgment Seat of Christ (Mark 8:35). He will experience spiritual impoverishment, that is, he will "die" spiritually (Romans 8:12-13). One choice leads to life, an enriched experience of life and reward, and the other leads to destruction.

WHAT IS MEANT BY "DESTRUCTION"?

> *Enter through the narrow gate; for the gate is wide and the way is broad that leads to destruction* [Gr *apōleia*], *and there are many who enter through it (Matthew 7:13).*

These travelers are faced with two different destinies, life or destruction. If they choose the broad way, they face destruction. What does this mean? There are two possibilities.

(1) "Destruction" *means final damnation.* Those who believe that the gate and the way refer to entrance into initial salvation followed by a life of sanctification naturally understand *apōleia*, "destruction" to mean damnation.

This is supposedly proven by the fact that a "true" believer would never follow the broad way. Those who believe that salvation can be lost also understand the "perishing" as eternal separation from God.[953]

(2) "Destruction" *means to experience* ***temporal*** *spiritual impoverishment and ruin as well as lowest status in the* ***future*** *Davidic theocracy.* Those who experience "destruction" are believers who do not persevere under persecution and hence will not receive the reward mentioned in 5:12 or store up treasure within heaven (6:21-20). These are believers who have become "saltless" (5:13). Their temporal spiritual lives are certainly ruined, but their eternal destination is not under discussion.

Which view is correct?

Those who hold that entering the broad gate are those who have chosen a path leading to eternal separation from God are faced with an obvious problem. If this is addressed to non-Christians, they are being exhorted to secure final entrance into heaven by means of works, that is, to persevere through trials in order to be saved.

On the other hand, if this text is addressed to Christians and if "life" means heaven and "destruction" means "eternal separation from God, then another problem arises. Jesus would be warning true believers about a fate which He knows will never happen to them, eternal separation from God. Realizing the problem this presents for his gospel view of the passage, Lloyd-Jones assures us that "every illustration has its limits."[954]

What do the broad gate and broad way signify? Broad gates are the ones that require great capital investment. They lead to something the majority of people would desire. They are spacious, well protected, roomy, and lead to things like the king's palace or somewhere else useful and frequently visited.

---

953 Arminian interpreters argue that the parable teaches that if true believers fail to obey or otherwise fall away, they will lose salvation. However, as we shall see, this is inconsistent with the meanings of the words "perish" and "life" as found in the gospel of Matthew. Furthermore this is difficult to harmonize with Jesus' specific statement elsewhere, "*This is the will of Him who sent Me, that of all that He has given Me,* ***I will lose nothing****, but raise it up on the last day*" (John 6:39; see also 10:27-29).

954 Lloyd-Jones, *Studies in the Sermon on the Mount*, 237.

But are those who follow the broad way on the highway to hell?[955] While it is common to understand "destruction" as a reference to eternal separation from God, and that use of the word is certainly found elsewhere,[956] it has a range of meanings.

The Gr word *apōleia* is used 18 times in the New Testament. It is used eleven times of damnation,[957] four times of temporal ruin and possibly physical death,[958] twice of ruin or physical waste,[959] and once in Matthew 7:13. Therefore while the sense of damnation is certainly possible, Matthew only uses the word one other time, and there he uses it in the sense of waste or the "needless squandering of a resource"[960] (Matthew 26:8; cf. Mark 14:4). Its variation in meaning elsewhere should give us pause in automatically assuming it means damnation in Matthew 7:13.

Perhaps the verbal form "to perish" (Gr *apollumi*), which is found 90 times in the New Testament and often in Matthew, will give us more to work with than the one reference to the noun, *apōleia*. The verb, *apollumi* does mean "suffer damnation" in a number of places outside of Matthew, and it has only one clear instance of that meaning in the Gospels.[961] What is of interest is that the verb is used nineteen times in seventeen verses in the Gospel of Matthew, and Matthew never uses it in the sense of damnation. It is used seven times of physical death.[962] For example, Peter was afraid of "perishing" by drowning (Matthew 8:25); Herod wanted to "destroy" Jesus (Matthew 2:13); the Pharisees likewise wanted to "destroy him" (Matthew 12:14). In one place it means "to ruin," where Jesus says that putting new wine into old wineskins "ruins" them (Matthew 9:17).[963]

The verb is commonly used of a temporal perishing or psychological and spiritual ruin of believers: "*Do not destroy* [Gr *apollumi*] *with your food him for whom Christ died*" (Romans 14:15); "*For through your knowledge he who is weak is ruined* [Gr *apollumi*], *the brother for whose sake Christ died*" (1 Corinthians 8:11).

Thus, it is clear that true believers can be "destroyed" in a spiritual/psychological sense. Paul speaks elsewhere of this possibility when he says, "*Remind them of these things, and solemnly charge them in the presence of God not to wrangle about words, which is useless,* and *leads to the ruin of the hearers*" (2 Timothy 2:14). In this passage, he uses the word *katastrophē* instead of *apōleia*. It refers in this instance to "a state of being intellectually upset to a ruinous degree."[964] For a more complete discussion of "destruction," see the excursus on "destruction" at the end of this chapter.

---

955 Citing Opeke, Carson asserts that the perishing in Matthew 7:13 refers to the plunge into hell. Opeke says, *apōleia* "is definitive destruction, not merely in the sense of the extinction of physical existence, but rather of an eternal plunge into Hades and a hopeless destiny of death." A. Opeke, "*apōleia,*" in TDNT, 1:396. However, Matthew does not use the term this way.

956 John 17:12; Romans 9:22; Philippians 1:28; 3:19; 1 Timothy 6:9.

957 John 17:12; Romans 9:22; Philippians 1:28; 3:19; 2 Thessalonians 2:3; 2 Peter 2:1, 3; 3:16 (twice); Revelation 17:8, 11.

958 Acts 8:20; 1 Timothy 6:9; Hebrews 10:39; 2 Peter 3:7.

959 Matthew 26:8; Mark 14:4.

960 Swanson, *DBLGNT*, s.v. GGK724.

961 E.g., John 10:28.

962 Matthew 2:13; 8:25; 12:14; 21:41 – he will "destroy those wretches" probably a reference to the judgment in time of AD 70 on the nation and not final damnation; Matthew 22:7; 26:52; 27:20.

963 See also Matthew 10:6; 18:13-14, "to go astray;" 12:14; 15:24; 22:7; 26:52; 27:20, etc.

964 BDAG, 528.

The wide gate leading to the broad way was the main thoroughfare into a city, the main avenue (Revelation 21:21; 22:2). It was the route followed by the merchants and was lined with shops. It was like entering a modern shopping mall. However, at its entrance one was met by the hated tax collectors who policed all the main thoroughfares of the empire.[965] The system of tax collection was corrupt and oppressive. When a traveler entered through the main gate, he expected to be fleeced, and he was.[966]

In this context we can see that Jesus warns His listeners to avoid the broad gate in spite of its worldly attractiveness and to seek the narrow gate. His point is that the broad way, while attractive and lined with shops and entertainment (like a contemporary mall) can be expensive in the sense of spiritual loss. He is using this as a metaphor for the loss that is entailed with the choice of the broad way.

The narrow way is costly as well, but in a different sense. It will cost the follower radical discipleship, but this loss has a positive outcome, a rich life now. Jesus is saying that just as men in this world will do everything reasonable to find a way into the city that would avoid financial ruin (they know that if they take the main gate, the broad one, they will be "ripped off") so the believer in Christ must avoid being damaged eternally by taking the broad gate. Instead, he must seek a way of entrance and a path to follow that will lead to true life, which is costly as well. But the broad and narrow gates are both choices set before the redeemed. These are not one-time choices, they are daily choices confronting believers throughout their lives.

So what does it mean in Matthew 7:13? The use of the words for destruction and life, and the broader context of the sermon as a call to discipleship (and not salvation) confirm the interpretation given above. The way is a way of life, and destruction is spiritual/psychological ruin.[967]

A Christian who takes the "broad way" is seeking a pleasurable, happy life of comfort and ease. What he will find, however, is loss of his final significance and meaning. This is what happened to the prodigal son. His father said of him, "*For this son of mine was dead, and has come to life again; he was lost, and has been found*" (Luke 15:24). He was once alive in

---

965 Recent archaeological excavations in Jordan have actually uncovered a free-standing, first-century city gate, which served as a customs tax collection station (Bible and the Spade, 11(1998), 74). These taxes in the Roman Empire were levied on all imports and exports and were "levied on the great public highways and in the seaports," Merrill F. Unger, *Unger's Bible Dictionary* (Chicago: Moody Press, 1961), 1073.

966 J. Duncan Derrett, "The Merits of the Narrow Gate," *JSNT* 15(1982): 24.

967 Additional evidence from the Old Testament supports the interpretation that "destruction" can mean the psychological/spiritual ruin and possible physical demise of one's temporal existence. The words "destroy" and "destruction" occur 512 times in the NKJV and represent 50 different Heb and Gr words, and none of them refers to perdition. Robert Morey, *Death and the Afterlife* (Minneapolis: Bethany House, 1984), 109., quoted by Jeff Spencer, "The Destruction of Hell: Annihilationism Examined," *Christian Apologetics Journal* 1, no. 1 (Spring 1998): 19. The Hebrew word behind this Greek word *apollumi* is *ʾābad*, which means, "become lost," "to go astray" (Psalms 2:12; 119:176; Jeremiah 50:5) "*ʾābad*," in HAL, 2-3 (e.g., 1 Samuel 9:3; Psalms 119:176; Proverbs 6:32; Jeremiah 50:6). The verb is a common word for "to die," or, in the case of things or reputation, etc., "to pass away," TWOT, 1:34. It means "to be lost, to perish, or to lose." See Derrett, "The Merits of the Narrow Gate," 23. It sometimes means "be in a state of wandering, in which the whereabouts of an object is unknown." See Swanson, *Dictionary of Biblical Languages with Semantic Domains: Hebrew* (Old Testament), DBLH 6, #3. It is often found in Old Testament passages referring to the physical destruction of a life (Psalms 9:5; 143:12; Proverbs 11:10). For example, we are told that the "*wicked will* ***perish*** *and vanish like smoke*" (Psalms 37:10) and that they will be totally "**destroyed**" (Psalms 37:38). This Hebrew word is most commonly translated by the Greek word *apollumi* in the Greek Old Testament. See EDNT, 1:135.

the sense of intimacy with his father, but due to his carnality, he became dead. When he was with the pigs, he was "lost" (Gr *apollumi*), not unsaved; he was still a son, but he was lost in the sense that his life was in ruins; he had gone astray; he was spiritually and psychologically ruined. The prodigal had taken the broad way and as a result he was "destroyed." But he came alive "again" (Gr *anazaō*, from *zaō*, "to live" and "*ana*" again, thus "be alive again"[968]).

Based on this evidence it is much more likely that the road leading to destruction is the road leading to the ruin of one's temporal and spiritual life, as was the destruction which came upon the prodigal son. It refers to one who has gone astray, not to one who has gone to the lake of fire. Those Christians who repeatedly choose this broad, roomy, and comfortable way have indeed entered the kingdom and are saved, but they will die spiritually in the sense of spiritual impoverishment and carnality (Romans 8:12); their temporal life will be ruined.[969]

WHAT IS MEANT BY "LIFE"?

The narrow way leads to "life." Does this refer to eternal life in heaven or a rich and meaningful life now? If the wide gate leads to the ruining of one's personal life as argued above, then the opposite "leading to life" would probably refer to a rich and meaningful life in the present, issuing in an abundant entrance into (2 Peter 1:11) the kingdom and not entrance into heaven. That initial impression is confirmed by the biblical evidence.

What is this "narrow" way? There are two different Gr words for the narrow (Gr *stenos*) gate, and the way that is narrow (Gr *thlibō*). The latter is a verb. Its noun form is *thlipsis* ("tribulation"), which almost always refers to persecution. *Stenos* means "squeezed or pressed and often refers to persecution or inner stress arising from external pressure.[970] Both the verb and the noun, when used of the present experience of believers, refer almost invariably to that which comes upon them from without."[971] The Gr word *thlibō* means "to squeeze together" or "to press" or "to crush."[972] The picture is of a traveler between two walls which "press together"[973] on him, causing affliction. Paul described his experience of

---

968 BDAG, 62.

969 Throughout the New Testament, Christians are exhorted not to love the world (1 John 2:15) lest they end up feeling "shame" at the Judgment Seat of Christ (1 John 2:28; Mark 4:24). The desire to gain the world will result in the loss of one's spiritual significance (Mark 8:36). Christians are to be in the world but not "of" it (John 17:16). Even though the Corinthian Christians were attracted to the world's wisdom, Paul declared it to be foolishness (1 Corinthians 3:19). The Christian is to "lay aside" any encumbrance that would keep him from his goal of Christlikeness and faithfulness (Hebrews 12:1). All those encumbrances will not fit through the narrow gate. Like a traveler with much extra baggage, he cannot squeeze through the opening. The broad way is the way of the world and its accoutrements. The narrow way shuns all this and pursues true life. But does the word "life" refer to "going to heaven when I die," or does it refer to a rich and abundant life now?

970 *Stenos* is often used in the LXX of the stresses and difficulties of inner and outer problems. It can speak of a narrow pass, to be squeezed or pressed. It is often found in topographical descriptions. Isaiah refers to bread eaten in "affliction" (Isaiah 30:20) to "denote a life under external pressure or psychologically in inner depression," Georg Bertram, "*stenos*," (TDNT, 7:605).

971 It has reference to sufferings because of the pressure of circumstances or the antagonism of persons (1 Thessalonians 3:4; 2 Thessalonians 1:6, 7; "straitened," in Matthew 7:14 [R.V.]; "throng," Mark 3:9; "afflicted," 2 Corinthians 1:6; 7:5 [R.V.]; 1 Timothy 5:10; Hebrews 11:37; "pressed," 2 Corinthians 4:8). VINE, 39.

972 Jacob Kremer, "*thlipsis*," in EDNT, 2:151.

973 BDAG, 457.

going through the narrow [Gr *stenos*] gate and walking on the narrow [Gr *thlibō*] way like this: "*we are afflicted* [Gr *thlibō*] *in every way, but not crushed* [Gr *stenochōreō*], *perplexed, but not despairing*" (2 Corinthians 4:8). The phrases describe the experience of a genuine believer and not of someone who has only professed faith but does not really possess it.

Suffering for Christ is a common theme in the New Testament, and Christ's disciples are frequently called upon to endure persecution.[974] It is also a common theme in Matthew.[975] This is hardly an appropriate call to an audience which includes unsaved people (without clarification to them).

Of particular interest is Acts 14:22, "*Strengthening the souls of the disciples, encouraging them to continue in the faith, and saying, 'Through many tribulations* [Gr *thlipsis*, cognate to the verb *thlibō* in 7:14] *we must enter the kingdom of God*.'" That believers must go through tribulations (the narrow gate and way) on their way to their entrance to the eschatological kingdom is clear from this passage and possibly explains Matthew 7:14.

If they chose this path, paradoxically, they will find "life." Jesus may well have had His Hebrew Scriptures in mind, where He would find "life" referring to flourishing spiritually in this life. For example, in the book of Proverbs the focus is on an experience of that life now. Sometimes it referred to the flourishing of one's affairs (Proverbs 15:15). In another place it seems to mean "to enjoy harmonious family life" (Proverbs 15:27).[976] Wisdom and discretion will result in "life to your soul and adornment to your neck" (Proverbs 3:22). Kidner notes, "The second of these phrases, pointing to a person's outward bearing, suggests that the first refers to the vitality of his whole being. This, he says, is clearly the meaning in Proverbs 14:30, where a "sound heart" (i.e., a tranquil mind) is "the life of the flesh but envy is rottenness of the bones."[977] Similarly, Torah teaches that one can have abundant life now by obeying the Law (Deuteronomy 4:1; Leviticus 18:5).

For fuller discussion of "life" see the excursus on "life" at the end of this chapter.

THE "TWO WAYS" IN THE OLD TESTAMENT

For an Old Testament model of the "two ways" doctrine for the people of God, the close parallel to Deuteronomy 30:15-16 is relevant.

> *See, I set before you today life and prosperity, death and* ***destruction*** (Gr *kakos*, ill, evil, trouble[978]). *For I command you today to love the* Lord *your God, to walk in his ways, and to keep his commands, decrees and laws; then you will* ***live*** *and increase, and the* Lord *your God will bless you in the land you are entering to possess.*

When Jesus was teaching on the "two ways" (Matthew 7:13-14), He very likely had this passage, as well as many similar verses in Proverbs, in mind. And if so, life and destruction refer to temporal experiences of the saved and not the eternal destinies of the saved and unsaved.

---

974 2 Corinthians 1:6; 4:8, 7:5; 1 Thessalonians 3:4; 2 Thessalonians 1:6, etc.

975 See Matthew 5:10-12, 44; 10:16-39; 11:11-12; 24:4-13.

976 Derek Kidner, *Proverbs: An Introduction and Commentary*, Tyndale Old Testament Commentaries (Downers Grove, IL: Intervarsity Press, 1975), 53.

977 Ibid., 53.

978 LSJ, 863.

The two-ways doctrine is also found in Jeremiah:

> *Furthermore, tell the people, "This is what the Lord says: 'See, I am setting before you the* ***way of life*** *and the* ***way of death****. Whoever stays in this city will die by the sword, famine or plague. But whoever goes out and surrenders to the Babylonians who are besieging you will live; he will escape with his life'" (Jeremiah 21:8-9).*

This passage obviously speaks of outcomes of physical death or physical life. Jeremiah calls upon the nation to walk in the "ancient ways."

> *Thus says the LORD, "Stand by the ways and see and ask for the ancient paths, where the good way is, and walk in it; and you will find rest for your souls. But they said, 'We will not walk in it'" (Jeremiah 6:16).*

Unless Matthew 7:13-14 is an exception, there is no place in the Bible where the ways of life and death are associated with heaven or eternal separation from God. In every case, when life or death this side of the grave are in view, they refer to either physical or psychological/spiritual conditions. Eternal destiny is never in view.[979]

Hear Solomon once more,

> *He who is steadfast in righteousness will attain to life, and he who pursues evil will bring about his own death (Proverbs 11:19).*

To be "steadfast in righteousness" is to enter the narrow gate daily and attain to a rich life in the present. To "pursue evil" is to take the broad way that ends in "death."

The disciple of Christ when faced with inevitable trial and persecution can be assured that if he "counts it all joy" and allows himself to be "trained by it," that the outcome will be a rich life indeed. This is what it means to follow the narrow way. How many believers in Christ actually find this way of living? According to Jesus, there are "few" (ὀλίγοι) who find it (7:14). John Nolland and Leon Morris both suggest that this word might better be

---

979 Finding "life" in this sense is impossible apart from divine assistance. Elsewhere, Jesus told His disciples that it is as difficult as getting a camel through the eye of the needle (Matthew 19:24). Apart from abiding in Him, this cannot be obtained. When Paul said to the Thessalonians, "*for now we really live, if you stand firm in the Lord*" (1 Thessalonians 3:8), he did not mean that if they continued to stand firm in the Lord then Paul and his companions would go to heaven when they die! Rather, he means that they would find true satisfaction knowing that their labors had not been in vain (v. 4). In the midst of their afflictions, it was a great encouragement to know that all their suffering was worth it. Their beloved disciples were doing well. This was "life" indeed. As Gene L. Green puts it, "For him and his companions the good news about this church was like a resurrection." Gene L. Green, *The Letters to the Thessalonians*, The Pillar New Testament Commentary (Grand Rapids: Wm. B. Eerdmans Publishing Co., 2002), 170. F. F. Bruce says, "The news of your unwavering faith and love is the very breath of life to us." Bruce, *The Epistles to the Colossians, to Philemon, and to the Ephesians*, 67. Jesus also spoke of "life" in two senses elsewhere, "*I have come that they may have life, and have it to the full*" (John 10:10). Faithful endurance and proper response to persecution or trial may lead to a rich life. 1 Peter 3:9; Mark 9:45; and Matthew 18:18 teach that one can find true life now only if he is willing to do whatever is necessary to follow Christ. Note 2 Corinthians 4:6-11 where persecution, properly responded to, results in the "life of Jesus" being manifested in the apostles (see also 2 Corinthians 1:6). "*All discipline for the moment seems not to be joyful, but sorrowful; yet to those who have been trained by it, afterwards* ***it yields the peaceful fruit of righteousness***" (Hebrews 12:11). "*Consider it all joy, my brethren, when you encounter various trials, knowing that the testing of your faith* **produces endurance***. And let endurance have its perfect result,* ***that you may be perfect and complete, lacking in nothing***" (James 1:2-4).

translated here (and in 22:14) as "fewer."[980] If they are correct, then our Lord's teaching is not that only a few will choose the path of discipleship but that fewer will choose this path than those who choose the broad way.

Summary

When Jesus challenges these regenerate disciples to enter by the narrow gate, He is not speaking of conditions for salvation. Entering is not a one-time event or a gospel invitation. Rather, He *speaks of entrance into a way of living*, a way that will ultimately issue in "life," and in the future greatness in the kingdom of heaven (Matthew 5:19-20). This way of living has been the subject of the Sermon on the Mount in the preceding two chapters. The two ways refer to the path of discipleship or the path of ease. In each day of a disciple's life, he is confronted with decisions to choose the broad or narrow way. These people have just heard an earth-shaking sermon. They are now exhorted to apply it, even though our Lord knows that doing so will lead to persecution and affliction.

As we repeatedly choose the way of discipleship, that is, as we daily choose to enter the narrow way, we will obtain not only a rich, meaningful life here but a rich welcome when we enter His kingdom when He returns. Conversely, to shy away from this demand, as did the lukewarm believers at Laodicea (Revelation 3:15-16) or the believers at Sardis who were "dead" and who had not "completed" their deeds (Revelation 3:2), will result in spiritual ruin and the loss of reward at that future day.

The command to "enter by the narrow gate" is similar in meaning to the command to take up one's cross *daily* (Luke 9:23) and follow Christ or to become "*fit for service*" (NIV) for the kingdom of heaven (Luke 9:62). It is a command to live out the way of life taught in the Sermon on the Mount. It is not a command to accept Christ as Savior or to validate that one already has.

Our Lord echoes the teaching of the Sage,

> *Now therefore, O sons, listen to me, for* ***blessed are they who keep my ways****. Heed instruction and be wise, and do not neglect it. Blessed is the man who listens to me,* ***watching daily at my gates, waiting at my doorposts****. For he who finds me finds life and obtains favor from the* Lord*. But he who sins against me* ***injures himself****; all those who hate me* ***love death*** *(Proverbs 8:32–36).*

To make this concept crystal clear, it is best that I conclude by clothing it with flesh and blood.

Collette had an agonizing decision to make regarding her failing relationship with her husband. After twenty-five years of marriage, she discovered he was someone very different from the man she had loved and trusted.

Collette's marriage had been shattered and for three years the shattered pieces had been left abandoned. She desperately needed God's wisdom. He spoke to her about those

---

[980] Nolland, *The Gospel of Matthew: A Commentary on the Greek Text*, 891. Leon Morris says, "It is possible to understand this passage [Matthew 22:14] to mean that the elect are fewer in number than those called; the actual number of the elect is then not in mind. Jesus is not saying whether the elect will be a tiny remnant or not; he is saying that not all the called will be finally chosen." See Morris, *The Gospel According to Matthew*, 552. These writers, being Experimental Predestinarians, relate the broad and narrow ways to pathways to hell or eternal life.

fragmented pieces from Exodus 34:1. God told Moses He would rewrite His Words on new tablets, replacing the tablets that had been shattered. Here are Collette's words.

> *I honestly did not know if new words could ever be written, replacing the fragmented vows of my marriage. But He then spoke again. "Trust Me."*
>
> *In fear and trembling, I pick up the shattered pieces of my heart that have sat dormant for these agonizing years, and I ask You, Jesus, to write on my heart new words that I can commit to. I cannot even begin to project a lifetime marriage statement, though my face is resolutely set toward a long obedience to my God, therefore to my husband. But I can commit to three months of purposeful, prayed over, "I wills."*
>
> *My Marriage Purpose Statement. January-March, 2010.*
>
> *I will forgive, and will ask for forgiveness, purposefully and prayerfully, each day. "As far as the east is from the west," I will not bring up forgiven hurts again. In my forgiving, I will release my husband of his "debts," so that he may walk in freedom and grow toward light.*
>
> *I will relinquish all judging, self-righteous attitudes, and my prideful heart. God alone is the righteous and Holy Judge. It is not my job.*
>
> *I will be present in body and spirit to my husband, actively engaging with his needs. I will not manipulate him with absence of spirit, lack of attention, or withdrawal.*
>
> *I will be respectful, accepting his leadership.*
>
> *I will not dwell on the darkness in him, nor fear it. Rather, I will live out Philippians 4:8:*
>
> *"Whatever is true, whatever is honorable, whatever is right, pure, lovely, whatever is of good repute, in my husband, excellent, worthy of praise, these are what I will discipline my mind to dwell on."*
>
> *I will be merciful to my husband, remembering the truth that my Father's mercies are new to us every morning.*
>
> *I will recognize, and celebrate, each decision for Life and Light my husband makes.*
>
> *I will not give up hope, for my hope is in God Himself, who is caring for me, and protecting me.*
>
> *These things, my Lord, I commit to You, fully understanding that it is only through Your Holy Spirit and by Your incredible grace to me that I can even pen these words. May You be praised!*

If you think the words Collette wrote flowed easily, you've never been in gut-wrenching pain. As I write, I can see Collette's eyes; they overflow with sorrow. In her grief, this woman of faith stripped off her old clothes of anger and resentment and put on her beautiful new wardrobe of kindness, compassion, and forgiveness.

Do you remember that Collette said she could not imagine committing to her "I Will's" for a lifetime? There is a P.S. to Collette's three-month Marriage Purpose Statement:

> *May 15, 2010. Today I declare that this Marriage Purpose Statement is till death do us part.*

What happened? Six months later my wife received an email from Collette.

> *Linda, you won't believe this but my husband and I are back in relationship and I actually miss him when he is traveling; I am excited for him to come home every day from work; and I am looking forward to a future together.*

Collette had entered the narrow gate and had chosen the narrow way and found life.

Excursus on "Destruction"

In extra-biblical Gr *apōleia* and *apollumi* never mean perdition or to go to perdition. Rather they commonly refer to waste by wear and tear or loss.[981] It is used over 100 times in the LXX and almost always in reference to a temporal calamity. In the New Testament, three times the verb (*apollumi*) means losing something, once it refers to losing one's reward,[982] and once it simply means "to ruin,"[983] twice it is used to describe "the lost sheep of the house of Israel,"[984] and in one place it may mean "damnation."[985]

Paul uses the word for the national "ruin" facing the nation of Israel whom he calls "vessels of wrath fitted for destruction" (Romans 9:22, Gr *apōleia*). The analogy with Pharaoh makes it clear that temporal destruction is in view. Pharaoh's servants said, "*How long shall this man [Moses] be a snare to us? Let the men go, that they may serve the Lord their God. Do you not yet know that Egypt is destroyed*?" (Exodus 10:8; LXX: "destroyed," Gr *apollumi*). According to Josephus, one million one hundred thousand people were "destroyed" (Gr *apollumi)* in the judgment of AD 70.[986]

When Jesus speaks of "destruction" and "life" in the Sermon, He is thinking in Old Testament wisdom terms. "The consensus that 'teacher of wisdom' is a central category for understanding the teaching of Jesus is the result of two closely related developments in the last two decades."[987] This is particularly noted in the Sermon on the Mount because of its many proverbial "one-liners," which are similar to the wisdom sayings of the book of Proverbs.

In the book of Proverbs, did *apōleia* refer to eternal condemnation or spiritual impoverishment in this life or physical death? It is found 14 to 16 times (depending on the variant readings).[988] In every instance it refers to a calamity of sort which occurs in time, not eternity. For example, "calamity" will come suddenly on the man who devises evil in his heart (Proverbs 6:15). "*He will be broken and there will be no healing.*"

> *The integrity of the upright guides them, but the unfaithful are destroyed* [Gr *apōleia*, LXX] *by their duplicity (Proverbs 11:3).*

---

981 Ibid., 23.

982 Matthew 5:29, 30; losing a reward Matthew 10:42.

983 Matthew 9:17.

984 Matthew 10:6; 15:24.

985 Matthew 10:28. However, this passage is addressed to the regenerate disciples, and it is doubtful that perishing in *Gehenna* is a warning to them that they will go to hell if they are unfaithful. Rather, as argued elsewhere (see pp.911 ff.), *Gehenna* probably does not refer to hell in this passage but instead speaks of the ruin and destruction of the true believer's life work at the Judgment Seat of Christ.

986 Flavius Josephus, "The Wars of the Jews," in *The Works of Josephus: Complete and Unabridged*, ed. W. Whiston (Peabody, MA: Hendrickson Publishers, 1987), VI, ix, 3.

987 Marcus J. Borg, "Jesus (Person)," in *The Anchor Yale Bible Dictionary*, ed. David Noel Freedman, Gary A. Herion, and David F. Graf (New York: Doubleday, 1996), 3:806. See also Gary A. Tuttle, "The Sermon on the Mount: Its Wisdom Affinities and their Relation to its Structure," *JETS* 20, no. 3 (1977): 213-30.

988 Proverbs 1:26; 6:15, 32; 10:11, 24; 11:3, 6; 13:1; 15; 16:26; 24:22; 27:20; 28:28.

In a passage speaking of the "way" of the wicked, similar to Matthew 7:13, we read:

Good understanding wins favor, but the ***way of the unfaithful is hard*** (Gr *apōleia) (Proverbs 13:15).*

He who obeys instructions guards his life, but he who is contemptuous of his ways will die (apollumi, Proverbs 19:16).

To obey instructions refers to maintaining a "way of life." To "guard" one's life means "to heed scrupulously." A failure to do so severs one's relationship of love and loyalty to God.[989] One can hear echoes of Jesus' reply to the rich young ruler here. The ruler was told that if he wanted to "live," he must obey the commandments. Eternal life can refer to a rich life now as well as to initial regeneration. "Ruin" will come upon those who do not obey the Lord and the king (Proverbs 24:21).[990]

In some places destruction leads to "death." "*There is a way that seems right to a man, but in the end it leads to death.*" (Proverbs 14:12; cf. 28:28). What is death? Is it final separation from God? The parallel with the next verse indicates that it is *psychological* and not eternal. It is "grief" (v. 14).[991]

One can hear Proverbs 1:20-22 echoing in the background of the parable of the narrow way. As the simpleton approaches the broad gate entering the city, Wisdom cries out with a distinct, ringing plea and with much emotion, "*How long, O naïve ones, will you love simplicity.*"

Wisdom shouts in the street, she lifts her voice in the square; at the head of the noisy streets she cries out; at the entrance of the gates in the city, she utters her sayings: "How long, O naive ones, will you love simplicity? And scoffers delight themselves in scoffing, and fools hate knowledge?" (Proverbs 1:20-22).

The *naïve* one is further warned, "*I will even laugh at your calamity; I will mock when your dread comes*" (Proverbs 1:26).

Lady wisdom greets the wayward believer and issues a warning. Unless the believer seeks wisdom, he will face "calamity" (Gr *apōleia*, Hebrew *›ābad*; 1:26). These calamities will come on him in his life like a whirlwind (v. 27). This is the danger facing the believer who continually chooses the broad gate. He is called a "fool" in Proverbs. The fool is not one who is stupid. Rather, he is one who is uncommitted; wandering, he believes anything (Proverbs 14:15); he is untaught and lacks moral discernment and is not interested in seeking it. He is like the Christians in Hebrew 5 who have become "dull of hearing;" are still "infants;" who "need milk and not solid food," and need to have their senses "trained to discern good and evil" (Hebrews 5:11-14). He is, according to Kidner, "no halfwit; he

---

989 Bruce K. Waltke, *The Book of Proverbs*, 2 vols. (Grand Rapids: Wm. B. Eerdmans Publishing Co., 2004), 2:110.

990 "To fear the Lord" does not mean "become a Christian." It means to obey the Lord.

991 "By death is meant a broad range of unhappy experiences, from simple adversity to one's (premature?) departure from this world. This saying makes room for the possibility of self-deception, and then the 'way' chosen in wisdom can turn out to be folly." Roland Edmund Murphy, *Proverbs*, Word Biblical Commentary (Nashville: Thomas Nelson, 1998), 104.

is a person whose instability could be rectified, who prefers not to accept discipline in the school of wisdom" (Prov 1:22-32).[992] He is, in the words of the Sermon on the Mount, a believer who prefers the broad gate.

Among the various usages of *ʾābad* and *apollumi,* which one is intended in Matthew 7:13-14? The usage of this Heb word in Jeremiah 50:6 and its corresponding translation as *apollumi* in the Greek Old Testament are relevant to this discussion and helps us narrow the options. There we learn that "to perish" often means "to go astray."

> *I have* ***gone astray*** [Heb *ʾābad;* Gr *apollumi,* LXX] ***like a lost sheep****; seek Thy servant, for I do not forget Thy commandments (Psalm 119:176).*

> *My people have become* ***lost sheep****; Their shepherds have led them* ***astray*** [Heb *ʾābad,* Gr *apollumi*]. *They have made them turn aside on the mountains; they have gone along from mountain to hill and have forgotten their resting place (Jeremiah 50:6).*

The fate of the wicked is "death," which is defined in the next line, not as eternal separation from God, but as going astray.

> *He will* ***die*** *for lack of discipline,* ***led astray*** *by his own great folly (Proverbs 5:23).*

> *His folly leads him astray, but not necessarily to eternal separation from God.*

Judith Volf cites many instances in the LXX where *apollumi* refers to subjective psychological destruction in this life. An evil wife, for example, "is rottenness to his [her husband's] bones" (Proverbs 12:4; cf. Proverbs 14:30). The LXX renders this as "destroys" (*apollumi*) her husband.[993]

The motif of God's people, not unbelievers, going astray like sheep is also found in Matthew:

> *What do you think? If any man has a hundred sheep, and one of them has gone astray* [Gr *planaō*], *does he not leave the ninety-nine on the mountains and go and search for the one that is straying? (Matthew 18:12).*

In verse 12 we are told that the lost lamb in the parable (Matthew 18:12) is one who has "gone astray (Gr *planaō*)."[994] But in verse 14, this "going astray" is equated with perishing (Gr *apollumi*). One of the priestly ministries of Christ is to deal gently with those are "ignorant and misguided" (Gr *planaō*, Hebrews 5:2).

> *So it is not the will of your Father who is in heaven that one of these little ones perish* (Gr *apollumi*) *(Matthew 18:14).*

Like those believers who chose the broad way in Matthew 7:13, one of these "little

---

[992] Kidner, *Proverbs: An Introduction and Commentary*, 39. He is aimless, inexperienced, drifting into temptation, in fact, almost courting it. In the LXX, *apōleia* is used to translate some 21 different Hebrew words. Here in 1:26 it translates *ʾēd* "distress, calamity."

[993] Judith M. Gundry Volf, *Paul and Perseverance: Staying in and Falling Away* (Tübingen: J.C.B. Mohr [Paul Siebeck], 1990), 96.

[994] We get the word "planets," wanderers in the heavens, from this word. BDAG, 643, "to lead astray."

ones" is in danger of perishing as well. Matthew's context is "pastoral care among believers, and the issue is the sheep of the community that go astray, since it is in a set of passages that deal with the behavior of believers (Matthew 18:6–11, 15–18)."[995] Although some may perish, this is not God's desire ("will", Gr *thelēma*).[996] This precise parallel suggests that "destruction" in Matthew 7:13 does not refer to eternal separation from God but to the same destruction that can happen to a regenerate believer, one of Christ's sheep, who wanders away from the fold. "Perishing in this context," according to Constable, "does not mean loss of salvation but the ultimate result of failing to achieve God's goal for him or her as a disciple, namely a wasted life."[997] Such a person loses his "life/soul."

This suggests that the believer who continually chooses throughout his life to enter the broad gate and walk on the broad way is not one who is on the highway to eternal damnation.[998] Rather he is a carnal Christian who has lost his way. Like the sheep to which Matthew later refers (Matthew 18:12-14), he has gone astray and his temporal and spiritual life is ruined.

Another parallel to our understanding of "perish" in Matthew 7:13 is found in 1 Corinthians 8:11.

> *For through your knowledge he who is weak is ruined [Gr apollumi], the brother for whose sake Christ died (1 Corinthians 8:11).*

What is the nature of this ruin/destruction? We are told it involves a negative, subjective, psychological impact, not eternal separation from God! Their conscience is "defiled" (v. 7) and "wounded" (v. 12, literally, "suffers a blow"). This "ruin" causes a "stumbling block," (v. 9), and causes a "brother" for whom Christ died (i.e., a true believer) to "stumble" (v. 13).[999] In the parallel passage in Romans 14:15 the weaker brother is "made to sorrow." In that passage we are exhorted "*Do not destroy* (Gr *apollumi*) *with your food him for whom Christ died.*"

Excursus on "Life"

Once again, we must consider the background of the sermon found in the wisdom literature of the book of Proverbs. Lady Wisdom says that if one will follow "my ways," he will find blessing and life (Proverbs 8:32-35). However, one who "hates me" in reality "loves death" (Proverbs 8:36). Both death and life refer to experiences in this life, not eternity.

We are specifically told that for the believer the fear of the Lord (obedience and trust) leads to life. "*The fear of the LORD leads to life: Then one rests content, untouched by trouble*" (Proverbs 19:23). "Life" is defined in the second phrase, not as heaven, but as spiritual

---

[995] Bock, *Luke 1-9:50*, 1300.

[996] BDAG, 447, "what one wishes to happen."

[997] Constable, *Tom Constable's Expository Notes on the Bible*, s.v. "Matthew 18:14."

[998] Contra, Albrecht Oepke, "*apollumi*," in TDNT, 1:396.

[999] The nature of this "perishing" is "stumbling" [Gr *skandalon*, Romans 14:13; 1 Corinthians 8:13], not final consignment to hell. It is "an action or circumstance that leads one to act contrary to a proper course of action or set of beliefs," (BDAG, 926). A *skandalon* was originally a trap to which bait was attached. In a close parallel of ideas, the false prophets of Matthew 7:15 are the "traps" that can derail the true believer as he follows the narrow way, the path of discipleship. In a similar way the puffed-up believers in 1 Corinthians 8:1-2 can become a "trap," and enticement to sin, to the weaker brothers at Corinth. The outcome in each case is not hell, but is, as Volf puts it, a "destruction [which] results from the disintegration of moral or psychological values and poses a fundamental existential threat to a person." Gundry Volf, *Paul and Perseverance*, 96.

contentment in this life. The KJV renders it, "*shall abide satisfied*." Certainly, this quality of life is only available to the regenerate. While that may be assumed, it is the daily experience of the believer, not his eternal destiny which is in view. One who lives by the Proverbs or by the Sermon on the Mount may find true life, a satisfying life, and the abundant *present* dimension of *eternal life* which Jesus promised (John 10:10).[1000] As Jesus tells His disciples, the sage tells his son, "*Make level paths for your feet and take only ways that are firm. Do not swerve to the right or the left; keep your foot from evil*" (Proverbs 4:26-70, NIV).

According to Solomon, the opposite of a rich life now is "death," "*He who is steadfast in righteousness will attain to life, and he who pursues evil will bring about his own death*" (Proverbs 11:19). To be "steadfast in righteousness" is to daily enter the narrow gate and attain to life. To "pursue evil" is to take the broad way that ends in "death."

"*He who guards his lips guards his life, but he who speaks rashly will come to ruin*" (Proverbs 13:3). The opposite of a rich life is "death" or "ruin" (Gr *ptoeō*, "to tremble, to dismay").[1001]

The "truly righteous" in Proverbs refers not to a man's state of justification, but to the fact that he lives well and has character and wisdom. The opposite of life is physical death or "ruin," that is, "dismay," which is the proverbial conclusion to a life lived out of fellowship with God.

Like the Sermon on the Mount, the "way of life" in Proverbs is not the way to heaven, but the way to a meaningful and full life now. For example, it is not found in the arms of an adulteress, "*None who go to her return or attain the paths of life*" (Proverbs 2:19); "*She gives no thought to the way of life; her paths are crooked, but she knows it not*" (Proverbs 5:6); "*For these commands are a lamp, this teaching is a light, and the corrections of discipline are the way to life*" (Proverbs 6:23); "*She [wisdom] is a tree of life to those who embrace her; those who lay hold of her will be blessed*" (Proverbs 3:18).[1002] Whoever finds wisdom "finds life" (8:35) and the one who does not find it "harms himself" and loves "death" (8:36). "Leave your simple ways," counsels the father, "and you will live" (9:5). Clearly, psychological/spiritual life and death, not heaven and eternal separation from God, are in view.

It is clear, says the psalmist, that the narrow way, the way of affliction has great benefits.

> *It is good for me that I was afflicted, that I may learn Your statutes (Psalm 119:71).*

The writer to the Hebrews agrees,

> *He disciplines us for our good, so that we may share His holiness. All discipline for the moment seems not to be joyful, but sorrowful; yet to those who have been trained by it, afterwards it yields the peaceful fruit of righteousness (Hebrews 12:10–11).*

To receive goodness from God and to share in His holiness is life indeed!

[1000] Wisdom's ways are pleasant and will "be life for you," and her "paths" as well. The Heb word for path is *netibah* and means "way of life, lifestyle, formally, path, i.e., conduct or behavior, with a focus on continuing behavior (Proverbs 1:15; 3:22)." Swanson, *Dictionary of Biblical Languages: Hebrew Old Testament*, DBLH 5986.

[1001] J. Lust et al., *A Greek-English Lexicon of the Septuagint* (Stuttgart: Deutsche Bibelgesellschaft, 1992), s.v. "πτοέω".

[1002] See also Psalms 16:11.

22

"I Never Knew You"

SEVERAL YEARS ago, the following incident was broadcast on a Christian radio station. The anchor was very excited to introduce his next guest, a man who had made "the trip." This particular program customarily focused on unusual spiritual experiences.

The anchor began, "Greetings, Dr. Jones (fictitious name), we are really looking forward to our time together. Thank you so much for being available to share the incredible things that God has done in your life."

"I am very glad to be here."

The interviewer continued, "I understand that you are among a number of people who have made the ultimate trip, a visionary experience in which you were transported to the third heaven."

"Yes, it was an amazing encounter with God the Father that led to some wonderful new revelations."

"Tell us about them."

When Dr. Jones described some words he received from God, the interviewer expressed wonder and amazement.

"What was the most significant revelation that you received?"

Being a medical doctor, Dr. Jones was particularly moved by one particular revelation.

He explained, "The human brain has twelve cranial nerves, and each of them is involved in specific functions of the brain. One nerve, the twelfth, is responsible for our sense of smell."

"When I was in the third heaven," he resumed, "I learned the purpose of God's twelfth cranial nerve. It enables Him to smell the sweet savor sacrifices specified in the book of Leviticus."

John MacArthur reports an account of another "prophet" who, while meditating by a lakeside, suddenly saw a picture of Jesus materialize in the water. He immediately photographed it, and in a brochure announced that for $19.95 he would send the picture to anyone who asked.

Another well-known "prophet" saw a vision of a 500-foot-tall Jesus who gave him a revelation that unless he received one million dollars in contributions to his ministry by December 31, 1987, he would die. Bumper stickers proliferated saying "Send [name] to heaven in 87, don't give him a dime." The evangelist did receive the one million dollars on time!

On a television program last night, I watched a TV evangelist offer "miracle water" which he would send in a small plastic bag. It was guaranteed to result in a miracle in your life. All you had to do was to provide your email and your address. On a different channel, another evangelist told his viewers that he believed that if they gave $1000 in seed money to his ministry, that all of their children and grandchildren would come to the Lord.

Dr. Jones and these other would-be prophets may be believers in Christ. Perhaps they did have some unusual spiritual experiences which were very real to them, and, no doubt, some may be very sincere and honest. However, when they, in collusion with the modern TV media, promulgate this kind of silliness, they denigrate biblical Christianity and make a mockery out of the Christian faith in the minds of millions of nonbelievers.

As we will see in this chapter, these kinds of "prophets" were common in New Testament times as well.

The Charismatic Teachers

Toward the end of the Sermon on the Mount, Jesus issues a warning to His disciples that they must enter through a narrow gate onto the narrow way (Matthew 7:13-14) and that only those who "do the will of the Father" will enter the kingdom of heaven (Matthew 7:21-23).[1003]

However, there is a danger. The next verses warn that there are two kinds of prophets who can threaten the disciples' intention to pursue the narrow way: false prophets from without (vv. 15-20) and deluded miracle workers from within (vv. 21-23). When this happens, the kingdom program "suffers violence" (Matthew 11:12), and many who have already entered the kingdom in a soteriological sense, are hindered from entering into discipleship.

Regarding the second group of prophets from within, when they apply for kingdom entrance, the Lord Jesus says, "*I never knew you, depart from Me you who practice lawlessness*" (v. 23). In this chapter we will discuss the identity and destiny of these supplicants. Contrary to the common understanding, we will argue that these are in fact true believers, and their destiny is not eternal separation from God, but temporal exclusion from Christ's presence, dramatic loss of reward, and a rebuke at the Judgment Seat of Christ. They will be "in the kingdom," but not "at the table."

But first we must discuss the two different groups in view; each can threaten the disciples' choices to walk along the narrow way. That Jesus intends us to understand that He had two different groups in mind is suggested by a structural feature which Matthew employs. The false prophets of 7:15-20 are set off from what follows by an *inclusio*: "*you will know them by their fruits*" (7:16), and, again "*you will know them by their fruits*" (v. 20). This feature distinguishes the false prophets from the group to follow in verses 21-23. Betz and Collins note, "One should keep the two sections as separate and not treat them

[1003] As discussed elsewhere, to enter into the kingdom in the Sermon on the Mount refers to entering into a kingdom way of life now resulting in higher status in the future millennium. "In the NT *hōdós* ("way") primarily refers to the way of life, the manner of life demanded by God (Acts 14:6; Rom 3:16f.; Js 1:8; 5:20; 2 Pet 2:15, 21)." Martin Völkel, "*hodos*," in EDNT, 2:491. These two passages (Matthew 7:13-14, 21-23) are parallel and explain each other. Therefore in the context Matthew 7, "to enter into the kingdom" should be understood as entering into a way of life, the narrow way, and should not be understood as "going to heaven when I die." As a result of one's entrance by the "narrow way," that person will be regarded as great in the kingdom when Christ returns (Matthew 5:20).

as one."[1004] Hagner has pointed out that this is a chiastic structure, further demarcating the false prophets of verses 15-20 from the charismatics of verses 21-23.[1005]

That these false prophets appear in sheep's clothing suggests that they outwardly appear to be Christian, but they are not. The fact that they are described as wolves in sheep's clothing tells at least two things: (1) they act like sheep, that is, they have good works; (2) they are really imposters, that is, wolves. These wolves are evidently unsaved heretics who come into the community of disciples from without.

The way one discerns a false prophet is by examining his fruit. Otherwise, detection is difficult. But what is this "fruit"? Elsewhere Matthew connects the fruit not only with behavior but also with their teaching. Indeed, their behavior was like sheep, it appeared good, so the more reliable way to discern whether or not they were false was by what they taught. Later Jesus said that "the tree is known by its fruit" (Matthew 12:33). In order to discern a prophet's true inner nature, one must attend to His words, "*For the mouth speaks out of that which fills the heart ... for by your words you will be justified, and by your words you will be condemned*" (Matthew 12:34, 37). Also the test of "fruit" is applied to those who claim to be prophets.

Some have applied this as a test of whether or not a certain person is truly born again.[1006] Throughout the New Testament, Christian leaders are held to a higher standard. This is not a test of salvation; it is a test of whether or not one who claims to be a prophet in the church is really speaking from God. In a nutshell, the test is that his inner character will be revealed by what he says. Both his life and his teaching must be examined.

What about the next group of people described in verses 21-23? What is their status at the judgment? The false prophets of verses 15-20 are described as "*coming to you,*"

1004 Betz and Collins, *The Sermon on the Mount: A Commentary on the Sermon on the Mount, Including the Sermon on the Plain (Matthew 5:3-7:27 and Luke 6:20-49)*, 539. James E. Davison, citing Betz, agrees, "There are two questions that we must face here. First, is it in fact correct to identify the false prophets in v 15 with the evildoers in v 23? Do the pericopes in vv. 15–20 and vv. 21–23 really speak of the same group of people?" Hill and Betz have recently argued strongly that the two do not, and I am inclined to agree with them. Further, the saying in verse 20, "You will know them by their fruits," repeats v 16 and serves to summarize the comparison of the false prophets to bad trees (verses 16–19). The following verses (21–23), which discuss the charismatics, are only loosely joined to the preceding group. The point of association is not the identity of the groups themselves, but the element that is common to both of them: the production of bad fruits. James E. Davison, "Anomia and the Question of an Antinomian Polemic in Matthew," *JBL* 104, no. 4 (Dec. 1985): 628.

1005 After the introductory warning of 7:15, this passage reveals a carefully designed structure, including a chiasm. Thus a (v 16a) corresponds verbatim to a′ (v 20) as an inclusio; b (v 16b) corresponds to b′ (v 19; this is the weakest part of the chiasm, although both elements refer to unfruitfulness); and c (v 17) corresponds exactly to c′ (v 18), which restates the thought negatively in terms of impossibility. Symmetry and parallelism are also to be found within certain elements of the larger structure. This is especially true of verses 17 and 18. Verse 17 contains two exactly parallel lines except for the very slight alteration in line 2, where the adjective *sapron*, "decayed," precedes the noun *dendron*, "tree." The two lines of verse 18 are exactly parallel except for the omission of the verb *dunatai*, "is able," in the second line. The parallelism of this passage probably derives from the form the material took in oral tradition, but the chiastic structure here probably derives from Matthew himself, as does the joining of this material to verse 15. This passage is quoted in abbreviated form in Justin, *Dialogue with Typho the Jew*. 35. 3 and *Apologia*. 1.16.12–13. See Hagner, *Matthew 14-28*, 182.

1006 Joseph K. Pak, "A Study of Selected Passages on Distinguishing Marks of Genuine and False Believers" (PhD diss., Dallas Theological Seminary, 2001), 50-54. In his fine dissertation Pak argues that I was wrong to identify "fruit" exclusively with words as I did in a former edition of this book. While "fruit" may elsewhere refer to character, in Matthew 7, words are in view. But the test is whether one is a true prophet. This is not a test of whether one is born again. In all likelihood these false prophets were unregenerate, but some of them may have been born again. We do not know.

which probably means they come from outside the church. In contrast to the self-deluded charismatics in the following verses (vv. 21-23), the false prophets were consciously putting on an act.[1007] That this group is distinguished from the first is held by several commentators.[1008]

Starting in verse 21 the scene changes. Now Jesus discusses those who are inside the Christian community, apparently those who have, in contrast to the false prophets, actually confessed Jesus as Lord. They proclaim a heartfelt, "*Lord, Lord*." As Calvin put it, "To *say that Jesus is the Lord,* is to speak of him in honorable terms and with reverence, and to extol his majesty."[1009] In view of the fact that Paul said no one can make such a heartfelt confession except by the Holy Spirit (1 Corinthians 12:3), a possible interpretation of this verse suggests that these people are regenerate. However, the fact that they are not admitted to the kingdom of heaven and that Jesus calls them "evildoers," saying "I never knew you," and demands that they depart from Him, has led many to understand that they only professed faith in Christ but in fact were not justified.[1010]

Jesus solemnly warns them in Matthew 7:21-23:

> *Not everyone who says to Me, "Lord, Lord," will enter the kingdom of heaven, but he who does the will of My Father who is in heaven will enter. Many will say to Me on that day, "Lord, Lord, did we not prophesy in Your name, and in Your name cast out demons, and in Your name perform many miracles?" And then I will declare to them, "I never knew you; DEPART FROM ME, YOU WHO PRACTICE LAWLESSNESS."*

Although Luther would certainly not accept the interpretation followed in this chapter, he asks the pertinent question, "What goes on here, that those who do miracles, and do them in the name of Christ, should still be numbered among the false Christians and among the evil and damned people?"[1011] Good question!

A problem for interpreters who view this second group as merely professing Christians (as Luther did) is that if they are non-Christians, then Christ is telling them that in order to enter heaven, they must perform good works, that is, "do the will of the Father" (v. 21).[1012] Would Christ lie to His hearers by telling them that they can work their way to heaven? While "doing the will of the Father" could possibly refer to believing in Christ for salvation (John 6:39), in the immediate context this refers to obeying the precepts of the Sermon on the Mount (see discussion below). These are believers who

---

1007 France, *The Gospel of Matthew*, p. 290.

1008 Stanley, *Did Jesus Teach Salvation by Works*, 176; David Hill, "False Prophets and Charismatics: Structure and Interpretation in Matthew 7:15-23," *Biblia* 57(1976): 327-48.

1009 Calvin, *1 Corinthians*, s.v. "1 Cor 12:3".

1010 Blomberg, *Matthew*, p. 132. A typical statement of this view is that a genuinely saved person is one who "does the will of my Father." The Greek present tense supposedly means that he is continually living in obedience to the will of God as the normal course of his life. He may fail at times, but his general course of consistency is to obey the will of the Father. Not only does this misrepresent the present tense (it does not necessarily show continuous action), but it is imposing a predetermined theological view on the passage. What is a "general course of consistency"? How much failure "at times" constitutes enough failure to establish that one is not born again? None of these concepts is hinted at in the passage.

1011 Luther, *Luther's Works*, 21:270.

1012 Some interpreters argue that Matthew here is in disagreement with the conclusion that salvation is by "faith alone" (e.g., Luz and Koester, *Matthew 1-7: A Commentary*, 379 and n50).

have not entered through the narrow gate, the way of discipleship, but instead have taken the broad way. They do not possess the surpassing inner righteousness required for entrance into the kingdom way of life (Matthew 5:20). They are believers who have lost their saltiness (Matthew 5:13), and have become carnal. As a result, they are cast aside and trampled on like garbage in an alley. They have not done the will of the Father as that will is defined in the Sermon on the Mount, namely, ethical adherence to the sermon's precepts. Like the carnal believers in 5:19, they will be "in" the kingdom, but lacking the necessary surpassing righteousness (i.e., doing the will of the Father), they will not be great there. They will not miss the kingdom, but they will miss ruling with Christ there.

If, in fact, they have cast out demons, how could they be doing this by the power of Satan? Unregenerate exorcists cannot cast out demons (Acts 19:14-16). These exorcists did.

> *Any kingdom divided against itself is laid waste; and any city or house divided against itself will not stand. If Satan casts out Satan, he is divided against himself; how then will his kingdom stand? ... But if I cast out demons by the Spirit of God, then the kingdom of God has come upon you (Matthew 12:25-26, 28).*

Christ never denies that they did in fact perform miracles in His name.[1013] He simply says that He never approved of their lifestyle and their distortion of the kingdom message.

Elsewhere in the New Testament, attempted exorcisms by the unregenerate are catastrophic failures. Acts 19:13-16 refers to unbelieving Jewish exorcists using the name of Jesus ("by Jesus whom Paul preaches") who were decidedly unsuccessful. The evil spirit responded to their commands by saying, "*I recognize Jesus, and I know about Paul, but who are you?*" (Acts 19:15). Then the evil spirit caused the demon-possessed victim to jump on these evil sons of Sceva and drive them away naked and wounded!

David Aune is therefore correct when he says, "They do not appear to have been Gnostics, Zealots, or Pharisees, but rather *Christians whom Matthew regarded as a dangerous threat to the order and integrity of the Christian communities.*"[1014]

Therefore it is probable that these false teachers who come from within the church (7:21-23) are regenerate people.[1015] This begs the question, "Can workers of iniquity be found in the kingdom of heaven?" An immediate illustration of the fact that lawless men can be found in the kingdom is Matthew 5:19. Jesus has already declared, "*Whoever then annuls one of the least of these commandments, and teaches others to do the same, shall be called least in the kingdom of heaven.*" Therefore when He says, "*Depart from Me, you who practice lawlessness*" (Matthew 7:23), we should not automatically assume that those who are addressed are unregenerate. Those described in 5:19 are clearly those who practice lawlessness and yet they are "in" the kingdom, saved people.

[1013] Clement seems to view them as Christians who lose their salvation. He says these prophets were "in my bosom," but they will not be saved at the last day (2 Clement 3.2-4).

[1014] David Edward Aune, *Prophecy in Early Christianity and the Ancient Mediterranean World* (Grand Rapids: Wm. B. Eerdmans Publishing Co., 1983), 223 (italics added).

[1015] Contra Davies and Allison who label them "counterfeit Christians." Davies and Allison, *A Critical and Exegetical Commentary on the Gospel According to Saint Matthew*, 1:704.

THE WILL OF THE FATHER

> *Not everyone who says to Me, 'Lord, Lord,' will* ***enter the kingdom*** *of heaven, but he who does the* ***will of My Father*** *who is in heaven will enter (Matthew 7:21).*

Because many interpreters have assumed without proof that "*enter the kingdom*" *always* means personal salvation, they cause Jesus to contradict Himself. In one place He says that bad people cannot be in the kingdom (Matthew 7:21), because they do not do the will of the Father, and in another He affirms they can (Matthew 5:19). Nolland is surely correct in stating that the "surpassing righteousness" of Matthew 5:20 is equivalent of "doing the will of the Father" in 7:21.[1016] Luz, knowing that the "will" is ethical obedience to the Sermon on the Mount, frankly admits that "doing the will of my Father is a condition of salvation."[1017] He asserts that Matthew "does polemicize sharply against the thesis that entering the kingdom of heaven is 'simply a matter of faith rather than along with faith also a matter of 'doing.'"[1018] And because in his view kingdom entrance (final salvation) is based in part at least on human effort, there can "be no certainty that one will enter the kingdom of heaven."[1019]

Luz is right in stating that the text asserts that works are a condition of entering the kingdom. But he is incorrect in his belief that entering the kingdom refers to final entrance into heaven. Rather, to enter the kingdom in Matthew 7:21 refers to more than physical entrance, it speaks of the outcome of entering onto the narrow way, greatness in the kingdom (Matthew 5:19-20). It is the abundant entrance into the kingdom concerning which Peter spoke (2 Peter 1:11).

During the last week of Christ's ministry on earth, John notes that many of the rulers, "believed in him" (John 12:42). In contrast to those who had hard hearts (vv. 40-41) and who did not believe in Him (v. 37), we are specifically told that "nevertheless many even of the rulers believed in him" (v. 42). Clearly, these saved "rulers" are being contrasted with the unsaved who did not believe. One is therefore surprised to read Carson's claim that this seems "to fit the pattern of inadequate, irresolute, even spurious faith that John repeatedly describes in this Gospel (e.g. 2:23–25; 6:60; 8:30ff.)."[1020] There is no "pattern" to fit. While their faith is certainly inadequate and irresolute, it is not spurious; in fact it is specifically contrasted with unbelief. Jesus said, "Whoever believes in him has eternal life," and since these rulers believed in Him, on the authority of Jesus Himself we can say that they have eternal life.[1021] Carson, of course, denies that their faith is genuine because the next phrase says, "*They were not confessing Him, for fear that they would be put out of the synagogue; for they loved the approval of men rather than the approval of God*" (12:42-43). Because Carson

---

[1016] Nolland, *The Gospel of Matthew: A Commentary on the Greek Text*, 339.

[1017] Luz and Koester, *Matthew 1-7: A Commentary*, 319.

[1018] Ibid., 379.

[1019] Ibid., 379.

[1020] Carson, *The Gospel According to John*, 450-51. Carson obviously interprets on the basis of his theological preunderstanding. We all bring theological preunderstandings to the texts we interpret (including the present writer), but one needs to understand what is often behind the interpretations of the commentators.

[1021] This phrase ("believed in Him") is easily shown to be John's way of speaking about saving faith in Christ. See John 2:11, "his disciples believed on him"; John 3:16, "whoever believes in him"; 3:18, "whoever believes in him is not judged"; 6:29, "this is the will of the Father, that everyone who beholds the Son and believe in him will have eternal life." See also 7:31, 39; 8:30; 9:36; 10:42; 11:45, 48.

"knows" that a person with genuine faith will always publicly acknowledge that faith and would never love the approval of men in place of the approval of God, these rulers *must* be examples of false faith.

But what does it mean to "do the will of the Father"? In the discussion above we have argued that it refers to ethical behavior consistent with the Sermon on the Mount. While some argue that to do the will of the Father means "believe on Christ for salvation,"[1022] in the context of the Sermon on the Mount this is highly unlikely. Clearly, Jesus is referring to what He has been talking about in the preceding two chapters, which is the ethical lifestyle of a disciple; the daily choices to enter through the narrow gate which, as argued elsewhere,[1023] refers not to believing on Christ for initial salvation, but to subsequent daily choices, the kingdom way of living. The main intent of the Sermon on the Mount is to define for Christ's disciples what the will of the Father is and to challenge them to live it. The will of the Father is the kingdom way of living that Jesus has been discussing in the preceding chapters.

The phrase "*will of the Father*" is used four times in Matthew (Matthew 7:21; 12:50; 18:14; 21:31) and three times in the gospel of John (John 4:34; 5:30; 6:40). The concept of God's will is variously expressed as "your will" (Matthew 6:10; 26:42; Luke 22:42), "the will of Him" (John 4:34), "his Master's will" (Luke 12:47), "His will" (John 7:17; 9:31); thus, it is found in many places in the Gospels. In no instance does it refer to belief for salvation but in each instance it speaks of doing works of obedience. In fact, in the Lord's prayer, Jesus instructs His followers to pray, "*your will be done*," that is, your standards of personal righteousness be fully implemented and displayed on the earth.[1024] Surely this defines the "will of the Father" in Matthew 7:21.

Often John 6:40 is cited to prove that the "will of My Father" is to believe on Christ.

> *For this is the will of My Father, that everyone who beholds the Son and believes in Him will have eternal life, and I Myself will raise him up on the last day (John 6:40).*

It is certainly God's will that everyone who believes on Christ will have eternal life. But is this the "will of the Father" of Matthew 7:21? It does not always mean that even in the Gospel of John.

Those who cite this verse as proof that the will of God in Matthew 7:21 refers to faith in Christ ignore the fact that they could have selected John 5:30 where the will of God relates to doing and not believing. In that passage Jesus defines the "will of God" as good works done in obedience. He says, "*I can do nothing on My own initiative. As I hear, I judge; and My judgment is just, because I do not seek My own will, but the will of Him who sent Me*" (John 5:30).

What about John 4:34 where Jesus says, "*My food is to do the will of him who sent me and accomplish his work*"? The will of God in that passage is not belief on Christ for salvation, it is good works done in obedience! Consider John 7:17 where Jesus says, "*If*

1022 See, for example, López, "The Pauline Vice List and Inheriting the Kingdom", 132.

1023 See discussion about the narrow gate and the narrow way in Chapter 21.

1024 In the *Grace New Testament Commentary*, for example, Hal Haller links "*your will be done*" with Isaiah 2:2-4, "*Let us go up to the mountain of the Lord, to the house of the God of Jacob; that He may teach us concerning His ways, and that we may walk in His paths*" (Isaiah 2:3–4). The will of the Father refers to "walking in his paths," ethical obedience to his will. Haller, "Matthew," 30.

anyone is willing to do His will, he will know of the teaching, whether it is of God or whether I speak from Myself" (John 7:17). Doing "His will," in this context, refers to obedience to Christ's teaching.

The Sermon on the Mount is about ethical obedience, the active lifestyle of the disciple. The context of the sermon is about living life, not gaining it, and this context is determinative in defining the meaning of "the will of God," not a single reference in John.

Furthermore, doing the will of God in Matthew 7:21 is the opposite of those "*who practice lawlessness*" (7:23); it is about obedience, not initial faith for salvation. The will of God in both Matthew 12:50 and Matthew 21:31 are most easily understood as obedience to His precepts. In the later reference doing the will of God refers to obedience to the Father (work in the vineyard). Matthew 12:50 says not one a word about faith in Christ for salvation. The easiest way to understand that passage is that Jesus refers to His instruction to disciples in the Sermon on the Mount. Obedience to the sermon is the "will of the Father," and while this is something *only those who are already believers can do*, not all believers do it. That is why Christ is giving this sermon! Earlier in the Sermon on the Mount, Christ referred to God's will as something that must be "*done on earth as it is in heaven*" (6:10). It involves doing, not just believing. The essence of entering the kingdom of God is that God is fully obeyed and His purposes accomplished.

Elsewhere in the New Testament, phrases similar to "the will of God" (e.g. *to thelēma tou theou, to thelēma autou, boulēmati autou*, etc.) never mean "believe on Christ for initial salvation." It often refers to God's plan for one's life.[1025] All other places it refers to obeying God. Paul relates it to a lifestyle of "*doing the will of God from the heart*" (Ephesians 6:6), and says it is "your sanctification" (1 Thessalonians 4:3; cf. Romans 12:2). Peter explains that "*it is God's will that by doing good you may put to silence the ignorant talk of foolish men*" (1 Peter 2:15). He says that the will of God is the opposite of living in the flesh (1 Peter 4:2). The writer to the Hebrews refers to the will of God as perseverance, "*For you have need of endurance, so that when you have done the will of God, you may receive what was promised*" (Hebrews 10:36).

In view of the fact that "the will of the Father" never means "believe on Christ for salvation in Matthew and only once in John, why do some evangelicals insist that it means this in Matthew 7:21? [1026] Robert Wilkin explains, "To some people this passage sounds like it is denying justification by faith alone."[1027] In other words, because they understand "enter the kingdom" as final entrance into the millennium or into heaven, they assert that the "will of the Father" *cannot* mean anything other than believe on Christ, or else a works salvation is taught.

Or, another possibility, of course, is that the Experimental Predestinarians are correct. They say that only those who do good works will be admitted into heaven, and, therefore, all "true" believers will do good works until the end of life. Thus, doing the will of the Father is not a condition of entrance, but is a characteristic of all who will enter.

For those who believe that the issue in Matthew 7:21 is final entrance into personal salvation, John Robbins gives a plausible explanation. He correctly points out that the charismatic prophets are pleading their good works as the basis for entrance, and that

---

[1025] Acts 13:36; Romans 1:10; 2 Corinthians 1:1; 8:5; Ephesians 1:1.

[1026] See for example, John W. Robbins, "Justification and Judgment," *JOGES* 15, no. 1 (Spring 2002).

[1027] Robert N. Wilkin, "Is Justification by Faith Alone," ibid.9, no. 2 (Autumn 1996): 9.

is why they are being rejected.[1028] However, his explanation in my opinion is inadequate because there is no good evidence that the "will of the Father" refers to faith for initial salvation. Robins says, "All of these extraordinary and wonderful works done in the name of Jesus are lawlessness, because they are done for the purpose of obtaining salvation."[1029] But, there is no evidence in the context that they were doing these works "for the purpose of obtaining salvation." We do not know from the context why they did them, but we do know from many first-century documents that charismatic prophets performed these works not for salvation but for money and personal glory.

Interpreters of Matthew should abandon the view that "enter the kingdom" refers to final entrance into heaven or the millennium. Instead, as many in the history of the church have argued, to enter the kingdom means to enter into the lifestyle of the Sermon on the Mount leading to high honor in the kingdom. The charismatic prophets were not seeking salvation in Matthew 7:21, they were seeking "greatness," and that is probably the motive they had in doing all these wonderful works. Because this entrance is based upon good works, Jesus is clearly not speaking of soteriology. to "enter the kingdom" refers to seeking surpassing righteousness and pursuing the journey along the narrow way, the path of discipleship. What Jesus has in mind here is not mere physical entrance into the kingdom but the abundant entrance the charismatic prophets thought they deserved (2 Peter 2:10-11), an entrance into greatness there (Matthew 5:19-20).

Those who are already saved are called on to enter into full discipleship by "*doing the will of the Father*" (Matthew 7:21), living out the Sermon on the Mount and by having a "righteousness [that] surpasses that of the scribes and Pharisees" (5:20). The outcome of personal salvation is regeneration and justification; the outcome of "doing the will of the Father" is "greatness" (5:19). The former refers to personal salvation, and the latter refers to application of the Sermon on the Mount, which leads to fullness of life and reward, a common theme in the Sermon (Matthew 5:12, 46; 6:1-6, 16, 18; 10:41-42). These believers in 7:21-23 may be "in" the kingdom, that is, saved people, but they will be "least" there.

But are they regenerate? Many doubt this.

FALSE CHRISTIAN PROPHETS

An early Christian writing, the *Didache*, warned about these false Christian prophets.

> *Whosoever therefore shall come and teach you all these things that have been said before, receive him; but if the teacher himself be perverted and teach a different doctrine to the destruction thereof, hear him not; but if to the increase of righteousness and the knowledge of the Lord, receive him as the Lord.*

The criterion of discernment is whether one's teaching leads to "the increase of righteousness." This is what Jesus called doing the will of God or applying the Sermon on

---

1028 John W. Robbins, "Justification and Judgment," ibid.15, no. 1 (Spring 2002): 68. Robbins says, "Their defense should be the imputed righteousness of Christ, not their works. Many will be sent to hell because they will not mention that they are sinners saved only by the righteousness of the Man Christ Jesus." Similarly Wilkin argues, "Jesus' point here is that no one can expect kingdom entrance on the basis of his or her works, or deeds. Far from contradicting justification by faith alone, He is proving it." Davison, "Anomia and the Question of an Antinomian Polemic in Matthew," 9.

1029 Robbins, "Justification and Judgment," 72.

the Mount to one's life. The *Didache* continues, "*Not every one that speaketh in the Spirit is a prophet, but only if he have the ways of the Lord. From his ways therefore the false prophet and the prophet shall be recognized.*"

This is reminiscent of our Lord's command to the believing disciples to enter by the narrow gate and embark on the narrow way. The "way" is a way of life and does not refer to the way to heaven or entrance into personal salvation.

The *Didache* understood these false prophets as Christian false prophets.

> *But let everyone that cometh in the name of the Lord be received; and then when ye have tested him ye shall know him, for ye shall have understanding on the right hand and on the left. If the comer is a traveler, assist him, so far as ye are able; but he shall not stay with you more than two or three days, if it be necessary. But if he wishes to settle with you, being a craftsman, let him work for and eat his bread.* ***But if he has no craft, according to your wisdom provide how he shall live as a Christian among you, but not in idleness. If he will not do this, he is trafficking upon Christ. Beware of such men.***[1030]

These are false *Christian* prophets. The *Didache* uses the Gr *christianos*, which is the common word for "a Christlike person," that is, a saved person (see Acts 26:28; 1 Peter 4:16). Even though they are genuine believers, these false Christian prophets are described as those "trafficking upon Christ" [Gr *christemporos*, "one who carries on a cheap trade in (the teachings of) Christ, a *Christmonger*"].[1031]

That this was a problem in the early church is clear from Paul's disclaimer to the Thessalonians:

> *For our exhortation does not come from error or impurity or by way of deceit; ... so we speak, not as pleasing men, but God who examines our hearts. For we never came with flattering speech, as you know, nor with a pretext for greed—God is witness—nor did we seek glory from men ... But we proved to be gentle among you, as a nursing mother tenderly cares for her own children (1 Thessalonians 2:3–7).*

Similarly, Paul exhorts Titus that those of the circumcision "*must be silenced because they are upsetting whole families, teaching things they should not teach for the sake of sordid gain*" (Titus 1:11).

We suggest that those to whom Jesus spoke in Matthew 7:21-23 were true believers who were "in" the kingdom but led lawless lives (Matthew 5:19). They spoke from impurity, deceit, and greed, and with flattering speech as a pretext for greed, "sordid gain." Like Simon the magician in Samaria who believed, was baptized, and who followed Philip (and was therefore regenerate), these superficial, charismatic believers of Matthew 7:21-23 may have seen a profit to be made and used their gifts for selfish purposes.[1032] Concerned for fame and fortune, Simon wanted to purchase the miracle-working power of the Holy Spirit with silver (Acts 8:18-24). He seemed to fall away after a lifestyle of doing spectacular things.

[1030] "Didache," in *The Apostolic Fathers: Greek Texts and English Translations of Their Writings*, ed. Joseph Barber Lightfoot, J. R. Harmer, and Michael W. Holmes (Grand Rapids: Baker Book House, 1992), (10:1-12:4), 233-34.

[1031] BDAG, 1090.

[1032] That Simon was in fact a regenerate saint is argued by Chay and Correia, *The Faith That Saves: The Nature of Faith in the New Testament*, 54-58. See discussion below pp. 528 ff.

What had happened to them? Why had they fallen into such lawless living? They apparently began well, performing miracles, casting out demons, and advancing the cause of the kingdom. But for some reason they fell into carnality. The text gives no explanation, but perhaps Paul's experience with the "thorn in the flesh" suggests a possible answer. Paul prayed three times that this thorn would be removed. But it was not. Why?

> *And because of the surpassing greatness of the revelations, for this reason, to keep me from exalting myself, there was given me a thorn in the flesh, a messenger of Satan to buffet me—to keep me from exalting myself! (2 Corinthians 12:7)*

Paul's prayer was denied because of the danger of spiritual pride! Billheimer is correct when he says,

> *Ego exaltation is probably the most dangerous and deadly of sins. It caused the downfall of Lucifer, with all its attending tragedies. It made the original earth a chaos, drowned in stygian darkness. It upset the balance of an entire planet. For any created being to make itself or any other thing but God the center of his world is catastrophic and self-destructive.*[1033]

Satan's heart was filled with pride, and this was the reason for his fall (Ezekiel 28:18). Paul recognized the same danger in appointing a youth to a position of authority (1 Timothy 3:6), and he also recognized that this danger could come on himself because of the "surpassing greatness of revelations" he had been privileged to receive.

We may be close to the explanation for their fall into lawlessness when we suggest that these believing leaders became enamored with their spiritual experiences. Surely, "I am the man," they thought. The miracles they performed served to exalt themselves. Being granted the privilege of prophesying in Christ's name, casting out demons, and performing miracles is heady stuff. If such things endangered the apostle, it could certainly endanger these believing prophets within the community. Pride leads to lawless living.

Ministering the gospel of Christ from base motives is discussed elsewhere in Scripture. While in prison, Paul notes that some preach Christ out of selfish motives,

> *Some, to be sure, are preaching Christ even from envy and strife, but some also from good will; the latter do it out of love, knowing that I am appointed for the defense of the gospel; the former proclaim Christ out of selfish ambition, rather than from pure motives, thinking to cause me distress in my imprisonment (Philippians 1:15–17).*

Paul refers to a group of self-centered teachers who plagued the Corinthian church:

> *Unlike so many, we do not peddle the word of God for profit [Gr kapēleuō]. On the contrary, in Christ we speak before God with sincerity, like men sent from God (2 Corinthians 2:17, NIV84).*

The word *kapēleuō* refers to a "huckster"[1034] who is motivated by financial remuneration for his preaching (2 Corinthians 11:20). Originally, this word referred to "the 'retailer' who sells on the market wares which he has bought from the ἔμπορος ('wholesaler'), and it

---

1033 Paul E. Billheimer, *Destined for the Throne*, rev. ed. (Minneapolis: Bethany House, 1975), 97.

1034 BDAG, 508.

means 'to engage in retail trade.' Both words carry with them the suggestion of trickery and avarice." It came to mean "to sell, to hawk deceitfully, at illegitimate profit."[1035] These hucksters were "suspected of corrupting by putting the best fruit on top of the basket."[1036] The problem was rampant with the traveling philosopher, and Paul says it was happening among Christian prophets as well. Apparently the word does not imply that these philosophers falsely misrepresented the wisdom.[1037] If that applies to the false Christian prophets Jesus rebukes at the judgment, then the issue may not only be the false content of their teaching but also their motives.

But how is it possible that Christ would allow true supernatural power from God to be used for purposes that might give credence to those who misuse it?[1038] One only has to turn to 1 Corinthians 12-14 where the supernatural gift of speaking in foreign languages not learned by the speaker (the "gift of tongues") was used in ways that caused unbelievers to think that the church was loaded with madmen (1 Corinthians 14:23), bringing discredit on the name of Christ. These men speak things "not understood" ("mysteries") by men but to God only, because He is the only one who could understand the foreign language. They were people who "build themselves up in the eyes of others" (edify themselves; 1 Corinthians 14:2; cf. 4:7-10; 13:4-5). Paul has just said that "love does not parade itself" and is not "puffed up" (cf. 1 Corinthians 13:4-5) but they were doing both. Consider Samson whom the Lord blessed (Judges 13:24) and who was carnal all his life (Judges 14:20; 16:1, 13), and yet he worked miracles by God's power (Judges 14:6, 19; 15:14; 16:28).

These prophets did these miracles "in my name." Elsewhere in Matthew's gospel, the phrase "in my name" is a marker of genuineness (Matthew 10:22; 18:5, 20). Even if they began well, they continued badly. They soon began to misuse them. As a result, their ministry was never approved by Christ. Christians, who have the gifts of pastor, teacher, or any other spiritual gift, can utilize them for selfish and unchristian purposes.

DEPART FROM ME

> *And then I will declare to them, "I never knew you;* DEPART FROM ME, YOU WHO PRACTICE LAWLESSNESS*" (Matthew 7:23).*

In Matthew 7:23 this terrible announcement is commonly understood by Matthew's commentators to mean exclusion from heaven and that Jesus is dooming them to eternal destruction."[1039]

These people, according to Hagner, "have shown by their conduct that they have not been chosen by Jesus,"[1040] that is, they are not of the elect. They are, in the words of

---

[1035] Windish, *kapēleuō*, in TDNT, 3:603.

[1036] WPNT, s.v. "2 Cor. 2:17."

[1037] MM, 321. Apparently Apollonius of Tyana, rebuked one of these huckster philosophers and "tried to wean him of his love of filthy lucre and of huckstering his wisdom." Ibid.

[1038] A current manifestation of the broad way is the "prosperity gospel," which promises a life of wealth, health, and ease to true disciples. Their shameful displays on TV of glossolalia and false prophecy and healings have caused many nonbelievers to mock the Christian faith. In addition, they have led countless believers into a false system of Christian living that has harmed the faith of many. It is these types of prophets that Jesus warns against.

[1039] Hendriksen and Kistemaker, *Exposition of the Gospel According to Matthew*, 377.

[1040] Donald. A Hagner, *Matthew 1-13*, Word Biblical Commentary (Dallas: Word, 2002), 188.

Jesus, "those who practice lawlessness" (7:23). Carson agrees, saying that the "essential characteristic of the true believer" is obedience. "True believers," he says, "will perform the will of their Father."[1041] Based upon the gospel of John, however, one would normally think that the "*essential characteristic*" of the true believer is faith in Christ. But, Carson "knows" that obedience is the essential characteristic, because he "knows" that the Reformed doctrine of perseverance is true.

It would seem that a careful reading of the Sermon on the Mount would surface an obvious problem with this interpretation. As mentioned above, in Matthew 5:19 Jesus speaks of saved people who are "in" the kingdom, and yet they clearly practice lawlessness. This creates a difficulty for Carson's interpretation when he further explains, "It is true, of course, that no man enters the kingdom because of his obedience; but is equally true that no man enters the kingdom who is not obedient. It is true that men are saved by God's grace through faith in Christ; but it is equally true that God's grace in a man's life inevitably results in obedience. Any other view of grace cheapens grace, and turns it into something unrecognizable."[1042] Really?! What about Solomon, Saul, and a myriad of other biblical examples of true believers who did not obey and persisted in their disobedience to the end of life?[1043] And of course, what about the persons in Matthew 5:19? These were "in" the kingdom, that is, "saved," in Carson's terms, and yet they lived lives of lawlessness.

As France points out, lawlessness is "a fairly general term for behavior displeasing to God."[1044] The people in 5:19 not only practice it themselves, refusing to obey even the least part of the Law, but they actively teach others to do the same. Clearly these regenerate saints of 5:19 are in the kingdom, but in the words of Jesus they have not done "the will of My Father," and hence they will not, according to Matthew 7:21, "enter the kingdom."[1045] Does this mean they will not go to heaven?

No! Those "least in the kingdom" are true Christians who never become disciples because, like the regenerate false prophets in Matthew 7:21-23, they loved the approval of men more than the approval of God. Davison is correct when he says, "Matthew's real target in the passages we have examined is the problem, common to every age of the Church—and to the Old Testament community of faith—of laxity in the moral life of believers.[1046] They are carnal Christians, and when they stand at the Judgment Seat of Christ, they will hear the terrible words, "*Depart from Me, you who practice lovelessness*" (v. 23). They will be in the kingdom (in a soteriological sense), but they will not be at the table. As a result, they will weep and gnash their teeth in profound regret for their wasted lives. For discussion of the meaning of "depart from me," see the "Excursus on the Ban Formula in the Talmuds" at the end of this chapter.

1041 Carson, *Jesus' Sermon on the Mount and His Confrontation with the World*, 139.

1042 Ibid., 139.

1043 See extensive proof of this in chapter 32.

1044 France, *The Gospel of Matthew*, 295. Contra Morris who says it is "basically the rejection of the law of God." Morris, *The Gospel According to Matthew*, 181.

1045 "'The will' refers to God's will as it has been revealed in the Sermon on the Mount." Davies and Allison, *A Critical and Exegetical Commentary on the Gospel According to Saint Matthew*, 711.

1046 Davison, "Anomia and the Question of an Antinomian Polemic in Matthew," 634. Disregarding the teaching of eternal security, Davison, of course, concludes that they will be damned.

I NEVER KNEW YOU

But it might fairly be asked, "If those in this second group in Matthew 7:21-23 are truly born again, why does Jesus say to them, 'I never knew you, depart from Me you who practice lawlessness'" (Matthew 7:23)? France admits that in Matthew addressing Jesus as Lord is usually a deliberate claim to a master/discipleship relationship and is thus an emphatic profession of faith.[1047] This observation is confirmed by the twenty-six uses of "Lord" as an address to Jesus throughout the gospel.[1048] Yet, it is common for interpreters to assert, without sound support, that these professors obtain only damnation.[1049] For some, the fact that Jesus says, "I *never* knew you," proves that they never had a saving relationship with Christ.[1050]

In this view, Matthew's purpose in citing these warnings and applying them to the believers in his community is either to impress upon them that works (even miraculous ones) do not save, or to warn those who have professed faith in Christ to consider the possibility that their faith in Christ is not genuine. They may think they are born again, but they are not. For example, Ridderbos says, "His warnings ... are loving admonitions to His disciples to see whether they have the fruits of faith, or most basically, whether they have faith itself. He admonishes them not to deceive themselves in their relationship with Him."[1051]

"Loving admonitions"?! One can hardly imagine a more horrible religious faith than one based on the need to examine one's whole life before knowing whether or not he lived well enough to establish that he is saved! Those holding this view have Jesus and His apostles continually warning their communities to wonder whether they achieved a sufficient amount of "doing the will of God" to establish to others and to their own conscience that they are in fact truly born again. This fear of eternal separation from God is supposedly a healthy fear that will motivate them to work hard to demonstrate that their faith is real and thus calm the claims of conscience. Of course, none of them can know for certain whether they will endure to the very end or that their works will be sufficient – until the end has come. Therefore, it follows from Ridderbos's premise that none of them can know if they are saved until they have persevered to the end. And they can only know that at the end; therefore, there is no real possibility of assurance in God's love until the final hour. Thus Reformed writer Joseph Pak can say, "Many of them will find out that their faith was not genuine on the day of judgment."[1052]

Is there a better understanding of this warning which is consistent with the grace of God taught throughout the New Testament? Yes, there is. There is no evidence that this rejection is final, as Ridderbos believes, or that it refers to damnation. To say otherwise is merely bare assertion.

1047 R. T. France, *Matthew*, Tyndale New Testament Commentaries (Grand Rapids: Wm. B. Eerdmans Publishing Co., 1985), 148.

1048 Matthew 8:2, 6, 8, 25; 9:28; 11:25; 13:27; 14:28, 30; 15:22, 25, 27; 17:4, 15; 18:21; 20:30, 31, 33; 25:11, 20, 22, 24, 37, 44; 26:22; 27:63.

1049 Karl Pagenkemper, "Rejection Imagery in the Synoptic Parables," *BibSac* 153, no. 611 (July-September 1996): 189.

1050 Robbins, "Justification and Judgment," 71.

1051 Herman Ridderbos, *Matthew*, trans. Ray Togtman, Bible Student's Commentary (Grand Rapids: Zondervan Publishing House, 1987), 157, quoted by Pak, "A Study of Selected Passages on Distinguishing Marks of Genuine and False Believers", 60.

1052 Pak, "A Study of Selected Passages on Distinguishing Marks of Genuine and False Believers", 61.

During their time of ministry on earth, they did not, Jesus says, enter into the kingdom way of living or of spreading its influence. This is in spite of the fact that they represented to others that their doctrine and practice was the doctrine and practice of the kingdom: prophecy, miracles (probably healings), and exorcisms. When they stand at the Judgment Seat of Christ and argue that they were manifesting a kingdom way of life and ministry, Jesus will say to them, "I never knew you." However, He obviously knew them in some sense, and He knew all about their ministry. What then does this mean?

The Gr word in verse 23 (I never "knew" you) is the common word for "to know" (*ginōskō*) found in the New Testament (222 times). It is usually more personal than the other word for know, *oida*, and communicates a "personal relationship between the one who knows and the one known."[1053]

Ginōskō has a broad range of meanings. It can mean to know,[1054] to learn, to be acquainted with, to have sexual intercourse with, to perceive, to recognize, to confirm, to be aware of, or even to understand (2 Corinthians 1:13).[1055] The psalmist said, "The Lord knows [LXX, *ginōskō*] the way of the righteous" (Psalm 1:6); that is, "The Lord *approves the manner of life* of the righteous."[1056] Translations vary: he "watches over it" (NIV, NRSV, NLT) or "approves" or "guards the way of the godly" (NET); "takes care of" (NCV); "protects" (CEV); "guided and protected" (GNT). The word is also commonly used to mean "to give recognition to."[1057] In secular Greek it can even mean "to verify."[1058] This meaning is found in the New Testament, where sometimes it can shade into the sense of "to confirm."[1059]

Elsewhere in the New Testament, we are told that God "knows" believers in the sense of finding favor with them, that is, He approves of them in the sense of choosing them for leadership (2 Timothy 2:19).[1060] The world, John tells us, "did not know" Christ, that is, they did not acknowledge Him for who He is (John 1:12). They did not approve of Him.

When Paul said, "*That which I do, I do not understand*" (Romans 7:15) [Gr *ou ginōskō*, lit. "I do not know"] it certainly does not mean "I do not know" or "I do not understand," as many translations render it. If there is anyone who knows and understands thoroughly

---

1053 E. D. Schmitz, "*ginōskō*" in NIDNTT, 2:398. However, it is not necessary to assume, as is often done, that the nature of this relationship is limited to personal salvation. It is clear that there is "knowing" and then there is "knowing." There are degrees. For example Paul said, "*If anyone supposes that he knows* (Gr *ginōskō*) *anything, he has not yet known as he ought to know* (Gr *ginōskō*)," (1 Corinthians 8:2). One can "know" but not really "know," that is, not know as he "ought to know." To know God can also refer to fellowship or, possibly, to understand Him more fully. An obvious illustration of the latter is Jesus' comment to Philip, "*Jesus said to him, 'Have I been so long with you, and yet you have not come to know Me, Philip? He who has seen Me has seen the Father; how can you say, "Show us the Father"?'*" (John 14:9). Here the word "know" means "to recognize who I am." Philip *did* know Christ in the sense of "being saved" but he did *not* yet fully understand who Christ really was.

1054 For the various categories and related verses, see BDAG, 199-200.

1055 Rudolf Bultmann, "*ginōskō*," in TDNT, 1:703.

1056 Adam Clarke suggests "Approveth the way." Adam Clarke, *Adam Clarke's Commentary*, Logos Library System electronic ed. (Albany, OR: Ages Software, 1999). Cf. Psalm 37:18. Many understand the word in Psalms 1:6 to mean "watches over" or "protects." However, the connection "way of life" more naturally suggests approval rather than guarding or protecting.

1057 Ibid, 2:399.

1058 Bultmann, "*ginōskō*," 1:691.

1059 Ibid. 1:703. Cf. Mark 6:38; 13:28-29; Luke 1:18; 1 Corinthians 4:19; 2 Corinthians 13:6.

1060 Adam Clarke suggests that the meaning here is to approve or watch over. Clarke, *Adam Clarke's Commentary*, 1233.

what he does, it is the apostle Paul! Rather, the meaning is "I do not approve," or as the KJV has it, "I allow not."[1061] Paul does not approve of what he does.

In a similar way Paul says, "*If anyone loves God, he is known by Him*" (1 Corinthians 8:3). To be "known" by God one must love Him. Jesus said, "*If you love Me, you will keep My commandments*" (John 14:15). The charismatic prophets did not keep His commandments, that is, the teaching of the Sermon on the Mount. As a result Jesus "never knew" them in the sense of knowing them as believers who had entered into the kingdom way of living. He never approved of them.

In 1 Corinthians 16:18 Paul urges, "Give recognition [i.e., "*know* such men," or "esteem highly," or "approve," Gr *epiginōskō*] to such men," that is, to colleagues who have shown their devoted service. The translations vary: "deserve notice" (GNT); "be proud that you have such people among you" (*The Message*); "deserve recognition" (TNIV); "are worthy of honor" (NIV); "give recognition" (NIV, NRSV). It may mean "to notice with approval" (cf. Ruth 2:10, 19). If this is the meaning of "know" in Matthew 7:23, then Jesus might be saying something like, "I never approved of your ministry," or "I never considered your work worthy of honor."[1062] The Lord will not "give weight to" or "approve" the claims of the carnal prophets in Matthew 7:23 to doing kingdom works in His name. In these instances *ginōskō* takes a meaning similar to the one usage of the other main word for "to know," *oida,* which can mean "esteem highly" or "appreciate" in 1 Thessalonians 5:12-13. Paul told the Corinthians that when he comes he will give no credence to the arrogant, that is, he will "*find out* [Gr *ginōskō*], *not the words of those who are arrogant but their power*" (1 Corinthians 4:19).

One lexicon suggests that in Matthew 7:23 "know" should be understood in the sense of "recognition of a claim."[1063] That could mean, of course, that Jesus does not recognize their claim to be true believers.[1064] However, the context is talking about their claim to be doing ministry in His name, not their claim to be regenerate. The meaning, in that case, might possibly be something like, "I never recognized your claim to be doing ministry in My name," or "I never approved of your ministry." This is the meaning used only two verses earlier when Jesus says in regard to the unregenerate false prophets "*You will know* [Gr *ginōskō,* i.e., recognize their claim to be true prophets] *them by their fruits*" (7:20). Jesus did not know them in the sense that he did not know or recognize their fruit! He knew that about them!

Of course Jesus knew them in one sense! But in comparison to those whose kingdom ministry represented His way of life, He never knew them. If the above references bear on Matthew 7:23, then Jesus is saying something like, "I never recognized and approved of your ministry," or possibly, "I never approved of you." He is using the word "know" not in the sense of an intimate saving relationship but of recognizing the validity of one's lifestyle or one's ministry. Jesus uses the related word *epiginōskō* in this sense in Matthew 17:12

[1061] Zodhiates, G1097. Leon Morris says, "The verb translated *understand* may point to Paul's perplexity as to why he does evil though he earnestly wants to do good. Or the word may be used in the sense 'acknowledge' or 'approve' (cf. 'the LORD knows the way of the righteous,' Psalms 1:6, RSV)." Morris, *The Epistle to the Romans,* 291.

[1062] 1 Corinthians 4:19, NIDNTT, 2:399. According to Barrett, Paul was "*unrecognized and yet recognized*" (i.e., disapproved yet approved, *ginōskō*) (2 Corinthians 6:9), C. K. Barrett, *A Commentary on the Second Epistle to the Corinthians* (New York: Harper & Row, 1973), 189.

[1063] ALGNT 99.

[1064] As Davies and Allison suggest, Davies and Allison, *A Critical and Exegetical Commentary on the Gospel According to Saint Matthew,* 1:717.

when He says that the scribes did not "recognize" (Gr *epiginōskō*) John the Baptist, that is, they did not acknowledge him as the promised Elijah, and so they treated him with contempt. They did not "approve" of him in the sense that they never recognized his ministry as authorized by God.

> *But I say to you that Elijah already came, and they did not recognize [epiginōskō] him, but did to him whatever they wished. So also the Son of Man is going to suffer at their hands (Matthew 17:12).*

Their lack of "knowing" was willful and involved more than mere lack of recognition; it was a moral failure to acknowledge him as a prophet of God (cf. Matthew 11:18; 21:23-27). The Gr *epiginōskō* in this context mens "to indicate that one values the person of another, acknowledge, give recognition to" (BDAG, 369). It is best translated as "approve or acknowledge." Just as the Pharisees did not acknowledge John the Baptist's prophetic ministry as being of God, Jesus will not acknowledge that the prophetic ministry of these lawless believers was of God.

The above discussion establishes the fact that to be known by God does not necessarily mean to be unconditionally elected to salvation from eternity past, as some assume.[1065] Rather, it can mean to have fellowship with Him; to be approved by Him, or even to be chosen by Him to participate in the wedding feast of the Lamb in the New Jerusalem during the tribulation.[1066] As Jesus put it, "*Many are called, but few are chosen*" (Matthew 22:14). Those "chosen" to participate in the feast are those clothed with the proper wedding garment (Matthew 22:12), the righteous acts of the saints (Revelation 19:8). They are chosen to participate in the messianic wedding feast to which all Christians are invited, but only the faithful are chosen to participate.[1067] Those faithful ones are "known" by God.[1068] Only the faithful are approved and will hear Him say, "Well done!"

If our proposals that such language is addressed to a justified saint seem extreme, one only has to turn to the Epistle to the Hebrews to see even stronger language addressed to believers. The writer of the epistle says that "*They are crucifying once again the Son of God to their own harm and holding him up to contempt*" (Hebrews 6:6, ESV). Crucifying again the Son of God! Holding Him up to contempt! No wonder these regenerate saints[1069] harm themselves. Apart from any temporal consequences, they will be severely "harmed" when the Lord Jesus says to them at the Judgment Seat of Christ, "*I never knew you, depart from me, you who practice lawlessness*" (Matthew 7:23). In the Old Testament they were not damned but killed (Deuteronomy 18:20).

1065 For a refutation of the unconditional election view see, Lawrence M. Vance, *The Other Side of Calvinism*, rev. ed. (Pensecola, FL: Vance Publications, 1991, 1999), 382-97.

1066 See chapter 51, The Parable of the Ten Virgins.

1067 Gregory P. Sapaugh, "A Call to the Wedding Celebration: An Exposition of Matthew 22:1-14," *JOTGES* 5, no. 1 (Spring 1992): 11-34.

1068 There is no need to understand Galatians 4:9 (where Paul says we are "known by God") as meaning we were elected in eternity past. Rather it means that we currently enjoy His loving fellowship and intimacy. Similarly, 1 Corinthians 13:12 means then we will perceive Him as fully as a creature can, just as he has perceived, loved, and understood us fully right now.

1069 For proof that those addressed in the Epistle to the Hebrews are regenerate saints, see chapter 41 and especially pp. 641 ff.

The issue at the Judgment Seat of Christ is ethics, not enthusiasm; character, not charismata; a way of life, not signs and wonders.[1070]

The passage in Matthew 7 (cf. Luke 6:26) may allude to Micah 2:11, where false prophets within Israel offered a "prosperity gospel." "The substance of the false teaching is the promise of material prosperity and blessings of the most sensuous character."[1071] These prophets "walk with the wind," not the Holy Spirit, says Micah. Their message is prosperity and wealth, "wine and beer," and not the strong moral demands of a true prophet.

When Jesus rejects their ministry, they will draw back in shame when they see the Lord Jesus in judgment (1 John 2:28).

DOES THIS CONTRADICT GRACE?

But it may be asked, "Is this not a violation of grace?" Did not Jesus die for all our sins?[1072] How can He then rebuke so severely those for whom He died and actually tell them to depart? Does this not put the average Christian under a burden of doubt and fear that he might face such a rebuke at the Judgment Seat of Christ instead of experience joy and reward?

No! It must be remembered that these severe warnings do not apply to all of Christians. We are explicitly told that they apply only to those who "practice lawlessness," that is, lawlessness is their habitual manner of life. They are "evil" servants (Matthew 24:48),[1073] who do not bother to prepare for the Lord's coming (Matthew 25:8),[1074] who care nothing about clothing themselves with righteous works (Matthew 22:10-14),[1075] and who abuse grace by doing little or nothing to commend their life work so that it is all burned up with the result that they are saved only through fire (1 Corinthians 3:15).

No Christian who is sincerely trying to follow Christ, or, to express it in biblical terminology, "fears the Lord," no matter how imperfectly, need fret about these warnings. They do not apply to him. For that believer, there is only anticipation of joy and reward.

> *He has not dealt with us according to our sins, Nor rewarded us according to our iniquities. For as high as the heavens are above the earth, So great is His lovingkindness toward those who fear Him. As far as the east is from the west, so far has He removed our transgressions from us. Just as a father has compassion on his children, so the LORD has compassion on those who fear Him. For He Himself knows our frame; He is mindful that we are but dust (Psalm 103:10–14).*

Jesus "knows our frame" and He is "mindful that we are dust." That is, He understands our weakness and failure and does not condemn us but loves and accepts us.

> *Therefore, since we have a great high priest who has passed through the heavens, Jesus the Son of God, let us hold fast our confession. For we do not have a high priest who cannot sympathize with our weaknesses, but One who has been tempted in all things as we are, yet without sin.*

[1070] Most modern-day "charismatics" would, of course, fully agree with this and do emphasize a kingdom way of life. There are extreme fringes among "evangelicals" as well.

[1071] J. M. P. Smith, W. H. Ward, and J. A. Bewer, *A Critical and Exegetical Commentary on Micah, Zephaniah, Nahum, Obadiah and Joel* (New York: Scribner's Sons, 1911), 63.

[1072] For discussion of the possibility of a negative judgment coming on true Christians, see vol. 3, chapter 59.

[1073] See elsewhere in vol. 3, chapter 51 for a discussion of "wicked" Christians.

[1074] For discussion of the foolish virgins' indifference to preparation for the Lord's return, see vol. 3, chapter 51.

[1075] For discussion of the parable of the wedding banquet, see vol. 3, chapter 49.

Therefore let us draw near with confidence to the throne of grace, so that we may receive mercy and find grace to help in time of need (Hebrews 4:14–16).

Summary

Jesus is telling these regenerate carnal Christians who never represented the Sermon on the Mount as the true manifestation of the kingdom way of life that He never approved of their ministry. He then announces the rebuke, "Depart from me." If this expression refers to the Talmudic ban formula, the *nezipha* and the *niddui* (see excursus in next section), then this does not refer to those who experience *a permanent separation, but only to a temporary separation.*[1076] In a similar way, these false teachers coming from inside the church (Matthew 7:21-23) are not assigned to eternal separation from God, but receive severe rebuke, millennial disinheritance, and exclusion from reigning with Christ in the fulfillment of human destiny, and the celebratory Marriage Banquet (the wedding supper of the Lamb) which occurs in the New Jerusalem prior to the second coming (Revelation 19:7-9). They will enter the "realm," but they will not enter the "reign."[1077] They will weep profoundly because of their exclusion from the final destiny of man in history. Elsewhere, this experience of exclusion is called "outer darkness." Their separation will not be permanent, but they will forfeit reward.[1078]

Because they did not enter the kingdom way of living in the sense of doing the will of the Father, they will not be His partners in the fulfillment of the creation purpose in the future. They will not "enter into high status in the kingdom" on that future day, that is, become great there (Matthew 5:19) and obtain the abundant entrance Peter spoke about (2 Peter 1:11). They will certainly be in it geographically and spiritually, but they will not enter it in the sense of reigning with Christ. They will not participate in Christ's royal authority in the coming age. They will not enter into rest (Hebrews 4:1-13) because they never completed their intended life purpose. As Paul says elsewhere, "*If we endure, we will reign with him*" (2 Timothy 2:15). They did not endure, and therefore they will not enter/reign.

Christ's warning regarding the claims of these believers that they have done works in His name is a reminder for all. Examples of this tendency to assign God's will to our own choices may be found everywhere. Recently, protesters from a Baptist church attended the funeral of a fallen soldier in the war in Afghanistan with signs saying, "God hates gays." Another man claimed to be doing God's will when he murdered an abortion doctor. We have all seen the abuses of many prominent TV evangelists who claim to speak in Jesus' name when they tell their gullible viewers to invest "seed faith" in their TV ministry with the guarantee that God will multiply their mite. They then purchase million-dollar homes, expensive cars, private jets, and bilk thousands in Africa out of their meager funds by soliciting donations for their "ministry." They may be confident of their actions today, but one day Jesus will say to them, "*I never knew you.*"

"I have no regrets." These were the last words of a well-known Christian leader as he lay dying in the hospital. Yet this man, who had "no regrets," had sexually abused his

---

1076 It may be that the phrases "I do not know" you and "depart from me" reflect a temporary exclusion and are a reference to the ban formula in the Talmuds. See Excursus on the Ban Formula at the end of this chapter.

1077 This interpretation differs from my former conclusions expressed in *The Reign of the Servant Kings* where I assumed that these charismatic leaders were in fact unregenerate and had never confessed Jesus as Lord during their lives, even though they were addressing Him as Lord at the judgment.

1078 For full discussion of the duration of remorse see pp. 326, 775 ff.

daughters and some others. His ten-year-old daughter was assured that it was all "in the will of God," because he was a father and a pastor, and he only did what God told him to do. If she resisted, she was told, she would be out of the will of God. However, one day, according to Matthew 7:23, he will learn what the "will of God" for him will be. He will know then what he surely knew in life, that he was not in the will of God, and the Lord will say to him, "Depart from me!"

Recently while speaking at a conference in a church, a small group gathered after dinner one night for interaction on the content of the messages. During the discussion, a significant application of the Lord's warning emerged that I had not formerly considered. A member of the group asked me about Matthew 7:23 and the Lord's strong rebuke to these "prophets" claiming to do ministry in Christ's name. When I explained that in my opinion the phrase "depart from me" was addressed to true believers who practiced lawlessness and who will face rebuke and shame at the Judgment Seat of Christ, a middle-aged woman named Sarah began to tear up. She said, "You have no idea how much this means to me. When I was a child I was severely sexually abused by a near relative. I have struggled with anger and bitterness for years and have worked hard to deal with it. However, all I ever heard from other Christians and from the church was that it was my responsibility to forgive. 'What about him?' I always thought. Does he just get away with it and enter into the kingdom with less reward than others? That does not seem just. To know that he will face this terrible rebuke somehow makes it easier for me to forgive."

This dear lady was finally able to personalize Paul's teaching, *"Vengeance is mine, **I will** repay, says the Lord"* (Romans 12:17). and Christ' example (1 Peter 2:23).

Some speculate about the fate of the unfaithful carnal Christian who dies in the first century. He has been in the blissful presence of Christ for two millennia. Why would Christ then punish him two thousand years later? Did not God promise that He will no longer remember the believer's sins? I answer that the carnal Christian who has committed apostasy, or sexually abused his daughters, and who crucified again the Son of God and held Him up to open shame (Hebrews 6:6), should have thought about those two thousand years of anticipated judgment before he denied Christ. God will remember those sins and will justly punish him by exclusion from the joy of the Wedding Banquet. The passages about God removing our trespasses from us (Psalm 103:12) or "casting sins behind [His] back" (Isaiah 38:17) do not apply to the believer who does not repent of his sins (1 John 1:9). As for the promise that He will "remember their sins no more" (Hebrews 8:12; 10:17), this refers to remembering them in the sense of applying the penalty of eternal damnation. Unconfessed sins within the family will be remembered as the rest of Scripture teaches (John 13:8; 1 Peter 4:7; 1 Corinthians 11:31-33; 2 Corinthians 5:10; 1 Tim 1:20; 1 Samuel 15:23; 2 Chronicles 26:20; Romans 5:12-14, etc.).

What about the fate of the unfaithful carnal Christian who dies in the first century? During many years in the blissful presence of Christ will he live in dread of punishment later? Unless one denies the possibility of any negative consequence at the Judgment Seat of Christ, this difficulty must be faced by all interpreters. Einstein has taught us that there is no such thing as absolute time. Furthermore, if reality is truly composed of seven extra dimensions (as current theory suggests) do we know how time in one dimension would be perceived by beings (i.e., resurrected saints) in another? Therefore, we should not dismiss the possibility that the perception of time in eternity relative to earth time differs dramatically. Two thousand years of time on earth may be perceived as a matter of days or weeks in the eternal state (2 Peter 3:8). The questions regarding the perception of time in the afterlife and how God perceives time, if He does, are the subject of considerable discussion. For example one might consult William Lane Craig's excellent book, *Time and Eternity: Exploring God's Relationship to Time.* Since God is not bound to measure time by the rotation of the earth, we cannot know the flow of time in eternity.

Early in our Christian lives my wife, Linda, and I met a man named Dick who claimed to be a prophet of God. One night he called us about 1:00 a.m. and told us that God had told him something in a "word of knowledge" which he needed to come over to our house immediately and communicate to us. When he arrived, we were informed that God had told him that if I went to seminary, I would be killed and that Linda would be eaten by lions. A year later we learned that Dick had received another prophecy from God which conveniently told him that he was not to pay taxes on his home. The judge was unimpressed.

While these examples are extreme, all of us must be careful that we do not fall into the same trap in our own lives. How often have we claimed to be doing the will of God when in fact we were simply fulfilling our own desires? The critical lesson that Jesus teaches here is that He is more interested in our daily adherence to the Sermon on the Mount than He is with external manifestations of His work in and through us. At the final day, all that will matter is that we made choices every day to enter the "narrow way," the way of kingdom living specified in the Discourse on Discipleship. He is more interested in who we are in our inner lives than He is in what we do for Him. He is more interested in our walk than our work.

Excursus on the Citation of Psalm 6:8

In Psalm 6:8, a sick and weary David demands that his wicked enemies depart from him. It may be that these enemies of David are in fact believers, and David hopes they will repent.[1079] He describes them as those who practice lawlessness.

> *Depart from me, all you who do **iniquity**, for the LORD has heard the voice of my weeping. The LORD has heard my supplication, The LORD receives my prayer. All my enemies will be ashamed and greatly dismayed; they shall **turn back**, they will suddenly be ashamed (Psalm 6:8-10).*

The Heb word for iniquity is ʾāwen, and "one of the basic meanings of ʾāwen is 'trouble.'"[1080] It does not necessarily refer to the essential identity of a person (unsaved); it can refer to his behavior. In the Psalms this is a common designation for the enemies of David or of God and is variously translated as "workers of iniquity," "those who do evil," or "evildoers." However, whether these evildoers are unbelievers or believers is usually not evident from the context. This reference has nothing to do with soteriology. Instead, it refers to political insurrection within the kingdom by usurpers from among the people of the covenant community.

Because the Experimental Predestinarian doctrine of the inevitable perseverance of the saints in holiness is "obviously" true, they naturally assume that enemies of the king must be unbelievers. But the notion that true believers could never be characterized as "troublemakers" or "workers of iniquity" not only flies in the face of common sense, but contradicts two thousand years of Christian experience, as well as the clear testimony of

---

[1079] That is, David desires that they will admit their guilt (repent) and then turn to God (bring forth the fruit of repentance).

[1080] Herbert Livingston, "**ʾāwen**," in TWOT, 23.

numerous passages in the Bible.[1081] To assume that ʾāwen applies only to the unsaved may be too hasty.

Consider what Samuel said to the previously appointed and regenerate, saved king Saul,[1082]

> *For rebellion is as the sin of divination, and insubordination is as iniquity [Heb ʾāwen] and idolatry. Because you have rejected the word of the* Lord*, He has also rejected you from being king (1 Samuel 15:23).*

Saul was an evildoer. Elsewhere in Scripture this epithet (*ʾāwen*) is applied to true believers. They can "speak wickedness" (Isaiah 58:9); the psalmist knows that it is possible that he might "regard wickedness in my heart" (Psalm 66:18) and that wickedness can possibly "have dominion over" him (119:133). He knows that his heart can practice "deeds of wickedness," and he prays that God will keep him from this (141:4). The fact is, it is not possible to know for certain whether a wicked person is an unbeliever or a believer.

As demonstrated elsewhere, the Exodus generation as a group was considered to be regenerate.[1083] They had believed in the Lord (Exodus 4:31; 14:31); had trusted in the blood of the Passover lamb (Exodus 12:27-28); and had believed in Christ (1 Corinthians 10:4-5). Yet the Lord says they are an "*evil* (Heb *raʿ*) *generation,*" and they will not see the good land of Canaan (Deuteronomy 1:34–35). True believers can be evil!

Later in the Psalms, David speaks of the iniquity (*ʾāwen*) of his enemies, and yet concerning one of them he says, "*But it is you, a man my equal, my companion and my familiar friend; we who had sweet fellowship together walked in the house of God in the throng*" (Psalm 55:13–14). This, of course, does not prove that this man was regenerate, but unless we "know" that anyone who opposes David is unsaved, it should give us pause. Neither does the identification "wicked" or "enemy" prove that a man in the Psalms was unregenerate. Soteriology was not on the psalmist's mind; rather, he was concerned about behavior, specifically, rebellion among those who were in the kingdom.

In Psalm 6:10 the NASB renders the Heb *shûv* as "turn back."

> *All my enemies will be ashamed and greatly dismayed; they shall turn back* [Heb *shûv*]; *they will suddenly be ashamed (Psalm 6:10).*

While this is certainly possible, it can also be rendered "return to."[1084] While the idea of the wicked turning from the king is certainly found in the Psalms (9:3; 51:9; 70:4), it is equally possible that in Psalm 6 David is praying to God that his enemies will "return to" God. While this would, of course include "turning back," to David, his burden was for their fellowship with God. The Heb word *shû*v is frequently used of sinners returning to God or of God returning to us. Earlier in the same psalm David prays to God,

> *Return [Heb shûv], O* Lord*, rescue my soul; save me because of Your lovingkindness (Psalm 6:4).*

1081 For extensive proof of this assertion, see vol. 2, chapter 32.

1082 For discussion of Saul's salvation see Zane C. Hodges, "A Voice from the Past: The Salvation of King Saul," *Grace in Focus* November-December 2011.

1083 For proof that the Exodus generation as a whole was viewed a regenerate see discussion on pp. 70 ff.

1084 The word occurs over 1,050 times in the Old Testament with "a rich variety of meanings, some ambiguity about direction (e.g., 'turn back from' or 'turn to')." VanGemeren, *NIDOTTE*, 4:56.

The parallelism is evident. Just as David wants God to "return" to him (v.4), he also prays that his enemies will "return to Him" (v. 10).[1085] The theme of those in rebellion returning back to God is found elsewhere in the Psalms in connection with the rebels in the wilderness.

When He killed them, then they sought Him, and returned [Heb shûv] and searched diligently for God; and they remembered that God was their rock, and the Most High God their Redeemer (Psalm 78:34–35).

In Psalm 51 David prays,

Then I will teach transgressors Your ways, and sinners will be converted [Heb shûv] to You (Psalm 51:13).

The word *shûv* is commonly used of the wicked; their return to God. They are exhorted to "*turn from your evil ways*" (2 Kings 17:13); to "return to the God of Abraham, Isaac, and Jacob" (2 Chronicles 30:6).[1086]

Many view the warning in this positive sense. Luther, for example, says, "He wishes that these, too, would have to experience the wrath of God, so that they would finally recover from their bold presumption and regain their senses."[1087] Adam Clarke concurs, "May they as deeply deplore their transgressions as I have done mine! May *they return*; may they be *suddenly converted*! The original will bear this meaning, and it is the most congenial to Christian principles."[1088] Spurgeon opined, "We pray *for* our enemies, not *against* them. God have mercy on them, and bring them into the right way."[1089]

There are good Old Testament parallels to this meaning of "to turn."[1090] For example, Hosea 3:5 says, "*Afterward the sons of Israel will return* [Heb *shûv*] *and seek the* Lord *their God and David their king; and they will come trembling to the Lord and to His goodness in the last days*" (Hosea 3:5). Jeremiah says, "*Therefore, thus says the Lord, 'If you return* (Heb *shûv*), *then I will restore you—Before Me you will stand*'" (Jeremiah 15:19). The psalmist cries, "*Restore* [Heb *shûv*] *to me the joy of Your salvation, and sustain me with a willing*

1085 John Donne argued that just as shame had been David's way back to God (Psalms 6:3), so also David prays that his enemies will be restored. (Cited by Charles Spurgeon, *The Treasury of David: In Three Volumes* (Grand Rapids: Zondervan Publishing House, 1966), 1:65.

1086 See also Jeremiah 3:22-42 and Ezekiel 14:6.

1087 "Selected Psalms III" in Luther, *Luther's Works*, 14:145.

1088 Clarke, *Adam Clarke's Commentary*, s.v. "Psalm 6:10."

1089 Charles Spurgeon, *The Psalms Vol. 1 and 2* (Wheaton, IL: Crossway Books, 1993), 20.

1090 The psalmist intended this warning "to turn" in either a negative sense (Judges 2:19; Psalms 28:4; 51:12; 56:9; 70:3) a positive sense (Pss. 22:28; 51;13; 78:34; 119:79; Hosea 3:5; 14:7; Jeremiah 15:19; 24:7). He says in Psalms 6:10 "All my enemies will be ashamed and greatly dismayed; they shall turn back, they will suddenly be ashamed" (NASB). These enemies are not consigned to eternal damnation but to dismay and shame in time. When David says that they will "turn back," he uses the Hebrew word shûv, which is the common word for "to turn." It is used 42 times in the Psalms. The word ἀποστρέφω, "to turn back, to turn away," in the LXX is used over 500 times and usually in spatial terms. It is used in some places of turning from sins (2 Chronicles 7:14) or conversion (Isaiah 30:15; Jeremiah 18:11; 23:14; 25:5; Jonah 3:8, 10; Zechariah 1:4). See Georg Bertram, "στρέφω, et. al.," TDNT 7:723. If the negative sense is implied, it could mean turn back in defeat; they stop bothering David (see Charles A. Briggs and Emilie Grace Briggs, *A Critical and Exegetical Commentary on the Book of Psalms*, 2 vols. (Edinburgh: T. & T. Clark, 1906). s.v. "Psalm 6:10"). This is the predominate view, and is succinctly expressed by Hans-Joachim Kraus, who says that God will "strike terror into the hearts of his [David's] enemies, so that they are put to shame and cease to trouble him." Hans-Joachim Kraus, *Psalms 1-59: A Continental Commentary* (Minneapolis: Fortress Press, 1993), 164.

spirit. Then I will teach transgressors Your ways, and sinners will be converted [Heb *shûv*] to You" (Psalm 51:12-13). Of course, God calls on people "to turn" (Psalm 90:3; Jeremiah 3:12; 18:11; 25:5; 35:15; Ezekiel 14:6; 18:30). He calls on the wicked to turn from sin, "*Say to them, 'As I live!' declares the Lord God, 'I take no pleasure in the death of the wicked, but rather that the wicked turn* [Heb *shûv*] *from his way and live,*" (Ezekiel 33:11).

I see no reason to deny this understanding in verse 8. David said of God that He was one who "restores [Heb *shûv*] my soul" (Psalm 23:1). God refreshes souls by turning them back to Him. Why would it be unreasonable to assume that David thus prays for his believing enemies?

Excursus on the Ban Formula in the Talmuds

We might add here the suggestion of Jeremias and others who note that the phrases "I do not know you" and "depart from me" may refer to a teacher's order (*neziphah*), forbidding the student access to the rabbi for seven days and means something like, "I will have nothing to do with you."[1091] John Nolland also suggests that the phrase is "reminiscent of a Jewish ban formula."[1092] Klyne Snodgrass, in his massive work on the parables, believes that the phrase "'I do not know you' in v. 12 may reflect a ban formula in which a disciple is forbidden access to a teacher."[1093] It is possible that the allusion here is to this Jewish custom of being put out of the congregation, a fate that fell on any Jew who confessed Jesus as messiah (John 9:22). However, all these parallels to Jewish literature are uncertain, because they are based mainly on references from the Talmuds in AD 400 to 600. It is debatable how much of this material reflects first-century Palestinian Judaism.

That said, there were three levels of excommunication. Edersheim states that "The first and lightest degree was the so-called *Neziphah* or *Neziphutha*; properly, 'a rebuke,' an inveighing. Ordinarily, its duration extended over seven days; but, if pronounced by the Nasi, or Head of the Sanhedrin, it lasted for thirty days."[1094] "In Palestine it was ordered, that an offending Rabbi should be scourged instead of being excommunicated."[1095] It is possible that this practice is behind the metaphorical reference to an unfaithful servant receiving many lashes (Luke 12:47-48).

The second level was called the *Niddui*, "excluded ones,"[1096] which, while very severe, was also temporary. It was issued for various offenses such as dealing unfairly with another, moral failure, or selfishness in seeking an undue advantage in business. The one who was

---

1091 Joachim Jeremias, *The Parables of Jesus*, 6th ed. (London: SCM, 1963), p.132. Jeremias is apparently referring to Marcus Jastrow, *A Dictionary of the Targumi, the Talmud Babli and Yerushalmi, and the Midreashic Literature* (New York: Judaica, 1985). "The Aramaic word … means a 'rebuke' and a 'lower degree of excommunication.' However, this Talmudic reference, written hundreds of years later, does not necessarily establish that this would have been the understood meaning of the word in Jesus' time." Paul Tanner, PhD, personal communication, July 5, 2005.

1092 John Nolland, *Luke 9:21-18:34*, Word Biblical Commentary (Dallas: Word, 2002), 734.

1093 Klyne Snodgrass, *Stories with Intent: A Comprehensive Guide to the Parables of Jesus* (Grand Rapids: Wm. B. Eerdmans Publishing Co., 2008), 510.

1094 Alfred Edersheim, *The Life and Times of Jesus the Messiah*, New American Edition ed., 2 vols. (Grand Rapids: Wm. B. Eerdmans Publishing Co., 1962). 2:183.

1095 Ibid., 2:183.

1096 From הָדְנ "separation, abomination, defilement," HAL, 673. The verbal form, הָדָנ, "to exclude, i.e. limit an association." Swanson, DBLH, 5611.

rebuked was to endure a 30, 60, or 90-day banishment, and when he turned from his conduct, the ban was terminated.[1097] According to the *Jewish Encyclopedia*,

> *He was forbidden contact with every person excepting his wife and children; and it was forbidden to sit at meals with him, or to count him in the ritual number (minyan) requisite for prayers. A person over whom niddui was pronounced was required to don the habiliments of mourning [possibly alluded to in the "wailing and gnashing of teeth" referred to in a number of passages in the New Testament].[1098] He was, moreover, forbidden to bathe, to cut his hair, and to wear footgear. The modus operandi was to pronounce niddui upon an offender for the period of thirty days, when, having repented* [that is, admitted his guilt] *his conduct, the ban terminated.*[1099]

The highest and most terrible form of the ban was the *cherem,* which was a ban of indefinite duration, but still temporary, if the person banned turned from his sins.

It is possible that Jesus is referring to the *Niddui* because in the Gospels this ban was associated with conduct of great mourning, "*wailing and gnashing of teeth.*" This expression, while used as a metaphor of the mourning of non-Christians in the lake of fire in a few instances, is often in the New Testament applied to the mourning of true Christians who experience rebuke and temporary rejection by Christ at the Judgment Seat of Christ.[1100] During this period of exclusion the *niddui* ("excluded ones") were to allow their beards to grow shaggy and their hair wild and never to bathe. One declared to be of the *niddui* was not admitted into an assembly of ten or more men. He was not allowed to eat and drink with others, and visitors had to maintain a distance of four cubits![1101] The exclusion from meals and table fellowship reminds us of the exclusion of the five foolish virgins from the Marriage Banquet (Matthew 25:1-13) or the refusal to be admitted to the Messianic Banquet with the great ones of Israel's history in Luke 13:25, as will be discussed in the next chapter.[1102] When they request permission to sit with Abraham, Isaac, and Jacob, the Lord pronounces them *niddui*, that is, "*I do not know where you are from.*" The intent of this action was not to consign the offender to eternal separation from God, but to exclude him from his sharing an inheritance with Israel's great ones.[1103] If this is behind the phrase "*I do not know where you are from,*" the exclusion is temporary.

1097 Jewish Encyclopedia, s.v. "anathema." See also discussion in Wolfgang Schrage, "*aposynagōgos,*" TDNT, 7:848.

1098 I will argue later (vol. 3, chapter 49) that this phrase can be applied to the experience of either the believer at the Judgment Seat of Christ or the non-believer in the lake of fire. The context must decide the issue. The expression occurs seven times (Matthew 8:12; 13:42, 50; 22:13; 24:51; 25:30; Luke 13:28). In five places it seems to apply to the experience of true believers when they face final assessment of their lives. In Pauline terms this is the Judgment Seat of Christ. On two instances it describes the experience of one of Christ's servants (Gr *doulos*, Matthew 24:45-51; 25:26-30), once of the "sons of the Kingdom" (Matthew 8:12), once of believers who have not prepared themselves for the Lord's return (Matthew 22:13), and, to those who are sent outside the banquet hall (Luke 13:28). In two other places it refers to the experience of the unregenerate eternally separated from God (Matthew 13:42, 50).

1099 Jewish Encyclopedia, s.v. "anathema."

1100 See discussion in vol. 3, chapter 49.

1101 Schrage, "*aposynagōgos,*" in TDNT, 7:848.

1102 See pp. 333 ff.

1103 Jewish Encyclopedia, s.v. "anathema." This purpose, of course, would not apply at the Judgment Seat of Christ because all believers have been cleansed and purified by the imputation of Christ's righteousness.

23

The Shut Door

WHEN JESUS said to the carnal charismatics, "*I never knew you!*" (Matthew 7:21), He announced their disinheritance and loss of reward in the millennial kingdom. This censure resulted from their lawless lives. On two other occasions He addresses unfaithful Christians at the Judgment Seat of Christ with this same phrase. In Matthew 25:12 He rebuked the foolish virgins, excluding them from the marriage banquet of the Lamb by saying, "I do not know you." The reason was their lack of preparation for His return.[1104]

In this chapter the third of these rejection sayings occurs at the door to the Messianic Banquet on earth which inaugurates the earthly reign of David's Greater Son. At this banquet the great ones of Israel's history will recline at table fellowship with their Messiah (Luke 13:28-29). Christ will take off His robes and serve this gathering of His Metochoi, His servant Kings, who will join with him in the final destiny of man. The wise and foolish virgins from the church age and all the resurrected saints from the Old Testament and Tribulation periods (Daniel 12:2; Revelation 20:4) will seek entrance into this celebration. Yet, for some of them, the door will be shut.

The Parable of the Shut Door

Luke introduces this parable in response to the question posed in verse 23, "*Lord, are there just a few who are being saved?*" The common view is that this refers to deliverance from final damnation.[1105] However, the context of Luke 13 suggests a different kind of salvation, deliverance from the catastrophe soon to fall upon the nation. In vv. 1-3, Jesus has told his listeners that unless they repent, they will experience the same **physical** destruction that the Galileans did. This repeats His theme of looming national destruction. Then in vv. 6-9, he compares the nation to an unfruitful fig tree and warns that if it does not produce fruit it will be "cut down."

> *And he said to the vineyard-keeper, "Behold, for three years I have come looking for fruit on this fig tree without finding any. Cut it down! Why does it even use up the ground?"* (Luke 13:7).

[1104] For discussion of the parable of the ten virgins, see vol. 3, chapter 51.

[1105] Mitzi Minor, "Luke 13:22-30 - The Wrong Question, The Right Door," *Review and Expositor* 91, no. 4 (Fall 1994): 552. Daniel S. Steffen, "The Messianic Banquet And The Eschatology Of Matthew's Gospel," *Global Journal of Classical Theology* 5, no. 2 (January 2006).

Therefore the meaning of the disciples' question was, "How many are joining our movement now in hopes that the nation will escape a future national calamity?"

The Lord does not directly answer their question. Instead, He says that the important question for the believers is not, "How many are being saved from this coming national catastrophe now?" To which His response would be,

"That is God's concern, not yours." The right question is, "How will those of you who are saved now live out your salvation."

Our Lord's application technique is also found in Acts 1:6 where the disciples, after 40 days of post-resurrection teaching on the subject of the kingdom of God, ask, "*Lord, is it at this time You are restoring the kingdom to Israel?*" (Acts 1:6). As in Luke 13:24, the Lord does not directly answer their question but applies the discussion directly to their lives. "*He said to them, 'It is not for you to know times or epochs which the Father has fixed by His own authority; but you will receive power when the Holy Spirit has come upon you; and you shall be My witnesses both in Jerusalem, and in all Judea and Samaria, and even to the remotest part of the earth*'" (Acts 1:7-8).

So in Luke 13:24, instead of answering their question about the number of being saved from the coming national catastrophe), Jesus' exhorted his disciples to "strive to enter by the narrow door."

> *Strive to enter through the narrow door; for many, I tell you, will seek to enter and will not be able* (Luke 13:24).

Notice the tense of the verbs. They are to *strive now* (present tense). Then at the Messianic Banquet they *will seek* (future tense) to enter. Their striving now apparently determines what will happen when they stand outside the door seeking entrance into the banquet (cf. v. 28). The image to follow describes a large group of believers who are in the kingdom and who also seek entrance into the festive celebration that will launch the reign of David's Greater Son.[1106]

Stauffer notes that this goal, which is entrance into the Messianic Banquet, "can be reached only with the full expenditure of all one's energies."[1107] However, this would be a decidedly novel way of obtaining the free gift of eternal life without cost (Revelation 21:6) and by faith alone apart from works (Ephesians 2:8-9)![1108] The imagery suggests that entering the Messianic Banquet by the narrow door is not the same as "going to heaven when one dies." Clearly the banquet is not the millennium, but is a metaphor for an aspect

---

1106 The banquet at the beginning of the messianic reign (Luke 13:22-30) is the "messianic banquet" which occurs "in the kingdom" (v. 29). I distinguish this from the Wedding Banquet in Matthew 22:1-10 which occurs in the New Jerusalem during the tribulation. See pp. 825.

1107 Ethelbert. Stauffer "*agonizomai*" in TDNT, 1:136.

1108 John MacArthur argues that this proves that submission to the Lordship of Christ is a condition for individual salvation. John MacArthur, *The Gospel According to Jesus* (Grand Rapids: Zondervan Publishing House, 1988), 182-83. Darrell Bock suggests, "The idea is not to work one's way to God, but to labor hard at listening and responding to his message. The concept is very much like passages in Proverbs that exhort one to incline the ear to wisdom and pursue it like riches (e.g., Proverbs 2:1–5)." Darrell L. Bock, *Luke 9:51-24:53*, Baker Exegetical Commentary on the New Testament (Grand Rapids: Baker Book House, 1996), 1234. While this view is possible, there is nothing in the context to suggest that a mental striving to understand is the issue. The striving elsewhere is to "do the will of the Father" (Matthew 7:21). One's moral behavior is what is at issue. Their problem is that they were evildoers (v. 27). This naturally suggests something different than striving hard to pay attention.

of the millennium which is obtained by striving and work. This is a parable which is a vehicle for carrying a central truth.[1109] Experimentalists often pass over this problem and leave the reader perplexed about how all this striving to be saved is to be harmonized with the simple gospel offer of believing in Christ through faith alone apart from works. For example, Joel Green says, "The tenses are important: Strive now, for seeking to enter in the future is futile. This places the emphasis on 'striving' in the present, using the athletic metaphor of 'struggle,' employed in Hellenism and Hellenistic Judaism with respect to the practice of virtue and obedience to the law of God."[1110] For Green, "entrance" is soteriological entrance into the kingdom and the condition is not faith alone, but striving with the intensity of an athlete in training and obedience to law. Unconcerned by what he has just taught his readers (another gospel), he moves on without comment.

Writers like Green who believe that entering the narrow door (Luke 13:24) refers to entrance into personal salvation are confronted with the problem that striving and obedience are necessary conditions of entrance.[1111] Of course, the question arises, "How much obedience is necessary for acceptance?" Pagenkemper neatly sidesteps this issue by asserting, "This question is simply not addressed in the text. But the necessity of preparation for acceptance into the kingdom is clear." He asks, "Is this preparation to be distinguished from faith in the work of Jesus on the cross? This is unlikely; although they are not identical, Matthew does not separate the two ideas."[1112] But Matthew *does* separate the two ideas. We see this directly in Matthew 5:19, where lawless false prophets are said to be "in" the kingdom (and therefore saved from damnation). Even though they had faith in Jesus' work on the cross, they had made no preparation for their final entrance into the kingdom, which is entrance into higher status (Matthew 5:20).[1113]

As pointed out above,[1114] while the Christian journeys toward the eschatological kingdom, he continually faces a choice between the broad way and the narrow way. Entering by the narrow way involves the call to discipleship and results in a rich life now and an abundant entrance into the kingdom. This striving is a struggle to live out the principles of the Sermon on the Mount, which requires committed discipleship. The Gr *agonizomai* ("strive") in Luke 13:24 was also used of an athlete putting forth strenuous effort to compete in the games,[1115] "agonizing" through self-discipline and self-denial to obtain the reward in the Isthmian games (1 Corinthians 9:27). This entrance, in contrast to final entrance into heaven, is achieved in part by man's ability (but, of course, by God's

---

[1109] For discussion of the present writer's approach to interpreting parables see pp. 780 ff.

[1110] Joel B. Green, *The Gospel of Luke*, New International Commentary on the New Testment (Grand Rapids: Wm. B. Eerdmans Publishing Co., 1997), 530.

[1111] For example, Mitzi Minor says that Jesus is "making use of the language of a contest or struggle so as to stress the effort needed from those who wish to be saved." Minor, "Luke 13:22-30 - The Wrong Question, The Right Door," 553.

[1112] Karl Pagenkemper, "An Analysis of the Rejection Motif in the Synoptic Parables and Its Relationship to Pauline Soteriology" (PhD diss., Dallas Theological Seminary, 1990), 142.

[1113] For discussion of Matthew 5:19-20 see pp. 279 ff. and 234 ff.

[1114] See elsewhere in this book pp. 291 ff.

[1115] "It denotes to contend in the public games" W. E. Vine, John R. Kohlenberger, and James A. Swanson, *The Expanded Vine's Expository Dictionary of New Testament Words* (Minneapolis: Bethany House, 1984). 2:94. It means to "contest in a struggle" EDNT. 1:25, or "to engage in a contest," BDAG, 17. There could hardly be a more inappropriate word to use for the means of salvation from damnation, for that involves none of this, only faith alone! See discussion of the entry requirements for the Isthmian games in vol. 3, chapters 61 and 65.

enablement, Philippians 4:13). As we shall see, this entrance is not about salvation but concerns reclining at table fellowship at the Messianic Banquet at the beginning of the millennium (Luke 13:29).

Those standing outside the door protest. They had attended meetings where Jesus preached and had had fellowship with Him. They claimed, "*We ate and drank in Your presence, and You taught in our streets*" (Luke 13:26). Does this not satisfy the requirements for entrance to the banquet? Many nominal church members today labor under the same delusion. But only the great ones in Israel's history can be found behind this shut door. This is a gathering of the firstborn, Christ's *Metochoi* ("partners"), and those believers shut out are called "evildoers" and are not permitted into this fellowship. They will be "cast out" from this community of the faithful with whom they are mingled and who are requesting entrance into the celebration.

"*I do not know where you are from*" (Luke 13:27) is our Lord's sobering response to those shut out. The point seems to be that a life of obedience and not just moments of fellowship are necessary for discipleship and entrance to the celebration. As discussed above, this may be an example of the Jewish ban in which disobedient students were *temporarily* banned from the presence of their teacher.[1116] Like the five foolish virgins in the parable of the Wedding Banquet of ten virgins,[1117] their request is denied. In this instance, it is because they are "evildoers," that is, they have performed activities that are "unjust" (Gr *adikia*).[1118] They have committed acts that "violate standards of right conduct."[1119] As discussed above, the citation of Psalm 6:8, in which they are called "wicked" or "evildoers," is not a reference to soteriology, but to one's behavior.[1120] True believers like Solomon, David, and many others[1121] *can* be "wicked" at times in their lives, but one day, they will be held accountable for their lifestyle.

To be called an "evildoer" does not refer to a few incidents of failure, but is a description of the life of the consistently disobedient Christian. The message is clear, sitting at table fellowship with Jesus is only for those who have believed in Him, but believing in Jesus is not enough to qualify one for entrance into the celebratory feast that inaugurates the kingdom. Only committed discipleship, "striving" (v. 24) to enter, qualifies one for this reward. The time is short. They cannot wait forever to make their decision to enter the narrow door, the life of discipleship. Some believers will and some will not.

They are then "cast out." "*There will be weeping and gnashing of teeth there when you see Abraham and Isaac and Jacob and all the prophets in the kingdom of God, but yourselves being cast out*" (Luke 13:28). Cast out of what? If one says they were cast out of the kingdom, that means they had been "in" it. They were not seeking kingdom entrance. They were seeking access to the banquet. Hauck suggests that this means "expulsion from the community"[1122] or to "expel someone from a group."[1123] If so, what group? Conceivably the

---

[1116] See pp. 330 ff.

[1117] See discussion of this parable in vol. 2, chapter 51.

[1118] Louw-Nida, 1:744.

[1119] BDAG, 20.

[1120] See elsewhere in this book pp. 326, 775 ff.

[1121] For extensive documentation of the existence of the permanently carnal Christian see chapter 32.

[1122] Friedrich Hauck, "*ekballō*" in TDNT, 1:158.

[1123] BDAG, 299. Cf Genesis 21:10; John 3:34; Galatians 4:30.

reference is to these disobedient believers being cast out of the total group of believers (all of whom are already in the kingdom and therefore saved) who were seeking entrance to the triumphant Messianic Banquet. Only the faithful are then admitted. The unfaithful are cast out from kingdom fellowship, that is, from reclining at table (v. 29) with the Messiah and His *Metochoi*. Also the word can be softened a bit and is elsewhere translated "led out" with no connotation of force[1124] (Matthew 12:20; Mark 1:12). Perhaps, they are being *sent away*. The following verse makes clear that they are being excluded from the "feast," the celebratory banquet that inaugurates the messianic reign.

The central thought of the parable is exclusion from the group of those who "recline at table," that is, from Christ's *Metochoi*.

What of those remaining? They will now gather at the Messianic Banquet: table with the King, "*And they will come from east and west, and from north and south, and will recline at table in the kingdom of God*" (Luke 13:29). There will be a great multitude of faithful saved people, who will gather from all over the world. Here the Lord refers to people who are not only in the kingdom (like those who are saved yet outside the door of the banquet hall) but to those who also "recline at the table" in the kingdom.[1125] Reclining at the table with the Messiah in His kingdom is a privilege granted only to a few, namely, "*those who have stood by Me in My trials*" (Luke 22:28-30). Note that they recline at the table *in the kingdom of God*. Just as treasure in heaven does not equal heaven, a banquet in the kingdom does not equal the kingdom. The banquet is a metaphor for a temporary time of rejoicing and celebration that inaugurates the kingdom but does not equal it.

In the former scene (Luke 13:24-27) the experience of the carnal believer was described. He experienced weeping and gnashing of his teeth. Here we are concerned with rankings in the kingdom. The Lord summarizes the second scene by saying, "*And indeed there are last who will be first, and there are first who will be last*" (Luke 13:30). This phrase is a common expression found elsewhere in the Gospels of rankings among believers based upon their servanthood in this life.[1126] There is a difference between being "in the kingdom" (v. 28) and being "at the table" (v. 29).[1127]

1124 BDAG, 237.

1125 The word rendered "recline (Gr *anaklithesomai*) at the table" often refers to reclining at a banquet, BDAG, 65. Danker relates it specifically to the messianic wedding banquet in this verse and connects it with Matthew 8:11. The banquet theme is evident even if it is not specifically mentioned. The same word for reclining at a banquet is used in Matthew 8:11 and Luke 12:37.

1126 Matthew 19:30; Mark 9:35; 10:31. See also 1 Corinthians 4:9; 15:8. For example, on Matthew 19:30, Allan H. McNeile says, "It is more probably a rebuke to Peter, and refers to **ranks** in the Kingdom" (p. 283). William Hendricksen says, "In view of the fact that Scripture clearly teaches that there are not only degrees of suffering in the lake of fire (Luke 12:47, 48) but also degrees of glory in the restored universe (1 Corinthians 15:42), the possibility must not be excluded that Jesus means that even among those ultimately saved there will be those who were 'first' in honor, prestige, etc., here, but who will be 'last' in degree of glory there. Similarly that among those ultimately saved there will be those 'last' in reputation here, who will be 'first' there." William Hendriksen, *Exposition of the Gospel According to Luke* (Grand Rapids: Baker Book House, 1978), 708.

1127 The separation in the scene between Luke 13:22-28 and 13:29-30 is further reinforced by the fact that Luke quotes two different scenes from two different chapters in Matthew's account and combines these two separate scenes into one continuous account in his gospel (i.e., Matthew 7:21-23 = Luke 13:22-28 and Matthew 8:11-12 = Luke 13:29-30).

Summary

Our Lord uses the theme of participation in a celebratory banquet in two ways in the Gospels. On two occasions it seems to refer to the Wedding Supper/Banquet of the Lamb that John mentions in Revelation 19:9. This is the marriage banquet of the Lord with His Church in the New Jerusalem during the tribulation (see Matthew. 22:1-14; 25:1-13). In Luke 13:22-30 and Matthew 8:11-12, however, He speaks of Messiah's celebration with the saints of all ages reclining with Abraham, Jacob and all the prophets in the Messianic Banquet that inaugurates the millennial kingdom.

The central point of the parable is the manner of entrance into the Messianic Banquet, and their resulting status (v. 30). One must enter by the narrow way. This is the way of discipleship, of perseverance, of total devotion to Christ and his way of life. This way of entrance requires striving like an athlete. This is the kind of kingdom entrance that we earlier called entering into Christ's way of life which leads to greatness in the kingdom. It is the abundant entrance about which the Apostle Peter spoke (1 Peter 1:11). The result of this strenuous effort is worth it. The faithful disciple will have the high privilege of joining with Abraham, Isaac, Jacob and the other great ones in Israel's history as co-heirs of Messiah in the final destiny of man.

Those believers, who did not choose the narrow way, but lived carnal, lawless lives, will be shut out when they seek entrance into the Messianic Banquet. They will be led away (Gr *ekballow*, "from a position, without force, send out/away, release," BDAG, 299.) Their argument will be that they had some degree of association with Jesus at His meetings and listened to his messages. Like some church members today, they will hear to sobering words, "I do not know where you are from." That is to say, "You may have been a neighbor, you may have been religious, but we never had fellowship."

So in answer to the question, "How many will be saved?", we offer this interpretive paraphrase of our Lord's response,

> *Don't worry about what will happen to others. Instead, focus on your own life and strive to enter by the narrow gate and pursue the narrow way of discipleship so that you might obtain a rich entrance into the Messianic Banquet. Your response to the call to discipleship involves eternal issues, your participation in the final destiny of man in the coming kingdom. If you chose the broad way, you will be excluded from your inheritance and reward in the great future. Only by choosing the narrow way throughout your life will you recline at a table with the great ones of Israel's history, and thus find final salvation in the fullest sense. There will be some startling reversals then. Some who are first now, will be last then.*

24

The Rich Young Ruler

FEW PASSAGES of Scripture have exercised the ingenuity of interpreters as much as those in which Jesus interacts in one case with a lawyer (Luke 10:25-29), and in the second, with a rich young ruler (Luke 18:18-30; Matthew 19:16-30). Both want to know, "*What shall I do to inherit eternal life*?" The latter's question is rephrased by Matthew, "*Teacher, what good thing shall I do that I may obtain eternal life?*"

In each instance Jesus' response to these questions involves something they must *do*, apparently implying that inheriting eternal life is achieved by works. If inheriting or obtaining eternal life refers to going to heaven when one dies, this seems to put Jesus in contradiction with Himself in the Gospel of John where he stressed that obtaining eternal life comes through faith and no other conditions are mentioned. And it also appears to throw Jesus into conflict with the rest of the New Testament.

Interpreters from all theological backgrounds have struggled with this difficulty. One writer posits that the rich young ruler was not asking about how to obtain salvation, but rather wanted to know how he could be assured of salvation.[1128] Some simply ignore the problem and leave the reader perplexed about the requirements to obey the Ten Commandments as a condition for obtaining eternal life.[1129] Others suggest that because he was seeking heaven on the basis of works, Jesus speaks to him from his viewpoint and tells him what he must do if he wants to pursue that approach. Thus Jesus is not endorsing his theology but is using the man's theology to show him his shallow understanding of the commandments. Obtaining heaven by works requires perfect obedience to the Ten Commandments.[1130] According to another interpreter, Jesus intended His words to show the young man that he lacked "the one all-comprehensive requirement of the law—the *absolute subjection of the heart to God,* and this vitiated all his other obediences."[1131] How this can be an explanation of the way to heaven as expressed in the rest of the New Testament, which is by faith and not by works, is never clarified! Another writer simply asserts, "Faith is assumed; judgment is on the basis of performance."[1132]

1128 Louis Barbieri, "Matthew," in *BKC: New Testament*, ed. John Walvord and Roy B. Zuck (Colorado Springs: Cook, 1996), 64.

1129 John L. McKenzie, "Matthew," in *The Jerome Biblical Commentary*, ed. Raymond E. Brown, Joseph A. Fitzmyer, and Roland E. Murphy (Englewood Cliffs, NJ: Prentice-Hall, 1996), 2:96.

1130 Hendriksen and Kistemaker, *Exposition of the Gospel According to Matthew*, 725.

1131 David Brown, "Matthew," in *Commentary Critical and Explanatory on the Whole Bible*, ed. Robert Jamieson, A. R. Fausset, and David Brown (Oak Harbor, WA: Logos Research Systems, 1997).

1132 Douglas R. A. Hare, *Matthew*, Interpretation: A Bible Commentary for Teaching and Preaching (Louisville: John Knox Press, 1993), 228.

Another commentator says that the purpose of Jesus' citation of the commandments was to show the young ruler that money was keeping him from making a saving commitment to Christ.[1133] Another writer avows that what Jesus teaches here is that the only way to enter the kingdom (i.e., go to heaven when you die) is via the route of discipleship. Like many others, this writer fails to explain theologically how this can be correlated with salvation by grace through faith, although, curiously, he denies that Jesus is here teaching that salvation can be gained by simple obedience to the commandments.[1134]

Within Reformed circles a new paradigm called Federal Vision or the Auburn Avenue Theology has emerged. This might be called "neonomism," the new legalism. In this view the rich young ruler is seeking salvation by works and that is what Jesus offers him. Salvation is a process of becoming eligible for final justification by means of non-meritorious works produced in the believer by God.[1135]

A recent scholar similarly leaves us perplexed by asserting that Jesus is calling upon the young man to become a genuine (in contrast to spurious) disciple and that all Christians are genuine disciples. Thus, we are again left wondering how this call to obedience can be related to the free offer of the gospel.[1136]

A recent scholarly work maintains that Jesus' intent was "to force the ruler to trust God and humbly rely upon him."[1137] Another commentator suggests that the intent of Jesus' words is not to teach salvation by works, which is impossible, but to test the sincerity of the young man's desire for eternal life (entrance into heaven when he dies).[1138]

A former professor and department head at Dallas Theological Seminary understands the young man to be asking about heavenly reward. However, before he can obtain reward, he must first be directed to trust the Good Teacher for initial salvation. For this to occur, the young ruler's self-righteous façade must be penetrated. Jesus does this by showing him that he emphatically has not kept all the commandments.[1139]

Obviously, there is no consensus on the meaning of Jesus' words. According to the traditional interpretation, a young man approached Jesus, sincerely wanting to know how to go to heaven and Jesus never tells him. Instead, Jesus leaves him with the impression that to obtain eternal life he must obey God; therefore, entrance into heaven would be predicated on works. In view of the fact that many of the interpretations leave us theologically unsatisfied, or contradict each other, perhaps it is time to consider a new approach.

Contextual Setting

The encounter with this young man (Luke 18:18-34; Matthew 19:16-30; Mark 10:17-26) occurs within the broader context of Jesus' final journey to Jerusalem (Luke 9:51-19:48).

[1133] Blomberg, *Matthew*, 229.

[1134] Hagner, *Matthew 14-28*, 558.

[1135] For example, Stanley, *Did Jesus Teach Salvation by Works*. See also Rainbow, *Way of Salvation*, 155-74.

[1136] Craig S. Keener, *A Commentary on the Gospel of Matthew* (Grand Rapids: Wm. B. Eerdmans Publishing Co., 1999), 476.

[1137] Bock, *Luke 9:51-24:53*, 1482.

[1138] Norval Geldenhuys, *The Gospel of Luke*, New International Commentary on the New Testament (Grand Rapids: Wm. B. Eerdmans Publishing Co., 1977), 459.

[1139] Hodges, *Absolutely Free! A Biblical Reply to Lordship Salvation*, 187.

A theme that occurs on several occasions during this section of Luke is the subject of humility as the route to significance.

The answer in the verses immediately preceding the encounter with the rich young ruler is the story of being like a little child as a condition of kingdom entrance. Like a child, one must assume lower status.[1140] The key characteristic of a small child is not his faith, but his insignificance. The teaching here is that "status in the kingdom is often inversely proportional to status in the world."[1141] A little child is the lowest rung on the social ladder. Keener notes that to "become as children, refers to assuming a child's low status rather than a characteristic like humility."[1142] Hagner agrees, "The child's humility is his lack of status, not his actions or feelings of humbleness."[1143] Our Lord teaches that "the kingdom of heaven *belongs* to such as these" (Matthew 19:14; Luke 18:16). In Luke's expanded version he seems to equate ownership of the kingdom with "receiving the kingdom" and both refer to obtaining high status there and do not relate to soteriological entrance.

> *And they were bringing even their babies to Him so that He would touch them, but when the disciples saw it, they began rebuking them. But Jesus called for them, saying, "Permit the children to come to Me, and do not hinder them, for* ***the kingdom of God belongs to such as these****. "Truly I say to you, whoever does not* ***receive the kingdom of God*** *like a child will not* ***enter it*** *at all"* (Luke 18:15-17; Matthew 19:13-15).

The issue is ownership of the kingdom ("belongs to"). Receiving the kingdom in Luke 19:15 = receiving royal authority there – it does not refer to receiving salvation. I suggest that "kingdom" means "royal authority."

> *When he returned,* ***after receiving the kingdom****, he ordered that these slaves, to whom he had given the money, be called to him so that he might know what business they had done (Luke 19:15).*

In Luke 18:17, Jesus says that if one does not receive the kingdom by taking the lowest status, he will not "enter" it. The words "at all" are not in the Greek text. The text should be read, ***"Whoever does not receive royal authority by taking the lowest status now will not enter into royal authority in the coming kingdom."*** "Entering the kingdom" does not refer to going to heaven when one dies; rather, it means to enter into the experience of ruling there, or to enter into greatness (Matthew 5:19-20). It is the successful conclusion of a life well-lived.

And immediately following this blessing on the children,

> *A ruler questioned Him, saying, "Good Teacher, what shall I do to inherit eternal life?"* (Luke 18:18; Matthew 19:16)

In Matthew's version we read,

1140 For fuller discussion of the story of Christ and the little children, see pp. 280 ff.

1141 Keener, *A Commentary on the Gospel of Matthew*, 447.

1142 Ibid., 447.

1143 Hagner, *Matthew 14-28*, 518.

And someone came to Him and said, "Teacher, what good thing shall I do that I may obtain eternal life?" (Matthew 19:16).

Apparently, inheriting eternal life and obtaining eternal life are the same thing.

The teaching that only the humble can obtain ownership (ruling authority) of the kingdom fits the broader context precisely, where we have been told twice that he who humbles himself will be exalted. High honor in the kingdom comes to those who adopt the lowest status now. As Jesus put it in Matthew's account, "*Whoever wishes to become great among you shall be your servant, and whoever wishes to be first among you shall be your slave*" (Matthew 20:26-27).[1144]

The encounter with the rich young ruler has a chiastic structure.

A	**RECEIVE KINGDOM AS A CHILD (MATTHEW 19:14)**
B	**RICH YOUNG RULER (MATTHEW 16-29)**
A'	**THE FIRST WILL BE LAST, AND THE LAST FIRST (MATTHEW 19:30)**

Lines A and A' bracket the encounter, setting it in a context of the requirement for humility if one is to "own" or "receive the kingdom" (that is, receive royal authority there). We shall see that the rich young ruler's question regarding inheriting eternal life is contextually linked with this *inclusio* and relates not to soteriology, but to the requirements for status.

Regarding "B" in the above, there are three requirements for inheriting eternal life, that is, becoming "complete" (Matthew 19:20), and obtaining treasure in heaven (v. 21). They are: (1) keep the commandments (Matthew 19:17); (2) sell all that you have and give to the poor (Matthew 19:21); and (3) come, follow me (Matthew 19:21). These do not look like conditions for obtaining personal salvation which comes to us by faith alone and without cost!

Matthew begins and ends the discussion with the theme of humility. He concludes the statement, "*But many who are first will be last; and the last, first*" a reference to status, not soteriology (Matthew 19:30, cf. Luke 18:14). Some writers, starting off with the false premise that the encounter is about soteriology, fall into serious theological difficulties regarding works as necessary condition for salvation; difficulties from which they often labor without success to extract themselves.[1145]

The structure of the passage tells us something else. The phrases "enter into life" and "if you wish to be complete" (Gr *teleios*) appear to be parallel to each other. Entering into life and becoming "complete" may be related ideas. *Teleios* is a common word for spiritual maturity of a full disciple. BDAG defines it as "being fully developed in a moral sense," (p. 996). Like its cognate, *telos*, it implies a goal. The sense of "accomplishment of a task" is

[1144] Matthew and Mark's reports of this encounter begin and end with the question of ranking in the kingdom. Luke omits the logion regarding "first and last," but the idea may be present in the promise of leaving all and receiving the reward of many times as much in the age to come (Luke 18:30).

[1145] For example Stanley says that works are a demonstration of salvation, "Jesus expected that anyone who will enter into life at the end of the age will have demonstrated a practical outworking of righteousness." Alan P. Stanley, "The Rich Young Ruler and Salvation," *BibSac* 649, no. 163 (January - March 2006): 58. There is nothing in the text that even hints at this. Works such as selling all that one has are not manifestations of salvation, they are conditions for obtaining it. This difficulty will be explained below.

found in many places. Passages in LXX illustrate this meaning. For example, Nehemiah refers to the fact that after the wall had been built, "*the work had been accomplished*" (Gr *teleioō,* Nehemiah 6:16; cf. 2 Chronicles 8:16).

Jesus apparently understands this young man to be asking about how to finish what he has begun. We will argue below that he wants to know how he can bring his initial belief to a successful conclusion. He wants to live with the end in view. He wants to know how he can *accomplish that goal.* He is asking a very significant question. This understanding is confirmed by Jesus' statement that if one does become "complete," his reward will be "treasure in heaven" (Matthew 19:21), something that is in addition to initial salvation.

Definition of Key Terms

The crux for understanding the story of the rich young ruler revolves around the meaning of some key phrases. In Matthew's account, the rich young ruler asks, "*What shall I do to obtain eternal life*" (Matthew 19:16)? Both Mark and Luke's accounts vary the query asking, "*What shall I do to inherit eternal life*" (Mark 10:17; Luke 18:18), and the lawyer in another encounter in Luke asks the same question (Luke 10:25). Turning to His disciples, Jesus commented about the rich young ruler, "*How hard it is for a rich man to enter the kingdom of God*" (Luke 18:25). By this phrase, the disciples understand that Jesus was explaining how difficult it is for a rich man to be "saved" (Luke 18:26). To the lawyer, Jesus simply says, "*Do this and you will live*" (Luke 10:28). In Mark and Matthew's versions, Jesus responds to the rich young ruler by saying, "*Go, sell whatsoever thou hast, and give to the poor, and you will have treasure in heaven. Then come, follow me*" (Matthew 19:21; Mark 10:21). Matthew alone adds the phrase that by selling all, the rich young ruler can become "complete" (Matthew 19:21), and in Luke Jesus says, "*One thing you lack*" (Luke 18:22).

The immediate impression is that the phrases "obtain eternal life," "inherit eternal life," be "saved," "be perfect," "enter the kingdom of God," "have treasure in heaven," and "you will live" are either equivalent or closely related concepts. The traditional interpretation correctly assumes this, but in my view, it is incorrect in assuming that all these terms mean "go to heaven when you die."[1146] When these terms are all understood in a soteriological sense, the method Jesus prescribes for obtaining eternal life ("do this," "keep the commandments," "sell that which you have," "love the Lord your God with all your heart, soul, and mind," etc.) creates an interpretive problem. Does Jesus teach in these passages that entrance into heaven is based on something a person must do in contradiction to what He has said elsewhere that salvation is by faith alone (John 3:16)?[1147]

A number of evangelical writers have concluded that we simply must abandon the Reformation *sola fide*, "by faith alone" and candidly admit that salvation is by faith plus

---

[1146] Contra Robert L. Thomas, "The Rich Young Man in Matthew," *GTJ* 3, no. 2 (1982): 258. Also, even though I disagree with Thomas Schreiner's interpretation of Mark 10:17-26, he is correct when he says, "Notice that the terms 'eternal life' (v. 17), 'kingdom of God' (vv. 24–25), and 'saved' (v. 26) are all synonyms in this text. There is no evidence whatsoever for distinguishing between them. Indeed, in this passage 'treasure in heaven' is also a term for eternal life (v. 21). See "Perseverance and Assurance: A Survey and a Proposal," 46.

[1147] "Reading Matthew 19:16–30 one might suppose that salvation is according to works: one must obey the Torah and Jesus Christ. But Matthew 20:1–15 disallows this simplistic interpretation. For it clearly teaches, albeit in a picture, that there is no necessary proportion between human work and divine reward." Davies and Allison, *A Critical and Exegetical Commentary on the Gospel According to Saint Matthew*, 76.

works.[1148] Like the Roman Catholics, however, they mean works of the Christian, not the works of the nonbeliever. Some who espouse this view understand these works of the nonbeliever as "works of law,"[1149] and they do not avail for salvation. However, the works produced by the Holy Spirit in response to faith, they say, are non-meritorious and are a "condition" for entering the kingdom of heaven.[1150] In this view salvation is a lifelong process, a pilgrimage,[1151] not an event, and justification occurs in two stages. Stage one is in response to faith and involves the "initial" justification. But stage two is in response to and is conditioned on good works and occurs at the Judgment Seat of Christ, which they equate with the Great White Throne Judgment.[1152] The account of the rich young ruler is a central passage to which their theology appeals.[1153] What do these phrases mean?

The young man's question and Jesus' answer have spawned volumes of ink; raising a number of interesting questions. Who was this young man? Was he a believer in Christ or a nonbelieving inquirer? What does he mean by getting "eternal life"? Is he asking how to go to heaven when he dies? Opinions differ and the discussion to follow will not settle the issue, but hopefully it will point the way toward a plausible solution to the many questions this encounter raises.

Before we can answer the question, "What does Jesus mean by 'life'?" we must first ask, "Who was this young man?" If he was a believer, then we know that he already has "life" in the sense of regeneration, and this would immediately change our understanding of his real question.

Who Was This Young Man?

Was this young man a believer? We do not know for sure, but there are indications that he may have been. We are told seven things about him. Luke says he was a ruler, probably meaning that he was an influential wealthy man or civic leader who was known for his piety.[1154] This is impressive. Not many rulers were drawn to Christ, but this young man was, and unlike Nicodemus, he was willing to come in the light of day, indicating courage. "Despite his high social standing he made no attempt to conceal his need and his

---

1148 For example, Stanley, *Did Jesus Teach Salvation by Works*, 166-293. See also Rainbow, *Way of Salvation*, 155-74. Stanley says, "It is evident that one's conduct evidently plays a role in determining one's eternal destiny" (p. 187), and "we cannot deny that Jesus demanded obedience to enter into eschatological life," 196. Stanley does not mean just that works are only an evidence of regeneration. He believes that they are an inferior cause of eternal life and that eternal life is a consequence of works (p. 198). He quotes Calvin with approval, Calvin, "Institutes," 3.14.21. From Luke 13:25-30 he derives the condition for salvation that one must "strain every nerve." He believes that salvation is "via endurance," and that endurance is a "condition" of salvation. Stanley is clear that texts speaking of endurance and "say nothing about endurance being a demonstration ... of salvation. Jesus does not say 'The one who endures to the end will demonstrate he is saved" (p. 248). Stanley confusedly does not feel that "condition" carries the baggage of "gaining merit or favor." Yet that "baggage" is what Jesus referred to when He spoke about the last being first and the first being last in his summary of the encounter (Matthew 19:30).

1149 Rainbow, *Way of Salvation*, 194.

1150 Stanley, *Did Jesus Teach Salvation by Works*, 197-98.

1151 "My point here is simply that Jesus understands salvation to be a pilgrimage," ibid., 142.

1152 Rainbow, *Way of Salvation*, 155-74.

1153 Stanley, *Did Jesus Teach Salvation by Works*, 188-219.

1154 Suggested by Bock, *Luke 9:51-24:53*, 1476.

admiration for Jesus."[1155] Also, he was young,[1156] extremely wealthy,[1157] and owned much property.[1158] His approach to Jesus was respectful and enthusiastic. He likely heard the Lord Jesus speak several times and wondered if He would answer his heart-searching question. This writer would assume that he believed Jesus to be the Messiah, just as many among the crowds did (John 7:31; 8:31). Seeing Jesus from afar, he came running to see him, and illustrating submission and respect, he knelt at Jesus' feet.[1159] He illustrates spiritual discernment and acknowledges Jesus as Lord by calling him "Good Master," which may be an indication that he believed Christ was the Messiah. He evidences a spiritual vitality and interest by asking, "What must I do to inherit eternal life?" He not only believes in God and sees Jesus as one sent from God, but he is morally upright. "*All these things*," he says, "*I have kept from my youth*." Jesus never challenges this claim. Furthermore he came with a spirit of obedience saying, "*What good thing must I do*," and with the spirit of a disciple desiring to be taught a matter of great importance he called Jesus "*Rabbi*," a respectful title.[1160] It should also be noted that Jesus "*loved him*."[1161] Apparently, then, the man was not insincere, as some have suggested. Here is a man who believes in God and Christ; he has both the character and the works that, according to Experimental Predestinarians, give evidence that his faith is real. Because he meets the required tests for genuine faith, Experimental Predestinarians should grant that he is a saved man.

Of significance is the fact that in Luke's account, after the ruler says, "*All these things I have kept from my youth*" Jesus replies, "*One thing you lack*" (Luke 18:22). Think of it – only "one thing"! Most of us could think of many things we lack. Baxter asks, "Could there be any finer commendation of this young man's character than for Jesus to say, 'One thing you lack?'"[1162] If inheriting eternal life means "get saved" and this young man lacks only one thing, surely He who came to die for our sins would say (as He did to Nicodemus), "*Whoever believes in him will never perish*." But He does not say that, because believing is not what he lacked nor was his question about how to obtain eternal salvation. Instead, Jesus gives this young man another work to do: "*Sell all that you possess, and distribute it to the poor, and you shall have treasure in heaven; and come, follow Me*." It is difficult to imagine that the Savior who "loved him" would leave this man hanging on the precipice of damnation with no hope, and tell him an untruth that by obeying commandments he can earn heaven. Therefore William Brown's assertion that "it is clear that the young man did not possess eternal life" is incorrect.[1163]

To explain why Jesus did not state that the way of salvation is by faith alone, Brown appeals to the other passages in the gospel of Matthew where kingdom entrance is conditioned on works (e.g., Matthew 5:20; 7:21) and asserts (without proof) that "faith is

---

1155 J. Sidlow Baxter, *Mark These Men: Practical Studies in Striking Aspects of Certain Bible Characters* (Grand Rapids: Zondervan Publishing House, 1960), 112.

1156 Matthew 19:20.

1157 Luke 18:23.

1158 Matthew 19:22.

1159 Mark 10:17.

1160 Luke 18:18.

1161 Mark 10:21.

1162 Baxter, *Mark These Men: Practical Studies in Striking Aspects of Certain Bible Characters*, 115.

1163 Brown, "The New Testament Concept of the Believer's Inheritance", 69.

implicit in the reception of Jesus' word and the appropriation of salvation."[1164] His problem is that he equates the "appropriation of salvation" (justification) which is by faith alone with inheriting the kingdom and entering life which, on the authority of the Lord Jesus in this passage, is obtained by faith plus works. The issue for the rich young ruler is sanctification and treasure (reward), not soteriology, as the following discussion will show.

Entering into Life

The first phrase requiring precise definition is "enter into life." What kind of life is in view, a full life now or final entrance into heaven?

> *And someone came to Him and said, "Teacher, what good thing shall I do that I may* ***obtain eternal life****? And He said to him, "Why are you asking Me about what is good? There is only One who is good; but if you wish* ***to enter into life****, keep the commandments" (Matthew 19:16, 17).*

The young man's question is variously reported as "*What good thing shall I do that I may obtain eternal life?*"[1165] or, in Mark and Luke's versions, "*What shall I do to inherit eternal life?*"[1166] In response to his question, Jesus replies, "*If you wish to enter into life, keep the commandments.*"[1167] Apparently "inheriting," "obtaining," and "entering" life refer to the same thing and relate to entering the kingdom as well.

THE HYPOTHETICAL "HIDDEN PREMISE" VIEW

Leon Morris assures his readers that by "life" Jesus "clearly meant life in the age to come, life in the final kingdom that God would set up."[1168] However, this is not clear. It results in Jesus teaching that entrance into heaven is obtained by means of works, a view that developed later in the Patristic writings. As will be demonstrated below, "life" does not mean heaven when one dies, but refers to a rich experience of life now *leading to* treasure (reward) *in* heaven.

The traditional view of the meaning of obtaining life is that it refers to final entrance into heaven. In agreement with Morris, Bock writes,

> *The ruler is asking, "How can I be sure I'll be saved in the final resurrection?" This is a basic soteriological question not referring to reward for service but to the eternal life that comes from being God's child. This is clear from the context: 18:17 discusses entry into the kingdom and 18:28–30 makes the point that basic spiritual benefits come in this life and the next.*[1169]

As we shall see, the context does not make this "clear" at all but in fact decisively argues against this viewpoint!

[1164] Ibid., 76.

[1165] Matthew 19:16.

[1166] Mark 10:17; Luke 18:17.

[1167] Matthew 19:16.

[1168] Morris, *The Gospel According to Matthew*, 489.

[1169] Bock, *Luke 9:51-24:53*, 1476.

Those, like Bock, who understand that the rich young ruler asks how he can be sure he will enter heaven when he dies run into difficulty because entering heaven would then be conditioned on keeping commandments and selling all one's possessions. Bock then adds, "*If* one is going to earn eternal life then acts of righteousness are required."[1170] Bock uses the word "if," but he has the burden of proof to establish this. Having stated that to "inherit eternal life" refers to personal salvation, Bock, in order to maintain his biblical commitment to faith alone as the only condition for personal salvation, feels he needs to introduce a word, "if," which is a hidden premise. However, this is not even hinted at in the text. This "hidden premise," that works would save *if* one could do them perfectly, is in direct contradiction to what Jesus specifically says (John 3:16). Bock suggests that Jesus is not saying works are a condition for inheriting eternal life. Instead, he believes this is only a misunderstanding by the rich young ruler.

Hendriksen and Kistemaker say, "If any human being would actually fulfill this law of love to perfection, he would indeed obtain everlasting life."[1171] Since no one can perfectly fulfill the law, they argue that Jesus is pointing out to the lawyer that no one can be saved using a legal approach. However, there is not even a hint in the passage that this is hypothetical. Inheriting everlasting life is clearly conditioned on works. Both of these writers end up contradicting the plain meaning of the text because they begin with the false premise that to "inherit eternal life" means "go to heaven when one dies." It is unclear how Jesus could have said it more plainly; *inheriting eternal life is indeed based on works*!

Wakefield, as cited in Chapter 13, vigorously objects to this "hypothetical view," noting that it involves Christ making a false promise. "And worse yet, that precise combination, the fact that God offers a promise which he most certainly knows can never be actualized, makes the promise seem not just false, but deceptive, the perpetration of a divine fraud."[1172] Raisanen agrees. When he explains Paul's use of the same phrase in Romans 10:5, he writes that Paul "gets involved in the cynicism that God explicitly provides men with a law 'unto life' while knowing from the start that this instrument will not work."[1173] Surely, there is a better way of handling this difficulty than contradicting the plain reading of the text![1174]

One can agree with the Catholics that there is no evidence in the context to support the Experimental Predestinarian interpretation that this is a hypothetical description of what one must do to be saved if one wants to be saved by works.[1175] The issue for this young man is not faith, rather "In the clearest language possible, Jesus teaches that the central issue is whether he has combined his faith with works of love sufficiently to gain eternal life."[1176] In fact this man claims he has obeyed the Law for the most part and Jesus does not challenge his claim. To the contrary, when Jesus hears him say, "*All this I have done since*

1170 Ibid., 1478. (italics added)

1171 Hendriksen and Kistemaker, *Exposition of the Gospel According to Matthew*, 592.

1172 Wakefield, *Where to Live: The Hermeneutical Significance of Paul's Citations from Scripture in Galatians 3:1-14*, 81.

1173 Raisanen, *Paul and the Law*, 265. Cited by Westerholm, *Israel's Law and the Church's Faith*, 101.

1174 For thorough discussion of the hypothetical view, see Chapter 13, "Excursus on the Hypothetical View."

1175 The Catholic apologist, Robert Sungenis, is quite right when he says, "In effect, they [Protestant interpreters like John MacArthur] say that Jesus is giving a misleading answer to the rich young man in an effort to show him that the Law cannot save him." Robert A. Sungenis, *Not by Faith Alone: The Biblical Evidence for the Catholic Doctrine of Justification* (Goleta, CA: Queenship Publishing, 1997), 179.

1176 Ibid., 181.

my youth," Jesus "*felt a love for him*" (Mark 10:20-21) and told him that "*There is only one thing you lack*" (Luke 18:22).

THE FAITH-PLUS-WORKS VIEW

Neonomians agree with Bock that "inherit eternal life" means "be saved from eternal damnation." For example, Alan Stanley argues that the ruler's question is about how he might obtain soteriological entrance into final salvation.[1177] Because Jesus said, "Keep the commandments," Stanley concludes that final entrance into heaven is conditioned upon works.[1178] He argues that the rich young ruler is asking about the final stage of salvation which, in Stanley's view, is obtained by the post-conversion non-meritorious works of the regenerate man.[1179]

If the above discussion is correct, both the Experimental Predestinarian hypothetical (Bock) and Neonomian (Stanley) solutions fail. They fail because they are both committed to the idea that to "inherit eternal life" means obtain final entrance into heaven. It does not. As the following context makes clear, inheriting eternal life and finding treasure/reward in heaven is obtained by means of becoming "complete" in one's commitment to discipleship; by saving one's soul.

ENTERING INTO A RICH LIFE NOW

Is there another alternative? This writer finds the Partner viewpoint quite compelling. If this young man was indeed regenerate, what does he mean when he says that he wants to "obtain" (Gr *echō*) or "inherit" eternal life? A regenerate man already has it. And why, in answer to his request, does Jesus tell him to obey the Law, sell all that he has, and follow Him?

[1177] Stanley, *Did Jesus Teach Salvation by Works*, 194-99. Stanley believes Jesus demands obedience to enter into eschatological life, that is, the glorified state (p. 196). Earlier, he defined eternal life, not only as the glorified state, but as a pilgrimage beginning with entrance and ending with perfection (ibid., 143). Eternal life, he says, is something to be enjoyed and experienced now (ibid., 142). A rich life now seems to be the focus in the encounter with the rich young ruler.

[1178] In his book, *Did Jesus Teach Salvation by Works,* Stanley is very explicit about this. He believes salvation is a "way of life rather than a one-time conversion experience" (ibid., 167), merging justification and sanctification, as did the Council of Trent. This way of life involves discipleship (ibid., 164). He says that when a person is initially justified, he may not yet be eligible to enter the kingdom on the last day (he feels this is soteriological entrance). But, "somewhere along the way converted sinners evidently become righteous and therefore eligible to enter the kingdom" (ibid., 175). He is clear that salvation is "via endurance" (ibid., 248) and that endurance is not a demonstration of salvation but is a condition (ibid., 248). Confusedly, he appears to contradict himself and says that "endurance does not cause salvation but is a demonstration of it" (ibid., 252). He argues that this contradiction is resolved because there is an "inseparable relationship" between faith and endurance (ibid., 253). Apparently, it is OK for works to be a condition of salvation so long as they do not cause it! Not only are works and endurance conditions of final salvation, according to Stanley, but how we treat others is also a condition. We must not have anger (ibid., 261-67); we must love our enemies (ibid., 267-73), and forgive others, or we will be condemned to "eternal damnation" (ibid., 288). He thinks he acquits himself of heresy by asserting that these works are impossible apart from divine enablement (ibid., 208) and that "condition" does not imply merit or favor (ibid.). But in the New Testament, it makes no difference who enables works, salvation is by faith alone apart from works (Ephesians 2:8-9). The key word is "alone." To drop this word, as some do, is to ignore the distinction between two entirely different kinds of religion.

[1179] For full discussion of this Neonomian view of salvation, see vol. 2, chapter 36-37.

The phrase "inherit eternal life" occurs four times in the New Testament.[1180] In each case, some kind of work or character quality is necessary if one is to inherit it. Therefore, it is doubtful that this has anything to do with personal salvation, which is by faith alone. We have discussed the meaning of "life" in detail in our earlier discussion.[1181] In the parable of the narrow way, entering life (Matthew 7:14) refers to entering into a kingdom way of living resulting in an abundant life now and greatness in the kingdom.[1182]

Because one who has placed his faith in Jesus Christ already has eternal life in the sense of regeneration, perhaps the common translation of *echō*, ("to have," or "to obtain") is not what the rich young ruler has in mind. This Greek word is used in some contexts in the sense of "to take hold of something" or "of holding fast to matters of transcendent importance."[1183] For example, Paul says one of the requirements for deacons is that they should be "*holding [echō] the mystery of the faith with a clear conscience*" (1 Timothy 3:9). Timothy is instructed by Paul to "*retain [echō] the standard of sound words which you have heard from me*" (2 Timothy 1:13). Then, to the Philippians he writes, "*holding fast (epechō) the word of life, so that in the day of Christ I will have reason to glory because I did not run in vain nor toil in vain*" (Philippians 2:16). The saved *good soil* "hold[s] fast" to the word of God. Like the good soil, the RYR wants to "*bear fruit with perseverance*" (Luke 8:15). In each instance, the idea is to hold onto a faith already in existence. This is similar to Paul's injunction, "*Fight the good fight of faith; take hold* [Gr *epilambanō*] *of the eternal life to which you were called, and you made the good confession in the presence of many witnesses*" (1 Timothy 6:12).

This view of "have" (Gr *echō*) explains why in Matthew's gospel the question is "What must I do to *have* eternal life?" whereas in Luke's gospel it is "*What must I do to inherit eternal life?*" Apparently "having" and "inheriting" are closely related. To "have" in English is to suggest a more passive acceptance, but to "take hold of" suggests an active choice. Similarly, "to inherit" something according to the New Testament involves the active choices of good works in order to obtain the inheritance as a reward (Colossians 3:24). Thus Jesus is telling the rich young ruler that he must take hold of eternal life now if he wants to inherit it in the future by means of good works.

The rich young ruler wants to be one who "has eternal life abiding in him" (1 Jn. 3:15). He wants a strong grip on it. In the discussion to follow, Jesus explains that the way the rich young ruler can "hold fast" is to obey the Law, give to the poor, and follow Christ as a disciple. This is the way he can "*have* eternal life."

If Jesus viewed the rich young ruler as an unsaved man, He would certainly have told him that "*whoever believes in him may have eternal life,*" and "*For God so loved the world, that He gave His only begotten Son, that whoever believes in Him shall not perish, but have*

1180 Matthew 19:29; Mark 10:17; Luke 10:25; 18:18.

1181 The related term "life" occurs 16 times in the Synoptics (Matthew 7:14; 18:8, 9; 19:16, 17, 29; 25:46; Mark 9:43, 45; 10:17, 30; Luke 10:25; 12:15; 16:25; 18:18, 30). In some places the term "life" is found outside of the expression "inherit eternal life" and the discussion with the rich young ruler. See Matthew 7:14; 18:8, 9; 25:46; Mark 9:43, 45; Luke 16:25. Some writers quote these passages without comment as if they prove that "life" means regeneration or "heaven when you die" (e. g. Brown, "The New Testament Concept of the Believer's Inheritance", 67), but it is questionable that any of these references refer to heaven or regeneration.

1182 See chapter 21 above.

1183 BDAG, 420.

eternal life" (John 3:15-16). One can "have" eternal life without cost by believing in Christ (Revelation 21:6). In these verses "to have eternal life" comes by faith alone and for no other reason. Yet in His answer to the ruler's questions about how he can have eternal life, Jesus tells him he must obey the Law, deny himself, and follow Christ as a loyal disciple. The simplest explanation of this disparity is that having eternal life is viewed from different perspectives: either (a) initial salvation, or (b) a fuller experience of life by which one matures and becomes complete in his faith.

Earlier in Luke's gospel, a lawyer asked the same question, "*Teacher, what shall I do to inherit eternal life*?" (Luke 10:25). However, the usual understanding of this passage is that the lawyer (scribe) was one of Christ's opponents and was an unsaved man. This is sometimes based on Luke's comment that the lawyer was attempting to test Jesus publicly and was also trying to "justify himself" (Luke 10:29).[1184] Bock understands the lawyer's question to be about "getting saved."[1185]

As he did with the rich young ruler, Jesus directs him to the Law and not to faith in the Son, saying, "*What is written in the Law? How does it read to you?*" (Luke 10:26). When the lawyer answers by saying one must love the Lord with all one's heart, soul, strength, and mind, and love his neighbor as himself, Jesus commends him saying, "*You have answered correctly; 'Do this and you will live*'" or, more clearly translated, "*Keep on doing this and you will live*"[1186] (Matthew 19:17; Luke 10:28).[1187]

However, it is likely that in this text Jesus does not mean "become regenerate" (or "obtain soteriological entrance into heaven," or "engage in a process of salvation leading to final justification"). Jesus is alluding to Leviticus 18:4-5:

> *You are to perform My judgments and keep My statutes, to live in accord with them; I am the* L*ORD your God. So you shall keep My statutes and My judgments, by which a man* ***may live*** *if he does them; I am the* L*ORD (Leviticus 18:4-5).*

Just like the response to the lawyer (Luke 10:25-29), Moses says that obedience to the commandments of God will result in "life." When Moses said, "Do this and you will live," was he promising heaven when one dies on the basis of obedience to the Law? No! All interpreters agree that Moses was promising a rich life now in response to faithful adherence to the Covenant. The "life" in view refers to a rich quality of life, not regeneration.[1188] According to Smick, "The verb *chāyâ* 'to live' involves the ability to have life somewhere on the scale between the fullest enjoyment of all the powers of one's being, with health and prosperity on the one hand and descent into trouble, sickness, and death on the other."[1189] Kaiser argues that in Leviticus 18:5 Moses tells them how to maintain fellowship with God and how to find a rich life now. He says, "The law has never served any purpose for

---

1184 Hendriksen and Kistemaker, *Exposition of the Gospel According to Matthew*, 591.

1185 Bock, *Luke 9:51-24:53*, 1023.

1186 Bock says that the present imperative ποίει (*poieō*, "do") speaks of an abiding love and action ibid., 1026.

1187 Through Ezekiel, Yahweh proclaimed the same truth, "I gave them My statutes and informed them of My ordinances, by which, if a man observes them, he will live" (Ezekiel 20:11).

1188 See Deuteronomy 4:1, 40; 5:29, 33. See also Hebrews 12:9-11 where submission to the Father, or as Jesus puts it, "follow Me," results in life abundant. See also Preston M. Sprinkle, "The Use of Genesis 42:18 (Not Leviticus 18:5) in Luke 10:28: Joseph and the Good Samaritan," Bulletin for Biblical Research 17, no. 2 (2007).

1189 Elmer B. Smick, "*chāyā*," in TWOT, 279.

justification; but it has an enormous contribution to make in the area of sanctification and living life to the fullest as God had intended his people to live [in the Old Testament, not today]."[1190] Similarly, the Mishnah counsels, "Lots of the Law, lots of life,"[1191] referring to the fact that study and application of the Torah leads to a rich life now under the covenant.

But are works of love toward one's God or one's neighbor the conditions for obtaining final entrance into heaven? Of course not! This is no problem for *sola fide* when one grants that "eternal life" is both personal salvation via faith alone and also a richer experience of that life that comes by faith plus works. In fact, most Reformed writers acknowledge this duality.[1192] That being so, it is much simpler to say that this particular lawyer was a saved man who wants to know how to experience a rich life now. However, because Jewish law defined "neighbor" as only the people of the covenant, he attempts to justify himself regarding the requirement of loving one's neighbor as himself. Since Jesus defines a neighbor as all people, the lawyer, like the Rich Young Ruler, seems to wonder if the price is too high.[1193]

According to some, the reason the Rich Young Ruler was being excluded from heaven is that he refused to part with his wealth.[1194] Surely this explanation cannot be taken seriously. The reason men are excluded from heaven is clearly stated elsewhere to be refusal to believe on the Son (John 3:18). The RYR did believe.

We conclude that if we are to understand the intent of the young man's question by how Jesus answers it, it appears that by the phrase, "inherit eternal life," Jesus understands him to be asking about how to live life to the fullest and obtain treasure in heaven (i.e., "inherit eternal life"), not "How can I become regenerate?" or "How can I be sure I will go to heaven?"[1195] Furthermore, by His answer Jesus affirms the common Jewish belief that

---

1190 Kaiser, "The Law as Guidance for the Promotion of Holiness," 397.

1191 m. Abot 2.7.

1192 E.g., Hendriksen, *Exposition of the Gospel According to Luke*. These Reformed writers say, "'Everlasting life,' how beautiful the term, and how superlatively precious the essence indicated by it! It refers to the kind of life that is not only endless in duration but also priceless in quality. It embraces such treasures as 'the love of God shed abroad in our hearts' (Romans 5:5), 'the peace of God that surpasses all understanding' (Philippians 4:7), 'joy inexpressible and full of glory' (I Peter 1:8), and 'fellowship with God the Father and with his Son' (John 17:3)," ibid., 591.

1193 To argue that this lawyer was unsaved because he wanted to publicly test Jesus and also wanted to justify himself requires us to believe that "true" believers would never want to test the Lord or be self-justifying. This is obviously not true. Furthermore, even though many of these lawyers were usually opponents of Jesus (Luke 11:45-52), some were genuinely saved or at least open to His message (Matthew 8:19, 21; 13:11,52; Acts 23:9; Titus 3:12). G. H. Twelftree says, "Also, when the scribes are depicted negatively they are always associated with another group, especially with the Pharisees." See G. H. Twelftree, "Scribes," in *Dictionary of Jesus and the Gospels*, ed. Joel B. Green, Scot McKnight, and I. Howard Marshall (Downers Grove, IL: InterVarsity Press, 1992), 734. This lawyer was obviously devout, and gave Jesus the correct answer. Jesus told him he was not "far from the kingdom of God" (Mark 12:34), and that if he did just one thing, as the Scriptures demanded, he would live abundantly.

1194 Stanley, *Did Jesus Teach Salvation by Works*, 199.

1195 Contra Stanley (ibid., 216) who quotes rabbinical writings, rather than quoting the Old Testament, to prove his thesis that to "enter life" means to go to heaven! However, none of the rabbinical writings he quotes even uses the phrase "enter life." Instead, they refer to entering life "in the world to come," a decidedly different concept than the Old Testament references to which Jesus refers. However, apart from the fact that these are questionable sources for understanding the gospel references, the Synoptic gospels never refer to "life in the world to come;" instead they refer to entering into life now, abundant life by being a disciple of Christ. Neither do the Pseudepigrapha or the Mishnah ever use the phrase "enter into life." Similarity does not equal

an inheritance is a reward for work done and is not a gift *obtained by faith alone.* This squares precisely with the way the words "inherit" and "inheritance" are used throughout the Scriptures (e.g., Colossians 3:24). It is also what Jesus teaches directly in the concluding summary of the passage, Matthew 19:29; Mark 10:30, and in Matthew 25:34-35.

We suggest, then, that N. T. Wright is absolutely correct when he says that the young man's question about inheriting eternal life has nothing to do with the modern question: "What must I do to go to heaven when I die?"[1196] Instead, according to Wright, the ruler wants to know "what must I do to have a share [inheritance] in the age to come."

If You Want to Be Perfect

The second key phrase which has a significant bearing on one's understanding of Christ's encounter with the young ruler is His response, "*if you wish to be complete,*" or "*if you want to be perfect*" (Matthew 19:21, NIV).

According to Matthew, the rich young ruler asked, "*What must I do to obtain eternal life?*" In His reply, Jesus understood him to be asking how to become "*perfect* [Gr *teleios*]" (Matthew 19:21). Apparently, Jesus understands the young man's question differently from the way in which modern interpreters understand it. Jesus understands him to be asking about how he can be complete, not how to enter heaven when he dies.

We must then ask, "What does it mean to be perfect?" The Greek *teleios* does not necessarily imply absolute perfection, that is, the kind of perfection needed to enter heaven when one dies, the perfect righteousness of Christ. More often it means "that which is fully accomplished—'complete, finished.'"[1197] In secular Greek it could refer to perfection in the various stages of learning, that is, beginner, advanced, and mature.[1198] The NASB nicely captures the sense by translating, "If you wish to be complete." In the New Testament

---

equality! Equating "enter life" and "enter life in the world to come" is an excellent illustration of Samuel Sandmel's definition of parallelomania: "Two passages ["enter into the world to come" in Pirke Aboth and "enter into life" in the Gospels] may sound the same in splendid isolation from their context, but when seen in context, reflect difference rather than similarity." See Sandmel, "Parallelomania," 3. It is common in the commentaries to find references in the Talmuds (400-600 years after the time of Christ) to prove this thesis. For example, b.Berakot 28b mentions "life in the future world" and b.Sotal 7b teaches that one can inherit "in the world to come." See Hebrews 2:5. These late references prove nothing about the meaning of "eternal life" in AD 30. In fact, one can find in the Pseudepigrapha a distinction between rich life in this world and life in the world to come. For example, Pirk Aboth, Sayings of the Fathers 6:7 says, "Great is Torah, for it gives to them that practice it **life in this world** and **in the world to come**; as it is said: 'For they are life to them that find them, and health to all their flesh.'" And "fairer is **one hour of repentance and good works in this world** than all the life of the world to come; and fairer is one hour of calmness of spirit in the world to come than all the life of this world." Entering into life and entering into life in the world to come are not necessarily the same thing. Frankly, these references are probably irrelevant, but so are those quoted to substantiate the point that entering life means the same as entering life in the world to come in rabbinic literature and then applying this to the incident of the rich young ruler. One can prove almost anything he wants by citing Talmudic sources dated 600 years after the time of Christ. The Mishnah would be a better source, but even here the Judaism of post–AD 70 was completely reconstructed at Jabneh. This discontinuity should caution us against the rush to all things rabbinic! The life in this world is a rich life now, and life in the world to come is soteriological entrance into the kingdom. See Charlesworth, ed. *The Old Testament Pseudepigrapha*, 2:711.

1196 Wright, *Jesus and the Victory of God*, 301. By sharing in the age to come, Wright means membership in the sense of having a possession there.

1197 Louw-Nida, 1:657.

1198 Gerhard Delling, "*teleios*," in TDNT, 8:67.

it refers to one who does the whole will of God. He is complete in his obedience, not absolutely perfect in it.

The immediate impression one receives from the account of the young man's running, kneeling, and calling Jesus "Good Rabbi," is of an enthusiastic, and perhaps, immature youth[1199] who has believed on Christ and now wants to know what is the next step. Jesus explains to him how he can be complete, undivided, or fully mature and, if he is, then he can obtain (or inherit) eternal life. He tells him what is necessary to "follow Him," not to become a Christian but to become a follower, that is, a fully committed disciple. By His answer, this seems to be how Jesus understands the young man's question. If that is so, the encounter is not about how to obtain personal salvation but how to be a complete, fully committed disciple. Why not understand the question the way Jesus did?

If becoming perfect is a condition for obtaining eternal life after this life, or entering the kingdom, or being "saved," then the requirement of selling everything and giving to the poor is perplexing. Beginning with this false assumption, most interpreters have concluded that "obviously He could not have meant that by literally and outwardly obeying this injunction, the young man would obtain a claim upon the kingdom of heaven."[1200] Why is this "obvious?" The most "obvious" interpretation is that this is precisely what Jesus meant! However, "obtaining a claim upon the kingdom of heaven" does not mean "enter into personal salvation." Rather, it refers to greatness in heaven in one's status and reward.

The passage presents the concept of two categories of Christians, those who are "complete" and those who are not. The rich young ruler wants to know how he can be among the former. Unfortunately, he views the price as too high.[1201]

That perfection here is to be understood as a higher level of discipleship is suggested by two factors. First, the parallel with obtaining eternal life and entering into life, as argued above, suggests that an enhanced quality of life is sought, not initial (or final) justification. Second, if one becomes complete, his reward is "treasure in heaven,"[1202] which is in addition to initial salvation. It refers to the believer's reward there. It is not "heaven," it is a treasure in heaven. Treasure in heaven is the same as our inheritance and to obtain it is the same as to "inherit eternal life" as a reward (Matthew 19:21; Mark 10:21; 25:34-35; Colossians 3:24).

Entering the Kingdom of Heaven

It is certainly true that inheriting eternal life is synonymous in this dialog with entering into the kingdom of God, as William Brown says.[1203] But entering into the kingdom of God, as discussed elsewhere, does not mean entering the future millennial kingdom in a soteriological sense. Rather, as discussed above, it refers to entering into future greatness,

---

1199 *Neaniskos* refers to a young man beyond the age of puberty, but normally before marriage, (Louw-Nida, 1:107). Paul often used the term in the sense of maturity. He desired to present every man "complete" (or mature) in Christ (Col 1:28). He contrasts *teleios* (mature) with its opposite *nēpios* (child) in Ephesians 4:13-14. Matthew tells us that this ruler was a "young man."

1200 John Peter Lange, "The Gospel of Matthew," in *Commentary on the Holy Scriptures, Critial, Doctrinal, and Hommelitical*, ed. John Peter Lange (Grand Rapids: Zondervan Publishing House, 1960), 345.

1201 This is similar to some lukewarm Christians (Revelation 3:15-16) throughout history who are carnal (1 Corinthians 3:3) and are "least" **in** the kingdom of heaven (Matthew 5:19).

1202 Luke 22:18.

1203 Brown, "The New Testament Concept of the Believer's Inheritance", 68.

sharing in the authority to rule in that kingdom by means of living out the Sermon on the Mount now.[1204] There is no place in Matthew's gospel where the "entry sayings" unambiguously refer to initial salvation.[1205] It is often simply assumed.[1206]

It is also argued that the metaphor of a camel going through the eye of a needle must refer to the impossibility of entering into initial salvation. Since becoming a believer in the first place is impossible unless God works a miracle in one's heart, entrance into the kingdom of heaven must, according to this interpretation, refer to regeneration. This presses the metaphor too far. The fact that it is impossible does not mean that getting into the kingdom is totally a work of God. It means that getting in is impossible without God's help. Furthermore, the saying about the camel through the eye of the needle is hyperbole; it *is a joke.* The surrounding crowds would have burst out laughing. Therefore, this is not a statement on which to build a doctrine of salvation. We might say today, "For it is easier for Congress to balance the budget than for a lukewarm Christian to become a fully committed disciple." While it seems humanly impossible for Congress to balance the budget, we would all agree that with divine assistance, this could happen! It is far more likely that Matthew has in view Jesus' teaching in which He said, "*Apart from me you can do nothing*" (John 15:5). The impossibility in view is not that of becoming a Christian by faith, but of persevering as a disciple and entering into greatness in the kingdom without Christ's help.

Who Then Can Be Saved?

Hearing that it is difficult for rich men to "enter the kingdom of God," (Matthew 19:23) the astonished disciples ask, "*Who then can be saved*?" (Matthew 19:25). While it is correct to say, "The Twelve give unmistakable evidence that they understand entering the kingdom and salvation to be one and the same thing,"[1207] one must ask, "Salvation from what?" It is doubtful that Matthew ever uses this word for salvation from eternal separation from God or of a process leading to heaven. Rather, in his gospel salvation refers to deliverance from some danger,[1208] from disease (i.e., being healed),[1209] from persecution,[1210] or from physical death.[1211]

[1204] See pp. 279 ff. above.

[1205] In Matthew's gospel there are 8 "entry sayings" including the two references to "entering into life" (Matthew 5:20; 7:13, 21; 18:3 [in verses 3 and 9 it is equated with entering into life]; 19:17, 23, 24; 23:13).

[1206] Matthew 7:21, of course, makes it clear that only those who do the will of the Father, that is, live out the Sermon on the Mount, will enter the kingdom of heaven in that day. However, "enter the kingdom" in Matthew 5:19-20 refers to entering into greatness in the kingdom by living out the Sermon on the Mount. The assumption is made that these false prophets must be non-Christians because they "practice lawlessness." Yet, earlier Jesus says that some who practice lawlessness are "in" the kingdom though they will be "least" there (Matthew 5:19).

[1207] Stanley, *Did Jesus Teach Salvation by Works*, 210.

[1208] Matthew 8:25; 14:30.

[1209] Matthew 9:22.

[1210] Matthew 10:22; 24:13.

[1211] Matthew 16:25; 24:22; 27:40, 42. There is one possible exception, "And she will bear a Son; and you shall call His name Jesus, for it is He who will save His people from their sins" (Matthew 1:21). However, even here it probably does not refer to salvation from damnation, but, as many have argued, the salvation in view is a national salvation, a return from the exilic judgment, restoration of the nation, a salvation from the consequences of their national sins. See Craig S. Keener, *The IVP Background Commentary* (Downers Grove, IL: InterVarsity Press, 1993), 48. While this conclusion is not shared by all, even if it should be applied to

The closest parallel to the salvation to which the astonished disciples allude (Matthew 19:25) is Matthew 16:24-26 where being saved is related to finding "life," or saving one's soul. As seen in a previous chapter, to save one's soul means to find a rich life now by self-denial, taking up one's cross, and following Christ, so that the believer is favorably recompensed at the Judgment Seat of Christ.

The rich young fool (Luke 12:19-23) stored up his goods so that his *psychē* ("life") could rest and be joyous.[1212] The paradox is that he must give up that selfish desire approach to a rich life now if he desires future-kingdom status. Instead, he must lose his life if he wants to be "saved." To "save the soul" in this sense is to secure for it eternal pleasures by living a life of sacrifice now. We are apparently, according to Jesus, developing an inner character that will be preserved (saved) into eternity. There is a connection between our life of sacrifice and our capability to enjoy and experience eternal fellowship with God.

Keeping this in mind clarifies the disciple's question to Jesus in Matthew 19:25, "Who then can be saved?" It may refer to an eschatological salvation,[1213] but if it does, it would not refer to entrance into heaven, but salvation in the sense of a reward for a life well lived. In any case, the proximity of Matthew 16:24 ff. and the use of "save" in Matthew argue against understanding "being saved" as deliverance from post-mortem condemnation to the lake of fire. The disciples are asking about how to find a rich life now and a high position in the age to come.

This interpretation fits very well with Peter's question, "*Behold, we have left everything and followed You; what then will there be for us*"" (Matthew 19:27). He is not asking, "How do we obtain heaven?" but rather he wants to know what reward they will receive for following Him. Jesus responds with an affirming answer, an answer that has nothing to do with salvation from eternal separation from God but everything to do with the subject under discussion in the preceding context, namely, rewards. He tells them they will sit on twelve thrones judging the twelve tribes of Israel, that they will benefit in this life, and that in eternity they will inherit eternal life (obtain a reward, Matthew 19:28-29). In fact, in regard to their ranking within the kingdom, they will be first in contrast to the rich young ruler, who will be last.

Treasure in Heaven

That the subject of the rich young ruler's question and the Lord's response is rewards to the believer and not final deliverance from eternal separation from God is further established by the fact that what is promised as a result of obeying the commandments is not heaven, but "treasure in heaven" (Matthew 19:21; Mark 10:21).

Some have understood this to mean the treasure "which is" heaven.[1214] This is argued from the near context where "eternal life," "saved," and "enter the kingdom" are

individual salvation, it is certainly not Matthew's general usage (e.g., Hagner, *Matthew 14-28*, 19.).

1212 For other passages where a similar thought is expressed, see Matthew 6:25; 12:18; 26:38; Mark 12:34; Hebrews 10:38.

1213 Hagner, *Matthew 14-28*, 561.

1214 Alfred Plummer, *A Critical and Exegetical Commentary on the Gospel according to St. Luke*, 5th. ed. (Edinburgh: T. & T. Clark, 1922), 424.

understood to refer to final salvation. However, this argument is circular. Rather than allow the earned reward, "treasure in heaven," to define the meaning of "inherit eternal life," they argue that "inherit eternal life" must define "treasure in heaven,"[1215] and therefore so is inheriting eternal life, which is parallel to this treasure. Elsewhere the treasure to be received is granted to those who obey His call to leave everything (Luke 18:29–30). It is a treasure that Jesus commands believers (not nonbelievers) to lay up "in" heaven (Matthew 6:20-21; cf. 1 Timothy 6:19; James 5:3). This fact of Lukan usage should have pointed the commentators toward interpreting phrases like "enter the kingdom," and "saved" in terms of "treasure" rather than regeneration or final entrance into heaven.[1216]

The notion that "treasure in heaven consists of deeds of love now,"[1217] must be rejected. How then, is it possible, that "no thief comes near and no moth destroys" them (Luke 12:33). The treasures are manifestly laid up in heaven as a result of deeds of charity done now.[1218] Jesus understands the man to be asking about earned reward in heaven, not initial entrance into eternal life.

Come Follow Me

Jesus' final command to the rich young ruler, after he had sold all he had and given the cash to the poor, was: "Come, follow me" (Matthew 19:21). We therefore disagree with Stanley when he says that Jesus is not placing an additional demand of discipleship beyond the faith requirement for salvation; that is precisely what Jesus is doing. Entering into discipleship is not synonymous with eternal life in the sense of "heaven when one dies."[1219] Rather, discipleship is the condition for entering eternal life in the sense of an enhanced experience of life, a rich life with God.

Summary

The rich young ruler was a regenerate man who had been impressed with the message of free grace in Christ and had believed on Him for eternal life. He now wants to know, "What is next?" He wants to have as high a place in heaven and as rich an experience of life as possible, and so he needs to know the terms. Consistent with the broader context, the issue under discussion is taking a lower status now if one wants to be exalted (receive authority) in the kingdom. Some will receive five cities, some will receive ten.

Jesus issues a stirring call to discipleship, "Sell everything and follow Me" and you will have rewards in heaven. He makes the concluding point that the issue for this young

---

1215 According to Luke's understanding of rewards, it is more likely that the treasure is something in addition to heaven. See Luke 6:35; 12:33-34 (cf. Matthew 6:19-20); 14:14; 16:10–11; 19:11–27.

1216 Curiously, Bock fails to do this. He grants that "treasure" is a reward in addition to salvation and that it parallels the terms "eternal life," "enter the kingdom," and "saved," but he does not take the obvious step of defining these parallel terms as something in addition to initial justification. He connects this treasure with rewards at the Judgment Seat of Christ, not final salvation. Bock, *Luke 1-9:50*, 481.

1217 Stanley, *Did Jesus Teach Salvation by Works*, 143. Stanley then appeals to Matthew 13:44 where the kingdom of heaven is likened to a treasure in a field. However, the kingdom is compared to a treasure and therefore a treasure in the kingdom cannot be the kingdom itself.

1218 In Judaism, "the interest on this may accrue to man in this life in the form of happy results, the capital will be kept in heaven to the Day of Judgment, and then it will be paid back." Friedrick Hauk, "*thesauras*," in TDNT, 3:137.

1219 Contra Stanley, *Did Jesus Teach Salvation by Works*, 144.

man was not initial entrance but status in the kingdom, "*But many who are first will be last; and the last, first*" (Matthew 19:30). The question for this young ruler was how to be "complete," that is, how to finish what he started.

I conclude this chapter with two examples of what it might mean to us to be "complete." My friend, Ney Bailey, read a missionary's prayer letter in which the missionary gave to God, "all that I am, all that I have, all that I do, all that I suffer." Ney wanted to finish well, so she got four pieces of paper and wrote one of these phrases at the top of each one. She then wrote down everything she could think of under each topic. For Ney, this defined what it would be if she were "complete."

Another woman, Phyllis Stanley, set Philippians 3:10 as her definition of "complete." For Phyllis, this meant she would live her life purposefully, faithfully, creatively, and paradoxically. To live purposefully meant regular review of Philippians 3:10. To live faithfully meant to believe God for what she could not see. To live creatively meant to create beauty and warmth in her home and in her Bible studies. And to live paradoxically meant she would go against her selfish nature and against our culture; giving more than she felt like giving.

25

Justification and Sanctification 1

ACCORDING TO Experimental Predestinarians a life of works is the necessary and inevitable result of genuine faith and conversion. As Luther put it, "It is therefore as impossible to separate works from faith as it is to separate heat and light from fire."[1220] In other words justification and sanctification are distinct but inseparable. More recently D. A. Carson wrote, "The salvation which God gives by grace is not static; it inevitably results in good works."[1221] Considerable attention is given to this point in their standard theology texts and will be analyzed in what follows. No one would question that God's intent is that believers should walk holy and blameless before Him in love. However, such a walk depends on their responses to God's love and grace. While justification is based on faith alone and is a work of God, sanctification is uniformly presented in Scripture as a work of man and God (Philippians 2:12-13) and is achieved by faith plus divinely enabled works.

Yet, in their misguided attempts to preserve at all costs the sovereignty of God (i.e., the "predestinarian" aspect of their teaching), Experimental Predestinarians have all but eliminated the contribution made by the new man in Christ to his own sanctification. Indeed, to even speak this way would cause them to cringe with fears that ancient "Pelagianism"[1222] is creeping into the evangelical church.

The inseparable unity of sanctification and justification is argued on many grounds. In the next four chapters we will discuss the evidence which Experimental Predestinarians cite in favor of their doctrine that faith and works (i.e., salvation and sanctification) are always inevitably and permanently linked and can never be separated in the life of one who has "truly" believed.

The Greater Righteousness

Recently the writer was privileged to spend a week at a seminar taught by one of the most articulate Experimental Predestinarian theologians in the United States. His approach to the Sermon on the Mount leads us into the inner workings of their system.

1220 Martin Luther, cited by *The Book of Concord and the Confessions of the Evangelical Lutheran Church*, ed. T. G. Tappert (Philadelphia: Mühlenberg Press, 1959), 553.

1221 Carson, *Jesus' Sermon on the Mount and His Confrontation with the World*, 124.

1222 In the conflict with Augustine, Pelagius, who stressed free will and moral ability, was the loser. Experimental Predestinarians seem to like to use the term Pelagianism. It gives them a sense of connection with history and with a battle in which they were on the winning side.

In order to establish that true faith will result in a life of works, he expounded Matthew 5:20,

> *For I say unto you, that unless your righteousness exceeds the righteousness of the scribes and Pharisees, you will by no means enter the kingdom of heaven* (Matthew 5:20).

In agreement with most scholars and with the present writer, he agrees that this surpassing righteousness is ethical behavior. Since, on Experimentalist assumptions, only ethically righteous people will be allowed into heaven, they believe that this text proves that sanctification always and necessarily follows justification.

After explaining that the righteousness of the scribes and Pharisees was not all bad but was, in fact, very scrupulous in spite of its externals, he concluded that, unless our lives manifest a practical righteousness which is quite high, we are not truly Christians at all and will be shut out of the kingdom on that fateful day.[1223] Thus, Jesus is not presenting a condition of entrance into heaven but is setting forth the characteristics of all who will.

Now, not only is this interpretation highly unlikely, but imagine the bondage this would place on the average Christian. How could anyone possibly know if his righteousness did, in fact, exceed that of the scribes and Pharisees? Assurance of salvation would be impossible unless the standards of the Pharisees were reduced to something less than what God requires. At the end of the lecture the speaker was asked, "Are you more righteous than the scribes and the Pharisees?" If he said, "No," then he would have no assurance, and yet the Bible says assurance is possible now. If he said "Yes," then one might ask, "How do you know for sure that you are righteous enough?"

If we assume the Pharisees were "foul,"[1224] then it would not take much to improve on their righteousness. If we assume their error was that they believed only in external righteousness, which may not be true,[1225] then any degree of internal righteousness would exceed theirs. If we assume their error was that they only practiced part of the Law, then if we practice more than part, we would exceed their righteousness. It is impossible for us to fulfill all the law. But these assumptions would not result in any great improvement in Christian behavior at all.

The degree of righteousness necessary for entrance into greatness in the kingdom is contrasted with the righteousness of the scribes and the Pharisees. But what is the point of the contrast? As we argued elsewhere, entering the kingdom most likely refers to a call to believers to enter fully into a kingdom way of living now resulting in greatness in the future millennium. Initial entrance for final salvation is not in view at all. Therefore the surpassing righteousness is not a characteristic of all who are saved. It is the characteristic of those among the saved who have embraced the kingdom way of living described in the Sermon on the Mount and will, as a result, obtain greatness in that future kingdom.

[1223] This view is expounded by Lloyd-Jones, *Studies in the Sermon on the Mount*, 208. See also Pink, *An Exposition of the Sermon on the Mount*, 61-66.

[1224] Pink, *An Exposition of the Sermon on the Mount*, 66.

[1225] See Richard Longenecker, *Paul, Apostle of Liberty* (New York: Harper and Row, 1964), 23, 71-85. He gathers much evidence regarding a genuine devotional and prophetic spirit present in Pharisaic Judaism and also in the Qumran community (e.g., John 3:1; Acts 15:8). See especially Sanders, *Paul and Palestinian Judaism*. This seminal work has caused New Testament scholars to completely reevaluate the nature of first-century Judaism.

Both Are Part of the New Covenant

Quoting the New Covenant of Jeremiah, Robert Dabney argues that both justification and sanctification are included in the New Covenant.[1226] Therefore all members always have both.

> *"This is the covenant I will make with the house of Israel after that time," declares the LORD. "I will put my law in their minds and write it on their hearts. I will be their God, and they will be my people" (Jeremiah 31:33).*

Dabney is struck by the words, "*I will put my law in their minds and write it on their hearts.*" However, he neglects to quote the next verse which helps us to know WHEN this will be fulfilled,

> *No longer will a man teach his neighbor, or a man his brother, saying, "Know the LORD," because they will all know me, from the least to the greatest (Jeremiah 31:34).*

Obviously, verse 34 is being fulfilled at the present time in only a preliminary manner. Certainly it is not true that all *know the Lord* and that there is no longer a need for personal evangelism. The New Covenant was inaugurated at the cross, and we enter into some of its benefits at the moment we believe. But its final fulfillment has not yet taken place and will not take place until the coming millennial kingdom and the eternal state. Then, and only then, will the statement in Ezekiel 36:27 be an experiential reality, "*And I will put My Spirit within you and cause you to walk in My statutes, and you will be careful to observe My ordinances.*"

When the new age dawns, God will "cause"[1227] His people to be obedient. Applying this verse to the current era when the context of Ezekiel applies it to the future one is not only experientially ludicrous, but it violates the context.

The ultimate writing of His law on our hearts and minds will be characteristic of the believer when he has achieved the goal of his justification, glorification. Being a member of the New Covenant community does not guarantee an inevitable link between justification and sanctification.

A Disciple Does the Will of God

Experimental Predestinarians often quote the numerous passages in the Gospels that refer to discipleship as proof that a man who is truly a Christian, that is, a disciple, is one who works and does not fall away. John Murray, for example, says in reference to John 8:30-32, "He [Jesus] set up a criterion by which true disciples might be distinguished and

---

1226 Dabney, *Lectures in Systematic Theology*, 664.

1227 The translation "cause" is from the Hebrew word for "to make or do," ʿāsāh. Keith Mathison incorrectly applies this verse to the current era when he says that "the Spirit will cause you kingdom people to walk in my statutes." See Keith Mathison, *Dispensationalism, Rightly Dividing the People of God?* (Phillipsburg, NJ: Presbyterian and Reformed Publishing Co., 1995), 89-90. Quoted in Ken Neff, *A Defense of Grace: An Examination of Saving Faith, Comparing Grace and Reformed Theology* (Available from prgneff@primeresearchgroup.com: Privately Published, 1996), 98.

that criterion is continuance in Jesus' word."[1228] This is true, and we will discuss this passage below. However, by way of prelimary response, let us note that being a disciple and being a Christian are not necessarily synonymous terms.

NOT ALL BELIEVERS ARE DISCIPLES

The basic meaning of "disciple" is "a learner" or "student."[1229] But are all Christians disciples? Jesus says that only believers who abide in His Word are disciples (John 8:31). To say that every Christian is a disciple contradicts the teaching of the New Testament. This alone alerts us to the fact that Jesus did not always equate being a "disciple" with being a Christian.

When Jesus calls a man to become a disciple, He is not asking him to accept the free gift of eternal life. Instead, He is asking those who have already believed to accept the stringent commands of discipleship. If being a disciple is a condition for becoming a Christian, why does Jesus exhort those who are already Christians to become disciples (Luke 14:26, 33)?

Many disciples left Jesus (John 6:66). If they were not Christians, then Experimental Predestinarians must acknowledge that being a disciple is not the same thing as being a Christian (or else give up their doctrine of eternal security!), and if they were Christians, then being a Christian does not inevitably result in a life of following Christ. When Paul and Barnabas went to Antioch, they encouraged the disciples to remain true to the faith (Acts 14:22). Disciples can be drawn away from the truth (Acts 20:30).

If being a disciple is not necessarily the same as being a Christian, then it is not logically or exegetically consistent to select passages that refer to discipleship and assume that they refer to the conditions for becoming a Christian or to the characteristics of all who are truly born again. One writer argues, "The word *disciple* is used consistently as a synonym for *believer* throughout the book of Acts." On this basis, he concludes, "Any distinction between the two words is purely artificial."[1230] But then he contradicts himself and says, "It is apparent that not every disciple is necessarily a true Christian."[1231] So, apparently this writer has concluded that a distinction between the words is not "purely artificial" but is grounded in the New Testament itself.[1232]

John MacArthur believes that "there is no more definitive statement on discipleship in the New Testament than Matthew 10:32-39." He believes that this proves that all "true" Christians are disciples, fully committed followers of Christ. As discussed elsewhere,[1233] Jesus is addressing His believing followers and warning them of the danger to the final significance of their lives by putting their own priorities, safety, comfort, and things of this world ahead of obedience to Christ. The passage has nothing to do with salvation. The disciples to whom He was speaking were already regenerate!

1228 Murray, *Redemption--Accomplished and Applied*, 151-52.

1229 See Mark 9:31; Luke 10:23; John 12:42.

1230 MacArthur, *The Gospel According to Jesus*, 196.

1231 Ibid., 196, n.2. As will be discussed in vol. 2, chapter 32, "The Carnal Christian," it is theologically impossible to hold this view of discipleship because the Bible teaches the existence of the permanently carnal Christian who persists in his rebellion to the point of physical death.

1232 See pp. 545 ff.

1233 See pp. 207 ff.

The conditions for becoming a disciple are different from those for becoming a Christian. One becomes a Christian, according to Jesus, on the basis of faith alone (John 3:16). We are justified "freely" (Romans 3:24) and receive regenerate life "without cost" (Revelation 22:17). But to become a disciple, something in addition to faith is needed, namely, works.[1234] A disciple is one who denies himself, is willing to leave his family, and follows Jesus (Mark 8:34). A disciple must love Jesus more than his own wife (Luke 14:26), hardly a requirement ever stated anywhere for becoming a Christian! The condition for discipleship is to forsake all and follow Christ (Luke 14:33). Consider Jesus' words:

> *If anyone comes to me and does not hate his father and mother, his wife and children, his brothers and sisters—yes, even his own life—he cannot be my disciple. Anyone who does not carry his cross and follow me cannot be my disciple (Luke 14:26-27).*

> *In the same way, any of you who does not give up everything he has cannot be my disciple (Luke 14:33).*

If being a disciple and being a Christian is the same thing, as some Experimental Predestinarians maintain, then are they not introducing a serious distortion into the gospel? In their view, to become a Christian, one must not only believe on Christ, but he must also (1) hate his father, mother, wife, children, and his own life; (2) carry his cross; (3) be willing to follow Jesus around Palestine; and (4) give up everything. Can any amount of theological sophistry equate these four conditions with the simple offer of a free gift on the basis of believing? Being a disciple and being a Christian cannot be the same thing! If we are justified "freely," how can the enormous cost of being a disciple be imposed as a condition of that justification?[1235]

The most famous discipleship passage in the New Testament makes it quite clear that becoming a disciple and becoming a Christian are two separate things. The Great Commission command is to "make disciples." In explaining how this is to be done, three activities are specified: going, baptizing, and teaching. "Going" means to go to them and explain the gospel. "Baptizing" identifies those who have responded publicly as new converts. "Teaching" is simply instruction in the Christian life. So there are three things involved in the production of a disciple: (1) the person must trust Christ; (2) he must be baptized; and (3) he must be taught to obey all that Christ taught. If being a disciple is the same as becoming a Christian, then in order to be saved, one must trust in Christ, be baptized, and must obey the commands of Christ. In other words salvation is by works.

A DISCIPLE CONTINUES IN HIS WORD

In the passage that Murray quotes to prove the doctrine of perseverance in holiness (John 8:30–32), Jesus is in fact teaching that a disciple will persevere in good works, but since all Christians are not necessarily disciples, the passage cannot be of much help to the Reformed doctrine of perseverance. Murray assumes his definition of a disciple and then

[1234] A few Experimental Predestinarians such as Thomas Schreiner and Ardel Caneday have argued that works are a condition of salvation but are nonmeritorious works. This subtlety is discussed in detail in vol. 2, chapter 37.

[1235] When MacArthur says that this is a "paradox," the writer would certainly agree. But it is more than a paradox; it is an irreconcilable contradiction. MacArthur, *The Gospel According to Jesus*, 140.

imports that assumption (disciple=justified saint) into his exegesis of John 8:31-32 without any comment.

In this "controversy" section Jesus is in the temple in Jerusalem confronting the Pharisees. Some of His hearers believed on Him and were born again. Jesus, in the verses Murray quotes, speaks to these who have believed and challenges them to discipleship. Then Jesus returns to the controversy.

> *As He spoke these things, many came to* **believe in Him** (perf. part dat.). *So Jesus was saying to those Jews who had believed Him, "If you continue in My word, then you are truly disciples of Mine; and you will know the truth, and the truth will make you free (John 8:30–32).*

After listening to Him for a time, some of the Jews, according to verse 30, "*believed on Him.*" The expression in Greek is *episteusan eis auton.* Similar constructions with the preposition *eis* are consistently used by John elsewhere for saving faith. For example:

> *Yet to all who received him, to those who* **believed in his name**, *he gave the right to become children of God, children born not of natural descent, nor of human decision or of a husband's will, but born of God (John 1:12-13).*

> *Everyone who* **believes in him** *may have eternal life. For God so loved the world that he gave his one and only Son, that whoever* **believes in him** *shall not perish but have eternal life (John 3:15-16).*

> *Whoever* **believes in me**, *as the Scripture has said, streams of living water will flow from within him (John 7:38).*

Examples could be multiplied.[1236] Even though Carson asserts that "whether or not their faith is genuine cannot be determined by the linguistic expression used by the Evangelist,"[1237] this is patently false. Debbie Hunn replies, "However, [John's] linguistic expressions are the final arbiters of what the Evangelist meant to communicate, and he consistently uses πιστεύω εις to indicate genuine faith in Jesus."[1238] Since these men in John 8:30 *believed on Him,* on the authority of Jesus Himself, we may say they are born again and have eternal life.

In John 8:31 Jesus turns to the "*Jews who had believed in Him*" (those mentioned in the preceding verse) and says, "*If you abide in My word, then you are truly disciples of Mine.*" Abiding in the word of Christ is a condition for being a disciple.

In this exchange, we might paraphrase Jesus saying in an aside to these new believers, "It is good that you have believed and are born again. Now, abide in My words and be a disciple!" It is to those who have already believed that He introduces a conditional relationship with Himself. Later, in John 15, Jesus will expand on the concept of abiding and explain that it is the condition of fruit-bearing in the Christian life and that it is characterized by obedience to His commands and love for the brothers in Christ.[1239]

[1236] See also John 2:11; 3:18, 36; 6:29, 35, 40; 7:39; 9:35, 36; 10:42; 11:25, 26, 45; 12:44, 46.

[1237] D. A. Carson, *The Gospel According to John* (Downers Grove, IL: InterVarsity, 1991), 348.

[1238] Debbie Hunn, "Who are "they" in John 8:33?," *CBQ* 66, no. 3 (2004): 390. Hunn has a full discussion of this passage and argues that the believers in v. 31 "truly believed" and are saved. Those in vv. 33, "they," do not refer to the believers in v. 31, but to an ongoing discussion between Jesus and the unbelieving Pharisees which began back in 12 and 19.

[1239] Those who object to this interpretation usually do so on the gratuitous assumption that John believes there is such a thing as spurious faith, often appealing to John 2:23. For example see Carson, *The Gospel According to*

At this point in the dialogue, Jesus' opponents challenge Him.

They answered Him, "We are Abraham's descendants and have never yet been enslaved to anyone; how is it that You say, 'You will become free'?" Jesus answered them, "Truly, truly, I say to you, everyone who commits sin is the slave of sin" (John 8:31–34).

"*They*" answered Him. While some argue that "they" refers back to verse 30 (i.e., to those who have believed in Him), the portrayal of those addressed in 8:33-59 renders this impression highly unlikely. Jesus says that they are slaves to sin; they are murderers; they have no belief in His word (v. 37); they want to kill Jesus; their father is Satan (v. 44); they are unable to hear what Jesus has to say (v. 43); they do not believe in Christ (v. 45); and they do not belong to God (v. 47). They in turn say that Jesus is demon-possessed (v. 48), and they picked up stones to stone Him (v. 48). This hardly sounds like the same group in verse 30, who, after hearing Him speak, "put their faith in him" (v. 30). Charles Bing is correct, "The abrupt change of tone from verses 30-31 resumes this motif, making it unnecessary to identify the speakers; the Jews had raised objections from the start of the dialogue (vs. 13, 19, 22, 25)."[1240] These critics, having heard Jesus' aside to the new Christians, respond in anger.

Similarly Charles Bing says, "The objection of v 33 is totally out of character with the inclination of those mentioned in verses 30–32, as is also the declaration that those opposing Christ are children of the devil (v 44)."[1241] The true believers of verses 31-32 are clearly not "children of the devil." It is therefore perplexing why Schreiner and Caneday call our interpretation "remarkable."[1242] It is not "remarkable" at all. It makes very good sense of the context and the general usage of the phrase "believe in" found in the rest of John's gospel.[1243]

In an extensive analysis, John Niemalä has shown that in John's Gospel there are 353 speaking verbs which introduce new speakers or re-introduce previously introduced ones. He determined that there are 78 such verbs which *do not have an explicit subject word* like "Jesus said" or "the Pharisees replied," etc. In all 78 instances the use of such verbs without a named subject ("they said," "they replied," etc.) these verbs *always indicated the re-introduction of a speaker who had spoken earlier in the context*. This suggests that the "they" of v. 33 probably does not refer to the believers in v. 31 who have never spoken in the preceding context and must refer to the Pharisees who have (see vv. 13, 14, 19, 22, 25, 33).[1244]

Long ago Augustine argued that "those who believed in him" are true, not spurious believers, and that the "they" of verse 33 refers to Christ's critics, not the true believers of

---

John, 347. However, we will argue later that passage refers to true believers, not spurious believers. See vol. 2, chapter 32.

1240 See Charles C. Bing, "The Condition for Salvation in John's Gospel," *JOTGES* 9, no. 1 (Spring 1996): 36.

1241 Bing, "The Condition for Salvation in John's Gospel."

1242 Schreiner and Caneday, *The Race Set Before Us*, 118.

1243 Does this violate the principle of the near antecedent? Should the "they" of verse 33 refer to those in verse 32 and not the Pharisees of verses 27-29? Not necessarily. The principle of the near antecedent is only suggestive and not absolute. What might be the nearest antecedent contextually might not be the nearest antecedent in the author's mind. For example in Acts 4:11 "He" refers to Christ in v. 10, but the near antecedent is "this man" in v. 10.

1244 John Niemalä, "Free at Last! Liberty in Jesus' Footsteps (John 8:30-32),"(2013). Niemalä's paper can be downloaded from http://www.mol316.com/pdfs/GES2013FreeAtLast.pdf.

verses 31-32.[1245] As Bernard and McNeile have noted, "Those who made the answer which follows were not the Jews who 'believed Him' (v. 31), but the Jewish objectors, with whom throughout the rest of this chapter Jesus is engaged in controversy. He could not have charged 'the Jews who believed Him' with seeking His life (vv. 37, 39)."[1246]

These angry unbelievers claim they are children of Abraham, but they are not willing to believe on Him as these others did. It is to these critics, not to those who have just believed that Jesus addresses the stinging rebuke, "*You belong to your father the devil*" (John 8:44). These critics, not the believers of verse 30, are the ones who "*picked up stones to stone Him*" (John 8:59).

We conclude then that the distinction between being a Christian and being a disciple has good foundation in the New Testament.

Colossians 1:22-23

Both Arminians and Experimental Predestinarians often appeal to this passage in support of their positions:

> *Yet He has now reconciled you in His fleshly body through death, in order to present you before Him holy and blameless and beyond reproach—if indeed you continue in the faith firmly established and steadfast, and not moved away from the hope of the gospel that you have heard (Colossians 1:22-23).*

Arminians find support here for their teaching that salvation can be lost if the Christian fails to continue in the faith.[1247] Some Reformed scholars argue that the Greek conditional clause here suggests certainty in the outcome. In other words, Paul could be saying, "If you continue in the faith, *and you will*, then you will be presented holy and blameless." To be presented "holy" in this view is to be presented clothed in the perfect righteousness of Christ.

Only those who continue in the faith will be presented as justified, that is, legally "blameless," having been clothed with the blameless righteousness of Christ. Therefore, they say, justification and continuance in the faith are always linked.

In Greek, this is technically a first class condition, that is, the condition is assumed to be true. This is said to mean the proof of the reality of one's faith is that one will continue in the faith. Or, to say it differently, "You will be presented holy and blameless because (or 'since') you will continue in the faith." Therefore, their argument is that only those who persevere are truly Christians in the first place.[1248]

This interpretation not only makes a gratuitous assumption that "holy and blameless" refers to absolute holiness and blamelessness (i.e., justification), which it does not (see below), but it is a total over-reach in the use of the Greek conditional clause. It is simply false to say that a first class condition guarantees that the conditional clause is certain.

[1245] Augustine, "Tractates on John," in *Nicene and Post-Nicene Fathers* ed. Philip Schaff (Oak Harbor, WA: Logos Research Systems, 1997), 7:230.

[1246] J. H. Bernard and A. H. McNeile, *A Critical and Exegetical Commentary on the Gospel according to St. John*, 2 vols. (Edinburgh: T. & T. Clark, 1928), 2:306.

[1247] For example, B. F. Westcott, *Colossians: A Letter to Asia*, reprint ed. (Minneapolis: Klock & Clock, 1914), 75.

[1248] William Hendriksen and Simon Kistemaker, *Exposition of Colossians and Philemon* (Grand Rapids: Baker Book House, 1964), 83-84.

Rather, as Wallace states: "The first class condition indicates *the assumption of truth for the sake of argument*. The normal idea, then, is *if—and let us assume that this is true for the sake of argument—then*."[1249] It does *not* always mean "since" as is sometimes assumed.[1250] But more importantly, the conditional clause in Colossians 1:23 does not begin with "if" (Gr *ei*), but with "if indeed" (Gr *ei ge*). That clause (*ei ge*) does *not* always assume a condition which is assumed to be true. Had Paul wanted to signal a higher degree of certainty, perhaps he would have used *ei*. Even so, it would only assume certainty for the sake of argument and not reality.[1251]

Neonomians view the matter similarly, but with their distinctive additional emphasis that one's eternal salvation *depends on* his faithfulness. Douglas Moo, for example, says,

> *He wants to confront the Colossians with the reality that their eventual salvation* ***depends on their remaining faithful*** *to Christ and to the true gospel. Only by continuing in their faith can they hope to find a favorable verdict from God on the day of judgment.*[1252]

Since this kind of statement would normally be understood as dangerously close to a works salvation, qualifications must be added. Moo explains that this is only the human responsibility side of the equation. On the one hand, Moo says that, God will work "to preserve his people so that they will be vindicated in the judgment; but, at the same time, God's people are responsible to persevere in their faith if they expect to see that vindication."[1253] However, this means that salvation is a joint effort between God and man: God's work by the Holy Spirit and man's work of perseverance, and that certainly looks like a works salvation.

One cannot escape from this conclusion unless he wants to argue that God "does it all" and that human effort contributes nothing. Naturally, Experimental Predestinarians will respond that their opponents do not understand the mysterious connectedness between divine sovereignty and human responsibility. But we do. We simply do not agree with their understanding of that connectedness. This retreat to the unexplainable and to "mystery" leaves the average Christian wondering, "How does this work?"

Apparently no answer is necessary. As Experimental Predestinarian Lorraine Boettner put it, the Calvinist is "under no obligation to explain all the mysteries connected with these doctrines."[1254] Such a response is simply a fig leaf for a system of theology which makes no rational sense and has little connection with the true believers' experience of Christ.[1255]

1249 Wallace, *Greek Grammar Beyond the Basics*, 690.

1250 Ibid., 690.

1251 Pak points out that "*ei ge*" does not really convey the condition which is assumed to be true. Cf. Gal 3:4. Pak, "A Study of Selected Passages on Distinguishing Marks of Genuine and False Believers", 271.

1252 Moo, *Colossians and Philemon*, 144.

1253 Ibid.

1254 Loraine Boettner, *The Reformed Doctrine of Predestination* (Pittsburg: Presbyterian and Reformed Publishing Co., 1932), 124.

1255 One can agree with Moo that this passage is indeed a real warning, but it is not a warning to examine oneself to see if he is truly born again. Instead, as will be shown below, it is a warning about the forfeiture of one's inheritance and reward; the incalculable loss that will be experienced by the Christian who does not persevere in faithfulness to Christ.

DOES PERSEVERANCE IN FAITH PROVE SALVATION?

Experimental Predestinarian Joseph Pak argues for this perspective in two ways. First, he says that (1) the conditional clause is "most likely" to be connected with the main verb, "be reconciled," (v. 22) and (2) the parallel passage in Ephesians 5:26-27 includes the believers' glorification (Gr *endochos*) with the nouns "holy, blameless and beyond reproach."

Regarding (1) above, does the conditional clause refer to "*in order to present you ... holy and blameless*," or to "*be reconciled*"? Pak thinks that it "is highly improbable that a conditional clause would not modify the main verb 'be reconciled.'"[1256] He continues, "A reasonable explanation is that Paul is presenting present continuation in the faith as a test of past reconciliation."[1257] Thus he says, "If you continue in the faith, then you have been reconciled."[1258] The difference is significant for the interpretation of the passage. If we are reconciled and presented before Him glorified only if we persevere in faith, that is one thing. However, if we are to be presented before Him holy and blameless and beyond reproach, only if we persevere in faithfulness, that is another. The Partners believe that all Christians will be presented before Him and be finally saved, but only some will be presented holy, blameless, and beyond reproach. The latter are Christ's *Metochoi*, His Servant Kings who will share in kingdom rule with Christ in the fulfillment of human destiny.

Pak gives no support for his assertion that the conditional clause should be linked to the main verb "reconciled" instead of the near antecedent infinitive, "in order to present you." In fact, there are many instances of a main verb, followed by an infinitive followed by a conditional clause in which the conditional clause is connected with the infinitive and not with the main verb.[1259] Douglas Moo (*contra* Pak) says, "The if clause is probably to be attached to the word 'present' in v. 22: 'God has reconciled you with the purpose of presenting you as holy before him—but you will, in fact, only be presented as holy before him if ...'"[1260] Similarly, Murray Harris observes that the phrase refers to "the future divine 'presentation' (but not the reconciliation)."[1261]

CHRIST PRESENTS THE BELIEVER HOLY AND BLAMELESS

Regarding Pak's second point (2), one must ask whether the purpose clause ("in order to present you ... blameless," etc.) refers only to the sanctification of believers without regard to their final stage, i.e. the glorification, or if it includes it. To support his interpretation that final glorification is included, Pak appeals to Ephesians 5:25-27.

He argues that "there is no compelling reason to conclude that Paul is excluding final glorification as the purpose of Christ's reconciliation of believers in v. 22."[1262] That may be true, but more importantly, there is no compelling reason to believe that the phrase includes

---

1256 Pak, "A Study of Selected Passages on Distinguishing Marks of Genuine and False Believers", 274.

1257 Ibid., 277.

1258 Ibid., 278.

1259 For example, Matthew 24:24; Mark 13:22; Acts 20:16; 1 Corinthians 16:7.

1260 Moo, *Colossians and Philemon*, 144.

1261 Murray J. Harris, *Exegetical Guide to the Greek New Testament: Colossians and Philemon* (Grand Rapids: Wm. B. Eerdmans Publishing Co., 1991), 60. Pokorny agrees, "The condition refers only to the final clause in 1:22b," Ptr Pokorny, *Colossians* (Peabody, MA: Hendriksen Publishers, 1991), 92.

1262 Pak, "A Study of Selected Passages on Distinguishing Marks of Genuine and False Believers", 275.

it. He says, "It is more probable that future glorification is also in view."[1263] Why is it "more probable"? Pak substantiates this in two ways. First he argues from Ephesians 5:26-27.

> *So that He might sanctify her, having* ***cleansed her by the washing of water*** *with the word, that He might present to Himself the church in all her glory, having no spot or wrinkle or any such thing; but that she would be holy and blameless (Ephesians 5:26–27).*

Pak says that the phrase "the church in all her glory" refers to the believers' perfected, resurrected bodies. But does the context suggest that?

The members of the church have been regenerated ("having cleansed her by the washing of water") and Christ's purpose is that He might (aorist subjunctive) also "sanctify her." The purpose of this sanctification is that He "might" (aor. subjunctive), present to Himself a church holy and blameless, etc. The subjunctives indicate uncertainty. Sanctification is a process involving both God and man. While it is certainly true that God's intention is that all believers be sanctified, it is obviously true that this does not always occur, because sanctification is not "all of God;" man's response is required. Pak admits this when he says, "Although sanctification invariably follows justification, it is difficult to describe the lives of certain believers as holy, blameless, and irreproachable."[1264]

He adds, "Since this happened while the lives of at least some of them [referring to the Corinthians] were still characterized by carnality (division in the church, immorality, idolatry, etc.), it would be difficult to say that in their lives, God's purpose of making them holy blameless and irreproachable has been accomplished." This glaring admission, buried in a footnote, not only negates his interpretation of Colossians 1:22-23 but invalidates his entire dissertation, which seeks to prove that the regenerate always have a life of works and always persevere in faith to the final hour.

Obviously, recognizing this problem, he explains,

> *It is also reasonable to view even these Corinthian believers reflected at least* ***some difference*** *in their lives from the lives of unbelievers in the city because when a member within [the] Corinthian church committed a serious sin in a defiant manner, not as an act of ignorance (1 Corinthians 5:1-15), Paul seems to have considered such a person as unsaved.*[1265]

But Paul does not say they are unsaved. He says they walk as "mere men" (1 Corinthians 3:3). Also the descriptions of their vices leave one perplexed about the "some difference" Pak sees between the Corinthians and the surrounding culture. According to Pak, on the one hand "sanctification invariably follows justification" but on the other hand it does not. Apparently all that is necessary for the believer to validate that he has been reconciled is that there is "some difference" between his life and that of nonbelievers.

Pak argues that because the word "glorious" is linked to being presented "holy and blameless" (Ephesians 5:27), the believer's glorification in a resurrection body is included.[1266] However, he confuses a theological idea, the glorification of the believer in a resurrection body, with the Greek word "glorious" (Gr *endochos*). This Greek word has no theological

---

1263 Ibid., 276.

1264 Ibid., 274, n. 78.

1265 Ibid., 274, n. 78.

1266 Ibid., 276.

connection to the concept of the believer's final transformation at the resurrection which Pak wants to draw from it.

Instead, it speaks of the relative glory and honor resulting from a well-lived life. To suggest that the goal of Christ's reconciliation is to provide His church with glorified bodies, removes the moral import of this context. His goal is to present the church brilliant in purity, mature, and composed of a people who have honored Him with their lives. The word "glorious" (Gr *endochos*), never refers to absolute perfection in the New Testament.[1267] Final glorification in Colossians 1:22-23 and Ephesians 5:25-27 is not included in the words for glory. Rather, the glory of a life lived faithfully to the end, pure, and unashamed is in view.

A more significant issue involves something Pak overlooks. In the marriage parallel there is no sense in which sanctification of the wife by the husband includes the notion of perfection. The whole context speaks of the husband's sacrificial love for his wife as being a relative purifying influence, not an absolute perfecting influence, on his wife. Sanctification is a setting apart in order to effect moral purity.[1268] Calvin correctly relates this passage not to final glorification (or including it) but to Christ's "inward work through which 'the fruits of that hidden purity become afterwards evident in outward works.'"[1269]

This passage teaches that just as Christ's sacrificial love for His church is intended to promote practical holiness and righteous acts (sanctification), so the husband's sacrificial love for his wife is intended to do the same. It would be a fiction to maintain that a husband's sacrificial love would result in perfect sanctification or include it. It is also fiction to assume that Christ's sacrifice results in absolute perfection in this life, and the context of Ephesians 5:26-27 is not about the resurrection body but about the moral perfection of the church. These verses parallel Colossians 1:28 where Paul says that his goal is to "present every man *complete* in Christ." Similarly, the goal of Christ is to "present to himself the church in all her glory." This is referred to in Revelation 19:8 as the "righteous acts of the saints." These acts will not be perfect, but they are commendable. Furthermore, just as the wife's growth in purity and blamelessness is also dependent on her responses (and not just her husband's love), so is the church's. The blamelessness in Ephesians 5:26-27 comes as a result of moral choices and is not the automatic purity of the resurrection body.[1270]

HOLY, BLAMELESS, AND WITHOUT BLEMISH

Probably, the major reason for understanding this passage with reference to salvation is that the words "holy," "blameless," and "without reproach" are taken absolutely. The focus here in Colossians 1:22-23 is on being presented holy, blameless, and beyond reproach. But does this refer to an absolute or a relative blamelessness? These are people who were "formerly alienated" from God and who are now reconciled (1:21-22). They are regenerate people who must "continue in the faith." Nonbelievers do not have faith in which to continue.

[1267] *Endochos* is used four times in the New Testament, once of the "glorious" garments of John the Baptist (Luke 7:25), once of being without "honor" (1 Corinthians 4:10) once in regard to the "wonderful" deeds of Christ (Luke 13:17), and here in Ephesians 5:27 of a "glorious" church.

[1268] Lincoln, *Ephesians*, 375.

[1269] Calvin, *Ephesians*, s.v. "Ep:5:27."

[1270] The idea that marriage partners by their godly behavior can effect change in one another is found in other places (1 Peter 3:1-2). Indeed, Christ, by His example (1 Peter 2:21), has led many a wayward lamb back into the fold (1 Peter 2:25).

At issue here is not arrival in heaven but whether believers will arrive there "holy, blameless, and beyond reproach."[1271] This is the goal toward which Paul labors (Colossians 1:28). This is a goal of sanctification, not salvation.

But what do the terms "holy," "blameless," and "irreproachable" mean in Colossians 1:22-23? Elsewhere in the New Testament the terms are used to describe imperfectly holy and imperfectly blameless Christians. Elders of the church, for example, are to be "beyond reproach" (Titus 1:6; 1 Timothy 3:10). When the 144,000 stand before the throne they are declared blameless, not because of their justification but because of their growth in progressive sanctification. There was no deceit in their mouth (Revelation 14:5). And believers are exhorted in 1 Corinthians 7:34 to be holy in both body and spirit. This obviously refers to an imperfect experiential relative holiness, not absolute justification. Also, Paul clearly relates these words when combined together to refer to a relative and not an absolute blamelessness.[1272]

> *Do all things without grumbling or disputing; so that you will prove yourselves to be **blameless** and **innocent**, children of God **above reproach** in the midst of a crooked and perverse generation, among whom you appear as lights in the world (Philippians 2:14–15).*

Paul's goal for them is not that they will attain sinless perfection (he knows that is not possible) but that they will be mature and experientially blameless, innocent, and above reproach in comparison to the rotten world in which they live.

Peter echoes a similar thought,

> *Therefore, beloved, since you look for these things, be diligent to be found by Him in peace, spotless and blameless (2 Peter 3:14).*

Becoming "spotless and blameless" does not come about through obtaining a glorified body, but by means of being "diligent" (Gr *spoudazō*, "take pains, make every effort").[1273]

The notion of being "blameless" in the sense of being experientially righteous is grounded in the Old Testament. "Blameless" never means perfectly blameless in the Bible. Beginning with Job we are told,

> *There was a man in the land of Uz whose name was Job; and that man was blameless, upright, fearing God and turning away from evil (Job 1:1).*[1274]

The Psalmist declares,

> *How blessed are those whose way is blameless, who walk in the law of the Lord (Psalm 119:1; cf. Deuteronomy 18:3).*

[1271] It is possible that this presentation is not eschatological at all. Lohse suggests that "the words 'before him' in Colossians do not primarily refer to the future day of the Lord. Rather, they express that the Christians' present lives are lived in God's presence." See Eduard Lohse, *Colossians and Philemon A Commentary on the Epistles to the Colossians and to Philemon*, Hermeneia (Philadelphia: Fortress Press, 1971), 65. This is also the view of Lightfoot, Ralph Martin, and C. D. F. Moule in their respective commentaries.

[1272] This is not to deny that Paul uses the term "holy" (Gr *hagios*) in the sense of absolute perfection in some contexts. We have been sanctified in an absolute way through the blood of Christ.

[1273] BDAG, 939.

[1274] The Heb *tōm* is translated *amemptos* in the LXX in this verse and variously translated elsewhere in the NASB as "guiltless" (Job 9:21), "blameless" (Psalms 37:37), "integrity" (Job 8:20). In no case is absolute perfection implied.

The Hebrew word for "blameless" [Heb *tāmîm*] in Psalm 119:1 (LXX Ps 118:1) was translated into Greek in the LXX as *amōmos*, the same word Paul uses in Ephesians 5:27 and Col 1:22. When the psalmist refers to a man who is blessed because his ways are blameless, he refers to the man's lifestyle: he does nothing wrong (v. 3), he observes God's statutes, and he seeks Him with all his heart (v. 2).

Similarly, David pleads for vindication saying,

> *Vindicate me, O Lord, for I have led a blameless [tōm] life; I have trusted in the Lord without wavering (Psalm 26:1).*

Elsewhere he refers to,

> *he whose walk is blameless [tāmîm] will minister to me (Psalm 101:6).*

Tāmîm is an adjective (also used as a substantive) that means "honest or devout" when applied to people. It refers to "purity, innocence, blamelessness, [one who] walked in *integrity*."[1275] Abraham was told that if he personally was to experience the blessings of the unconditional Abrahamic covenant, he must be "blameless." Waltke defines this as "wholeness of relationship and integrity rather than no sin."[1276] This is not the absolute blamelessness of justification, but the experiential and relative blamelessness of one who is mature and walks in God's ways.

In Pauline thought to be "blameless" is to be relatively pure and mature. He says,

> *That we may present every man complete [Gr* ***teleios****] in Christ. And for this purpose also I labor (Colossians 1:28-29).*

Most interpreters of the New Testament understand Paul's use of *teleios* to refer to maturity. This is the completeness to which James referred when he said we must endure trials joyfully so that we will be "perfect and complete, lacking in nothing" (James 1:4). This is the "mature man" to which Paul refers elsewhere when he says:

> *Until we all attain to the unity of the faith, and of the knowledge of the Son of God, to a mature [Gr teleios] man, to the measure of the stature which belongs to the fullness of Christ. As a result we are* ***no longer to be children****, tossed here and there by waves, and carried about by every wind of doctrine, ... but speaking the truth in love, we are* ***to grow up in all aspects*** *unto Him (Ephesians 4:13-15).*

In other words, while his goal is to produce "mature" (Gr *teleios*) Christians, he certainly knows that this will not always happen. But he presses on to promote the growth of his converts so that they will be relatively holy, relatively blameless, and relatively beyond reproach when they stand before the King at the Judgment Seat of Christ. These terms do not refer to the believer's future glorification. They refer to his present sanctification.

In conclusion, it is better to understand Colossians 1:22-23 not as a proof that those who are truly reconciled will necessarily continue in a life of holiness to the final hour. Rather, it is a passage that teaches that believers will be presented blameless and beyond reproach only if they remain steadfast, unmovable, and firmly established in their faith.

1275 Swanson, *Dictionary of Biblical Languages: Hebrew Old Testament*, #9448, s.v. "tom".

1276 Waltke, *Genesis: A Commentary*, 259.

Some will and some will not, but all who are genuinely born again will arrive in heaven when they die regardless of their faithfulness in this life.

1 Corinthians 15:1-2

Like Colossians 1:23, something in the experience of the Corinthians is conditioned on their holding fast:

> *Now I make known to you brethren, the gospel which I preached to you, which also you received, in which also you stand, by which also you are saved,* ***if you hold fast the word*** *which I preached to you, unless you believed in vain (1 Corinthians 15:1-2).*

Experimental Predestinarians find fodder in this passage for their doctrine that holding fast in the faith is the proof of the reality of saving faith and their teaching that justification and sanctification are always connected and cannot be separated. Kistemaker says, "They must hold on to that gospel and so demonstrate this in their conduct. Otherwise their faith will be hollow and worthless."[1277] Thus they translate the conditional clause "if you hold fast" as "if, as I assume to be the case, you hold fast."[1278] In other words we might paraphrase as follows,

> *If you are holding fast, this is proof that you are in fact born again and that you are saved now and if you continue to hold fast, you will be saved in the future. Should you stop holding fast, this would only prove that you were never born again.*

This interpretation is sometimes argued from the notion that the first-class conditional clause indicates reality, which as discussed above, is a very thin reed on which to lean.[1279]

Their interpretation also depends on the meaning of not believing "in vain." Some Experimental Predestinarians understand this to mean that there is a possibility that some believed spuriously, that they did not "truly" believe or have "genuine" faith. Calvin took this position: "He warns them that they had needlessly and uselessly professed allegiance to Christ, if they did not hold fast this main doctrine."[1280]

However, to "believe in vain" is not about their initial belief being spurious; it is about the object of their faith. Paul makes this clear a few verses later: "*If Christ has not been raised, then our preaching is vain, your faith also is vain*" (1 Corinthians 15:14). The Corinthians' faith would be groundless if the resurrection had not in fact occurred. Gundry Volf says, "If one has believed a message which cannot save, one would have believed in vain."[1281] (It is also possible that to "believe in vain" means to believe with no outcome of a sanctified life).

Arminians, of course, see this as another text that supports their doctrine that salvation can be lost if one fails to hold fast. "The expression 'believed in vain' would be meaningless [they say] unless someone who had actually believed could fail to receive the

---

1277 Kistemaker, *Exposition of the First Epistle to the Corinthians*, 257.

1278 Gundry Volf, *Paul and Perseverance*, 273.

1279 For full discussion of first-class conditional Greek clauses see James L. Boyer, "First Class Conditions: What Do They Mean?," *GTJ* 2, no. 73-114 (Spring 1981).

1280 Calvin, *1 Corinthians*, 313. R. E. Ciampa and B. S. Rosner, assert that "those who believe in the doctrine of the perseverance of the saints and those who reject that doctrine both agree that people who do not persevere in the gospel have no true claim on its promised blessings and benefits. See R. E. Ciampa and B. S. Rosner, *The First Letter to the Corinthians*, Pillar New Testament Commentary (Grand Rapids: Wm. B. Eerdmans Publishing Co., 2010), 744. See also, Fee, *The First Epistle to the Corinthians*.

1281 Gundry Volf, *Paul and Perseverance*, 274.

final salvation."[1282] Adam Clarke puts it this way: "Your future salvation, or being brought finally to glory, will now depend on your *faithfulness* to the grace that ye have received."[1283] Marshall says,

> *Salvation depends upon continuing to hold fast to the apostolic message, and to give up belief in one essential item of it, viz. the resurrection, as some of them apparently had done, was to give up hope of final salvation. Paul's principal point here is that attainment of salvation depends upon continuance in the apostolic faith.*[1284]

If the Experimental Predestinarian interpretation was correct, a past or future tense would be more appropriate. If the Arminian interpretation was correct, a future tense would make it clear, and we would translate, "*by which you will be saved if you hold fast*."

The Partner view offers another possibility.

Since the verb "saved" is a present tense, it is possible that salvation in this verse is not salvation from damnation but is a salvation that may take place throughout the Christian's life. While it could refer to "being in a present state of salvation from damnation," elsewhere in 1 Corinthians, when Paul speaks of salvation from damnation, he usually uses the past tense.[1285] Paul refers to salvation in the present in 1 Corinthians 1:18, where he speaks of the believing Corinthians who are in the process of being saved now (sanctification) in contrast to those who are "perishing" now, that is, falling further and further into corruption. The former will eventually enter heaven; the latter will eventually experience damnation. Those who are perishing now are those described in Romans 1:18-32, where a process of being given over to corruption results in continual degradation in time (Paul wrote Romans while he was in Corinth).[1286] See also 2 Corinthians 2:15; Romans 10:9-10.

This consistency of usage suggests that Lowery is correct when he says that the "tense of the verb saved focuses on sanctification."[1287] In this view one would translate, "*by which you are currently being saved, if you hold fast*," (cf. NET, ESV)[1288] and Paul's point is that "they are being saved now in the sense of progressive sanctification as long as they hold fast."[1289]

1282 Brenda B. Colijn, "The Three Tenses of Salvation in Paul's Letters," *Ashland Theological Journal* 22(1990): 34.

1283 Adam Clarke, "First Corinthians," in *Clarke's Commentaries* (Albany, OR: Ages Software, 1999), s.v. "1 Cor. 15:2", 1120.

1284 Marshall, *Kept by the Power of God: A Study of Perseverance and Falling Away*, 118. See also Hanse, "*katechō*," in TDNT, 2:829 "Only by this holding fast can present possession become eternal and heavenly possession," although Neonomians like Thomas Schreiner and Alan Stanley would say the same thing.

1285 1 Corinthians 1:21; 5:5; 10:33.

1286 Moo, *The Epistle to the Romans*, 2.

1287 David Lowery, "1 Corinthians," in *BKC: New Testament*, ed. John F. Walvoord and Roy B. Zuck (Colorado Springs: Cook, 1996), 2:542. Strangely, even though Thistelton says that "saved" is a "continuous present," he nevertheless asserts that it refers to "what is being done for them for the future." Thiselton, *The First Epistle to the Corinthians: A Commentary on the Greek Text*, 1185.

1288 Aldrich translates, "Through which also you are being saved, if you keep holding fast what I preached to you, except you believed in vain." Willard Maxwell Aldrich, "Perseverance," *BibSac* 115, no. 457 (January - March 1958): 12. Faussett agrees when he says, "Ye are being saved," A. R. Fausset, "The First Epistle of Paul the Apostle to the Corinthians," in *Commentary Critical and Explanatory on the Whole Bible*, ed. Robert Jamieson, A. R. Fausset, and David Brown (Oak Harbor: Logos Research Systems, 1997), s.v. "1 Cor. 15:2", 326.

1289 Martin Luther understood the salvation here to be salvation from the false teachers who were leading them astray in regard to the doctrine of the resurrection. Martin Luther, "1 Corinthians 7, 1 Corinthians 15, 1 Timothy," in *Luther's Works*, ed. J. J. Pelikan, H. C. Oswald, and H. T. Lehman (Philadelphia: Fortress Press, 1973), 28:66.

This present salvation is contingent on two things: (1) that they keep on believing; and (2) that the resurrection of Christ actually happened, that is, they did not "believe in vain."

Let's consider more closely the word "saved" and the word "hold fast" in their usage in the New Testament.

We have already established that the word "save" does not always mean saved from final damnation. In fact, in a number of places it refers to a present salvation in the sense of sanctification or deliverance from some present difficulty. For example,

> *For whoever wishes to save his life will lose it, but whoever loses his life for My sake, he is the one who will save it (Luke 9:24).*

As discussed elsewhere,[1290] to "save" one's soul means to find a rich life now by self-denial, taking up our cross, and following Christ, so that we will be favorably recompensed at the Judgment Seat of Christ.

Earlier in 1 Corinthians, Paul linked salvation not to damnation but to being saved "through fire" at the Judgment Seat of Christ (1 Corinthians 3:15). In 1 Timothy 2:4, Paul says he desires that all wayward believers may be saved in the present and return to knowledge of the truth. He says that women can be saved through childbearing (1 Tim 2:15). And he exhorted to Timothy,

> *Pay close attention to yourself and to your teaching; persevere in these things, for as you do this you will ensure salvation both for yourself and for those who hear you (1 Timothy 4:16).*

To "pay close attention" and to "persevere in these things" are equivalent to "hold fast," and the result is sanctification in this life and reward in the future, not escape from damnation.

Elsewhere in the New Testament believers are challenged to "hold fast" (Gr *katechō*) in order to bear fruit or to obtain reward. For example,

> *But the seed in the good soil, these are the ones who have heard the word in an honest and good heart, and* ***hold it fast*** [Gr *katechō*]***, and bear fruit*** *with perseverance (Luke 8:15).*

Holding fast *to the message of Christ* is not a condition of escape from final damnation but is a condition for bearing fruit.

Similarly, the writer to the Hebrews says,

> *Let us hold fast* [Gr *katechō*] *the confession of our hope without wavering, for He who promised is faithful (Hebrews 10:23).*

He then explains the outcome of holding fast:

> *Therefore, do not throw away your confidence, which has a great reward. For you have need of endurance, so that when you have done the will of God, you may receive what was promised (Hebrews 10:35–36).*

The word "hold fast" is used seventeen times in the New Testament, and unless 1 Corinthians 15:2 is an exception, there is no place where it means "hold fast in order to prove that you were saved initially" or "hold fast or you will lose your salvation."

We conclude, therefore, that when Paul tells the Corinthians that they are being saved

---

[1290] See discussion in chapter 15 above.

now if they hold fast the word which he preached, he is speaking of their being saved from the corruptions of their past life and the salvation to the temporal blessings of salvation, sanctification. He is not warning these believers that they might not have "truly" believed, or that they might lose their final salvation. He is warning them that they will no longer experience the present blessings of sanctification and the future blessings of ultimate reward at the Judgment Seat of Christ (1 Corinthians 3:15) if they depart from the gospel of Christ's resurrection, as some of them have done.

Aldrich summarizes,

> *The primary thought in the verse [1 Corinthians 15:2] has to do with present deliverance from sin, and this is conditioned upon continuous faith in Christ. The verse does not have to do with the ultimate condition of the soul. Present-tense salvation is somewhat of a variable. In this life we never find complete deliverance from the sin nature and its eruptions into the leprous sores of outbroken sin, but deliverance comes in the measure that we trust the Savior.*[1291]

Summary

Experimental Predestinarians have argued vigorously for their view concerning the inevitable and necessary permanent connection between justification and sanctification. If the above analysis is correct, they have not argued convincingly. Their claim that a person must have "greater righteousness," that is, a life of good works, if he desires to enter the kingdom of heaven, is correct. However, entering the kingdom and being saved are two different things. To enter the kingdom is to enter into a kingdom way of living leading to high honor in the kingdom. The subject is sanctification and reward, not soteriology.

It is also argued that because believers are under the New Covenant they will be caused to persevere, because the law of God is written on their hearts. The New Covenant also promises, however, that "all will know the Lord." The New Covenant has been inaugurated but clearly not yet completely fulfilled. It will not be fulfilled until the millennium. When the new age dawns, and only then, will God's promise be fulfilled, that is, to "cause" His people to obey.

While it is true, as Experimentalists claim that a disciple does the will of God, the Partners maintain that not all Christians are disciples.

Paul says that Christ's desire is to present the Colossians holy and blameless at the judgment. He will achieve this aim only if they "continue in the faith." In Reformed thinking, if they are truly saved, God will guarantee that they will continue. These writers say that continuance in the faith is not a condition of salvation, but a characteristic of all who are perfectly sanctified, that is, saved. However, it *is in fact a condition* and to be "holy and blameless" does not refer to absolute perfection, but to a relative sanctification and maturity as all other references to it established. It is true, that believers will be presented mature and full of good works if they persevere. Colossians 1:22-23 does not relate to soteriology, it refers to sanctification and rewards.

Finally, the argument from 1 Corinthians 15:2 that all true believers "hold fast" because only those who "hold fast" will go to heaven is not convincing. A more likely understanding is that being saved in this passage refers to present sanctification and not to future entrance into heaven. When one "holds fast," one is growing as a Christian in the present.

[1291] Aldrich, "Perseverance," 14.

26

Justification and Sanctification 2

MANY OTHER arguments are sometimes offered for the teaching that the New Testament connects justification and sanctification as an inseparable unity.

The New Creation

Experimental Predestinarians are properly impressed with the fact that Paul says any man in Christ is a new creation:

> *Therefore if any man is in Christ, he is a new creature; the old things passed away; behold new things have come (2 Corinthians 5:17).*

From this passage Iain H. Murray concludes, "So Calvinism says that Christ's work for us—that is the legal, forensic side of salvation—is never without Christ's work in us. Wherever there is a true change in a man's relation to God there is also a change in his subjective, moral, personal state. Thus, on this understanding, faced with the question, 'Do I belong to Christ?' the Christian is permitted to argue, 'Yes I do belong to Christ because I find in myself changes which He alone can work and changes which only His unbought love prompted Him to work.'"[1292]

What is the new creation? While some, like Iain Murray, have interpreted this to refer to subjective internal moral renewal, this is by no means the prevalent view.[1293] The fact that Paul connects the new creation with our being "in Christ" points us to a positional status rather than an experiential one.[1294] As Martyn Lloyd-Jones says, "We must differentiate between what is true of our position as a fact and our experience."[1295] By position, Lloyd-Jones means what a Christian is as a new man, perfect in Christ. The crucifixion of the old man (Romans 6:6) like the creation of the new man, is not experiential knowledge. Lloyd-Jones objects strongly to Charles Hodge on this point: "My entire exposition [of Romans 6:1-11] asserts the exact opposite and says that it is not experiential; and that to

1292 Iain H. Murray, "Will the Unholy Be Saved?," *The Banner of Truth* no. 246 (March 1984): 4.

1293 See, for example, George E. Ladd, *Theology of the New Testament* (Grand Rapids: Wm. B. Eerdmans Publishing Co., 1974), 479. He rejects the idea that this passage should be interpreted "in terms of subjective experience."

1294 The "new creation" is commonly interpreted as a kind of proleptic anticipation, an assurance here and now of something that will happen experientially in the last day. Then we are perfect. See H. H. Esser, "Creation," in NIDNTT, 1:385.

1295 Martin Lloyd-Jones, *The Sons of God: Exposition of Romans 8:5-17* (Grand Rapids: Zondervan Publishing House, 1975), 21.

take it experientially produces utter confusion. This is not experiential knowledge; it is the knowledge of faith, it is the knowledge which is revealed in the Scripture, and of which faith is certain."[1296]

The new creation of the heavens and the earth (Revelation 21:1; Isaiah 65:17; 66:22) does not refer to a renovation of the old creation, but the creation of a new order. Peter tells us to look for the total destruction of the present order (2 Peter 3:12) and the creation of a new heavens and a new earth (2 Peter 3:13). Similarly, the "old man" was crucified. He no longer can inevitably dominate the new man in Christ, and each believer is a new man in Christ.

The new man in Ephesians 4:24 is the regenerate self (Colossians 3:3-4). In no sense is he the old self made over or improved.[1297] The new self is Christ "formed" in the Christian.[1298] He is the new nature united with one's personality.

The new nature is a new metaphysical entity, created perfect by God at regeneration. It is a "creation." In Ephesians 4:24 we learn that the new man was created *kata theon*, "according to the standard of God," in righteousness, and in *hosiotēs*, "holiness, piety" of truth. It appears that this new self is as perfect as God is, just as it is as righteous as God is (2 Corinthians 5:21). The perfection and righteousness are ascribed to the believer by nature of his being "in Christ." The fact that it has been "created" means that it has no sin in it. God would not create something with sin in it. Does this mean that the person is perfect in experience? No. The person, the "ego," lives in either his new capacity or his old. The person always has both and is always sinful. But when viewed from the single perspective of the person as united to the new creation, that is, the new man, he is perfect. That union, that identity is man as God intends man to be. However, no person will ever live life as the perfect new creation until his old nature is experientially as well as forensically gone at the resurrection.

Finally, in Colossians 3:10 we are told to "put on the new man which is being renewed."[1299] The "new self" is being renewed in knowledge in the image of the Creator.[1300] How can a perfect new man in Christ be "renewed"? The renewal is "into" (*eis*) knowledge and "according to" (*kata*) the image of God. The new man, while without sin, is not mature. In the same way, Jesus, who was perfect, was "made perfect" (Hebrews 2:10) through suffering. Like Jesus, the new man, who really is in Christ, is renewed through suffering (2 Corinthians 4:16).[1301]

Paul refers to the perfect new creation in Christ when he says:

> *So now, no longer am I the one doing it, but sin which indwells me (Romans 7:17).*
>
> *But if I am doing the very thing I do not wish, I am no longer the one doing it, but sin which dwells in me (Romans 7:20).*

[1296] Ibid., 61.

[1297] 2 Corinthians 5:17; Galatians 6:15; Ephesians 2:10; Colossians 3:10.

[1298] Galatians 2:20; 4:19; Colossians 1:27; 1 John 4:12.

[1299] Or "Seeing … you have put on the new man."

[1300] "Renewed" translates *anakainoumenon*, from anakainoō, the same word used in 2 Corinthians 4:16, "inwardly we are being renewed day by day." Paul refers to the new creation in Galatians 6:15, where he says that only walking consistently is the rule of the new creation.

[1301] "Jesus grew in wisdom and stature" (Luke 2:52).

His meaning is transparent when seen in this light. The sin in the believer's life is not a product of the new creation! The new creation is sinless and created according to righteousness. Sin is no longer part of our true identity. Lloyd-Jones finds further evidence for the perfect, sinless, new man in Christ in these verses. He notes that Paul will say, "I am not doing this or that, it is this sin that remains in my members that does so. Sin is no longer in me; it is in my members only. That is the most liberating thing you have ever heard. Our old self is gone, we should never think of ourselves in those terms again."[1302]

Therefore, when Paul says that we are now a new creation in Christ, he is not saying that we have been experientially transformed and will inevitably manifest a life of good works. In fact, he repeatedly asks us to act like who we really are. He tells us to "reckon ourselves dead to sin" and to present ourselves to God "as those alive from the dead" (Romans 6:13). He commands us to "put on the new man" (Ephesians 4:24; Colossians 3:10). His meaning is that we are to be in experience what we already are in Christ. If it is automatic and inevitable that this will happen, why command it? More to the point, nowhere does the Bible assert that, just because a person is a new creation, he will act like who he is in Christ to the final hour.

The Christian Cannot Live in Sin

Any discussion of the relationship between God's free gift of the justifying righteousness of Christ and the life of works which should follow cannot ignore the central passage on the subject, Romans 6. Experimental Predestinarians quote it often in support of their view.

As is generally recognized, the context begins with Romans 5:20, where Paul concludes that sin produces more grace to cover it up. He marvels at the grace of God! As might be expected, however, such a doctrine would be open to the charge that it logically leads to a life of license. Paul puts the words of the imaginary objector into his epistle and opens Romans 6 with his complaint: "*What shall we say, then? Are we to continue in sin that grace might increase?*" (Romans 6:1). His opening statement should have alerted the Experimental Predestinarians to their misunderstanding of the passage. He is not discussing whether it is possible for a believer to continue in sin but whether such a lifestyle is logically derived from the premise that grace abounds where sin increases.

His answer to this objector is one of horror, "*May it never be! How shall we who died to sin still live in it?*" Once again, he does not ask, "How could those who died to sin have the capability to live in sin?" Whether true believers have this capacity to fall into sin is not Paul's question. He is refuting the notion that a life of sin is a logical outcome of the gospel of grace. Paul's response is that such a lifestyle is in no way a logical deduction from his doctrine.

Experimental Predestinarians derive three arguments from this passage (Romans 6) to justify their notion that sanctification necessarily follows justification. First, they are struck with the words "dead to sin." A "decisive breach" with sin has occurred. Second, Paul assures his readers that "sin shall not have dominion over them." Third, the contrasts between what they were before becoming Christians and what they are now in Christ (6:15-23) imply, it is thought, that Christians cannot be characterized by the things of the old man.

[1302] Lloyd-Jones, *The Sons of God: Exposition of Romans 8:5-17*, 83.

DEAD TO SIN

Central to the understanding of this important passage is the significance of the concept of being "dead to sin." While some have argued that it means "death for sin" and teaches that we died for our own sins in Christ,[1303] most have concluded that a break with the sin nature's authority, and not sin's penalty, is in view. What is the nature of this break?

Some teach that Paul's meaning is that our death to sin is "positional." By this they mean this truth is not necessarily experienced but is absolutely true in the reckoning of God. It is "true" truth.[1304] Just as we did not experience dying with Christ, so we did not experience our death to the sin nature. The practical effect of this positional death to sin is that we are no longer obligated to obey it as our master.

John Murray uses the word "actual" instead of "positional" in commenting on Romans 6:

> *And this victory is actual or it is nothing. It is a reflection upon and a deflection from the pervasive New Testament witness to speak of it as merely potential or positional. It is actual and practical as much as anything comprised in the application of redemption is actual and practical.*[1305]

He says this victory over the power of sin was achieved "once and for all" and is not achieved by a process, nor by our striving or working to that end. Yet he differs from perfectionism in three ways:

1. They (perfectionists) fail to recognize that this victory is possessed by everyone who is born of God.
2. They portray it as freedom from sinning or freedom from conscious sin, but the Bible says it is a freedom from the power and love of sin.
3. They say this victory is a second blessing distinct from the state of justification.

Murray hardly makes it clear how an actual, practical, and real break with the sin nature's power and authority, achieved once for all, can leave us with the daily struggle. The terms used in Romans 6 describe, as Murray admits, something decisive and total. They are "absolute-death" to sin. But if this total break is real, actual, and practical, then there should be no daily struggle. Since there is a daily struggle because of indwelling sin, according to Murray, how can he claim that the death to sin is "real" in the experiential sense? Murray's "death to sin" is real in the heavenlies but not real on earth unless we act on what is real up there. If it is real here, then there is no indwelling sin that has any power over us. He says that "there must be a constant and increasing appreciation that though sin still remains it does not have the mastery."[1306]

He is therefore admitting that it is not real, practical, nor actual "once and for all" in our experience. Could we even say, then, it is potential in our experience? That is what

---

[1303] William G. T. Shedd, *Commentary on Romans*, reprint ed. (Grand Rapids: Zondervan Publishing House, 1967), 146.

[1304] Watchman Nee, *The Normal Christian Life* (Fort Washington, PA: Christian Literature Crusade, 1957), 59.

[1305] John Murray, "Definite Sanctification," in *Collected Writings of John Murray* (Edinburgh: Banner of Truth Trust, 1977), 142. *Accomplished and Applied*, 142.

[1306] Murray, *Redemption--Accomplished and Applied*, 145.

many mean by positional truth. By using the word "actual" in order to justify his doctrine of perseverance in holiness, Murray is trying to make the text say that believers will never live in sin.

> *There is a total difference between surviving sin and reigning sin, the regenerate in conflict with sin and the unregenerate complacent to sin. It is one thing for sin to live in us: it is another for us to live in sin. It is one thing for the enemy to occupy the capital; it is another for his defeated hosts to harass the garrisons of the kingdom.*[1307]

This is great rhetoric, but does it really say anything? Apparently our death to sin was sufficient to overcome reigning sin, but our union with Christ was not sufficient to overcome remaining sin. Where is the difference between "reigning sin" and "remaining sin" found in Scripture? Is there really any difference between sin living (i.e., expressing itself in life) in us and our living in sin? The fact that as believers we are no longer complacent to sin does not mean that sin is not very much alive or incapable of taking the capital again if we do not submit to the Lord of the kingdom.

But why does Paul say, "How can we who died to sin, continue to live in it?" Paul is refuting an objection. His statement is very definite and absolute. He is not saying we partially died. He says that we completely died to sin. If this death is an experiential death, then a serious problem develops. Who in the Calvinist tradition claims that his experiential death to sin is absolute and total? This passage can be harmonized with the Experimental Predestinarian doctrine of perseverance only by watering down Paul's absolute statements to say that we died to sin a little bit experientially and that we become deader as we mature. Yet the passage is not saying that. We died to sin (absolute); we have been "justified from sin" (absolute); indeed, our relationship to sin is as total a severance and death as that of Jesus Himself, which is absolute (Romans 6:9-10). As Paul put it, we have died to sin "once for all" (6:10).

Therefore we must ask, "Is this death to sin actual in our experience or actual in the reckoning of revelation?" The fact that Paul says in Romans 6:7 that the man who has died is "justified" from sin implies that for Paul this death to sin is legal, forensic, and positional, and not automatically real in experience; it is absolute, not partial. It is ours *in heaven* because of the *blood of Christ* and our unity in His death. The Gr *dikaioō* is his normal word for the legal justification of the sinner.[1308] It is a forensic and not a "real in experience" term. In fact, after pages of adjectives describing our "decisive breach" with sin, Murray comes to the same conclusion! When he is finally forced to state exactly what he means by a "real decisive breach" with sin, we are told that on the basis of Romans 6:7, Paul's meaning is that it is "forensic and juridical."[1309] Now this is the common meaning of positional truth, the very doctrine which Murray assails.

Death to sin is real in our position but not necessarily experienced in this life. Paul's commands to believers, to present themselves to righteousness and to reckon themselves dead to sin, imply that some might not necessarily do this. As Howe put it, "If the believer's death with Christ described in Romans 6:1-10 is 'actual' [in experience], then

---

[1307] Ibid.

[1308] BAGD, 196.

[1309] Murray, "Definite Sanctification."

exactly what is meant by Romans 6:11? If death means cessation of existence actually, then why does Paul urge believers in that verse to reckon (count, consider as true, realize, believe) themselves dead to sin?"[1310] We should do this, but there is the possibility of negligence. However, if we do this, we will be successful, because we present ourselves "as those who are alive" and because "sin will not have dominion."

SIN WILL NOT HAVE DOMINION

When Paul tells his readers that "sin will not have dominion over you" (Romans 6:14), John Murray concludes that this means that sanctification inevitably follows from justification. But is it not obvious that this victory is conditioned on what he has just said? Sin will not have dominion in the future *if we do what Paul says we should do—reckon and yield right now*. This is a promise of success if we apply the God-appointed means, and not a statement of reality irrespective of those means.

The text does not say that sin does not have dominion. It says sin *will not have dominion* (*kyrieusei*, future tense, in contrast to the aorist and perfect tenses of the context), *if we reckon and yield*. If a believer does not reckon and yield, then sin can have dominion in his life. The fact that believers have died to sin does not automatically mean they will reckon and yield. It means that, if they do reckon and yield, they will be successful.

Paul continues, "*For just as you presented your members as slaves to impurity and to lawlessness, resulting in further lawlessness, so now present your members as slaves to righteousness, resulting in sanctification*" (6:19). It is true that they "became obedient from the heart" (6:17), but now they must continually make choices regarding which master they will serve, whether sin or Christ. The victory is that they no longer have to obey sin, and if they choose not to, they will be successful. But if they do not so choose, they will not be successful, and sin will have dominion over them.

Paul is refuting a logical argument against grace. It logically follows, the objector says, that we should continue to sin to make more grace abound. Paul says this is illogical, but not impossible. He asks, "Do you not know?" He appeals to an intellectually apprehensible fact of the divine reckoning. It is illogical because grace not only includes (1) the forgiveness of sin but also (2) the removal of sin's legal dominion and (3) the impartation of life. Because we are united with Christ in His death, sin no longer has the legal right to rule us. Since we are united with Him in resurrection, we have new life within us that gives us the power to overcome sin and the motivation to want to overcome it. Because we died to sin, we no longer have to sin, and since we live in Christ, we no longer want to sin. A man who does not have to do what he does not want to do does not normally do it. Thus the objection is fully answered. The fact that a believer could subsequently quench the Spirit, become carnal, stop growing or fall away does not strengthen the objector's case. Logically, the gospel does not lead to a continuance in sin; instead, it encourages a cessation from it. Any gospel that breaks a person from sin's power and gives him new life, the divine enablement to resist sin, and motivation not to sin is not subject to the charge that it logically results in license, even if an individual Christian resists the positive influences of grace.

[1310] Frederick R. Howe, "A Review of Birthright by David Needham," *BibSac* 141, no. 161 (January-March 1984): 71.

SLAVES OF RIGHTEOUSNESS (ROMANS 6:16-23)

In Romans 6:16-23, some find evidence that justification and sanctification are inextricably connected. In verse 18, we read, "*and having been freed from sin, you became slaves of righteousness.*" Reformed theologians say that all "true" believers are free from sin and have become "slaves of righteousness." Shedd concludes, "A will which, by regeneration, has been powerfully determined and inclined to holiness, is unable to sin, in the sense in which Christ intends when he says, that 'a good tree cannot bring forth evil fruit.'" Then, of course, the qualification begins, "But it means that the regenerate will be unable to sin in the manner that the unregenerate will: i.e., impenitently and totally."[1311]

The fact that a man may not reckon and yield to sin is indicated by the existence of the commands to do so. Those from an Experimental Predestinarian persuasion feel, of course, that this proves nothing. The commands, they say, are one of God's means for securing obedience,[1312] and it is certain that the thrust of the life will be one of obedience. However, it is evident that the commands do not *always* secure obedience. While our Reformed friends are certain that the commands and warnings will keep the elect from falling away, there are numerous biblical illustrations that contradict this belief.[1313]

The contrasts in the latter half of Romans 6 must be seen in this light. They were "slaves of sin," but now they have "*become obedient from the heart to that form of teaching to which you were committed*" (Romans 6:17). They were "slaves to sin" and are now "slaves to righteousness" (Romans 6:18). They have been "freed from sin" and are "enslaved to God" (Romans 6:22). Paul explains that we are only slaves of the person we obey:

> *Do you not know that when you present yourselves to someone as slaves for obedience, you are slaves of the one whom you obey, either of sin resulting in death, or of obedience resulting in righteousness (Romans 6:16).*

Slavery to sin leads to death (spiritual and psychological ruin), and obedience leads to moral righteousness, a rich experience of eternal life. Death for the non-Christian is both temporal (ending of this physical life) and, of course, eternal and final. For the Christian, death is temporal judgment and spiritual impoverishment as in Romans 8:13. A person becomes a slave when he repeatedly submits himself to a master. While Paul may have physical death in mind, his concept of death is much broader. As he explains in Romans 7:8-13 and 8:6-13, death can be the experience of the Christian in this life. It is the spiritual impoverishment or sin unto death which can come upon the carnal Christian.[1314]

These Roman Christians had not only received the righteousness of Christ through faith alone, but in addition, they had submitted themselves to the Lordship of Christ subsequent

---

1311 Shedd, *Commentary on Romans*, 166.

1312 They cite, for example, Paul's account of the shipwreck at sea (Acts 27:22-25) to prove the exhortations and warnings are the means of achieving the inevitable perseverance of the saints in good works. I address this fully in vol. 2, chapter 36.

1313 For substantiation of this statement see vol. 2, chapter 32.

1314 James agrees, "When tempted, no one should say, 'God is tempting me.' For God cannot be tempted by evil nor does he tempt anyone; but each one is tempted when by his own evil desire he is dragged away and enticed. Then, after desire has conceived, it gives birth to sin; **and sin, when it is full-grown, gives birth to death"** (James 1:13-15).

to saving faith and had become obedient from the heart. Their obedience was producing moral righteousness:[1315]

But thanks be to God that though you were slaves of sin, you became obedient from the heart to that form of teaching to which you were committed (Romans 6:17).

They were already committed to the "form [Gr *tupos*] of teaching."[1316] They were already Christians. But in addition to being Christians, they became obedient from the heart, that is, they obeyed sincerely. They not only believed in Christ but they also submitted to Christ's Lordship. They became obedient to truth to which they had already committed themselves.

And having been freed from sin, you became slaves of righteousness. I am speaking in human terms because of the weakness of your flesh. For just as you presented your members as slaves to impurity and to lawlessness, resulting in further lawlessness, so now present your members as slaves to righteousness, resulting in sanctification [Gr *hagiasmos*, "holiness"] *(Romans 6:18-19).*

When they were non-Christians, they were slaves to impurity. Now they are Christians, and Paul wants them to keep on presenting their members to righteousness. If they do, the result will be personal holiness ("sanctification"). It is not automatic that they will keep on presenting themselves as slaves. They have made a good beginning, and Paul wants them to continue it:

For when you were slaves of sin, you were free in regard to righteousness. Therefore what benefit were you then deriving from the things of which you are now ashamed? For the outcome of those things is death (Romans 6:20-21).

When they were non-Christians, they received no benefits from their profligate lifestyle. The result of it was death. By "death" Paul means emptiness of life, that is, spiritual and psychological impoverishment.

Paul does not want them to return to that:

But now having been freed from sin and enslaved to God, you derive your benefit [Gr *karpos*, "fruit"]*, resulting in sanctification, and the outcome, eternal life (Romans 6:22).*

They were positionally freed from sin and enslaved to God when they became Christians (Romans 6:6-7). What is the benefit ("fruit")? Is it not the acts of God legally freeing them from sin and legally enslaving them to God? The fruit is their legal union with Christ.

The benefit of this legal union is growth in sanctification. The "fruit" ("benefit," Gr *karpos)*" is not sanctification itself, but rather is that which leads "to" sanctification. Fruit and sanctification are clearly distinguished. It is a fruit "to" (Gr *eis)* sanctification, not fruit "which is" sanctification. Sanctification here refers to the increase in ethical renewal and growth.[1317] The fruit is their positional and legal freedom from sin and slavery to God.

[1315] Paul has said earlier that "if Abraham was justified by works, he has something to boast about" and "to the one who does not work, but believes in Him who justifies the ungodly, his faith is reckoned as righteousness" (Romans 4:2, 5). Forensic righteousness comes by faith alone; moral righteousness comes by works of obedience.

[1316] This means "a kind, class, or thing that suggests a model or pattern." BDAG, 1020.

[1317] The noun *hagiasmos* occurs in the New Testament eight other times (v. 22; 1 Corinthians 1:30; 1 Thessalonians

This is the basis of sanctification, but does not necessarily result in it. Furthermore, their growth in sanctification has a wonderful outcome, eternal life. We suggest that by "eternal life" Paul refers to that enriched experience of life which comes as a result of progressive sanctification and not final entrance into heaven which comes by faith alone.

We were "enslaved" (passive voice, Romans 6:22) to God. This enslavement was legal and positional as the preceding context makes clear. A person may be the slave of a new master, but he may be a disobedient slave. This is a restatement of verse 16, "*Do you not know that when you present yourselves to someone as slaves (active voice) you are slaves of the one whom you obey?*" If one does not obey, he may be a slave of his new Master, but he is not acting like one. All Christians are born again as servants of their new Master. But they are not necessarily obedient servants unless they choose to be. Paul had already made it clear that experiential slavery to righteousness is a personal choice, and nowhere does he say it is the necessary or inevitable outcome of their regeneration. He says, "*Present yourselves to God, as those alive from the dead*" (Romans 6:13). He also says, "Present your members as slaves to righteousness" (Romans 6:19). We *are* slaves, whether we present our members or not. We *are* alive from the dead, whether we act like it or not!

If we continue to present ourselves for His service and continue as obedient slaves to Him, then, and only then, will we receive the benefit which is sanctification.

What about the "outcome," which is "eternal life"? Since eternal life is a result of personal holiness, that is, sanctification, Paul must have the enriched experience of eternal life in mind. This was a part of his opening statement in the epistle, "*Now the one who is righteous, by faith shall live*" (Romans 1:17).

Paul now summarizes the two principles he has been making in the entire context. For believers, sin leads to death, holiness leads to a rich experience of eternal life now.

> *For the wages of sin is death, but the free gift of God is eternal life in Christ Jesus our Lord (Romans 6:23).*

Death is the final wage for sin. The word for "wages" (Gr *opsōnion*) means payment or compensation. It refers to "whatever is bought to be eaten with bread, as fish, flesh, corn, meat, fruits, and salt were given the soldiers instead of pay."[1318]

While this verse certainly has application to nonbelievers and is a favorite verse used by many in gospel presentations, technically this context is speaking of sanctification and not soteriology all through Romans 6-8. Thus Paul speaks here of the wages of sin for Christians. It is "death," that is, spiritual and psychological ruin. But the free gift of eternal life blossoms into a rich life now as we follow Paul's prescription in the preceding verses.

The sequence is:

1. Positional death to sin's power – We must reckon this to be true.
2. Progressive sanctification by perseverance in faith and obedience – We must yield ourselves to obedience.
3. An enriched experience of eternal life as the result of 1 and 2.

4:3, 4, 7; 2 Thessalonians 2:13; 1 Timothy 2:15; Hebrews 12:14; 1 Peter 1:2). In each instance it seems to refer to God's transforming work in the believer. In contrast to being "freed from sin" and "enslaved to God," it is a process rather than a state.

1318 Joseph Thayer, *A Greek-English Lexicon of the New Testament* (New York: American Book Co., 1898), 471.

Eternal life begins with regeneration by faith alone. But to enjoy it fully, we must persevere in faith and obedience. James agrees (James 1:17-18, 21).

The "wages of sin" is ultimately eternal death, but Paul has in mind the temporal experience of psychological/spiritual ruin. He echoes James, "*But each one is tempted when he is carried away and enticed by his own lust. Then when lust has conceived, it gives birth to sin; and when sin is accomplished,* ***it brings forth death***" (James 1:14–15). If James and Paul are referring to eternal death, there should be a lot of dead Christians around! But as Paul says later, death can also be experienced by carnal believers as temporal spiritual ruin (Romans 8:13). He refers over and over again to the temporal "death" that he himself experienced while trying to live the Christian life by means of law (Romans 7:5, 8-11, 24). Such death is not final damnation, it is spiritual/psychological ruin! In agreement with this writer, Dunn relates "eternal life" in this context not to final entrance into heaven (although it includes that) but to the experience of that life which we must receive as a gift every day. It must, he says, be "entered ... ever and again throughout life in this mortal body."[1319] Paul is still speaking of sanctification, not soteriology. Eternal life is given to us initially through faith alone, but then developed into a rich experience of God in the present by continually presenting ourselves to our new Master. Nothing in Romans 6 requires the interpretation that a Christian will inevitably persevere in good works up to the point of physical death.

By Their Fruits You Shall Know Them

Probably, the most commonly recognized statement that is thought to support the Reformed doctrine of perseverance is Jesus' warning, "By their fruits you shall know them" (Matthew 7:16). They assume that Christ meant that one can discern whether or not another person is truly a Christian by examining the evidence of good works in his life. If there is good work (fruit) present, it must be a good tree, that is, regenerate. If good character qualities are not obvious, then the tree must be bad, he is unregenerate. This initial impression, they believe, is reinforced by Christ's stinging rebuke to these false teachers, "*I never knew you,*"[1320] and by His explanation that only the person "*who does the will of My Father who is in heaven will enter the kingdom of heaven*" (Matthew 7:21).[1321]

Before considering this interpretation in more detail, let us make an obvious point. The Scriptures are perfectly clear that a good tree *can* produce bad fruit and that a bad tree *can* produce good fruit (e.g., Romans 2:14-15). As James said, out of the mouth of a believer can come both blessing and cursing (James 3:10). James expects a negative answer in response to his question, "*Does a fountain send out from the same opening both fresh and bitter water?*" (James 3:11). James' point is not that this *cannot* be, but that "*these things ought not to be*" (v. 10). Since it is obvious that good trees can on occasion produce bad fruit (e.g., David or carnal Christians at Corinth), what does Christ mean in Matthew 7:16? The sense is that the *person who is walking in fellowship with Christ*, that is, a good tree, will not act this way. Chrysostom (347-407) said,

[1319] Dunn, *Romans 1-8*, 357.

[1320] For discussion of this phrase see pp. 318-22 ff.

[1321] For discussion of the phrase, "will of the Father," see pp. 312 ff.

But Christ saith not this, that for the wicked there is no way to change, or that the good cannot fall away, but that so long as he is living in wickedness, he will not be able to bear good fruit. For he may indeed change to virtue, being evil; but while continuing in wickedness, he will not bear good fruit.

He gives the example of David who certainly did not commit evil while he was walking "in the habit of virtue."[1322] The good tree is the believer who is abiding in Christ, and the bad tree is the man who is not (either non-Christian or Christian). This does not necessarily refer only to an ontological difference, that is, his essential nature, but rather to his current habit of life. These false prophets claimed to be good trees, but because of their lack of "fruit," it was clear that their claims were false.

To return to the central question, "Is Jesus suggesting that one must obey Him in order to enter the kingdom of God in a saving sense (i.e., "go to heaven when one dies")? Such an interpretation obviously contradicts the clear teaching elsewhere that entrance into the kingdom of heaven is based on faith alone. To resolve this difficulty Experimental Predestinarians inject their theological system into the passage and say that since all believers persevere in holiness to the end of life, it is certainly true that only those who do the Father's will, will enter the kingdom. If a person fails to do this, this proves he was not a Christian at all.[1323]

The Partners view the matter differently. After exhorting His disciples to enter the kingdom by the narrow way, that is, the way of discipleship, Jesus now warns them that there are false teachers present who would lead the sheep to the wrong gate and path. These men come in "sheep's" clothing, but inwardly they are "ravenous wolves." Today, one might think of Bible teachers and theologians who deny the essentials of Christianity and destroy the faith of many. Warnings about this are common in the New Testament. I remember, as a college student, listening to religion professors debunk the historicity of the Gospels and deny Jesus' resurrection.

Yet, what a person is on the inside is not obvious, and thus a test is needed to determine his nature.

You will know them by their fruits. Grapes are not gathered from thorn bushes, nor figs from thistles, are they? (Matthew 7:16)

To what does the " fruit" refer? We suggest that for Matthew, "fruit" involves two things, life and doctrine. In this passage it could refer to their deeds as in Matthew 3:2, but the parallel passage in chapter 12 suggests that the doctrine of the false teachers was in view, not their lifestyle:

And whoever ***shall speak a word against the Son of Man****, it shall be forgiven him, but whoever* ***shall speak against the Holy Spirit****, it shall not be forgiven him, either in this age or, in the age to come. Either make the tree good, and its* ***fruit*** *good, or make the tree bad, and its* ***fruit*** *bad; for* ***the tree is known by its fruit****. You brood of vipers, how can you, being evil,* ***speak what***

1322 John Chrysostom, "Homilies on Matthew," in *A Select Library of the Nicene and Post-Nicene Fathers of the Christian Church, First Series, Volume X*, , ed. P. Schaff (New York: Christian Literature Company, 1988), s.v. "Matthew 23:8," 10:164.

1323 Stanley D. Toussaint, *Behold the King* (Portland, OR: Multnomah Press, 1980), 115-19.

> ***is good?*** *For the mouth speaks out of that which fills the heart. The good man out of his good treasure brings forth what is good; and the evil man out of his evil treasure brings forth what is evil. And I say to you, that every careless word that men shall speak, they shall render account for it in the day of judgment.* ***For by your words you shall be justified, and by your words you shall be condemned*** *(Matthew 12:32-37).*

Their lifestyle seems to indicate they are Christians. They are called sheep; they look like Christians. Works are therefore not determinative as an indicator of one's salvation or what one believes and teaches.

Lange, Calvin, Jerome, and others viewed the fruit as the false teaching of the false prophets. Lange points out that the fruit in view is not that of ordinary professors of Christianity but of false teachers. Their fruit is their destructive doctrine.[1324] These are no doubt related at points to their character and may often be revealed by behavioral abnormalities, but frequently that is not obvious for many years, and sometimes never in this life. What is obvious is what they say. Even though their character is clothed in sheep's garments, and they are "gentle and meek in their outward appearance," their incorrect teaching is evident to all.

We should not be surprised that Jesus tells us that the teaching of a false prophet is the fruit by which we can discern his true identity. By asserting this, He is aligning Himself firmly with Moses and the prophets who continually stressed that the way one discerns a true prophet from a false one is by giving attention to what he says:

> *If a prophet or a dreamer of dreams arises among you and gives you a sign or a wonder, and the sign or wonder comes true, concerning which he spoke to you, saying, "Let us go after other gods (whom you have not known) and let us serve them," you shall not listen to the words of that prophet or that dreamer of dreams; for the LORD your God is testing you to find out if you love the LORD your God with all your heart and all your soul. You shall follow the LORD your God and fear Him; and shall keep His commandments, listen to His voice, serve Him, and cling to Him (Deuteronomy 13:1-4).*

Moses commands his readers to listen to what these false prophets say and to compare it with the commands and voice of the Lord, the Torah, and not to pay any attention to what they do. In fact, these false prophets, according to Moses, like those in Matthew 7, performed signs and wonders. Words, not works, are the basis for the discernment.

When faced with a people who sought help in mediums, Isaiah gave similar advice:

> *And when they say to you, "Consult the mediums and the spiritists who whisper and mutter," should not a people consult their God? Should they consult the dead on behalf of the living?* ***To the law and to the testimony. If they do not speak according to this word it is because they have no dawn*** *(Isaiah 8:19-20).*

The teaching of these false prophets is to be compared to *the law and the testimony.* If they *do not speak according to this word*, that is, if their fruit reveals they are not true prophets, it is because they have no revelation.

[1324] Lange, "The Gospel of Matthew," 8:144.

The idea that a false prophet can be discerned by comparing what he says with Scripture is widespread in the Bible,[1325] and it is surprising that the Lord's comments about fruit are not always read in this light. The fruit by which we may discern these false prophets is their doctrine. Their works were good. They looked and acted like sheep and even performed miracles. Satan himself "*disguises himself as an angel of light. Therefore it is not surprising if his servants also disguise themselves as servants of righteousness, whose end will be according to their deeds*" (2 Corinthians 11:14–15).

To examine only their works would have led to the wrong conclusion!

Only Believers Go to Heaven

In support of their contention that justification and sanctification are inextricably related, Experimental Predestinarians often point to the passages in which we are told that "whoever believes in Him" (John 3:16) will have eternal life. They say this implies that a person who has believed in the past and then has stopped believing will not go to heaven because only "believers" go to heaven.

Yes, we may well doubt the salvation of any person who has believed in Christ in the past and then, for some reason, no longer believes. Furthermore, such an individual, even if he is regenerate, can have no assurance of his salvation because faith is the assurance of things hoped for, and if he no longer believes the things hoped for, he no longer has faith or assurance.

As will be demonstrated in chapter 32, it is possible for a born-again person to fall away from the faith and cease believing.[1326] He is called a carnal Christian and will be subject to severe divine discipline. If final apostasy is not possible, then the warnings are empty of meaning, as will be discussed in a later chapter.[1327] However, Experimental Predestinarians are often impressed with the fact that in many of these verses the present tense of the verb "to believe" is used or the participle is an articular present participle meaning "the one who believes." The fact that these verbs are in the present tense, they say, implies that Jesus meant that "whoever continues to believe" has everlasting life.

Thus, the simple offer of the gospel on the basis of faith has become, for Experimental Predestinarians, something entirely different. When Jesus said, "Whoever believes in Him will have everlasting life," the Experimental Predestinarians say His true meaning was "whoever believes in Him and continues to believe in Him up to the point of physical death and who also manifests evidence of having truly believed by practical works of holiness and has persevered to the end of life has everlasting life." The woman at the well, and even Nicodemus, the teacher of Israel himself, would have been perplexed.

The argument from the articular present participle is simply wrong. It is sometimes true that a durative/progressive aspect is associated with the present tense. However, the aspect can be overridden by a host of other factors (lexical meaning, limited verbal choices, context, etc.) and is usually non-existent or nearly so in the articular participle.

The adherents of perseverance are reading into the term "believe" the meaning "believe at a point of time and continue to believe up to the point of physical death." This is not

---

1325 See Jeremiah 26; Galatians 1:6-9; 1 John 4:2ff.

1326 See vol. 2, chapter 32.

1327 See vol. 2, chapter 33.

only foreign to normal Greek usage but to English usage as well. We might say, "Whoever believes that Rockefeller is a philanthropist will receive a million dollars." At the point in time a person believes this, he is a millionaire. However, if ten years later, he ceases to believe, he is still in possession of the million dollars. Similarly, if a man has believed in Christ, he is regenerate and in possession of eternal life, even if he ceases to believe in God in the future.

The verses that promise heaven on the condition of belief simply do not logically imply that the real condition is that you continue in belief up to the end of life.

The notion that the present tense *requires* the sense "he who continually and habitually believes has everlasting life" is not supported by Greek grammar.[1328] For example, Moulton and Turner comment, "Thus in Greek, one seldom knows apart from the context whether the present indicative means, I walk or I am walking."[1329] Often the present has a punctiliar meaning.[1330]

Moulton and Turner call attention to the fact that the personal present articular participle "the one who believes" is often used "where we would expect aorist."[1331] When used that way, they say "Action (time or variety) is irrelevant and the participle has become a proper name."[1332] Wallace illustrates from Matthew, "Thus, for example, in Matthew 5:28, 'everyone who looks at a woman' with lust in his heart does not mean 'continually looking' or 'habitually looking,' any more than four verses later 'everyone who divorces his wife' means 'repeatedly divorces!'"[1333]

Perhaps 1 Thessalonians 1:10, "Jesus who delivers us from the wrath to come," is relevant here. The intent is to describe deliverance from the tribulation wrath. He is not saying that Jesus is the One who continually delivers us from the tribulation wrath. A deliverance once accomplished does not need to be habitually repeated.

In his discussion of the articular present participle Moulton makes a similar point.[1334] This form has in fact, he says, become a noun and is not a verb at all. For example, "the destroyer of the temple" of Matthew 27:40 is not "the one who continually destroys the temple." John the Baptist is called *ho baptizōn*, "the baptizer" (Mark 6:14, 24), not the one who continually baptizes people. Similarly, Robertson observes, "The participle with the article sometimes loses much of its verbal force."[1335]

1328 For a good discussion of this grammatical error see Chay and Correia, *The Faith That Saves: The Nature of Faith in the New Testament*, 45-53.

1329 James H. Moulton and Nigel Turner, *A Grammar of New Testament Greek, Volume 3: Syntax*, reprint ed. (Edinburgh: T. & T. Clark, 1963), 3:60.

1330 For example, Matthew 5:22, 28; 9:2 ("Your sins are forgiven"); 14:8; 26:63; Mark 2:5; Luke 7:8; 12:44; John 5:34; 9:25; Acts 8:23; 9:34 ("He heals you," not "is continually healing you"); 16:18; 26:1.

1331 Moulton and Turner, *A Grammar of New Testament Greek, Volume 3: Syntax*, 3:150. See esp. Mark 5:15-16, *ho daimonizomenos*, even after his healing.

1332 Ibid. See also Philippians 3:6 and Hebrews 7:9. Moulton and Turner cite several examples of this aoristic punctiliar use of the articular present participle: Matthew 26:46; 27:40; Mark 1:4; 6:14, 24; John 1:29 (the sin bearer); 6:63; 8:18; Acts 17:17; Romans 8:34; Ephesians 4:28; Galatians 1:23.

1333 Wallace, *Greek Grammar Beyond the Basics*, 616. In spite of Wallace's recognition that with gnomic present articular participles "we would be hard-pressed to make something more out of them—such as a progressive idea," he allows his theology to intervene in the case of *ho pisteuōn* in John (see Wallace, 616; 620-621).

1334 James Hope Moulton, *Grammar of New Testament Greek: Prolegomena*, reprint ed., 3 vols. (Edinburgh: T. & T. Clark, 1963), 1:126.

1335 A. T. Robertson, *A Grammar of the Greek New Testament in the Light of Historical Research*, reprint ed.

Summary

While it is horrible to contemplate, possible apostasy and cessation of belief is a very real danger set before the readers of the New Testament, particularly in the book of Hebrews. Though it is possible that a person who professes belief once and then rejects the faith is not a Christian, it is also possible that he is genuinely born again. Saving faith is "the act of a single moment whereby all the benefits of Christ's life, death, and resurrection suddenly become the irrevocable possession of the individual, per se, despite any and all eventualities."[1336] If a person is born again, what he forfeits when he "falls away" is not his eternal destiny but his opportunity to reign with Christ's *Metochoi* in the coming kingdom. "And he who overcomes and he who keeps My deeds until the end, to him I will give authority over the nations" (Revelation 2:26).

(Bellingham, WA: Logos Bible Software, 2006), 892. Acts 2:47, *tous sōzomenous*, and Galatians 4:27, *hē ou tiktousa, hē ouk ōdinousa*.

[1336] Robert Shank, *Life in the Son: A Study of the Doctrine of Perseverance* (Springfield, MO: Westcott Publishers, 1961), 195. However, Shank does not agree with this sentence.

27

Justification and Sanctification 3

IN THIS chapter we will continue our discussion of several passages in Paul's epistles that have often been cited to prove that justification and sanctification are always linked and can never be separated.

The Implied "All"

A number of passages ascribe to the saints, in apparently inclusive terms, the benefits of the future kingdom. For example:

> *Do you not know that the saints will judge the world (1 Corinthians 6:2)?*
>
> *Then the righteous will shine forth as the sun in the kingdom of their Father (Matthew 13:43).*
>
> *You have made them to be kingdom of priests to serve our God, and they will reign on the earth (Revelation 5:10).*
>
> *And to her it was granted to be arrayed in fine linen, clean and bright, for the fine linen is the righteous acts of the saints (Revelation 19:8, KJV).*

Experimental Predestinarians read these passages to mean that "all" the saints will judge the world, that "all" the righteous will shine forth, and that "all" members of the bride are arrayed with "righteous acts."

However, obviously this is reading the word "all" into these texts. The word "all" is not in the Greek text, and there is nothing in the contexts of these passages that requires that the word "all" be there. True, the saints will judge (reign), but Paul elsewhere clarifies that only those saints who are faithful will reign with Christ (2 Timothy 2:12). Only those saints who "overcome" will have authority over the nations.

Furthermore, it is clear that not all believers will function as priests:

> *Now if you obey me fully and keep my covenant, then out of all nations you will be my treasured possession ... You will be for me a kingdom of priests and a holy nation (Exodus 19:5-6).*

Only those believers who obey Him are priests. God's intent is that we all attain to that privilege both here and in the coming kingdom, but to say that a disobedient believer has obtained that privilege is contradicted by common sense and by the passages above. This is seen in the book of Hebrews.

> *We are his house, if we hold on to our courage and the hope of which we boast (Hebrews 3:6).*

Being part of Christ's priestly house is not automatic to all Christians. It is the intent, the ideal, but it is "actual" only in the lives of those faithful Christians who persevere in holiness.

True, the righteous will shine, but nowhere does the Bible say that "all" of them will. Furthermore, to be "righteous" in Matthew does not necessarily mean to be in possession of the forensic legal righteousness of Christ, as in Paul, but rather, "to possess a righteous life."[1337] It cannot be proved that justifying righteousness is in view in the passages listed in the footnote below. Only those saints who live righteous lives will shine in the kingdom. The unfaithful will not.[1338]

As for the claim that the wedding garment is for "all" the saved, this is simply a misreading of the text. Revelation 19:8-9 says only that the wedding garment, that is, righteous acts, adorn the individual saints of which she is composed. Each saint makes various contributions (righteous acts) to the bride's wedding garment, and some may not make any at all. Nothing in the passage teaches otherwise.

Another passage that is sometimes thought to be all-inclusive is 1 Corinthians 4:5:

> *Therefore do not go on passing judgment before the time, but wait until the Lord comes who will both bring to light the things hidden in the darkness and disclose the motives of men's hearts; and then each man's praise will come to him from God.*

Paul's statement in this verse has led some Experimental Predestinarians to conclude that all who are saved will be rewarded. When Paul says, "Then each man's praise will come to him from God," they understand this to mean each man without exception will receive praise. Yet Paul has just said that some will enter eternity with their work "burned up" (1 Corinthians 3:15). He evidently does not intend to teach that all without exception will receive praise. Instead, he is saying that each man who has earned praise will receive it.

Furthermore, the context is not talking about praise coming to the Corinthians at all. Rather, as verse 6 suggests, the praise coming to "each man" refers to *Paul's and Apollos' praise,* not to Christians in general.[1339]

Christians Have Crucified the Flesh

> *Now those who belong to Christ have crucified the flesh with its passions and desires (Galatians 5:24).*

Many say this passage affirms that all Christians have crucified the flesh. This is, of course, true. However, the event referred to is not self-crucifixion of the flesh by the believer but, the co-crucifixion of the believer with Christ at the point of saving faith. There is nothing here about a believer's determination to subdue the flesh as a part of the saving transaction. This verse simply refers to the positional crucifixion of the flesh mentioned in Galatians 2:20 and Romans 6:1-11.

[1337] See, for example, Matthew 1:19; 5:45; 9:13; 10:41; 13:17; 20:4; 23:28, 29; 23:35.

[1338] The "shining" could simply refer to the glory of the resurrection body which will, of course, be manifested by all saints.

[1339] "When verse six says that Paul applies these things to himself and Apollos figuratively, the *us* portions refer to Paul and Apollos, but the *you* aspect of the passage still applies to the Corinthians." John Niemelä, "If Anyone's Work is Burned: Scrutinizing Proof Texts," *Chafer Theological Journal* 8, no. 1 (2002): 136.

Galatians 6:14 refers to a positional crucifixion of the world to Paul. That is, it is dead to him and he is dead to it. Furthermore, Galatians 5:24 refers to the *crucifixion* of the flesh, not a daily struggle with it. The word connotes a decisive death and not a continuing battle. The aorist tense is not to be translated "are crucifying" the flesh but "have crucified." That is, the event occurred in the past. This makes the notion of an experiential crucifixion intrinsically unlikely here. In view of the fact that nowhere else in the Bible is such an experiential crucifixion referred to and the fact that in many places the believer's once-and-for-all co-crucifixion with Christ is found in Pauline theology, it seems best to take it this way here.

How did they bring about this crucifixion? They did it by believing in Christ. When they did this they made a response that resulted in the crucifixion of the flesh by joining themselves with Christ in His death, burial, and resurrection.[1340]

He Who Began a Good Work

Reflecting with joy on the spiritual vitality of his church at Philippi, Paul says of them:

> [*I thank you*] *for your fellowship* [*koinōnia*] *in the gospel from the first day until now, being confident of this very thing, that He who has begun a good work in you will complete it until the day of Jesus Christ (Philippians 1:5-6, NKJV).*

Some Experimental Predestinarians have understood this to teach that God will continually work to sanctify all who are truly born again until the point of physical death or until the return of Christ and that His work will inevitably be successful. The lack of the continuing transformation of life, is then, supposed proof that a man is not born again. Final failure is not possible according to this verse, they say.

However, as many commentators acknowledge, the "good work" to which Paul refers is probably not sanctification or regeneration but financial contributions or a more general assistance and partnership, including financial help, in the cause of Christ.[1341] This was their "fellowship in the gospel" (v. 5) for which he thanks them now and also later in the letter (4:15-17). The sense of "financial contributions" fits the context of the epistle well. Elsewhere, Paul speaks of "fellowship" (Gr *koinōnia*) in terms of financial aid,[1342] and he certainly refers to this in 4:15-17 where he uses the verbal form of *koinōnia*, "to share."

If this is the meaning, then Hawthorne's suggestion that the phrase be rendered "fellowship in order to make it possible to spread the gospel" would make good sense. Hawthorne sees the "fellowship" as financial contributions.[1343] He also believes that the phrase, "a good work," cannot be shaken loose from its immediate context and be interpreted primarily in terms of "God's redeeming and renewing work" in the lives of the

---

1340 It is also possible to take the phrase "belong to Christ" as a genitive of source and not of possession. The Greek is "of Christ." This would mean that those who are "of Christ" in their behavior crucify the flesh. Some Christians are, and some are not. Paul does use the genitive "of Christ" elsewhere in the sense of source (1 Corinthians 1:1, 12; 11:1; 2 Corinthians 1:1; 3:3; 4:4; 5:14; 10:7 [see v. 2]; 11:13; 12:9). From this perspective then, those who crucify the flesh are those Christians who are led by the Spirit and who walk by the Spirit.

1341 John Eadie, *A Commentary on the Greek Text of the Epistle of Paul to the Philippians* (Grand Rapids: Zondervan Publishing House, 1953), 83.

1342 For example, Romans 12:13; 15:26; 2 Corinthians 8:4; 9:13; Galatians 6:6; 1 Timothy 6:18; Hebrews 13:16.

1343 Gerald F. Hawthorne, *Philippians*, Word Biblical Commentary (Waco, TX: Word Books, 1983), 19.

Philippians.[1344] Rather, he insists, it is the sharing of their resources to make possible the proclamation of the gospel.

The "completion" of this "good work" would then be either (1) its continuation; (2) its consummation in being rewarded at the day of Christ; or (3) its achievement of its final aim - multiplied fruit in the lives of others through Paul's defense and confirmation of the gospel.[1345] Indeed, Paul tells them that as a result of their contributions they have become partners with him in this defense and confirmation of the gospel (v. 6). It is easy to see how this latter kind of participation could be carried on to "completion" until the day of Christ. It is difficult to see how Paul could be teaching that their financial contributions could continue until that time. Paul in effect is saying, "I am sure that God will finish what He started. Your financial sacrifice has not been and will not be in vain. God will complete it."

In other words, like many missionaries who followed, Paul is assuring his supporters that the good work of giving which they began will be completed by God with significant impact for Christ through Paul's ministry to others. God will take their contributions and use them mightily!

Because You Have Kept the Word of My Patience

The great promise to the church at Philadelphia has sometimes been used by Experimental Predestinarians to support their views on perseverance.

> *I will make those who are of the synagogue of Satan, who claim to be Jews though they are not, but are liars—I will make them come and fall down at your feet and acknowledge that I have loved you.*
>
> *Since [or "because"] you have kept my command to endure patiently, I will also keep you from the hour of trial that is going to come upon the whole world to test those who live on the earth (Revelation 3:9, 10).*

This passage, as is well known, has been at the center of the discussion regarding the time of the rapture, an issue which we cannot consider here.[1346]

For those holding to a pretribulational view of the rapture, this passage presents a difficulty. Since participation in the rapture is the inheritance of all the saved, to condition this participation on faithful endurance suggests that only those who faithfully keep his word of patience will be saved. In other words, only those who faithfully persevere are truly born again. At the turn of the century, Robert Govett propounded this idea emphasizing that rapture was a reward for steadfast discipleship.[1347]

[1344] Ibid., 21.

[1345] The result of the cash gift in the lives of others is alluded to in 1 Corinthians 9:13, where the result of giving was that men would praise God.

[1346] This writer holds to a pretribulational rapture view. While this view of Revelation 3:10 has been challenged, notably by Robert Gundry, David G. Winfrey offers a spirited defense of Revelation 3:10 as a central passage supporting the pretribulational view. See David G. Winfrey, "The Great Tribulation: Kept 'out of' or 'through'?," *GTJ* 3, no. 1 (1982). Ibid., 3-18; Thomas R. Edgar, "Robert H. Gundry and Revelation 3:10," *Grace Theological Journal* 3, no. 1 (Spring 1982).

[1347] This is sometimes known as the "partial rapture" theory. Only those Christians who are faithful will experience the rapture prior to the tribulation. The rest must wait until the end of the millennium, thus missing the kingdom. See Robert Govett, *Govett on Revelation*, 2 vols. (Miami Springs, FL: Schoettle Publishing, 1981), 1:189.

However, in a *tour de force*, John Niemelä demonstrated that the common punctuation of these verses is undoubtedly incorrect. The earliest Greek manuscripts had no punctuation. According to Niemelä, a better translation would be:

> *I will make those who are of the synagogue of Satan, who claim to be Jews though they are not, but are liars—I will make them come and fall down at your feet and acknowledge that I have loved you because you have kept my command to endure patiently.*
>
> *I will also keep you from the hour of trial that is going to come upon the whole world to test those who live on the earth (Revelation 3:9-10).*

The phrase, "because you have kept my command to endure," goes with verse 9 and not verse 10.[1348] Therefore there is no statement here marking true Christians as those who necessarily persevere in faith and works (or of a partial rapture).

If Possible (Matthew 24:24)

Experimental Predestinarians sometimes quote Matthew 24:24 in defense of their doctrine that justification and sanctification are necessarily inseparable, and that final failure or apostasy is therefore impossible.

> *For false Christs and false prophets will arise and will show great signs and wonders, so as to mislead* [Gr *planaō*], *if possible, even the elect (Matthew 24:24).*

William Hendriksen is typical of this line of thought when he says, "The implication is that to successfully mislead God's elect, so that until the day of their death they would permit themselves to resemble wandering stars [Gr *planaō*, 'to lead astray,' used of planets wandering in their orbits], is impossible."[1349] "The implication is," says A. T. Robertson, "that it is not possible."[1350] Hagner agrees saying, "The implication of the ... 'if possible,' is that the 'elect'... are in the care of their Father and that it is therefore not within the power of these enemies to accomplish their purpose."[1351]

Blomberg similarly assures his readers, "Here emerges another indirect testimony to the truth that those who do give up believing demonstrate that they never truly were Christ's followers." However, in his very next sentence he subtly nuances his interpretation (with no support) and says, "But despite Christ's warning (v. 25) believers can be misled in *other ways, such as looking for him in some remote or hidden place*" (v. 26, italics added).[1352] He is trying to imply there are two types of deception: one regarding who the real Christ is and another regarding where He is located. Apparently, according to Blomberg, the first type

---

1348 See John Niemelä, "For You Have Kept My Word," *Chafer Theological Journal* 6, no. 1 (January 2000): 1-26. Niemalä notes that the coordinating conjunction, *hoti* ("because"), only exceptionally goes with a dependent clause to follow (16 out of 180 times in the New Testament). *Hoti* normally connects with and explains a preceding clause. David Aune noted the same problem with the traditional punctuation, "The ὅτι clause that begins this sentence is in an unusual position, since in the vast majority of instances dependent clauses follow the main clause." David E. Aune, *Revelation 1-5*, Word Biblical Commentary (Dallas, TX: Word Books, 1997), 231, n.10.

1349 Hendriksen and Kistemaker, *Exposition of the Gospel According to Matthew*, 860.

1350 WPNT, s.v. "Matthew 24:24."

1351 Hagner, *Matthew 14-28*, 706.

1352 Blomberg, *Matthew*, 361.

of misleading is impossible but the second is possible. He substitutes "give up believing" with the word "misled." But to be misled does not necessarily imply "give up believing." Even if it did, the verse gives no support to Experimental Predestinarian assumptions that true believers could never commit apostasy. Of course they can, and there are numerous examples of this in both the New and Old Testaments (e.g., Solomon).[1353]

The key phrase "if possible" only suggests possibility. It may be an ellipsis for a fourth class condition which is absorbed by the third class (maybe yes, maybe no). It does not necessarily imply that deception cannot happen.[1354] It is incorrect for Blomberg to assert that this is really a rhetorical statement expressing the extreme unlikelihood that this deception could occur.[1355] The verse only says that the condition ("if possible") could be likely or unlikely for the sake of argument. It in no way requires that it is certain that deception will or will not occur.[1356] To quote this passage in support of their doctrine is to lean on a broken reed and surely is a result of reading one's theological bias into the verse.

The implication is **not** *that it is impossible but that it **is** possible.* This fits better with the entire warning thrust of the context. The possibility that disciples can be misled is specifically stated in verse 4, where Matthew uses the same word, *planaō*: "see to it that no one misleads [Gr *planaō*] you."

The Mark of the Beast

During the reign of the Antichrist, terrible persecution will come on all believers. This world leader will require everyone to receive a mark on his right hand or forehead, and without this mark no one will be able to buy food for their families (Revelation 13:16-17). Anyone who receives this mark will show that he is unregenerate, and he will be forever condemned (Revelation 14:9-11). For a believer who can never accept the mark, some degree of faithfulness is evident.

It is clear that during the tribulation the love of many will grow cold (Matthew 24:12), that there will be unfaithful Christians during this time, and some will live to the end. How can one have a sufficient degree of faithfulness to reject the mark, and yet an insufficient degree to avoid coldness and rebuke and loss of reward when the King returns? Like the unpardonable sin, the sin of accepting the mark is frightening. Unfaithful, cold Christians will not accept this mark for three reasons; (1) some may be afraid to; (2) they will be prevented from it; (3) or they will die before accepting it. So, many believers who refuse the

---

1353 See chapter 32 for proof.

1354 There is an evident allusion to Deuteronomy 13:2 here, where the possibility *not* the impossibility of being deceived by false prophets is warned against. The LXX uses the same word, *planaō*, "mislead" (32:6).

1355 He says, "If that were possible" (εἰ δυνατόν) is probably an ellipsis for the protasis of a fourth-class condition (εἰ δυνατόν ἔη) used in an indirect rhetorical question, thus implying that it is not probable that the elect will be deceived," (Blomberg, 359). But why is it not probable? My guess is that he needs it to be that to support his doctrine that true saints cannot apostatize. Nowhere in the New Testament does εἰ δυνατόν imply something that is impossible (cf. Matthew 24:24; 26:39; Mark 14:35; Acts 20:16; Romans 12:18; Galatians 4:15).

1356 Robertson says, "The difference between the third and fourth class conditions is just that between the subj. and the opt. They are both modes of *doubtful, hesitating affirmation* [emphasis added], but the optative is more remote and the subj. in this type the premise is not assumed to be either true or untrue." Robertson, *A Grammar of the Greek New Testament in the Light of Historical Research*, 1004-05. If Matthew wanted to say that "if possible" really means "not possible," he could easily have used the second class, contrary-to-fact condition, which would have more clearly stated things the way Experimental Predestinarians want them to be stated.

mark will remain cold, go underground, and live out of fellowship with God but will refuse the mark. It is not the love of Christ that causes them to say, "No," but fear that He will carry out His threats. Since they are elect, God will either work in their hearts or circumstances so that they avoid accepting the mark, or He will take them to be with Him before they do.

The entire period involves special occurrences of divine and human wrath, the deceptions by Satan, and a removal of the restraining influence of the Holy Spirit against sin in the world. To grant a special work of God during these times to prevent true believers from accepting the mark of the beast in no way justifies the inference that the doctrine of the saints' perseverance in holiness is scriptural.

Summary

All the major passages supporting the teaching that justification and sanctification are necessarily united have been examined. None of these passages requires the meaning that sanctification will necessarily follow justification. Since none of them requires this meaning and since the rest of the New Testament warns Christians that they may not be faithful to the end of their lives, the Experimental Predestinarian view of perseverance is falsified.

While it is true, as the preceding chapters have argued, that perseverance in good works is not the inevitable outcome of salvation, nevertheless, they are still necessary as our duty on the way to final salvation. Here are 13 reasons why:

1. They are the basis for our future reward (1 Timothy. 4:7-8).
2. They are God's means to make our Christian lives secure against falling into sin (2 Peter 1:10).
3. They are a defense against sin and corruption (Ephesians 6:14-16).
4. They are necessary by debt and obligation (Romans 8:12).
5. They are commanded by God as the will of God (1 Thessalonians 4:3).
6. They are necessary for us to feel that we have pleased God and know that he is therefore pleased with us and also glorified in us. (Ephesians 5:8-10; Hebrews 13:21; 1 John 3:22).
7. They are necessary for us to maintain intimacy with God (1 John 1:9).
8. They are necessary if we are to fulfill our obligation to be salt and light in the world (Matthew 5:16).
9. They are the intended goal of our faith and justification (1 Timothy 1:5).
10. They are necessary for us to maintain a vital and living faith in contrast to a dead one (James 2:17).
11. They are necessary to save us from the downward spiral of lust, sin, and spiritual ruin (James 1:14-15, 21; 2:14).
12. They are our reasonable and necessary acts of spiritual sacrifice to God (Romans 12:1-2).
13. They guarantee that at the judgment we will not have our life-work rejected (1 Corinthians 3:15); that we will not draw back from him in shame (1 John 2:28); and that we will not lose reward (2 John 8).

There is one passage that has played a most important role in the discussion of faith and works, James 2:14-26. Did not James say, "*Faith without works is dead*"? Our attention is directed to this important passage in the next chapter.

28

Faith without Works Is Dead

WHEN JAMES said, "*Faith without works is dead*" and "*A man is justified by works, and not by faith alone*" (James 2:24), he no doubt was completely unaware of the volumes which would be written in the history of the church that would attempt to harmonize his words with those of the apostle Paul. This verse led Luther to conclude that James wrote "an epistle of straw."[1357] James would also be surprised to learn that many would misconstrue his words to mean that those who have "true saving" faith will necessarily evidence this by a life of works and that, if they lack works, this proves their faith is not genuine, that is, not "saving" faith.

The apparent contradiction between James and Paul can be seen as follows:

> *Paul: "For we maintain that a man is justified by faith apart from works of the Law" (Romans 3:28).*
>
> *James: "You see that a man is justified by works and not by faith alone" (James 2:24).*

One can readily see the problem. By focusing on five key words: salvation, faith, justification, "dead faith," and works, different writers have suggested alternative solutions by proposing that Paul and James were defining or using these terms in different ways.

Calvin famously explained this contradiction by saying, "It is therefore faith alone which justifies, and the faith which justifies is not alone."[1358] As we shall see, there is no basis for this cliché in James 2.

Faith in the Book of James

> *What use is it, my brethren, if someone says he has faith but he has no works? **Can that faith save him?** If a brother or sister is without clothing and in need of daily food, [16] and one of you says to them, "Go in peace, be warmed and be filled," and yet you do not give them what is necessary for their body, what use is that? (James 2:14-16)*

Can that faith save him? Apparently it cannot, because the question expects a negative answer. We must ask two questions, "What is *that* faith?" and "Salvation from what?"

By inserting the word "that" in front of "faith," the translators are saying that there are different kinds of faith, true faith that would save him and "that" faith which does not.[1359]

[1357] Martin Luther, "Preface to the New Testament," in *Word and Sacrament*, ed. Theodor Bachman (Philadelphia: Fortress Press, 1960), 35:362.

[1358] John Calvin, *Acts of the Council of Trent: with the Antidote*, 6th Session, can. 11.

[1359] Commentaries routinely insert "that" in front of faith reflecting their Reformed bias rather than the actual

There *are* two kinds of faith in James, but not as Experimental Predestinarians imagine. In their view there is a faith that saves a person from final damnation, and a false faith which does not. The way one identifies this false faith, in their view, is that it does not result in a life of works. However, the text says nothing about faith that saves from eternal damnation versus a faith that does not. Rather, the focus in James is between a regenerate person who says he has a *walk of faith* but gives no evidence of it in his life; between what Paul called a living faith (Galatians 2:20), and what James called a "useless" faith (James 2:20)

Faith in the book of James (as will be demonstrated below) does not refer to the initial act of faith through which one is saved from damnation. It refers to the ongoing walk of faith which can save one from the pathway to "death." "Death" however, is the progression to psychological, spiritual, or, possibly, the physical sin unto death resulting in a negative assessment of one's life at the Judgment Seat of Christ.

But does the Bible speak often of faith as a walk in distinction from faith as the initial event which procures salvation? Yes it does. Consider:

> *Now that no one is justified by the Law before God is evident; for, "The righteous man* ***shall live by faith****" (Galatians 3:11).*
>
> *If we* ***live by the Spirit****, let us also* ***walk by the Spirit*** *(Galatians 5:25).*
>
> *Therefore* ***as you have received*** *Christ Jesus the Lord* [i.e., by faith], ***so walk*** *in Him (Colossians 2:6).*
>
> *For* ***we walk by faith****, not by sight (2 Corinthians 5:7).*
>
> *But he who doubts is condemned if he eats, because his eating is not from faith; and whatever* ***is not from faith*** *is sin (Romans 14:23).*
>
> ***Fight the good fight of faith****; take hold of the eternal life to which you were called, and you made the good confession in the presence of many witnesses (1 Timothy 6:12).*
>
> *Nor to pay attention to myths and endless genealogies, which give rise to mere speculation rather than* ***furthering the administration of God which is by faith*** *But the goal of our instruction is love from a pure heart and a good conscience and a* ***sincere faith*** *(1 Timothy 1:4-5).*
>
> *Not boasting beyond our measure, that is, in other men's labors, but with the hope that* ***as your faith grows****, we will be, within our sphere, enlarged even more by you (2 Corinthians 10:15).*
>
> *For in Christ Jesus neither circumcision nor uncircumcision means anything, but* ***faith working through love*** *(Galatians 5:6).*

Faith in the sense of an ongoing piety and trust and not just in the sense of the act which procures initial salvation is found throughout the Bible. Faith is not only an initial act; it is also a walk, a way of life for the Christian by which he furthers his sanctification,

---

reading of the Greek. For example, with no proof or discussion Davids calls it "a certain faith" and that the person in 2:14 is only "claiming to have faith," Peter H. Davids, *The Epistle of James: A Commentary on the Greek Text* (Grand Rapids: Wm. B. Eerdmans Publishing Co., 1982), 120. He then points to the prophets' protests against ritual piety which this passage is not even discussing.

grows, lives richly, and stands firm. Scores of passages could be cited.[1360] Indeed, the entire eleventh chapter of Hebrews is devoted to the life of faith, rather than faith that is credited as justification. The saints mentioned,

> *By faith conquered kingdoms, performed acts of righteousness, obtained promises, shut the mouths of lions, quenched the power of fire, escaped the edge of the sword, from weakness were made strong, became mighty in war, put foreign armies to flight (Hebrews 11:33–34).*

All these benefits were obtained by the ongoing life of faith, "*by faith*," and not the initial act whereby they were saved from damnation. Their faith was not "useless" or "dead," to use James' words, but was useful and alive and was "true piety, genuine devotion."[1361]

What does James refer to when he speaks of "faith"? Is the initial act in view or the ongoing life of trust, the walk of faith, his subject? Usage in the epistle indicates the latter is his theme. James uses the word "faith" fifteen times.[1362] In the first instance, 1:2-4, it is used of a faith related to testing and enduring trials; initial faith is not in view. Instead, the faith that endures testing is the subject. Next, James wrote of a faith that is to be exercised during a trial in which a believer asks for wisdom. One "must ask in faith without any doubting" (1:6). Once again ongoing faith, that is, trusting God in one's daily walk, is the subject, not trusting Christ for deliverance from eternal damnation.

Next, in 2:1, James speaks of holding one's faith in Christ with an attitude of impartiality. Obviously, the continuing exercise of faith, "holding" it, is in view and not initial inception. James speaks of the poor who are "rich in faith and heirs of the kingdom" (2:5). To be "rich in faith" is not a reference to the initial act of faith that procures salvation from damnation; instead, it refers to being "rich in the sphere of faith,"[1363] the ongoing experience of their walk with God. The prayer "offered in faith" is not a prayer of the initial act of saving faith, but a prayer that emerges from a life of faith and genuine piety (James 5:15).[1364]

If the above analysis of faith in James is correct, this will have significant impact on how phrases like "faith without works is dead," or "can that faith save him?" are interpreted.

Salvation in the Book of James

James says, "*Can that faith save him*?" The question in Greek requires a negative answer, "No, it cannot." As argued above, a "walk of faith" which does not manifest itself in deeds of charity and a life of obedience, is not a walk of faith at all; it is an illusion. Such a Christian may claim he is living the Christian life, but he is not, and he is warned that his

---

[1360] Romans 11:20; 14:1, 22; 1 Corinthians 10:15; 2 Corinthians 5:7; Ephesians 3:17; Philippians 1:25; 1 Thessalonians 5:2, 5, 7; 2 Thessalonians 1:3, 11; 1 Timothy 1:19; 6:10 (wandered away from true devotion to Christ); Philemon 6; Hebrews 6:12; 10:38.

[1361] BDAG, 819.

[1362] For example, see James 1:3, 6; 2:1, 5, 14 (2x), 17, 18 (3x), 20, 22, 24, 26; 5:15.

[1363] Martin Dibelius and Heinrich Greeven, *James: A Commentary on the Epistle of James*, 11th rev. ed., Hermeneia (Philadelphia: Fortress Press, 1975), 124.

[1364] In order to maintain his idea that faith means faith for initial salvation in James 2:14, Joseph Pak gratuitously argues, "In this passage faith means acceptance of revelation without corresponding behavior." He offers no proof beyond mere assertion, an assertion necessary to maintain his interpretation of James, which says that faith apart from works is not genuine. See Pak, "A Study of Selected Passages on Distinguishing Marks of Genuine and False Believers", 250.

version of a walking faith cannot save. As James puts it, "*He deceives himself*" (James 1:26). This begs the question, "Save from what?"

There is extremely strong resistance to the idea that salvation can refer to anything else other than deliverance from post-mortem condemnation to the lake of fire. In rejecting the idea that "save a soul" refers to a temporal deliverance (a view which will be argued below), Schreiner writes, "The lengths to which advocates of this view will go to preserve their theology are remarkable and ... [To take 'save' to refer to a deliverance from physical death] is an astonishing move since salvation and justification are typically associated in the New Testament with entering heaven."[1365]

However, there is nothing "remarkable" or "astonishing" about this at all. In fact, salvation is associated with entering heaven only 40 percent of the time in the New Testament[1366] and not even once in the Old Testament.[1367] The context demands, as we will demonstrate below, that we understand "saved" as salvation from some temporal trial leading to psychological/spiritual or physical death now and ultimately to salvation from negative judgment at the Judgment Seat of Christ (see discussion below).

It appears that Schreiner's unsubstantiated theological assumption that initial faith must always result in a life of works in order to be "genuine" has obscured what the context is begging him to see. The word "save" is used five times in James, and, unless 2:14 is an exception, in none of the other usages does it refer to salvation from eternal damnation.[1368]

SALVATION OF THE SOUL FROM "DEATH" (JAMES 1:21)

The first mention of "to save" (Gr *sōzō*) in James is used of the salvation of the soul.

> *Therefore, putting aside all filthiness and all that remains of wickedness, in humility receive the word implanted, which is able to save your souls (James 1:21).*

[1365] Thomas R. Schreiner, "Perseverance and Assurance," *SBTJ* 2, no. 1 (1998): 45. Schriener appeals to Jesus' encounter with the rich young ruler to support his thesis that salvation always means deliverance from final damnation.

[1366] For proof of this see elsewhere in this book, 155 ff.

[1367] See elsewhere in this book, pp. 153 ff.

[1368] Alan Stanley disagrees. He may be unaware of the evidence presented below (see p. 405, FN 1372), that "salvation of the soul" never refers to salvation from eternal damnation, and cites 1 Peter 1:9 as proof. This of course proves nothing unless one already agrees with his incorrect assumption about the meaning of the "salvation of a soul." He strangely argues that because "eschatological salvation is clearly in view" in Matthew 25:44-46, it must be in view in James 2:14. There is no evident connection between the passages. He then says that the use of "*dunamai*" ("to be able") in 2:14 "orients the discussion toward the future." While it may be true that there is a future aspect, Stanley never proves that damnation is in view. It is best to see the future dimension as reward or rebuke at the Judgment Seat of Christ. Furthermore, this does not necessarily require an eschatological future, as Stanley implies. Any time future to the implanting of the Word that is able to save one's soul from the trials of life will do (1:21) and protect the believer from temptation. Rather than being future oriented, this exhortation would refer to a present and ongoing need in the believer's life. Stanley continues saying that "the entire epistle is set within the context of eschatological hope (1:12; 5:7-8; cf. 4:10) and judgment (4:11-12; 5:9; 12)." None of the verses he cites prove that the outcome of that judgment is escape from final damnation. Finally, he argues that the immediate context of 2:14 refers to the eternal damnation (v. 13). This view will be has shown to be false below. The immediate context is speaking of a judgment on the believer's works or lack of them at the Judgment Seat of Christ, and eternal damnation is not even mentioned. See Stanley, *Did Jesus Teach Salvation by Works*, 162.

While the phrase "save your soul" is often understood as a reference to salvation from eternal damnation, the author has been unable to find any biblical evidence which supports this.[1369]

When Pak asserts that "salvation in the New Testament predominately denotes deliverance from condemnation in hell," this is not only false, but irrelevant.[1370] As already noted, this is the meaning in 43 percent of the instances in the New Testament. Normally (57% of the time) salvation refers to deliverance from a temporal difficulty, death, disease, or a meaningless life.[1371]

In every instance in the Old Testament to save a soul refers to being saved from some temporal danger (usually physical death) and not an eternal one.[1372] Stanley admits that "salvation" does not necessarily refer to deliverance from damnation but can refer to a temporal deliverance but says "the context is usually very clear when this is the case."[1373] And, in this case, the context is very clear; the salvation in view is the salvation from temporal disaster in the Christian life which, of course, leads to salvation from a negative

---

1369 Dibelius and Greeven state that this is "an expression which here quite clearly must be understood eschatologically." Dibelius and Greeven, *James: A Commentary on the Epistle of James*, 113. Later, James uses the word in a way which does include an eschatological dimension. However, the reference is to the Judgment Seat of Christ, and not, as Dibelius suggests, to judgment in heaven or eternal damnation. This will be discussed below.

1370 For example, Pak makes this unfounded assertion with poor supporting evidence, Pak, "A Study of Selected Passages on Distinguishing Marks of Genuine and False Believers", 244. He cites only three other passages that do not necessarily refer to salvation from damnation (Matthew 10:28; John 12:25; 1 Peter 1:9). All of these have been dealt with elsewhere (see footnotes above). Pak sees the phrase about keeping one's soul for eternal life as something the believer does by means of hating the world (John 12:25). This is a novel way of guaranteeing one's arrival in heaven. It is better to understand keeping for eternal life as persevering and enhancing one's intimacy with God now and on into heaven when we die. Only by faithfulness can that intimacy be "kept" and thus experienced abundantly in heaven. As Billy Graham puts it, "Everyone's cup will be full, but the cups will be different sizes." Jesus referred to this "keeping" elsewhere as laying up treasures for ourselves in heaven. Pak also argues from Matthew 10:28 that killing the "soul" in *Gehenna* refers to final condemnation. That is doubtful because those addressed are Jesus' believing disciples and *Gehenna*, the Valley of Hinnom, does not refer to eternal damnation, but to a negative assessment of one's life at the Judgment Seat of Christ. This will be demonstrated elsewhere (see chapter 57 herein). Pak understands 1 Peter 1:9, "obtaining the goal of your faith—the salvation of your souls," as a reference to final entrance into heaven. However, as pointed out elsewhere (see elsewhere in this book, p. 216), "obtaining" in Gr refers to receiving something as a recompense and the salvation in view is being experienced now. It is a deliverance from the struggles his readers fight against in the present and has sanctification as one of its foci.

1371 See elsewhere in this book, pp. 153 ff. and esp. p. 155.

1372 This phrase or similar ones are found 14 times in the LXX (Genesis 19:17, 20, 32:30; Judges 12:3; Psalm 3:3; 6:5; 34:3; 42:11; 68:2; 73:13; 85:2; Job 33:28; Amos 2:14, 16). In each case the phrase suggests the notion of preserving one's physical life. In Genesis 19:17 the LXX translates, "save your soul"; and in Genesis 32:30, Jacob, after his struggle with the Angel of the Lord, exclaims, "My life (LXX Gr *psyche, "soul"*, Heb *nepeš*) has been preserved (i.e., "saved," Gr *sōzō*, Heb *nāṣal*)." In one passage it refers to delivering the needy from social injustice (Psalm 72:13) by preserving their lives. Even the warrior, declares Amos, will "not save his life" in the coming invasion Amos 2:14, 16). In Psalm 42:11 (LXX, 41:12), David's soul ("life" Gr *psychē*), is in despair so he turns to God for "help of my countenance," which in the LXX is "salvation (Gr *sōtēria*) of my countenance." In 1 Samuel 19:5, 1 Kings 19:5 LXX), David took his life (Gr psyche) in his hand and killed Goliath, and this resulted in salvation (Gr *sōtēria*) of all Israel, including, of course, David. Salvation from enemies is the meaning. Similarly, in Psalm 3:2 David once again finds many enemies saying that God will not save (LXX Gr *sōzō*) him. In Psalm 35:3, he asks the Lord to save his soul (LXX Gr *psychē*), and God responds, "I am your salvation (Gr *sōtēria*)." He wants deliverance from those who are his enemies and who fight against him (v. 2).

1373 Stanley, *Did Jesus Teach Salvation by Works*, 161.

assessment of one's life at the Judgment Seat of Christ (James 2:12-14). The danger in the immediate context from which the soul needs to be saved is temporal.[1374] This is stated in verse 15.

> *Then when lust has conceived, it gives birth to sin; and when sin is accomplished, it **brings forth death** (James 1:15).*

The danger is that for the Christian believer, the sequence beginning with lust and then sin might lead to "death." This is an analysis of the experience of temptation in the life of a Christian (1:3) whose "faith" is being tested by trials (temptation is one of the trials). James makes the same point in the last verse of his epistle,

> *My brethren, if any among you strays from the truth and one turns him back, let him know that he who turns a sinner from the error of his way will **save his soul from death** and will cover a multitude of sins (James 5:20).*

The "saving of a soul" in James 1:21 is the saving of one of the "brethren" from a path that leads to death. James is writing to Christians.[1375] He calls his readers "brothers" 15 times and specifically the kind of brothers in whom the Word of God has been implanted (1:21) and who possess "*faith in our glorious Lord Jesus Christ*" (2:1). These beloved brethren are those who know that they are born again! This epistle is addressed to those who are born again and not those who have merely professed faith in Christ but are not saved from damnation.

It is evident that a born-again believer can experience some kind of death.[1376] Thus, while it is clear that such a life can lead to judgment at the Judgment Seat of Christ (James 2:12-13), it is astonishing that Stanley says that this salvation is "eschatological" (in the sense of escaping damnation or not entering into heaven). While it only is eschatological in the sense of reward or rebuke at the Judgment Seat of Christ, the immediate context of James 1:21 begs us to see death's temporal aspect.[1377]

[1374] Stanley argues that the contrast between the implanted word (i.e., regeneration) and salvation suggests a contrast between the beginning of salvation and the end (i.e., final entrance into heaven). This is, according to Stanley, "especially the case since the intervening verses (vv. 1:19-20) deal with matter subsequent to regeneration – listening, anger, righteous living." However, those intervening verses prove precisely the opposite. The salvation in view is progressive sanctification. Furthermore, the following verses describe the outcome of this process as "doing the word" which yields "blessing" and not deliverance from eternal damnation (1:25).

[1375] James refers to his readers as "brothers" (1:2) who have been "brought forth by the word of truth" (1:18) and who already have faith to hold on to (2:1). See also 1:16, 19; 2:5, 14; 3:1, 10, 12; 5:12; 19. I have argued elsewhere that "death" is the spiritual death but in the sense of the spiritual ineffectiveness of the Christian, and not a reference to eternal damnation. See pp. 385, 425, 722, 725.

[1376] Norman Sellers has observed, "Death from sin, then, could be physical death, for believers or unbelievers. It could be spiritual death—separating a believer from fellowship with God." C. Norman Sellers, *Election and Perseverance* (Miami Springs, FL: Schoettle Publishing Co., 1987), 105.

[1377] Stanley, *Did Jesus Teach Salvation by Works*, 61. Stanley ignores two passages in James that appear to refute the idea that the salvation of a soul refers to eternal salvation (5:15, 20). He says, "I will leave them out (it matters little to our discussion)"!! However, it matters a lot. These verses seem to refute Stanley's view. Stanley says, "The use of *dunatai* (able) in 2:14 orients the discussion toward the future" (ibid., 162). But, we ask, "What aspect?" Elsewhere he says, "Needless to say it is clear that James 2:14 is speaking of eschatological and eternal salvation" (ibid., 308). Stanley, like Pak, is correct in saying that this passage may include an

Likewise, when Pak asserts that the salvation in James 2:14 is "eschatological," we believe he is only partially correct.[1378] It is eschatological in the sense that it includes the eschatological assessment of the believer's life at the Judgment Seat of Christ (vv. 12-13). The believer who is not self-deluded and who has a growing and mature faith will be saved from a negative assessment of his life, rebuke, loss of inheritance, and from the shame of being exposed as unfaithful. We will discuss this passage later in this chapter.

Just as it is possible to "save" one in whom the Word has been implanted (James 1:21), it is also sometimes necessary to "save" one who is of the "brethren" and is "among us." A man who is already saved in the sense of having judicial deliverance from final damnation needs only to be saved from death in this life. The death here may be the "sin unto death" referred to in Genesis 38:7, Ezekiel 3:20; Acts 5:5, 1 Corinthians 11:30 and 1 John 5:16.[1379] Certainly, this is the ultimate consequence of divine discipline brought on the sinning Christian. However, in the immediate context (vv. 15, 21), it appears that the salvation of a soul is salvation from temptations of sin that lead to spiritual death (broken fellowship) of the Christian.

A similar thought is found in 1 Corinthians,

> *No temptation has overtaken you but such as is common to man; and God is faithful, who will not allow you to be tempted beyond what you are able, but with the temptation will provide the way of escape also, so that you will be able to endure it (1 Corinthians 10:13).*

The "way of escape" is the same salvation of which James speaks; a salvation that is a way of escape from the path leading to spiritual danger.

James appears to be echoing the book of Proverbs when he speaks of salvation from the paths of sin. "*Wisdom,*" Solomon said, "*will save you from the ways of the wicked, from the adulteress ... from the wayward life*" (Proverbs 2:12, 16).

It is probable that James is using the term "salvation" in this sense when we consider the context in which his statement is placed. As discussed above, James describes the deathly consequences of sin in the life of the believer:

> *Let no one say when he is tempted, "I am being tempted by God"; for God cannot be tempted by evil, and He Himself does not tempt anyone. But each one is tempted when he is carried away and enticed by his own lust. Then when lust has conceived, it gives birth to sin; and when sin is accomplished, **it brings forth death**. Do not be deceived **my beloved brethren** (James 1:13-16).*

In view of the possibility of death in our Christian life, what should one do to prevent this catastrophe? James responds by saying:

> *Therefore, putting aside all filthiness and all that remains of wickedness, in humility receive the word implanted, which is able to save your souls (James 1:21).*

---

eschatological salvation, but the immediately preceding verses associate it with the Judgment Seat of Christ on genuine believers and not with the damnation or salvation of the unsaved. The immediate context of James 5:20 argues against his interpretation that salvation in James 2:14 refers to deliverance from eternal separation from God.

1378 Pak, "A Study of Selected Passages on Distinguishing Marks of Genuine and False Believers", 242.

1379 See Charles Ryrie, *The Ryrie Study Bible: New American Standard Translation* (Chicago: Moody Press, 1978), 1863. As pointed out in on pp. 260 ff., it always has this meaning in every other use in the LXX or New Testament.

Believers are to turn from sin and "receive" (Gr *dechomai*, "welcome with open arms") the "word implanted." The Word of God has been implanted in these believers, that is, they have been born again. If they want to save their souls from the temptations leading to spiritual impoverishment, they must welcome it as the implanted word that can protect them from temptations. One commentator puts it this way, "You must be humble and accept the message that God has planted [or, placed] in your hearts."[1380] This means to respond to instruction in the Word of God, or as James says in the next verse, they "*must be doers of the word and not hearers only*" (James 1:22).

These are "*beloved brethren*" who have been "*brought forth by the word of truth*" in whom the Word has been "*implanted.*" James says that these "brethren" are those who have "*faith in our glorious Lord Christ*" (James 2:1). Note that he says, "*Brought* ***us*** *forth by the word of truth*" (v. 18), thus including his readers along with **himself** as regenerate. He then refers to them as "beloved brethren" in v. 19 and says, "this you know [that is, you were 'brought forth'], my beloved brethren." These beloved brethren are those who know that they are born again! Therefore, commentators making unsubstantiated statements like "it is common for apostolic writers to include in letters addressed to churches stern warnings for those whose profession of faith was questionable"[1381] may safely be ignored. Also, Pak's curious statement, that it is "unlikely" that a true believer could be described as a mere hearer and one who deceives his own heart, is to be rejected.[1382] It is not unlikely at all. That believers can only hear and not do and can deceive themselves is taught in this very passage and surely corresponds with numerous warnings in both the Old and New Testaments as well as two thousand years of Christian experience!

The readers are saved people in the sense of having final deliverance from eternal damnation. However, these saved people need "salvation," which is defined as a deliverance from the death-producing effects of sin and ultimately salvation from loss and rebuke at the Judgment Seat of Christ (James 2:12-14). It is likely that Paul had a similar idea in mind when he exhorted Timothy, "*Watch your life and doctrine closely. Persevere in them, because if you do, you will save both yourself and your hearers*" (1 Timothy 4:16).

Any believer who becomes a doer will be blessed, that is the positive side of salvation. James continues,

> *But one who looks intently at the perfect law, the law of liberty, and abides by it, not having become a forgetful hearer but an effectual doer,* ***this man shall be blessed in what he does*** *(James 1:25).*

Like Timothy, he will save himself (1 Timothy 4:16). Once again, it is quite likely that James is thinking in Old Testament terms here. Solomon, for example, frequently contrasted the life-enriching benefits of righteousness with the death-producing effects of sin:

> *The truly righteous man attains life,*
> *But he who pursues evil goes to his death (Proverbs 11:19).*

[1380] Leon Morris, *The Gospel of John*, The New International Commentary on the New Testament (Grand Rapids: Wm. B. Eerdmans Publishing Co., 1995), 46.

[1381] John MacArthur, "Faith According to the Apostle James," *JETS* 33, no. 1 (March 1990): 29.

[1382] Pak, "A Study of Selected Passages on Distinguishing Marks of Genuine and False Believers", 246.

The terms "life" and "death" are contextually defined in Proverbs 11 as "abundant life" and "carnality," to use contemporary terms. In a series of contrasts he defines death as "being trapped by evil desires" (Proverbs 11:6); physical death and loss of hope (11:7); overwhelmed with trouble (11:8); destroying one's neighbor (11:9); destruction of a city by evil actions (11:11); a lack of judgment and a deriding of one's neighbor (11:12); and a lack of guidance resulting in the fall of a nation (11:14). Life, on the other hand, is defined as having a "straight way" (11:5); being delivered from evil snares (11:6); being rescued from trouble (11:8); giving blessing to a city (11:11); and sowing righteousness (11:18). Contrasts such as these define life and death not as entrance into heaven and final commitment to eternal damnation but as relative qualities of life now, qualities that depend on the faith-vitalizing property of good works.[1383]

In Solomon's terms it is rescue from trouble or the trap of evil desires. It is not final deliverance from eternal damnation. The parallelism between James 1:21-27 and 2:14-26 enables us to see how these passages explain each other. In 1:21-27 James tells us we will be "saved" by being doers and not just hearers of the word. In 2:14-16, we can now see that his meaning is the same. They will be saved in the sense of finding deliverance from the spiritually impoverishing consequences of sin if they energize their faith by works of obedience.

In Psalm 116, we find a remarkable parallel. The psalmist says the "*cords of death*" encompassed him. He equates "death" with distress and sorrow. He then calls on the Lord saying, "*Save my life*" (Heb *nephesh*, "soul," Psalm 116:1-4). The salvation of a soul in the psalm is from spiritual distress, and not final damnation.

The psalmist continues, "*For Thou hast rescued my soul from death, My eyes from tears, my feet from stumbling*" (Psalm 116:8). This rescue is from tears and stumbling, that is, from psychological/spiritual death. A key to the psalmist's deliverance was a determination to "*walk before the Lord*," that is, to do good works (v. 9) and to have a steadfast faith (v. 10), even in the midst of affliction. In other words, the salvation of which the psalmist speaks is like that of James. It is a temporal salvation from distress and trouble (death) and is obtained by faith plus works.

The salvation of a soul in James 1:21 is the deliverance *from* the spiritually impoverishing consequences of sin and *to* the experiential blessing of God now. (See p. 405, FN 1372). Because Jesus, James' Half-Brother (the Lord Jesus Christ), used the same phrase (Matthew 16:24-27), we can safely assume that for James, this salvation comes from self-denial, taking up our cross and following Christ, so that we will be favorably recompensed at the Judgment Seat of Christ.[1384]

SALVATION FROM LOSS AT THE JUDGMENT SEAT OF CHRIST

Just before saying, "Can that faith save him?" (2:14), James says,

> *So speak and so act as those who are to be judged by the law of liberty. For judgment will be merciless to one who has shown no mercy; mercy triumphs over judgment (James 2:12-13).*

[1383] See also Proverbs 10:27; 12:28; 13:14; 19:16.

[1384] See discussion on the salvation of the soul in chapters 15 and 16.

These believers are warned that "*judgment will be merciless to one who has shown no mercy*." This judgment will fall on the justified saint (James 2:1) who has not responded to James' exhortation to humbly accept the implanted Word by becoming a doer and not just a hearer (1:22-25), and thus save his soul from death (1:15, 21).

Some writers suggest that the judgment in verse 13 "*will be merciless to one who has shown no mercy*" means that the judgment of eternal damnation must be in view.[1385] Moo interprets the passage differently: "With these commands, James returns to the dominant theme in this section of the letter: the need for believers to *validate* ['doing' the word (1:22)]."[1386] However, there is nothing here in the context about validating one's initial "saving" faith. Moo should have followed through on his statement that "the Greek text puts even more emphasis on the need for *Christians* [italics added] to regulate their conduct with an eye on the judgment to come."[1387] Professing Christians who are not born again are not in view at all.

What is the "law of liberty" by which the Christian will be judged? In view of the many parallels between James and the Sermon on the Mount, it is easy to understand this as the precepts of Christ as taught in that magnificent sermon. When Christians ask, "What is the basis by which I will be judged at the judgment seat; how can I obtain reward there?" the answer is, "You will be judged by how you have applied the Sermon on the Mount to your life!"

If believers show partiality toward the rich and neglect the poor, they violate the "*royal law*" of Scripture: "*You shall love your neighbor as yourself*" (James 2:8).

Hart makes two points in favor of the idea that this judgment is a judgment on true believers. First, he notes that "James challenges his readership to act like those who have been forgiven and freed from guilt. But unbelievers or false believers cannot act like they have been freed from guilt."[1388] This judgment is based on the "law of liberty," which is something believers look into (James 1:21). This law, which gives freedom, is a law that, for those who know the truth, sets them free (John 8:31-32). Second, Hart notes that "2:12–13 corresponds to 3:1 as an *inclusio*. Therefore, the judgment mentioned in 3:1 corresponds with the judgment mentioned in 2:12–13. But in 3:1, James himself states that he will experience this judgment, and that it will involve greater strictness for him and for all teachers. '*Let not many of you become teachers, my brethren, knowing that as such* ***we*** *will incur a stricter judgment.*' Can anyone suppose that James thought of himself as appearing before God to determine his eternal destiny? Was heaven held in the balance for him? Absolutely not!"[1389]

1385 Gale Z. Heide, "The Soteriology of James 2:14," *GTJ* 12, no. 1 (Spring 1991).

1386 Douglas J. Moo, *The Letter of James*, The Pillar New Testament Commentary (Grand Rapids: Wm. B. Eerdmans Publishing Co., 2000), 116.

1387 Ibid.

1388 John F. Hart, "How to Energize Our Faith: Reconsidering the Meaning of James 2:14-26," *JOTGES* 12, no. 1 (Spring 1999): 52.

1389 Ibid., 52. Robert Wilkin agrees, "The verses immediately before and after James 2:14–26 are dealing with genuine believers. They are called 'my brethren' (2:1, 5; 3:1). These are not 'brethren' in the sense that all Jews refer to each other as brothers, but these are brothers in whom the Word has been implanted ('accept the word planted in you, which can save you,' James 1:21). These are brethren who have 'faith in our glorious Lord Jesus Christ' (James 2:1). Only believers will be at the Judgment Seat of Christ, to which James refers. James would never warn unbelievers to be cautious about becoming teachers in the church. Nor would he warn unbelievers of the need to be merciful to believers in the church." Robert Wilkin, "Another View of Faith and Works in James 2," *Journal of the Grace Evangelical Society* 15, no. 2 (Fall 2002): 20.

James also refers to the Judgment Seat of Christ at the end of the epistle. "*Do not complain, brethren, against one another, so that you yourselves may not be judged; behold, the Judge is standing right at the door*" (James 5:9). The salvation obtained by faith plus works is not soteriological entrance into heaven. Rather, it is a salvation of "brethren" (regenerate believers) from the temporal, psychological, spiritual, or physical consequences (sin unto death) of a nonworking faith resulting in a negative assessment of one's life at the Judgment Seat of Christ.[1390]

We are on familiar ground here. Elsewhere, Paul warns of judgment good and bad which can fall on the regenerate saint at the Judgment Seat of Christ (2 Corinthians 5:10) and John warns of the danger of losing what one has worked for (2 John 8; cp. Matthew 4:25). James' point is that faith without works cannot save one from the negative consequences of a lifestyle of sin leading to death (1:21) and the resultant negative judgment at the Judgment Seat of Christ.

In fact, "save" is related by James, not only to deliverance and perseverance in trial, i.e., sanctification but also to obtaining an "advantage" at the Judgment Seat of Christ. James teaches, "*And one of you says to them, 'Go in peace, be warmed and be filled,' and yet you do not give them what is necessary for their body, what use is that?*" (James 2:16). Faith without works is of no "use." The word "use" (Gr *ophelos*), refers to an "advantage,"[1391] or an additional benefit or "increase."[1392] The preceding context relates this to an advantage or increase of benefit at the Judgement Seat of Christ (2:12-13), where James warns his readers that one day they will be held accountable for how they treat others. Immediately after saying, "*Judgment will be merciless to one who has shown no mercy; mercy triumphs over judgment,*" James asks, "*What advantage do you have if you do not do good works?*"[1393]

SALVATION FROM SIN'S PENALTIES (JAMES 4:12)

The next instance of the word "save" in James (besides 2:14) is in 4:12, where we read of the divine Lawgiver, who is able to "save or destroy."[1394]

> *There is only one Lawgiver and Judge, the One who is able to save and to destroy; but who are you who judge your neighbor? (James 4:12)*

There is no need to assume, as Douglas Moo does, that "James ... is thinking of 'judging' in terms of determining the ultimate spiritual destiny of individuals."[1395] By "ultimate

1390 Heide says, "The judgment that he has in mind does not look at the accomplishments of the person, rather it inspects the person's sinful transgression and judges upon that basis. This type of judgment is not with a view to reward, but with a view to convict and punish." Heide, "The Soteriology of James 2:14," 89. Apparently in Heide's theology, no negative could happen to the sinful believer at the Judgment Seat of Christ. All are to be happy there. The biblical idea that true believers can face "shame" (1 John 2:28) does not seem to dawn on her.

1391 Louw-Nida, 1:624. The word is used only three times in the New Testament (James 2:14, 16; 1 Cor 15:32).

1392 BDAG 743.

1393 J. B. Hixson, *Getting the Gospel Wrong* (Longwood, FL: Xulon Press, 2008), n100, 78.

1394 Alan P. Stanley assures his readers that "eschatological salvation is in view" because only God is able to save and destroy. However, this context is about temporal destruction and not damnation. Stanley, *Did Jesus Teach Salvation by Works*, 161. He cites Matthew 10:28, "Do not fear those who kill the body but are unable to kill the soul; but rather fear Him who is able to destroy both soul and body in hell (Gr *Gehenna*)." But there is nothing here about salvation. Furthermore, *Gehenna*, as argued elsewhere, does not refer to damnation but is a metaphor for a negative assessment of one's life at the Judgment Seat of Christ. See extensive discussion of *Gehenna* elsewhere in this book in chapters 54-57.

1395 Moo, *The Letter of James*, 199.

spiritual destiny" Moo means the lake of fire. But, this is a bare assertion. There is nothing here about judging a man's state of redemptive salvation. Rather, James speaks of judging a fellow believer's behavior.

While it is true that God has the power to send one to heaven or eternal damnation, "to save or destroy," these terms in the immediate context are linked to temporal salvation and destruction. Consider the following comments by Zane Hodges on verses 13-17, where James speaks of physical death, "life is a vapor."

> *God is certainly the only One who determines our eternal destinies, but this determination is already made: believers are already free from final judgment and condemnation (John 3:18; 5:24). But here a reference to this truth is not as natural as a reference to physical life or death (as also in 1:21; 2:14; 5:15, 20). The idea will then be that though we may condemn our brothers verbally, it is God alone who determines whether to save them from sin's penalty of death (1:15; 5:20) or whether to destroy their lives as an act of chastening (cf. Acts 5:1–11; 1 Corinthians 11:30).*[1396]

The reference to slandering one's brother and God's response of destroying the one who slanders is too close to be coincidental. The Hebrew concept for destruction uses the word *ṣāmat*. It is found 15 times in the Old Testament. Although it is not translated by *apōllumi* in the LXX, it never refers to the destruction of eternal damnation. Rather is refers to some temporal consequence.[1397] In some places it means to have one's reputation "destroyed" (Psalm 69:4), and this fits the context of James. In one instance it refers to the spiritual and psychological destruction that can come upon a believer; like David, when he sins (Psalm 88:16).

When James says that the divine Lawgiver is able to "destroy," it is evident from the context that he does not have eternal destruction in view.[1398] The kind of destruction in this context is temporal, not eternal. This view is confirmed by his statement in verse 11, "*Do not slander one another,*" and the exhortation, in which James asks, "*Who are you to judge your neighbor?*" James, who was a careful student of the Old Testament, likely has Psalm 101:5 in mind.

> *Whoever secretly slanders his neighbor, him I will destroy* (LXX, *Gr ekdiōk*); *No one who has a haughty look and an arrogant heart will I endure (Psalm 101:5).*

Only God has the right to destroy someone's life or reputation, or on the other hand, to exalt him (v. 10). A sinning brother is God's responsibility, and although his fellow believers can exhort and encourage him, they are not to slander or judge him.

Paul taught the same thing,

> *Never take your own revenge, beloved, but leave room for the wrath of God, for it is written, "Vengeance is Mine, I will repay," says the Lord (Romans 12:19).*

1396 Zane C. Hodges, *The Epistle of James: Proven Character Through Testing: A Verse by Verse Commentary* (Irving, TX: Grace Evangelical Society, 1994), 99.

1397 Cf. Psalms 18:40; 143:12.

1398 The phrase "save or destroy" [Gr *apollumi*], may echo Jesus' statement to the Pharisees in Mark 3:4, "And He said to them, Is it lawful to do good or to do harm on the Sabbath, to save a life or to kill? [Gr *apokteinō*]." The Gr words are different but the sentiment is the same, "to save a soul" or "to destroy it."

Only God has the right to revenge. Only God has the right to destroy someone. When the believers James addresses slander one another and judge one another, they assume a right they do not have. It is God's responsibility to deal with one's offender. To "save," in this context, means to deliver from the temporal consequences of sin which can be spiritual and psychological ruin, physical illness (5:15), or possibly physical death (5:19-20).

Clearly, James has in mind his Half-Brother's teaching given in His famous Sermon on the Mount where He said,

> *Do not judge so that you will not be judged. For in the way you judge, you will be judged; and by your standard of measure, it will be measured to you. Why do you look at the speck that is in your brother's eye, but do not notice the log that is in your own eye? Or how can you say to your brother, "Let me take the speck out of your eye" and behold, the log is in your own eye? You hypocrite, first take the log out of your own eye, and then you will see clearly to take the speck out of your brother's eye (Matthew 7:1–5).*

It is God's responsibility to "destroy" a sinning brother in this sense and only God can ultimately save him from this kind of "destruction," that is, from spiritual and psychological ruin from a possible judgment unto physical death, or from a damaged reputation. Salvation, once again, has nothing to do in James with deliverance from damnation!

SALVATION FROM DISEASE (JAMES 5:15)

In the final chapter of his epistle, James uses the word *sōzō* two more times.

> *And the prayer offered in faith will restore* [Gr *sōzō*] *the one who is sick, and the Lord will raise him up* [Gr *sōzō*, "save"], *and if he has committed sins, they will be forgiven him (James 5:15).*

Clearly, salvation in this verse refers to salvation from disease, that is, physical healing. The one who is healed is a member of the congregation who believes in Christ and who calls on the elders of the congregation to pray for healing. He may need, as James suggests, forgiveness and restoration to fellowship with God. As Paul explained, sometimes a physical illness can be a divine discipline for a carnal life (1 Corinthians 11:30).

SALVATION FROM PHYSICAL DEATH (JAMES 5:19-20)

Finally we read in James 5:19-20,

> *My brethren, if any among you strays from the truth and one turns him back, let him know that he who turns a sinner from the error of his way will save [Gr sōzō] his soul from death and will cover a multitude of sins.*

Once again we see the phrase "save a soul," which as demonstrated above never in the Bible means salvation from eternal damnation. But even if one does not grant this, it is clear that a temporal deliverance is in view. John Niemelä asks,

> *Can an unbeliever wander away from that which he has never believed? The very absurdity of such a proposition is easily envisioned in geographic terms: Unless a person has been in China, how can he wander away from it? Likewise, can a person be turned back to China, if he has never set foot in China? Indeed, James 5:19 speaks of anyone who left the truth that regenerated him, and is now turned back by a someone.*[1399]

[1399] John Niemelä, "Faith Without Works: A Definition 1," *Chafer Theological Seminary Journal* 6, no. 2 (April 2000): 11.

At the risk of repetition, let me say again, James is not talking about the initial act of faith. Instead, he speaks of the ongoing life of faith, so there is no conflict at all with Paul's faith-apart-from-works Gospel.[1400] Only a life of maturing faith can "save" in the sense in which James is using the word "save."

James is well within the theology of the Old Testament when he warns against the shortening of life which occurs when a man lives a life of debauchery or bitterness or sin. Indeed, his point has been commonly observed by mankind throughout the ages and confirmed by modern medical science. Many of our ailments have psychosomatic origins. Emotional stress brought on by a life of guilt and bitterness is perhaps the major cause of physical death in the Western world.

Faith without Works Is Dead

James continues,

Even so faith, if it has no works, is dead, being by itself (James 2:17).

Just like the body is dead if its spirit has departed, so the believer's walk of faith becomes dead if works depart. This is what happened to the prodigal son. His father said, "*For this son of mine was dead, and has come to life again* [Gr *anazaō*]*; he was lost, and has been found*" (Luke 15:24). He was once alive in the sense of intimacy with his father, but because of his carnality, he became dead. When he was with the pigs, he was "lost" (Gr *apollumi*), not unsaved. He was still a son, but he was lost in the sense that his life was in ruins. His life had been destroyed, impoverished, psychologically and spiritually, and in that sense, he was dead. But he came alive "again" (Gr *anazaō*, from *zaō*, "to live," and "*ana*" again, thus "be alive again"[1401]). Of course, this means that he was alive before, but because of his lack of works he had become dead.

Apparently some of the Christians to whom James was writing were deluding themselves (James 1:22). They imagined that their faith was "living" and that they were walking in a life of faith even though it was not in accord with acts of charity. They had justifying faith, but they did not have the living faith with which the epistle is concerned. This is a typical situation faced by many pastors today. There are some justified saints in their congregations who are lukewarm or even carnal, but they think all is well and that they are in fact living the Christian life when in fact they lack some of the essential attributes of a living faith. This was the problem John faced in 1 John. "*If we say that we have fellowship with Him and yet walk in the darkness, we lie and do not practice the truth*" (1 John 1:6).[1402] Also, John's readers faced a negative assessment of their lives at the

---

[1400] This point negates most of Joseph Pak's refutation of the Partner view of James. Starting from the unfounded premise that "faith" refers to genuine soteriological faith instead of genuine walking faith, Pak is led to conclude, erroneously, that initial genuine "saving" faith which is not followed by a life of works is not really genuine saving faith (notice all the adjectives which one must add to clarify Pak's discussion!). See Pak, "A Study of Selected Passages on Distinguishing Marks of Genuine and False Believers", 224 and 50 ff.

[1401] BDAG, 62.

[1402] As demonstrated elsewhere, the theme of 1 John is not tests of salvation, but tests of whether one is walking in fellowship. Like James, there were those among John's readers who had deluded (James 1:22) themselves and were walking in darkness (1 John 2:9) even though their sins had been forgiven (1 John 2:12). See discussion

Judgment Seat of Christ when some of them would draw back in shame (1 John 2:28).

Faith by itself (or "faith alone" which is not vitalized by works) is useless in the sense that it is of no value to the believer in living his Christian life, or to others who need practical assistance rather than platitudes, or for receiving any benefits at the Judgment Seat of Christ. The word "dead" is explained by James 2:20, where this faith is called "useless" (Gr *argos*) which means "idle" or unproductive, or "unemployed."[1403] In all of the uses of *argos*, it is talking about something that is existent but not functioning as intended.[1404]

Dialogue with the Objector

The words of an objector are now introduced in 2:18-19.[1405] It is confusing from our English translations where the words of the objector end and James begins to respond to his objection. The quotation marks are attempts by the translators to indicate their preference. In the Greek text when James wrote, there were neither punctuation marks nor lower/upper case letters. Any insertion of such distinguishing marks is an addition by much later editors or the various translators, and, as is often the case, is often informed by their prior theological bias.

Let's consider some of the most prominent suggestions as to where the quotation marks should be placed and how this placement affects the understanding of the text.[1406] The traditional understanding is reflected in the translation of NIV, ESV, and the NKJV. It looks like Table 1 below.

TABLE 1	
JAMES:	But someone will say (2:18a)
OBJECTOR:	"You have faith; I have deeds" (2:18b).
JAMES:	"Show me your faith without deeds, and I will show you my faith by what I do (2:18b). You believe that there is one God. Good! Even the demons believe that—and shudder (2:19). But are you willing to recognize, you foolish fellow, that faith without works is useless?" (2:20).

of the tests of 1 John elsewhere in this book in chapter 31.

1403 BDAG 128.

1404 Wendall Hollis notes, "One of the other uses is in Matt 12:36-37. In v. 36 he speaks of 'careless' words, and then in 37 says 'by your words you will be justified [or condemned].' The Greek words and construction are the same as James 2:20. Yet here 'justified' almost certainly does not have a forensic meaning but something like 'vindicated.' That would seem to give a foundation for the view that faith in James 2:14-26 talks about an actual faith that is useless if it doesn't work rather than a nonexistent faith." Personal Communication, March 10, 2011.

1405 A structural observation, not often commented on, suggests that the objector's comments extend through verse 19. James' reply, then, begins in verse 20 with "you foolish fellow." The evidence for this point that the objector's comments terminate there is that this is clearly a Greek diatribe (debate format). As John F. Hart notes, "These parallel stylistic structures make it nearly impossible to take the text in any other way than that 2:18–19 is a complete unit—the entire words of an opponent to James." See Hart, "The Faith of Demons," 50.

1406 For an excellent discussion of the issues surrounding this dialogue, see Fred Lybrand, *Back to Faith: Reclaiming Gospel Clarity in an Age of Incongruence* (Lakewood, FL: Xulon Press, 2009), 92-109.

The first question to be addressed is "Why would an objector make this comment? What is his point when he says to James, 'You have faith, I have deeds'?" If he is arguing that works are unnecessary, it seems strange that he would claim to have the very thing he says is unnecessary, works![1407]

Also, how would James' response in verse 18b ("show me your faith without deeds") have any meaning? The objector would just say, "But, James, I told you I do have deeds!"[1408] As Martin has pointed out, "The clauses that follow the words 'You have faith; I have deeds' do not oppose James' thoughts but in fact support his position."[1409] On this view the objector's statement is that James has faith and the objector has works, a statement to which James never responds,[1410] and which makes no sense.

Because of the difficulty of identifying "you" with James, and "I" with a particular opponent, many suggest that the pronouns do not refer to James and the objector, but are equivalent to "one" and "another," and are merely a more picturesque mode of indicating two imaginary persons.[1411]

On this view the argument looks like this:

James: *Faith alone cannot save a person (v. 14).*

Supposed objector: *Some have faith others have works and both are legitimate in living the Christian life (v. 18a).*

James' response: *A life of faith and works cannot exist separately (vv. 18b-19).*

Yet there is a difficulty for this viewpoint which is not easily overcome. The pronouns "you" (Gr *su*) and "I" (Gr *kai egō*) are never used in the New Testament in the sense of "some" and "others."[1412] It is interesting that some interpreters believe that this

1407 Not only is the objector's "objection" irrelevant (in the Reformed view), James' response make no sense. No doubt the objector would agree with James (in 18b), not disagree, that faith cannot be seen apart from works. He would also believe that faith cannot be seen with works. Faith, according to the objector, cannot be seen at all. It is invisible and has no connection with behavior. Furthermore, the objector has already said, I have works. So James' response in verse 18b would be pointless. As Lybrand put it, "The objector says he has works, but according to the NASB, James is demanding that he show his faith without his works. 'Show me your faith without your works' could easily be followed by the objector's interruption and clarification, 'But, James, I just said I have works!'" Fred Lybrand, "Does Faith Guarantee Works? Rethinking the Cliché" (DMin diss., Phoenix Theological Seminary, 2007), 79.

1408 Peter H. Davids has James responding to the objector saying, "Prove to me this (so-called) faith of yours apart from deeds." Davids, *The Epistle of James: A Commentary on the Greek Text*, 124. The difficulty with Davids' view is that the objector says that he (the objector) has deeds. Davids has completely reversed the phrase. In other words, if James is the speaker in the phrase beginning with "show me" ("prove to me"), then James is completely ignoring the objector's argument.

1409 Ralph P. Martin, *James*, Word Biblical Commentary (Dallas: Word, 2002), 48.

1410 It is therefore doubtful that Alan Stanley's view that this is a statement of James could be correct. Stanley places this statement in the lips of James and not the objector. Stanley, *Did Jesus Teach Salvation by Works*, 236-37.

1411 J. H. Ropes, *A Critical and Exegetical Commentary on the Epistle of St. James* (New York: Scribner's Sons, 1916), 208.

1412 Apparently, according to Ropes, there are places in extra-biblical Greek where *su* is used as an equivalent to *tis* "some" or "someone," but in the New Testament *su* is found 174 times in 161 verses. It never means "some."

interpretation has "the least difficulty"[1413] but others feel it is "the least likely."[1414]

Another punctuation commonly accepted by Experimental Predestinarians is that found in the NASB. See Table 2.

TABLE 2	
JAMES:	But someone will say (2:18a).
OBJECTOR:	"You have faith; I have deeds. Show me your faith without deeds, and I will show you my faith by what I do" (2:18b).
JAMES:	You believe that there is one God. Good! Even the demons believe that—and shudder (2:19). But are you willing to recognize, you foolish fellow, that faith without works is useless? (2:20).

In this view the objector asserts that he has works and he is challenging James to show his faith without works. The objector is saying that he can demonstrate that he has faith by means of his works. This places the Reformed cliché ("faith alone saves, but the faith that saves is not alone") on the lips of the objector, not James! It is difficult to see how this is an objection to James' viewpoint if James' viewpoint is, as the Reformed authors claim, that genuine faith always results in works. That is precisely what the objector is saying, so how can this be an objection?

In this view, James sarcastically says, "You believe that there is one God. Good! But so do demons." The word "good" (Gr *kalos*) should be rendered "You do well" (see discussion below). The demons believe in God, and they do not do good works, instead, they shudder. Since both the objector and the demons believe in God, and yet one works and one does not, then James (not the objector) is the one who would be saying there is no connection between belief and action in direct contradiction to the Reformed view of the passage. Since the objector says, "I have deeds," James' response that "faith without works is useless" is illogical. The objector would say, "James, I just said I have good works!" Why would James make such an irrational argument?

To avoid this dilemma a final way of punctuating the passage is to place the final quote at the end of verse 19, thereby indicating that verses 18a-19 are all on the lips of the objector. See Table 3 on the next page.

The markers beginning with "someone" in verse 18a and "you foolish fellow" in verse 20 form a unit demarcating the boundaries of the objector's comments. In other words, verses 18b and 19 are all part of the objector's response.

In the NASB translation above, it is the objector who seems to be saying that faith can be shown by works, a point with which James would agree! So does the apostle John who says, "*By this the children of God and the children of the devil are obvious: anyone who does not practice righteousness is not of God* [that is, he is not "of God" in the sense that the

Also, the phrase "and I" (Gr *kai egō*) is found 80 times in 84 verses and never refers to "others." It always means "and I." Ibid., 209.

1413 Pak says this view "seems to have the least difficulty." Pak, "A Study of Selected Passages on Distinguishing Marks of Genuine and False Believers", 233.

1414 Ralph Martin says, "No one interpretation is free from problems, but it seems that the third interpretation is the least likely." Martin, *James*, 86.

source of his behavior is not "of God"[1415]], *nor the one who does not love his brother*" (1 John 3:10). How then is this an objection?[1416]

TABLE 3	
JAMES:	But someone will say (2:18a).
OBJECTOR:	"You have faith; I have deeds. Show me your faith without deeds, and I will show you my faith by what I do. You believe that there is one God. Good! Even the demons believe that--and shudder" (2:18b-19).
JAMES:	But are you willing to recognize, you foolish fellow, that faith without works is useless? (2:20).

A sound solution to the problem is recognizing that James is definitely using a common Greek debating technique called diatribe.[1417] Elsewhere in the New Testament where this fully developed format with its "objection/reply" format is used, it is marked by the objection and then the reply beginning with "O man" or "you fool," or something similar (cf. Romans 9:19-20; 1 Corinthians 15:35-36). Thus the diatribe begins with "O Man," the objector is speaking (in 2:18a-2:19), and quotation marks should be placed around those verses.

This Greek rhetorical device, which is acknowledged by many interpreters, requires that the objector is disagreeing, not agreeing. Paul uses this approach on several occasions. "In using it, the apostle simulated objections to his argument, or drew false inferences from it, both of which he subsequently refuted (1 Corinthians 15:35–37; Galatians 2:17). In effect, the diatribe furnished him with a method of creating dialogues between himself and imaginary interlocutors (Romans 3:27–4:2)."[1418]

To restate the problem, the objector seems to say, "*Show me your faith apart from* [Gr *chōris*] *works*." If this is an objection, then the objector is assuming that this cannot be done. Yet this is James' point as well. So how can this be an objection?

If this is the correct reading, then the objection makes sense. The objector begins by saying,

---

[1415] See discussion on pp. 500.

[1416] Rather than interact with all the issues here, the writer will set forth his interpretation and the reasons for it. "When do the objector's comments terminate and James' reply begin?" As punctuated above, we believe the objector's comment extends to the end of verse 19. However, if the objector's comments extend to verse 19, how can his reply be construed as an objection? It appears that he agrees with James when he says, "Show me your faith, without the works," implying, with James, that this cannot be done! The issues are very complex and beyond the scope of this book. Those interested in deeper understanding might check the excellent commentaries by Peter Davids and Ralph Martin, and in particular the excellent article by Hart, "The Faith of Demons," 39-54. See also Lybrand, *Back to Faith: Reclaiming Gospel Clarity in an Age of Incongruence.*

[1417] Martin, *James*, 59, 79, 90.

[1418] Werner H. Kelber, "Oral Tradition, New Testament," in *Anchor Yale Bible Dictionary*, ed. David Noel Freedman, et al. (New York: Doubleday, 1992), 5:33. Stanley K. Stowers, "Diatribe," in *Anchor Yale Bible Dictionary*, ed. David Noel Freedman, et al. (New York: Doubleday, 1992), 2:191. According to Essel, "From a study of its literary forms J. H. Ropes concluded that the Epistle reveals many of the characteristics of the diatribe — the short moral or ethical address developed initially by the Stoics and Cynics. Certain stylistic features of the Epistle are similar to the peculiar style of the diatribe: dialogue (2:20); brief questions and answers (5:13f); rhetorical questions (2:14); harsh speech (2:20; 4:4); the introduction of an opposing speaker with "but someone will say" (2:18); etc. The choice of illustrations, especially in 3:2–12, is significant." W. W. Essel, "James - Literary Character - Diatribe Theory," in *NISBE*, ed. G. W. Bromiley (Grand Rapids: Wm. B. Eerdmans Publishing Co., 1988), 2:961.

You have faith and I have works.

This is not his objection, but is the premise upon which his objection is built. It is as if he said,

Okay James, let's say you have faith and I have works. Let's start there.

At this point he is not contradicting James but stating an opening premise upon which he will build his objection. The objection does not begin until the interlocutor says, "*Show me.*"

Show me your faith by means of your works [which I do not believe can be done because there is no connection between faith and works], and I will show you my faith by means of my works [which also cannot be done].

The opening words, "show me." signal that the statement to follow is an objection. Thus the challenge to "show me" your faith by your works when placed on the lips of the objector imply that such a demonstration cannot be done because there is no connection between faith and works.

To put this in modern terms, John Hart says,

In modern terms, the imaginary objector might have said, "James, you start with a doctrinal point, and show me what good work proves you believe this. If you can do that, I'll do the reverse. I'll name a good work and show what doctrine must be behind it. It's impossible! For example, James, you believe that the body is the temple of the Holy Spirit. And you have a monogamous marriage. But the Mormons believe that too, and some of them are polygamous. So works can't show us anything about a person's faith. No one can see faith."[1419]

There is a textual issue bearing on this difficulty which is noted by Martin. In the first half of verse 18 "there is a weaker yet well-attested alternative to this textual reading."[1420] While most translations render this like the NASB, "show me your faith without (Gr *chōris*) the works, and I will show you my faith by (Gr *ek*) my works,"[1421] the alternative text would be translated, "show me your faith 'from' or 'by' [Gr *ek*] your works and I will show you my faith 'from' (or 'by', Gr *ek*) my works." This reading is found in the Majority Text and the Textus Receptus (but omitted from the KJV).

Douglas Moo objects saying, "However, quite apart from its dubious textual basis, the irony necessary to sustain this view is simply not evident."[1422] Why Moo says the irony is insufficient is unclear. It is quite obvious that there is irony and even sarcasm in the argument. The objector mocks saying, "Even the demons believe!"

As far as Moo's claim that the textual tradition is insufficient, Fred Chay carefully

---

1419 Hart, "The Faith of Demons," 51.

1420 Martin, *James*, 76.

1421 The Latin Vulgate translates from Greek using *sine* which means "without" suggesting that the Greek text before Jerome had the word *chōris* (without), not *ek* (from or by). The text of Westcott and Hort uses *chōris* and the Majority Text uses *ek*. The Syriac Peshitta renders it, "Show me your faith with no works," indicating it was translated from a Greek manuscript that had *chōris*.

1422 Moo, *The Letter of James*, 129.

analyzed this issue and demonstrated that the reading "from/by" (Gr *ek*) rather than "without" (Gr *chōris*) has very good manuscript support and may be preferable.[1423] The basis, however, for selecting *ek* rather than *chōris*, are the internal requirements of the context, not just the fact that many manuscripts have this variant.

Two compelling contextual factors are these: first, only the reading "*by works*" (Gr *ek*) makes the objector's retort an objection, and second, the severity of the rebuke in verse 20 must be noted. If the reading "*apart from works*" (or "*without*," Gr *chōris*) is accepted, then the objector is saying, as discussed above, that faith cannot be shown apart from works, a viewpoint which James holds, and is therefore not an objection to James. But if the objector is saying "show me your faith '*by*' (*ek*) works," he is saying this cannot be done, because faith cannot be shown "*by works*" (or *from* works) because there is no connection between faith and works at all. In fact, according to the objector, all that is needed is the Shema, "*God is one*" (v. 19). The point is that if "apart from works" is the translation, there is no real objection and no basis for James saying, "You foolish man!"

When the contextual factors are considered,[1424] and one accepts *ek* as the correct reading, then we might consider Weymouth's translation as follows:[1425]

> *Nay, someone will say, "You have faith, I have actions; prove to me your faith* ***from*** [Gr *ek*] *corresponding actions and I will prove mine to you* **by** [Gr **ek**][1426] *my actions. You believe that God is one, and you are quite right: evil spirits also believe this, and shudder." But, idle boaster, are you willing to be taught how it is that faith apart from obedience is worthless? (James 2:18-19).*[1427]

The objector's proof of his claim that works cannot demonstrate faith is that the demons believe there is one God and tremble; James believes the same thing but does good works.[1428] Each have different behavioral outcomes from the same creed.

1423 See Chay and Correia, *The Faith That Saves: The Nature of Faith in the New Testament*, 141-48. See also Peters, "The Meaning of Conversion." Zane C. Hodges, "Light from James 2 from Textual Criticism," *BibSac* 120, no. 480 (October-December 1963): 341-50. Lybrand, "Does Faith Guarantee Works? Rethinking the Cliché". Hart, "The Faith of Demons." These writers oppose the view of Pak, "A Study of Selected Passages on Distinguishing Marks of Genuine and False Believers", 228-30.

1424 Martin himself accepts the Nestle-Aland Text, *chōris*, but notes that the discussion of R. W. Wall has merit. Wall says, "The issue of a correct reading must be decided on internal grounds, namely, that in order to account for the severity of the rebuke (in v 20: ὦ ἄνθρωπε κενέ, 'you foolish man!'), it is necessary to have the objector say more than the simple statement that there are two [equally] competing claims to authentic religion: You have faith, I have deeds (v 18a)." For Wall, "this is followed by an interlocutor's second remark which is not tautological, that there are two beginning points of 'true religion' (1:27)—faith and deeds—that are 'not only mutually exclusive; they have no logical interplay as well.' The upshot of the objector's position is that 'believers' may choose to have either faith or works and still be classed as true to religion. Hence the parallelism ἐκ τῶν ἔργων … ἐκ τῶν ἔργων (by works …. by works, accepting TR). The interlocutor also is responsible for the affirmation καλῶς ποιεῖς, lit., 'You do well,' which he borrows from James' earlier remark (2:8, καλῶς ποιεῖτε, 'you are doing well,') about obedience to the royal law. He also cites the monotheistic formula as the epitome of his faith, seeking James' concurrence along with what he regards as the essence of faith. According to this reconstruction, based on the text-critical issue, James' reply begins in v 20 with a stinging invective." R. W. Wall, "Interlocutor and James, James 2:18–20 Reconsidered." Unpublished article, cited by Martin, *James*, 76.

1425 Richard F. Weymouth, *The New Testament in Modern Speech* (London: James Clark and Co., 1905). See also Williams, The New Testament (1986 ed.); and Young's Literal Translation (1898).

1426 *Gr ek* can be translated "by" or "from".

1427 F. H. A. Scrivener's and Steven's Textus Receptus (1550) and the Byzantine/Majority Textform Greek New Testament all support this textual variant on which Weymouth's translation is based.

1428 Hart, "The Faith of Demons," 51.

You believe that there is one God. Good! Even the demons believe that—and shudder (James 2:19).

It is typical to hear, based upon this verse, that simple faith in Christ is not enough. Even demons believe, so something more than faith is needed—repentance (defined as surrender or turning). However, the demons do not believe in the Gospel of Christ. The demons are not resting in Christ for their forgiveness of sins. The demons believe one thing, God is one, that is, they are monotheistic. That is not saving faith. Muslims and Jews believe that God is one.

When the objector says, "Good" (Gr *kalōs poieis*), his meaning is not "Good for you" or "that is a good thing" but literally, "You do well." The same phrase is found in verse 8, "*If you really keep the royal law of Scripture, 'Love your neighbor as yourself', you are doing right*"[1429] [Gr *kalōs poieite*]. The objector is therefore saying, "James, you believe in God, good for you ("you do well")! The demons also believe in God, but they shudder. The conclusion is, there is no necessary connection between faith and good works."

Such an argument is ludicrous, and appropriately James begins his response in verse 20 by calling his interlocutor a "*foolish man*" and tells him that the walk of faith, unless it is vitalized and matured by a life of works, is not only a delusion, it is dead; it is a faith that has no effect. The objector apparently imagines that one can live the Christian life by a faith which is not energized by works, and that this alone is adequate for an abundant life and for the fulfillment of all obligations to God. However, James counters that faith without works is useless as far as sanctification and deliverance through trials are concerned (2:20; cf. 1:21; 2:14). Furthermore, faith without works has no benefit before the Judgment Seat of Christ (vv. 13-14). There is a connection between faith and works but not the connection imagined by the Reformed doctrine of perseverance.

In the final analysis, this writer prefers the punctuation of the dialogue followed by Weymouth. Notice that the Partners and the Experimental Predestinarians agree that faith without works is dead. They also agree that true faith should express itself and include a life of works. Furthermore, they agree that faith alone cannot save. The disagreement centers on the meaning of the words "faith," "dead," and "save." "True" faith or "that" faith in James never means the "initial act of faith whereby one is justified freely by His grace." It always refers to the walk of faith that follows initial salvation. Also, for James, "save" never means deliverance from eternal damnation. Rather, it speaks of the temporal salvation from a path leading to spiritual/psychological or physical death and the resultant negative judgment on one's life at the Judgment Seat of Christ. Finally, for James, for faith to be "dead" does not mean it never existed, it means it is not vital or living; or, to use James' words, it has no "benefit."

The Maturing of Abraham's Faith

As proof of the worthless nature of a life of faith apart from works, James now cites the illustration of Abraham:

Was not Abraham our father ***justified by works*** *when he offered up Isaac his son on the altar? You see that faith was working with his works, and as a result of the works, faith was*

[1429] This meaning of the phrase is found in several places in the New Testament (Luke 6:27; Matthew 12:12; James 4:17).

perfected; and the Scripture was fulfilled which says, "AND ABRAHAM BELIEVED GOD, AND IT WAS RECKONED TO HIM AS RIGHTEOUSNESS," and he was called the friend of God. You see that a man is justified by works and not by faith alone" (James 2:21–24).

What Paul asserts is that Abraham was not justified by works (Romans 4:2), whereas James says he was (James 2:21). But, surely James' readers knew that Abraham had been declared righteous before God long before he offered Isaac on the altar. The offering of Isaac occurred in Genesis 22:9, but he had surely been declared righteous earlier (Hebrews 11:8; Acts 7:4) when he left Ur, as confirmed in Genesis 15:6, which was 20 to 30 years earlier. Abraham was already a saved man when he was "justified" in Genesis 22:9.

Paul Rainbow and others[1430] have argued that the resolution is to be found in a distinction between pre-conversion and post-conversion works. They say, pre-conversion works cannot save but post-conversion works can! This raises the question, "When does this post-conversion justification happen?" Stanley argues that the justification here occurs "not as the entry point of salvation but the end point, that is final justification at the future judgment."[1431] Stanley understands final justification as the result of a process where "somewhere along the way converted sinners become righteous and therefore eligible to enter the kingdom."[1432] This eschatological view of justification conflicts directly with what James says regarding the justification of Abraham. It occurred when he offered up Isaac (James 2:21). It was *temporal* not eschatological.

Two phrases in James 2:21-24 are key to resolving the apparent contradiction between James and Paul.

- "A person is justified by what he does, and not by faith alone" (v. 24).
- "His faith and actions were working together" (v. 22).

In the former phrase, the word "alone" (Gr *monon*) is crucial. While it is often translated as an adjective, there is no noun in the sentence that agrees with it in gender and number. So it most likely should be understood as an adverb[1433] modifying "justified" rather than as an adjective modifying "faith."[1434]

The resulting difference brings out more clearly what all translations imply.

If *monon* is an adjective modifying "faith" we translate:

"A person is justified by what he does and not by faith alone."

On the other hand if monon is an adverb modifying "justified," we translate:

[1430] See Rainbow, *Way of Salvation*, 213-23. Stanley, *Did Jesus Teach Salvation by Works*, 308. Stanley draws a distinction between pre-conversion works which cannot justify, and post-conversion works which can. According to Stanley, Paul speaks of the entry point of justification and James speaks of justification as an acquittal or declaration of righteousness at the end (p. 309). Justification at the beginning is by faith alone but justification at the end is by faith plus works.

[1431] Stanley, *Did Jesus Teach Salvation by Works*, 309.

[1432] Ibid., 175. This is, of course, the view taken by Rome. See, for example, Catholic apologist, Sungenis, *Not By Faith Alone*, 223.

[1433] Martin, *James*, 95.

[1434] See John Niemelä, "James 2:24: Re-translation Required (Part 1 of 3)," *CTSJ* 7, no. 1 (January 2001): 2-15, no. 1 (January 2001).

A man ***is justified*** *by works, and [****is****]* ***not*** *[****justified****]* ***only*** [*monon*] *by faith.*[1435]

Or, more simply expressed in English,

A man is not only justified by faith, but also by works.

This is the preferable translation and brings out more clearly that James has two different kinds of justification in view: one by works, and one by faith.[1436] In other words James is not suggesting that there are two conditions for justification, faith plus works, but there is a justification by faith and another one by works, and they are not the same kind of justification.

This is his point in verse 24, when he refers to a justification by works that differs from the justification by faith alone mentioned by Paul. Abraham's justification in James 2:24 was a vindication-justification before God. His justification in Genesis 15:6 was a soteriological-justification before God. In the former, God pronounced, "Well done!" But in the latter He announced, "Acquitted." The word "justify" is being used in James 2:23-24 in the sense of declaring that someone is righteous in behavior (Matthew 11:19).[1437] This declaration is based upon James 2:18 and 3:13, "*Who is wise and understanding among you? Let him show it by his good life, by deeds done in the humility that comes from wisdom.*" Abraham was already justified before God when he left Ur (Hebrews 11:8; Acts 7:4) 30 or more years earlier, but was later vindicated before God by his righteous life when he offered Isaac.

And what was the outcome of this justification by works? It was not personal salvation as the Neonomians believe, or proof of genuine faith as the Experimental Predestinarians believe. Abraham's faith was strengthened, matured, and perfected by his obedience. To use James' words, it "was made complete" (*eteleiōthē*, "matured," "perfected") by what he did. Recall the opening words of the epistle where James sets out a major goal, maturity, James 1:4, "*And let endurance have its perfect result, so that you may be perfect [teleios] and complete [holoklēros], lacking in nothing.*" "The point of v. 22 is not the substantiation of faith but the maturation of it."[1438]

How was this outcome achieved? According to James, Abraham's "*actions were working together, and his faith was made complete by what he did.*" It was not achieved by faith alone but by a life of faith working together (Gr *synergeō*) with works (v. 22). *Synergeō* signifies "to engage in a cooperative endeavor,"[1439] or "work together with, cooperate, assist."[1440] For example, "*all things work together for good*" (Romans 8:28). James is saying that actions work together with faith; it says nothing about whether the good works inevitably result from a supposed genuine faith.

[1435] Ibid., 13.

[1436] Contra Stanley who sees the justification of Abraham as "an acquittal or declaration of righteousness," Stanley, *Did Jesus Teach Salvation by Works*, 308. Joseph Pak similarly overlooks this point of grammar and thus his claim that "James cannot mean two different justifications" is not supported by the text. The text explicity teaches two different kinds of justification! See Pak, "A Study of Selected Passages on Distinguishing Marks of Genuine and False Believers", 236.

[1437] BAGD, 197.

[1438] Hart, "How to Energize Our Faith: Reconsidering the Meaning of James 2:14-26," 44.

[1439] BDAG, 969.

[1440] Wolf-Henning Olbrog, "*suneros*" in EDNT, 3:303.

This passage also contradicts the Catholic assumption that claims that the result of this "working together" is final entrance into heaven. The text says nothing about heaven, rather it speaks of being made "complete."[1441] To be made complete is to become mature in one's faith. Lybrand is correct when he says, "The combination of faith plus works is not to secure salvation from hell to heaven, but to propel the spiritual growth of the already-saved by giving fullness to a faithful walk with God, and a warning for avoiding 'death' through the failure to add works to one's faith."[1442]

Abraham was already saved, but the vitality and maturity of his faith could only be accomplished by works. Such an obedient response resulted in his being called God's friend,[1443] a vindication-justification. Similarly, Jesus said, "*You are My friends, if you do what I command*" (John 15:14). There was no question about the disciples' regenerate state, but there was a question about whether they would continue to walk in fellowship with their King and be His "friend." When James says Abraham was justified by cooperative working of faith and works together, he means that Abraham was declared to be morally righteous, not that he was saved.

Thus James 2:24 is not in disagreement with Paul. James is simply saying that justification by faith is not the only kind of justification there is. Justification by faith alone secures our eternal standing, but justification by works results from our obedient behavior and secures our final vindication-justification before God. Our final justification is our vindication before God at the Judgment Seat of Christ if he declares that we have lived Christ's way of life. It is equivalent to hearing the Master say, "Well done!" James referred to this final justification when he spoke of being "saved" at the Judgment Seat of Christ (James 2:14) because we have obeyed "the perfect law of liberty" (James 1:25; 2:12). That law is the law of the Spirit of life in Christ Jesus (Romans 8:3), which enables us to live out the Sermon on the Mount. Justification by faith alone secures our right standing before God; justification by works demonstrates our moral character as vindicated (justified) before God.

James's point then is not that works are the necessary and inevitable result of soteriological-justification. Rather, he is saying that, if works do not follow our

---

1441 In this instance we agree, in part, with the Roman Catholic view of this passage. Catholics also see this as a synergy and not a sequence. See Sungenis, *Not By Faith Alone*, 153. Sungenis protests that no one was around to "see" this vindication before men! (ibid. 125). However, James refers to the necessity of demonstration in 2:18-19. Sungenis also objects (ibid. 125) that James could have used a word that clearly does mean vindication "rather than a word commonly understood to refer to salvific justification." However, the verb *dikaioō* is used 39 times in the New Testament and commonly means "proved to be right" or "vindicated" (Matthew 11:19, 12:37; Luke 7:29, 35; 10:39; 16:15; 18:14, "proved to be right"; Romans 3:4; 6:7, "freed from sin," sanctified; 1 Corinthians 4:4; 1 Timothy 3:16). Thus, outside of James, the word is used 11 of 36 times in ways other than soteriological salvation or 33% of the time. If one adds the three usages in James 2, then it is used 14 of 39 times in a non-soteriological sense or 36%. So when Sungenis claims that "prove to be right" or "vindicate" is not a common sense of the word, he is incorrect. Sungenis admits that the word often has a non-soteriological meaning (ibid. 126-27). Furthermore, Sungenis assumes that the context of James is soteriological. He bases this on one verse, 2:14, "*Can that faith save him.*" He never answers the question "Save from what?" The context is about salvation from the spiritual/psychological death and a negative assessment of one's life at the Judgment Seat of Christ (1:14, 15, 21; 2:13). Sungenis makes a valid observation that in some of these instances, the nature of the context eliminates the possibility of it meaning soteriological justification (e.g., Matthew 11:19), and therefore, it is illegitimate to cite these passages against his Catholic view.

1442 Lybrand, "Does Faith Guarantee Works? Rethinking the Cliché", 85.

1443 2 Chronicles 20:7; Isaiah 41:8.

soteriological-justification, our faith will shrivel up and die; we are in danger of spiritual impoverishment, "death." Nor does he say that the failure to work will result in the loss of our salvation. This is not a passage to prove the inevitable connection between forensic justification and progressive sanctification at all! Rather, it proves the desirable connection.

The Faith of Rahab

> *In the same way, was not Rahab the harlot also justified by works when she received the messengers and sent them out by another way? (James 2:25)*

Like Abraham, Rahab was vindicated or shown to be ethically righteous by her works working together with her faith. There is nothing said here about her act being the result of faith. Rather, her act was combined with a faith she already had.

Dead Faith?

> *For just as the body without the spirit is dead, so also faith without works is dead (James 2:26).*

In this analogy, the body is parallel to faith, and the spirit is parallel to works. Just as the spirit animates the body, so works animate faith. This obvious point is missed by Experimental Predestinarians because for centuries their thinking has been dominated by the idea that faith animates works. While that is true, it is also true, as this text says, that works animate faith. Hart is correct when he says, "James is teaching that faith without works is simply a cold orthodoxy, lacking spiritual vibrancy. Practically speaking, we might think of a 'dead church.' This is not to say that those gathering as part of this assembly are not Christians. As noted earlier James' concerns are more practical than theological. The real issue for these believers is the absence of a freshness, vitality, and energy in their faith. When a Christian engages in practical deeds to benefit others, James says our faith comes alive."[1444]

The important question to ask in understanding this passage is to consider what James meant when he used the term "dead faith." The use of the term "death" to describe what can happen to Christians is not uncommon in the Bible:

> *For if you are living according to the flesh, **you must die**; but if by the spirit, you are putting to death the deeds of the body, you will live (Romans 8:13).*

> *But she who gives herself to wanton pleasure is dead even while she lives (1 Timothy 5:6, NASB).*

> *And to the angel of the church in Sardis write: He who has the seven Spirits of God, and the seven stars, says this: "I know your deeds, that you have a name that you are alive, but you are dead" (Revelation 3:1).*

In each of these passages, the notion of death included a rather obvious point—they were once alive! Death is *always* preceded by life, and in common biblical usage this is

[1444] Hart, "How to Energize Our Faith: Reconsidering the Meaning of James 2:14-26," 48.

always true. There is no reason to assume that James viewed it any differently. The dead faith to which James refers was unquestionably alive at one time, or it could not have died! This is not pressing the metaphor beyond its intent. It is an explicit implication of this same metaphor used elsewhere in the New Testament as the above passages reveal. As mentioned above, the experience of the prodigal son who was once alive and became dead is the kind of death to which James refers (Luke 15:24).

Furthermore, James seems to say this is the idea he intends to convey by the analogy he uses, "*For just as the body without the spirit is dead, so also faith without works is dead*" (James 2:26). The body dies, according to the Bible, when the spirit departs (John 19:30). Just as the body dies when our spirit departs, even so our faith dies when our works depart! Just as the spirit is the animating principle which gives the body life, so work is the animating principle which gives faith "life."

When believers do not animate their faith with works, James does not say their faith is nonexistent; he says it is useless, that is, it is of no value to others or themselves. This helps define what he means by "dead" because he describes it as *useless* in verse 20 (Gr *argos*). This Greek word means that it does "not accomplish anything."[1445] One lexicon translates it as "unemployed."[1446] The whole point of James 2:14-26 is to exhort believers who already have faith to add works to it.

The passage is strikingly similar in this regard to 2 Peter 1:5-9.

> *Now for this very reason also, applying all diligence, in your faith supply moral excellence, and in your moral excellence, knowledge, and in your knowledge, self-control, and in your self-control, perseverance, and in your perseverance, godliness, and in your godliness, brotherly kindness, and in your brotherly kindness, love. For if these qualities are yours and are increasing, they render you neither useless nor unfruitful in the true knowledge of our Lord Jesus Christ. For he who lacks these qualities is blind or short-sighted, having forgotten his purification from his former sins (2 Peter 1:5-9).*

These believers are to add works (like self-control, kindness, love, and so forth) to their faith, and if they do, they will not be "useless" (Gr *akarpos*, "without fruit"). That is a good synonym for a dead faith, one which was once alive but is now "unemployed," having lost its vitality because it was not animated by a life of good works.

Summary

An interpretive paraphrase of James 2:14-26 might go something like this:[1447]

> *What good is it dear brothers and sisters if you say you have faith but do not add works to it. Can that kind of walk of faith deliver you from the temptations and trials of life which lead to spiritual impoverishment and negative judgment at the Judgment Seat of Christ? Suppose you see a brother or sister with no clothing or food and you say, "Have a good day, hope things get better for you," but you do not give them what they need, food and clothing. What good*

1445 LN 1:452.

1446 BDAG 128.

1447 Adapted from Lybrand, *Back to Faith: Reclaiming Gospel Clarity in an Age of Incongruence*, 93.

does this do? Thus, faith, when it is alone and not animated by good works is useless to others and only leads to spiritual impoverishment in your Christian life and rebuke from Christ.

But someone will object. "Faith and works are two different things and they have no necessary relationship together in the Christian life. Some have faith, and some have works. James, just as you cannot show me your faith by your works I cannot show you my faith by my works. Let me prove this to you. James, you believe that there is one true God and you have good works. However, the demons also believe in one true God, and they have no works; in fact, they only tremble. So, this proves that there is no necessary connection between faith and works at all."

Now, I James, say to you that you are a foolish man for claiming there is no relationship between faith and works. Can't you see that faith without works is useless? Here is my proof. Let's look at Abraham. Don't you remember that Abraham grew in his faith to the point that he was vindicated before God and man as a righteous believer? He showed this openly when he offered Isaac his son on the altar long after he was saved. So you can see that his faith and works cooperated together and caused him to grow in faith and become mature. In this story we are told that "Abraham believed God and it was accounted to him for righteousness." As a result others, seeing this, called Abraham the friend of God. So you can see that justification by faith alone is not the only kind of justification there is. There is also a justification by works which is a public demonstration of one's inner fidelity and maturity in the Lord.

Consider another example, Rahab the harlot. She animated her faith by saving the lives of God's messengers by sending them out another way. In this way she too was shown to be a follower of God. Her faith was not dead or useless.

In conclusion let me give you a final analogy. When the physical body dies, it no longer has a spirit. The body becomes useless and dead, though it was once alive. In the same way, if you have faith in God but do not animate your faith with a life of works, your faith is no longer vital, it is useless, and your life will be spiritually impoverished.

Volume 2

Assurance

Introduction

EVANGELIST PAUL Washer strode back and forth across the platform. He was addressing over 2,000 high school students on the subject of assurance of faith and how one can know if he has "truly" believed. What followed was one of the most depressing and biblically inaccurate presentations of grace I have ever heard.[1448]

He began by solemnly saying,

> *I speak as a dying man to dying men. You will not like me when I finish. Many of you will hate me and reject everything I am saying.*

After this encouraging introduction, he waded in.

> *There is only one thing which gives me a sleepless night. Within a 100 years a great majority in this building will be in hell. Many who confess Jesus as Lord will be in hell.*

He is quite certain of the eternal destiny of many in his audience because many of them "*laugh at the same jokes the world laughs at, and the girls wear sensual clothing.*"

> *"So many Americans," he says, "are deceived into believing that because they prayed a prayer one time they are going to heaven. The greatest heresy in the American church is that if you pray and ask Jesus into your heart you will be saved."*

Imagine that! Believing on Christ and assuming that you are therefore saved is a heresy?

He quickly clarifies,

> *True faith is followed by repentance. The Bible says to examine yourself to see if you are in the faith.*

To be truly saved, he believes, one must enter the narrow gate and way, that is, Jesus (John 14:6). What is required?

> *To get through the gate we must repent and believe the Gospel and continue to do it. It means to spend the rest of your life repenting of your sins.*

[1448] The quotes to follow are taken from a message given by Paul Washer. It is available at http://www.sermonaudio.com/sermoninfo.asp?SID=52906154239

The "error" the evangelist is attempting to correct is what he believes to be the "heresy" of the carnal Christian.

He continues,

> *The doctrine of the carnal Christian is unbiblical—there is no such thing. Those who are carnal are not in danger of losing reward, but are going to hell. There is not only a narrow gate but a narrow way. If you are not on it, you will go to hell. If you are genuinely born again you will walk in the way of righteousness as a style of life.*
> *When you step off those paths as we all do, God comes for you and puts you back on the path. One of the greatest evidences that you are born again is that God will not let you talk as you might want to talk. God will not let you dress as the sensual world and the sensual church allows you to dress. God will not allow you to listen to the things the world listens to.*
> *You must be permanently changed.*
> *How many times do you rededicate your life over and over again and your decisions last only a week. If it lasts it is of God, otherwise it is only emotion.*
> *If there is no fruit—you are cut down and thrown into the fire—this is the judgment which will fall upon the world.*
> *By looking at the fruits in your life and by doing the will of the Father a person can obtain personal assurance.*

He says,

> *The way you can have assurance is that you do as a style of life the will of the Father.*

There are also tests you can apply to see if you are *not* really born again.

> *If you can play around in sin and love the world and if your heroes are world people, there is a good chance you do not know God, and you do not belong to Him.*
> *If you made a decision to be saved, if it was genuine, it will last, and even if you try to run away from it, you will not be able to do it.*

Mr. Washer often wept as he excoriated these young people and threatened them with eternal damnation if they did not change their lifestyle, obey Christ completely, and in this way prove that they are really saved.

This method of motivating Christians to live as they should is not just confined to popular youth evangelists; one finds similar threats emerging from leaders in the Experimental Predestinarian movement. As mentioned in volume 1, John Piper sternly warned his congregation one morning saying, "*If you are not fighting lust, you will go to hell forever. And that's a long, long time.*"

Other Experimentalists, whom I termed Neonomians in volume 1, take a more nuanced approach. These scholars teach that salvation is based upon faith plus God-produced non-meritorious works. There is little daylight between this new approach and that of Rome. The outcome is the same; assurance can only be obtained by being righteous enough to show that your initial belief in Christ was genuine. Because this tide is rising, we will give it considerable attention in the chapters to follow.

In volume 1 of this series, we dealt with many of the questions which relate to how one becomes a Christian. We now move on to questions of how one can know if he is saved. We will consider the many passages which the New Testament addresses to all believers that challenge them to live lives with the end of life in view. We will see that there is no basis in the New Testament for a life of "fruit-inspection" and thereby proving to one's conscience or to others that a person has done "the will of the Father" to a sufficient degree to establish conclusively that he is on the highway to heaven. We will learn about the biblical path to full assurance that a child of God may possess giving him confidence that one day he will meet Christ and departed love ones in heaven.

The warning passages of the New Testament have been commonly misunderstood by the Experimentalists. In their view, God is continually threatening disobedient Christians with damnation in the lake of fire in order to motivate them to live well. Of course, they do not say it so boldly. Rather, they speak of their doctrine as an encouragement to examine one's self to see if one is really born again.

In this volume we will address these issues and a number of related questions.

- Where did the idea originate that the test of the reality of the faith is perseverance in good works to the end of life? Is this biblical?
- Does the Bible really teach us to examine ourselves to see if our faith is genuine?
- What about the "tests" of life in 1 John? Are these criteria for discerning one's saved status or are they tests whether or not we are walking in fellowship with God?
- Like most Experimental Predestinarians, the youth evangelist mentioned above asserts that there is no such thing as a carnal Christian. Really? What does the Bible say about this? Can true Christians commit apostasy?
- What is the purpose of the warnings in the New Testament? Are they God's means of securing our perseverance in good works so that we can prove we are born again? Or are they God's means of motivating genuine believers to live in the manner described in the parable of the vine and the branches? Is the warning in Hebrews 6 against falling away directed toward genuine believers?
- What is the relationship between faith and assurance? Does faith include repentance and a commitment to obey?
- If we have failed in the Christian life, what is the Father's attitude? Is He sternly sitting on the throne warning us that we might not really be saved, or is He like the pursuing father in the parable of the prodigal son?
- What is the way of restoration and return to fellowship?
- What is the role of the Holy Spirit in our lives which enables us to live lives pleasing to God?
- How do we "walk by the Spirit"?
- Can salvation be lost as some have taught? If not, what about the many problem passages which seem to suggest our justification can be forfeited?
- What is the biblical proof of the doctrine of eternal life, the doctrine which teaches that salvation cannot be lost?

As one can see, there are many difficult questions ahead! We will begin with some perspectives from church history regarding the development of the doctrine of assurance from Calvin to the Westminster Assembly in 1643.

29

From Calvin to Westminster

JOHN DUNCAN was born in 1796 in Aberdeen, Scotland, the son of a shoemaker.[1449] Although not well known, his influence on Jewish missions was great. He was affectionately called "Rabbi" Duncan because of his immense knowledge of Hebrew literature and his espousal of the cause of the Jews. In fact, when he applied for the Chair of Oriental Languages in the University of Glasgow, there was no one who was qualified to examine him. He read fluently in Syriac, Arabic, Persian, Sanskrit, Bengali, Hindustani, and Marathi, as well as Latin, German, French, Hebrew, and Greek!

While studying in Budapest, he met a brilliant Jewish scholar, whom he led to Christ. This man was later to become the most learned writer on the life of Christ in the nineteenth century. His name? Alfred Edersheim.

Becoming a Christian was not easy for Rabbi Duncan, and believing that he was saved was even harder. He struggled so desperately with doubt concerning his salvation that on one occasion, at a prayer meeting of professors and students, Duncan, who was presiding, broke down and wept, saying that God had forsaken him.[1450]

In his quest to find subjective assurance that he was truly born again, Duncan turned repeatedly to Caesar Malan, through whom he was converted. Malan was ordained to the ministry in Geneva and apparently preached with great power and evangelical zeal. Malan's pastoral method of helping Duncan find assurance was through the use of a faith-based practical syllogism. He asked Duncan to consider the following logic:

MAJOR PREMISE: He who believes that Jesus is the Christ is born of God.
MINOR PREMISE: But I believe that Jesus is the Christ.
CONCLUSION: Therefore I am born of God.

As the implications of this reasoning dawned on his consciousness, Duncan said he sat still for hours, without moving, as many sermons he had preached came to his memory. The contemplation of the syllogism transformed his life, for a while. His new joy lasted for only two years and was followed by a time of terrible darkness. He says he prayed for the Holy Spirit and tried vainly to believe in Christ but could not. He then quarreled

[1449] This historical information is from John E. Marshall, "Rabbi Duncan and the Problem of Assurance (I)," *Banner of Truth*, no. 201 (June 1980): 16-27.

[1450] John E. Marshall, "Rabbi Duncan and the Problem of Assurance (II)," *The Banner of Truth*, no. 202 (July 1980): 27.

with God for not giving him His Holy Spirit and then rebuked himself for doing this. He thought that perhaps he was reprobate.

He pursued another version of the syllogism. He reasoned that those who are born of God will produce the fruits of regeneration.

MAJOR PREMISE: Those who are born again will necessarily produce the fruits of regeneration in their lives.
MINOR PREMISE: I have the fruits of regeneration.
CONCLUSION: Therefore, I am born again.

Duncan's problem was with the minor premise. He simply could not be convinced that there was sufficient evidence of the fruits of regeneration in his life for him to draw the necessary conclusion that he was indeed born of God.

He wrote one more time to his spiritual mentor, Caesar Malan. Once again he told Duncan to reflect on his faith and scolded him for not believing the promises of the gospel. Malan told him that the fruits of regeneration can come only after we have received assurance.

This did not help Duncan at all, and his struggles remained with him until his deathbed. In fact, his doubts were renewed with terrifying intensity: "I was in a terrible agony last night at the thought of a Christless state, and that I might be in it. The fear of it exhausted my faculties."[1451]

He asked that the following words be published after his death:

> *I can't put a negative upon my regeneration. I don't say I can put a positive. Sometimes hope abounds, and at the worst I have never been able dogmatically to pronounce myself unregenerate ... Sometimes I have strongly thought that what is formed between Christ and me shall last forever. At other times I fear I may be in hell yet. But if I can't affirm my regeneration, I can't deny it; my self-examination can go no further.*[1452]

No doubt Duncan's healthy fear of taking the grace of God for granted (antinomianism) contributed to his emotional state, but the methods employed to secure confidence are foreign to the New Testament. **Nowhere are we commanded to look to faith or to fruits to determine if we are born again.** We look only to God's promises in Christ as declared in His Word for that kind of assurance.

The incident highlights two things about the Experimental Predestinarian view of assurance. First, in order to know whether a person is saved, he must employ what they called the practical syllogism. It goes something like this:

MAJOR PREMISE: All who have believed and who have the fruits of regeneration are saved.
MINOR PREMISE: I have believed and have some fruits.
CONCLUSION: Therefore, I am saved.

[1451] Ibid., 28.

[1452] John Duncan, quoted in Marshall, ibid., 27.

The implementation of this faith-fruit syllogism occurred during what they called the reflex act of faith, in which a person reflects on his belief and fruits and concludes that he is among God's elect. This was in contrast to the so-called direct act of faith in which the person trusts in Christ for justification.

Second, according to Experimental Predestinarians faith and assurance are separate acts of grace. Assurance is not part of saving faith but is a reflex act of faith which comes later. Even though the advocates of this view bear the name of Calvin, they have completely departed not only from him in their view of faith and assurance but, in our opinion, from the New Testament as well.

Possibly, for many within the Experimental Predestinarian position this will be the most important discussion in this book. It would not be surprising if they skipped over the previous and following chapters in the search for the answer to the question, "What does the author say about assurance?" For the Puritans and their modern followers, assurance of salvation is their magnificent obsession, 2 Peter 1:10 their life verse, and the faith-fruit practical syllogism their chief practice. When Peter wrote, "*Be all the more eager to make your calling and election sure*," he unwittingly gave them a basis for hundreds of years of introspection. Indeed, this verse could aptly be used to summarize a key struggle in the roughly one hundred years between the Reformation and the Westminster Confession (1649).[1453]

If God has elected some to salvation and passed over others, how can a person be sure that he is among the elect? Our churches today are full of people who claim to be Christians. In fact, according to a Gallup survey over fifty million people in the United States believe they are born again. In view of the seeming lack of influence or cultural relevance of these people as far as the gospel is concerned, one naturally asks, "Are they really saved?" It would be a terrible tragedy to "give assurance"[1454] to someone who is not justified by faith alone. We would then be assuring a man that all is well with his soul, when in fact he is on the road to eternal damnation. This concern seems to motivate the modern heirs of the Puritan tradition.

This is a book of exegetical, not historical, theology. However, since many who share these views of assurance seem to feel they stand in the tradition of the early Reformers, and of John Calvin in particular, it is of interest to note that those who bear Calvin's name have widely departed from Calvin in this central fact. For Calvin, assurance was not a reflex act of faith but is part of the direct act of saving faith itself. Our assurance, Calvin said, does not come from reflecting on our faith; it comes from reflecting on Christ.

The period leading up to the assembly at Westminster produced many notable theologians in both England and Scotland. The contributions of several of these key figures reveal that Solomon was right, "There is nothing new under the sun" (Ecclesiastes 1:9). The same struggles with assurance and perseverance that are present today are clearly manifested in their writings.

[1453] This writer is indebted to R. T. Kendall for discussion of the development of this theme among the English Puritans in Kendall, *English Calvinism*. For similar development in Scotland, see M. Charles Bell, *Calvin and the Scottish Theology: The Doctrine of Assurance* (Edinburgh: Handsel Press, 1985). Their contributions to this chapter are gratefully acknowledged.

[1454] One of the great errors of Experimental Predestinarians is that they seem to think they have either the responsibility or the right to ascertain another person's eternal destiny. Better is the attitude of the apostle Paul, "Do not go on passing judgment before the time" (1 Corinthians 4:5).

John Calvin (1509-1564)

SAVING FAITH

If Calvin were to be asked, "Where do we get faith?" he would have answered that its source is the intercessory prayer of Christ. We receive the gift of faith because Christ prayed to the Father and asked Him to give it to us. Faith is thus located in the mind and is not an act of the will; it is passively received. With unusual insight this towering theologian of the Reformed faith put his finger on the heart of the matter. Faith and assurance go together. We do not agree with him that faith is a gift, but his understanding of assurance and faith is significant. It is true that faith is "passively received." Faith "happens" to us as we contemplate Christ and the gospel promises. But, Calvin is correct when he says,

> *We shall now have a full definition of faith if we say that it is a firm and sure knowledge of the divine favour toward us, founded on the truth of a free promise in Christ, and revealed to our minds, and sealed on our hearts, by the Holy Spirit.*[1455]

A firm and sure knowledge that we are saved is thus of the essence of faith itself and is not the result of later reflection on whether we have believed or whether there are fruits of regeneration in our lives.[1456] Calvin devotes several sections in the *Institutes* to explain and clarify this definition.[1457] For Calvin faith is knowledge. It is not obedience. It is a passive thing received as a result of the witness of the Holy Spirit. It is "recognition" and "knowledge."[1458] It is illumination[1459] and knowledge as opposed to feeling; it is certainty, firm conviction,[1460] assurance,[1461] firm assurance,[1462] and full assurance.[1463] In all these descriptions the idea that faith is an act of the will is absent.[1464]

Calvin correctly asserts that works are not required to verify faith's existence in the heart. He insists, "For, in regard to justification, faith is merely passive, bringing nothing of ourselves to procure the favor of God, but receiving from Christ everything we want."[1465] It is the instrument for receiving righteousness,[1466] a kind of pipe through which the knowledge of justification is transmitted.[1467]

This doctrine of faith leads to a view of assurance which would be quite foreign to much modern discussion. The idea of "giving assurance" or of obtaining assurance by

---

1455 Calvin, "Institutes," 3.2.7.

1456 Of course, there should be fruits of regeneration in our lives, but our assurance is not based on their presence or absence.

1457 See Calvin, "Institutes," 3.2.14, 15, 28, 29, 31, 32, 33.

1458 Ibid., 3.2.14.

1459 Ibid., 3.1.4.

1460 Ibid., 3.2.2.

1461 Ibid.

1462 Ibid.

1463 Ibid., 3.2.22.

1464 While that is true in the sense that we cannot will faith, Calvin's belief in unconditional election has led him to the error that there is nothing we do to obtain faith. However, there certainly is something we do. We turn our attention to Christ and the gospel promises.

1465 Ibid., 3.13.5.

1466 Ibid., 3.11.7.

1467 Ibid.

reflection on our works would have seemed to Calvin like entrance into another culture. Assurance is faith, and faith is assurance. You cannot have one without the other. For Calvin faith is a perception of full assurance that God's mercy applies to us. While it is true that at times this persuasion can be lost, weakened, or strengthened, faith is not a matter of rational deduction, or of willing oneself to believe, but something we know within ourselves.[1468] Faith "happens" to us as a result of contemplation on the object of faith—Christ and the beauty of the gospel promise. Calvin will go so far as to say that, if a person has no assurance, he is not a true believer,[1469] a view that seems rather extreme.

THE BASIS OF ASSURANCE

What then is the basis of assurance, according to Calvin? Christ is the source of our assurance. How? It is on the basis of His atoning work. We look for peace "solely in the anguish of Christ our Redeemer."[1470] We are to look to Christ who is the "pledge" of God's love for us.[1471] When we look to Him, He pledges eternal life to us. Unless we cling steadfastly to Christ, we will "waver continually."[1472] Bell explains that while acknowledging that the Scriptures call on us to examine our lives, Calvin maintains that this is never to discern whether or not we are Christians:

> *When we so examine ourselves, however, it is not to see whether our holiness, our works, or the fruit of the Spirit in our lives warrant assurance of salvation. Rather, it is to determine that such assurance rests on the proper foundation of God's mercy in Christ. Because of the phenomenon of temporary faith, we see that our feelings are an unreliable test of our standing with God. Therefore, if we are to be sure of our salvation, we must always direct our gaze to Christ, in whose face we see the love of God for us fully displayed.*[1473]

We are not to ask, "Am I *trusting* in Christ?" but "Am I trusting in *Christ*?" In other words, for Calvin the object of self-examination is not to see if we are saved but to be sure that we are trusting in Christ and not our works for our assurance.

According to Calvin, faith is the principal work of the Holy Spirit.[1474] Calvin goes so far as to say that "unless we feel the Spirit dwelling in us," we can have no hope of our own future resurrection.[1475] In this experience the believer understands that the Spirit is God's earnest and pledge of adoption. This, in turn, gives us a sure persuasion that God loves us and is our gracious heavenly Father.[1476] In this way the Holy Spirit seals or guarantees our salvation.[1477] Calvin conceded that believers struggle against doubts, but the outcome is sure because of the Spirit's work.

[1468] Ibid., 3.2.15; 3.20.12.

[1469] Ibid., 3.2.16.

[1470] Ibid., 3.13.4.

[1471] Calvin, *John*, s.v. "Jn. 15:9".

[1472] John Calvin, *Joshua*, electronic ed., Calvin's Commentaries (Albany, OR: Ages Software, 1998), s.v. 3:10.

[1473] Bell, *Calvin and the Scottish Theology: The Doctrine of Assurance*, 30.

[1474] Calvin, "Institutes," 3.1.4.

[1475] Ibid., 3.2.39.

[1476] Calvin, *Galatians*, s.v. "Gal. 4:16".

[1477] Calvin, "Institutes," 3.1.3; 3.2.36.

Calvin said that we should not seek our assurance in the doctrine of election, even though the decree of election does bring comfort and confidence in our salvation. Indeed, he says, until we know of God's decree of election, we will never know assurance of "the free mercy of God."[1478] This is so because election means that our salvation depends not on us but on God.

However, we should not involve ourselves in questions as to whether we are elect. Bell says, "When concern for our salvation arises, we must not look to God's secret counsel, which is hidden from us. We must not ask whether we are chosen. Rather, our concern must be related to Christ, since all that pertains to our salvation is to be found in him, and while, indeed, we are elect from the foundation of the world, yet this election is 'in Christ.'"[1479] Thus Calvin speaks of Christ as the "mirror" of our election:

> *But if we are elected in Him, we cannot find the certainty of our election in ourselves; and not even in God the Father, if we look at Him apart from the Son.* ***Christ, then, is the mirror in which we ought, and in which, without deception, we may contemplate our election.*** *For since it is into His body that the Father has decreed to ingraft those whom from eternity He wished to be His, that He may regard as sons all whom He acknowledges to be His members, if we are in communion with Christ, we have proof sufficiently clear and strong that we are written in the Book of Life.*[1480]

Or as he put it elsewhwere:

> *But if we have been chosen in Him, we shall not find assurance of our election in ourselves; and not even in God the Father, if we conceive Him as severed from His Son. Christ, then, is the mirror wherein we must, and without self-deception may, contemplate our own election.*[1481]

In other words, if we doubt our salvation, we are not to look to ourselves to find evidences of justification, but we should look to Christ, who is a mirror reflecting back to us those persons who are elect. As we look at Him, we see ourselves in the reflection and have assurance of our salvation.

Calvin feels strongly about this. He not only asserts that faith is assurance, but conversely he states that we cannot find assurance by examining our works.

> *Doubtless, if we are to determine by our works in what way the Lord stands affected towards us, I admit that we cannot even get the length of a feeble conjecture: but since faith should accord with the free and simple promise, there is no room left for ambiguity. With what kind of confidence, pray, shall we be armed if we reason in this way—God is propitious to us, provided we deserve it by the purity of our lives?*[1482]

If we are not to trust in our works for justification, why should we trust in them for our assurance? While acknowledging that regeneration has its fruits, such as love, he avows

---

1478 Ibid., 3.21.1.

1479 Bell, *Calvin and the Scottish Theology: The Doctrine of Assurance*, 27.

1480 Calvin, "Institutes," 3.24.5.

1481 Ibid.

1482 Calvin, "Institutes," 3.2.38.

that the presence in our hearts of love for our neighbor is an "accessory or inferior aid to our faith."[1483] He insists that "if we are elected in Him, we cannot find the certainty of our election in ourselves."[1484] In his commentary on 1 Corinthians he says, "When the Christian looks at himself he can only have ground for anxiety, indeed despair."[1485]

There is no doubt that Calvin would see good works as helpful to convince the believer that he is among the children of God, but they do so as confirmations of salvation and not as the basis of assurance. They bring secondary encouragement to the mind which already has assurance. He argues that the fruits of regeneration are the evidence that the Holy Spirit dwells in us, but only to the person who is already deriving his assurance from contemplation of Christ. When present, they reveal salvation, but when absent, they prove nothing. The evidences of holiness in our lives have no assuring value except to the mind which has already "perceived that the goodness of God is sealed to them by nothing but the certainty of the promise."[1486] He continues:

> *Should they begin to estimate it [assurance of their salvation] by their good works, nothing will be weaker or more uncertain; works, when estimated by themselves, no less proving the divine displeasure by their imperfection, than His good-will by their incipient purity.*[1487]

While our obedience confirms our adoption, it is only a supporting factor of our assurance. Our good works, Calvin says, give a "subsidiary aid to its confirmation,"[1488] Love is an inferior aid, a prop for our faith (*Commentary*, 1 John 3:19). But even with this concession he insists that we must never "look to our works for our assurance to be firm."[1489] If we want to know if we are elect, we must be "persuaded" that Christ died for us. We know this by a direct act of faith. We do not look for testimonies of good works in our lives. Thus Calvin affirms: "If Pighius[1490] asks how I know I am elect, I answer that Christ is more than a thousand testimonies to me."[1491]

Saving faith, according to Calvin and the New Testament, is a passive thing located in the mind. It is not mere assent to a proposition but includes the additional elements of confidence, trust, persuasion, inner conviction, and assurance. This basic idea is still held today by many within the Experimental Predestinarian tradition,[1492] but confusedly. While attempting to hold onto the New Testament doctrine that faith is assurance, they have attempted to add that good works are the necessary and inevitable result of faith, and some even define faith as obedience or submission. As long as any works are *necessary* to establish that a person is of the elect, then, practically speaking, works become the basis

---

1483 Calvin, *1 John*, s.v. "1 Jn. 3:19; 3:14".

1484 Calvin, "Institutes," 3.24.5.

1485 Calvin, *1 Corinthians*, s.v. "1 Cor. 1:9".

1486 Calvin, "Institutes," 3.14.19.

1487 Ibid.

1488 Calvin, *Joshua*, s.v. "Josh. 3:10".

1489 Calvin, *1 John*, s.v. "1 John 3:19".

1490 Albertus Pighius was a strong Catholic opponent of Calvin. He died in 1526 shortly after writing a book against Calvin and the other Reformers. He objected strongly to Calvin's doctrine of absolute predestination and believed it led to moral indifference.

1491 Jean Calvin and John Kelman Sutherland Reid, *Concerning the Eternal Predestination of God* (Louisville, KY: Westminster John Knox Press, 1997), 130.

1492 For example, Berkhof, Voss, and Warfield.

of his confidence instead of Christ. Calvin himself confused the issue with his doctrine of temporary faith (see discussion below) and with his insistence that repentance necessarily follows faith. As soon as some specific fruit of regeneration is said to *necessarily* follow faith, then it becomes difficult to avoid asking, "Do I have this fruit to a sufficient degree to establish that my faith is real?" Clearly, as indicated above, Calvin warned against this, and the doctrine of *necessary works* compromises his central, and biblically correct, belief, namely, that assurance is the essence of faith.

Furthermore, if works are necessary for assurance, then it is impossible for a person to have assurance until works have been manifested in his life. This leads to the absurd conclusion that one can believe in Christ but not know that he has believed. In fact, he cannot really know if he has believed until he finds himself believing at the "final hour." Then, and only then, have his works finally verified his faith to be that of the elect and not that of the reprobate.

Calvin also taught that the reprobate can have similar feelings and evidences of regeneration as the elect. How then does one know if he is of the reprobate? Some means of discrimination are immediately thrust on the Christian mind: Is my faith only temporary? How can I know if my faith is saving faith? Wherein do they differ? Having opened the door to a possible separation between assurance and faith (which he himself vigorously denied), his followers drove a truck through it and separated them forever.

It seems that Calvin's stress on the passive nature of faith is a valid biblical insight. It does appear that faith is something that happens to us as a result of contemplation on Christ and the beauty and wonder of the Gospel promises. We are responsible to believe[1493] in the sense that we are responsible to look to Christ, not conjure up faith. Clearly, faith is not located primarily in the will, as Calvin observed, for we often are forced to believe things against our will (the death of a loved one, for example). Also, it seems that for some people they would give the world to believe, but for some reason they cannot. To tell them that they can is to violate their conscience.

CALVIN'S DOCTRINE OF TEMPORARY FAITH

The scandal of the Experimental Predestinarian tradition, which the divines at Westminster passed over, was the doctrine of temporary faith. The origin of this odious doctrine is to be traced to Calvin himself. He based it on misinterpretations of the parable of the sower,[1494] the warnings in Hebrews,[1495] and the Lord's warning, "By their fruits you shall know them."[1496]

The central claim of this teaching is that God imparts supernatural influences to the reprobate[1497] which approximates, but does not equal, the influences of effectual calling. The reprobate is illuminated, he tastes, he grows, and he has similar feelings as the elect.

[1493] See also John 5:43; 1 John 5:1; John 3:16, 36.

[1494] This will be discussed elsewhere (see p. 653). Each of the last three are regenerate as evidenced by the obvious fact that even the one with "temporary faith" (i.e., the stony ground) evidenced life and growth.

[1495] These warnings are addressed to true Christians and present the danger of millennial disinheritance. This is what they potentially may fall away from. (See chapters 41 and 42.)

[1496] The fruit in view is not the character/quality of professing Christians but the false doctrine of the false teachers. False doctrine, not immoral lives, is the fruit. See vol. 1, chapter 22.

[1497] Those predestined to damnation.

However, it seems God is deceiving this man into believing he is elect so that God can be more than just in condemning him when he finally falls away. After all, the man had these "tastes."

Calvin taught three kinds of grace. First, *common grace* enabled a man to do physics, produce a *Summa Theologica*, a Mass in B Minor, a painting, or a *Hamlet*. This is due to the general grace of God.[1498] Second, *effectual grace* is that ministry of the Holy Spirit whereby, according to Calvin, the unregenerate are *infallibly* acted on and inclined to believe and be saved.[1499] Third, *ineffectual grace* (the writer's term) is due to the ministry of the Spirit in imparting "transitory" faith or temporary faith.[1500] Calvin argues this from Scripture on the basis of Hebrews 6:4-5:

> *I know that to attribute faith to the reprobate seems hard to some, when Paul declares it (faith) to be the result of election. This difficulty is easily solved. For ... experience shows that the reprobate are sometimes affected by almost the same feeling as the elect, so that even in their own judgment they do not in any way differ from the elect.*[1501]

Calvin does not think it absurd that the reprobate should have "a taste of the heavenly gift—and Christ" (Hebrews 6:4-5), because this makes them convicted and more inexcusable. This is a consequence of a "lower" working of the Spirit, which he later seems to term an "ineffectual" calling.[1502] "There is nothing strange in God's shedding some rays of grace on the reprobate and afterwards allowing these to be extinguished."[1503] This, according to Calvin, was "an inferior operation of the Spirit," the whole purpose of which is "the better to convict them and leave them without excuse."[1504]

His discussion is worthy of extensive quotation:

> *Experience shows that the reprobate are sometimes affected in a way so similar to the elect, that even in their own judgment there is no difference between them. Hence it is not strange, that by the Apostle a taste of heavenly gifts, and by Christ Himself a temporary faith, is ascribed to them. Not that they truly perceive the power of spiritual grace and the sure light of faith; but the Lord, the better to convict them, and leave them without excuse, instills into their minds such a sense of His goodness as can be felt without the Spirit of Adoption.* ***Should it be objected, that believers have no stronger testimony to assure them of their adoption, I answer, that though there is a great resemblance and affinity between the elect of God and those who are impressed for a time with fading faith, yet the elect alone have that full assurance which is extolled by Paul, and by which are enabled to cry, Abba, Father.*** *Therefore, as God regenerates the elect only forever by incorruptible seed, as the seed of life once sown in their hearts never perishes, so He effectually seals in them the grace of His adoption, that it may be sure and steadfast. But there is nothing to prevent an inferior*

1498 Calvin, "Institutes," 2.2.16.

1499 The present writer is a "zero point" Calvinist and rejects the notion of efficacious grace. The Holy Spirit works in the heart of all who respond to common grace and inclines them to believe, yet that inclination can be resisted.

1500 Calvin, "Institutes," 3.2.11.

1501 Ibid.

1502 Calvin, *Luke*, s.v. "Luke 17:13".

1503 Calvin, "Institutes," 3.2.12.

1504 Ibid., 3.2.11.

> *operation of the Spirit from taking its course in the reprobate. Meanwhile, believers are taught to examine themselves carefully and humbly, lest carnal security creep in and take the place of assurance of faith. We may add, that the reprobate never have any other than a confused sense of grace, laying hold of the shadow rather than the substance, because the Spirit properly seals the forgiveness of sins in the elect only, applying it by special faith to their use. Still it is correctly said, that the reprobate believe God to be propitious to them, inasmuch as they accept the gift of reconciliation, though confusedly and without due discernment; not that they are Partners of the same faith or regeneration with the children of God; but because, under a covering of hypocrisy, they seem to have a principle of faith in common with them. Nor do I even deny that God illumines their minds to this extent, that they recognize His grace; but that conviction He distinguishes from the peculiar testimony which He gives to His elect in this respect, that the reprobate never obtain to the full result or to fruition. When He shows Himself propitious to them, it is not as if He had truly rescued them from death, and taken them under His protection. He only gives them a manifestation of His present mercy.* ***In the elect alone He implants the living root of faith, so that they persevere even to the end.*** *Thus we dispose of the objection, that if God truly displays His grace, it must endure forever. There is nothing inconsistent in this with the fact of His enlightening some with a present sense of grace, which afterwards proves evanescent. Although faith is knowledge of the divine favor towards us, and a full persuasion of its truth, it is not strange that the sense of the divine love, which though akin to faith differs much from it, vanishes in those who are temporarily impressed. The will of God is, I confess, immutable, and His truth is always consistent with itself; but I deny that the reprobate ever advance so far as to penetrate to that secret revelation which Scripture reserves for the elect only. I therefore deny that they either understand His will considered as immutable, or steadily embrace His truth, inasmuch as they rest satisfied with an evanescent impression;* ***just as a tree not planted deep enough may take root, but will in the process of time wither away, though it may for several years not only put forth leaves and flowers, but produce fruit.*** *In short, as by the revolt of the first man, the image of God could be effaced from his mind and soul, so there is nothing strange in His shedding some rays of grace on the reprobate, and afterwards allowing these to be extinguished.*[1505]

Aware of the obvious objection that the Spirit of God is lying to the reprobate, leading them to believe they are elect when they are not, Calvin continues:

> *Nor can it be said that the Spirit therefore deceives, because He does not quicken the seed which lies in their hearts, so as to make it ever remain incorruptible as in the elect.*

However, this is simply an answer by assertion and no answer at all!

Calvin says (1) the reprobate may have "almost the same feeling as the elect"; and (2) this is "but a confused awareness of grace." He goes on to say that the reprobate "believe that God is merciful toward them, for they receive the gift of reconciliation, although confusedly and not distinctly enough." Moreover, they seem "to have a beginning of faith in common" with the elect.[1506]

Calvin recognizes the obvious objection that a true believer could suspect his own faith to be that of the reprobate:

[1505] Ibid., 3.2.11-12.

[1506] Ibid., 3.2.11.

> *Should it be objected that believers have no stronger testimony to assure them of their adoption, I answer that there is a great resemblance and affinity between the elect of God and those who are impressed for a time with fading faith, yet the elect alone have that full assurance which is extolled by Paul, and by which they are enabled to cry, Abba, Father.*[1507]

This answer would be of little comfort to someone who was struggling with assurance. In fact, it would just add to their fear. Obviously, a true believer can become discouraged and imagine that his faith is simply a "confused awareness" which the reprobate have. Kendall observes:

> *And if the reprobate may experience "almost the same feeling as the elect," there is no way to know finally what the reprobate experiences. Furthermore, if the reprobate may believe that God is merciful towards them, how can* **we** *be sure our believing the same thing is any different from theirs? How can we be so sure that our "beginning of faith" is saving and is not the "beginning of faith" which the reprobate seem to have?*[1508]

Thus, when Calvin bases his doctrine on an inner assurance given by the Spirit and then affirms that the reprobate can have a similar sensation, he ruins his argument.

Calvin has said that the reprobate cannot discern the difference between their experience and that of a born-again Christian. They believe God to be propitious to them and to have given them the gift of reconciliation. Since both the reprobate and the saved can have these feelings, how can one know if he is saved? Calvin seems to be saying that the unsaved man has these feelings, but they are more intense in the elect and enable them to say, "Abba, Father."

He feels, however, that the differences between the reprobate and the elect are more important than the similarities. The primary difference is that the faith of the reprobate is temporary. Eventually it fails and they fall away. The true believer is sustained.[1509] A second difference is that the reprobate never enjoy a "living feeling" of firm assurance.[1510]

Part of Calvin's problem goes back to his misinterpretation of the parable of the soils. The last three are all true believers and are not reprobate.[1511] Therefore, there is no "temporary" non-regenerating faith taught here. Similarly, Hebrews 6 refers to Christians, not mere professors, and the doctrine of temporary non-regenerating faith is not found there either. Since the Bible does not address the subject of a supernaturally imparted temporary faith, should we speculate about it? Calvin's doctrine of perseverance (to which he was driven in order to defend the Reformation against the Catholic attack that it was antinomian) forced him to interpret these passages in a way contrary to their obvious meaning. We should assume that those who produce fruit, who take root, who grow, who are illumined, and who have tasted the heavenly gift are genuinely born again, even if they do fall away in the future. We will see them in heaven if they genuinely believed. We do not know if they have, but a lack of enduring fruit does not prove they are reprobate.

1507 Ibid.

1508 Kendall, *English Calvinism*, 24. (Emphasis his)

1509 Calvin, "Institutes," 3.2.17-18.

1510 Calvin, *The Harmony of the Gospels: Calvin's Commentary on Matthew, Mark, and Luke*, s.v. "Mt. 13:20".

1511 See discussion of this parable on pp. 532 ff.

In the final analysis, Calvin has thrown away the possibility of assurance, at least until the final hour. When he grants that the only certain difference between the faith of the elect and the faith of the reprobate is that the faith of the former perseveres to the end, he makes assurance now virtually impossible. As Shank has insisted:

> *Obviously, it can be known only as one finally perseveres (or fails to persevere) in faith. There is no valid assurance of election and final salvation for any man, apart from deliberate perseverance in faith.*[1512]

Those who bear Calvin's name in the Reformed faith have, of course, come to a similar conclusion. Charles Hodge, for example, says:[1513]

> *Election, calling, justification, and salvation are indissolubly united; and, therefore, he who has clear evidence of his being called has the same evidence of his election and final salvation … The only evidence of election is effectual calling, that is, the production of holiness. And the only evidence of the genuineness of this call and the certainty of our perseverance, is a patient continuance in well doing.*

In other words, the only real evidence of election is perseverance, and our only assurance of the certainty of persevering is—to persevere! So on this ground there is no assurance at all! As John Murray put it, "The perseverance of the saints reminds us very forcefully that only those who persevere to the end are truly saints."

The Experimental Predestinarian cannot really ever offer security and is, in fact, teaching a flat contradiction in this regard, as can be seen by the following:

PROPOSITION A: It is possible for a person to have assurance before the end of life that he will go to heaven when he dies.

Yet the following syllogism leads to proposition B:

MAJOR PREMISE: I am saved now if I persevere in faith to the end of life.
MINOR PREMISE: It is possible that I will not persevere to the end of life.
CONCLUSION: Therefore, I may not be saved now.

This inevitably leads to:

PROPOSITION B: It is not possible for man to have assurance before the end of life that he will go to heaven when he dies.

Since A cannot equal non-A, since both proposition A and proposition B cannot be true at the same time, the Calvinist system flatly contradicts itself. Some Calvinists might reply, "This is not a contradiction, only a healthy tension."[1514] The word "healthy" is used to imply that there is value in wondering whether or not one is saved. His doubts and

---

1512 Shank, *Life in the Son: A Study of the Doctrine of Perseverance*, 293.

1513 Charles Hodge, *St. Paul's Epistle to the Romans*, reprint ed. (Grand Rapids: Wm. B. Eerdmans Publishing Co., 1950), 212.

1514 Berkouwer uses the word "tension" as a substitute for the more obvious word "contradiction." See G. C. Berkouwer, *Faith and Perseverance* (Grand Rapids: Wm. B. Eerdmans Publishing Co., 1958), 110.

resultant fears may motivate him to live a godly life. However, the word "tension" is simply a circumlocution for a blatant contradiction. Others, like D. A. Carson, retreat to the word "mystery." He says we must "appreciate the undergirding mystery that stands behind Christian assurance."[1515] So, if one's theology yields a logical contradiction, just call it a mystery (supposedly in a legitimate manner like the human and divine natures of Christ) and move on. Unfortunately, believers struggling with their personal assurance of salvation will be left behind.

It is disturbing that Experimental Predestinarians are able to continue to believe these contradictory things. One is reminded of the Red Queen in Lewis Carroll's story of Alice in Wonderland. When Alice protested that there is no use trying to believe impossible things, the Queen said:

> *I dare say you haven't had much practice. . . . When I was your age I did it for half an hour a day. Why, sometimes I've believed as many as six impossible things before breakfast.*[1516]

Furthermore, the idea that God intends to motivate His children to godly living by desiring that they wonder if they have only temporary faith like the reprobate, and that they must persevere to the end to find out, is so far removed from the apostles' statements of grace and love that one wonders how anyone could ever find it in the New Testament. Yet, such perspectives are not uncommon in Experimental Predestinarian writings.

Maurice Roberts, for example, exhorts his readers to hold two contradictory notions in their minds at the same time: "We may cling tenaciously to the doctrine of Final Perseverance and yet at the same time we may legitimately view our own personal profession of faith with something akin to uncertainty."[1517] So we are to believe in the Reformed doctrine of perseverance in a general sense but doubt that we in particular are necessarily saved! Roberts finds justification for this travesty of grace in the apostle Paul's statement that he worries that he himself should be a castaway (1 Corinthians 9:26-27). As demonstrated elsewhere, the word translated "castaway" (Gr *adokimos*) does not mean final rejection to hell but to be disqualified for the prize, to forfeit reward.[1518] But then Roberts makes it worse: "More positively we may say that this fear of being *adokimos* or castaway is one of the great hallmarks of those who are elect and who finally do persevere. All who lack it are possessed of a sickly presumption which needs correcting from the pulpit or which—may God forbid—they will have to unlearn by the sad experience of falling."[1519]

For most, however, the certainty of their final salvation does not lead to license. On the contrary, it leads to a wonderful security and sense of gratitude that promotes true religion and godliness. Is it not indisputable that our children are more likely to behave well in an atmosphere of unconditional parental acceptance than in an atmosphere of uncertainty? Can it ever be "healthy" for a child to cherish doubts about his parents' long-term acceptance of him? If it is true that earthly parents must strive to communicate unconditional and permanent acceptance regardless of failure, would it not be even more true of our heavenly parent?

1515 Carson, "Reflections on Christian Assurance," 28.

1516 Lewis Carroll, *Through the Looking-glass* (New York: Duell, 1959), 100.

1517 Maurice Roberts, "Final Perseverance," *Banner of Truth Trust*, no. 265 (October 1985): 10.

1518 See pp. 463 below.

1519 Roberts, "Final Perseverance," 11.

To teach that a "hallmark" of the saved person is that he carries about the "fear of being a castaway" is absurd and obviously contradicts the promises of assurance found in the New Testament. Roberts is simply taking the Experimental Predestinarian view to its logical, ridiculous conclusion: there is no real certainty of perseverance, because you may not be one of the elect, and to have such certainty is a "sickly presumption." Few thoughtful readers of the New Testament would ever glean such a view from the apostles' letters!

Theodore Beza (1519-1605)

Calvin grounded assurance in the death of Christ and included it in saving faith itself. However, Calvin's successor at Geneva, Theodore Beza (1519-1605), departed from Calvin and grounded assurance in evidences of fruit in the life. Beza's starting point was his doctrine of limited atonement. Calvin, according to Kendall, held to unlimited atonement.[1520] If Christ died for all, Beza argued, then all would be saved. He developed a system that became known as supralapsarianism. In that system the order of elective decrees is as follows:

1. Decree to elect some to be saved and to reprobate all others.
2. Decree to create men, both elect and nonelect.
3. Decree to permit the fall.
4. Decree to provide salvation for the elect.
5. Decree to apply salvation to the elect.

The view is to be rejected because it assumes that the decree of election and preterition have reference to an, as yet, uncreated entity. The Scriptures uniformly represent the decrees of election as involving some actually created beings from which to select (e.g., Romans 9:18, "On *whom* He will, He hath mercy, and *whom* He will, He hardens"). Thus the first decree must be the decree to create. God must bring into existence before He can decide what man will do or what his final destiny will be. The Scriptures represent the elect and nonelect as taken out of an aggregate of beings.[1521]

Calvin said that men are chosen from a corrupt mass, but Beza says men are chosen from a mass "yet unshapen." By basing his system around predestination, Beza gave election and reprobation priority over creation and the fall. However, his predestination refers to the destinies of men not yet created, much less fallen.

Beza logically works out his system so that Jesus is the Savior of the elect before their

---

[1520] Kendall, *English Calvinism*, 13-18. He cites Calvin, "Institutes," 3.1.1., Commentary on Isaiah, s.v. "Isaiah 53:12"; Commentary on Hebrews, s.v. "Hebrews 9:28." In both places Romans 5:15 is referred to, and Calvin says "many" equals "all." In "Concerning the Eternal Predestination of God," p. 148, he says, it is "incontestable that Christ came for the expiation of the sins of the whole world." In his commentary on John 1:29, he observes, "And when he says *the sin of the world* he extends this kindness indiscriminately to the whole human race." "For God commends to us the salvation of all men without exception, even as Christ suffered for the sins of the whole world" (Sermons on Isaiah's Prophecy, 141). See also the extensive comment on this point in Bell, *Calvin and the Scottish Theology: The Doctrine of Assurance*, 13-19. Bell negatively critiques Paul Helm's response to Kendall in Paul Helm, "Article Review: Calvin, English Calvinism and the Logic of Doctrinal Development," *Scottish Journal of Theology* 34, no. 2 (1981).

[1521] John 15:19. Also, the elect are chosen to sanctification (Ephesians 1:4-6; 1 Peter 1:2). They must, therefore, have already fallen and been created before that.

creation or fall. Assurance is thus grounded in two things: the election of God and the knowledge that we are among the ones who have been offered a Redeemer, for not all have. For Beza, if we can obtain the knowledge that Christ died for us, then we may be certain that we will not perish, because God will not demand a double payment for sin.

This doctrine led to the division between assurance and faith which differed from Calvin. For Calvin, Christ was the "mirror" in whom we contemplated our election. By this he meant we look to Christ for assurance and not ourselves. But for Beza we have no certainty that we are elected because we do not know for sure that we are one of those for whom Christ died. "He insisted upon a theory of limited atonement ... a conclusion which could be drawn from Calvin's premises, but that Calvin himself refused to draw."[1522] If Christ died for all, then we could know that we are elect (if we persevere, according to Calvin), but if He died only for the elect, it is presumptuous for us to trust in Christ's death (even if we currently are persevering). In fact, it would be dangerous for the nonelect to trust in Christ:

> *We could be putting our trust in One who did not die for us and therefore be damned. Thus we can no more trust Christ's death by a direct act of faith than we can infallibly project that we are among the number chosen from eternity: for the number of the elect and the number for whom Christ died are one and the same. The ground of assurance, then, must be sought elsewhere than in Christ.*[1523]

Beza, knowing this, suggests that we should look within ourselves for the evidence that Christ died for us. We cannot comprehend God's eternal decrees, but we can see if He is at work in our lives. "Beza directs us not to Christ but to ourselves; we do not begin with Him but with the effects, which points us back, as it were, to the decree of election. Thus, while Calvin thinks looking to ourselves leads to anxiety, despair (Calvin, *1 Corinthians*, s.v. "1 Cor. 1:9"), and belief that one is damned (*Institutes* 3.2.295), Beza thinks otherwise; sanctification, or good works, is the infallible proof of saving faith."[1524]

Beza's doctrine requires the use of the faith-fruit practical syllogism in order for one to be persuaded he is one of those for whom Christ died. Conversion includes two works of grace: faith and then sanctification. The first, however, is invalid if not ratified by the second.

He also taught the doctrine of temporary faith, which is contradictory to a theology that grounds assurance in works. He says that the unregenerate may receive an ineffectual calling. The reprobate may have the appearance of virtue, called moral virtue, but such are different from the works of the children of God governed by the Spirit of regeneration. According to Kendall, Beza does not state what these differences are. We might justly fear that our good works are simply the moral virtues of the unregenerate. Thus, contradictory to his statement that sanctification yields assurance, our sanctification can yield little comfort. Even the reprobate can have the evidences of life. So what is the solution? Ultimately, Beza says that the only true evidence that Christ died for you is if you persevere in holiness. He turns to 2 Peter 1:10 and argues that assurance of election is

[1522] Justo L. González, *From the Protestant Reformation to the Twentieth Century*, rev. ed., vol. 3, A History of Christian Thought (Nashville: Abingdon Press, 1975), 271.

[1523] Kendall, *English Calvinism*, 32.

[1524] Ibid., 33.

based on a good conscience. We make our election sure by good works. These works, he says, are a testimony to our conscience that Christ lives in us, and thus, we cannot perish, being elected to salvation.

William Perkins (1558-1602)

According to Kendall, William Perkins is "the fountainhead of the experimental predestinarian tradition." He developed a system of assurance built around an interpretation of 2 Peter 1:10, which says we must prove our election to ourselves by means of good works. He is the third member of the Calvinist Trinity (Calvin, Beza, and Perkins), and by the end of the sixteenth century his works were more published and read more than those of Calvin. He was a supralapsarian, and his famous work *A Golden Chain* brings this out forcefully.

According to him, before one can become a Christian, the heart must be made malleable by four hammers: the Law, the knowledge of sin, a sense of God's wrath, and a holy desperation. 2 Peter 1:10 teaches us to prove to ourselves that we have faith by means of a good conscience. Justifying faith is that by which a person is persuaded in his conscience. The will to believe does not yield assurance, but the conscience, reflecting on the fruits of regeneration, can give assurance.

Because he accepts Calvin's doctrine of temporary faith and since the only way one can know if he is elect is by works, Perkins must have a way of distinguishing the faith of the reprobate from that of the elect. He concludes that the reprobate believes that some shall be saved but not that he himself shall be saved. The reprobate, however, can acknowledge his sin, feel God's wrath, be grieved for sin, and feel he deserves punishment, acknowledge that God is just in punishing him, desire to be saved, and promise God he will repent, and God can even answer his prayers.[1525] The problem, of course, is that all these graces are characteristic of the elect as well.

Perkins set the stage for the syllogistic reasoning by saying:

MAJOR PREMISE: He that believes and repents is God's child.
MINOR PREMISE: I believe in Christ and repent: at the least I subject my will to the commandment which bids me repent and believe: I detest my unbelief, and all my sins: and desire the Lord to increase my faith.
CONCLUSION: Therefore, I am a child of God.[1526]

The minor premise involves the graces of sanctification, which Perkins says are essential if you are of the elect. He expands upon this fact and lists nine effects of sanctification that must be present:[1527]

1. Feelings of bitterness of heart when we have offended God by sin.
2. Striving against the flesh.
3. Desiring God's grace earnestly.

[1525] Ibid., 68.

[1526] Ibid., 71 (spelling modernized).

[1527] William Perkins, *The Works of that Famous and Worthy Minister of Christ in the University of Cambridge*, 3 vols. (Cambridge: John Legatt, 1612), 1:115, quoted by Kendall, *English Calvinism*, 72.

4. Considering that God's grace is a most precious jewel.
5. Loving the ministers of God's Word.
6. Calling on God earnestly and with tears.
7. Desiring Christ's second coming.
8. Avoiding all occasions of sin.
9. Persevering in the effects to the last gasp of life.

Each of these points, except for desiring Christ's second coming, is imputed to the reprobate also. When we read Perkins, we may be drawn to the sincere desire for holiness and attracted to the intense practical concern for assurance. However, it is superficial to be drawn to this without realizing the terrible theological bondage and misunderstanding that underlies his concept of the grace of God. The reprobate are characterized by ineffectual calling. This calling will fail in the end. This is really the only way one can tell if he is saved or not, which is no way at all.

Perkins' advice to the troubled Christian is to seek the assurance promised in 2 Peter 1:10 by practicing the virtues of the moral law in 2:24. For Perkins sanctification is the ground of assurance.

He himself acknowledges that we must "descend into our own hearts"[1528] to know our assurance. Apart from a special revelation, there is no way to know if we are one of those for whom Christ died. Therefore, we must do certain things, and if we do them, we can reflect on the fact that we have done them and from this infer we are of the elect. Apparently, Perkins left this world in a spiritual conflict of troubled conscience. And it is no wonder in view of the doctrine he held.

Perkins said two works of grace are necessary: initial faith and perseverance. Only the second ultimately proves that the first is valid. If godliness is the means by which we make our calling and election sure, then the Experimental Predestinarians reasoned we had better give a list of what it means to be godly and how to become godly. This led to the legalism for which Puritanism is noted, and the heavy sobriety and lack of joy which is so proverbial in their churches.

Various Puritan divines discerned varying bases for assurance. For some it was keeping a pure heart. Others based it on a feeling, others on being in love with godliness, others on being sincere, and others in keeping the Law. One thing they all agree on, and seem to think is noble, is that full assurance is not obtained easily.

Jacobus Arminius (1559-1609)

Jacobus Arminius studied under Beza at Geneva in 1581. After taking a pastorate in Amsterdam in 1587, he was asked to defend Beza's doctrine of predestination in the light of a pamphlet circulating against it. However, after studying the matter further, he became a convert to the very opinions he had been asked to refute. The general belief was that the man in Romans 7:14-21 was regenerate. Arminius began to question this. When Perkins' book on predestination appeared in Holland, Arminius read it eagerly because he was an admirer of Perkins. He prepared a refutation, but out of respect for Perkins' death he did not publish it. He was appointed professor of theology at the University of Leiden and was made a doctor of theology.

[1528] Perkins, *The Works of that Famous and Worthy Minister of Christ in the University of Cambridge*, 1:290.

His doctrine of predestination was simple: God predestines believers (who will persevere). If one believes (perseveringly), he is elected; if he does not believe (perseveringly), he is not elected. Once God has seen that he chooses to look to Christ, then God moves on his heart. Paradoxically, this is precisely the view held by Experimental Predestinarians as illustrated in Perkins. Faith for them follows repentance, and a man prepares himself for Christ by the four hammers and then chooses to believe when the heart has been softened enough. However, Arminius did believe that faith is a gift. He said, "A rich man bestows, on a poor and famishing beggar, alms by which he may be able to maintain himself and his family. Does it cease to be a gift, because the beggar extends his hand to receive it?"[1529] "Arminius ties election (though based on foreseen faith) to man's will to believe; the Experimental Predestinarians make the will to believe the proof of election."[1530] The similarity is in the nature of saving faith.

Arminius believes salvation can be lost. He affirms dogmatically that it is impossible for believers to decline from salvation. What he means, however, is that they cannot decline as long as they remain believers. Thus, both Arminius and the Experimental Predestinarians agree that those who apostatize or reject the gospel are reprobates. "The Experimental Predestinarians explain that believers persevere because they were elected; Arminius says God elects believers whom He foresees will persevere."[1531]

Arminius challenged Perkins on his two works of grace. If perseverance must be achieved to prove that faith is real, then there is no practical difference between their positions. Kendall concludes, "If Perkins holds that the recipient of the first grace must obtain the second (perseverance) or the first is rendered invalid, there is no practical difference whatever in the two positions. If the believer does not persevere (whether Arminius or Perkins says it), such a person proves to be non-elect."[1532]

The difference between the two is not in the issue of whether men fall, but rather, what is the theoretical explanation behind the event. Like the Experimental Predestinarians, Arminius places faith in the will and says that faith is obedience. He says that there are three parts to it: repentance, faith in Christ, and observance of God's commands.[1533] His doctrine of assurance is also the same as that of his opponents. Assurance comes from the fruits of faith. Arminius' views were rejected at the international Synod of Dordrecht (Dort) on May 29, 1619.

The Westminster Assembly Theology

Those invited to the Westminster Assembly were completely unified from the beginning in their doctrine of saving faith. No representative of the viewpoint of Calvin was there, and the breech between faith and assurance was now given creedal sanction. The assembly is, therefore, to be seen as the creedal conclusion of the Experimental Predestinarian tradition.

1529 Jacobus Arminius et al., *The Works of James Arminius*, London, reprint ed., 3 vols. (Grand Rapids: Baker Book House, 1986), 2:52.

1530 Kendall, *English Calvinism*, 143.

1531 Ibid., 144.

1532 Ibid.

1533 Arminius et al., *The Works of James Arminius*, 1:589.

The theology of Westminster completely reversed the doctrine of Calvin. Calvin often used such synonyms for faith as persuasion, assurance, knowledge, apprehension, perception, or conviction. The Westminster theology used terms like accepting, receiving, assenting, resting, yielding, answering, and embracing—all active words. Man's will is not eliminated as it was in Calvin. Saving faith is not only believing that God's Word is true, but it is "yielding obedience to the commands, trembling at the threatenings, and embracing the promises of God for this life, and that which is to come. But the principal acts of saving faith are accepting, receiving, and resting upon Christ alone."[1534] For Calvin faith was an instrument of our justification, but it was *God's* instrument, not ours. It was the instrument of God's act whereby He opens our blind eyes. For the assembly at Westminster, however, faith is *man's* act.

Surprisingly, there is no mention in the Westminster Confession of Calvin's doctrine of temporary faith. Perhaps it was because these divines sensed the latent contradiction such a teaching would bring into their Experimental Predestinarian system. It seems obvious that, if assurance is to be grounded in sanctification, the doctrine of temporary faith had to be eliminated. The reprobate simply cannot experience the graces of sanctification, or there would be no way to distinguish between the reprobate and the saved. Hence, there would be no basis for assurance. Therefore, if a man is doing good, he cannot be reprobate.

In regard to assurance, the Westminster representatives clearly stated that "assurance of grace and salvation, not being of the essence of faith, true believers may wait long before they obtain it."[1535] Calvin asserted that the "least drop of faith" firmly assures. Seeing Christ, even afar off, assures; Christ is the mirror of our election. "But holding out Christ as the ground of assurance as a direct act seems not to have been regarded as an option by the Westminster divines."[1536] Rather, our assurance is based on three things:[1537]

1. The divine truth of the promises of salvation.
2. "The inward evidence of those graces unto which these promises are made."
3. The testimony of the Spirit of adoption that we are children of God.

In the second statement, assurance is promised only to those who have evidence of regeneration in their life. The problem, of course, is how much evidence is required? The Hodges answer, "Hence, when these graces are possessed in such a degree, strength, and purity, that we are conscious of their genuineness, shall the conclusion be immediate and irresistible, that we are in union with Christ, and have a right to appropriate the promises to ourselves."[1538] A sensitive soul, like Rabbi Duncan, will never have graces in sufficient degree so that he is conscious of their genuineness.

When Experimental Predestinarians try to draw a distinction between this approach and the first so-called "Covenant of works" made with Adam, their theology gets murky.

1534 *Westminster Confession of Faith*, ed. Philip Schaff (Grand Rapids, MI: Baker Book House, 1985), 3:630; s.v. "14.2".

1535 Ibid., 3:368; s.v. "18.3".

1536 Kendall, *English Calvinism*, 203.

1537 *Westminster Confession of Faith*, 3:638; s.v. "18.2".

1538 Archibald Alexander Hodge and Charles Hodge, *The Confession of Faith: With Questions for Theological Students and Bible Classes* (Simpsonville, SC: Christian Classics Foundation, 1992), Chap.18, 2.

The Adamic covenant promised salvation on the basis of a "perfect and personal obedience," [1539] and the new is promised on the condition of faith. Yet, when faith is defined as "yielding obedience to the commands,"[1540] we are left without a clear understanding of the difference. Kendall concludes that "the difference seems to be that perfect obedience was required" under the Adamic covenant and "doing our best" is required under the new.[1541] Even though they posit faith as the condition of salvation, when they describe faith as an act of the will and submission to the commands of God, they come close to making salvation, or at least our personal assurance of it, the reward for doing good. The responsibility for salvation, in the final analysis, is put back on our shoulders.

Believers can lose their assurance because it is based on their performance. How one's conscience feels about one's performance as he reflects on his recent behavior is certainly subject to fluctuation. Assurance is encouraged by reflection on our sincerity. Supposedly, our good works do not need to be perfect, only sincere.[1542] This leads to the inevitable conclusion, however, that perseverance and sanctification are not based on a response to God's love but upon one's intense desire to ensure his salvation.

It is certainly true that the assembly at Westminster could never be charged with antinomianism. That in itself would make its theology suspect. Had the apostle Paul espoused their doctrine, it is inconceivable that he would have ever been misunderstood as saying, "Let us continue in sin that grace may abound." Paul was susceptible to the charge of antinomianism, but Westminster could not be. There must be a difference, therefore, between the Westminster theology and that of the apostle.

But such a deviation from Paul and Calvin in the interests of protecting the church against antinomianism has its own dangers, which Calvin often warned against: endless introspection, constant self-analysis, and legalism. When they endorsed the experimental way of thinking, they embraced a much more complex theology than Calvin's simple idea that "Christ is better than a thousand testimonies to me."

Faith for Calvin was never a condition. He felt it was a passive work to which "no reward can be paid."[1543] Calvin would never accept the idea that God gives Christ to us on the condition of faith because for Calvin the very seeing that God gave Christ to us is faith. He pointed men not to personal revelations by the Spirit to know they had faith but to Christ's death. This was God's pledge that we are chosen. For Calvin the promise of salvation was "made" in reference to our persuasion that Christ died for us, and not, to use the language of Westminster, to "the inward evidence of those graces (works)" manifested in our lives.

The paradoxical thing is that the doctrines of Arminius and Westminster, which are supposedly opposed to one another, are much the same. With Westminster, Arminians would agree that: (1) there is a separation between faith and assurance; (2) there is a need for two acts of faith, the direct and reflex acts; and (3) assurance comes by means of the faith-fruit practical syllogism.

[1539] *Westminster Confession of Faith*, 7.2.

[1540] Ibid., 3:630; s.v. "18.4".

[1541] Kendall, *English Calvinism*, 206.

[1542] *Westminster Confession of Faith*, 3:639; s.v. "18.4".

[1543] Calvin, *John*, s.v. "John 6:29".

Furthermore, in the question of perseverance, there is virtually no practical difference either. If a man who has professed Christ dies in a fallen condition, neither Arminius nor Westminster would grant that he is elect. Both agree that it is only the persevering believer, after all, who can certainly be said to be elected.

Summary

The road from Calvin to Westminster was to be expected. Even though he taught that assurance was of the essence of faith, Calvin's doctrine of temporary faith obviously led to the need for some criteria other than perseverance to determine which faith was temporary and which was real. It was Theodore Beza, with his doctrine of limited atonement, who made the quest for assurance based on works a necessity. Since Christ did not die for all men, it would not be proper to direct men to Christ for assurance, as Calvin taught, because Christ may not have died for that particular man. Therefore, according to Beza, assurance must be based on works. As he reflected deeply on this problem, William Perkins concluded that the best means of arriving at personal assurance was by means of the faith-fruit practical syllogism. The divines of Westminster codified these conclusions in creedal form.

It is now necessary to look more carefully at some of the biblical passages that have been discussed along this journey. What does the Bible say about faith, assurance, and the need to examine ourselves?

30

Self-examination and Assurance

EXPERIMENTAL PREDESTINARIANS assume, often without discussion, that the Bible obviously calls on believers to "examine themselves" in order to discern whether they are actually Christians. To this writer's knowledge only four passages (other than the so-called "tests of life" in 1 John) have ever been adduced in support of this contention. Yet these passages lend little support for their doctrine. In this chapter these passages will be discussed.

The Scriptural Admonitions

HEBREWS 6:11

The NKJV translation of Hebrews 6:11 reads:

> *And we desire that each one of you show the same diligence to the full assurance of hope until the end.*

The text has often been used to establish the notion that we can prove our election to ourselves by means of good works, and thus through examination of them become assured of our salvation. Indeed, they say, it is our duty to be diligent to find assurance.[1544]

ά ere are several factors in this verse that make this interpretation questionable. First, the word translated "full assurance" (Gr *plērophoria*), is always used in a passive sense in the New testament,[1545] so that it means "fullness" and not "fulfilling." If it meant "fulfilling," the phrase might be translated, "show diligence for the fulfilling of hope." Predestinarians prefer "fulfilling," claiming that we should be diligent to obtain assurance by producing more and more good works in our lives. However, if it is rendered passively, as it is elsewhere in the New testament, then the translation is, "Show diligence with respect to the fullness of hope." ά is would mean that we should be diligent regarding something already obtained.

Next, the preposition "to" in the phrase "to the full assurance" is the Gr *pros*. Based on its spatial sense of motion and direction, it is often used in a psychological sense of

---

1544 "These verses [Heb. 6:11; 10:22; Colossians 2:2] obviously imply that there are degrees of assurance, and that Christians should never be satisfied with little assurance but should always be striving for greater degrees of grace" (Marshall, "Rabbi Duncan and the Problem of Assurance (I)," 2).

1545 Westcott, *The Epistle to the Hebrews*, 156.

"in view of," "with a view to," "in accordance with," and "with reference to."[1546] Arndt and Gingrich say the meaning in this verse is "as far as ... is concerned, with regard to."[1547]

Considering only the lexical meanings of *pros* and *plērophoria* together, the author of Hebrews would appear to be exhorting his readers to "show diligence with regard to the fullness of assurance of hope that you now have to the end."[1548] Or, more simply, "Be faithful to the end of life."

But, as is usually the case, contextual and biblical factors ultimately decide an issue. In favor of this rendering of *pros* are: (1) The context of the warning passage and related passages in Hebrews are about holding your confidence, your confession of Christ, firm to the end of life (3:6, 14; 6:6, 15; 10:35). (2) The passage is parallel to Hebrews 10:32-36. Verse 10 is expanded in 10:32-34 (the external works) and verse 11 is expanded on in 10:35-36 (the internal maintenance of one's confession). (3) The other usage of *plērophoria* in Hebrews refers to an assurance that comes as a result of trusting in the cross for forgiveness, not an assurance which is arrived at later in life through diligent attention to the fruits of regeneration (Hebrews 10:22). (4) The word *plērophoria* always has a passive, never an active, meaning in the New Testament and is not found in classical Greek. (5) It appears from 1 Thessalonians 1:5 that this fullness of hope is not the result of a reflex act of faith later in the Christian's life but is included in one's initial belief in Christ.

His meaning is that, just as they have shown diligence in regard to these external matters (loving others, v. 10), he wants them to show diligence in regard to this internal matter (maintaining their assurance of hope to the end). He is not fearful that they will lose their salvation. He is fearful they will lose their testimony, their faithfulness, and their perseverance.

Thus the meaning of the passage is completely unrelated to finding out if one is a Christian by means of perseverance. Rather, it is an exhortation to be diligent in regard to one's sure hope of salvation as he has already been diligent in his love for his brothers. In other words, it is an exhortation to persevere to the end.

2 PETER 1:10

The central verse of the Experimental Predestinarian tradition is 2 Peter 1:10-11:

> *Therefore, my brothers, be all the more eager to make your calling and election sure. For if you do these things, you will never fall, and you will receive a rich welcome into the eternal kingdom of our Lord and Savior Jesus Christ.*

What does it mean to "make your calling and election sure"? Arminians see it as an exhortation to guarantee that we do not fall fatally and lose our salvation.[1549] Experimental Predestinarians generally have understood the passage to apply to the conscience. In other

[1546] Murray J. Harris, "Prepositions and Theology in the Greek New Testament," in *NIDNTT*, ed. Colin Brown (Grand Rapids: Zondervan Publishing House, 1986), 3:1024.

[1547] BAGD, 717.

[1548] This use of *pros* is found in Hebrews 5:1: "in things pertaining to (God)." Note also Hebrews 1:7: "in regard to (the angels)"; Romans 10:21: "in regard to (Israel)"; Luke 12:47: "(that slave did not act) in accord with (his master's will)."

[1549] For example, R. C. H. Lenski, *The Interpretation of the Epistles of St. Peter, St. John, and St. Jude* (Minneapolis: Augsburg Publishing Co., 1966), 277.

words, by the doing of good works, by the adding of the various qualities of the preceding context to faith (1:3-7), we prove to our conscience that we really are saved people. As the troubled conscience reflects on the presence of these qualities in life, it is supposedly quieted and assured. Salvation, they say, is sure from the viewpoint of the counsels of God, but from the human side it is "insecure unless established by holiness of life."[1550] We must "produce a guarantee of [our] calling and election"[1551] or "make your calling and election secure."[1552] Others, such as Calvin, do not connect this with conscience but simply with the need for some external evidence as proof that we are saved.[1553] Thus no subjective sensation of an assured conscience is meant.

This interpretation of Peter's words is unlikely for several reasons. For one thing, it suffers from the fact that the immediate context defines the "sureness" as a *bulwark against falling, and not a subjective confidence to the heart* that one is saved. Peter says that the way we make one's calling and election sure is by "doing these things." This evidently refers back to 1:3-7 where he exhorts believers to add various virtues to their Christian lives. The apostle is concerned, not with their assurance, but with their perseverance and their fruitfulness. He says:

> *For this very reason, make every effort to add to your faith goodness; and to goodness, knowledge; and to knowledge self-control; and to self-control, perseverance; and to perseverance, godliness; and to godliness, brotherly kindness; and to brotherly kindness, love (2 Peter 1:5-7).*

He wants his readers, having begun well, to finish well. He explains why:

> *For if you possess these qualities in increasing measure, they will keep you from being ineffective and unproductive in your knowledge of our Lord Jesus Christ (2 Peter 1:8).*

Being effective and productive in our knowledge of Christ will result in our calling and election being "sure," morally impregnable against falling into sin. Rather than calling into question the salvation of those who may lack these qualities, as the Experimental Predestinarians do, Peter does just the opposite. He affirms they are saved.

> *But if anyone does not have them, he is nearsighted and blind, and has* ***forgotten that he has been cleansed from his past sins*** *(2 Peter 1:9).*

The absence of these qualities does not necessarily cast doubt on one's justification. It only points out that a believer has forgotten the motivating benefits of the grace of God. Elsewhere Peter expressed a similar thought:

> *But resist him, firm in your faith, knowing that the same experiences of suffering are being accomplished by your brethren who are in the world. And after you have suffered for a little while, the God of all grace, who called you to His eternal glory in Christ, will Himself perfect, confirm, strengthen and establish you (1 Peter 5:9-10 NASB).*

1550 Henry Alford, "2 Peter," in *The Greek Testament* (Chicago: Moody Press, 1966), 4:394.

1551 R. J. Strachan, "The Second General Epistle of Peter," in *The Expositor's Greek Testament*, ed. W. Robertson Nicoll (New York: George H. Doran, 1967), 5:128.

1552 For example, Alford, "2 Peter," 4:394.

1553 Calvin, *2 Peter*, s.v. "2 Peter 1:10".

The goal, says Jude, is to keep ourselves in the love of God (probably "love for God,"[1554] Jude 20-24) by means of building ourselves up and praying in the Spirit (Jude 20). As we do that, God keeps us from stumbling (Jude 24) or falling into sin.

The result of doing these things is that we will not stumble and fall. This immediately suggests that sureness is a sureness that prevents stumbling and not a sensation of assurance or proof of salvation. Peter's exhortation follows an Old Testament pattern. "*Those who love Thy law have great peace, And nothing causes them to stumble*" (Psalm 119:165). To love God's law is a statement of Peter's exhortation that believers should be "doing these things." As a result, they will not stumble.

Furthermore, the general thrust of the book, as summed up at the end in 2 Peter 3:17, is concerned with perseverance, not assurance. The Gr word for "sure," *bebaios*, never has a subjective sense in biblical or extra-biblical Gr. Indeed, it is often used elsewhere in the New Testament of an external confirmation[1555] or of something legally guaranteed.[1556] A few verses later Peter refers to the prophetic word which is "more sure" (*bebaios*) than the subjective experience Peter enjoyed in witnessing the transfiguration of the Lord on the mountain (1:19).

The Experimental Predestinarian interpretation assumes that Peter addresses his readers as professing Christians and not as true Christians. In this view Peter wants his readers to prove that they are Christians by living a godly life. Yet this directly contradicts what Peter has just said in the preceding verse (1:9). There he assured them that, even if they lack these Christian virtues, it means only that they have forgotten they have been cleansed from sin. Forgetting forgiveness does not mean that a person does not have it! If they lack these virtues, as stated in the next verse (1:10), does this mean they have not been cleansed from sin?

Bebaios is often a technical term for a legally guaranteed security,[1557] but that is probably not the sense here. In classical Gr bebaios and related words[1558] meant "fit to tread upon" or a "firm foundation." The words are used in two ways in the New Testament:[1559] (1) "to confirm or validate" and (2) "to strengthen, to establish, to make firm, reliable, durable, unshakeable."[1560] Experimental Predestinarians prefer the former, but the context seems to be strongly in favor of the latter.

Of particular interest is the *Metochoi* in Hebrews 3:14: "*We are partners* [Gr *Metochoi*] *of Christ if we hold 'firm' the beginning of our assurance firm* [Gr *bebaios*] *to the end.*" The similar contexts seem to suggest that to hold one's assurance firm (*bebaios*) is similar to the idea, to "make your calling and election sure." In other words, to make our calling and election sure is simply another way of saying persevere to the end. It has the simple sense of "remain firm" or "be strong." This is the meaning of the verbal form in Colossians 2:7 where Paul exhorts his readers to be rooted and built up in him and "strengthened [Gr

[1554] The imperative requires an action on our part.

[1555] Hebrews 2:2.

[1556] Hebrews 6:19; 9:17.

[1557] MM, 107. It is common in the juristic sense: "if I make a claim or fail to guarantee the sale, the claim shall be invalid" or "[I] will guarantee the sale with every guarantee" (108).

[1558] *Bebaioō*, "to establish," and *bebaiōsis*, "confirmation."

[1559] H. Schoenweiss, "Firm, Foundation, Certainty, Confirm," in *NIDNTT*, 659.

[1560] Ibid.

bebaioō] in the faith." "It is good," says the writer of the Epistle to the Hebrews, "for the heart to be strengthened [*bebaioō*] by grace" (Hebrews 13:9). It is important to notice that in two passages Peter himself seems to explain what he means by "make sure."

We are to make our calling and election "sure" as a protection so that we will never stumble in our Christian lives (1:10). The word "stumble" (Gr *ptaiō*) is never used of damnation; it refers instead to personal failure in the Christian life. It means "to lose one's footing." As James put it, "for we all stumble in many ways" (James 3:2). Jesus had a similar idea in mind when He said that when a believer "walks in the day, he does not stumble [Gr *proskoptō*]" (John 11:9). The thought of stumbling is central to Peter's epistle and is brought out again at the end: "*You therefore, beloved, knowing this beforehand,* be on your guard *lest, being carried away by the error of unprincipled men, you* **fall from your own steadfastness**" (2 Peter 3:17). To "be on your guard" is a parallel thought to "make your calling and election sure." "Fall from your own steadfastness" is manifestly the same as "to stumble" in 1:10.

To "make [our] calling and election sure" means to guarantee by adding to our faith the character qualities in 2 Peter 1:5-7 that our calling and election will achieve their intended aim. What is that?

> *But as He who* ***called*** *you is holy, you also* ***be holy in all your conduct*** *(1 Peter 1:15, NKJV).*

> *But when you do good and suffer for it, if you take it patiently, this is commendable before God. For* ***to this you were called*** *(1 Peter 2:20-21, NKJV).*

> *Not returning evil for evil or reviling for reviling, but on the contrary blessing, knowing that* ***you were called to this****, that you may inherit a blessing (1 Peter 3:9, NKJV).*

We have been called to be holy and that we might be obedient (1 Peter 1:1-2), and that we might proclaim His name (1 Peter 2:9). Because the Thessalonians already knew they were chosen of God, they lived consistently with the intended purpose of the election and became examples to the believers in Macedonia and Achaia (1 Thessalonians 1:4-7).

The aim of our calling and election is holiness in this life, perseverance in suffering, and inheriting a blessing in the life to come. "Calling and election" in 2 Peter 1:10 are united under the same article. This sometimes signifies that the nouns in such a structure may have some relationship to one another. Calling and election are very practical and experiential concepts in the New Testament. Our Reformation heritage has perhaps caused us to overemphasize the basic meaning of the words instead of their intended aim. We often talk of *election* rather than *election to be holy*. We speak of an efficacious call rather than a call to suffer and persevere. In other words, we discuss the initial event, calling and election, separately from the intended effect, a holy, obedient life.[1561] First-century readers would have seen the terms as signifying the totality of their Christian experience. To them it is probable that the two words taken together are a merism representing their Christian lives or the intended aim of calling and election.[1562]

1561 The concepts of calling and election are so profound and problematic that they fully justify such a treatment. But readers of the New Testament would not do this. They saw the ideas of initial event and intended result as all part of the same term, "calling and election."

1562 This phrase has merismic tendencies in that it seems to be looking at the Christian life as a totality by using the words that signify the beginning and the end of the process. For further explanation of merism, see A. M. Honeyman, "Merismus in Biblical Literature," *JBL* 71(1952): 11-18.

Peter's meaning is that we must make our Christian lives impregnable against falling into sin by adding the virtues in the preceding context to our foundation of faith. We must strengthen our lives. This will make us unshakable and firm in the midst of suffering. To say it differently, "to make our calling and election sure" is to purpose that they will achieve their intended aim: a holy life, perseverance in suffering, and inheriting a blessing.

The experimentalists say that to make our calling and election sure is to discover if we are elected by looking at our works. But Peter is saying something different. To make our calling and election sure is to add virtues to our faith so that we (1) build a firm foundation, impregnable against falling into sin, and (2) obtain a rich welcome when we enter the kingdom.

2 CORINTHIANS 13:5

The exhortation to " examine yourselves" has found a prominent place in the theology of the Experimental Predestinarians:

> *Examine yourselves to see whether you are in the faith; test yourselves. Do you not realize that Christ Jesus is in you—unless, of course, you fail the test (2 Corinthians 13:5).*

Here, the apostle tells his readers that self-examination can result in knowledge as to whether or not one is "in the faith" [Gr *en tē pistei*]. A failure of this test is proof that Christ Jesus is not "in you." If having Christ "in you" refers to salvation, then this passage would seem to lend credence to the idea that we should examine our lives to determine if there are sufficient evidences present to establish that we are in fact among the elect. However, it does not mean this.

The word "yourselves" is first in order in the Gr sentence; it is emphatic. He is referring back to verse 3, in which he wrote, "You are demanding proof that Christ is **speaking** through **me**." Then, in verse 5, Paul turns the thought around on them: "You, yourselves, should test yourselves to see if he is really **speaking** ***in you***." Before discussing the phrase "in you," note first that the object of this examination is not to find out if they are Christians but to find out if they are "in the faith" (v. 5). Why do some assume that being "in the faith" is the same thing as being regenerate? In other uses of this phrase, it refers to living according to what we believe, or, possibly, living consistently with the fundamental doctrine of the Christian faith. For example, in the LXX it is found in 1 Chronicles 9:31:

> *And Mattithiah ... **was entrusted with the responsibility** [Gr en tē pistei, 'in the faith'] for baking the offering bread.*

The verse could be translated, "And Mattithiah was in the faith for baking the offering bread," that is, he was to have responsibility for baking or to be faithful in doing it.[1563] Earlier in this same epistle, Paul uses the term in the sense of "standing firm" in the faith, that is, in one's Christian walk, not in the sense of possessing salvation.

[1563] Keil renders it "on good faith," that is, "faithful." See "1 Chronicles" in C. F. Keil and F. Delitzsch, *Commentary on the Old Testament*, reprint ed. (Peabody, MA: Hendrickson Publishers, 2002), 3:481. Curtis renders it "in the office of trust." See E. L. Curtis and A. A. Madson, *A Critical and Exegetical Commentary on the Books of Chronicles*, International Critical Commentary (New York: Scribner Sons, 1910), 177.d.

> *Not that we lord it over your faith, but are workers with you for your joy;* ***for in your faith you are standing firm*** *(2 Corinthians 1:24).*

In 1 Corinthians 16:13 Paul says, "Be on the alert, stand firm *in the faith* [Gr *en tē pistei*], act like men, be strong." Being "in the faith" here seems to mean something like "live consistently with what you believe." Paul spoke elsewhere of fellow Christians who are "weak in the faith"[1564] (Romans 14:1), that is, "weak in living according to what one believes." Paul wants believers to be "sound in the faith"[1565] (Titus 1:13, possibly, "sound in doctrine"), and Peter urges Christians to be strong in resisting the devil, "steadfast in the faith"[1566] (1 Peter 5:8-9). In each case being "in the faith" refers to *consistency* in the Christian life, not *possession* of it.

But what about the expression "Jesus Christ is in you"? While this could mean Christ is in them in the sense that they are saved, Paul's reference to Christ "through me" in verse 3 does not refer to salvation but to demonstration of powerful speech and deeds. Similarly, the test they are to perform to see if Christ is "in you" (2 Corinthians 13:5) is not to discover if they are saved but whether Christ is manifesting Himself in their words and deeds. Paul, of course, doubts that Christ is in them in this sense. Salvation is not in view at all.

Christ is in them, unless they fail the test, that is, unless they are *adokimos*, "unapproved." This word is used eight times in the New Testament (Romans 1:28; 1 Corinthians 9:27; 2 Corinthians 13:5, 6, 7; 2 Timothy 3:8; Titus 1:16; Hebrews 6:8). Blomberg opines that those who disagree with his own understanding of this word do so because they have "a too simplistic understanding of 'eternal security.'" Blomberg says he is surprised that many Christians would "doubt that Paul could have seriously considered not 'making it to heaven'. But true Reformed doctrine," he says, "recognizes that saints are those who persevere."[1567] So, in Blomberg's view, even the apostle Paul was not certain he would go to heaven. One wonders, therefore, if Blomberg is correct, how any Christian in the history of the church could ever know for certain that God was his Father!

The word *adokimos* is found in the often quoted passage in 1 Corinthians 9:27, where the apostle himself fears he might become *adokimos*. Its basic meaning is "not standing the test, rejected."[1568] According to Sauer, it "is the technical term for a runner not standing the test before the master of the games and therefore being excluded at the prize-giving."[1569] Similarly, Thiselton argues that this does not mean loss of salvation, but "the test reveals failures of an unspecified nature, not utter rejection."[1570] The meaning of *adokimos* is simply "to fail the test." It is used of Christians five times in three passages (1 Corinthians 9:27; 2 Corinthians 13:5-7; Hebrews 6:8), and of the damnation of the lost three times (Romans 1:28; 2 Timothy 3:8; Titus 1:16). The result of their failure is determined by the context. In 1 Corinthians 9:27, Paul uses *adokimos* to express his concern that his works could be disapproved at the end of his life. In a similar fashion

---

1564 Gr *tē pistei,* dative case with no preposition (*en*)—different construction, same meaning.

1565 Gr *en tē pistei.*

1566 Gr *tē pistei,* dative case with no preposition (*en*).

1567 Blomberg, "Degrees of Reward in the Kingdom of Heaven?," 163.

1568 Abbott-Smith, 10.

1569 Sauer, *In the Arena of Faith: A Call to a Consecrated Life*, 162.

1570 Thiselton, *The First Epistle to the Corinthians: A Commentary on the Greek Text*, 717.

the athletes in the Isthmian games could be "disqualified" and fail to win a prize.[1571] He says, "*I know whom I have believed and I am convinced that He is able to guard what I have entrusted to Him until that day*" (2 Timothy 1:12, NASB95). Unlike the Experimentalists, Paul has no doubts about his sonship!

In Hebrews 6:8, *adokimos* is used of an unproductive field to picture the unfruitful believer. It is a worthless crop of thorns and thistles and is close to being cursed. Paul's passionate goal for the end of life was to be found by the Lord *dokimos* ("tested in battle, reliable, trustworthy)."[1572] The danger which concerned him was failure to obtain the prize (v. 24). The prize would be his reward, something in addition to redemptive salvation. "But the prize is not in all cases the same: God gives to each according to his merit."[1573]

Morris is correct in this explanation:

> *Castaway is too strong for* ***adokimos****. The word means "which has not stood the test," and in this context refers to disqualification. Paul's fear was not that he might lose his salvation, but that he might lose his crown through failing to satisfy his Lord (cf. 3:15).*[1574]

In 2 Corinthians 13:5 to "fail the test" is to (1) fail the test that Christ is mighty in them in the sense of mighty words and deeds; and (2) to fail to stand firm in the faith. This was their charge against Paul in 2 Corinthians 13:3. He now turns it around on them.[1575]

1 CORINTHIANS 11:28-32

A command to examine ourselves is also found in 1 Corinthians 11:28-32 (NKJV):

> *But let a man examine himself, and so let him eat of that bread and drink of that cup. For he who eats and drinks in an unworthy manner eats and drinks judgment to himself, not discerning the Lord's body. For this reason many are weak and sick among you, and many sleep. For if we would judge ourselves, we would not be judged. But when we are judged, we are chastened by the Lord, that we may not be condemned with the world.*

Experimental Predestinarians cite this passage to prove that unless we examine ourselves (judge ourselves), we risk damnation, that is, being "condemned with the world." Such self-examination is necessary within their view, because it is possible that if we have sin in our lives, we may have only professed faith in Christ and are not saved.

The passage raises two questions: What kind of self-examination is commanded? What is the consequence of failure in this test?

[1571] In view of the following passages, it is very difficult to believe that the Apostle Paul had any doubt about the certainty of his salvation: Romans 1:1; 4:23-25; 8:38-39; 1 Corinthians 1:1; 3:9-15; 2 Corinthians 1:1; 5:1-21; Galatians 1:1; 2:16; Ephesians 1:1; Philippians 1:7; Titus 3:5.

[1572] Grundman, "*dokimos* et al," in TDNT, 2:255.

[1573] Archibald Robertson and Alfred Plummer, *A Critical and Exegetical Commentary on the Second Epistle of St. Paul to the Corinthians*, International Critical Commentary (Edinburgh: T. & T. Clark, 1915), 193.

[1574] Leon Morris, *The First Epistle of Paul to the Corinthians: An Introduction and Commentary*, The Tyndale New Testament commentaries (Grand Rapids: Wm. B. Eerdmans Publishing Co., 1983), 140.

[1575] For a full discussion of the viewpoint presented here, see Perry C. Brown, "What is the Meaning of 'Examine Yourselves' in 2 Cor. 13:5?," *BibSac* 154, no. 614 (April-June 1997): 175-88.

In answer to the first question, Paul says that this examination is about judging the body of Christ rightly, that is, to discern that the elements are sacred and figuratively represent the body of Christ. The NIV translates it as, "Recognizing the body of the Lord." To partake of the Lord's Supper in a worthy manner is to partake with a consciousness of what it truly signifies: His death for our sins.[1576] This should cause us to avoid careless indifference or irreverence.

Conversely, to partake in an unworthy manner is to go to the Lord's Table with an indifferent attitude about what it signifies. The self-examination here is apparently for the purpose of finding sin in the life and to determine whether our minds are sufficiently centered on Christ so that when we partake, we do so with full appreciation for the significance of the elements. Paul's readers are not commanded to examine themselves to see if they are Christians, but to see if they are properly comprehending the body of Christ.

The consequences of failure to do this are severe indeed. Some of them were sick, and some had fallen asleep (died) in the Lord. While it is sometimes said that the judgment which can come on the believer here is the final judgment of the lake of fire,[1577] the passage seems to say precisely the opposite—it is a discipline in time (Gr *paideuō*) (11:32).

We go through these disciplines in time "in order that" we might not be condemned with the world. If the condemnation of the world refers to its current condemnation in time (e.g., Romans 1:18), this may mean that if a Christian responds properly to discipline, he will confess and submit to the Lord and avoid the judgments in time that commonly come on the wicked.[1578]

It is significant that Paul uses the verb "to sleep" (Gr *koimaō*) to describe their physical death. This is the common Christian term for the death of a believer (e.g., 1 Thessalonians 4:14).[1579] Paul appears to be thinking in Old Testament terms of blessing and cursing. Moses spoke of the temporal judgments which would come upon Israel if they disobeyed the Old Covenant (Deuteronomy 27-30). Paul has already said that the experiences of the Exodus generation were a model for believers today (1 Corinthians 10:6). The condemnation of the world from which they can escape refers to the terrible ills which come upon men because of their sin, drugs, alcohol, aids, etc., all which can lead to an untimely death—the sin unto death. Chrysostom said, "I mean, since many question one with another, 'whence arise the untimely deaths, whence the long diseases of men;' he tells them that these unexpected events, many of them, conditional upon certain sins."[1580]

1576 I am aware that there are other plausible views of the meaning of the phrase "the body of the Lord." This could refer to the church, the body of Christ, or, possibly, it refers to both the elements of the Lord's Supper and the church. See good discussion in Keith R. Krell, *Temporal Judgment and the Church: Paul's Remedial Agenda in 1 Corinthians* (Dallas: Biblical Studies Press, L.L.C., 2011), 200-05.

1577 Frédéric Louis Godet, *Commentary on First Corinthians*, reprint ed. (Grand Rapids: Kregel Publications, 1977), 597. See also Robertson and Plummer, *A Critical and Exegetical Commentary on the Second Epistle of St. Paul to the Corinthians*, 254.

1578 Physical death as a form of chastisement is found in the LXX (e.g., Psalm 6:2, 6 "O Lord, do not rebuke me in Thine anger, nor chasten me in Thy wrath … For there is no mention of Thee in death; in Sheol who will give Thee thanks?").

1579 This word is used in the New Testament only of physical death (Acts 7:60; 1 Corinthians 15:6, 18, 20, 51; 1 Thessalonians 4:13-15; 2 Peter 3:4).

1580 John Chrysostom, "Homilies on First Corinthians," in *A Select Library of the Nicene and Post-Nicene Fathers of the Christian Church, First Series, Volume XII: Saint Chrysostom: Homilies on the Epistles of Paul to the Corinthians*, ed. Philip Schaff (Buffalo, NY: Christian Literature Company, 1989), 28.2, p. 163.

This refutes the idea that just because the chastisement is pedagogical in nature, all true believers will respond to this chastisement, repent, and thus escape final condemnation. These believers did not repent before they died, yet they are "asleep" and thus are going to heaven. By using the Christian word for death, Paul suggests that "even if the guilty had failed to repent before death, their physical deaths would not have entailed eschatological or spiritual death."[1581]

Furthermore, the fact that Paul calls this a "chastisement" (Gr *paideuō*) is evidence that those who are objects of God's love are in view, that is, believers.[1582] They are being chastised because they are believers (e.g. Hebrews 12:8). What then is the purpose of the chastisement of believers? Is it to secure their repentance so that they will not finally be condemned to the lake of fire? Not at all. Rather, the purpose is to lead them, His children, to repentance. He disciplines because He loves them (Hebrews 12:5). Their status as one of His children marks discipline as distinct from condemnation of the world.

What about the purpose clause? Paul clearly stated that this chastisement is "in order that" they might not be condemned with the world. The purpose of this discipline is to steer the sinning Christians away from the path of discipline which can lead to spiritual and psychological ruin and ultimately physical death. The fact that they are disciplined for this purpose is evidence they are true children of God and not those who have merely professed faith.

> *For those whom the Lord loves He disciplines, And He scourges every son whom He receives. It is for discipline that you endure; God deals with you as with sons; for what son is there whom his father does not discipline? (Hebrews 12:6–7)*

Paul is not saying, if they repent in response to chastisement, they will be exempt from final condemnation (as Arminians and Experimental Predestinarians maintain); rather, he asserts that because they are indeed God's children, they will in no way experience the temporal judgment of God which comes upon the reprobate (Romans 1:18).

Conclusion

No part of Experimental Predestinarian teaching is potentially more damaging to Christian growth than their misguided notion that assurance is based on evidences of works in the life. Gerstner, for example, insists that the only way one can know he is saved is by knowing that he is being sanctified.[1583] In this he echoes the harmful counsel of Eliphaz who told Job, "*Should not your piety be your confidence and your blameless ways your hope*?" (Job 4:6). The view of Gerstner and Eliphaz was soundly rejected by Calvin when he said, "Doubtless, if we are to determine by our works in what way the Lord stands affected towards us, I admit that *we cannot even get the length of a feeble*

1581 See the excellent discussion by Gundry Volf, *Paul and Perseverance*, 106-7.

1582 The term Paul uses for chastisement, *paideuein*, means "train, educate, discipline, punish." See discussion in Bertram, "*paideuō*" TDNT, 5:622. Note also Proverbs 3:12; Psalm 94:12 (LXX Psalm 93:12); Revelation 3:19.

1583 John H. Gerstner, *Wrongly Dividing the Word of Truth: A Critique of Dispensationalism*, 1st ed. (Brentwood, TN: Wolgemuth & Hyatt, 1991), 233.

conjecture."[1584] Their continual insistence on self-examination to verify one's state of salvation cannot be found in the New Testament.

It would be a hateful father who entered into the following conversation with his son:[1585]

Son: "Dad, am I *really* your son?"

Father: "Well, young man, it depends on how you behave. If you really are my son, you will show this by doing the things I tell you to do. If you have my nature inside you, you can't help but be obedient."

Son: "But what if I disobey you a lot, Dad?"

Father: "Then you have every reason to doubt that you are truly my son!"

A child's greatest need when faced with doubt about his acceptance is to have his father's unconditional love reaffirmed. No human father would treat his child as Experimental Predestinarians imagine our divine Father treats His!

Assurance Is of the Essence of Faith

The writer of the Epistle to the Hebrews tells us,

> *Now faith is the assurance of things hoped for, the conviction of things not seen (Hebrews 11:1, NASB95).*

In this statement we learn that faith and assurance are intimately connected. The early Reformers understood this to mean that assurance is of the essence of saving faith. One cannot have saving faith without having assurance that one is saved. Robert Dabney and many later Experimentalists disagree.

ROBERT DABNEY AND THE ASSURANCE OF FAITH

Robert L. Dabney was one of the best minds the Reformed faith has ever produced. His *Lectures in Systematic Theology*[1586] are filled with valuable theological insight. He served under General Stonewall Jackson during the Civil War and was a professor at Union Theological Seminary. This Southern Presbyterian from Virginia was an articulate spokesman for the Experimental Predestinarian views of assurance and faith. One of the best ways, then, to critique their position is to interact with his discussion.

Dabney acknowledges that Calvin and the early Reformers united assurance and faith as one direct act of faith.[1587] Interestingly, in 1878 Dabney attacked this doctrine as an "error" of the "early" Reformers and their "modern imitators."[1588]

Dabney objected to the doctrine of the Reformers that assurance is part of the essence of faith on three grounds.[1589] First, saints in the Bible often seem to lose their assurance. If

---

1584 Calvin, "Institutes," 3.2.38.

1585 This illustration is adapted from Hodges, *Absolutely Free! A Biblical Reply to Lordship Salvation*, 17.

1586 Dabney, *Lectures in Systematic Theology.*

1587 Ibid., 699.

1588 Ibid., 703.

1589 Ibid., 702-4.

assurance is of the essence of saving faith, how, Dabney asks, can these verses be explained (Psalms 31:22; 77:2, 5; Isaiah 50:10)? The lack of this assurance can easily be explained, however, by the fact that the Christian is not looking biblically to Christ and the gospel promise. Saved people often lose their perspective and stop relying on Christ as the conscious object of their faith. They are emotionally troubled. This does not mean they are not saved. It only means that at that moment they are not exercising the biblical faith they did at first and hence have no assurance. This answer would not have occurred to Dabney because his Westminster Calvinism has taught him that any true Christian always believes. Such a position is not only contrary to Scripture but is also contrary to Christian experience.

Second, Dabney objects that Calvin's view adds something to the object of saving faith. Thus a man is not saved until he has come to believe that Christ has saved him, but it is only by believing that he is saved to begin with. This definition of faith, Dabney maintains, requires the effect, being saved, to precede the cause, faith.

Dabney argues that a man knows he is saved only if he meets the conditions.

MAJOR PREMISE: All who believe are saved.
MINOR PREMISE: I have believed.
CONCLUSION: Therefore, I am saved.

"Now my point is: that the mind cannot know the conclusion before it knows the minor premise thereof."[1590] He would, therefore, reject the faith-based syllogism.

But is this not theological hair-splitting? Calvin would reply that a persuasion that Christ has saved you is saving faith and is therefore not something you must have before you have saving faith. Furthermore, the state of salvation occurs at the same time when faith "happens" to us as a result of contemplation on the Object of faith. If faith includes assurance (and it does; Hebrews 11:1), then assurance is given with faith.[1591]

Dabney objects to Calvin on the grounds that the scriptural exhortations to self-examination refer not only to our moral life but also whether we are truly saved.[1592] Dabney argues that if assurance of grace was an essential part of faith, then believers would not be commanded to examine their faith and settle the question. In fact, if assurance is of the essence of saving faith, then the need to examine faith proves that we are not Christians at all! The biblical calls to self-examination were examined above. It is sufficient to say here that none of Dabney's proof texts establish his point. **Nowhere in the Bible is a Christian asked to examine either his faith or his life to determine if he is a Christian.** He is told only to look outside of himself to Christ alone for his assurance that he is a Christian. The Christian is, however, often told to examine his *walk of faith* and life to see if he is walking in fellowship and in conformity to God's commands.[1593]

1590 Ibid., 703.

1591 We disagree with the Reformed view that the gift of faith is included in regeneration. Rather, it is imparted before regeneration in the act of illumination.

1592 He refers to John 15:14; Romans 5:4; 1 Corinthians 11:28; 2 Corinthians 13:5; 2 Peter 1:10; 1 John 3:14, 19.

1593 Near the time of his death Dabney himself suffered from lack of assurance according to an "Our Daily Bread" article by Haddon Robinson, dated January 28, 1995 (http://www.rbc.org/devotionals/our-daily-bread/1995/01/28/devotion.aspx). A former student of Dabney's pointed him to the promise, and he found help.

ASSURANCE AND FAITH

Since faith is located primarily in the mind and is received as a gift of God, there are no necessary actions of the will or good works required to verify its presence. A man knows he has faith in the same way he knows he loves his wife and children. And if he has faith, then he has justification and assurance. He does not have to wait until his will "kicks in" weeks or months later to produce a few evidences of regeneration. Rather, he can accept the gospel promise that "whosoever believes in Him will not perish" and know at the instant he believes that his eternal security is definite. Yes, in spite of ridicule to the contrary, all that is necessary is to "believe at a point in time."

Berkhof properly distinguishes objective and subjective assurance. Objective assurance is "the certain and undoubting conviction that Christ is all He professes to be, and will do all He promises. "It is generally agreed that this assurance is of the essence of faith,"[1594] but, surely, there is a subjective element as well.

Warfield insists that faith is given a formal definition in Hebrews 11:1, "It consists in neither assent nor obedience, but in a reliant trust in the invisible Author of all good."[1595] According to Warfield assurance is part of saving faith.[1596]

Various views of personal assurance have been held in the history of the church.[1597] In contrast to Calvin and Warfield, the Westminster Confession asserts that assurance does not belong to the essence of faith: "This infallible assurance doth not so belong to the essence of faith, but that a true believer may wait long, and conflict with many difficulties before he be a Partner of it. Therefore it is the duty of every man, to give all diligence to make his calling and election sure."[1598] The modern Calvinists accept the doctrine of

---

1594 Berkhof, *Systematic Theology*, 507.

1595 Benjamin B. Warfield, "Faith in Its Psychological Aspects," in *Biblical and Theological Studies* (Philadelphia: Presbyterian and Reformed Publishing Co., 1968), 422.

1596 Ibid., 427.

1597 The Roman Catholic view denies that personal assurance belongs to the essence of faith. Believers can never be sure (except in special instances where assurance is given by special revelation, such as to Stephen and Paul). This had great impact in keeping people under the control of the church. Only through such means as indulgences, masses, and priestcraft could a person have a chance of heaven. The Reformers, on the other hand, held that personal assurance was in the essence of saving faith. They did not deny that true children of God may struggle with doubt. The Reformed confessions, however, vary. The Heidelberg Catechism teaches that the assurance of faith consists in the assurance of the forgiveness of sin and is included in saving faith. But the Canons of Dort say that assurance comes from (a) faith in God's promises; (b) the testimony of the Spirit; and (c) the exercise of a good conscience and the doing of good works and is enjoyed according to the measure of faith. For the Pietists assurance belongs not to the being but to the well-being of faith, and it can be secured only by continuous and conscientious introspection. Like the Experimental Predestinarians, the Pietists emphasized self-examination. Methodists hold that one can have assurance that he is saved now, but not assurance that he will be saved ultimately. Wesley and the later Arminians believed that, while final assurance is impossible, present assurance is. A man can be assured of his present conversion and have some hope of his final salvation. This present assurance comes through an immediate impression of the Holy Spirit. This mystical direct witness seems to have come through the Moravians to Wesley. Wesley was also a great admirer of the mystic Thomas à Kempis and may have been influenced by him as well. The Reformed Presbyterians deny that faith itself includes assurance. Yet Kuyper, Bavink, and Vos correctly hold that true faith is trust and carries with it a sense of security, which may vary in degree. There is also an assurance of faith which is the fruit of reflection. It is possible, they say, to make faith itself an object of reflection and thus arrive at a subjective assurance that does not belong to the essence of faith. In that case we conclude from what we experience in our lives that the Holy Spirit dwells within us.

1598 *Westminster Confession of Faith*, 3:638 (18.3.21-32).

Westminster. The assurance of hope, they say, is not of the essence of saving faith. A man may be justified without having assurance. Assurance, they say, is based on the witness of the Spirit and a comparison of one's life with Scripture and should be the goal sought by every believer.

That Calvin, Warfield, Berkhof, and the Heidelberg Confession are more in alignment with Paul than the Experimental Predestinarians and Neonomians in the matter of faith and assurance is evident for several reasons.

First, some assurance must always be part of faith. There must always be some hope where there is faith or belief in the heart. Assurance of faith and assurance of hope are therefore both ingredients of faith.[1599]

But, second, an assurance that is based on the believer's own spirituality does not deserve to be called assurance. It is too subjective and uncertain.

In addition, since faith and hope have the same object, the death of Christ for sin, and the same basis, the promises of God, a close relationship is certainly to be expected.

Third, if assurance is separate from faith, then the basis of our assurance is not our trust in Christ but our trust in Christ plus reflection on the fruits of regeneration in our lives. We are therefore ultimately trusting for assurance in self and not in the promises of scripture.

Fourth, the Bible explicitly and implicitly affirms that assurance is part of saving faith. The writer to the Hebrews unambiguously declares this to be true when he says, "Faith is the assurance of things hoped for" (Hebrews 11:1). But in addition, the scores of passages that tell us that "whosoever believes has eternal life" surely imply that a person who has believed has eternal life. If he is not assured of that fact, how is it possible that he has believed the promise? Belief and assurance are so obviously inseparable that only the interest of preserving the Experimental Predestinarian doctrine of perseverance can justify their division.

EXPERIMENTAL PREDESTINARIAN RESPONSE

Dabney responds:[1600]

> *The promises are assuredly mine, provided I have genuine faith. But I know that there is a spurious faith. Hence, although I have some* ***elpis*** *[hope] from the moment I embrace that truth, I do not have the* ***plērophoria elpidos*** *[full assurance of hope]; until I have eliminated the doubt whether my faith is, possibly, of the spurious kind.*

However, Dabney's reference to *plērophoria elpidos* reflects a misunderstanding of these words.

> *And we desire that each one of you show the same diligence so as to realize the full assurance of hope until the end (Hebrews 6:11).*

[1599] Dabney, *Lectures in Systematic Theology*, 699. Dabney responds that of course there is assurance with all faith, but not *plērophoria elpidos*, "full assurance of hope." The assurance of hope, according to Dabney, is grounded on gospel promises, testimony of the Spirit, and evidences of fruit. He answers by assertion, rather than by biblical reference. He says they are united because any true faith requires it, but he gives no reason for the distinction.

[1600] Ibid., 699.

He intends "full assurance of hope" to mean the "fulfilling of hope," that is, the finding of assurance, rather than "fullness of hope," as its usage elsewhere suggests. *But the way we determine whether our faith is spurious is not by examining our faith or our works but by examining the object of our faith and the biblical presentation of the gospel promise.* A man looking biblically at the person of Christ as presented in the Scriptures does not have a spurious faith.

Dabney's logical syllogism may once again be stated:

MAJOR PREMISE: All who believe are saved.
MINOR PREMISE: I have believed.
CONCLUSION: Therefore, I am saved.

The troubled believer must focus his attention on the minor premise, how do I know if I have truly believed? It seems obvious that this would cause him to base his assurance on the results of the self-examination of his faith, a point which Dabney elsewhere tells us we must do.[1601] Nevertheless, Dabney claims this does not mean we are trusting in ourselves for assurance.[1602]

> *When that same God tells him that there are two kinds of believing, only one of which fulfills the terms of that proposition, and that the deceitfulness of the heart often causes the false kind to ape the true; and when the humble soul inspects his own faith to make sure that it meets the terms of God's promise, prompted to do so by mistrust of self, it passes common wit to see, wherein that process is a "trusting in self instead of God's word."*

It may "pass common wit" for Dabney, but most would see a serious problem here which Dabney merely answers by assertion. As Dabney says elsewhere, faith is a product of looking at the object of faith and not at faith itself. If a believer tries to determine whether he is saved by examining his faith, he is, in effect, placing his *faith in faith* instead of in Christ. His examination will always turn up an impurity, insincerity, or incompleteness in his believing. Rather, the Bible calls us to look to the object of faith, and this act of "looking" **is** faith if we are looking scripturally and objectively at the God-man who paid the penalty for all sin. As long as we focus our thoughts on Him and His justifying righteousness and rest on that wholeheartedly, we have not only objective assurance but also the subjective feelings of the "full assurance of faith." Saving faith never comes from a self-examination, but it is part of a "Christ examination." Christ is the mirror in which we contemplate our salvation. As we look at Him, we see our own image reflected back to us.

Also, it must be remembered that it is not so much the amount of faith (faith the size of a mustard seed will do!) but the existence of faith which "is the evidence of things hoped for." The mere presence of faith in the life is the evidence of regeneration. Yet the Bible never asks us to examine the quality or amount of our faith, as Dabney and the Puritans insist. Rather, like Calvin, it directs us to reflect upon Christ, not faith, in order to find our assurance.

1601 Ibid., 704.

1602 Ibid., 705.

If a person has believed, he knows it, and if he has believed, he has eternal life and therefore knows it; that is, he has assurance. Consciousness attends all the operations of the soul. Therefore, no man can believe (resulting in salvation) without being conscious that he has believed (resulting in salvation). To say otherwise leads to the absurd conclusion that a person can believe in Christ and not know if he has done so.

Dabney responds by noting that, when the mind is troubled or confused, a remembered consciousness is obscured, or even lost. Thus, it is possible to believe and not be conscious of it. Dabney confuses what occurs at the point in time a person believes for salvation with doubts that may arise later. It is impossible at the point of saving faith to believe and not know one has believed. Dabney here introduces the common distinction between objective assurance and subjective assurance. It is obviously true that a man can know objectively with his mind that he is saved by focusing outwardly on Christ and the gospel promise and yet, because of a troubled heart or psychological state, not enjoy the "feelings" of assurance. With this the writer agrees, but this is not the point. We are not dealing with the troubled state of a Christian sometime after he has believed but with the gospel offer to the nonbeliever. Is it not generally true, apart from psychological disturbance of some kind that a person can believe and know that he has done so? If he cannot, then the gospel promise is no promise at all. But, Dabney says that a person can believe falsely, and his faith must be examined. If his faith must be examined, then, says Dabney, so must his consciousness.

> *If a man thinks he believes aright, he is conscious of exercising what he thinks is a right faith. This is the correct statement. Now, if the faith needs a discrimination to distinguish it from the dead faith, just to the same extent will the consciousness about it need the same discrimination.*[1603]

But a self-examination of faith once again puts our *faith in faith*. We do not examine faith, but we look to Christ and rest in Him, and that act is true faith. *The Bible nowhere commands us to examine whether or not our faith is true or false.* It calls on us to look to Christ, to believe on Him. The act of doing this is faith itself. Assurance is intrinsically involved in such an act, if faith and the finished work of Christ are properly understood. Dabney everywhere assumes that a man must struggle with the question of whether or not he has believed correctly.

The Bible never raises this issue which dominated three hundred years of English Puritan theological debate and which Dabney vainly tries to defend. Does a man struggle to know if he loves his child? Does he struggle to know if he has trusted the courts of law? Does he struggle to know if he has chosen a particular profession? These things are obvious as soon as the decision is made. *We know we have believed aright if we have believed according to biblical truth.* We do not know it by the results; we know it by the act of believing in the biblically understood object. If the object is correctly understood and we place our faith in the object, then our faith is correct, and we have assurance.

The way we come to accurate knowledge of the object of faith is called preaching the gospel. If the gospel is incorrectly preached, as with the Mormons, for example, then the

---

[1603] Ibid.

faith in that object is false. But if the object is correctly perceived and believed and trusted in, the faith is correct, the consciousness of having believed is valid, and the assurance associated with trusting in that object is valid assurance. We are not called on in Scripture to examine our faith but to examine Christ, the object of our faith.

As mentioned above, a Christian can obviously have objective assurance in the sense that he believes the gospel promise and yet not always have the subjective feelings of assurance because of some psychological state. The solution is not to direct him to the evidences of works in his life, but to continue to focus on Christ and the beauty of the gospel promise until the feelings gradually align with the facts. For some, this struggle may affect them throughout their entire lives, but to direct them to the vicissitudes of their current state of good works is sure emotional damnation. No amount of good works will satisfy the claims of a sensitive conscience.

The issue is not a rational examination of our faith as to whether we have believed correctly, as Experimental Predestinarians insist. Rather, the issue is a rational examination of the object of faith, Jesus Christ, and the gospel offer.

Yet in spite of the fact that assurance is of the essence faith, it is true that in the course of their journey to the Kingdom of God, some believers struggle with personal assurance.

Obtaining Assurance

How then is assurance to be obtained, according to Experimental Predestinarians? If it is not part of the essence of faith and does not come as we look at Christ, then it must come from looking at Christ plus something else. This leads to an examination of one's works to see if they are adequate. This is an impossible standard that causes even a wonderful Christian like John Piper to wonder if he is really saved. In response to a question about our imperfectness in this life, Piper responded,

> *I know people, and I would say this about myself, for whom the greatest threat to my perseverance and my ultimate salvation is the slowness of my sanctification. It's not theoretical questions like "Did He rise from the dead?" or the problem of evil. I've got answers. But why I sin against my wife the same at age 62 that I did at age 42 causes me sometimes to doubt my salvation or the power of the Holy Spirit ... This question is not theoretical.*[1604]

Different writers have different criteria. For Piper, one criterion is how he treats his wife, but all advocates of the Reformed doctrine of perseverance agree that self-examination of certain fruits of regeneration is necessary in order to verify the presence of saving faith. John Murray insists that finding or obtaining assurance is a duty.[1605] By "grounds of assurance" he means "the ways in which a believer comes to entertain this assurance, not of the grounds on which his salvation rests." He expands the grounds of assurance to

[1604] John Piper, "Why God is Not a Megalomaniac in Demanding to be Worshipped" 60th Annual Meeting of the Evangelical Theological Society. Recording available through ACTS Conference Products, # EV08487 (www.actsconferenceproducts.com/merchant/ev0108b.pdf.

[1605] Murray, "Definite Sanctification," 2:264. He cites Romans 6:11, 17-19; 8:15-16, 35-39; 2 Corinthians 1:21-22; Ephesians 1:13-14; 4:30; 2 Timothy 1:12; Hebrews 6:11, 17-19; 2 Peter 1:4-11; 1 John 2:3; 3:14, 18-19, 21, 24; 5:2, 5, 13.

five.[1606] First, there must be intelligent understanding of the nature of salvation. Second, we must recognize the immutability of the gifts and calling of God. Our security rests in the faithfulness of God and not in the fluctuations of our experience. Third, we must obey the commandments of God. Fourth, there must be self-examination. He cites 2 Peter 1:10 and 2 Corinthians 13:5. Fifth, our assurance is based on the inward witness of the Holy Spirit.[1607]

He concludes by saying, "Assurance is cultivated, not through special duties ... but through faithful and diligent use of the means of grace and devotions to the duties which devolve on us in the family, the church and the world."[1608]

Lloyd-Jones has a different list. He rests assurance totally on evidences of fruit in the life. He even goes so far as to say that our certainty of salvation is increased according to the number of tests we pass.[1609]

His tests are:

1. My outlook on life will be spiritual (1 Corinthians 2:12).
2. I will love the brethren.
3. I will seek God's glory: "A man who is led by the Spirit of God, is, by definition, a man who desires to live to God's glory."
4. A man led by the Spirit always has a desire within him for greater knowledge of God, and a greater knowledge of our Lord and Saviour Jesus Christ.
5. Anyone led by the Spirit is always concerned about his lack of love for God and for the Lord.
6. Anyone led by the Spirit has an increasing awareness of sin within.
7. A man led of the Spirit is increasingly sensitive to every approach of sin and evil and to temptation.
8. Are we putting to death the deeds of the body?
9. He is aware in himself of desires for righteousness and holiness. Do you long to be holy?[1610]
10. Are we manifesting the fruit of the Spirit (Galatians 5)? (He actually considers this as nine additional tests! How much joy do you have? How much peace do you have, etc., he asks?)

Lloyd-Jones asks, "Are we testing ourselves as we should?" Then he begins to qualify his requirements. "I am not asking whether you are perfect with respect to any one of the questions. I am simply asking–and I do so to encourage you. Do you find in yourself any evidence of these things? If you do, you are Christian. If there is but little, a mere trace, you are a very small infant and you have perhaps only just been formed. That is a beginning. If there are but glimmerings of life in you, it is sufficient."[1611] So apparently, only a "little" evidence, even a "trace," is all that is necessary. Of course, traces are found in the reprobate

---

[1606] Ibid., 2:270.

[1607] Romans 8:15-16; Galatians 4:6; 1 Corinthians 2:12; 2 Corinthians 1:21; 5:5; Ephesians 1:13-14.

[1608] Murray, "Definite Sanctification," 2:274.

[1609] Lloyd-Jones, *Romans Chapter 8:17-39: The Final Perseverance of the Saints*, 185-92.

[1610] Lloyd-Jones misquotes the Beatitudes here, which apply to rewards for perseverance and not tests of holiness.

[1611] Lloyd-Jones, *Romans Chapter 8:17-39: The Final Perseverance of the Saints*, 193.

with their temporary faith and in disobedient Christians as well. Therefore, Lloyd-Jones' assurance gives no basis for distinguishing one's faith from that of the nonelect. In other words, his excruciating introspection will yield no assurance at all.

This is the problem: How much evidence do you need? How much is "any evidence"? How much is a "glimmering"? A person might be very carnal for life and have "glimmerings" and "some evidence." If that is all he means, then how is his regeneration to be validated?[1612]

Dabney suggests three things a person must do to obtain Assurance: (1) We must be sure we are true Christians. (Why he includes this is perplexing. Obviously if we are sure we are true Christians, we would not need assurance. That is the point of his self-examination!) (2) We should endeavor to live godly lives in accord with Scripture. (3) We should make a comparison between the Bible description of a Christian and our own heart and life.[1613]

This is, of course, the root of the matter. According to Experimentalists, we are to examine our moral attributes and see if they correspond with the Scriptures, that is, conduct an "experiment." Dabney acknowledges, however, that this is only an "indirect means of assurance." This is what Calvin called a secondary means and not the basis of assurance. If that is all Dabney means, then he differs from Calvin not at all! Yet throughout his discussion he has emphasized that self-examination is the basis, not the "indirect means," of assurance.

He hastens to warn of the dangers of introspection.

> *For a faithful self-inspection usually reveals so much that is defective, that its first result is rather the discouragement than the encouragement of hope. But this leads the humbled Christian to look away from himself to the Redeemer; and thus assurance, which is the reflex act of faith, is strengthened by strengthening the direct act of faith itself.*[1614]

With this he seems to throw away his entire discussion and states that assurance comes only by looking to Christ after all! However, that alone, he confusedly adds, is not sufficient. There must be evidence of fruit in the life. How much? Dabney feels that, if there is "little" evidence, this would not be sufficient.[1615] Lloyd-Jones, however, feels that a "trace" or "glimmer" would suffice. How much then? Dabney never answers. He only says that, if the "soul finds evident actings of such graces as the Bible calls for," then he has assurance. But Dabney has already acknowledged the existence of a temporary faith, which

---

1612 Rosscup seems trapped in the same ambiguity which he tries to overcome by forceful assertion rather than logic. Rosscup, "The Overcomers of the Apocalypse," 281-86. He says the demonstration of regeneration must be "in some vital degree" (ibid., 268), or as he later qualifies, "at least in some degree" (ibid., 273). So he has reduced the qualifications from a "vital" degree to only "some" degree. But this helps the sensitive soul not at all. What degree is "vital"? What degree is "some"? "He follows in the direction of faith toward God in the thrust of his life" (ibid., 268). These statements are not found in Scripture and give little help. How much following "in the direction of faith toward God" is necessary to establish that the "thrust of his life" is one of "following"? Rosscup acknowledges that believers can die in carnal rebellion but then contradicts himself and says, "The truly saved ones are the brand of people who, when they sin, confess, seek God's forgiveness and cleansing, and desire to live in the light with God" (ibid., 270). Certainly, the saved believer who dies in carnal rebellion as did the regenerate Solomon would not fit in this category.

1613 Dabney, *Lectures in Systematic Theology*, 708.

1614 Ibid.

1615 Ibid.

has similar evidences. *How can the believer know whether his faith is temporary?* How much evidence would be adequate to give him assurance? Only with Christ in the forefront of the believer's mind and as the direct object of his faith can there be any assurance at all. As soon as we begin to examine our love for Christ, we substitute another object. This results in a reduction of our love for Him by the very act of measuring it. As the love for Christ subsides through self-examination, the introspection is more and more likely to return a negative verdict. How then can assurance ever be attained by self-examination?

Some Experimental Predestinarians have higher requirements than others for determining the saved condition of another Christian. Consider, for example, how Pink evaluates things that are absent in the life of a person who claims to be a Christian but who in reality is not:

> *We will mention some things which, if they are absent, indicate that the "root of the matter" (Job 19:28) is not in the person. One who regards sin lightly, who thinks nothing of breaking a promise, who is careless in performance of temporal duties, who gives no sign of a tender conscience which is exercised over what is commonly called "trifles," lacks the one thing needful. A person who is vain and self-important, who pushes to the fore seeking the notice of others, who parades his fancied knowledge and attainments, has not learned of Him who is "meek and lowly of heart." One who is hypersensitive, who is deeply hurt if someone slights her, who resents a word of reproof no matter how kindly spoken, betrays the lack of a humble and teachable spirit. One who frets over disappointments, murmurs each time his will is crossed and rebels against the dispensations of Providence, exhibits a will which has not been Divinely subdued.*[1616]

Such a list would surely call into question the salvation of every believer since the dawn of time, including even Pink himself! His listing is completely arbitrary. How careless in our duties must one be? How lightly is sin regarded? How vain is too vain? If the professing Christian is too sensitive, he is not really saved. Yet if he is not sensitive enough, if his conscience is not tender enough, then this proves that "he lacks the root of the matter."

The whole quest for assurance based on self-examination is doomed for a seemingly conspicuous reason. How can a man know that the good works he produces are in fact produced by the Holy Spirit flowing from a regenerate nature and not by his unregenerate flesh? There is no evident way to distinguish them outwardly, and yet it is to these outward evidences that assurance allegedly is promised. Thankfully, the apostle Paul specifically forbids such attempts at discrimination when he commands the Corinthians to postpone such judgments until the Judgment Seat of Christ (1 Corinthians 4:1-5). For if there is no infallible way to discern whether the works are the product of the Holy Spirit or the product of the flesh, then is it not impossible to have assurance based on works?

Obviously, these questions cannot be answered on the premises of the Experimental Predestinarian. Since the premises of this view of assurance logically make assurance now impossible, those premises must be contrary to Scripture, which says it is possible now. The only way to achieve the full assurance, which the Scriptures promise, is to ground it completely outside the believer's subjective experience and emotions but rather objectively in the person and work of Christ. The Reformation attempt to establish the

[1616] Arthur Pink, *Eternal Security* (Grand Rapids: Baker Book House, 1974), 67.

fact that justification was an external righteousness, rather than infused, was, according to Richard Lovelace, thwarted in part by Puritan and Pietist legalism and their stress on self-examination. "An unbalanced stress on auxiliary methods of assurance—testing one's life by the inspection of works and searching for the internal witness of the Spirit—obscured Luther's teaching on assurance of salvation through naked reliance on the work of Christ."[1617]

To argue that we must derive our assurance by observing qualities in ourselves that could only be wrought by sovereign grace is specious. The only quality that reliably and finally distinguishes temporary faith from saving faith is that saving faith is not temporary! And according to Experimental Predestinarians one cannot know if his faith is temporary until the final hour. In which case, contrary to Scripture, no one can have assurance until the end of life.

The major objection to all views of assurance is that they could become occasions of spiritual indolence and carnal security. According to the Partner view of assurance, though, a person living in sin may or may not be genuinely saved. If he is, the Scriptures give him no comfort. He faces serious warnings of divine discipline now and severe rebuke and disinheritance at the Judgment Seat of Christ. If he has departed from the faith, he has no assurance of salvation because he is no longer looking to Christ, and assurance comes only from conscious reflection on the object of faith. Hence the Partner view of assurance can never lead to false security. Yet, paradoxically, those within the Experimental Predestinarian tradition have promulgated a view of security that lends itself to the false security they abhor. By looking to some work in their lives, some people might be led to believe they are born again when in fact they are on the highway to eternal separation from God. As they look to Lloyd-Jones' "glimmer" or "trace," they conclude all is well with their soul. But if a man is asked to look biblically to Christ for his assurance, false security is impossible because looking biblically to Christ makes a life of sin logically inconceivable.

In answer to the question, "Would you give assurance to someone who is living a profligate life?" the answer is, "No." Neither should assurance be given to someone who is living a godly life. There is no illustration or teaching in the Bible of one believer ever "giving assurance" to another, that is, pronouncing him saved. Only the Holy Spirit gives subjective assurance in the heart, in response to looking to Christ, the mirror of our election and contemplating the beauty of the Gospel promises: "The Spirit himself testifies with our spirit that we are God's children" (Romans 8:16).

So if a person living an inconsistent life and claiming to be a believer, asks, "Am I saved?" The only answer can be, "You can only find assurance of salvation by looking to Christ. You cannot find it in the subjective opinions of others. However, if you are saved, your present lifestyle is inconsistent with the faith you claim to profess." We cannot pronounce on the eternal destiny of anyone in this situation. We simply explain the gospel and leave the conviction to the Holy Spirit. We have not left him with a "carnal security."

External fruit is evidence to others that a person is saved, and it is certainly a secondary confirmation to the believer of the reality of God in his life, but it is never presented in Scripture as the basis for personal assurance or the means for obtaining subjective assurance. When a person lives a profligate life, we have no observable evidence that he

[1617] Richard F. Lovelace, *Dynamics of Spiritual Life: An Evangelical Theology of Renewal* (Downers Grove, IL: InterVarsity Press, 1979), 100.

is a believer. "*This is how we know who the children of God are and who the children of the devil are*" (1 John 3:10). Since a life of good works reveals who the children of God are, one can only wonder about the genuineness of a person's faith if he reveals no good works. However, an unbeliever can live a loving life full of good works, so this kind of testimony is of little value apart from knowledge of what the person believes and in whom he trusts for justification.

It must be candidly admitted that a person who has lived for Christ for many years and who one day rejects Him could theoretically enjoy a hypothetical assurance. He could reason, "If Christianity is really true, I will be in heaven even though I do not presently believe it." Frankly, this seems absurd. Furthermore, it must be admitted that a man who continues to believe and yet persists in sin could theoretically reason, "I can continue in sin and grace will abound." Indeed, Paul's doctrine was criticized at this very point. Any doctrine of assurance which is not open to this charge is not biblical. This would seem to exclude the Experimental Predestinarian view of assurance.

But, we must ask, would such responses be typical? Would this be a normal response to love and grace? No! These theoretical possibilities do not represent the normal Christian life. Is it not true that a major objection to the Partner's view is that it is too narrowly focused on the few who might abuse grace rather than the many who do not? Grace can be abused and taken for granted, or it is not really grace, that is, "without cost."

The secrets of a man's heart are known only by the Spirit of God. We do not know one's hidden struggles. Neither can we know of an underlying genuine faith which for a lengthy time does not manifest itself in righteous living. It is not for us to judge. In fact, the entire preoccupation with "giving assurance" is presumptuous. The apostle Paul specifically refrained from giving or denying assurance: "*Therefore judge nothing before the appointed time; wait until the Lord comes. He will bring to light what is hidden in darkness and will expose the motive of men's hearts*" (1 Corinthians 4:5). He specifically left the giving of assurance to the Holy Spirit.

How, then, are we to comfort the troubled soul who lacks assurance of salvation? There is perhaps no better way than to follow the method employed by the apostle Paul in Romans 8:31-39. Here the apostle asks four questions, each beginning with the word "who."

1. "*Who can be against us?*" (v. 31). His answer is *no one*, because Christ gave Himself for all of us, and therefore God will graciously give us all things (v. 32).
2. "*Who will bring any charge against those whom God has chosen?*" (v. 33). His answer is *no one*, because God, the only One who could bring such a charge has already rendered His verdict, justified (v. 33).
3. "*Who is he that condemns*?" (v. 34). His answer is *no one*, because Christ has paid the penalty for sin and is at the right hand of God right now interceding for us.
4. "*Who shall separate us from the love of Christ?*" (v. 35). His answer is *no one*, because Christ's love for us is not conditioned on our loving Him (Romans 5:8).

What is striking about all four of these answers is that Paul never asks the believer to look inwardly and test for evidences of regeneration, as the Experimentalist requires. Rather, in answer to all four questions Paul directs him to Christ. "How does this bring assurance? It does so objectively because it provides the answers to my deepest doubts and fears. . . . From such a premise, only one conclusion is possible. It is the conclusion of assurance."[1618]

A believer may lack subjective assurance because of doubt, trials, or even an inconsistent Christian life. But for the sincere Christian the Bible does not ask him to examine his life but to look to Christ. Attention must be focused on Christ and the answers Paul gives to the four questions above. This gives the objective foundation from which subjective feelings of assurance can flow. Assurance can be felt to greater or lesser degrees, but it is the product of looking at the "mirror of our election."

The Bible says, "Faith is the assurance of things hoped for" (Hebrews 11:1). How else could a biblical writer make it plainer that assurance is the essence of faith?

Summary

It is very important that Christians regularly "examine themselves." However, nowhere in the New Testament is such an examination demanded in order to discern whether one is really saved. Instead, we much examine ourselves to see if we are in the faith as a way of life; to see if Christ is really expressing His life through us.

The four passages that are commonly cited to demonstrate that seeking full assurance is a Christian duty have been shown to challenge us to see if we have lives that are steadfast, impregnable against falling, and which will one day obtain an abundant entrance into the eternal kingdom of our Lord and Savior Jesus Christ

Paul counseled his readers to seek assurance by looking outward to Christ and the beauty of the gospel promise. After all, if Christ is for us, he pointed out, who can be against us? As Calvin put it, one finds assurance not by examining one's works, but by looking to Christ who is the mirror in which we contemplate our election.

[1618] Sinclair B. Ferguson, "The Assurance of Salvation," *The Banner of Truth*, no. 186 (March 1979): 5-6.

31

The Tests of Fellowship

THE SO-CALLED "tests" of 1 John have caused difficulty for all interpreters. Despairing of an exegetically sound interpretation of these passages that could emerge naturally out of the words themselves, scholars from all theological backgrounds have resorted to bringing in their theological system to explain the passages. How does one deal with such absolute statements as, "*No one who is born of God sins, because His seed abides in Him; and he cannot sin, because he is born of God*" (1 John 3:9)?

Advocates of the Reformed doctrine of perseverance understand 1 John to provide several tests by which a professing believer or others can discern whether he is truly born again. Once again, Experimentalists tell us the experiment with which introspection must be conducted. The believer is commanded to look within, to fruits in his life to discern whether he is one of the elect. Since only those who pass these tests are born again, justification and sanctification must necessarily and inevitably be connected. In their understanding of 1 John, "fellowship" is equivalent to personal salvation; to "know" God means to be born again; and "abiding in Him" is the same as what the Apostle Paul called being "in Christ."[1619] However, in this chapter we will argue that "fellowship" refers to walking in the light, not personal salvation; "knowing God" refers to a deep communion, not salvation; and "abiding" refers to remaining obedient and trusting.

To properly interpret the "tests of life" in 1 John, three introductory considerations must first be settled. (1) Was the epistle written to Christians or professing Christians? (2) What was the nature of the Gnostic heresy being confronted? (3) What was the intended purpose of the book?

The Readers of 1 John

Some have maintained that the readers of this epistle were a group of professing Christians, and in some cases the apostle doubts their regeneration. However, there are a number of verses which teach otherwise. John says of his readers that they are "*little children*" whose sins had been "*forgiven for His name's sake*" (1 Jn 2:12). He calls them "*fathers*" who "*have known Him from the beginning,*" and he writes to the young men who "*have overcome the evil one*" and in whom "*the word of God abides*" (1 John 2:13-14). They are specifically contrasted with the non-Christian, Gnostic antichrists who departed from them. Furthermore these people have received an "anointing," the Holy Spirit (1 John

[1619] For good discussion of these tests, see Gary W. Derickson, "What is the Message of 1 John?," *BibSac* 150, no. 597 (January-March 1993): 88-94.

2:20). This anointing, John says, "*abides in you and you have no need for anyone to teach you*" because His anointing teaches you (1 John 2:27).

It is obvious that John views his readers as regenerate when he says, "*I have not written to you because you do not know the truth, but because you do know it.*" He is confident that the truth is presently "abiding" in them, and he wants it to continue to abide in them (1 John 2:24). He specifically affirms of them that "*we should be called children of God;* ***and such we are***" (1 John 3:1). Furthermore, they are now "children of God," and when Christ returns, he affirms of his readers that they "*shall be like Him, because we* [he and them] *shall see Him just as He is*" (1 John 3:2).

They are "*from God*" and have overcome antichrists, because "*greater is He that is in you than he who is in the world*" (1 John 4:4). In contrast to his regenerate readers, the next verse refers to those who are "*from the world.*" His understanding of the saved state of his readers is further clarified when he says of them, "*These things I have written to you who believe in the name of the Son of God*" (1 John 5:13). For John, when a person has believed on the name of the Son of God, he is born again (John 3:15-16). In fact, one who has believed in the Son of God has *overcome the world* (1 John 5:5). Finally, while the world "*lies in the power of the evil one,*" "*we know that we are of God*" (1 John 5:18).

Throughout the epistle he uses the term "we"[1620] and includes himself in the same spiritual state and faces the same spiritual dangers as his readers. We must ask, "If John wanted to assert that his readers were in fact born again in contrast to the world, how could he make it clearer?"

If John believed his readers were saved people, we must understand these tests not as tests of salvation but tests of something else.

The Gnostic Heresy

The readers were plagued by false teachers who had introduced an incipient form of Gnosticism into the church. It is difficult to draw final conclusions as to the nature of the heresy, but specific references in the text of 1 John itself that strive to refute it give us some clues. One thing we do know is that they believed that there was a "mixture" in God of good and evil, light and darkness, and therefore a new creation in Christ could similarly have a mixture of good and evil and still be holy. This justified the Gnostic notion that sin was permissible for the Christian. John reacts in horror to this notion by saying, "*God is light, and in Him there is no darkness at all*" (1 John 1:5). The word order in the Greek text places emphasis on the negative here, "God is light, and in Him there is *absolutely no* darkness, *not any whatsoever*!"[1621] He may be responding to a peculiar Gnostic notion of God in this passage.

What was Gnosticism? There were a number of varieties, but basically it was an attempt to combine Christianity with various pagan and Jewish philosophies. It seems to have come from two basic sources: Alexandrian philosophy and Persian Zoroastrianism.[1622]

1620 1 John 1:1, 3, 5, 6, 7, 8, 9, 10; 2:1.

1621 The phrase "at all" (Gr *oudemia*) in conjunction with *ouk* is emphatic, "absolutely not at all." Apparently, the author wants to emphasize God's complete separation from any kind of darkness.

1622 John Rutherford, "Gnosticism," in *ISBE (1915)*, ed. James Orr (Albany, OR: Ages Software, 1915), 2:1241-42.

Alexandrian philosophy is seen in the attempt by Philo to expound the Old Testament in terms of Plato's thought. A line was drawn between God and the material world. God does not exert any direct action on the material world; He operates only through intermediaries, that is, angels and demons. Each soul existed before birth and is now imprisoned in the flesh. To be "saved," one must break out of the flesh.

In the ancient Eastern philosophy of Zoroastrianism, the world was viewed as a battleground between good and evil spirits. It was a dualistic view of the cosmos, common in many Eastern faiths. Thus, Gnosticism was built on the Greek opposition between spirit and matter and the Persian dualism between good and evil.

The essential question for the gnostic was, "What is the origin of evil?" He did not ask, "What must I do to be saved?" but "What is the origin of evil?" In the answer to this question, redemption was to be found. Rutherford lists other essential beliefs:

1. The initiated have a special knowledge. They are more enlightened than ordinary Christians.
2. There is a strict separation between matter and spirit, and matter is essentially evil.
3. The demiurge is the source of evil. He is the creator of the world and is distinct from the supreme Deity. Intermediate beings between God and man formed the universe and were responsible for evil. This, of course, only located the source in the demiurge but does not explain how part of him became evil in the first place.
4. They denied the true humanity of Christ. His sufferings were unreal.
5. They denied the personality of a supreme God and the free will of man.
6. Practical application focused on asceticism and antinomianism.
7. There was a combination of Christianity with pagan thought.
8. The Old Testament Scriptures were a product of a demiurge, or an inferior creator of the world, the God of the Jews.[1623]

These teachings led, paradoxically, to both asceticism and antinomianism. Asceticism developed from the thought that if matter and spirit are completely distinct and matter is evil, then sin and evil are inherent in the material substance of the body. The only way one can achieve perfection is to punish the body. By the infliction of pain and the mortification of the flesh, the region of pure spirit may be reached, and a person may become like God.

The antinomian expression of Gnosticism developed in the following manner. If the soul and body are separate entities and have nothing in common, then one should let the soul go its own way, the way of the spirit, and let the body go its own way as well. If the soul and the body are completely distinct and separate, then nothing that the body does can corrupt the soul, no matter how carnal and depraved.[1624] Ignatius said of them, "They give no heed to love, caring not for the widow, the orphan or the afflicted, neither for those who are in bondage, or for those who are released from bonds, neither for the hungry nor the thirsty." This sounds strikingly like certain references to their teaching in 1 John 2:9; 3:14; 4:7-8. In 1 John many of these tendencies are evident:

[1623] Ibid.

[1624] Ibid., 2:1242.

1. Higher knowledge—John refers to them claiming to be "in the light," abiding in Christ, and knowing God, and yet they are without love and obedience. Only by walking as Jesus did could they claim to be abiding (1 John 2:6).
2. Its loveless nature—They had only intellectual head knowledge and no love for the brethren; whereas, John stressed the need for love (1 John 4:7-11).
3. Docetism—God cannot have contact with matter. Therefore, the incarnation of the Supreme God is not possible, and, therefore, Jesus only appeared to have a human body. John stressed the physical presence of God in Jesus (1 John 1:1; 2:22-23). Jesus only appeared to have a human body.
4. Antinomianism—The Gnostics alleged that sin was a thing indifferent in itself. For the Gnostics, "It made no difference to the spiritual man whether he sinned with his body or not,"[1625] but John pointed out the incongruity of sin in the life of the Christian (1 John 1:8-9; 3:9).

The precise form of Gnosticism that John counters is not known. However, from references in his other writings and references by Polycarp, we can be certain of some of its broad outlines. In the book of Revelation, John alludes to Satan's so-called "deep secrets" (Revelation 2:24). This phrase, "to know the depths (deep secrets)" was common in the Ophite Gnostic sect. "From this language we may, I think, infer the existence of an Ophite sect, boasting of its peculiar gnosis."[1626] Gnosticism, before reaching its full development, was fully represented by the Ophite sects or systems. "Ophite" stems from the word *ophis*, "serpent," to which they paid honor as the symbol of intelligence. "They held that the creator of the world was an ignorant and imperfect being, Ialdaboth, the Son of Chaos, and that it was a meritorious act when the serpent persuaded Adam and Eve to disobey Him."[1627] Some in this sect even chose as heroes persons whom the Bible condemns, such as Cain and the men of Sodom.

We know from Polycarp that the apostle John vehemently opposed Cerinthus, a well-known Gnostic heretic of the first century. Polycarp says that they encountered each other at Ephesus and that, when John discovered that Cerinthus was in the same building with him, a public bath, he instantly left, exclaiming that he could not remain while Cerinthus, the enemy of God and of man, was there.[1628] Central to Cerinthus's teaching, like that of the Ophites, was that the God who created the world was an inferior power and that the incarnation was docetic. He taught that there would be a millennium of sensuality.

Thus the Ophites "ascribed the origin and the working of evil to God."[1629] That is why John calls their "depth" the depths of Satan (Revelation 2:24). He is being sarcastic.

God is the "unfathomable Abyss." The fullness (*plērōma*) of deity flows out from him as emanations, or "*aeons*," all of which are necessarily imperfect. Each of these emanations, *aeons* or angels [was] more spiritual than the grade immediately below it.[1630] At the end of the chain is the world of man. "Life continues to be unfolded in such a way that its successive

[1625] Ibid., 2:1243.

[1626] Ibid.

[1627] Ibid., 2:1246.

[1628] Ibid.

[1629] Ibid., 2:1243.

[1630] Ibid., 2:1244.

grades sink farther and farther from the purity of God, the life is feebler the nearer they come to matter, with which, at length, *they blend*. Such, according to Gnosticism, is the origin of evil."[1631]

Opposing this notion of an imperfect Creator, a demiurge with a mixture of good and evil, John says, "*This is the message we have heard from him and declare to you: God is light; in him there is no darkness at all*" (1 John 1:5). There is no blending of good and evil in God!

Therefore, if a believer claims to be in the light, walking in fellowship with Christ, and abiding in Him, but has sin in his life, his claims to have communion with God are spurious.

The Purpose of the Epistle

Many writers say that the purpose of John's epistle is given in his closing words:

> *These things I have written to you who believe in the name of the Son of God, in order that you may know that you have eternal life (1 John 5:13 NKJV).*

According to the Experimental Predestinarian interpretation, John writes 1 John to give the church several tests by which they can determine whether members are truly saved. If they pass these tests, then they can be confident that they have eternal life. However, such a view of the purpose of the epistle depends on the nature of the tests. Are these tests of life, that is, tests of whether one is born again, or tests of whether one is walking in fellowship with God?

The verse above is written to those "who believe," that is, to regenerate people. How do born-again people acquire assurance that they are born again? Experimentalists say that it is by submitting to the tests of life in this epistle. They ask, "Are good works and character evident in the person's life?"

John's usage of the same phrase elsewhere ("I write this," or "I write to you," or "I am writing") always locates the antecedent in the immediately preceding context.[1632] The immediate antecedent to "these things" says, "The one who believes in the Son of God has the witness in himself" (1 John 5:10). He who believes has the Son, and "*he who has the Son has life*" (1 John 5:12). In John 5:24, John makes it plain that the only conditions for knowing that you have eternal life is that you have heard and believed, and it is belief alone that is the subject of the preceding (1 John 5:9-12).[1633]

What then is the purpose of 1 John? The purpose is found where one would often find a purpose statement in a book or letter, namely, in the opening paragraph (1 John 1:3):

[1631] Ibid.

[1632] See 1 John 2:1, which refers to 1:5-10, and 2:26, which refers to 2:18-25. Because 2:1 refers only to 1:5-10 and not to all of chapter 1, it will not do to protest that this cannot parallel 5:13 because only chapter 1 had been written before 2:1. The phrase "I am writing" (or "I write to you") found in 2:7, 8, 12, 13, 14 does not refer to all of the verses before these, but only to the verses that immediately precede them.

[1633] Michael Eaton has suggested another interpretation. "Knowing" that one has eternal life may not refer to assurance of final deliverance from final damnation. He suggests that all that is meant is that true believers may know that they are experiencing eternal life in the sense of having abundant life. See Michael Eaton, *Living Under Grace* (Nashville: Word Publishing, 1994), 110.

> *What we have seen and heard we proclaim to you also,* ***that you may have fellowship with us****; and indeed our fellowship is* ***with the Father****, and* ***with His Son Jesus Christ*** *(NASB).*

Could John make it any clearer? "The manifest purpose of the apostle [is] to preserve his readers in the fellowship with God."[1634] He is not writing to test their salvation; he is writing so that his "joy may be made complete" (1 John 1:4). His joy was present; it had "begun" because they had been born again. But he wants this joy to be complete by seeing them walk in fellowship with Christ. The completion of his joy does not refer to his desire to obtain assurance that they are really saved, but as the apostle himself explains, "*I have no greater joy than this, to hear that my children are walking in the truth*" (3 John 4). He wants to rejoice that his saved children are walking in the truth!

Jesus used the term in the same way when He addressed His regenerate disciples: "*If you love Me, keep My commandments. . . . These things I have spoken to you, that My joy may be in you, and that your joy may be made full*" (John 15:11-12). To have one's joy "made full" is not to become a Christian but, being a Christian already, to act like it!

How can he know they are walking in the truth, and how can they know it in the face of the confusion introduced into their midst by the Gnostics? The Gnostics were maintaining that a child of God could have sin in his life, still be in fellowship with Christ, and therefore be abiding in Him—all at the same time! The remaining portions of the letter present several tests of whether a Christian is walking in fellowship with God, tests by which the falsity of the Gnostic teaching could be discerned. They are not tests of whether the readers are Christians.

The Experimentalists believe that 1 John presents four primary experiments which one can use to test whether or not he is a "true" Christian. In the discussion to follow, we will explore their understanding of these tests and the Partner response.

Test 1: True Christians Never Depart from the Apostles' Teaching

In 1 John 2:19-20, the apostle declares, "*They went out from us, but they did not really belong to us. For if they had belonged to us, they would have remained with us; but their going showed that none of them belonged to us.*" Lloyd-Jones says, "The fact that they had gone out proves that they had never really belonged; they were merely within the realm of the church, and appeared to be Christian."[1635]

Lloyd-Jones is identifying "us" with all Christians. However, elsewhere in the epistle John distinguishes between "us," that is, the apostolic circle, and "you," the believers to whom he is writing. For example, in 1:3 he says, "***We*** *proclaim to* ***you*** *what* ***we*** [the apostles] *have seen and heard.*" And in 1:5 he asserts, "*This is the message* ***we*** *have heard from Him and declare to* ***you*** *that* ***you*** *may have fellowship with* ***us****.*" And in 4:6 he says, "***We*** [i.e., the apostles] *are from God, and whoever knows God listens to* ***us****; whoever is not from God* [like Cerinthus and other false apostles] *does not listen to* ***us****.*" The "us" of 2:19-20 is, therefore, a reference to the apostles in particular and not the readers of the epistle in general.

Experimental Predestinarians often correctly point out that the "we" of 1:3, 5, where it refers to the apostles, is also used for all Christians. This, however, misses the point. When

---

[1634] Karl Brain, *The First Epistle General of John*, ed. J. P. Lange, et al., electronic, reprint ed., A Commentary on the Holy Scriptures: 1, 2, 3, John (Bellingham, WA: Logos Research Systems, 2008), 15.

[1635] Lloyd-Jones, *Romans Chapter 8:17-39: The Final Perseverance of the Saints*, 285.

"we" or "us" are contrasted with "you," it *always* distinguishes the apostolic circle from the larger body of Christians. And this is the situation in 2:19, where the "us" is placed in contrast once again to the larger body of Christians ("you") in verse 20.

The fact that these antichrists departed from the apostolic circle is proof that they were never apostles even though they, like Cerinthus, claimed to be. If they were true apostles, they would have joined with John and "listened to him."

If these false teachers had left the church to which the readers belonged, it is difficult to see why they would be a problem. Why would John need to refute them? They would no longer be there troubling the believers. If, on the other hand, they were claiming to have authority from Jerusalem, with roots in that apostolic circle, then the verse makes sense.

There is no statement here that true believers will persevere to the end. Nor is there the statement that, if a person departs from the faith, this proves he was never a Christian in the first place. What is taught is that, if these so-called apostles were really apostles, they would have listened to the apostle John and would have continued in fellowship with the Twelve. Diligent attention to the apostles' teaching is required for believers.

> *As for you, let that abide in you which you heard from the beginning. If what you heard from the beginning abides in you, you also will abide in the Son and in the Father (1 John 2:24).*

If the apostles' teaching abides in them, then believers abide in the Son and in the Father. They have fellowship with them.

> *Jesus answered and said to him, "If anyone loves Me, he will keep My word; and My Father will love him, and We will come to him and make Our abode with him" (John 14:23).*

The first test, then, that a believer is walking in fellowship with Christ is that he is attentive to apostolic teaching.

Test 2: If We Really Know Him, We Obey Him

The Gnostics claimed to " know God," and yet their indifference to sin in the body led them to disobey God's commands. How can such people claim to "know God"? John says:

> *And by this we know that we have come to know Him, if we keep His commandments. The man who says, "I have come to know Him," and does not keep His commandments is a liar, and the truth is not in him; but whoever keeps His word, in him the love of God has truly been perfected. By this we know that we are in Him. The one who says he abides in Him ought himself to walk in the same manner as He walked (1 John 2:3-6).*

Two tests of fellowship are given in these verses:

- keeping His commands
- abiding in Him

If a believer does these two things, he "knows" God. What does it mean to "know God"? Does it mean to be a Christian, or does it refer to something beyond the initial reception of eternal life?

Experimental Predestinarians have used these passages to prove their doctrine of perseverance in holiness. True Christians, that is, those who "know God," they say, are those who keep His commands and who have love for their brethren. The absence of obedience or love in the life of a professing Christian is proof, they say, that he is not a Christian at all. He does not know God!

But for John, in this passage, knowing God is to walk in fellowship with Him. It does not refer to the entrance into eternal life at justification but to the continuing experience with Christ called fellowship. What is in focus here is not whether they are regenerate but whether God's love has been "*perfected in them*." God's love cannot be brought to completion ("perfected") in one who does not have it at all! In fact, in 1 John 2:4-6 John equates "knowing God" with "abiding in Him."[1636] He is not discussing their justification; he is discussing their "walk."

John's usage here is illustrated by his usage in John 14. There he quotes Jesus as saying to Philip:

> *If you had known Me, you would have known My Father also; from now on you know Him, and have seen Him (John 14:7).*

Philip naturally wants to be shown the Father. But Jesus says:

> *Have I been so long with you [plural], and yet you [singular] have not come to know Me, Philip? (14:9).*

Jesus addresses all the disciples and then focuses on one. What did Jesus mean when He said that Philip did not know Him? Of course, Philip did know Jesus in a saving sense.[1637] He had believed and followed Christ (John 1:43). But he did not know Him in some other sense. He did not seem to know how fully the Son had manifested the Father. This knowledge comes only as the disciples obey Him (14:21). In other words, we come to know Him in a deeper sense as we obey Him, that is, "abide in Him."

The term "abide" is his word for something conditional in the believer's relationship with Christ, fellowship within the family. The conditional nature of the abiding relationship is brought out where Jesus says, "*If you keep My commandments, you will abide in My love*" (John 15:10). His foremost command, which must be obeyed if we are to abide in Him, is the command which John discusses in 1 John, the command to love one another (John 15:12). Only if we love one another, do we remain in friendship (fellowship) with Christ! "*You are My friends, if you do what I command you*" (John 15:14).

> *And the one who keeps His commandments abides in Him, and He in him (1 John 3:24).*

[1636] As will be discussed below, the "abiding" relationship refers to the believer's walk of fellowship and not to one's experience of regeneration.

[1637] The fact that the word "know" can mean *know* in a saving sense is completely irrelevant. The issue is, "What does it mean in this passage?" To assume that just because "know" can mean "be saved" in some passages and then to carry that meaning into all passages is another manifestation of the error of illegitimate totality transfer.

By this statement John signals clearly that the abiding relationship is conditioned on obedience, in contrast to the regeneration experience which comes through faith alone (1 John 5:10-11).

This is the same as John's thought expressed as having " fellowship with Him" in 1 John 1:6-7:

> *If we say that we have fellowship with Him and yet walk in the darkness, we lie and do not practice the truth, but if we walk in the light as He Himself is in the light, we have fellowship with one another.*

There is a difference between being born again and knowing God. Knowing God is a matter of degrees, while being born again, like physical birth occurs in an instant. The word "know" has the same latitude in Greek that it does in English.

A wife may complain, "Even though we have been married for ten years, my husband does not know me." She does not mean that they have never become acquainted but that her husband has never taken the time to know her in the sense of intimate fellowship. If a Christian claims to know God experientially but does not obey God's commandments, he is lying. John continues by saying that we know we are "in Him" and "abide in Him" by walking as He walked (1 John 2:5-6). His meaning is simply that we know Christ in our experience; our experience is Christlike only if we are walking as Jesus walked.

The apostle Paul used the word "know" in a similar sense when he said, "*I want to know Christ and the power of His resurrection and the fellowship of His sufferings*" (Philippians 3:10). Paul already knows Christ in the sense of possessing justification, but he wants to know Him intimately, to have continual fellowship with Him.

Recently I received this email from a friend.

> *I'd been a Christian for fifteen years, and while I often enjoyed sweet, deep fellowship with God, I could not deny that on many occasions a restless undercurrent pervaded my life. I didn't understand this. Jesus promised to give me a peace which surpassed all understanding, so why wasn't I experiencing this?*
>
> *The answer was revealed through separate events. The first happened one morning as I was reading the Word. In John 14:9, Jesus and Philip are having a discussion in which Philip makes a rather foolish comment (this I could relate to). Jesus responds by asking, "Don't you know me, Philip, even after I have been among you such a long time?" The verse pierced me as Jesus seemed to ask the same thing of me, "Don't you know Me, Lorraine, even after so many years of walking with Me?" The question hung in the air— I didn't know what to do with it. I knew a lot about Jesus, but did I really, really know Him? Something was missing in our relationship.*[1638]

Lorraine knew God in the sense of being born again. However, it was fifteen years later before she came to know Him intimately. John is speaking about the experience of more intimate fellowship, like that of Lorraine's, not of regeneration.

What a beautiful thing to be known at the end of life as a person who really "knew" God and who was truly "God's friend" (James 2:23).

[1638] Lorraine Pintus, Monument, CO, personal communication, March 2005.

Therefore, the second test of having a life of fellowship with God is an experiential knowledge of God which is the result of abiding in Him.

Test 3: We Are Able Not to Sin and Refuse to Sin

The third test of fellowship is the absence of sin in our lives. The Gnostics disagreed. They said that since, in their view, God is imperfect, and possesses good and evil in His nature, then sin may be a matter of some indifference. For this reason John says, "*in Him is no sin*" (1 John 1:5). As stated earlier, this is very emphatic in Greek: "no sin, none at all!" He seems to be countering this Ophite heresy of the imperfect God. If there is a mixture of good and evil in God, the Gnostics reasoned, there is also a mixture of evil and good in the creation which emanates from Him, the new man in Christ, who is at the bottom end of the emanations from the Deity. The new man in Christ, then, instead of being the perfect sinless creation of a perfect God, is a "blend" of good and evil. Sin is therefore of no great concern. John strongly reacts to this belief saying,

> ***No one who is born of God practices sin**, because His seed abides in him; and he cannot sin, because he is born of God (1 John 3:9).*

This absolute rebuttal has raised questions. In view of the fact that John specifically tells us that "*If we say that we have no sin, we are deceiving ourselves and the truth is not in us*" (1 John 1:8), and "*If we say that we have not sinned, we make Him a liar, and His word is not in us*" (1 John 1:10), how is it possible for him to say two chapters later that a Christian cannot sin?

THE PRESENT-TENSE SOLUTION

This passage (1 John 3:9) is problematic for all interpreters.[1639] How can it be that one "born of God" never sins? Of the many different approaches, one of the most popular (and favored by many Experimental Predestinarians) is to understand the present tense here as continuous. This theology is reflected in the NASB translation above, "*No one who is born of God **practices** to sin.*" These translators understand John as saying that the Christian may sin once in a while, but he will not continually sin. If he does, this simply proves he is not a Christian at all. As Kruse explains, "The author uses a present tense form of the verb 'to sin' (*hamartanō*), indicating that it is sinning as an ongoing action that he has in mind here as impossible for those born of God."[1640]

[1639] For a good discussion of the various solutions see Colin G. Kruse, "Sin and Perfection in 1 John," *Southern Baptist Theological Journal* 23, no. 1 (Fall 2005): 20-30. Kruse's approach is to say that the sin in view is the sin of rebellion. "It is this sin which believers cannot commit because God's 'seed' remains in them. The children of God do sometimes commit sins (2:1), but the one thing they do not do is commit anomia, the sin of rebellion, the sin of the devil." Ibid., 30. But is not all sin rebellion against God? Did not David, Solomon, Saul, and a host of others rebel against God at one time or another? Griffith writes, "Those who are born of God do not apostatize, because God's offspring (σπέρμα) remain in him, indeed they cannot apostatize [sic], because they have been born of God. Thus, 1 John 3:9 restates in even stronger terms the thought of 3:6: 'No-one who lives in him apostatizes.'" Terry Griffith, "A Non-Polemical Reading of 1 John: Sin, Christology, and the Limits of Johannine Christianity," *Tyndale Bulletin* 49, no. 2 (1998): 252-76. Certainly Solomon committed apostasy, rejecting Yahweh, and turning to idols. Why do the Scriptures include many warnings against apostasy (e.g., Hebrews 6) if it is impossible to apostatize? For discussion of apostasy and the believer see chapter 33.

[1640] Colin G. Kruse, *The Letters of John*, The Pillar New Testament Commentary (Grand Rapids: Wm. B. Eerdmans Publishing Co., 2000), 124.

This understanding of the present tense is aspectually plausible, but it depends upon the context and cannot be assumed. It does seem to fit the context of 1 John 1:9. J. P. Louw doubts that continuous action is indicated by the present tense, it merely indicates that an action occurs, "Donna is working."[1641]

However, for at least five reasons, the present tense solution is unlikely.

(1) Sakae Kubo and many others have pointed out that the present tense solution does not adequately address the background of the Epistle.[1642] As pointed out above, the Gnostics believed that there may be some sin in their god, the Logos, and also in the abiding believer. John is making an absolute statement that there is no sin in God (1 John 1:5); the Logos, that is Jesus (1 John 35), and also in the believer (1 John 3:6-9).

(2) Based upon point one above, the Gnostics argued that one could sin and still be in fellowship with God. The habitual present interpretation favored by many Reformed interpreters agrees, saying only that continuous habitual sin would be impossible. However, this would hardly be a refutation of Gnosticism, which taught that a man can sin a little and still be in fellowship with God. The present tense solution is too ambiguous. Does only "habitual sin" prove the one is not really justified (as Experimentalists believe)? If so, then a professing believer who sins less than "habitually" may be a "true" Christian. How much is habitual? Furthermore, the gnostic believed that sin was ignorance and was not a moral issue. Like our media today says, sin is a "mistake." That is why John is careful to define sin as "lawlessness."[1643]

(3) Thirdly, John says, the reason the Christian does not sin is because "*His* [God's] *seed* abides *in him; and he cannot sin*" (3:9). In the habitual present-tense view, the seed of God is powerful enough to prevent habitual sin, but it is not powerful enough to prevent a *little* sin.

Surely this cannot be John's meaning. Neither can we say that the seed is powerful enough to prevent only the sin of unbelief but not powerful enough to prevent moral sins of other kinds. That would only mean that the seed of God could prevent a Christian from denying Christ but could not prevent his committing daily acts of sin. The Gnostics would have favored that view of the seed. It kept them believing in Christ, which they thought they did anyway, but it did not interfere with their committing some acts of sin. Smalley shares our objection to the habitual understanding, saying, "If God, whose nature remains in the Christian (3:9) and keeps him safe (5:18), can be said to protect the believer from habitual sin, why can he not preserve him as well from occasional sins?"[1644]

In agreement with the above objections, Experimentalist writer John Murray argues against the present-tense interpretation on two grounds: (1) The meaning of "habitual"

1641 In "scholar-speak" he says, "it is the zero tense of factual actuality." See J. P. Louw, "Verbal Aspect in the First Letter of John," *Neotestamentica* 9(1975): 103. Wallace says it is a "customary present," GGBB, 522.

1642 Sakae Kubo, "1 John 1:9: Absolute or Habitual," *Andrews University Seminary Studies* 7, no. 1 (January 1969): 49.

1643 Ibid., 50.

1644 S. S. Smalley, *1, 2, 3 John*, Word Biblical Commentary (Dallas: Word Inc., 2002), 160.

is not precisely defined; and (2) this view leaves too much room for a loophole which contradicts the incisiveness of John's teaching. It allows the believer to commit certain sins, but not to do so habitually. "This would contradict the decisiveness of such a statement that the one begotten of God does not sin and cannot sin."[1645]

(4) A fourth objection to the present tense solution is that it makes chaos of the uses of the present tense in relation to sin in other parts of the epistle. Consider 1 John 1:8,

> *If we say that we have no sin, we are deceiving ourselves, and the truth is not in us (1 John 1:8, cf. 1 Kings 8:46).*

The phrase "have [Gr *echō*] no sin" is present tense in Greek. If we are to render this as continuous action then the verse would be translated, "*If we say that we continually have no sin, we are deceiving ourselves, and the truth is not in us*." This leaves open the door that if one is not sinning *continually*, the truth might be in such a person. So a little sin is okay, but continuous sin would prove that the truth is not in him. This is absurd. *Any* sin in the life of a believer reveals that the truth is not in him. In fact, is it not true that all believers sin every day? Isn't "every day" equal to continually?

The continuous rendering of the present tense in v. 8 would also place 1:8 in contradiction with 3:9. The "we" and "us" includes the apostle John.

> **1:8** *If we say that we continually have no sin, we are deceiving ourselves, and the truth is not in us.*
>
> **3:9** *No one born of God continues to sin.*

Thus, v. 8 says believers like John ("we") might continually sin, but 3:9 says we cannot. Also in this regard, consider 1 John 5:16,

> *If anyone sees his brother committing a sin [present participle] not leading to death, he shall ask and God will for him give life to those who commit sin not leading to death. There is a sin leading to death; I do not say that he should make request for this (1 John 5:16).*

Here we are told that a "brother" can commit a sin not leading to death. If the present tense is rendered as continuous, then this verse says a brother can continually commit sin, but 3:9 says he cannot! As Christopher Bass points out, "it would assert that a habitual sin does not lead to death." [1646]

[1645] Murray, "Definite Sanctification," 2:283. Murray's own view is that the absolute terms can, and perhaps do, refer to some specific sin in the Gospel of John. He mentions John 9:41 (the sin of self-complacency and self-infatuation); John 9:2-3 (the specific sin the man might have committed that resulted in blindness); and John 15:22 (the sin of rejecting Jesus and His Father). Murray points out there must be a radical difference between the sin unto death and the sin not unto death in 1 John 5:16-17. He says the believer may commit the sin not unto death, but he could not commit a "sin unto death" (1 John 5:16). "Since, according to 3:6-9; 5:18, the regenerate do not commit sin, it is surely justifiable to conclude that the sin he does not commit is the sin unto death" (ibid.). However, John says that a "brother" is potentially capable of committing this sin (cf. John 5:16-17). The "sin unto death," with the death being an act of punishment within the family, is illustrated elsewhere (Acts 5:5; 1 Corinthians 5:5; 11:30). Similarly, Raymond Brown rejects the "habitual" translation which says that Christians "do not or cannot sin habitually even though there are occasional lapses." He argues that it rests upon "fragile ... grammatical subtlety. Would the readers perceive such a subtlety?" Raymond Edward Brown, *The Epistles of John*, 1st ed. (Garden City, NY: Doubleday, 1982), 414.

[1646] Christopher D. Bass, *That You May Know: Assurance of Salvation in 1 John*, ed. E. Ray Clendenen, NAC Studies in Bible & Theology (Nashville: B & H Publishing Group, 2008), 136.

(5) Fifthly, if John wanted to communicate in 3:9 that continuous sin was the object of his concern, he would not have based it on a subtlety of Gr grammar. It is more likely that he would use some type of adverbial modifier to bring out the continual aspect. Zane Hodges says,

> *But the introduction of ideas like "continue to" or "to go on doing" require more than the Greek tense to make them intelligible. For this purpose there were Greek words available which are actually used in the New Testament. For example, dia pantos occurs in Luke 24:53: "... and [they] were continually in the temple praising and blessing God." The same word occurs in Hebrews 13:15: "Therefore by Him let us continually offer the sacrifice of praise to God." (See also: Mark 5:5; Acts 10:2; 24:16; Romans 11:10; Hebrews 9:6).*[1647]

Most grammarians reject the present-tense solution. Wallace classifies this use of the present tense as "gnomic," not continuous. The gnomic present is common in proverbial expressions and general maxims. It does not say that something is continually happening; it only says that it does happen.[1648]

For example when the writer to the Hebrews says, "Every house is built [present tense] by someone" (Hebrews 3:4), he is not saying, "Every house is continuously built by someone."

THE NEW MAN IN CHRIST CANNOT SIN

A second understanding of John's statement that a born-again person cannot sin takes the absolutes seriously. He cannot sin at all! Those holding this view understand John to say that "anyone born of God does not sin, even one time, not at all." Yet since he has already said that a man who says he never sins is a liar (1:8), he must be viewing the sinning Christian from a particular point of view. The Christian, viewed as a man born of God, and particularly as abiding in Christ, does not sin even once. For the Gnostics, a man could be born again, and be abiding in Christ, and yet sin could still be in his life because sin is from the body and is a matter of indifference. Therefore, the new man in Christ was a "mixture" of light and darkness, like the Gnostics' god.

John counters that a person who is born of God does not sin even once because "God's seed abides in him." God's seed is the regenerate new nature given to each believer when he is born again (John 1:13). Elsewhere, Paul refers to this perfect new nature as the "new self" (Ephesians 4:24) or "new man" (Colossians 3:10).

Brooke explains, "The fact that he has been begotten of God excludes the possibility of his committing sin *as an expression of his true character*, though actual sins may, and do, occur, in so far as he fails from weakness to realize his true character."[1649]

This means that sin cannot be a product of the regenerate life, contrary to the Gnostics.

1647 Zane C. Hodges, *The Epistles of John: Walking in the Light of God's Love: A Verse by Verse Commentary* (Irving, TX: Grace Evangelical Theological Society, 1999), 143.

1648 Wallace, *Greek Grammar Beyond the Basics*, 524.

1649 A. E. Brooke, *Critical and Exegetical Commentary on the Johannine Epistles* (New York: Scribner's Sons, 1912), 89. Emphasis added.

Zane Hodges is a forceful exponent of this view: "The divine seed (Greek: *sperma*) of that life remains (or, "abides," "stays" [Greek: *menō*]) in him who is born again, making sin an impossibility at the level of his regenerate inward self."[1650]

In a similar vein, according to Hodges, Paul declares:

> *But if I am doing the very thing I do not wish,* ***I am no longer the one doing it,*** *but sin which dwells in me. I find then a principle that evil is present in me, the one who wishes to do good. For I joyfully concur with the law of God in* ***the inner man,*** *but I see a different law in the members of my body, waging war against the law of my mind, and making me a prisoner of the law of sin which is in my members. Wretched man that I am! Who will set me free from the body of this death? Thanks be to God through Jesus Christ our Lord! So then, on the one hand* ***I myself*** *with my mind am serving the law of God, but on the other, with* ***my flesh*** *the law of sin (Romans 7:20-25).*

Paul, in some sense, understands that the true Paul, the real Paul, "I myself," does not serve sin. If, when he sins, the true Paul, the "inner man," the new creation in Christ, is not the one doing it, then who, we might ask, is doing it? The source of that sin is in the "flesh" and is not in the new creation in Christ, the regenerate new nature. The first step toward victory over sin is to be absolutely convinced, as Paul and John are, that it is completely foreign to our true new identity in Christ.

Paul also says, "*I have been crucified with Christ; and it is no longer I who live, but Christ lives in me; and the life which I now live in the flesh I live by faith in the Son of God, who loved me and delivered Himself up for me*" (Galatians 2:20). If a Christian sins, his sin cannot be an expression of who he really is, because his true life is that of Christ in him.

But according to the Gnostics, sinning can be a possible expression of the born-again person, and this is the precise heresy John is opposing. For them an imperfect demiurge can create an imperfect new creation. Furthermore, for the Gnostics sin was a matter of the body and not of the spirit, and so sin could be ignored because the spirit was the only thing of importance. Since there is a strong separation between spirit and matter, the sins of the body, according to the Gnostics, do not corrupt the spirit.

This second interpretation allows us to take the absolutes seriously and fits well with the context and is explainable in light of the Gnostic heresy being refuted.

The same phrase is repeated in 1 John 5:18 with the qualifying thought, "The one who was born of God keeps him, and the evil one cannot harm him" (author's translation).

> *We know that no one who is born of God sins; but He who was born of God keeps him and the evil one does not touch him (NASB).*

While this view is plausible, there are reasons for rejecting it. Essentially, it boils down to saying, "The old nature may continue to sin, but the new nature 'cannot.' In that sense the Christian does not sin, and is incapable of doing so."[1651] However, this could hardly be an adequate refutation of the Gnostics. Smalley correctly objects to this view, "The Christian may be controlled by the promptings of the flesh or the Spirit; but when it comes to acting upon those promptings, it is the *same person* who is involved. Thus the subject of the verb

---

[1650] Hodges, *The Epistles of John: Walking in the Light of God's Love: A Verse by Verse Commentary*, 141.

[1651] Smalley, *1, 2, 3 John*, 160.

hamartanein ('to sin') throughout is personal ('he'), and not impersonal ('it,' a nature)."[1652] As long as the total person sins, then it cannot be said that the total person cannot sin as those holding this view maintain and in 1 John 3:9, the whole person is doing the sin and is responsible for it, not, as Hodges suggests, just "his regenerate inward self."

A more nuanced view of Hodges' position is possible. One could argue that when the Christian is viewed as one "born of God," the reference is evidently to his true identity as a new man in Christ. The new man is sinless (Ephesians 4:24; Colossians 3:10), and no sin in the life of the Christian ever comes from who he really is, a new creation.

If a person sins, it is not an expression of his character as a new creation.[1653] It is as if someone says, "The president cannot break the law." Now, it is acknowledged that as a man he can, but *in his position as president* he cannot. If he does, that is not an expression of his character as the president. If someone says, "A priest cannot commit fornication," one cannot deny that as a man he can commit it; but priests, functioning as priests, do not do those things. The Bible uses language in a similar way, "*A good tree cannot produce bad fruit*" (Matthew 7:18). Of course, a good tree can produce bad fruit (James 3:1), but not as a result of what it really is, a good tree. Also Jesus said that men "cannot" fast while the bridegroom is with them (Mark 2:19). They can fast, but to do so is incongruous and unnatural and not consistent with the reality that the bridegroom is present.[1654]

Similarly, when John says, "No one born of God sins," he is saying that the person, as a man born of God, does not sin. If he sins, it is not an expression of who he is as one who has been born of God. It is not compatible with "abiding in him" (abide = obey, 1 John 3:6). If one is obeying God, he does not sin. The Gnostic said just the opposite: One could obey God ("abide in Him") and sin.

This modified view of Hodges' position seems plausible to me. However, there is another possibility.

THE NEW MAN IN CHRIST REFUSES TO SIN

Rudolf Bultmann suggested that the phrase "cannot sin" be understood as the possibility and not the certainty of not sinning.

> *The resolution of the contradiction [between 1:8, 10 and 3:9] lies in the fact that the "abiding" of the "seed" is understood as the gift of God's "love," 3:1, which remains for the believer a possibility not to be lost, so that he can always call upon that gift, even though he in fact sins. Οὐ δύναται ἁμαρτάνειν ("he is not able to sin") is therefore to be understood* ***as the possibility of not sinning.***[1655]

To rephrase Bultmann, we would translate the phrase "*he is not able to sin*" by "*he does not need to sin,*" or more simply, he "*refuses to sin because he does not have to.*" Similarly,

---

1652 Ibid., 160-61.

1653 Zane Hodges says, "This much-discussed text simply means that the regenerate person, as such, cannot sin. Since God's law is written in his heart, his regenerate self never produces sin. Sin, as Paul teaches us in Romans 7, is the work of the sinful flesh as it operates in and through our yet-to-be transformed physical bodies." Zane C. Hodges, "Regeneration: A New Covenant Blessing," *JOTGES* 22, no. 42 (Spring 2009): 77.

1654 Horatius Bonar, *God's Way of Holiness* (Chicago: Moody, n.d.), 90.

1655 Rudolf K. Bultmann, *The Johannine Epistles: A Commentary on the Johanine Epistles*, Hermeneia (Philadelphia: Fortress Press, 1973), 53. (Emphasis added).

Smalley says, "Our conclusion is that John has in view throughout the present passage the Christian's *potential* state of sinlessness."[1656] Viewed theologically, man has been partially restored to his original estate. Adam was able not to sin; similarly, the new man in Christ is able not to sin.[1657] Of course, the new man in Christ has a disability that Adam never had, namely, a sin nature.

While it is true that the word order in Greek (*ou dunatai hamartanein, "not able to sin"*) would not normally be understood to mean "*able not to sin,*" there are a number of illustrations where this phase does reflect the sense of possibility of not doing something and not the absolute inability of doing something. A possible example in the New Testament might be "*The world cannot hate* [*ou dunatai*] *you, but it hates Me because I testify of it that its works are evil*" (John 7:7, NKJV). Obviously, the world *can* hate the disciples and Jesus says it does (John 15:19; 17:14). However, it is true that the world is *able not to hate* them, and in fact the world does not always hate believers.

That said, we think the best translation of *ou dunatai hamartanein* is not "cannot sin" but "refuses to sin." Consider the following examples from the Septuagint.

> *For my wrath [Gr psychē, Heb nephesh, "soul"] cannot [Heb māʾēn, "to refuse", " Gr ou dunamai, LXX] cease; for I perceive my food as the smell of a lion to be loathsome" (Job 6:7).*[1658]

Clearly, his wrath about the food can cease, but because of its repugnance his anger still burns. God's wrath "is not able to cease," or "refuses to cease."

> *And the Lord could no longer [ou dunamai] bear you, because of the wickedness of your doings, and because of your abominations which ye wrought; and so your land became a desolation and a waste, and a curse, as at this day" (Jeremiah 44:22; LXX 51:22).*

The Lord certainly could bear them forever. However, "the Lord was not able [refused] to bear" them any longer.

> *For we [elders] shall not be able [LXX, ou dunamai] to give them wives of our daughters, because we swore among the children of Israel, saying, "Cursed is he that gives a wife to Benjamin" (Judges 21:18).*

The elders could give them wives of their daughters, they were able to do this, but they "refused," or perhaps they "dared not" do it.

> *And the kinsman said, I shall not be able [ou dunamai] to redeem it for myself, lest I mar my own inheritance: do thou redeem my right for thyself, for I shall not be able to redeem it (Ruth 4:6).*

[1656] Smalley, *1, 2, 3 John*, 172.

[1657] As Norman L. Geisler says, "Now, by God's grace we are able not to sin," Norman L. Geisler, *Systematic Theology*, 4 vols. (Minneapolis: Bethany House, 2002), 3:242.

[1658] The NASB translates "*My soul refuses* [Heb "*māʾēn* "to refuse" *] to touch them; They are like loathsome food to me*" (Job 6:7), Walter C. Kaiser, "*māʾēn,*" in TWOT, 488. If *ou dunamai* ("not able") in 1 John 3:9 was translated "refuses," the verse would make good sense. The translation would be, "No one born of God sins, because His seed abides in him; and he *refuses to sin*, because he is born of God."

The kinsman was able to redeem Elimelech's property, but he "did not need to" and refused to do so because he did not want to mar his inheritance.[1659] The believer is able to sin, but he refuses to do so because he is born again and God's seed abides in him.

> *And he poured it out for the men to eat: and it came to pass, when they were eating of the pottage, that lo! They cried out, and said, "There is death in the pot, O man of God." And they could not [LXX, ou dunamai] eat (2 Kings 4:40; LXX 4 Kingdoms 4:40).*

They could eat and they were able to eat, but they "did not need to" and refused to eat it because the food was rotten. Similarly, the child of God *can* sin but he *refuses* to do so. He is able not to and chooses not to because he is a child of God.

> *So I sent messengers to them, saying, I am doing a great work, and I shall not be able [LXX, ou dunamai] to come down, lest the work should cease: as soon as I shall have finished it, I will come down to you (Nehemiah 6:3).*

Nehemiah *could* go down, but he "did not need to" and refused to do so. Since the word *dunamai* in extra-biblical Gr can refer to moral possibility, this could be translated, "I dare not."[1660] The child of God *can* sin but he refuses to do so.

All these references in the LXX show that the phrase *ou dunamai*, "not able to," are sometimes used in the sense of potential. The words, "I shall not be able to come down," mean "There is a possibility I will not come down," or, better, "I am able not to come down and I won't," or in better English, "I am able to stay away, but I will not."

When the text says, "they could not eat," it means they "are not able to eat," but because of its repugnance. They refuse to eat. They could eat but they refuse to eat because the there is "death" in it.

As the examples above demonstrate, the phrase *ou dunami* does not always suggest inability; it can mean the possibility (not the certainty) of not doing something. What it means depends on the context. In the context of 1 John, it cannot mean that it is impossible for a believer to sin because John clearly says it *is* possible. In fact, he says, if a believer says he cannot sin he is a liar (1:10), and the truth is not in him (1:8).

It is therefore clear that the word "cannot" is not always used in a pure, absolute sense but, as the above illustrations suggest, it can be used in a relative or conditioned sense. Let's say that you were in Iraq and were walking through a field, and you sensed that you had just stepped on a mine but had not yet lifted your foot. You knew that the minute you lifted your foot, it would blow you up. Your buddy says, "Come on, we have to get back to the base," and you say, "I can't." Of course, you can. It isn't merely that you refuse to lift it; you cannot, unless you want to get blown up.

Or suppose a traveling salesman promised his wife he would be faithful while on a trip away from home. While on the trip he was propositioned by a woman to sleep with her. Besides the fact that he does not want to, he might say, "I can't." Of course he can, but his

---

[1659] In extra-biblical Gr the word *dunamai* sometimes takes the meaning "to enjoy a legal right," LSJ, 452. There are no examples in biblical Greek of this meaning, but it is tempting because of the parallel with Romans 6:7, "Anyone who has died has been freed [lit., 'justified'] from sin." That is, he no longer has any legal obligation to obey the sin nature; he is dead to it.

[1660] Ibid.

promise to his wife bound him to deny her request. He does not need to sin and "refuses" the request, and he is "able not to" accept it.

When John says in 1 John 3:9 that the child of God cannot sin, he means, "the child of God has the possibility of sinning, but is able not to, he does not need to, and he refuses to sin," because it violates who he is as a child of God. Children customarily obey their parents. Because a believer has God's seed in him abiding in him, one normally expects him to obey. Thus, we understand John to say in 3:9,

> *Whoever has been born of God does not sin, for Christ* [or the Holy Spirit?] *abides in Him; and he refuses to sin, because he has been born of God.*

It is not that sinning is impossible, but that he refuses to sin. Why does he refuse? In this understanding of the passage, John gives his readers three reasons ("*for*," Gr *hoti*, "because") why believers refuse to sin: (1) God's seed abides in them, and therefore due to this abiding relationship they have the resources for overcoming sin, and they do not have to sin (John 15:5; 1 John 3:9; Romans 6:1-11); and (2) they are born of God, and therefore they are new people with new inclinations, and they do not want to sin. When a person does not have to do what he does not want to do, he does not normally do it. John makes it clear that he will do it sometimes, but this would not be his normal behavior and would not occur at all if he is abiding.

However, note a very important qualifier. John clearly says that there is a third crucial factor: "*No one who abides in him sins, no one who sins has seen him or knows him*" (v. 6). Simply having the resources to overcome sin, and the motivation not to sin, is not enough. A person must respond to this inclination and appropriate these resources. In other words, he must choose to "abide in Him" as the branch abides in the Vine. The third reason (3) believers are able not to sin and do not need to sin and refuse to sin is that as they abide in Christ, sin will not result.

Let us consider this third point in more detail. We are in familiar territory here. The believer who does not abide in Him (walk in fellowship with Him) "has not seen him or knows him" (v. 6). These Greek tenses describe a current state and not necessarily a past event (not seen or knows). Thus, we translate, "sees him or knows him." The words "see" and "know" are words for fellowship and not regeneration. The perfect tense *of a stative verb* expresses an intensified present state. Thus, Dave Anderson translates, "to know intensively, or intimately," and to "see very closely." He concludes that these are verbs of close fellowship with the Savior.[1661] The person who is in fellowship does not sin. The Gnostics said he could and John is refuting this heresy.

When John states that the reason the believer is able not to sin is because God's "*seed abides* [Gr *menō*] *in him*" (1 John 3:9), he no doubt has in mind Jesus' words from the Upper Room Discourse on the vine and the branches. In that wonderful analogy the Lord Jesus says, "*Abide in Me, and I in you. As the branch cannot bear fruit of itself, unless it abides in the vine, neither can you, unless you abide in Me*" (John 15:4, NKJV). He continues,

[1661] David R. Anderson, *Maximum Joy: First John - Relationship or Fellowship* (Irving, TX: Grace Evangelical Society, 2005), 148. Stative verbs describe a state of belief, emotion, sensation, measurement, possession, etc. There is no movement. Louw is skeptical of the intensive perfect (Louw, "Verbal Aspect in the First Letter of John," 101). However, Wallace says, "The perfect may be used to *emphasize* the results or present state produced by a past action." See GGBB, 574.

I am the vine, you are the branches. He who abides [Gr menō] in Me, and I in him, bears much fruit; for without Me you can do nothing (John 15:5, NKJV).

If you abide [Gr menō] in Me, and My words abide [Gr menō] in you, you will ask what you desire, and it shall be done for you (John 15:7, NKJV).

Again the words "abide in Me" correspond to 1 John 3:6:

*No one who **abides in Him** sins; no one who sins has seen Him or knows Him (NASB).*

In 1 John 3:9 the words "remains [Gr *menō*] in him" are the same as "abides [Gr *menō*] in him." This expression corresponds to Jesus' words in John 15 where he said, "I in you," "I in him," and "my words abide [Gr *menō*] in you."

This *mutual* abiding enables the believer not to sin (1 John 3:9) and to bear much fruit (John 15:5).

This understanding of the passage totally refutes the Gnostics. They claimed that a person who is abiding in Christ sins and that such sin was a matter of moral indifference because there is darkness in God and in the Logos. John says that sin is absolutely not part of the abiding experience.

Believers are able not to sin and refuse to sin when they appropriate the divine Seed which dwells in them. As Lewis Sperry Chafer said, "The Word of God teaches that, by the power of the indwelling Spirit, the child of God, though ever and always beset in this life by an evil disposition, may be *able not to sin*."[1662]

Another factor that supports this translation is the prevailing New Testament understanding that sanctification involves both God and the believer (e.g., Philippians 2:12-13). God's part is universally presented as encouragement, strengthening, motivation, and command, and the believer's part is to abide in Him, to trust, and to obey.

The context of 1 John 3 nicely brings this synergism together in verses 6-10. Believers do not sin because "*whoever abides in Him does not sin*" (the believer's part, v. 6) and because God's seed "*abides in him*" (God's part, v. 10). As long as the believer is abiding in Christ, he is able not to sin because God's seed abiding in him gives him the resources he needs to overcome sin. This gift is a manifestation of God's love that John mentions in 1 John 3:1: "*Behold what manner of love the Father has bestowed on us, that we should be called children of God*" (NKJV). Because we are "children of God," we are "born of God" (v. 9), and therefore we have the resources of God's "seed" within us to motivate (Philippians 2:13) and strengthen us (Philippians 4:13).

John concludes his discussion by saying, "*By this the children of God and the children of the devil are obvious*" (1 John 3:10a). This verse becomes a bridge between his discussion of righteousness and the expression of it in practical love in the following section.

The Greek text reads, "By this are the children of God and the children of the devil revealed [Gr *phanēros*, 'visible, plainly seen']."[1663] He is referring to the following statement,[1664] "*Anyone who does not do what is right is not of God; nor is anyone who does*

1662 Lewis Sperry Chafer, "The Doctrine of Sin: Part 5," *BibSac* 93, no. 369 (January-March 1936): 25.

1663 BDAG 1047.

1664 According to Brooke, "It is more probable, and more in accordance with the writer's usual custom, that the

not love his brother." Earlier he said, "*He who does what is right is righteous, just as he is righteous. He who does what is sinful is of the devil*" (1 John 3:8).

When a Christian is "*of the devil*," John means that, when he commits even one sinful act, in the doing of that act, even though the ultimate source was his sin nature, he has yielded to satanic influence. Or, more simply, he is acting like Satan would want him to act; according to his values. Christ exhorted us to pray that we might be delivered from the "evil one" (Matthew 6:13), and Paul warned us that our battle is not against flesh and blood but against "principalities and powers of darkness," and the flaming darts of "the evil one" (Ephesians 6:12, 13). Even though the source of all sin is the heart and our own lusts (James 1:14), it is possible for Christian behavior to be inspired and enabled by Satan who pours gasoline on the flame. For example, Ananias' and Sapphira's hearts were "filled" by Satan. They were "of the devil" when they lied to the Holy Spirit. When Jesus told Peter, "*Get thee behind me, Satan*" (Mark 8:33), it was evident that Peter's behavior was "of the devil" (characterized by Satan's influence) in that one act.

John has just said that a Christian is not permitted to sin at all, not even once. Now he continues as if to say, "In fact, the absence of sin in the life of a Christian is one way he reveals by his actions that he is a Christian. Furthermore, the presence of sin in the life of a non-Christian is how he reveals that he is a non-Christian." However, when a Christian sins (and John believes he can and will, 1 John 2:1), in that act he is behaving like a child of Satan. Who he really is, is not being made evident. To use Paul's words, he is walking like a "mere man" (1 Corinthians 3:4).

But John does *not say* what the Experimental Predestinarians say. He does not say that the presence of sin in the life of a Christian proves that he is not a Christian at all. He only says that when a Christian does not do what is right, in that act he is not "of God [*ek tou theou*]" (1 John 3:10b). In other places in John's epistle, when that phrase stands by itself, as it does here, it means that the believer is not of God in the sense that the source of his behavior is not of God; it does not mean that he is unregenerate. For example, the apostle in reference to the apostolic band says, "We are of God [*ek tou theou*]" (1 John 4:6). He means their actions and source of authority are God.[1665] In a similar way we might say today, "That man is of God," or "We really feel this suggestion is of God" or "It seems evident that this situation is of God."

John knew that Christians sin. But when a Christian sins, there is no evidence, at least in that act, of his regenerate nature; it is in effect concealed. The only way others can tell whether we are born again is if we make it clearly seen (Gr *phanēros*) by our actions. If we do not reveal it by our actions, that does not mean we are not born again, but it does mean that our Christian commitment is not evident.

This third test of fellowship is the test of sin in the believer's life. If while sinning, he claims to be in fellowship with God, his claim is false.

---

reference is to what follows, the achievement of, or the failure to achieve, righteousness and love (cf. 2:3)." Brooke, *Critical and Exegetical Commentary on the Johannine Epistles*, 90.

[1665] See also 1 John 4:1, 3, 6, 7.

Test 4: Love for the Brethren

The final test of whether a believer is walking in fellowship with Christ is love.

Whoever does not love does not know God, because God is love (1 John 4:8).

John introduces the idea that practical Christianity expresses itself in love for other Christians and that hatred of a fellow Christian is incompatible with the Christian faith. He does not say that a Christian who hates his brother is not a Christian, but, rather, he "abides in death" and does not have "eternal life abiding in him":

We know that we have ***passed out of death into life****, because we love the brethren. He who does not love abides in death. Everyone who* ***hates his brother*** *is a murderer; and you know that no murderer* ***has eternal life abiding in him*** *(1 John 3:14-15).*

Can a true Christian "hate his brother"? Of course he can. David is a good example of a justified man who not only hated but followed up the murder in his heart with murder in reality by killing Uriah the Hittite (2 Samuel 12:9). Even Peter acknowledges that it is possible for a Christian to "suffer as a murderer" (1 Peter 4:15). Who has not felt anger in his heart at some time and is thus, on the authority of Jesus, a murderer (Matthew 5:21-22)?

When we harbor anger in our hearts, John says, we are in effect murderers, and we abide in death, the very sphere from which we were delivered when we became Christians. We walk as "mere men" (1 Corinthians 3:3), that is, as if we were still unregenerate. We are "carnal Christians" who are " walking in darkness" (1 John 2:11) and are in danger of losing our reward (2 John 8); losing what we have (Mark 4:25) and shrinking back in shame at the Judgment Seat of Christ (1 John 2:28). Jesus Christ is not at home in such a heart. He does not abide there.

The phrase "passed from death to life" is found elsewhere in John:

Most assuredly, I say to you, he who hears My word and believes in Him who sent Me has everlasting life, and shall not come into judgment, but has passed from death into life (John 5:24, NKJV).

It is possible that passing from death into life in both passages refers to the experience of regeneration. If so, then John would be saying that we "know" (Gr *oida*, "recognize") that we are regenerate by the fact that we have love for our brothers in Christ in our hearts. Then, in no uncertain terms, love for the brothers is an evidence of sonship! But this in no way proves the Experimental Predestinarian assertion that justification and sanctification are inevitably united. The passage does not say what Experimental Predestinarians say. It does not say that an absence of love is proof that one is not a son. Instead, it says that he is abiding in death, that is, living in the sphere from which he has been delivered. It does not say that if a person is born again, he will *always* manifest love. It does say that the presence of love is a way one can recognize a Christian's regeneration. The work of the Holy Spirit as evidenced in our love for the brethren is a secondary confirmation to our hearts that we are born again, but is not the basis of our assurance.

The abiding relationship is not the regeneration experience. Rather, it refers to the degree of intimacy and fellowship with the Lord which is possible for those who continue to obey His commands. For John, Jesus Christ is "the eternal life" which abides in us (1 John 1:2). To have Christ abiding in us (1 John 3:15, i.e., to have "eternal life") is not the same thing as being regenerate. Frequently, eternal life for John in this epistle is about the **quality** of the life being lived out in our lives, the very life we have been given.[1666] It is a conditional relationship referring to Christ's being at home in the heart of the obedient Christian who loves his brother.

In passage after passage, the writers of the New Testament warn Christians about the possibility of failure. Unfortunately, our Experimental Predestinarian friends have taught that the warnings only apply to Christians in the sense that they warn them that they may not be Christians after all if they do not obey the warning. They are primarily addressed to those who have professed Christ but have not possessed Him in the heart. This has, in no small way, contributed to the general loss of a sense of final accountability observed in many of our churches. This will be the subject of the next chapter.

The fourth test of a life of walking in fellowship with Christ is the test of love for one's fellow Christians.

Summary

The "tests of life" in 1 John do not refer to tests by which a church can discern whether one of its members is "truly" born again. Instead, they are directed against the Gnostic heresy that a believer can be walking in fellowship with Christ and yet still manifest sin and disobedience in his life. The Gnostics believed that God Himself was a mixture of good and evil, and therefore the new man in Christ which he created was also a mixture. To refute this error John gives four tests of whether a believer is walking in fellowship with God.

1. The first test that a believer is walking in fellowship with Christ is that he is attentive to apostolic teaching.
2. The second test of whether one has fellowship with God is whether he is experiencing a knowledge of God, that is, intimacy, as a result of abiding in Him.
3. This third test pertains to sin in the believer's life. If while sinning, he claims to be in fellowship with God, his claim is false.
4. The fourth test of whether one is walking in fellowship with Christ is if he has love for his fellow believers.

The error that John addresses has been common in the church since the first century. There are many lukewarm or even carnal believers who think all is well and that they are in fact walking with Christ when in fact they are disobedient to Him. Their lives differ little from the values of the world around them. They are not attentive to the apostolic teaching; they spend little or no time with Christ; they sin often and say they cannot help it; and they seem to enjoy the fellowship of the world more than quality time with other believers.

[1666] In 1 John 5:11-13, of course, eternal life is a soteriological concept.

32

The Carnal Christian

EXPERIMENTAL PREDESTINARIANS deny that the Bible teaches the existence of so-called "carnal Christians." Yet the Bible is more realistic than some of its modern adherents. It accepts the woeful fact that failure is possible.

By "carnal Christian" the writer means a Christian who is knowingly disobedient to Christ for a period of time. He is a Christian who walks as if he were a "mere man," that is, as an unregenerate person (1 Corinthians 3:3). Occasional lapses of sin are not the subject of this chapter. The focus is the apparent persistence in sin by regenerate people. In remote cases it is even possible that such people will publicly renounce Christ and persist in either sin or unbelief to the point of physical death. However, if they were truly born again in Christ, they will go to heaven when they die.

The Westminster Confession comes very close to the view in this book with the exception of the length of time a carnal Christian can persist in carnality. The Westminster Confession reads as follows:[1667]

> *Nevertheless they may, through the temptations of Satan and of the world, the prevalence of corruption remaining in them, and the neglect of the means of their preservation, fall into grievous sins [Matthew 26:70, 72, 74];* ***and for a time continue therein*** *[Psalms 51:14 and title]; whereby they incur God's displeasure [Isaiah 64:5, 7, 9; 2 Samuel 11:27], and grieve his Holy Spirit [Ephesians 4:30]; come to be deprived of some measure of their graces and comforts [Psalm 51:8, 10, 12; Revelation 2:4; Song of Songs 5:2, 3, 4, 6]; have their hearts hardened [Isaiah 36:17; Mark 6:52; 16:14; Psalm 95:8], and their consciences wounded [Psalms 33:3, 4; 51:8]; hurt and scandalize others [2 Samuel 12:14]; and bring temporal judgments upon themselves [Psalm 134:31-32; 1 Corinthians 11:32].*[1668]

Apparently, the Westminster divines believed that the Holy Spirit's power was capable of preventing apostasy or persistence in sin to the point of death. Was He not quite strong enough to prevent it "for a time"? It is interesting to note, however, that they acknowledge that one of the judgments in time is physical death (1 Corinthians 11:30). There, the length of time in which a person can "continue therein" is for the rest of his life! Here we have the precise position of this book!

[1667] *Larger Catechism of the Westminster Standards,* ed. M. H. Smith (Greenville, SC: Presbyterian Theological Seminary Press, 1996), s.v. Answer: Question 195.

[1668] Scripture references in square brackets in this quote are written as footnotes in the confession itself.

Objections to the Teaching of the Carnal Christian

Terry Chrisope argues that the "permanently carnal Christian" is a figment of the imagination.[1669] He says a Christian may have carnal moments, but if he does not have meaningful character growth, he is not a Christian. By "carnal Christian" Chrisope means "a professing Christian who shows no practical evidence of conversion."[1670] If you have one sin, you can apparently still be a Christian. But to have many, or, as he says, to remain in a state of "constant and total" carnality, you are not a Christian.

How does one draw the line? What is "constant" and what is "total"? Apparently one sin is not total. How about two or three? In fact, the Corinthians were involved in "constant and total" sin. Paul came to them in AD 52, and four years later they are "yet" carnal. They had remained in constant divisiveness for at least four years. The rest of the book documents other aspects of their carnality: jealousy, quarreling (1 Corinthians 3:3), toleration of incest (5:1), lawsuits against brothers (6:1), fornication (6:18), indifference to weaker brothers (chapters 8-9), drunkenness (11:21), and egotistical use of spiritual gifts (14:4). Certainly the description of these believers is one of "total and constant" carnality. In at least two cases their carnality could or did persist unto physical death (5:5; 11:30), and their physical death was a divine judgment on them for their refusal to respond to the exhortations of the apostle.

The opponents of the Partner viewpoint have lodged three major objections to the teaching that carnal Christians exist.

IT LEADS TO ANTINOMIANISM

One well-known theologian, R. C. Sproul, objects to the existence of the carnal Christian on two grounds. First, it can lead to antinomianism.[1671] By this he means that those espousing the carnal Christian believe that one can receive Christ as Savior but not necessarily as Lord. He says, "It assumes faith without obedience." He incorrectly feels that this is what James referred to as a "dead faith," that is, a non-saving faith. However, James is referring to the faith of a believer which is not vital, or living, or productive.

This theologian believes that "if a person manifests a life of pure and consistent carnality, he is no Christian."[1672] But how much carnality is "consistent" carnality? If "pure" carnality is required, then a person could have a lot of carnality short of "pure," but apparently this theologian would be willing to acknowledge him as a believer. What of

---

1669 Terry A. Chrisope, *Jesus is Lord: A Study in the Unity of Confessing Jesus as Lord and Saviour in the New Testament* (Welwyn, Hertfordshire, UK: Evangelical Press, 1982), 89.

1670 Chrisope gives the following reasons for rejecting the carnal Christian view, ibid.: (1) The New Testament teaches that a Christian is one who has made a definite break with the ruling power of sin. As argued elsewhere, however, Romans 6 is not teaching that this break is automatic and experientially inevitable. Otherwise, why would Paul tell them to reckon and yield? Unless the possibility of not doing it is present, then the command is meaningless. (2) Chrisope also argues incorrectly from 1 John. He camps on the black-and-white portrait of the believer and unbeliever (1 John 1:6; 2:4, 9; 3:6-10; 4:8; 5:18). But 1:6 and 2:4 refer to "know" in the sense of "walk in fellowship with." A Christian who claims to walk in fellowship with Christ and who sins is a liar and is not walking in fellowship with Christ. Any pastor knows of Christians who feign spirituality and who at the same time are engaging in acts of disobedience. Their spirituality is a lie, but they are Christians. See chapters 26-28 above for full discussion.

1671 R. C. Sproul, *Pleasing God* (Wheaton, IL: Tyndale House, 1988), 152.

1672 Ibid., 153.

Solomon, what of Saul and many others in the Bible (which we will extensively document below) who did live lives of "consistent and pure carnality" and yet were regenerate?

FALSE ASSURANCE

A second concern of those who object to the teaching that there are two categories of Christians (carnal and spiritual) is the fear that "people begin to think that all that is required to be saved is a *profession* of faith."[1673] What Sproul apparently intends to imply is that those who are not Christians will think that a mere profession of acceptance of some facts has saved them. He has in his cross-hairs here the oft-repeated scenarios where someone is invited to come forward in a church, prays a prayer, thinks he has a ticket to heaven, and then lives like a profligate, giving no evidence of any change in life. Many Experimentalists, like Sproul, believe that this is either the teaching of the Partner viewpoint or is a necessary result of it.

But the Partners do not say that a profession saves. Nor does the Partner believe that all persons living a carnal life are Christians. What the Partners do say is that he may be a Christian but that is for God who knows the heart to judge. But if a person did make such a profession that was invalid, it would be a result of an incorrect presentation of the gospel and in no way flows logically out of the teaching of the possible existence of a carnal Christian. The real peril is that those who espouse the Experimental Predestinarian view and who are in fact non-Christians will be in danger of thinking they are truly saved because their carnality is not "pure" and "consistent." Thus their teaching could possibly promote the very carnality which they reject.

Can such people have assurance of their "ticket to heaven"? Such people, of course, may theoretically enjoy a "carnal assurance," that is, falsely believe they are saved, but they cannot enjoy biblical assurance. If faith is a looking to Christ for forgiveness of sin, then a life of sin is psychologically, spiritually, and, of course, ethically contradictory to such faith. Since faith includes assurance, such people can have no biblical assurance of their final destiny. Therefore, to assert that the Bible teaches the existence of the carnal Christian is not the same thing as "giving assurance" to a person who has professed faith in Christ but has no evidence of such faith. The only way one can assume that a man is saved is by his claim that he has believed in Christ and by the evidences of such belief in perseverance. But only God knows the reality. Many who say they are saved are not.

Because Experimental Predestinarians ground assurance, in part, in the observation of works in one's life, there is a danger of a false assurance. The subjective nature of such a personal examination leads some to believe they are Christians when in fact they are not. Since the precise amount of work necessary to verify the presence of saving faith is impossible to define, many who are not regenerate at all may believe (on the basis of some imagined "good works" in their lives) that they are saved. This danger is much less likely to be present among those who, like the Partners, ground assurance in looking to the cross and to Christ. Such a looking is incompatible with a life of sin and with the resultant carnal security about which both Experimental Predestinarians and Partners are properly concerned.

1673 Ibid., 52 (emphasis in original).

Realizing the threat to over three hundred years of tradition, the discussion of the carnal Christian strikes a "raw nerve" in those committed to God-produced, non-meritorious works as a means of obtaining final entrance into heaven, that is, to perseverance in holiness. Their fear that somewhere, somehow, a person who is not a Christian might be assured that he is saved so dominates their consciousness that the grace of God which saved them seems to be forgotten. Is it possible that some of them have forgotten that they too are presently imperfect? Have they forgotten that there is not a purely sincere motive in any of our hearts? Have they forgotten that there is no unsullied act any believer commits? Have they forgotten their cleansing from former sins (2 Peter 1:9)? Or is only the obviously inconsistent Christian the subject of their concern? We are all sinful. Sin is in the heart of the sincere saint who lives inconsistently and persists in it. Indeed, who of us does not "persist" to the final hour in mixed motives, in pride, in hypocrisy, in greed? The only difference between the most sincere saint and the most carnal one is a matter of degree. Hear the apostle Paul:

> *For that which I am doing, I do not understand; for I am not practicing what I would like to do, but am doing the very thing I hate.*
>
> *For the good that I wish, I do not do; but I practice the very evil that I do not wish (Romans 7:15-19).*

The apostle is certainly not a carnal Christian, but he recognizes that in his life there is sin and a mixture of good and evil, and that this persists to the end of life. *If we say that we have not sinned, we make Him a liar, and His word is not in us* (1 John 1:10).

The evident impossibility of drawing a line across this continuum to divide those who are saved from those who only claim to be is, no doubt, what has caused Experimental Predestinarians to push assurance of salvation to the final hour—a consistency that is invalidated by the fact that the Bible offers assurance *now*.

The preoccupation with where to draw the line has historically resulted in the need for external objective standards. This explains the legalism present in both Reformed and Arminian circles. Whatever they disagree on, on this one point they are united: a person who is not living the Christian life is not a Christian. This requires an objective definition of "the life" which must be lived. In some circles this has led to such views as a woman who wears make-up is probably not saved, and a man who drinks or smokes surely could not be.[1674]

TRUE FAITH ALWAYS INCLUDES SUBMISSION TO THE LORDSHIP OF CHRIST

Another common error of the Experimentalists is to confuse the idea of Lordship as a condition for salvation with perseverance in holiness. Some seem to think they will solve the problem of carnality in our churches by teaching (1) that obedience is part of saving faith, and (2) that in order to be saved a person must turn from all known sin and submit himself to the Lordship of Christ.

But it should be obvious that, even if this is granted, which it is not, the act of submitting to the Lordship of Christ at the point of saving faith in no way guarantees that

[1674] These viewpoints are common in some conservative churches in Eastern Europe. Spurgeon is reported to have said, "I will smoke my cigar for the Glory of God."

a person will continue to submit to the Lordship of Christ throughout the rest of his life. Thus books written to eliminate the problem of dead Christianity by frontloading the gospel with lordship salvation are not only wrong biblically, but logically they provide no answer at all.[1675] Only *perseverance in godliness* will solve the problem, not a decision at a point in time. Therefore, the issue of lordship salvation is logically irrelevant to the whole discussion.

Biblical Proof of the Doctrine of the Carnal Christian

The theory of the saints' perseverance in holiness is, in principle, falsifiable. If the Bible offers illustrations of individuals who have persisted in sin for a lengthy period of time, the theory of the saints' perseverance is simply wrong. No amount of special pleading that these are simply "descriptions of the failure of one man" rather than the "teaching" of Scripture will do. If one man who is born again fails to persevere in holiness, then the Scriptures cannot teach that *all* who are born again will persevere in holiness.

In fact, not just one or two passages describe such failing believers. Scores of them are seen in both the Old and New Testaments. One such illustration would be sufficient to falsify the Reformed doctrine of perseverance, but the existence of many of them leaves the theory in shreds.

SPIRITUAL DULLNESS

A central passage in the New Testament on the subject of the carnal Christian is Hebrews 5:11-14. The writer has just referred to the Melchizedekian priesthood of Jesus Christ when he realizes that the spiritual state of his hearers prevents him from explaining it in detail:

> *Concerning him, we have much to say, and it is hard to explain, since you have become dull of hearing (5:11).*

They had "become" dull. That is, they were not always so. They had fallen from a former state. There are two Greek words for "dull." The first is *bradus*, which simply means "slow." It is a person who is not to blame for his dullness, and so he has no moral fault. But the word used here is *nōthros*. This word means slowness of perception due to moral laxness or irresponsibility.[1676] It goes much deeper and reflects a moral deficiency. In classical Greek it was used as an epithet for the mule who stubbornly refuses to obey.

> *For though by this time you ought to be teachers, you have need again for someone to teach you the elementary principles of the oracles and you have come to need milk and not solid food (5:12).*

> *For everyone who partakes only of milk, is not accustomed to the word of righteousness, for **he is a babe** (5:13).*

[1675] See, for example, Chrisope, *Jesus is Lord: A Study in the Unity of Confessing Jesus as Lord and Saviour in the New Testament.*

[1676] Richard Chenevix Trench, *Synonyms of the New Testament*, reprint ed. (Grand Rapids: Wm. B. Eerdmans Publishing Co., 1953), 382.

> *But solid food is for **the mature**, who because of practice have their senses trained to discern good and evil (5:14).*

Here, one of the chief characteristics of the "carnal" (*nōthros*) Christian is persistence in sin for a period of time, the very thing many Experimental Predestinarians say cannot happen in the life of a Christian. The contrast in these verses is not between Christians and non-Christians, but between the "babes" in Christ and the "mature" (5:13-14). The writer of Hebrews wants them to move from infancy to maturity.

In a popular commentary one popular Bible teacher has suggested that "the maturity being called for in Hebrews 5:14 is not that of a Christian's growing in the faith, but of an unbeliever's coming into the faith—into the full-grown, mature trust and blessing of the new Covenant."[1677] However, *nowhere* else in the Bible is the movement from death to life described as a movement from infancy to maturity. This is indeed a novel way of maintaining the Experimental Predestinarian interpretation of Hebrews! The contrast between the infant (Gr *nēpios*, 5:13) and the mature (Gr *teleios*, Hebrews 5:14) is elsewhere between the immature and the mature Christian and never between the non-Christian and the Christian (Ephesians 4:13-14).

The writer mentioned above bases this on the fact that the biblical writer wants his readers to become "mature," and the Greek word *teleios* in its verb form, *teleioō*, is used in 10:1 and 10:14 of perfect positional sanctification (that which is received at salvation). However, in Hebrews 5:14, *teleios* refers to maturity and not positional sanctification. The contexts are completely different. In chapter 10, the writer is discussing being qualified to worship by means of the one perfect sacrifice Christ made. In chapter 5, the subject is encouragement to press on to maturity. The mature have been trained by the practice—application of the Word in their lives—such that they can handle the "meat" of the Word and can discern between good and evil. Importing the contextual flavor of the verb *teleioō* in chapter 10 into chapter 5 is another illustration of Barr's illegitimate identity transfer. The meaning of *teleioō* in chapter 10 has as much relevance to the context of chapter 5 as the meaning of the "stock" purchased on Wall Street has to the cattle sequestered on a cattleman's ranch.[1678] The lexicon says that *teleios* in chapter 5 refers to people who are "full-grown, mature, adult."[1679] No instantaneous movement from death to life is in view. Instead, the writer to the Hebrews is urging progress to maturity by the proper exercise of spiritual disciplines over a period of time.

The problem with these Christians has apparently been a willful refusal to grow. They have had time to mature but have chosen not to. The carnal Christian is characterized by:

1. Refusal to grow for a period of time.
2. A lack of skill in the use of the "word of righteousness."
3. Ability to absorb only milk and not solid food.
4. Spiritual dullness because of a lack of "meat."

[1677] John MacArthur, *Hebrews* (Chicago: Moody Press, 1983), 129.

[1678] Another term for such cattle is "stock." This example is suggested by Louw, *Semantics of New Testament Greek*, 34-35.

[1679] BAGD, 817.

These four things would aptly describe a person whose faith is "dead" (James 2:17). The Bible abounds with illustrations of genuine believers who have become carnal Christians, dull of hearing (*nōthroi*).

JACOB'S SONS

We must include the founders of the nation of Israel in our discussion of the permanently carnal Christian. We cannot prove that they were born again, but since God selected them as founders of His people, the burden of proof surely would be on those who deny their regenerate state. Jacob's sons were in a state of willful sin for over eleven years.[1680] They first considered murdering Joseph without any sense of regret (Genesis 37:20-35). Then, at Judah's suggestion, they decided to sell him in the slave trade into Egypt (Genesis 37:27), and then they lied to their father claiming he was killed by a ferocious animal (37:33). They jointly persisted in this lie for eleven years, in the face of their parents' intense grief (37:34-35). Today, if we met a man who claimed to be a Christian, and found out that he had sold his sister into the slave trade, then reported to his parents that she was drowned, pocketed the money, and persisted in this perfidious sin, even in the face of the pain and anguish of the parents, and did nothing to get the sister back and gave no indication of repentance until he was caught, we would, of course, deny he was ever a Christian. Yet this is the state of the born-again sons of Jacob.

COMMUNITY LEADERS

What are we to make of the 250 "well-known community leaders "who had been appointed members of the council" (Numbers 16:2)? These leaders who joined Korah and his associates in the rebellion are called "leaders of the congregation, representatives of the congregation, men of renown" (16:2). They are defined in Numbers 1:16 as the distinguished or illustrious. They were renowned for the wisdom of the age and therefore were called on for consultation in matters of importance pertaining to the tribes. When the people selected them, they perceived them to be "wise, understanding, and experienced men." Moses approved them also, believing them to be "wise and experienced men" (Deuteronomy 1:11-15). Since they had believed on the Lord (Exodus 14:31) and given evidence that their faith was "genuine" by being "wise, understanding and experienced," Experimental Predestinarian criteria for true saving faith seems to have been met. They seem to consist of a national council of a representative character.[1681] They led the nation in the offering of sacrifices (Numbers 7), were set apart for the work of the tabernacle (Numbers 8), and observed the Passover (Numbers 9). These men are evidently the regenerate leaders of the nation! Are we to seriously believe that all these appointed leaders were not really believers in the one true God (and justified by faith), but only pretended to be?

Yet, they "opposed" Moses and Aaron (16:2-3) and "gathered against the Lord" (16:11), and God destroyed all of them (16:30-32).[1682]

1680 Genesis 39 = 1 year + 41:2 = 2 years in prison + 41:30, 53 = 7 years of abundance + 42:3 = 1 year, trips to Egypt for food during the famine and back, etc. = a total of more than 11 years.

1681 For discussion see George Bush, *Notes, Critical and Practical, on the Book of Numbers* (Minneapolis: Klock & Klock, 1981), 19.

1682 For more discussion of their regenerate state and their rebellion, see pp. 539 ff.

SAUL

Saul was clearly regenerate. He was anointed by the Lord as ruler over God's inheritance (1 Samuel 10:1, 24), the Spirit of the Lord had come on him "*mightily*," and he prophesied and had been "*changed into another man*" by means of the Spirit (vv. 6-11). The Spirit of the Lord came on him on one occasion, provoking him to righteous anger (1 Samuel 11:6). He expelled all the mediums and spiritualists from the land (1 Samuel 28:3). Even in his carnality he remembered that God had answered his prayers in the past (1 Samuel 28:15), and he had some faith and inclination to goodness (1 Samuel 24:16-21). He still prayed (1 Samuel 28:6), and he could still repent. All these things would, of course, indicate to the Experimental Predestinarian that Saul was regenerate (1 Samuel 26:21, 25). Yet his continued favor with God was conditioned on his obedience (1 Samuel 12:14, 25). There was the possibility that he would fall away from the Lord. Becoming regenerate was not viewed as a guarantee of his perseverance in holiness.

Now here was a man who met all the conditions which the Experimentalists say are necessary for true salvation. The evidence above shows that he had believed and he had manifested his faith in a life of good works. Yet Saul became carnal. At first, he was repentant, a further evidence, according to Experimentalists, of his regenerate state (1 Samuel 15:24-25). But he became disobedient and forfeited his rulership over the kingdom (1 Samuel 13:13-14). This precisely parallels the experience of the carnal Christian who, like Saul, forfeits his inheritance and will not rule over the kingdom, that is, will not inherit it. He became deceptive (1 Samuel 18:21). He continually persisted in his anger and sin (1 Samuel 18:29). There was no perseverance in holiness. The Lord disciplined him by sending an evil spirit on him (1 Samuel 19:9). Saul murdered the priests of the Lord (1 Samuel 22:17-18). When the writer of Chronicles summarized Saul's life, he said, "*Saul died because he was unfaithful to the LORD; he did not keep the word of the LORD and even consulted a medium for guidance, and did not inquire of the LORD. So the LORD put him to death and turned the kingdom over to David son of Jesse*" (1 Chronicles 10:13-14).

Saul was a regenerate man who became carnal. Furthermore, he persisted in his carnality to the point of physical death. Any doctrine that teaches that all who are regenerate will necessarily and inevitably persevere in a life of good works up to the point of physical death is falsified if only **one** regenerate person fails to do so. The life of Saul obviously falsifies the Experimental Predestinarian theory of perseverance.

BALAAM

Balaam, the wicked prophet of the Old Testament, is a classic illustration of the permanently carnal, regenerate saint. "Balaam became proverbial for the false teacher who, for money, influences believers to enter into relationships of compromising unfaithfulness, is warned by God to stop, and is finally punished for continuing to disobey (Numbers 22:7; Deuteronomy 23:4; Nehemiah 13:2; 2 Peter 2:14–16; Jude 5–12)."[1683]

But was he really regenerate? Opinion is divided. Augustine thought so, but not Irenaeus, Tertullian, or Jerome.[1684] God comes to him and speaks to him, so we might

---

[1683] G. K. Beale, *The Book of Revelation: A Commentary on the Greek Text* (Grand Rapids: Wm. B. Eerdmans Publishing Co., 1999), 249.

[1684] Irenaeus, "Fragments from the Lost Writings of Irenaeus," in *The Ante-Nicene fathers. Translations of the*

conclude that Balaam was in communion with God (Numbers 22:8-9). When God tells him not to go back with the elders of Midian, who wanted him to curse Israel, he says, "The Lord refused to let me go with you" (Numbers 22:13). In his reply to these men, he says, "*I could not do anything, either small or great, contrary to the command of the LORD my God*" (v. 18).

He waits on the Lord "*to find out what else the LORD will speak to me*" (v. 19). Then Balaam disobeyed the Lord and went with the elders anyway, and the Lord sent an angel to block his way (v. 23). Balaam then repented of his sin saying, "*I have sinned, for I did not know that you were standing in the way against me. Now then, if it is displeasing to you, I will turn back*" (v. 34). God meets with Balaam (Numbers 23:4) and "*put a word in Balaam's mouth*" (Numbers 23:5, 16). He stands for the Lord's point of view, refusing to curse Israel, "*How shall I curse whom God has not cursed? And how can I denounce whom the LORD has not denounced?*" (v. 8). He indicates a commitment to obey the Lord by saying, "Must I not be careful to speak what the LORD puts in my mouth?"(v. 12). He was a man "whose eye is opened" (Numbers 24:3) and "who hears the words of God" (v. 4). He blesses Israel as commanded by God in his prophecy from Peor (v. 3-9). Balaam prophesied of the coming Messiah, "*I see him, but not now; I behold him, but not near. A star will come out of Jacob; a scepter will rise out of Israel*" (v. 17).

In Balaam we have a man who swears, "*I could not do anything contrary to the command of the LORD, either good or bad, of my own accord. What the LORD speaks, that I will speak*" (Numbers 24:13). He was finally killed by the Lord's command, along with the other enemies of Israel (Numbers 31:8), apparently having committed a sin unto death. He caused the sons of Israel to trespass in the matter of Peor, possibly by telling them to inter-marry with the Midianites, and as a result a plague came on the congregation of Israel (Numbers 31:16). The Lord refused to listen to Balaam (Deuteronomy 23:5). He was a diviner (Joshua 13:22), and yet he was a prophet of God instructing Balak, the king of Moab that he "might know the righteous acts of the Lord" (Micah 6:5).

While it is true God revealed Himself to unbelievers such as Abimelech, king of Gerar, in Abraham's time (Genesis 20:6-7), a Pharaoh in dreams (Genesis 41:25), and to Nebuchadnezzar in a dream and in visions (Daniel 4:1-18), this does not mean that Balaam was unregenerate. On Experimentalist assumptions, Balaam was a believer, for he believed in Yahweh and sought to obey him while these other men did not. But he was overcome by his carnal desires. He believed God would speak to him directly, and in the following context the communications come by direct revelation from God (Numbers 24:5, 16).

From these references and others Adam Clarke concludes:[1685]

1. "It appears sufficiently evident from the preceding account that Balaam knew and worshipped the true God.
2. That he had been a true prophet, and appears to have been in the habit of receiving oracles from God.
3. That he practiced some illicit branches of knowledge, or was reputed by the Moabites

Writings of the Fathers down to A.D. 325, ed. Philip Schaff (Grand Rapids: Wm. B. Eerdmans Publishing Co., 1962), 15:571.

1685 Adam Clarke, "Numbers," in *Adam Clarke's Commentary* (Albany, OR: Ages Software, 1999), s.v. "Numbers 24:25".

as a sorcerer, probably because of the high reputation he had for wisdom; and we know that even in England, in the fifteenth and sixteenth centuries, persons who excelled their contemporaries in wisdom were reputed as magicians.

4. That though he was a believer in the true God, yet he was covetous; *he loved the wages of unrighteousness.*
5. That so conscientiously did he act in the whole business, that as soon as he found it displeased God he cheerfully offered to return; and did not advance till he had not only the permission, but the authority of God to proceed.
6. That he did seek to find out the will of the true God, by using *those means* which God himself had prescribed, viz., supplication and prayer, and the sacrifice of the clean beasts.
7. That though he knew it would greatly displease Balak, yet he most faithfully and firmly told him all that God said on every occasion.
8. That notwithstanding his allowed covetous disposition, yet he refused all promised honors and proffered rewards, even of the most extensive kind, to induce him to act in any respect contrary to the declared will of God.
9. That God on this occasion communicated to him some of the most extraordinary prophetic influences ever conferred on man.
10. That his prophecies are, upon the whole, clear and pointed, and have been fulfilled in the most remarkable manner, and furnish a very strong argument in proof of Divine revelation."

Balaam was a believer, even though he was a diviner and a conjuror (Revelation 2:14) and loved money (2 Peter 2:14; Jude 11). He was double minded, serving Yahweh on the one hand but coveting the reward Balak offered him on the other. There is no reason to deny that Balaam was regenerate except the prior theological assumption read into these Old Testament descriptions of his character that he could not have been. Why? According to Experimental Predestinarians, the fiction of the perseverance of the saints in holiness to the end of life must be true. This one example falsifies the Reformed view of perseverance.

THE CARNAL WILDERNESS GENERATION

According to Moses, the Jews who left Egypt in the Exodus were believers who worshiped the Lord.

> *And they believed. And when they heard that the Lord was concerned about them and had seen their misery, they bowed down and worshiped (Exodus 4:31).*

They believed in the Lord and as a reflection of it, they worshiped Him. They not only believed and worshiped, but they also put their trust in the Lord and feared Him.

> *And when the Israelites saw the great power the Lord displayed against the Egyptians, the people feared the Lord and put their trust in him and in Moses his servant (Exodus 14:31; cf Jeremiah 2:1-3).*

This is why Paul viewed them as true believers saying:

They were all baptized into Moses in the cloud and in the sea. They all ate the same spiritual food and drank the same spiritual drink; for they drank from the spiritual rock that accompanied them, and that rock was Christ (1 Corinthians 10:2–4).

The psalmist tells us,

Then they believed His words; they sang His praise (Psalm 106:12).

We should say, then, that the Jews of the Exodus generation were believers. They "drank" from the "spiritual rock," that is, they *believed* on Christ. That is not to say every single one of them was born again, but as a group, Moses and Paul declared they were saved people.

Yet this group of saved people displeased the Lord and also developed hardened hearts (Hebrews 3:7-11).

Nevertheless, God was not pleased with most of them; their bodies were scattered over the desert (1 Corinthians 10:5).

They were, "a stubborn and rebellious generation, whose hearts were not loyal to God, whose spirits were not faithful to him" (Psalm 78:8). Can regenerate people be called "evil"? That is what God called the saints of the Exodus generation (Deuteronomy 1:35).

Once again, the Experimental Predestinarian doctrine of the inevitable and necessary connection between genuine faith and a life of good works is falsified. Here is a group of true believers who worshiped, trusted, and feared the Lord but fell away and became disloyal, rebellious, evil, and unfaithful—and they died in that state. Their "bodies were scattered over the desert." They not only fell away from Yahweh; they also persisted in their unfaithfulness to the end of their lives, precisely what the Reformed doctrine says cannot happen.

SOLOMON

1 Kings 1-10 describes Solomon's glory and his dedication to God. The Lord granted his request for wisdom with discernment between good and evil (1 Kings 3:9). His childlike humility (1 Kings 3:7), his intimacy with the Lord (1 Kings 3:11-12), his prayer of dedication (1 Kings 8:23-53), and his God-given wisdom and administration all confirm that he was regenerate. He wrote three books of Scripture, which reveal divine wisdom available only to the regenerate mind.

But beginning in 1 Kings 11, he forsook the Lord. He began to love foreign wives (1 Kings 11:1), even though God had forbidden intermarriage (11:2). These wives turned his heart to "other gods," and his heart was no longer fully devoted to God (11:2). He became an idolater and worshiped the Ashtoreth, the moon-goddess of the Sidonians and female counterpart to Baal, and Molech, the detestable god of the Ammonites (11:5) to whom children were sacrificed in the Valley of Hinnom (*Gehenna*). He did evil in the eyes of the Lord and did not follow the Lord completely (11:6). He kept neither the Lord's covenant nor His decrees (11:11), and he became a worshiper of other gods. God began to bring divine discipline. He removed the kingdom from his house (11:11, 34). He raised up adversaries,

Hadad the Edomite (11:14); Rezon; Hadadezer, king of Zobah; and others (11:23). Solomon tried to kill Jeroboam (11:40). Solomon was unrepentant and in carnality up to the point of his death. The kingdom was split because of his sin (12:1-33).

A popular Jewish legend indicates that he wrote the Song of Songs when he was young, Proverbs when he was middle age, and then fell away and returned and wrote Ecclesiates *when he was old.* Yet the Scriptures specifically say, "*For it came about* ***when Solomon was old****, his wives turned his heart away after other gods; and his heart was not wholly devoted to the* L*ORD his God, as the heart of David his father had been*" (1 Kings 11:4). The writer of 1 Kings summarizes his life saying, "*And Solomon did what was evil in the sight of the* L*ORD, and did not follow the* L*ORD fully, as David his father had done*" (1 Kings 11:6), and "*Now the* L*ORD was angry with Solomon because his heart was turned away from the* L*ORD, the God of Israel, who had appeared to him twice*" (1 Kings 11:9).[1686] No evidence indicates that he repented. In fact, as Solomon grew older, he went farther away from God (1 Kings 11:33).

If we met a man today who had professed faith in Christ, been a well-known spiritual leader for years, manifested incredible divine wisdom and published numerous journal articles and Christian books of high spiritual caliber, we would conclude he was a Christian. If that same man then rejected the Lord and began to worship idols, got involved in witchcraft and the New Age Movement, Experimental Predestinarians would say he was never justified to begin with. Yet this is what happened to Solomon who was a born-again believer in Yahweh. Once again, the Experimental Predestinarian's theory of the saints' perseverance is wrong.

THE KINGS OF ISRAEL AND JUDAH

REHOBOAM. Rehoboam was the son of Solomon and Naamah and was the last king of the united kingdom and the first king of Judah (931-913 BC). Tired of the severe burdens imposed on them by Solomon, the elders counseled him to lighten the load so that the people would follow him (1 Kings 12:6-7). Foolishly, he took the counsel of some young men with whom he grew up and imposed greater burdens (12:8-11). As a result, united Israel split into the northern kingdom of Israel and the southern kingdom of Judah. The true Israel was now in Judah.

At the beginning of his reign, he was obedient to Yahweh (1 Kings 12:24). Rehoboam maintained the worship of Yahweh and the temple services in Jerusalem, and as a result the true followers of Yahweh left the north and migrated to Judah (2 Chronicles 11:13-17). Those who set their hearts on seeking the Lord, the God of Israel, followed the Levites to Jerusalem to offer sacrifices to the Lord (11:16). For three years Rehoboam and his followers "walked in the ways of David and Solomon" (2 Chronicles 11:17).

Yet he abandoned the Lord, possibly because of the influence of his foreign wives and also because of his associations with ungodly youth and his youthful indecisiveness (2 Chronicles 13:7). He allowed pagan worship to prosper in Judah (1 Kings 14:22-24). As a result, Yahweh raised up Shishak to destroy the kingdom. The Chronicler says, "*When the kingdom of Rehoboam was established and strong, he and all Israel with him forsook the law of the* L*ORD*" (2 Chronicles 12:1). If he "forsook" the law of the Lord, that means he

---

1686 For a detailed discussion of Solomon's apostasy see Wayne A. Brindle, "The Causes of the Divisions of Israel's Kingdom " *BibSac* 141, no. 563 (July-September 1984): 230-33.

formerly followed it. So God declares, "*This is what the* Lord *says, 'You have abandoned me; therefore, I now abandon you to Shishak.'*" When the Egyptian king Shishak threatened invasion, Rehoboam listened to God's prophet, Shemiah, repented and humbled himself before Yahweh, and as a result a catastrophe was averted (2 Chronicles 12:6-7). Therefore, the Lord promised that His wrath would not be poured out on Jerusalem through Shishak but that Judah would become subject to the Egyptians so that they might "learn the difference between serving me and serving the kings of other lands" (2 Chronicles 12:8). In summarizing his life the Chronicler wrote, "*He did evil because he did not set his heart to seek the* Lord" (2 Chronicles 12:14).

On Experimental Predestinarian grounds, this man was not regenerate. He believed, he maintained the worship of Yahweh, he obeyed the Lord, he repented, and he humbled himself. Yet he "abandoned" the Lord, and the Lord abandoned him, something Experimental Predestinarians say cannot happen to a truly regenerate person.

Jehu. Jehu was the son of Jehoshaphat and reigned as the 10th king of the northern kingdom of Israel for 28 years (842-815 BC, 2 Kings 10:36). He was appointed as king by the Lord (2 Kings 9:2-3) at the hand of Elisha the prophet (2 Kings 9:1-13). Does God directly anoint unbelievers to rule His people? He stamped out the worship of Baal in Israel (2 Kings 10:10-28).

Yet he continued to worship the golden calves at Bethel and Dan (2 Kings 10:29-31). Jehu was a believer in Yahweh and was appointed to the throne by the Lord's prophet. Because he destroyed Baal worship, "*The* Lord *said to Jehu, 'Because you have done well in accomplishing what is right in my eyes and have done to the house of Ahab all I had in mind to do, your descendants will sit on the throne of Israel to the fourth generation'*" (2 Kings 10:30). He bears all the evidence of being born again, but he did not keep the law "with all his heart." "*Yet Jehu was not careful to keep the law of the* Lord, *the God of Israel, with all his heart. He did not turn away from the sins of Jeroboam, which he had caused Israel to commit*" (2 Kings 10:31). This man's life proves that the Experimental Predestinarian refusal to acknowledge the differing categories of believers presented in Scripture is simply ill-informed. Here, we have a believer who did not keep the Law of the Lord "with all his heart." He was a carnal believer.

Joash. That a king can be a follower of the Lord, genuinely saved, and yet compromise in aspects of his reign is a repeated refrain in the books of Kings and Chronicles. For example, "Joash *did what was right in the eyes of the* Lord *all the years Jehoiada the priest instructed him*" (2 Kings 12:2). For 23 years during this time, "*he did what was right in the eyes of the* Lord" (2 Chronicles 24:2), for he was under the influence of the devout priest, Jehoiada. Yet after Jehoiada died, the princes of Judah came to Joash and asked for greater freedom in worship, and Joash granted their request (2 Chronicles 24:16-18). After idols and Asherim were set up all over the country, God sent a prophet, Zechariah, to warn the king. Because Joash had "forsaken the Lord," Zechariah said, "he has forsaken you" (2 Chronicles 24:20).

Joash responded by having Zechariah stoned. God brought judgment on him by bringing the army of Aram, leaving Joash severely wounded and his army defeated (2 Chronicles 24:24). His own officials conspired against him and killed him while he lay in his bed. He reigned from 878 to 838 BC. Here is an example of a regenerate man who did what was right in the eyes of the Lord for 23 years, but who then, like Solomon, abandoned the Lord and was subjected to the sin unto death. Experimental Predestinarians and Neonomians will say, "Well, the fact that he abandoned the Lord, is proof that he never knew the Lord in a saving sense to begin with." That, however, is a theological premise read into the text and would not arise in the mind of a ninth century BC Israelite unfamiliar with Calvin's response to the Catholic Counter-Reformation, twenty-three centuries later.

AMAZIAH. Amaziah, who reigned over Judah for 29 years, "*did what was right in the eyes of the LORD*" (2 Kings 14:3). Yet, he did not do it "*as his father David had done*." In fact, he never removed the high places, and he allowed the people to continue to offer sacrifices there (2 Kings 14:4). The Chronicler says that though he did what was right in the eyes of the Lord, he did not do it "wholeheartedly" (2 Chronicles 25:2). He turned away from following the Lord and apparently persisted in it unto death. Had he reversed himself, his fortunes would have been changed (2 Chronicles 25:27). This further establishes the doctrine that there are two categories of regenerate saints, those who wholeheartedly do what is right in the eyes of the Lord and those who do not, in contradiction again, to Experimental Predestinarian doctrine. Azariah, another king of Judah, "did what was right in the eyes of the Lord," yet he did so incompletely because he too allowed the people to continue to offer sacrifices "at the high places" (2 Kings 15:3-4). As a result, the Lord afflicted him with leprosy until the day he died. He was a permanently carnal believer (2 Kings 15:5).

UZZIAH. King Uzziah did what was right in the eyes of the Lord (2 Chronicles 26:4) in the early years of his reign. Around 767 BC he became the 10th King of Judah. "*He sought God during the days of Zechariah, who instructed him in the fear of God. As long as he sought the LORD, God gave him success*" (2 Chronicles 26:5). So here is a king who did what was right in God's eyes, who sought the Lord and who feared the Lord. But, in another falsification of Experimental Predestinarian doctrine, when he became powerful, because of pride he fell into sin (2 Chronicles 26:16) and became unfaithful to the LORD. As a result, while he was burning incense in the temple, which was a ministry reserved only for the Levites, he was struck with leprosy on his forehead (2 Chronicles 26:19-20). He had leprosy until he died, lived in a separate house, and was excluded from the temple of the Lord. The rulership of his kingdom was given to Jotham, his son.

ASA. A classic illustration of a regenerate man who falls into permanent carnality and dies in that condition is Asa, the third king of the southern kingdom, Judah (956–916 BC) and Rehoboam's grandson. The first ten years of his reign were prosperous and peaceful (2 Chronicles 14:1). Experimental Predestinarians must admit that he was clearly regenerate, for we are told that "*Asa did good and right in the sight of the LORD his God*" (2 Chronicles 14:2). As further evidence of his regenerate state, the Chronicler attests that he "*commanded Judah to seek the LORD*" (2 Chronicles 14:4). He removed the high places and introduced many reforms (14:5; 15:8).

When the country was in danger he

> *Called to the LORD his God, and said, "LORD, there is no one like you to help the powerless against the mighty. Help us, O LORD our God, for we rely on you, and in your name we have come against this vast army. O LORD, you are our God; do not let man prevail against you" (2 Chronicles 14:11).*

> *He sought the Lord with all his heart and soul and his heart "was fully committed to the LORD all his life" (2 Chronicles 15:17).*

However, as his life wore on, he began to waver in his trust in the Lord (2 Chronicles 16:7). When God's prophet, Hanani, rebuked him for trusting in men rather than God, Asa became angry and put him in prison. Also, Asa at this time began to brutally oppress his people (2 Chronicles 16:10). In his later years, he became severely ill with gout, and yet "*even in his illness he did not seek help from the LORD, but only from the physicians*" (2 Chronicles 16:12). He died in his carnality. Once again, the Experimental Predestinarian assumption that those who are truly regenerate will persevere in a life of holiness to the final hour is shown to be false.

In contrast to these kings (Rehoboam, Jehu, Joash, Amaziah, Uziah, and Asa), Hezekiah "*did what was right in the eyes of the LORD*" (2 Kings 18:3), "removed the high places, and smashed the sacred stones and cut down the Asherah poles" (18:4). Here, we have what Experimental Predestinarians say do not exist, two classes of believers, carnal and spiritual. At the beginning they believed, and did what was right in the eyes of the Lord, but in the end they fell into permanent carnality. Therefore, according to Experimental Predestinarians they were never saved in the first place. However, this kind of argument brings a theological premise into the story that would never have occurred to the contemporaries of these disobedient believers who were not familiar with post-reformation polemics.

LOT

Lot was called "just" (Gr *dikaios*, "righteous") by Peter (2 Peter 2:7). Had Peter not said this, we probably would not have thought Lot was saved. He willingly entered a corrupt city, choosing Sodom where the men were "wicked and were sinning greatly against the LORD" (Genesis 13:12-13). He offered his own daughters for the sexual pleasures of its inhabitants in order to save his guests from a homosexual attack (Genesis 19:8). The last mention of him in the Bible is when he was old, and drunk with wine, his decadent daughters slept with him (Genesis 19:33). To maintain the false notion that believers inevitably persevere in holiness, John Gerstner says that Lot's "daughters had to trick him into drunkenness" in order to involve him in incest.[1687] Lot was not exactly the kind of fellow one would want for a neighbor. That said, it appears that Abraham considered him morally righteous (Genesis 18:23-32) and Peter describes him as "godly" (v. 9). While Lot's behavior cannot be cited as a decisive refutation of the Reformed doctrine perseverance, his moral failures certainly prove that true faith does not always result in a life of works.

TWO CATEGORIES OF BELIEVERS

Although Experimental Predestinarians are offended by the concept and consider it unbiblical, the Bible explicitly describes two categories of believers. We are told, as mentioned above, that King Hezekiah walked before the Lord with a "whole heart" (2 Kings 20:3), but Amaziah "did what was right in the sight of the Lord yet not with a whole heart" (2 Chronicles 25:2). Of Solomon it is said, "For when Solomon was old, his wives

[1687] Gerstner, *Wrongly Dividing the Word of Truth: A Critique of Dispensationalism*, 221.

turned his heart away after other gods; and his heart was not *wholly devoted* to the LORD his God, as the heart of David his father *had been*" (1 Kings 11:4). From this we learn that there are regenerate saints who are wholly devoted to the Lord, like David, and those who are not, who like Solomon finished his life worshiping Baals. Jehu was "not careful to walk in the law of the LORD, the God of Israel, with all his heart" (2 Kings 10:31). Some believers are careful to walk in the Law of the Lord with all their hearts, and some are not. So according to the Bible there are two classifications of Christians: those who follow the Lord wholeheartedly and those who do not, precisely what the Experimental Predestinarians say is fiction.[1688]

In the New Testament Paul teaches the same thing. Instead of referring to those who follow the Lord wholeheartedly and those who do not, he refers to the two categories of Christians as vessels for honor and for dishonor.

> *Now in a large house there are not only gold and silver vessels, but also vessels of wood and of earthenware, and some to honor and some to dishonor. Therefore, if a man cleanses himself from these things, he will be a vessel for honor, sanctified, useful to the Master, prepared for every good work (2 Timothy 2:20–21).*

In 1 Corinthians 3:15, Paul speaks of two kinds of Christians, those who produce works of gold, silver, and costly stones, and those who produce works of wood, hay, and straw. The latter are called to cleanse themselves (2 Timothy 2:21). Experimental Predestinarians customarily understand this as a "call to conversion" and "the division of true and false believers."[1689] But the call to saving faith is not a call to cleanse oneself from sin; it is a call to believe on Christ for eternal life. Paul is addressing believers who have gone astray and asking them to amend their ways and seek forgiveness within the family. Lea and Griffin are correct,

> *In using the expression "articles ... of gold and silver," Paul referred to worthy, commendable Christians. In using the expression "articles ... of wood and clay [2 Timothy 2:20]," he spoke of unworthy Christians, who were to be avoided. Paul was suggesting that the church contained both faithful and unfaithful believers; some served for desirable ends, and others accomplished shameful ends.*[1690]

SALTLESS

> *You are the salt of the earth; but if the salt has become tasteless, how can it be made salty again? It is no longer good for anything, except to be thrown out and trampled underfoot by men (Matthew 5:13).*

Salt had many uses in the ancient world. It was a seasoning for food (Job 6:6; Colossians 4:6), and it was associated with purity (Exodus 30:35; 2 Kings 2:19-22). Newborn babies were rubbed down with it for a cleansing (Ezekiel 16:4). It was also considered a

---

1688 Two categories of Christians are also taught in 1 Corinthians 8:11, the weak and the carnal. Paul refers to the carnal man, who is arrogant through his superior spiritual knowledge and who thus ruins his weaker brother. In so doing, he sins against Christ (8:12).

1689 For example, Philip H. Towner, *The Letters to Timothy and Titus*, New International Commentary on the New Testament (Grand Rapids: Wm. B. Eerdmans Publishing Co., 2006), 543.

1690 Thomas D. Lea and Hayne P. Griffin, *1, 2 Timothy, Titus*, New American Commentary (Nashville: Broadman & Holman, 2001), 218.

preservative. It is difficult to know exactly how salt in the life of the believer is an analogy. However, Christianity has been a preservative for civilization.[1691]

Because the chemical nature of salt is stable, the exact nature of this proverb has been problematic. Possibly, the salt in view here is what is derived from the Dead Sea by evaporation. The residue is impure and contains other minerals. Thus, salt becomes "saltless" when it "acquires easily a stale and alkaline taste"[1692] because of the presence of these foregoing elements. Apparently, believers can lose their saltiness and as a result are "no longer good for anything." The word translated "tasteless" (Gr *mōros*, "dull, sluggish, stupid, foolish") in its verbal form means to play the fool, to become foolish, or of salt to become tasteless, insipid (Mark 9:50).[1693]

Furthermore, they can then be "thrown out" into the alleys and trampled on like garbage (Matthew 3:13). The foolish man is the failed Christian. It seems quite likely that the "foolish man" who built his house on sand (Matthew 7:24-27) and the five "foolish" virgins (Matthew 25:1-13) are pictures of the same lifestyle portrayed here. Both were salt, that is, believers, who became saltless, foolish.[1694] As a result, they are "thrown out and trampled underfoot by men."

The saltless metaphor is most likely a metaphor for uselessness. The negative consequence suggests the negative assessment of a useless and wasted life at the Judgment Seat of Christ when "saltless Christians" will lose their reward (2 John 8) and draw back in shame from Christ. At that time saltless Christians will be shamed (1 John 2:28); be judged for the "bad" they have done (2 Corinthians 5:10), and lose what they have been given (Mark 4:25). These are Christians whose faith is not vital, living, and productive (i.e., it is dead), whose faith lacks the energizing influence of good works (James 2:14) and is "useless" for sanctification (James 2:20).

Vincent suggests this historical background:

> *A merchant of Sidon, having farmed of the government the revenue from the importation of salt, brought over a great quantity from the marshes of Cyprus — enough, in fact, to supply the whole province for many years. This he had transferred to the mountains, to cheat the government out of some small percentage of duty. Sixty-five houses were rented and filled with salt. Such houses have merely earthen floors, and the salt next to the ground was in a few years entirely spoiled. I saw large quantities of it literally thrown into the road to be trodden under foot of men and beasts. It was "good for nothing."*[1695]

When the salt becomes mixed with impurities, it loses its savor. When Christians allow their lives to be mixed with "dirt," they become saltless. The supposed inevitable and

---

1691 See the extensive documentation of this fact in Schmidt, *Under the Influence: How Christianity Transformed Civilization.*

1692 Friedrich Hauk, "ἅλας," in TDNT, 1:228. It is interesting to see how one Experimental Presdestinarian commentator misquotes Hauk to imply that the gypsum which is mixed with the salt is then mistaken for the salt itself. Thus the reference is (supposedly) not to salt, but to gypsum which is said to have lost it saltiness, Hagner, *Matthew 14-28*, 99.

1693 WPNT, s.v. "Matthew 5:13."

1694 Suggested by Betz and Collins, *The Sermon on the Mount: A Commentary on the Sermon on the Mount, Including the Sermon on the Plain (Matthew 5:3-7:27 and Luke 6:20-49)*, 159.

1695 Marvin R. Vincent, *Word Studies in the New Testament* (Grand Rapids: Wm. B. Eerdmans Publishing Co., 1946), 1:38-39.

necessary connection between genuine faith and a life of good works is refuted by this passage alone.

How do Experimental Predestinarians respond? Some argue that the salt here refers to the Pharisees! Others say that when salt loses it flavor this refers to "those who were trained in the knowledge of the truth but who then resolutely set themselves against the exhortations of the Holy Spirit and become hardened in their opposition [and] are not renewed unto repentance (Matt. 12:32; Hebrews 6:4–6)."[1696] This of course is mere assertion; an assertion that flatly contradicts the text. The disciples, that is, "*you*," can "*become*" saltless. What was at one time salt can *become saltless*.

Others simply avoid the issue. Craig Blomberg, for example, while avowing that the reference to being trampled on by men "neither affirms nor denies anything about eternal security," nevertheless states that "believers who fail to arrest corruption become worthless agents of change and redemption."[1697]

LEAST IN THE KINGDOM (MATTHEW 5:19)

In Matthew 5:19 we read, "*Whoever then annuls one of the least of these commandments, and so teaches others, shall be called least in the kingdom of heaven.*" The man in this verse is "in" the kingdom, but he not only disobeys even the least of the commandments (possibly the teaching of the sermon to follow),[1698] but he actively teaches others to the do the same! In other words he actually causes little ones to stumble (as in Matthew 18:6), but he is saved, he is "in" the kingdom! To teach others something that is contrary to what God has said is the ministry of a false prophet. Yet these false prophets are "in" the kingdom. Thus, while we agree that a carnal Christian without works is a monstrosity, Shepherd's statement that "Faith alone justifies but a justified person with faith alone would be a monstrosity which never exists in the kingdom of grace,"[1699] contradicts the teaching of Christ. Clearly, such monsters can exist "in" the kingdom of God.

THE CARNAL CHRISTIAN (1 CORINTHIANS 3:1-4)

In no uncertain terms Paul makes it clear that it is possible for true believers to "*walk like mere men*" (1 Corinthians 3:3), something Experimental Predestinarians say cannot happen. Of course they insert the qualifier, "for a limited period of time but not for the rest of their lives." If that is so, why, then, is it possible for one's life work to be burned up at the Judgment Seat of Christ (1 Corinthians 3:15)? How is it possible that a believer can persist in known sin up to the point of physical death (1 Corinthians 11:27-30)?

In dealing with this passage it is common for Experimental Predestinarians to create a straw man regarding what the Partner position actually teaches. For example, Carson believes that those who disagree with him introduce "an ontological distinction in the congregation."[1700] Ontological? With this he caricatures his opponents as believing there

---

1696 Hendriksen and Kistemaker, *Exposition of the Gospel According to Matthew*, 283.

1697 Blomberg, *Matthew*, 102.

1698 "Thus, the phrase 'the least of these commandments' refers to the final and full meaning of the law, but taken up and interpreted by Jesus." Hagner, *Matthew 14-28*, 108.

1699 Shepherd, "Justification by Faith Alone," 88.

1700 Carson, "Reflections on Christian Assurance," 8.

is a category of Christians whose *very essence* is carnal; that is, there is an "absolute, qualitative disjunction between those who are carnal and those who are spiritual." Having been involved in the Free Grace movement for many years, I am unaware of anyone who believes this. Then Carson goes on to give the "true" meaning of 1 Corinthians 3 by asserting that the carnal man in this chapter is not ontologically different, but his behavior, not his essential being is carnal. Since this is precisely the Partner position, it is not clear where Carson derived his opinion of the Partner viewpoint. He gives no documentation.

But by "carnal" Carson adds an additional nuance. The carnal Christian in 1 Corinthians 3, he says, is not "someone who made a profession of faith at an evangelistic rally, followed the way of Christ for a few months, and then lived in a manner indistinguishable from that of any pagan for the next fifteen years, despite conscientious pastoral interest."[1701] However, we insist that if he appears at the Judgment Seat of Christ, then he *is* a believer. Carson is arguing in a circle. He "knows" this man cannot be a believer because the Reformed doctrine of the perseverance in holiness is true.

Apparently, Carson thinks that the Partners believe that anyone who makes a superficial commitment at an evangelistic rally and then lives like a pagan for fifteen years is a Christian. Supposedly, this is the Partner view of carnality. What we do say, and what Carson does not believe, is that a carnal person *may* be a believer, but only God knows his heart. Carson thinks fifteen years of carnal behavior would be sufficient to demonstrate that this man was not a genuine believer. Why not ten, or five, or how about one year? For how long would this man's carnality have to endure before Experimental Predestinarians would feel free to announce that he was definitely not a Christian?

The Partner interpretation is that 1 Corinthians 2:14–3:4 describes three categories of Christians: the spiritual (mature) Christian (2:14), the immature Christian (3:1, "babes in Christ"), and the carnal Christian (3:3). There is also an "ontological distinction" between the "natural man" who is an unbeliever, and the three types of Christians who are believers.[1702]

FALL OF A RIGHTEOUS MAN

> *But if a righteous man turns from his righteousness and commits sin and does the same detestable things the wicked man does, will he live? None of the righteous things he has done will be remembered. Because of the unfaithfulness he is guilty of and because of the sins he has committed, he will die (Ezekiel 18:24).*

Ezekiel clearly states that it is possible for a "righteous man," a justified man, to do "the same detestable things that a wicked man does." Once again, the Experimental Predestinarians are refuted by the clear meaning of the text. Arminians, understandably, view this as strong evidence that a regenerate person can indeed lose his salvation, that is, "die."

But of course their view depends on the contextual usage of the word "die." Does the prophet have eternal or temporal death in view? The context clearly favors a temporal calamity and not an eternal forfeiture of salvation. The man who lends money on interest

---

1701 Ibid.

1702 For more detail on this view see Stanley D. Toussaint, "The Spiritual Man," *BibSac* 125, no. 498 (April-June 1968): 139-46.

and takes increase, will he live? He will not live! He has committed all these abominations, he will surely be put to death; his blood will be on his own head (Ezekiel 18:13).

The death in view here is a temporal calamity; eternal destiny is not in question at all. "Life," on the other hand, is not regeneration in this instance but a rich walk with God based on obedience. Life comes to the person who does not oppress anyone, who gives bread to the hungry (Ezekiel 18:7), who does not lend money on interest, and who walks in God's statutes and ordinances (v. 9). The man who does these things "will surely live" (v. 9). Since life in the sense of regeneration comes on the basis of faith alone, we are justified in concluding that the prophet has life in the sense of physical life or spiritual vitality in view. Its opposite, death, is not loss of salvation but physical death or spiritual impoverishment.

Here is a regenerate man who fell into sin, who did the same things the wicked do, and who persisted in sin up to the point of physical death. This directly contradicts the central thesis of the Experimental Predestinarian position.

1 CORINTHIANS 5

An extreme case of the "consistently carnal Christian" is found in 1 Corinthians 5:5. Apparently, a member of the congregation was involved in an incestuous relationship with his stepmother (5:1)! Paul hands this carnal Christian over to physical death, but he notes that he will be saved at the day of the Lord Jesus.

> *I have decided to deliver such a one to Satan for the destruction of his flesh, that his spirit may be saved in the day of the Lord Jesus (NASB).*

In describing this incestuous brother and other immoral Christians like him, some have emphasized the NIV translation which describes him as one "who calls himself a brother" (1 Corinthians 5:11). The implication, of course, is that this man is not truly a regenerate person; he only claims to be.[1703] This meaning, however, is very unlikely. This man is contrasted with the heathen in 5:1 and with those of the world and "those outside the church" in 5:12 (cf. 5:9-10, 12-13). He is, therefore, being contrasted with non-Christians and not equated with them. His similarity to them is in his behavior.

Also, in no other New Testament passage does the Gr word *onomazō* ("called") carry the sense of doubt as to whether the person being "named" is something other than what he is called.[1704] Of course, that does not mean it *cannot* mean "so-called" in this passage, but there is no contextual reason that requires this. Regardless of the theological difficulties involved, the exegetical data is on the side of the view that a regenerate man is in view. Indeed, if it were not for the Experimentalist's theological problems, it probably would not be doubted.

[1703] G. G. Findlay, *St. Paul's First Epistle to the Corinthians*, ed. W. Robertson Nicoll, reprint ed., The Expositor's Greek Testament (Grand Rapids: Wm. B. Eerdmans Publishing Co., 1967), 2:813.

[1704] Did Jesus doubt that those He "designated" (*onomazō*) apostles really were (Mark 3:14)? Of course, one of the apostles was not regenerate, Judas, but he was truly an apostle. Did the Jews in their attempts to drive out evil spirits invoke the "so-called" name of Jesus (Acts 19:13)? When Paul says he wants to preach the gospel in places where Christ is not known (*onomazō*), did he imply that Christ may have been known but he was not sure (Romans 15:20)? Is Jesus far above every "so-called" title that can be given as if there is some doubt about the validity of these titles (Ephesians 1:21)? Is the Father's family only "named" His family but is not really His family (Ephesians 3:15)? Is Paul concerned only about a "so-called" hint (*onomazō*) of immortality among the Ephesians or a real and actual hint (Ephesians 5:3)?

We are told that this man was turned over to Satan for the *destruction of his flesh* "*that his spirit*" might be "*saved on the day of the Lord*." The phrase is difficult to interpret. The Greek is *hina* ("in order to") plus a verb in the subjunctive mood, which normally expresses a purpose clause. In fact, in the other uses of this phrase with structure using the word "save" in Paul's writings, it is a purpose clause (e.g., 1 Corinthians 9:22; 10:33; 1 Thessalonians 2:16). However, this translation yields a very difficult sense in 1 Corinthians 5:5. How can a man be turned over to Satan for the purpose that he will be delivered from damnation at the final hour? A possible explanation is that the turning over to Satan is remedial in nature. It is sometimes pointed out that this was God's purpose in allowing Satan to afflict Job. Paul himself viewed his thorn in the flesh as a messenger of Satan that God used to keep him humble (2 Corinthians 12:7). In fact, there is a specific parallel in 1 Timothy 1:20 where Hymenaeus and Alexander were turned over to Satan for a remedial purpose that they would learn not to blaspheme. If this is the sense, then the passage means: "Turn him over to Satan for the divine discipline in order that through this disciplinary process he might be humbled and repent of his sins and be saved at the day of the Lord."

However, there is a problem with this view. While a turning over to Satan for remedial purposes is found in the Bible, this verse specifically says that this turning over is not for instruction but for destruction! Nowhere else does Paul speak of the destruction of the flesh as being a humbling of the sinful nature.[1705] In the three other uses of this word "destruction" (Gr *olethros*), something final and sometimes eternal is in view.[1706] In those examples it does not take a remedial sense.[1707] Indeed, such a thought is without parallel in the New Testament. Isn't this reading too much into the text?

Probably, the main reason for taking this passage in a remedial sense is the presence of the purpose clause, "in order that." The purpose of this "turning over" is for the sinner's ultimate salvation. This would seem to require an additional assumption that this turning over was intended to bring about the repentance and ultimate salvation of the sinner. However, this is not likely because this man is probably viewed as regenerate already, and, in any case, Satan's "ministry" here is specifically declared *not* to be remedial but that of physical destruction. Is there another option?

Another possibility is that the salvation in view is corporate, not individual. In other words, Paul's point is that they must remove this yeast from the congregation so that the public testimony of the church is not ruined.[1708] Because a little yeast can leaven the whole dough (1 Corinthians 5:6), the salvation of the church is in view. This is cleaning out the old yeast, which in this interpretation is the destruction of the flesh, the self-centered orientation of the Corinthians (note their "arrogance" in v. 2). "The spirit to be saved is not that of the offender but the corporate life of the church lived in union with God

---

1705 Contra Fee who says, "What Paul was desiring by having this man put outside the believing community was the destruction of what was 'carnal' in him, so that he might be 'saved' eschatologically," that is, go to heaven when he dies. See Fee, *The First Epistle to the Corinthians*, 212. Thistelton understands "destruction of the flesh" to mean "the 'fleshly' *stance of self-sufficiency*" and not the sin nature per se, "Hell," in *Dictionary of Biblical Imagery*, ed. Leland Ryken, Jim Wilhoit, and Tremper Longman (Downers Grove, IL: InterVarsity Press, 2000), 396.

1706 See 1 Thessalonians 5:3; 2 Thessalonians 1:9; 1 Timothy 6:9.

1707 Arndt and Gingrich say that the passage refers to the physical death of the sinner and not a remedial activity (BAGD, 566).

1708 Barth Lynn Campbell, "Flesh and Spirit in 1 Cor 5:5: An Exercise in Rhetorical Criticism of the NT," *JETS* 36, no. 3 (1993): 331-42.

through the Holy Spirit. The apostle desires that life to be preserved and thus found intact in the Day of the Lord. Thus it will be saved."[1709] The formal acceptance of gay marriage in some denominations today makes this warning very relevant.

Another view suggests that the salvation of the individual is in view, but the salvation is to be equated with a rich entrance into His presence (Mark 8:35). This would be a reference to the "saving of a soul" and 2 Peter 1:11, which speaks of an "abundant" entrance into the kingdom if the individual responds to this "destruction" of his sinful ways by repenting.

A final option notes that the use of *hina* plus the subjunctive in a sense of *result*, though questioned by some, occurs in some passages in the New Testament. For example, in Romans 11:11 Paul says of Israel, "*Did they stumble so as to fall beyond recovery?*" They did not stumble for the purpose of falling beyond recovery, but that was the *result* of their stumbling.[1710] There are several clear illustrations in the Pauline literature of *hina* followed by a verb in the subjunctive mood with a sense of result.[1711]

If this is the correct meaning, then the verse would be rendered, "Hand this man over to Satan, so that his body ("flesh") may be destroyed, with the result that [*at least*] his spirit will be saved on the day of the Lord." This has the advantage of taking *olethros* in its normal sense of total ruin, "flesh" in a very common sense (physical body), and requires that nothing be read into the passage at all. In fact, it explains nicely the contrast between flesh and spirit. His body will be destroyed (the sin unto death), but his spirit will be saved. Furthermore, this fits well into the well-known New Testament teaching of a sin to physical death (e.g., in the same epistle, 1 Corinthians 11:30).

All in all, this seems to be the most plausible interpretation of the apostle's meaning, and it does not require a reading of secondary ideas into the passage. It emerges simply from the words themselves. Here, then, is another example of a carnal Christian who might persist in his carnality to the point of physical death. Even though he will not persevere in a life of good works to the final hour, his spirit will be saved when the Lord returns. Fortunately, in this instance the man repented and was returned to fellowship. We will see him in heaven.[1712]

RECEIVING THE GRACE OF GOD IN VAIN

As is well known, Paul was quite concerned about the carnality of many within the Corinthian church. At one point he wonders if their justification (1 Corinthians 6:11), reconciliation (2 Corinthians 5:18), and enjoyment of the gifts of the Holy Spirit will come to nothing. He says,

> *And working together with Him, we also urge you not to receive the grace of God in vain (2 Corinthians 6:1).*

1709 Ibid., 340.

1710 See also John 6:7; Luke 1:43; Galatians 5:17.

1711 For example, Romans 3:19; 11:11; 15:32; 1 Corinthians 7:29; 2 Corinthians 1:17; Galatians 5:17; and 1 Thessalonians 5:4.

1712 Keith Krell has come to a similar conclusion. For thorough discussion of the various viewpoints, see Krell, *Temporal Judgment and the Church: Paul's Remedial Agenda in 1 Corinthians*, 110-26.

On Experimentalist premises, this statement is perplexing. According to them the receipt of personal salvation can never ultimately come to nothing, yet Paul seems to be worried that this could happen to the Corinthians. They had received the grace of God, they were saved, and yet their moral life might come to nothing (Gr *kenos*). The adjective refers to "fruitlessness and inefficacy."[1713] As Thrall notes, Paul fears "that their moral lives might in the end become a contradiction and rejection of the divine grace bestowed upon them."[1714] In light of Paul's emphasis on the Judgment Seat of Christ (2 Corinthians 5:10-11) it is likely that ultimately to receive the grace of God in vain means that "it has not produced the desired results."[1715] Barrett is correct, "It is no forgone conclusion that all will cease to live to themselves and live henceforth for Christ."[1716] Thus, we have two categories of Christians: those who receive the grace of God with the desired result and who consequently will be rewarded at the Judgment Seat of Christ, and those who receive the grace of God without the desired result of final perseverance.

UNDISCIPLINED, LAZY, BUSYBODIES

Paul instructed the church at Thessalonica not to associate with certain "brothers" who disobeyed his instructions.

> *For we hear that some among you are leading an undisciplined life, doing no work at all, but acting like busybodies. Now such persons we command and exhort in the Lord Jesus Christ to work in quiet fashion and eat their own bread. But as for you, brethren, do not grow weary of doing good. And if anyone does not obey our instruction in this letter, take special note of that man and do not associate with him, so that he may be put to shame. And yet do not regard him as an enemy, but admonish him* ***as a brother*** *(2 Thessalonians 3:11-15).*

GALATIANS

Can a Christian lose his joy (Galatians 4:15)? Yes! Can a Christian count an apostle as his enemy (Galatians 4:16)? Yes! Can Christians put themselves under the law (Galatians 4:21), fall from the grace-way-of-life, and become alienated from Christ (Galatians 5:4)? Yes! Is it possible for a Christian to use his freedom in Christ to "indulge the sinful nature" (5:13)? Yes. If it were not possible, there would be no point in warning them not to do something they could never do. Christians can "destroy" each other by their biting and devouring of each other (5:15). Christians are capable of expressing the fruits of either the flesh or of the Spirit. The works of the flesh are warned against (Galatians 5:21). If they persist in them, they will not inherit the kingdom. If there is no possibility of their living like this, why warn them against it?

1713 NIDNTT, 1:547.

1714 Margaret E. Thrall, *A Critical Exegetical Commentary on the Second Epistle of the Corinthians*, International Critical Commentary (New York: T&T Clark, 2004), 452. Experimental Predestinarian writer, Simon Kistemaker, says "An inactive response to God's word is worthless and unprofitable." Yet according to his theology in a "true" Christian there can never be an "inactive response" leading to that which is "worthless and unprofitable." Simon J. Kistemaker and William Hendriksen, *Exposition of the Second Epistle to the Corinthians*, New Testament Commentary (Grand Rapids: Baker, 2001), 209-10.

1715 Martin, *2 Corinthians*, 166.

1716 Barrett, *A Commentary on the Second Epistle to the Corinthians*, 183.

Now if Christians can do all these things, how are they to be distinguished from the carnal Christian, which many Experimental Predestinarians say does not exist?

If a Christian sows to please his flesh, he will reap destruction: divine discipline, possibly physical death, and certain loss of reward (Galatians 6:8). If he sows to please the Spirit, he will reap eternal life. When eternal life is put in the future, as it is here, it is often viewed as something earned, that is, a reward.[1717]

JOHN 2:23

Many people saw the miraculous signs and *episteusan eis to onoma autou* ("believed on His name"). Yet Jesus would not *episteuen auton autois* ("entrust Himself to them") because He "knew all men." While some have called this "spurious" faith,[1718] this concept of believing on His name is used throughout John for saving faith. In fact, the first usage of the phrase in the book contradicts the view that it refers to a spurious faith.

> *Yet to all who received him, to those who* ***believed in his name****, he gave the right to become children of God—children born not of natural descent, nor of human decision or a husband's will, but born of God (John 1:12-13).*

> *Whoever believes in him is not condemned, but whoever does not believe stands condemned already because he has not* ***believed in the name*** *of God's one and only Son (John 3:18).*

The phrase *pisteuō eis*, "believe in," is John's standard expression for saving faith. One believes "on Him" or "in His name."[1719] When Calvin[1720] says that they did not have true faith but were only borne along by some impulse of zeal which prevented them from carefully examining their hearts, he is therefore flatly contradicting John's consistent usage in the rest of his writings. This illustrates "theological exegesis."

Martin Lloyd-Jones falls into the same error. He feels that those who "believed in His name" "did not truly believe in Him. They gave a kind of intellectual assent, they seemed to believe in Him; but He knew that they had not believed in Him in reality, and that is why He did not commit Himself to them."[1721] He cites John 6:60-66, where Jesus says there were some disciples "that believe not" and concludes that this explains the people in John 2:25. But isn't this directly contradicting the very words of John? John tells us that in John 2, contrary to the unbelieving disciples in John 6, these people specifically *did* believe. On what authority does Lloyd-Jones say they did not? How else could John say it if his intent was to indicate saving faith? Nowhere in the New Testament are adverbs, such as "truly" or "really" ever used to modify "believe" in a soteriological context. These adverbs are frequently inserted in front of the word "believe" in Experimental writings in order to sustain the fiction of the final perseverance of the saints in holiness to the final hour.

The fact that these believers became believers in response to signs in no way requires that their faith was superficial. John makes it clear that he believes that signs are *a* cause that

---

[1717] See chapter 17, "Inheriting Eternal Life."

[1718] Carson, *The Gospel According to John*, 184.

[1719] See John 6:40; 7:39; 8:30; 10:42; 11:25, 26; 12:11.

[1720] Calvin, "Institutes," 3.2.12.

[1721] Lloyd-Jones, *Romans Chapter 8:17-39: The Final Perseverance of the Saints*, 282.

may lead to faith, and he would be most perplexed to read in many modern commentaries that a faith that is generated in response to signs is not genuine. *"Jesus did many other miraculous signs in the presence of His disciples, which are not recorded in this book. But* ***these are written that you may believe that Jesus is the Christ,*** *the Son of God, and that by believing you may have life in His name"* (John 20:30-31). In fact, John viewed a lack of response to signs as sinful rebellion! *"Even after Jesus had done all these miraculous signs in their presence, they still would not believe in Him"* (John 12:37). John would never reject a faith based on signs; in fact, he would applaud it! However, it is true that a more mature faith, a more virtuous faith, does not rest on visible signs (John 20:29).

What then does it mean that "Jesus was not entrusting Himself to them?" Debbie Hunn cites several examples from the first century which suggest that "entrusting oneself to another, then, in the examples known in the Greek of John's day, referred not to disclosure of truth, intimacy, or belief in the sayings of another, but to personal security."[1722] This idea nicely fits the context of John 2:24. After driving out the traders from the temple, Jesus for the first time announced His coming death (John 2:18-22).

Others see the expression as suggesting that He chose not to become "intimate" with them as in John 15:14-17.[1723] After the departure of Judas, the Lord turns to the disciples and says, "You are my friends if you do what I command" (John 15:14). Friendship with Christ is *not* a free gift; it is conditional. The result of such friendship is that Jesus commits Himself to His friends. He does this in the sense of imparting to them additional truth. *"I no longer call you servants because a servant does not know his master's business. Instead, I have called you friends, for everything that I learned from My Father I have made known to you"* (John 15:15). When Jesus says He did not commit Himself to them, there is no need to conclude they were unregenerate. Rather, it means He was not their friend and did not reveal to them additional truths learned from the Father.

The text does *not* say, "Many *said* they believed in his name." *John* says they *"believed in his name."* The word "believe" followed by "in the name" occurs only two other places in the Gospel of John. In John 1:12, it says the ones who believe in His name are children of God, and John 3:18 states that one who believes in His name is not condemned. In the only other places in the New Testament where "believe" is followed by "in the name," saving faith is indicated. In John 3:24, God commands people to believe in the name of Jesus, and 1 John 5:13 states that believing in the name of Jesus gives assurance of having eternal life.[1724]

JOHN 12:42

Many of the leaders among the Pharisees *episteusan eis auton*, "believed on Him," and yet they refused to confess their faith for fear of being put out of the synagogue (John 12:42). This technical term for saving faith proves they were born again. Even so they had not submitted to the Lordship of Christ or persevered in a life of good works. In fact, *"they loved the praise of men more than praise from God"* (12:43). If one did not "know"

1722 Debbie Hunn, "The Believers Jesus Doubted: John 2:23-25," *TJ* 25, no. 1 (Spring 2004): 19-21.

1723 Zane C. Hodges, "Problem Passages in the Gospel of John: Untrustworthy Believers," *BibSac* 135, no. 538 (April 1978): 146-47.

1724 See Hunn, "The Believers Jesus Doubted: John 2:23-25," 17.

before he came to the text that it is impossible for regenerate people to be characterized by such behavior or attitudes, he would assume John 12:42 applies to true Christians. Only a theological system can negate the consistent usage of this phrase in John. Could not these hypocritical Pharisees, these secret Christians, be called "carnal Christians"? Similarly, it is written of Joseph of Arimathea, at the time of Christ's burial, that he "*was a disciple of Jesus, but secretly because he feared the Jews*" (John 19:38-42).

CHRISTIANS WHO HAVE NO PART WITH CHRIST

Two kinds of Christians are referred to by the Lord in John 13:8:

> *Peter said to Him, "Never shall You wash my feet!" Jesus answered him, "If I do not wash you, you have no part with Me" (NASB).*

> *He who has bathed need only to wash his feet, but is completely clean (John 13:10).*

Jesus refers to Christians who are "bathed" (Gr *louō*), who are "completely clean," that is, regenerate (Titus 3:5). But a bathed, regenerate person sometimes needs washing (Gr *niptō*). In fact, if he does not go through this washing (*niptō*) he has no part with Christ. To wash (*niptō*) means to wash in part, and to bathe (*louō*) means "to wash all over."[1725] The former refers to cleansing from daily sin by confession (1 John 1:9), whereas the latter refers to regeneration. Christ teaches here that, if a person who has been bathed refuses daily washing, he will have no part with Him. This is what is meant by a carnal Christian.

SIMON MAGUS

Under the preaching of Philip, a sorcerer named Simon Magus believed and was baptized (Acts 8:13). In addition, "he continued on with Philip." According to Luke, if a man believes and is baptized, because he believed, he is saved (Acts 2:38; 16:31-33). Experimental Predestinarians say that Simon Magus could not have been saved because he did not persevere. Over one hundred years ago James Inglis forcefully rejected this view:

> *Those who regard Simon as a hypocrite must own, that on the supposition that he was a true believer, it would have been impossible to state it more plainly than in the language of the passage, which records not merely the fact of his public profession of the faith, followed by the natural evidence of his sincerity, but the express testimony, "Simon himself believed also."*[1726]

The gift of the Holy Spirit, however, was delayed in Samaria until Peter and John arrived. When the Spirit was given, apparently the external manifestations which Simon saw motivated him to try to purchase the gift of being able to impart the Holy Spirit by the laying on of hands (8:18). Because of his sin, the apostle Peter responds:

> *May your silver perish with you, because you thought you could obtain the gift of God with money! You have no part or portion in this matter, for your heart is not right before God.*

1725 Trench, *Synonyms of the New Testament*, 161-62.

1726 James Inglis, "Simon Magus," *Waymarks in the Wilderness* 5(Spring 1867): 35-50. Reprinted in JOTGES 2 (Spring 1989): 45-54.

Therefore repent of this wickedness of yours, and pray the Lord that if possible, the intention of your heart may be forgiven you. For I see that you are in the gall of bitterness, and in the bondage of iniquity. But Simon answered and said, "Pray to the Lord for me yourselves, so that nothing of what you have said may come upon me" (Acts 8:20-24).

What was Simon's sin? It was selfish ambition. "Give this authority to me as well, so that everyone on whom I lay my hands may receive the Holy Spirit." Peter concluded that he wanted to buy the power to pass on the gift of the Holy Spirit with money and that his heart was not right with God. Surely the presence of prideful ambition is not a basis for concluding that a man is not saved! Who among us has not at one time or another been tempted in this way? Unholy rivalries and ambitions often plague relationships between true Christians. To say the presence of this sin invalidates the claim to regeneration is unrealistic.

The punishment for Simon's sin is that he will "perish." This refers to physical death. His money is to perish with him, and the perishing of his money is obviously temporal. This is another illustration of the sin unto physical death.[1727] If Simon repents, "perhaps" he will be forgiven. But there is no "perhaps" in the gospel offer to the unregenerate. "Believe in the Lord Jesus Christ, and thou shalt be saved," not "perhaps thou shalt be saved." There is uncertainty, however, as to whether the divine parent will punish (and how severely) His sinning child in the course of time. Often the intent of family discipline is accomplished best by listening to the cry of the erring child.

Here is a man who believed and was baptized and who, for a while, continued with Philip (Acts 8:13), thus entering into discipleship. And yet he became carnal. It is important to note that both the Samaritans and Simon "believed" (vv. 12-13). If the former were saved, on what basis can one argue that Simon was not? Luke makes the point regarding Simon very emphatic, "Even Simon himself believed; and after being baptized, he continued on with Philip."[1728]

Peter warns him that he may perish (die physically) in such a state if he does not repent. Peter is therefore holding out the possibility of failing to persevere to the end of life.

CHRISTIANS WHO SLEEP

Paul rebukes the Corinthians because many of them were coming to the Lord's Table drunk and as a result many were ill and some were asleep (1 Corinthians 11:29-32). To "sleep" (Gr *koimaō*) was the Christian term for death.[1729] The passage speaks of rebellious believers who were drunks, who apparently failed to respond to other forms of divine discipline ("illness"), and whom God eventually took to be with Him. That is the meaning of sleep. Remember, the theory of the saints' perseverance requires that all regenerate people will necessarily continue in a life of good works until the final hour. If one person who is regenerate fails in this, then the theory must be wrong. Here was a group of people who failed and persisted in their failure up to physical death.

[1727] See also 1 Corinthians 8:11, where the perishing of the weaker brother has the same effect. See elsewhere in this book, pp. 545 ff.

[1728] For good discussion of this passage, see Chay and Correia, *The Faith That Saves: The Nature of Faith in the New Testament*, 54-58.

[1729] See Acts 7:60; 1 Corinthians 15:51; 1 Thessalonians 4:13-17.

Another use of " sleep" (but using a different word) is found in Paul's words to the Thessalonians:

> *For God has not destined us for wrath, but for obtaining salvation through our Lord Jesus Christ, who died for us that **whether we are awake or asleep** [Gr katheudō], we may live together with Him (1 Thessalonians 5:9-10).*

The wrath in this context is the tribulation wrath of the day of the Lord (5:2-3). The references to being "awake" and "asleep" do not refer to being alive and dead but, rather, to being watchful for our Lord's return or being indifferent to it. The word for sleep (*katheudō*) differs from the word for sleep in 1 Corinthians 11:30, which refers to death. Earlier in 1 Thessalonians 4:14, when referring to physical death, he used the word *koimaō*. *Katheudō* often has an ethical connotation[1730] in the New Testament and always does in every other use in Paul,[1731] but *koimaō* never does:[1732]

> *So then let us not sleep as others do, but let us be alert and sober. For those who sleep do their sleeping [Gr katheudō] at night, and those who get drunk get drunk at night (1 Thessalonians 5:6-7).*

Jesus used the same word, *katheudō*, in a similar context in the parable of the doorkeeper (Mark 13:33-37). Like the exhortation in 1 Thessalonians 5, the exhortation is to spiritual watchfulness in contrast to "sleep" in view of the uncertainty of the Lord's return:

> *Take heed, keep on the alert; for you do not know when the appointed time is. It is like a man, away on a journey, who upon leaving his house and putting his slaves in charge, assigning to each one his task, also commanded the doorkeeper to stay on the alert. Therefore, be on the alert—for you do not know when the master of the house is coming, whether in the evening, at midnight, at cockcrowing, or in the morning—lest he come suddenly and find you asleep [katheudō]. And what I say to you I say to all, "Be on the alert!" (NASB).*

Apparently Paul has this same parable in mind in 1 Thessalonians 5 when he warns them about the sudden and unexpected nature of the Lord's return (5:2), tells them to be alert (5:6), and warns them against sleeping (*katheudō*), or spiritual insensitivity.[1733] The opposite of spiritual insensitivity is to be awake (Gr *grēgoreō*). This is the verb Paul uses of spiritual alertness in 5:6 ("be alert"), and it is the same word he uses as the opposite of

---

[1730] Matthew 13:25; Mark 13:36.

[1731] Ephesians 5:14; 1 Thessalonians 5:6, 7.

[1732] See BAGD, 438.

[1733] Tracy Howard objects. He feels that Paul's selection of *katheudō* is due to an unintentional, unnatural repetition of a word or phrase that was used naturally in the immediately preceding context. He acknowledges that to use *katheudō* for physical sleep would be contradictory to the preceding context. Paul used *katheudō* instead of *koimaō* because *koimaō* was still on Paul's mind when he wrote verse 10. See Tracy L Howard, "The Meaning of 'Sleep' in 1 Thessalonians 5:10 - A Reappraisal," *GTJ* 6, no. 2 (1985): 342. However, this kind of reasoning seems to be completely negated by the fact that Paul obviously has the parable of the doorkeeper in his mind, and that the parable, with its use of *katheudō* as spiritual insensitivity, would have a far more determinative force in his selection of words. *Katheudō* was the word his Lord used in describing the same situation, namely spiritual insensitivity at the second advent!

katheudō in 5:10. Had Paul intended *katheudō* to refer to physical death in 5:10, he would have used the usual word for physical life, *zaō*, as its opposite.[1734]

Some object that such a view of 5:10 negates the ethical exhortation in the preceding context. The meaning is something like this: "Although I desire you to maintain spiritual alertness in view of the imminent *Parousia*, Jesus died so that whether or not we are spiritually alert, we might still live with Him."[1735] However, abhorrent this may be to those steeped in experimental ways of thinking, this is precisely the teaching of the New Testament and is in complete harmony with the rest of Scripture, as this book has been attempting to show. The Bible does teach in numerous places that there are believers who will be with the Lord whether they are vigilant or not. The motivation for vigilance is to be found in the desire to hear the Master say, "Well done," and the fear of disapproval when He returns. The sudden and unexpected nature of the Lord's return can leave believers unprepared and shrinking away from Him in shame at that day. Paul knows that and his readers know that. We may safely assume that the general teaching of the apostle on this subject had already been imparted to them as to them as it was to other churches. It is possible to take the grace of God for granted, and that is the very thing about which he is warning them!

This passage contradicts the theory of the saints' perseverance to death because it declares that sleeping carnal Christians will live together with Christ. However, the sleeping Christian is the carnal Christian, the one who is indifferent to the Lord's return, who is spiritually insensitive, and who spends his time in drunken hedonism.[1736]

ACCEPTING ANOTHER GOSPEL?

> *For I am jealous for you with a godly jealousy; for I betrothed you to one husband, so that to Christ I might present you as a pure virgin. But I am afraid that, as the serpent deceived Eve by his craftiness, your minds will be led astray from the simplicity and purity of devotion to Christ. For if one comes and preaches another Jesus whom we have not preached, or you receive a different spirit which you have not received, or a different gospel which you have not accepted, you bear this beautifully (2 Corinthians 11:2-4).*

Here is a group of people who have been betrothed "*to one husband*." They are true believers, "professing" but also "possessing." Paul wants to present them as a pure virgin at the Judgment Seat of Christ. But he has some concerns. He fears that:

- Their minds will be led astray from devotion to Christ.
- They might receive a different spirit (probably a "worldly" spirit).

1734 For this reason, Hogg and Vine insist that the passage teaches that whether believers are spiritually alert or not, they will all live with the Lord. They say, "*Gregoromen* is not used elsewhere in the metaphorical sense of 'to be alive' and as *katheudō* means 'to be dead' in only one place out of two-and-twenty occurrences in N.T., and never elsewhere in Paul's epistles, there does not seem to be sufficient justification for departing from the usual meaning of the words, i.e., vigilance and expectancy as contrasted with laxity and indifference" C. F. Hogg and W. E. Vine, *The Epistle to the Thessalonians* (Grand Rapids: Kregel Publications, 1952), 172.

1735 This is Howard's phraseology (Howard, "The Meaning of 'Sleep' in 1 Thessalonians 5:10 - A Reappraisal," 344.)

1736 For a discussion of a view similar to that taken here, see Thomas R. Edgar, "The Meaning of 'Sleep' in 1 Thessalonians 5:10," *JETS* 22, no. 4 (December 1979): 345-49.

- They might receive a different gospel.
- They might accept this easily and with no sense of guilt or conviction ("you bear this beautifully"—Paul is being sarcastic).

According to the Experimental Predestinarian, no true Christian could be characterized by these four things. One receiving a different gospel is "accursed," by which they mean "damned" (Galatians 1:6-7). A worldly spirit is one devoid of power, love, joy, peace, patience, kindness, goodness, faithfulness, gentleness, and self-control (1 Corinthians 2:4-5; Galatians 5:22–23). Experimental Predestinarian Simon Kistemaker admits, "Now the people are in danger of accepting a different gospel. They can hear the echo of Galatians 1:6–7, where Paul writes, 'I am astonished that you are so quickly ... turning to a different gospel—which is really no gospel at all.'"[1737] If it is possible for Christians to embrace another gospel, fall away from the faith, fall into worldliness, and do so with no sense of guilt or conviction, how can the Experimental Predestinarian's doctrine of the denial of the carnal Christian have any basis in fact? The initial Galatian reception of the gospel is a virtual synonym for a salvation experience. Luke, as well as Paul, refers to the way in which the Thessalonians "*received the word with great eagerness*" (Acts 17:11). This was a salvation experience. When Luke argues to prove that the salvation of the Samaritans (Acts 8:14) and the Gentiles (Acts 11:1) was a genuine experience of the Holy Spirit (and not a superficial one), he says that it was similar to that at the outpouring of the Holy Spirit at Pentecost (see Acts 11:15-18). He says that they "received the word." Luke equates it with saving faith when he refers to the conversion of the three thousand at Pentecost, noting that they had "*received His word.*" Surely most would agree with Link when he says, "In the early Christian communities the phrase *ton logon dechesthai*, to receive the word, became a technical term for *the believing acceptance of the gospel.*"[1738]

Luke 8:11-15—The Four Soils

The parable of the four soils presents four differing responses to the gospel. Experimental Predestinarians and Arminians are once again united in their belief that only the person represented by the fourth soil, the one who produces fruit, will ultimately arrive in heaven. They believe this because they "know" that justification and sanctification are always united and therefore the first three soils could not possibly be saved people. The difference is that the Calvinist maintains that the first three soils were never born again in the first place, while the Arminian maintains that the rocky soil and that which was choked by thorns were both saved and then lost their salvation.

In the following discussion I will argue that there are three categories of people mentioned in this parable, the nonbeliever ("those by the road"), the carnal Christian ("those on the rocky soil," and "those which fell among the thorns"), and the mature fruit-bearing Christian ("the seed in the good soil").

In Matthew, chapters one through twelve, Jesus presents Himself to Israel as her Messiah. In the twelfth chapter an official delegation is sent by the religious leaders to

[1737] Kistemaker and Hendriksen, *Exposition of the Second Epistle to the Corinthians*, 362.

[1738] H. G. Link, "Take," in NIDNTT, 3:746. He cites Luke 8:13; Acts 8:14; 11:1; 17:11; and 1 Thessalonians 1:6 and 2:13 as proof.

inspect His claims. Their conclusion: He is a demon from hell! (Matthew 12:24). A natural question arises. If Jesus is truly the Messiah, how do you explain this rejection by His own people? The parables of Matthew 13 seem to be given to answer this question. The first one faces it squarely. The reason for this rejection is that there are various responses to the gospel message, depending upon the heart condition of the recipient.

Once again John Murray is typical of those holding to the Reformed view of the parable.[1739] Murray defines apostasy as falling away from a profession of faith and not from true faith.[1740] He supports his doctrine of a false faith from this parable. The man on rocky ground (the second soil) is, according to Murray, a man with false or temporary faith. He is a mere professor but not a true possessor of Christ. Facing the difficulty of his position directly, Murray says:

It is possible to give all the outward signs of faith in Christ and obedience to him, to witness for a time a good confession and show great zeal for Christ and his kingdom and then lose all interest and become indifferent, if not hostile, to the claims of Christ and of his kingdom. It is the lesson of seed sown on rocky ground—the seed took root, it sprang up, but when the sun rose it was scorched and brought forth no fruit to perfection.[1741]

Murray ruins his argument when he acknowledges that "there is not only germination; there is growth." How can there be growth and germination if there is no regeneration, new life? Murray explains this as a result of the nearness of the "supernatural forces that are operative in the kingdom of God." This is Calvin's old doctrine of temporary faith.[1742]

> *The scripture itself, therefore, leads us to the conclusion that it is possible to have a very uplifting, ennobling, reforming, and exhilarating experience of the power and truth of the gospel, to come into such a close contact with the supernatural forces which are operative in God's kingdom of grace that these forces produce effects in us which to human observation are hardly distinguishable from those produced by God's regeneration and sanctifying grace and yet be not partaker of Christ and heirs of eternal life.*[1743]

Confusion abounds in every phrase. There is no scriptural evidence of which the writer is aware that a non-Christian can experience all the supernatural changes and hardly be distinguishable from Christians. Unless, of course, these two passages teach it (Luke 8:11-15; Hebrews 6). Unfortunately for Murray's reasoning, that is the very point in

---

1739 John Murray, *Redemption Accomplished and Applied* (Grand Rapids: Eerdmans, 1955), pp. 151-53.

1740 He cites John 8:31-32 to prove that the only true disciple is the one who continues to the end. We agree. But, as discussed in chapter 8, a disciple is not the same as a Christian. All disciples are Christians, but not all Christians are disciples, as John 8:31-32 proves! He also refers to Matthew 10:22, "He who endures to the end will be saved." Murray does not discuss whether or not "save" means "to deliver from hell" or "preserve physical life" or "salvation/reward at the Judgment Seat of Christ." Neither does he discuss his assumption that all Christians are disciples. Since these are the very points at issue, his argument is specious. He also cites Hebrews 3:14 as proof that endurance in the faith is the only evidence of the reality of the faith. But as demonstrated in vol. 1, chapter 11, this passage refers to loss of a Christian's participation in the messianic partnership, the final destiny of man. He quotes John 15:6 and misconstrues it as a test of whether or not a man is truly saved instead of an issue of fruit bearing among those who are saved. See discussion in chapter 39 below.

1741 Murray, *Redemption—Accomplished and Applied*, 152.

1742 He cites Hebrews 6:5-6 as proof. But those enlightened, etc., in Hebrews 6, as discussed in vol. 2, chapter 41, are true Christians.

1743 Murray, *Redemption—Accomplished and Applied.*

question! The subjects of Hebrews six seem to be Christians, and it would be questionable to deny the same status to those who have "germinated and grown," that is, been regenerated. There is nothing in the parable to suggest that this experience of germination and growth was not really germination and growth but only an appearance of it. Isn't this reading a theological view into the parable unsupported by the plain statements of our Lord?

Not only did the individual represented by the rocky soil germinate and grow, but we read that he "*received the word with joy*" (Luke 8:13). This can hardly be the description of a superficial profession based on emotion.[1744] Elsewhere in the New Testament receiving the word with joy often refers to saving faith (e.g., 1 Thessalonians 1:6). In fact, "joy" (Gr *chara*) is never used in the New Testament of a superficial and insincere excitement. For Luke it is joy the Shepherd (the Father) feels at finding one of His lost sheep (Luke 15:5ff.), the joy of true Christians because their names are written in heaven (10:20), and the joy of the disciples after the ascension (24:52).

Furthermore, for Luke and the other gospel writers, the phrase "*receive the word*" is a virtual synonym for a salvation experience. Luke, as well as Paul, refers to the way in which the Thessalonians "received the word" with great eagerness (Acts 17:11). This was a salvation experience. When Luke argues to prove that the salvation of the Samaritans (Acts 8:14) and the Gentiles (Acts 11:1) was a genuine experience of the Holy Spirit (and not a superficial one), similar to that experienced with the outpouring of the Holy Spirit of Pentecost (see Acts 11:15-18), he says that they "received the word." Luke equates it with saving faith when he refers to the conversion of the three thousand at Pentecost, noting that they had "received His word." Surely most would agree with Link when he says, "In the early Christian communities the phrase *ton logon dechesthai*, to receive the word, became a technical term for *the believing acceptance of the gospel*."[1745]

Luke tells us that in regard to the first soil the devil came and took the word away lest he should believe and be saved (8:12). In contrast to this the second soil did believe and was therefore saved. The meaning of "believe" in v. 12 is clearly "saving faith." Why should the meaning in the next verse be changed to "false faith"? The fact that he only believed "for a time" in no way denies that he was truly regenerate, unless one knows before he begins his exegesis that the Experimental Predestinarian doctrine of perseverance is true!

Sellers is impressed with the fact that the parable says in v. 13 that they "*have no root*."[1746] The rendering of the NASB, however, more correctly catches the sense, "they have no *firm* root." The intent of the phrase is probably not to suggest there was no root at all but only that it was not firm enough and deep enough to sustain a life of perseverance. That is the central point of the parable (Luke 8:15). Anytime there is germination and growth, there must of necessity be some root to the plant. This is simply a fact of botany. The Lord's point is that those represented by the second soil believe, are saved, and then fall away due to testing. But all of this is beside the point. The evidence of life in a plant has nothing to do with the presence or absence of a firm root system. The presence of life is indicated by germination and growth.

[1744] Geldenhuys, *The Gospel of Luke*, 244.

[1745] H. G. Link, "Take," in NIDNTT, 3:746. He cites Luke 8:13; Acts 8:14; 11:1; 17:11; and 1 Thessalonians 1:6 and 2:13 as proof.

[1746] Sellers, *Election and Perseverance*, 85.

If one were to argue that the passage teaches the absence of a root and that the root indicates being soteriologically implanted into Christ, then he must reckon with the fact that in Matthew 13:29 the saved person can be uprooted, that is lose his salvation. But if the root means deeply grounded and walking in close intimacy with Christ, then both the root and the possibility of it being uprooted are easily explained. To use Paul's phrase, they are not "*rooted* (Gr *rizoō*) *and grounded in love*" (Ephesians 3:17; cf Colossians 2:6-7).

In Matthew's version we are told that the man represented by the first soil "does not understand" (Matthew 13:19). In contrast, the fruit-bearing believer, the fourth soil, does understand and produces a crop. Does the fact that it is not said that the second and third soil understand mean that the person represented here had not believed or had not experienced any joy? While some have argued this way, such a conclusion is unwarranted. We might as well ask: Does the fact that the fourth soil is not said to have "received the word with joy" mean that he had not believed or had no joy? Does a parable have to say everything about each man? Is it not probable that a man who receives the word with joy and believes (Luke 8:13) has understood the meaning of the gospel and rejoiced in it even if the text does not specifically state that he understood? Is it possible to believe the gospel and yet not understand the gospel? Nowhere are we told that the second or third seeds represent those with no understanding. It appears that little can be made of this one way or the other.

The issue in the parable is fruit bearing (Luke 8:8), and progression to maturity (8:14), and not just salvation. But from what did he fall? There is not a word about heaven and hell in the parable. The most plausible interpretation of the phrase is simply to fall away from that progression which leads to maturity, to fruit bearing, and become a dead and carnal Christian.

	NON BELIEVER	CARNAL CHRISTIAN	MATURE CHRISTIAN
Parable of the Sower (Luke 8:12-15)	By the wayside (8:12)	Rocky and thorny soils (8:13-14)	Good soil (8:15)
Exhortation to Corinthians (1 Cor. 2:14-3:3)	Natural man (2:14)	You are still carnal (3:3)	You who are spiritual (2:14)

The good fruit comes from lives which hold on to the Word of God and which persevere. Falling away is not the same as losing one's salvation. Instead it means to fall from being "rooted," that is, falling from walking in intimacy with Christ.

Summary

Obviously something is amiss with a doctrine that cannot account for many contradictions to its main tenet, the impossibility of perseverance in carnality. But the problem becomes even more acute when numerous passages describe not only persistent moral carnality by regenerate people but also final apostasy and rejection of the faith altogether.

The argument for the Reformed doctrine of perseverance has been disputed in the previous chapters. Their claim that a regenerate person will necessarily and inevitably persevere in a life of good works is refuted on all counts.

First, they lack any convincing biblical evidence that the Bible teaches this. The passages commonly cited to prove that justification and sanctification are united prove nothing (see chapters 25-28). Second, the Bible specifically warns true Christians about the possibility of failure. We will discuss this issue in some detail in the chapters to follow. These warnings are a mockery, unless the possibility carnality exists, and only the strained theological exegesis can assign them to the unregenerate (see chapters 34-37). Third, the Bible promises assurance now, included in faith itself. Yet the Experimental Predestinarians cannot logically grant assurance before the final hour. Thus their doctrine contradicts Scripture (see chapters 29-31). Finally, the conclusive refutation of the Reformed view is that the Bible cites numerous instances of people who have in fact been born again but who later fell into sin as this chapter has documented. Some persisted in it to the end of life.

33

Apostasy and Divine Discipline

PERSECUTION WAS a common experience in the early church as it is in many countries of the world today. If you lived in the third century AD, how would you respond if you were asked to sacrifice to the emperor, particularly if you knew that simply a pinch of incense sprinkled on the coals of a Roman altar could save your life, family, and property? What would you do if you were put on trial as Bishop Cyprian[1747] was in the middle of the third century?

The proconsul Galerius Maximus ordered Cyprian to be brought before him ....

> Proconsul: "Are you Thascius Cyprianus?"
> Cyprian: "I am."
> Proconsul: "Have you allowed yourself to be called 'father' of persons holding sacrilegious [that is, Christian] opinion?"
> Cyprian: "I have."
> Proconsul: "The most sacred emperors have ordered you to sacrifice [to the emperor as a god]."
> Cyprian: "I will not do it."
> Proconsul: "Have care for yourself ...."
> Cyprian: "Do as you are bid. There is no room for discussion when the issue is so clear."
> Proconsul: "You have lived for a long time holding sacrilegious opinions. You have gathered a large number of accomplices around in your blameworthy conspiracy. You have proved an enemy to the Roman gods and their sacred worship. Nor have the pious and most sacred Emperors Valerian and Gallienus, the Augusti, and Valerian, the noble Caesar, been able to recall you to the observance of their rites. And so since you have been convicted as the instigator and ringleader in most atrocious crimes, you shall be an example to the accomplices in your crime. Your blood shall be shed in accordance with the law."

After saying this, the proconsul read the verdict from his tablet: "We command that Cyprianus be executed by the sword." Bishop Cyprian said, "Thanks be to God."[1748]

[1747] Cyprian was Bishop of Carthage in the middle of the third century. He suffered martyrdom in the persecution of the Emperor Valerian, AD 260. Cyprian is one of the finest characters we meet in the history of the early church; and his letters may still be read with profit.

[1748] Illustration from Christopher Hall, "Rejecting the Prodigal," *Christianity Today* (October 26, 1998): 73.

Cyprian refused to compromise and deny Christ by offering a sacrifice to the Roman gods. He received the "crown of life."

But what about those who lapsed in their faith and offered a sacrifice to the emperor? Experimental Predestinarians would say that such a lapse at the end of life would prove that even if they had faithfully served Christ all their lives, as Cyprian did, this would prove that they had not really been born again.

Within Experimental Predestinarian circles, writers differ in how they treat the possible existence of the carnal Christian. Some would not allow that the Scriptures even teach such a thing. Others would say that a Christian can be carnal but only for a limited period of time. If his carnality continues past this subjective limit, this proves he is not truly a Christian at all. What all agree on, however, is that a Christian will not persist in carnality to the point of physical death and that no Christian can ever commit the sin of public repudiation of his faith in Christ. Had Cyprian done that, this would have proven he was never born again.

In the previous chapter it was seen that the theory of the saints' inevitable perseverance in good works to the final hour is proven false by the many examples of carnality in the Bible. Now, however, we must direct our attention to biblical data that seems to suggest that a Christian can actually commit apostasy as well as be carnal.

Illustrations of Apostasy

APOSTASY OF HYMENAEUS AND ALEXANDER

In some specific cases the possible became actual!

> *Keeping faith and a good conscience, which some have rejected and suffered shipwreck in regard to their faith. Among these are Hymenaeus and Alexander, whom I have delivered over to Satan, so that they may be taught not to blaspheme (1 Timothy 1:19-20).*

These two men had "faith" and "a good conscience," but they rejected both and experienced shipwreck in their faith. The Experimentalists, of course, will simply bring their theological system into the passage and say that the fact they rejected the faith proves they never had "true" faith to begin with.[1749] Once again, however, this is the point in question. The spiritual state of these people must be determined from 1 Timothy 1 and not from a theological system. I. Howard Marshall argues, "The language suggests a violent rejection of the claims of conscience, and the metaphor of shipwreck implies the loss of a faith once held."[1750]

Three things are said about these two men: (1) they had believed; (2) they had given the internal evidence of regeneration in a good conscience; and (3) they needed to be taught not to blaspheme. If it were not for the third point, one would conclude on the premises of

---

[1749] Sometimes this is done by translating the word "their" (Gr *tēn*) as "the." Then the sense is that they became shipwrecked in regard to the objective faith and not in regard to their subjectively appropriated faith. However, the subjective sense agrees better with the previous verse as well as with the stress on faith in the whole book. Supporting "the faith" would also be the phrase *peri tēn pistin* (1 Timothy 6:21 and 2 Timothy 3:8 which seem clearly objective) and *peri tēn alētheian* (2 Timothy 2:18) which is clearly objective. The 2 Timothy passage seems conclusive enough that Hymenaeus was a believer who had gone astray.

[1750] Marshall, *Kept by the Power of God: A Study of Perseverance and Falling Away*, 128.

the Experimental Predestinarian that they were saved people. They had believed, and they had given some initial evidence of it.

However, even the third point paradoxically substantiates the thesis that they are regenerate. When Paul says they must be handed over to Satan, he calls to mind the only other illustration in the New Testament of a man being handed over to Satan, which is recorded in 1 Corinthians 5:5. In that passage a member of the congregation was involved in incest (5:1). However, even though he is obviously carnal, he will be saved in the day of Jesus Christ.[1751]

Hymenaeus and Alexander needed to be "taught" (Gr *paideuō*). In its other usages in the New Testament, this verb is commonly used of the divine chastening or discipline of the regenerate (1 Corinthians 11:32; Titus 2:12-13; Hebrews 12:5-6).

The exegetical evidence seems to present these men as genuine Christians who have fallen away from the faith. Paradoxically, even Martyn Lloyd-Jones acknowledges that these men were saved, but "with respect to their belief, and their statement of their belief, they were in a state of chaos, shipwreck, utter muddle. The apostle does not say they were reprobate; all he says is that they have got in to this indescribable muddle, a shipwreck, a shambles, call it what you will."[1752] We call it a carnal Christian who has denied the faith.

APOSTASY OF HYMENAEUS AND PHILETUS

Hymenaeus is the same individual referred to in 2 Timothy 2:17-19.

> *And their talk will spread like gangrene, among whom are Hymenaeus and Philetus, men who have gone astray from the truth saying that the resurrection has already taken place, and thus they upset the faith of some. Nevertheless, the firm foundation of God stands having this seal, "The Lord knows those who are His," and "Let everyone who names the name of the Lord abstain from wickedness" (NASB).*

These men have "gone astray from the truth," that is, they once held to it. Hymenaeus had such an impact on the faith of some believers that he actually "upset" the faith of some. The Greek word is a bit stronger than "upset." It means to "cause to fall, overturn, destroy."[1753] In direct contradiction to our Lord's words (John 6:39), they asserted that the resurrection had already occurred, and they thereby destroyed the faith of some.

When Paul says, "The Lord knows those who are His," he is not saying that the Lord knows those who are truly regenerate in contrast to those who are not, implying that Hymenaeus was not regenerate. Paul quotes from the LXX (substituting *kurios* for *theos*). The translation of the Hebrew text of Numbers 16:5 reads: "*Tomorrow morning the Lord will **show who is His** and who is holy, and will cause him to come near to Him*" (NKJV). The incident is instructive. Korah led a rebellion against Moses. The point at issue seems to be that Korah felt that since Israel was a community, all were in equal authority, and therefore it was only presumption, not God's appointment, that led Moses to assume the leadership of Israel. Furthermore, Moses had taken away the right of the firstborn of every household to be a member of the priesthood of Israel and had instead invested that right in a branch

---

1751 See discussion in preceding chapter.

1752 Lloyd-Jones, *Romans Chapter 8:17-39: The Final Perseverance of the Saints*, 284.

1753 BAGD, 62.

of his own family, the sons of Aaron,[1754] his brother.[1755] Surely, Korah reasoned, Moses was merely presuming on God.

Three grounds for the revolt are stated (Numbers 16). First, Moses and Aaron had set themselves above the rest of Israel (vv. 3, 13); second, Moses had failed to bring Israel to the Promised Land (v. 14); and third, he and Aaron had arrogated the priesthood to themselves (vv. 7-11). The LXX of Numbers 16:5 reads, *"And he spoke to Korah and all his assembly, saying, God has carefully considered and known* [Gr *ginōskō*] *those that are his and who are holy* (Gr *agios*, prob. "consecrated to the service of God," BDAG. 10), *and has brought them to himself."* The Hebrew text has *yadah* in the hiphil which means "to make known, declare." The idea is, *"The Lord will consider the situation and declare whom He has dedicated to the service" (v. 10, 28).* So when Paul says to Timothy that God "knows" those who are His, Paul is not saying "God knows who is a Christian." He is saying that God acknowledges who His appointed leaders are, and that they are not Hymenaeus and Philetus. We understand that *ginōskō* here means "know, *acknowledge, recognize*."[1756] God recognizes those whom He has appointed for leadership.

If this interpretation is correct, the passage has nothing to do with distinguishing who is saved and who is not, that is, those "known by God" are saved in contrast of the leaders, who are not. Instead, God knows whom He appointed as leaders, and these leaders, like Hymenaeus and Alexander, are saved people who committed apostasy against God and His appointed leaders, that is, Moses and Paul.

APOSTASY IN HEBREWS

Apostasy is a real danger, just as the writer to the Hebrews warned in chapter 10:

> *But My righteous one shall live by faith; and if he shrinks back, My soul has no pleasure in him. But we are not of those who shrink back to destruction, but of those who have faith to the preserving of the soul (Hebrews 10:38-39).*

The "preserving of the soul" is a common term for maintaining physical life. It never means "go to heaven when you die."[1757] Instead of experiencing "destruction," they will "live." The word "destruction" (Gr *apōleia*) is the common term for "loss" or "destruction" in secular Greek.[1758] It is not a technical term for eternal damnation. Sometimes it means "waste" (Mark 14:4) and sometimes "execution" (Acts 25:16).[1759] The context (Hebrews 10:26-38) refers to the possible execution of judgment in time on the sinning Christian. The judgment may include physical death or even worse (10:28). To avoid the possibility of experiencing physical death as a result of sin (discipline resulting in ruin of one's physical life), one must persevere in faith. The danger is that he will not. And if that occurs, that is, if "he shrinks back," then God will have no pleasure in him. This is an understatement (litotes), for "God will be very angry with the Christian who behaves this way."

[1754] See Numbers 3:10.

[1755] Moses and Aaron were both Levites and were brothers (Exodus 7:1).

[1756] BDAG, 200, 7. See John 1:10, "the world did not *acknowledge*" Him.

[1757] For proof, see discussion in vol. 1, chapter 16.

[1758] MM, 73.

[1759] Majority Text.

Apostasy here is not theoretical; it is a real possibility. This is the apostasy of God's "righteous one," the regenerate child of God who has received the imputed righteousness of Christ.[1760]

APOSTASY IN GALATIANS

In Galatians 6:12, Paul refers to those who are true believers who have denied the faith:

> *Those who desire to make a good showing in the flesh try to compel you to be circumcised, simply that they may not be persecuted for the cross of Christ.*

To avoid persecution, these believers denied the cross. Submission to circumcision indicated cessation of faith in Christ (Galatians 2:17-21). In fact, it meant that a believer viewed Christ's death as vain, had severed himself from Christ (Galatians 5:2), had fallen from grace (Galatians 5:4), and was liable to judgment (5:10). To be severed from Christ and to fall from grace logically required a former standing in grace and connection with Christ from which to fall and be severed! Those who are regenerate may possibly deny the faith and forfeit their share in the coming kingdom. There is no need to assume that they lose their salvation, as the Arminian maintains. Rather, as John tells us, "*Watch yourselves that you do not lose what you have accomplished, but that you may receive a full reward*" (2 John 8).

APOSTASY IN THE LAST DAYS

The apostle Paul specifically declares in 1 Timothy 4:1-3 that it is possible for believers to depart from the faith:

> *But the Spirit explicitly says that in later times some will fall away from the faith, paying attention to deceitful spirits and doctrines of demons.*

Now if the Spirit "explicitly says" that apostasy from the faith is possible, by what right do Experimental Predestinarians deny this? These people who fall away are believers and are contrasted with the liars who have a seared conscience (v. 2). These non-Christians led these believers into apostasy. Marshall observes that the use of *aphistēmi* ("fall away") "implies a departure from a position once held and therefore refers to apostasy from the faith by those who once held it."[1761]

DENIAL OF THE FAITH

When a man refuses to care for his household, he has in effect denied the faith:

> *But if anyone does not provide for his own, and especially for those of his household, he has denied the faith, and is worse than an unbeliever (1 Timothy 5:8).*

[1760] The reference to Habakkuk 2:3-4 is more of an allusion than a citation. The writer to the Hebrews has modified it slightly to fit the context of what he wants to say.

[1761] Marshall, *Kept by the Power of God: A Study of Perseverance and Falling Away*, 129.

This verse suggests that it is possible for a Christian to deny the faith and to be worse than a non-Christian. This is an apostasy in life, if not in lips, and therefore equally serious! If it is possible for a believer to be worse than an apostate, then could he not be at least as bad as one as well?

APOSTASY OF WIDOWS

Paul specifically says that some younger widows had departed from the faith and followed Satan:

> *Therefore I want younger widows to get married, bear children, keep house, and give the enemy no occasion for reproach, for some have already turned aside to follow Satan (1 Timothy 5:14-15).*

Of course, this may only mean that they have turned aside from the Christian way of life, not that they finally denied Christ.

APOSTASY DUE TO GNOSTIC DECEPTION

False teachers are often the cause for the departure from the faith by those who are truly regenerate:

> *O Timothy, guard what has been entrusted to you, avoiding worldly and empty chatter and the opposing arguments of what is falsely called "knowledge"—which some have professed and thus gone astray from the faith (1 Timothy 6:20-21).*

Some under Timothy's care in the church had gone astray from the faith. It does no good to argue that they could not have been Christians in the first place because, in counterpoint, Timothy, a Christian, is being warned against this very possibility.

APOSTASY OF DEMAS AND OTHERS

Toward the end of his life, Paul found himself deserted by many of his fellow laborers. Among them were Demas, Phygelus and Hermogenes (2 Timothy 1:15), and a number of unnamed people (2 Timothy 4:16).

Demas, according to Paul, was a "fellow worker" (Philemon 24). He is listed along with Luke as a traveling companion of the apostle (Colossians 4:14). Yet he "deserted" the imprisoned Paul (possibly for bribe)[1762] and went to Thessalonica because he came to a point where "he loved this present world" (2 Timothy 4:10).

In 2 Timothy 2:24-26, Paul refers to those who are "in opposition." Who are they?

> *With gentleness correcting those who are in opposition, if perhaps God may grant them repentance leading to the knowledge of the truth, and they may come to their senses and escape from the snare of the devil, having been held captive by him to do his will.*

[1762] This is based on a questionable reference in the apocryphal Acts of Paul. Florence Morgan Gillman, "Demas," in *The Anchor Bible Dictionary*, ed. David Noel Freedman (New York: Doubleday Co., 1992), 2:134.

While the phrase about repentance leading to a "knowledge of the truth" certainly could refer to the conversion of non-Christians, the parallel usage (Titus 1:1) refers to the knowledge necessary for those who already are Christians, so that they can live godly lives. Furthermore, as Marshall points out,[1763] the parallel passage about being ensnared by the devil clearly refers to believers (1 Timothy 3:7). It appears, then, that the lapse of regenerate people is in view in 2 Timothy 2:24-28. They have fallen from the faith and become opponents of the apostle Paul!

CONCLUSION

Other passages could be cited which establish the fact that true Christians can become carnal and even persist in their carnality up to the point of physical death.[1764] Reference has already been made to the warnings in the New Testament. Each warning implies the possibility of failure, and almost all of them are specifically addressed to regenerate people.[1765]

The Partner's contention is that the combined weight of the warning passages, the passages illustrating the fact of the carnal Christian, and the specific biblical illustrations of apostasy firmly establish the possible existence of the permanently carnal Christian. We maintain that it is obvious that this is true and that only prior adherence to a theological system could possibly yield another result after careful examination of the biblical data.

One simply cannot successfully argue that Scripture guarantees that those who believe will be kept in a state of belief to the final hour. What is guaranteed by Scripture is that God's faithfulness is independent from man's faith. "If we are faithless, He will remain faithful."[1766]

The sense of moral revulsion that God would allow a sinning Christian to enter heaven betrays not only a lack of appreciation for the grace of God in our own lives, as well as those of carnal Christians, but is also the probable motive behind much Experimental Predestinarian exegesis.

SPIRITUAL CONSEQUENCES

Documenting the moral failures above is an unpleasant but necessary chore. Until the possibility of ultimate failure is clear, the warnings against it have little relevance. Equally distasteful is the task of explaining the consequences of carnality, and they are severe indeed. Once a person is born again in Christ, he is now in God's family, and as any human father would do, our divine Father takes a more personal interest in the moral behavior of those who belong to Him than to those who are outside the household of faith. The Scriptures set forth three consequences of sin: discipline, death, and disinheritance.

DIVINE DISCIPLINE

The principle of judgment on believers is found in many passages of the Old Testament (2 Samuel 7:14-15). If Solomon, for example, were to be disobedient, he would be

---

1763 Marshall, *Kept by the Power of God: A Study of Perseverance and Falling Away*, 130.

1764 1 Timothy 5:5-6, 11-15; 2 Timothy 2:22-26; James 1:12-16; Revelation 12:11.

1765 See Chapter 32, "The Carnal Christian."

1766 He remains faithful to His promise to save us, not, as some have incredibly stated, "to condemn us"!

disciplined with "*the rod of men, with floggings inflicted by men.*" This may suggest God would use the instrumentality of men to discipline. But God says that He would not remove His love as He did from Saul. To "remove love" refers to 1 Samuel 13:13-14, where Saul is told that if he had obeyed the Lord, God "would have established your kingdom over Israel for all time. But now your kingdom will not endure." In contrast, the houses of David and Solomon would maintain their right to the throne, that is, would endure, even if David and Solomon disobeyed. This refers not to loss of salvation but to loss of the right to rule. The principle is that discipline results in judgment in time or forfeiture in eternity, but not loss of redemptive salvation from damnation.

In Psalm 89:30-36, God promised to discipline the sons of David if they refused to follow His statutes. But "I will not take my love from him [i.e., I will not deny my promise to establish his throne forever]." In 2 Samuel 12:10-12, God disciplined David. He was to reap what he had sown (Galatians 6:7-8) and would experience punishment worse than death (Hebrews 10:29). God says that He would take his wives and give them to someone close to him and that person would lie with his wives "in broad daylight." David repented of his adultery with Bathsheba and murder of Uriah before the baby was born (2 Samuel 12:13), but God took the baby (one reaps what one sows). The future of the kingdom went downhill with murder and intrigue as a result of his sin with Bathsheba.

In extreme forms it is possible for a true believer to be forsaken by God:

> *And if you seek Him, He will let you find Him; but if you forsake Him, He will forsake you (2 Chronicles 15:2).*

A true believer can forsake God! These words were addressed to Asa, king of Judah. He is a king who led the people in a brief revival. He responded to Azariah's prophecy with faith and good works. He removed the abominable idols from all the land of Judah and rebuilt the altar of the Lord (15:8). He had believed and manifested his faith in actions. He led the people to seek the Lord, and as a result of the fact that they sought the Lord, they were rewarded (2 Chronicles 15:7) and found rest (15:15). Failure to seek the Lord or evidence of forsaking Him resulted in punishment in time (15:12-13), capital punishment. Asa, however, did not continue to seek the Lord and died seeking the help of physicians instead of trusting the Lord to cure his severely diseased feet (16:12).

King Uzziah, mentioned above, fell into sin, and as a result he experienced divine discipline.

Hezekiah was a godly king. He did what was right in the eyes of the Lord (2 Chronicles 29:2; 31:21). Yet, in a moment of pride, he fell into sin. The Lord disciplined him with "wrath." Hezekiah repented of the pride in his heart and as a result the Lord's wrath did not come on Jerusalem (2 Chronicles 32:24-26).

The central passage in the Bible on the subject of divine discipline is Hebrews 12:3-11. Here, we are told that God's purpose in discipline is to correct by punishment. He disciplines us for our good so that we may share in His holiness (Hebrews 12:10). Every child of God will sooner or later experience this. His purpose is always to correct, the definite aim of which is "for our profit that we might be partners of His holiness." Without this holiness "no man will see the Lord" (Hebrews 12:14). To see the Lord means to fellowship with Him. Job, for example, said, "But now my eyes have *seen* you" (Job 42:5).

The parallel is precise. As a result of divine discipline, Job came to "see" the Lord. The writer to the Hebrews, steeped in the Old Testament as he was, apparently had this passage in mind.

THE SIN UNTO DEATH

The second consequence of carnality in the life of a believer is physical death. A number of passages already alluded to suggest that when a believer fails to respond to discipline, God may take him home. For example:

> *My brethren, if any among you strays from the truth, and one turns him back, let him know that he who turns a sinner from the error of his way will save his soul from death, and will cover a multitude of sins (James 5:19-20).*

It is apparently possible for a "brother" who is "among" us to stray from the truth and be in danger of death (cf. Gen. 37:7). Regenerate people are certainly in view here. The reference to covering a multitude of sins is used elsewhere of covering the sins of the regenerate (1 Peter 4:8).

These sheep within the fold have "wandered" (Gr *planaō*). The word means to become lost, to lose one's way. Our word "planet" comes from this word and suggests the idea that the planets, in contrast to the stars, were not fixed but wandered about the heavens. The restoration of carnal Christians is in view. The intent is to "save his soul from death," that is, to intercept his downward path before the Lord brings the discipline of physical death. We recover a "sinner" (a backslidden brother) in this way, by intercession and exhortation (cf. Hebrews 3:13; 1 Thessalonians 5:14-15). We are intercessors with God, as was Moses (Exodus 32:30).

Another passage that refers to the sin unto death is 1 John 5:16-17: "There is a sin leading unto death." Physical death is in view because it is contrasted with physical life. Elsewhere in the epistle, when "eternal" life is meant, the adjective "eternal" is included. Second, John instructs his readers to pray for their "brother" that he might experience "life," not death. How can a brother be prayed for that he might obtain "eternal life"? A "brother" already has eternal life. But if abundant life is meant, then the phrase not only makes sense but fits well with the thrust of the epistle: fellowship and joy (1 John 1:3-4). Also, it makes good sense to pray that God will spare a sinning brother and restore him to fellowship. There is no reason to suggest that by the term "brother" John means "professing" brother, no reason except a prior commitment to the Experimental Predestinarian view of perseverance! Had John meant professing brother, he could have said so.

Paul explained that some of the Corinthians who had come to the Lord's Table drunk were "weak and sick, and a number sleep" (1 Corinthians 11:30). The brother in 1 Corinthians who was caught in adultery with his stepmother was turned over to Satan "for the destruction of his flesh, that his spirit may be saved in the day of the Lord Jesus" (1 Corinthians 5:5). No doubt, Ananias and his wife Sapphira, regenerate members of the early church, experienced the sin unto physical death when they lied to the Holy Spirit (Acts 5:1-11). There are, then, ample biblical parallels to justify the doctrine of the sin unto physical death.

Paul's warnings to the Corinthians in 1 Corinthians 10:1-13 contain one of the more obvious refutations of the Experimental Predestinarian's view of the carnal Christian. With warnings from Israel's history, he admonishes the Christians at Corinth that they face the possibility of sin unto physical death just as the believing, regenerate nation of Israel did. He addresses this warning to "brothers" (10:1) in whose lives God can work and give them a way out of every trial (10:13). These "dear friends" are urged to flee idolatry (10:14). That the wilderness generation is similarly viewed by Paul as mostly regenerate is indicated by the fact that he says they experienced God's leading (v. 1); they were baptized unto Moses (v. 2); and they "ate" and "drank" of Jesus Christ (v. 4). These phrases are used elsewhere of regenerate people (John 6:55-56).

Yet the wilderness generation experienced the sin unto physical death. The regenerate Corinthian brothers are warned not to set their "hearts on evil things as they did" (v. 6). It is apparently possible for brothers in Christ to set their hearts on evil things! They are warned not to become involved in sexual immorality (v. 8), and not to test the Lord (v. 9), or to grumble (v. 10). Paul says, "These things happened to them as examples and were written down as warnings for us" (v. 11). Paul apparently thinks these warnings imply a real danger, a danger that can come upon regenerate "brothers." What was the danger? In each case it was the sin unto death! Because of various acts of persistent rebellion, the wilderness generation experienced the death of twenty-three thousand in one day. Some were killed by snakes (v. 9), and some were killed by the destroying angel (v. 10).

When a Christian is judged by God and experiences the sin unto physical death, it is evident that he has not only sinned but that he has persisted in sin unto the final hour, precisely what the adherents of the Reformed doctrine of perseverance say cannot happen!

MILLENNIAL DISINHERITANCE

The final consequence of protracted carnality is forfeiture of reward and stinging rebuke when the King returns to establish His rule. No tragedy could be greater for the Christian, saved by grace and given unlimited possibilities, than for him to forfeit all these blessings and fail to participate in the future reign of the servant kings. The loss of reward at the Judgment Seat of Christ is often referred to, but rarely specifically defined:

> *For we must all appear before the Judgment Seat of Christ, that each one may be recompensed for his deeds in the body, according to what he has done,* ***whether good or bad*** *(2 Corinthians 5:10).*

That there are negative consequences at the Judgment Seat of Christ is usually glossed over, and then a somewhat nebulous reference to crowns is alluded to in popular presentations. But there are negative consequences too! This is what the apostle Paul referred to when he said:

> *For we shall all stand before the judgment seat of God. For it is written, "As I live, says the Lord, every knee shall bow to Me, and every tongue shall give praise to God." So then each one of us shall give account of himself to God (Romans 14:10-12).*

Obviously it is better for us to deal with our sin now, rather than then.

The Way of Recovery: Confession

The recovery of the carnal Christian requires that he "repent" (2 Corinthians 7:10; Revelation 2:5). Elsewhere this repentance is called confession (1 John 1:9).

While some say that Christians do not need to confess, that God takes no notice of our sins because they are buried in the sea of forgetfulness, the Bible seems to say otherwise. True, the Lord does not impute sin to us (Psalms 32:1-2; Romans 4:7-8), but that refers to our eternal standing. If God does not expect confession, why did Jesus say, "Forgive us our trespasses" (Matthew 6:12)? We would be confessing what God cannot see. Also the Lord said, "If ye forgive not men their trespasses, neither will your Father forgive your trespasses" (Matthew 6:15).

There are two kinds of forgiveness in the New Testament. One pertains to our eternal salvation (justification by faith), and the other to our temporal fellowship with the Father. Just as children in our family may sin, so the believer in God's family may sin. Our child is always our child, but until he confesses, our fellowship is not good. In God's family the same principle applies. There is a forgiveness for salvation and a forgiveness for restoration. The Lord referred to this second kind of forgiveness when He said to Peter, "If I do not wash you, you have no part with Me" (John 13:8). Peter told the Lord to wash him all over if that was the case. To this Jesus replied, "He who has bathed needs only to wash his feet, but is completely clean" (John 13:10). Forgiveness related to restoration of fellowship is parallel in thought with the cleansing of the feet of the already bathed, regenerate man.

In 1 Corinthians 11:31 we are told, "If we would judge ourselves, we should not be judged." The meaning is plain: if we deal with our sin now, we will be spared from His fierce judgment later on.

Summary

The first time this writer assembled these verses together, he was surprised to discover that the Scriptures seemed to teach something he had always assumed to be impossible, namely, that Christians can commit apostasy. However, the Bible is quite realistic. It teaches that final failure is possible. Indeed, this is constantly warned against in the New Testament.

No doubt this conclusion will be one of the most problematic for many who read this book. It is possible that part of the problem is that many assume that it is faith which saves us. If that is so, then if we stop believing, we would no longer be saved. Imagine a man at the top of a burning building. He notes that the firemen have gathered below with a large net. With a leap of faith (literally!) he trusts himself into the hands of the firemen and jumps off the building. He crashes into the net, it holds, and he is saved. Now did his faith save him? No. It was the firemen holding the net. Leaping into the net did not save him either. Many have jumped to their deaths by leaping out of windows. No! It was not faith, not leaping, but the net that saved him.

After going through an experience like this, the man would probably be encouraged to trust in firemen should he ever find himself again on top of a burning building. Let us imagine, however, that his faith in firemen fails. He has still been saved from crashing to the pavement even if he stops believing.

Even though the man could theoretically be faced with another fire, and because of his loss of faith in firemen he could face a deadly peril, the believer in Christ faces no such danger. There are no more fires from which we have to escape!

The danger of apostasy is clear. Many readers of this book have known people who once believed, who witnessed, who prayed, who read their Bibles, and yet did not finish their course. To say they were never saved to begin with begs the question and in many instances contradicts our personal knowledge of those people.

No! The danger is real, and we must stay close to Christ, or we too can face the prospects of discipline and disinheritance. The Christian life is not easy, and believing God in the midst of trials and suffering is the most difficult of all. Many have abandoned their faith because of their disappointment with God. The New Testament warns all of us about the danger of millennial disinheritance.

In view of the danger of becoming a carnal Christian and the possibility of final apostasy, it is not surprising that the New Testament writers repeatedly and forcefully warn their believing readers not to fall away. If one's mind was not saturated with post-Reformation, anti-Catholic polemics, the normal reading of these numerous warnings would be that it is possible that true believers could in fact fall into carnality or deny the faith altogether. Because this would contradict their doctrine of the inevitable and necessary perseverance of the saints in holiness to the end of life, Experimental Predestinarians have devoted considerable attention to this apparent decisive refutation to their system. The warnings, they say, are God's means to motivating true believers to persevere in the faith. We will discuss this central tenet of Reformed thinking in the next four chapters.

34

The Warnings: The Possibility of Failure

THE REFORMED doctrine of perseverance not only lacks scriptural support for its view of sanctification, but it also flies in the face of the numerous warnings against falling away repeated in nearly every book of the New Testament. Arminian theologians have pressed the warning passages vigorously on their Calvinist friends, and in the judgment of this writer, with telling force. Unless it is possible for a believer to fall away, it is difficult to see the relevance of these passages that seem to be directly applied to him by the New Testament writers.[1767] The New Testament is replete with passages which argue convincingly and decisively against the Reformed doctrine of the perseverance of the saints in holiness to the final hour.

The Warning Passages

In order to set the Experimental Predestinarian difficulty in the full glare of the New Testament witness, it will be helpful at this point to peruse a few of these so-called warning passages and observe their importance for this discussion.

Few passages have entered more frequently into the discussion of perseverance than John 15:6:

> *If anyone does not abide in Me, he is thrown away as a branch, and dries up; and they gather them, and cast them into the fire, and they are burned (NASB).*

The difficulty for the Experimental Predestinarians is that Jesus is referring to branches which are "in Me," who do not bear fruit (15:2). It seems to be possible for people "in Christ" to be unfruitful and to be cast into the fire and burned. Abiding in Christ involves more than clinging to Christ alone for salvation.[1768] It includes obedience (1 John 3:24).[1769]

Speaking to the Colossians, the apostle Paul warns:

> *And although you were formerly alienated and hostile in mind, engaged in evil deeds, yet He has now reconciled you in His fleshly body through death, in order to present you before Him holy and blameless and beyond reproach—**if indeed you continue in the faith firmly***

1767 As will be argued elsewhere, the term "fall away" does not refer to falling away from eternal salvation. It refers, rather, to a falling away from the path of growth, or forfeiture of eternal reward.

1768 Schreiner says that the warning passages are "nothing other than a call to continue to believe." Thomas R. Schreiner, *Run to Win the Prize: Perseverance in the New Testament* (Wheaton, IL: Crossway Books, 2010).

1769 See also John 15:10, 14; 1 John 2:6, 10; 3:6, 15, 17.

> ***established and steadfast, and not moved away from the hope of the gospel*** *which you have heard (Colossians 1:21-23).*

The real danger here is that of not being presented blameless before Him![1770] On the Reformed premises, there can be no real danger to a "true" Christian because all "true" Christians will continue in faith and will not be moved away from the hope of the gospel. Paul also warns believers about the danger of "not holding fast to the head" (Colossians 2:19) and of being taken "captive through philosophy and empty deception" (Colossians 2:8).

The salvation of the Corinthians seems to be conditioned on their holding fast:

> *Now I make known to you brethren, the gospel which I preached to you, which also you received, in which also you stand, by which also you are saved,* ***if you hold fast the word*** *which I preached to you, unless you believed in vain (1 Corinthians 15:1-2).*

Young Timothy is challenged to guard against the danger of "wandering from the faith":

> *For the love of money is a root of all sorts of evil, and some by longing for it have wandered away from the faith, and pierced themselves with many a pang. But flee from these things, you man of God; and pursue righteousness, godliness, faith, love, perseverance and gentleness. Fight the good fight of faith; take hold of the eternal life to which you were called, and you made the good confession in the presence of many witnesses (1 Timothy 6:10-12 NASB).*

Obviously, perseverance involves more than merely continuing to believe; a life of works is included. Paul apparently does not believe that perseverance is the necessary and inevitable result of saving faith. Otherwise, why would he warn this regenerate man of the danger of wandering from the faith, and why would he exhort him to "fight the good fight"? On Experimental Predestinarian premises, all true Christians will necessarily and inevitably fight the good fight, and they will not wander from the faith. They will persevere in faith up to the point of physical death. (Of course, I am aware that Experimentalists argue that the warnings are the means by which God secures perseverance. We will discuss this in chapters 36-38.)

According to James, it is possible for a Christian to stray from the truth:

> *My brethren, if any among you strays from the truth, and one turns him back, let him know that he who turns a sinner from the error of his way will save his soul from death, and will cover a multitude of sins (James 5:19-20).*

The "sinner" to which James refers is evidently a Christian brother. The conditional clause implies that it is by no means inevitable that he will always be turned back.

Likewise, the apostle Peter makes it clear that Christians can "fall":

> *Therefore, my brothers, be all the more eager to make your calling and election sure. For if you do these things, you will never fall, and you will receive a rich welcome into the eternal kingdom of our Lord and Savior Jesus Christ (2 Peter 1:10-11).*[1771]

[1770] As argued in a previous chapter, this refers to the promise of being presented before Christ relatively blameless and mature if they hold fast to their faith. It does not refer to the absolute perfection of glorification in the resurrection body. See vol. 1, chapter 25.

[1771] To make one's calling and election sure means to make one's Christian life impregnable against stumbling by adding to one's faith the virtues in 2 Peter 1:3-7. See pp. 458 ff.

The conditional participle, "if you do" (Gr *poiountes*), holds forth a real danger to the readers of this epistle. They might "fall" and forfeit their rich welcome into the eternal kingdom. Earlier, he suggested that they can become "ineffective and unproductive" in their knowledge of Jesus Christ (1:8). In fact, he teaches the need to have certain character qualities manifested in "increasing measure." He then teaches that Christians may not have this increasing measure of growth and are nearsighted, blind, and forgetful of their being cleansed from former sins (1:8-9). Yet, according to the Experimental Predestinarians, Christians will always have an increasing measure of growth and will never permanently fall.

The danger of falling away is repeated later in the same epistle:

> *His [Paul's] letters contain some things that are hard to understand, which ignorant and unstable people distort, as they do the other Scriptures to their own destruction. Therefore, dear friends, since you already know this, be on your guard so that you may not be carried away by the error of lawless men and fall from your secure position. But grow in the grace and knowledge of our Lord and Savior Jesus Christ (2 Peter 3:16-18).*

Once again, the danger of falling away is something real for Christians. Ignorant and unstable people have distorted the epistles of Paul, and this act resulted in their "destruction." That the same result can come on these "dear friends" seems to be stated when he warns them "not to be carried away by the error of lawless men and fall from your secure position." Why would this warning be addressed to these "dear friends," if in fact it was not possible for them to experience this danger?

Consistent with the other passages studied, the apostle Jude affirms a similar danger:

> *These are men who divide you, who followed mere natural instincts and do not have the Spirit. But you, dear friends, build yourselves up in your most holy faith and pray in the Holy Spirit. Keep yourselves in God's love as you wait for the mercy of our Lord Jesus Christ to bring you to eternal life (Jude 19-21).*

In contrast to the nonbelievers, who do not have the Holy Spirit and who have caused division, these "dear friends" are warned that they must keep themselves in God's love. These are born-again people who possess the "most holy faith." If being kept in God's love is the necessary and inevitable result of regeneration, why are they commanded to keep themselves? Surely the command implies that they may not. And if they may not,[1772] then the Experimental Predestinarian position is fiction.

The danger of failing to abide in Him is clearly in the mind of the apostle John when he writes to his "little children," that is, his regenerate sons and daughters in the faith:

> *If what you heard from the beginning abides in you, you also will abide in the Son and in the Father. . . . And now little children, abide in Him, so that when He appears, we may have confidence and not shrink away from Him in shame at His coming (1 John 2:24-28).*

[1772] I am aware of the Experimental Predestinarian response that the warnings are God's means for keeping them. We will discuss this below.

We continue to abide in Him only if what we heard from the beginning abides in us. Failure to continue to abide is very real, not hypothetical, and will result in shrinking away from Him in shame at His coming.

According to the apostle, there is a danger that a Christian can "die":

Therefore, brothers, we have an obligation—but it is not to the sinful nature, to live according to it. For if you live according to the sinful nature, you will die; but if by the Spirit you put to death the misdeeds of the body, you will live (Romans 8:12-13).

It goes without saying that the possibility that a "brother" could live "according to the sinful nature" is assumed. If a born-again brother does so, however, he will "die." He becomes dead spiritually; he is a carnal Christian, his faith is no longer living and vital, it has become dead.

In the same book Paul issues another emphatic warning, a warning against the possibility of being "cut off":

But they were broken off because of unbelief, and you stand by faith. Do not be arrogant, but be afraid. For if God did not spare the natural branches, he will not spare you either. Consider therefore the kindness and sternness of God; sternness to those who fell, but kindness to you, ***provided you continue in this kindness.*** *Otherwise,* ***you also will be cut off*** *(Romans 11:20-22).*

In no uncertain terms Paul affirms a real danger of being in some sense "cut off" if we fail to "continue in His kindness."[1773]

In this famous passage the apostle himself acknowledges the possibility of failure:

Do you not know that in a race all the runners run, but only one gets the prize? I beat my body and make it my slave so that after I have preached to others, I myself will not be disqualified for the prize (1 Corinthians 9:24, 27).

The prize for which Paul strives is not salvation, it is rewards. The context is an athletic contest at the Isthmian games.[1774] He warns them, by inference, concerning the danger of similarly being disqualified.

In 1 Corinthians 10:1-21 Paul warns the Corinthians against the danger of failure. The whole passage is instructive. As demonstrated earlier, the majority of the Israelites were born again, and yet the majority did not persevere in holiness.

So if you think you are standing firm, be careful that you don't fall. No temptation has seized you except what is common to man. And God is faithful; he will not let you be tempted beyond what you can bear. But when you are tempted he will also provide a way out so that you can stand up under it (1 Corinthians 10:12-13).

He tells them that the experience of the forefathers was intended as a warning for us (10:11). It is clear that he has Christians in view. If we are "truly" saved, what is the danger

[1773] This passage will be discussed fully later. See pp. 627 ff.

[1774] I will establish this conclusion later and also show that *adokimos*, "disqualified," does not refer to consignment to "the lake of fire," but refers to loss of reward. See pp. 463 ff.

to "us"? Experimental Predestinarians teach that salvation cannot be lost. Some say that if they are truly born again, this is only a "conceivable danger," not a real one.

Few verses seem to have impacted popular consciousness as frequently as Paul's famous warning about "falling from grace":

> *Stand firm, and do not let yourselves be burdened again by a yoke of slavery. . . . Mark my words! I, Paul, tell you that if you let yourselves be circumcised, Christ will be of no value to you at all. . . . You who are trying to be justified by law have been alienated from Christ; you have fallen away from grace (Galatians 5:1-4).*

Marshaling his full authority as an apostle, Paul tells these Galatians that it is possible for believers to fall from grace, come under the yoke of slavery, and become alienated from Christ! These strong words fly directly in the face of the Experimental Predestinarian claim that believers cannot fall and could never become alienated from Christ because they will persevere in faith to the end of life.

The possibility of failure to "continue" is stressed by Paul in the famous passage where he worries that he may have labored "for nothing":

> *Therefore, my dear friends, as you have always obeyed—not only in my presence, but now much more in my absence—continue to work out your salvation in fear and trembling ... in order that I may boast on the day of Christ that I did not run or labor for nothing (Philippians 2:12-16).*

These are "dear friends" who previously have "always obeyed." They are born again. Yet there is a possibility of their failure to "continue to work out their salvation," resulting in the apostle's labor among them being "for nothing." There is nothing inevitable and necessary about their perseverance.

Can a true Christian fail to persevere and thus forfeit the prize?

> *Do not let anyone who delights in false humility and the worship of angels disqualify you for the prize (Colossians 2:18).*

A true believer can, by his life, deny the faith and become worse than an unbeliever:

> *If anyone does not provide for his relatives and especially for his immediate family, he has denied the faith and is worse than an unbeliever (1 Timothy 5:8).*

This person who denies the faith is contrasted with the "unbeliever." Clearly, Paul is saying that a believer can be described in this way.

The love of money can cause Christians to wander from the faith:

> *People who want to get rich fall into temptation and a trap and into many foolish and harmful desires that plunge men into ruin and destruction. For the love of money is the root of all kinds of evil. Some people, eager for money, **have wandered from the faith** and pierced themselves with many griefs (1 Timothy 6:9-10).*

The "people" to whom Paul refers includes those who have wandered from the faith, that is, those who have faith but are not in some way persevering in it. The result of this is much grief. In contrast to these Christians who wander, Timothy is told to "take hold of the eternal life to which he was called" (1 Timothy 6:12).

That there is something conditional in the believer's future and that he faces a danger of not persevering necessarily and inevitably to the end of life could hardly be made plainer than it is in these verses:

Here is a trustworthy saying:

> *If we died with him,*
> *we will also live with him;*
> *if we endure,*
> *we will also reign with him;*
> *If we disown him,*
> *he will also disown us;*
> *if we are faithless, yet*
> *he will remain faithful,*
> *for he cannot disown himself (2 Timothy 2:11-13).*

The possibilities of failure to endure, of disowning Christ, and of being faithless are stark realities. To say that Christians do not face these dangers seems contradictory to passages such as this.

Without question, the center of the controversy in theological discussion has swirled around the warnings of Hebrews. These passages clearly reveal the weakness of Experimental Predestinarian exegesis. It is sometimes claimed that these verses apply only to those who have professed Christ, and not to those who have really believed. Or, if they are believers, the warning is God's means of keeping them from falling away. Furthermore, if they are believers, God will guarantee that they will not fall away. These assertions will be responded to in a later chapter,[1775] but first let us consider the warnings themselves:

> *We must pay more careful attention, therefore, to what we have heard, so that we do not drift away. For if the message spoken by angels was binding, and every violation and disobedience received its just punishment, how shall we escape if we ignore such a great salvation? (Hebrews 2:1-3)*

Notice that "we" are in danger. The author includes himself as an object of this warning. Unless there are some contextual indicators to suggest this is an "editorial" *we*, there is no obvious justification for concluding anything else but that truly born-again people are the subject of the warning. It is possible for these Christians to drift away and as a result to receive a punishment.

The apostle exhorts believers against the danger of a failure to enter rest:

> *Therefore, since the promise of entering his rest still stands, let us be careful that none of you be found to have fallen short of it (Hebrews 4:1).*

It is possible that a Christian will not enter rest. Real danger, not hypothetical danger, is here.

[1775] See discussion of Hebrews 6 in chapter 41 and on the other warning passages in Hebrew in chapter 42.

The warning becomes more forceful in this well-known passage:

It is impossible for those who have once been enlightened, who have tasted the heavenly gift, who have shared in the Holy Spirit, who have tasted the goodness of the word of God and the powers of the coming age, if they fall away, to be brought back to repentance, because to their loss they are crucifying the Son of God all over again and subjecting him to public disgrace (Hebrews 6:4-6).

These born-again people are those who **have** fallen away. That they are born again is evident from the descriptive phrases applied to them.

There is no warning in the New Testament which is more forceful and direct than this caution against sinning willfully:

If we deliberately keep on sinning after we have received the knowledge of the truth, no sacrifice for sins is left, but only a fearful expectation of judgment (Hebrews 10:26-27).

But are genuine Christians the objects of this warning or are the warnings directed to mere professors in Christ who were never really born again? Several things characterize those being warned.

First, they have "received the light" (Hebrews 10:32). To be "enlightened" (*phōtizomai*) means to be born again and to have truly and inwardly experienced the heavenly gift and the personal ministry of the Holy Spirit.[1776]

Second, they "stood [their] ground in a great contest in the face of suffering" (10:32). These people had not only responded to the gospel; they had also suffered for it and persevered in their suffering for Christ's sake.

Third, they "were publicly exposed to insult and persecution; and at other times stood side by side with those who were so treated" (10:33). The public nature of their confession of Christ resulted in public ridicule and persecution. But far from backing away, they pressed on and joined with others who were similarly treated.

Fourth, they sympathized with those in prison (Hebrews 10:34). Risking danger to their own lives, they visited persecuted brothers and sisters in prison, thereby publicly identifying themselves to hostile authorities as Christian sympathizers.

Fifth, they "joyfully accepted the confiscation of [their] property" (10:34). Furthermore, they accepted this confiscation for the right motives, "because you knew that you yourselves had better and lasting possessions." They were focused on the eternal inheritance which the faithful will acquire.

Sixth, he specifically says they have been "sanctified":

How much severer punishment do you think he will deserve who has trampled under foot the Son of God, and has regarded as unclean the blood of the covenant ***by which he was sanctified****, and has insulted the Spirit of grace? (Hebrews 10:29)*

Sanctification in Hebrews looks at the righteousness of faith of Christ from the vantage point of being qualified to enter the presence of God to worship and seek help in time of

1776 This will be substantiated in chapter 41.

need (Hebrews 10:10, 14, 19). It is possible for men who have been the recipients of this sanctification to trample underfoot the Son of God and insult the Spirit of grace.

Does the writer of this epistle doubt their salvation? No! What he worries about is their loss of reward. He says:

> *So do not throw away your confidence; it will be richly rewarded. You need to persevere so that when you have done the will of God, you will receive what he has promised (Hebrews 10:35).*

That he does not consider them mere professors in Christ is proven by the six things he says are true of them. In addition, one does not warn professing Christians about the loss of reward but about their eternal destiny to eternal damnation. One does not tell non-Christians to persevere in the faith so that they will receive a reward. Instead, he tells them to believe the gospel.

The exegetical and theological weakness of the Experimental Predestinarian position is clearly seen by the following facts. In their system of assurance a man can know he is a Christian by reflecting on the truth that (1) he has believed; (2) he has the evidences of works in his life; and (3) he has internal witness of the Holy Spirit. Now, in the case of these people, whom many Experimental Predestinarians maintain are not really Christians at all, all three criteria of their own introspective system are fully met. These people have believed (10:35, their "confidence"); they have evidenced their belief by perseverance in trials and good works (10:32-34); and they have the inner testimony of the Spirit ("enlightened," 10:32; 6:4). If they are not Christians, then the Reformed view of assurance is false; and if they are Christians, the doctrine of the perseverance of the saints is fiction.

Only a few of the many warnings of the New Testament have been considered.[1777] This lengthy presentation, however, has been necessary in order to force a consideration of the breadth of the Experimental Predestinarian problem. This theological system cannot be dismissed by plausible exegesis of a few difficult passages; it is contradicted by the entire New Testament.

The Reformed faith has produced some of the most outstanding Christian scholars in the history of the church. Their contribution to the theological stability and apologetic defense of Protestant Christianity has been enormous. Yet the proverb remains true: "Brilliant men confuse things brilliantly." Many of these brilliant men are aware of the numerous passages that can be quoted against their position, and they have spilt no small amount of ink in attempts to defend their view of the warnings in the light of the passages cited above.

In response to these passages that seem to imply that the Christian is in some kind of danger, that there is something contingent about his future destiny, the Experimental Predestinarians have replied that either (1) the passages are addressed to professing but not true Christians; or (2) they are addressed to Christians but are simply a means God uses to guarantee that they will persevere; or (3) they are conceivable but not actual consequences that could fall on the true believer. In this system, the evidence of the reality of the faith is perseverance in holiness to the end of life. All who are saved will persevere, and those who

---

[1777] Other relevant passages are: 2 Peter 3:16-17; 2 John 6-9; Revelation 2:7, 10-11, 17, 18-26; 3:4-5, 8-12, 14-22; 12:11; 22:18-19.

persevere, and those alone, are the truly saved. True apostasy is possible only for those who have never entered into a saving relationship with Jesus Christ.

Summary

Repeatedly in the New Testament, writers address justified saints with warnings about possible post-mortem judgment. If this judgment is condemnation to the lake of fire, why would God threaten His saints with a destiny He knows will never befall them? If these warnings apply only to those who have professed faith in Christ who do not possess the real item, then how does one explain the fact that in each warning context, there is compelling evidence that those addressed are not mere professors but are in fact born again?

As mentioned on the preceding page, the Reformed understanding of these warnings is threefold, depending on the Reformed interpreter's understanding of the saved state of those to whom he thinks the warnings are addressed. Some understand the intended readers to be merely professing Christians who are not saved (option 1). Others believe that those addressed are true Christians (options 2 and 3). In the next chapter we will discuss the former view, and in chapter 36, our attention will be directed to the latter views.

35

The Warnings: Addressed to Professing Christians?

THE TRADITIONAL way in which Experimental Predestinarians respond to the problem of the warning passages in Hebrews is to claim that they are addressed to professing believers, not possessing believers.[1778] As Martyn Lloyd-Jones explains, "The primary purpose of the warning passages is to test our profession of faith in order that we may know whether it is true or spurious. They are given to warn us against the terrible danger of having a false profession."[1779]

Dabney says the Arminian would conclude from his backsliding that he had fallen from grace and the Calvinist would conclude that he never had any salvation to begin with, a fear that Dabney believes is "much more wholesome and searching than the erring Arminian's":

> *For this alarmed Calvinist would see, that while he had been flattering himself he was advancing heavenward, he was, in fact, all the time on the high road to hell; and so, now, if he would not be damned, he must make a new beginning, and lay better foundations than his old one (not like the alarmed Arminian, merely set about repairing the same old ones).*[1780]

Often Calvinists appeal to the wheat and the tares, the example of Judas, and the rejection of those who say, "Lord, Lord," and yet He never knew them as proof that the writers of the New Testament viewed their readers as a group of professors and not possessors.

Are Warnings Addressed to Professing Believers?

This approach to the warning passages has largely fallen from favor among most biblical scholars. The majority now agree that the warning passages are in fact addressed to believers as God's means of securing their final perseverance in faith and holiness to the final hour. However, in this brief chapter we will respond with five objections to this common view that those addressed are a professing but not possessing subgroup in the early church.

[1778] Joseph Pak argues for a category of false believers in the New Testament in Pak, "A Study of Selected Passages on Distinguishing Marks of Genuine and False Believers", 9-36.

[1779] Lloyd-Jones, *Romans Chapter 8:17-39: The Final Perseverance of the Saints*, 307.

[1780] Dabney, *Lectures in Systematic Theology*, 697.

DIFFERING CONTEXTS

First, this view ignores the differing contexts intended by the Lord's references to the wheat and tares and the New Testament house fellowships that were in the mind of the writers of the New Testament. When the Lord referred to wheat and tares, He was speaking of a theoretical situation in the church in general. When the writers of the New Testament address their readers as "saints," "brothers," "brethren," and "little children," they are speaking not to the unknown masses of Christendom at large but to their intimate friends to whom they have ministered and often led to the Lord. We must not read into the first-century church the present situation of large, twentieth-century churches, many with over one thousand people, many of whom are not known at all by the preacher on Sunday morning. These first-century churches were small, personal "table fellowships," consisting of several families who knew each other well. Participation in the Lord's Supper involved, therefore, a commitment to the other families.[1781] Additionally, the presence or possibility of persecution made attendance at these meetings no casual thing. Indeed, they often had to meet together secretly in order to avoid persecution. Each house fellowship was presided over by an appointed elder. So the intended audience is more intimate, definitely Christian, and known by the writers. Richard Lovelace comments:

> *Unlike most modern congregations the early Christian church was an integrated community centered around the worship of God and the advancement of his kingdom. Economically it was a commonwealth, which meant that its members were not being pulled apart from one another by the pursuit of individual goals of success; they were devoting everything they were and owned to the strengthening of one another and the cause of Christ. Worshiping and eating together, the members were in constant communication. . . . Little time or distance separated the members of this body, so there was an unhindered communication of the gifts and graces of each one to the others.*[1782]

It is emphatically *not* the same situation a preacher in the twentieth century faces when he climbs into the pulpit before several thousand professing Christians. We are, therefore, fully justified in concluding that, when a New Testament writer uses a term like "brethren," he is not thinking that some may and some may not really be brothers, but he assumes that all his readers are in fact born again. He knows these people, has led some of them to the Lord, has discipled them, and has maintained contact over the years by repeated visits and letters.

REQUIRES UNUSUAL DISCRIMINATION

Second, if all the letters were addressed to a mixed group of saved and unsaved people, then both wheat and tares would need to be discriminating in their reading of the epistle. The wheat must come to all the *warnings* and realize that they apply only to the tares, and the tares must realize that all the *commands* are addressed only to believers and that the real issue for them, as tares, is to believe. Such a requirement almost guarantees that the epistles would be frequently misunderstood by their intended audience.

1781 Johannes Behm, "*deipnon*," in TDNT, 3:801.

1782 Lovelace, *Dynamics of Spiritual Life: An Evangelical Theology of Renewal* 161.

THE WRITERS ASSUME REGENERATION

The writers rarely draw the distinction between wheat and tares in the very epistles supposedly addressed by intent to those kinds of groups. In nearly every case the distinction must be read into the text and read into the author's mind. Nowhere, for example, does the writer to the Hebrews say, "How can we who claim to be Christians (and may not really be) escape if we neglect so great a salvation?" The writers never qualify the warnings and never introduce the distinction that the Calvinist view specifically requires. Since the writers themselves never explicitly say that they believe their audience is a mixture and since they everywhere make statements to the effect that they are talking to genuine Christians, we have no warrant for reading into their otherwise clear statements qualifications they themselves never make.[1783]

The issue is not the theoretical existence of wheat and tares but to whom is the writer addressing; that is, does the writer assume that his readers are born again? That he can speak to wheat, tares, or both does not mean that he is. We can only discern his intended audience by studying the terms and themes he discusses in describing them. Everywhere he uses terms like "brethren," "sanctified," "holy brethren," and "children" and describes them as having believed and manifested a life of works (Hebrews 10:35ff.). While it is possible that mere professing Christians are in the audience, he does not seem to have them in his thinking at all. The existence of these kinds of people in the New Testament fellowships was not an issue of conscious concern reflected in the writings of the New Testament writers. The fact that they may exist does not logically require that the writer included them in his intended audience.

Against this view Experimental Predestinarians might cite 2 Corinthians 5:20,

> *Therefore, we are ambassadors for Christ, as though God were entreating through us; we beg* ***you*** *on behalf of Christ,* ***be reconciled*** *to God.*

Notice the word "you." The problem for Experimental Predestinarians is that this word is not in the Greek text. Paul is not exhorting the Corinthians ("you") to be reconciled to God as if he was addressing a subgroup within the church who had merely professed faith but did not really possess it. Paul is describing *his* ministry *to the world.*[1784] When Paul gets up every morning, this is what he thinks about, fulfilling his mandate to call the world to be reconciled to God. He is describing the ministry God has given him. The Corinthians were clearly a carnal group of believers, but they were believers. Paul says so in 2 Corinthians 3:3,

---

1783 Schreiner admits that the New Testament warnings "specifically address believers." Schreiner, *Run to Win the Prize*, 111.

1784 Some translations include it based upon the fact that "be reconciled" (Gr *katallagēte*) is 2nd person plural imperative. However, the context demands that this is Paul's message to nonbelievers and the "you" should be translated "people." See Murray J. Harris, *2 Corinthians*, ed. Frank E. Gabelein, et al., The Expositor's Bible Commentary, Volume 10: Romans Through Galatians (Grand Rapids: Zondervan Publishing House, 1976), 354. Thrall says, "This call for response is most naturally seen as a quotation of the apostolic message to the unconverted rather than as addressed to the Corinthian readers of the letter." Thrall, *A Critical Exegetical Commentary on the Second Epistle of the Corinthians*, 438. If the imperative is addressed to the Corinthians, Paul is strangely commanding people who have already been reconciled (because they have previously believed in Christ) to be reconciled. Obviously, this command is related to "people" and concerns what Paul says to nonbelievers as part of his ministry.

And you show that you are a letter from Christ delivered by us, written not with ink but with the Spirit of the living God, not on tablets of stone but on tablets of human hearts (2 Corinthians 3:3, ESV).

N. T. Wright is surely correct when he says, "Paul is not appealing to the Corinthian Christians to be reconciled." Instead this verse "is a description of what Paul characteristically does."[1785] He says, Christ died for us, we persuade others (2 Corinthians 5:11), and we therefore make this appeal, "be reconciled." Paul is therefore Christ's ambassador, he has the authority of the King. He has needed to establish his credentials throughout the preceding chapters because there were those who denied it.[1786]

THE WARNINGS EXHORT BELIEVERS NOT TO SURRENDER A FAITH THEY ALREADY POSSESS

I. Howard Marshall has correctly pointed out that, "if the Calvinist theory were true, the warnings would necessarily take such forms as: 'Make sure that you really were converted.' 'Beware lest what you think is an experience of salvation by faith is really nothing of the kind.'"[1787] Instead, the authors of the various warning passages take the salvation of their readers for granted. These warnings, contrary to Martyn Lloyd-Jones, cannot be construed as tests to determine if one is saved. The warnings are everywhere presented to saved people, exhorting them to continue in the faith or to face some danger. They are warned against giving up a faith they already possess.

The warnings are never presented as positive commands to begin to be a genuine believer. They are meant to challenge believers to persevere and continue in the faith which one already has. They are never told to go back to the beginning and start over by becoming true Christians; instead, they are warned to hold fast to their faith to the end of life. Marshall summarizes:

The New Testament takes for granted a present experience of salvation of which the believer is conscious. Here and now he may know the experience of Christian joy and certainty. He is not called to question the reality of this experience on the grounds that it may be illusory because he was never truly converted; rather, he is urged to continue to enjoy salvation through abiding in Christ and persevering in faith.[1788]

Summary

If the discussion above is correct, there is little reason to doubt that believers were the ones being warned about the consequences of not persevering. This is now generally accepted by most of the modern commentaries. However, such a claim raises a number of serious questions.

[1785] Wright, *Justification: God's Plan and Paul's Vision*, 162.

[1786] It is also possible that Paul could be applying the doctrine of reconciliation to the strained relationships between the believers in Corinth. They are carnal, and they are therefore fundamentally out of fellowship with God and need to be restored to fellowship with Him. In this understanding of the text, Paul is asking them to live out their reconciliation in terms of their relationship with one another and with him. At any rate, there is no justification in this passage for the claim that Paul is directing the exhortation to a minority group of unbelievers who have only professed faith.

[1787] Marshall, *Kept by the Power of God: A Study of Perseverance and Falling Away*, 201.

[1788] Ibid., 202.

If believers are being warned about possible damnation if they do not persevere, how can they ever have assurance of salvation? Why would God warn His children of a destiny He knows will never happen to them? For the Christian who is fully assured of his salvation, how would the warnings have any effect on him? What is the purpose of the warnings if they are addressed to those who are already saved?

It is to these questions and other related issues we will direct our attention in the chapters to follow.

36

The Warnings: A Means of Perseverance 1?

OUR JOURNEY through the intricacies of the Reformed doctrine of the perseverance of the saints now brings us to the headwater of Experimentalist thinking, the warnings to "true" believers. To understand why this is so, let us summarize briefly some of our conclusions and some problems the Reformed camp has attempted to address in their response to the problem that the warnings seem to some to suggest works are a condition of final salvation.

- We have shown that the future inheritance is a reward (Colossians 3:24) and will be granted to those who are not disobedient (1 Corinthians 6:9-10) and who provide charity to those in need (Matthew 25:34-35).
- In order to "enter life" one must "keep the commandments" (Matthew 19:16) and persevere in doing good works (Romans 2:7).
- If one desires to enter the kingdom, he must possess a lifestyle defined by the standards of the Sermon on the Mount (Matthew 5:20) and must "do the will of the Father" (Matthew 7:21).
- One of the requirements for being affirmed by Christ at the Judgment Seat of Christ is a steadfast refusal to deny Christ even in the face of martyrdom (Matthew 10:32).
- If one desires to be "saved," that is, find true life and reign with Him, he must commit himself to persevere to the end of life (Matthew 24:13)
- If one is to avoid final condemnation to *Gehenna*, he must avoid adultery (Matthew 5:27) and never call a brother a "fool" (Matthew 5:22).

In the preceding chapter we discussed a common Experimentalist view that the New Testament warnings are intended as a kind of test directed at professing Christians. If they heed the warnings, one can assume they are Christians. However, if their current lifestyle is one of disobedience and they refuse to heed the warnings, Expermentalists assume they were never born again to begin with. As these warnings regarding the possibility of final damnation fall on the deaf ears of Christian congregations, self-examination is enjoined. Those who have not met the standards set by Experimental Predestinarians to establish, with some certainty, that one is born again are to reexamine whether their faith is "genuine" and whether they have "truly" believed. Usually, this exhortation is ignored because the Experimentalist view of the Christian life is simply too impossible to believe.

A much more plausible Reformed approach to the warning passages is to admit that they are directed to true Christians. In that case, their purpose is to exhort those who know

Christ to continue to persevere to the final hour. However, since perseverance to the final hour means perseverance in good works as well as faith, then the questions arises, "Are good works a condition of final entrance into heaven?"

Experimentalists suggest the warnings are the means God uses to motivate and guarantee that believers will never fall into permanent sin and will never commit the sin of final apostasy from Christ. Furthermore, all "true" Christians will heed these warnings, because God will work in them to guarantee that they will respond and finish life still believing and manifesting some degree of holiness and good works. Genuine faith and a life of works are inextricably united. One cannot claim to have the former and not manifest the latter. Faith without works is dead, that is, nonexistent. As Calvin expressed it, "We are saved by faith alone, but the faith that saves is not alone." [1789]

However, this raises an important existential question, "What is the consequence of failure to heed the warnings?" Experimental Predestinarians say that the danger is final damnation because such a failure proves that the "believer" was not a "true" believer.[1790]

Before examining this viewpoint and the evidences adduced to support it, let us first clearly define it from the writings of its adherents.

The Reformed View of the Warnings

Those within the Reformed tradition insist that works are the result of regeneration, the evidences of life. They are the "fruit," and saving faith is the "root." They are the manifestation that arises out of the essence of the new man in Christ. In this Experimental Predestinarians are, of course, partially correct. If a person is truly born again, he will normally manifest evidence of such rebirth. Works are a natural, desirable, and logical result of saving faith.[1791] The issue, however, is whether or not all believers will inevitably continue in these good works to the end of life.

However, not all Experimental Predestinarians have been content to leave the matter there. Many believe that since the warnings are addressed to believers and exhort them to persevere in faith and good works to the end of life or risk damnation, the warnings necessarily entail the idea that salvation is by works. They have made perseverance a condition of salvation, and not just an evidence of it. In this they are either taking the Reformed doctrine to a logical conclusion, or they are boldly stating what it really means: salvation is by faith plus God-produced, non-meritorious works. We have called them Neonomians.

The Neonomian view of perseverance seems to have support in the Westminster Shorter Catechism.

> *Ques. 90. How is the Word to be read and heard, that it may become* ***effectual to salvation?***

[1789] John Calvin, Acts of the Council of Trent, 3:152.

[1790] Partners say the danger is divine discipline, possible sin unto death, millennial disinheritance, and loss of final rewards. Christians who do not heed the warnings will not hear the King say, "Well done." They will draw back in shame at His coming and they will not experience the full degree of intimacy with Christ they could have enjoyed in the kingdom and in the eternal state.

[1791] What is being argued in this book is that this manifestation is an inadequate base upon which to build assurance and will not necessarily continue to the final hour.

Ans. That the Word may become effectual to salvation, ***we must*** *attend thereunto with* ***diligence, preparation, and prayer****; receive it with faith and love, lay it up in our hearts, and* ***practice it in our lives.***[1792]

They make it clear that works are required when they say,

That we may escape the wrath and curse of God due to us by reason of the transgression of the law, he requireth of us repentance toward God, and faith toward our Lord Jesus Christ, ***and the diligent use of the outward means whereby Christ communicates to us the benefits of his mediation.***[1793]

Steeped as we are in the Reformed tradition, which teaches salvation by grace alone, through the instrumentality of faith alone and apart from works, we naturally recoil at such words and wonder, "Could they really have meant this?" It appears that they did mean this. Any ambiguity here has been removed in the writings of some later Experimental Predestinarians.

For example, Arthur Pink teaches that God requires that true Christians must "keep themselves" or risk eternal damnation.[1794] Yet he unequivocally maintains the "absolute and eternal security of the saints."[1795] He is attempting to show that God preserves His children through means, that is, by works. He quotes John Owen, that prince of the Puritan expositors, with approval who taught that works are a means of salvation:

But yet our own diligent endeavor is such an ***indispensable means*** *for that end, as that without it, it will not be brought about. . . . If we are in Christ, God hath given us the lives of our souls, and hath taken upon Himself, in His covenant, the preservation of them. But* ***yet*** *we may say, with reference unto the* ***means*** *that He hath appointed, when storms and trials arise,* ***unless we use our diligent endeavors, we cannot be saved.***[1796]

Elsewhere Pink asserts,

Holiness in this life is such a part of our "salvation" that it is a ***necessary means*** *to make us meet to be partners of the inheritance of the saints in heavenly light and glory.*[1797]
They [good works] are requisite as part of the ***means*** *which God has appointed: they are the* ***means of spiritual preservation.***[1798]

R. C. Sproul agrees with this,

Endurance in the faith is a ***condition*** *for future salvation. Only those who endure in the faith will be saved in eternity.*[1799]

1792 Philip Schaff, "Westminster Shorter Catechism," in *The Creeds of Christendom: With a History and Critical Notes* (Grand Rapids: Baker Book House, 1985), Q. 90, 3:696. See also ibid., Q. 85, 3:694.

1793 *Larger Catechism of the Westminster Standards*, ed. M. H. Smith (Greenville, SC: Presbyterian Theological Seminary Press, 1996), s.v. "Question 153".

1794 Pink, *Exposition of Hebrews*, 601.

1795 Ibid., 599.

1796 John Owen, *Hebrews*, quoted in Pink, *Exposition of Hebrews*, 600.

1797 Arthur Pink, *The Doctrine of Sanctification* (Swengel, PA: Reiner Publications, 1975), 28.

1798 Pink, *An Exposition of the Sermon on the Mount*, 349.

1799 R. C. Sproul, *Grace Unknown:The Heart of Reformed Theology* (Grand Rapids: Baker Book House, 1997), 198.

Similarly, Thomas Schreiner writes,

Believers obtain eschatological salvation by continuing to believe until the end and by heeding the warnings given to them.[1800]
The summons to persevere and the initial call to believe are conditions that must be fulfilled to be saved.[1801]

In their comment on the Westminster Confession, Hodge and Hodge say,

This doctrine teaches, not that persistent effort on our part is not necessary in order to secure perseverance in grace to the end, but that in this effort we are certain of success; for it is God that works in us both to will and to do of his good pleasure (Philippians 2:13).[1802]

The double negative is confusing. In plain English the first sentence reads, "Persistent effort *is* necessary in order to secure perseverance in grace to the end." According to Hodge and Hodge, although God initiates, motivates, and enables, it is obvious to Paul and common experience that *we do* persevere. If such perseverance is not achieved, then the person will not be saved. Thus in spite of themselves, the Hodges affirm that salvation is achieved through something we do!

One might be tempted to explain this by saying, "Well, what Pink and others really mean is that because works are the necessary fruit of regeneration, we can understand them to mean that they are only a means in the sense of verifying that true faith has occurred." However, that is not what they mean. Pink clearly says, "That good works are neither the chief nor the procuring cause of salvation is readily admitted, **but that they are no cause whatever, that they are simply 'fruits' of salvation and not a means thereto, we definitely deny.**"[1803] "Faith obtains the title [to salvation], good works secure the actual admission into the full and final benefits of redemption."[1804] So according to Pink, works are "a" cause. "The doing of good works," he says, "is indispensable in order to the securing of full and final salvation, that is, in order to an actual entrance into heaven itself."[1805]

In their book, *The Race Set Before Us*, Neonomian writers Schreiner and Caneday boldly declare that works are a condition of salvation with much less hesitation than most within the Experimental Predestinarian tradition:

We must run the race with dogged determination to obtain the prize of eternal life, and it takes remarkable discipline and training to make it to the end.[1806]

1800 Schreiner, *Run to Win the Prize*, 109.

1801 Ibid., 104. Schreiner continues to confuse his readers by also saying, "Heeding warnings is not the basis of our salvation," thus we obtain eschatological salvation "by heeding warnings" but heeding warnings is not the basis. So the warnings are not a "basis" of salvation but they are a "condition" and a means of salvation. I think I understand what Schreiner is getting at, but this nuanced use of language explains why some believe he is in fact teaching a works righteousness even though he strongly denies it. I am also doubtful that a first-century fisherman or readers of Paul's epistles in the first century could comprehend this subtle defense of post-Reformation theology!

1802 Hodge and Hodge, *The Confession of Faith: With Questions for Theological Students and Bible Classes*, 235.

1803 Pink, *An Exposition of the Sermon on the Mount*, 343.

1804 Ibid., 349.

1805 Ibid.

1806 Schreiner and Caneday, *The Race Set Before Us*, 314.

> *Note [Paul] does not say, "You are saved. Now work for your reward, which is in addition to salvation." He summons the Philippians to bring to accomplishment their salvation! Effort, toil and energy are all communicated in this phrase ["work out your salvation"]. We are to use all the resources at our disposal in order to be saved on the last day. We must obey, pray, resist the flesh and yield to the Spirit to inherit salvation. No theology is acceptable that diminishes this call to work out our salvation.*[1807]

They are saying that the initial justification does not "accomplish their salvation." Instead the Philippians themselves must do this.

Roy Zuck responds,

> *A problem with this view is the authors' contradictory statements about works in relation to salvation. They "categorically deny that salvation can be earned by works" (p. 86). And yet in the very next sentence they write, "The prize to be won is eternal life ... and we must strive to win that prize." When they say that "good works and following Jesus (Romans 2:6–7; Mark 10:29–30) are also necessary to obtain eternal life on the last day" (p. 67), is this not making salvation dependent on one's works? How can a gift be a gift if one must strive to attain it? Is this not illogical?*[1808]

"How," Zuck pointedly asks, "can the authors say they are not adding a condition to salvation (p. 153), when they repeatedly say that 'the promise of eternal life is conditional' (p. 166), that 'God's promise of salvation is conditional' (p. 167), and that '*if* we fail to persevere we will perish' (p. 206, italics added)? Is it not adding a condition to salvation to say, 'We must obey, pray, resist the flesh and yield to the Spirit to inherit salvation' (p. 315)?

Schreiner and Caneday would reply, "Yes, but praying, resisting the flesh, and yielding to the Spirit are God-produced, non-meritorious conditions, and therefore no works-righteousness is involved in obtaining our final entrance into heaven. Works are involved, but not works-righteousness. Thus, God-produced non-meritorious works are a condition of salvation, and God will produce these works in the lives of those who have 'truly' believed."

As the reader can see, Schreiner and Caneday have a very specific definition of a "condition." For hundreds of years, evangelical scholars have understood the addition of the condition of works to salvation as adding works-righteousness as a "condition" for final arrival into heaven. However, Schreiner, Caneday, Stanley, Rainbow, and other Neonomians use this commonly understood term, with a long history and subtly change the meaning. For them, the condition of works is NOT a condition of works-righteousness because the work is produced by God in the believer's life and is therefore non-meritorious. So what they mean by "conditions" is non-meritorious, God-produced works. We will explore this idea of a non-meritorious condition in the next chapter. Nevertheless, they have added a new condition for arrival into heaven, a condition which evangelicals in accordance with one reading of the Westminster Confession of Faith have rejected for centuries. In their commentary on the Westminster Confession, Hodge makes this crystal clear, "The *single condition of salvation* demanded in the Scriptures is that we should 'believe in' or on Christ

---

1807 Ibid., 315.

1808 Roy B. Zuck, "Book Review of The Race Set Before Us: A Biblical Theology of Perseverance and Assurance by Thomas R. Schreiner and Ardel B. Caneday," *BibSac* 160, no. 638 (April-June 2003): 242.

Jesus. And salvation is promised absolutely and certainly if this command is obeyed. (John 7:38; Acts 10:43; 16:31; Gal. 2:16.) To believe in or on a person, implies trust as well as credence" (emphasis added).[1809]

In their preoccupation with means to the end, these writers, in effect, make God-produced, non-meritorious works a condition of salvation. When they repeatedly deny that they are teaching that works is a condition and claim that they are being misunderstood, it is because readers do misunderstand their particular definition of works.[1810] Thus, in their view, it is a particular kind of works which are the means by which the final end, bliss in heaven, is achieved. But the New Testament declares that the only means to bliss in heaven is faith alone apart from any human effort, God enabled or not. Pink, Schreiner, Caneday, Sproul, and others have, in effect, added another condition beyond simple faith for becoming a Christian—persevering by means of God enabled, non-meritorious, positive responses to the warning passages.

Sensing the apparent difficulty of his position, Pink shifts the terms. He says those who apostatize are not really Christians at all; they were mere professors![1811]

Schreiner does the same thing. He wants it both ways. He says those addressed in the warning passages are "true believers,"[1812] but some may fall away proving they were not true believers.[1813] He summarily dismisses the view that the warnings are related to loss of reward.[1814] Of course, if they are not, well then, they are not. But that is the point in question.

In his exposition of the book of Hebrews, Pink began his discussion by saying that Hebrews 10 applies to true Christians, and then, faced with the fact that the warnings are real and that final damnation is in view, he shifts to calling them professing Christians.

Pink rails against the "carnal security" offered by "dead" preachers who have led people to believe that "guilt can nevermore rest upon them, and that no matter what sins they commit, nothing can possibly jeopardize their eternal interests."[1815] Of course, if they are eternally secure in the purpose of God, which Pink believes, nothing can! He says that some Christians sin with a high hand because all they have to lose is "some millennial crown or reward."

Then he defiantly declares, "The blood of Christ covers no sins that have not been truly repented of and confessed to God with a broken heart." If all he means is that if Christians do not confess their sins, they will not be restored to fellowship with God, then all would agree. But he does not mean that. He means that a Christian who does not repent is really not a Christian at all and is "hastening to Hell as swiftly as time wings its flight."[1816]

1809 Archibald Alexander Hodge and Presbyterian Church in the U.S.A. Board of Publication, *A Commentary on the Confession of Faith: with Questions for Theological Students and Bible Classes* (Philadelphia: Presbyterian Board of Publication, 1926), 207.

1810 They say, however, that these works are non-meritorious.

1811 Pink, *Exposition of Hebrews*, 618.

1812 Schreiner, *Run to Win the Prize*, 110.

1813 Ibid., 105.

1814 Ibid., 113.

1815 Pink, *Exposition of Hebrews*, 618.

1816 Ibid., 618.

Perhaps Pink has forgotten the promise in the book on which he wrote his commentary, "*Their sins and lawless acts I will remember no more*" (Hebrews 10:17). Indeed, he seems to have forgotten the gospel itself. He would have us believe that Hebrews 10:26 applies to true Christians and to professing Christians at the same time. The only reason for shifting to the fact that they must be professing Christians is the demands of his theology.

It is interesting that an Arminian, Robert Shank, agrees with Pink and Schreiner and Caneday on this point, that salvation must be obtained by attention to the means of its attainment, namely, faithful perseverance.[1817]

Another statement of perseverance as a condition of final entrance into heaven comes from Christian Friedrich Kling. He comments on 1 Corinthians 9:27, which reads, "*but I discipline my body and make it my slave, so that, after I have preached to others, I myself will not be disqualified* [Gr *adokimos*]."

He views *adokimos*, "disapproved," as meaning loss of salvation. He says,

> *A sound belief in the doctrine of the saints' perseverance is ever accompanied with a conviction of the possibility of failure and of the absolute necessity of using our utmost endeavor in order to final success. No experiences of Divine favor in the past, no circumstances, however advantageous, furnish such a guarantee of salvation as to warrant spiritual repose. There is no perseverance without conscious and determined persevering, and the requisite effort can be put forth only under the influence alike of hope and fear. And he who apprehends no danger of being ultimately a castaway through neglect or transgression, will lack the motive necessary to urge him triumphantly to the goal.*[1818]

His point is that while we may be saved by faith, we are kept saved by works exactly as much Arminian theology requires (of course, Arminians would deny this). Kling thinks that the Christian must be continually in fear of eternal damnation if he is to be sufficiently motivated toward a godly life.

Maurice Roberts, a contributor to the Experimental Predestinarian journal, *The Banner of Truth*, writes, "There are conditions to be fulfilled if Heaven is to be ours."[1819] His condition is perseverance. This condition, however, is to be fulfilled by God's effectual work in the regenerate. But we must cooperate with God in this work. So salvation in this system is initial belief coupled with a lifelong synergism of human and divine work.[1820] Only when the condition is fulfilled, can heaven be ours. But since the condition of perseverance cannot be fulfilled until we have persevered, we can have no certainty of our perseverance, and hence of our salvation, until the final hour. A doctrine leading to this conclusion flies in the face of the numerous biblical statements that offer assurance now.

Pink, Owen, Kling, Schreiner, Caneday, Sproul, and Roberts are simply being honest about the real meaning of the Reformed doctrine of perseverance. Their concern about antinomianism and Scriptures that contradict their system have boxed them into a distortion of their own doctrine. They start out by saying that the warnings are the means

---

[1817] Shank, *Life in the Son: A Study of the Doctrine of Perseverance*, 299.

[1818] Kling, *The First Epistle of Paul to the Corinthians*, 10:210.

[1819] Roberts, "Final Perseverance," 11.

[1820] Sproul says, "As part of the process of our sanctification, perseverance is a synergistic work." The title of Sproul's book is revealing! See also Gerstner, *Wrongly Dividing the Word of Truth: A Critique of Dispensationalism*, 210.

of securing perseverance and end up by saying that it is our obedience to those warnings that finally saves us. They subtly make this shift because they are undoubtedly aware that merely warning a man will not guarantee he will obey. Thus one needs to make his actual obedience the necessary ingredient for obtaining heaven. This indeed shuts out all possibility of antinomianism, and for this they are to be commended. But is this really the gospel?

Even though the above writers make perseverance in faith and good works a condition and not just an effect of salvation, we must agree with Experimental Predestinarians that the warnings are a means of motivating God's people toward perseverance. But the outcome of perseverance in response to the warnings is not entrance into heaven. Instead, perseverance in faith leads to rewards, greater intimacy with Christ, and inheritance in the kingdom. Furthermore, the warnings do not inevitably and necessarily guarantee perseverance in faith and holiness. Perseverance depends on the believer's choices to pursue a full assurance firm to the end (Hebrews 3:14). We do not agree that grace and warnings are tightly correlated so that grace always secures the positive outcome which the warnings imply might be lost.[1821] We insist there is a disjuncture between them, and grace does not inevitably secure perseverance. Rather, grace makes it possible, but the believer must choose.

Warnings: Conceivable Consequences but Not Probable Ones

Experimentalist problems with the warnings involve more than the difficulty of a works-righteousness. They also face the "tension" that, on the one hand, believers are promised that their eternal destiny is secure, but, on the other hand, the warnings about damnation (in their view) suggest that salvation could be lost.

WARNINGS CONCERN CONCEIVABLE CONSEQUENCES

In a highly nuanced and confusing (to this writer) defense of the Experimental Predestinarian view, Neonomians Schreiner and Caneday explain that the warnings are God's means of saving His people,[1822] but that we must not view the warnings as implying a probable danger to the believer "but only a conceivable one." "Warnings and admonitions," they say, "express what is capable of being conceived with the mind. They speak of things conceivable or imaginable, not of things likely to happen."[1823] Of course, one might respond, "If they are not likely to happen," this necessarily implies that they "might" happen. They further assure their readers that "the truthfulness of a warning or admonition does not depend on whether or not the thing supposed may come to pass."[1824]

1821 For example John Murray in his comment on Romans 11:22 argues, "The conditional clause in this verse 'if thou continue in his goodness,' is a reminder that there is no security in the bond of the gospel apart from perseverance. There is no such thing as a continuance in God's favor in spite of apostasy; God's saving embrace and endurance are correlative." Murray, *The Epistle to the Romans*, 2:88. Yet this contradicts the teaching of Christ and Paul. Jesus said that a carnal man can be "in" the kingdom (Matthew 5:19), and Paul said, "If we are faithless, he remains faithful—for he cannot deny himself" (2 Timothy 2:13, ESV). Thus, contrary to Murray, God's saving grace and endurance are not necessarily correlative.

1822 Schreiner and Caneday, *The Race Set Before Us*, 38.

1823 Ibid., 207.

1824 Ibid., 209.

Their book is well written, irenic, and for the most part it accurately presents the viewpoints with which they disagree. Both are very capable scholars. Tom Schreiner's outstanding commentary on Romans has helped many. Yet there are a number of points where we respectfully differ from their conclusions.

If I understand them correctly, Schreiner and Caneday's logic might be summarized as follows:

A. The promises say, "Salvation cannot be lost."
B. The warnings say, "It is possible and conceivable that salvation can be lost but not likely."

A and B, they say, are in "tension." This dialectical approach to theology might appeal to logicians, but first-century fishermen were not philosophers. Most readers of this book (*their* book as well) would probably not view this as a "tension" but a blatant contradiction. As they further explain this "tension," things become more confusing. Consider this statement:

> *Conditional warnings in themselves do not function to indicate anything about possible failure or fulfillment. Instead, the conditional warnings appeal to our minds to conceive or imagine the invariable consequences that come to all who pursue a course of apostasy from Christ.*[1825]

So, dividing their explanation into two propositions yields something like this:

A. Conditional warnings do not indicate a possibility of failure.
B. Conditional warnings bring to mind the invariable consequences (read, "failure") of apostasy.

Thus proposition A says there is no possibility of failure, and proposition B says there is (read *invariable* consequences!).[1826] When our minds recoil at this logic, we are assured that "Biblical writers presuppose that the two stand compatibly together." Schreiner and Caneday explain that those who disagree with them "misunderstand the nature of perseverance and treat it in isolation from its correlation with faith."[1827]

However, we do not misunderstand the nature of perseverance at all. We understand that perseverance is for rewards, not for final salvation. When one accepts this biblical premise, all these contradictions and tensions in the Experimental Predestinarian system evaporate.

To seek to help the reader understand this mystifying logic, they offer this illustration.[1828]

> *As we drive along highways, we make decisions that affect our safety. Signs along the highway warn of curves ahead or of slippery bridges or of falling rocks.*

[1825] Ibid., 199.

[1826] For a more detailed refutation of Schreiner and Caneday's view that the warnings are a means of salvation see Ken Keathly, "Does Anyone Really Know if They are Saved?," *JOTGES* 15, no. 1 (Spring 2002): 51.

[1827] They quote Berkouwer here as we did above in responding to this same point. See Berkouwer, *Faith and Perseverance*, 110.

[1828] Schreiner and Caneday, *The Race Set Before Us*, 208.

So far so good. We normally think of these road signs warning us of a danger, and if we refuse to heed them, there is a possibility that we will experience a crash.

According to Schreiner and Caneday, however, this is a misunderstanding of the function of road signs. Instead, they say,

> *Their function is not to call into question my ability to drive by frightening me that I might crash.*

"Call into question my ability to drive?" Who would have ever thought this was their function? But most would assume that their function is indeed to frighten us that we might crash (if we do not heed the sign). Is it not strange reasoning to say that a warning sign along a mountain curve does *not* mean it is possible to crash if we refuse to obey it?

They continue,

> *Rather, warning signs project cautions concerning various road hazards, and these projected cautions appeal to my capability to imagine the consequences of failing to heed the warning.*

But what are the consequences of failing to heed the warning? A crash! But this is the very thing, according to these writers, that the warnings do not warn about! As Schreiner says, "It does not logically follow that the warning lacks force if the threat does not come to pass."[1829] Notice how Schreiner phrases this, "if the threat **does not** come to pass." In order for his statement to make any sense it should be phrased, "If the threat **cannot** come to pass." If the threat "cannot" come to pass, it is obvious that the warning would have no force. In the soteriological parallel, the believer is promised that these supposed threats of damnation cannot come to pass. Ergo, these are not threats of damnation or else God is lying to "true" believers about a fate which He knows can never happen to them. However, if these warnings are real and concern loss of reward and disinheritance, the regenerate man knows they can come to pass and takes them seriously.

Schreiner adds, "The elect escape the threatened judgment precisely by heeding the warning. And I would contend that all the elect heed the warning, and hence will never face the final judgment."[1830] The present writer, however, would respond that the Bible teaches that "the elect" do not always heed the warnings.[1831] Schreiner asserts that the certainty of the outcome does not render the means superfluous. This, of course, is true, but that is not the issue. If the outcome depends in any way on our perseverance, then salvation by faith alone is lost.

The illustration about the road sign is supposed to help clarify their view of the biblical warnings. Like road signs on a mountain road, they do function to warn of consequences likely to happen. However, as soon as they use the phrase "not likely to happen," we are confronted with the alternative that these warnings function to warn us about something that "might" happen. But these writers refuse to state the obvious, because it would destroy their whole argument. It would mean that salvation can be lost.

When one tries to unravel the logic of their position and fails, Neonomians like Schreiner admit, "Some have misunderstood what we were arguing for in *The Race Set*

[1829] Schreiner, *Run to Win the Prize*, 96.

[1830] Ibid.

[1831] For proof of this, see chapter 32.

Before Us."[1832] The fact that so many do misunderstand should be a signal to them. In spite of professor Schreiner's irenic spirit and obvious scholarship, the reason he is misunderstood is that his position is simply not understandable. It is difficult to imagine that believers throughout the centuries would ever grasp these subtleties, and certainly Galilean fishermen would be perplexed.

SALVATION IS "ALREADY" BUT "NOT YET"

To maintain their idea that the warnings in fact do imply some danger we can imagine or conceive but not necessarily experience, Schreiner and Caneday need to resort to the Roman Catholic method of looking at justification and forgiveness. Justification, they say, is granted to "persistent" faith. Thus if our faith does not persist, we will not be justified. Confronted with the obvious fact that many New Testament passages say we are already justified when we believe, they need a way to say we are justified but we are not yet justified. They believe that "there seems to be a tension between biblical texts that warn and admonish us and texts that promise us great confidence and salvation."[1833] To arrive at their solution to this apparent tension, they claim that "justification remains fundamentally the *eschatological* verdict of acquittal."[1834] If we have already been justified and acquitted, their argument is weakened. By pushing justification to the end point of our salvation, they can argue, in agreement with Rome, that salvation is a process occurring over a lifetime and is not completed until the final day.[1835] Salvation is promised not in response to an act of faith, but, they say, only to "persistent" faith.[1836] If by "salvation" they mean "sanctification," we would agree. But this is not what they mean. While they include sanctification in their concept, sanctification is necessary to complete the task of delivering a person from final damnation. It is difficult to see any difference between this and Roman Catholic theology.

Stanley also argues that a final forensic judicial acquittal is rewarded only to "persistent" faith.[1837] This is an eschatological justification. Confronted with the obvious fact that many New Testament passages say we are already justified when we believe, Stanley argues that those passages refer to our initial justification, but until we have manifested a life of works

---

[1832] Schreiner, *Run to Win the Prize*, 9.

[1833] Schreiner and Caneday, *The Race Set Before Us*, 141.

[1834] Ibid., 161.

[1835] The Partners, of course, agree that certain aspects of salvation, namely, sanctification, do involve a process that culminates at the last day. But we do not agree that justification and positional forgiveness are part of that process.

[1836] Schreiner and Caneday, *The Race Set Before Us*, 43. This formulation leads them to typical Experimental Predestinarian doubletalk. "The Scriptures call on those who are wandering to repent and to turn again in order to be saved! Such an admonition does not necessarily lead to the conclusion that these people were not saved before! The admonition, however, is directed to where a person is now in his or her walk with the Lord." One might think that they are saying that this person, who may already be saved, needs to be saved again! However, what they mean is that salvation is a process beginning with initial faith and ultimately culminating in glorification. Certain aspects of salvation are "already" but some aspects are "not yet." Faith embraces the whole process, if it is saving faith, and persists from beginning to end.

[1837] If we are justified by "persistent" faith, then it is impossible to say for certain that anyone is justified now, because no one's faith has yet persisted! Justification is already complete, the future acquittal before the judge is based on this fact. For an excellent and coherent discussion of the nature of salvation see Earl Radmacher, *Salvation* (Dallas: Word Publishing, 2000), pp. 5 ff.

we will not be finally justified, and this final justification has its "basis" (his term) in our works.[1838]

As others have observed, "They never make it crystal clear … what it means for salvation to be already present, but not yet realized."[1839] Paul, says, "*For we maintain that a man is justified by faith apart from works of the Law*" (Romans 3:28). But when is this justification accomplished—at the point in time one believes, or at the last day? Paul answers that Abraham was declared righteous at the moment he believed. "*For what does the Scripture say? 'AND ABRAHAM BELIEVED GOD, AND IT WAS RECKONED TO HIM AS RIGHTEOUSNESS*'" (Romans 4:3).

Schreiner and Caneday confusedly say, "Until that day, we now stand justified in God's courtroom by faith only."[1840] By this they mean that when we believe we are justified, but the certainty of this is a "secret"[1841] which will only be revealed to us as reality on the last day. A secret!? The operative word is "by faith," by which they mean "persistent" faith. Of course, one can never know his faith is "persistent" until it has persisted! Schreiner and Caneday admit that "in the vast majority of instances righteousness is said to belong to believers now."[1842] This obviously sets up a contradiction that destroys the whole thesis of their book. If we are justified by "persistent" faith, then it is impossible to say for certain than anyone is justified now, because our faith has not yet persisted! How do they resolve this contradiction?

These writers appeal to a supposed "tension" between the "already" and "not yet." "There are," they say, "*indications* … that righteousness should be included in the already-but-not-yet tension that informs New Testament soteriology."[1843] And what are these "indications"? They appeal to passages that say we will be declared righteous on the final day (Romans 2:13; 3:20).[1844]

Their view might be rephrased this way: We are justified by faith plus (non-meritorious) works. Initial justification is contingent on final justification (or judgment according to works); these two are one. These are two aspects of the same justification. They are the "already" and "not yet" aspects of justification. Thus, in their confusing double-talk our "single justification by faith," the "already" of justification is not made complete until the *eschaton* on the condition that we persevere in faith to the end of life.

However, as Karlberg (a Reformed, covenant, amillennial theologian) has observed, "This statement of the doctrine is both unclear and misleading. How can the 'already' (the fixed, once-for-all) aspect of justification await future completion? The implication … is that faith must persevere in order for genuine faith to justify. But such a formulation is flatly contradictory."[1845]

Paul's statement to the Galatians has a significant role to play in their thinking:

[1838] Stanley, *Did Jesus Teach Salvation by Works*, 311.

[1839] Robert N. Wilkin, "Striving for the Prize of Eternal Salvation: A Review of Schreiner and Caneday's *The Race Set Before Us*," *JOTGES* 15, no. 1 (Spring 2002): 7.

[1840] Schreiner and Caneday, *The Race Set Before Us*, 162.

[1841] Ibid., 162.

[1842] Ibid., 78.

[1843] Ibid., 79 (italics added).

[1844] See extensive discussion of this point of view in this book on pp. 225 ff.

[1845] Karlberg, "JETS," 569.

> *For we through the Spirit, by faith, are waiting* (Gr *apekdechomai*, "eagerly await") *for the hope of righteousness (Galatians 5:5).*

Are we "waiting" for the "hope" that we might be saved? This passage provides their basis for the "already—not yet" view of justification.[1846] However, I can see no objection to understanding (Gr *elpis*) in its normal biblical usage of the certain Christian expectation of final arrival in heaven. It refers to a confident assurance which contains no element of uncertainty.[1847] It is a close synonym for faith adding the nuance of confident expectation. Also, the phrase "by faith" need not refer to "by persevering faithfulness." It could simply mean confident assurance and trust that we will one day be declared righteous (justified) because we have already been justified at the point in time we believed.

It is possible to understand "justification" ("righteousness") in this passage in the other well-known biblical sense of "vindication." As argued elsewhere there are two kinds of justification in the Bible: a justification by faith alone (Romans 3:28; 4:5) and a justification by works (James 2:24; Romans 2:13). The former secures acquittal before the bar of justice and guarantees final entrance into heaven. The latter results in "praise from God" for a life well-lived (Romans 2:29; 1 Corinthians 4:5).[1848] That said, I prefer to understand the phrase as the time when we will be perfectly conformed to God's will, that is, our glorification.

Both of these alternatives to Schreiner's "already-not yet" tension are plausible. One could either throw Paul in contradiction with himself, as Schreiner and Caneday do, calling the contradiction a "tension," or one could take the more obvious approach and say that a believer will be acquitted (soteriological-justification) on the final day because he was previously justified when he believed,[1849] or that he will be vindicated (vindication-justification) by God for a life of persevering faith.

While soteriological-justification certainly has a future manifestation, according to this writer's understanding of the New Testament, that future soteriological declaration is based on the fact that a person was justified at the very moment he believed. We do not wait to be justified; we wait to stand before the divine tribunal as already acquitted. Forensic justification is already complete; the future acquittal before the judge is based on this fact.[1850]

> *THEREFORE having been justified by faith, we have peace with God through our Lord Jesus Christ (Romans 5:1).*

1846 VanLandingham understands the righteousness which we await to be the age of righteousness, and not personal justification. However, he bases this on Quman references and not the New Testament. See Chris VanLandingham, *Judgment & Justification in Early Judaism and the Apostle Paul* (Peabody, MA: Hendrickson Publishers, 2006), 315-19.

1847 For example Romans 4:18; 8:20; 12:12; Ephesians 1:18; 1 Peter 1:21; Titus 1:2.

1848 See vol. 1, chapter 17 for discussion of final justification in Romans 2:5-13 and vol. 1, chapter 28 for the two kinds of justification alluded to in James 2:24. See pp. 422 ff.

1849 They manufacture a similar "tension" between the fact that we are already forgiven of our sins (p. 76) and we must continue to confess or we will not be saved (p. 77). Since the theme of 1 John is stated in the opening verses to be "fellowship," it is much simpler to say that ongoing confession and forgiveness are for fellowship and not salvation from eternal damnation!

1850 For an excellent and coherent discussion of the nature of salvation see Earl Radmacher, *Salvation* (Dallas: Word Publishing, 2000), 5 ff. See also David R. Anderson, *Free Grace Soteriology* (Lakeland, FL: Xulon Press, 2010).

Justification for salvation is a past event and does not await the future for its completion. We already have the peace with God, which flows from justification completed (Romans 5:1).

And whom He predestined, these He also called; and whom He called, these He also justified; and whom He justified, these He also glorified (Rom 8:30).

Justification precedes glorification and occurs in this life:

And such were some of you; but you were washed, but you were sanctified, but you were justified in the name of the Lord Jesus Christ and in the Spirit of our God (1 Corinthians 6:11).

The Corinthians had already been justified and were not awaiting its completion on the last day. Similarly, Paul tells the Galatians,

Nevertheless knowing that a man is not justified by the works of the Law but through faith in Christ Jesus, even we have believed in Christ Jesus, that we may be justified by faith in Christ, and not by the works of the Law; since by the works of the Law shall no flesh be justified (Galatians 2:16).

When a man believes he *is* justified. The Bible does not say, "He will be."[1851]

Shipwreck at Sea

In the above discussion, we saw repeatedly that Experimental Predestinarians believe that the warnings are the means by which one is motivated to persevere to the end of life in order to secure soteriological benefits. Among the many problems they must encounter in maintaining this position, there is one difficulty that lies at the heart of their theology. If God has promised eternal life to believers and assured them that they cannot lose it, why then does He issue warnings to them that tell them they can? As pointed out above, Experimentalists argue that those who raise this objection simply do not understand the correspondence between warning and assurance. To explain this mystery, they often point to the incident in the book of Acts where Paul was shipwrecked at sea. Caneday and Schreiner develop this notion fully in their carefully nuanced discussion of this event.

On the way to Rome as a prisoner, the ship on which Paul sailed entered into a violent storm at sea. After several days of struggling against the wind, they began to lose control of the ship and the sailors lost all hope of survival. At this point God gave a prophecy to Paul though an angel.

And yet now I urge you to keep up your courage, for there shall be no loss of life among you, but only of the ship. For this very night an angel of the God to whom I belong and whom I serve stood before me, saying, "Do not be afraid, Paul; you must stand before Caesar; and behold, God has granted you all those who are sailing with you." Therefore, keep up your courage, men, for I believe God, that it will turn out exactly as I have been told. But we must run aground on a certain island (Acts 27:22-26).

In this passage the apostle Paul is promised that he will not perish, but he warns the men in the boat that, unless they attend to the means of saving themselves from the storm,

---

[1851] See Titus 3:7.

they will perish. On the one hand, Paul says, "There shall be no loss of life among you" (Acts 27:24), and on the other hand, when the sailors tried to escape the boat he says, "Unless these men remain in the ship, you yourselves cannot be saved" (Acts 27:31).

Paul assured them that no life will be lost *if* they stay on the ship and allow it to run aground. Obviously, if they decided not to meet the conditions of the promise and jump ship and not allow the ship to naturally run aground, they would be lost. Caneday and Schreiner admit this.[1852] They continue, "God accomplishes his purposes by the use of means. Paul understood this. He recognized that God's promise included both the end (all lives will be saved) and the means (run aground on an island)."[1853] But there is no certainty in this promise if they fail to use the means. So far, so good, the Partners agree. Schreiner then makes a big leap from this incident to assuming that the warnings regarding loss to the Christian are about losing salvation. However, in our view a legitimate application of the shipwreck at sea incident to salvation would look like the table below.

	SHIPWRECK AT SEA	REWARDS
PROMISE	There shall be no loss of life among you.	Reward and no loss at the Judgment Seat of Christ
MEANS	Stay on board and let the ship run aground.	Persevere in faith and good works to the final hour.

Schreiner and Caneday are certainly correct that God achieves His ends through means. Their false application is that they assume, without discussion, that the incident of the shipwreck at sea should be applied to salvation and not to rewards. Their application of this incident to salvation cannot be correct because the means for obtaining salvation is faith alone apart from works, and salvation comes to us "without cost."

They incorrectly assume that inheritance, future salvation, and a full experience of eternal life all refer to final entrance into heaven and not reward and an enhanced experience of life, as has been fully documented elsewhere in this book. With this false assumption in play, they apply it to the promises of salvation. Their logic goes like this:

1. Salvation is promised to all who believe.
2. Inheritance, eternal life, crowns, the prize, and reward are promised to faith plus works.
3. Inheritance, crowns, the prize, eternal life, and reward equal salvation in the sense of entrance into heaven.
4. Believers are warned that they will not inherit (i.e., go to heaven) without persistent faith and a life of works.
5. Therefore, salvation (in terms of entering heaven) is promised to faith but conditioned on works.

The problem is that points (3) and (4) are unbiblical (or are merely assumed to be a legitimate application of the incident in Acts), and therefore the conclusion (5) which follows is false.

1852 Schreiner and Caneday, *The Race Set Before Us*, 210.

1853 Eight years earlier, Schreiner viewed works only as a "mark" of salvation. See "Did Paul Believe in Justification by Works? Another Look at Romans 2," *Bullietin for Biblical Research* 3(1993). Now he views them also as a "means."

If God were to make a promise that salvation is free, making it clear that it is "without cost," and then say, "It is not free, it will cost you everything," then would not God have been lying when He made the initial promise? God did make such an unconditional promise in relationship to final salvation in many passages, but He did not in the shipwreck at sea.[1854] Of course, Experimental Predestinarians disagree that God made a promise of salvation "without cost." That is because they view rewards, the prize, inheritance, and so forth as relating to final entrance into heaven, which we have refuted earlier. In regard to the shipwreck at sea, God promised physical salvation *on the condition that they stay on the ship*. To cite this one non-soteriological instance as a counter example fails.

Summary

As seen in this chapter, Experimentalists reduce the warnings to a "bluff." They are empty threats regarding a danger that will never befall the true believer. When warnings are referred to as "conceivable consequences," it is difficult to see how they are even conceivable. If in fact, the believer has received the imputed righteousness of Christ, as these writers say, how is it possible that the believer is in danger of damnation? Schreiner and Caneday are not Arminians; they do believe that salvation cannot be lost.

Experimentalist explanations for the warning passages have led us to a theological dead end. The contexts of these passages do not allow us to assign the warnings only to professing believers. That the intended audience of these warnings is believers is now commonly accepted.

But if believers are in view, and if according to the warnings, they must persevere in good works in order to be saved on the final day, as Experimentalists contend, how does this differ from a works salvation? As explained in this chapter, Experimental Predestinarians argue that, understood in this manner, the warnings lead to the conclusion that good works are a condition for final salvation.

How can this be? In their desire to remain faithful to the Reformation *sola fide*, they have cleverly nuanced their teaching in an unsuccessful attempt to claim they are within the framework of traditional Protestant orthodoxy. These works, they say, are non-meritorious conditions and not causes.

The next chapter explores how they deal with the charge that they teach a works-righteousness.

[1854] Contra Schreiner who objects, "One could also object that the example adduced from Acts 27 relates to physical life, not to spiritual salvation. Such an objection is not compelling, for the principle of how warnings function applies in both spheres." See Schreiner, *Run to Win the Prize*, 97. Schreiner misunderstands the objection to his view. The issue is not the different spheres (physical and spiritual) but the different conditions.

37

The Warnings: A Means of Perseverance 2?

THE EXPERIMENTAL Predestinarian viewpoint on the warning passages in the New Testament leads to the conclusion that works are a condition for obtaining heaven. The Neonomian wing of the Reformed faith often makes this shocking claim as an attention-getting challenge to orthodox evangelicals who cherish the Reformation's *sola fide*.

Advocates of this position say they are being misunderstood. The problem, they say, is that readers are not hearing their strong assertions that salvation comes by faith alone and are misrepresenting them. In order to clarify their position, they argue in two ways that what they teach is not a works-righteousness.

First, they say that although works are indeed a condition for obtaining final salvation, because they are non-meritorious works, there is no contradiction with *sola fide*. Since these works are produced by God and not the believer, these works *can* save. Works produced by nonbelievers cannot save. Second, they argue that works are only a condition, but not a cause of salvation.

This chapter addresses these two responses to their problem of a works-salvation, and in the following chapter we will discuss the biblical evidence that refutes their system.

"Works are a Nonmeritorious Condition"

Faced with the troubling implications of their view, many Experimental Predestinarians respond, "Yes, works are a condition of salvation but they are a nonmeritorious condition."[1855] For example, Neonomian writer Ed Neufeld asserts, "If God can graciously enable saving faith, he can also graciously enable saving obedience."[1856]

[1855] This formulation has a long history, going back to Calvin himself. Illustrating again the Experimental Predestinarian penchant for wearying their opponents with double talk, Calvin says, "There is nothing to prevent the Lord from embracing works as inferior causes. But how so? In this way: Those whom in mercy He has destined for the inheritance of eternal life, He, in his ordinary administration, introduces to the possession of it by means of good works. What precedes in the order of administration is called the cause of what follows. For this reason, He sometimes makes eternal life a consequent of works; not because it is to be ascribed to them, but because those whom He has elected He justifies, that He may at length glorify (Romans 8:30); He makes the prior grace to be a kind of cause, because it is a kind of step to that which follows. But whenever the true cause is to be assigned, He enjoins us not to take refuge in works, but to keep our thoughts entirely fixed on the mercy of God." Calvin, "Institutes," 3.14.21. So instead of calling works a meritorious cause, they simply re-label them and call them an inferior one! But regardless of what they call these works, they are still saying that works cause final entrance into heaven, which is, if words mean anything, another gospel.

[1856] Neufeld, "The Gospel in the Gospels: Answering the Question 'What must I do to be saved?' From the Synoptics," 268.

"Saving obedience"!? What is this saving obedience? For that writer saving obedience is an obedience "rising from that same dynamic of God's grace and meritless human response."[1857] In other words, it is meritless because God does it in the believer.

Thomas Schreiner agrees, and, because of this, he believes that he has been misunderstood when critics say he teaches "works-righteousness." In both of his books[1858] he explains what he means. A works-righteousness, he says, is characterized by two things: (1) it is a righteousness produced by human effort, and (2) it is meritorious. Such righteousness Schreiner strongly asserts cannot save. In agreement with other Neonomian writers, he believes that works are a condition for salvation but not a meritorious cause of final entrance into heaven. This distinction between a condition and a cause seems obvious to these writers.

Chuck Lowe puts it this way, "Romans 6–8, no less than 8:1–2, indicate that good works are a precondition for—albeit not the meritorious cause of—eschatological salvation."[1859]

Why are these works non-meritorious? Schreiner and Caneday explain.

> *The teaching of God's election and God's prior work in our lives also demonstrates that the thesis propounded in this book cannot be dismissed as works-righteousness, **for any good work we do comes from God's work in us:** We love because he first loved us (1 John 4:19).*[1860]

But how can this view escape the charge that this contradicts Paul's doctrine that salvation is apart from works? Would it make any difference to Paul whether the work in us is produced by God or produced by man? Do works produced in us save? Of course, salvation by human works contradicts Paul, but so does salvation by works produced in us, whether worked by God or by man. Their view is the same as Rome's response to the Reformation assertion that Rome was teaching a works-righteousness.

We respectfully disagree for two reasons. First, works in a believer's life are produced *both by God and man*, and not by God alone, and second, they *are* meritorious. Paul asserts, "*I can do all things through Him who strengthens me*" (Philippians 4:13). Paul is the one doing the work, and Christ helps (cf. Hebrews 4:16), and Paul said that at the judgment seat he could boast about what he had done (1 Corinthians 9:15-18; 1 Thessalonians 2:20).

Accordingly, Schreiner and others are teaching salvation that is achieved by a synergism of human and divine works. Faith, in their view, is not the "alone" instrument of justification, in spite of their claims to the contrary. It is difficult to distinguish this viewpoint from classical Arminianism or Rome, which also say that final arrival to heaven is conditional.

Neonomians claim that because good works are the result of God's prior work, one's work cannot be called a works-righteousness. But is this accurate? Contrary to their thesis, we suggest that since we have a part in the work of sanctification, it is NOT *all* God's work; some of it is our work (Philippians 4:13).[1861] Therefore, according to their

---

1857 Ibid., 268.

1858 Schreiner and Caneday, *The Race Set Before Us*. Schreiner, *Run to Win the Prize*.

1859 Chuck Lowe, "There Is No Condemnation (Rom. 8:1): But Why Not?," *JETS* 42, no. 2 (June 1999): 246.

1860 Schreiner and Caneday, *The Race Set Before Us*, 330.

1861 "The heart of the issue lies in the efficacy of God's grace: is God's grace intrinsically efficacious or extrinsically efficacious? According to the classic doctrine of perseverance, God's grace is intrinsically efficacious in producing its result, that is to say, grace infallibly causes its effect. But according to Molina, divine grace is

view the believer's work does contribute to his final salvation. Accordingly, they do teach that salvation is by works, regardless of how strongly they deny it.

But there is another problem with this viewpoint. How can the works of a believer be considered non-meritorious when the Bible clearly presents them otherwise?

ARE THE BELIEVER'S WORKS MERITORIOUS?

According to Hoehner, they are not: "Although salvation is based on grace (unmerited favor), it might appear that rewards imply merit. But on the contrary, rewards from God are not payment for services but a gracious gift from a generous God. They are independent of human achievement."[1862] Hoehner argues this from the parable of the laborers[1863] in the vineyard where those who had worked one hour received the same pay as those who worked the entire day. However, contra Hoehner, merit certainly was involved. They were paid equally, some were paid over generously, but all were "paid."

All the Greek words used in this connection imply merit of some kind. For example Jesus says, *"For you will be repaid at the resurrection of the righteous"* (Luke 14:14). The word for "repay" is *antapodidōmi* and means, "to pay something back to someone as the result of an incurred obligation."[1864] God, it seems, has graciously agreed to obligate Himself to pay us "wages."

Jesus repeatedly refers to the works of the regenerate man as meriting compensation by using another common term for "wage" (Gr *misthos*) and applying it to the believer's reward in heaven.[1865] Seven Greek words are translated "reward," and twenty-nine passages having theological significance in the New Testament use *misthos* or cognate Gr words.[1866] The basic idea of this word group means payment for work done. For example, *"He who receives a prophet in the name of a prophet shall receive a prophet's reward* [Gr *misthos*]*; and he who receives a righteous man in the name of a righteous man shall receive a righteous man's reward"* (Matthew 10:41). The righteous man's "reward" is a *misthos*, "remuneration for work done, *pay, wages*."[1867] It is in addition to heaven!

In Romans 4:4 Paul explicitly says that a "wage" is an obligation which is owed to the worker, *"Now to the one who works, his wage* [*Gr misthos*] *is not reckoned as a favor, but as what is due* [*Gr opheilēma*]*"* (Romans 4:4). An *opheilēma* ("what is due") is a "debt" or "obligation."[1868] Clearly then, God has agreed to place Himself in debt to the faithful Christian when He calls the reward granted a *misthos*. God has obligated Himself to reward work!

---

extrinsically efficacious, that is to say, it becomes efficacious when conjoined with the free cooperation of the creaturely will. On Molina's view, God gives sufficient grace for salvation to all men, but it becomes efficacious only in the lives of those who respond affirmatively to it." William Lane Craig, "Lest Anyone Should Fall: A Middle Knowledge Perspective on Perseverance and Apostolic Warnings," *International Journal for Philosophy of Religion* 29, no. 2 (1991): 69.

1862 Harold W. Hoehner, "Rewards," in *New Dictionary of Biblical Theology*, ed. T. D. Alexander and B. S. Rosner (Downers Grove, IL: InterVarsity Press, 2001).

1863 To be discussed later, see pp. 996.

1864 Louw-Nida, 1:574. See Colossians 3:24.

1865 Matthew 5:12, 46; 20:28; Luke 6:23; 1 Corinthians 3:14; 2 John 8.

1866 Hoehner, "Rewards."

1867 BDAG, 653.

1868 Louw-Nida, 1:670.

Another Greek word for reward is used in Hebrews 10:35. *"Therefore, do not throw away your confidence, which has a great reward* [Gr *misthapodosia*]*"* (Hebrews 10:35). *Misthapodosia* also refers to "recompense…a payment of wages."[1869]

On several occasions Paul refers to a crown the believer may receive at the Judgment Seat of Christ. The victor's crown is obtained only as a result of exceptional performance. He says, *"Everyone who competes in the games exercises self-control in all things. They then do it to receive a perishable wreath, but we an imperishable"* (1 Corinthians 9:25). The word for "wreath" is *stephanos*, and it refers to an "award or prize for exceptional service or conduct, *prize, reward.*"[1870]

Paul speaks of the reward he hopes to obtain at the Judgment Seat of Christ as a *brabeion* in Philippians 3:4, *"Do you not know that those who run in a race all run, but only one receives the prize* [Gr *brabeion*]*?" "Run in such a way that you may win"* (1 Corinthians 9:24). According to the lexicon, a *brabeion* is "an award for exceptional performance, prize, award."[1871]

Paul also says that the inheritance of the believer is a reward (Colossians 3:24), calling it an *antapodosis*, which means "that which is given to someone in exchange for what has been done, *repaying, reward.*"[1872] The writer of the Epistle to the Hebrews tells us that God is a "rewarder" of those who believe Him (Hebrews 11:6). The Greek word *misthapodotēs* means "one who pays wages."[1873]

All these Greek words (*misthos, antapodidōmi, misthapodosia, stephanos, brabeion, antapodosis, misthapodotēs*) express the idea of something obtained by means of effort, remuneration for work done, wages, or payment. They are singularly inappropriate terms to describe a "condition" for final entrance into heaven which comes apart from payment, wages, work done, or remuneration but is obtained *"without cost"* (Revelation 21:6; 22:17). It is therefore lexically impossible to say, as some Experimental Predestinarians do, that while believers are judged according to their works, their works have no "merits, but in that they are the effects of faith."[1874] Certainly, they are the effect of abiding in the Vine but they are also the effect of the believer choosing to abide and to do.

And how do Experimental Predestinarians respond to this? They do so in two ways. First, consider once again, Schreiner and Caneday,

> *Though it is true that the word used in this verse [Hebrews 10:35] literally means "one who pays wages" (misthapodotēs), the author of Hebrews does not mean that we achieve the reward by meriting it.*[1875]

1869 BDAG, 653. See also Hebrews 11:6, 26.

1870 BDAG, 944. Schreiner and Caneday say, "Each of the crowns is a metaphor for obtaining the heavenly inheritance." Schreiner and Caneday, *The Race Set Before Us*, 83. The Partners, of course, agree. However, contrary to these writers, the heavenly inheritance is not final entrance into heaven as they believe, but, as has been demonstrated in earlier chapters, the inheritance refers to rewards received there.

1871 BDAG, 183. See also Philippians 3:14.

1872 BDAG, 87.

1873 BDAG, 653.

1874 William G. T. Shedd and Alan W. Gomes, *Dogmatic Theology*, 3 vols. in 1 ed. (Phillipsburg, NJ: Presbyterian and Reformed Publishing Co., 2003), 802.

1875 Schreiner and Caneday, *The Race Set Before Us*, 90.

They directly contradict the writer to the Hebrews by saying, "God's reward for us is not earned wages." In view of the well-established meaning of the word *misthapodotēs* and the other words for reward, how can they make this claim? They explain that this is to be understood as a metaphor. Of course, they are correct, but this does not mean that one can change the meaning of the words used. Simply dismissing the verses in which *misthos* is used as metaphorical will not do. The metaphor is a metaphor with an intended meaning. It clearly stands for payment in the sense of reward, as all the lexicons attest. Romans 4:4-5 refutes this plainly.[1876]

> *Now to the one who works, his wage [Gr misthos] is not reckoned as a favor, but as what is due. But to the one who does not work, but believes in Him who justifies the ungodly, his faith is reckoned as righteousness (Romans 4:4-5).*

Schreiner and Caneday labor to show that in the context of Hebrews 10 and 11, reward cannot mean "payment for work done." How can they be so sure? They say, "According to Hebrews 11:6, and the context, the reward which God gives them is commendation, the verdict of righteousness."[1877] They understand this to mean the imputed righteousness of Christ of which Paul spoke. Noah's "reward" was the verdict of righteousness, and since that verdict (in their view) is personal salvation, the reward here must be personal salvation.

How did Noah obtain this verdict of righteousness? He obtained it because he "*in reverence prepared an ark for the salvation of his household, by which he condemned the world*" (Hebrews 11:7). He obtained it by works. Noah was already a believer before he built this ark. Before he even struck the first nail, God said of him, "*But Noah found favor in the eyes of the Lord*" (Genesis 6:8). He displayed his saved status when he worshiped God "in reverence" as he hammered every nail. Thus this verdict of righteousness was something added to a salvation which he already possessed.

What does it mean that Noah became "an heir of the righteousness which is according to faith" (Hebrews 11:7)? What is this "faith" and this "righteousness?" Paul Tanner argues that in Hebrews 11 "faith" does not refer to the initial transaction through which we are born again, rather, "faith" in this chapter refers to the *walk of faith* in every instance.[1878] He further points out that the word "righteousness" is used six times in Hebrews and never of imputed righteousness. In each instance it refers to the moral quality of righteousness.[1879] Tanner concludes,

> *Since "faith" in Hebrews 10-11 is not "saving faith," and since "righteousness" in Hebrews is not "forensic imputed righteousness," this verse is probably talking about something else. Noah was a man of faith, and as Genesis 6:8 teaches us, he was a "righteous and blameless man." So what did that gain him? It qualified (or led to) him becoming an "heir."*

Thus, when the writer says Noah inherited the righteousness which is according to faith, we paraphrase, "Noah inherited the moral righteousness corresponding to [his] faithfulness," that is, he became a possessor of a lifestyle which God commended because he lived by faith.

[1876] For extensive discussion of this passage, see pp. 77 ff.

[1877] Schreiner and Caneday, *The Race Set Before Us*, 90.

[1878] Paul Tanner, personal communication, May 27, 2012.

[1879] See Hebrews 1:9; 5:13; 7:2; 11:33 and 12:11.

We can see, then, that when Schreiner and Caneday assert that "God's reward for us is not an addition to salvation,"[1880] the very context of Hebrews 11 they are using to prove this claim says precisely the opposite.

Even some Reformed theologians, such as Charles Hodge, vigorously refute the idea that a reward is equivalent to heaven when one dies and is secured by faith alone. Instead, they say, it is something owed to the believer.

> *It is, however, clearly recognized in Scripture that a laborer is worthy of his hire. To him that worketh, says the Apostle, the reward is not reckoned of grace, but of debt. It is something due in justice. This principle also is universally recognized among men.*[1881]

A second response by Experimentalists is to argue that since faith is a condition and is obviously non-meritorious, conditions do not necessarily entail merit. Shedd argues this way: "After this statement of the inseparability of good works from faith it is important to observe carefully that the works which naturally issue from faith are not the cause or ground of justification any more than the act of faith itself is."[1882] He goes on to say, "Both of these are regarded as constituting a unity that has two phases or aspects, so that works are faith in operation and faith is works potentially."[1883]

However, does not Scripture refute this idea in place after place where it describes works as meriting reward?

Of course, works contribute nothing to a believer's justification. Why? Because they are polluted and because they are inadequate (Galatians 3:10). A violation in one part of the law, James says (James 2:10), makes us guilty of all, and perfect obedience is required. Furthermore, if works figure into the equation at all, then the total sufficiency of what Christ did (Hebrews 7-10) is nullified. That is why the agency through which we obtain salvation is punctiliar faith, which is passive acceptance and non-meritorious. Even God's work in the believer does not produce adequate or unpolluted works because God's work through the Holy Spirit involves a synergism in which God and man cooperate in the production of the works.[1884] Naturally, this does not mean that God rewards polluted works. As argued elswhere, God accepted Abraham's faith as a fully adequate substitute for perfect obedience. He does this both in regard to our salvation and to our daily walk.[1885]

The means by which we obtain rewards is not only initial faith but also faithfulness (Matthew 5:19; 1 Corinthians 4:2). A perfect obedience (impossible for us but provided freely by the justifying righteousness of Jesus the Christ, 2 Corinthians 5:21) is required

---

1880 Schreiner and Caneday, *The Race Set Before Us*, 91.

1881 Hodge, *Systematic Theology*, 3:343.

1882 Shedd and Gomes, *Dogmatic Theology*, 808.

1883 Ibid., 808.

1884 This is not to say that God rewards polluted works! As Calvin acknowledged, He justifies those works which we contributed every time we have come to Him in faith throughout the rest of our lives.

1885 See pp. 78, 82. This "vindication-justification" is referred to in Genesis. 15:6?, Romans 4:22; and James 2:23. Calvin has a different view. He says, "As we ourselves, when we have been engrafted in Christ, are righteous in God's sight because our iniquities are covered by Christ's sinlessness, so our works are righteous and are thus regarded because whatever fault is otherwise in them is buried in Christ's purity, and is not charged to our account." See Calvin, *Romans*, 345. This "vindication-justification" is referred to in Genesis. 15:6?, Romans 4:22; and James 2:23.

for justification, but faithfulness is required for reward. The works of the believer are the means by which we obtain reward and thus *are* meritorious. Therefore, it is a *non sequitur* to say that because saving faith is a condition that does not entail merit, that in a similar way, the works of the believer for salvation or rewards are conditions that entail no merit.

The Neonomian wing of Experimental Predestinarian theology believes these works are conditions for obtaining salvation. But Partners argue that they are conditions for obtaining rewards. The problem for Experimental Predestinarians is that these works are continually presented in the New Testament as meritorious, the very thing they are trying to avoid.[1886]

IS GOD UNDER OBLIGATION?

Part of the Neonomian concern is that if these works are meritorious, that means that God is in some way under obligation to reward us or to save us by works. That would mean that their doctrine of non-meritorious works as a condition for salvation is false. They recoil in horror at any idea of God being obligated to man. According to them, that is a Roman Catholic error.[1887] Yet this is precisely why rewards are gracious. The point is that God freely chose to enter into a relationship with the believer in which He would reward him for work done. God was under no obligation to enter into this relationship. That He chose to do so is an act of grace. If it be argued that this means "God becomes indebted to man,"[1888] we agree, but He willingly and freely chose to become indebted and was in no way obligated to obligate Himself.

Paradoxically, many within the Reformed faith have no problem with the fact that God may obligate Himself to provide assurance to the believer. For example, Joel Beeke, says, "Consequently, the believer may plead for the fulfillment of the covenant on the ground that God is obliged to act in accord with his covenant-promises."[1889] There is no denial of grace in asserting that God obligates Himself if He chose to do so when He did not have to.

Also consider how Experimental Predestinarians often argue in regard to their proposed "Adamic" Covenant, that "by *covenant* the Creator voluntarily bound himself to owe the creature eternal life, upon the condition of perfect obedience."[1890] The Partner argues that God has in fact done this in regard to rewards, but not in regard to works for eternal life. No one should be surprised at this because God continuously does this sort of thing throughout Scripture in relationships called conditional covenants, not to mention the scores of promises which He obligates Himself to honor (Hebrews 6:16-18).[1891]

Writers from this Reformed persuasion often assert that they are being misrepresented. When one quotes their precise words, they complain that they are taken

---

[1886] Sometimes faith is referred to as a non-meritorious condition, and the works of the regenerate are a "wage," a meritorious condition. Actually, faith is NOT a condition for salvation at all. It is represented in Scripture as a means. We are saved "through" faith and not "by" faith (e.g., Ephesians 2:8, 9).

[1887] Berkouwer, *Faith and Perseverance*, 126.

[1888] Ibid., 126.

[1889] Joel Beeke, "Personal Assurance of Faith and Chapter 18:2 of the Westminster Confession," *WSJ* 55, no. 1 (Spring 1993): 30.

[1890] Hodge and Hodge, *The Confession of Faith: With Questions for Theological Students and Bible Classes*.

[1891] Andrew H. Wakefield has pointed out, "The fact that God offers a promise [if you work you will be saved—the Adamic Covenant] which he must certainly know can never be actualized, makes the promise seem not just false, but deceptive, the perpetration of a divine fraud." Wakefield, *Where to Live: The Hermeneutical Significance of Paul's Citations from Scripture in Galatians 3:1-14*, 81.

out of context or that the totality of their work must be considered. True, their statements should not be taken out of context. Yet it is the responsibility of these proponents to make themselves clear. Schreiner later realized that in a book he earlier coauthored with Ardel Caneday that some "have thought that we [Schreiner and Caneday] were proposing works-righteousness."[1892] It is easy to see why some "misunderstood" him. But did they really misunderstand? As a result of the confusion, he felt it necessary to write a second book to provide "a fresh and somewhat different angle to the questions explored in the *Race Set Before Us*." He says this second effort was written to provide "further clarification of some controversial issues."[1893]

However, his point of view, which many cannot comprehend and which seems to state what they say they do not mean, does breed confusion in the minds of many. This view sounds so similar to Roman Catholic theology espoused at the Council of Trent that it is no wonder that some readers have been led "back to Rome" after reviewing their book. One example of this is found on the Amazon.com website, where a former Calvinist says, "I read this book [*The Race Set Before Us*] as a Calvinist nearly a month before my conversion to the Catholic Church, ironically. The authors make a superb biblical analysis of the process of salvation, and it not being just a onetime event." Interestingly, not just their *opponents* "misunderstand" what they are saying!

"Works Are a Condition of Salvation but Not a Cause"

CONDITIONS AND CAUSES

Some Experimental Predestinarians say that a believer's works are a *condition* for salvation, but not a *cause* of it. Historically, as far as I can determine, we owe this distinction to Jonathan Edwards. Summarizing Edwards' teaching on this point, Logan says, "The fact that a certain reality is not a cause does not mean, however, that it may not be a condition. Very simply, all causes are conditions but not all conditions are causes. Evangelical obedience is thus fully a condition of justification, but clearly is not a cause of justification."[1894] So works and not faith alone are a condition for final entrance into heaven after all! But are they also a cause?

Their logic goes like this:

MAJOR PREMISE: Works are not the cause of our entrance into heaven.
MINOR PREMISE: Works are necessary for entrance into heaven.
CONCLUSION: Therefore, the works of a believer *must not* be a *cause* of entrance into heaven but only a *condition*.

The minor premise has been refuted by biblical evidence presented in previous chapters that "carnal" Christians will go to heaven and that true believers can fail (see chapter 32).

[1892] Schreiner, *Run to Win the Prize*, 11.

[1893] Ibid., 11.

[1894] Samuel T. Logan, "The Doctrine of Justification in the Theology of Jonathan Edwards," *WTJ* 46, no. 1 (Spring 1984). Other Experimental Predestinarians have been similarly very forthright on this point. "Logically, then," Nicoll says, "Good works must be a condition of justification." W. Robertson Nicoll, "Faith and Works in the Letter of James in Essays on the General Epistles of the New Testament," *Neotestamenticia* 9(1975): 22. Cited by Hodges, *Absolutely Free! A Biblical Reply to Lordship Salvation*, 214.

Note, for example, 1 Corinthians 3:15 (works burned up, saved through fire, etc., so heaven apparently *can* be obtained without works). Jesus taught that works are *not* necessary for entrance into heaven (Matthew 5:19), but they are necessary for reward (Matt. 5:12, 46; 6:1, 4, 6, 18; 10:41-42; 19:27-30; Luke 6:35, etc.).

In the view of Neonomian writer, Alan Stanley, salvation is a complicated affair. In fact, he has recently published a book entitled *Salvation Is More Complicated Than You Think.*[1895] If, as Stanley maintains, the works of the Christian are not meritorious, what is the precise relationship between works and final entrance into heaven in Stanley's soteriology? Are they a cause of salvation, a demonstration, a condition, or none of the above? Stanley answers this way, "If endurance looks *back* onto salvation that has already occurred, then it is clearly a demonstration of that salvation. If endurance looks *forward* to salvation yet to occur, then it is clearly a condition for salvation." So, in Stanley's soteriology, works are either a demonstration or a condition, but they are not a cause. Stanley maintains he is not teaching faith plus meritorious works as two different conditions for salvation. However, as will be demonstrated below, the logic of his position suggests that he is.

This writer found Stanley's discussion confusing and contradictory. While the statement above lifts some of the fog, a mist still remains. On the one hand, Stanley says he agrees with Luther that "works are not the cause of one's salvation but the result,"[1896] but, on the other hand, Stanley says he agrees with Calvin that works are an "inferior cause."[1897] On the one hand, he states "that salvation to be attained in eternity is secure right now though not complete." But on the other hand, he says, "There are passages that teach the possibility of forfeiting salvation through lack of endurance."[1898] On the one hand, he tells us that endurance is a "condition because salvation hasn't occurred yet." On the other hand, he says, "It is incorrect to say that endurance is an addition to the gospel."[1899] On the one hand, he says that "endurance [i.e., post-conversion, God-produced, nonmeritorious, work] does not, in agreement with the Reformers' viewpoint,[1900] cause [final] salvation," but is only a

[1895] Alan P. Stanley, *Salvation Is More Complicated Than You Think* (Colorado Springs: Paternoster, 2007).

[1896] Stanley, *Did Jesus Teach Salvation by Works*, 321. Stanley would probably say that Luther is speaking of pre-conversion works, leaving open whether post-conversion works save. However, Luther would maintain that no works of any kind, pre or post-conversion, can save. Stanley quotes Luther as saying, "For we perceive that a man who is justified is not yet a righteous man, but is in the very movement or journey toward righteousness." Martin Luther, *The Disputation Concerning Justification*, ed. J. J. Pelikan, H. C. Oswald, and H. T. Lehman, Luther's Works (Philadelphia: Fortress Press, 1999), 23. However, what Luther meant by "journey toward righteousness," is not, as Stanley implies, a journey toward final salvation from eternal damnation, rather it is the journey of progressive sanctification, becoming righteous in experience just as we are by forensic imputation. Here is what Luther actually said: "23. For we perceive that a man who is justified is not yet a righteous man, but is in the very movement or journey toward righteousness. 24. Therefore, whoever is justified is still a sinner; and yet he is considered fully and perfectly righteous by God who pardons and is merciful. 25. Moreover, God forgives and is merciful to us because Christ, our advocate and priest, intercedes and sanctifies our beginning in righteousness. 26. His righteousness, since it is without defect and serves us like an umbrella against the heat of God's wrath, does not allow our beginning righteousness to be condemned." Ibid. 23-26. One possesses a full and perfect righteousness when he believes, but he must make it experiential.

[1897] Stanley, *Did Jesus Teach Salvation by Works*, 322. See below where it will be argued that this was not Calvin's view.

[1898] Ibid., 327.

[1899] Ibid., 252-53.

[1900] Ibid., 320.

"constituent part" or "intrinsic aspect" of it.[1901] On the other hand, he agrees with Calvin's supposed view that works are a "minor" cause.[1902] On the one hand, he insists that entering the kingdom is by faith alone, but, on the other hand, he says "Somewhere along the way converted sinners become righteous and therefore eligible to enter the kingdom."[1903] On the one hand, he maintains that there is a distinction between a condition and a cause[1904] and that salvation is not "caused" by works, while, on the other hand, he states that final salvation is a "consequence" of works,[1905] is "based" on works,[1906] and has works as a "minor cause," thereby seemingly closely relating the ideas of condition and cause. He says works are a condition for (final) salvation but not a demonstration of it because final salvation has not occurred yet, but then he says works are a condition of final salvation in the sense that they are a demonstration of initial salvation. One gets lost in all these fine distinctions and wonders how a fisherman in the first century would ever have understood Jesus. Drawing a line between a "condition," a "consequence," a "basis,"[1907] a "cause," a "constituent part" or an "intrinsic aspect" would appear to many to be distinctions without significant differences. Stanley admits that some of these contrasts "seem" to be contradictory and there is a "tension" here. One is reminded of the man who throws ash up in the air, and as it cascades around him complains, "I cannot see."[1908]

Imagine the following dialogue as an advocate of Stanley's views (as set forth in his book, *Salvation Is More Complicated Than You Think*),[1909] shares the gospel with an unbeliever, whom we will call Bill.

[1901] Ibid., 252. Notice all the qualifiers one must insert to make Stanley's views clear. How would any reader of the New Testament pick up on all these subtleties?

[1902] Ibid., 51, 322. Admittedly, Calvin spoke rather opaquely. Calvin, "Institutes," 3.14.6. But it is not clear that Calvin is defining "cause" the same way Stanley defines it. Calvin asserts, "What precedes in the order of administration is called the cause of what follows." It is not really a cause but is only "called" that because works precede entrance into heaven. Calvin explicitly clarified what he meant when he said, "There are inferior causes, but these depend on free justification, which is the only true cause why God blesses us. These modes of expression designate the order of sequence rather than the cause." For Stanley, "cause" means "something which brings about an effect," but it is likely that Calvin simply means "something which precedes something else in a sequence."

[1903] Stanley, *Did Jesus Teach Salvation by Works*, 175.

[1904] Stanley asserts that works are a "condition" of salvation, but then he begins to qualify that statement: "It is unfortunate that the term 'condition' carries with it all sorts of negative connotations, for Jesus does not mean condition here in the sense of gaining merit or favor." He then says that by condition he means that "one must continue in their already existing relationship with God if they are to be finally saved." Ibid., 248.

[1905] Calvin, quoted by ibid., 322.

[1906] Stanley says, "People will be judged on the basis of their works vis-à-vis their final destiny." Ibid., 311.

[1907] Stanley says that the eschatological judgment (entrance into heaven) is "based on works." Ibid., 133.

[1908] Stanley might explain these seeming discrepancies this way: "If a person is truly saved, he will have post-conversion works. These works must be there from beginning to end of the salvation process before a person can enter heaven. But during the process the same works are viewed from two different perspectives, depending on which way a person is viewing salvation: (1) looking back on initial salvation, these works are a demonstration of faith, because salvation has been attained; (2) looking forward to final salvation, these works are a condition of salvation because that final salvation hasn't been attained yet. In other words, works are at the same time a demonstration and a condition, depending of the perspective. Demonstration points to successful accomplishment; condition points to potential accomplishment. In either case, the works have to be there before a person can claim to be saved. Conditional works are demonstration of works waiting to happen." (Suggested by Wendall Hollis, personal communication, April 7, 2008).

[1909] Stanley, *Salvation Is More Complicated Than You Think*.

Counselor: Bill, I would like to share with you the wonderful good news of God's free offer of eternal life that comes "without cost."

Bill: How can I obtain this free gift without cost? Please explain the gospel to me? How can I become a Christian?

Counselor: You must believe on the Lord Jesus Christ and if your believing is sincere you will be saved.

Bill: How will I know if I am sincere enough?

Counselor: You will progress to a point where you possess surpassing righteousness, and then you will be eligible to enter the kingdom.

Bill: What does that involve?

Counselor: Well, you will need to obey all the commands, sell your wealth and give it to the poor, always forgive others, be a peacemaker, completely deny yourself to the point of possible martyrdom, obey everything the Bible teaches, develop a personal character that surpasses the highest known standards of character in Jesus' day, always struggle against lust, never develop anger as a pattern of life, do acts of kindness toward others, strive to be perfect, abandon everything to follow Christ, and a few other things.

Bill: Do I have to make a commitment to do all these things in order for my faith to be genuine?

Counselor: That seems to be what Jesus is teaching. You must commit to live out the principles of the Sermon on the Mount.

Bill: I thought you said salvation is by faith alone, is a gift, and is offered to me without cost.

Counselor: Well, Bill ... salvation is more complicated than you think.

What is a "cause"? According to Webster it is "something that brings about an effect or a result; a person or thing that is the occasion of an action or state; an agent that brings something about."[1910] The online dictionary defines a *cause* as a "person or thing that acts, happens, or exists in such a way that some specific thing happens as a result; the producer of an effect."[1911] The Lexicon Wesbster Dictionary defines it as, "That which produces an effect; that which brings about a change; that from which anything proceeds; and without which it would not exist."[1912] What is a "condition"? Webster says, "Something essential to the appearance or occurrence of something else."[1913] One can see that while the words do mean different things, there is a close conceptual connection between them.

When Stanley says that salvation is a "minor cause," a "consequence of works," and is "based on works," how does this differ from Webster's definition of a "cause" as "an agent which brings something about"? When Pink says that works are the "indispensable means" and that unless we use our "diligent endeavors we cannot be saved," [1914] how does this differ practically from "***we,***" at least in part, being a cause? Similarly when Thomas Schreiner tells us, "*Believers obtain eschatological salvation by continuing to believe until the end and by heeding the warnings given to them,*"[1915] and "*The summons to persevere and the initial call to believe are conditions that must be fulfilled to be saved,*"[1916] how do

[1910] *Merriam-Webster's Collegiate Dictionary*, (Springfield, MA: Merriam-Webster, Inc., 2003), s.v. "cause".

[1911] http://dictionary.reference.com/browse/cause?s=t&ld=1087.

[1912] *The Lexicon Webster Dictionary: Enclyclopedic Edition* (English-Language Institute of America, Inc., 1976), 160.

[1913] *Merriam-Webster's Collegiate Dictionary*, s.v. "condition".

[1914] Owen, *Hebrews*. Quoted in Pink, *Exposition of Hebrews*, 600.

[1915] Schreiner, *Run to Win the Prize*, 109.

[1916] Ibid., 104. Schreiner continues to confuse us by also saying, "Heeding warnings is not the basis of our salvation." Thus we obtain eschatological salvation "by heeding warnings," but heeding warnings is not the

these requirements differ in any practical way from "***believers***" being a cause and from Webster's definition of a cause, "that which produces an effect"? When they tell us that if we are to be saved, "*We must run the race with dogged determination to obtain the prize of eternal life, and it takes remarkable discipline and training to make it to the end,*"[1917] would not most understand that our "dogged determination" and "remarkable discipline and training" are not just conditions but are actions that "exists in such a way that some specific thing happens as a result."[1918] Are they not causes which, as they say, "***we***" must do, and not just conditions, of our final arrival in heaven?

Stanley responds saying that a "condition" is another word *for a demonstration which has not yet occurred*. If all he means is that one is only saved on the condition that his current lifestyle demonstrates that his initial faith was genuine, this would be nothing new and would be consistent with the traditional views of Westminster Calvinism. However, he seems to mean more than that. He says that a condition means "one must continue *in their already existing relationship with God* [i.e. endure] if they are to be admitted to heaven."[1919] Presumably, he would say that this means that if one does not continue in their already existing relationship with God, this means they were never saved initially because endurance in the faith is the proof of the reality of the faith. The problem is that Stanley has just said this person *does* have a "*relationship with God*." If he fails to persevere that means he can lose it. Would not this mean a saved person could lose his salvation? In Stanley's view, since salvation is a process and has not yet been completed, one cannot technically speak of losing a salvation which has not yet been attained.

But even granting that these works are technically not a "cause," they are so closely related conceptually that this is how many would understand him. For example, if the coach of the New York Yankees says to his team, "If you win this next game, you will go to the World Series." The condition for going to the World Series is winning the game. It is semantically true that winning did not "cause" their entrance into the series, but would anyone not wrapped up in post-reformation polemics see much difference?

Because the Experimentalists have assumed that works are necessary for final entrance into heaven, they are logically forced to conclude that because the works of the believer *cannot* be a cause, they must be something else, a condition, and then they must distinguish a condition from a cause, as if in the final analysis it makes any theological difference.

It should be noted, however, that some in the Neonomian wing of the Reformed faith do believe that faith and the works produced in our lives by the Holy Spirit are "causes" of salvation. The latter, they say, is an "instrumental" cause and the former is an "efficient"

---

basis. So the warnings are not a "basis" of salvation, but they are a "condition" and a means of salvation. I think I understand what Schreiner is getting at, but this nuanced use of language explains why some believe he is in fact teaching a works-righteousness even though he strongly denies it. I am also doubtful that a first-century fisherman or readers of Paul's epistles in the first century could comprehend this subtle defense of post-Reformation theology!

[1917] Schreiner and Caneday, *The Race Set Before Us*, 314.

[1918] http://dictionary.reference.com/browse/cause?s=t&ld=1087.

[1919] Stanley, *Did Jesus Teach Salvation by Works*, 248.

cause.[1920] But, if anything is plain from the New Testament, works have NOTHING to do with a person's arrival in heaven either as a cause or a condition.

But if it is by grace, it is no longer on the basis of works, otherwise grace is no longer grace (Romans 11:6).

But to the one ***who does not work****, but believes in Him who justifies the ungodly, his faith is reckoned as righteousness (Romans 4:5).*

For by grace you have been saved through faith; and that not of yourselves, it is the gift of God; not as a result of works, that no one should boast (Ephesians 2:8-9).

He saved us, not on the basis of deeds which we have done in righteousness, but according to His mercy, by the washing of regeneration and renewing by the Holy Spirit (Titus 3:5-7).

As these passages make clear, one cannot mix faith and works in the plan of salvation and be faithful to the New Testament. If works are introduced, grace is no longer grace.

DOES SALVATION DEPEND ON RESULTS FOR WHICH WE ARE RESPONSIBLE?

If it does, then salvation is in some sense "caused" by our own works and is not just a condition of final arrival in heaven. Who does these works? *If man has a part in their production, it would seem that man, in the final analysis, is responsible for his ultimate arrival in heaven.*

As an example of the Experimentalist approach to the warnings, consider Paul's famous athletic metaphor for Christian discipleship.

Do you not know that those who run in a race all run, but only one receives the prize? Run in such a way that you may win. Everyone who competes in the games exercises self-control in all things. They then do it to receive a perishable wreath, but we an imperishable. Therefore I run in such a way, as not without aim; I box in such a way, as not beating the air; but I discipline my body and make it my slave, so that, after I have preached to others, I myself will not be disqualified (1 Corinthians 9:24–27).

In a recent sermon by Piper, he appears to have embraced the conclusions of the Council of Trent in regard to final salvation by faith plus works.[1921] He understands Paul to be uncertain of his final destiny in 1 Corinthians 9:27. Paul is concerned that he might be "disqualified," which Piper understands to mean, sent to the lake of fire. According to Piper, "If Paul says somewhere along the race, 'I am through, I am tired of living for the gospel, I am tired of doing what you say I must do,'—if that happens, then Paul would not share

---

1920 Pink, *An Exposition of the Sermon on the Mount*, 347. Pink provides a classic illustration here of how Experimental Predestinarians weary their opponents with their endless distinctions and "clarifications." Because of their manifold qualifications, definitions, and refinements, they can always say, "You do not understand what the Reformed faith teaches." Even Peter and Paul might be confused! For example, we learn from Pink that there are five "causes" of salvation: (1) the original cause, God's sovereign election; (2) the meritorious cause, the mediatorial work of Christ; (3) the efficient cause, the work of the Holy Spirit in "making them meet for the inheritance of light; (4) the ministerial cause, the preaching of the Word; and (5) the instrumental cause, faith."

1921 Piper, *Beyond the Gold.*

in the gospel [go to heaven when he dies]."[1922] He misunderstands Paul to say, "If I do not pummel my body, if I give way to flesh … I could go to the lake of fire."

In proof of this denial of the grace of God, Piper quotes 2 Corinthians 13:5. "*Test yourselves to see if you are in the faith; examine yourselves! Or do you not recognize this about yourselves, that Jesus Christ is in you—unless indeed you fail the test?* [Gr *adokimos*]." Piper is impressed with the fact that the same word "disqualified" (Gr *adokimos*) is used both in 1 Corinthians 9:27 and in this verse. He misunderstands the phrases "in the faith" and "Jesus Christ is in you" as referring to personal salvation. As argued elsewhere, "in the faith" does not refer to the state of salvation but to being in a faith-way-of-life or as we say today, "being in fellowship." The phrase "Christ in you," in context, does not refer to the indwelling of Christ in regeneration but to the manifestation of Christ's power in one's life. The test and examination has nothing to do with finding out if one is really saved. Rather, it refers to testing to see if Christ is really working in them as they have just denied that Christ is working in Paul (2 Corinthians 13:3).[1923]

Because Paul speaks of receiving an imperishable wreath (Gr *stephanos*, "crown"), Piper turns to 2 Timothy 4:7-8 for a parallel because both passages, he correctly notes, speak of a race, a fight, and a crown. The crown in 2 Timothy 4:8 is called "the crown (Gr *stephanos*) of righteousness." In spite of the fact that a different crown is referred to in 1 Corinthians 9:25, Piper equates them and understands the crown of righteousness to refer to "the righteousness which fits us for heaven," that is, the justifying righteousness of Christ. True, according to the New Testament, a believer receives that righteousness the moment he believes but the crown of righteousness in 2 Timothy 4:8 will be awarded upon his arrival into heaven. It is quite unlikely that the crown of righteousness has anything to do with the justification of Christ. The crown of righteousness most likely is the crown of "right behavior." It is a crown of vindication whereby Jesus says, "You have lived faithfully and well."[1924]

If one is to achieve final salvation, Piper asks his listeners to consider, "Do you run the race because heaven is at stake in your life, do you fight and pummel your body and deny yourself and crucify the flesh because heaven is at stake in your life or do you play games with God?"[1925] But in response we must ask our readers, "Is this the salvation by faith alone taught in the New Testament?"

No doubt an evangelical like Piper does not want to be understood to mean that works save us. In order to avoid this he says, "What is at stake is the demonstration that Christ is in you." So if one does not pummel his body and exert the discipline, the demonstration would not be adequate enough to establish to others (presumably) and to oneself that he is saved. Thus, on the one hand, Piper can argue that all these works are part of what is necessary to obtain salvation, and, on the other hand, they are merely a demonstration of a salvation already received. Only a theologian ensconced in post-reformation polemics could either think of or understand all this. Certainly, Galilean fishermen and the Corinthian readers of Paul's letter would have no idea what he was talking about. This is classic theological exegesis in full flower, adjusting the text in order to make it consistent with a particular system of theology.

1922 Ibid.

1923 For discussion of this passage see pp. 462 ff.

1924 For discussion of the Crown of Righteousness see pp. 967 ff.

1925 Piper, *Beyond the Gold.*

The subtlety of the Experimental Predestinarian argument is rarely perceived. Works are not, we are told, a condition of salvation but a necessary result of saving faith. We shall see, however, in the discussion to follow that this "necessary result" is a result for which we are responsible, thus making final entrance into heaven our responsibility and therefore ultimately caused, at least in part, by the believer. These writers will claim, of course, that God assumes responsibility to guarantee that believers will in fact perform these works, thus ultimately placing our final destiny in God's hands.

Reflect for a moment on the simple statement, "If you want to arrive in Los Angeles, you must drive a car." A correct understanding of the gospel offer is more like a train. The train carries us to our final destination with no participation from us. We only sit. The driving of a car requires our diligent effort.

CONDITION: Drive a car
RESULT: Arrive in Los Angeles

To draw the parallel with gospel, we would say, "If you want to go to heaven, you must believe."

CONDITION: Believe
RESULT: Arrive in heaven

The person who drives a car to Los Angeles knows, however, that driving a car involves many things: turning on the ignition, use of the brakes, turning wheels, filling up with gas, and signaling with turn signals. All of these things "cause" the car to arrive in LA. Now it is true that use of brakes and turning of wheels are necessary aspects (results?) of driving a car. If one does not use the brakes and does not turn the steering wheel, he will never achieve the intended result, arrival in Los Angeles. All understand, therefore, that these necessary aspects are really conditions of arriving in Los Angeles. They are all assumed as part of the general condition, driving a car, and thus it is the driver's responsibility to get the car to Los Angeles. In fact, they are the "causes" of arrival in LA as well. These actions cause the engine to turn on and the wheels to stay on the correct roads.

But the gospel does not include all these additional items in the word "believe." "Believe" is not a general term for a life of good works, even if driving is a general term for a number of works involved in navigating an automobile. This is the precise point at which the Reformed argument fails. To believe is to trust and includes nothing else. If anything is clear in the New Testament, whatever belief is, it is totally exclusive of works:

> *Does He then, who provides you with the Spirit and works miracles among you, do it by the works of the Law, or by hearing with faith? (Galatians 3:5).*

> *But to the one who does not work, but believes in Him who justifies the ungodly, his faith is credited as righteousness (Romans 4:5, NASB95).*

When Paul and Jesus connect faith with hearing and looking, they are trying to throw it into the strongest possible contrast with anything connected with working. Hearing and looking are receptive functions. One sees when light happens on the eye. One hears when sound happens on the ear. *Faith does not include a life of works! Faith "happens" to us as a result of contemplation of the Object of Faith, the Lord Jesus, and the beauty of the gospel promise.*

But to pick a human illustration, let us explore the parallel with physical birth. We might say, "A condition for growing old is to be born." Now, on Experimentalist assumptions, certain kinds of results of birth are necessary for a person to grow old, such as eating. Hunger is a possible result of being born, and satisfying hunger is a necessary condition for and cause of growing old. Furthermore, unlike breathing, eating is a result for which we are responsible. Moreover, we can say that eating does cause growth and is not just a result of birth. We can choose to eat or not to eat. Here we can lay down a self-evident principle,

> *A necessary result for which we are responsible and which must be present for another result to occur is no different from an additional condition and cause for the achievement of that second result.*

In the analogy of physical birth, therefore, two conditions are necessary for growing old, birth and eating, the former making the latter possible and the latter making old age possible. In other words, there is no difference between a result for which we are responsible and a condition! And if a "cause" is something that brings about an effect or a result and if eating brings about the "result" of growing old (according to Webster), there is little practical difference between a cause and a condition in the birth analogy.

Now a person who has been born physically might do a lot of things like brush his hair, shave his beard, and brush his teeth. None of these things, however, are conditions for or causes of growing old, and none of them are necessary results of birth. However, any result of birth which is a necessary condition for growing old and for which we are responsible is in fact a second cause and condition, added to birth, for growing old.

Imagine, after reflecting on this illustration regarding birth, you say to a friend, "Eating is a cause of growing old." Steeped in Experimental Predestinarian ways of thinking, your friend replies, "No, that is not true. Eating is not a cause of growing old but a necessary result of birth." Your reaction would understandably be one of amazement. Eating is both a condition and a cause.

Therefore, when Experimental Predestinarians use such phrases as "faith alone saves a man, but the faith that saves is not alone," they are in fact saying that works are a cause of salvation. When terminology like "It is therefore faith alone which justifies, and yet the faith which justifies is not alone,"[1926] the cleverness of the prose serves to conceal that fact. Proverbial sayings like this have been passed on in theology textbooks for centuries. They seem to have explanatory power, and they certainly left opponents of the Experimental Predestinarian system speechless, but in reality they are not only empty of meaning but are also contradictory and confusing. If the works are a necessary result of faith and if a person cannot be saved without them, then the works are in fact a condition for and a cause of salvation, and the person is responsible to save himself. If they are not present, he will perish. Necessary results for which we are responsible are the same as conditions.

The above illustrations spoke of necessary results "for which we are responsible." Let us consider this point more carefully. There are some necessary results of spiritual and physical birth for which we are not responsible. Physically, we may think of such things as breathing, heartbeat, and transmission of neurons across brain synapses. Spiritually, we may think of

[1926] John Calvin, Acts of the Council of Trent, 3:152.

the creation of the new man, our death to sin, our justification, and the gift of all spiritual blessings in Christ. But there are many spiritual effects of the new birth for which we are jointly responsible with God.

The Reformed faith maintains, and we certainly agree, that, while salvation is a work of God, sanctification is a work of God in which believers cooperate.[1927] For example, Experimentalists declare,

> *There is no perseverance without man* ***working out his own*** *salvation.*[1928]
> *Authorities maintain that sanctification is not an autonomous human work* ***but a divine-human (concursive)***[1929] ***operation*** *initiated by God.*[1930]
> *Scripture also teaches that the people of God are called to strive after sanctification of life … For while it is God that worketh in them both to will and to do they are nevertheless called to walk in obedience and to* ***work out their own salvation*** *in fear and trembling.*[1931]

The vast majority of Reformed theologians would agree with Lewis and Demarest that while God's part in sanctification is to initiate, enable, motivate, and warn, there is still a sense in which "we sanctify ourselves."[1932] We must take action; we must separate ourselves from immoral influences; we must initiate acts of love. Erickson puts it this way, "So while sanctification is God's work, the believer has a role as well, entailing both removal of sinfulness and development of holiness." It is not, he says, "A completely passive matter on the believer's part … the believer is constantly exhorted to work and to grow in the matters pertaining to salvation."[1933]

As Reformed theologian Charles Hodge said, "It must be remembered that while the subject is passive with respect to that divine act of grace whereby he is regenerated, *after he is regenerated he cooperates with the Holy Ghost in the work of sanctification.*"[1934] The entire responsibility for our sanctification cannot be laid on God.[1935] As these Reformed theologians and Scripture together testify, if man is responsible for works, he must cooperate with the Holy Spirit to produce them. Thus, his works must be a "cause." Because they think that the outcome of this work is salvation and not reward, the Neonomians must wordsmith the meaning of cause and condition.

The Experimentalists will reply that in their view the warnings in Scripture are a means of guaranteeing that believers will strive and work in order to enter heaven. But this confuses sanctification with salvation, and reduces salvation to an outcome obtained, in part, by human effort.

We must, of course remember that God is represented in Scripture as the source, the motivator, and the one who enables, but we are the ones who must act. We do it, and He

1927 Berkhof, *Systematic Theology*, 534. He says, "Man is privileged to co-operate with the Spirit of God," and elsewhere that these kinds of works (i.e., those following regeneration), "are deserving of approval" and since a reward is attached to them are "sometimes called meritorious works," ibid., 542.

1928 Leonard J. Coppes, *Are Five Points Enough? The Ten Points of Calvinism* (Denver: the author, 1980), 55.

1929 That is, referring to a cooperation or combination of agents.

1930 Lewis and Demarest, *Integrative Theology*, 3:185.

1931 Herman Hoeksema, *Reformed Dogmatics* (Grand Rapids: Reformed Free Publishing Association, 1966), 524.

1932 Lewis and Demarest, *Integrative Theology*, 3:207.

1933 Erickson, *Christian Theology*, 2:971.

1934 Hodge, *A Commentary on the Confession of Faith: with Questions for Theological Students and Bible Classes.*

1935 G. Walters, "Sanctification, Sanctify," in *New Bible Dictionary* (Grand Rapids, MI: Wm. B. Eerdmans Publishing Co., 1962), 1141.

strengthens (Philippians 4:13). The Bible calls the unbeliever to do one thing, believe (Acts 16:31). But the calls to the believer are to work: we are to flee fornication (1 Corinthians 6:18), present our bodies as living sacrifices (Romans 12:1), and make every effort to enter rest (Hebrews 4:11), to mention just three. Yes, the warnings, the commands, and the exhortations of the New Testament make it clear that the believer as well as God is responsible for the believer's sanctification. We must respond to God's promptings and appropriate the help He gives. Berkhof puts it this way, "Though man is privileged to co-operate with the Spirit of God, he can do this only in virtue of the strength which the Spirit imparts to him from day to day."[1936] Shedd says that the regenerate "*cooperate* with the Holy Spirit."[1937]

But if man must cooperate, then he must choose to do this. If he does not choose to cooperate, then he will not be sanctified. The numerous biblical illustrations of failure prove that a believer may not so choose (see chapter 32 above). It is therefore incorrect to say, as Berkhof does, that man deserves no credit. He certainly does deserve credit, and the Lord everywhere acknowledges that man will be rewarded for it in the future.

Now, what shall we call this "cooperation" of man? What shall we call his decisions to pursue godliness? Could we not call them works for which he is responsible? Could we not call them "causes" of our ultimate arrival in heaven? And if so, could we not call the outcome of these works a wage earned based on meritorious effort? And if we can call them that, then are they not additional works necessary to obtain heaven? If they are not done, according to Experimental Predestinarians, the person will perish. If a person is responsible to do these works and if that person may choose not to (and both Scripture and experience confirm that he may), are not these works a condition for and cause of his salvation? If works are demanded as an essential part of the agreement which secures our final arrival in heaven, how does this differ from works being a condition or a cause? Indeed, the dictionary defines a condition as "something demanded as an essential part of an agreement"[1938] and a cause as "something that brings about an effect or a result."[1939]

It is at this point that Experimental Predestinarians often feel that those who argue against their position do not really understand their position. "Do you not believe in mystery?" they will often say, "Are you unaware of the mysterious working of the Holy Spirit with the human will in such a way that the result can be declared God's work and not man's?" Experimental Predestinarians tend to retreat to "mystery" when the arguments against their view become too pointed or logical.

The writer remembers teaching a seminar to a group of Reformed students, and after giving some of the illustrations above, one of the professors asked, "I still don't see why the results of regeneration are necessarily works necessary for salvation. Regardless of what you have just said, it seems to me that these works are merely evidences of true faith, and not conditions of salvation." That professor misunderstands the Reformed faith he professes. No one states it better than Pink. "They [good works] are requisite as *a condition* of the possession of full salvation."[1940]

[1936] Berkhof, *Systematic Theology*, 535.

[1937] Shedd and Gomes, *Dogmatic Theology*, 807.

[1938] Lexicon Webster Dictionary, s.v. "Condition," 1:211.

[1939] *Merriam-Webster's Collegiate Dictionary*, s.v. "cause".

[1940] Pink, *An Exposition of the Sermon on the Mount*, 349. (Italics his.)

The professor was thinking of the Reformed teaching that any evidential works are worked in the believer by God. But if we are responsible for these works and they are partly a result of our own efforts, then it is faith plus meritorious human works that are necessary for our arrival in heaven. Some of our Reformed friends will reply, "You continue to misunderstand. We do not teach that works are necessary for arrival in heaven. We teach they are necessary demonstrations that one has genuine faith and it is faith alone that is necessary for arrival in heaven." While this response seems plausible, it is confusing, easily misunderstood, and, to the present writer, appears to be another gospel. Of course our Reformed friends would deny this conclusion but, nevertheless, their view (1) logically requires that salvation is by faith plus works (as argued above and in the next chapter); (2) it contradicts the biblical teaching that works are *not* a necessary demonstration that faith is genuine (see chapters 30-32); and (3) it makes biblical assurance impossible because the amount and duration of the required works are subjective.

That said, many within the Reformed faith go further. As John Owen pointedly insists, "But yet our own diligent endeavor is such an *indispensable means* for that end, as that without it, it will not be brought about. . . . *Unless we use our diligent endeavors, we cannot be saved* [emphases added]."[1941] It appears to this writer that attempting to call diligent effort a condition and not a cause of salvation is to make a distinction with no difference. Owen was not making a careless statement when he said this. He was simply stating the real meaning of the Reformed doctrine of perseverance. If these resulting works are *all* of God, then no human work would be involved, but it is still a works salvation. But if the resulting works are part God's and part ours (as the Reformed faith and Scripture teach), then a man may choose not to do them as Solomon and other regenerate men in the Bible often did. If he may choose not to do them, then true faith will not necessarily result in a life of works.

Even acknowledging that God through "mystery" secures the cooperation of the human will, *man is still responsible and must do good works*. This means that works *are* a condition for and cause of entrance into heaven whether worked in us or done by divine aid, and heaven is earned by meritorious works. After all, Paul did not say, "***Christ** can do all things through me*," but "***I** can do all things through Christ*." Paul does the work, and Christ "strengthens." However, in the Experimental Predestinarian view, faith itself includes this life of works for which we are responsible (e.g., driving a car to Los Angeles), and therefore faith is not simple reliance and conviction but belief plus obedience. In other words, salvation by faith is actually by faith plus works.

Summary

While we must certainly submit to the mysteries of God's providence, that doctrine does not really appear to be relevant to the discussion. The issue is quite simple. According to Experimental Predestinarians:

1. Perseverance in works is the means of obtaining heaven.
2. Because they are the means, they are both a condition and a cause.
3. We are responsible for doing these works and a necessary result for which we are responsible and which must be present for another result to occur is no different from

[1941] Owen, *Hebrews*, 600.

an additional condition and cause for the achievement of that second result.

4. These works, according to the New Testament, are conditions required for us to obtain a reward or payment (Gr *misthos*) for work done, that is, they are meritorious.
5. A commitment to perform these works is included within saving faith.

Therefore, even though Schreiner denies it, if my arguments above are correct, he teaches a works-righteousness as a condition for salvation.

If, on the other hand, perseverance in works is not necessary for entrance into heaven and is not included within the compass of the word "faith," then the gospel of pure and free grace has been maintained.

As explained above, the "means of salvation" view of the warnings faces the following objections.

First, according to the New Testament, the works of the believer are meritorious. All these Greek words (*misthos, antapodidōmi, misthapodosia, stephanos, brabeion, antapodosis, misthapodotēs*) express the idea of something obtained by means of effort, remuneration for work done, wages, or payment. Therefore, in spite of their protests to the contrary, Neonomians are in fact teaching a salvation based upon merit.

Secondly, the distinction between condition and a cause, while semantically valid, is theologically without relevance in regard to the requirements for final salvation. It is clear that these works cause *"something"* related to our final destiny. Because Experimentalists view that "*something*" as heaven, they must carefully define their terms in ways that not only differ from common theological usage but confounds readers of their books. That is why, as they say, they are so often misunderstood. The Partners do not have any problem with these post-salvation works because the outcome obtained by these works is, in the Partner viewpoint, rewards and not final entrance into heaven.

Third, they say that believers are saved by works performed in their lives by God. Yet this is still salvation by works, a wage earned, a synergism of human and divine work, and therefore a meritorious works-righteousness. "Perseverance," they say, "is a necessary means that God has appointed for attaining final salvation."[1942] With this, they fall into the cross hairs of the canon fire that Calvin launched at the Council of Trent: "According to them [i.e, the Council], man is justified by faith as well as by work, provided these are not his own works, but gifts of Christ and fruits of regeneration."[1943]

We now turn to the specific biblical evidence that refutes the Experimental Predestinarian view of the warnings.

1942 Schreiner and Caneday, *The Race Set Before Us*, 152.

1943 Calvin, "Institutes," 3.11.14.

38

The Warnings: Objections to the Reformed View

IN THE preceding chapters we have argued that the Reformed view of the warnings leads to a works-righteousness in spite of their protests to the contrary. In addition, three decisive existential objections oppose their entire system.

It Fails the Test of Human Consciousness

First, because God's Word assures believers that Christ will not forsake them, that they can never be taken out of the Father's hand, and that He will lose none of them, the Experimentalist view of the warnings leads to serious practical psychological problems.

Calvinism has often enjoyed the sanctuary of the philosopher's hall. It revels in theoretical speculation and theological argument. When one reads Calvin's *Institutes* on the subject of election and reprobation, one often feels that some of the arguments are abstract and unconvincing. Sadly, but probably consistent with the spirit of the day, when he responds to his opponents, Calvin assails their character in direct proportion to the weakness of his arguments. When confronted with the perplexing questions of God's justice in the face of election and reprobation, Calvin gives one strained answer after another, and then, in each case, as if sensing the futility of his arguments, he falls back on the standard refrain, "*Who art thou, O Man, who repliest against God*" (Romans 9:20). Indeed, that section of his masterpiece could be appropriately renamed, "One Hundred Ways to Use Romans 9:20 To Refute Opponents of Our System."

However, in contrast to the doctrine of election, with its doctrine of perseverance, Calvinism must emerge from the halls of academia and submit itself to the test of the consciousness of men. If it is true that the warnings are to produce sincere alarm, then one must concede that it is impossible not to know whether he experiences sincere alarm. And since apostasy is said to be impossible, how can one be sincerely alarmed by the warnings against apostasy? Shank observes, "The folly of their contention is seen in the fact that, the moment a man becomes persuaded that their doctrine of unconditional security is correct, the warning passages immediately lose the very purpose and value which they claim for themselves."[1944]

The only way one could think he may commit apostasy would be if he was uncertain that he was one of the elect. Thus the only way this system of motivation could ever work would be if a person throughout his life maintains the possibility that he may not persevere. In other words, he can never know he will persevere until he has! Furthermore,

---

[1944] Shank, *Life in the Son: A Study of the Doctrine of Perseverance*, 164.

as the believer regularly sees inconsistencies in his life, the Reformed teaching exhorts him to examine himself and to consider the possibility that he may not be one of the elect.

And how is this uncertainty to be corrected? According to Schreiner a believer can "escape the threat of judgment by heeding the warning."[1945] "Heeding warnings," he says, "is one of the means by which the promise of final salvation is obtained on the last day."[1946] "By heeding the warnings, believers gain assurance in their lives."[1947] One can see how far Schreiner has drifted from the biblical view that assurance comes (as Romans 8:28-39 teaches) through contemplation of Christ and the beauty of the gospel promises. Not only are works a "condition" of salvation, but in Neonomian theology they are also a condition of assurance.

Berkouwer explains how this works in practice.

> *Anyone who would take away any of the tension, this completely earnest admonition, this many-sided warning, from the doctrine of the perseverance of the saints would do the Scriptures great injury, and would cast the Church into the error of carelessness and sloth.*[1948]

This statement correctly stresses that the warnings imply a real danger, and not Schreiner's "conceivable" danger. However, Berkouwer then tells his readers,

> *The doctrine of the perseverance of the saints can never become an* ***a priori*** *guarantee in the life of believers which would enable them to get along without admonitions and warnings.*[1949]

According to these theologians, the promises of God that we are justified, redeemed, forgiven, and guaranteed eternal life are not guarantees that the believer will never be damned. But how can this be? Final perseverance, Berkouwer believes, "is something that comes to realization only *in the path of faith*."[1950] By using the word "path" he wants us to understand that only persistent faith throughout one's life will guarantee that we will arrive in heaven when we die. But how can God promise us eternal life without cost, and then tell us it will only be ours if we persevere? Berkouwer answers this question this way:

> *To think of admonition and perseverance as opposites, as contradictories, is possible only if we misunderstand the nature of perseverance and treat it in isolation from its correlation with faith. For the correct understanding of the correlation between faith and perseverance, it is precisely these admonitions that are significant, and they enable us to understand better the nature of perseverance.*[1951]

He is saying that the nature of the correlation between faith and perseverance explains the presence of the admonitions. "True" faith perseveres, and the warnings are God's means of guaranteeing that it will. But paradoxically, the admonitions help us

---

[1945] Schreiner, *Run to Win the Prize*, 96.

[1946] Ibid., 101.

[1947] Ibid., 102.

[1948] Berkouwer, *Faith and Perseverance*, 110.

[1949] Ibid.

[1950] Ibid., 111.

[1951] Ibid., 110.

understand the nature of the correlation between faith and perseverance! He is arguing in a circle; although, typical of Berkouwer, his circularity is veiled in complex language. This is the point at issue. Do the admonitions "enable us to understand better the nature of perseverance," or do they help us understand the impossibility of this Experimental Predestinarian doctrine?

We ask, if we have become sufficiently enlightened to understand that perseverance is inevitable and does not depend on us in any manner or degree, how are we to become alarmed by these admonitions and warnings?

The only way we could become alarmed would be if we began to doubt our salvation because of sin. Thus in the final analysis the Reformed view boils down to their dangling the threat of eternal damnation over a believer's head every time he fails "for a period of time" (how long?) in order to motivate him toward perseverance. One can never know if he is saved until the final hour when it is proven that he has persevered.

According to Berkouwer our faith must "always direct itself anew to this confidence. In this perspective it always discovers a fresh consolation, after it has allowed itself to be earnestly admonished."[1952] But how can there be "confidence" and "fresh consolation" if one's status before God is determined by how well he is behaving? Sensitive souls would, and have, died a thousand deaths of introspection under this frightening approach to intimacy with the Lord.

So is a believer to be first alarmed by the warnings and afterwards consoled by the promise of final perseverance? If so, a person cannot accept all of Scripture at face value at the same time. "He must oscillate between two contradictory persuasions, both of which are supposedly equally warranted by the Scriptures."[1953] A person cannot be motivated by the warnings until he has abandoned the promise that perseverance is inevitable and apostasy is impossible. Until he comes to the conclusion that his faith may not be "genuine," he will have no alarm. How is he supposed to determine if his faith is genuine? The answer is that he must heed the warnings.

Berkouwer, like many Calvinists, appeals to irresistible grace. The warnings do not prove that the elect are in danger of apostasy, but the warnings are necessary to prevent the elect from apostasy. The elect cannot fall because they are elect, and God keeps them from falling by giving them exhortations to which they will infallibly respond. However, contra Berkouwer, we know that from Genesis to Revelation, believers do not always respond to God's exhortations.[1954]

The Partners also take the warnings seriously but find no contextual justification for the Arminian conclusion that these warnings threaten loss of salvation. Rather, in each instance a millennial disinheritance or a judgment in time is forecast.

Would not the Experimentalist approach to assurance lead to unhealthy introspection? Schreiner does not think so. He believes that the real danger is that believers will become prideful. He says that for a believer to come to an assurance that he is among the elect, he must give attention to the quality of his works. He must reflect on them to ascertain whether they are of sufficient quality to indicate that he is truly saved. "The paradox here is quite striking. If we concentrate on the quality of our works, we are

---

[1952] Ibid., 122.

[1953] Shank, *Life in the Son: A Study of the Doctrine of Perseverance*, 167.

[1954] See the biblical evidence for the permanently carnal Christian in chapter 32 above.

apt to become consumed with ourselves and our righteousness. Their pride is therefore opened to pride and self-delusion."[1955]

I am not sure to whom he refers. Perhaps there is some pride of this nature in extreme Experimentalist circles where there is a tendency to judge the behavior of others. The present writer has been a missionary, evangelist, and disciple maker for over forty years, and I have never met one person who, when concentrating on his character qualities, fell into Schreiner's paradox of self-delusion and pride. What I have met are confused Christians who have sat under Neonomian and Experimentalist teaching and wonder whether they have heeded the "means" of assurance (i.e., responded to warnings) sufficient in degree to justify that they are truly saved. To have assurance a believer must not focus on the quality of his works. Instead, he must look to Christ who, as Calvin expressed it, is the mirror in which we contemplate our election.

It seems strange that Schreiner believes that his view of the warnings should not lead to unhealthy introspection. Why not? He proceeds to contradict himself in two ways. First he says that "the warning passages are none other than a call to continue to believe."[1956] Yet throughout his books he has been stating that the warnings are calls to obey. Certainly, one must continue to believe to heed the warnings. But the warnings involve more than believing. They are chock full of commands to obey, to work, to do, to strive, to persevere. They are much more than a call to continue to believe.

Secondly, Schreiner has been stressing that the way a person finds assurance is by heeding warnings. But then he says, "The call to persevere, however, should be understood in a radically different way. We are summoned to look to Christ rather than to ourselves, to put our hope in Christ's death and resurrection, to remind ourselves daily that our only hope at the day of resurrection is in what Christ has done for us."[1957] Thus Schreiner contradicts himself. Is he not merely pasting the "right words" on top of a theology of works? If so, the glue does not stick. Earlier, citing Jonathan Edwards with approval, he says, "It is not God's design that men should obtain assurance *in any other way* than by mortifying corruption, and increasing in grace, and obtaining the lively exercises of it."[1958] On page after page he told his readers that the way one finds assurance is by good works, heeding warnings, and persevering. Now he says that assurance is found the way Paul taught us, by contemplation on Christ. Which is it?

Neonomian Calvinism fails the test of human consciousness. Is it not ridiculous to tell a person that the only way he can be sure of his salvation is to persevere in good works to the final hour and then to tell him that he can find assurance only by looking to Christ? Is it not ridiculous to assume that a person living under such a system could escape introspection and a negative view of a wrathful God? How can believers be alarmed by warnings if they have already been consoled by the promise that they are secure? How can they be alarmed about something which could never happen to them unless they are to live in continual doubt that they may be in danger of final damnation? Calvinism fails the test of human experience.

[1955] Schreiner, *Run to Win the Prize*, 109.

[1956] Ibid., 104.

[1957] Ibid., 74.

[1958] Ibid., 109.

Is it not also debatable to say that men are to hold two contradictory sets of Scriptures in their minds at the same time and switch back and forth depending on whether their need is for consolation or admonition? They are unable, on the Experimentalist view of the warnings, to view the whole of Scripture with equal sincerity at the same time. Even Calvin fell into this trap:

> *As far then as Christians are illuminated by faith, they hear, for their assurance, that the calling of God is without repentance; but as far as they carry about them the flesh, which wantonly resists the grace of God, they are taught humility by this warning, "Take heed lest thou be cut off."*[1959]

In this view when a person is "illuminated by faith," he knows that the calling of God is without repentance. But in his struggle with the flesh, a person is supposed to fear going to the lake of fire. So, on-the-one-hand, we are to have a consciousness that we are eternally secure (if we work hard enough to satisfy the claims of conscience that our faith is real), and, on the other hand, because of our flesh we are to be aware that we might be damned. On these premises, even if a believer is currently heeding the warnings and hence is "making his calling and election sure" and is fulfilling his duty to find "full assurance," he cannot know for sure that he will continue to do so. He cannot know that he will finally persevere until he has. Even though he may be confident at a particular point in his Christian life that all is well, he must always hold in his consciousness the possibility, however remote, that he might not continue to believe. Otherwise, the warnings about this possibility would have no influence. But how can a person hold these two contradictory states in his mind at the same time? Being conscious of either one logically and subjectively excludes the other.

It Is Logically Contradictory

Not only do the warnings fail the test of human consciousness in the Experimental Predestinarian system, but also their view of the warnings is logically contradictory. In the previous section we stressed the psychological and practical aspects of this contradiction. This section examines in more detail the contradiction itself.

According to the Experimentalists, on one hand, we are told that our eternal destiny is secure and that we will persevere in holiness to the final hour. On the other hand, we are told that there is no guarantee we will because, if we are living an unfaithful life, we may not be "truly" saved. We cannot be sure that we are saved until we have heeded the warnings. As Schreiner says, "By heeding warnings, believers gain assurance in their lives."[1960] If this is all Schreiner meant, we would agree. But this is not all. He means that unless we obey the warnings, we are not truly Christians. In the final analysis, no matter what Schreiner claims to the contrary, for the struggling Christian this casts aside Christ as the mirror in which he contemplates his election and it substitutes works,[1961] and his final arrival in heaven is in his own hands.

[1959] John Calvin and John Owen, *Commentary on the Epistle of Paul to the Romans*, Calvin's Commentaries (Bellingham, WA: Logos Bible Software, 2010), s.v. Rom. 11:22-24, p. 433.

[1960] Schreiner, *Run to Win the Prize*, 102.

[1961] For discussion on how the believer obtains assurance according to Paul, see chapter 44.

Berkouwer objects, saying there is no factor in man that may determine the issue of perseverance, for "in this way the consolation of perseverance would most certainly be lost, because the final outcome would be put again in the hands of persevering man."[1962] Yet later, as quoted above, he said, "the doctrine of the perseverance of the saints can never become an a priori guarantee in the life of believers which would enable them to get along without the admonitions and warnings."[1963]

Shank correctly objects:

> *But if the "consolation of perseverance" is the assurance that the final outcome is not in the hands of persevering man, does not this "consolation" constitute "an* ***a priori*** *guarantee" of perseverance for all who embrace it? If it does not constitute such a guarantee, just what does it constitute? And if the final outcome is in no way in the hands of persevering man, then how can "the alarming admonitions" be sincere?*[1964]

How is this theological pre-understanding applied to specific warning passages? Arthur Pink illustrates this in his commentary on Hebrews 10:26.[1965]

> *For if we go on sinning willfully after receiving the knowledge of the truth, there no longer remains a sacrifice for sins, but a terrifying expectation of judgment and* THE FURY OF A FIRE WHICH WILL CONSUME THE ADVERSARIES *(Hebrews 10:26–27).*

We will discuss the Partner approach to this difficult passage later.[1966] Our burden here is to explore the inadequacies of the Reformed approach.

First, Pink correctly refutes the position that Hebrews 10:26 refers to unregenerate professors of Christ.[1967] For Pink the fact that the apostle uses "we" proves that regenerate believers are in view. Now he wades in: "If it be impossible for truly regenerated people to ever perish, then why would the Holy Spirit move the apostle to hypothetically describing the irremediable doom **if** they should apostatize?"[1968] Good question. He now gives his "answer." The Christian, he says, must always be viewed from two perspectives:

1. As he exists in the purpose of God—eternally secure.
2. As he exists in himself—in need of solemn warnings and exhortations.

In Hebrews 10:26-27, according to Pink, we see the Christian as he "exists in himself," and not in the eternal purpose of God. He explains that we must consider the relationship between God's eternal plan and the predetermined means to bring it about:

> *God has eternally decreed that every regenerated soul shall get safely through to Heaven, yet He certainly has not ordained that any shall do so whether or not they use the means which*

[1962] Berkouwer, *Faith and Perseverance*, 220.

[1963] Ibid., 110.

[1964] Shank, *Life in the Son: A Study of the Doctrine of Perseverance*, 168.

[1965] Pink, *Exposition of Hebrews*, 614-24.

[1966] See pp. 661 ff.

[1967] Pink, *Exposition of Hebrews*, 615.

[1968] Ibid.

> *He has appointed for their preservation. Christians are "kept by the power of God through faith" (I Pet 1:5)—there is the human responsibility side.*[1969]
>
> *To say that real Christians need no such warning because they cannot possibly commit that sin, is, we repeat to lose sight of the connection which God Himself has established between His predestined ends and the means whereby they are reached. The end to which God has predestined His people is their eternal bliss in Heaven, and one of the means by which that end is reached, is through their taking heed to the solemn warning He has given against that which would prevent their reaching Heaven.*[1970]

Once again we see the Neonomian teaching that good works, not faith alone, is said to be the means God uses to bring a person to heaven. And again we are told that the Christian is to hold two contradictory ideas in his mind at once: viewed from God's perspective, a believer is eternally secure, but viewed from his own perspective, that is "in himself," he is not.

Instead of calling the contradiction between God's preservation and the necessity of our perseverance a "tension," as Berkouwer does, an "already and not yet" as Schreiner does, or "differing perspectives," as Pink does, Experimentalist writer J. A. Tosti prefers the word "symmetry."[1971] Tosti correctly observes that the Reformed doctrine of perseverance is extremely dangerous: "It requires one to walk along the knife-edge of truth; a path so narrow that even the slightest move to the left or right will cast one into an abyss of pernicious error."[1972] To move to the "left," he says, robs the children of God of assurance, and to move to the "right" encourages laxity and slothfulness. The antidote to these dangers is to maintain what he calls "biblical symmetry." It is, however, impossible to maintain symmetry between contradictory concepts. Our eternal security either depends solely on God's guarantees in Scripture, or it depends on those guarantees plus our perseverance. If both are necessary, this is not a "tension" or "symmetry" but a contradiction. If the latter is necessary, it is a salvation by works. Only an eternal security based on the promises of God and completely unrelated to the necessity of the believer's perseverance in holiness can possibly be reconciled with the scores of passages that state the freeness of salvation in Christ.

Tosti's logic, like Berkouwer's, is curious. He correctly assumes that the Bible promises eternal security on the basis of the promises of God. He then correctly assumes that the warnings are directed to true Christians. However, since Tosti, Berkouwer, Schreiner, and Stanley agree that the warnings imply a danger of loss of salvation, an obvious contradiction is set up. How can God promise eternal security on the basis of the death of Christ and at the same time warn those He has promised that their eternal security is secured by their faithful perseverance? They may not, in the end, be saved after all! Unless, of course, they are elect, in which case God will guarantee that they will persevere, even though they can have no confidence that they will (unless they infallibly know they are elect, which the Reformed view of the warning disallows). Otherwise, there would be no real warning. But how can a believer have confidence in God's promises of eternal security since he cannot

---

1969 Ibid., 616.

1970 Ibid.

1971 J. A. Tony Tosti, "Perseverance: The Other Side of the Coin," *The Banner of Truth Trust* 259(1985): 13.

1972 Ibid., 11.

know that these promises apply to him until the final hour, when sufficient evidence of perseverance has finally been demonstrated?

One would normally think that a believer is either eternally secure or he is not. Also one would normally think that such an approach to the warning passages is doubtful. Would the Lord of grace motivate believers in this way? Does this ring true? Would the Bible contradict itself in so many passages on an issue so fundamental to our Christian lives? Tosti simply leaves the contradiction open and says, "For the Scriptures, then, there is apparently no unbearable tension or opposition between the gracious faithfulness of God and the dynamic life; because it is in the thick of the dynamic of the actual struggle of life that Scripture speaks of perseverance in grace. If this is the way the Word of God treats the subject, **dare we do anything different?**"[1973] When our minds naturally revolt at such contorted theology, Tosti states that these are "apparent difficulties" because our minds are yet fallen!

Of course, if this is "the way the Word of God treats the subject," we would have to bow in humble submission. Fortunately, for our emotional health and our intellectual integrity, the Word of God does not treat the subject in this way. A contradiction of this magnitude could only be accepted by one who has a prior agenda, that is, a commitment to maintain the fiction of the saints' perseverance in holiness against all logic and Scripture which teach otherwise!

At least the Arminians are consistent. There is no mysterious tension or symmetry ("contradiction") in their theology. The regenerate man, they say, will be saved if he perseveres, but he can lose salvation as the warnings clearly (they say) teach. Neither is there a contradiction in the position of the Partner. What is in view in the warnings is not a loss of justification or proof that one was saved but a loss of reward at the Judgment Seat of Christ.

To walk on Tosti's "knife-edge" would require a fairly high degree of theological knowledge and reflection. Surely, few would ever be able to believe such contradictory things! The Bible, however, was written to the unlearned and prosaic mind.

It Involves God in a Falsehood

If God has decreed that His elect will finally persevere in holiness and if warnings are a means He uses to secure that perseverance, then God is threatening His elect with a destiny He knows will never befall them. He is telling them they might lose their salvation and He says this to motivate them by fear (read "healthy tension" or "wholesome fear") to persevere. How can a God of truth use lies to accomplish His purpose of holiness in His elect?

Consider how Calvin interprets Paul's famous warning to the Romans:

> *Behold the kindness and severity of God; to those who fell, severity, but to you, God's kindness, if you continue in His kindness; otherwise you also will be cut off (Romans 11:22).*

[1973] Ibid., 16.

In his commentary on Romans 11 he says:

> *We understand now in what sense Paul threatens those with excision whom he has already asserted to have been grafted into the hope of life through God's election.* ***For, first, though this cannot happen to the elect, they have yet need of such warnings****, in order to subdue the pride of the flesh; which being strongly opposed to their salvation, needs to be terrified with the dread of perdition. As far then, as Christians are illuminated by faith, they hear, for their assurance, that the calling of God is without repentance; but as far as they carry about them the flesh which wantonly resists the grace of God, they are taught humility by this warning, "Take heed lest thou too be cut off."*[1974]

Calvin's "interpretation" here is not only empty, but it borders on blasphemy. He is saying that, even though God knows the sinning Christian is elect and therefore saved, God terrifies him with "the dread of perdition" to teach him humility! Lest this be considered simply an aberration of the sixteenth century, listen to Andrew Fuller as quoted approvingly by Arthur Pink:

> *It is necessary for those whom the Lord may know to be heirs of salvation, in certain circumstances, to be threatened with damnation, as a means of preserving them from it.*[1975]

So God, on the one hand, knows Christians will never go to the lake of fire, but, on the other hand, He tells them they might go to the lake of fire if they do not respond to the warnings! Doesn't this mean that God is lying to them, telling them something God Himself knows to be false?

Experimental Predestinarians say, "God threatens the world with damnation, knowing that the elect will never experience it. Is this a lie?" The truth is that God has never promised eternal life to anyone who has not accepted Christ. And the elect, prior to their acceptance of Christ, are subject to damnation. But once a person has become a child of God, born into His family, and told that he can never lose his salvation, an entirely different ethical situation is present. Prior to becoming a Christian, the elect are damned, but after becoming Christians, they are not! It is therefore one thing to warn a non-Christian (even if he is elect) that, if he does not believe, he will perish. That is a true statement. But it is another thing for God to tell that same person, now that he is saved, that if he does not obey, he will be damned, when God knows he is now justified and will never be condemned for his disobedience.

Some Experimental Predestinarians illogically argue that this proposition can be true (i.e., "if you do not persevere, you will be damned") even if it is spiritually impossible for one to fall away. In other words, God is not lying because regardless of whether the person perseveres, it is still true that "if he does not persevere, he will be damned." The problem is that God then gives the impression that it is possible that the person will not persevere even if he does not explicitly say it. Thus God is leaving a false impression, and He knows it, and thus the God of truth is a liar.

[1974] Calvin, *Romans*, s.v. "Rom. 11:22".

[1975] Pink, *An Exposition of the Sermon on the Mount*, 88.

Summary

In this chapter we have argued that the Reformed doctrine of the perseverance of the saints in holiness to the end of life fails the test of human consciousness, is logically contradictory, and involves God in a monstrous falsehood.

This doctrine fails the test of human consciousness because it demands that the believer must hold two contradictory concepts at the same time and must regulate his life with God by maintaining this so-called symmetry. On the one hand, he is to believe he is eternally secure, and on the other he is to consider the warnings as possible indications that he is not. This is emotional schizophrenia.

This approach is not only existentially devastating, but it is also logically contradictory. When one tries to apply this theological pre-understanding to particular passages, it becomes very difficult to interpret them consistently. One must start by assuming that the warning passages are directed to true Christians, and then one must work in the idea that this is healthy for Christians to consider the possibility of eternal damnation, which illogically implies that it does not apply to "true" believers.

Third, most horribly, this Reformed view implies that the God of truth is using a falsehood to motivate His children to obey Him. Even though God knows that the believer is saved, God warns the believer that he might be damned if he does not obey.

It would be unwise to leave this topic without a brief comment concerning the implications of the views of Alan Stanley and Thomas Schreiner on the relationship between works and salvation and rewards. In their system the God-produced works for salvation are necessarily the same works God produces in the believer for sanctification. Thus, degrees of reward are granted on the basis of God-produced works. However, this leads to the question, "How is God glorified in awarding to Himself a lesser reward than is possible?" Some get more reward some get less, but God alone, supposedly, produced them all. If the believer had any role in these works then salvation is ultimately based on works. We can see that the experimentalist doctrine of salvation and rewards involves a conundrum. It actually makes no sense at all. Which is perhaps why preaching and teaching about heavenly rewards is rarely found in their communities. They only make sense within a synergistic view of sanctification, which, paradoxically, many of them embrace but then deny in their doctrine of salvation even though, in their system, it is the same works which apply to both!! They want it both ways. According to them, these works are produced by God alone when they talk about justification but the same works, when they speak of sanctification are produced by God and the believer.

Throughout the preceding chapters of this book, we have assumed, that the Bible teaches that salvation cannot be lost. All Experimental Predestinarians agree with this. The following chapters address the false doctrine of conditional security taught by Arminians.

39
The Vine and the Branches

FEW PASSAGES have been quoted so often and, in my view, incorrectly as John 15. The beautiful and profound analogy of the vine and the branches has been a source of wonderful encouragement to believers throughout the centuries, but it has also become, unfortunately, a controversial passage regarding the eternal security of the saints.

The Last Supper has been completed, and Jesus and His disciples have crossed the Kidron Valley, east of Jerusalem, and are proceeding up the slopes of the Mount of Olives. As they pass by the many grape vines lining their path that have been lifted up and tied to the supporting trestles in the vineyards, Jesus says, "I am the true vine and my Father is the vine dresser."

The disciples have just received some frightening news. Their Master was going to be killed, and they were to be left alone! In John 15-17, Jesus compassionately addresses these fears. Just as these vines have been lifted up, He wants to lift them up, spiritually and psychologically, and to prepare them for the difficulties ahead. His counsel in John 15 is to "abide in the vine" and if they do, they will experience enablement, fruit bearing, and answers to prayer; they will be His "friends."

There has been much difference of opinion about the meaning of this passage. Some of the difficulty is related to the fact that the analogy emerges from an agrarian economy that is not familiar to those of us in the industrialized West. Consequently, cultural and historical data will help us understand some of the key terms and concepts.

15:1 *I am the true vine, and My Father is the vinedresser.*
15:2 *Every branch in Me that does not bear fruit, He takes away, and every branch that bears fruit, He prunes it, that it may bear more fruit (John 15:1-2).*

Because Jesus is the true vine, He commands His disciples to "abide in Me," and if they do, they will bear much fruit:

> *Abide in Me, and I in you. As the branch cannot bear fruit of itself unless it abides in the vine, so neither can you unless you abide in Me (John 15:4).*

Before we discuss the meaning of John 15 in more detail, let us first digress a bit and answer three critical questions that have significant bearing on the interpretations suggested on the following pages. Is Jesus speaking about nonbelievers or believers? What is a branch "in Me"? What does "abide in Me" mean?

To Whom Is Jesus Speaking?

Is Jesus describing those who have only professed faith in Christ, or is He thinking of His regenerate disciples? Most expositors agree that the branches that bear fruit and are pruned represent true Christians. However, some believe that the branch "in Me" that does not bear fruit is not a true Christian; that is, it refers to one who professes faith but does not possess it in the heart. In this view the kingdom is a mixture of true and false believers.[1976] As Bishop Ryle put it:

> *It cannot be shown that a branch in Me must mean a believer in Me. It means nothing more than a "professing member of My Church, a man joined to the company of My people, but not joined to Me."*[1977]

Often justification for this interpretation is found by going outside of John to the analogy of the vine in Isaiah.[1978]

> *Let me sing now for my well-beloved a song of my beloved concerning His vineyard. My well-beloved had a vineyard on a fertile hill. He dug it all around, removed its stones, and planted it with the choicest vine. And He built a tower in the middle of it and also hewed out a wine vat in it; then He expected it to produce good grapes, But it produced only worthless ones (Isaiah 5:1–2).*

The divine Vinedresser tenderly cared for Israel, the vineyard. His intention was that this vineyard would produce good grapes, but it produced only worthless ones. Experimental Predestinarians refer to this passage to explain John 15 because Israel, the vineyard, was His covenant people and not everyone under the Old Covenant was necessarily born again. But is this relevant to John 15? Even admitting that the vineyard in Isaiah 5 may have been composed of both believers and unbelievers, that is irrelevant to the New Covenant under which those addressed in John 15 would live. Under the New Covenant, which was "not like the covenant" (Jeremiah 31:32-34) God made with Old Testament Israel, Yahweh says, "*all will know Me*" (Jeremiah 31:34). John 15 never mentions Israel and its irresponsibility. Instead, the focus is on the disciples and their fruit bearing as a result of intimacy with Christ and the care of the Vinedresser.

Furthermore, what is the most likely thought or event that would have suggested to Christ's mind the analogy of the vine and the branches? What would this metaphor have suggested to the disciples? While it is possible that they would think back to Old Testament references to Israel as a vineyard, is it not more likely that some immediate incident would suggest this metaphor? The immediately preceding event was the Last Supper at which Christ and His disciples enjoyed the fruit of the vine together. Remember also that they have just entered a vineyard on the Mount of Olives. Is it not much more likely that these two factors were prominent in the Master's mind as He taught on the vine and the branches? We can very easily imagine Him passing through the vineyard, and pointing to the vines and the branches and saying: "I am the true vine and my Father is the Vinedresser" (John 15:1).

1976 Charles R. Smith, "The Unfruitful Branches in John 15," *Grace Journal* 9, no. 2 (Spring 1968): 10.

1977 J. C. Ryle, *Expository Thoughts on the Gospels* (Grand Rapids: Zondervan Publishing House, n.d.), 4:334.

1978 See also Romans 11:16-24 and Jeremiah 5:10a.

The Meaning of "in Me"

To whom does the branch "in Me" refer? The literature on the "in Christ" relationship is immense. The phrase "in Me"[1979] is used sixteen times in John's gospel.[1980] In each case it refers to true fellowship with Christ. A review of the sixteen usages in John suggests that when He used this phrase, the Lord referred to a life of fellowship, a unity of purpose rather than an organic connection. If this is correct, it is not possible to take it as "the sphere of profession."[1981] A person "in Me" is always a true Christian. While the word "in" (Gr *en*) is often "used to designate a close personal relation,"[1982] we must ask, "What kind of relationship is meant?" Salvation or fellowship? In no other place in John's writings does "in Me" refer specifically and only to salvation.[1983]

For example, in John 10:38 "in Me" speaks of the fellowship between Christ and the Father:

> *If I do not do the works of My Father, do not believe Me; but if I do them, though you do not believe Me, believe the works, that you may know and understand that the Father is* ***in Me, and I in the Father*** *(John 10:37-38).*

Christ obviously does not mean that the Father is inside of Him and He is inside the Father. The figure is of a relationship between them. The works He performs enable His followers to understand the nature of the relationship. Certainly, observation of miracles does not prove to the observer that the Lord is of the same essence as the Father, organically connected with Him. If that were so, then whenever a disciple performed a miracle, it would show that the disciple was also of the same essence. Christ's miracles prove that God is "with Him." They prove that what God does, Christ does, and what Christ does, God does. They prove that the Son and the Father are likeminded and speak the same things. Therefore, we are to believe what the Son says because what He says is the same as what the Father says. So the "in Me" relationship speaks not of organic connection or commonality of essence but of commonality of purpose and commitment.[1984] The application of the analogy of the vine and the branches is that those "in Me" are not those who are organically connected to Christ, that is, all true Christians, but it refers to Christians who are in fellowship, who are abiding. All believers are organically connected to Christ, but not all abide in Him.

Consider also John 14:30 where the Lord insists that the ruler of this world has nothing "in Me"; that is, he has no relationship or part with Jesus, no communion of purpose.[1985]

[1979] Gr *en emoi*, first person, singular, dative, personal pronoun *egō*.

[1980] John 6:56; 10:38; 14:10(2x), 11, 20, 30; 15:2, 4(2x), 5, 6, 7; 16:33; 17:21, 23.

[1981] Contra Carson, *The Gospel According to John*, 515.

[1982] BAGD, 259.

[1983] It should be noted that this is different from Paul's usage of the concept of "in Christ." While Paul did use the phrase "in Christ" (not "in Me") in this way, he often used it in a forensic (legal) sense referring to the believer's position in Christ or to his organic membership in His body (e.g., 1 Corinthians 12:13). But John never does this. For him, to be "in him" is to be in communion with Him and not organically connected in union with Him.

[1984] In John 14:10, the words "in Me" refer to a close working relationship between Christ and the Father, a unity of purpose.

[1985] In 14:20 the Lord says that in "that day" they will know that He is in them and they are in Him. The sense seems to be that, when they see Him in resurrection, they will know again the fellowship they have with

The Lord is not teaching that the ruler of this world has no part of His essence (who would have thought that?), but that they are not like-minded.

The experience of peace in the midst of persecution will come only to believers who are obediently walking in His commandments and who are aligned with His purposes (John 16:33). "*These things I have spoken to you, so that in me you may have peace*" (John 16:33). He has spoken these words so that "in Me" they can have peace. This peace comes through fellowship "with Him." John's writings and the rest of the New Testament confirm that being "in him" in a saving way does not automatically result in an experience of peace in the midst of trials. Only when believers are "in him" in the sense of walking in fellowship with Him do they have peace.

That "in Me" means oneness of purpose and not organic connection is further brought out in John 17:21. Here Christ prays for the same kind of oneness among the disciples that He enjoys with the Father, a oneness of love and fellowship.

> *That all of them* ***may be one****, Father,* ***just as you are in me and I am in you.*** *May they also be in us so that the world may believe that you have sent me. I have given them the glory that you gave me, that they* ***may be one as we are one: I in them and you in me. May they be brought to complete unity*** *to let the world know that you sent me and have loved them even as you have loved me (John 17:21-23).*

The "in me and I in you" relationship that Christ enjoys with the Father is explicitly taught to be the same as the experience of oneness, unity, and fellowship for which Christ prays for all His followers. How then can the "in Me" relationship refer to organic connection? Why would Christ pray that organic connection between Him and His disciples be achieved if it supposedly had already been established the moment they had believed.

The Father is in the Son, and the Son is in the Father. This prayer describes not an organic connection, but a life of communion, a oneness of purpose. Jesus wants them to have an experience of unity because that observable unity will prove to the world that they are His disciples, models of Christian love (17:23). If being "in him" referred only to an

---

Him now. "That day" could refer to either the coming of the Holy Spirit at Pentecost or the appearances of the resurrected Christ to His disciples. The preceding verse seems to connect it with the resurrection appearances. This is confirmed by John 16:16 where He also speaks of the fact that in a little while they will no longer behold Him and then in a little while they will see Him, a reference to His appearance in resurrection. The meaning then is that when they see Christ in resurrection, they will understand fully some things they do not understand fully now. What they will understand is that Christ was "in the Father" and that they are in Christ and He is in them. The objective knowledge of the resurrected Christ will bring about this clear perception. At this time they will see clearly that Christ has been operating in complete unity of purpose with the Father and that they are in complete unity of purpose with Him. Apparently, they will know something they do not know now. They are already regenerate, but there is something they either do not know at all or only know imperfectly. What brings about the change? The text does not say, but later John states that before the disciples did not understand that He had to rise from the dead (John 20:9). Apparently seeing Christ in His resurrected state brought a flood of understanding concerning the Old Testament predictions and Christ's unity of purpose and obedience to the Father, and this solidified their commitment to Him. The resurrection forever removed doubts regarding who He was and resulted in a change that lasted the rest of their lives. They committed themselves fully to follow Him forever. That commitment, brought about by their seeing Christ in His resurrected state on "that day," resulted in their total unity of purpose and obedience to Him. That is when they knew the experience of unity and fellowship, "you in me and I in you," with their resurrected Lord.

organic connection, it would prove nothing. But if it refers to an observable experiential unity of purpose and fellowship, this would have great testimonial impact. It is a unity they do not yet have but must be "brought to." For John, to be "in Me" is simply to have unity of fellowship and purpose with Him, not organic connection or commonality of essence.

In John 3:21, Jesus refers to the fact that His works have been done "in God." Arndt and Gingrich correctly observe that this means that His works were done in communion or fellowship with God.[1986] Being "in God" does not refer to an organic relationship but to a relationship of commonality of purpose.

In spite of the consistent use of "in Me" to refer to those who are born again, D. A. Carson is not convinced. He believes that "it is more satisfactory to recognize that asking the *in me* language to settle such disputes is to push the vine imagery too far. Supposedly, the transparent purpose of the verse is to insist that there are no true Christians without some measure of fruit. Fruitfulness is an infallible mark of true Christianity; the alternative is dead wood, and the exigencies of the vine metaphor make it necessary that such wood be connected to the vine.[1987]

Apparently, Carson feels that it is "more satisfactory" not "to push the vine imagery too far" because to do so would conflict with his Experimentalist theology. Of course, all would agree that fruitfulness is "*a*" mark of salvation, but we would not agree that it is an "infallible mark." Professing believers, even as Experimental Predestinarians themselves acknowledge, often manifest the same marks. But what Carson really means is that a *life of fruitfulness* is "the" infallible mark of regeneration. Carson does not think the phrase "in Me" necessarily refers to one who is regenerate. However, as shown above, a person "in Christ" in the New Testament is *always* a true believer. Also, Carson's "infallible mark" is shown to be not so infallible because only two verses later Jesus says it is possible for a true believer not to "abide in me" (v. 4).

Experimental Predestinarian Carl Laney has suggested another possibility. He points out that the phrase "in Me" can either be taken adjectivally with the noun "branch" or adverbially with the verb "bearing." If it is rendered adverbially, then the translation is,

Every branch not bearing fruit in me he takes away.

Most translations, however, render the verse,

Every branch in me that does not bear fruit he takes away (ESV).

If Laney is correct, the phrase "in Me" is the sphere of enablement and fellowship in which fruit bearing can occur.[1988] The view is exegetically possible. Laney understands "to be taken away" as final damnation.[1989] He believes that a branch "in Me" is only a branch who professes Christ but may or may not be born again. But is it likely that in Johannine usage, the "in Me" phraseology refers only to one who professes faith in Christ? The passages cited above refute this.

[1986] BAGD, 259.

[1987] Carson, *The Gospel According to John*, 515.

[1988] J. Carl Laney, "Abiding Is Believing: The Analogy of the Vine in John 15:1-6," *BibSac* 146, no. 582 (January-March 1989): 64.

[1989] He says, "The fruitless branches represent 'disciples' who have had an external association with Christ that is not matched by an internal, spiritual union by personal faith and regeneration." Ibid., 61.

More examples could be cited, but this is sufficient to establish that the use of the phrase "in Me" in John does not require the sense of organic connection often found in Paul. To be "in Me" is simply to be in fellowship with Christ, living obediently and with a common purpose. Therefore, it is possible for a true Christian not to be "in Me" in the Johannine sense. That this is true seems evident from the command to "abide in Christ." Believers are to remain in fellowship with their Lord. If all Christians remain "in me," then why command them to remain in that relationship?[1990] It must be possible for them not to remain. This leads us to a discussion of one of John's favorite terms, "abide" (Gr *menō*).

The Meaning of "Abide"

According to Webster, the English word "abide" means (1) to wait for; (2) to endure without yielding, to withstand, to bear patiently, to tolerate; (3) to remain stable or in a fixed state, to continue in a place.[1991] Thus it is similar in meaning to the Greek word *menō*.

The lexicons are unanimous in saying that the verb *menō* means "to remain."[1992] It is used often in John, and in **every** instance it means to remain, to stay, to continue, or to endure.[1993] Christ commands His disciples to remain in Him. What does it mean to "remain"?

A number of things are characteristic of those who remain in him. First, they are those who eat His flesh and drink His blood (John 6:56). Elsewhere (vv. 40, 50) believing and eating are equated and result in eternal life.[1994] The references to blood and flesh point to the cross. One must believe in Christ for the forgiveness of sins if he is to receive life, that is, regeneration. Also, those who have believed in Him for salvation are [normally] those who also continually abide in Him for abundant life (John 10:10b). Believing refers to soteriology and abiding to sanctification. To equate them results in a tautology, "He who believes in me, believes in me."

In John 15:10 the apostle records Jesus as saying,

[1990] The Reformed notion that this is the means by which God uses to secure their abiding is unsatisfactory as discussed in the preceding chapter.

[1991] Webster's Ninth New College Dictionary (Springfield, MA: Merriam-Webster, Inc. 1987), p. 44.

[1992] For example, Friedrich Hauck says it means "to stay in a place." Figuratively "to remain in a sphere," "to stand against opposition, to endure, to hold fast" (Friedrich Hauck, "*menō*," in TDNT, 4:574-88). The word is used of the permanence of God in contrast to human mutability. God's counsel "endures" (Romans 9:11), His Word endures (1 Peter 1:23, 25), the New Covenant endures (2 Corinthians 3:11), and faith, hope, and love endure (1 Corinthians 13:13). Paul uses *menō* of the perseverance of believers in the faith (1 Timothy 2:15; 2 Timothy 2:13, 15). If we endure, we will reign with Him. If we are faithless, He "remains" faithful. Karlfried Munzer says it is used metaphorically to mean to hold fast, or remain steadfast, that is, in a teaching (2 Timothy 3:14; 2 John 9), in fellowship with (John 14:10), to pass the test when one's works are judged (1 Corinthians 3:14). See Colin Brown, "remain," in NIDNTT, 3:224.

[1993] For example, John 1:32, 38, 39; 2:12.

[1994] The reference to eating His flesh and drinking His blood refer to the initial act of appropriation of Christ and the resultant gift of regeneration (6:50, 51, 54, 58). Regarding the metaphors for eating, Carson correctly notes that verses 54 and 40 are closely parallel: 'Whoever eats my flesh and drinks my blood has eternal life, and I will raise him up at the last day' (v. 54); '... everyone who looks to the Son and believes in him shall have eternal life, and I will raise him up at the last day' (v. 40). D. A. Carson, *The Gospel According to John* (Downers Grove, IL: Intervarsity, 1991), 298.

That said, it does not necessary follow that, as Carson says, everyone who "continues in saving faith and consequent transformation of life." Only those believers who obey him experience the fellowship relationship called "abiding" (John 15:10).

If you keep My commandments, you will abide in My love; just as I have kept My Father's commandments and abide in His love (NASB).

If remaining and believing are the same, then believing is obeying commandments, a thought far removed from John's gospel of faith alone. If *menō* ("abide") means "believe," a works gospel would be taught. It is therefore doubtful that the word "remain" could ever mean "to accept Jesus as Savior,"[1995] as some Experimentalists maintain.

Consider John 15:4,

Abide in Me, and I in you. As the branch cannot bear fruit of itself unless it abides in the vine, so neither can you unless you abide in Me (NASB).

If "abide" means "believe," then Jesus would be saying, "If you believe in Me, and I believe in you (i.e., 'I abide in you'), you will bear much fruit." This is hardly a sensible statement! Even if one could successfully argue that *menō* in one place could mean "believe," one cannot allow a possible meaning in one place to govern the clear meaning in so many others![1996]

Everyone who hates his brother is a murderer; and you know that no murderer has eternal life abiding in him (1 John 3:15).

"Eternal life" in this epistle is a metaphor for Jesus Christ. The phrase is precisely the same as saying, "No murderer has Jesus Christ abiding in him." As discussed above, this means, "No murderer remains in fellowship with Jesus Christ." This is made clear by the following verse.

The one who keeps His commandments abides in Him, and He in him. We know by this ***that He abides in us****, by the Spirit whom He has given us (1 John 3:24.)*

In order to "remain in Him," we must keep His commandments.

Like his Master, the Apostle John often linked abiding in Him with loving others.

No one has seen God at any time; if we love one another God abides in us, and His love is perfected in us (1 John 4:12).

1995 Edward A. Blum, "John," in *BKC: New Testament*, ed. John F. Walvoord and Roy Zuck (Colorado Springs: Cook, 2002), 325.

1996 Alan Stanley commits this error. After discussing only three instances of *menō*, John 6:56, 8:31 and 1 John 2:10-11, he declares, "I have already shown that *menō* in 6:56 is synonymous with eternal life." Stanley, *Did Jesus Teach Salvation by Works*, 256. When one reads his discussion of *menō* on p. 154, it is evident that he has shown little. Curiously, he says that *menō* is "often used synonymously for life." Even if abiding in Him were a synonym in this one passage for "believing," it is never a synonym for life! Also, there is no need to assume, as Stanley does, that walking in darkness means "be an unbeliever." Believers can walk in darkness, and abiding in the light in this passage is more naturally understood as continuing in fellowship, not becoming or proving that you are born again. Nor does it refer to a process by which one ultimately achieves final salvation. It is a simple statement of fellowship with God, the purpose of the book (1 John 1:3). In regard to John 8:31, "If you remain in My word, then you are truly disciples of Mine" (NASB), Stanley misses a key contextual element which negates the point he makes. He says that those who "believed him" (John 8:31) are only "so-called" believers because in verse 44 he calls them sons of the devil. Stanley misses the point that verse 31 is an aside to those who had believed, and in verse 44 Jesus resumes His broadside attack against the Pharisees by referring to them, not those who had believed, as "belong to" their "father, the devil." I have discussed this passage more fully on pp. 361ff.

Only if we love one another, does the love of God "remain in us" (1 John 4:12). In order for the love of God to remain in us, it must first have been in us to begin with. As elsewhere, "remain" never signifies the initiatory event of saving faith but the enduring fellowship of walking in communion. The very meaning of the word "remain" implies staying in a position already obtained or entered into, and not entering into a position or state for the first time. If a nonbeliever should ask, "What must I do to be saved," it would be wrong for anyone to say, "Remain in Christ."[1997] We remain in Christ (i.e., remain in fellowship) by keeping His commandments *after* we have been saved.

God remains in fellowship with us only if we love one another (1 John 4:12). We become Christians, however, by faith alone. Through the Holy Spirit we enjoy the fellowship of the Father and He with us (4:13). The Holy Spirit is the source from which we draw to sustain fellowship. As John wrote in 1 John 3:24: "We know by this that He abides in us, by the Spirit whom He has given us" (NASB).

In 2 John 8-9 the apostle declares,

> *Watch yourselves, that you might not lose what we have accomplished, but that you may receive a full reward (v. 8).*
>
> *Anyone who goes too far and does not abide ["remain"] in the teaching of Christ, does not have God; the one who abides ["remains"] in the teaching, he has both the Father and the Son (v. 9).*

Because "abide" means "remain" or "continue," it is evident that there are those who were once in the teaching of Christ who did not continue in that teaching (v. 9). John is following up on his warning in the preceding verse (v. 8) about the danger of losing their rewards at the Judgment Seat of Christ.

When John refers to one who deviates from the teaching of Christ as one who "does not have God," he is still referring to a believer. The context is "abiding," not "being regenerate." He simply means that God was not involved in this defection from pure doctrine. There is no exegetical evidence of which this writer is aware that "having God" ever means "be saved" in Johannine literature. It is roughly equivalent to our saying, "He has [a walk with] God," or "He has God with him in this." This is functionally the same as having "eternal life in him" which, for John, means "having Jesus Christ remain in fellowship with him" (1 John 3:15).

1. We must love our brothers (1 John 2:10).
2. We must walk as He walked (1 John 2:6).
3. We must be strong in the faith (1 John 2:14).
4. We must do the will of God (1 John 2:17).
5. We must hold to the truth we learned when we first became Christians (1 John 2:24).
6. We must not hate our brother (1 John 3:15).
7. We must keep His commandments (1 John 3:24; John 15:10).
8. We must love one another (1 John 4:12).
9. We must publicly confess Christ (1 John 4:15).

The rewards for meeting all these conditions are great. First, we will truly be His disciples (John 8:31). But most of all, such a life will enable us to stand before Him with

---

[1997] Hence, the present writer prefers the Partaker perspective mentioned above. See pp. 616.

confidence rather than shame when He returns (1 John 2:28) and receive our "full reward" (2 John 8).

It is not possible, therefore, to equate abiding with believing. Abiding involves all these works such as obedience, avoiding hatred, having love, publicly confessing Christ, remaining strong in the faith, holding on to truth first learned, and continuing in His word. Whatever belief is, it is not conditioned on works, nor does it consist of works (Galatians 3:5).

Taken Away

If the above discussion is correct, we have established that to be "in Me" means to be walking in fellowship with Christ and does not refer to merely professing a relationship with Christ. Also, to "abide" does not refer to believing but refers to remaining in a belief that one has already initiated at salvation. The way one "remains" is by obedience and faithfulness. Jesus says,

> *Every branch in Me that does not bear fruit, He* ***takes away*** [Gr *airō*]; *and every branch that bears fruit, He prunes it so that it may bear more fruit (John 15:2).*

What does He mean when He says He "takes away" the unfruitful branch?

This consequence has been understood three different ways. However, first we must consider the context in which these words were spoken. Jesus is addressing the believing disciples and preparing them for their work after His departure. It is a time when they need encouragement. Would Jesus spend time warning them that unless they bear fruit, they will prove not be true Christians and be cast into the lake of fire, as Experimental Predestinarians maintain? The disciples were to be the leaders of the early church. Yet now they are about to lose their leader whom they love, and their world will be turned upside down. The need is encouragement and lifting up. Indeed, as Jesus addresses this issue in verse 2, He says that He "takes away" these branches. This phrase has been understood in three ways.

VIEW 1: THEY LOSE SALVATION

The Arminian view of the destiny of the branches is that they lose their salvation. However, even if the verb means "remove" and not "lift up," the loss of salvation is not in view. Jesus repeatedly taught that it could not be:

> *This is the will of Him who sent Me, that of all that He has given Me* ***I lose nothing, but raise it up on the last day.*** *For this is the will of My Father, that everyone who beholds the Son and believes in Him will have eternal life, and I Myself will raise him up on the last day (John 6:39–40).*

And also,

> *My sheep hear My voice, and I know them, and they follow Me; and I give eternal life to them, and they will never perish; and no one will snatch them out of My hand. My Father, who has given them to Me, is greater than all; and no one is able to snatch them out of the Father's hand (John 10:27–29).*

Christ emphatically says that He will "*lose nothing*" and "*no one will snatch them out of My hand.*"

The figure of the vine and the branches does not signify regeneration; it pictures fellowship. To cease to abide in Him does not mean to cease to be organically related to Him but only to fail to remain in fellowship. The context is about fruit-bearing, not justification. Thus removal here refers simply to removal from fellowship and fruit-bearing due to failure to abide.

VIEW 2: THEY ARE SEPARATED FROM SUPERFICIAL CONNECTION WITH CHRIST

A second view is that "takes away" refers to the separation of professing Christians from a superficial connection with Christ.[1998] This view has problems too. A branch connected to the vine is an illustration of the believer in fellowship with Christ. If "in Me" means to be in fellowship with Me, as Laney says,[1999] then the branch connected with the vine must be a branch in fellowship with the vine, a true not merely a professing, Christian. This raises the fundamental problem with Experimental Predestinarian exegesis. To whom is this addressed? Experimental Predestinarians say that the fruitless branches are only professing Christians. On this view the passage's only application to the disciples would be to threaten them with damnation if they do not prove to be true Christians, hardly a likely interpretation in this atmosphere of encouragement and tenderness on their last night together!

Therefore, some suggest that the analogy of the vine and the branches is intended to give the disciples instruction *concerning those to whom they would minister* and who did not bear fruit.[2000] Yet the text itself gives every evidence that in its entirety it was addressed *to the disciples* to tell *them* how they could bear fruit in their lives. He wants His followers to bear fruit and in this way "be" (aorist, middle subjunctive of *ginomai*) disciples (15:8).

> *My Father is glorified by this, that you bear much fruit, and so prove to be My disciples (John 15:8, NASB, ESV).*

The phrase "prove to be" is an interpretive translation of one word, "*ginomai*," which means "come into being." Thus, in the act of fruit bearing, we *come into being* as a disciple. This is difficult to translate in English, but the sense is that in the act of bearing fruit, we become disciples. Therefore, a better translation is,

> *My Father is gloriãed by this, that you bear much fruit, and so become My disciples (NRSV, NAB, CEV, ASV, GNB).*

One becomes a Christian by faith alone; one becomes a disciple by bearing fruit.

There is a warning and an encouragement here to the disciples. In their desire to maintain the doctrine of eternal security and salvage their doctrine of perseverance, Experimental Predestinarians have been forced into the exegetically difficult position of maintaining that the disciples of Christ are not the subject of the warning. Indeed, this is

---

[1998] For example, Laney, "Abiding Is Believing: The Analogy of the Vine in John 15:1-6," 61. See also Stanley, *Did Jesus Teach Salvation by Works*, 257.

[1999] Laney, "Abiding Is Believing: The Analogy of the Vine in John 15:1-6," 64.

[2000] Ibid.

the only way, within their paradigm, they can maintain the idea of the saints' perseverance and the truth of eternal security at the same time.

For example, one scholar argues that when Jesus says in verse 3, "*You are already clean because of the word I have spoken to you,*" He is contrasting the disciples with those in the preceding verse who are only professing Christians. We disagree. As will be shown in the following section, in verse 2 there are two kinds of Christians mentioned: those who are in fellowship with Him who have not yet produced fruit, and those in fellowship with Him who have produced fruit. The former need to be lifted up by the Vinedresser so they can become fruitful, and the latter need to be pruned (Gr *kathaireō*) so that they will bear more fruit.[2001] The disciples have already been "pruned" (they are "clean," same Gr word, *kathaireō*) through the word which was spoken to them. The disciples are now given instruction on how they, not those to whom they will minister, can continue to bear fruit. They will continue to bear fruit if they remain in fellowship with Him (i.e., abide in Him).

> *Abide in Me, and I in you. As the branch cannot bear fruit of itself, unless it abides in the vine, so neither can* ***you*** [not those to whom the disciples will minister], *unless you abide in Me (15:4).*

It would seem obvious that it is possible for a Christian through disobedience to remove himself from Christ's influence and enablement. That seems to be the danger the Lord is warning about in this very passage. But that in no way implies that the one being warned is not a Christian. In fact, since he is commanded to remain in that sphere of influence and enablement, we may safely assume he was in it already and hence was regenerate.

VIEW 3: THEY ARE LIFTED UP AND ENCOURAGED

A third understanding of the words "takes away" in verse 2 coheres more satisfactorily with the context. The Greek word *airō* used in verse 2 and translated "takes away" is used twenty-six times in the Gospel of John. It frequently means "to take away" or "to remove."[2002] Also, it can mean "to lift up." For example, Jesus said to the paralytic, "*take up [airō] your bed and walk*" (John 5:8), and then the man "*took up [airō] his bed and walked*" (5:9). The Pharisees "*picked up*" [*airō*] stones to throw at Christ (John 8:59).

R. K. Harrison argues that the word translated "takes away" (Gr *airō*) is best rendered "lifts up" in John 15:2, as it is five times in John's gospel.[2003] He says that it was a common practice to lift with meticulous care vine branches that had fallen and to allow them to heal.[2004] When the branches matured enough to be able to bear fruit, "they were raised above the ground on supports (Ezekiel 17:6),"[2005] and "the end of the vine-stock is raised by means of a cleft stick a foot or more above the surface."[2006]

2001 Pliny notes that "every part [of the vine] is pruned off that has borne fruit the previous year." See Pliny, "The Culture of the Vine and the Various Shrubs which Support It," in *The Natural History* (Medford, MA: Taylor and Francis, 1855), 17:35.

2002 John 1:29; 2:16.

2003 John 5:8, 9, 11; 12; 8:59.

2004 R. K. Harrison, "Vine," in *NISBE*, 4:986.

2005 R. K. Harrison and F. N. Hepper, "Vine, Vineyard," in *The New Bible Dictionary*, ed. D. R. W. Wood and I. H. Marshall (Downers Grove, IL: InterVarsity Press, 1996), 1225.

2006 E. W. G. Masterman, "Vine," in *ISBE*, ed. James Orr (Albany, OR: Ages Software, 1999).

The writer has observed this practice himself in the vineyards behind his home in Austria. *Airō* was commonly used in classical Greek to mean "to lift for the purpose of carrying."[2007] The standard lexicons commonly mention this translation of the word. It is sometimes translated "to lift from the ground," or "to lift up,"[2008] or "to raise to a higher place or position, to lift up, take up, pickup;"[2009] not "to take away."

Carson rejects this interpretation saying,

> *Yet in the context of viticulture it is not the most natural way to take it. Despite arguments to the contrary, there is no good evidence of which I am aware to confirm that lower stalks of grapevines were seasonally "lifted up" from the ground.*[2010]

Apparently, Carson is not aware of a good amount of evidence on this viticultural practice. Pliny refers to "the vine that is propped and requires a single cross-piece, and the vine that requires a trellis of four compartments."[2011] Evidently, this practice was quite common in Palestine. Gary Derickson cites a number of sources that describe the common viticultural practice of trellising where the vines were lifted up to keep them from contact with the soil and to provide more air, thereby enabling them to dry more quickly.[2012]

It seems curious that Alan Stanley would say, "The problem with this interpretation is that it relies more on historical background than on the context of the passage."[2013] However, historical background is part of the "context of the passage." Furthermore, the entire context of the passage shows that *airō* means "lift up." The need was encouragement for the disciples, not damnation if they fail! This is what much of the Upper Room Discourse is about.

The word "*pheron*" (bear) is a present participle. Many of the translations translate, "*does not bear fruit*" (ESV, NKJV, NAB, NET, etc.), or "*bears no fruit*" (NIV, NRSV). While these translations are perfectly accurate, they are not the only manner in which one would translate a present participle. To render it "does not" is more absolute than the present participle requires. That translation might infer that this branch never has and never will bear fruit; that it is the *characteristic* of this branch. This translation, of course, fits nicely with the Reformed view. However, the present participle may also be translated "not bearing" or "is not bearing" fruit. It does not say that it never did.[2014]

True, this branch is not currently bearing fruit, but the text does not imply that this is its essential characteristic or that it never will (or never has). Thus an acceptable rendering is "*every branch in me not bearing fruit*" (Darby, *Young's Literal Interpretation*).

Therefore we translate,

> *Every branch in fellowship with Me that is not bearing fruit, he lifts up, and every branch that bears fruit, he prunes it so that it may bear more fruit.*

[2007] LSJ, 14.

[2008] Joachim Jeremias, "*airō*" in TDNT, 1:185.

[2009] BDAG, p. 28.

[2010] Carson, *The Gospel According to John*, 518.

[2011] Pliny, "The Culture of the Vine and the Various Shrubs which Support It," 17:35, p. 3499.

[2012] Gary W. Derickson, "Viticulture and John 15:1-6," *BibSac* 153, no. 609 (January-March 1996).

[2013] Stanley, *Did Jesus Teach Salvation by Works*, 256.

[2014] The time of the present participle is coincident with the present tense of *airō* and thus present.

This verse is a divine promise that every unfruitful Christian who is not bearing fruit and *yet is walking in fellowship,* that is, is "in me," will be lifted up, that is, receive divine encouragement. This fits extremely well with the whole context of this last night of Christ with those whom He loved. This was a time when the disciples needed encouragement, not a time of threatening them with damnation if they do not prove to be true believers! They "have grief now" (John 16:22) and are full of "sorrow" (v. 1). He wants them to know that in the coming weeks, after His crucifixion and departure, the Vinedresser will tenderly care for them and lift them into the light on the trellises where they can bear fruit, even if they lay fruitless on the ground like grape vines.

Derickson and Radmacher have also brought to our attention another relevant fact from a knowledge of the viticulture of the era. The vinedresser knew and cared for each vine individually as a shepherd cares for his sheep. Their discussion is worth quoting in full.

> *The vinedresser's grape vines remain with him for decades. He comes to know each one in a personal way, much like a shepherd with his sheep. He knows how the vine is faring from year to year and which ones are more productive or vigorous than others. He knows what they respond to and what special care certain one's need. Every vine has its own personality. And the vinedresser comes to know it over the years. The vinedresser cares for each vine and nurtures it, pruning it the appropriate amount at the appropriate times, fertilizing it, lifting its branches from the ground and propping them or tying them to the trellis, and taking measures to protect them from insects and disease. So, when Jesus calls His Father the Vinedresser, He is describing Him in terms of His relationship and attitude as well as His actions in the lives of the disciples. We cannot stress enough how important it is to recall the attributes and actions of the Father from the previous context. To call Him a Vinedresser is to tell them He cares for them personally and is wise to know exactly what to do to make them fruitful. With such a Vinedresser, the branches can experience complete confidence and security.*[2015]

It is possible for a Christian to be in fellowship with God and yet not be bearing fruit for an extended period of time. John of the Cross called it "the dark night of the soul," and the practical treatises by the Puritans on sanctification are full of discussions of how to trust God during this time.

Cast Out

> *If anyone does not abide in Me, he is cast out [Gr ballō exō] as a branch and dries up; and they gather them, and cast [Gr ballō] them into the fire, and they are burned (John 15:6).*

In this verse, Jesus states what happens to a Christian who does not "abide in me." In verse 2, Jesus spoke about the believer who is "in me," that is, the believer who is in fellowship with Christ. Now, in verse 6, He states what happens to a believer who does not "remain in me" that is, who does not *remain* in fellowship with Christ. He is "cast out" (Gr *ballō exō*). This destiny is decidedly different from that of the believer who is "in me" and is not yet bearing fruit (v. 2). That believer is lifted up and encouraged.

[2015] Gary W. Derickson and Earl D. Radmacher, *The Disciplemaker: What Matters Most to Jesus* (Salem, OR: Charis, 2001), 152.

Alan Stanley argues that verses 2 and 6 are saying the same thing; verse 2 says the Lord "takes away" the fruitless branch, and verse 6 says the fruitless branch is "thrown away." He says, "For the one who does not remain (v. 6) is clearly the one who does not produce fruit (vv. 4, 5). And the one who does not produce fruit is the one who is also cut off."[2016] However, this assumes that *airō* must mean "remove." It does not. It means "to lift up." It also contradicts the encouraging note of the context.

Furthermore, the branch in verse 2 is specifically called a branch "in me," that is, a branch in fellowship with Christ. The branch in verse 6 is specifically said to be a branch that does "not abide in me," that is, is not in fellowship with Christ. Verses 2 and 6 are referring to two different branches and two different outcomes. They do not refer to the same process.

Verse 6 states that a branch that does not abide is "cast out" (Gr *ballō exō*, not the word *airō*, "lifted up"). This suggests that the heavenly Vinedresser first encourages the branches and lifts them in the sense of loving care to enable them to bear fruit. If, after this encouragement, they do not remain in fellowship with Him and bear fruit, they are then cast out. Therefore, verses 2 and 6 do not have to be parallel. Verse 2 refers to encouragement, and verse 6 refers to divine discipline.

The Lord is saying that, if a Christian does not remain in fellowship with Him, he will be thrown away (Gr *ballō exō*, "cast out"). One Experimental Predestinarian writer, ensnared again in the illegitimate identity transfer makes the point that a compound form of the same word is used in John 6:37 where Jesus promises that "*the one who comes to Me I will certainly not cast out* [Gr *ekballō*]."[2017] Once he is saved, he will never be cast out from that saving relationship. However, John 6:37 refers to an unbeliever coming to Christ for salvation. That is a contextually derived nuance like "box in the attic" or "the circumference of a tree" are identical (both are "trunks"). John 15 is speaking of abiding for fellowship, not coming to Christ for salvation. The believer who is already saved but who fails to abide in Him will be cast out *from usefulness to Christ, from fellowship*.

The metaphor from viticultural practice (to be "thrown away as a branch") refers to being a useless Christian, not an unbeliever. Pliny the Elder says, "The vine throws out a great number of shoots. In the first place, however, none of them are ever used for planting, except those which are useless, and would have been cut away as mere brushwood."[2018] One pushes the analogy too far to assert that the verse means "to be cast away from a saving relationship with Christ" (Arminian view), or from "a professing relationship with Christ" (common Reformed view). We need go no further than Jesus' instruction to His believing disciples in the Sermon on the Mount in order to understand this phrase.

> *You are the salt of the earth; but if the salt has become tasteless, how can it be made salty again? It is no longer good for anything, except to be thrown out [Gr ballō* exō*] and trampled under foot by men (Matthew 5:13).*[2019]

[2016] Stanley, *Did Jesus Teach Salvation by Works*, 256.

[2017] Crenshaw, *Lordship Salvation: The Only Kind There Is - An Evaluation of Jody Dillow's The Reign of the Servant Kings and Other Antinomian Arguments*, 157.

[2018] Pliny, "The Culture of the Vine and the Various Shrubs which Support It," 17:35, p. 3497.

[2019] Cf. Mark 9:50; Luke 14:34.

A branch in the Vine which does not produce fruit has become, in some ways, similar to salt that has become saltless. It is no longer good for anything.[2020]

What is the ultimate fate of the believer who does not remain in fellowship? We know from other Scripture that he faces divine discipline in time, possibly physical death, and loss of rewards at the Judgment Seat of Christ. This was the view propounded by Lewis Sperry Chafer and fits the context well.[2021]

John 15:6 concludes,

They gather them, and cast [Gr *ballō*] *them into the fire, and they are burned (NASB).*

We do not know for sure who "they" are. It cannot refer to Christ or to the Father because the pronoun is plural, not singular. It may refer to men. Derickson and Radmacher suggest that this may refer back to John 13:35: "*By this all men will know that you are My disciples, if you have love for one another.*" Possibly, the "they" of John 15:6 is the same as the unbelieving world, that is, "all men" in 13:35. The meaning would be that when nonbelievers see believers acting inconsistently with what they profess to believe; it is a terrible hypocrisy, and the unbelieving world simply dismisses Christianity because of the testimony of those who profess it.[2022] These hypocrites are "cast out"; that is, they dry up and are useless.

To what does the fire refer? Experimental Predestinarians often associate fire with damnation. However, fire is also a common symbol in the Bible for the judgment on God's people in time (e.g., Isaiah 26:11),[2023] or a negative assessment of one's life at the Judgment Seat of Christ (1 Corinthians 3:15). In fact, in the only reference in the Old Testament to a vine being cut and burned refers to a temporal judgment on the people of God for their disobedience (Psalm 80:16). Only rarely and exceptionally is it associated with the lake of fire.[2024] The outcome of their failure to remain in fellowship therefore may be divine judgment in time.

It is quite possible that John was thinking of something similar to Paul's comment in 1 Corinthians 3:9. The bearing of fruit may have registered in his mind just like the idea of ministry as producing buildings did for Paul. In both cases, the quality of work and what the believer produces are things that will be submitted to fire at the Judgment Seat of Christ (1 Corinthians 3:15). It seems like mere quibbling to say that in 1 Corinthians 3:15 the fire is applied to believer's works and in John 15:6 it is applied to the believer himself and therefore that John 15:6 and 1 Corinthians 3:15 could not refer to the same event.[2025] Paul

---

2020 For a fuller discussion of what it means for a believer to become "saltless," see pp. 518.

2021 Lewis Sperry Chafer, *Systematic Theology* (Dallas: Dallas Seminary Press, 1947), 7:4.

2022 See Derickson and Radmacher, *The Disciplemaker: What Matters Most to Jesus*, 179-84.

2023 It is used this way in Amos 1:4, 7, 10, 12, 14; 2:2, 5. See also Isaiah 9:10; Jeremiah 21:12-14; 22:6-7; 48:45; Ezekiel 15:1-8; Hosea 8:14; Nahum 1:6; Zephaniah 1:18.

2024 Alan Stanley argues that "the fire imagery in John 15:6 suggests eternal rather them temporal judgment." Stanley, *Did Jesus Teach Salvation by Works*, 257. To establish this thesis he cites a few passages in the Old Testament such as Ezekiel 15:4-6 which do not even refer to eternal judgment. It refers to judgment in time. He then jumps to the Synoptics and cites Matthew 3:8-12 which has nothing to do with eternal damnation but is a warning addressed to the nation regarding a coming national catastrophe, in AD 70 if they do not come to national repentance and stop distorting the law. See my discussion on this in vol. 1, chapter 3.

2025 Laney, "Abiding Is Believing: The Analogy of the Vine in John 15:1-6," 61.

says that the believer is the building and that the building is built up with various kinds of building materials and that the fire is applied to the building. The apostle obviously sees an intimate connection between the believer and his work. To apply the fire of judgment to the believer is the same as applying it to his work. Indeed, the believer's works are simply a metonymy for the believer himself.[2026]

The issue in John 15 is sanctification, not soteriology; fruit bearing, not justification; and friendship with Christ, not proof of salvation. In His summary Jesus says,

> *You are My friends, if you do what I command you. No longer do I call you slaves, for the slave does not know what his master is doing; but I have called you friends, for all things that I have heard from My Father I have made known to you (John 15:14–15).*

Carson opines, "This obedience is not what *makes* them friends; it is what *characterizes* his friends."[2027] It is certainly true that obedience characterizes friends of Christ. However, not all believers are characterized as friends; it depends on whether they are obedient to His commands. Obedience *does* make them friends. How could Christ have made it plainer?

Summary

The analogy of the vine and the branches is a metaphor for some kind of relationship to Christ. There are three possibilities: (1) the relationship professing Christians sustain to Christ; (2) the relationship any Christian sustains to Christ; (3) a relation which only mature or growing Christians sustain with Christ. Experimental Predestinarians favor the first; Arminians the second, and Partners the third. As argued above, the first view is impossible, and the second view misinterprets the sense of "in me." That phrase refers not to organic union but to fellowship. Not all Christians walk in fellowship with Christ at all times. The analogy signifies not an organic connection, but a dynamic fellowship. A branch "in Me" is not portraying an analogy of a branch organically connected to Him as a literal branch is organically connected to a vine. Instead, a branch "in Me" is portraying a branch deriving its sustenance from Christ and living in fellowship with Him (as a literal branch derives sustenance from a literal vine). This is proven by the fact that "in Me" means "in fellowship with Me." The analogy is used to illustrate the "in Me" relationship.

John 15 tells us that when a believer is in fellowship with Christ but is not bearing fruit because of immaturity or injury, our Lord lovingly lifts him up so that he can bear fruit. The believer who is in fellowship with Christ and who is bearing fruit is pruned so that he can bear more fruit. The analogy of the vine and the branches signifies fellowship with Christ, not organic connection with him. The believer who does not remain in fellowship because of disobedience is deemed to be of no more value to Christ than are dried up branches useful to the Vinedresser. He withers spiritually, faces severe divine discipline in time, and loss of reward at the Judgment Seat of Christ. Nothing in this passage demands that this refers to loss of salvation. Neither is there anything here to suggest that all believers will always bear fruit. Only believers who remain in fellowship will bear fruit.

[2026] A metonymy is a figure of speech consisting of the use of the name of one thing for that of another of which it is an attribute or with which it is associated.

[2027] Carson, *The Gospel According to John*, 522.

40

Conditional Security: Paul's Letters

THE DOCTRINE of the eternal security of the saints is, in my opinion, a fundamental belief that all believers must hold if they are to walk in the fullness of resurrection life in Christ. Experimental Predestinarians teach that believers are to continually examine their own works to verify that they are saved. Arminians encourage this continual self-examination to verify they have not lost their justification. Thus in the final analysis it makes no difference whether Calvin or Arminius says it. A professing believer who is living sinfully is on the highway to eternal separation from God.

In many parts of the world, Bible teachers affirm that unless believers are threatened with final damnation in the lake of fire, they will not have sufficient motivation to persevere in holiness to the end of life. Several passages have been brought forth by Arminians to establish their doctrine that salvation can be lost, that is, that salvation is conditional. In this chapter, four of these passages are examined.

Romans 11:22

> *Behold then the kindness and severity of God; to those who fell, severity, but to you, God's kindness, if you continue in His kindness; otherwise you also will be cut off (Romans 11:22).*

What does Paul mean when he says some of his readers may be "cut off"? Does he mean that it is possible for a true believer who was once a partaker of the Abrahamic promise to be cut off from it and lose his salvation? This passage has understandably troubled many readers. It is seemingly a contradiction to a central claim of this book, that eternal salvation cannot be lost.

Before looking at this verse in particular, let's view the context. For two chapters Paul has been focusing on God's purpose for national Israel. Now he explains that even though the kingdom has been temporarily taken from Israel (Matthew 21:43) and even though the nation is no longer at the center of God's purposes (temporarily), one day His plans for His chosen people will be realized. One day they will no longer be an object of His divine displeasure, and they will experience "salvation" when "the Deliverer will come from Zion," and "remove ungodliness from Jacob" (Romans 11:26).

In the first ten verses of Romans 11, Paul makes it clear that God has not rejected His people (v. 1). This, he says, is proven by the fact that there is a remnant of which Paul and other Jewish believers are a part. But was Israel's fall final? Does national Israel still have a future? Apparently, some of the readers of this epistle answered, "No." Paul viewed this Gentile viewpoint as "arrogant" (cf. Romans 11:20).

In Romans 11:11 Paul makes explicit the fact that Israel's fall is temporary.

Again I ask, Did they stumble so as to fall beyond recovery? Not at all! Rather, because of their transgression, salvation has come to the Gentiles to make Israel envious.

Because Israel has been temporarily set aside in the purposes of God, "salvation" has come to the Gentiles. Does this mean that Gentiles can now experience personal salvation from damnation but formerly they could not? Of course not! It does mean that the message of salvation in Christ is now spreading throughout the Gentile world but far more than personal rescue from damnation is implied.

He calls this salvation, "riches for the Gentiles."

But if their transgression means riches for the world, and their loss means riches for the Gentiles, how much greater riches will their fullness bring! (Romans 11:12)

What are these "riches"? The Gentiles already had salvation from eternal separation from God available to them.[2028] Those riches would come to Gentiles through the agency of the descendants of Abraham is a common theme of the Old Testament.[2029] This is the messianic salvation we discussed earlier.[2030] This was part of God's plan to bless the world through Israel. God's faithfulness to finally implement this plan and bring it to a successful eschatological conclusion is called "God's righteousness" (Romans 10:3).[2031]

The blessings to the Gentile world through the influence of "Gentile" biblical Christianity is well documented.[2032] Slaves have been freed, public schools came into existence, child labor laws were abolished, and the status of women elevated. On account of the gospel, millions of Gentiles have experienced "salvation." This salvation is deliverance from the *present* display of God's wrath (Romans 1:17, "is" revealed, not "will be") in the social, moral, economic, and material destitution that has come upon the Gentile world because of sin. God had given them over to the consequences of sin (Romans 1:22-32).

Because Israel had changed the righteousness of God from God's plan to bless the world through Israel to a plan that God would bless Israel alone (and in order for Gentiles to participate they must first become Jews), God set the nation aside, and in the current era He is implementing messianic salvation through the Gentile church.

Furthermore, because they have been grafted into the "olive tree" (Romans 11:17), Gentiles have been exposed to and have embraced the Jewish Scriptures. Riches indeed! As a result the Gentile world has been reached for Christ, and millions have been born again.

This came about because of Israel's "loss." What did they lose? Paul is not speaking of the loss of individual salvation. Instead, he is speaking in national term. *What the nation Israel as a group lost was their role as the centerpiece of God's purposes in history.*

[2028] A discussion of salvation in the Old Testament is beyond the purpose of this book. However, it is evident that many Gentiles in the Old Testament were saved people. Consider, for example, Balaam, Rahab, and the Ninevites.

[2029] Isaiah 60:1-3; 62:1-3; Micah 4:1-4; Zechariah 8:11-13, 20-23.

[2030] See pp. 165 ff.

[2031] See discussion of "the righteousness of God" pp. 182 ff.

[2032] For extensive documentation of the riches to the world which have come through the influence of the gospel see Schmidt, *Under the Influence: How Christianity Transformed Civilization.*

As expressed in the promises to Abraham, it was God's intent that through Israel blessing would come to the nations. This loss, however, is temporary.

Paul continues,

> *But if some of the branches were broken off, and you, being a wild olive, were grafted in among them and became partaker with them of the rich root of the olive tree, do not be arrogant toward the branches; but if you are arrogant, remember that it is not you who supports the root, but the root supports you (Romans 11:17–18).*

Why does Paul use the metaphor of an olive tree? The metaphor is very appropriate. Israel was to be a channel of blessing to the entire world.[2033] This was God's promise to Abraham (Genesis 12:1-3). Throughout the Old Testament, the olive tree is a common metaphor for divine blessing and fruitfulness.[2034] The fruit of the olive was used in almost every aspect of Jewish life. An abundant oil harvest signified divine blessing (Joel 2:24; 3:13). The loss of the olive oil was a loss of blessing. Israel was to endure in faith in the face of the loss of this valuable agricultural product (Habakkuk 3:17). Olive wood was used for fuel and by carpenters; olive oil was used for food and medicine; olives were picked and eaten.[2035] A fruitful person enjoying God's favor is "like a green olive tree in the house of the Lord" (Psalm 52:8). Here is the point:

> *The metaphor of the olive tree speaks of blessing and fruitfulness and not final entrance into heaven or deliverance from hell.*

As Solomon put it, "*But the root of the righteous yields fruit*" (Proverbs 12:12). In Romans 11, Abraham is the root, and the olive tree is the fruit. The olive tree is God's channel of blessing to the world. Israel has been temporarily removed from being that blessing, and the Gentiles have been grafted in to assume the role of being God's channel of blessing to the nations.

In Romans 11:13-25, Paul begins to rebuke Gentile Christians because of their presumptuous boasting that they had replaced Israel as the channel of God's blessing to the world (v. 18). Apparently, Gentile Christians in Rome not only misunderstood their place in the divine plan to bless the world, but they also misunderstood God's dealings with His chosen people. Because the majority of Jews had failed to accept Paul's gospel, the Gentile Christians erroneously concluded that God's rejection of the nation was permanent. Furthermore, they saw themselves as displacing the broken-off branches and boasted in their newfound status.[2036]

[2033] Isaiah 60:1-3; 62:1-3; Micah 4:1-4; Zechariah 8:11-13, 20-23.

[2034] Deuteronomy 6:11; Judges 9:8-9; Hosea 14:6; Haggai 2:19.

[2035] Packer, Tenny, and White, *Illustrated Manners and Customs of the Bible*, 251.

[2036] W. S. Campbell summarizes, "Paul uses the olive tree analogy to make several important points. (1) The branches remain in, or are incorporated into, the tree only by faith (not because of ethnic or any other qualities). (2) The branches, even those grafted in, do not support the root but are entirely dependent on it; the life is in the root, branches of themselves can never constitute a tree. (3) The branches grafted in are brought in to share (Rom 11:17) the richness of the root—not to monopolize it or to displace all the other branches. (4) The in-grafted branches are not different in kind from the other branches because if they do not live in humble dependent faith they too will be broken off. (5) Even the broken-off branches (normally destined to wither or even to be burned), if they do not continue to disobey will be grafted in again—a truly

God had said to Abraham and his seed, "*In you all the families of the earth will be blessed*" (Genesis 12:3). But they failed to fulfill that role, and, as Jesus put it, "*Therefore I say to you, the kingdom of God will be taken away from you and given to a people, producing the fruit of it*" (Matthew 21:43).[2037]

Unnatural branches, the Gentiles, were grafted into the place of Abrahamic blessing. Israel has been set aside and now God is using the Gentiles as the instruments of His purposes in history.[2038]

If, because of Jewish national rejection of Messiah, the Gentiles were grafted into the place of blessing, think what will happen when the Jews return to the Messiah. It will be like "life from the dead," a magnificent universal righteousness in the coming thousand-year kingdom of God.

> *You will say then, "Branches were broken off so that I might be grafted in." Quite right, they were broken off for their unbelief, but you stand by your faith. Do not be conceited, but fear; for if God did not spare the natural branches, He will not spare you, either (Romans 11:19–21).*

For centuries Gentiles have conceitedly concluded that they have permanently replaced Israel, and that the Gentile church is the "New Israel." However, we know from the book of Revelation, that one day 144,000 believing Jews will be sent out to evangelize the world. One day God will restore Israel as His channel of blessing. We can already see that Gentile Christendom is falling away from the teaching of Paul. Not only is the difference disappearing between the church and the surrounding culture (primarily in the West), but also the message of Paul is no longer preached.

Paul warns the Gentiles that just as the Jewish nation was "cut off" nationally, so they too can be "cut off." They believed that Israel had been permanently replaced by the Gentile church/mission. This suggests that there were Gentiles in the Roman church advocating that viewpoint.

> *Behold then the kindness and severity of God; to those who fell, severity, but to you, God's kindness, if you continue in His kindness; otherwise you also will be cut off. And they also, if they do not continue in their unbelief, they will be grafted in, for God is able to graft them in again (Romans 11:22-23).*

---

unnatural, even miraculous activity. The function served by the analogy here is primarily that of deflating the pompous self-image of the Gentile Christians, to insist that arrogance stands in contradiction to faith, to reaffirm the divine election of Israel and to maintain the unity of all God's people whether Jew or Gentile." W. S. Campbell, "Olive Tree," in *Dictionary of Paul and His Letters*, ed. Gerald F. Hawthorne, Ralph P. Martin, and Daniel G. Reid (Downers Grove, IL: InterVarsity Press, 1993), 643.

[2037] However, as Paul makes clear in the following verses, this taking away of the kingdom of God is not permanent. One day the kingdom will be restored to Israel (Acts 1:6) and the natural branches will be grafted into the Abrahamic promises (Romans 11:25-27) and Israel will fulfill her destiny to bless the nations.

[2038] This is Paul's teaching in Ephesians when he reveals that Gentiles have been made "fellow heirs" of the promises (Ephesians 3:6; cf. 2:11-22). "For if their rejection be the reconciliation of the world [removal of enmity between Jew and Gentile], what will their acceptance be but life from the dead." These two groups, Jews and Gentiles, who were formerly enemies, have been reconciled in one body in Christ. The enmity between Gentiles and Jews, because of the Gentile rejection of the Law, has been removed by eliminating the Law so that "He himself is our peace, who has made the two one and has destroyed the barrier, the dividing wall of hostility, by abolishing in his flesh the law with its commandments and regulations" (Ephesians 2:14-15). Now those who were "aliens" and "far off" and "strangers to the covenants of promise" are brought near (2:12).

Cut off from what? The Gentiles will one day no longer be the center of God's plans on earth. Because they will fail to "continue in His kindness," God will once again return His chosen people as His agency to bless the world as the Old Testament Scriptures abundantly predict. The natural branches (Israel) will again be grafted into the place of centrality in God's purposes.

Currently, the Gentiles experience the "kindness" of God. They are currently the channel through whom He works. Israel has been set aside. But like national Israel, they too can be "cut off," removed from the olive tree. It is evident that the Gentile church has departed from Christianity, just as the Jews in Paul's day had departed from the true Jewish faith.

The olive tree is not a metaphor for "being saved." As pointed out above, it is a metaphor for being the channel of blessing to the world. This passage has absolutely nothing to do with the idea that individuals can lose salvation.[2039]

The danger then to which Paul refers is that the believing Gentiles as a group, like national Israel, can be cut off from the current position they now enjoy. Harrison notes,

> *This should not be understood on an individual basis as though Paul were questioning their personal salvation. The matter in hand is the current Gentile prominence in the church made possible by the rejection of the gospel on the part of the nation of Israel as a whole. Let Gentile Christians beware. Their predominance in the Christian community may not last!*[2040]

What applies to the church in general can, of course, be applied to individuals within it. The Lord Jesus spoke of dead or useless branches being of no more value than dead wood and are cast out of the place of communion and fruit bearing (John 15:6). The writer of Hebrews warns his readers that we are Partners, sharers in the final destiny of man as co-heirs with Christ, only if we "*hold fast the beginning of our assurance firm until the end*" (Hebrews 3:14). All Christians will be in the kingdom, but only those who persevere in faith will inherit the kingdom, that is, rule with Christ there.

Experimental Predestinarian exegesis of this passage is severely deficient. In their equation of the wild olive tree with personal salvation, they give the argument away to those of an Arminian perspective. The proof, they say, that a man is truly born again is that he "continues in His kindness."[2041] The problem, however, is that, if he does not, he is cut off from the olive tree. To be cut off from it obviously implies that one was once part of it.[2042]

[2039] Experimental Predestinarians and Neonomians see evidence for their view that only those who persevere to the end are actually saved initially. For example Schreiner says, "One should never conclude from Paul's teaching on divine election that he downplayed the necessity of human beings continuing to exercise faith in order to obtain eschatological salvation. Those who do so impose an alien system upon the Pauline writings. The warnings are grammatically hypothetical but are seriously intended for believers. Those who do not continue in faith will face God's judgment. Neither would it be correct to conclude that some of those that God elected will fail to continue in the faith. Murray (1965: 88) observes rightly that 'God's saving embrace and endurance are correlative.'" Schreiner, *Romans*, 608. However, Paul is not talking about individual salvation from damnation or its loss. He is talking about groups of people, national Israel and the current Gentile church, participating in the glories of the Abrahamic promise as the channel of messianic salvation.

[2040] Harrison, "Romans," 10:122.

[2041] For example, R. H. Mounce says, "There is no security for those who by their lives show that the grafting process of faith was apparent rather than real." Mounce, *Romans*, 222.

[2042] For example, Douglas Moo says, "For the goodness of God is not simply a past act or automatic benefit on

In other words, he had salvation and lost it, which is precisely the view of many Arminian interpreters. However, both Arminians and Experimental Predestinarians have missed the point of the context, which has nothing to do with individuals gaining and losing heaven. The context relates to the nations gaining and losing the privilege of being God's channel of blessing to the world.

1 Corinthians 3:15-17

In 1 Corinthians 3:15-17 the apostle Paul declares:

> *If any man's work is burned up, he will suffer loss; but he himself will be saved, yet so as through fire. Do you not know that you are a temple of God and that the Spirit of God dwells in you? If any man destroys the temple of God,* ***God will destroy him****, for the temple of God is holy, and that is what you are (1 Corinthians 3:15-17).*

The phrase "God will destroy him" has been understood by some to prove that there may be a kind of sin that a believer could commit that would result in the loss of his salvation.[2043] The sin in question is the destruction of God's temple, that is, the local assembly of believers, not the individual Christian.[2044] Paul has been speaking in the context of the building up of that local assembly by various ministers (3:5-8): Paul, Apollos, and Peter. He is concerned that the divisions in Corinth will affect the building up of this local assembly. He says:

> *For we are God's fellow workers; you are God's field;* ***God's building.*** *By the grace God has given me, I laid a foundation as an expert* ***builder****, and someone else is building on it. But each one should be careful how he* ***builds*** *(1 Corinthians 3:9-10).*

He gives a warning, "Be careful how you build this building." The assembly was rife with divisions and carnality. Fights and lawsuits among Christians were disrupting the unity of the believers and threatening the destruction of the "temple," that is, the building, the believers who composed the local church in Corinth. The city was full of pagan temples, but the local body of believers was the "temple of God" (1 Corinthians 3:3-4).

The "temple" in 1 Corinthians 6:19 is the individual Christian, and the temple in 1 Corinthians 3:16 is the building, the body of believers, which Paul and the other laborers have been building and which is threatened with division because of the carnal Christians in its membership.[2045] This "destruction" was a real danger in Corinth as the assembly

---

which the believer can rest secure; it is also a continuing relationship in which the believer must remain. 'Otherwise'—that is, if the believer does not continue in the goodness of God—the believer will, like the Jew, be 'cut off'—severed forever from the people of God and eternally condemned. In issuing this warning, Paul echoes a consistent New Testament theme: ultimate salvation is dependent on continuing faith; therefore, the person who ceases to believe forfeits any hope of salvation (cf. also Romans 8:13; Colossians 1:23; Hebrews 3:6, 14)." Moo, *The Epistle to the Romans*, 706-07.

2043 For example, VanLandingham, *Judgment & Justification in Early Judaism and the Apostle Paul*, 188-92. VanLandingham views the temple as the church and not the individual, but the individual can be destroyed, condemned to the lake of fire.

2044 Some have argued from the use of "temple" in 1 Corinthians 6:19, which refers to individual Christians, that the sin referred to in 1 Corinthians 3:16 is the sin of suicide!

2045 This view of the "temple" is widely accepted because it flows naturally out of the context. For example,

was divided, full of jealousy and quarreling, and the believers were behaving like non-Christians.

Their divisive party spirit was threatening the destruction of the church, the temple of God in Corinth. What are the consequences? Paul solemnly warns, "If anyone destroys God's temple, God will destroy him; for God's temple is sacred, and you are that temple."

To what does this "destruction" refer? Some understand this destruction to refer to eternal damnation.[2046] While there are several places in the New Testament where it probably means that,[2047] there are many places where it simply means "to cause harm in a physical manner or in outward circumstances, destroy, ruin, corrupt, spoil."[2048]

A more plausible view in this context is that the "destruction" refers back to verse 15, which states that the works of the believer will be "burned up" and that he will "suffer loss." Stumpff argues that it means to suffer loss of reward.[2049] This "loss of reward" is what is meant by the believer being "destroyed." The same idea is expressed by the Apostle John, "*Watch yourselves, that you do not lose what we have accomplished, but that you may receive a full reward*" (2 John 8).

The destruction facing the one who destroys the unity of a local church is not eternal. It refers either to the sin unto physical death (1 Corinthians 5:5) or the forfeiture of his eternal reward. [2050] In any event "he himself will be saved" (1 Corinthians 3:15), but all that he has built has been of wood, hay, and straw and will be consumed with fire—destroyed at the Judgment Seat of Christ. As a result, he will be disinherited by his coming King.

In conclusion, there is no justification in this passage for the teaching that a believer can commit some sin, even suicide, which can in any way affect his eternal destiny. A carnal believer who "destroys the temple of God" faces the fact that "God will destroy him." Causing division in the local church is a serious matter. However, the sinning Christian's eternal destiny is secure because it does not depend on what he does but on what Christ has done for him. Jesus declared that He will lose "none" of those whom the Father has given to Him (John 6:39-40). If we have "looked to the Son and believed," we

---

Archibald Robertson and Alfred Plummer have observed, "There is but one Temple, embodied equally truly in the whole Church, in the local Church, and in the individual Christian; the local Church is meant here." Robertson and Plummer, *A Critical and Exegetical Commentary on the First Epistle of Paul to the Corinthians*, 66.

[2046] VanLandingham, *Judgment & Justification in Early Judaism and the Apostle Paul*, 189-92.

[2047] Jude 10; 2 Peter 2:12. BDAG assign this meaning to 1 Corinthians 3:17.

[2048] BDAG, 1054. See 2 Corinthians 7:2, "to ruin financially."

[2049] "Loss, or the missing of the reward, is the result" Albrecht Stumpff "*zēmioō*," in TDNT, 2:890.

[2050] Keith R. Krell notes that the Roman Catholic notion that this refers to purgatory is not valid for several reasons. He says, "Roman Catholic scholars of another era have interpreted the 'fire' as a purging fire that the worker must encounter in purgatory. Certain factors argue against the idea of purgatory from the usage of fire in 1 Corinthians 3:13 and 15: (1) The purpose of the 'fire' is not to purge but to test for reward. The saved were already cleansed through Christ's blood. The 'fire' that tests the 'work' is not aimed at 'improving the character' (Hillyer 1970: 1056). (2) No punishment is in view. Christ bore all the punishment for every believer (Rom 8:1). His judgment of the saved is to reward for good and diminish reward, not condemn for bad. (3) 'Fire' here affects all who do work on the true foundation; it is not exclusively for work that is worthless. (4) The text does not teach explicitly or implicitly a remission of sins at this testing. It does not deal with changing a person's lot but revealing it (cf. 1 Corinthians 3:13). There is no suggestion of a later improvement after death in a purgatorial fire. Contemporary exegetical warrant was developed at a much later time in the history of Christianity." Krell, *Temporal Judgment and the Church: Paul's Remedial Agenda in 1 Corinthians*, 76.

have eternal life, and Christ will never lose any of us! However, the burning up of his life work at the Judgment Seat of Christ, that is, being "destroyed" by God, is what he must anticipate.

Galatians 5:4

> *You have been severed from Christ, you who are seeking to be justified by law; you have fallen from grace (Galatians 5:4).*

Many people fear they have "fallen from grace"; that is, they think they may have lost eternal salvation. However, usually people who use the term this way are only vaguely aware of its source or to what it originally referred.

To understand this phrase correctly, we must first consider the background of the book of Galatians. Paul was dealing with a group of false teachers who had greatly disturbed the faith of his readers. They apparently taught that salvation was to be found by means of faith in Christ coupled with keeping of the Law. Furthermore, sanctification could only be fully accomplished if they went back under the Law (Galatians 3:3; 5:7). This conflict later led to the Jerusalem council in Acts 15. They seemed to have a particular fixation on the rite of circumcision. The danger his readers faced was not loss of salvation or even lapse into immorality, but a return to the bondage of the Law as a way of life and a way of justification.

While the words, "fallen from grace," have often been misunderstood to teach that regeneration can be lost, the context suggests that Paul speaks of falling from a grace-way-of-living. Paul wants to prevent believers from returning to the Law as a way of life.

"*Christ will be of no benefit to you*" (v. 2). When Paul warns them about this, he is telling them that their Christian lives will be back under the legalistic system of the Mosaic code from which they have been liberated. The whole context, indeed the entire thrust of the epistle, is that the "benefit" in view is the freedom of the Christian who is walking under the grace-way-of-life. To return to the Law forfeits the freedom from Law which Christ's death accomplished. It does not forfeit eternal salvation.

"*You have been severed from Christ*" (v. 4a). This clause in the Greek could be rendered, "You have been made to receive no effect from Christ," (Gr *katargeō*, "to cause something to lose its power," BDAG, 525, # 2). But what "effect" is he speaking of, sanctification or justification? In verse 5 Paul shifts from "you" to "we," and to a new subject, our final complete sanctification at the Parousia into which we are now growing (sanctification). At that time our progressive righteousness will become perfect righteousness and glorification. "Hope" in the New Testament refers to something that will one day be certainly realized but now is in process. This righteousness (both progressive and future) is distinguished from their legalistic approach, which is of no benefit. Just as our final glorification is by faith and through the Spirit, so is our growth toward it.

"*You have fallen from grace*" (v. 4b). It is doubtful that the word "grace" (Gr *charis*) is ever used in the New Testament of the "state of salvation."[2051] Thus a fall from the state of salvation is not in view in verse 4. S. Lewis Johnson comments, "Let us note what it says. In the first place, Paul does not say that, if the Galatians were seeking to be justified by the

[2051] A possible exception is Romans 5:2.

law (by the rite of circumcision), they would fall from *salvation*. He says that they would fall from *grace* (cf. Acts 13:43)."[2052] Appealing to Galatians 1:6; 2:21, and Ephesians 2:8-9, Johnson argues that "grace" refers not to a state of salvation, but to the method of obtaining salvation. The Galatian believers have not fallen from salvation, but they have fallen into a false teaching that says the method of salvation requires a return to the Mosaic Law. As Betz puts it, the issue was more like a change of denominations.[2053]

While Johnson's view is plausible, I prefer to understand the fall from grace as a fall from the grace way of living. Two different ways of living the Christian life are being contrasted in Galatians 5, not two differing eternal states. To "fall from grace" is to fall from the grace way of living the Christian life and into a lower, legal way of living it. What has Paul been contrasting? Grace and law. Therefore, to fall from grace is to fall into law, not into damnation.

2 Timothy 2:12

The somewhat measured and rhythmical structure of 2 Timothy 2:11-12 has suggested to many that it is a first-century Christian hymn:

> *It is a trustworthy statement:*
> *For if we died with Him, we will also live with Him;*
> *If we endure, we will also reign with Him;*
> *If we deny Him, He also will deny us;*
> *If we are faithless, He remains faithful, for He cannot deny Himself.*

Here, the promise of reigning with Him, that is, being rewarded in the coming millennial kingdom, is in the forefront. Those who are victorious in suffering, who persevere to the end, will enjoy a joint participation with Christ in His future reign. This theme is taught extensively in the New Testament (Matthew 16:24-27; 19:28-29; Luke 22:28-30; Romans 8:17; Revelation 2:26-27; 3:21).

Notice in the preceding verse, Paul says,

> *I endure all things for the sake of those who are chosen, so that they also may obtain the salvation which is in Christ Jesus and with it eternal glory (2 Timothy 2:10).*

Paul endures for the sake of "those who are chosen," that is, the elect. This could mean that he endures for those who are not yet saved so that he can get the gospel to them in order that they can be saved from damnation. Or it could mean that he endures for the sake of those who are already saved so that they can obtain the messianic salvation, that is, sanctification and ultimate sharing in the reign with Christ. "Eternal glory" could mean the glory of the resurrection body and heaven when one dies, or it could mean eternal honor awarded to Christ's Partners in the final destiny of man. One's theology, Reformed or Partner, affects one's view.

[2052] S. Lewis Johnson, "Freedom in Christ versus Falling from Grace: An Exposition of Galatians 5:1-12," *Emmaus Journal* 15, no. 2 (Winter 2006): 32.

[2053] Hans Dieter Betz, *Galatians: A Commentary on Paul's Letter to the Churches in Galatia*, Hermenia (Philadelphia: Fortress Press, 1979), 261.

However, as noted earlier, the word "salvation" does not necessarily mean "final deliverance from the lake of fire." Indeed, in this context such a meaning would be most inappropriate. Paul has been discussing the rewards for perseverance: "If anyone competes as an athlete, he does not win the prize [lit., "is not crowned"] unless he competes according to the rules" (2 Timothy 2:5). This salvation is an additional crown that is given to those who are already saved. For the believer there should be *no doubt* that he will experience eternal life (the testimony of Jesus guarantees it!), but there is doubt as to whether he will compete lawfully and "be crowned." Therefore, the context suggests that it is not salvation from damnation for which Paul labors on behalf of the elect, but that they might also possess "eternal glory," that is, "receive honor." This coheres nicely with the promise in verse 12 that if we "endure" (as Paul did), we will "reign with Him."

Therefore, to "reign with Him" is the reward, the salvation, the crown promised to those who persevere.

In 2 Timothy 2:12 Paul wrote, "If we deny Him, He also will deny us." But in what sense can believers "deny" Him? To deny Christ is the opposite of "enduring" in the preceding phrase. To deny Him then is to fail to persevere in faith to the final hour. As a result He will "deny us." There is nothing in the context or anywhere else in the New Testament that suggests that His denial of believers refers to their being excluded from heaven.

Obviously, "we" and "us" in verse 12 refer to believers. These regenerate people may actually deny Christ! There is nothing here that says, "This proves they were not Christians in the first place," as Experimental Predestinarians suggest. Paul clearly has in mind other warnings made by our Lord to Christians, such as the warning in Matthew 10:33, where the context refers to those who know Christ.[2054]

In what sense will Christ deny the believer? That seems to be defined by the contrast with the preceding phrase.

> *If we endure, we will also reign with Him;*
> *If we deny Him, He also will deny us.*

If the opposite of enduring is to deny Him, then the opposite of reigning with Him is that He will deny us the privilege of reigning with Him. Christ will deny the unfaithful Christian the reward of reigning with Him. Nothing is said here about loss of salvation.[2055]

The Arminians are correct, however, in saying that it is possible for true Christians to deny Christ. This is brought out further in the next phrase when Paul asserts that it is possible for Christians to be "faithless." The Greek word is *apisteō* and means either to "be "unbelieving" or to "be unfaithful." Danker suggests that in this context *be unfaithful*" means to be neglecting of one's obligations.[2056] The problem with these believers is not that they are now unbelievers; instead, they failed in their obligation to endure to the end.

Yet even when a believer is like this, "He remains faithful." Paul teaches here that Christians can become unfaithful or unbelieving, but even when this happens, Christ will not be unfaithful to His promises to give them of eternal life. As Patrick Fairbairn has observed:

[2054] For discussion of Matthew 10:33, see pp. 920 ff.

[2055] See Brad McCoy, "Secure, Yet Scrutinized: 2 Tim 2:11-13," *JOTGETS* 1(Autumn 1988): 21-33.

[2056] BDAG, 103.

> *Finally if we are unbelieving* [Gr *apistoumen*], *not merely prove unfaithful in times of trial, shrink from confessing what we inwardly feel to be the truth concerning Him, but, rejecting or quitting our hold of the truth, pass over entirely into the region of unbelief,—if we should thus estrange ourselves from the common ground of faith, still He abides faithful—remaining perfectly true to His declarations and promises, whether we accredit them or not. To disown this, therefore would to deny Himself; and that is impossible.*[2057]
>
> *For He cannot deny Himself.*[2058]

Summary

Somewhat ironic is the notion that Paul, the apostle of grace, should be interpreted as teaching that salvation could be lost. The great apostle of liberty has given the clearest possible exposition of the grace of God and the absolute security of the justified. We will explore his teaching on this subject in more detail in a later chapter.[2059]

In Romans 11, Paul warns Gentiles that because of their arrogant assumption that Israel has been replaced permanently, and that now the Gentile church is the Israel of God (the true heirs of the messianic salvation), they too can be "cut off." Just as Israel was temporarily set aside because they changed God's plan to bless the world through Israel into a plan to bless Israel only, so the Gentile church can be cut off as well. The prevalence of laxity in the church, its compromise with the world, and the drift of institutional Christianity into denial of the inerrancy of the Bible and the deity of Christ suggests that this "cutting off" is close at hand. Romans 11 has nothing to do with individuals being cut off from personal salvation, it speaks in national, institutional terms.

When Paul warns that believers who destroy the unity of a local church might also be "destroyed" (1 Corinthians 3:15), the context shows that the destruction in view is spiritual and psychological ruin and loss of reward at the Judgment Seat of Christ, not loss of personal salvation.

But can believers "fall from grace"? Of course they can, but nowhere does the Bible suggest that "grace" refers to the state of personal salvation. What believers can fall from is the grace way of life and a return to the Law as a means of sanctification. That was the issue in Galatia.

What did Paul mean when he said, "If we deny Him, He will deny us"? We have shown from the context that Jesus' denial of a believer has nothing to do with a denial of that person's entry into heaven. Rather, it speaks of a denial of the right to reign with Him. It cannot mean denial of final salvation because for Jesus to deny salvation to believers would mean that He had denied Himself, which He cannot do. He would never renege on His promise that He will lose none of them.

An interpretive paraphrase might be worded something like this:

> *If we have died with Him (and every believer has), then we will live with Him (both now and in His presence after death). If we are faithful to Him through the course of our lives, then we will also govern with Him in His kingdom. If we are unfaithful to Him, then He will deny us the privilege of reigning with Him. But even if we are unfaithful, even then He remains faithful to us. We can never lose salvation, and we will go to heaven when we die.*

[2057] Patrick Fairbairn, *Pastoral Epistles*, reprint ed. (Minneapolis: Klock & Klock, 1980), 341.

[2058] McCoy, "Secure, Yet Scrutinized: 2 Tim 2:11-13," 33.

[2059] See chapter 47.

Experimental Predestinarian theology may be aghast at this, being mired as they are in works as proof of salvation, but this is what the text says.

Arminians can find little support for their doctrine of conditional security in these passages. In the General Epistles, however, they often feel their case is secure, particularly in the warning in Hebrews 6. This passage is quoted more than any other by Arminians in defense of their doctrine of conditional security. The next chapter examines this passage in some detail. We will see that the danger of falling away refers not to loss of salvation, but instead to a loss of the opportunity to enter into our inheritance-rest in the coming kingdom. Because of the complexity of the passage and the frequency with which it is quoted in defense of the Arminian view, an entire chapter will be devoted to that passage.

41

Conditional Security: Hebrews 6

THE READERS of the Epistle to the Hebrews are believers who are contemplating "leaving the race" because of the difficulties they are encountering. John described such people as dried branches (John 15:6), and Jesus called them salt that has lost its saltiness (Matthew 5:13; Luke 14:34). The writer of this epistle says that they are a field that has produced thorns.

About forty years have passed since the Ascension. Christianity has spread widely throughout the Roman Empire. A reaction has begun to set in. Who are these people who have "love feasts," and why do they not worship the Roman gods? Are they traitors to Rome? Persecutions broke out. Nero impaled believers on poles, covered them with tar, and used them as torches to light the streets of the city.

Hadn't Jesus said that in "this generation" He would return? About a generation had passed and things were not looking promising for the Christian movement.

At least Judaism was legal. So some of the recipients of the epistle to the Hebrews said, "Perhaps we should return to it."

The Epistle to the Hebrews was written to the Hebrews to teach the Hebrews that they should no longer be Hebrews (religiously). The writer devotes his epistle to encouraging them in the battle, to promising reward if they are faithful, and to warning them of the dangers of denying Christ.

One of those warnings is the subject of this chapter, the warning about falling away.

Hebrews 5:11-6:12

Few passages have had greater impact on Arminian thinking than this fearful warning about falling away and entering into such a spiritual state that it is impossible to be renewed to repentance. If we had only the Arminian and Calvinist views of this passage from which to choose, it seems that the Arminian view is much more defensible. However, the Partners offer another suggestion.

THE EXHORTATION (6:1-3)

> *Therefore let us leave the elementary teachings about Christ and go on to maturity, not laying again the foundation of repentance from acts that lead to death, and of faith in God, instruction about baptisms, the laying on of hands, the resurrection of the dead, and eternal judgment. And God permitting, we will do so (Hebrews 6:1-3).*

The opening word "therefore" refers to the preceding verses (5:11-14) as a whole. Because of their spiritual dullness, they need to commit themselves to learning and applying the truth and to press on to maturity. They need to be able to "distinguish good from evil" (5:14), and he wants to help them by stretching their minds and steeling their wills. He wants them to move from "milk" (5:12-13), that is, receiving the most elementary biblical truths, to "solid food" (5:12, 14), that is, understanding and applying the more advanced concepts of biblical truth.

In the midst of his discussion regarding the Melchizedekian priesthood of the Lord Jesus Christ (Hebrews 5:1-10) the author pauses, rebukes them for their spiritual stupor (Hebrews 5:11-14), exhorts them to press on to maturity (6:1-2), warns them about the danger of falling away (6:4-6), illustrates the danger with an analogy from nature (6:7-8), and encourages them regarding confidence in their spiritual status and their need to finish what they have begun (6:9-12). He then returns to his main theme, the Melchizedekian priesthood of Christ in chapter 7.

Now it is plain and almost universally acknowledged that the author's burden here is for true Christians to grow to maturity.[2060] These people "ought to be teachers" (5:13), but they are "*slow to learn*" (5:11). They "*need milk, not solid food*" (5:12). They "live," but they live on "milk" this is a frequent metaphor in Paul's writings, who also contrasts "babes" (*nēpioi*) with the mature (*teleioi*), as in 1 Corinthians 2:6, Galatians 4:3, and Ephesians 4:13-14.[2061] The infants in Hebrews 5:11 are not non-Christians, but believers who have refused to grow even though sufficient time for growth to maturity has elapsed. The "maturity" in view is the same as that described in the preceding verses. This is not just spiritual understanding, that is, advanced mental perception. It is experiential righteousness and discernment (5:14). The opening word "therefore" in 6:1 connects maturity in that verse with 5:14: "*But solid food is for the mature, who by constant use have trained themselves to distinguish good from evil.*" "Therefore," he says, "*let us go on to maturity* [Gr *teleiotēs*]."

Obviously, the author addresses "true" Christians and not merely "professing" Christians. One who is only a professing Christian may not be a Christian at all. Being an unbeliever, he cannot grow in his ability to experientially apply the word of righteousness to daily life and have his spiritual senses trained in spiritual discernment.

These believers are to go beyond the foundation of repentance and the elementary teachings about Christ and faith in God. But which foundation is meant, Jewish or Christian? I agree with those who believe that the foundational truths are the basic doctrines which these Jewish believers embraced as they began their journey in new life in Christ.[2062] There are three parts to the foundation: repentance, faith, and teaching. The teaching is further defined as consisting of teaching about baptism, laying on of hands, the resurrection, and eternal judgment. He says they have experienced all of this at the beginning of their Christian journey. These people have clearly exercised faith toward God (6:1) and have repented and been baptized and are therefore regenerate.

He says, "And God permitting, this we will do" (v. 3). The Greek word order reads, "This we will do, God permitting." What is it that we will do, "God permitting"? The

[2060] For example, Marcus Dodds, "The Epistle to the Hebrews," in *The Expositor's Greek Testament*, ed. W. Robertson Nicoll (Grand Rapids: Wm. B. Eerdmans Publishing Co., 1967), 4:292. B. F. Westcott, *Saint Paul's Epistle to the Ephesians* (New York: Macmillan & Co., 1909), 135. Bruce, *The Epistle to the Hebrews*, 108.

[2061] Farrar, *The Epistle of Paul the Apostle to the Hebrews*, 78. See also 1 Corinthians 2:6 with 3:1 and 14:20.

[2062] Sauer, "A Critical and Exegetical Examination of Hebrews 5:11-6:8", 176 ff. Sauer has given a full and convincing argument that the foundations of the Christian, not Jewish, faith are in view.

immediate antecedent of "this" is obviously "going on to maturity."[2063] The writer is telling them that they are to press on to maturity if God permits them to do so. In phrasing it this way, he is preparing them for the warning to follow. God may not permit it just as He did not permit the Exodus generation to enter into their inheritance-rest, the land of Canaan (Hebrews 3:18)![2064]

THE WARNING (6:4-6)

> *[For] it is impossible for those who have once been enlightened, who have tasted the heavenly gift, who have shared in the Holy Spirit, who have tasted the goodness of the word of God and the powers of the coming age, if they fall away, to be brought back to repentance, because to their loss they are crucifying the Son of God all over again and subjecting Him to public disgrace. (Hebrews 6:4-6)*

The NIV translation above omits the introductory "for." This word, however, establishes a causal link with what he has just said about going forward to maturity, God permitting. What is the precise nature of this link? It refers back to the phrase "this we will do," that is, press on to maturity. Thus the writer explains by this warning why we must press on to maturity. If we do not, we are in danger of falling away, and it will be impossible for us to be renewed to repentance.

Because this warning seems to suggest the possibility of a return to the Jewish faith and the sacrificial system and is therefore a denial of the sufficiency of the final sacrifice of Christ (which amounts to denial of Christ or apostasy), many Experimental Predestinarians have labored to demonstrate that true Christians are not the subject of the warning. For this reason, it is important that we pause here to consider whether the original recipients of this epistle were Christian or non-Christian? Typically, Reformed exegesis consists of an attempt to prove that the phrases "enlightened," "tasted the heavenly gift," "shared in the Holy Spirit," and "tasted the good Word of God and the powers of the coming age" do not necessarily refer to regenerate people. Instead, Calvinists say the phrases could refer to those exposed externally to the influences of the gospel through association with Christians and through sitting under the preaching of the Word of God. However, most commentators in the history of the church have found little difficulty in understanding that these warnings in Hebrews are addressed to regenerate people. Marshall is correct when he says the vast majority of scholars view them as genuine Christians.[2065]

Several things are said of these people who are capable of falling away. Glen Riddle has pointed out that the Greek structure is giving five adjectival descriptions of the same people, all five aorist participles are tied by the te-kai-kai-kai structure under the one article with the first participle (enlightened).[2066]

[2063] The antecedent of "this" cannot be "laying again the foundation" because then the writer would be saying, "Let us go beyond the foundation, and we will lay the foundation, if God permits." This of course is nonsense.

[2064] Marshall objects that this interpretation is in conflict with what follows. In verses 4-5 the impossibility of renewal to repentance is in view, and not going forward to maturity. But surely this is quibbling. The first step toward restoration of lost love for Christ and progression to maturity is to confess one's sin, that is, repent (Revelation 2:5). See Marshall, *Kept by the Power of God: A Study of Perseverance and Falling Away*, 141.

[2065] Ibid., 142.

[2066] Glen Riddle, personal communication, July 16, 2012.

Four phrases following the participle translated "those who have been enlightened" define what it means (6:4-5):

1. te . . . and have tasted the heavenly gift
2. kai . . . and have shared in the Holy Spirit
3. kai . . . and have tasted the goodness of the word of God and the powers of the coming age
4. kai . . . and have fallen away.

Since all five adjectival participles[2067] (enlightened, tasted, shared, tasted, and fallen away) are united under the same article (Gr *tous*), there is no valid reason for taking number 5 as conditional (i.e., "if they fall away"). The first four are not conditional, and neither is the fifth.

What do these five descriptions mean?

Who have been enlightened. The word *phōtisthentas* ("enlightened") is common in the New Testament. Experimentalists customarily point to John 1:9. Here, the apostle John uses it of Christ as the true light who enlightens every man. However, all this shows is that some kind of general enlightenment short of actual conversion is possible.[2068] In Hebrews, however, this is not likely. The addition of "once for all" and the defining phrases show that the enlightenment of conversion is probably meant here.

The apostle Paul applies the word "enlightened" to Christians when he prays that the "*eyes of your heart may be enlightened in order that you may know the hope to which He has called you, the riches of his glorious inheritance in the saints*" (Ephesians 1:18).[2069] The author of the Epistle to the Hebrews uses the same word of his readers' initial reception of the gospel: "*Remember those earlier days after you had received the light*" (Hebrews 10:32). Those who received this light are those who have confessed Christ (10:35), who have given evidence of their regeneration by a life of works and their hope of heaven (10:32-34), who have been sanctified (10:29), and who possess the imputed righteousness of Christ (10:38). In other words in its only other use in Hebrews, the verb "enlightened" is clearly used of the conversion experience. Sauer correctly observes:

> *The word* ***photizesthai*** *occurs again in 10:32. The illumination both here and there, is referred to the decisive moment when the light was apprehended in its glory. . . . Inwardly this crisis of illumination was marked by a reception of the knowledge of the truth (10:26) and outwardly by the admission to Christian fellowship.*[2070]

Elsewhere in the New Testament receiving the light is commonly used for regeneration:

> *The god of this age has blinded the minds of unbelievers, so that they cannot see the light of the gospel of the glory of Christ, who is the image of God. . . . For God who said, "Let light shine out of darkness" made His light shine in our hearts to give us the light of the knowledge of the glory of God in the face of Christ. But we have this treasure in jars of clay (2 Corinthians 4:4-7).*

[2067] Participles with the article must be adjectival. Articular participles cannot be adverbial.

[2068] It may also refer to the particular enlightenment of "every man who is elect."

[2069] See also Ephesians 2:1-5; 8, 11-13, 19; 4:1; 5:8.

[2070] Sauer, "A Critical and Exegetical Examination of Hebrews 5:11-6:8", 142.

The similarity between the clause "*made His light shine in our hearts to give us the light*" (2 Corinthians 4:6) and "*who have once been enlightened*" (Hebrews 6:4) is possible evidence that the latter means the same as the former, and the former is obviously conversion.[2071]

The writer of the epistle to the Hebrews says that they have been *hapax phōtisthentas* ("once for all enlightened"). The word *hapax* often has a sense of finality in it. It provides a conceptual contrast with "again" (*palin*) in 6:6. The writer also uses it of Christ's "once-for-all" appearance at the end of the age to do away with sin (Hebrews 9:26; 10:2) and of the finality of death that comes on all men (9:27). *Hapax* is applied to the "once-and-for-all" taking away of sin by Christ's sacrifice (9:28). Danker (BDAG, 97) lists Hebrews 10:2 under the meaning "once for all" and also Jude 3 where Jude uses it of the faith, which has been "once-and-for-all" delivered to the saints.

These people, then, have been "once-and-for-all" enlightened. This is not a mere mental awareness, a mere first introduction, but a "final" enlightenment.

This once-for-all inward enlightenment and reception of the gospel is hardly consistent with the thesis that these people were not truly born again. Its use "would be strange if the reference was merely to the reception of a course of instruction" in contrast to actual conversion as some experimentalists maintain.[2072] Furthermore, assuming that the structural arrangement of the passage outlined above is correct, the word is then defined in the immediate context as "having tasted the heavenly gift" and as "having become partners of the Holy Spirit."[2073]

Who have tasted the heavenly gift. This enlightenment is, first of all, explained as involving "having tasted" of the heavenly gift (Gr *dōrea*). The parallel with John 4:10 is noteworthy. In His comments to the Samaritan woman Jesus said:

> *If you knew the gift [Gr dōrea] of God and who it is that asks you for a drink, you would have asked him and he would have given you living water.*

Every usage of *dōrea* in the Bible refers to the bestowal of some divine gift, spiritual and supernatural, given to man. In each case, unless Hebrews 6 is an exception, the receiver of this gift is either regenerate already, or the gift itself is regeneration.[2074] In Romans 5:17 it is the gift of righteousness; in Ephesians 3:7 it is the gift of the grace of God; in Acts 2:38 it is the gift of the Holy Spirit. Regeneration is, of course, not part of the semantic value of the word. The precise nature of the gift must be determined from its sense in the context of Hebrews 6. There it is qualified as a "heavenly" gift, or a gift that comes from heaven. The phraseology is so suggestive of the numerous other references to the gift of Christ, the Holy Spirit, or righteousness that comes from heaven, that this must surely be the first thought

---

2071 In 1 Peter 2:9, coming out of darkness into light is described as conversion. Indeed, the movement from darkness to light is a popular theme in the apostle John's writings for the movement from death to life, that is, conversion (John 5:24). Jesus called Himself the light of the world and said "*I have come into this world so that the blind will see*" (John 9:39).

2072 Sauer, "A Critical and Exegetical Examination of Hebrews 5:11-6:8".

2073 John MacArthur tries to blunt the force of this by referring to a usage of *photizō* in the LXX in Isaiah 9:1-2 which refers to people in darkness who saw a great light; cf. Matthew 4:16. This is irrelevant to the usage in the New Testament where it specifically refers to the spiritual enlightenment of regeneration and where the context describes it as *hapax*, final, once-and-for-all enlightenment. See MacArthur, *Hebrews*, 142.

2074 John 4:10; Acts 2:38; 8:20; 10:45; 11:17; Romans 5:15, 17; 2 Corinthians 9:15; Ephesians 3:7; 4:7; Hebrews 6:4.

that would come to the minds of first-century readers.[2075] As Paul said, "*The gift is not like the trespass. For if the many died by the trespass of the one man, how much more did God's grace and the gift that came by the grace of the one man, Jesus Christ, overflow to the many!*" (Romans 5:15). To taste the heavenly gift is to experience regeneration, to taste salvation itself.

The word *geuomai*, "taste," is not used of an external association but of an internal taste. Some have argued that the choice of the word "taste" means that the gift was not really received; it was only sampled, not feasted on.[2076] Even Calvin "vainly attempts to make the clause refer only to 'those who had but as it were tasted with their outward lips the grace of God, and been irradiated with some sparks of His light.'"[2077] Farrar correctly insists, "This is not to explain Scripture, but to explain it away in favour of some preconceived doctrine. It is clear from 1 Peter 2:3 that such a view is untenable."[2078]

A contemporary writer pursues the idea of pressing a distinction between "eating" and "tasting." Only by "eating" does one obtain eternal life, he says, not by tasting. But on the contrary, the word "taste" includes within its compass the sense of eating:

He became hungry and wanted something to eat (geuomai, Acts 10:10).

Then he went upstairs again and broke bread and ate (geuomai, Acts 20:11).

In both biblical and secular Greek this verb means to eat or to "partake of" or to "join."[2079] One papyrus manuscript refers to a man who went to bed without eating (*geuomai*) his supper, and another refers to a group who "joined in" (*geuomai*) the praise of another.[2080]

Eating and tasting can be used as synonymous terms and either verb in this case imply believing in Christ, resulting in regeneration and eternal life. This is very similar to Christ using "eating" His flesh and "drinking" His blood as terms that both mean "partake of My life." Only the particular context determines whether this is a matter of partaking for temporal benefit or eternal gain.

Jesus was not externally associated with death. We are told that "*because of the suffering of death crowned with glory and honor, so that by the grace of God He might taste* (Gr *geuomai*) *death for everyone*" (Hebrews 2:9). He did not merely sample it, He experienced it to the full! The full experience of death was the tasting itself and not something that followed tasting. How does one taste death and then fully experience it after dying? Tasting is full experience!

[2075] The gift of God is the gift of regeneration (2 Corinthians 10:15) and the gift of the Holy Spirit (Acts 10:44-46). Elsewhere in the New Testament the references to the gift of God refer to salvation and the forgiveness of sins. "It is the whole gift of redemption, the new creation, the fullness of life eternal freely bestowed, and made known freely, to the enlightened." Dodds, "The Epistle to the Hebrews," 4:296.

[2076] MacArthur, *Hebrews*, 143.

[2077] Farrar, *The Epistle of Paul the Apostle to the Hebrews*, 82.

[2078] Ibid. "The construction with the genitive (instead of the accusative as at ver. 5) does not warrant the interpretation made in the interests of Calvinism, of a mere tasting with the tip of the tongue." Carl B. Moll, *Hebrews*, ed. J. P. Lange, reprint ed., *A Commentary on the Holy Scriptures* (Bellingham, WA: Logos Bible Software, 2008), 11:114.

[2079] M-M, 125; BAGD, 156.

[2080] M-M, 125.

Tiedtke is surely correct when he says:

The emphasis in tasting is not that of taking a sip, as Calvin thought. In Hebrews 2:9 Christ "tasted death" in the sense that He experienced its bitter taste to the full. The amount consumed is not the point, but the fact of experiencing what is eaten. The Christians to whom this is addressed have already experienced something of the future age.[2081]

Peter uses it of the experience of Christians, of newborn infants:

Like newborn babies, crave the pure spiritual milk, so that by it you may grow up in your salvation, now that you have tasted [geuomai] that the Lord is good (1 Peter 2:3).

These are not people who have been superficially exposed to external Christian influences. On the contrary, they have internally experienced them through regeneration. As Westcott insists, "Geusasthai expresses a real and conscious enjoyment of the blessing apprehended in its true character." He then cites John 6:54 as a parallel.[2082]

It is often related to the spiritual experience of the regenerate:

Taste and see that the Lord is good (Psalm 34:8).[2083]

The regenerate to whom Peter writes have "tasted [*geuomai*] the kindness of the Lord" (1 Peter 2:3). The experience of tasting is not that of those who do not know Christ but of those who have come to know Him.

For these reasons most recent scholars agree with Behm that the amount consumed is not intended by the word "tasted."[2084]

Who have shared in [have become partners of] the Holy Spirit. The second qualifier of enlightenment is that it includes being "partners" of the Holy Spirit. This is the same word used in 3:14, *Metochoi*, "partners," Christians.

But in what sense are these people partners with the Holy Spirit? The ministry of the Holy Spirit in the book of the Hebrews is described in various ways. There is no consistent notion, as Sauer argues, that He only communicates information and testimony.[2085] Rather, He is the Spirit who imparts grace (10:29), that is, justification and regeneration; and He imparts spiritual gifts (2:4) to the *regenerate*! In view of the fact that they are partners of the Holy Spirit and that in all other references to partners true Christians are in view, there is no reason here not to assume that it does not mean something like close partnership or spiritual fellowship, which is possible only to the regenerate.

In each reference to *Metochoi* in the book of Hebrews, regenerate people are in view.[2086] In Hebrews 12:8 because they are true sons, regenerate, they are partners (*Metochoi*) in discipline. In 1:9 they are regenerate companions (*Metochoi*) of the King. In 3:1 they are regenerate "holy brothers" who are partners (*Metochoi*) in the heavenly calling. In 3:14, as

2081 Erich Tiedtke, "Hunger," in NIDNTT, 2:270.

2082 Westcott, *The Epistle to the Hebrews*, 149.

2083 See also Job 20:18. The ESV translates "swallow it down [Gr *geuō*]."

2084 Johannes Behm, "*geuomai*," in TDNT, 1:675-77; LSJ, s.v. "*geuomai*."

2085 Sauer, "A Critical and Exegetical Examination of Hebrews 5:11-6:8", 223.

2086 Hebrews 1:9; 3:1, 14; 5:13; 6:4; 7:13; 12:8.

discussed in chapter 5, they are partners with Christ in the final destiny of man, ruling over the millennial earth.[2087] Thus the Partner view is certainly to be preferred.

Who have tasted the goodness of the word of God. The third qualifier of the word "enlighten" is "tasting the goodness of the word of God." This may be viewed as a continual tasting of the Word of God (cf. 1 Peter 2:2-3). Farrar, justifiably, has little patience with Calvin's exegesis on this point: "There is no excuse for the attempt of Calvin and others, in the interests of their dogmatic bias, to make 'taste of' mean only 'have an inkling of' without any deep or real participation."[2088]

Who have tasted the powers of the coming age. This refers to the miracles of the New Testament era, which are a foretaste, a preview, of the miraculous nature of the future kingdom of God. The ministry of the Holy Spirit authenticated the gospel with "powers," as mentioned in 2:4. The writer apparently knows of some of his readers who have fallen, and he writes to warn the rest against the danger of such failure in the future. In what way did these who are in danger of falling away taste these mighty works? Sauer argues that they only externally tasted the Spirit's authenticating ministry through miracles as taught in 2:4. While it is true that they experienced this external authentication, it is also true that they received the spiritual gifts of the Holy Spirit, which are given only to the regenerate. At any rate, the taste was not superficial. It was a full taste just as Jesus tasted death. A personal experience with the Holy Spirit is implied, not just the observation of His performing miracles. These people had personally and internally experienced the power of God in their lives.

Who have fallen away. The Greek word *parapiptō* means "to fall by the wayside." It is used only here in the New Testament. The Egyptian papyri manuscripts have examples of the word where it means "to fall by the wayside."[2089] And a frequent meaning in the LXX is "to fall in one's way, befall."[2090] Glen Riddle has pointed out that since this participle must be an attributive,[2091] any English translation reading "*if* they fall away" is simply not reflecting the Gr grammatical structure. Such a translation would only be valid for an adverbial participle. Actuality, not mere potentiality, is under review. Not only does the grammar require that we understand the author is thinking of those who *have in fact* fallen away, but the logic of the passage also demands this. How can one need renewal to a state from which they have not fallen or lost? While some may debate this conclusion (that actual apostasy has in fact occurred), what is *very clear* in the Greek text is that for those who have fallen in this way, *as long as they are in that condition*, it is impossible for them to be renewed to a state of fellowship and a path of growth toward maturity.

2087 Glen Riddle notes, "We have a perfect analogy to this in our government. The President does not rule alone; he has a cabinet of trusted individuals who are given great authority, trust, and responsibility to share in the ruling of the country. Ancient rulers had similar *Metochoi* to assist in administration and rule. It is often overlooked by New Testament exegetes that in Mark 10:32-40 (and parallel passages elsewhere) Jesus did not deny there would be such positions in His kingdom. In fact, vs. 40 clearly says *there will be* such positions!" Glen Riddle, personal communication, July 16, 2012.

2088 Farrar, *The Epistle of Paul the Apostle to the Hebrews*, 82.

2089 M-M, p. 489, where the untranslated German word *verlorengehen* means "become lost, wander astray."

2090 Abbott-Smith, 342.

2091 "When the article is used there is no doubt about the participle being attributive," and "all articular participles are, of course, attributive." Robertson, *A Grammar of the Greek New Testament in the Light of Historical Research*, 1105. Glen Riddle, personal communication, October 2012.

These believers were considering a relapse into Judaism, and some already have. Indeed, the whole book was written to demonstrate the superiority of Christianity to Judaism and hence to prevent such a relapse. In addition, the central sin, the sin of throwing away their confidence in Christ as the sufficient sacrifice for sin, is what is warned about in 10:26. Throughout the epistle the writer urges his readers to hold fast to their confession of faith (10:23). The danger of persistence in this fallen state is the point of the warning. That would lead to final apostasy.

He is aware, however, that the decisive act of apostasy has precursors. This results from a period of hardening of heart that crystallizes at a particular moment. It is preceded by "neglect" of our great salvation, by hardness of heart (3:12), and by refusal to grow (5:11-14). The reference to "going astray" in Hebrews 6 probably refers not only to apostasy but also to the preceding process which can lead to it.

The verses in the immediate context have been referring to the need to grow from infancy to maturity. The readers have been exhorted to "go on to maturity." Thus the meaning of "fall away" must include the opposite of "going on to maturity." As they "go on," as they press to that goal, there is a danger that some will "go astray, fall away," that they will fail to persevere. He is not speaking of falling away from eternal salvation at all. He is talking about wandering from the path that is leading to maturity (a path that is only possible when one recognizes the sufficiency of the sacrifice of Christ—New Covenant worship requires this), from that progression in the Christian life that results in their ultimate entrance into rest, the achievement/completion of their life work (Hebrews 4:11). Nor is he speaking about falling away from a mere profession of faith, because these people possessed saving faith in Christ. They were regenerate. If they did not decide to press on to maturity, they are in danger of denying the faith altogether. At least, this is the real concern of the epistle.

Later he tells them:

> *So do not throw away your confidence; it will be richly rewarded. You need to persevere so that when you have done the will of God, you will receive what he has promised (Hebrews 10:35-36).*

He has before his mind the failure of the largely regenerate Exodus generation[2092] who did not achieve their intended destiny of entrance into the inheritance-rest of Canaan.[2093] A failure to go on to maturity typically results from a spiritual lapse, a hardened heart, and unbelief (Hebrews 3:7, 12). Just as the wilderness failure to persevere did not result in the loss of salvation of two million Jews, neither would the potential failure of the Hebrews result in their loss of salvation. What is in danger is the forfeiture of their position as Christ's *Metochoi*, those who will partner with Him in His future reign.

How does one know when a believer has "gone astray"? Several things seem to be involved in the lives of those who are moving in this direction. They "neglect" their great salvation; that is, they are not interested in their glorious future (not to mention all the blessings of the spiritual life in the Body of Christ now), and they have a sense

---

[2092] For proof that the Exodus Generation was largely regenerate see volume 1, chapter 4, p. 68 ff.

[2093] See volume 1, chapter 11 inheritance rest of Hebrews and a demonstration that this refers to the believer's ultimate reward in heaven, not his final deliverance from damnation.

of "drift" in their Christian lives (Hebrews 2:2-3). A gradual hardness of heart appears. This is associated with an unbelief that results in turning away from, instead of toward, the living God (Hebrews 3:12). Spiritual dullness sets in, and there is no evidence of growth (Hebrews 5:11). As a natural consequence a person traveling along this road no longer desires the fellowship of other Christians, and he habitually stops meeting with other Christians (Hebrews 10:25), refusing to join with those who live by faith and desire to persevere (Hebrews 4:1-2). He may even find the company of nonbelievers or carnal believers more pleasant. If the Exodus generation is our parallel, this may suggest that an age of accountability is involved. Only those who were twenty years and older were in danger of the certain severe divine judgment for this behavior pattern (Numbers 14:29).

These are only the initial symptoms. The writer to the Hebrews knows of such people to whom he is writing. His concern goes far deeper, however. He worries that they will commit apostasy and finally reject the faith altogether. This is his meaning when he warns them "not to throw away their confidence" (Hebrews 10:35) and not to "deliberately keep on sinning" (Hebrews 10:26). He does not want them to take this final step and be among those who "shrink back and are destroyed" (Hebrews 10:39). It seems evident from these warnings in Hebrews that it is possible for Christians to commit apostasy, to publicly reject Christ.

The consequence of such an apostasy, however, is not loss of salvation but loss of inheritance, as he illustrates from the example of Esau (Hebrews 12:17). Likewise, in Hebrews 3 and 4 he warns them extensively through the example of Israel's failure to obtain their inheritance-rest.

The impossibility of renewal. For those who have "gone astray," "it is impossible to renew them again to repentance."[2094] The phrase "*since they again crucify to themselves the Son of God*" (NASB, ESV, NKJV) is a present participle (Gr *anastaurountas*, "crucify again"). The NASB translates it "since they crucify again." However, it can just as easily be a temporal participle translated "while they crucify again" and simultaneous with the impossibility of renewal. In other words, it is impossible for God to renew them *as long as they continue to crucify Him again.*[2095]

It is *ethically* impossible for God to restore to fellowship one of His children *while/because/if and when* that child is refusing to acknowledge the sufficiency of the blood of Christ. A person praying the Rosary 50 times in the Catholic church, thinking that doing so will pay for his sin, *cannot* be restored to fellowship with God while they are depending on their own works to bring that restoration. Neither can giving money, nor attending a church meeting, or any other human effort be considered a condition for union by those who are experiencing communion. Restoration to fellowship and New Covenant worship in the heavenly sanctuary is *only possible* through the completed and sufficient work of Christ.

[2094] The usage of *adunatos* ("impossible") in other places in the book excludes the idea that it could simply be rendered "very difficult." It is impossible for God to lie (6:18), impossible for the blood of bulls and goats to take away sin (10:4), and impossible to please God without faith (11:6).

[2095] The note in the NET bible reads, "Or 'while'; *Gr* 'crucifying ... and holding.' The Greek participles here ('crucifying ... and holding') can be understood as either causal ('since') or temporal ('while')." This point was suggested to me by Glen Riddle, personal communication, July 2012.

There will come a time when his opportunity to progress as a Christian may be terminated by God. Encouragement falls on deaf ears. When that happens, they, like the wilderness generation, will die and never enter into rest. It must be remembered that God declared an oath: "*In My anger, they shall never enter My rest*" (Hebrews 3:11). The writer probably has in mind Yahweh's terrible words to the believing[2096] Israelites in the wilderness who had believed in the Lord (Exodus 4:31; 14:31); had trusted in the blood of the Passover lamb (Exodus 12:27-28); and had believed in Christ (1 Corinthians 10:4-5): "*Then the Lord heard the sound of your words, and He was angry and took an oath, saying, 'Not one of these men, this evil generation, shall see the good land which I swore to give your fathers'*" (Deuteronomy 1:34–35). True believers can reach a point where God will not allow them to go on to maturity!

This is why the writer says that progression to maturity (6:1) can only continue, "God permitting" (6:3). God will not permit it as long as they continue to shame His Son and deny the sufficiency of His final sacrifice. God may draw the line and disinherit them as He did with the Exodus generation. Once we withdraw from God's house of worship and forsake fellowship with other Christians, we are beyond the opportunity to respond to their encouragement, and we risk loss of reward at the Judgment Seat of Christ.

But what is the precise object of "renew"? It is "to repentance." The readers of Hebrews had experienced repentance before and cannot be renewed again to it. This creates some problems for Experimental Predestinarian exegesis. Normally, within the Experimentalist perspective, repentance in the sense of submission to the Lordship of Christ is viewed as one of the conditions for salvation (in addition to faith alone). If these apostates have repented, then they are saved. Yet on these Calvinistic assumptions, if they are saved, they cannot be mere professors, as the Experimentalist exegesis of the passage requires. Experimental Predestinarian Roger Nicole is acutely aware of his problem here:[2097]

> *This characteristic ... appears to confront us with greater difficulties than any of the other descriptions. For if the repentance that these apostates had experienced was not true godly sorrow (2 Corinthians 7:10), it is hard to see why it would be desirable to renew it. And if this repentance is the genuine sorrow of the penitent believer, as the word metanoia ordinarily denotes, then regeneration appears presupposed as the only adequate fountain for such an attitude.*[2098]

Experimental Predestinarians have adopted two ways to explain this problem. The typical approach, represented by Nicole for example, argues that the repentance these apostates originally exercised was a false, non-saving repentance, an approach Nicole himself acknowledges is "not entirely free of difficulty."[2099] He admits that the reason he adopts it is that the alternative is that "regenerate individuals may be lost."[2100] Surely, there is a better alternative!

2096 For proof that the Exodus generation as a whole was viewed as regenerate see discussion on pp. 70 ff.

2097 Roger Nicole, "Some Comments on Heb. 6:4-6 and the Doctrine of Perseverance of God with the Saints," in *Current Issues in Biblical and Patristic Interpretation*, ed. Gerald G. Hawthorne (Grand Rapids: Wm. B. Eerdmans Publishing Co., 1975), 361.

2098 Ibid.

2099 Ibid.

2100 Ibid.

A similar approach, represented by Sauer, is to say that the repentance was real but that repentance plus faith are necessary for salvation and that the readers are only said to have repented in 6:6:

> *The fallen had repented. That is, they underwent a change of mind about their sinful life, the validity of Christianity, and the continuing worth of Judaism. . . . This repentance was to be followed up and supplemented by conversion. But the expected epistrophe, or turning to God through faith in Christ, is not said to have occurred.*[2101]

But it *does* say it has occurred! In 6:1 we are told that they repented and exercised faith toward God. In 10:23 they had professed "hope," Trust in the person of Christ. They had "confidence" in Christ (10:35) and had been "sanctified by the blood of the covenant" (10:29). Furthermore, the descriptive phrases mentioned in 6:4-6, as argued above, are in fact best interpreted as descriptive of regenerate people.

The Partners also see the repentance of these Jewish believers (cf. Acts 2:37-38) as genuine admission of guilt which lead to faith in Christ. As discussed in chapter 3, "repentance" does not refer to turning from sin, but rather admission of guilt, a need for a savior, and a willingness to change. The Partners see the repentance of these Jewish believers in 6:1 as a reference to Jewish-Christian repentance from trusting in the dead works of the Levitical sacrifices (9:14) as the means for fellowship with God, after beginning their new life in Christ. To trust in them is a denial of the all sufficiency of Christ's final sacrifice. Here the author thinks of the Christian reaching a state where he cannot be restored to that state of trust in the sufficiency of Christ's sacrifice alone he had at the beginning. He cannot admit guilt and desire to change. In this sense of the word it is very similar to "confession." The application of repentance (Gr *metanoia*) to the regenerate is common in the New Testament (cf. Luke 17:3; 2 Corinthians 7:10; 2 Corinthians 12:21; 2 Timothy 2:25; Revelation 2:5, 16). His point is that a regenerate man can get into such a psychological and spiritual state that he is hardened (Hebrews 3:13), *and as long as he remains in that state* (as the Exodus generation did), as long as he continues to crucify the Son of God and hold him up to open shame, his perspective cannot be renewed. This is not a renewal to salvation from sin's penalty of final damnation It is a renewal to the state of mind that trusts only in the sufficiency of Christ's sacrifice for fellowship and admits that trust in the Levitical system is wrong. Without it, there can be no growth in sanctification. This "renewal" is illustrated in 2 Corinthians 7:10-11:

> *Godly sorrow brings repentance that leads to salvation. . . . See what this godly sorrow has produced in you: what earnestness, what eagerness to clear yourselves, what indignation, what alarm, what longing, what concern, what readiness to see justice done.*

The salvation here is equivalent to experiential sanctification, moral victory, deliverance from sin's power. But the godly sorrow is the same as the renewal or repentance of Hebrews 6:6. It is a renewal that produces earnestness, eagerness to clear yourself, alarm over sin, and readiness to see justice done (2 Corinthians 7:11). When that state of mind is achieved, a man can repent, change his mind about sin, and confess it. Repentance here is not saving faith but confession of sin by the Christian.[2102]

2101 Sauer, "A Critical and Exegetical Examination of Hebrews 5:11-6:8", 250.

2102 Repentance can mean "change of mind." It is used this way of Esau in Hebrews 12:17. He sold his birthright

Crucifying the Son of God. The reason given for the impossibility of renewal to repentance is that they crucify the Son of God and subject Him to public shame (Hebrews 6:6). While many believe that the verb "crucify" (Gr *anastauroō*) does not necessarily mean "crucify again," [2103] according to Danker "the context seems to require the fig. mng. crucify again (ἀνά=again), and the ancient translators and Gr fathers understood it so."[2104] Louw-Nida agrees, "In Hebrews 6:6 ἀνασταυρόω is used figuratively of believers whose sin causes Christ to be crucified again in the sense of exposing Christ to public shame by virtue of the misdeeds of his professed followers."[2105] This crucifixion is not literal but is "for themselves," yet not as the NIV puts it, "to their loss." If they are falling back into dependence on animal sacrifices, they are doing it "for themselves" (dative of advantage).[2106] They think offering such sacrifices will get them back into fellowship with God. Such thinking is a denial of the total sufficiency of the work of Christ (so fully developed by the author in chapters 7-10). Such dependence on human effort will undoubtedly be assayed negatively at the Judgment Seat of Christ.

It is therefore clear how such actions put Christ to open shame. There were only two possible interpretations of His death. He was either crucified justly as a common criminal (the Jewish view), or He was crucified unjustly as the Son of God, an innocent man. When a Christian refuses to grow and lapses into carnality, he is in effect saying that the Jewish view was correct, Christ was a blasphemer deserving of capital punishment. Paul makes a similar observation regarding those who partake of the Lord's upper *"in an unworthy manner."* He says they are *"guilty of the body and the blood of the Lord"* (1 Corinthians 11:27). In other words, they align themselves with those who killed the Lord and are liable for his death. In this sense, the believer holds Christ up to public shame. Furthermore, for the Hebrews to return to Jewish sacrifices, would proclaim that the sacrifice of Christ was insufficient!

But why does crucifying the Son of God mean that renewal to repentance is impossible? It is impossible *as long as he continues to crucify the Son of God and hold Him up to open shame.* God cannot ethically restore one to fellowship who continues in sin and trusts in dead works. It is probable that this pattern of life has become habitual. Later, he says that the neglect of communal worship has become *"the habit of some"* (Hebrews 10:25). This action of crucifying the Son of God is in process. They cannot be renewed to repentance while they continually crucify the Son of God. The hardness associated with any continued state of sin makes repentance psychologically and spiritually impossible. Because of their hardness they are in danger of final apostasy, and some may already have gone that far.

Also, as already mentioned, it is likely that from the divine side, repentance is not

for a meal, and afterward he could bring about no change of mind (from his father, Isaac), though he sought it with tears. Isaac could only tell him that it was too late to get back the firstborn birthright blessings that had already been given to Jacob. Even in 6:1, which refers to the repentance of non-Christians, the meaning is to change one's mind about the value of dead works.

2103 Dodds, "The Epistle to the Hebrews," 4:298. See also Bruce, *The Epistle to the Hebrews*, 124. Although Arndt and Gingrich favor the view of the older translators, "crucify again," they acknowledge that in Greek it always means simply "to crucify," BAGD, 60. This is also the rendering of Brandenburger. See "Cross," in NIDNTT, 1:397.

2104 BDAG, 72.

2105 Louw-Nida, 1:236.

2106 According to Farrar this is a dative of disadvantage, Farrar, *The Epistle of Paul the Apostle to the Hebrews*, 84. It is disadvantage if looked at from God's perspective; it is advantage if looked at from the perspective of those who are doing the activity – they *think* what they are doing is advantageous.

allowed while they continue in this behavior. The writer has stated that progression to maturity is possible only if God permits. However, those who have been hardened by sin (3:13) and who have unbelieving hearts that have turned away from God (3:12) are, like the Exodus generation, not permitted to go on. They will not advance to maturity and share in the great salvation promised to those who by "faith and patience will inherit the promises" (Hebrews 6:12).

THE SAVED CONDITION OF THE APOSTATES

Before continuing our discussion of the falling away, it is necessary that some summary points regarding the regenerate nature of these apostates be made.

First, most expositors acknowledge that the writer has in mind the experience of the Exodus generation in the wilderness. Just as they failed to enter rest, so New Testament believers are in danger of not entering by "following their example of disobedience" (Hebrews 4:11). The majority of the Exodus generation was regenerate, but they did not enter into rest; that is, they did not finish their work of possessing Canaan. As stressed in Hebrews 11, the "rest" in Hebrews is not heaven but the reward of joint participation with Messiah in the final destiny of man. To enter into rest is not to go to heaven when we die but to finish our life work (4:4; 10:36), to persevere to the final hour. Some Christians will, and some will not. Those who do are "Partners of Christ," that is, partners of the Messiah in His messianic purposes.

Since the analogy of the regenerate Exodus generation is in his mind and since their failure was not forfeiture of heaven but forfeiture of their reward, there is no reason to assume that the readers referred to in Hebrews 6:4-6 will forfeit more. And there is no reason to assume they are unregenerate.

Second, it is impossible to view the believers of verses 4-6 as unregenerate. Why? Because they are being urged to go on to maturity, and unregenerate non-Christians cannot mature in Christ. The maturity of 6:1 is not just advanced doctrine but is defined by the reference to 5:14 as mature character in exercising discernment between good and evil. Solid food is only appropriate for those who are mature, namely, those who have their perceptions trained "because of" (dia + accusative) practice (practical application of God's Word) with the result that they are able to discern good and evil. Even if it was "advanced doctrine," unregenerate professing Christians, lacking spiritual ability to understand spiritual truth (1 Corinthians 2:14), being blind (2 Corinthians 4:4), and being dead in trespasses and sins (Ephesians 2:1-3), can hardly be expected or exhorted to understand the Melchizedekian priesthood of Jesus Christ!

Third, the writer assumes their regeneration. He never asks them to examine themselves to see if they are Christians. If he doubted their salvation, he would certainly have placed this question before them. Instead, he tells them that these "holy brothers" (3:1) are partners of Christ only if they persevere. As most commentators now agree, being a partner and being a Christian are not synonymous. All partners are Christians, but not all Christians are partners. Only those who persevere to the final hour are *Metochoi* (Hebrews 3:14).

Fourth, it seems exegetically questionable to detach the references to believers in the warning contexts from the warnings themselves. Experimental Predestinarians acknowledge that believers are obviously being addressed in the broader context of the warning passages.[2107] Hebrews 6:4-8 is no exception. It is certainly circumscribed by exhortations to believers in 5:11-6:3 and 6:9-12. Is it exegetically plausible to switch addressees in the middle of the warning context? There is nothing in the warning itself to suggest that such a change has been made. Indeed, in the other warnings it would be almost impossible to draw such a distinction.[2108] Furthermore, even Nicole admits that our "most immediate impulse would be to interpret this cluster of statements [the references to "enlightened," etc.] as describing regenerate persons."[2109]

THE THORN-INFESTED GROUND (6:7-8)

The only possible result of their failure to persevere on the path to maturity and their return to Judaism is divine discipline and judgment. The writer now explains this by an analogy from nature in Hebrews 6:7-8:

> *Land that drinks in the rain often falling on it and that produces a crop useful to those for whom it is farmed receives the blessing of God. But the land that produces thorns and thistles is worthless and is in danger of being [or, "close to being"] cursed. In the end it will be burned (Hebrews 6:7-8).*

The "land" refers to the individual regenerate person, the Christian. It is not permissible, as some have done, to speak of two different parcels of land: one that produces a good crop and one that produces thorns (i.e., regenerate and unregenerate). Only one plot of land is mentioned or discussed here.[2110] What is in view is two differing crops resulting from different responses to the blessings of God (rain) which falls upon them.

That this "land" represents a regenerate person is proven from the descriptive phrases applied to it in 6:1-3.[2111] As the rain falls on this land, it stimulates the land to produce a useful crop, picturing a life of perseverance in good works. Or, as expressed in verse 10, the useful crop is "your work and the love you have shown him [God] as you have helped his people and continue to help them." The rain refers to the "free ... bestowal of spiritual impulse; the enlightenment, the good word of God, the energetic indwelling of the Holy Spirit, which the Hebrews had received and which should have enabled them to bring forth fruit to God."[2112] In sum, the "rain" points back to the blessings described in 6:4-5 (enlightenment, tasting the Word of God, partnership with the Holy Spirit, and tasting the heavenly gift).

Furthermore, the land "drinks" these blessings. The produce useful for the farmer and land owner pictures the fruitful life of the believer who is progressing beyond the initial

---

2107 For example 3:1, 12; 6:9; 10:19.

2108 Note the "we" in 2:1 and 10:19, 26 and the fact that those warned have been "sanctified" in 10:29.

2109 Nicole, "Some Comments on Heb. 6:4-6 and the Doctrine of Perseverance of God with the Saints," 356. Nicole honestly admits that he rejects this impulse because he has determined beforehand that it cannot mean this since the doctrine of perseverance is "powerfully grounded" elsewhere.

2110 Once again, Glen Riddle helps us, "This is shown in the Greek text by the structure: 'land' plus article which governs the participle 'drinks' plus *kai* plus the participle 'producing' plus contrastive *de* plus the participle 'bearing.' Thus, the three participles are all united with *kai/de* under one article, all three describing the 'land.'" Glen Riddle, personal communication, July 16, 2012.

2111 See also 6:10; 10:14, 32-34.

2112 Dodds, "The Epistle to the Hebrews," 4:229.

stages of infancy. Coming into the Christian life, he was enlightened and tasted good things from God, and was being prepared for the glorious day when he would be a partner in ruling with King Jesus (2:10). This person does not remain lazy in hearing the Word of God or continue in a state of "fallen away" from fellowship in the Body of Christ. The important difference pictured in this passage is the kinds of produce resulting *when* the land is drinking the rain. The blessing is similar to the obedient believer in James who presses on to maturity: the believer preserves his own life with blessing; he in turn provides blessing to the orphans, widows, the naked, the hungry as he treats everyone without prejudice and shows God's compassion to them, *and he stores up blessing at the Judgment Seat of Christ*—resulting in further blessing in the Lord's kingdom.

It is clear in the Greek text that this "land" is described several ways: (1) it drinks in the rain; (2) it produces a useful crop; (3) it is farmed; (4) it receives blessing; but, the *same* land can (5) bear thorns and thistles; (6) lack approval; (7) be nearing a cursing; and (8) face a destructive fire in the end (verse 8).[2113] Sauer correctly observes that "the writer's aim is to point out the diversity of results that can arise from the same field under equally favorable conditions."[2114] The phrase "that drinks" stresses that the rain does not merely fall on the ground but is actually absorbed by it. This soil was not hard and unreceptive, as in the case of the first soil in Jesus' parable of the soils.[2115] This is not a picture of the rain falling on the surface but not being absorbed. These people not only were enlightened and were partners of the Holy Spirit and recipients of the heavenly gift, but they also drank and absorbed it.[2116]

This crop is useful to God, the "owner." Probably, Christian ministers and teachers are the farmers (1 Corinthians 3:9). However, the same land may not produce this useful crop. It may also produce "thorns." Obviously, the writer of Hebrews does not believe that a life of perseverance is the necessary and inevitable result of regeneration. The Lord taught the same thing in the parable of the soils. The final three soils all represent regenerate people as proven by the fact that even the one with no mature root did grow and hence did manifest regenerate life. But it did not produce fruit, and the thorny one did not produce mature fruit.[2117]

When the land produces a good crop, it receives additional blessing from God. This blessing is divine approval, entrance into "rest" (Hebrews 4:11), the receiving of rewards, and various unspecified temporal blessings as well. The only other use of "blessing" in Hebrews is of Esau forfeiting his inheritance (Hebrews 12:17). That seems to confirm the interpretation that the blessing from God is a reward at the Judgment Seat of Christ. As demonstrated elsewhere, the inheritance-rest of Hebrews, indeed inheritance in the New Testament, is always, when conditioned on obedience, a reward in heaven and not heaven itself.[2118]

2113 The participles are all governed by the definite article preceding "drink" (*hē piousa*).

2114 Sauer, "A Critical and Exegetical Examination of Hebrews 5:11-6:8", 273.

2115 See pp. 532 ff.

2116 The word "drinks" (Gr *pinō*) is commonly used elsewhere of saving faith (John 4:13; 6:54; 7:37-38). These "holy brothers" (Hebrews 3:1) who are in danger of apostasy have all drunk of the water of life (i.e., believed), and on the authority of Jesus they will be raised on the last day.

2117 See discussion of this parable on pp. 532 ff.

2118 See volume 1, chapters 4-11.

But Experimental Predestinarians insist it is not possible for the same soil to bring forth both a good and a bad crop. They say it can bring forth only one or the other. But this contradicts the author's plain statements in other parts of the epistle. These regenerate people have produced a "crop" of patience in suffering and commendable good works (10:32-34). But some have also produced the "crop" of dullness and spiritual lethargy (5:11-14); some of these "brothers" are in danger of hardness of heart (3:12), and many have stopped meeting together with other Christians (10:25). The same land that produces a crop of perseverance in patience also produces a crop of initial righteousness that then falls into transgression. That is the whole point of the book.

In order to substantiate their thesis that the same regenerate heart cannot produce righteousness for a while and then fall into unrighteousness, Experimental Predestinarians have to go outside of Hebrews. They refer to Matthew 7:16, where the Lord says, "*You will know them by their fruits*" and verse 18 where He says, "*A good tree cannot bear bad fruit and a bad tree cannot bear good fruit.*" Or, as James tells us, "*Can both fresh water and salt water flow from the same spring? My brothers, can a fig tree bear olives, or a grapevine bear figs? Neither can a salt spring produce fresh water*" (James 3:11). But surely little can be argued for their case from these verses, for three reasons.

First, these are proverbial sayings. A proverb is a general maxim for which there are exceptions. It is generally true that a good tree cannot bear bad fruit, but a plain fact of agriculture is that sometimes good trees do bear bad fruit. While living in Austria, the writer had sixty-seven good apple trees in his backyard that sadly testified to this fact!

But second, James is hardly saying that regenerate people cannot produce bitter water. He is saying that they are inconsistent with their faith when they do. In the verses immediately preceding, he says, "*With one tongue we praise our Lord and Father and with it we curse men who have been made in God's likeness. Out of the same mouth come praise and cursing. My brothers,* ***this should not be***" (v. 10). James' point is not that these things *cannot be* (he has just said they can), but rather that they *should not be*.

Third, since the entire Bible presents numerous illustrations of truly regenerate people, such as Saul and Solomon, who in fact did produce a crop of righteousness and then began to produce unrighteousness, Hebrews 6:6-8 cannot be teaching something otherwise, or it is in contradiction with the rest of Scripture.[2119] The grammar and syntax of the passage do not require this "either/or" interpretation at all, and since the rest of the Bible prohibits it, there is no reason other than an a priori commitment to the Reformed doctrine of perseverance to accept it!

However, if the heart of the regenerate man produces thorns, three phrases describe his uselessness to God.[2120] He is "worthless," "in danger of being cursed," and "will be burned" (Hebrews 6:8).

THEY ARE USELESS TO GOD. The word *adokimos*, "worthless," means "disqualified" or "useless." Experimental Predestinarians, of course, prefer the translation, "spurious," which, while possible, is not the opposite of the "useful" of verse 7. The opposite of "useful" is not "false" or "spurious" but "useless" or "worthless." The writer's point is that because some of these

---

[2119] See chapter 32 above.

[2120] See Kem Oberholtzer, "The Thorn Invested Ground in Hebrews 6:4-12," *BibSac* 145(July - September 1988). Thomas ibid., 319-28.

believers are producing thorns, they are useless to the farmer. The author is not saying that the production of thorns proves that the man's profession of faith is spurious. That Christians can lead useless lives and fail to finish their work is the central warning of the epistle. The land upon which the blessings fell is "worthless." The Exodus generation, which is in the writer's mind, was not unregenerate but useless. They never accomplished the task of conquering Canaan in spite of the many blessings God poured on them.

Paul used this concept of himself in 1 Corinthians 9:27, when he said that his goal was that at the end of life he would not be found "disqualified [*adokimos*] for the prize." As discussed elsewhere,[2121] Paul has no doubt about the fact that his eternal salvation is secure! He is burdened that he finish his course and hence receive the reward. Similarly, the believer who produces thorns in Hebrews 6 is not subject to damnation, but his disobedient life will disqualify him at the judgment seat and will make him useless for the purposes of God now.

THEY ARE IN DANGER OF BEING CURSED. The second phrase, "in danger of being cursed" is more literally, "*close* (Gr *eggus*, "to being close in point of time, *near*"[2122]) *to being cursed*" (NASB). It is possible, but not likely, the curse refers back to Genesis 3. There the thorns were a result of the curse, but here the curse is a result of thorns. Preferable is seeing the Jewish background of the readers and looking to Deuteronomy 28-30 where Moses taught that obedience resulted in temporal blessing and disobedience resulted in temporal cursing.[2123] If this is the meaning, the reference directs us back once again to the temporal curse that fell on the Exodus generation that included hardship and physical death. That God sometimes brings this judgment on His regenerate people is taught elsewhere in Hebrews (Hebrews 12:5-11), and the sin to physical death is taught throughout the New Testament.[2124]

While the immediate reference is certainly to divine discipline in time, the writer of the epistle probably has the future consequences of this cursing in mind as well. He often speaks of the need to persevere and hence to receive reward.[2125] He has this thought in view in the immediate context when he says, "Imitate those who through faith and patience inherit what has been promised" (Hebrews 6:12). Conversely, those who do not persevere in faith and patience will be cursed, that is, disinherited like Esau was (12:17). The cursing does not refer to loss of salvation.

THEY WILL BE BURNED. It seems that the antecedent of "it" ("it" is not in Gr but implied) in verse 8 is "the land" in verse 7. Because it is worthless (Gr *adokimos*) the land is in danger of being burned. What is meant by this burning? Some have argued that the burning is a purifying rather than a destroying fire. Apparently, there was a common agricultural practice behind this. When a field was overgrown with weeds and thorns, it was customary to burn it in order to cleanse the field and restore its fertility. It still is. Every year you can see sugar cane fields in Hawaii having the old stalks along with the weeds being burned off. Many Americans do this to their lawns; it adds nitrogen to the soil. If this is the meaning,

---

[2121] See discussion on pp. 463 ff.

[2122] BDAG, 271.

[2123] Note Deuteronomy 29:22-28; 30:15-30.

[2124] 1 Corinthians 5:5; 11:30; James 5:19-20; 1 John 5:16-17.

[2125] Hebrews 10:36; 11:6, 10, 15, 16, 26.

then the result of the apostate's denial is severe divine discipline with a corrective intent. Justification for this might be found in Hebrews 12:5-11.

But the purifying intent is doubtful here in Hebrews 6. The parallel of the Exodus generation's failure and their destruction in the wilderness is the controlling thought of the warnings. It is impossible to renew them to repentance as long as they persist in their laziness and immaturity. In fact, if they continue, they can become so hardened that they fall into apostasy. So the burning is divine judgment in time. This is the thought of 10:27, which refers to the "raging fire that will consume the enemies of God."[2126]

Paul wrote that a believer's dead works will be burned at the Judgment Seat of Christ (1 Corinthians 3:10-15), with negative as well as positive consequences that will accrue to believers at that time (2 Corinthians 5:10). So we are not without scriptural parallel if we interpret Hebrews 6:8 from that perspective. The burning of the thorns then refers to the burning of the believer's works.

This helps explain the statement that "in the end" the works of the unfaithful believer [the produce of the field] will be "burned" (Hebrews 6:8). There is no reference to damnation here but rather to the burning up of the believer's life work at the Judgment Seat of Christ. Even though the fire consumes his house of wood, hay, and stubble (= "land," metonymy for "thorns and thistles," in Hebrews 6:8), yet this carnal Christian "will be saved, but only as one escaping through the flames" (1 Corinthians 3:15).

CONSOLATION AND ENCOURAGEMENT (6:9-12)

Having warned them, the writer's pastoral heart now emerges, and he turns to consolation in Hebrews 6:9-12. He is confident, he says, that their lives are characterized by "the better things...that accompany salvation." He affirms to them that they began well. Salvation in Hebrews, as discussed elsewhere,[2127] does not necessarily refer to final entrance into heaven, which is based on faith alone, but to the future participation in the future messianic salvation (Hebrews 1:14; 2:5), which is conditioned on obedience (Hebrews 5:9). The inheritance they will obtain refers not to heaven, which is theirs through faith alone, but to their reward in heaven, which comes only to those "who *through* ['by means of'] faith and patience inherit what has been promised" (Hebrews 6:12). Since the "promise" in Hebrews usually refers to the millennium (e.g., 4:1; 6:13, 15; 7:6; 11:9, 11, 13, 17; 12:26), to "inherit the promise" means to rule in the millennium and parallels the phrase "inherit the kingdom," which does not mean merely entering the kingdom but to own it and rule there.[2128]

Summary

For many years the author has had the privilege of traveling and teaching the Bible in Russia and Eastern Europe. In nearly every Bible conference, numerous questions were raised about the doctrine of eternal security. This doctrine is not popular in that part of the world. People fear that, if it is taught, believers will become lax in their Christian

---

[2126] See pp. 662–664 above for proof that the judgment in view is temporal and not eternal.

[2127] See volume 1, chapter 12.

[2128] See volume 1, chapter 5.

lives. On one occasion, while teaching this material, a pastor who was attending the session became quite upset. Even though no reference was made to the doctrine of eternal security, the fact that Hebrews 6 was being taught in such a way that removed it as a defense for conditional security caused him great distress. Why? Because church leaders often use this passage to motivate their congregation to fear God and obey the Scriptures.

In one situation, after the author had taken forty hours teaching through the book of Hebrews with fourteen pastors in Bucharest, Romania, many of them were quite intrigued with the approach to the passage described above. They were so interested that they asked this writer to return for a special three-day conference on the subject of eternal security. They had never been exposed to anyone who believed salvation could not be lost. At the end of three days of wonderful interaction, all of them but one had embraced the doctrines of grace.

Interesting things happened, however, when they returned to their congregations and began to preach this. One of them was threatened with his job, and another was talked to sternly by the deacons in the church.

A colleague of mine teaching in Asia reported something similar. After thoroughly presenting the Biblical case for the eternal security of God's salvific promises, one of the national leaders admitted "this has to be true, and it is extremely encouraging; but we could never teach this to our congregants without losing control over their behavior . . . it would really diminish the way our people are motivated to live the way they should."

People are often afraid of grace. There is a fear that if the doctrine of eternal security is taught, moral failure will follow.

Hebrews 6, like the other warnings in the book, is addressed to Christians and not those who have merely professed faith. They are not warned about eternal separation from God. Instead, the writer appeals to a much more challenging and ennobling danger: forfeiture of the inheritance-rest. From the way he describes them, they have obviously received much encouragement from God. Much rain has fallen on their fields, and he wants them to produce fruit, not thorns. If they fail to do so, they face severe discipline in time and loss of reward at the Judgment Seat of Christ.

In conclusion, there is no reference in Hebrews 6 to either a falling away from salvation or perseverance in holiness. This passage is a dreadful warning to those with hardened hearts, but it is not a passage to apply to persevering Christians who are "in the battle."

42

Warnings in Hebrews, Peter, and Revelation

TWO OTHER warning passages in the book of Hebrews must be considered: the warning about departure from God's house and the warning regarding willful sin. Peter also warns carnal Christians that their final state might be worse than their earlier one. Do these passages refer to the possibility of loss of eternal salvation?

Hebrews 3:1-6

The writer of the Epistle to the Hebrews told his readers that they are Christ's "house" only *if* they "hold fast":

> *Now Moses was faithful in all His house as a servant, for a testimony of those things which were to be spoken later (Hebrews 3:5).*
>
> *But Christ is faithful as a Son over God's house. And we are his house, if we hold on to our courage and hope of which we boast (Hebrews 3:6).*

To Arminians the word "if" suggests that it is possible that a true Christian may cease being part of the house of God, the community of the saved, and lose his salvation. Experimental Predestinarians see this passage as further proof of their doctrine of perseverance. Only those who have courage and who hold on to the hope of which we boast are members of the saved community.

But does "house" refer to the community of the saved? The term has been understood in different ways. Experimental Predestinarians normally understand this to refer to all the elect. One writer bases this on the fact that in Hebrews 2:10-13 the references to "sons," "brothers," and "children" refer to the elect.[2129] However, this is completely irrelevant. This is a classic illustration of an illegitimate totality transfer. The writer has read the "theological idea" of "the elect" into the concept of being a member of the "house of God." Just because all "sons" are elect does not mean that the house of God equals all the elect.

We would agree that these terms refer to the saved and that all the saved are the intended readers. However, there is no logical reason for saying that because "sons" refers to "all Christians," therefore "house of God" must also mean "all Christians." It does not. The "house of God" refers to those believers who do not withdraw from the worshiping community.

[2129] John J. Collins, "Sibylline Oracles," in *Anchor Bible Dictionary*, ed. David Noel Freedman (New York: Doubleday, 1922), 206.

Most commentators note that the faithfulness of Moses over his house in Hebrews 3:5 refers to Numbers 12. According to Michel, the term "house of God" (Gr *oikos theou*) was a fixed term for the sanctuary in the Septuagint.[2130] Lange observes:

> *It is better to understand by "my house" the Tabernacle, including the economy that it represents. The Apostle's reference to this phrase in Hebrews 3:2-6 is quite consistent with this, and most of all his words: "whose house we are."*[2131]

The apostle is speaking of the place where Moses' priestly activity occurred. He says, "Moses was faithful in all God's house" (Hebrews 3:2). Just as Moses was faithful in the tabernacle in the wilderness, we too are to be faithful in the New Testament "house." The Old Testament house was a tent in the wilderness; the New Testament house is the worshiping community, functioning in their capacity as priests (Exodus 19:4-6; 1 Peter 2:9), who have made a decision about "*not forsaking our own assembling together, as is the habit of some, but encouraging one another; and all the more as you see the day drawing near*" (Hebrews 10:25). We are His "*house ... if we hold fast.*"

Paul Tanner has noted the similarities between Hebrews 3:1-6 and Hebrews 10:19-25.[2132]

- Both passages refer to our "confidence" (3:6b; 10:19).
- Both are addressed to "brethren" (3:1; 10:19).
- Both emphasize Christ as the high priest (3:1; 10:21).
- Both emphasize the "house" (3:6; 10:21).
- Both say Christ is over the house (3:6a; 10:21).
- Both mention our "confession" (3:1; 10:23).
- Both mention our "hope" (3:6b, 10:23; cf. 4:14).
- Both are concerned that the readers "hold fast" (3:6b; 10:23).

Unless the similarities are purely coincidental, they suggest that the house in both sections refers to the same thing. In Hebrews 10, the house is the believers who are gathered together and functioning in their roles as priests, in contrast to some believers who chose not to gather with the rest. In Hebrews 10, the author's desire is not that his readers get saved, but that they draw near, hold fast, and stimulate one another to good works.

This leads to the conclusion that the "house" is not all Christians but is only those Christians who have not withdrawn from the rest and who hold fast their confession of Christ. The "house" consists of those members of the believing community who continue to assemble in worship and function in their royal priesthood. Some have habitually neglected this gathering and therefore are no longer members of the worshiping community. This says nothing about their saved status unless one "knows" that anyone who falls into the habit of forsaking regular worship with other believers is quite simply not a believer.

Peter tells us that believers "as living stones, are being built up as a spiritual house" is actually *functioning* in a priestly role as pictured in the New Testament.

2130 Otto Michel, "*oikos*," in TDNT, 5:120.

2131 Robert W. Yarbrough, "Chapter 3: Jesus on Hell," in *Hell under Fire: Modern Scholarship Reinvents Eternal Punishment*, ed. Christopher W. Peterson (Grand Rapids: Zondervan Publishing House, 2009), 3:39.

2132 Tanner, "Hebrews," 2:786.

You also, as living stones, are being built up as a spiritual house for a holy priesthood, to offer up spiritual sacrifices acceptable to God through Jesus Christ (1 Peter 2:5).

Yet it is inconceivable that a believer who is no longer fulfilling his priestly function of offering up spiritual sacrifices is actually part of the New Testament "holy priesthood." He may be saved, but he is not part of Christ's worshiping and priestly community.

Yahweh said the same thing to the Old Testament worshiping community:

Now then, if you will indeed obey My voice and keep My covenant, then ... you shall be to Me a kingdom of priests and a holy nation (Exodus 19:5–6).

Israel would be a kingdom of priests and a holy nation only if they obeyed God's voice and kept His covenant.

When we withdraw from the exercise of our New Testament priestly worship, we are no longer fellowshipping with other believers. But this does not mean we are not saved or that we had salvation and lost it.

Hebrews 10

The warning against deliberate sin in Hebrews 10:26-39 has understandably given rise to doubt in the minds of some as to whether the doctrine of eternal security is in the Bible. Arminians may be forgiven for being unimpressed with Experimental Predestinarian exegesis which labors under the impossible burden of claiming that the readers to whom the warning is addressed may not be regenerate. As demonstrated in the discussion of Hebrews 6 in chapter 41, it is evident that the author of this epistle intends to address his readers as regenerate and not as merely professing Christians.

THE REGENERATE NATURE OF THE READERS

The fact that the readers are viewed as regenerate is evident from several considerations in Hebrews 10 as well. First, they are the same group addressed in Hebrews 6. If the arguments there for the saved condition of these people are valid, then the case is settled.[2133] However, in addition, these people have already been "made perfect" according to verse 14,

---

[2133] For compelling proof that saved people are the subject of the warnings in Hebrews see James Fyfe, *The Hereafter: Sheol, Hades and Hell, the World to Come, and the Scripture Doctrine of Retribution According to Law* (Edinburgh: T. & T. Clark, 1890); Kenneth J. Morgan, "The New Testament Use of *Gehenna*: Its Historical Background and Its Significance for the Doctrine of Eternal Punishment," (May 1975), http://rediscoveringthebible.com/Geenna.pdf. The following facts show that the people addressed in Hebrews are regenerate and justified. (1) They have been enlightened and have tasted the good Word of God. They had an initial conversion followed by Christian experience as discussed above. (2) They were called "holy brothers" and "partners of the heavenly calling" (Hebrews 3:1). (3) The writer warns that an "evil heart of unbelief" can be present in a "brother" (Hebrews 3:12) and that such a person risks falling away from the living God, just as did the born-again nation of Israelites in the wilderness. (4) He does not warn them as if they were still unbelievers, but rather as Christians who are in danger of falling away (Hebrew 3:12; 4:1). (5) He specifically says that he believes they are Christians. He feels they possess the things that accompany salvation (Hebrews 6:9-12). He acknowledges "the work and love" which they "have shown toward His name." He does not exhort them to become Christians, but rather he assumes they are and says, "And we desire that each one of you show the same diligence so as to realize the full assurance of hope to the end." He says that they have "fled for refuge in laying hold of the hope set before us."

are called "sanctified" in verse 29, and are described as "righteous" in verse 38. Furthermore, they have confessed Christ (v. 35) and have demonstrated their faith: by remaining true to Christ in the midst of reproach and tribulation (v. 35) by showing sympathy to other Christians who had been imprisoned for their faith, by joyfully accepting the confiscation of their property, and by hoping in a better possession, an abiding one (v. 34).

On Experimental Predestinarian premises these people must be saved. They have confessed Christ, are declared to be righteous and sanctified, and have proven it by a life of good works. If they are not saved, then the Experimental Predestinarian view of works as a necessary evidence of salvation is false. But if they are saved, then their view of perseverance is fiction!

THE CONSEQUENCES OF WILLFUL SIN (10:26-27)

> *For if we go on sinning willfully after receiving the knowledge of the truth, there no longer remains a sacrifice for sin, but a certain terrifying expectation of judgment, and the fury of a fire which will consume the adversaries (10:26-27).*

These words serve as a real warning to Christians. There is a danger here for all who know Christ. To sin "willfully" (Gr *ekousiōs*) means to sin "without compulsion" (1 Peter 5:2). This willful sinning continues after having received "full knowledge" (Gr *epignōsis*) of the truth. This word is used of the knowledge of salvation in 1 Timothy 2:4. No contextual reason suggests that a knowledge less than salvation is intended here.

Probably, the writer has a particular sin in view, the sin of not holding fast their confession, against which he has just warned (10:23): "*Let us hold fast the confession of our hope without wavering ... for if we go on sinning willfully....*"[2134] He is warning them against the sin of wavering in regard to their confession. Such wavering could lead to a denial of it altogether, that is, apostasy. The writer of Hebrews apparently thinks it is possible for righteous ones—who are sanctified, perfected forever (v. 14), and who have proven their confession by works—to finally depart from the faith and return to Judaism. However, distasteful such a view is or however contradictory it is to the Reformed doctrine of perseverance, should not biblical data determine our theology rather than the other way around?

When a person takes this step, "*there no longer remains a sacrifice for sins.*" The sacrifice of Christ, of course, certainly remains in one sense, but it no longer remains in the sense that avails to protect him from the judgment of God. Why? Because they have rejected it and gone back to Jewish sacrifices. When a person sins, the only basis for restoration to fellowship is the blood of Christ. That sacrifice is all-sufficient, once-for-all, and permanent. There is nothing that can be added to it. There is no longer any additional sacrifice that can be made for anything.

But what kind of judgment is in view? To answer that question, we must turn to the Old Testament passages to which the writer is referring. What was willful sin?

In the Old Testament, sacrifices were provided for unintentional sin (Numbers 15:27, 29). However, if an Old Testament believer sinned willfully, no sacrificial protection was provided.

[2134] The verse opens with "for," which connects the thought with 10:23.

But the person who does anything defiantly, whether he is a native or an alien, that one is blaspheming the L*ORD; and that person shall be cut off from among his people. Because he has despised the Word of the* L*ORD and has broken His commandment, that person shall be completely cut off; his guilt shall be on him (Numbers 15:30-31).*

The Hebrew phrase translated "defiantly" (*ekousiōs*) in Hebrews 10:26 is the translation of a two-word Hebrew phrase that means "with a high hand" (Numbers 15:30). It is used in Numbers of a person "acting in deliberate presumption, pride, and disdain."[2135] When the Hebrews left Egypt, they left with a "high hand"; that is, they left boldly and defiantly against Pharaoh (Numbers 33:3).

For the readers of the Epistle to the Hebrews to similarly sin like this against God, there was no sacrificial protection from the judgment. To be "cut off" in Numbers 15:31 was to undergo capital punishment.

Therefore you are to observe the sabbath, for it is holy to you. Everyone who profanes it ***shall surely be put to death****; for whoever does any work on it, that person shall be* ***cut off*** *from among his people (Exodus 31:14 NASB; cf. Deuteronomy 17:12).*

This phrase "cut off" is often used of capital punishment or of severance from the covenant community but never of eternal separation from God.[2136] Therefore, when the writer of the Epistle to the Hebrews speaks of the consequences of willful sin, he means that there is no sacrificial protection from the *temporal* consequences of sin. Having rejected the sacrifice of and returned to Jewish sacrifices, there is no protection. He has in view the judgment of God in time, not in eternity, as these Old Testament references show.

While it is acknowledged that the writer cites Old Testament passages that apply to judgment in time, Experimental Predestinarians object that the Old Testament had an underdeveloped doctrine of the judgment in the afterlife. Therefore, they say, these Old Testament passages are to be understood as pointing to a final judgment of which the temporal one was only a type.

What kind of argument is this? In essence they are saying that, since there was a poorly developed doctrine of the afterlife in the Old Testament, we must interpret some references to temporal judgment as final damnation! Of course, it is possible that an Old Testament temporal reference does have an application to an eschatological judgment. We will argue this is the case in regard to the judgment of the valley of Hinnom in later chapters. However, in Hebrews 10:26-27 there is no contextual indication that an eschatological application of the phrase "fury of fire" is intended. This phrase is often used of temporal judgments upon God's people.

The context of Hebrews 10 is about the application of Christ's death to daily sins for temporal not eternal forgiveness. The writer has already said they have protection from the judgment of eternal damnation: "By this will we have been sanctified through the offering of the body of Jesus Christ *once for all*" (Hebrews 10:10). He has already told them that God will remember their sins and lawless deeds "no more" (Hebrews 10:17) and that "by one

---

2135 "Dung," in *The Eerdmans Bible Dictionary*, ed. Allen C. Myers (Grand Rapids: Wm. B. Eerdmans Publishing Co., 1987), 2:830.

2136 See Genesis 17:14; Leviticus 7:20; 17:4; 20:2, 4-5; Numbers 19:13, 20.

offering He has perfected for all time those who are sanctified" (Hebrews 10:14). Would he now turn around and contradict himself in verses 26-30? Our eternal position before the Father is in view in verse 17, while verses 26-30 refer to our temporal relationship to Him. The believer today who sins through ignorance and weakness is protected from temporal judgment in time (if he repents) by the blood of Christ. The blood of Christ, however, will not protect the believer who sins willfully. He is in danger of judgment after the Old Testament pattern, a judgment in time that may include physical death or worse.

If a believer abandons his confession of Christ, that is, returns to Judaism, there is no place he can go for sacrificial protection from the judgment of God. There is only one thing left—"*a certain terrifying expectation of judgment, and the fury of a fire which will consume the adversaries*" (Hebrews 10:27).

This judgment is said to be a "*fury of fire that will consume the adversaries*." The writer quotes Isaiah 26:11 which refers to the physical destruction of Israel's enemies in time, not eternity. The mention of "fire" unnecessarily evokes images of hell in our minds. Normally, it simply symbolizes some kind of judgment, either in time or eternity. Here, as the Old Testament citations prove, judgments in time are in view.[2137]

Severe consequences may befall a Christian who sins in this way.

THE MORE SEVERE PUNISHMENT (10:28-29)

> *Anyone who has set aside the Law of Moses dies without mercy on the testimony of two or three witnesses.*
> *How much severer punishment do you think he will deserve who has trampled underfoot the Son of God, and has regarded as unclean the blood of the covenant by which he was sanctified, and has insulted the Spirit of grace? (10:29).*

The *severer punishment* is a punishment even worse than physical death. Death without mercy in the Old Testament was God's punishment for idolatry based on the testimony of two or three witnesses.[2138] One such example of a more severe punishment was Saul's mental anguish. He became mentally ill and was tormented by evil spirits (1 Samuel 16:14-15). Here was a man who was depressed and was consumed with hatred, whose fate was far worse than physical death. As discussed previously,[2139] he was a regenerate man. A more severe punishment could be a prolonged illness, being kept alive by artificial means, or insanity. Many people in insane asylums today would testify to the truth of this torture. Lacking the courage to take their own lives, they endure a pain far worse than physical death. One thinks of David's sin and the resultant consequence, the loss of his child. David would be the first to affirm that his punishment was more severe than physical death. No doubt the writer of Hebrews views millennial disinheritance which is a result of a failure to *complete one's life work*, that is, enter into rest (the literal intended meaning of the Old Testament text in Gen. 2:2), as more severe than physical death as well.

[2137] See Charles C. Bing, "Does Fire in Hebrews Refer to Hell?," *BibSac* 167, no. 667 (July-September 2010): 350-56.

[2138] Deuteronomy 17:2-7. The death penalty in the Old Testament was given for blasphemy (Leviticus 24:11-16), murder (Leviticus 24:17; Numbers 35:30), false prophecy (Deuteronomy 18:20), and rejection of the decree of the court (Deuteronomy 18:20).

[2139] See chapter 32.

The writer certainly has loss of reward in view as well (v. 35). A punishment which might include physical death, emotional and spiritual ruin, and loss of reward for all eternity is certainly "more severe" than the Old Testament judgment of temporal death alone.

The seriousness of this step is described in three ways. First, such a man "*tramples the Son of God underfoot.*" The sinning Christian here obviously does not literally trample on the Son of God, but that is the effect of his life. The term is used in Matthew 7:6 of pigs trampling spiritual truth underfoot. In the writings of Homer, "to trample underfoot" apparently referred to the breaking of an oath.[2140] This meaning would fit well with the present context, a denial of one's oath that was expressed in baptism, that is, a denial of Christ. In Zechariah 14:2, Jerusalem is described as a stone trampled on by all the nations. The city will be scorned. In conclusion, then, the term "trample under foot" signifies a strong rejection and actual denial of one's confession of faith in Christ either by life or by an actual verbal denial.

Suppose a family of four is out in a rowboat and a terrible storm breaks out. It soon becomes clear that the boat can hold only two people and that two will have to jump overboard to save the other two. As the water continues to pour into the boat and the danger becomes acute, the parents, in order to save the children, dive overboard and are drowned. Before they did this, however, they ask the older brother in the boat to take care of his little sister. They say, "We love you both. We are going to die so that you can live. Please commit to us that you will take care of your little sister." The older brother tearfully commits to do so. As the years go by, he becomes involved in other concerns and does not want to be bothered with this little child. He renounces his commitment and sends her off to an orphanage. In effect he has just "trampled" his parents under foot. He has scorned the sacrifice they have made. He is, however, still a son. He is in their family. He entered that family by physical birth just as we enter God's family by spiritual birth. Neither process can be reversed!

Second, these sinning Christians regard "*as unclean the blood of the covenant.*" This blood of the New Covenant has made forgiveness of sins available; it is therefore holy blood. There are only two possible meanings of the death of Christ. It could have been the death of a common criminal. He would then have received his just reward—he was merely a man. His sin of blasphemy for claiming to be God was, according to the Old Testament, punishable by death. Or it could have been the death of the God-man, a sacrifice for the sins of the world. If Christ was a criminal, then His blood was "unclean." The man who denies Christ by his life or his lips is in effect saying, "Christ's blood is the blood of a common criminal." A person is being inconsistent if he says that Christ's blood is holy blood, shed for the forgiveness of sins, and then he abandons his confession. If Jesus is not the Son of God, then there is only one other conclusion—the Jews and Romans were right—He was a criminal.

The blood of the covenant has *sanctified* this person who tramples Christ underfoot. Here is true evidence of this person's regenerate nature. MacArthur, however, suggests that the one sanctified is Jesus Christ. The person could not, he says, refer to a Christian because the apostate is "regarding the blood as unclean." The reference therefore must be to Christ being sanctified.[2141] But is it impossible for true believers to count the blood of

[2140] Bruce, *The Epistle to the Hebrews*, 259.

[2141] John MacArthur, "Gehenna," in *Tyndale Bible Dictionary*, ed. Walter Elwell and Philip Wesley Comfort

Christ as unclean and apostatize from the faith? Unfortunately, for MacArthur's position, that is the very point in question! MacArthur has already told his readers that there is a positional, as well as a practical, sanctification. The former is perfect, but the latter is not. By MacArthur's own admission the sanctification by the blood elsewhere refers to positional, and not experiential, sanctification.[2142] It is therefore possible on MacArthur's premises, and the Bible's as well, to be perfectly sanctified in one's position but still have sin in one's life.[2143] There is no need to go to a remotely different context like John 17:19, where Christ speaks of sanctifying Himself to find the meaning of "sanctify" in Hebrews 10. The word is defined in the book of Hebrews itself. In this book, to be "sanctified" always refers to Christians made qualified to worship (positional sanctification); it never refers to Christ.[2144] Why did MacArthur not go to the use of the word in Hebrews instead of jumping to the Gospels?[2145]

Third, the seriousness of trampling underfoot the Son of God is seen in that this is an insult "to the Spirit of grace." This action presumes on the grace of God, taking the grace of God for granted. Severe consequences can be expected.

THE LORD WILL JUDGE HIS PEOPLE (10:30-31)

For we know Him who said, "Vengeance is Mine, I will repay." And again, "The Lord will judge His people. It is a terrible thing to fall into the hands of the living God (Hebrews 10:30-31).

The clause "Vengeance is Mine" is quoted from Deuteronomy 32:35. Experimental Predestinarians and Arminians are invited to read that chapter and see if they can find any indications that the punishment of eternal separation from God is in view. Rather, judgments on the people of God *in time* are the subject. The principle the writer is affirming is that when a Christian fails to persevere and denies Christ, he is no different from rebellious people of God in the Old Testament and can only expect a similar fate—judgment in time.

The second phrase "*the Lord will judge His people*" is taken from Deuteronomy 32:36. In Deuteronomy, however, it reads, "The Lord will vindicate His people." Bruce comments, "This certainly means that He will execute judgment on their behalf, vindicating their cause against their enemies, but also that, on the same principles of impartial righteousness, He will execute judgment against them when they forsake His covenant."[2146] Thus either "vindicate" or "judge" are proper renderings of the Hebrew rendered "vindicate" in Deuteronomy 32:36, and both are consistent with the contexts of Deuteronomy 32 and of Hebrews 10.

(Wheaton, IL: Tyndale House, 2001), 279.

2142 Ibid., 263. He refers to 9:14.

2143 Ibid.

2144 See 2:11; 9:13; 10:10, 14, 29; 12:14; 13:12.

2145 T. Hewitt and John Owen grant that the sanctification is of the apostate, but they refer it to an external rather than an internal sanctification. See T. Hewitt and John Owen, "Corruption," in *Dictionary of Biblical Imagery*, ed. Leland Ryken, Jim Wilhoit, and Tremper Longman (Downers Grove, IL: InterVarsity Press, 2000). This "is to read a subtle meaning into the text which is not there, elsewhere in Hebrews sanctified is a description of true Christians" and not just those who are externally so (Marshall, *Kept by the Power of God: A Study of Perseverance and Falling Away*, 149. See also the references in the preceding footnote.

2146 Bruce, *The Epistle to the Hebrews*, 262-63.

God said of Israel, "*You only have I known of all the families of the earth: therefore I will visit upon you all your iniquities*" (Amos 3:2). Greater privilege means greater responsibility and greater discipline because of failure to follow the Lord. This was true with the Old Testament people of God on a corporate level, and according to the writer to the Hebrews, it is also true for Christians under the New Covenant. So F. F. Bruce writes, "These words have no doubt been used frequently as a warning to the ungodly of what lies in store for them unless they amend their ways, but their primary application is to the people of God."[2147] This is how the writer of the Epistle to the Hebrews applies the passage. Nothing here speaks of eternal damnation and nothing suggests that the "more severe punishment" implies a loss of salvation.

EXHORTATION TO PERSEVERE (10:32-39)

Obviously, the writer believes that his readers are Christians, for they have confessed Christ and have demonstrated the reality of their faith by many good works:

> *But remember the former days, when after being enlightened, you endured a great conflict of sufferings, partly, by being made a public spectacle through reproaches and tribulations, and partly by becoming sharers with those who were so treated. For you showed sympathy to the prisoners and accepted joyfully the seizure of your property, knowing that you have for yourselves a better possession and an abiding one (Hebrews 10:32-34).*

But possibly this great beginning will not be continued.

> *Therefore do not throw away your confidence, which has a* ***great reward****. For you had need of endurance, so that when* ***you have done the will of God****, you may receive what was promised (Hebrews 10:35-36).*

Entrance into heaven is promised to no one on the basis of doing the will of God. What is promised here refers to the "great reward" for perseverance to the final hour. Facing tremendous persecution, these Christians were contemplating rejecting the faith. The danger is not that they would lose eternal salvation but that they would lose their reward. They will not be among the *Metochoi*, the Partners, and will not share in the final destiny of man, to rule and have dominion. There is nothing here about their not having "trusted in His Son fully"[2148] for initial salvation. In the New Testament a man either believes or he does not. Adjectives such as "fully," "genuinely," or "truly" are never found as modifiers of "faith" in the New Testament. They are found only in the writings of Experimental Predestinarians. These people are clearly regenerate, or language has lost its meaning. To say that "they had not done the will of God fully because they had not trusted His Son fully"[2149] is to subvert the obvious meaning of the text and the context in the interest of forcing the passage to fit into a preconceived system of theology. The text says they had not done the will of God fully *because they had not yet endured.* Their endurance in the faith, not their justification, is the subject of the passage.

[2147] Ibid., 263.

[2148] MacArthur, "Gehenna," 282.

[2149] Ibid.

The writer to the Hebrews then cites an Old Testament warning from Habakkuk:

*For yet in a very little while, He who is coming will come, and will not delay. But **My righteous one**, shall live by faith; and **if he shrinks back**, My soul has no pleasure in him (Hebrews 10:37-38).*

God's "righteous one," the regenerate Christian, may "shrink back." But the writer encourages them away from that option:

But we are not of those who shrink back to destruction, but of those who have faith to the preserving of the soul (Hebrews 10:39).

We have shown in a previous chapter that the saving of one's soul means to find a rich life now by self-denial, taking up one's cross, and following Christ, so that the believer will be favorably recompensed at the Judgment Seat of Christ.[2150] The Greek word *sozō*, "to save," is not used here. Instead, the writer uses a synonym for the noun *sōtēria*, *peripoiēsis*, which means a "*keeping safe, preserving, saving.*"[2151]

Instead of experiencing "destruction," they will save their souls. The word "destruction" (Gr *apōleia*) is the common term for "loss" or "destruction" in secular Greek,[2152] it is not a technical term for damnation. Sometimes it means "waste" (Mark 4:4) and sometimes "execution" (Acts 25:16, Majority Text). The context (Hebrews 10:26-38) refers to the possible execution of judgment in time on the sinning Christian. The judgment may include physical death or even worse (10:28). To avoid the possibility of this sin to physical death—God's discipline resulting in ruin of one's physical life—the believers must persevere in faith. The danger is that he will not. And if that occurs, that is, if "he shrinks back," then God will have no pleasure in him. This is simply an understatement (litotes) for "God will be very displeased with the Christian who behaves this way."

CONCLUSION

It is best to interpret Hebrews 10 as a warning against the failure to persevere to the end. The consequences of this failure are, according to the Old Testament references quoted, not a loss of salvation but severe divine discipline in time. The God of grace may not always execute these judgments, but experience shows that the results of willful sin in emotional life can be more severe than death. The most severe punishment, however, is that God will have "no pleasure in Him." When the carnal Christian stands before his Lord in the last day, he will not hear Him say, "Well done, good and faithful servant. Enter into the joy of your Lord."

2 Peter 2:20-22

*For speaking out arrogant words of vanity they entice by fleshly desires, by sensuality, **those who barely escape** from the ones who live in error, promising them freedom while they themselves are slaves of corruption; for by what a man is overcome, by this he is enslaved.*

[2150] See discussion in chapters 15 and 16.

[2151] BDAG, 804.

[2152] M-M, p. 73.

> *For if they have escaped the defilements of the world by the knowledge of the Lord and Savior Jesus Christ, they are again entangled in them and are overcome, then the last state has become worse for them than the first. For it would be better for them not to have known the way of righteousness, than having known it, to turn away from the holy commandment delivered to them. It has happened to them according the true proverb, "A dog returns to its own vomit," and, "A sow, after washing, returns to wallowing in the mire" (2 Peter 2:18-22).*

Peter seems to be speaking of true believers in these verses. The fact that they escaped (Gr *apopheugō*) the corruptions of the world "by knowing [Gr *epiginōskō*] our Lord and Savior Jesus Christ" certainly points in that direction. In addition, they knew the way of righteousness (righteous living). This word "know" suggests that they possessed a *full* knowledge of Christ's way of life..[2153]

Throughout the context Peter has been talking about false teachers who deny the Lord (2:1) and who are unbelievably corrupt. Second Peter 2:10-19 shows that these are the same people whom Jude was talking about in Jude 4. They "deny Jesus Christ," and their condemnation was written about "long ago" (Jude 4). They are non-Christians, never saved initially.

Who are "they" in 2 Peter 2:20? One possibility is that "they" refers to the false teachers of verse 19. However, there is good reason to suggest that the pronoun refers to the new Christians who have been corrupted and led astray by the false teachers in verse 18b.

> *They entice people who are just escaping* [Gr apopheugō*] from those who live in error (2:18b).*

Here the reference is to people who are "just escaping," that is, new converts. The new believers have been led astray by the immoral libertines described in the preceding verses of the chapter. The connection between verses 20 and 18 seems certain because Peter brings us back, after a parenthesis in verse 19, to the fact that they "escaped," using the same Greek word in both verses (*apopheugō*). The word is used of believers having escaped the world's corruption in 1:4. Furthermore, the false teachers do not know Christ, as argued above, yet those addressed in verse 20 have "knowledge of our Lord and Savior Jesus Christ." It is not possible to find an explicit example of a person having "knowledge" (Gr *epignōsis*, "a full and accurate knowledge") who is unregenerate in the New Testament.[2154] This suggests that the new Christians of verse 18 are in view.

Peter says, "The last state has become worse for them than the former" (2:20). If "last" and "former" are to be taken absolutely, then the meaning is "their final condemnation to eternal separation from God is worse than their former life of sin." This is banal. It is better to take the terms "latter" and "former" as references to time periods in the person's current temporal life. Then "latter" refers to their current condition, a condition which is in some sense worse than the condition they were in before they were saved.

When Peter says, "For it would be better for them not to have known the way of righteousness," we must ask, "Why would it be better?"[2155] It expresses a wish, a potential.[2156]

2153 The Greek word does not always mean saving knowledge. See Ruldof Bultmann, "*ginoskō*," in TDNT, 1:703. Contra Shank, *Life in the Son: A Study of the Doctrine of Perseverance*, 175.

2154 Note the usage in 1 Peter 1:2, 3, 8, 20 and of the verb in 2:21. They all seem to refer to the regenerate.

2155 The new believers who have been led back into the worldly life from which they had escaped would have been better off as far as their experience *in this life* was concerned if they had never known Christ at all.

2156 Kenneth O. Gangle, *2 Peter*, ed. John F. Walvoord and Roy Zuck, reprint ed., Bible Knowledge Commentary

However, Peter is not talking about eternal destiny. As far as the spiritual condition in this life, if someone knows the way of righteousness (which Luke defines as the kingdom way of living, Luke 3:10-14), and *then* falls back into the sewer of the old life, they will be far more miserable than if they'd never set foot on the narrow way. They will experience severe divine discipline like that which Saul experienced. That he refers to their misery in this life, and not eternal damnation, is clear from Peter's quotation of Proverbs 26:11:

> *Of them the proverbs are true: "A dog returns to its vomit," and, "A sow that is washed goes back to her wallowing in the mud" (2:22).*

These newborn infants, babies, who were washed by the bath of regeneration, have returned to the "mud." The most miserable people are sometimes Christians under severe divine discipline. As far as their enjoyment of this life is concerned, they would be far better off never to have known the way of righteous living than to endure such correction.

Peter opens this chapter by warning that the church will face severe difficulties when and if false teachers enter their congregations (2:1-3). He then describes the characteristics and behavior of these teachers (2:4-17). Finally, he applies the warning to those most likely to fall into their clutches, new Christians who have just recently escaped the pollutions of the world (2:18-22). He warns them that they will find misery in returning to sin after having enjoyed knowledge of the way of righteousness. Indeed, they will be more miserable than they were before as far as their happiness in this life is concerned. In terms of their earthly experience, it will be better for them not to have known the way of righteousness at all than to fall into a life of carnality after having known the joy of walking with Christ. Turning back to such a state of affairs is like a dog eating its own vomit or a washed pig wallowing in mud.

The passage is a severe warning to those being enticed to return to their former ways of sin, but there is nothing here about loss of salvation.

Summary

When the writer of the Epistle to the Hebrews exhorted his readers to continue to hold fast and not to give up faith in Christ, he used a metaphor that would have powerful associations for a "messianic" Jew— the tabernacle in the wilderness. That, he pointed out, was God's house; a place where the people of God worshiped. But today, he desires that they understand that God's house is no longer a building nor is it found in a particular place. God's "house" under the New Covenant is composed of those believers *who continue to gather together to confess His name and worship Him.* He tells them, "*Whose house we are, if we hold fast our confidence and the boast of our hope firm until the end*" (Hebrews 3:6). Only those who "hold fast" are part of the worshiping community and entitled to reward (Hebrews 10:36).

Should these believers fail to remain part of the worshipping community, they are not in danger of losing their eternal salvation but are in danger of temporal judgment like what came on the Exodus generation. God swore that generation would never enter His rest, that is, they would not finish the life task assigned to them, the conquest of Canaan.

(Colorado Springs: Cook, 1996), 49. However, Gangle incorrectly assumes that the "former state" was damnation.

Instead, they faced terrible temporal judgment in the wilderness. Similarly, the believers addressed in this epistle, face judgment in time.

This judgment is made very explicit in Hebrews chapter 10. For those believers who do not hold fast but sin willfully by denying Christ, a certain expectation of judgment awaits them. The particular judgment mentioned is a judgment in time. Nothing in Hebrews 10 pertains to loss of eternal salvation.

When Peter said that for those who have escaped the defilements of the world and then return to them and that their "last" state is worse than their former, he does not mean they had salvation and lost it. The "last state" is not damnation but is the misery, discipline, and spiritual and psychological poverty that God brings on the carnal Christian. In terms of their current experience (not their final destiny), it would be better never to have known the way of righteousness, that is, the way of righteous living in this life.

We now turn to the last book of the Bible. On seven occasions, John refers to the overcomers and uses language that suggests to many Arminians that there is something conditional about their eternal destiny. The following chapter explores that conditionality and notes that one's final arrival in heaven is not in view. Instead, John warns of their loss of reward, inheritance, intimacy with Christ, and opportunities to serve Him in the millennium and on into eternity.

43
The Overcomers

IN REVELATION 2:26, a thrilling promise is held out to those Christians who remain faithful to Christ to the end of life:

> *And he who overcomes, and he who keeps My deeds until the end, to him I will give authority over the nations (Revelation 2:26).*

In seven other places in the final book of the New Testament, similar promises are made to this select company. But who are they?

The Greek word translated "to overcome" is *nikaō*. In a legal sense it means "to win one's case." The verb was commonly used of the victor in the Greek athletic games or referring to the Caesars, "of our all victorious masters the Augusti."[2157] The noun *nikē* means "victory." *Nikē* was the name of a Greek goddess who is often represented in art as a symbol of personal superiority. To be an overcomer was to be victorious in athletic, military, or legal combat.[2158]

Three views of the overcomers are held by expositors. (1) Arminians view them as believers who may lose their justification if they fail to continue in the faith.[2159] (2) Experimental Predestinarians and Neonomians view them as Christians who will necessarily and inevitably overcome. For them all Christians are overcomers.[2160] (3) Partners view overcomers as faithful Christians, in contrast to those Christians who are not.[2161]

Are all Christians Overcomers?

Are all Christians overcomers? Experimental Predestinarians, Arminians, and Neonomians think so, but the Partners do not. Four reasons are frequently given in support of the view that all Christians are overcomers.

2157 M-M, p. 427.

2158 W. Guenther, "Fight," in NIDNTT, 1:650.

2159 Marshall, *Kept by the Power of God: A Study of Perseverance and Falling Away*, 174-75.

2160 Rosscup, "The Overcomers of the Apocalypse," 261-68.

2161 Donald G. Barnhouse, *Messages to the Seven Churches* (Philadelphia: Eternity Book Service, 1953), 38.

THE OVERCOMER IN 1 JOHN

First, in 1 John 5:4-5 we are told:

For whatever is born of God overcomes the world; and this is the victory that has overcome the world—our faith. And who is the one who overcomes the world, but he who believes that Jesus is the Son of God?
You are from God, little children, and have overcome them (1 John 4:4).

I am writing to you, young men, because you have overcome the evil one (1 John 2:13).

Experimentalists believe that this proves that in John's first epistle the overcomer is a regenerate saint. If he is a saved person then, consistency, they say, requires that the overcomer in Revelation also refers to the saved. These writers argue[2162] as follows. If "whatever" is born or God overcomes the world and if the "one who overcomes the world" is the person who believes that Jesus is the Son of God, then all who believe in Jesus must overcome the world.

But John refutes this notion in this very epistle. He says that at the second coming some believers will "shrink away in shame" (1 John 2:28). Obviously, they did not overcome the world in a practical, daily sense, and they persisted in this failure all the way to the end. Furthermore, John specifically says, "*But the one who hates his brother is in the darkness and walks in the darkness, and does not know where he is going because the darkness has blinded his eyes*" (1 John 2:11). A believer (a "*brother*") can hate "his brother" and "walk in the darkness" (nonbelievers do not have Christians as "brothers").[2163] We have shown in chapter 32 that the thesis that all "genuine" believers will persevere in a life of works is biblically unsustainable. Thus, the argument that all Christians are overcomers in their daily lives is false. So when John says, "Whatever is born of God overcomes the world," he clearly does not mean that everyone born of God will necessarily and inevitably overcome the world in practice. Whoever is born of God will overcome the world in the practical sense described in Revelation, if, and only if, that person abides in Christ. Some will and some will not, as the entire Bible and church history affirm.

John is concerned not only with the initial act of faith by which victory is achieved over the world, but also with the continuing exercises of faith by which the believer continues to have victory over the world. A person who is born of God "overcomes the world" now (present tense); not just in the past. Each act of faith appropriates the power of God to be victorious over the world, its temptations, and its power to destroy the Christian's life.

Realizing the difficulty his interpretation raises, James Rosscup says, "Does every saved person in fact overcome in the Christian struggle? In the biblical sense, yes."[2164]

2162 Marshall says, "Everyone born of God has overcome the world." I. Howard Marshall, *The Epistles of John*, New International Commentary on the New Testament (Grand Rapids: Wm. B. Eerdmans Publishing Co., 1978), 227.

2163 Of course, Rosscup would say that calling one his "brother" in no way implies that the one doing the calling is really born again, it is only the language of courtesy and not of fact. But that is a theological assertion, not established from the context, necessary to maintain the falsehood of the saints' inevitable perseverance in good works.

2164 Rosscup, "The Overcomers of the Apocalypse," 264.

And what is this "biblical sense?" It turns out that the "biblical sense" involves invisible "attitudes of commitment that continue."[2165] Are these invisible attitudes supposed to result in visible works? Yes. How much? Rosscup says that the "thrust of his life" will be towards faith in God.[2166] Of course, only God could know the heart. Rosscup "allows the possibility that some may for a time be thought to be true believers, yet not heed the warnings, and end up unsaved. This does not reveal that they *lost* salvation but that they *lacked* it all along."[2167] This requires that all "true" believers will heed the warnings, a viewpoint that is demonstrably false according to the biblical records.[2168] The upshot of this theology is that no one can know if he is a "true" believer until the "thrust of his life" can be demonstrated to have been "towards faith in God" all his life. In other words, no one can know if they are saved until they have persevered to the end, and no one can know if they have persevered to the end until the end!

It is true that only those who believe that Jesus is the Son of God (1 John 5:5) overcome the world. However, it is also true that one must continue to exercise faith in Christ if he is to continue to obtain victory. All of the references in 1 John refer to present victory in the Christian life and not just past victory in the sense of initial salvation.

Let us suppose, for the sake of argument, that the Experimentalists are correct that all believers are overcomers in 1 John and that the particular kind of overcoming in 1 John is believing in Christ (1 John 5:1). Even so, this in no way means that all believers are overcomers in practice in Revelation. The fact that all believers are overcomers ontologically in virtue of being born again through faith alone, in no way implies that all believers are overcomers in daily practice by continuing acts of faith. The meaning of overcomer in Revelation must be determined by its usage in that book, where it is used in a decidedly different way. In the book of Revelation, John unambiguously has in view a victorious perseverance in the midst of trials by which a Christian merits special rewards in eternity, not the initial act of becoming a Christian in which sense all Christians have "overcome the world" by believing.

It is certainly true that all Christians are overcomers in the sense that all overcomers have believed in Christ and are therefore justified. Even if it was true that 1 John 5 speaks of the overcomer in this manner. However, as argued above, not all who are overcomers in the sense of personal salvation live like overcomers in their practical lives. In the book of Revelation, John addresses all true Christians, and challenges them to become Christians who overcome, and challenges them to live like who they are, promising them rewards if they do, and in five instances, loss if they do not.[2169]

THE OVERCOMER INHERITS THESE THINGS

A second argument Experimental Predestinarians bring forth to establish their doctrine that all Christians are overcomers in practice as well as standing is based on the promise that those who overcome inherit "these things." In Revelation 21:7, the apostle writes:

[2165] Ibid.

[2166] Ibid., 268.

[2167] Ibid., 270.

[2168] See discussion of the Carnal Christian in chapter 32.

[2169] Both are trunks.

He who overcomes shall inherit these things, and I will be his God and he will be My son (NASB).

The one who overcomes will not only enter into the new heavens and the new earth, but he will also "inherit" it. As discussed elsewhere, it is one thing to enter someone's house, but it is quite another to inherit it. Consistent with its usage throughout the Bible, the word "inherit" is a reward for faithful service (e.g., Colossians 3:24).[2170] Contrary to Rosscup, the context does not "convey the natural impression that blessings the overcomer inherits are for any saved person."[2171] Rather, "these things" are those obtained by means of "overcoming"; unlike eternal life, they are not given "without cost" (Revelation 21:6).

The things the overcomer possesses refer to ownership in contrast to residence in the New Jerusalem. The New Jerusalem, in the present writer's opinion, will be inhabited by all the saints, but only the overcomers will rule there.[2172] They are the ones who receive special honor.

In Revelation 21:6-8, John presents three classes of humanity. [2173]

The first class is specified in verse 6 where we read of a promise to all the saints:

I am the Alpha and Omega, the beginning and the end. I will give to the one who thirsts from the spring of the water of ***life without cost*** *(Revelation 21:6 NASB).*

Eternal life is free, a gift that comes solely by means of believing in Christ. John employed similar imagery in recounting the Lord's offer of the free gift of life to the woman at the well (John 4:10, 14) in response to thirst. This offer is of grace; it is a gift; it is, as John says, "without cost." Throughout Revelation eternal life is offered freely, without cost (1:5; 7:14; 21:6; 22:17), but the reward that comes to the overcomer costs him everything. This is consistent with the rest of the New Testament, as has been argued in the preceding chapters.

In Revelation 21:7, John addresses a second group within those of verse 6, to whom he holds out the possibility of inheriting, of earning a reward by victorious perseverance:

He who overcomes shall inherit these things, and I will be his God and he will be My son [huios, mature son] (Revelation 21:7).

This outcome costs much, a life of discipleship. Eternal life is absolutely free, but a life of discipleship may cost everything. Is it not obvious that the reference is to those among the saints of verse 6 who have not only received the free gift without cost but have, in addition, persevered faithfully to the final hour?

[2170] This has been thoroughly documented in chapters 4-12 above.

[2171] Rosscup, "The Overcomers of the Apocalypse," 265.

[2172] There are two other alternatives consistent with the Partner paradigm. Marty Cauley suggests that residence within the city is a reward available only to those who overcome. The city itself is a reward. Unfaithful believers will not have a residence or access to the city either in the millennium or in eternity future. See Cauley, *The Outer Darkness*, 530, 653-54. Bob Wilkin agrees that residence in the city is a reward but that those who do not overcome will nevertheless have access, but not residence. See http://www.faithalone.org/magazine/y1993/93nov3.html. For the present writer's discussion of entrance by the gates into the city, see pp. 974 ff.

[2173] Lang, *Firstborn Sons: Their Rights and Risks*, 122.

This thought is consistent with the rest of the book of Revelation. While John occasionally contrasts Christians with non-Christians,[2174] his major burden in the book is to challenge overcomers in standing to become overcomers in practice by laying before them the magnificent future they can inherit if they are faithful to the end. Repeatedly, the contrasts in this book are between the faithful overcomer and the unfaithful Christian.[2175] Since this is so, is not such a contrast to be expected here in this way as well?

The phrase "I will be his God and he will be My son" is defined elsewhere as a statement of special honor, not of regeneration. The Davidic Covenant promised to David's son, Solomon, "*I will be a Father to him and he will be a son to Me*" (2 Samuel 7:14). The intent of the phrase was to signify installation as the king.

On His resurrection from the dead, Jesus was invested with the title "Son" (Acts 13:33), and this was because His humility involved total obedience to the Father's will (Philippians 2:5-10). Similarly, we arrive at the state of full sonship (Gr *huioi*, not *tekna*, "children") by a life of obedience. Our union with Him, according to the writer of the Epistle to the Hebrews, means that our path to glory is the same as His. Because of His obedience He was entitled to the designation "Son of God," King of Israel. "*Thou hast loved righteousness and hated lawlessness; therefore God, thy God, has anointed thee with the oil of gladness above thy companions*" (Hebrews 1:9).

A similar thought regarding sonship is expressed in Hebrews 11:16, "*Therefore God is not ashamed to be called their God.*" Of course, in the heavenly city God will be the God of all, both faithful and unfaithful Christians (Revelation 21:3), but it is apparently possible for us to live life in such a way that God is *proud to be called* our God. Evidently the writer has the title "*I am the God of Abraham, Isaac, and Jacob*" in mind. This sense fits well the conditional aspect of sonship in Revelation. John's meaning is simply, "Because you have lived a life of constant fellowship with Me," God will say, "I am proud to be known as your God."

The idea here is that God is "proud" to be known as "our God," because we have persevered to the final hour in contrast to other Christians who are sons but not obedient sons, and who will draw back from Him in shame at His coming (1 John 2:28) and lose what they have accomplished (Mark 4:25; Revelation 3:11).

Finally, in contrast to the two classes of believers in Revelation 21:6-7, John describes the fate of the nonbeliever:

> *But for the cowardly and unbelieving and abominable and murderers and immoral persons ... their part will be in the lake that burns with fire and brimstone which is the second death (Revelation 21:8).*

There is no evidence here that everyone who is saved overcomes.[2176] Rather, he who overcomes is a believer who has merited an eternal inheritance, ownership in the heavenly city.[2177]

[2174] For example Revelation 21:26-27; 22:14-15.

[2175] For example, Revelation 2:16 versus 2:7; 2:14-16 versus 2:17; 2:18-23 versus 2:24-29; 3:1-3 versus 3:4-6; 3:11 versus 3:12; 3:14-19 versus 3:21.

[2176] Rosscup, "The Overcomers of the Apocalypse," 265.

[2177] Some Experimental Predestinarians object that there are no distinctions among believers in the heavenly city mentioned in 21:3-4. But is this not an argument from silence? The fact that these distinctions are not

BELIEVERS AND OVERCOMERS PARTAKE OF THE TREE OF LIFE

He who has an ear, let him hear what the Spirit says to the churches. To him who overcomes, I will grant to eat of the tree of life, which is in the Paradise of God (Revelation 2:7).

Blessed are those who wash their robes, that they may have the right to the tree of life, and may enter by the gates into the city (Revelation 22:14).

A third proof given by Experimental Predestinarians that all Christians are overcomers in practice is derived from the fact the overcomers partake of the tree of life (Revelation 22:14). According to Experimental Predestinarians, all believers will partake of the tree of life because "tree of life" means eternal life and heaven when one dies. However, a more careful investigation into the question, "What is this 'tree of life?' is prudent.

THE TREE OF LIFE. The phrase "the tree of life" is found first in Genesis 3:22, 24. All of its other uses in the Old Testament are confined to the book of Proverbs. There the fruit of the morally upright (Proverbs 11:30), a desire fulfilled (Proverbs 13:12), a gentle tongue (Proverbs 15:4), and wisdom (Proverbs 3:18) are all called a "tree of life." This usage suggests a quality of life—rich fellowship with God—rather than the notion of regeneration. It "symbolizes the enrichment of life in various ways."[2178] It speaks not of obtaining life, but of living it. According to 22:12 it is a reward (Gr *misthos*) and not a gift to all. It is not freely given. This fits well with the context of Revelation. Regenerate life comes to all "without cost" (Revelation 22:17), but "the tree of life" is presented as a conditionally earned and merited reward going to those who have not only received eternal life without cost but who also, at great cost to themselves, have overcome and persevered to the final hour.

Since partaking of the tree of life in 22:14 is based upon doing good works, it should be understood as conditional in 2:7 as well:

*Behold, I am coming quickly, and My **reward** is with Me, to **render to every man according to what he has done**. . . . Blessed are those who wash their robes, that they may have the right to the tree of life and may enter by the gates into the city (Revelation 22:12, 14).*

Grant Osborne, an Experimental Predestinarian, believes that "the one unifying theme is the necessity of remaining true to the Lord in order to participate in the resurrection to eternal life."[2179] He begins well, saying that the overcomer's victory is "achieved through perseverance." To eat from the tree of life requires "faithfulness and a determination that we will place living for him alone above all earthly things." He adds, "To be an overcomer in the eschatological war demands a day-by-day walk with God and dependence on his strength."

---

mentioned in these verses does not necessarily imply that they are not real. Many who hold this position acknowledge that there are distinctions in terms of greater and lesser degrees of reward. Are we to deny this truth, too, simply because it is not mentioned? Every verse cannot say everything. In fact, it is common in Hebraic literature to make a general statement and then repeat the same discussion with more detail following. The most obvious illustration of this are the so-called "two creation accounts." But Genesis, chapter 1, is a general statement and Genesis 2 covers the same ground and develops numerous details about the creation of man. Similarly, Revelation 21:3-6 gives a survey of the new order, and 21:6-8 then reviews the survey but gives more detail.

2178 "Tree of Life" in *Tyndale Bible Dictionary*, ed. Walter A. Elwell and Philip Wesley, Tyndale Reference Library (Wheaton, IL: Tyndale House, 2001), 1274.

2179 Grant Osborne, *Revelation*, Baker Exegetical Commentary on the New Testament (Grand Rapids: Baker Academic, 2002), 789.

With these statements one would assume that the victory is a reward to works and could not be salvation or heaven when one dies because entrance into heaven is ours by faith alone.

However, we are soon disappointed to learn that this is not Osborne's meaning. We are told that the "tree of life" is the cross of Christ. He says this even after admitting that this tree in the Old Testament refers to temporal life giving qualities of wisdom (Proverbs 3:18; 11:30; 13:12; 15:40) and refers to refreshment which comes from rich fellowship with God (Ezekiel 47:12; cf. Revelation 22:2).

As is often the case in Experimentalist writings, he never explains this contradiction with his belief in faith alone apart from works as the only means of final salvation. No doubt he would say something like, "Well, since we know for a fact that faith and works are inextricably related, and the latter always follows the former, we do not need to explain that the phrase 'in order that' does not mean this is a condition of entrance but is only to be understood as a characteristic of all who enter." Yet the text says nothing about this being a characteristic of all believers. It is doubtful that a first-century reader unfamiliar with post-Reformation debates would ever understand it this way. The phrase "wash their robes" may refer to initial salvation, but more likely it refers to a lifestyle of cleansing from sin by a life of repentance. Some believers do not do this, but the overcomers do, and they will be rewarded accordingly.

What is the paradise of God? It appears that Christ revealed to John when the plan of salvation will be completed. Beginning with the original paradise in the Garden of Eden where the original tree of life was located, it will reach its consummation in the final Paradise of God, the new heavens and the new earth. There the final tree of life will provide much more than temporal immortality. It will reward those who overcome with a special privilege, an enhanced intimacy with God. The original tree of life would have provided immortality on earth in mankind's natural bodies had Adam not sinned and been expelled (Genesis 3:22). This future tree of life will provide an enhanced experience of life in the new heavens and the new earth.

The tree of life will yield fruit monthly throughout all eternity:

> *And on either side of the river was the tree of life, bearing twelve kinds of fruit, yielding its fruit every month; and the leaves of the tree were for the healing of the nations (Revelation 22:2).*

It seems possible, therefore, to understand participation in the tree of life and eating of this monthly fruit as a picture of the regular experience of fellowshipping with God. It is inconceivable that a Christian, in whom eternal life dwells, must continually eat from a tree to obtain final entrance into heaven or maintain his presence there. Therefore, eating of the tree of life cannot refer to regeneration.

It is impossible that the tree of life refers to final entrance into heaven. Why? Because we are told in Revelation 2:5 that the condition for obtaining the right to eat of this tree is based upon "doing," that is, on works. Final salvation comes to us by faith alone apart from works. In Revelation 22:19, Jesus says that if anyone takes away from the words of the prophecy, "*God will take away his portion* (Gr *meros*) *from the tree of life and from the city.*" As Marty Cauley has observed, "Obviously one cannot lose something one does not have.... Genuine believers are in danger of losing their right to this tree; unbelievers have no right to this tree to lose."[2180]

[2180] Cauley, *The Outer Darkness*, 510.

Thus both verses refer to special privileges reserved only for faithful believers. As Barnhouse correctly notes,

> *Some have said that eating from the tree of life was the equivalent of receiving eternal life, but this is most evidently a false interpretation. Eternal life is the prerequisite for membership in the true Church. Eating of the tree of life is a reward that shall be given to the overcomer in addition to his salvation. . . . He receives over and above his entrance into eternal life, a place in the Heavens in the midst of the paradise of God.*[2181]

Wash their robes. According to Revelation 22:14, the privilege of eating from the tree of life is granted to those who have "overcome" (Revelation 2:7) and who have washed their robes (Revelation 22:14). This phrase "wash their robes" is used only two times in Revelation (7:14; 22:14).

> *These are the ones who come out of the great tribulation, and they have washed their robes and made them white in the blood of the lamb. For this reason, they are before the throne of God and they serve Him day and night in His temple (Revelation 7:14-15).*

> *Blessed are those who wash their robes, that they may have the right to the tree of life, and may enter by the gates into the city (Revelation 22:14).*

Does this refer to the washing of regeneration or sanctification? The washing of regeneration depends upon God alone. Therefore this washing, involving believers' efforts, probably refers to the daily confession of sin and cleansing, that is, progressive sanctification.[2182] They have lived faithful and persevering lives and will be rewarded.

While the NASB translation of Revelation 22:14 reads, "*Blessed are those who wash their robes,*" the Byzantine Majority text reads, "*Blessed are those who keep My commandments*" (NKJV). This suggests that some early editors understood washing robes to mean keeping commandments and not regeneration.

Obedience to His commands, then, is necessary in order to obtain His promised reward. Obviously, eternal salvation cannot be in view because a few verses later John makes it clear that regeneration and eternal life are available freely and "without cost" (Revelation 22:17).

The church at Sardis had a few people who had "not soiled their garments" (Revelation 3:4).

> *But you have a few people in Sardis who have not soiled their garments; and they will walk with Me in white; for they are worthy (NASB).*

2181 Donald Grey Barnhouse, *God's Last Word: Revelation; an Expository Commentary* (Grand Rapids: Zondervan Publishing House, 1971), 43-44. For a similar view see Richard R. Benedict, "The Use of *Nikaō* in the Letters to the Seven Churches of Revelation" (Th.M. thesis, Dallas Theological Seminary, 1966), 11.

2182 The word Jesus used for the washing of regeneration was *louō* (John 13:10). The writer to the Hebrews also used the word this way (Hebrews 10:22). However, this is not decisive. Beale connects this washing with "the process of perseverance" and comments, "The same preparation is pictured in 7:13–15. There 'they washed their robes and made them white in the blood of the Lamb' means that, despite resistance, the saints continued believing in and testifying to the Lamb's death on their behalf (see further on 7:14). 'The blood of the Lamb' is the only means of 'washing' their robes. Yet, the washing metaphor itself includes reference to saints identifying themselves with the Lamb in his death by both their faith and their works, which demonstrate the genuineness of their faith." See Beale, *The Book of Revelation: A Commentary on the Greek Text*, 943.

This passage lends support to the suggestion above that washing one's robes refers to the cleansing needed for our daily walk, and not to regeneration; to living life, not gaining it.[2183] Additional confirmation that washing one's robes refers to sanctification and not justification is found in the immediate context of Revelation 22. Christ says that He is "*coming quickly, and My reward is with Me, to render to every man according to what he has done*" (Revelation 22:12). The context is about "rewards" (Gr *misthos*), that is, payment for work done!

ENTERING BY THE GATES. Before leaving our discussion of the great privilege granted to overcomers (to eat of the tree of life), some comment on the fact that they "enter by the gates" is needed.

Revelation 22:14 states that they "*may enter by the gates into the city.*"

Does this mean that all believers will receive this blessing? We will discuss this passage in more detail later. However, the emphasis in the Greek text is on the phrase "by the gates," that is the path of honor. Some believers will enter "by the gates" and some believers will not.[2184]

ALL BELIEVERS RULE

A final argument Experimental Predestinarians give for saying all Christians are overcomers is found in Revelation 22:5, which assures that believers will "*reign forever and ever*" (NASB). Marshall says that since *all* believers will rule, therefore all believers are overcomers.[2185] However, neither this verse nor the rest of the book of Revelation teaches that *all* believers will rule over the millennial earth. Only the crowned and rewarded church in heaven will rule (cf. Revelation 4:10 and 5:10). While it is true that believers will "*reign forever and ever*" (Revelation 22:5), the text does not say that *all* believers will reign forever.[2186]

Only Faithful Christians Are Overcomers

The teaching espoused by Experimentalists, that all Christians are overcomers, lacks adequate scriptural support. There are at least four objections to this theory.

(1) IF ALL ARE OVERCOMERS, THE WARNINGS BECOME TESTS OF SALVATION

If all overcomers are also overcomers in their daily lives, it is difficult to see how the warnings have any relevance to them. Rosscup asserts that true faith heeds God's warnings,

2183 That Christians are in view in Revelation 3:4 is evident from His command to "*wake up and strengthen the things that remain, which were about to die; for I have not found your deeds completed in the sight of My God*" (Revelation 3:2). One does not tell non-Christians that their deeds are incomplete and that they are to become Christians by strengthening the things that might remain which were about to die. The death here is, as elsewhere (Romans 8:13), a possibility for true Christians. It refers to spiritual impoverishment and sin of which the believer needs to repent. Probably, the corporate death of the congregation, that is, the lampstand's removal, is in view, which is why he tells them to repent in Revelation 3:3. Many of these Christians had apparently soiled their garments. They had not "washed their robes" by confessing their sin and performing the righteous acts of the saints.

2184 For full discussion see pp. 974 ff.

2185 For example, Marshall, *Kept by the Power of God: A Study of Perseverance and Falling Away*, 254.

2186 Revelation 5:10; 20:4, 6.

enabling the believers to "gain victory (1 John 5:4-5), and forge on with Him."[2187] However, to the prosaic mind, a warning which every believer heeds in order to obtain a reward which every believer receives is nonsense.

Perhaps sensing the obvious objection to his views, Rosscup then says that his view "allows the possibility" that some are non-Christians.[2188] He says, "Failure to inherit the kingdom due to tolerating a sinfully indulgent life-style must mean that one will turn out not to be saved."[2189] He cites 1 Corinthians 6:9-10; Galatians 5:21; and Ephesians 5:3-5, which do not prove his point unless we already know that "inherit the kingdom" means to "go to heaven." As has been demonstrated elsewhere, this equation is simply false.[2190]

He wants the warnings to be real and realizes they are not real if there can be no failure. So he shifts to the standard response that those who do not respond to the warnings are revealing that they are not truly saved.[2191] For those among the group being warned who are truly saved, the warnings serve to cause them to examine themselves to see if in fact they are true overcomers and hence regenerate. They must, on Rosscup's premises, reason that if they do not heed the warnings, they must not be justified and are on the highway to hell. Is this how the New Testament presents God's fatherly, priestly, and shepherding relationship with those for whom His Son died? Are believers required to live life under the fear that if they do not heed a warning they are going to hell? Is this how God wants Christians to live?

(2) IF ALL ARE OVERCOMERS, THEN NONE CAN LOSE THE CROWN

If all are overcomers, then all believers will receive rewards. James Rosscup says, "All of the genuinely saved will turn out to be overcomers and receive the reward Christ promises them."[2192] Yet, we know from Scripture that this is not true. Some will receive no reward at all, and their works will be burned up (1 Corinthians 3:15).

If it is true that all the saved will receive the crown, as Rosscup argues, then, how can the specific warning "*I am coming quickly; hold fast to what you have, in order that no one take your crown*" (Revelation 3:11) have any meaning if one cannot in fact lose the crown? Rosscup responds, "Revelation 3:11 more probably refers to an unsaved persecutor who can take the crown from a person who has only a professed relationship with Christ and His church."[2193] This is refuted by the plain words of the text, "*Hold fast to what you have.*" Surely, he is not asking non-Christian professors of Christ to hold fast to their false profession, lest even that be taken from them! Rather, he is talking to true Christians and telling them to hold fast to their genuine faith so that they will receive the reward of perseverance.

2187 Rosscup, "The Overcomers of the Apocalypse," 270.

2188 Ibid.

2189 Ibid., 271.

2190 See chapters 4-12.

2191 He quotes Matthew 7:16, which helps him not at all. As demonstrated elsewhere, the "fruit" in Matthew 7:16 is the fruit of "false prophets," not believers in general. He also cites 1 John 2:19, but this refers only to departure from apostolic company by nonbelieving false teachers, and not departure from the profession of the faith by non-Christian professors of Christianity.

2192 Rosscup, for example, says, "All of the genuinely saved will turn out to be overcomers and receive the reward Christ promises them." Rosscup, "The Overcomers of the Apocalypse," 263.

2193 Ibid., 272.

(3) IF ALL CHRISTIANS ARE OVERCOMERS, THEN JOHN IS TEACHING SALVATION BY WORKS

Rosscup continues his reasoning as follows, "Often New Testament passages which address believers weave in warnings that … appeal even to the unsaved."[2194] But wouldn't this yield a different gospel message? The message to non-Christians would not be "believe on the Lord Jesus Christ and you will be saved" but "overcome by returning to your first love (2:5), suffering for Christ (2:10), and keeping Christ's deeds unto the end (2:26)." In other words, Rosscup logically should end up saying that John, the apostle of belief, is now offering salvation to non-Christians on the basis of works.

Grant Osborne says what Rosscup only implies, final salvation is by works. He asserts, "To be an 'overcomer' in the eschatological war demands a day-by-day walk with God and dependence on his strength."[2195] The result of this daily perseverance is access to the "tree of life" which Osborne understands to mean heaven. He seems to veil his ambiguity by conflating "rewards or 'gifts'"[2196] which are obtained by the overcome as a result of a life-work of perseverance and are equivalent to final entrance into heaven. But these two words obviously mean entirely different things.

If these warnings are addressed to non-Christian professors of Christianity, the readers of the book would not only have to be very discriminating but also understand that non-Christians become Christians by works. This is incompatible with the gospel offer and would certainly confuse the supposedly non-Christians among the readers. Rosscup suggests that this is not incompatible because John the Baptist called on non-Christians to bring forth fruit in keeping with repentance.[2197] But the Baptist *first* asked them to "repent" and *then* live lives of fruitfulness. Also, as demonstrated elsewhere,[2198] John's call to repentance is not a call to personal salvation but is a call to the nation Israel to admit national guilt and be willing to do something about it in order to escape temporal, not eternal, judgment. His command is clear: as individuals repented and joined the messianic expectation, they were to live lives that reflected it. Yet, in Rosscup's interpretation of the overcomer, the overcomer is asked to live like a Christian and therefore become one!

(4) IF ALL CHRISTIANS ARE OVERCOMERS, THERE IS NO POSSIBILITY OF FAILURE

If all Christians are practical overcomers, there is no room for total failure in the Christian life. Yet the New Testament presents failure of such magnitude that a true Christian can persist in it to the point of physical death (see Genesis 38:7, Ezekiel 3:20; 1 John 5:16; 1 Corinthians 11:30).[2199] Such a man is hardly an "overcomer" in the sense John describes it in Revelation.

In order to allow for some degree of failure, Rosscup waters down John's definition of what it means to overcome. Some, he says, will overcome to a higher degree than

---

2194 Ibid., 271.

2195 Osborne, *Revelation*, 123.

2196 Ibid.

2197 Rosscup, "The Overcomers of the Apocalypse," 273.

2198 See discussion in vol. 1, chapter 3.

2199 See discussion in chapter 32.

others. There is, of course, biblical truth in this statement. There are distinctions between persevering believers (five cities and ten cities, etc). However, the overcomer in Revelation is a man who either does or does not overcome in relation to certain tests. What is in view is not relative degrees of maturity or fruit but overcoming or not overcoming. A man has either repented of his lack of love for Christ, or he has not (Revelation 2:5). He has either kept the faith to the point of death, or he has not (Revelation 2:10). He has either rejected the teaching of the "depths of Satan," or he has not (Revelation 2:23). He has either repented of sin (3:3), or he has not. He has either persevered under trial, or he has not (3:10).

Rosscup's doctrine of final perseverance requires that all will persevere. Yet, it is impossible to maintain that (a) all true Christians will repent and return when they backslide and at the same time maintain that (b) some true Christians will backslide and remain in that state until physical death. Yet this is the conundrum found in Experimentalist writings. On the one hand, Rosscup says, "The truly saved ones are the brand of people who, when they sin, confess, seek God's forgiveness and cleansing, and desire to live in the light with God (1 John 1:5-9)." But then he says, on the other hand, "If they are negligent here, God may take them home early."[2200] Thus, they can remain in this state of sin and lack of repentance until the point of physical death. Marty Cauley is correct, "To say that negligent believers who live in a backslidden condition until they die are, in fact, overcomers (in the way John uses that term in Revelation 2-3) reduces Rosscup's argument to saying, "all genuine believers overcome except for all those genuine believers who do not overcome.'"[2201]

The Overcomer in Revelation 3:5

In Revelation 3:5, the overcomer is promised that his name will not be blotted out of the book of life:

> *He who overcomes will, like them, be dressed in white. I will never blot out his name from the book of life, but will acknowledge his name before my Father and his angels.*

This raises three questions: Who is the overcomer? What is the book of life? What is meant by being removed from the book of life? Arminians find in this passage evidence that a believer can lose his salvation. They have understood that the passage implies it is possible for a believer to have his name removed and hence to lose his justification.[2202]

WHAT IS THE BOOK OF LIFE?

In the ancient Near East the book of life was a list of the members of a community. Apparently, in all Greek and Roman cities of the time, a list of citizens was maintained according to their class or tribe. Those unworthy of the city were removed from the book, and new citizens were continually added.[2203] When a criminal's name was removed from this book, he lost his citizenship.[2204]

2200 Rosscup, "The Overcomers of the Apocalypse," 270.

2201 Cauley, *The Outer Darkness*, 502.

2202 J. B. Smith, *A Revelation of Jesus Christ* (Scottsdale, PA: Mennonite Publishing House, 1961), 329-31.

2203 W. M. Ramsay, *The Letters from the Seven Churches of Asia* (London: Hodder and Stoughton, 1904), 385.

2204 Mounce, *The Book of Revelation*, 113.

In ancient Israel the book of life was the legal register of citizens, not a list of those who would go to heaven when they die. To "erase his name" meant either (1) physical death (Deuteronomy 29:20) or (2) removal of the memory of a person (Exodus 17:14; Deuteronomy 25:19). It never referred to the loss of salvation. In Exodus 32:32, Moses asked to be blotted out of the book that God had written if God would not forgive Israel. This is an emotional outburst expressing his deep love for his people. He was asking that God take his physical life, not that he forfeit his eternal destiny. In Psalm 69:28, David asked that the nonbelievers be blotted out of the book and not be listed with the righteous.[2205] David asked that they be physically put to death.

In Revelation, however, the book of life is the register of the saved. Daniel 12:1 says that everyone who is recorded in the book will be delivered from the great tribulation of the end time. This seems to refer to the elect and, in contrast to the other references, seems to refer to direct teaching about their eternal security.

> *And at that time your people, everyone who is found written in the book, will be rescued. (Daniel 12:1)*

Revelation refers to the elect whose names have been recorded in the book since the foundation of the world (Revelation 13:8; 17:8; 21:27).

WHAT IS MEANT BY REMOVAL OF ONE'S NAME FROM THE BOOK OF LIFE?

> *He who overcomes shall thus be clothed in white garments; and I will not erase his name from the book of life, and I will confess his name before My Father, and before His angels (Revelation 3:5).*

The answer to that question depends upon the meaning of "name." Arndt and Gingrich list five major usages of *onoma*: name, title or category, person, reputation or fame, and office.[2206] They ascribe the meaning "reputation" to *onoma* in Revelation 3:1,[2207] and that is how it is translated in the NIV.

What then does it mean to have one's name erased from the book of life? There are two suggestions which do not require the interpretation that it refers to the loss of one's justification.

First, one view is that this verse is giving a promise that the overcomer's reputation will not be blotted out. This view is suggested by William J. Fuller, who gives five reasons for this view.

1. If name always means "person," then a difficult tension is set up between Revelation 3:5 and Revelation 13:8; 17:8; and 21:27. In 13:8; 17:8; and 21:27, we are told that if our name is recorded in the book of life, it was so recorded from the foundation of the world. In other words, it is an absolute and unchanging thing. But in Revelation

---

2205 This could mean that David wants them removed from a heavenly book of life, but there is no mention of a heavenly book of life in the Old Testament. More likely, he is asking that they be removed from the book of the living, that is, die. One writer holding this viewpoint is M. E. Tate, *Vol. 20: Psalms 51-100: Word Biblical Commentary* (Dallas: Word, Inc., 1998). Tate says, "Let them be 'be removed from the book of the living,' i.e., removed from those who are preserved alive by God (for the scroll of the living, cf. Ps 109:13–14; Exod 32:32; Isa 4:3; Mal 3:16; Dan 12:1; *1 Enoch* 47.3, 108.3; Rev 3:5)."

2206 BAGD, 573-77.

2207 BAGD, 577.

3:5 we are told that a person's name can be present at one time and absent at another. One emphasizes the permanence of the name and the other the possibility of temporal removal. This is easily harmonized by the simple assumption that "name" means "person" in Revelation 13:8, 17:8, and 21:27, and "reputation" in 3:5. The childless but faithful eunuch will have a better posterity—an "everlasting name [reputation] that will not be cut off"(Isaiah 56:5).

2. The overcomer can achieve a new name (2:17; 3:12), that is, a spiritual reputation in the sight of God. He will have a reputation in heaven which conformed to his earthly faithfulness. Here "name" cannot mean "person," and the theme of "reputation" is clearly the subject of Revelation 3:1-12.
3. In Revelation 3:1 a name is a reputation. It is descriptive of the person's life and faithfulness. Why should the meaning be different in Revelation 3:5?
4. Throughout Revelation the life of good works produces a reputation in heaven (Revelation 2:2, 19; 3:1, 8, 19). In turn a good reputation results in an honorable eternal identity, a new name (2:17; 3:12).
5. The Old Testament often referred to the name of a man as his reputation and honor. In Proverbs 22:1 a good name is to be desired more than great riches.[2208] Job 30:8 notes that those who had a bad reputation were called "nameless." Being nameless is to be compared with having one's name blotted out of the book of life.[2209]

If "name" in Revelation 3:5 refers to a reputation or title, then God is saying, "I will not erase his title or reputation from the book of life." A name in the sense of "title" or "reputation" may be blotted out but not in the sense of person. God will remember and preserve the *onoma* of the Christian who overcomes, implying a peculiarly close relationship between God and the believer. The quality of eternal life is determined by one's faithfulness.

If someone objects that God has promised He will not forget the believers' labor of love (Hebrews 6:10), it could be replied that He *will* forget it in the lives of those who have not overcome and who have never repented. As far as I can tell, final failure cannot be reversed. There is no second chance:

> *But if a righteous man turns from his righteousness and commits sin and does the same detestable things the wicked man does, will he live?* ***None of the righteous things he has done will be remembered*** *(Ezekiel 18:24).*

> *I tell you that to everyone who has, more will be given, but as for the one who has nothing, even what he has will be taken away (Luke 19:26).*

What may be promised, then, in Revelation 3:5 is a unique and honorable eternal identity. This promise makes endurance through these trials possible. The unfaithful Christian will find, however, that at the second coming, he will be ashamed of his name

---

[2208] See Isaiah 56:4-5. Isaiah speaks of "eunuchs" who (1) keep the Sabbath; (2) choose what pleases God; and (3) hold fast to God's covenant. As a reward for these works of obedience, God says He will give them a memorial and a name within His temple and its walls: "I will give him an everlasting name that will not be cut off" (Isaiah 56:6). "Name" is used here in the sense of "reputation" or "memorial." This reputation will be eternal, as a memorial to a faithful life.

[2209] Fuller, "I Will Not Erase His Name from the Book of Life (Revelation 3:5)," 299.

(Matthew 10:33; 2 Timothy 2:12). John is saying that, even if we are ridiculed and ultimately killed for our faith here on earth so that our name is dishonored and forgotten, we will, if we persevere, enjoy a heavenly reputation for all eternity. Our name will never be blotted out in heaven. No Christian will ever have his person blotted out of the book of life, even carnal ones. The overcomers are being reminded that, even though others can destroy them on earth, they cannot ruin the believer's heavenly name.

But there is a second way of interpreting this verse. Martyn Lloyd-Jones has approached the passage from the assumption that "name" always means person throughout the book.[2210] This has the advantage of consistency over the previous interpretation. He explains the apparent contradiction between Revelation 13:8 and Revelation 3:5 by saying 3:5 is an illustration of a figure of speech known as litotes.

After the financial catastrophe which hit the US economy in 2008, a certified financial planner sent this in an email to his clients, "It was not one of the market's finest performances." This is a litotes which says, "It was one of the market's worst performances." In this figure "an affirmative meaning is expressed by denying its opposite."[2211] When we refer to "an artist of no small stature," we mean he is an outstanding artist. When Paul says of the rebellious wilderness generation, "God was not pleased with most of them" (1 Corinthians 10:5), he means that God was extremely displeased with all but two of them! When Paul says, "I am not ashamed of the gospel," he really means that he is very proud of it. Or, when Luke says the believers were "not a little comforted" at the restoration of Eutychus to life (Acts 20:12), he means they were "exceedingly comforted."[2212]

These examples reveal the key to understanding a litotes. The negative idea is not central. Rather, the interpreter must focus on the positive idea to which the negative refers. Thus, when the Lord says, "*I will not blot his name out*," He is not implying that there is such a possibility, but He is saying emphatically that He will keep his name in the book. The point is that what happens in Greek and Roman cities, that is, removal of one's name, can never happen in regard to the book of life.

Not only will his name be kept in the book, not only is his eternal security guaranteed, but also his name will be acknowledged by Christ before His holy angels.

The statement is parallel to our Lord's famous words:

I tell you, whoever acknowledges me before men, the Son of Man will also acknowledge him before the angels of God (Luke 12:8).

Whoever acknowledges me before men, I will also acknowledge him before my Father in heaven. But whoever disowns me before men, I will disown him before my Father in heaven (Matthew 10:32-33).

Only those Christians who acknowledge Christ now will be acknowledged by Him then. Only those Christians who are overcomers now will have their names acknowledged

---

2210 Lloyd-Jones, *Romans Chapter 8:17-39: The Final Perseverance of the Saints*, 314 ff.

2211 The Lexicon Webster Dictionary, s.v. "litotes."

2212 Cited by AS, p. 289, as an illustration of litotes. When the writer to the Hebrews says, "God is not unjust to forget your work and labor of love" (Hebrews 6:10), he is saying that God most certainly will not forget it. When Jim Elliot said, "He is no fool to give up what he cannot keep to obtain what he cannot lose," the phrase "is no fool" means "is very wise."

before the Father and His angels (Revelation 3:5). But having one's name "acknowledged" is not the same as being declared saved. Rather, it refers to the public testimony by the Son of God to the faithful life of the obedient Christian. Conversely, not having one's name acknowledged is to forfeit the Master's "Well done."

In summary, then, we note that three blessings accrue to the overcomer: (1) he will be dressed in white; (2) his name will never be blotted out of the book of life; and (3) his name will be acknowledged by Christ to the Father in the presence of the holy angels. The first is a special honor to those who are worthy (Revelation 3:4). It may consist of some special token of the purity of their lives. In other uses it refers to righteous acts and not justification (Revelation 19:8, 14). The second is a reminder that no matter what they do to him on earth, he will emphatically not lose his eternal security. And finally, he is assured that he will be publicly acknowledged before the Father in contrast to the unfaithful Christian who will not.

Both interpretations are exegetically sound, and Arminians can therefore find no necessary argument here for their doctrine of conditional security.

Revelation 22:18-19

The apostle John's solemn warning about not adding any words to the book of Revelation has understandably been used by advocates of the doctrine of conditional security:

> *I warn everyone who hears the words of the prophecy of this book: If anyone adds anything to them, God will add to him the plagues described in this book. And if anyone takes words away from the book of prophecy, God will take away from his share in the tree of life and in the holy city, which are described in this book (Revelation 22:18-19).*

However, to have a share in the tree of life and in the holy city does not, as discussed above, refer to going to heaven. Rather, it refers to the privileged position of Christ's *Metochoi*. The danger is disinheritance and not loss of salvation. A share in the tree of life is always in Scripture an additional blessing that comes to those who are already saved.

44

Reflections on Faith

IN CHAPTER 29 the relationship between faith and assurance from Calvin to Westminster was described. The complete departure from Calvin's simple idea that faith is located in the mind and is basically "belief" and assurance was noted. Now our attention will be turned to the biblical and theological issues. While historical theology yields interesting perspective, the final issue is, what does the Bible teach? Not what did Calvin, Beza, Perkins, or Westminster teach? This brings us immediately to the relevant texts that have been used to establish the Westminster tradition.

The Definition of Faith

It is somewhat perplexing how this simple, universally understood, and commonly used term "faith" has been so freighted with additional meanings.[2213] Notions like obedience, yieldedness, repentance, and a myriad of other terms are continually read into this word in order to make it serve the purpose of some particular theological system. This is perplexing because the lexical authorities are virtually unanimous in their assertion that faith, *pistis*, means belief, confidence, trust, or persuasion. The verbal forms all mean the same—to believe something, to give assent, to have confidence in, or to be persuaded of.[2214]

It can be clearly demonstrated that the word "faith" simply means to believe that something is true resulting in trust in the person of Christ. One may object that he thinks more is included, but it can safely be said that this is the historic view of the matter.[2215]

[2213] For extensive lexical, grammatical, and syntactical documentation that the verb "to believe" and the noun "faith" refer only to believing assent and have absolutely nothing to do with submission to the Lordship of Christ or obedience, see the excellent discussion in Chay and Correia, *The Faith That Saves: The Nature of Faith in the New Testament*, 22-53.

[2214] The verb *peithō* means "to convince, persuade, be convinced, be sure, come to believe, be persuaded" (BAGD, 644-45). The remote meaning "to obey" (only 4 out of 50 instances, Romans 2:8; Galatians 5:7; Hebrews 13:17; James 3:3), is noted but is not relevant to the soteriological usage in the New Testament, just as the meaning "elephant's nose" is not relevant to a discussion about a box in the attic. Abbott-Smith asserts that it means to apply persuasion, to persuade, to trust, to be confident, to believe, or to be persuaded (pp. 350-51). Otto Michel says that the active form of *peithō* "always has the meaning of persuade, induce, and even to mislead or corrupt" ("Faith, Persuade, Belief, Unbelief," in NIDNTT, 1:589). "Soon you will persuade [*peithō*] me to become a Christian" (Acts 26:28). The passive form always means to be persuaded, to be convinced. Similarly, the word *pistis* simply means "belief, conviction, or assent," and the verb, *pisteuō*, means "to believe" (ibid., 1:599-605). Abbott-Smith concur that the sense is belief, trust, or confidence, and to believe something (pp. 361-62).

[2215] Augustine defined faith as belief in propositions only and failed to include the biblical requirement of reliance, or trust. He says, "Faith is nothing else than to think with assent." Augustine, "On the Predestination

The Greek word *pisteuō* does not include the notions of obedience, desire, or willingness to change one's life and desist from sin in any soteriological contexts. When Jesus said to the woman at the well, "*Woman, believe Me, an hour is coming when neither in this mountain nor in Jerusalem will you worship the Father*" (John 4:21), He was telling her, "Believe what I say."

In his extensive philological comment on faith, Benjamin Warfield does not offer one suggestion that faith includes obedience.[2216] He would say it results in reliant trust in the person of Christ. He would say it results in reliant trust in the person of Christ."[2217]

Warfield continually stresses that faith is a mental matter rather than a matter of obedience:[2218]

> *The central movement in all faith is no doubt the element of assent; it is that which constitutes the mental movement so called a movement of conviction. But the movement of assent must depend, as it always does depend, on a movement, not specifically of the will, but of the intellect; the assensus issues from the notitia. The movement of the sensibilities which we call "trust," is on the contrary the produce of the assent. And it is in this movement of the sensibilities that faith fulfills itself, and it is by that, as specifically "faith," it is formed.*

This view of faith has strong historical precedent in the Lutheran confessions. Indeed, this is one of the principal areas of disagreement between Lutheranism and the English Puritans. The Puritan view of faith, like that of many modern Experimental Predestinarians, is virtually the same as Rome's. By adding words like "submission" and "obedience" to the concept, they have aligned themselves with their opponents. The Council of Trent declared, "If anyone should say that justifying faith is nothing else than trust (*fiducia*)[2219] in the divine compassion which forgives sins for Christ's sake, or that we are justified alone by such trust, let him be accursed."[2220] Lutheranism, in agreement with Calvin, has traditionally defined faith as "personal trust, or confidence, in God's gracious forgiveness of sins for Christ's sake."[2221] It is viewed as a passive instrument for receiving the divine gift. The will is not involved in producing faith. Faith, according to Lutheran theologian John Mueller, "merely accepts the merits that have been secured for the world by Christ's obedience."[2222] He calls it a passive act or a passive instrument.

It is passive "hearing" in contrast to a volitional decision.

> *Does He then, who provides you with the Spirit and works miracles among you, do it by the works of the Law, or by hearing with faith? (Galatians 3:5)*

---

of the Saints," in *The Nicene and Post-Nicent Fathers of the Church - Anti pelagian Writings*, ed. Philip Schaff (Grand Rapids: Wm. B. Eerdmans Publishing Co., 1956), 499.

2216 Warfield, "Faith in Its Psychological Aspects," 444.

2217 Ibid., 436.

2218 Ibid., 403.

2219 *Fiducia* means "confidence, trust, assurance" and has nothing to do with commitment of the will, submission, or obedience as some Experimental Predestinarian writers assert. See the Latin Dictionary, http://www.archives.nd.edu/cgi-bin/lookup.pl?stem=fiducia&ending.

2220 Session 6, Can. 12 quoted in John T. Mueller, *Christian Dogmatics* (St. Louis, MI: Concordia Publishing House, 1955), 324.

2221 Ibid., 329. For a good discussion of the Lutheran view of faith and how it differs from Experimental Predestinarians, Arminians, and Catholicism, see ibid., 321-35.

2222 Ibid., 327.

In this verse, for example, Paul speaks of God working miracles among them because "you believe what you heard,"[2223] and he sets this in contrast to works of obedience. Whatever faith is, it certainly does not include within its compass the very thing with which it is contrasted, namely, obedience! In Romans Paul is equally clear:

But to one who does not work, but believes in Him who justifies the ungodly, his faith is reckoned as righteousness (Romans 4:5).

For we maintain that a man is justified by faith apart from works of the law (Romans 3:28).
*He who **believes in the Son has eternal life**; but he who does not obey the Son will not see life, but the wrath of God abides on him (John 3:36).*

*Jesus said to them, "I am the bread of life; he who comes to Me will not hunger, and **he who believes in Me** will never thirst" (John 6:35).*

*For this is the will of My Father, that everyone who beholds the Son and **believes in Him** will have eternal life, and I Myself will raise him up on the last day (John 6:40).*

*And everyone who lives and **believes in Me** will never die. Do you believe this? (John 11:26).*

*He who has the Son has the life; he who does not have the Son of God does not have the life. These things I have written to you **who believe** in the name of the Son of God, so that you may know that you have eternal life (1 John 5:12-13).*

*For God so loved the world, that He gave His only begotten Son, that **whoever believes in Him** shall not perish, but have eternal life (John 3:16).*

*But these have been written so that you may believe that Jesus is the Christ, the Son of God; and that **believing** you may have life in His name (John 20:31).*

Experimental Predestinarians claim that in their view works are not added to faith as an additional condition of salvation.[2224] Works, they say, are a necessary expression of genuine faith. However, they certainly appear to contradict themselves when some say that even though works are not added to faith, they are "implicit [involved in the nature or essence of something][2225] in the faith from the beginning."[2226] John Gerstner avows, "Again, this fundamental failure to comprehend is evident. Lordship teaching does not 'add works,' as if faith were not sufficient. *The 'works' are part of the definition of faith.*"[2227] However, if faith is apart from works of obedience (law), by what mental alchemy can one seriously argue that while faith is apart from works of obedience, faith itself includes works of

---

[2223] Gr *akoēs pisteōs*, "the hearing which is faith." Faith is totally passive, a "hearing" of the gospel!

[2224] Experimental Predestinarian clarifications of what they mean by faith confuse most people. In his comment on Isaiah 55:1-2, John Martin explains faith this way: "By coming they indicate that they are trusting in and relying on Him for salvation and are agreeing to obey His commandments. The blessings God gives them are available *without cost***.** Salvation is a free gift of God, whether it refers to spiritual redemption or physical deliverance." So, on the one hand, salvation is granted to those who rely on Christ and is available "without cost" to the one who comes. But on the other hand, in the very the same sentence he says, it is granted to all who "are agreeing to obey." Martin, "Isaiah," 1110.

[2225] *Merriam-Webster's Collegiate Dictionary*, s.v. "implicit".

[2226] For example Gerstner, *Wrongly Dividing the Word of Truth: A Critique of Dispensationalism*, 216.

[2227] Ibid., 257 (Italics added).

obedience in its nature or essence![2228] If faith plus works does not save, then one cannot include obedience as a part of faith and then say faith alone saves when you mean that faith plus works saves![2229]

In Bultmann's article[2230] on "faith" he repeatedly says that faith is reliance, trust, and belief, and then claims that faith includes obedience. In a good example of searching for the "theological idea" rather than the semantic value of a word, Bultmann strings three verses together:

> *Through whom we have received grace and apostleship to bring about the obedience of faith among all the Gentiles (Romans 1:5).*
>
> *What Christ has accomplished through me, resulting in the obedience of the Gentiles by word and deed (Romans 15:18).*
>
> *For the report of your obedience has reached to all (Romans 16:19).*

Now, even though the word *pisteuō* is not used in Romans 15:18 or 16:19, Bultmann uses these verses to prove that *pisteuō* can sometimes mean "to obey." In Romans 1:5 Paul's efforts resulted in the "obedience of faith among all the Gentiles." Since an "obedience" was the result of his ministry to Gentiles in 15:18 and 16:19, Bultmann concludes that faith in this passage is equal to obedience. He has a theological idea in mind, that salvation is by means of works, and feels no contextual restraint in equating the three verses. But Romans 1:5 means "the obedience that can and should be produced by faith,"[2231] not a faith which equals obedience.

Paul wanted to bring about both kinds of obedience, the obedience that consists of believing assent resulting in trust in Christ, and the life of works. But the verb "believe" refers only to the former and not to the latter. Furthermore, only the former, according to the rest of the epistle, is the means of eternal salvation (Romans 3:28; 4:5).[2232] This is the only evidence Bultmann gives that faith is equal to obedience!

MacArthur similarly misunderstands the nature of faith and, like Bultmann (whom he quotes), equates it with obedience.[2233] For example, he cites W. E. Vine in his

---

2228 The "faith of a mustard seed" is certainly not obedience, nor does it include the idea of obedience (Luke 17:6).

2229 If Warfield is one of the leading lights of the Reformed faith in the twentieth century, surely Archibald Alexander would be considered by many to be the leading Reformed thinker of the nineteenth century. He was professor of theology at Princeton Seminary from its beginning in 1812 to his death on September 7, 1851. Dr. Charles Hodge, also of Princeton fame, said of Alexander that he was the greatest man he had ever met. He was known not only for his wide learning but also for his devout piety. In his classic discussion of the practical Christian life, *Thoughts on Religious Experience*, he has a very interesting discussion of faith. Unlike Warfield, he insists that "faith is simply a belief of the truth." Warfield would add that it involves trust. "Similar to John Calvin he explains that faith "is a firm persuasion or belief of the truth, apprehended under the illumination of the Holy Spirit." Archibald Alexander, *Thoughts on Religious Experience to which is added an appendix containing "Letters to the aged"* (Philadelphia: Presbyterian Board of Publication, 1844), 64.

2230 Rudolf Bultmann, "*pisteuō*," in TDNT 6:205.

2231 Zane C. Hodges, *Romans: Deliverance from Wrath,* ed. Robert N Wilkin and John H. Niemelä (Corinth, TX: Grace Evangelical Society, 2013), 29.

2232 Bultmann also cites Hebrews 11; Romans 1:8; 1 Thessalonians 1:8; 10:3; and 2 Corinthians 9:13, all of which are irrelevant and suggest only that works are a proper result of salvation but not that obedience is intrinsic to faith or even that obedience is a necessary result of faith.

2233 MacArthur, *The Gospel According to Jesus*, 172-78.

discussion of the words *peithō* and *pisteuō*. "*Peithō* and *pisteuō*, 'to trust', are closely related etymologically; the difference in meaning is that the former implies the obedience that is produced by the latter. *Peithō* in the New Testament suggests an actual and outward result of the inward persuasion and consequent faith."[2234] However, Vine commits the root fallacy. The fact that both words come from the same root ("to bind") is irrelevant. One does not determine word meanings by tracing them back to their root.[2235]

MacArthur adds that "the real believer will obey," and he states, "The biblical concept of faith is inseparable from obedience."[2236] However, possible, or even inevitable, consequences of faith are not to be equated with faith itself. Faith does *not* mean "to obey." It is *not*, as MacArthur says, "the determination of the will to obey the truth."[2237] In asserting this he has adopted the Catholic view that the Reformers labored to refute.[2238] Faith is believing, acceptance of the facts of the gospel,[2239] and reliance upon Christ for the forgiveness of sins. As mentioned above, to import notions of obedience into the word "faith" is contrary to the teaching of the apostle Paul.

What, then, is saving faith? As has been argued above, saving faith is simply believing something is true and resting confidently in the object of faith. It involves knowledge about the object and then belief and acceptance of that knowledge as valid.

But the most important characteristic of faith is the content of what is believed. What makes faith saving, is not whether it results in obedience but what is the content of that which is believed. J. B. Hixson precisely defines saving faith by saying,

> *Saving faith is the belief in Jesus Christ as the Son of God who died and rose again to pay one's personal penalty for sin and the one who gives eternal life to all who trust Him and Him alone for it.*[2240]

2234 VINE, 2:124.

2235 See Chay and Correia, *The Faith That Saves: The Nature of Faith in the New Testament*, 22-24.

2236 In this writer's opinion, it is not true that, as MacArthur maintains, faith includes the idea of repentance (p. 172). The call to repentance is national; it is for the nation of Israel so that they may avoid a temporal catastrophe, namely, the destruction of Jerusalem in AD 70. Also repentance is something believers do to return to fellowship with God. When the writer to the Hebrews says, "The just shall live by faith," he means that the modus operandi of life of the regenerate man is faith. He does not mean that we must believe (= obey) for the rest of our lives to become Christians or to prove that we already are. True a believer is a Partner with Christ only if he holds firm to the end, but being a Partner and being a Christian are different things. (See elsewhere in this book, pp. 351 ff.) The work that God will complete in the lives of the Philippians (Philippians 1:6) is not sanctification but their participation in the gospel with Him, which will continue up to the Lord's return. Paul expected the Lord to return in his lifetime.

2237 MacArthur, *The Gospel According to Jesus*, 173.

2238 Orchard, a Roman Catholic, understands faith as follows: "Omission causes no difficulty if faith be understood in the sense of dogmatic faith, which accepts all the doctrines of the Gospel as true and obeys all its precepts as divine commandments. For in this faith sacraments and good works are included." Bernard Orchard, *A Catholic Commentary on Holy Scripture* (Nashville: Thomas Nelson, 1953), 1049.

2239 MacArthur quotes passages like Hebrews 11, which describe how people accomplished great things by faith, as proof that faith itself is the determination to accomplish great things. He has taken a contextual nuance, obedience, read it into the semantic value of the word *pisteuō*, and then interpreted *pisteuō* to mean "to obey" in its other usages in the New Testament. Such a procedure is not exegesis but is reading theological ideas into words. This has no place in legitimate New Testament interpretation. Nor does it have any place in the presentation of the gospel. The gospel according to MacArthur is so confusing that a non-Christian would have to be a theologian to comprehend it. Gone is the simple offer of eternal life on the basis of faith apart from works. MacArthur presents a faith that consists of works, and yet does not consist of works.

2240 Hixson, *Getting the Gospel Wrong*, 84.

It does not include anything else: no repentance (in the sense of turning from sin), no obedience, nothing. To add to this is to preach another gospel.

The Role of the Will in Faith

Actions of the will arise from faith, but the will itself is not involved in the production of faith. This may seem surprising to some, but a moment's reflection will substantiate the commonly understood notion that faith is located in the mind and is persuasion or belief. It is something that "happens" to us as a result of our reflecting on sufficient evidence. We can no more will faith than we can will feelings of love, or will to hear, or will to see. Hearing "happens" when sound waves fall upon our eardrums and seeing "happens" when light from an object falls upon our eyes.

That faith is passive, and not active, is evident when Paul says:

Did you receive the Spirit by works of law, or by hearing with faith? (Galatians 3:2)

As he often does, Paul throws faith into the sharpest contrast possible with works and describes its function as "hearing." There is something different about "hearing." In Paul's mind, it does not involve work. "Hearing with faith" is apparently a passive receptivity. In choosing the word "hearing" (instead of "obeying"), he is not only stating that faith is a passive reception, but he is also aligning himself with his Master who taught that faith was "looking"[2241] and "drinking"[2242] and with the writer to the Hebrews who described it as "tasting."[2243] All these terms assign a passive, receptive function to faith. The will chooses to turn up the volume, to lift a fork to one's mounth, and to direct attention to an object. That is the role of the will. But the resultant hearing, tasting, and seeing is not willed. Similarly faith cannot be willed, it happens to us as a result of contemplation of the object of faith.

The conclusion that faith is a persuasion resulting in reliant trust in the person of Christ, is completely within the mainstream of the Reformed faith, and there is no better discussion of it than Benjamin Warfield's article "On Faith in Its Psychological Aspects."[2244]

Warfield eliminates a role for the will in producing faith when he says:

The conception embodied in the terms "belief," "faith," is not that of an arbitrary act of the subject's; it is that of a mental state or an act which is determined by sufficient reasons.[2245]

This, of course, rules out any notion of obedience in the production of faith, which is located in the will not the mind. He continues:

[2241] John 3:14-15; compare Numbers 21:9 where "looking" resulted in living.

[2242] John 4:14; 7:37-38. It is true that sometimes "drink" can have ideas such as "surrender" (e.g., Matthew 20:22; John 18:11), but it does not have such a meaning in soteriological passages. It is a figure of speech, and its meaning must be derived from each context in which it is used. In Revelation 5:5, Jesus is called a lion, but in 1 Peter 5:8 Satan goes about like a lion. If the intent of a figure is always the same, irrespective of context, we would be forced to say that Jesus is Satan!

[2243] Hebrews 6:4.

[2244] Warfield, "Faith in Its Psychological Aspects," 376 ff.

[2245] Ibid., 376.

That is to say, with respect to belief, it is a mental recognition of what is before the mind, as objectively true and real, and therefore depends upon the evidence that a thing is true and real and is determined by this evidence; it is the response of the mind to this evidence and cannot arise apart from it. ***It is, therefore, impossible that belief should be the product of a volition;*** *volitions look to the future and represent our desires; beliefs look to the present and represent our findings.*[2246]

He says that faith cannot be created by the will willing it. It is a product of evidence.[2247] This statement conforms to common experience. On many occasions this writer has spoken with non-Christians who simply cannot believe. To tell such a man that he can is a mockery. In some cases he sincerely wants to, but for some reason the evidence necessary for such a reflection has not yet been presented to his mind for faith to arise, or he is blind to it. No faith is possible without evidence or what the mind takes for evidence. We may safely conclude, on the authority of Christ Himself, that the will of man has absolutely no direct role in producing saving faith. We cannot will faith. Since obedience or repentance are matters of the will, they cannot be part of the saving transaction which is by faith alone. Rather faith "happens" to us when we contemplate the object of faith, the Lord Jesus Christ and the wonder of the gospel promises and results in reliant trust in the person of Christ.

But as many as received Him, to them He gave the right to become children of God, even to those who believe in His name, who were born, not of blood nor of the will of the flesh ***nor of the will of man****, but of God (John 1:12–13).*

If the will/obedience is not involved in the **production** of faith, why do some Experimentalists curiously insist that it is implicit in the **nature** of faith and includes repentance? This is often because they incorrectly understand the noun *fiducia* (confidence) to mean "to entrust" (a verb) and then incorrectly understand "to entrust" as an equivalent to "obey." In the Protestant confessions, *fiducia* means to "have trust or confidence" in the free mercy of God for forgiveness.[2248] All admit that faith includes *fiducia* in this sense. However this is not submission to His Lordship. We also agree that works **should** arise **from** faith. Experimentalists also argue that when the word "faith" is followed by a preposition such as "into," "in," or "on" that changes the meaning of the verb and requires us to incorporate notions of allegiance into it.[2249] In his article on faith, Bultmann is clear that adding prepositions to the word "faith" like "believe into," or "believe in," do not change the fundamental meaning. These constructions mean the same thing as "believe that."[2250] Clark has shown that the presence of a noun or pronoun (e.g. "Jesus" or "me") following the Greek verb *pisteuō* changes nothing in the meaning of the verb.[2251] It means to have confidence in what that person says.[2252]

2246 Ibid.

2247 Ibid., 379.

2248 William. Cunningham, "Sec.IV: Justification by Faith," in *Historical Theology: A Review of the Principal Doctrinal Discussions in the Christian Church Since the Apostolic Age* (Edinburgh: T&T Clark, 1864), 57. Warfield denies that even "preparedness to act," that is, willingness to obey, is part of the meaning of pisteuo." Benjamin B. Warfield, "Faith in Its PsychologicalAspects," in *Biblical and Theological Studies* (Philadelphia: Presbyterian and Reformed Publishing Co., 1968), 317.

2249 For example Berkhof, *Systematic Theology*, pp. 494-95.

2250 Bultmann, "*pisteuō*," in TDNT, 6:203.

2251 Gordon Haddon Clark, *What Is Saving Faith?* (Jefferson, MD: Trinity Foundation, 2004), 143.

2252 See discussion in Hixson, *Getting the Gospel Wrong*, 108 ff.

If, indeed, faith is a mental and not a volitional thing, then two problems immediately come to mind. First, if the will is not involved in producing faith, then why is it that faith is everywhere presented in Scripture as something for which people are responsible? Second, how can such a view of faith be distinguished from mere intellectual assent? Certainly, Satan assents mentally to the proposition that Jesus is God. Does this mean that he has faith?

Regarding the role of the will in producing faith, Warfield explains that there are two factors involved in the production of faith: (1) the evidence, or the ground on which faith is yielded, and (2) the subjective condition by virtue of which the evidence can take effect in the appropriate act of faith.

> *Evidence cannot produce belief, faith, except in a mind open to this evidence, and capable of responding to it. A mathematical demonstration is demonstrative proof of the proposition demonstrated. But even such a demonstration cannot produce conviction in a mind incapable of following the demonstration.*[2253]

Something more is needed to produce faith. Faith is not a mechanical result of the presentation of evidence. Good evidence can be refused because of the subjective nature or condition of the mind to which it is addressed. This is the ground of responsibility for belief or faith: "it is not merely a question of evidence but of subjectivity; and subjectivity is the other name for personality." Warfield continues,

> *If evidence which is objectively adequate is not subjectively adequate, the fault is in us. If we are not accessible to musical evidence, then we are by nature unmusical, or in a present state of unmusicalness. If we are not accessible to moral evidence then we are either unmoral, or being moral beings, immoral.*[2254]

Since this is true, it is easy to see that a sinful heart which is at enmity to God is incapable of the supreme act of trust in the person of Christ apart from the illumination of the Holy Spirit.

Faith comes to a person when (1) he directs his attention to the evidence for and towards the object of, faith; and (2) when the Holy Spirit illumines his mind and creates an empathy toward, and understanding of, that evidence. Faith is made possible by illumination, softening of the heart, and a quickening of the will. As a result, a person is enabled to believe on the basis of the evidence submitted to him in the Gospels. He does not "will it." It "happens" to him as a result of sympathetic reflection on the Object of faith. His faith was simply a response to the evidence the Holy Spirit enabled him to see clearly and sympathetically.[2255]

[2253] Warfield, "Faith in Its Psychological Aspects," 397.

[2254] Ibid., 398.

[2255] Thus faith is not a "gift" in the Experimental Predestinarian sense of God regenerating a man before he believes. Reformed writers sometimes quote 1 John 5:1 as proof that regeneration precedes faith. "Whoever believes that Jesus is the Christ, is born of God." In doing this they mistakenly connect the present participle, "whoever believes" with the perfect tense main verb "is born." But the present participle is adjectival and articular and thus "this participle can be broadly antecedent to the time of the main verb, especially if it is articular." Wallace, *Greek Grammar Beyond the Basics*, 626. The present participle is modified by "whoever" (Gr *pas*).

Warfield goes further than this writer is willing to go when he concludes that regeneration precedes faith.[2256] To the contrary, faith, according to the New Testament is the condition for receiving salvation and is not a result of it.

When the Bible teaches that we are responsible for believing (e.g., Acts 16:31), the meaning is plain. We are responsible for directing our sight to Christ and to an openness to consider the evidence. The evidence for faith is good—the revelation of God in the Bible—and to reject it is a moral, not an intellectual, problem. The refusal of man to do this precludes the possibility that he will come to faith. It is in this that the responsibility for faith lies. In this way we can see that faith itself is not volitional, as it is so often described. It is a mental act.

Is Faith a Gift?

If the will is not directly involved in producing of faith, then is faith a gift? Warfield would say, "Yes," and along with other Calvinists cites Ephesians 2:8-9 as proof.

> *For by grace you have been saved through faith; and that* (Gr *touto*) *not of yourselves, it is the gift of God (Ephesians 2:8).*

According to Paul "*that*" is not of ourselves but is a gift. While this seems plausible in English, it is not so in Greek. The Calvinist interpretation depends largely upon the English word order which suggests that the near antecedent of "*that*" is "faith." Thus, faith is a gift. However, the Gr word, *touto*, is inflected as a nominative, singular, neuter, demonstrative pronoun. Faith is feminine, and thus Gr grammar suggests that *toutos* probably does not refer to faith because the pronoun and the noun to which it refers must be the same gender. However, because there is no preceding feminine noun ("saved" is a verb), this grammatical point is not fatal to the faith-is-a-gift view, but it does make it less probable. Calvinists typically say that "*that*" (*touto*) refers to salvation plus faith, but to link it with faith is unlikely. We prefer to translate, "It is by grace you have been saved, and that [salvation] is not from yourselves, [this salvation] is the gift of God."[2257] "That" refers to the entire plan and provision of salvation through grace.

The spiritual illumination which must precede faith is a result of the unbeliever choosing to direct his attention to the object of faith with an attitude of receptivity. God then grants the illumination necessary for spiritual perception. Thus, faith is not willed nor is it a work.

Faith and Knowledge

But if faith is merely a mental act, a persuasion based on evidence, how is it distinguished from mere knowledge, which the demons possess? Are we to say that saving faith is simply the acceptance of a set of propositions about the deity of Christ and the atonement? No! It includes the act of trusting in the person of Christ. Did not the demons have faith? Were they saved? Did not James' opponent say,

> *You believe that God is one. You do well; the demons also believe, and shudder (James 2:19).*

[2256] Warfield, "Faith in Its Psychological Aspects," 399.

[2257] For discussion of this verse see Jerry L. Walls and Joseph Dongell, *Why I am not a Calvinist* (Downers Grove, IL: InterVarsity Press, 2004), 77.

It is important to note that the faith of the demons in James 2:19 is not saving faith. And even when faith does "save," only the context answers the question: "Save from what?" Their demonic faith is simply a faith that God is a unity. God is One. Muslims and Jews believe that. That kind of faith will not save because the content of the faith is not in the Son of God who died for our sins. Furthermore, it is not James who is making the statement that "*You believe that God is one. You do well; the demons also believe, and shudder*" (James 2:19). It is the objector making this claim.[2258] The objector's foolish point is that faith in and of itself has no connection with obedience.

Two things differentiate saving faith from mere knowledge. The first may be stated as a persuasion resulting in reliance on the person of Christ. Persuasion is deeper than knowledge. Furthermore, persuasion will always result in a degree of trust in the Object. The Greek word *pistis*, "faith," includes the idea of reliability, trustworthiness. It refers to "that which evokes trust."[2259] If there is faith, there is also trust. Similarly, to "believe" (Gr *pisteuō*) means to consider something "to be true and therefore worthy of one's trust."[2260] It is one thing to intellectually accept certain propositions; it is another to be in a state of reliant trust. It is one thing to believe that God is one, it is another to believe that Jesus is that God and by reliance on Him as one's Savior one can escape the penalty for sin.

The story has been told of a man who pushed a wheelbarrow across the Grand Canyon on a tightrope wire. For five dollars one could daily watch his death-defying performance. At the finale he would ask his assistant to get into the wheelbarrow, and he would push her across in front of him. Now imagine you are watching this performance, and a man turns to you and says, "Do you believe he can push his assistant across the Grand Canyon on the wire?"

"Of course," you reply. "I have watched him do it every day for a week."

"Then get in!"

To believe that he can push the wheelbarrow across without accident is knowledge. To have an inward conviction and reliant trust that you could "get in" is not only knowledge but faith.

But there is a second characteristic of true faith which separates it from mere knowledge or intellectual assent. True faith, according to Archibald Alexander, is distinguished from historic faith in the differing evidence on which it is based.[2261] The ground of historical faith, or assent, is only the deductions of reason or the prejudices of culture and education. It is based upon cultural familiarity (i.e., "I am a Christian because I am an American," etc.) or intellectual acceptance of logical conclusions based on reasonable data. Biblical faith, however, differs from this. Faith in the Bible is not based on cultural convenience or a deduction of reason. It is based on a perception of the beauty, glory, and sweetness of divine things as revealed in Scripture and the gospel promise. The object of biblical faith is the saving work of Christ and the gospel offer. The evidence on which it rests is the promises of Scripture.

2258 For extensive discussion of this passage see chapter 28.

2259 BDAG, 818.

2260 BDAG, 816.

2261 Alexander, *Thoughts on Religious Experience to which is added an appendix containing "Letters to the aged"*, 66.

Neither Alexander, Warfield, nor a host of other Reformed theologians including Calvin himself, ever taught as Westminster did that faith included obedience. They would all, no doubt, be surprised to learn that some modern-day Experimental Predestinarians would view their teaching as unhistorical or antinomian! What they did teach was that true faith always results in a life of obedience, a conclusion that is simply untrue to Scripture, as earlier chapters of this book have shown.[2262]

Faith and Profession

Closely related to the question of faith and knowledge is the question, "How is a saved man to be distinguished from one who professes to be saved but in fact is not?" Or, "How is a false profession of faith in Christ to be distinguished from a true one?" If the preceding train of thought is granted, then it is clear how we do not *reliably* discern a false profession. We do not discern this by an examination of his fruits or an assessment of his grief over sin or a measurement of his desire to have fellowship with God.[2263] Rather, the presence of a false profession is best discerned by asking questions that will reveal whether a man understands the gospel and has Christ as the conscious object of faith and whether he believes it. We ask questions to reveal whether a person understands the gospel, believes it, and is trusting in Christ for salvation. While such an examination can never yield the certainty that the Experimental Predestinarian judges seem to desire, one should realize that their method of examining fruit yields no certainty at all. Indeed, the whole quest for others to ascertain with certainty the inner life of a believer is ill-founded. Paul warned us to judge no man before the time (1 Corinthians 4:5).

Only the individual can know if he has believed. No one can externally know this for him. Certainly the lack of fruit in a person's life raises the question, "Does he possess the Spirit at all, or if he does, has he quenched Him?" But as Calvin argued, just as the presence of fruit cannot prove whether a person is a Christian, neither can its absence deny it (*Institutes*, 3.14.19).

Additional citation of authorities or of biblical references is unnecessary.[2264] Any concordance will abundantly confirm the conclusions of those already cited. It may be dogmatically stated that Calvin was correct. Faith is located in the mind. It is primarily a mental and not a volitional act. It differs from mere assent in that it has the additional idea of confidence or persuasion and reliance. It is, as the writer to the Hebrews insisted, an inward conviction, "a conviction of things hoped for" (Hebrews 11:1).

2262 See chapter 32.

2263 As suggested by Darrell L. Bock, "A Review of *The Gospel According to Jesus*," *BibSac* 146, no. 581 (January-March 1989): 31-32.

2264 MacArthur refers to John 10:27 and says the sheep "follow." MacArthur, *The Gospel According to Jesus*, 178. This supposedly means that those who are saved follow Him to the end of life. Yes, those who believe in Christ will normally follow Him. But to insist, as MacArthur does, that they will always do so or inevitably and necessarily do so to the end of life lacks biblical support as chapter 32 above demonstrates. The illustration of the little child coming to Jesus does indicate humility in the sense that a believer must be converted and take the lowest status if he desires to enter into greatness in God's kingdom. But Matthew 18:3 is addressed to disciples and has nothing to do with personal salvation. See discussion on pp. 280 ff.

Summary

Faith involves believing assent to the facts of the Gospel and a personal reliance upon the person of Christ as a Savior from sin. It is a persuasion that leads to trust. It is not a product of volition; it "happens" to us as we contemplate the Object of faith and the wonder and beauty of the Gospel promises. While some who hold variations of the Partner viewpoint on perseverance maintain that faith is only believing something to be true, the Partners disagree. As Warfield has shown, saving faith, involves trusting in *the person of Christ* and does not include obedience. It is believing assent resulting in trust. Mere mental agreement with facts about Christ is not genuine saving faith. Biblical faith is distinguished from mere assent in that it includes *"the assurance of things hoped for"* (Hebrews 11:1-2) and reliance upon the person of Christ.

The Partners also agree that for faith to be genuine, it is necessarily preceded by repentance. However, as demonstrated in Chapter 3 above (see pp 33-38), to repent (Gr *metanoeō*) does not mean "turn from sin." Based on its use in the LXX it means "to regret, to feel sorry for, to admit one is guilty." One cannot come to Christ as a Savior from sin until one first of all admits he needs a Savior, that is, he stands as a guilty sinner under the judgment of God.

The Protestant confessions have correctly spoken of faith as *fiducia*. However, sometimes this word has been misunderstood to mean surrender of one's life in the sense of obedience to Christ. It does not mean that. It means to have reliant trust in the person of Christ for the forgiveness of sins.

Warfield's persuasive argument that faith cannot be produced by willing it, but instead "happens" to us as we reflect the person of our gracious Savior and the promises of Scripture, contributes to the Partner view of assurance. Like initial faith, assuring faith comes by looking outward to the person of Christ and the biblical promises as discussed in Chapters 29-30 above. It cannot be willed into existence.

Furthermore, if saving faith is not a product of the will, this implies that the will is not involved in the saving transaction. While Warfield would not agree, that would exclude his notions of turning from sin or commitment to obey as necessary aspects of genuine faith.

While good works are an indicator of whether or not a profession of faith is genuine, ultimately they are unreliable (consider Solomon!). No one but God knows the heart. The best route to helping a person understand whether or not his faith is real is to clarify the beauty and certainty of the Gospel promise of security. Let us hear Calvin once again.

> *Should they begin to estimate it [assurance of their salvation] by their good works, nothing will be weaker or more uncertain; works, when estimated by themselves, no less proving the divine displeasure by their imperfection, than His good-will by their incipient purity (Calvin, "Institutes," 3.14.19).*

> *And indeed we do not deny that the faith which justifies us is accompanied by an earnest desire to live well and righteously; but we only maintain that our confidence cannot rest on anything else than on the mercy of God alone (Calvin, John, s.v. "John 5:29).*

45
The Prodigal Son

THERE WAS a shepherd who lived in the highlands above Glasgow, Scotland, with his daughter. This shepherd had been married for a number of years, and he and his wife had one daughter. His wife had passed away, and so now it was the loving responsibility of the father to raise his one child, his one daughter.

The father and daughter loved to take walks together along the mountain paths in the hills of Scotland. Then they would go down into the valleys, and as they walked, this shepherd father used to call out with a beautiful voice for the sheep. And more than seemingly anything else, the daughter loved to hear the voice of the shepherd father calling out for the sheep.

Well, in time this little girl grew into an attractive young woman, and she bade farewell to her father, promising to write, and she moved to Edinburgh and then to Glasgow. At first she wrote her father every week, but then the letters came less frequently—she wrote only about once a month, and then the letters stopped coming. No longer was there any word from the daughter to the shepherd father.

A young man on one occasion saw the daughter in Glasgow, and, knowing the father, he went up and visited the father in the highlands. He communicated to the father that the daughter was now living a lifestyle of overt immorality and sin. She was working in a bar, she was drinking heavily, and she was living with another man.

The shepherd father put on his shepherd garb, his cloak and sandals, and he walked down into the streets of Glasgow. The citizens of Glasgow observed this strange looking character, this shepherd who had walked down from the hills. But he did not mind their stares because he was there for a purpose; he was looking for his daughter. He walked first through the main streets, then the avenues and the boulevards and through the byways of Glasgow, but he could not find his daughter. So then he ventured into the alleys and into the slums and into the poorest sections of the city and still his daughter was not to be found.

And finally one night, as he had been lying awake all night, it came to him in the early morning that perhaps he should get up and call out to his daughter with his shepherd's voice, that voice that his daughter loved to hear all the years she had been growing up together with him in the hills of Scotland. And so he got up that morning, and he began to call out in that beautiful shepherd's voice. A short time after he had been calling out, his daughter heard the beautiful voice of her father.

There she was, sleeping with a man. She jumped up, pushed open the windows, and saw her father walking down this back alley. She had been sleeping in this room above a bar. She ran downstairs, pushed open the doors of the bar, and ran into the arms of her father. The first words that came from the lips of her father as he embraced her were, "I forgive you. I love you."

He picked her up in his arms, and he carried her for a while and then set her down. Arm-in-arm they walked back to their home in the hills, where he restored her to her faith in Jesus Christ. And she came once again to love the Lord with all her heart. She married a Christian man and raised a Christian family.

As the years passed, and the time of her death drew near, she communicated that she wanted only one word on her gravestone. She wanted only one word because she had been so impacted by the example of her father. If you go to Scotland today, you can see that gravestone. On it you will see the name of the woman, the date of her birth, the date of her death, and in large letters on the gravestone is the one word, "*Forgiven*". That's all it says. "*Forgiven*".

The past few chapters in this book have been dark. We have elaborated in some detail on the neglected theme of the negatives that can happen to the carnal believer at the Judgment Seat of Christ. It is important to note that all is not lost! The Father grieves for the believer's broken fellowship and longs for his return. Like the father of the prodigal son described in this chapter, he daily looks down the road, eagerly anticipating a restoration to fellowship.

It is most important that the way back and the compassion, love, and acceptance of the Father now be brought into focus. The best way to do this is to expound the Parable of the Prodigal Son.

The Sinners and Tax Collectors

The context opens with a complaint from the Pharisees, "This man receives *sinners* and eats with them" (Luke 15:2). But who are these sinners? Opinions differ. Many assume this is a reference to the "godless" who often in the Old Testament opposed the Lord.[2265] However, in this context, in which the Pharisees are disturbed by Jesus' associations, a more likely candidate is the *am ha'arets*, "the people of the land." These were the common people considered by the Pharisees to be "sinners" because they did not follow all the pharisaic rules regarding cleanliness, and other traditions.[2266] Many in that multitude were

---

[2265] Bock, *Luke 9:51-24:53*, 1299.

[2266] Moore says that the *am ha'arets* are the "common people." The term was often used to describe the masses in contrast to the scholars. The common man was one who did not observe the Pharisees' religious rules (BDAG, 51). The educated class looked down on them, viewing them as rude, ill-bred, and dirty. An educated man would never marry a woman of this class. Those contrasted in the Parable of the Prodigal Son are the Pharisees and the *am ha'arets*. A Pharisee would not travel with one of these "sinners" nor would he ever have dinner at his table. George F. Moore, "The Am-ha-arets (the people of the land) and the Haberim (Associates)," in Foakes-Jackson et al., *The Beginnings of Christianity : The Acts of the Apostles*, 1:440 ff. This view of "sinners," of course, is not shared by all. E. P. Sanders rejects it. See Sanders, *Jesus and Judaism*, 175-211; Sanders, *Paul and Palestinian Judaism*, 152. Karl H. Rengsdorf, "*harmartōlos*," in TDNT, 1:327 notes that the word "sinners" can refer to the wicked, that is, nonbelievers (the view he prefers in Luke 15:1), or to one who does not subject himself to Pharisaic ordinances. We prefer the latter in this context because the parables are specifically against the Pharisees (15:2). See Wright, *Jesus and the Victory of God*, 264-68. "'Sinners' may carry the more technical sense of those whose lack of observance of legal regulations placed them outside the 'pure' company which Pharisees kept (Mann here translates 'nonobservant Jews'), but the term is probably used in a more general sense, with the focus at least as much on moral as on ritual offence." France, *The*

followers of Jesus. In fact, most of Jesus' followers were from this group, and we may safely assume that these are "believing" *am ha'arets.* Mark tells us, "*And it happened that He was reclining at the table in his house, and many tax collectors and sinners were dining with Jesus and His disciples; for there were many of them, and they were following Him*" (Mark 2:15). These sinners and tax collectors associated with Jesus are those who "were following Him." The phrase identifies them not as those casually interested, but as His followers who have come to His home for what we might call "follow-up." Regarding them, Jesus said earlier, "*Truly I say to you that the tax-gatherers and harlots will get into the kingdom of God* [i.e., the kingdom way of living] *before you*" (Matthew 21:31). As discussed elsewhere, these "crowds" in Mark and Matthew are viewed as believers.[2267] Jesus said they are "*my brother and my sister and my mother*" (Matthew 12:49-50).

But the Pharisees saw the matter differently. They considered themselves to be members of a group that scrupulously observed the laws of Levitical cleanliness. As comrades among these religious elite, they would not sell anything to the *am ha'arets;* they would buy nothing from them (for fear of it being levitically unclean); they would not accept hospitality from them, and they would never receive them as guests.[2268] The clothing of the *am ha'arets* was considered unclean.[2269] Their contempt for the *am ha'arets* was clear, "But this multitude which does not know the Law is accursed" (John 7:49).

According to E. P. Sanders, though, based on the Hebrew word *resha ʿim,* translated *harmatōloi* in much of Hebrew literature, the word "sinners" (Gr *harmatōloi*) is a technical term for the wicked, unrepentant nonbeliever.[2270] Bruce Chilton challenges Sanders on this point, saying "the argument that 'the wicked' is a technical term appears strained."[2271] But, more importantly, Sanders is refuted by the New Testament. Peter called himself a sinner, "*But when Simon Peter saw that, he fell down at Jesus' feet, saying, 'Depart from me, for I am a sinful man (Gr harmartōlos), O Lord!'*" (Luke 5:8). A sinner is a person, believer or nonbeliever, who commits sins. But even if Sanders is correct, and he is not, it is immaterial. Matthew places the word "sinners" in the lips of the Pharisees, not Jesus. This only indicates what the Pharisees think them to be and is irrelevant in telling us anything about their saved status. In fact, this could support the view that they are believers; the Pharisees thought of Jesus and His disciples as "sinners"!

Recall our Lord's mission statement, "*I have not come to call the righteous but sinners to repentance*" (Luke 5:32). Does this mean that Jesus' ministry was directed toward the hardened unrepentant "wicked"? Of course not! He would never throw his pearls before swine (Matthew 7:6). As argued earlier, repentance is fundamentally an admission of guilt and some degree of regret about it. Repentance does not save, but it can lead to saving faith. But more often repentance is applied to those who are already saved; for them it is a call to

---

Gospel of Mark: A Commentary on the Greek Text, 132. Recently Dwayne Adams has argued extensively that Luke views the "sinners" as "repentant Jewish sinners" and "repentant Gentile followers" of Jesus, and they represent a fulfillment of God's promise of universal salvation. See Dwayne H. Adams, *The Sinner in Luke* (Eugene, OR: Pickwick Publications, 2008).

2267 See pp. 271 ff. above.

2268 "m.Demai 2:3" in Jacob Neusner, *The Mishnah: A New Translation* (New Haven, CT: Yale University Press, 1988), 37.

2269 "m.Hagigah 2:7" in ibid., 331.

2270 Sanders, *Jesus and Judaism*, 177.

2271 Bruce D. Chilton, "Jesus and the Repentance of E. P. Sanders," *Tyndale Bulletin* 39, no. 1 (1988): 10.

confess their sin and be restored to fellowship with Christ. Calvin called the Christian life a life of repentance. There is no reason to deny the likelihood that the "sinners" gathered in Jesus' home in the parables of Luke 15 are believing sinners (see below). Frequently, repentance is addressed to those who are already saved but, having wandered astray, need to return to the Shepherd.[2272] Some, perhaps, have been hindered by the Pharisees from entering into the full teaching of Christ, a rich experience of kingdom life (Matthew 23:13).

When Jesus refers to the "righteous" in Luke 5:32, it is unlikely that He is being ironic, meaning "those who think they are righteous." In order to maintain the parallelism, that would require that "sinners" are only those who think they are sinners.[2273] No, the ninety-nine righteous persons in Luke 5:32 and 15:7 are healthy believers. Jesus said they have no need of repentance.

The Lord responds to the Pharisees' protest about eating with sinners by saying,

> *What man among you, if he has a hundred sheep and has lost one of them, does not leave the ninety-nine in the open pasture, and go after the one which is lost, until he finds it? (Luke 15:4)*

Notice, this man "has" a hundred sheep. These sheep belong to the Shepherd. The sinners with whom Jesus has table fellowship similarly "belong" to Him. They are saved people.

The sinners dining with Jesus are new followers of Christ, the *am ha'arets*. Many of them are confused, some are just beginning the journey, and all of them need to make major decisions about the direction their lives are taking; they need to repent in the sense of changing their mind about their sin and confessing it. They need to enter into full discipleship.

The Shepherd rejoices when even one of these lost sheep that belong to Him repents,

> *And when he comes home, he calls together his friends and his neighbors, saying to them, "Rejoice with me, for I have found my sheep which was lost!" I tell you that in the same way, there will be more joy in heaven over one sinner who repents, than over ninety-nine righteous persons who need no repentance (Luke 15:6–7).*

That the sinners are believing sinners is proven by three things: (1) they are salt which has become saltless; (2) like the prodigal son in the parable to follow (with whom they are identified), they were sons of the father *before* they were lost; and (3) they have been invited to table fellowship at the Lord's home.

SALT THAT HAS BECOME SALTLESS

First, a point not often noticed is the connection between Luke 15:1 and the last verses of Luke 14, "Therefore, salt is good; but if even *salt has become tasteless*, with what will it be seasoned? It is useless either for the soil or *for the manure pile; it is thrown out*"(Luke 14:34-35). The reference is to disciples, believing "sinners," who have lost their saltiness, who have become carnal and useless for the cause of the kingdom. As a result, they are thrown out of service; they are in a true sense, "lost." At the moment we are born again, we

---

[2272] For full discussion of the meaning of repentance in the New Testament, see Chapter 3 above.

[2273] Robert A. Guelich, *Mark 1-8:26*, Word Biblical Commentary (Dallas: Word Books, 2002).

are fully equipped, inclined, and empowered to be salt. Yet some become "saltless." The fact that Mark does not include the parables about the lost sheep, the lost coin, and the lost son right after this same saying (Mark 9:50) raises the question, "Why did Luke include them here?" Probably, he is expanding on the theme just mentioned: believers who have lost their saltiness are "lost" in the sense that they are no longer useful for kingdom work. Why did they lose their saltiness? The text does not say. We do know, however, that there were many who had believed, but because of Pharisaic opposition and distortion they became confused and never entered fully into kingdom living (Matthew 23:13). We also know that the cares of this world or the trials of life (Matthew 13:20-22) can choke the new life of those born again and justified.[2274] It is also possible, even likely, that many of the *am ha'arets* who heard Jesus and believed on Him for eternal life, lacking any immediate follow-up, fell back into their old patterns. A major part of Jesus' ministry was challenging these new followers to live out the Sermon on the Mount, becoming fully committed disciples.

THE SHEEP, THE COIN, AND THE SON BELONG TO THEIR OWNER

Second, the sheep, the coin, and the son belonged to the owner/shepherd/father *before they were lost.*[2275] The sheep was a member of the shepherd's flock before it was lost; it did not become a member of the flock only after it was found.[2276] The prodigal was a son of his father before he was lost and did not become a son after he repented—he was already a son. Since the "sinners" of verse 2 are illustrated by the lost lamb, the lost coin, and the lost son, these three metaphors identify the saved status of the sinners. The sheep and the coin belonged to their owner, and the son was truly a son.

David prayed,

> *I have gone astray like a lost sheep; seek Your servant, for I do not forget Your commandments (Psalm 119:176).*

David was one of the Shepherd's sheep, he was born again, but he had gone astray. So he asks the Shepherd to seek him out. This is the situation in the Parable of the Lost Sheep.

INVITED TO TABLE FELLOWSHIP

Finally, as Jeremias points out, "it is important to realize that in the east, even today, to invite a man to a meal was an honor. It was an offer of peace, trust, brotherhood, and forgiveness; in short, sharing a table meant sharing life. Table fellowship means fellowship before God. The eating of a piece of broken bread by everyone who shares in the meal brings out the fact that they all have a share in the blessing which the master of the house

---

2274 See discussion of the Parable of the Soils on pp.532 ff.

2275 E. P. Sanders turns these passages upside down and uses them to prove that the "sinners" in Luke 15:2 were eternally damned, "lost." He does this by assuming that "lost" equals "damned." Sanders, *Jesus and Judaism*, 179. Yet in the parable those "lost" belonged to the shepherd, the woman, and the father, before they were lost! Thus "lost" does not mean damned but means "gone astray," and therefore the "sinners" are not unbelievers but are believers who have gone astray, who are saltless.

2276 The word "lost" does not necessarily refer to damnation. Elsewhere in Matthew, instead of calling the sheep "lost," he says they have gone "astray" (Matthew 18:12).

had spoken over the unbroken bread."[2277] He concludes that the sharing of a meal with the sinners had a deeper significance than mere social courtesy. It was an expression of Jesus' mission (Matthew 8:11; Mark 2:7) and anticipates the celebratory messianic feast that will inaugurate the kingdom. "The inclusion of sinners in the community of salvation, achieved in table fellowship, is then a most meaningful expression of the message of the redeeming love of God."[2278] These sinners are saved people!

One can imagine consternation of the Pharisees when Jesus ignores all their prohibitions and enjoys eating a meal with these "sinners." In fact, the majority of those responding to Jesus all over Palestine were from this group. That they are saved people is confirmed by Matthew 18:12-14, where the lost lamb is equated with one of Christ's "little ones."

These considerations should lead one away from the common misunderstanding of the parable that those "lost" are those eternally damned. Rather, as Matthew's account states, the parable represents believing sheep who have "gone astray" (Matthew 18:12) and thus are like those who have "become saltless."

In Luke's version, Jesus says they are "lost."

> *What man among you, if he has a hundred sheep and has lost [Gr apollumi] one of them, does not leave the ninety-nine in the open pasture, and go after the one which is lost, until he finds it?" (Luke 15:4).*

Elsewhere the disciples are called "sheep" (Matthew 10:16). As noted above, in the Greek Old Testament, the psalmist describes himself as one who has "gone astray" saying, "*I have gone astray like a lost* [LXX, *apollumi*] *sheep; seek Your servant, for I do not forget Your commandments*" (Psalm 119:176).[2279] The Hebrew word *ta 'ah* ("gone astray") does not mean "damnation"; it means "*err, wander, go astray,*"[2280] "to stumble, stagger, to totter."[2281] The LXX translates this Hebrew by the Gr word *planaō,* "to cause to go astray."[2282] Having gotten off track, the regenerate and justified psalmist asks the Shepherd to "seek" him. This is what has happened to the *am ha'arets* gathered with Jesus, as He expounds to the objecting Pharisees in the parables of the lost sheep, coin, and son.

Like the psalmist, the sinners and tax collectors are regenerate saints who have either already wandered from their initial response to Christ or have not taken the next steps necessary for kingdom living. They are listening to the Good Shepherd who is seeking them. Some may have already entered the kingdom in the sense of entering the kingdom way of

---

[2277] Joachim Jeremias, *New Testament Theology* (New York: Charles Scribner's Sons, 1971), 115.

[2278] Ibid., 116. Jeremias points out that throughout the Gospels Christ's followers are called "publicans and sinners" (Mark 2:16), "publicans and prostitutes" (Matthew 21:32), or simply "sinners" (Luke 7:27; ibid., 109). It is significant that these phrases were coined by Jesus' opponents. Ibid., 109. Sanders objects to Jeremias's thesis on two grounds. Sanders admits that the "wicked" do not include the *am ha'arets,* but he believes the wicked refer to sinners, and the sinners are not the *am ha'arets*. See Sanders, *Jesus and Judaism*, 179-80.

[2279] Curiously, E. P. Sanders claims that the Gr "*harmartōloi*" always means "the wicked, those who sinned willfully and heinously and who did not repent." Sanders, *Jesus and Judaism*, 177. According to Sanders, Jesus' mission was directed toward these hardened unrepentant people in Palestine. Ibid., 179. This is evangelistically and psychologically absurd, as well as biblically false. Jesus devoted His time to those who wanted to hear and not those who were hardened. Jesus said that He does not cast pearls before swine.

[2280] TWOT, 977.

[2281] BDB, 505.

[2282] BDAG, 821.

living, and others are on the path. They are gathered at a meal with Him. The Pharisees cannot believe that such people are really saved. In fact, however, these "people of the land" were in the kingdom in a saving sense but need to move on beyond the fundamentals of Christ (cf. Hebrews 6:1-2) and "enter the kingdom," in the sense of entering into the rich experience of kingdom life, that is, become "salt," useful for kingdom work (Matthew 23:13).

The Parable of the Prodigal Son

Muslim scholars love to quote this parable as evidence against Christianity and Christians. The reason is that here is a son who is lost, who is freely and graciously welcomed back by his father. They say there is no need for an incarnation, a cross, or an atonement. Furthermore, there is no mediator between them. He simply returns home and his father accepts him. Therefore, Jesus was a good Muslim![2283]

The very title by which this parable is known in the church declares the parable's clear intent. This is the story of a son who has wandered away from his father! The New Testament does not disclose any sense in which unregenerate people may be considered as "sons of God." That high honor is granted only, according to John 1:12-13, "to those who have received him." It follows, therefore, that the reference is to a Christian who has gone astray, just as the lost sheep and the lost coin have exactly the same reference.

THE SON'S REQUEST (LUKE 15:11-12)

And He said, "A certain man had two sons; and the younger of them said to his father, 'Father, give me the share of the estate that falls to me.' And he divided his wealth between them" (Luke 15:11-12).

The younger son requests his inheritance while his father is still alive and in good health. In traditional Middle Eastern culture, this means, "Father, I am eager for you to die!"

Ken Bailey notes that for over fifteen years he has talked with people in the Middle East today, from Turkey to the Sudan, about the implications of the son's request for an inheritance while the Father is still alive.[2284]

The conversation goes like this:

"Has anyone ever made such a request in your village?"

"Never!"

"Could anyone ever make such a request?"

"Impossible!"

"If anyone ever did, what would happen?"

"His father would beat him, of course!"

"Why?"

"This request means—he wants his father to die!"[2285]

[2283] Kenneth E. Bailey, "The Pursuing Father," *Christianity Today* (October 26, 1998): 34.

[2284] Kenneth E. Bailey, *Poet and Peasant and through Peasant Eyes: A Literary-cultural Approach to the Parables in Luke* (Grand Rapids: Wm. B. Eerdmans Publishing Co., 1983), 161-62. Most of the cultural background in the discussion to follow is taken from Bailey's excellent exposition of this parable.

[2285] Bailey cites two exceptions in the hundreds of times he asked this question. In one instance, a believer reported in anguish, "My son wants me to die!" The man's pastor discovered that the son had broached

Bailey concludes, "If the father is a traditional Middle Eastern father, he will strike the boy across the face and drive him out of the house. Surely, anywhere in the world this is an outrageous request. The prodigal is not simply a young boy who is 'off to the big city to make his fame and fortune.' Rather, this young son makes a request that is unthinkable, particularly in Middle Eastern culture. The father is expected to refuse—if he is an oriental patriarch! In fact, he is not, which brings us to the second point."[2286]

THE FATHER'S GIFT (LUKE 15:12)

And he divided his wealth between them.

Remarkably, the father grants the young son's request, gives him his inheritance, and the right to sell it for cash. Five times in the parable the father does not behave like a traditional oriental patriarch. This is the first instance. "In the Middle Eastern milieu the father is expected to explode and discipline the boy for the cruel implication of his demand [i.e. 'I wish you were dead']. It is difficult to imagine a more dramatic illustration of the quality of love which grants freedom even to reject the lover, than is given in this opening scene."[2287]

"The inheritance is substantial. This is a wealthy family that has a herd of fatted calves and a herd of goats. House servants/slaves appear. The house includes a banquet hall large enough to host a crowd that will eat an entire fatted calf in one evening. Professional musicians and dancers are hired for that banquet. The father is respected in the community, and thus the community responds to his invitation."[2288]

And not many days later, the younger son gathered ***everything*** *together and went on a journey into a distant country (v. 13).*

Furthermore, the prodigal "gathered all he had." This means that he is selling his part of the family farm. He "turns it into cash" (NEB).[2289] However, according to local law at the time of Jesus, the son did not have the right to sell the property until his father died.[2290] Yet, he does it anyway.

As that happens, this horrendous family breakdown becomes public knowledge, and the family is shamed before the entire community. Jewish law of the first century provided

---

the question of the inheritance. "Three months later, the father, a Hebrew Christian (a medical doctor), in previously good health, died. The mother said, 'He died that night!' meaning that the night the son dared ask for the inheritance, the father 'died.'" The shock to him was so great that life was over that night. Ibid., 162.

2286 Bailey, "The Pursuing Father," 35.

2287 Bailey, *Poet and Peasant and through Peasant Eyes: A Literary-cultural Approach to the Parables in Luke*, 164.

2288 Bailey, "The Pursuing Father," 35.

2289 A relevant passage in the Mishnah is often cited here. "He who writes over his property to his sons has to write, 'From today and after death,'" the words of R. Judah. R. Yose says, "He does not have [to do so]." He who writes over his property to his son [to take effect] after his death, the father cannot sell the property, because it is written over to the son, and the son cannot sell the property, because it is [yet] in the domain of the father. [If] the father sold [it], the property is sold until he dies. [If] the son sold the property, the purchaser has no right whatever in the property until the father dies. The father harvests the crops and gives the usufruct to anyone whom he wants. And whatever he left already harvested—lo, it belongs to his heirs. See Baba Batra 8:7, in Neusner, *The Mishnah: A New Translation*.

2290 Jeremias, *The Parables of Jesus*, 128.

for the division of an inheritance (when the father was ready to make such a division), but it did not grant the children the right to sell until after the father's death.

In a second departure from the expected norm, the father grants the inheritance and the right to sell, knowing that this right will shame the family before the community.

Thus, from the opening lines of the parable, it is clear that Jesus does not use the typical oriental patriarch as a model for God. Rather, he has broken all the bounds of Middle Eastern patriarchy in creating this image of a different kind of Father. No human father is an adequate model for God. Knowing this, Jesus elevates the figure of father beyond its human limitations and reshapes it for use as a model for God.

THE HURRIED SALE (LUKE 15:13)

> ***And not many days later***, *the younger son gathered everything together and went on a journey into a distant country, and there he squandered his estate with loose living (v. 13).*

The prodigal sells quickly ("not many days later"). He is probably obliged to do so. Because he has shamed his father and his extended family; the villagers are angry and would most likely rise up against him. According to Jewish law, a healthy father may continue to farm the land during his lifetime. As a result, he has to conclude the sale and get out of town as quickly as possible. As mentioned above, Jewish law did not permit such a sale. The prodigal does not care.

EXPENSIVE LIVING (LUKE 15:13)

> *And not many days later, the younger son gathered everything together and went on a journey into a distant country, and there he squandered his estate* ***with loose living*** *(v. 13).*

Many translations and many commentaries have accused the prodigal of "loose living" or "riotous living." The Gr adverb, *asōtōs*, in this phrase, however, does not imply immorality. Jesus gives no hint as to how the prodigal wasted his money. We are only told that he was a spendthrift. At the end of the story, the older son publicly accuses his brother of spending the money on harlots. But the older son has just arrived from the field and knows nothing. He clearly wants to exaggerate his brother's failures. The Gr *asōtōs* "loosely, recklessly, wastefully" refers to behavior which is senseless; living without thinking, a spendthrift and wasteful lifestyle.[2291] The thought is of a disorderly life rather than an immoral one. However, admittedly, for a believer just wasteful spending would be a moral problem. It certainly would not reflect the wisdom of Proverbs nor would it show good stewardship of what really belongs to the Master.

THE *QETSATSAH* CEREMONY

We know from the Dead Sea Scrolls that the Jews of the time of Jesus had a method of punishing any Jewish boy who lost the family inheritance to Gentiles. It was called the "*qetsatsah* ceremony." Shameful behavior, such as that of the younger son, made it certain that he would face *qetsatsah* ceremony if he dared to return to his home village. What

[2291] One ancient writer illustrates this senseless waste by citing as an example of ἀσωτία provision for the washing of feet with spiced wine. BDAG, 148

was the *qetsatsah*?[2292] The villagers would bring a large earthenware jar, fill it with burned nuts and burned corn, and break it in front of the guilty individual. While doing this, the community would shout, "So-and-so is cut off from his people." From that point on, the village would have nothing to do with the wayward lad.

The Amish have something similar to this today, it is called the "shun."

However, the *qetsatsah* ceremony was much worse, it prohibited any further contact with the village again. The one shunned by the Amish can at least eat at a separate table.

The son knows that the greatest dishonor would be to lose this money among the Gentiles. He does and, furthermore, works for someone who owns pigs.

THE PRODIGAL BECOMES A PIG HERDER (LUKE 15:14-15)

> *Now when he had spent everything, a severe famine occurred in that country, and he began to be in need. And he went and attached himself to one of the citizens of that country, and he sent him into his fields to feed swine.*

Ten recorded famines in and around Jerusalem were recorded between 169 BC and AD 70. A lone Jew in a Gentile country would be particularly desperate during such a time. Now his inheritance has ended up in the hands of Gentiles. The *qetsatsah* definitely awaits him should he ever return home. Normally, after spending everything, a son would return home, but the prodigal cannot until he pays back the lost inheritance. So he makes two unsuccessful attempts to find employment. The first attempt is working at feeding pigs. To avoid the *qetsatsah* ceremony, he must get back the money he has wasted and pay it back.

So he attaches (Gr *kollaō*) himself to a citizen of that country. The Greek word is quite strong. He closely unites himself to this citizen.[2293] He is now an indigent and looks for any benefactor who will take care of him. Having come to the community with money and then losing it in reckless living, he has lost the respect of his new community. The normal way a polite Middle Easterner gets rid of unwanted "clingers" is to assign them a task he knows they will refuse.[2294] For a Jew, no fall from favor could be more catastrophic. Becoming a pig herder was the extreme opposite of enjoying the father's favor and blessing. The Jews did not like pork! But his money is spent, and even though he naturally desires to return home, he has broken the rules. He knows that the *qetsatsah* ceremony awaits him if he returns to the village. As he sinks further into psychological and spiritual despair and takes a despised job, he could not be more "lost."

> *And he was longing to fill his stomach with the pods that the swine were eating, and no one was giving anything to him (v. 16).*

2292 "What is kezazah? R. Jose b. Abin answered: If a man sold his field to a Gentile, his relatives used to bring barrels full of parched corn and nuts and break them open in the presence of children, and the children would gather them and proclaim, 'So-and-so is cut off from his inheritance.' If it was returned to him, they used to say, 'So-and-so has returned to his inheritance.' And likewise if a man married a woman who was not fitting for him, his relatives use to bring barrels full of parched corn and nuts and break them open in the presence of children, and the children would gather them and proclaim 'So-and-so is lost to his family.' When he divorced her, they used to say, 'So-and-so has returned to his family.'" See Midrash Ruth in *Midrash Rabba*, ed. Rabbi H. Freedman and Maurice Simon, trans. Rabbi L. Rabinowitz, 10 vols., vol. 8 (London: Soncino Press, 1939), 8:87.

2293 MM, 352.

2294 Bailey, *Poet and Peasant and through Peasant Eyes: A Literary-cultural Approach to the Parables in Luke*, 170.

But becoming a pig herder does not work. The text deliberately affirms, "No one gave him anything." As a pig herder, the prodigal is fed but not paid. What did he eat? The text does not say that he actually *ate* "pods" (Gr *keration*), but it does say that he had reached such a destitute situation that "he was desiring to eat" the pods. For a Jewish young man to reach the point of herding pigs was bad enough. To reach the point of even thinking about eating their food was abhorent indeed! These pods were of two kinds. One was a sweet bean from the carob plant which had a flavor similar to that of chocolate. The other was a bitter harsh tasting berry that grew on another kind of carob tree.[2295] The former was widely eaten and readily available and could easily satisfy hunger. In view of the fact that this was a time of famine, it is likely that the latter pod is meant. The prodigal says in the next verse, with a bit of hyperbole often used by those in such a situation, that he is "dying" of hunger.

THE PRODIGAL REPENTS (LUKE 15:17-19)

But when he came to his senses, he said, "How many of my father's hired men have more than enough bread, but I am dying here with hunger! I will get up and go to my father, and will say to him, 'Father, I have sinned against heaven, and in your sight; I am no longer worthy to be called your son; make me as one of your hired men'" (vv. 17-19).

The prodigal finally "comes to his senses." He repents. It is notable that even in the far country where the prodigal squanders his resources, he is fully conscious of his sonship. We are given his thoughts about what he will tell his father: "*I am no longer worthy to be called your son. Make me as one of your hired servants*" (Luke 15:17-19). These are not the words of one who is not a son, as if it pictures an unsaved person.

Even after squandering the resources his father had placed in his hands, the prodigal is still fully aware that he is his father's son. He is also aware of the lofty privilege of being a son, but he now feels that his conduct makes him unworthy of such a status. He intends to tell his father to reduce him to the level of a hired servant, not because he is not a son, but because he feels that he should tell his father, "*I am no longer worthy to be called your son.*" We hear an echo of these words in the lovely statement in 1 John 3:1, "*Behold what manner of love the Father has bestowed upon us, that we should be called children of God!*" The prodigal feels he has fallen far below the privilege of being called a child or son of his father.

The prodigal steels his nerves for his humiliating entrance into the village. He remembers the *qetsatsah* ceremony and braces himself to endure its shame. The painful interview with his father will not be any easier. The prodigal is expected to return with generous gifts for the family. Instead, he has not only offended his entire home village, but he has lost all of his father's money to Gentiles. It is likely that his return to the village will be accompanied by hostility toward him for having insulted his father.

THE FATHER'S AMAZING LOVE (LUKE 15:20)

And he got up and came to his father. But while he was still a long way off, his father saw him, and felt compassion for him, and ran and embraced him, and kissed him.

[2295] Bock, *Luke 9:51-24:53*, 1311.

But what of his father? Hoping that his son will return to his senses, the father waits day after day, staring down the crowded village street to the road in the distance along which his son disappeared with arrogance and high hopes. He knows what the son faces when he returns—public rejection and disgrace. Knowing this, the father decides in advance to go out to meet his son before the boy reaches the village. If the villagers see the reconciliation between father and son in public, no one in the village will treat the son badly and suggest that the *qetsatsah* ceremony be enacted.

Finally, seeing his son afar off, for the third time, the father departs from the cultural norms. Taking the bottom edge of his long robes in his hand, he runs to welcome his pig-herding son. Because of these robes, an oriental gentleman would never run like this in public. To do so would be humiliating. Then the father falls on his son's neck and kisses him before hearing the son's prepared speech! The father does not demonstrate love in response to his son's confession. Rather, out of his own compassion he empties himself, assumes the form of a servant, and *runs* to welcome his estranged son.

Here we see what the Lord Jesus did. He emptied Himself and took the form of a servant, running toward His "sons" to restore fellowship (Philippians 2:5-11).

In the parable a traditional oriental patriarch would be expected to sit in grand isolation in the house to hear what the wayward boy might have to say for himself. The mother, but not the father, could run down the road and shower the boy with kisses.[2296]

THE SON'S CONFESSION (LUKE 15:21)

The son's confession is genuine, but he underestimates the fullness of his father's forgiving grace.

So he says,

Father, I have sinned against heaven and in your sight,

but he also adds,

and am no longer worthy to be called your son (Luke 15:21).

Here we have genuine repentance. He has been overwhelmed by grace and he responds appropriately.

THREE REASONS FOR THE BANQUET (LUKE 15:22-27)

But instead of rebuking the son, the father throws a banquet in celebration of his return!

But the father said to his slaves, "Quickly bring out the best robe and put it on him, and put a ring on his hand and sandals on his feet; and bring the fattened calf, kill it, and let us eat and be merry; for this son of mine was dead, and has come to life again; he was lost, and has been found." And they began to be merry (Luke 15:22-24).

The servants are ordered to dress the son, a command that ensures that the servants will respect him. They would naturally be awaiting some signal from the father as to how

[2296] In the Old Testament God is often presented as a Father who acts with the tender compassion of a mother (Deuteronomy 32:18; Psalm 131; Isaiah 42:14; 66:13).

they were to treat this pig-herding young man. He is to be dressed with the "best robe." This is most certainly a robe belonging to the Father which he wore on feast days.[2297] When the guests see the boy enter the banquet wearing his father's robe, this will ensure acceptance by the community.

What is the significance of killing a fatted calf? This may reflect an ancient Middle Eastern custom of granting high honor to the invited guest. To slaughter a calf means at least 100 people are invited; otherwise the meat will spoil. A calf was slaughtered for the marriage of the eldest son or for the visit of the governor of a province.

There are three reasons given for the banquet. The first is offered by the father, the second by a little boy in the courtyard of the home, and the third by the older brother.

The Father's reason ...

1. Because my son was once dead and is alive again. Brushing aside all notions of his son's unworthiness, the father says,

> *Bring out the best robe and put it on him, and put a ring on his hand and sandals on his feet for this son of mine was* ***dead and has come to life again; he was lost and has been found*** *(15:23-24).*

The father orders a banquet. He says, "Let us eat and celebrate; for [now comes his reason] *this son of mine was dead and is alive again; he was lost and is found!*" Both in terms of his treatment of the prodigal, as well as by his direct announcement, the father proclaims that the returning young man is his son. But who found him? It was the father. He found him at the edge of the village. Just like the shepherd went and found his lost sheep and the woman went and found her lost coin, so the father, now, possibly merged into a symbol of Christ, went and found his lost son.

But it should be noted carefully that he is not just now becoming his son. On the contrary, this same son previous to this had been "dead" and "lost," but is now "alive" and "found." These words of course do not mean that this son had somehow literally lost his life. Instead, they describe his period of separation from his father. On the level of the entirely human experience in this parable, the father has felt the absence of his son as deeply as if he had died, because he had totally lost contact with him. Their reunion is like a glorious coming to life and a joyful rediscovery of the shared father-son experience. Any father who has long been separated from a son whom he loves dearly can fully relate to these words.

The father's actions are a model for all of us. In returning to God, particularly after a long separation from Him, repentant Christians are likely to experience a deep sense of unworthiness. They may feel that they have disgraced the Christian name and they may be all too aware of bringing disrepute to God their heavenly Father. Such Christians need to be reassured of the full and gracious acceptance God extends to them when they return. Their forgiveness is complete, and they need not feel as if they are forever second-class Christians, as if they now serve God as mere hired servants. Instead, they should be encouraged to enjoy all the privileges of sonship, symbolized by the robe, the ring, and the sandals.

[2297] Bailey, *Poet and Peasant and through Peasant Eyes: A Literary-cultural Approach to the Parables in Luke*, 185.

But as is transparent from the story, though the prodigal returns to the full experience of sonship, he does not get back the possessions he has foolishly squandered. Restoration for the straying Christian is real, but the loss of time, potential, and opportunity is equally real. The portion of any Christian's life that is spent away from God as well as the rewards that might have been earned during that time are permanently lost.

The little boy's reason ...

The second reason for the banquet is given by the little boy.

2. Because he has received him back safe and sound.

> *Now his older son was in the field, and when he came and approached the house, he heard music and dancing. And he summoned one of the servants* (Gr *pais*, "little boy") *and began inquiring what these things might be. And he said to him, "Your brother has come, and your father has killed the fattened calf,* ***because he has received him back safe and sound****" (Luke 15:25-27).*

The older son comes in from the field and on hearing the music calls to a servant, a *pais*. This Gr word can mean any of three things. The first is "son," which does not fit this text. The second is "servant," which also does not fit, because all the servants are busy in the house serving the huge banquet. The third option is "young boy." Middle Eastern Syriac and Arabic versions have always chosen this third alternative. As the older son approaches his family home in the center of the village, he naturally meets a crowd of young boys who are not old enough to recline with the elders at the banquet, but are outside the house dancing in tune to the music and enjoying the occasion in their own boisterous manner.

The older son asks him what the party is all about and the lad says, "*Your brother has come, and your father has killed the fatted calf, because* (now comes the second reason for the banquet) *he* (the father) *received him* (the prodigal) ***healthy and sound*** (i.e. with peace!)."

The word translated here as "sound" is the Gr *hugiainō*. This means "to be in good health." But in the Greek Old Testament (the Septuagint), this same Greek word appears 14 times, and without exception it translates the Hebrew *shalōm* "peace."[2298] When a first-century Jew used the word *hugiainō*, he or she mentally translated the Hebrew word *shalōm*, which includes "good health" but means so very much more, harmony and wholeness.

Probably, Jesus used the word *shalōm* in the story. The point is that the banquet is celebrating restored harmony (*shalōm*) between the father and his estranged son, and the community has come to participate in that celebration. Rather than a *qetsatsah* ceremony of rejection, they are participating in the joy of a restored fellowship between the father and the prodigal.

The language of the young boy, "He received him" (and plans to eat with him), reminds the listener of the Pharisees' complaint, "This fellow [Jesus] welcomes sinners and eats with them." "The young boy's speech confirms that the father has clearly evolved into a symbol for Jesus. Jesus receives sinners and eats with them. In this parable, the father does the same."[2299]

[2298] A verb is supplied as in Genesis 29:6, "is he well" (LXX). The Hebrew says, "is it well to him.

[2299] Bailey, "The Pursuing Father," 40.

THE OLDER SON'S ANGER (LUKE 15:28-30)

The older brother's reason ...
But what is the older brother's explanation for the banquet?
3. So that the younger son might celebrate with his friends.

But he became angry, and was not willing to go in; and his father came out and began entreating him. But he answered and said to his father, "Look! For so many years I have been serving you, and I have never neglected a command of yours; and yet you have never given me a kid, ***that I might be merry with my friends****; but when this son of yours came, who has devoured your wealth with harlots, you killed the fattened calf for him" (Luke 15:28-30).*

The older son believes that the banquet is being given to *reward the prodigal* for his successful efforts to return home. He has completely missed the point. The banquet is given to celebrate the *joy of the father* in that he has found his son!

Why won't the older brother go in? If the banquet were only a celebration of the prodigal's return, he would most likely join in the festivities. But it was more than that. *It was* ***shalōm****, a restoration of fellowship.* If this had only been a celebration of the prodigal's return, the festival would not have bothered the older son, the details of his sin could be worked out later. But this is a celebration of restoration to fellowship with no need to pay for his sins. The little boy has explained that it is all over. The father has already reconciled with the son, and the son did not have to pay for his sins! This is why the older brother is angry.

The older son is furious at this unconditional acceptance. His younger brother should be punished, but instead the father showers him with a banquet! The older brother is so angry, he takes the radical step of breaking his fellowship with his father; he refuses to go into the banquet. For a son to be present and to refuse participation in such a banquet is an unspeakable public insult to the father. A cultural equivalent might be the case of a son in the West who has a heated public shouting match with his father in the middle of a wedding banquet after a large family wedding. A shouting match is not unthinkable, but not in public at such a banquet.[2300]

THE FATHER'S RESPONSE TO THE OLDER BROTHER (LUKE 15:31)

For a fourth time the father departs from the normal response of a Middle Eastern patriarch. For the second time in the same day he offers a demonstration of unexpected love. However, on this occasion he accepts the older son, who has publicly insulted him. Local culture would require that the Father proceed with the banquet and ignore the public insult. He could deal with the older son later. Instead, in painful public humiliation, the "father came out and began entreating him" (Luke 15:28), urging him to join in the banquet. In other words, he goes out and seeks one more lost son!

Then, for a fifth and final time, patriarchy is transcended. The father is expected to explode and order a public beating of the older son because of his insults. Instead he compassionately and gently says,

And he said to him, "My child, you have always been with me, and all that is mine is yours" (Luke 15:31).

[2300] Ibid.

This remarkable father is a symbol for God, whose goodness, love, forgiveness, care, joy, and compassion have no limits at all. Jesus presents God's generosity by using all the imagery that His culture provides. The father continues,

> *But we had to be merry and rejoice, for this brother of yours was dead and has begun to live, and was lost and has been found (Luke 15:32).*

The older son had referred to his brother as "this son of yours," but the father reminds him, he is your "brother." He was "lost" [Gr *apollumi*], but now he has been "found." This common word is used 90 times in the New Testament.[2301] Its most general meaning is "to ruin, destroy."[2302] A frequent meaning is to die physically.[2303] In other contexts it refers to the loss of reward.[2304] It is also a term in some contexts for eternal damnation.[2305] On a number of occasions, this word is found in verses containing the great paradox, "He who has found his life will lose [*apollumi*] it, and he who has lost [*apollumi*] his life for My sake will find it" (Matthew 10:39).[2306]

What does it refer to in the parable of the lost sheep (Luke 15:6), the lost coin (Luke 15:9), and the lost son (Luke 15:24, 32)? Because the term is used in a father/son relationship, the lost son is still a son, and we therefore are not dealing with a person lost in the sense of eternal damnation but lost in the sense of broken fellowship with one's father. The most likely meaning in Luke 15 is found in the passages regarding the finding and losing of one's life. To lose one's life in Luke is not final damnation; rather, it is the spiritual and psychological ruin that comes on the Christian who sets out to find a rich life by means of material benefit and security (Luke 9:24-25; 17:33), and avoidance of hardship. *This is a precise parallel to what the younger son did.* He was not damned when he went to the far country (instead he was "ruined"), and he did not become a son when he returned and was found. In the words of Jesus the son *thought* he was going to find "life," through money and pleasure, but in actuality he found a great loss of life; he experienced "death"—death of goals, fulfillment, success, and family fellowship. Of course, when Jesus says that He came to save the unsaved "lost," like Zacchaeus (Luke 19:9-10), His "salvation" also included spiritual restoration as well as deliverance from judgment (v. 10).

However, unlike Zacchaeus, the Prodigal was not lost in the sense of being on the highway to hell. Rather, he was lost in the sense of spiritual backsliding. Then he was "found," restored to fellowship with his father. While living senselessly and almost coming to the point of eating pig food, he was truly "dead," living a life of carnality. But on his return, he came to life again, enjoying true life in fellowship with his father (John 10:10; 17:3).

The father lavishes a great feast on the younger son but no banquet was ever held in honor of the faithful older brother. How can this be fair? The point of the parable is *grace.*

2301 For full discussion of *apollumi*, see pp. 294 ff.

2302 BDAG 115. Luke 5:37; James 1:11.

2303 Matthew 2:13, 8:25, 21:41; Mark 3:6; Luke 13:3, etc.

2304 Matthew 10:42; 2 John 8.

2305 2 Thessalonians 2:10. If *Gehenna* always refers to eternal damnation, then Matthew 5:29-30 would apply. However, as argued elsewhere, it is doubtful that *Gehenna* refers to eternal damnation in this passage. It is more likely that it refers to being burned alive in the garbage dump outside of Jerusalem as the final disgraceful death of an unfaithful Christian life. See elsewhere in this book, pp. 904 ff.

2306 Matthew 16:25; Mark 8:35; Luke 9:24; 17:23.

The older brother and many of us today have trouble accepting and understanding this. It is simply unbelievable. The Pharisees are completely refuted; they understood nothing of the grace of God.

This parable is a portrayal of the goodness, love, compassion, and acceptance of God toward wayward Christians whom He loves and seeks.

"If the older son accepts the love now offered to him, he will be obliged to treat the prodigal with the same loving acceptance with which the father welcomed the pig herder."[2307] Just as the older son needs to become compassionate like the father in the parable, so the Pharisees who have criticized Jesus for eating with "sinners" must change their attitudes toward "sinners" and welcome them with the love of God. Are they willing? We are not told. More importantly the question is, "Are *we* willing?"

Summary

Robert Robinson was a poet and hymn writer. Many of us have sung his hymns. Perhaps his most beloved hymn was "Come Thou fount of every blessing, tune my heart to sing Thy grace." If you read through that hymn, you will observe in the third verse that Robert Robinson very vulnerably shared about a tendency in his own life, one that pictures struggles that can occur in any believer's life.

He wrote, "Prone to wander, Lord I feel it. Prone to leave the God I love. Here's my heart, Oh take and seal it, seal it for Thy courts above." Robert Robinson was prone to wander. He was prone to defect. He was prone to leave the God he loved. In fact he did drift from the all-sufficiency of a Christ-centered faith. He took a step back, and then another, and then another and soon he was leading an openly hedonistic evil life, in opposition to the gospel of Jesus Christ. For years he walked away from the Lord.

Then one day Robert Robinson was in a carriage traveling from one city to another.[2308]

There was one stop along the way. On the stop a young woman got on the carriage, and, as they were traveling together, this young woman was reading a book of poems and hymns. She came to a particular poem that she did not understand. As she was reading it, she handed the book of poems over to the man and said, "Excuse me, sir. Could you explain this poem, this hymn to me?"

Robinson looked at the poem, and it began by reading, "Come Thou fount of every blessing, tune my heart to sing Thy grace." He couldn't talk for a long time. Then he began to weep, tears streaming down his face. Finally, he said, "I wrote this poem. I wrote this hymn. I once believed these words, but no more."

And this woman, being guided by the Holy Spirit, took back the book and after a moment gently replied, "But then, remember what else you wrote? 'Prone to wander, Lord I feel it, prone to leave the God I love.' That's what you've done. You've wandered, you've drifted. But remember how you ended your poem. 'Here's my heart, Oh take and seal it, seal it for Thy courts above.'"

On that day Robert Robinson came back to the faith. Robert Robinson was prone to wander. He was prone to drift like many of us, perhaps like all of us.[2309]

[2307] Bailey, "The Pursuing Father," 40.

[2308] P. Eckert, *Steve Green's MIDI Hymnal: A Complete Toolkit for Personal Devotions and Corporate Worship* (Bellingham, WA: Logos Bible Software, 1998), s.v. "Come Thou Fount of Every Blessing".

[2309] K. W. Osbeck, *101 Hymn Stories* (Grand Rapids: Kregel Publications, 1982), 50.

Readers of this parable must ask, "Where are you?" "Do you need to return?" What is Jesus' attitude toward you in your wandering? The parable helps us. It teaches us that God is waiting and watching with great love and anticipation. God is the father in the parable arising every morning and looking toward the horizon along the path leading to his home. He is not the God of Experimentalist theology, sternly warning the sinning believer that he may not be saved, and that unless he looks again to his foundations, he might go to hell. Jesus is praying for your return today. He intercedes to the Father for us. We are told this in Hebrews that He is not ashamed to call us brothers (Hebrews 2:11), yet, He is our compassionate High Priest.

Suddenly, God sees you in the distance, and His heart leaps with joy. Like the father in the parable, He does not sit and wait for you to make your way to the home. He bounds down the path with heart leaping inside Him and embraces you, and exclaims, "Welcome home."

Notice:

- His eyes of mercy; He sees you from afar off.
- His emotions of compassion for you as His lost son.
- His feet of grace. He ran. Grace takes the initiative. It responds before we ask.
- His arms of love. He embraced his son in love.
- His kiss of forgiveness. The Father's kiss not only assured the prodigal of His welcome, it also sealed his pardon.

Yes, the Pharisees got it right, "This man receives sinners and eats with them."

46
Life in the Spirit

IN ROMANS 8 the apostle turns from the struggle in Romans 7 and explains the source and method of living abundantly. It is by the Spirit of God and the use of certain spiritual weapons that our Christian experience can be increasingly characterized by "life and peace." Indeed, persistence in using the means of grace will result not only in a vital Christian life but also joint heirship with the Messiah in the final destiny of man.

Although these verses have often been understood to present a contrast between persons who have "genuine" faith and those who merely profess it, in the following exposition we will suggest that two categories of believers are in view, those who walk by the Spirit and those who walk by the flesh.

Freedom from Sin's Power (8:1-7)

THE TWO WALKS (8:1-5)

Paul begins with a thrilling proclamation. There is *no condemnation*!

> *There is therefore now no condemnation for those who are in Christ Jesus (Romans 8:1).*

The majority of Greek manuscripts, add the phrase, "*who do not walk according to the flesh, but according to the Spirit*" (Romans 8:1, NKJV). While this may be an interpolation from Romans 8:4, it has good manuscript support[2310] and fits the sanctification context well. Only those who walk by means of the Spirit are free from "condemnation." But what kind of condemnation is in view? Many scholars view the condemnation in view here as final condemnation to the lake of fire.[2311]

[2310] This phrase is found in the KJV (which was based on later manuscripts because the earlier manuscripts available now were not known at that time) and the majority of Greek manuscripts (most of much later dates). It is not in the two earliest Greek manuscripts of Romans 8: Aleph, original hand, B (fourth century); the original hand of D (sixth century for Pauline epistles), and a significant number of other manuscripts from a wide geographical distribution; it is omitted in most modern translations. However, the phrase does reflect an early fifth century view (A) and sixth century (D for Pauline epistles), and, more importantly, it fits the sanctification context well. See the similar statement in 8:4.

[2311] See Moo, *The Epistle to the Romans*, 473. See also Schreiner, *Romans*, 399. While this is possible, the word itself properly speaks of an unspecified penalty for sin, that is, the consequence of sin. We argue that the penalty in view here in 7:24 is not damnation, "Wretched man that I am. Who will set me free from the body of this death?" Paul felt condemned to serve sin; this is the penalty in view, and the condemnation is spiritual and psychological "death." The subject in Romans 8 is sanctification, which is Paul's answer to Romans 7.

The word "condemnation" (Gr *katakrima*) is best understood to mean "penal servitude."[2312] Deissman suggests, "It signifies a burden issuing from a judicial pronouncement— a servitude," and he believes this meaning "is particularly suitable in Romans 8:1."[2313]

The word "*therefore*" in Romans 8:1 refers back to the preceding verse, "*Thank God*" (Romans 7:25). Paul thanks God that deliverance from the penal servitude to sin is available to overcome what he described in 7:24 ("*wretched man that I am! Who will set me free from the body of this death*"). This condemnation is called "death" in Romans 8:13. It refers to spiritual/psychological death that befalls the believer who walks according to the flesh.

> *For the law of the Spirit of life in Christ Jesus has set you free from the law of sin and of death (Romans 8:2).*

Deliverance from this kind of condemnation (spiritual and psychological "death") is achieved through progressive sanctification by means of *a new and higher principle of life* which Paul calls the "*law of the Spirit of life*."[2314]

The escape from condemnation in this chapter is not through the penal substitution of Christ, but, according to verse 2, is through transformational righteousness, that is, progressive sanctification[2315] made available to us through the work of the Holy Spirit in our lives. This higher law has set believers free from the lower law, the law of sin and death.[2316]

> *For what the Law could not do, weak as it was through the flesh, God did: sending His own Son in the likeness of sinful flesh and as an offering for sin, He condemned sin in the flesh (8:3).*

The problem was not with the law but with the flesh. It was too weak to obey. So God solved this problem by releasing the flesh from its sin master at the point in time we believed. This occurred upon our union with Christ in His death and resurrection (Romans 6:1-11).

Why did God condemn sin in the flesh? His purpose was,

2312 Bruce, *Romans: An Introduction and Commentary*, 159. Arndt and Gingrich say that *katakrima* signifies "not condemnation, but the punishment following a sentence," BAGD, 412. Murray agrees. Condemnation is the opposite of justification but what aspect of justification? He says that the context is talking about sanctification and not expiation. "Hence what is thrust into the foreground in the terms 'no condemnation' is not only freedom from the guilt but also freedom from the enslaving power of sin" (John Murray, The Epistle to the Romans, NICNT, 2 vols. in one, 6-1:275).

2313 G. Adolph Deissman, *Bible Studies*, reprint, 1923 ed. (Winona Lake: Alpha Publications, 1979), 265.

2314 The term is defined by looking at its contrast. The law of the Spirit of life is the opposite of the law of sin and death. What is the law of sin and death? In 7:21 it is a principle (same Greek word), namely, a law. F. F. Bruce says the law of the Spirit of life refers to the principle of the Spirit which is life. See F. F. Bruce, *The Letter of Paul to the Romans: An Introduction and Commentary*, 2nd ed., Tyndale New Testament commentaries (Grand Rapids: Wm. B. Eerdmans Publishing Co., 1985), 160. John Murray says that the law refers to a regulating and actuating power as well as a legislating authority. It is the regulating and actuating power of the Holy Spirit as the Spirit of life. It is the power of the Holy Spirit operative in us to make us free from the power of sin which is unto death. Murray, *The Epistle to the Romans*, 276.

2315 For an excellent discussion of this chapter proving this point see Lowe, "There Is No Condemnation (Rom. 8:1): But Why Not?" However, Lowe eventually adopts the Neonomian idea that the works of the believer are non-meritorious and are a condition for salvation (p. 246).

2316 This cannot refer to the Law of Moses because that was holy (7:12) and spiritual (7:14) but to "the inward rule of the sin principle." H. P. Liddon, *Explanatory Analysis of St. Paul's Epistle to the Romans* reprint ed. (Minneapolis: James and Klock, 1977), 127.

In order that the requirement of the Law might be fulfilled in us, who do not walk according to the flesh, but according to the Spirit (8:4).[2317]

Christ condemned sin in the flesh so that the Law might be fulfilled in us, but Paul clarifies that those among us who will experience the fulfillment of the Law are those "*who walk not according to the flesh but according to the Spirit.*" He therefore presents two possibilities for "us," that is, Christians: we can walk according to the flesh (like non-Christians) or according to the Spirit. Paul has told us elsewhere that it is possible for Christians to walk *kata anthrōpon*, "as mere men" (1 Corinthians 3:3).

The phrase "*who walk not according to the flesh but according to the Spirit*" has been understood in several ways. Experimentalists understand this as a descriptive phrase characteristic of *all* who are regenerate.[2318] Others, including the Partners, understand this to describe the manner in which the law is fulfilled, if the condition of walking by the Spirit is met.[2319] There are three factors, however, which make it clear that not all genuine believers meet this condition!

First, the context says that true life is conditioned on "*putting to death the deeds of the body*" and that this is not automatic. It is possible for Christians to "die" (Romans 8:12). Second, the inclusion of the phrase "who do not walk according to flesh" seems to suggest that there are two possibilities, not one, for the regenerate person. Fitzmeyer agrees:

The Greek uses a participle with the negative mē which gives almost a proviso or conditional force to the expression, "provided we walk not according to the flesh." It thus insinuates that Christian living is not something that flows automatically, as it were, from baptism.[2320]

As Liddon insists, "The condition of retaining this freedom from sin is the cooperation of the regenerate will."[2321]

Third, it seems evident that Paul is referring here to what he has taught elsewhere. "*Walk by the Spirit and you will not carry out the desires of the flesh*" (Galatians 5:16). There, the walk is not automatic for all Christians but is conditional. The contexts appear very similar. Paul also says, "*If we live by the Spirit, let us also walk by the Spirit*" (Galatians 5:25). He is obviously saying that, while all Christians live by means of the Spirit, not all necessarily walk that way.

[2317] It is important to note that the requirement of the Law is to be fulfilled "in us" (i.e., in sanctification) and not "to us" or "on our behalf" (i.e., soteriology). Elsewhere, the requirement which is to be fulfilled is the sum of the Law, to love one another (13:8).

[2318] See, for example, William G. T. Shedd, *A Critical and Doctrinal Commentary on the Epistle of St. Paul to the Romans*, reprint ed. (Grand Rapids: Zondervan Publishing House, 1967), 232. He argues that the clause indicates the necessary effect of justification. He takes the preceding verse to refer to justification: "Those to whom Christ's work is imputed (4:24), and in whom the requirement of the law is thereby completely fulfilled (8:4), and to whom there is consequently no condemnation (8:1), are a class of persons who are characterized by a pious life, though not a sinless and perfect one. The imputed righteousness or justification, spoken of in vv. 3 and 4, is accompanied with the inherent righteousness or sanctification, spoken of in v. 2. The former does not exist without the latter. St. Paul conjoins them and mentions both, in proof that the believer is not in a state of condemnation" (p. 233).

[2319] Sanday, *A Critical and Exegetical Commentary on the Epistle to the Romans*, 385.

[2320] Fitzmeyer, "Romans," 2:315.

[2321] Liddon, *Explanatory Analysis of St. Paul's Epistle to the Romans*, 128. Bruce similarly agrees that two possible kinds of walks for a Christian are being described. See Bruce, *The Letter of Paul to the Romans: An Introduction and Commentary*, 157.

For those who are according to the flesh set their minds on the things of the flesh, but those who are according to the Spirit, the things of the Spirit (Romans 8:5).

Two kinds of Christians are contrasted in this verse: believers who walk according to flesh and believers who walk according to the Spirit. A Christian can have his mind set either upon what the flesh desires or upon what the Spirit desires.

Verses 4-7 and later in 12-17 continue this contrast. The descriptions of the two kinds of Christians can be seen in the following table.

	SPIRITUAL CHRISTIAN	CARNAL CHRISTIAN
8:4	walks according to the Spirit	walks according to the flesh
8:5	sets mind on the Spirit	sets mind on the flesh
8:6	life and peace	death
8:7		hostile to God not subject to God unable to obey God
8:12	puts to death the deeds of the body	lives according to the flesh
8:13	those being led by the Spirit of God life	those who walk according to the flesh death
8:17	those who suffer with Christ joint-heirs of Christ	those who do not suffer with Him heirs of God

Paul summarizes the first twelve verses with the statement, "*So then,* ***brethren,*** *we are under obligation, not to the flesh, to live according to the flesh*" (Romans 8:12). He is saying that it is possible for "brethren" to walk according to the flesh. It is possible for brethren to be characterized by the things on the right hand side of the chart. The result is that they, Christians, will "die."

The other alternative summarizes the items on the left side of the chart and in v. 13 says they are described as "*by the Spirit putting to death the deeds of the body.*" The result of this activity is that these brethren will "live." Thus, truly abundant life is meant and not just regeneration.

That it is possible for these brothers to avoid putting to death the deeds of the body is obvious because he says, "If." Paul's picture here is of a battle. A Christian must choose life or death, fellowship with God or spiritual impoverishment. Paul evidently has in mind his own struggle in the verses Romans 7:14-25.

THE TWO MINDS (8:6-7)

What does it mean to walk "according to the flesh" (Gr *kata sarka*)? Paul explains that it means to set one's mind on the things of the flesh. To walk according to the Spirit, means to set one's mind on the things of the Spirit. These two kinds of walks begin in the mind:

For the mind set on the flesh is death, but the mind set on the Spirit is life and peace (Romans 8:6).

A mind set on the flesh is death. By "death" here he means the opposite of "life and peace." Peace in Romans means either peace with God as a result of reconciliation (Romans

1:7; 5:1) or peace in the sense of wholeness, harmonious relations, and mental health (Rom 2:17; 14:17, 19; 15:13, 33; 16:20). The connection with "joy" and harmonious interpersonal relations (Romans 14:17, 19) fits well with the sanctification context of Romans 8 and is the meaning here.

"Life" (Gr *zōē*) is often used of an abundant quality of life beyond regeneration, which is the possession of those who "persevere in doing good" (Romans 2:7).[2322] The "reign in life" of the believer (Romans 5:17) is called "much more" than the reign in death. Therefore, abundant life, which is a vibrant experience with Christ, is the subject here; it is "newness of life" (Romans 6:4).

Death, being the opposite of life and peace, is not final commitment to the lake of fire. It is the life of anxiety and emptiness which comes to anyone (believer or nonbeliever) who sets his mind on the wrong things:

> *Because the mind set on the flesh is hostile toward God; for it does not subject itself to the law of God, for it is not even able to do so (Romans 8:7).*

Here, we have a key to the seeming inability of many Christians to flourish in their Christian lives. When a Christian sets his mind on the flesh, he is hostile to God and is cut off from the Holy Spirit and therefore is unable to obey. Successful Christian living begins in the mind, our thought life. One clear way to set our minds on the things of the Spirit obviously involves daily time in prayer, meditation on Scripture, and our moment by moment choices to direct our thoughts to God and His way of Life (2 Cor. 10:5; Philippians 4:8; Romans 12:1-2; Proverbs 23:7; Matthew 5:8; 15:19). The way a Christian walks by the Spirit is to set his mind on the things of the Spirit, and daily committing all situations into His hands in prayer.

To say that these verses refer to a contrast between Christians and non-Christians rather than between two kinds of Christians not only contradicts the facts of Christian experience but the rest of the New Testament as well. On this view all Christians "walk according to the Spirit" (8:4), have their minds "set upon ... the things of the Spirit" (8:5), and have their minds "set upon the Spirit" (8:6). This contradicts Paul's teaching elsewhere that walking in the Spirit is not automatic or inevitable (Galatians 5:16). In addition, it is refuted by the conditionality of this walk in the immediate context of Romans 8. In verse 13 the possibility of a rich spiritual experience ("life") is conditioned on putting to death the deeds of the body. It is not the automatic possession of each Christian. To say these things are true of all Christians does not accurately represent the past two thousand years of Christian experience.

[2322] See, for example, 1:17: the just shall live by faith—abundant life, vital fellowship with God; 6:2: continue to live in sin—a present experience of life; 7:9-10: he was alive apart from the law once, but when sin came, he died; 10:5: Moses says that the man who practices the righteousness based on law will live by that righteousness—have a rich and meaningful life; 14:8: if we live, we live for the Lord; 2:7: eternal life—enriched experience of it as a result of works; 5:17: reign in life—abundant life; 6:4: walk in newness of life—a rich experience of life now, not regeneration; 6:22: the eternal life that comes as a result of works—enriched experience of life; 7:10: the commandment was to result in life—abundant life, but it resulted in death (Murray admits that life here is life in the path of moral righteousness.); 8:2: the Spirit of life is the Spirit who brings true life—release from the struggle in chapter 7; 8:6: mind set on the Spirit is life and peace. See Murray, *The Epistle to the Romans*, 1:252.

Freedom from Sin's Sphere (8:8-11)

IN THE FLESH (8:8)

Those who are in the flesh cannot please God (Romans 8:8).

Paul now reminds them of their situation when they were "in" the flesh, that is, when they were non-Christians. The verse opens with the conjunction *de*, variously translated "and" (NASB; RSV), "so then" (NKJV), "moreover" (Wuest), and is left untranslated by the NIV.[2323] Having spoken of the inability of Christians to obey when their minds are set on the flesh, he now reminds them that, when they were unsaved ("in the flesh"), they had no possibility of knowing the fulfillment of the Law in them. But they *are* saved, and they therefore not only have the possibility of this experience but the obligation (8:12) to live on this new plane. Because verse 9 contrasts sharply with verse 8, they are to be joined together. Thus verse 8 is not a continuation and exposition of v. 7 but is to be connected to verse 9. The most contextually accurate rendition is to translate *de* by "now," or "now then," signifying that a new paragraph has begun.

That a transition to a new subject is intended is further substantiated by Paul's shift from "*according to the flesh*" to "*in the flesh*" in verse 8. Being "in the *flesh*" (Gr *en sarki*) is a different concept than walking "according to the flesh" (*kata sarka*) of verses 1-7. The New Testament avows that it is possible for Christians to walk as mere men (Gr *kata anthrōpon*).[2324] It is possible for Christians to make plans according to the flesh (*kata sarka*, 2 Corinthians 1:17). In an instructive non-ethical usage of "flesh,"[2325] Paul draws a sharp distinction between being "in the flesh" (*en sarki*), that is, in the sphere of bodily existence, and walking "according to the flesh" (*kata sarka*), that is, walking according to a standard of weakness (2 Corinthians 10:2-3). The fact that Paul distinguishes between *en sarki* and *kata sarka* in this non-ethical passage lends support to the distinction that is drawn here. It is one thing to be "in the flesh," to be in that sphere of life with only those weak resources (i.e., to be unregenerate) and quite another to be in the sphere of the Spirit.

We therefore disagree with Moo[2326] and Schreiner[2327] and concur with Dunn that the contrast is not between Christians and non-Christians. Christians may be "determined by the flesh,"[2328] even though they are no longer in that sphere.[2329] It is one thing to be "in the flesh," but it is another thing to walk "according to the flesh." These terms are not synonymous in the New Testament. Christians can walk "according to the flesh," but they are never described in the New Testament as being in that sphere of life, "in the flesh."

[2323] This is a flexible conjunction and can often express a contrast or a transition to a new subject. Abbott-Smith, 98.

[2324] 1 Corinthians 3:3.

[2325] As far as this writer can tell, the expression is used only in a non-ethical sense outside of Romans 8 with the possible exception of 2 Corinthians 1:17. See Romans 1:3; 4:1; 9:3, 5; 1 Corinthians 1:26; 10:18; 2 Corinthians 1:17; 5:16; 10:2; 11:18; Galatians 4:23, 29; 5:17; Ephesians 6:5; Colossians 3:22; 1 Peter 4:6; John 8:15. The usage in Romans 8, however, seems to be distinctly ethical in view of verses 5-7.

[2326] Moo, *The Epistle to the Romans*, 487.

[2327] Schreiner, *Romans*, 411.

[2328] Dunn, *Romans 1-8*, 425.

[2329] See chapter 32 for documentation of this point.

In verse 13 Paul says that it is possible for Christians to "live according to the flesh." In that verse he returns to his use of the expression "according to flesh" (*kata sarka*) after the parenthetical contrast between Christians and non-Christians in verses 8-11. Even though it is possible for Christians to walk "*according* to the flesh," it is emphatically asserted here that Christians can never be "*in* the flesh."[2330]

IN THE SPIRIT (8:9-11)

In sharp contrast to their former life in the flesh, Paul asserts they are no longer in that sphere. They are now in a new sphere and thus able to live Christ's way of life due to the presence of the indwelling Spirit.

> *But you are not in the flesh but in the Spirit, if indeed the Spirit of God dwells in you. Now if anyone does not have the Spirit of Christ, he is not His. And if Christ is in you, the body is dead because of sin, but the spirit is alive because of righteousness. But if the Spirit of Him who raised Jesus from the dead dwells in you, He who raised Christ Jesus from the dead will also give life to your mortal bodies through His Spirit who indwells you (Romans 8:8-11, NKJV).*

We would not go astray if we asserted that the apostle is here teaching that not only does the indwelling Spirit revive and revitalize our spirit (8:10), but indeed, as Christians walk with an orientation toward the Spirit, the Holy Spirit will impart spiritual life, sanctifying their bodies. A future physical resurrection is not the subject in this context. The Holy Spirit overcomes the state of death which characterizes our mortal bodies and instead expresses new life in Christ through them.

Freedom to Really Live (8:12-17)

To this point Paul has taught the Romans that God has released them from their penal servitude to sin (or power of sin) and has made that freedom experientially available to those who walk according to the Spirit (8:1-7). Then, in a parenthetical aside, he reminded them that they are no longer unsaved, that is, living in the *sphere* of the flesh. Indeed, all believers have the promise that one day we will be done with sin altogether in the resurrection (8:8-11).

Returning to his original topic, Paul concludes that because we have been delivered from penal servitude, we have therefore no obligation to live in accordance with the flesh (*kata sarka*). He introduces *kata* again because he is now back to the subject of Christians walking "according to" either flesh or the Spirit. Instead, we are now free to be as God intended us to be. We are free to experience true life.

THE TWO OBLIGATIONS (8:12-13)

In order to live abundantly, we must realize that we have no obligation to the sin principle any more. Furthermore, we must accept our obligation to live according to the Spirit:

> *So then, **brethren**, we are under obligation, not to the flesh, to live according to the flesh—for if you are living according to the flesh, you must die [thanatoō] but if by the Spirit you are putting to death the deeds of the body, you will live (Romans 8:12-13).*

[2330] The phrase is used in Romans 7:5 where it means to be a non-Christian.

If Christians ("brethren") live *kata sarka*, they will die. "Death" is the opposite of life. "Life" in this verse comes as a result of "putting to death the misdeeds of the body" as Christians live ***kata** pneuma* (the *kata* must be supplied, but it is necessary from the parallelism with ***kata** sarka*). John Calvin emphasizes, "Paul implies that the baptized Christian could still be interested in the 'deeds, actions, pursuits' of a man dominated by *sarx*." Hence, he exhorts him to make use of the Spirit received; this is the debt that is owed to Christ."[2331] "The life of the flesh is the death of man and the death of the flesh is the life of man."[2332]

We therefore disagree with Schreiner who claims that "death" refers to final damnation.[2333] That kind of "death" is the result of Adam's sin and our identification with him. But "death" in this passage is the result of something we do. It is a spiritual/psychological death that results from a carnal lifestyle. Since Schreiner does not believe that a "carnal lifestyle" is possible for a "true" Christian, his system will not allow the text to speak for itself.

Experimental Predestinarians have great difficulty with this passage. It seems that " life" comes as a result of perseverance in works. Schreiner and Caneday say that death means damnation, and therefore its opposite in their system, "life," must mean justification. They believe that "life" refers to heaven when we die. In support of their thesis, they quote Galatians 6:8 which refers to "eternal life," and then they import their incorrect understanding of life in that passage into Romans 8:13. They apparently think it is obvious that eternal life is best understood as a state of existence in heaven and not a dynamic fellowship that believers now have and which varies in degree. Schreiner and Caneday incomprehensibly argue that there is no uncertainty reflected in the "if clause" in verse 13. Rather, they say, this is a "warning to resist the temptation to live according to the way of the flesh and die in the last day."[2334] Of course, that is false. There is no danger of eternal death for believers on the last day (John 6:39-40), but it appears that Schreiner and Caneday have contradicted themselves and agreed that there is uncertainty after all. What their system does not allow is that there can be uncertainty as to whether a "true" Christian will persevere in walking in the Spirit to the end of life. A "true" Christian in their system could never "die."

Sellers boldly calls a spade a spade. "The one who does keep his salvation does so by mortifying the deeds of the flesh *through the Holy Spirit*."[2335] Thus, ultimately, he is saying that we obtain heaven by means of works.[2336] Nowhere in Romans does Paul suggest that heaven is obtained by means of putting to death the misdeeds of the body. That would, in fact, be contrary to the entire thrust of the epistle where he is trying to separate works as far as possible from the means of obtaining eternal life, which is by faith alone (Romans 4:5).[2337]

[2331] Fitzmeyer, "Romans," 2:135.

[2332] Calvin, *Romans*, s.v. "7:9-10".

[2333] Schreiner, *Romans*, 421.

[2334] Schreiner and Caneday, *The Race Set Before Us*, 175. I have read and reread their chapters on the warnings and find their viewpoint incomprehensible.

[2335] Sellers, *Election and Perseverance*, 99.

[2336] In their system, of course, all Christians will put to death the deeds of the body. They do not allow for final failure. But the plain words of the passage confute this.

[2337] Death is the spiritual destitution and impoverishment that comes as an ingredient of divine discipline on the sinning Christian. This is the sense in verse 6 where it is the opposite of "life and peace." This is also the meaning for pre-Christian Paul's experience of death and spiritual depression as a result of his attempts to find life by means of law (Romans 7:9-11). "Life" here, as in all of Romans, is abundant life, and not regeneration

When Paul says that we are to put to death the deeds of the body, he says we are to do it "by the Spirit." What does Paul mean? The context talks about a warfare, a war between our new inclinations and the sin principle within—the flesh. That sin principle is completely foreign to who we are as new people in Christ. We must fight this foreigner, this enemy, by the Spirit. To "fight" by the Spirit means that we must use spiritual weapons against this enemy instead of weak, bodily ones. Too often in our thinking of this passage, and of similar ones, we have thought in terms of using the Spirit as a person to fight the battle.[2338] We do not "use" the Spirit, we appropriate His help. The emphasis in the New Testament is normally on using the weapons with which he has equipped us. Consider:

> *For though we walk in the flesh, we do not war according to the flesh, for the weapons of our warfare are not of the flesh, but divinely powerful for the destruction of fortresses (2 Corinthians 10:3-4).*

The "fortresses" are "lofty things raised up against the knowledge of God" (2 Corinthians 10:5). In order to fight this battle, Paul says we are destroying speculations and "are taking every thought captive to the obedience of Christ." Once again the spiritual mind is central in our warfare with the enemy, the flesh. To take captive every thought is the same as setting our minds on the things of the Spirit instead of on the things of the flesh.

THE WEAPONS OF OUR WARFARE. What are the weapons of this warfare by the Spirit against the flesh? Romans gives us three. First, we attack the enemy by settling in our minds who we really are in Christ and then battle from that viewpoint. We present our bodies as those who are dead to sin and alive in Christ. We are to refuse to present our members as instruments of unrighteousness (Romans 6:13). Rather, we are to present our bodies as instruments of righteousness. "Instruments" (Gr *hoplon*) was often used as a military term, as it clearly is here; these instruments are weapons. We are to present our lives as weapons. We are new men in Christ. The enemy is not part of us. He is foreign to who we really are at the deepest level in Christ. Furthermore, he will not win. He will not have dominion if we war against him from that perspective (Romans 6:1-11).

The second weapon Paul mentions is the spiritual mind, the mind that fills itself with spiritual thoughts. This suggests that we need to have minds transformed by meditation on Scripture (Romans 12:1-2). "Out of the heart (mind)," says Solomon, "come the issues of life." We must not have our mind set on the things of the flesh if we are to win. We must take every thought captive.

Our final weapon for warfare by the Spirit is faith. This is the central theme of the epistle: "*But the righteous man shall live by faith*" (Romans 1:17). The meaning is that those who are already justified shall find a rich experience of life only as they trust God. The life of faith is the subject of Ephesians 6, where faithfulness is called our shield. Paul tells us that the power of the Spirit, His indwelling presence, is ours by faith.

---

or heaven. It is the same life that Paul found when Timothy returned from his visit to Thessalonica with the good news of the Thessalonians' faith and love. Paul could say, "Now we *really* live" (1 Thessalonians 3:8, NIV). The Greek simply says, "We live," but the translators understand this to mean we live richly. We "really live."

[2338] "The dative [*pneumati*] is not to be taken to imply that the Holy Spirit is to be a tool in the hands of Christians, wielded and managed by them. A safeguard against such a misunderstanding is afforded by *pneumati theou agontai* in the next verse." Cranfield, *A Critical and Exegetical Commentary on the Epistle to the Romans*, 394.

That He would grant you, according to the riches of His glory, to be strengthened with power through His Spirit in the inner man; so that Christ may dwell in your hearts through faith (Ephesians 3:16-17).

These, then, are our weapons: the new man, the new mind, and the new principle—the life of faith. As the flesh attacks, we are to bring this battery to the war. We are to say to ourselves, "I am a new man in Christ. I do not have to obey sin. This flesh is not an expression of who I really am but is a foreigner. I will obey Christ; I am alive in Him. I reckon myself dead to sin." Then we focus our mind on spiritual things. We set the mind on the things of the Spirit and refuse to allow the mind of the flesh to gain the upper hand. We take every thought captive. Then we trust the situation to the Lord in a word of prayer and ask that He might strengthen us in the inner man and that Christ might be the dominate influence in this situation.

These are powerful weapons. The use of them is what Paul means by putting to death the deeds of the flesh.

THE LEADING OF GOD'S SONS (8:14-15)

Paul now explains that a "son of God" is one who is "led by the Sprit." This is the person who is putting to death the deeds of the body and who is walking by the Spirit as described in v. 13. To be a "son" in this sense is to be a Christian who reflects the character of his Father.

For all who are being led by the Spirit of God, these are the sons of God (8:14).

This verse raises three questions: (1) Who is led? (2) Where are they led? (3) How is this leading accomplished?

WHO ARE THE SONS OF GOD? Christians can be "sons of God" in two senses in the New Testament. Of course, all Christians are sons of God by faith in Christ (Galatians 3:26). But in Romans 8:14 Paul speaks of sonship in a different sense. This designation refers to something beyond being a son in the soteriological sense. A son is one who *has the characteristics of his father*. D. A. Carson says "In Jewish thought, 'son' [*huios*] often bears the meaning; 'partaker of the character of.'"[2339]

Who calls us a son? Are all Christians peacemakers and therefore called sons? What is a peacemaker? These are all interesting questions. But also true is the fact that the word *huios* ("son") can take a different emphasis depending on the context. In Matthew 5:45, we are to do the work of loving our enemies *in order that we may become sons*. In Matthew 5:9, we need to be peacemakers before we can be *called* sons of God.

A peacemaker is the person who does not inject harmful words into a conversation and who does not retaliate when he is attacked. He is the kind of person whom one likes to have around in the midst of controversy. He is able to smooth things out. He has control of his emotions, and his presence helps bring opponents together. In the final analysis, God must call a person a "peacemaker," but he may be called such by other believers. But how can one be called a son when he is already a son? Or how can one become a son if he is already a son?

[2339] Carson, *Jesus' Sermon on the Mount and His Confrontation with the World*, 28.

When we act like peacemakers we are reflecting how Jesus and the Father would act in that situation. There is no obvious reason to believe that this is a test of whether one is "truly" a son in a soteriological sense or that it is characteristic of all children of God. After all Matthew 5:9 and 45 are addressed to the disciples (Matthew 5:1-2). When a disciple acts like a peacemaker, he is called a son because he is acting as His heavenly Father would act. This is what John referred to, "*He who overcomes will inherit these things, and I will be his God and he will be My son*" (Revelation 21:7). The overcomer, who is already a born-again son of God, can, like the peacemaker in the Sermon on the Mount, become God's son in another sense. When he overcomes, he acts like his Father.

Obviously, acting like a peacemaker is not a condition for becoming a son of God in the sense of being saved. It is possible for those who are already sons, according to these three verses (Matthew 5:9, 45; Revelation 21:7), to "become sons." In the parable of the prodigal son, Jesus makes a distinction between being a son and one who is *worthy* to be called a son (Luke 15:19). Is it not obvious that the Lord's meaning in Matthew 5:45 quoted above is something like "sons indeed"? In other words, if we love our enemies and function as peacemakers, we are not only sons in fact, but we act like it and are therefore called sons.

In agreement with Schreiner, many interpreters from the Experimental Predestinarian tradition understand "sons of God" in a restrictive sense, which means these who are led by the Spirit of God, and none other, are sons of God.[2340] However, many interpreters have understood the phrase in a more general sense. Liddon, for example, says, "This sonship, although a product of God's grace, depends for its continuance on man's passive obedience to the leading of the Holy Spirit."[2341] Similarly, Godet argues, "The reference is therefore to a *more advanced stage of the Christian life*. You have a right to the title of sons as soon as ye let yourselves be led by the Spirit. Though one becomes a son by justification, he does not possess the filial state; he does not really enjoy adoption until he has become loyally submissive to the operation of the Spirit. The meaning is therefore this: 'If ye let yourselves be led by the Spirit, ye are *ipso facto* [by that fact itself, in reality, indeed] sons of God.' The verb may be taken as passive, 'are driven,' or middle, 'let themselves be driven.'"[2342]

When Paul says "if we are children we are heirs" in v. 17, he uses the word *tekna* ("children)" instead of *huioi* ("sons"). A distinction between the words has often been noted by commentators. The former refers to a "born one," or simply offspring, but the latter speaks of adult, mature, and understanding sonship.[2343] Alford observes, "*huios* of God differs from *teknon* of God, in implying the higher and more mature and conscious member of God's family (see Galatians 5:1-6)."[2344] Godet concurs, "In the one what is expressed is the position of honor [*huios*], in the other the relation of nature [*teknon*]."[2345] We therefore

---

2340 For comments representing this position see Murray, *The Epistle to the Romans*, 1:295. See also Moo, *The Epistle to the Romans*, 499. Of course, Paul sometimes uses "son" in the sense of "offspring," and in those passages the distinction disappears. However, when both words are found in the same context, the presumption would normally be that he probably intends his readers to understand the basic difference in meaning. This distinction seems evident in Romans 8 and is commonly noted by many commentators.

2341 Liddon, *Explanatory Analysis of St. Paul's Epistle to the Romans* 132.

2342 Godet and Cousin, *Commentary on St. Paul's Epistle to the Romans*, 2:309.

2343 E.g., Newell, *Romans: Verse by Verse*, 314.

2344 Henry Alford, "Romans," in *Alford's Greek Testament: An Exegetcial and Critical Commentary* (Bellingham, WA: Logos Bible Software, 2010), 2:391.

2345 Godet and Cousin, *Commentary on St. Paul's Epistle to the Romans*, 311.

disagree with Schreiner's position in which he asserts that "the terms [*tekna* and *huioi*] are synonymous here and should not be distinguished."[2346]

All Christians are "born ones," children of God, that is, sons of God in a soteriological sense. The Spirit of God testifies to the heart of all that they are His offspring. But not all Christians are sons in the sense of those who go on to maturity, who maintain a personal relationship with Christ, who suffer with Him, and as a result will one day share in His inheritance-kingdom, being honored with Him there.

This meaning fits well with the context of Romans 8. Those Christians who are "putting to death the deeds of the body" are *sons in behavior as well as in nature*. Some Christians allow themselves to be led by the Spirit of God, and some do not. Those who do are "sons indeed." To be led by the Spirit is the same as walking by the Spirit. The sense of the passage is, "For all who are walking by the Spirit are sons indeed."

That Paul may have such a distinction in mind between being a son and behaving as a son is reinforced by the fact that he connects the sonship of verse 15 with having the spirit of "adoption" (Gr *huiothesia*), which is different from being a son by birth:

> *For you have not received a spirit of slavery leading to fear again, but you have received a spirit of adoption as sons by which we cry out, Abba! Father! (Romans 8:15)*

We have received a spirit of adoption, *huiothesia* (Romans 8:15).[2347] The method of adoption intended by Paul is somewhat in dispute. In Hebrew practice[2348] the firstborn received a double portion. Even though the Hebrews apparently did not have the practice of adoption as a legal act, Cranfield inclines toward the idea that Paul may have had the Jewish view very much in mind.[2349] The Old Testament references to adoption and the rights of the firstborn,[2350] and Paul's use of the same word in reference to the Israelites "to whom belong the adoption [Gr *huiothesia*] as sons" in Romans 9:4 may suggest that it was the Jewish practice to which Paul referred. This view is reinforced by the fact that adopted sons address God using the Aramaic expression "Abba."

The Roman method of adoption was very severe and binding. The emphasis was on the father's power, and the son was almost a slave. The son was transferred to the power and control of the adoptive father. The transfer was like a sale. According to Ball, "St. Paul exchanges the physical metaphor of regeneration for the legal metaphor of adoption. The adopted person became in the eye of the law a new creature. He was born again into a new family."[2351] All received an equal share of the inheritance. The fact that the epistle was written to the "Romans" has led some interpreters to conclude that the Roman method must be in view.[2352]

2346 Schreiner, *Romans*, 423.

2347 For discussion of adoption see A. H. Leitch, "Adoption," in *The Zondervan Pictorial Encyclopedia of the Bible*, ed. Merrill C. Tenney (Grand Rapids: Zondervan Publishing House, 1975), 1:61-63.

2348 Lloyd-Jones, *The Sons of God: Exposition of Romans 8:5-17*, 401.

2349 According to Sanday and Headlam, *A Critical and Exegetical Commentary on the Epistle of the Romans*, 203.

2350 For example Genesis 14:12-14; Exodus 2:10; 4:22-23; 2 Samuel 7:14; 2 Chronicles 28:6; Esther 2:7; Psalms 2:7; 89:26-27; Jeremiah 3:19; Hosea 11:1.

2351 Ball, *St. Paul and Roman Law and Other Studies on the Origin and Form of Doctrine*, 6.

2352 Lloyd-Jones, *The Sons of God: Exposition of Romans 8:5-17*, 401-02. See also Ball, *St. Paul and Roman Law and Other Studies on the Origin and Form of Doctrine*, 4-12. Ball gives a thorough and fascinating discussion of the Roman adoption practices and believes this is what is behind Paul's thinking in Romans 8.

A problem with the Roman view is that the ceremony of adoption included a drama in which "the adopter, it may be supposed, has died: and the adopted son claims the inheritance."[2353] However, God the Father never died, so the parallel is imprecise. Plus, the stilted formal ceremony and the forensic atmosphere which so dominated the Roman adoption is noticeably absent from and contrary to the warm and more family feeling of Romans 8 where the adoptee cries, "*Abba Father*."

Among the Greeks, however, a more warm and familial attitude prevailed. A man might adopt a child for various reasons: a desire to extend his possessions; a relationship that resulted in deep affections for a child; religious reasons. He could do so in his lifetime or by his will he could extend to a son of another family the privileges of his own family in perpetuity. "There was a condition, however, that the person adopted accept the legal obligations and religious duties of the new father."[2354] Paul used the word in both senses, depending on what he wanted to emphasize. "He found readily at hand the Roman idea when he was emphasizing man's release from the slavery of sin and found the Greek idea congenial when he was emphasizing the relationships and gifts of sonship."[2355] The emphasis on the warm familial relationship with the words "Abba, Father" and the fact that "the idea, like the word [Gr *huiothesia*], is native Greek"[2356] have led many to think of the Greek adoptive practices. Also favoring the Greek view is the fact that unlike the Roman laws, the Greek practice involved conditional acceptance of the laws, and Romans 8:17 also stipulates a condition for co-heirship. These two factors: (1) the warm familial "Abba" and (2) the "if clause" which implies that the sons referred to are likely those who are fulfilling the conditions of the adoption (Greek inheritance) lend support to the Greek view.

All Christians are adopted sons by virtue of our spiritual birth and the legal ransom paid, but not all adopted sons fulfill the requirements of adoption even though God has done His part. Adoption is of grace, and we are adopted regardless of whether we fulfill the requirements (Galatians 4:5), but only those who do so are worthy of the name "son" and will finally obtain the inheritance rights. Even in the Hebrew view, the double portion of the inheritance which comes to the firstborn son is his at birth, based on grace. But he must value and honor that right. He must not, like Esau (Hebrews 12:16-17), treat it lightly and therefore lose it. In Romans 8:17, Paul specifies the condition necessary for maintaining the status and honor of being a firstborn son—we must suffer with him.

Only the faithful Christians are "sons indeed" (cf. Deuteronomy 32:20). These "sons indeed" allow themselves to be "led of the Spirit of God." They are the ones who are "putting to death the deeds of the body" and who, as a result, will truly live. It is impossible to think of one being led without his submitting to being led. They are two sides of the same coin. An obedient son is one who allows himself to be led, and in so doing, puts to death the deeds of the body.

WHERE ARE THE SONS OF GOD LED? As to where this leading takes them, the preceding context makes it clear that it is to holiness. It finds its object in the putting to death the

---

[2353] Ball, *St. Paul and Roman Law and Other Studies on the Origin and Form of Doctrine*, 8.

[2354] Leitch, "Adoption," 61.

[2355] Ibid.

[2356] Sanday and Headlam, *A Critical and Exegetical Commentary on the Epistle of the Romans*, 203.

deeds of the body. Indeed, the verse is a kind of summary of deliverance from sin and to "life and peace" just described. When this ministry of the Holy Spirit is viewed with reference to the end of the whole process, we call it sanctification. When we consider it with reference to the process itself, we call it spiritual leading.[2357]

The meaning of being led by the Spirit of God is to put to death the deeds of the body:

> *For all who are being led by the Spirit of God, these are the sons* [Gr *huioi,* mature sons] *of God (Romans 8:14).*

As others have observed,[2358] verses 13 and 14 seem to be precisely parallel and explain each other. Therefore:

- putting to death the things of the body = led by the Spirit
- you will live = to be a son of God.

In these words we find one of the central passages of the New Testament on the subject of the leading of the Spirit. The introductory "for" goes back to verse 13 and clarifies what Paul means by life, leading us to the first aspect of the meaning of "life." To be led by the Spirit is not the same as our Lord's promise that, when the Holy Spirit comes, He will "guide" us into all truth. Galatians 5:18 is parallel to Romans 8:14, "*But if you are led by the Spirit, you are not under the law.*" There (Gal. 5:18) the leading is into a holy life:

> *But I say, walk by the Spirit, and you will not carry out the desire of the flesh. . . . But if you are led by the Spirit, you are not under the Law (Galatians 5:16, 18).*

The phrases are parallel and explain one another. To be led by the Spirit is the same as walking by the Spirit. The difference may be that it throws the emphasis on God's part rather than man's. But both sides are true. A man cannot be led into sanctification unless he allows himself to be, that is, unless he walks by the Spirit.

Certainly, God can providentially guide His people through Scripture, counselors, and circumstances. But this passage says nothing of this. Nor does it speak of supernatural direction someone may have received.

HOW ARE THE SONS OF GOD LED? Finally, an examination of the word for "lead" (Gr *agō*) suggests how these sons of God are being led. Warfield observes that it should be emphasized that, in all of the uses of the word "led," the self-action of the object being led is involved. The man may lead the horse to drink, but the horse must under his own energy walk up the hill to the water trough. Had Paul wanted to teach that the leading of the Spirit involved only God's work, he had another word he could have used, "move, carry" (Gr *pherō*).

Peter uses this word to explain how the prophets received their message: "*For no prophecy was ever made by an act of human will, but men moved (pherō) by the Holy Spirit spoke from God*" (1 Peter 1:21). The word "moved" suggests that the power and the work are done completely by the mover, not the will of the prophet. If Paul had wanted to

[2357] Warfield, "The Leading of the Spirit," 546.

[2358] For example John R. Stott, *Men Made New* (Downers Grove, IL: InterVarsity Press, 1966), 92.

imply that in the sanctification process we are taken up by God and carried to this goal of holiness with no effort or cooperation on our part, he would have used this word. But he passed over it and used "led" (*agō*). This suggests that the Holy Spirit determines the goal and the way of arriving there, but it is by our effort and cooperation that we proceed.

The prophet is "moved," and the child of God is "led." The prophet's attitude in receiving revelation is completely passive and purely receptive; he adds nothing to it and has no part in it. He is only the mouthpiece through which God speaks. The child of God, however, is not passive in the hands of the sanctifying Spirit. He is not "moved" but "led." His own efforts enter into the progress made under the controlling influence of the Spirit. As Warfield put it,

> *He supplies, in fact, the force exerted in attaining the progress, while yet the controlling Spirit supplies the entire directing impulse.*[2359]

For this reason, no prophet could be urged to work out his own message with fear and trembling. It was not left for him to work out. But the believer is commanded to work out his own salvation with fear and trembling because he knows that the Spirit is working in him both the willing and the doing according to His own good pleasure. This is a:

> *leading of an active agent to an end determined indeed by the Spirit, and along a course which is marked out by the Spirit, but over which the soul is carried by virtue of its own power of action and through its own strenuous efforts. . . . It is His part to keep us in the path and to bring us at length to the goal. But it is we who tread every step of the way; our limbs that grow weary with the labor; our hearts that faint, our courage that fails.*[2360]

We have, then, in these two verses (8:13-14), God's part and man's part in the process of sanctification. Verse 13 states that man's part is to "put to death the things of the body" and enjoy true life. Verse 14 states that God's part is to lead Christians along the path of sanctification and that those who allow themselves to be so led are sons, or "sons indeed," who enjoy true life.

Another passage that seems to parallel this is Philippians 2:12-13. To "work out your salvation with fear and trembling" is another way of saying that we should put to death the deeds of the body. And to say that God is "at work in you, both to will and to work for His good pleasure" is to say we are led by the Spirit of God.

The believer who submits to this leading (who is "being led"), who perseveres to the goal, is earlier described as a believer who walks according to the Spirit or who sets his mind on the things of the Spirit. He is in the company of the *Metochoi*, a Partner, and will be a co-heir with Christ, inheriting the kingdom. Furthermore, as he responds to the Spirit's sanctifying leading, he need no longer fear the condemnation of the Law.

Finally, Paul says that we "*have not received a spirit of slavery leading to fear again*" (8:15). By spirit of slavery, Paul may mean disobedience to God's leading and hence entrance into a walk that could be described as slavery. Perhaps, he means simply that

---

[2359] Warfield, "The Leading of the Spirit," 553.

[2360] Ibid., 555.

the Holy Spirit is not a Spirit of bondage but of adoption.[2361] This Spirit does not lead to fear again. This fear can plausibly be understood as the opposite of the certainty of adoption. An adopted son knows he is in the family. He is secure forever. The fear that we are excluded from the family of God and the experience of bondage to sin are no longer necessary to those who are in Christ Jesus. As Godet puts it, "The Spirit which ye have received from God is not a servile spirit throwing you back into the fear in which ye formerly lived."[2362]

THE TWO HEIRSHIPS (8:16-17)

> *The Spirit Himself bears witness with our spirit that we are children of God; and if children, heirs also, heirs of God, and fellow-heirs with Christ if indeed we suffer with Him in order that we may also be glorified with Him (Romans 8:16-17).*

In these verses, Paul explains that there are two categories of Christians: those who are heirs of God, and those who are fellow-heirs with Christ. Being a co-heir of Christ is conditional, "*if indeed*." In other words, some believers will be co-heirs of Christ and some will not.[2363] This distinction fits well with the preceding context where he has spoken of those who walk by the Spirit and those who walk by the flesh; those who put to death the deeds of the body and those who do not; those who are *tekna* (children of God) and those who are also *huioi* (mature, obedient sons); and those who "live" and those who "die"; those who are led by the Spirit and those who are not.

The condition for being a fellow-heir with Christ is to persevere in all trials to the end of life. This is a theme and condition found in many discussions in previous chapters of this book. Because I have discussed these verses in considerable detail in volume 1, chapter 5, I will not repeat that material here.

Our Final Assurance (8:18-30)

The apostle continues,

> *For I consider that the sufferings of this present time are not worthy to be compared with the glory that is to be revealed to us (Romans 8:18 NASB).*

The glories of the reign of the Messiah are still in view. The "for" refers back to the salvation and glory of the messianic kingdom. The verse explains why we should suffer with Him in order to be glorified with Him. This is because the blessings of the messianic era are beyond description. What a tragedy it would be not to have a share in all of them!

These glories are to be revealed to us (Gr *eis hēmas,* "in" or "to") and not necessarily "in us," as some translations read.[2364] The wonders of the great future will be revealed to

---

[2361] Cranfield, *A Critical and Exegetical Commentary on the Epistle to the Romans*, 396.

[2362] Godet and Cousin, *Commentary on St. Paul's Epistle to the Romans*, 309. Cf. 2 Timothy 1:7; and 2 Corinthians 1:12.

[2363] For discussion of this interpretation, see pp. 84 ff.

[2364] This phrase is used eight times in the New Testament: Acts 3:4; Romans 5:8; 8:18; 2 Corinthians 1:5; 1:11; Ephesians 1:8, 9; Hebrews 2:3). In each instance the meaning is "toward, to, or upon us." It never means "in" in the sense of "within."

all, but they will be shared in (inherited) only by those who persevere in suffering. Our own glorification-resurrection, while certainly included in this glory, is probably not yet specifically in view here. The apostle would have used *en hēmin*, "in us," had he intended this.

> *For the anxious longing of the creation waits eagerly for the revealing of the sons of God (Romans 8:19).*

The "sons of God" are properly those who have allowed themselves to be led by the Spirit. They are those who have walked by means of the Spirit and who have set their minds on the things of the Spirit. They are the "sons indeed" referred to in verse 14. Not all Christians are sons (Gr *huioi*) of God in this sense, but all are children of God (Gr *tekna*). The "revealing of the sons of God" is then the making known to all creation who these faithful believers are. It refers to their installation as the co-heirs and co-rulers with Messiah in the final destiny of man. The entire creation longs for the future reign of the servant kings!

> *For the creation was subjected to futility, not of its own will, but because of Him who subjected it, in hope that the creation itself also will be set free from its slavery to corruption into the freedom of the glory of the children of God (Romans 8:20-21).*

The introductory "for" informs us that this verse explains why the creation longs for this future reign of Christ's servant kings. When that future reign dawns, it will include a physical transformation of the creation itself. The creation has endured a subjection to futility for many ages. This subjection creates within itself a sense of hope for something better. That "something better" is a transformation similar to what will occur for all Christians, "the freedom of the glory of the children of God." This glory is part of, but not equal to, the "glory that is to be revealed to us" (v. 18). The former is a general term for the glories of the messianic era. The latter is the glory of a transformed body which all Christians will share in the day of resurrection.

The creation does not share in all aspects of the future glory. It will never be set free to rule with Christ, the revealing of the sons of God. No inanimate thing can share in the reign of Christ's servants. But the creation will share in an aspect of the future glory common to all the children of God, physical transformation. For this reason, Paul changes from "sons" (v. 19) to "children" of God in verse 21. All children of God will be transformed, but only the "sons" will rule with Christ.[2365]

> *And not only this, but also we ourselves, having the first fruits of the Spirit, even we ourselves groan within ourselves waiting eagerly for our adoption as sons, the redemption of our body (Romans 8:23).*

The verse presents an interpretive problem in that it seems to contradict verse 15. There we are told we have been adopted, but here we are told we await our adoption. The

[2365] Henry Alford has observed this same distinction here, Alford, "Romans," 2:395. Galatians 4:7 is not necessarily in contradiction to this. Paul there uses the word "son" in the sense of an adopted child. All adopted children have the full rights of being heirs of God. Only those adopted children who suffer with Christ will be co-heirs of Christ, a subject not addressed in Galatians.

solution may be that this verse refers to the completion of our adoption, which consists in the reception of our resurrection bodies.[2366]

Finally, there is good reason for Sanday and Headlam's distinction between the co-glorification with Christ in verse 17 and the glorification of the believer in verse 30. The former they equate with sharing with Messiah in His inheritance[2367] and the latter with participating in His divine perfection.[2368] For Cranfield the former is primarily the outwardly manifest glory of the final consummation, and the latter is primarily internal, our ultimate conformation to His glory.[2369]

That two different aspects of the one future glorification are in view seems probable because of the contextual contrasts between them. In verse 17 the glorification is conditional and only for those who suffer with Christ, but in verse 30 it is unconditional and is for all who are justified. In verse 17 it is a sharing in the glory of Messiah, but in verse 30 it refers to our own glorification. In verse 17 the verb is "be glorified with" and in verse 30 the verb is "glorified." In verse 17 it refers to the wonders of the messianic era, but in verse 30 it refers to our ultimate conformity into the image of Christ at the resurrection of the body. In verse 17 the verb is in a purpose clause implying intent and not necessarily certainty. But in verse 30 it is an indicative verb, implying the certainty of a presently achieved fact. Verse 17 is in a context that stresses exhortation. It is a challenge to persevere in order that we might share in Christ's glory. But verse 30 is a statement of fact that we have already, in a proleptic and anticipatory sense, entered into that glory. René López summarizes,

> *Thus, Paul teaches here that all believers upon regeneration become heirs of God, but only those who suffer will "be glorified with Him." This "glory" "revealed in" the "sons of God" (vv. 18-19) refers to the faithful believers' participation in the glorious honor, prestige, and reward of co-reigning with Christ over creation (vv. 18-23; cf. Hebrews 1:8-9; 2 Timothy 2:12; Revelation 2:26-28). When a king was crowned (for his faithfulness to the kingdom for which he served; cf. Heb 1:5-9), he was glorified. So believers (as His cabinet members who stay the course with Him) will also be crowned (1 Corinthians 9:25; Philippians 4:1; 1 Thessalonians 2:19; 2 Timothy 4:8; James 1:12; 1 Peter 5:4; Revelation 2:10; 3:11) and glorified (for their faithfulness) with many rewards. In this context especially, it appears that this glorification refers to the reward of exercising dominion over creation with Christ (8:18-23; cf. 2 Timothy 2:12; Revelation 2:26-27).*[2370]

All believers share in the latter aspect of that glory, the final resurrection, but only those who put to death the deeds of the body will share in the former, the future reign of the servant kings.

[2366] Sanday and Headlam call it the "manifested, realized, act of adoption, a public promulgation." Sanday and Headlam, *A Critical and Exegetical Commentary on the Epistle of the Romans*, 209.

[2367] Ibid., 202.

[2368] Ibid., 215.

[2369] Sanday, *A Critical and Exegetical Commentary on the Epistle to the Romans*, 433.

[2370] René A. López, "The Pauline Vice List and Inheriting the Kingdom" (PhD diss., Dallas Theological Seminary, 2010), 189.

Summary

Romans 8 is a magnificent presentation of the life that is led by the Spirit and the final outcome of such a life in sharing with Messiah in the final destiny of man. It is a challenge to us Christians to live that life by putting to death the deeds of the body by the use of their spiritual weapons. It contrasts two categories or descriptions of Christians and does not contrast the Christian and the non-Christian.

47

The Doctrine of Eternal Life

WE COME at last to the specific biblical evidence for the eternal security of the believer. The Arminian denies that the child of God is eternally secure, and the Experimental Predestinarian insists that, if the believer does not persevere in holiness, he was never regenerate in the first place.

The Partner, however, teaches that, if he is a child of God, he is "obligated" to persevere (Paul's word, Romans 8:12), but he may not. If he does not, he does not forfeit salvation or demonstrate that he never had it, but he faces divine discipline in time and loss of reward at the Judgment Seat of Christ.

R. T. Kendall put it this way; "A man who is truly saved will go to heaven when he dies no matter what work (or lack of work) may accompany such faith. This is not unbecoming of the gospel, *it honors it*!"[2371]

This doctrine is called eternal security, or the *preservation* of the saints. While the Experimental Predestinarians prefer the term *perseverance*, the Partner favors "preservation." "*Perseverance*" implies that our ultimate arrival in heaven is dependent on our faithfulness plus God's work, but "*preservation*" depends on God alone.

It is important to stress some points of clarification:

1. This doctrine does not teach that a person who prays a prayer, walks down the aisle, or folds the corner of an invitation card at an evangelistic meeting is necessarily going to heaven. Mere intellectual acceptance of Christ with no acknowledgment of one's sinfulness before God is not saving faith.
2. This doctrine does not teach that those who act like believers outwardly, who attend church, are necessarily going to heaven. We only assert that among those who have outward Christianity are those who have it inwardly as well. Those, and only those who have this principle of life within them, will never lose it and will be saved in the end.
3. This doctrine does not condone the existence of carnal and dead Christians in our churches. On the contrary, the Partner view of the doctrine of eternal life includes the highest possible motivations for godly service, that is, the gift of unconditional acceptance, and the strong desire to hear the Master's "Well done!" The fact that some may take advantage of the grace of God does not nullify that grace. Our doctrine stresses that God will discipline the child of God who persists in sin, and that the sinning child risks severe punishment in this life and the fearful possibility of future disinheritance (Hebrews 3:12-1; 4:1, 11; 10:35). This is a powerful incentive toward a faithful life.

[2371] Kendall, *Once Saved, Always Saved*, 41.

4. This doctrine does teach that those whom God has regenerated to new birth through the Holy Spirit and declared justified in Christ can never lose salvation but shall be preserved in a state of salvation to the final hour and shall be eternally saved.

A belief in conditional security necessarily leads to consideration of what sin or sins are necessary to forfeit salvation. If we entertain even the remotest possibility that there is something we can do or not do which can nullify the value of the blood of Christ, we will focus our attention on our obedience, and not Christ's sacrifice for us and the beauty of the gospel promises. This is the way human nature works. This explains the high degree of legalism in Arminian circles. If ninety-nine percent of saved people cannot be lost, but one percent can, we have no sense of security, ever. We would constantly be worried as to whether or not we were one of the one percent. We would need to know what kind of sin or disobedience it is that endangers the one percent. Whatever that sin may be, we would live in constant horror that we just might, one day, commit such a sin.

From Genesis to Revelation, salvation is presented as a work of God. God the Father purposes, calls, justifies, and glorifies those who believe on Christ. God the Son became incarnate that He might be a Kinsman-Redeemer and die a substitutionary death. He rose to be a living Savior, both as Advocate and Intercessor, and as Head over all things to the church. God the Holy Spirit administers and executes the purpose of the Father and the redemption which the Son has wrought. Therefore, all three persons of the Godhead have their share in preserving to fruition what God has determined.

Our salvation and eternal security depends on God the Father, God the Son, and God the Holy Spirit. Since it depends upon Him and not upon us, it cannot be lost.

Eternal Security Depends on God the Father

From eternity past God's firm purpose has been established. The Scriptures tell us that before the foundations of the world He elected those who would believe to salvation in Christ and predestined us to glory.[2372] It is therefore clear that our eternal security depends, first of all:

ON HIS SOVEREIGN PURPOSE

PREDESTINED TO GLORY. God's eternal purpose cannot be defeated in the realization of all He intends, and bringing His redeemed to glory is a major aspect of His divine purpose. That eternal purpose is declared in Ephesians 1:11-12:

> *In Christ we too have been claimed as God's own possession, since we were predestined according to the one purpose of him who accomplishes all things according to the counsel of his will (Ephesians 1:11, NET).*

We have been "*claimed as God's own possession*" since we were predestined to this privilege. The Greek could be translated, "*We were made a heritage*."[2373] If those who

[2372] He chose the church before the foundation of the world and predestined those who responded by faith to glory in conformity to the image of His Son.

[2373] For discussion of this verse, see vol.1 chapter 9.

believe in Christ have been predestined to become God's heritage, it is certain that we will, in the final outcome of things, be His heritage.[2374]

Ephesians 1:4-6 adds:

> *Just as He chose us in Him before the foundation of the world, that we should be holy and blameless before Him. In love He predestined us to adoption as sons through Jesus Christ to Himself, according to the kind intention of His will, to the praise of the glory of His grace, which He freely bestowed on us in the Beloved (NASB).*

His choice of us is not to salvation but to be "holy and blameless," that is to His purpose that we grow in grace in this life. As a result we will increasingly become relatively holy and blameless. There is an element of contingency here. While such growth in sanctification is one of the reasons He chose us, the Bible teaches us elsewhere that such growth does not always occur.[2375] I prefer the translation of the Gr verb "to be" as "*should be* holy and blameless" (ESV, NKJV, NET "may be," KJV, RSV, ASV, DARBY). There is a difference between what we *should be* and what we inevitably will be, that is, *would be.* Thus the passage harmonizes with the present author's understanding of Colossians 1:22. Nevertheless, regardless of the degree of our daily sanctification, the next phrase promises that salvation cannot be lost.

If those who believed are predestined to adoption as sons, as well as to being made a heritage, it is not possible that we will not be adopted as sons. Notice, predestination does not refer to predestination to salvation, but refers to our destiny as Christians.[2376] God does not lose those He has inherited and adopted through the death of His Son. The "adoption as sons" refers to the end point of our salvation (Romans 8:23) when we enter glory. Those initially adopted when they believed are guaranteed that God will bring the adoption to a conclusion at the resurrection. Otherwise, God's predestination would fail. All depends on whether God can accomplish His intentions.

2374 We do not agree with the Calvinists that this predestination is unrelated to foreseen faith. We agree with the Arminians that God predestinates those who will believe and those who believe do so freely and not as a result of efficacious grace. The Experimentalist view is a blasphemous conception of God which says that in eternity past He predestined the vast majority of the human race to eternal torment before they were even born and had a chance to accept or reject Him.

2375 See chapter 32.

2376 Experimental Predestinarians believe in a personal, eternal, sovereign, unconditional, pre-temporal predestination of some to salvation and some to damnation. Calvin himself called this the *Decretum horrible* (horrible decree); Calvin, *Institutes,* book 3, chapter 23, section 7. For thorough refutation of this doctrine see Vance, *The Other Side of Calvinism,* 241-404; esp. 354-64. God chose, those who would believe in Christ, to be "in him" and hence to experience all spiritual blessings. In other words, before time, God determined that all those who are in Him by faith alone would be blessed, adopted, and go to heaven. Obviously, those who are not in Him, would not be so blessed. The verse does not say that God chose us to be in Him before the foundation of the world. It says that God chose that whoever is in His Son will be holy and blameless before Him. How does one get "in him"? It is through faith alone (Ephesians 2:8-9). Paul's point is not pre-temporal election, but that all blessings come "in Him" and set it up this way before the world began. It is ridiculous to say, as Calvinists sometimes do, that the unsaved were "in Him," before the foundation of the world. One does not get "in Him" until he believes. It is clear that the unsaved were not in Him but were "dead in trespasses and sins" and were "children of wrath" (Eph. 2:1-3). The Calvinist scenario leads to this absurdity: (1) the elect were in Christ before the foundation of the world; (2) the elect then fell out of Christ and became lost in Adam; (3) the elect then got back into Christ when they believed!

THE GOLDEN CHAIN. Theodore Beza, Calvin's successor at Geneva, argued persuasively that Romans 8:28-30 describes an unbreakable chain consisting of five links:

> *For whom He **foreknew**, He also **predestined**, and these He also **called**; and whom He called, these He also **justified**; and whom He justified, these He also **glorified**.*

Note the terms, "whom" and "these also." These five terms link, as in a chain, the history of the same group of people from foreknowledge to glorification. The same group that was foreknown will also ultimately be glorified.

1. Foreknowledge
2. Predestination
3. Calling
4. Justification
5. Glorification

The word "foreknowledge" could mean, as our Experimentalist friends maintain, "prior choice."[2377] However, there is no obvious reason for rejecting the more common meaning—simple prior knowledge of future events. God knows who will believe and, based on this prior knowledge, He predestines them to salvation. To predestine is simply to plan in advance.

The call referred to here is the efficacious call to come to Him. Jesus said, "*My sheep hear My voice and they follow Me*." All those whom God foreknew would believe are predestined. Because God foreknew they would believe, He calls them efficaciously. All those who are predestined are called, and all those who are called are justified. This calling is an effectual calling. And all those who are justified will be glorified. This refers to the redemption of our bodies at the last day (Romans 8:23).

The two-verse chain with its fivefold unbreakable links, "those whom … He also," is a clear statement of the eternal security of the saints.

John Wesley, in the face of such a passage, finally resorted to reading phrases into the text which are not there in order to salvage his doctrine of conditional security.

> *And whom He justified—**provided they continue in His goodness**, Romans 11:22, He in the end glorified—St. Paul does not affirm, either here or in any other part of his writings, that precisely the same number of men are called, justified, and glorified. He does not deny that a believer may fall away and be cut off between his special calling and his glorification, Romans 11:22. Neither does he deny that many are called who are never justified. He only affirms that this is the method whereby God leads us step by step towards Heaven.*[2378]

[2377] For example, in Amos 3:2 God says of Israel, "Only thee have I known of all the nations of the earth." Obviously God has knowledge of the other nations, but only Israel was chosen. It is a personal, loving, and intimate prior choice. Obviously, the present writer accepts what is known as Middle Knowledge, which in no way denies the ultimate sovereignty of God. See Craig, "Lest Anyone Should Fall: A Middle Knowledge Perspective on Perseverance and Apostolic Warnings," 65-74.

[2378] John Wesley, Explanatory Notes upon the New Testament, 1754, cited by Marshall, *Kept by the Power of God: A Study of Perseverance and Falling Away*, 103.

But God certainly does affirm that "precisely the same number of men are called, justified, and glorified." He affirms it in this passage. To deny it is like the philosopher who looks into a well and upon seeing his own reflection writes about what he sees, or a man who looks at the sun and says, "There is no light!" With respect to John Wesley, it is evident that he is deliberately contradicting the clear intent of the passage in the interests of his belief that the justified can lose salvation. He offers absolutely no exegetical proof whatsoever for his view. Paul *does* say that all who are called in this sense are justified. That there is an ineffectual call is acknowledged by all, including John Wesley, but this one is an effectual call!

But our eternal security depends not only on His sovereign purpose, but also ...

ON HIS "MUCH MORE" LOVE

The preservation of the saved flows from the free and unchangeable love of the Father. It was God's love, not the Christian's worthiness, which was the reason for his salvation in the first place. The Scriptures make it plain that God saved no man because He observed some good, attractive, or meriting attribute in an individual sinner. Rather, He saved us because we believed.

> *Not only that, but Rebecca's children had one and the same father, our father Isaac. Yet, before the twins were born or had done anything good or bad—in order that God's purpose in election might stand: not by works but by Him who calls—she was told, "The older will serve the younger." Just as it is written: "Jacob I loved, but Esau I hated" (Romans 9:10-13).*

Now since the cause of the sinner's salvation had nothing to do with any imagined merit or goodness in the sinner, neither does the preservation of the saint. Since God was not motivated to impart saving grace based on good works, the subsequent absence of those works would be no new motive for Him to withdraw His grace. God knew when He saved us that we were sinful, and therefore any new manifestation of sin in our lives after our conversion cannot be any motivation for God to change His mind and withdraw salvation.

Consider:

> *He who did not spare his own Son, but gave him up for us all—how will he not also, along with him, graciously give us all things? (Romans 8:32)*

> *For I am convinced that neither death nor life, neither angels nor demons, neither the present nor the future, nor any powers, neither height nor depth, nor* ***anything else in all creation,*** *will be able to separate us from the love of God that is in Christ Jesus our Lord (Romans 8:38-39).*

The fact that God's intent to bring His elect to glory is grounded in His infinite love for them is clearly brought out in Romans 5:6-10:

> *You see, at just the right time, when we were still powerless, Christ died for the ungodly. Very rarely will anyone die for a righteous man, though for a good man someone might possibly*

dare to die. But God demonstrates his own love for us in this: While we were still sinners, Christ died for us. Since we have now been justified by his blood, how much more shall we be saved from God's wrath through him! For if, when we were God's enemies, we were reconciled to him through the death of his Son, how much more, having been reconciled, shall we be saved through his life!

If God will do all this for us when we were His enemies, He will surely do much more now that we are His friends. If He did the harder thing (die for us) when we were His enemies, He will surely do the easier thing (save us from the coming wrath) now that we are His friends. Love has removed every barrier to eternal security which sin had erected, and the "much more" love will surely keep those whom He has chosen before the foundation of the world.

Finally, eternal security is grounded in the Father's faithfulness; it does not depend on us. Rather, it depends …

ON HIS PROMISE TO KEEP US

He has promised to keep us saved. In no uncertain terms our Lord declares:

And this is the will of him who sent me, that ***I shall lose none of all that he has given me,*** *but raise them up at the last day. For my Father's will is that everyone who looks to the Son and believes in him shall have eternal life, and I will raise him up at the last day (John 6:39).*

It is not God's will that Christ will lose any of those the Father gave to Him.[2379] Consider:

My sheep listen to my voice; I know them, and they follow me. I give them eternal life, and they shall never perish; no one can snatch them out of my hand. My Father, who has given them to me, is greater than all; no one can snatch them out of the Father's hand (John 10:27-29).

Many Arminians explain all these passages by asserting that all gospel promises have implied conditions. Thus, it is to be understood that the promises will be fulfilled only if the believer remains faithful to the final hour. This, however, is simply an assertion not supported by these texts. One can read all kinds of conditions into these precious promises, but the promises themselves, as stated, are unconditional, and one is dangerously close to adding words to the Scripture when he argues this way.

Robert Shank points out that the phrase, "*and they follow me*" (John 10:27) must be included in the promise. He says that only those who hear and follow will never perish. He argues that "follow" implies a second condition in addition to faith that is necessary if one is to obtain eternal life, life of obedience,[2380] or that following is a characteristic of all who believe. Sheep, according to Jesus, follow.

However, one must ask, "What is the meaning of *follow* in the Gospel of John?" In the preceding verse Jesus says,

---

[2379] Judas was a "son of perdition." He was never "given" by the Father to the Son; he was unregenerate.

[2380] Shank, *Life in the Son: A Study of the Doctrine of Perseverance*, 56. John MacArthur takes a similar view. MacArthur, *The Gospel According to Jesus*, 178.

But you do not believe, because you are not of My sheep (John 10:26).

Christ's sheep, however, do hear and they do believe. Many have noted that hearing stands alone to represent faith in 10:3, 8, and 16 and is used elsewhere by John to speak of faith (cf. 5:24–25; 8:43, 47).[2381]

This might suggest that by "follow" Jesus means "believe." Sheep believe (v. 26), and sheep "hear" and "follow" (v. 27), ergo, "hear" and "follow" equal "believe." Thus, "to follow" might not mean "to obey." This is suggested by the fact that sheep will not follow the voice of an unknown shepherd. They fear the voice of strangers (vv. 4-5). The act of "following" *is the act of trust*. This could be supported by the fact that eternal life is the result of following. One might argue that it is intrinsically unlikely that "follow" is a metaphor for obedience because elsewhere in John eternal life is the result of faith alone. The use of "hear and believe" in John 5:24 might support our interpretation:

Truly, truly, I say to you, he ***who hears My word, and believes*** *Him who sent Me, has eternal life; and does not come into judgment, but has passed out of death into life (John 5:24).*

Hearing and believing according to John 5:24 result in eternal life. "Hearing and following" in John 10:27 result in eternal life. Therefore, "hearing and believing" could equal "hearing and following." This means that "to follow" may be another of John's metaphors for "to believe." He has also used "look," "taste," "eat," and "drink."[2382] Are literal eating, looking, tasting, and drinking necessary for eternal life? Hardly! Neither, it could be argued, is literal following. To follow the Shepherd, in this view, is to believe on Him.[2383]

Experimentalists as well as Arminians are confounded by the passage. Their doctrine states that God *first* gives eternal life and faith and as a result the sheep follow. But assuming that hear = believe, and follow = discipleship (as they believe), Jesus says just the reverse. The sequence is hear and follow and then one obtains eternal life. Furthermore, if "follow" means to obey Christ all one's life, then it is not possible to obtain eternal life until one has obeyed all his life. In other words, it cannot be received as a gift now, contrary to the gospel promise (John 17:3). Of course, Experimentalists will say that following (i.e., lifelong obedience) is the characteristic of all who "truly" believe and is not a condition. But obedience is not a characteristic of all who believe, as Scripture clearly teaches.[2384]

There is another possible way of understanding the phrase, "they follow me." It could be that Jesus is saying that "true" believers *do* follow Christ in discipleship as an expectation and general characteristic. In that case this is a general statement about the normal character of the saved. However, this is not saying what the Experimentalist says. He is not saying that "true" believers inevitably and necessarily follow Him to the final hour. In fact, He has said earlier that *many* true believers who began well, take the broad

---

2381 Bing, "The Condition for Salvation in John's Gospel," 40.

2382 See discussion of the various metaphors which Jesus uses to illustrate saving faith in ibid., 30-31.

2383 I see no problem in saying that "true" believers do follow Christ in discipleship as an expectation and general characteristic. Jesus is making a general statement about the character of the saved. However, this is not saying what the Experimentalist says. He is not saying that "true" believers inevitably and necessarily follow Him to the final hour. He is not saying that a commitment to follow is a precondition for saving faith. Jesus spoke of "lost sheep." All sheep do not follow, but most do and all are expected to do so. Thus it is perfectly proper to call believers, "followers."

2384 See discussion in chapter 32.

road leading to destruction (Matthew 7:13).[2385] He is not saying that a commitment to follow is a precondition for saving faith. Jesus spoke elsewhere of "lost sheep" (Luke 15). All sheep do not follow, but most do, and all are expected to. Thus it is perfectly proper to call believers, "followers." He is using synecdoche, the part for the whole. The faithful believers for all believers.[2386] When the news media report, "The White House said," we do not understand this to mean everyone in the White House said it. We understand that the president or one of his senior advisors said it. When Jesus said "My sheep follow me," He did not mean all of the sheep inevitably and necessarily always do, but that the faithful sheep will follow.

Returning to John 10:27, Jesus says, "*They shall never perish.*" Arminian interpreters understand this promise as "assurance from the divine side; but it is entirely consistent with a conditioning fidelity on the human side."[2387] How so? Miley continues, "This is utterly without proof of an absolute final perseverance, except on the assumption of an absolute sovereignty of grace in every instance of a personal salvation."[2388] Well … of course. Essentially he is saying that this is without proof unless the doctrine of eternal security is true. He is arguing in a circle.

The phrase "shall never" is a double negative in Greek (*ou mē*). It is very emphatic. It is often claimed that the text only promises that someone else cannot snatch the believer out of the Father's hand. The believer, it is said, can snatch himself out of the Father's hand by unbelief or sin. But is that all these precious words mean? If so, then they mean nothing. To any person who really knows his own heart, these implied conditions would nullify the promises. What kind of security is it that offers no security against our own weakness?

If our enjoyment of the promise of eternal security depends on our continued ability to persevere, as Arminians maintain, then the loss of our justification is not only possible but probable. Are we to suppose that Christ's meaning is that no one can snatch us out of the Father's hand provided we do not choose to allow ourselves to be snatched away? Are we to suppose that Christ did not know the common biblical truth that the only way any spiritual danger can attack a soul successfully is by persuasion; that unless the adversary can get the consent of the believer's free will, he cannot harm him? Is there any other way a soul can be snatched away other than by the consent of the soul itself? Dabney observes, "Surely Jesus knew this; and if this supposed condition is to be understood, then this precious promise would be a worthless and pompous truism." It would then mean only this:

> *You can never be snatched away except by the only way anyone can be snatched away.*
>
> or
>
> *No one can take you out of the Father's hand except, of course, by the only means anyone can take you out of the Father's hand.*
>
> or

[2385] For discussion of the broad and narrow way, see chapter 21.

[2386] For discussion of this figure of speech, see pp. 844 ff.

[2387] John Miley, *Systematic Theology*, originally published by Hunt & Eaton, 1893 ed., 2 vols. (Peabody, MA: Hendrickson, 1989), 2:269.

[2388] Ibid.

You can never fall unless, of course, you do.

or

You can never fall as long as you stand up.

God's purpose to ultimately save His elect is based not only upon His infinite power. It also depends:

ON HIS ANSWER TO THE PRAYER OF HIS SON

The saved are called many things in Scripture: saints, believers, sheep, Christians, partners of the heavenly calling, and others. But the title most dear to the heart of Christ is repeated seven times in His high priestly prayer—"*those whom You have given Me.*"[2389] This phrase, according to John 17:20, includes all who would believe in Him throughout the ages:

> *Holy Father, keep them in Thy name, the name which Thou has given Me, that they may be one, even as We are. While I was with them, I was keeping them in Thy name which Thou has given Me; and I guarded them and not one of them perished but the son of perdition (John 17:11-12).*

Jesus asks the Father to keep them from damnation. As shown elsewhere these Gr words translated "*perished*" and "*perdition*" do not refer to damnation (see p. 293 ff.). Jesus kept them from *apōleia* on earth when he was "with them." This was a keeping from spiritual ruin and being lost like the Prodigal Son keeping that is, a keeping from losing one's life, not damnation. All Twelve had been given to Him, including Judas. Jesus had warned His disciples about the danger of losing their lives (Matthew 16:25). Judas was the son of "ruin and lostness" destined for "loss and ruin," which probably meant ruin in this life as well as damnation. That said, Judas, of course, was not saved. All Eleven will be kept by the Father for eternal life.

The Son asks the Father to keep saved those whom the Father has given to the Son. Even if the Father had no personal interest in keeping them saved, which He does, He must respond to the prayer of the Son, whose prayers are always answered (John 11:42). Jesus prays that we will be kept from hell (John 17:15) and that we will be with Him in heaven (John 17:20, 24). Will not the prayers of the Son of God be answered?

Not only has God the Father committed Himself by oath to guarantee the eternal security of His elect, but God the Son, through His active and passive obedience has made our final arrival into heaven certain. Our eternal security does not depend on us.

Eternal Security Depends on God the Son

The apostle Paul specifically raises the question of eternal security in his magnificent conclusion to Romans 8:

> *What, then, shall we say in response to this? (8:31)*

Paul has just finished presenting the "golden chain" (8:29-30). These five unbreakable links guarantee the believer's eternal destiny. What shall we say in response to this "golden chain," he now asks?

[2389] John 17:2, 6, 9, 11-12, 20, 24.

> *If God is for us, who can be against us? He who did not spare his own Son, but gave him up for us all—how will he not also, along with him, graciously give us all things? Who will bring any charge against those whom God has chosen? It is God who justifies (Romans 8:31-33).*

Paul's argument is that, if God has already justified the one who believes in Jesus (Romans 3:26; 8:30), how can He lay anything to the charge of His justified one? He sees the Christian's failures and imperfections. He does not shut His eyes to these failures but disciplines His children because of them.

However, justification comes from the imputed righteousness of Christ and is legally ours. It is not a subject of merit, and its loss cannot be a subject of demerit. Like a human father, God can and does correct His earthly sons, but they always remain sons.

The truth is that God, having justified the ungodly (Romans 4:5), will not and cannot contradict Himself by charging them with evil. To do so amounts to reversing their justification. Christ either died for our sins and has justified those who believe or He has not. The Arminian cannot have it both ways. God is the only one ultimately who could bring a charge against His elect, and, as Paul says, God has already rendered His verdict—justified. Therefore none can, or ever will again, bring a charge of guilt against the believer as far as his eternal standing is concerned.

In his answer to the second question, Who is the one that condemns? (Romans 8:34), Paul gives four answers. Each of the answers affirms the absolute security of the believer as unconditionally safe forever: (1) Christ died, (2) He is risen, (3) He advocates, and (4) He intercedes. Because of these four ministries of Christ, "*nothing will be able to separate us from the love of God*" (8:39), that is, cause us to forfeit our justification. These four ministries of Christ are taught elsewhere in Scripture, but all are gathered together in one verse here to support the unconditional security of the believer. Paul declares, first of all, that our eternal security depends...

ON HIS SUBSTITUTIONARY DEATH

Paul's first answer is "Christ has died!" Who can condemn us, he says, if the penalty for our sins has already been paid? The greatest proof of eternal security is justification by faith. Justification refers to how God sees us, and not the way we see ourselves or how others see us. Justification is "exterior" to us. It lies utterly outside us. The interior change is due to regeneration. Justification is forensic; it is entirely a legal matter. This is how God will judge us. We have been declared righteous. It was on the basis of Christ's death for sin that we were saved initially, and it is now on that basis that no one can condemn us.

By Christ's death a holy God was freed to pardon every sin that was or ever will be, with respect to its power to condemn. If we can lose salvation, then we must conclude that there is some sin which is sufficiently serious to cause us to forfeit it—perhaps adultery, drunkenness, or denial of Christ. This assumes that we were less worthy of salvation after having committed this sin than before, and it reduces salvation down to the human ability to merit it. Our eternal security does not depend on our moral worthiness. If it did, none of us would be saved. Rather, it depends on the fact that Christ's death has rendered God free to save us in spite of our moral imperfection and that God's power is capable of keeping us saved.

In Colossians 2:14, Paul refers to the accumulation of sin as a "certificate of debt":

He forgave us all our sin, having cancelled the certificate of debt, with its regulations, that was against us and that stood opposed to us; he took it away, nailing it to the cross.

In the ancient world when a debtor owned money, the indebtedness was recorded on a "certificate of debt." Paul seems to use this as a metaphor for our certificate of accumulated debt due to our sin. Over a lifetime every man accumulates a massive "certificate of debt." Imagine an extremely pious man who sins only five times a day. Then his certificate of debt would record:

5 sins/day x 365 days x 70 years = 127,750 sins!

Now God knew about all these sins against us when He saved us in the first place. All these sins, past, present and future, were paid in full by the death of Christ. Recall Christ's last words on the cross, "it is finished (Gr *tetelestai*)"[2390] (John 19:30). With His sacrificial death, Jesus had completed the work the Father gave Him to do. One is tempted to suggest a secondary meaning of the verb Christ used. *Tetelestai* can mean, "It is paid in full."[2391]

Either Christ's death for sin actually paid the penalty, or it did not. If it did, then the believer cannot be condemned for the very sins for which Christ died. All sins that we would ever commit were future from the death of Christ. If our sins are a ground of judgment against us, then Christ's death was not propitious. If it was propitious, then our sin is no longer a ground of condemnation. It is either one or the other, and the Bible is quite clear that Christ has paid the penalty.

However, when Christ canceled the certificate of debt, it was not just for sins prior to our imprisonment but for all sin. In contrast to the temporary atonement we might make for our own sin by imprisonment or that a priest might make by offering sacrifices, Christ made an eternal redemption. The writer of the Epistle to the Hebrews says:

He did not enter by means of the blood of goats and calves; but he entered the Most Holy Place once for all by His own blood, having obtained ***eternal redemption*** *(Hebrews 9:12).*

But when this priest had offered ***for all time*** *one sacrifice for sin, he sat down at the right hand of God (Hebrews 10:12).*

Because by one sacrifice ***he has made perfect forever*** *those who are being made holy (Hebrews 10:14).*

Dabney asks:

Can one who has been fully justified in Christ, whose sins have been all blotted out, irrespective of their heinousness, by the perfect and efficacious price paid by Jesus Christ, become again unjustified, and fall under condemnation without a dishonor done to Christ's righteousness?[2392]

When Christ our Priest finished His sacrificial work, He "sat down." The notion of a seated priest was foreign to the Jewish economy. In fact, there were no chairs in the

[2390] Gr *tetelestai*, to complete an activity, BDAG, 996.

[2391] BDAG, 997. Moulton and Milligan cite instances in the commercial world where the verb means, "to pay," MM, 630.

[2392] Dabney, *Lectures in Systematic Theology*, 691.

tabernacle because a priest's work was never done. But here is a Priest who has finished His work. He sat down! There is nothing more to do as far as paying the penalty for sin is concerned. We have an eternal redemption. Our sin has been paid for all time, and we have been perfected forever!

Shank attempts to put verses 10 and 14 together and say that the phrase "once for all" in verse 10 and "for all time" in verse 14 both refer to Christ's offering, and not to the believer's permanent status before God.[2393] However, it is obvious that the recipients of the perfection in verse 14 are "those who are sanctified," and not the "one offering." In verse 14 the phrase "those who are sanctified" is an accusative participle and the phrase "one offering" is dative singular. The accusative case is the case of a direct object. It is those who are sanctified who receive the action of the main verb, "made perfect." The dative is properly rendered, "by means of." Thus we translate: "By means of one sacrifice He made those who are sanctified perfect forever." Shank's version would read something like, "One sacrifice has been made perfect forever, for those who are being sanctified." But this is simply impossible from Greek grammar.

Christ guaranteed our eternal security not only by means of His substitutionary death but also by means of His substitutionary life. Our eternal security depends …

ON HIS SUBSTITUTIONARY LIFE

Paul does not bring in this aspect of Christ's substitutionary work in Romans 8:31-34, but it is the subject of a large body of Scripture. Christ was our Substitute by His death, His so-called passive obedience, but He was also our Substitute by His life, His so-called active obedience. The Law required both a penalty for disobedience and a standard of perfect obedience. We can and could do neither. But by His righteous life Christ obeyed for us. In fact, we have been saved, according to some interpreters, by the faith *of* Christ as well as by faith *in* Christ.[2394]

There is a material cause and an instrumental cause of our salvation. The material cause is the active and passive obedience of Christ, His death, and His faith. The instrumental cause is our faith. We are justified by His blood and saved by His life (Romans 5:9-10). The righteousness the Law required is imputed to us when we believe.

Christ's active obedience is His perfect performance of the requirements of the moral law. There is atoning, or expiatory, value in the active obedience in the sense that His obedience was part of His humiliation. However, His active obedience relates mainly to the Law as precept, and not as penalty. The chief function of His active obedience was to win the reward of heaven for the believer.

This is necessary because to merely atone for past sin would not be a complete salvation. It would provide forgiveness but would not make him fit for heaven. He would be delivered from the law's punishment but not entitled to the law's reward. The law required perfect obedience. The mediator, then, must both pay the law's penalty, as well as obey the law in man's stead if he is to do for man everything the law requires:

2393 Shank, *Life in the Son: A Study of the Doctrine of Perseverance*, 122. "By this will we have been sanctified through the offering of the body of Jesus Christ *once for all*" (Hebrews 10:10).

2394 See Kendall, *Once Saved, Always Saved*, 64.

He made Him who knew no sin to be sin on our behalf, so that we might become the righteousness of God in Him (2 Corinthians 5:21)

His righteous life was credited to us. He obeyed on our behalf and as a result that obedience is now counted as our obedience.

Christ is the end of the law for righteousness to everyone who believes (Romans 10:4).

This means that Christ completely fulfilled the Law for the believer, but the Law requires obedience to its precepts as well as endurance of its penalty:[2395]

For as through the one man's disobedience the many were made sinners, even so through the obedience of the One the many will be made righteous (Romans 5:19).

And in Him you have been made complete (Colossians 2:10).

This is another basis of eternal security. If Christ has already perfectly obeyed the Law for us, and if His obedience has been imputed to us, then our eternal destiny is secure. However, if we base our eternal security on the degree of holiness or the perseverance in holiness in this life, we will be filled with the fear of uncertainty:

If I am a Christian for fifty years and have become increasingly godly with every passing year (which I hope would be true), I will still be judged by the same righteousness that was imputed to me when I first believed.[2396]

"If only Christ's passive obedience is put to our account, it follows that we must produce sufficient works on our own in order to be finally saved. This would mean that the death of Christ forgives our sins, but, since Christ's active obedience is not imputed to us, we must, from the moment of our conversion, live a life worthy of eternal life to be saved in the end. It therefore becomes absolutely crucial to know whether the active obedience of Christ, as well as the passive obedience of Christ, is imputed to us."[2397] Because Christ has already obeyed for us, we have a right to eternal life. Our own obedience secures reward but not life. Christ's obedience secures our right to heaven, and our obedience determines the degree of our reward there.

Christ died for us, but He also lives today to intercede for us. Paul emphasizes this in Romans 8:34 when he mentions that Christ is seated in heaven. There is a man representing us in heaven today! Because of His work of intercession, our eternal security depends …

ON HIS PRESENT SESSION

Paul also bases our eternal security on the fact that Jesus rose from the dead and is seated at the right hand of God. He is our Advocate and Intercessor (Romans 8:34). This is sometimes called the present priestly ministry of Christ, or His present session. In this role Jesus pleads our case as our Advocate, our defense attorney in the heavenly courtroom:

2395 Shedd and Gomes, *Dogmatic Theology*, 2:430-33.

2396 Kendall, *Once Saved, Always Saved*, 73.

2397 Ibid., 71.

My little children, I am writing these things to you that you may not sin. And if anyone sins, we have an Advocate with the Father, Jesus Christ the Righteous, and He Himself is the propitiation for our sins; and not for ours only, but also for those of the whole world (1 John 2:1-2).

Arminians have feared that this doctrine will tend to sin. John says that there is a motivation in this doctrine not to sin. The heavenly courtroom is opened. Satan, "the accuser of the brethren" (Revelation 12:10), brings the sinning Christian before the divine tribunal. In his role as prosecuting attorney he presents a compelling and irrefutable case before the bar of justice. This Christian has sinned, and justice requires that the penalty be paid. His accusations are correct. God is just. As the gavel is about to sound "Case closed" and the sinning Christian dismissed to punishment, our Advocate, Jesus Christ the Righteous, approaches the bar and begins His wonderful work of intercession:

Father, it is correct, as the Satan says, this brother of Mine has sinned and Your justice requires his condemnation. But Father, remember, I am the propitiation for his sin. By My death on the cross I have forever satisfied the claims of Your justice.

When the Father hears this intercessory prayer, He responds:

Case dismissed!

Christ could argue our case in various ways. He could make excuses. He could plead for leniency, but the Father, being holy and just, cannot be lenient with sin. However, our Attorney argues differently. Rather than make excuses or plea for mercy, He reminds the Father of the work He performed which earned Him the title, Jesus Christ the Righteous.

The title refers, first of all, to the fact that He is made to us the righteousness of God. He is the source of the imputed righteousness of Christ, the one by whom the Christian is saved and in whom he stands forever:

He made Him who knew no sin to be sin on our behalf, that we might become the righteousness of God in Him (2 Corinthians 5:21).

But, second, in 1 John 2:2 we are told that this Righteous One is righteous because of His work for us. He is the propitiation for our sins. Thus when the Father withholds condemnation, He is just. Jesus the Righteous has satisfied every claim against the sinning Christian. His advocacy is presented under the picture of His entrance into the heavenly sanctuary in Hebrews 9:24:

For Christ did not enter a holy place made with hands, a mere copy of the true one, but into heaven itself, now to appear in the presence of God for us (Hebrews 9:24).

It is obvious that, while God will exercise parental discipline (Hebrews 12:3-15), His child will never be condemned to the lake of fire because our Advocate has satisfied the claims of justice. Satan can never again bring a case to the bar of justice which will win. It is Christ who bore our sin who appears in heaven on our behalf, and Christ is the very righteousness in which the Christian is accepted before God. There is therefore no sin we can ever commit that will cause us to lose our salvation because of the advocacy and propitiation for all sin provided by Jesus Christ, the Righteous One:

And the former priests, on the one hand, existed in greater numbers, because they were prevented by death from continuing, but He, on the other hand, because He abides forever, holds His priesthood permanently. Hence, also, He is able to ***save forever*** *those who draw near to God through Him, since He always lives to make intercession for them (Hebrews 7:23-25).*

He is able to save forever, or to the "uttermost," because He lives forever to pray for us. Our eternal security is made to depend on the advocacy and intercession of Christ.[2398] Through His offering for sin and intercession we are "perfected for all time" (Hebrews 10:14).

Not only does the eternal security of the believer depend on God the Father and God the Son. It also ...

Eternal Security Depends on God the Holy Spirit

The ministry of the Holy Spirit toward the believer in Christ is also devoted to keeping him saved forever. Three specific works of the Holy Spirit are related to the issue of eternal security. Our eternal security depends, first of all, ...

UPON HIS MINISTRY OF REGENERATION

The ministry of the Holy Spirit in regeneration results in the birth of a new person and the gift of eternal life. Both of these effects imply irreversible change and a permanent new condition.

SPIRITUAL BIRTH. When Jesus told Nicodemus, "You must be born again," He taught that there are certain similarities between physical and spiritual birth. In each a new thing is created:

He saved us, not on the basis of deeds which we have done in righteousness, but according to His mercy, by the washing of regeneration and renewing by the Holy Spirit (Titus 3:5).

When this happens, a new thing is produced, the new creation:

Therefore if any man is in Christ, he is a new creature; the old things passed away; behold new things have come (2 Corinthians 5:17).

This new creation is His workmanship and unites us with the divine nature itself:

For we are His workmanship, created in Christ Jesus for good works (Ephesians 2:10).

Arminians, of course, point out that there are important differences between spiritual birth and physical birth and conclude, from the differences, that none of the similarities can be pressed. However, this surely takes the matter too far. It is obvious, as Arminians point out, that the subject of physical birth has no prior knowledge of his birth, but the subject of spiritual birth does have prior knowledge and is accountable. The real question, however, is, "Are there aspects of the physical birth analogy which do carry over into spiritual birth?"

[2398] "Forever" is *pantelēs* in Greek and can mean "for all time" or "completely" (BAGD, 63).

If so, which ones? It seems that the fundamental idea of the creation of a new thing, a new creation (2 Corinthians 5:17) called a "son" (Galatians 4:6), who is an heir of God (Romans 8:17), allows us, indeed requires us, to stress the point that a son cannot become a non-son and a created new man cannot be uncreated. New birth is clearly irreversible.

In the case of human generation, a being comes into existence who did not exist before, and this being will go on living forever. An earthly parent imparts a nature to a child, and that nature endures forever. Thus, to a much higher degree, our divine parent similarly creates a new man in Christ who will live forever. The earthly nature we inherit from our earthly parent never dies; it endures forever. Logic requires that the divine nature we inherit from our heavenly parent will similarly endure forever.

Can a man be unborn? Of course he can die, but this in no way reverses the fact of his sonship and his birth. Both physical and spiritual birth are one-time events with permanent consequences. Even death does not reverse it. Our conscious existence never ends, and one day all will be raised from the dead (John 5:28-29).

The son of a human parent may rebel and disobey, but he is still of the nature of his parent. That never changes. God similarly has created a new man; He gave birth to us. We may rebel, and God may disinherit us, as an earthly father can, but we will never cease to be His sons.

There is nothing, then, that can be done to reverse regeneration. Even if we decided we did not want to be God's children any longer, it would do no good. Spiritual and physical birth cannot be reversed. Furthermore, we cannot give salvation back. Is it not obvious that one cannot give his physical birth back to his human parent? Neither can he give his spiritual birth back to his divine parent. If that were possible, then the gospel promise would be contradicted. Then a person who had believed in God's Son would perish and not have everlasting life after all (John 3:16). Then a person who possesses eternal life *would* come under judgment in direct contradiction to John 5:24.

ETERNAL LIFE. Not only are we born into His family, but through regeneration we receive the gift of eternal life. Eternal life implies endless existence. Shank counters by stressing that eternal life is a quality of existence.[2399] With this, of course, all would agree. But that in no way diminishes the obvious biblical testimony to the fact that eternal life is eternal, endless. All of the lexicons include the notion of "endless existence" in the semantic value of the word "eternal."[2400]

Shank insists, however, that eternal life can only be shared with men, not permanently possessed by them.[2401] However, if a man has eternal existence, he will live endlessly. Eternal life is owned permanently the moment it is given. It is a characteristic of the new creation. To be given the gift of eternal life, according to Shank, is to be given the gift of living forever until you die and no longer live forever! This is an absurdity. Jesus Himself argued that eternal life was first of all the promise that a believer will rise from the dead after he physically dies (John 11:25-26). But He also says that a Christian has eternal life right now and this means he cannot cease to live:

2399 Shank, *Life in the Son: A Study of the Doctrine of Perseverance*, 21-22.

2400 E.g., see BAGD, 28; MM, 16.

2401 Shank, *Life in the Son: A Study of the Doctrine of Perseverance*, 52.

Jesus said to her, "I am the resurrection and the life, he who believes in Me shall live even if he dies, and everyone who lives and believes in Me shall never die."

He says we have eternal life now, and as a result (1) we will rise from the dead in resurrection, and (2) we will *never* die. For Jesus, at least, the gift of eternal life meant far more than sharing the life of God now. It was also a guarantee of endless existence with Him. We will never die! Over and over again the Savior stresses the permanent nature of the gift of eternal life. He told the woman at the well that, if she were to just take a drink of the water He would give, she would "never thirst" (John 4:14). He said, "I am the bread of life; he who comes to Me shall never hunger, and he who believes in Me shall never thirst" (John 6:35). Eternal life is permanent. "All that the Father gives Me shall come to Me, and the one who comes to Me I will certainly not cast out" (John 6:37). The Christian will "certainly not" be cast out! How else could the Lord say it? Eternal life is not only "without cost," it is permanent!

Second, our eternal security depends …

ON HIS BAPTIZING MINISTRY

In 1 Corinthians 12:13 Paul tells us:

For by one Spirit we were all baptized into one body (NASB).

Through the baptizing ministry of the Holy Spirit, we are brought into organic union with Christ. Paul develops this further in Romans 6:

Or do you not know that all of us who have been baptized into Christ Jesus have been baptized into His death? (Romans 6:3).

In this famous passage on sanctification, Paul explains that Christ's history has become ours. His death to sin has become ours. But there are permanent effects of this union:

Now if we have died with Christ, we believe that we shall also live with Him, knowing that Christ, having been raised from the dead, is ***never to die again****; death no longer is master over Him. For the death that He died,* ***He died to sin, once for all****; but the life that He lives, He lives to God (Romans 6:8-10).*

Because of the baptizing work of the Holy Spirit, uniting us to Christ, what is true of Him has become true of us. One thing that is true of Him is that He died to sin "once and for all" and that He will "never die again." Paul specifically tells us that this is true of us as well:

Even so consider yourselves to be dead to sin, but alive to God in Christ Jesus (Romans 6:11).

What is true of Him is declared to be true of us. We are eternally secure because we are in a permanent union with Christ.

Finally our eternal security depends …

ON HIS SEALING MINISTRY

There are three references to the sealing ministry of the Holy Spirit:

Who also sealed [sphragizō] us and gave us the Spirit in our hearts as a pledge [arrabōn] (2 Corinthians 1:21-22).

In Him, you also, after listening to the message of truth, the gospel of your salvation—having also believed, you were sealed [sphragizō] in Him with the Holy Spirit of promise, who is given as a pledge [arrabōn] of our inheritance, with a view to the redemption of God's own possession, to the praise of His glory (Ephesians 1:13-14).

And do not grieve the Holy Spirit of God, by whom you were sealed [sphragizō] for the day of redemption (Ephesians 4:30).

Two things stand out in these verses: (1) the Holy Spirit has sealed us (*sphragizō*), and (2) the Holy Spirit is the pledge (*arrabōn*).

The ancient practice of using seals is behind the figurative use of the word here. A seal was a mark of protection[2402] and ownership. The Greek word *sphragizō* is used of a stone being fastened with a seal to "prevent its being moved from a position."[2403] In fact, this was apparently the earliest method of distinguishing one's property. The seal was engraved with a design or mark distinctive to the owner. The seal of ownership or protection was often made in soft wax with a signet ring. An impression was left on the wax signifying the owner of the thing sealed. When the Holy Spirit seals us, He presses the signet ring of our heavenly Father on our hearts of wax and leaves the mark of ownership. We belong to Him. He certifies this by His unchangeable purpose to protect and own us to the day of redemption.[2404]

In Ephesians 1:13-14, we are told that the Holy Spirit Himself is the seal. He is impressed upon us, so to speak. His presence in our lives is thus a guarantee of God's protection and that we are owned by God. A broken seal was an indication that the person had not been protected. The Holy Spirit cannot be broken. He is the seal of ownership. In Ephesians 4:30, we are told that we are sealed *unto the day of redemption*. This sealing ministry of the Spirit is forever and guarantees that we will arrive safely for the redemption of our bodies and entrance into heaven (Romans 8:23). He is the seal that we are now owned and protected by God until the day of redemption.

We are forever protected from wrath. We cannot lose our salvation any more than we can break the seal. We would have to have greater power to lose salvation than the Holy Spirit has to keep us saved. About all Arminian Robert Shank can do is to weakly object, "But the Holy Spirit can do nothing for those who refuse His ministry."[2405] But He certainly can! That is precisely what these verses are saying. It seems that Shank is looking right at the verse and simply refusing to accept what it says and actually reverses its plain meaning. Shank lists various experiential ministries which the believer can refuse to accept as proof, such as the filling of the Spirit (Ephesians 5:18), and he points out that we can

---

[2402] E.g., Matthew 27:66, where the tomb of Christ was made secure by sealing the stone.

[2403] BAGD, 803.

[2404] F. B. Huey, "Seal," in ZPED, 5:319.

[2405] Shank, *Life in the Son: A Study of the Doctrine of Perseverance*, 186.

grieve the Spirit (Ephesians 4:30). "But," as Sellers correctly points out, "those ministries are experiential ministries; sealing and pledging are not."[2406] Nowhere are believers asked to allow the Spirit to seal them or to become their pledge. These are things that happen to all believers at the time they believe: "having also believed, you were also sealed" (Ephesians 1:13).

Then Why Not Sin?

"Well then," one might ask. "If I am eternally secure and cannot lose salvation, what motivation is there to keep me from sinning?" Lewis Sperry Chafer answers,

> *Because you should act like a child of God. Sinning brings loss of fellowship, and as children of God we should desire fellowship with Him.*
>
> *Because grace is a trust to us. It [sin] puts us out of fellowship with God and to be out of fellowship is a stormy state, not to be lost but to lose those blessings which are not receivable while out of fellowship.*
>
> *Because His grace-gift does not give us a license.*
>
> *Because we are placed on the greatest honor anyone could be placed on. To sin would cause grief to God who provided so great salvation for us. We are to walk in a new life-principle guided by the Holy Spirit. We are to serve God but not sin.*
>
> *God's grace and love given to me are the great incentive for me to please Him: "Grace teaches us…to live godly" (Titus 2:11–12), "the love of God shed abroad in our hearts" (Rom 5:5), "If a man love me, he will keep my words" (John 14:23), "How shall we that are dead to sin, live any longer therein?" (Rom 6:2).*
>
> *Because it is not in accordance with His will, and the Christian has a desire to live pleasing to Him. This also would be dishonoring to Him and the Christian has the desire to honor Him. To sin is to disobey God, grieve the Holy Spirit, and dishonor the Son.*
>
> *Because we are dead to the sin nature and it has no more dominion over us (Rom 6:1–14).*
>
> *Because we are saved by grace, we are to yield ourselves servants to obey Christ, not sin (Rom 6:15). Being made free from sin, we become the servants of righteousness (Rom 6:18). (I should not sin since I am secure, because I am grateful for my salvation and I want to evidence this by a life that pleases God.)*
>
> *Because (1) we lose our fellowship with the Father and the Son; (2) it affects our testimony before the unsaved; (3) it affects our service for God; and (4) it requires Christ to advocate for us when Satan accuses us before God.*
>
> *In Christ we are complete, having partaken of His divine nature, and to sin would be contradicting and bringing dire insult to such a possession. Also, fellowship with Him is too sweet; why should I want to break such a sweet relationship with a careless life?*
>
> *Sin has an effect upon God and saint (according to 1 John 1 and 2). For the latter it means loss of fellowship, loss of joy, powerlessness in prayer, and lack of assurance.*
>
> *Because we are dead to sin—"Shall we continue in sin that grace may abound? God forbid. How shall we that died to sin live any longer therein?" (Rom 6:1–2).*
>
> *I can't sin as if I had a license to sin, and live a life in keeping with the position in Christ which God has given me.*
>
> *Ephesians 4:1: "Walk worthy of the vocation wherewith ye are called."*[2407]

[2406] Ibid., 187.

[2407] Lewis Sperry Chafer, "The Sins of Christians," *BibSac* 109, no. 433 (January-March 52): 4.

Finally, we must add a significant reason which Dr. Chafer omitted.

Because if I fail to follow Christ as a disciple, I face shame, profound regret, rebuke, millennial disinheritance, and vastly reduced intimacy with Christ, service for Christ, and honor from Christ in the millennium and in the eternal state (see volume 3).

We now turn to this theme in the next chapter.

Summary

If our eternal security depends on anything in us, it is certain that it is not secure. However, the Scriptures teach that our final entrance into heaven is guaranteed by the work of the Father, the Son, and the Holy Spirit. Since it depends on an infinite Person, who is faithful and true, it is inconceivable that the salvation of any child of God could ever be lost.

Volume 3

Destiny

Introduction

SPECIAL DAYS like birthdays, Mother's Day, anniversaries, etc., are big around our house. After missing Valentine's Day during the first year of our marriage, I learned how *really important* they are! Therefore, on our anniversary a few years ago when my wife outdid her previous efforts and surprised me with a Scientific American cruise in the Caribbean, this was true to form.

This was a cosmology cruise. There were about 2500 guests on the ship, and 120 participants in special lectures given by various experts in astrophysics and the origin of the universe research. Those attending included university professors, engineers, scientists, teachers … and me.

Monday morning with great anticipation (I love to study cosmology) I went into the lecture room where Lawrence Krauss was giving the first lecture. Professor Kraus is a brilliant atheist who often writes for *Scientific American*. He is a recognized authority on cosmology and questions of the origin, nature, and structure of the universe. It is simply impossible for him to write a book that is not interesting, profound, and totally engaging. A recent example of his remarkable literary and scientific abilities is his book entitled *A Universe from Nothing: Why There Is Something Rather Than Nothing.*

Krauss began his lecture with these words, "My purpose this week is to convince you that there is absolutely no ultimate meaning to human existence. The universe is pointless." I was reminded of the quip reportedly made by a Russian physicist, "Cosmologists are often wrong, but never in doubt."

After that opening salvo I knew I was in for an interesting week, and I was not disappointed. I was there, not to disagree, but to learn from these scientists what they really believe.

Realizing that there is considerable evidence emerging which points to the fact that the universe was designed for life, had a beginning, and emerged out of nothing, Dr. Krauss admits that "thoughtful people" consider this as evidence for a First Cause (God).[2408] He summarily dismisses this, however, with the tired riposte, "Who created the Creator? After all," he says, "what is the difference between arguing in favor of an eternally existing creator versus an eternally existing universe without one?"[2409] With respect to Dr.

[2408] For a fascinating summary of the scientific evidence that the universe appears to be designed for man, see Guillermo Gonzalez and Jay W. Richards, *The Privileged Planet: How Our Place in the Cosmos Is Designed for Discovery* (Washington D.C.: Regnery, 2004).

[2409] Lawrence M. Krauss, *A Universe from Nothing: Why There Is Something Rather Than Nothing* (New York: Free Press, a Division of Simon & Schuster, 2012), s.v. "Preface". The answer to Krauss' objection is that he incorrectly assumes that everything needs a cause. Everything does not need a cause, unless of course, it does,

Krauss, plenty! An eternally existing Creator who designed the universe for life leads to the conclusion that we have significance, our lives do matter, and that one day we will be held accountable before that Creator for how we have lived. A universe that popped into existence out of nothing, has no meaning and no purpose, and neither do we.

Krauss recognizes the difficulty of positing the notion that something came out of nothing. After all, this contradicts one of the fundamental laws of physics, the first law of thermodynamics which says that mass and energy are always conserved and can never be created or destroyed. Something, therefore, cannot emerge from nothing. Therefore, he addresses his attention to the meaning of "nothing." The prosaic mind would understand this to mean the absence of anything— no mass, no energy, no fields, nada, zip. Not so, says Krauss, "nothing" may not be "nothing." In fact, it is full of virtual particles. These particles pop into existence out of a pervasive field of dark energy and endure for 10^{-44} seconds. The energy is the so-called "vacuum energy" of free space and is part of the "fabric" of free space. It is equivalent to Einstein's cosmological constant. Therefore, he says, "getting something from nothing is not a problem. Indeed, something from nothing may have been required for the universe to come into being. Moreover, all signs suggest that this is how our universe could have arisen."[2410]

In fact, Krauss says, "'nothing' is every bit as physical as 'something,' especially if it is to be defined as the 'absence of something.'"[2411] If one wants to invoke God to explain the origin of the new "nothing," Krauss objects that one who does this "is merely intellectually lazy." Besides, "Theologians," he says, "are experts in nothing."[2412]

Whether this theory of the pre-big-bang state is correct or not, it is clearly not "nothing," and it does not answer the question, "Who created the virtual particle?" "Who created the dark energy?" This, then, is where Krauss's thinking has led him, debating the meaning of the word "nothing"! In the end, it is "something" after all!

As I write these words I am camping with Linda at beautiful Mueller State Park southwest of Colorado Springs. My choice of reading for the week is Miguel de Cervantes' classic masterpiece, *Don Quixote*. It is the story of a man who after years of reading histories and stories of knights-errant, became so enmeshed in this fantasy world that he became mad. With his squire, Sancho, Don Quixote sets out on many adventures to right wrongs, save damsels in distress, and establish his credentials as the gallant knight of La Mancha, the village where he lived. At one level the book is a satire about the standards of chivalry of the era. But at a deeper level Don Quixote was in search for meaning in his life.

which is the point in question and which Krauss blandly assumes. "However," as Norm Geisler explains, "This dilemma is based on a misunderstanding of the principle of causality, which does not state that 'everything needs a cause' but only that 'every *finite* (or contingent) thing needs a cause.' A being that is not finite (viz., is infinite) does not need a cause, nor does one that is not contingent (viz., is necessary). Since the physical universe is finite, it does need a cause. Likewise, not everything that is eternal needs a cause (e.g., God) but everything that has a beginning does need a cause. Since the physical universe had a beginning, it must have had a Cause." See Geisler, *Systematic Theology*, 566. Also, an infinite regress, that is, and infinite series of causes is logically impossible. Geisler explains, "An ungrounded infinite regress is tantamount to affirming that the existence in the series arises from nonexistence, since no cause in the series has a real ground for its existence. Or, if one cause in the series grounds the existence of the others, then it must be a First Cause (and hence the series is not infinite). Otherwise, it turns out to be a cause that causes its own existence (which is impossible), while it is causing the existence of everything else in the series." Ibid., 569-70.

[2410] Krauss, *A Universe from Nothing: Why There Is Something Rather Than Nothing.*

[2411] Ibid.

[2412] Ibid.

He found it in living out a fantasy, a made-up world in which he was the gallant knight-errant. The final reference point in his world is himself and the valiant exploits he could achieve. God is not in the picture.

Don Quixote is the story of every man. Having rejected the God of the Bible, mankind has become adept at manufacturing fanciful ideas such as Krauss's universe created out of nothing. That worldview does indeed, as Krauss suggests, yield a conclusion that human life is pointless. Considerable creative thought is required if one is to find meaning and significance in this pointless universe without God.

Krauss, however, is perfectly willing to take up the challenge. His solution to the apparently meaningless existence he endures is that the quest for understanding of the cosmos "whatever the outcome, provides its own reward."[2413] He explains,

> *A universe without purpose or guidance may seem, for some, to make life itself meaningless. For others, including me, such a universe is invigorating. It makes the fact of our existence even more amazing and it motivates us to draw meaning from our own actions and to make the most of our brief existence in the sun, simply because we are here, blessed with consciousness and with the opportunity to do so.*[2414]

Excuse me! We are supposed "*to draw meaning from our own actions*"!? Like Don Quixote, this brilliant scientist has manufactured a fantasy world in which the final reference point is himself. There is no God to whom he is finally accountable and from whom he can derive personal significance. All revolves around (1) him and his search for knowledge; and (2) his actions. These actions, however, have no value other than the value which Krauss assigns to them. No one but Krauss himself can adjudicate their ultimate meaning.

But is the universe pointless? What is the final significance of man? Why are we here? Why did God create us, and what is our role in His eternal purpose? From an eternal perspective God has made it clear that the ultimate purpose of all creation is the manifestation of His own glory. This, of course, is not egotistical, but it is the highest conceivable good. If God is infinitely holy, just, and loving, there is no higher purpose than for these magnificent attributes to be fully demonstrated.

Where does man fit into God's eternal purpose? In this final volume of the three-volume series, we will address this question in considerable detail. In volume 1, chapters 15 and 16, we summarized Jesus' answer to this question as to the "salvation of our soul." By this we do not mean final entrance into heaven or escape from the lake of fire. Rather, "to save one's soul" (Gr *sōsai tēn psychē*) is an idiom which clearly means "to preserve one's physical life." There is the connotative meaning in some New Testament contexts of "find rich life now by self-denial, taking up our cross and following Christ, with the result that we will be favorably recompensed at the Judgment Seat of Christ."[2415]

If a person is to seek the final significance of his life in hearing the Master's "Well done!" there must also be a consequence if one's life does not receive that wonderful affirmation. Final accountability and true purpose involve blessing for faithfulness and rebuke for willful failure. Therefore, we must consider both outcomes if we are to truly

---

[2413] Ibid., 182.

[2414] Ibid., 181.

[2415] See discussion in volume 1, chapters 15 and 16.

understand and be motivated by the biblical solution to the meaning of life.

This discussion will lead us onto many paths and raise significant questions.

- What is the Judgment Seat of Christ, and how do we obtain a favorable account there?
- The "darkness outside" is presented as a dreadful fate. Is it possible that this is a metaphor for a negative assessment of a believer's life?
- Several parables in Matthew 24, the wicked servant, the ten virgins, and the unfaithful servant, all describe a negative judgment for an unfaithful life. To whom do they apply, believers or nonbelievers?
- At the judgment of the sheep and the goats in Matthew 25, the sheep are awarded kingships and eternal life on the basis of their acts of charity to the poor. Does this indicate that heaven is obtained by good works?
- Jesus refers to *Gehenna* eleven times. On a number of occasions, He warns believers that they might be consigned to this place. How are we to understand these warnings if *Gehenna* refers to final damnation as the traditional view maintains?
- If Christ is the propitiation for the sins of the whole world, how can any believer experience a negative appraisal at the Judgment Seat of Christ? Hasn't the penalty for all his sins already been paid?
- The Bible speaks of the possibility that believers might obtain treasures in heaven. What are they, and how can we receive them?
- Is the pursuit of rewards a legitimate motivation for Christian living? Does not the Bible teach us that "love seeks not its own"? Shouldn't we do good works simply for the sake of the good itself or because we love God?
- If God will reward us on the basis of our works, how do we explain that this is a merited reward? Isn't this spiritual commercialism?
- In Philippians chapter 3 Paul expresses some uncertainty as to whether or not he will attain to the resurrection from the dead. Does this mean that believers should be in doubt regarding their final destiny? Paul says that he strives to obtain the "upward call." What is this call? Is it the call to enter heaven or the call to obtain treasures in heaven, awarded to a faithful life?
- Many of the interpretations suggested in these volumes depart from traditional views. How can a person be comfortable with these viewpoints when he has never heard them before?
- What is the final significance of man?

48

Tragedy or Triumph

AT LAST!" cried Michael's colleague as he rushed into the archangel's presence. "Did you hear the trumpet?"[2416]

Excitedly, Michael replied, "Of course, my friend. It is time for the beginning."

For centuries the long and arduous course of human history had unfolded. It had been the Father's purpose during that time to prepare a race of servant kings who would fulfill the final destiny of man. During that brief moment between eternity future and eternity past called Time, the futility of independence had been made evident to all. The Satan's lie had been answered. It was now time for the righting of all wrongs, the final accounting. The reign of the *Metochoi* ("partners") was about to begin.

"We have been preparing for this moment for thousands of years," said Michael. "We have constructed the city exactly according to the King's specifications."[2417]

"And what a magnificent structure it is," his angelic helper replied. "The King Himself supervised every detail in anticipation of the ultimate arrival of His servants. Did you see the joy on His face as He saw the completed project?"

"Yes, it thrilled my heart. He has devoted centuries to preparing these mansions for His followers on earth."

Suddenly, there was a sound like the rush of a great wind. In an instant millions of people abruptly appeared in the heavenly city. The dead in Christ had risen. Those still living had received resurrection bodies, and all had been transported to heaven to be with the Lord.[2418] But the hosts of heaven were ready; their work was done. Dwellings for each were ready to be inhabited.

"Yes, our King has kept His promise to them; it is now time to honor those who have kept their promises to Him."[2419]

"Come, let us proceed to the square in the center of the city."

On arrival, Michael and his colleague saw multitudes of men and women surrounding a raised platform in the city square. Brilliant lights splashed outward in all directions. Beautiful music created a sense of anticipation. The atmosphere was electric with expectation.

2416 1 Thessalonians 4:16.

2417 Hebrews 11:16.

2418 1 Thessalonians 4:17.

2419 Romans 8:17.

Seated on the jewel-studded throne, the King named Wonderful[2420] gazed smilingly and compassionately on the hushed throng. It was the Judgment Seat of Christ.[2421]

For centuries the angels had been preparing for this event. Not only had they labored to build the city, but each had been assigned to assist a particular man or woman in his personal struggle to inherit salvation.[2422]

One-by-one the members of the vast multitude were summoned to the Judge's throne. A man appeared before the King. He had wasted his life, and it was now all too evident that he had searched for meaning in the wrong places. He had become a Christian at an early age but had never followed the path of discipleship. "Next year," he had always said. "Next year, I will get serious about my Christian faith." But "next year" had finally come, and it was too late. He had married a committed Christian girl, but his real marriage was to his work and himself. For years he had thought of nothing but material success and high position on the corporate ladder. His Christian commitment extended to avoidance of gross sin. He had attended church regularly and had often gone to various Christian meetings. His heart, however, was never focused on eternity. Instead of laying up treasure in heaven, he had chosen to lay up treasure on earth. Bible reading was boring, and his prayer life was nonexistent.

"Come, servant of Mine," thundered the voice from the throne. The eyes of the Wonderful Counselor were no longer smiling.

There was a shuffling among the throng. Suddenly, everyone was quiet, and many were looking down, unable to endure the searing eyes of the King.

"Yes, Lord, I ...." For the first time in his life he was speechless. All the excuses which had so easily postponed serious commitment no longer mattered. In an instant his entire life was somehow miraculously paraded in front of his mind.

As he remembered all the opportunities he had wasted, he winced in pain. This was heightened in intensity because of the greater sensitivity to sin of the resurrection body. He thought of the great Christian home from which he had come and how his mother had taught him to live for eternity, but the things at school always seemed more attractive. He thought of God's gift to him of a loving wife who had truly modeled Christianity before him. He had never joined her in her desire for a truly spiritual relationship in marriage. Yet, outwardly he appeared Christian, and the underlying inconsistencies were not evident.

"Servant of Mine," the voice from the throne interrupted his thoughts. "I warned you often that there is nothing covered up that will not be revealed and hidden that will not be known."[2423]

"Lord, I am so sorry," he cried, realizing that momentarily he would face the eternal consequences of his life.

"You have presumed on My grace and have lived for yourself," the King continued. "I have given you much and told you that to everyone who has been given much, much will be required."[2424]

Turning His face upward, the one called the Word of God said, "Father, I bring this servant of Mine before You. He has denied Me by his life on earth, and I now deny him before You. He will not join with My *Metochoi* as one of My servant kings. He has lost his inheritance!"

[2420] Isaiah 9:6.

[2421] 2 Corinthians 5:10.

[2422] Hebrews 1:14.

[2423] Luke 12:2.

[2424] Luke 12:48.

Then with a stern look on His face, the King rebuked His unfaithful follower, "Depart from Me, you wicked, lazy slave."[2425]

"Noooo ...," the lazy servant screamed. But the angels came and led him to the darkness outside the city square where he began to weep and gnash his teeth in profound regret.[2426]

Another man appeared before the judgment seat. This one stood with joyful countenance and tearful expectation. The eyes of the King called Wonderful softened with compassion and delight.

"Come, servant of Mine," said the King.

Jimmy had faithfully served his master throughout his eighty years. It had been the King's purpose that this man would uniquely display God's power and grace. The King had allowed terrible skin cancer to ravage his body for all of his adult life. Over two hundred painful operations had grotesquely lacerated his once handsome face. No one knew the silent, daily humiliation Jimmy had felt, having to conduct business appointments, teach Sunday school classes, and otherwise be exposed to the public eye. Yet, he had never complained or doubted God's sovereign purpose in his life.

Once, when a non-Christian friend was provoked by Jimmy's pain and appearance to doubt the existence of God, Jimmy responded, "Could it be that God allowed this to happen to me so that I would have the privilege of revealing to others how a true Christian deals with tragedy?"

Yet, now he stood before his King whole and without pain. His once handsome face had been restored and now radiated with exhilaration at being in the presence of the Master he had so greatly pleased. There were no more tears and no more pain.

Once again with tears in His eyes, the King called Wonderful summoned the man, "Come, servant of Mine."

"Why is he hesitating?" said Michael's colleague. "If I were he, I would be bounding upward to join the King."

"This has been typical of Jimmy all his life," Michael replied. "In every case those servants who are most worthy of the King's honors are the most humble and self-effacing."

Then the multitude gasped. The King did something He only rarely did. He got off the throne and came down to the man and embraced him.

"Jimmy," the King said, "I want to thank you for never complaining and for fulfilling the purpose I have designed for your life. You have been faithful in little things. I am now going to make you ruler over many.[2427]

"Thank you for the many cups of water you have given to Me."

"But, Lord," Jimmy replied, "when did I ever give You a cup of water."

"Do you remember when you used to take food to the poor on Christmas day? Do you remember the young Korean girl you took into your home? Do you remember the many gifts you gave to charity and to world evangelization? Do you remember the young couples you and Mallory adopted as spiritual children and before whom you modeled My life? Do you remember the many destitute people who came to you for financial and practical counsel and how you were always available and always helpful in representing My view of life? Do you not remember the wise counsel you gave as a board member of many

---

2425 Matthew 25:26.

2426 Matthew 25:30.

2427 Matthew 25:21-26. While this passage applies to the 2nd coming, I assume that the same standard applies to the Judgment Seat of Christ.

Christian organizations and how you participated at your own expense, even though you were physically in great pain and very weary?"

Jimmy was now very embarrassed but quietly pleased that the One for Whom he labored remembered everything.

"Lord," Jimmy replied, "thank You for remembering all that, but I am just your unworthy servant. I have only done my duty."[2428]

"Jimmy, what you say is true," the King called Wonderful replied, "but whatever you did for one of the least of these brothers of Mine, you did for Me.[2429]

"Because you have honored Me on earth, I will now honor you in heaven. Your new name shall be 'Courageous.'[2430] You have been courageous in faith in the midst of personal difficulty. You have lived courageously and faithfully to the end. You have fought a good fight. You have kept the faith. You have now finished your course. You have longed for My return. I now give you the crown of righteousness."[2431]

Then, taking Jimmy by the arm, the King escorted him up to the platform to join Him around the throne.

Turning His face upward, the King called Wonderful said, "Father, I now bring before you My faithful servant Jimmy. He has finished his life with his flag at full mast. He has been faithful in the small things. I will now honor him with many things."[2432]

With joy in His eyes the King turned to His faithful servant and said, "Well done, good and faithful servant, enter into the joy of your Lord. You will now inherit the kingdom."

> *I, the Lord, search the heart, I test the mind, Even to give to each man according to his ways, according to the results of his deeds (Jeremiah 17:10).*

The New Testament everywhere avows that each believer will one day face an accounting for the stewardship with which we have been entrusted. Apparently, and fortunately for us, our lives will not be evaluated according to the world's criteria of success but God's. At issue will be our faithfulness.[2433] For those who have been faithful to their Lord throughout life, it will be a day of great triumph, of reward, and of hearing the Master say, "Well done."

However, a different fate awaits those Christians who have failed to persevere, who have not remained faithful to their Lord. In an instant, as they stand before their King, their entire lives will be seen to have been wasted. There can be no greater tragedy than to hear the words, "Too late."

Yes, the Judgment Seat of Christ will be a time of either tragedy or triumph. We will discuss the triumph of the faithful in later chapters, but in this chapter we will address the tragedy of those who are not.

What is the nature of the Judgment Seat of Christ? Will there be distinctions in heaven? How can those for whom Christ died receive any negative consequence at the final tribunal? How can the New Testament doctrine of rewards be reconciled with the doctrine of unmerited favor? It is to these and other questions we now direct our attention.

[2428] Luke 17:10.

[2429] Matthew 25:40.

[2430] Revelation 2:17.

[2431] 2 Timothy 4:7-8.

[2432] Luke 19:17.

[2433] 1 Corinthians 4:1-2.

The Judgment Seat

Travelers to the archaeological excavations of the city of Corinth have seen the famous judgment seat in the town square. There is little doubt that this was the very forum in the apostle's mind when he wrote:

> *For we must all appear before the Judgment Seat of Christ, that each one may receive what is due him for the things done while in the body, whether good or bad (2 Corinthians 5:10).*

The judgment seat (Gr *bēma*) in Corinth was a large, richly decorated rostrum, centrally located in the marketplace. It was the place where rewards were given out for victory at the Isthmian athletic games. These rewards consisted of garlands, trophies, crowns, and special social benefits, such as exemption from income tax. But punishments were also administered here.

Apparently this judgment deals with the negative as well as the positive. Paul says that we will be judged according to both the good and the bad things we have done while in the body. We tend to gloss over this, yet the Lord warned, "For there is nothing covered that shall not be revealed; neither hid, that shall not be known" (Luke 12:2-3).[2434] Paul spoke of God bringing to light the hidden things of darkness (1 Corinthians 4:3-5), and Peter spoke of the fact that judgment must begin with the household of God (1 Peter 4:17-18). Paul's reaction to the Judgment Seat of Christ was, "Knowing therefore the terror of the Lord" (2 Corinthians 5:11).

Paul refers to our life work as a building that will be subjected to a careful examination (1 Corinthians 3:14-15). He warns us that all will appear for this accounting (Romans 14:10-12). Therefore, we should not judge others now, for the Lord will judge the hidden motives then (1 Corinthians 4:5). He often compared the Christian life to that of the athlete who pursues the victor's crown (1 Corinthians 9:24-27; 2 Timothy 2:5).

From this very judgment seat, the Bēma, Gallio passed judgment on the apostle Paul (Acts 18:12). It was to this raised platform that Paul referred when he said, "We must all appear before the Judgment Seat of Christ" (2 Corinthians 5:10).

[2434] Note also Matthew 10:26; Mark 4:22; Luke 8:17.

Jesus continually exhorted His fellows to full discipleship by reminding them that one day they will face an accounting for their stewardship.[2435] He challenged them to pursue rewards[2436] and treasure in heaven.[2437]

Throughout the New Testament this theme repeatedly emerges:

> *My brethren, let not many of you become teachers, knowing that we shall receive the stricter judgment (James 3:1, NKJV).*

> *For the time has come for judgment to begin at the house of God; and if it begins with us first, what will be the end of those who do not obey the gospel of God? (1 Peter 4:17, NKJV).*

> *Love has been perfected among us in this: that we may have boldness in the day of judgment (1 John 4:17, NKJV).*

The Criteria of Judgment

It is vitally important that we understand precisely what Christ will look for in our lives. If we are to be evaluated, what are the criteria for passing the test? There seem to be three: our deeds, our faithfulness, and our words.[2438]

OUR DEEDS

In the Partner view of eternal security, it is impossible to take lightly our responsibility to perform good works. The Scriptures everywhere stress their importance:

> *Each one's work will become manifest, for the Day will declare it, because it will be revealed by fire, and the fire will test each one's work,* ***of what sort it is*** *(1 Corinthians 3:13, NKJV).*

> *For we must all appear before the Judgment Seat of Christ, that each one may receive the things done in the body,* ***according to what he has done, whether it is good or bad*** *(2 Corinthians 5:10, NKJV).*

> *And I will give to each one of you* ***according to your works*** *(Revelation 2:23, NKJV).*

The issue will not be just the amount of work but "of what sort it is" and whether it is "good or bad." How does one determine whether his work is good or bad? The Scriptures give two criteria.

They must be according to Scripture. No work will be accepted which does not pass this test:

> *Do you not know that those who run in a race all run, but one receives the prize?* ***Run in such a way that you may obtain it*** *(1 Corinthians 9:24).*

2435 Matthew 10:26-42; 16:27; 24:45-51; Mark 8:38; Luke 12:42-48.

2436 Matthew 5:11, 46; 6:1-6, 16-18.

2437 Matthew 6:19-21; 19:21; Mark 4:24-25; Luke 12:13-21; 16:1-13.

2438 The following discussion is borrowed from Ken Quick, "The Doctrine of Eternal Significance" (DMin diss., Dallas Theological Seminary, 1989).

*And if anyone competes in athletics, he is not crowned unless he **competes according to the rules** (2 Timothy 2:5, NKJV).*

In some instances there may be differing interpretations of Scripture. This introduces a degree of ambiguity. Suppose our interpretation was wrong, and we did a work consistent with an incorrect interpretation? This is why the Lord looks deeper than the interpretation, to our inward motives. Who among us has not been guilty of interpreting the Bible to fit what we wanted to do? Who of us has not been guilty of twisting the Bible to fit our doctrinal system? The purpose here is not to discuss the various social issues of the day. But we are all aware of the new interpretations of the Bible being given by evangelicals regarding women's roles, abortion, marriage, government (e.g., theonomy), and the definition and nature of the church.

When deeds are performed based on a particular interpretation of Scripture, the Lord will look to the person's motive in arriving at that interpretation. Was the true motive to discern the single intent of the original author of Scripture? Was the true motive to find out what the Bible truly said, and do it no matter what the cost? Or was the person making the Bible fit into a belief system he had accepted elsewhere? Was he, in reaction to something about the Christian community that hurt him in his past, using the Bible falsely? These questions lead us to the second criterion used to test "what sort of work" we have done: motivation.

THEY MUST EMERGE FROM A MOTIVATION TO BRING HONOR TO GOD. A work done has two aspects to it: the deed itself, and the motive behind it. Is it not true that we often begin good projects for the Lord but they become total failures? Conversely, sometimes some of the works that outwardly are the biggest and most public were done for the wrong motives. When our Lord evaluates our lives, He will look deeper than the works themselves. He will search "the minds and hearts" (Revelation 2:23).

Consider:

Therefore judge nothing before the time, until the Lord comes, who will both bring to light the hidden things of darkness and reveal the counsel of the hearts; and then each one's praise will come from God (1 Corinthians 4:5, NKJV).

Jesus too emphasized that inner motivation determines the value of a deed:

Take heed that you do not do your charitable deeds before men, to be seen by them. Otherwise you have no reward from your Father in heaven. Therefore when you do a charitable deed, do not sound the trumpet before you as the hypocrites do in the synagogues and the streets, that they may have glory from men. Assuredly I say to you, they have their reward. But when you do a charitable deed, do not let your left hand know what your right hand is doing, that your charitable deed may be in secret; and your Father who sees in secret will Himself reward you openly (Matthew 6:1-4, NKJV).

In one of the most sobering passages of the book of Hebrews, we are told that one day we will have to give an accounting. At this time "the thoughts and intents of the heart" will be the crucial issue:

For the word of God is living and powerful, and sharper than any two-edged sword, piercing even to the division of soul and spirit, and of joints and marrow, and is a discerner of ***the thoughts and intents of the heart****. And there is no creature hidden from His sight, but all things are naked and open to the eyes of Him to whom we must give account (Hebrews 4:12-13, NKJV).*

The Word of God is able to penetrate to the very core of a man and will reveal to all what his real motivations have been!

The Lord will primarily want to reveal whether what we did was motivated by a desire to bring honor to Christ and out of a sincere heart which fears ("honors") God:

Servants obey in all things your masters according to the flesh, not with eye service, as men-pleasers, but in sincerity of heart, fearing God. And whatever you do, do it heartily, as to the Lord and not to men, knowing that from the Lord you will receive the reward of the inheritance, for you serve the Lord Christ. But he who does wrong will be repaid for the wrong which he has done, and there is no partiality (Colossians 3:22-25, NKJV).

Therefore, whether you eat or drink or whatever you do, do all to the glory of God (1 Corinthians 10:31, NKJV).

To our ears the word "glory" communicates a somewhat resplendent and even mystical aura. Perhaps a word like "honor" is more understandable. Was our motive in what we did or said to bring honor to God?

This is of course, difficult to discern. We all operate with mixed motives, and this leads us to the issue of faithfulness. In the final analysis the overriding consideration seems to be how faithful we have been. Have we given God our best?

OUR FAITHFULNESS

Who then is a faithful and wise servant, whom His master made ruler over His household? (Matthew 24:45, NKJV)

His Master said to him, "Well done, good and faithful servant; you have been faithful over a few things, I will make you ruler over many things. Enter into the joy of your Lord" (Matthew 25:23, NKJV).

He who is faithful in what is least, is faithful also in much (Luke 16:10, NKJV).

Moreover it is required in stewards that one be found faithful (1 Corinthians 4:2, NKJV).

Be faithful until death, and I will give you the crown of life (Revelation 2:10, NKJV).

A faithful man is of high value to God. Solomon asks, "Who can find a faithful man" (Proverbs 20:6). In the final analysis this will be the "bottom line." God will not judge us on the basis of our success but on the basis of our faithfulness. This is an excellent approach to mental health. We cannot all be successful, but we all can be faithful.

Here is a man who struggles with emotional problems that were either chemically or environmentally induced. His struggle against sin in certain areas may never be as successful as the struggle in that area that another man has. But God knows the heart. He looks at faithfulness and not only victory. Thus, even though he was less successful, it is conceivable that he will be more highly rewarded. There will be many reversals in heaven. The first will be last, and those seemingly destined for high honor will be distant from the throne. Those unknown to history, who were perhaps insignificant in this life but who were faithful servants, will reign with the servant kings in the coming kingdom.

OUR WORDS AND THOUGHTS

The third major criterion the Lord will employ to evaluate the worthiness of our lives is the words we have spoken. This is appropriate because words are often reflections of the motives and attitudes in our hearts:

> *But I say to you that for every idle word men may speak, they will give account of it in the day of judgment. For by your words you will be justified, and by your words you will be condemned (Matthew 12:36-37).*

> *For there is nothing covered that will not be revealed, nor hidden that will not be known. Therefore whatever you have spoken in the dark will be heard in the light, and what you have spoken in the ear in the inner rooms will be proclaimed on the housetops (Luke 12:2-3, NKJV).*

This is a sobering thought. We should be ever mindful of the fact that there is a third party present in every conversation, the Holy Spirit. The Scriptures have much to say regarding the tongue and the impact of our words. Control of the tongue is presented as evidence of depth of character in the books of James and Proverbs. But, as the apostle says, it is a fire and difficult to tame. Those who succeed in taming it, however, God will reward greatly.

No doubt these hidden things refer also to our thoughts, and not just our spoken words.

> *For nothing is hidden that will not become evident, nor anything secret that will not be known and come to light (Luke 8:17).*

This warning is followed by another:

> *So take care how you listen; for whoever has, to him more shall be given; and whoever does not have, even what he thinks he has shall be taken away from him (Luke 8:18).*

This proverbial saying is found in many places in the teaching of Christ.

> *For whoever has, to him more shall be given; and whoever does not have, even what he has shall be taken away from him (Mark 4:25).*

> *For whoever has, to him more shall be given, and he will have an abundance; but whoever does not have, even what he has shall be taken away from him (Matthew 13:12).*

While some understand this statement to refer to nonbelievers (based upon Matthew 13:13) and suggest that what this person "does not have" is personal salvation, this makes little sense. How can salvation be taken away from someone who does not have it in the first place? The subject matter is the mysteries of the kingdom and spiritual understanding of these mysteries. Many believers had some understanding but were not following through with actions. That being so, even the minimal spiritual insight they had would be taken from them, and they would become spiritually dull and ineffective. The reference to the Pharisees in verses 11-15 is a parenthesis. But in verse 16 He returns to the exhortation to the disciples and says, "But blessed are *your* eyes" (emphatic in Greek) in contrast to the Pharisees. His followers have some understanding and are blessed because of it. The danger is that like the second and third soils mentioned in the parable of the soils, they may not grow to maturity and then they will lose spiritual capacity and become useless and dull.

In Matthew and Mark it simply says *"what he has"* will be taken from him. But how can something be taken away from a man who has nothing? There would be nothing to take away! There is no indication that this servant is unsaved. "What he has" is a low level of understanding and reward. In order to make the passage logically coherent, we must understand the phrase "does not have" in relative terms.

> *Therefore take away the talent from him, and give it to the one who has the ten talents. For to everyone who has, more shall be given, and he will have an abundance; but from the one who does not have, even what he does have shall be taken away. Throw out the worthless slave into the outer darkness; in that place there will be weeping and gnashing of teeth (Matthew 25:28-30).*

The talents in the parable represent opportunities for service. That unfaithful slave was given an opportunity. However, because he did not make use of it, he will have no opportunity to serve with Christ in the restored Davidic theocracy known as the millennium. In this passage, the proverb is applied eschatologically, referring to the loss of reward and millennial disinheritance in the coming kingdom.[2439]

> *Then he said to the bystanders, "Take the mina away from him and give it to the one who has the ten minas." And they said to him, "Master, he has ten minas already." "I tell you that to everyone who has, more shall be given, but from the one who does not have, even what he does have shall be taken away. But these enemies of mine, who did not want me to reign over them, bring them here and slay them in my presence" (Luke 19:24-27).*

The saying in Luke also seems to be an eschatological reference, describing what will happen at the Judgment Seat of Christ. This passage is addressed to believers. On the one hand he speaks of a servant of Christ, a slave, who "does not have" and then says, "Even what he has will be taken away" from him. Again, we ask, How can something be taken away from someone who had nothing to take away? Obviously, Jesus is speaking in relative terms. The believer with the one mina (a metaphor for a lesser degree of ability and service) will lose even that minimal opportunity to serve with Christ in the coming kingdom. He will be in the kingdom but will not reign there.

[2439] As argued elsewhere, the phrases "outer darkness" and "weeping and gnashing of teeth" refer to (1) exclusion from the joy of the final gathering (the messianic wedding banquet) and (2) the profound regret the carnal Christian will feel at the Judgment Seat of Christ when he faces rebuke and exclusion from the privilege of reigning with Christ in the fulfillment of human destiny.

While many doubt that the third servant in Luke 19:20-26 and Matthew 25:24-30 is actually saved, Luke seems to make it clear that he is. He distinguishes the third servant from his enemies, saying, "*But these enemies of mine, who did not want me to reign over them*" (Luke 19:27). The third servant is not an unbeliever, he is specifically distinguished from with the unbelievers who Jesus says are "enemies of mine."

Returning to Luke 8:18, the phrase "take care how you listen" refers to paying close attention to what is said and then doing it. The disciples are warned that what they have can be taken from them. It all depends on "how you listen." Darrell Bock turns the text around and says that "you" refers to the nonbelieving hearers of the gospel message.[2440] Since the passage is directly addressed to the believing disciples, it is difficult to understand Bock's conclusion. He appeals to the parable of the soils where he apparently believes the first three are nonbelievers. But, as argued elsewhere, the last three are all regenerate and justified.[2441]

What is it that these believers have or think they have that may be taken from them or that they may receive more? The context is talking about knowledge and spiritual illumination in Luke 8:18; Mark 4:25; and Matthew 13:12. This believer is apparently self-deceived. He seems to have minimal understanding and opportunities for service. But in Luke we are told that even what little he has will be taken from him. Often the carnal Christian is self-deceived. He thinks all is going well. Perhaps he attends church; he believes the Bible and the gospel message, but he has little interest in moving to maturity. But the fact that a disciple has the truth in the sense of having heard it is not what matters. Only careful hearing and doing will count at the Judgment Seat of Christ or advance his spiritual maturity and fruitfulness in this life. This verse is a summary of the preceding verses (Luke 8:11-15). In the parable of the soils, three kinds of Christians are described, and only the one who bears mature fruit, who hears and does, will be rewarded.

But what does it mean that what they thought they had would be taken? While it is tempting to link this saying with the Pharisees who think they are righteous but who are not,[2442] the contexts in all these passages are referring to true believers, the disciples. The interpretation of this saying is difficult, but the central message is clear. The believer who listens carefully will be granted more and more spiritual insight and opportunities for service. All who know Christ have not only experienced this reality, but have seen it in others as they have observed their spiritual growth to maturity. However, when a believer in Christ does not listen, he becomes spiritually dull (Hebrews 5:11) and loses what he had, his ability to discern (Hebrews 5:14). Paul warned elsewhere, "Therefore let him who thinks he stands take heed that he does not fall" (1 Corinthians 10:12).

But what of those who fail in this way? What of those whose works are burned? What of those who lose what they have? Will they endure an eternity of regret? No.

The Duration of the Remorse

In the next chapter we will discuss in detail the theological implications of negative judgment falling on the believer at the Judgment Seat of Christ. As discussed above, for

2440 Bock, *Luke 1-9:50*, 746.

2441 See elsewhere in this book, pp. 532 ff.

2442 As suggested by François Bovon and Helmut Koester, *Luke: A Commentary on the Gospel of Luke* (Minneapolis: Fortress Press, 2002), 1:315. These writers cite Luke 15:7 and 18:9 as possible parallels.

some it will be a time of great remorse. However, the Scriptures give us no reason to assume that these unfaithful Christians will spend their eternity in remorse and regret. Those unfaithful Christians who did not repent in life will repent then. In fact, at His name every knee will bow (Philippians 2:10).

Paul specifically applies this very saying to Christians and not just nonbelievers in Romans 14:10-12:

> *You, then, why do you judge your brother? Or why do you look down on your brother? For we will all stand before God's judgment seat. It is written: "As surely as I live," says the Lord, "every knee will bow before me; every tongue will confess to God." So then,* ***each of us will give an account of himself to God.***

We are told here that all Christians, faithful and unfaitbful, will bow down and confess. When a Christian confesses, he is forgiven. "*If we confess our sins, He is faithful and righteous to forgive us our sins and to cleanse us from all unrighteousness*" (1 John 1:9). Therefore, the view that unfaithful believers will not be restored seems unlikely.[2443]

In view of the glorious promises of heavenly life promised to justified saints, we can be assured that this remorse cannot continue throughout the millennium or eternal state. All will be "*with Him*," and not in the "outer darkness" (John 14:3). In fact we will "*always be*" with Him (1 Thessalonians 4:17). The glories experienced by all saints are so incredible that they have never "*entered the heart of man*" (1 Corinthians 2:9), and they are available to all "*who love Him*," that is all who are justified. The nature of heaven itself precludes unending remorse.

And having confessed their sin, like the prodigal son they will be restored to eternal fellowship with their King. We are told that in the new heavens and new earth (Rev 21:1); "*the former things will not be remembered, nor will they come to mind*" (Isaiah 65:17).[2444] Regrets over a failed life will be erased.

Just as an earthly father rejoices over the repentance of his rebellious son (Luke 15:21-24), so we have every right to expect that the Lord will rejoice in the tardy repentance of those for whom He died. "*For his anger lasts only a moment, but his favor lasts a lifetime; weeping may remain for a night, but rejoicing comes in the morning*" (Psalm 30:5, NIV). If Christ will redeem lost sinners, how much more will He do for His born-again sons:

> *Much more then, having been justified by His blood, we shall be saved from the wrath of God through Him. For if while we were enemies, we were reconciled to God through the death of His Son, much more, having been reconciled, we shall be saved by His life (Romans 5:9-10).*

The exclusion from the banquet is a temporary act of divine discipline and cannot be an eternal exclusion from fellowship with the King. Yet, it is true that we will reap what we sow (Galatians 6:7). There will be for some a time of profound sorrow.

[2443] For a defense of this view see Cauley, *The Outer Darkness*, 520.

[2444] This general amnesia of "former things" includes "past troubles" (Isaiah 65:16). "Not be remembered" refers to the conscious contents of memory, come to mind, to memories suddenly roused. "The awareness will be of a total newness without anything even prompting a recollection of what used to be. The divine forgetfulness of verse 16 ff. will be matched by general amnesia." Motyer, *The Prophecy of Isaiah: An Introduction and Commentary*, s.v. "Isa. 65:17".

Of course even the finest of Christians will find things in their lives for which they are ashamed and for which they feel remorse when seen in the light of God's unapproachable holiness. Hoyt speculates that the millennium will be like a graduation ceremony. There is some measure of disappointment and remorse that one did not do better and work harder. However, the central emotion at such an event is joy, not sadness. The graduates did not leave the auditorium weeping because they did not receive better grades. Rather, they are thankful they graduated, and they are grateful for what they did achieve. Hoyt is correct, "To overdo the sorrow aspect of the Judgment Seat of Christ is to make heaven into hell. To underdo the sorrow aspect is to make faithfulness inconsequential."[2445]

Whatever the time period of remorse during their exclusion from the marriage banquet in the New Jerusalem during the tribulation, we are told that even in the kingdom that unfaithful saints of all ages will know the experience of weeping because of being excluded from the Messianic Banquet (Luke 13:28). One can imagine the Lord at some time after the beginning of the millennium, forgiving and restoring to fellowship all those unfaithful Christians for whom He died and for whom His loving heart still desires. There is no millennium of weeping and remorse. While some may disagree,[2446] this is what I believe. However, they will miss the joy of the fellowship of the *Metochoi*, and they will forfeit the right to "reign with Him" in the thousand-year kingdom to follow. As Luke expresses it, they will not "*recline at the table*" (Lk. 13:29). They will be in the kingdom but not at the table.

It could be argued, as Karl Pagekemper does, that the Partaker view of a temporary rather than an eternal duration of the remorse reduces the negative aspects of the Judgment Seat of Christ to a "*temporary inconvenience*."[2447] This is a startling assertion! Of course it is true that a carnal believer could think, "Well, this feeling of tears will only last for a few years (or whatever), so I will continue to live my carnal life now and just endure this 'temporary inconvenience' in the future." It is true, as Paul has taught us, and our own daily experience confirms, that grace can be taken for granted and abused (Romans 6:1). However, the expectation of the Lord and the New Testament writers is that, for most, the incentives of special intimacy, opportunities for service, higher honor,[2448] and the fear of hearing the Lord's rebuke, along with the other motivations indicated in Scripture[2449] will be greater than the incentive to take the grace of God for granted. This is certainly true in the writer's life.

We must not forget that when we stand before Him at that day, we will be in resurrection bodies. Because of the absence of sin and the experience of the maximum fullness of human potential, our ability to deal with the emotion of grief will be heightened and immeasurably more mature. At that time we will finally exist as man was intended to be, mature and without sin. There is a cycle to all grief—it is dealt with, and then it passes.

2445 Samuel L. Hoyt, "The Judgment Seat of Christ in Theological Perspective, Part 2: The Negative Aspects of the Christian's Judgment," *BibSac* 137, no. 546 (April 1980): 131.

2446 Cauley, *The Outer Darkness*, 519-64.

2447 Pagenkemper, "An Analysis of the Rejection Motif in the Synoptic Parables and Its Relationship to Pauline Soteriology", 113. See discussion in the next chapter on pp. 791 ff.

2448 For full discussion of the motivational influence of the rewards of greater intimacy, opportunities for service, and high honor see chapters 60-62 below.

2449 For discussion of six powerful biblical motivations for living Christ's way of life see pp. 1010 ff. and pp. 757 ff.

There is no reason that this would not be the case in the kingdom. However, because of our heightened state the cycle will be abbreviated in comparison to our present experience.

Differences in honor, service, reward, and intimacy with Christ will, however, remain throughout eternity. Spurgeon in his famous parable of Noah's ark, argued that all believers will be in the ark, but not all will be on the upper decks.[2450] Billy Graham is reported to have expressed it this way, "Everyone's cup will be full, but the cups will be of different sizes."

This is *grace*!

Summary

One day we will all face an accounting for our lives. Too frequently, in evangelical circles, the possibility of a negative consequence is simply ignored. Surely, many believe, God would never punish or rebuke or disinherit any of His born-again and adopted sons. All was covered by the cross of Christ so that the only negative that could possibly be experienced would be loss of reward.

This chapter and the chapters to follow argue that this viewpoint is not true. Once our lives have been reviewed based on the criteria of our deeds, our faithfulness, and our words and thoughts, there will not only be joy for most, but, for some, sadness and remorse. This remorse will not last throughout eternity, but it will affect our degree of intimacy with Christ and opportunities to serve Him throughout eternity future. Our experience at the Judgment Seat of Christ will either be one of triumph or one of tragedy.

In the following chapters we will explore in more detail what that tragedy entails.

[2450] Spurgeon, *Spurgeon's Sermons*, Vol 53, "The Parable of the Ark," No. 3042.

49

The Darkness Outside

THE FESTIVE gathering had commenced. From the East, West, North and South they had come. It was a gathering of the church of the first born and the friends of the Bridegroom. They were there to celebrate the Wedding Feast of the Lamb in the New Jerusalem during the tribulation. As the guests filed into the banquet hall, the King fixed His gazed on one of the attendees. He was inappropriately dressed. The King known as "Wonderful" rose from the table and slowly moved toward the massive oak doors of the banquet hall. As He walked His countenance saddened, knowing the fearful pronouncement He must make.

"Greetings, Lord," the guest began.

The entrants were those for whom the King had died and whom the Father had chosen before the foundation of the world that they might be holy and blameless before Him. Good works had been prepared for them, but for various reasons, some of them had chosen not to walk in those good works. While the other entrants were clothed in fine linen called the "righteous acts of the saints," this man did not have the proper attire.

He had accepted the invitation to the feast; he had believed in Jesus. However, he never really sank his roots deeply into his Lord. When affliction or persecution arose because of the world, he compromised and did not persevere in his walk to the end of life.

Many are like this man, who began well, but were overcome by the worries of this world and the deceitfulness of riches. The seed which the King had planted in them was choked, never yielding fruit in their lives.

In this life all of them had an excuse, but none of them had been faithful. Now they stand speechless. The day of reckoning had come. The King had warned them all saying,

> *For whoever wishes to save his life will lose it; but whoever loses his life for My sake will find it. For what will it profit a man if he gains the whole world and forfeits his soul?*

As discussed in chapter 15, to "save one's soul" translates Greek the idiom which means to find a rich life now by self-denial, taking up our cross and following Christ, so that we will be favorably recompensed at the Judgment Seat of Christ.

The guest at the Great Supper had not done this.

With a broken heart, for He loved him deeply, and with a tear in His eye, the King called Wonderful replied with these dreadful words:

"Please escort those who are not prepared for My supper into the darkness outside the banquet hall."

Three places in the Gospels Jesus refers to the "darkness outside." In this chapter we will discuss two of them—the fate of the unprepared guest at the Great Supper (Matthew

22:1-14) and the fate of the "sons of the kingdom" who lived with anemic faith (Matthew 8:12).

Parable of the Wedding Banquet (Matthew 22:1-14)

In the parable of the wedding banquet in Matthew 22:1-14, a great celebration is described. However, not all will participate in that joy. Jesus describes this lamentable fact in His parable of the unprepared wedding guest.

A King has invited all to attend a great feast which one day will take place in his Palace (possibly, in the New Jerusalem) during the time of the Great Tribulation.[2451] The parable identifies four responses to his invitation. The first two are negative and represent those on earth during the present era who reject the King's invitation to participate in this heavenly banquet. One group was merely indifferent and made excuses why they could not attend (Matthew 22:5; Luke 14:18-20). Perhaps, this represents many in Israel who did not believe Jesus was the Messiah. A second group, possibly directly referring to the Pharisees, was openly hostile (Matthew 22:6-7). Both of these groups represent nonbelievers who totally rejected the free offer to come to the feast.

But there are two more groups who do accept the King's invitation while on earth and now appear at this Marriage Banquet in the New Jerusalem. One group enters the banquet wearing the appropriate wedding clothes (Matthew 22:10) and another appears at the banquet completely unprepared, lacking the life of good works required to share in the joy of the king and his other guests (Matthew 22:11). In Matthew 25:1-13 this second group are described in another parable as foolish virgins who similarly were unprepared. These two groups represent two categories of Christians.

Before proceeding, it is important that I set forth my approach to the interpretation of parables. Because a parable is essentially a similitude[2452] or an extended metaphor,[2453] I do not believe that all the details have significance. If parables were allegories, and they are not, Blomberg correctly points out that allegories "are more complex stories which require numerous details in them to be 'decoded.'"[2454] Thus, details of the wedding banquet, where it was located, and how it would be possible to serve millions of people a dinner are matters best left to speculation. Similarly, questions regarding the spatial locations relative to the banquet hall, such as the darkness outside, are irrelevant to the major points of the parable. The classical view of parabolic interpretation is that one should seek the one central point of the parable. Blomberg has correctly argued that there may be several points, not just one, but the details do not have independent significance. Ramm says, "A parable is not like an allegory for in the latter, most of the elements have meaning." He continues, "A Parable is a truth carried in a vehicle. Therefore there is the inevitable presence of accessories which are necessary for the drapery of the parable, but are not part of the meaning. The danger in parabolic teaching at this point is to interpret as meaningful what is drapery."[2455]

[2451] For discussion of the location and the time of this banquet, see Chapter 51, pp. 818 ff.

[2452] A. Berkley Mickelsen, *Interpreting the Bible* (Grand Rapids: Wm. B. Eerdmans Pub. Co., 1963), 212-15.

[2453] Bernard Ramm, *Protestant Biblical Interpretation* (Boston: W. A. Wilde Co., 1956), 254-65.

[2454] Craig Blomberg, *Interpreting Parables* (Downers Grove, IL: InterVarsity Press, 1990), 30.

[2455] Ramm, *Protestant Biblical Interpretation*, 261.

WARNING TO THE PHARISEES (MATTHEW 22:1-10)

The parable opens as follows,

> *And Jesus answered and spoke to them again in parables, saying, "The kingdom of heaven may be compared to a king, who gave a wedding feast for his son" (Matthew 22:1-2).*

These words identify those addressed as "them," as a reference to the Pharisees and others who had rejected Christ in the preceding context. Jesus has just explained that the kingdom would be taken from them and given to a nation producing the fruit of it (Matthew 21:43).[2456] ἀese hypocrites are the subject of verses 1-10.

Some interpreters equate the wedding banquet in this parable with the entire kingdom era. However, as I will suggest later, the Marriage Banquet of the Lamb in Matthew 22 is not the same as the Messianic Banquet.[2457] The former refers to the marriage of Christ to His Bride, the church, and is a specific event. The latter is a metaphor for the rejoicing among Christ's *Metochoi* at the beginning of the millennial era. It goes too far to say with Nãgelsbach that the feast is "everlasting entertainment."[2458]

Regarding the Marriage Banquet in Matthew 22, we would disagree with Karl Pagenkemper who asserts, "The temporary imagery within the kingdom is not clearly drawn and to make a distinction between the banquet and the kingdom itself is overly subtle."[2459] ἀe phrase "the kingdom of heaven may be compared to" does not necessarily suggest that the kingdom of heaven "is the same as" a wedding banquet. Instead, as discussed elsewhere, it suggests that there is an aspect of the kingdom of heaven, that is, preparation for its arrival by a life of works and a time of judgment, that can be compared to a wedding banquet.[2460]

This is the marriage supper of the Lamb (Revelation 19:7-9) and is parallel to the parable of the ten Virgins (Matthew 25:1-13) It occurs immediately after the pre-tribulation rapture in the New Jerusalem (probably) in heaven while the tribulation transpires on earth.

With this background in mind let us consider this parable about the Marriage Banquet which celebrates Christ's marriage to the church. As we shall see, the point of the parable is that just being invited does not guarantee blessing. In verses 1-7, the Pharisees were invited but did not respond by believing on Christ as their Messiah. Instead, their city was burned (Matthew 22:7). Then in verses 8-10, we are introduced to those who were invited to the Marriage Banquet and who did respond. However, in verse 11 a guest appears who was at the banquet but was not dressed in suitable attire for such a royal celebration.

> *And he sent out his slaves to call those who had been invited to the wedding feast, and they were unwilling to come. Again he sent out other slaves saying, "Tell those who have been invited, 'Behold, I have prepared my dinner; my oxen and my fattened livestock are all butchered and everything is ready; come to the wedding feast'" (Matthew 22:3-4).*

[2456] The plural "parables," has suggested to some that there are two parables, vv. 1-10 and another one in vv. 11-13.

[2457] For discussion of the distinction between these two banquets see pp. 825 ff.

[2458] Carl Wilhelm Eduard Nãgelsbach, "The Prophet Isaiah," in *Lange's Commentary on the Holy Scriptures* (Grand Rapids: Zondervan Publishing House, n.d.), 280.

[2459] Pagenkemper, "An Analysis of the Rejection Motif in the Synoptic Parables and Its Relationship to Pauline Soteriology", 115. See also Pagenkemper, "Rejection Imagery in the Synoptic Parables," 308-31.

[2460] For discussion of what the kingdom of heaven "is like" or what it may be compared to see pp. 817.

A great banquet is naturally hosted by a great man. The initial invitation had already been sent out. This double invitation is common in the Middle East. The first invitation identifies who can come and how much meat is needed. Then the host kills and butchers the meat. He decides how much meat is needed based on the number of accepted invitations. However, once he has killed the meat, the countdown begins and cannot be stopped.[2461] The animal has been killed and must be eaten that night. The guests who have "RSVP'd" the invitation are duty bound to appear. The hour of the wedding banquet has arrived. Suddenly, there is a surprising turn of events. Those invited insult the host and refuse to come!

In the parable this first call refers to the call issued through the Old Testament prophets to national Israel to come to the feast to which they had previously been invited. In the context of Christ's ministry, this invitation involves the call to the nation to repent of their national sins, receive national forgiveness, and then bring forth fruit in keeping with that forgiveness. What applied on a national level, of course, applied to individual Israelites as well. All must believe on the Messiah and then live lives expressing such faith.

Some of the invited guests, the unbelieving Pharisees, ignore the summons.

But they paid no attention and went their way, one to his own farm and one to his business (Matthew 22:5).

Each had an excuse for not coming. Some had farms to work, and others had businesses to attend to. In a separate parable relating not to the Marriage Banquet, but to the kingdom era, the Messianic Banquet, Luke fills in some detail.[2462] Regarding the one who "had a farm to work" Luke says, "*I have just bought a field, and I must go and see it. Please excuse me*" (Luke 14:18). Any Israelite in a first-century culture would have viewed this as ridiculous and insulting. The purchaser had already seen it, thoroughly investigated the property, and carefully scrutinized the contract before signing. What is the point of looking at a field after one has already done all this and signed the contract? To believe that this farm had "just" been bought and now must be seen is highly unlikely. A contemporary parallel might be the case of a neighbor who cancels a dinner invitation by saying, "I have just bought a new house over the phone; I must go and have a look at it and at the neighborhood." The excuse is paper-thin, and no one would believe it.[2463]

Matthew tells us that the second individual excused himself because he had to go "to his business." Jesus told a similar story regarding His present offer of kingdom blessings and their rejection in Luke 14. One man declined His offer to sit at His dinner (experience kingdom blessings now) by saying "*I have just bought five yoke of oxen, and I'm on my way to try them out. Please excuse me*" (Luke 14:19). One would never buy ten oxen without first testing them before he buys! The buyer would always go to the seller's field and observe them first. He would watch animals pull the plows back and forth across the field to be

---

[2461] The cultural material to follow is taken from "Through Peasant Eyes" in Bailey, *Poet and Peasant and through Peasant Eyes: A Literary-cultural Approach to the Parables in Luke*, 94-113.

[2462] Blomberg argues convincingly that these two parables are not parallel but refer to separate events. Craig L. Blomberg, "When is a Parallel Really a Parallel? A Test Case: The Lucan Parables," *WTJ* 46, no. 1 (Spring 1984).

[2463] Bailey, *Poet and Peasant and through Peasant Eyes: A Literary-cultural Approach to the Parables in Luke*, 96.

assured of their health and strength. Then, and only then, would he begin to negotiate a price and buy the oxen. The excuse is a transparent fabrication.

In our time the neighbor mentioned earlier might say to his wife, "I cannot make it home tonight for dinner, because I just signed a check for ten used cars that I bought over the phone. I am on my way down to the used car lot to find out their age and model and to see if they will start."

Essentially, the second guest has said, "These animals are more important to me than my relationship with you!"

But the response of the third guest is even more shocking, some of the people of God actually murdered the king's servants, that is, the prophets.

> *And the rest seized his slaves and mistreated them and killed them (Matthew 22:6, NASB).*

Jesus refers to the fact that nation had executed God's messengers throughout their history. Naturally, the King is quite angry about this.

> *But the king was enraged and sent his armies, and destroyed those murderers, and set their city on fire (Matthew 22:7).*

This probably refers to the coming destruction of Jerusalem which Jesus would speak about a few chapters later (Matthew 24:2): "*Truly I say to you, not one stone here will be left upon another, which will not be torn down.*" This occurred in AD 70, when the Roman armies under the general Titus burned and sacked the city.[2464] Jerusalem is no longer God's city, it is now called "their" city because they have turned away from God.[2465]

The King concludes that many among His people, Israel, were not worthy to attend the wedding feast. They were unworthy because they did not believe in Christ. So He opens up the invitation to all, not just those who are descended from Abraham:

> *The wedding is ready, but those who were invited were not worthy. Go therefore to the main highways, as many as you find there, invite to the wedding feast. And those slaves went out into the streets, and gathered together all they found, both evil and good and the wedding hall was filled with dinner guests (Matthew 22:8-10).*

They are to go to the "main highways." This probably refers to "the place where a principal thoroughfare crosses a city boundary and extends into the open country 'where a main street leaves the city.'"[2466] In other words, go beyond the boundaries of Israel and invite all men to come.

[2464] Luz says, "In my judgment the strange v. 7 makes sense only if it was prompted by the destruction of Jerusalem in 70 CE." See Ulrich Luz and Helmut Koester, *Matthew 21-28: A Commentary*, Hermeneia (Minneapolis: Augsburg Publishing Co., 1989), 53. "'Definitive judgment' is not to be understood in the sense of the last judgment that, according to Matt 25:31–46, comes to every individual person. It is, rather, a judgment within history," ibid., 54.

[2465] One must suspend chronological belief here. Snodgrass notes, "A military expedition takes place while the banquet is ready to eat." Snodgrass, *Stories with Intent: A Comprehensive Guide to the Parables of Jesus*, 319. One must remember this is a story and must not press the details. The point is that a banquet has been prepared and those who refuse to enter it will encounter judgment.

[2466] Louw-Nida, 2:63.

The former invitees were either "not worthy" (Matthew 22:8) or did not want to come (22:3).[2467] Those now gathered at the feast are *therefore worthy and do want to come.* In order to enter the Marriage Banquet, only one thing is required, the imputed righteousness of Christ. However, to be "worthy" to enter the banquet two things are necessary: (1) believing on Christ; and (2) following Him as a disciple. These individuals do enter the banquet. Therefore, they not only believed on Christ but also lived lives worthy of that belief. The fact that the king's servants gathered "all they found" does not mean that everyone without exception they contacted responded to the gospel and filled the wedding hall (v. 10). Rather, the thought is that they gathered "all kinds" of people, both good and bad, both Jew and Gentile.[2468]

While it is certain that the call described in the preceding verses, which now goes out far beyond the boundaries of Israel, is a call to salvation, it involves much more. Jesus never invites someone only to salvation. His call includes that, but in addition, it is a call to become a disciple and live out the principles of the Discourse on Discipleship (Matthew 5-7), the Sermon on the Mount. When he says that those "*both evil and good*" were invited, he "means that Jesus accepts people the Jewish establishment would regard as evil (tax collectors and harlots) and therefore totally unacceptable."[2469] Jew and Gentile apparently respond, are saved, and now appear at the wedding banquet.[2470]

APPLICATION TO THE GATHERED GUESTS (MATTHEW 22:11-14)

At this point some interpreters have assumed that because the details here are so different from verses 1-10, that these verses may introduce a separate parable.[2471] The break is strong. In verses 1-7 an invitation goes out and is rejected and in verses 8-10 a second call went out and many accepted. Then in verse 11 Jesus shifts from the "them" of verse 1 to the "gathered" of verse 10.[2472] Those gathered are the invited guests who responded to the call of salvation in verse 10 and who lived lives worthy of that call. In Pauline terms, they now face the King at the Judgment Seat of Christ.

This suggests that the Pharisees of the earlier part of the chapter are no longer the focus. Having rebuked the Pharisees, Jesus now addresses the gathered believers.[2473] He

[2467] They "were unwilling to come" (Gr *thelō*, "wish, desire"). BDAG, 447.

[2468] "He probably means 'all' in a different sense: evil and good people are to be invited." Luz and Koester, *Matthew 21-28: A Commentary*, 55.

[2469] Morris, *The Gospel According to Matthew*, 551.

[2470] It is also possible that it means he accepts all kinds of people; both prostitutes and ethical Gentiles like Cornelius.

[2471] For example, Snodgrass, in his outstanding commentary on the parables, says, "The most difficult question for me, one about which I remain ambivalent, is whether 11:11-14 belonged originally to the parable." Snodgrass, *Stories with Intent: A Comprehensive Guide to the Parables of Jesus*, 320. This has actually led some interpreters to say that the parable is not a unit and Matthew has simply added material to Luke's original source. For discussion see Nolland, *The Gospel of Matthew: A Commentary on the Greek Text*, 889.

[2472] It is commonly acknowledged that this parable has two parts. Verses 1-10 clearly refer to the Pharisees. "On the other hand," Olshausen notes, "another part of the parable is not applicable to the Pharisees, namely, that which speaks of the guest who did not wear the wedding garment." Hermann Olshausen, *Biblical Commentary of the New Testament*, trans. A. C. Kendrick, reprint ed. (Bowling Green, OH: Guardian of Truth Foundation, 2005), 2:168.

[2473] For further evidence of this shift in focus, see the *Excursus on Salt Unfit for the Dunghill* at the end of this chapter.

does not want His disciples to take their status for granted, and so He points out that they too will face a final accountability for their lives. There are two categories of believers at the Marriage Banquet of the Lamb, those properly attired and those who are not. After the feast begins, the King notes that there is one saved man who entered who should not be there:

> *But when the King came in to look over the dinner guests, He saw there a man not dressed in wedding clothes, and He said to him, "Friend, how did you come in here without wedding clothes?" And he was speechless (Matthew 22:11-12).*

To show up at such a banquet without the proper attire was a sign of disrespect for the king. That is all that can be made of his lack of clothing. To imply that these garments were given to guests and therefore refer to the imputed righteousness of Christ given to believers is to stretch the detail far beyond anything suggested in the context.[2474] As Hagner notes, "The idea that the host provided the proper garment for the wedding feast is both difficult to substantiate and moreover irrelevant to Matthew's point."[2475] Carson agrees, "There is no historical foundation for Augustine's suggestion that *wedding clothes* were provided by the host."[2476]

It is rather obvious that the wedding clothes could not possibly be something provided by the host. If they were, the man would never have been permitted to enter the banquet at all. Imagine the servants approaching this man, and he says he will come and then they give him the wedding clothes that the host requires and the man refuses to wear them. Would the servants have allowed him to enter the banquet? Certainly not! No, the wedding garment must be something the man himself finds and puts on. After accepting the invitation he would return to his house, put on his "tuxedo," and then go to the banquet. Some of these verses don't even have "righteousness" in them.[2477]

What then is the indispensable wedding garment mentioned in verse eleven? The nature of the garment is made explicitly clear in Revelation 19:7-8: "*Let us rejoice and be glad and give the glory to Him, for the marriage of the Lamb has come and His bride has made herself ready. And it was given to her to clothe herself in fine linen, bright and clean; for the fine linen is the* ***righteous acts of the saints.***" Ezekiel also links these garments with purity. All who enter at the "gates of the inner court" shall be "clothed with linen garments" (Ezekiel 44:17), a symbol of purity.

[2474] Contra Hendriksen and Kistemaker, *Exposition of the Gospel According to Matthew*, 798.

[2475] Hagner, *Matthew 14-28*, 631.

[2476] D. A. Carson, "Matthew," in *The New Bible Commentary: 21st Century Edition*, ed. D. Guthrie and J. A. Motyer (Downers Grove, IL: InterVarsity Press, 1994), s.v. "Matthew 21:28".

[2477] Some link these garments with the garments of salvation and the robe of righteousness of Isaiah 61:10. They assert, without basis, that the "robe of righteousness" is the imputed righteousness of Christ. Yet, there is not one use of "righteousness" in Isaiah that refers to imputation. The overwhelming use is moral or ethical righteousness. For example, Isaiah 5:7, 16; 9:7; 10:22; 28:17; 32:16; 45:23; 46:12; 48:1; 57:12; 58:2; 59:14; 63:1; 64:5. It is far more likely that the righteousness referred to, to be consistent with Isaiah's use of the term is the righteousness of those who are living by God's standards (cf. Isa 58:8; 60:21). Martin, "Isaiah," 1116. This is how "garments" are symbolically used in many places in the Old Testament (e.g., Job 29:14; Psalm 132:9; Isaiah 11:5). It is also possible that "righteousness" in Isaiah 61:10 refers to "legitimacy." The speaker is an unnamed administrator [possibly Artaxerxes]. John D. W. Watts, *Isaiah 34-66*, Word Biblical Commentary (Dallas: Word, 2002), 301. "The ruler-administrator fits the role of Artaxerxes and his renewal of the decree of restoration (Ezra 7:12–28)." See Jeremiah 51:10, "vindication", and 2 Samuel 19:28 in the sense of "entitlement."

These practical, righteous acts (Revelation 15:4) do not refer to the act of the Son of God in declaring us righteous (justification). This garment must be put on by the believer himself. When the invitation went out to *all* in verse 10, it was indicated that in order to enter the banquet one must have a life of works; that is, in addition to responding in faith to the invitation, they must also be "worthy." Elsewhere, Jesus said, "*the laborer is **worthy** of his wages*" (Luke 10:7, NKJV). This guest was not worthy of reward, and, as we shall see, he will be excluded from the banquet.

It is unwarranted to say, as Hendriksen does that the wedding garments refer to both imputed and imparted righteousness. He claims, "Although these two must be distinguished, they must not be separated.[2478] But as this book has shown, most definitely they must be separated to maintain a coherent message throughout God's Word. Here is a man who is at the Marriage Banquet, but was not worthy to attend the banquet. We are plainly told that he entered the banquet. The king said to him, "how did you *come in* here" (Gr *eiserchomai*, "enter into"), Matthew 22:12; therefore, he must have been regenerate (John 3:3). Yet he does not have a life of good works, the *righteous acts of the saints*. This text plainly proves that a saved man may not inevitably lead a life of progressive sanctification, and yet Hendriksen argues that because he has not led a life of progressive sanctification he must not be saved![2479]

Another writer says, "The symbolism is of someone who presumes on the free offer of salvation by assuming that therefore there are no obligations attached, someone whose life belies their profession: faith without works. Entry to the kingdom of heaven may be free, but to continue in it carries conditions."[2480] This boils down to saying that salvation is not free, but is finally secured by faith plus works. France notes that "even though this man belongs to the new group of invitees, he is one who produces no fruit, and so is no less liable to forfeit his new-found privilege than those who were excluded before him."[2481] It is questionable to argue that because they did not produce fruit they were never saved unless one "knows" before looking at the text that the Experimental Predestinarian system of interpretation is true. In contrast to the hostile Pharisees who wanted to kill him (Matthew 21:46), Jesus calls this man, "Friend." According to Leon Morris, "'*Friend*' is a kindly word, and there is something of an appeal about it."[2482] Nolland agrees, "It is a conventional way of addressing someone whose name is not known, but only when this is to be in a friendly manner."[2483] It would seem rather inconsistent of Christ to use this term and then in the following verse to consign the man to eternal damnation.[2484] It better fits an address to one of His regenerate saints than to the sons of disobedience.

2478 Hendriksen and Kistemaker, *Exposition of the Gospel According to Matthew*, 799.

2479 Hendriksen then falls into the typical Experimental Predestinarian quandary of trying to quantify how much progressive sanctification is necessary to establish that one's faith was in fact genuine. He concludes that there "must be a complete turnabout, a thorough-going renewal" (ibid.). It is of course doubtful that any person since the dawn of time has ever had a "complete" turnabout or a "thorough-going renewal." No doubt if one pressed Hendriksen on this, he would begin to nuance the terms until they die a death of a thousand qualifications.

2480 France, *The Gospel of Matthew*, 827.

2481 Ibid.

2482 Morris, *The Gospel According to Matthew*, 552.

2483 Nolland, *The Gospel of Matthew: A Commentary on the Greek Text*, 890.

2484 Admittedly, though, Jesus referred to the unsaved Judas as a "friend" also (Matthew 26:50).

This text refutes their system. Here is a guest who is in the New Jerusalem at the wedding supper of the Lamb, and thus on the authority of Jesus Christ he is born again (John 3:5) but has produced no fruit. Clearly, faith does not always produce a life of works. This man's appearance in dirty clothes was not only an insult to his host, it is also a refutation of the Reformed view of perseverance.

But how did he get into the wedding banquet in the first place? The fact that he is present establishes that he is born again (John 3:3-5).[2485] The point is that there are distinctions among the saved (the gathered guests), and one day those differences in faithfulness will be adjudicated. What follows in the parable is an illustration of what will occur at the Judgment Seat of Christ, when all believers will be rewarded for the things they have done, "good and bad" (2 Corinthians 5:10). The man without the proper clothing represents all those who are saved, but who have no business being at the Marriage Banquet to celebrate with Christ's *Metochoi*. His removal is a metonymy for the removal of all of them.

Note, the man was "speechless" (v. 12), literally "muzzled" (cf. 1 Corinthians 9:9; 1 Timothy 5:18). At this judgment there will be no attempt at self-defense. There will be no more excuses, no more rationalizing. Everyone there will realize that the assessment he receives is just and fair.

What the friend at the wedding banquet lacked was not justification but a life of righteous acts. He had responded to the invitation (v. 10); that is, he had believed in Jesus, but he had not lived for Christ. The consequences are terrible.

"BIND HIM HAND AND FOOT"

> *Then the king said to the servants, "Bind him hand and foot, take him away, and cast him into outer darkness; there will be weeping and gnashing of teeth" (Matthew 22:13, NKJV).*

Several questions are raised by this striking warning. Is the servant *really* a saved man? To what does the "darkness outside" refer? What is the meaning of "wailing and gnashing of teeth"?

The main reason for denying that this man is saved even though he is "in" the New Jerusalem and at the banquet is the judgment that comes on him in verse 13.[2486] Because Experimental Predestinarians do not believe that a true Christian can ever lose salvation and because they interpret "outer darkness" and "wailing and gnashing of teeth" as descriptions of final damnation, they conclude, that this man could not have been saved. Let it be stated again, but in a different way. This man was not removed from the banquet because he lacked faith or because his profession was not genuine. He was removed because he lacked a life of good works. Good works qualified one to enter the banquet. Therefore, entering the banquet is not the same as being saved. Being saved is without cost, with no need of good works, and is by faith alone.

What then is the meaning of the metaphors "bind him hand and foot," "outer darkness," and "weeping and gnashing of teeth?"

[2485] The foolish virgins also, who were born again, never enter through the door, and yet this man does. Why? The answer is that even though he is saved, he should not have gotten in. Probably, all the details of the parables should not be pressed.

[2486] Pagenkemper, "An Analysis of the Rejection Motif in the Synoptic Parables and Its Relationship to Pauline Soteriology", 109.

The man is to be bound "hand and foot." Whatever the illustration of binding pictures, it must be very severe and causes the cessation of all meaningful activity. Perhaps the point is that while the servant kings will participate in man's final destiny, this bound one will not be free to do so. The binding of the hands and feet is a metaphor for exclusion from the activity of reigning with Messiah, and joy and light are metaphors for the joy of the faithful as they unite with their King and receive their rewards (cf. Hebrews 1:8-9). This is a parable, a story, and may not refer to literal events.

CAST OUT

The king says, "Cast him" into the outer darkness. The term "cast out" (Gr *ekballō*) is sometimes loaded with violence and negativity. Actually, while that nuance is contextually derived in certain contexts (e.g. "casting out" demons), there is no negativity of compulsion inferred by the basic meaning of the Greek word. For example, Jesus asked that we pray that the Lord of the harvest would "send out" (Gr *ekballō*) laborers into the harvest (Mark 9:38). Does the good man "*cast out*" good things from his treasury (Matthew 12:23, *ekballō*)? No! He brings them out (NASB). Jesus Himself was "led out" or "sent" (Gr *ekballō*), into the wilderness by the Holy Spirit (Mark 1:12); the English "cast out" gives the wrong impression (see *New Century Bible, NIV)*. In fact, in Luke's version we are told that Jesus "was led [Gr *agō*] by the Spirit in the desert" (Luke 4:1). The Greek word *agō* means "to lead."[2487] He "sent forth" His own (John 10:4), and Rahab the harlot did not "cast out" or "compel" the spies, she "sent [them] out" by another way (James 2:25).[2488]

Another more enlightening parallel is found in Mark 1:43. After compassionately healing a leper, Jesus "*sternly warned him and immediately sent him away*" (Gr *ekballō)*. Jesus did not cast him out!

We are to imagine, then, that there comes a point in the opening of the festivities where Christ says something like, "Please, lead outside the banquet those who have not endured with Me." No doubt, the King who loved them had tears in His eyes as He said this.

THE DARKNESS OUTSIDE

But where are they sent? The term, "the darkness outside" is often associated in Experimental Predestinarian thinking with final damnation and torture.[2489] The phrase is associated with eschatological judgment in three places (Matthew 8:12; 22:13; 25:30).

A related phrase, "weeping and gnashing of teeth," is used seven times; the phrase "darkness outside" is used three times. The phrase "furnace of fire," which does refer to damnation, is used only twice and never in association with the darkness outside. Why? The simplest suggestion is that they refer to two different experiences. The furnace of fire is clearly the experience of eternal separation from God, which will be the fate of the "sons of the devil" (the tares, Matthew 13:48) and of the bad fish (the wicked, Matthew 13:47-50). The darkness that is outside is a metaphor for exclusion from the joy of the light of the wedding festivities which occur in the New Jerusalem during the tribulation (Matthew

---

2487 BDAG, 16. This text, however, may refer to Jesus' being led around in the wilderness after He arrived there.

2488 Louw-Nida, 51-56.

2489 For the most comprehensive study of the "outer darkness" in print, see Marty Cauley's extensive treatment of the subject that decisively rejects the notion that it always refers to damnation. Cauley, *The Outer Darkness*, 1220..

22:13; 25:30) or from the Messianic Banquet at the beginning of the millennium (Matthew 8:12; Luke 13:27-30).[2490]

	FURNACE OF FIRE	DARKNESS OUTSIDE	WEEPING
MATTHEW 8:12		●	●
MATTHEW 13:42	●		●
MATTHEW 13:50	●		●
MATTHEW 22:13		●	●
MATTHEW 24:51			●
MATTHEW 25:30		●	●
LUKE 13:28			●
	LAKE OF FIRE	DISINHERITANCE	

Banquets in the Middle East were held at night. The key phrase in Greek is *to skotos to exōteron*, simply translated "the darkness outside." If there is anything to be made of the word order, it would be that the adjective "outside" is specifying either the kind or the location of the darkness. This is not the farthest darkness, that is, the lake of fire. John Nolland is correct in saying, "'The darkness outside [the building which has the banquet hall]' fits the imagery better than 'the farthest darkness.' We are to think of an evening banquet well lit inside but surrounded by darkness outside."[2491]

Experimental Predestinarians need the darkness outside to refer to final damnation in order to fit the passage into their theology. Thus, they translate it "outermost darkness," in order to emphasize this. In this discussion we choose to render the phrase as "the darkness outside," rather than "outer darkness," for two reasons. One is to keep this specifying aspect before us. The second relates to the connotation of the phrase "the outer darkness." Because it has come to be strongly associated with judgment in the lake of fire,

2490 The Partner interpretation of the "outer darkness," while not common, is found among a number of evangelicals. Warren Wiersbe, for example, says, "Some feel that this unprofitable servant was not a true believer. But it seems that he *was* a true servant, even though he proved to be unprofitable. The 'outer darkness' of Matthew 25:30 need not refer to hell, even though that is often the case in the Gospels (Matt. 8:12; 22:13). It is dangerous to build theology on parables, for parables illustrate truth in vivid ways. The man was dealt with by the Lord, he lost his opportunity for service, and he gained no praise or reward. To me, that is outer darkness." See Warren W. Wiersbe, *The Bible Exposition Commentary* (Wheaton: Victor Books, 1996), s.v. "Matthew 24:25". Spiros Zodhiates says, "In the first two instances, 'outer darkness' refers to the place of suffering for the unbelievers contrasted to the light where the believers dwell. . . . The expression 'outer darkness' in Matthew 25:30 occurs at the end of the parable of the talents, a parable to show the necessity of serving Christ faithfully according to His investment in us. Therefore, in this instance, the 'outer darkness' must mean a place of far less reward for the servants who proved themselves less diligent than those who used and exercise their talents to the fullest." See Spiros Zodhiates, *Hebrew-Greek Key Word Study Bible* (Chattanooga: AMG Publishers, 2008), 1270-71. Marty Cauley alerted me to these two citations. See Cauley, *The Outer Darkness*, 453.

2491 Nolland, *The Gospel of Matthew: A Commentary on the Greek Text*, 357. However, Nolland equates this darkness with damnation. To prove this Nolland cites references to darkness in the Pseudepigrapha, *Wis.* 17:21; *Pss. Sol.* 14:9; and the Apocrypha, Tob. 14:10 with possible allusions to 2 Peter 2:17; Jude 13. The only justification is that when one sees the word "darkness," it must mean final damnation. Is this not reading one's theology into the passages?

it makes an objective consideration of this passage more difficult.

"Darkness" (*skotos*) can simply refer to physical darkness (Luke 23:44-45).[2492] The notion of "judgment in the lake of fire" is not part of the semantic value of the word. To read this idea into it is again to commit the illegitimate identity transfer. It does sometimes refer to the judgment of the lake of fire, but only when associated with the "furnace of fire," but, in Matthew 22, it is associated with the relative darkness outside of a banquet hall.[2493]

Some argue against the above interpretation by suggesting that there is an incongruity between a true believer who is a "son of light" and who no longer remains in darkness (John 12:46; cf. Matt 5:14, 16; Luke 16:8) and the scene in the parable.[2494] This is a classic usage of the illegitimate identify transfer where the term "darkness" in John 12:46, meaning a lost state, is imported into the meaning of the word and then brought into a completely unrelated context by a different author who wrote 30 or 40 years earlier. John himself understands that true believers, when they are angry with their brothers, are "in the darkness" and walk around "in the darkness" (1 John 2:9-11). He says,

> *Anyone who claims to be in the light but hates his brother is still in the darkness. Whoever loves his brother lives in the light, and there is nothing in him to make him stumble. But whoever hates his brother is in the darkness and walks around in the darkness; he does not know where he is going, because the darkness has blinded him (1 John 2:9-11, NIV).*

To be in darkness is used here as a metaphor for exclusion from fellowship with the Lord.[2495]

By using the phrase "the darkness outside" rather than "outer darkness," we are freed from traditional usage that might color our thinking, enabling us to more easily discern what the phrase means in context. When we do that, it becomes highly probable that this phrase refers to the darkness outside the relative light of the banquet hall.[2496]

Presumably, *in the story* this is a local area immediately outside the banquet hall. The phrase is a metaphor for an experience of exclusion from the joy. If it has a spatial inference, it refers to a region in the New Jerusalem in heaven which is outside the banquet hall where the wedding festivities occur. This does not mean they are on the "edge of the kingdom,"

2492 See also Matthew 27:45; Mark 15:33; Acts 13:11.

2493 Only Christ uses the term, and it is found only in Matthew 8:12; 22:13; 25:30. The region in view is simply outside some other region, contiguous to it. As Matthew puts it, it is in "that place." In two of the references, a house of feasting is in view. In these passages the King comes into the banquet hall, and then some guests are sent out of it. The banquet hall is brilliantly lit up, but, by contrast, the gardens around them are in black darkness. All that is meant is "darkness which is without, outside the house."

2494 Pagenkemper, "An Analysis of the Rejection Motif in the Synoptic Parables and Its Relationship to Pauline Soteriology", 114.

2495 No doubt Isaiah had the same idea in mind when he said, "Who among you fears the Lord and obeys the word of his servant? Let him who walks in the dark, who has no light, trust in the name of the Lord and rely on his God" (Isaiah 50:10, NIV). This passage appears to be a call to a true believer to cease from walking in the dark and to start trusting in God and rely on Him.

2496 Thayer seems to agree when he says the phrase refers to "the darkness outside the limits of the lighted palace." Joseph H. Thayer, *Thayer's Greek-English Lexicon of the Greek New Testament* (Grand Rapids: Associate Publishers and Authors, 1889), 226.

but they are outside the celebration.[2497] This is a parable and it is inappropriate to speculate regarding all the details and then draw inferences from them. The present writer doubts there is a spatial inference. Rather this is a metaphor for the experience of exclusion.

If one chooses to take all the details literally, significant problems arise. For example, it is hard to imagine that there is a literal table with food set for a hundred million faithful believers (or however many millions) in some gigantic banquet hall. Imagine ten people at each table. This would require ten million tables! Yet if one chooses to press for spatial inferences to the outer darkness in this parable, it would be inconsistent to deny that spatial inferences regarding the banquet can lead to absurdities. This parable is a story with two main points—exclusion/regret or joy/celebration. In my opinion one over interprets by insisting a literal spatial location for the darkness outside. That said, it *is a metaphor for an **experience** and any spatial reference is an incidental inference.* As Walvoord has stressed, "It should be remembered that this will not be a literal feast with millions of people attending, but it is a symbolic concept where the guests, or friends, of the bride and the bridegroom will join in on the celebration of the marriage of the bridegroom and the bride."[2498]

Experimental Predestinarians say this man is being tortured in the lake of fire.[2499] We disagree. The expression implies nothing about the damnation of the one who "weeps and wails." Charles Stanley correctly states, "To be in the 'outer darkness' is to be in the kingdom of God but outside the circle of men and women whose faithfulness on this earth earned them a special rank or position of authority."[2500]

Karl Pagenkemper rejects the Partner interpretation of this parable, in part, on the grounds that if the punishment is experienced by the carnal Christian, it is not severe enough. He asserts, "To suggest that the expulsion from the banquet into the 'outer darkness' refers *only* to missing the initial banquet at the beginning of the [millennial] kingdom is to suggest that such a lack of faith simply is a *temporary inconvenience*."[2501]

"*Only*" missing the initial banquet!? *Simply* a "*temporary inconvenience*"!? Behind this shocking perspective is the notion that only a threat of the lake of fire is adequate to motivate a Christian who does not live up to the demands of discipleship. Apparently,

---

[2497] Darrell Bock, in his commentary on Luke, misunderstands this when he says, "Outer darkness does not mean being on the edge of the kingdom or on the edge of light, excluded only from participating in kingdom administration. It means totally outside. The kingdom is light, so one cannot be in darkness and in the kingdom at the same time, much less in outer darkness!" Darrell L Bock, Luke 9:51-24:53. Baker Exegetical Commentary on the New Testament (Grand Rapids: Baker Books, 1996) 1183. Also, sinful people who are lawless can certainly be "in" the kingdom; see Matthew 5:19, Revelation 20:7-10. They are not "totally outside" in a geographical sense, but they are certainly totally outside the company of the *Metochoi* and co-heirship with Christ.

[2498] John F. Walvoord, *The Prophecy Knowledge Handbook* (Dallas: Dallas Seminary Press, 1990), 618. Similarly Marty Cauley places this supper on earth after the revelation and opines that it lasts "throughout the millennial age," Cauley, *The Outer Darkness*, 970.

[2499] Leon Morris cannot bring himself to say "final damnation," so he describes this as a place of "uncomfortable lodging of those who are rejected." Morris, *The Gospel According to Matthew*, 552.

[2500] Charles Stanley, *Eternal Security: Can You Be Sure?"* (Nashville: Oliver Nelson, 1990), 126.

[2501] Pagenkemper, "An Analysis of the Rejection Motif in the Synoptic Parables and Its Relationship to Pauline Soteriology", 113. In the interpretation given in this chapter, we do not suggest that this exclusion is from "the initial banquet at the beginning of the [millennial] kingdom." The banquet at the beginning of the messianic reign (Luke 13:22-30) is the "Messianic Banquet" which occurs "in the kingdom" (v. 29). I distinguish this from the Wedding Banquet in Matthew 22:1-10 which occurs in the New Jerusalem during the tribulation. See pp. 780 ff. and 825 ff.

having the Savior dismiss the totality, or even the majority of one's life work as worthless is a matter of little consequence. Is it really reasonable to think that to face rebuke by Christ, to be excluded from the Marriage Banquet of the Lamb and then to be denied the privilege of co-reigning with Him **throughout the thousand year millennium and eternity** are only *temporary inconveniences*? Eternity is not temporary! Nor are such privileges merely conveniences! Would Pagenkemper actually have us believe that hearing Christ say, "Well done" and granting us rulership with Him are insignificant results? He slights the Savior's promises when he loses sight of their significance by calling their loss nothing more than *temporary inconveniences.* The Scripture says that it will be a time of "weeping and gnashing of teeth," that is, profound regret.[2502] There is something strangely disturbing about a viewpoint of eternity that can dismiss as unimportant, greater capacity for intimacy with God and opportunities to serve Him, simply because, by the grace of God there will be no regrets or comparison in the new heavens and the new earth.[2503]

Matthew therefore leads us to imagine a feast of great rejoicing. All the faithful Christians of the church are there to celebrate their wedding feast with their King. This joyful banquet is portrayed by the Lord as occurring in the evening in a brightly lit banquet hall. Outside the banquet, where the shining lights of the feast are not present, into *that place,* where the evening darkness prevails, the unfaithful will be led. This is a metaphor for the relative physical darkness. This darkness is not literal, but is a metaphor for the exclusion of the carnal Christian from the glorious reign of the *Metochoi.* It is not the darkness of eternal exclusion from heaven.

WHAT IS THE MEANING OF "WAILING AND GNASHING OF TEETH"?

Those Christians who do not possess the garment of righteous acts, who lack wedding garments at the wedding banquet, will not only be excluded from the joy of the banquet but will also experience profound regret, "wailing and gnashing of teeth."[2504] The expression occurs seven times (Matthew 8:12; 13:42, 50; 22:13; 24:51; 25:30; Luke 13:28).

But aren't these expressions unusually strong to describe the experience of a true Christian at the Judgment Seat of Christ? Strong phrases like "wailing and gnashing of teeth" portray extreme pictures to the Western mind, which cause us to freight them with meanings like the lake of fire, when all that is meant is strong remorse.[2505] To give this phrase a technical meaning for the torments of the unregenerate in the lake of fire

2502 See the section on the Duration of Remorse in chapter 48, pp. 775. See also p. 327.

2503 For example, Craig Blomberg says, "If such gradations are not perceptible or do not matter, why introduce them in the first place? And if they are imperceptible and do not matter, then how can they be motivation for a life that pleases God now?" Blomberg, "Degrees of Reward in the Kingdom of Heaven?," 162.

2504 McComiskey notes that there are no parallels to the expression "weeping and gnashing of teeth" in either secular Greek or Jewish literature. Thus its meaning must be derived contextually from the specific New Testament occurrences. He further observes, "While it is true that in many instances the usage of *bruchō* (gnash) in the expression 'to gnash the teeth' connotes anger, the association of the word with κλαυθμὸς (weeping), and the figure of torment that accompanies the term in Matt 13:42, 50 seem to indicate that the gnashing of the teeth is not an indication of rage but of extreme suffering and remorse." Thomas McComiskey, "'Lament, Sorrow, Weep, Groan,' *bruchō*'" in NIDNTT, 2:421 and Hermann Haarbeck, "*klaiō* "in ibid., 2:417. Rengstorf believes that the terms refer to exclusion from the kingdom. Karl H. Rengstorf, "*bruchō* in TDNT 1:641. We disagree. They refer to exclusion from partnership with Messiah there and to remorse felt over a wasted life.

2505 "It may be important, however, to suggest the significance of this symbolic action, namely, 'gnashing their teeth in suffering' or 'to suffer so much as to gnash the teeth.'" Louw-Nida, 1:253.

is to turn Semitic passion into theological prose, making the Bible a sword, in the words of Bellarmine, "which can be thrust into any scabbard."[2506] "The Hebrews did not restrain themselves (as modern Westerners characteristically do) from expressing emotion through weeping."[2507] For example, it was customary to hire professional mourners at a burial.

The poetic symbolism of the book of Lamentations illustrates this oriental characteristic. Jeremiah says the Lord instructed him to summon the women most skilled at mourning to compose and sing dirges (Jeremiah 9:17-22). Amos speaks of men skilled in lamentation and wailing (Amos 5:16). Special clothing was often used. A black garment made of goat's hair, coarse in nature and similar to a grain sack, was called a sackcloth (Genesis 37:34; Jeremiah 6:26).[2508] Rending the garments by tearing them from top to bottom was a universal sign among the Hebrews signifying grief and distress. Gregory says, "The capacity of the Hebrew for tears is immense, though the psalmist probably is using hyperbole when he speaks of flooding his bed every night with tears" (Psalm 6:6).[2509] As Kraus says, "Near Easterners have a way of depicting distress of soul with a lively fantasy."[2510]

David notes that his eyes shed "rivers of water" (Psalm 119:136), and Jeremiah says that his eyes are a "fountain" of tears (Jeremiah 9:1). Loud cries are frequently associated with weeping as a sign of grief (Ruth 1:9; 2 Samuel 13:36). Accompanying these cries is the characteristic action of beating the breast. The sprinkling of ashes, dust, or dirt on oneself and then wallowing in it was a common way to express grief over a personal tragedy (2 Samuel 1:2; 13:19, 31; Esther 4:1-3; Ezekiel 27:30). Amos says there was "wailing in all the plazas," saying "alas, alas," and he speaks of "professional mourners to [or 'for'] lamentation" (Amos 5:16).[2511]

Lang summarizes this well:

> *It were but an event to be expected that an Oriental despot, of royal or lesser rank, if offended with one of the slaves, should order that he be bound and thrown into the garden. There the unfortunate man, with the common Eastern emotionalism, would bewail the dark and the cold, and the danger from hungry dogs and jackals, and would gnash his teeth at being deprived of the pleasures forfeited.*[2512]

2506 For example, consider the phrase "behold, days are coming" (Heb *hinneh yamim ba'im*) in the book of Jeremiah. It occurs sixteen times in reference to days of judgment that are coming on Judah and the surrounding nations (e.g., Jeremiah 7:32; 9:25; 16:14; 19:6). However, it occurs nine times in reference to a time of future blessing for Israel in the kingdom (e.g., Jeremiah 30:3; 31:27, 38; 33:14; 49:2). This is the same phrase, but it has a different meaning, because of the context.

2507 A. Macalister, "Tear, Tears," in *International Standard Bible Encyclopedia, Revised*, ed. G. W. Bromiley (Grand Rapids: Wm. B. Eerdmans Publishing Co., 2002), 4:745.

2508 T. M. Gregory, "Mourning," in *Zondervan Pictorial Encyclopedia of the Bible*, ed. Merrill C. Tenny (Grand Rapids: Zondervan Publishing House, 2009), 4:306.

2509 Ibid., 4:304.

2510 Kraus, *Psalms 1-59: A Continental Commentary*, 161.

2511 Johnson describes this characteristic mourning: "Mourners would weep, tear their clothes, wear sackcloth, uncover and/or dishevel their hair, cover themselves with dust, sit and sleep on the ground, walk barefoot and fast." Philip S. Johnston, *Shades of Sheol: Death and the Afterlife in the Old Testament* (Downers Grove, IL: InterVarsity Press, 2002), 48.

2512 Being sent out to the garden outside the banquet hall is a completely different destiny from that of the tares, the sons of the evil one (Matthew 13:38), being cast into the furnace of fire, eternal damnation, where there will also be wailing and gnashing of teeth (Matthew 13:42). "Such obviously distinct pictures must be viewed

The phrase "wailing and gnashing of teeth" is a proverbial expression for remorse. As such, it can be applied to different situations, and one should not read the situation in which the mourner is placed into the meaning of the proverb.[2513] For example, when Jesus says, "*No one, after lighting a lamp, puts it away in a cellar nor under a basket, but on the lampstand, so that those who enter may see the light*" (Luke 11:33), the light refers to His message. It should not be hidden under a lampstand. However, the same proverbial expression in Matthew 5:14-16 refers to the believer's walk as a light that should not be hidden.[2514] Proverbial expression can have different referents depending on the context.

But does not all this weeping connect the experience with the lake of fire? No. God says, through Jeremiah, that there will be weeping and lamentation because of the conduct of His people (Jeremiah 9:10). The Greek noun for "weeping" in the LXX (9:9) is *kopetos*. It refers to violent grief, often accompanied by a beating of the breast.[2515]

The Hebrew noun (*bĕkî*) means "a lamentation" or "weeping" cf. Jeremiah 31:15. The Hebrew verb (*bākâ*)[2516] means "to weep, cry, shed tears"[2517] (cf. Deuteronomy 34:8)."[2518] Isaiah wept bitterly (Heb *bākâ*) over Israel (Isaiah 22:4). Peter wept bitterly (same expression) over his denial of Christ (Matthew 26:70). If God can weep bitterly, violently, and with tears over our sin (Jeremiah 10:10),[2519] why cannot the carnal Christian do the same at the Judgment Seat of Christ? Bitter weeping is not confined to remorse in the lake of fire. After denying the Lord three times, Peter, full of shame and remorse, "went out and *wept bitterly*" (Luke 22:61–62).

While there is an understandable tendency among many commentators to assume that these sobering words could not possibly describe the experience of true believers, we must ask, "Why not?" To assume that this phrase speaks of damnation is an assumption imported into the passage. Spiros Zodhiates correctly observes, "These terms may be applied to believers who have failed the Lord in their service. 'Outer darkness' may be a

as distinct, and distinct meanings be sought." Owen L. Crouch, *Expository preaching and teaching : Hebrews* (Joplin, Mo.: College Press Pub. Co., 1983), 306.

2513 A possible illustration from the Gospels might be, "He who is not against you is for you" (Luke 9:50). Yet in Luke 11:23 Jesus seems to apply the proverb in a contradictory way, "He who is not with me is against me." Bock notes, "Only commitment to Jesus allies one to him. Some attempt to argue that this Luke 11 saying stands in contradiction with the one here, but that fails to note their distinct contexts. In fact, the variant form in a fresh context shows that Jesus used the concept proverbially and repeatedly. It was a major theme, whether stated positively or negatively." Bock, *Luke 1-9:50*, 898.

2514 Manson, *The teaching of Jesus: Studies of its Form and Content*, 93.

2515 Rengsdorf, "*kopetos*," in TDNT, 3:832.

2516 Qal imperfect verb.

2517 TWOT, 107.

2518 HAL, 130.

2519 "The concept of a God who suffers is rejected by many because it implies that He is weak and finite. The impossibility of God suffering is a central teaching in some of the great world religions and is even advocated in some Christian circles. However, the notion of a God who cannot suffer, while perhaps making theology more manageable, nevertheless leaves it placid and spiritless. If the love of God is more than an empty metaphor, then the suffering of God must also be regarded as real. This passage has traditionally been emended in such a way as to make the prophet, and not God, the sufferer. It seems best, however, to leave the text as it is and to interpret it as the response of God to the unyielding stubbornness of his people." See Peter C. Craigie, Kelly Page H., and Joel F. Drinkard, *Jeremiah 1-26*, Word Biblical Commentary (Dallas: Word Books, 1991), 145. .

reference to a place or position of far less rewards for the servants who proved themselves less diligent than those who used and exercised their talents to the fullest."[2520]

The phrase "wailing and gnashing of teeth" means "to grieve." The location where the grieving occurs must be determined by the context and not by the necessities of Experimental Predestinarian theology. The Reformed theologians simply beg the question and assume what they consider to be a foregone conclusion. When Arminian I. Howard Marshall makes a statement like, "This is obviously a reference to the judgment on the wicked,"[2521] there is nothing "obvious" about his interpretation at all. It is only obvious to him because he has assumed before looking at the evidence that true Christians could never experience such a negative rebuke at the Judgment Seat of Christ.[2522]

At the Judgment Seat of Christ carnal Christians will indeed experience such remorse. This is taught in many passages. For example, we are told that when the Lord comes, He will reward us "good and bad" (2 Corinthians 5:10) and that some may draw back in "shame" at His coming (1 John 2:28). Some will lose what they have accomplished and never receive the full reward (2 John 8). Some Christians will be saved "*but only as one escaping through the flames*" (1 Corinthians 3:15). It seems that these verses adequately explain the experience of profound regret for the unfaithful Christian that Matthew calls "wailing and gnashing of teeth."

How long will this grief and regret last? We addressed this issue previously,[2523] but a brief comment is needed here. Pagenkemper, who believes the darkness outside refers to eternal damnation, obviously needs the experience of profound regret to last for eternity. He suggests that "the argument about the temporal nature of the Messianic Banquet is not really supported by the text of Scripture." He believes that the Partner interpretation is "forced" to assume the temporary nature of this punishment due to the false idea, in his view, that the carnal believer will miss the banquet and yet enjoy the kingdom.[2524] Actually, it seems that it is Pagenkemper who is forced to assume the banquet lasts forever

---

2520 Spiros Zodhiates, *The Complete Word Study New Testament: King James Version* (Chattanooga: AMG Publishers, 1991), 25. This writer does not agree that "outer darkness" is a place, but it may be a metaphor for a "position."

2521 I. Howard Marshall, "Who is a Hypocrite?," *BibSac* 159, no. 634 (April-June 2002): 142.

2522 That a true Christian could never face a "judgment" from God lies at the heart of the resistance to this interpretation suggested above. Yet, Paul told the Thessalonians that judgment can come on believers: "The Lord is the avenger" of those who are defrauded (1 Thessalonians 4:6). This word, "avenger" (Gr *ekdikos*) refers to "justice being done so as to rectify wrong done to another, punishing." BDAG, 301. As Green notes, "The Lord is the avenger 'in all these things,' whether or not the protagonists are members of the church!" Green, *The Letters to the Thessalonians*, 197. This is a distinctly legal term. The verbal form, is found six times in the New Testament and refers to "punishment" (e.g., 2 Corinthians 10:6; Revelation 6:10; 19:2; Romans 12:19). See discussion by Shrenk, "ἐκδικέω, ἔκδικος, ἐκδίκησις," in TDNT, 2:443 ff. The Lord is the one who "inflicts punishment." James Everett Frame, *A Critical and Exegetical Commentary on St. Paul's Epistles to the Thessalonians* (New York: Scribner's Sons, 1912), 154. As explained elsewhere (see discussion on pp. 946 ff.), the atonement of Christ has forever satisfied the claims of justice so far as the believer's eternal destiny is concerned. It is also the basis for the believer's forgiveness for restoration of fellowship within God's family (1 John 1:9-2:2). However, forgiveness within the family is extended only on the basis of confession and repentance (1 John 1:9; Revelation 2:5-6).

2523 See elsewhere in this book, p. 326, 775.

2524 Pagenkemper, "An Analysis of the Rejection Motif in the Synoptic Parables and Its Relationship to Pauline Soteriology", 114.

because of his theological bias. He assumed that a professing Christian who is not living the life is in fact not a Christian at all and will spend eternity in the lake of fire.

MANY ARE CALLED, BUT FEW ARE CHOSEN

Jesus summarizes the Parable of the Marriage Banquet with His well-known saying,

For many are called, but few are chosen (Matthew 22:14).

According to the Lord, many are called to personal salvation and to enter the banquet, but only the faithful will be admitted to the wedding feast of the Lamb. This is apparently the meaning of the saying, "*Many are called, but few are chosen.*" This ancient proverb means that while all, both Christians and non-Christians, are invited to salvation and to the banquet, only those wearing the wedding garment are chosen to participate in it. While it is true that Matthew uses the term "chosen" as a general term for the elect (Matthew 24:22), he also recognizes that there are distinctions within the elect; some will be deceived due to some moral fault of their own, and some will not (v. 24). Some writers bring in Pauline perspectives here and argue that since Paul seems to equate the chosen and the elect, Matthew must do so as well.[2525] If the above interpretation is true, however, the context is about being chosen (based upon righteous deeds) to participate in a celebration, and the issues of election and predestination are not in view at all. The banquet does not refer to the kingdom or to the sphere of personal salvation. It is the time of rejoicing at the marriage of the Lamb and His Church. All are invited, "called," but only those possessing the righteous acts of the saints will be "chosen" to participate in the marriage banquet.[2526]

Those Christians who fail to persevere to the end, who are carnal, will experience three negatives at the future judgment: (1) a stinging rebuke (Matthew 24:45-51);[2527] (2) exclusion from the wedding banquet (Matthew 22:1-14; 25:1-13);[2528] and (3) millennial disinheritance (Matthew 25:14-30).

The Centurion's Faith

A key passage where the phrase "darkness outside" is used is in the account of the centurion's great faith (Matthew 8:5-13). One day after entering his hometown of Capernaum, a Roman centurion approached Jesus with a request. His servant was paralyzed, and he begged Jesus to heal him. When Jesus offered to go to his home, the man replied that this was unnecessary because Jesus could just speak the word and his servant

---

2525 Ibid., 118.

2526 Adam Clarke suggests that the phrase may come from the ancient Roman practice of recruiting armies. "No one in ancient Rome was forced to serve in the army. They were chosen for the privilege. All were citizens, but only some were chosen to participate in the armed forces. Rome could have recruited her armies from volunteers from such a mass of well-educated and hardy youth. Instead, each tribe submitted candidates to twenty-four Roman military tribunes, chosen each year, and the honor of being chosen to serve in the wars was the reward of the accomplishments shown by the citizens. When the legions were thus completed, the citizens who had been called, but not chosen, returned to their respective employments, and served their country in other capacities." All were citizens of the empire, but only some were chosen to be in the army. Adam Clarke, *Matthew*, Clarke's Commentary (Albany, OR: Ages Software, 1999), s.v. "Matthew 20:16".

2527 See discussion on pp. 804 ff.

2528 Clarke, *Matthew*, s.v. "Matthew 20-:16".

would be healed. He said he was not worthy to have Jesus come to his house and that he, like Jesus, was a man with authority. Therefore, Jesus could exercise His authority remotely. Our Lord was amazed.

> *Now when Jesus heard this, He marveled, and said to those who were following, "Truly I say to you, I have not found such great faith with anyone in Israel. "And I say to you, that many shall come from east and west, and recline at the table with Abraham, and Isaac, and Jacob, in the kingdom of heaven; but* ***the sons of the kingdom*** *shall be cast out into the outer darkness; in that place there shall be weeping and gnashing of teeth." And Jesus said to the centurion, "Go your way; let it be done to you as you have believed." And the servant was healed that very hour (Matthew 8:10-13).*

The setting of this parable is different from the setting of the parable of the Wedding Banquet. This parable occurs "in the kingdom" when the faithful "recline at the table with Abraham, Isaac, and Jacob." This is the Messianic Banquet on earth mentioned in Isaiah 25:6; Luke 13:22-30; and, possibly, though unlikely, Luke 14:16-24[2529] and not the Marriage Banquet of the Lamb which occurs in heaven during the tribulation. It is doubtful that this is a literal banquet with millions of tables in a gigantic banquet hall. Rather it is a metaphor for the time of rejoicing of Christ's Metochoi from all ages, not just the church, as the kingdom begins.

It seems likely that anyone would have wanted such a popular teacher as Jesus to come directly to his home to perform the healing. Yet this man knows this is unnecessary. All Jesus has to do is speak the word, and his servant will be healed. Impressed, Jesus acclaims his "great faith."

What is this "great faith"? It obviously refers to believing something that is very difficult to believe. This is illustrated by the faith of Abraham who was a man justified before God. Yet, in Romans 4:19-21 we are told that Abraham, even though Sarah's womb was dead, continued to believe the word of God's promise that he and Sarah would have a son. "*He did not waver in unbelief, but grew strong in faith, giving glory to God.*"

If one knows that Jesus is the Messiah and the Savior, it is easy to believe on Him for the forgiveness of sins. But as we all know, it is more difficult to believe for a healing or to trust Him in the midst of a trial or a difficulty. As Christ says elsewhere, "*Which is easier, to say to the paralytic, 'Your sins are forgiven'; or to say, 'Arise, and take up your pallet and walk'?*" (Mark 2:9).

The issue at stake in the words to follow is "great faith" and not saving faith. He now describes a scene that occurs shortly after He returns. Abraham, Isaac, and Jacob, and many others are reclining together at a great feast,[2530] the eschatological banquet.[2531] Having just spoken of the great faith of the centurion, Jesus takes us forward to that final day when our lives will be evaluated.

Who are these "sons of the kingdom"? This point is relevant to the understanding of "the outer darkness" because these sons experience this anguish. These "sons of the kingdom" do not have the great faith of this Gentile centurion, and that will be noted at

---

[2529] It is possible that this parable refers to entering into current kingdom blessings and is not eschatological.

[2530] The Greek for "recline" (Gr *anaklinō*) often means "recline at the meal" (Louw-Nida, 1:83, BDAG, 65).

[2531] Johannes Behm, "*deipnon, deipneō*," in TDNT, 2:34-35.

the judgment. That is not to say they have none at all or that they are unregenerate. This is not a contrast between a Gentile with faith and an Israelite without faith.[2532] It is obvious that the Lord did find faith in Israel. Indeed, thousands believed in Him, although many superficially, but many nevertheless believed genuinely. What dismayed Him was that, in comparison with the Gentile centurion, there was rarely an instance of "great faith" within Israel. The contrast is between a Gentile who had great faith and the sons of the kingdom who should have had great faith but did not. That is clearly what the parable says, and to argue that the sons of the kingdom were unsaved is simply reading one's theology into the passage.

Note that the setting is "in the kingdom." We are told that it is at this time that faithful believers will recline at table with Abraham, Isaac, and Jacob (cf. Luke 13:29). This is not the Marriage of the Lamb of Matthew 22 but the Messianic Banquet, a celebration at the beginning of the millennium (cf. Isaiah 25:6)[2533]

Note that they are "sons" of the kingdom. We must remember that there are sons, and there are also "sons indeed." This is similar to the fact that the Captain of Our Salvation was the eternal "Son of God" in one sense (Galatians 4:4) and then was declared "Son" in another sense when He sat down at the right hand of the throne of majesty. It was because of His perseverance and faithfulness (Hebrews 1:5; Psalm 2:7) that He obtained the right to that position. His brothers, who are already sons (Galatians 3:26), can also become "sons" in another sense through suffering with Him. All believers are sons by faith in Christ, but Matthew uses the term in some places in the sense of "sons indeed," when He says we must perform good works in order to become "sons of God" (Matthew 5:9, 44-45). Similarly, Jesus says in Luke, "*But love your enemies, and do good, and lend, expecting nothing in return; and your reward will be great, and you will be sons of the Most High; for He Himself is kind to ungrateful and evil men*" (Luke 6:35).

There is nothing in this verse about proving that one is "truly" a son (in the sense of being born again) by a life of works. Rather, this future tense suggests that one who is already a son in one sense can become a son in another. The phrase "son of" is common as a Jewish idiom for "one who is like one's Father." This is how the phrase "son of righteousness" means "a righteous person" or "sons of thunder" means "violent men." To be a "son of something" means to share the characteristics of the "father." When we love our enemies, we are like our Father in that instance, and in this sense we become "sons indeed." One becomes a son of God by spiritual rebirth (John 3:5); accordingly, we "become children of God" by receiving Him (John 1:12-13). But there is evidently a difference between being a son of God and living like one and thus being publicly revealed as such, that is, "called" or *recognized as* a son. Those who are peacemakers and who love their enemies are not only sons but are also "sons indeed."

But are these "sons of the kingdom" saved people? Yes! That these "sons of the kingdom" are justified saints is specifically stated in Matthew 13:38: "*As for the good seed, these are the sons of the kingdom; and the tares are the sons of the evil one.*" It is evident that

---

[2532] Contra Pak, "A Study of Selected Passages on Distinguishing Marks of Genuine and False Believers", 17. One will search in vain here for a statement that the sons of the kingdom had no faith or were unbelievers. Pak is simply asserting this probably because it fits his Experimental Predestinarian prior assumption.

[2533] For discussion of the duration of this remorse see pp. 326, 775 ff.

the sons of the kingdom are "the good seed," that is, believers. These "sons of the kingdom" are the children of the kingdom. They are those who have humbled themselves like a little child and were converted (Matthew 18:3-4).[2534]

That Gentiles would be sitting down with the patriarchs, and yet some of the Jewish sons of the kingdom would not, must have been very shocking to Jesus' hearers. Similarly, it is shocking to people today to hear that while all Christians will be in the kingdom, not all will be at the table.

The account of the sons of the kingdom cast into the darkness outside and experiencing "wailing and gnashing of teeth" in Matthew 8:12 for an unspecified period of time informs us of the identity of those lacking the proper wedding attire in Matthew 22:13 for admission into the Marriage Banquet in the New Jerusalem prior to the second coming.[2535] If the regenerate sons of the kingdom can experience this remorse, there is no objection to those lacking the wedding garment experiencing the same thing.

Summary

For many readers, this chapter may be one of the most difficult in this book. It is certainly sobering and definitely contrary to much teaching that something negative could occur at the Judgment Seat of Christ. The common view is that it is a happy time for all believers regardless of the kind of life they have led. Yet, Paul specifically says that at this judgment believers will receive a recompense (Gr *komizō*, "receive what is due")[2536] for what we have done "*whether good or bad*" (2 Corinthians 5:10). The guests at the wedding banquet, like some believers today, will look back at a life lacking in good works. Some of the "sons of the kingdom" will have had an anemic faith.

These parables give a response to a common objection to the Partner defense of eternal security. Objectors are prone to say something like, "You mean to say that a person can believe in Christ and then live a life of sin and still go to heaven?!" The inference is that unless there is a danger of final damnation, believers will fall into lives of sin. Perhaps an even more preposterous inference is that only those who are *good enough in themselves* will escape eternal damnation because of the moral level they have achieved. This is indeed the creed of both Arminians and Neonomians. Opponents of the Partner view accuse us of having no final accountability.

Au contraire! The Partner viewpoint introduces serious accountability in its understanding of the biblical passages of negative consequences that may befall the unfaithful believer at the final assize. To fall back on the threat of final damnation as the only completely adequate means of motivating the carnal believer to climb out of the sewer is a poor concept of biblical motivation. Does it adequately substitute for the more ennobling incentive of hearing the Master's "Well done," or conversely, fearing the rebuke and the darkness outside? Believers confronted with the threat of the lake of fire should simply ignore it.

2534 There is no implication here that this is a "stock phrase" or a "technical term." The point is that the only defined usage of the term in Matthew ascribes it to the good seed and the wheat, true believers. Therefore, the burden of proof is on those who want to understand it in a different way in Matthew 8:12.

2535 See discussion of "wailing and gnashing of teeth" above on pp. 792 and ff.

2536 BDAG, 557.

At the Judgment Seat of Christ, we will all have regrets. But not all will weep and gnash their teeth, and the regrets will be overcome by the Savior's embrace in unconditional love and the rewards He will grant.

As we think about this future day of reward, two passages of Scripture should be kept in mind.

> *For I am conscious of nothing against myself, yet I am not by this acquitted; but the one who examines me is the Lord. Therefore do not go on passing judgment before the time, but wait until the Lord comes who will both bring to light the things hidden in the darkness and disclose the motives of men's hearts; and then each man's praise will come to him from God (1 Corinthians 4:4-5).*

"Do not," Paul says, "go on passing judgment before the time." Applying this to ourselves, he is telling us not to be introspective in a condemnatory fashion. If known sins appear, we need to confess them and move on, knowing that one day our praise will come from God and that He is perfectly fair, just, and loving.

Remember too that mercy triumphs over judgment.

> *For judgment will be merciless to one who has shown no mercy; mercy triumphs over judgment (James 2:13).*

If I want mercy, I must be a merciful person. I can prepare for the future by becoming an increasingly merciful individual. This can be very hard—we always run into people who wound us and rub us the wrong way, but this helps us get off the introspective track.

Excursus on the Gathering of the Firstborn

This theme of a failure to endure is central to the book of Hebrews. For an instructive passage which seems to parallel the parable of the wedding banquet in Matthew 22:1-14, let us consider Hebrews 12:22-23:

> *But you have come to Mount Zion and to the city of the living God, the heavenly Jerusalem, and to myriads of angels, to the general assembly and church of the firstborn who are enrolled in heaven, and to God, the Judge of all, and to the spirits of righteous men made perfect (NASB).*

The reference to "the church of the firstborn" picks up a reference in the preceding context to Esau, the firstborn of Isaac and Rebekah. The "firstborn" in Jewish culture had certain inheritance rights. He could, however, forfeit them and must maintain certain protocols to keep them. Esau, the firstborn of Isaac, gave up his inheritance rights. A major concern of the epistle is that the Hebrews might fail to persevere and thus forfeit their inheritance rights as well.

This "general assembly" consists of those who, unlike Esau (Heb 12:16-17), *will* obtain the inheritance rights. "This company consists of those who persevere in faith and so secure the inheritance and the objective blessings associated with it."[2537] These are the

---

[2537] William L. Lane, *Hebrews 9-13*, Word Biblical Commentary (Dallas: Word, Inc., 2002), 469 "companions" (Gr *Metochoi*) mentioned in Hebrews 1:9. This future vision is the basis for the warning of Hebrews 12:25: "*See to it that you do not refuse Him who is speaking. For if those did not escape when they refused him who warned them on earth, much less will we escape who turn away from Him who warns from heaven*" (NASB).

The phrase "general assembly" is from the Greek for "a happy, joyous festivity" (*Gr panēguris*).[2538] This word differs from the word *ekklēsia* (translated "church") which follows, in that *panēguris* refers to a festival of rejoicing while *ekklēsia* refers to any gathering in general.[2539] Thus, like Matthew 8, this is a festive gathering of those with "great faith, who have endured, and therefore are qualified to obtain the inheritance rights of firstborn sons, the company of the *Metochoi*.

Those escorted to the darkness outside the banquet hall will experience weeping and gnashing of teeth, an expression for profound regret over a wasted life.

[2538] Louw-Nida, 1:528.

[2539] Trench, *Synonyms of the New Testament*, 6. BDAG, 754.

50
The Wicked Servant

WITH A series of parables in the Olivet Discourse, Jesus makes applications arising from His dramatic prophetic announcements in the preceding verses. In the discussion to follow we will suggest that the first three of these parables apply to a future time in which the Lord appears without prior notice, unexpectedly; at a time when no one knows the time of His arrival.

The final parable, however, occurs when the Son of Man appears in His glory with all His angels and sits on His glorious throne (Matthew 25:31). The first three occur at the beginning of the *Parousia*, the rapture of the church, while the Parable of the Sheep and the Goats occurs at the second coming, seven years later. The first three parables deal with the assessment of the lives of believers in this age in regard to servant leadership, spiritual preparation for His return, and faithfulness. The last parable deals with an assessment of those living in the tribulation period. The key issue is how they treat Christ's "little ones," the messengers of the Gospel during that era.

After describing the totally unexpected judgment which comes on the world, our Lord now applies this to His followers. First, He stresses the unexpected nature of the Lord's return, like a thief in the night. In view of this, He warns them to always be prepared "for you do not know which day your Lord is coming" (Matthew 24:42).

> *Therefore you also be ready, for the Son of Man is coming at an hour when you do not expect Him (Matthew 24:44, NKJV).*

The coming of the Son of Man in this verse obviously cannot refer to the second coming because all can know the precise day and hour of the Second Advent. It will occur precisely 1260 days (Revelation 11:3) after the abomination of desolation. There is nothing unexpected about it.[2540]

Four parables follow:

- the faithful vs. the unfaithful servant (Matthew 24:45-51),
- the wise vs. the foolish virgins (Matthew 25:1-13),
- the faithful vs. the wicked and lazy servant (the parable of the talents, Matthew 25:14-30),
- the faithful sheep vs. the unbelieving nations (Matthew 25:31-46).

[2540] We will discuss this issue in more detail in the chapter to follow, *The Ten Virgins*.

The Evil Servant

The rapture of the church is unexpected. Because it can occur at any moment without any signs preceding, Jesus says,

> *Who then is a faithful and wise servant, whom his master made ruler over his household, to give them food in due season? (Matthew 24:45, NKJV)*

He says, "Who ***then***" is a faithful servant. In view of the fact that the Lord Jesus can return at any moment in the pretribulation rapture, we need to always be prepared.

In the parable of the wise servant, the evil servant is after all a "servant." If the wise servant is saved, there is no exegetical basis for implying that the evil servant is not. In fact, the Greek text indicates that only one servant, not two, are in view. Then the Lord says, "But if that (Gr *ekeinos*) evil slave says …" (24:48). He is speaking of that same servant, the wise one of the preceding verses. This one servant may conceivably follow two different courses in life.[2541] Luke's version of the parable makes the same point (Luke 12:45): "if *that* slave"—same slave, different choices.

The wicked servant is not an unbeliever. He genuinely believes in the return of "his" master. He is a "true" Christian but has become carnal and walks as "mere men" (1 Corinthians 3:3). His indifferent attitude is due to the fact that his Lord's return has been delayed. A non-Christian could hardly be called a "servant" of Christ. Like the parallel passage in Luke 12:41-46 where a similar parable was told on a different occasion, this man is entrusted with responsibility over the household of God and is promised to be blessed if he is faithful (Luke 12:44). Would Jesus entrust spiritual ministry to a nonbeliever? The blessing probably refers to positions of administration in the future kingdom (Luke 19:17; 1 Corinthians 6:2–3). While crowds are listening (in Luke's account), the passage is likely addressed to leaders of the church, those responsible for local congregations. This seems evident from Peter's question in Luke 12:41, "*Lord, are you telling this parable to us, or to everyone?*" In the Lord's answer He applies this to Peter and the Twelve, as stated in verse 22, "And he said *to his disciples,*" and there is no indication of a change of audience in the verses to follow.

According to Frederick Danker, the Pauline parallel to this judgment is found in 1 Cor. 3:10-4:5 where regenerate leaders for the church will be similarly judged at the Judgment Seat of Christ, and some will make it as through fire.[2542] I agree. Thus, the warning to follow (Matthew 24:42-46) is for true believers. An evil servant is *a servant*. There is nothing here that says he was a "so-called" servant. Rather, the parable acknowledges a common fact of Christian experience. Some servants of Christ are faithful and wise, and some who start out serving their master become indolent. Indeed, if his "fellow servants" are believers, he must be saved too. Fellow servants in Matthew are called "brethren" (Matthew 18:28, 29, 31, 33, 35). There are not two different servants in this parable, as

---

2541 Some interpreters mistakenly parallel this parable with the parable of the two sons in Matthew 21:28-32; wherein one was saved and one was not. But there are two sons in that parable and one servant with two possible lifestyles in this one.

2542 Suggested by Frederick W. Danker, *Jesus and the New Age: A Commentary on St. Luke's Gospel*, completely rev. and expanded. ed. (Philadelphia: Fortress Press, 1988), 256.

indicated in the parallel passage in Luke 12:45..[2543] There is one servant who can make two different choices.[2544]

> *But if that evil slave says in his heart, "My master is not coming for a long time," and shall begin to beat his fellow slaves and eat and drink with drunkards; the master of that slave will come on a day when he does not expect him and at an hour which he does not know" (Matthew 24:48–50).*

This servant conducts himself in a manner that earns him the title "evil servant" (Matthew 24:48). He drinks with drunkards, beats his fellow servants, and is completely unprepared for his master's return. One need not suppose that he spends most of his life in a bar getting drunk and beating up on fellow believers. "Elsewhere 'drunkenness' symbolizes the recklessness that no longer thinks in 'sober' terms of responsibility in the eyes of God."[2545]

When his master does return, this servant is "cut in pieces" and assigned a place "with the hypocrites" where there is " weeping" and "gnashing of teeth" (Matthew 24:51).

> *And shall cut him in pieces and assign him a place with the hypocrites; weeping shall be there and the gnashing of teeth (Matthew 24:51).*

It is understandable that interpreters have difficulty in imagining that this could be the experience of a born-again child of God. Part of the problem is the extreme phrases used: "cut in pieces" and "weeping and gnashing of teeth." As explained in the previous chapter, however, "weeping and gnashing of teeth" is oriental symbolism for profound regret,[2546] and "cut in pieces" is a metaphor for judgment.[2547]

In Luke's version, there are apparently three levels of punishment for this born-again carnal Christian: (1) severe, "cut in pieces" (Luke 12:46); (2) less severe, "severe beating," (v. 47); and (3) least severe, "will receive but a few [floggings]" (v. 48). These scales of punishment do not refer to degrees of "suffering in hell"[2548] but to degrees of rebuke at the Judgment Seat of Christ.

If we were to ask, "What is the specific nature of this most severe judgment?," the figure "cut in pieces" possibly suggests "the sword of the Spirit, which is the Word of God" (Ephesians 6:17). This view is reinforced when we read that, when the Lord returns in judgment, "from His mouth comes a sharp sword" (Revelation 19:15).

That the Word of God could be considered an instrument capable of "cutting" in a judgmental sense is further affirmed by Hebrews 4:12:

2543 Hagner admits that "in Luke, the same servant who is thought of as entertaining an altogether different train of thought and engaging in a very different behavior (Luke 12:45)." Hagner, *Matthew 14-28*, 724. Then, curiously, he argues that the same parable in Matthew's vision speaks of two different servants.

2544 "The same servant (ἐκεῖνος), however, may act otherwise. As time passes, he may think that his master is away for some time, and that he can take advantage of this to act as he please." Marshall, *The Gospel of Luke: A Commentary on the Greek Text*, 539.

2545 See Eduard Schweizer, *The Good News According to Matthew* (Atlanta: John Knox Press, 1975), 462.

2546 See elsewhere in this book, pp. 792 ff.

2547 BAGD, 159. Arndt and Gingrich say *dichotomeō* is "metaphorical in Luke 12:46, 'to punish with utmost severity,' like the modern threat 'I will tan your hide.'"

2548 Contra Hendriksen, *Exposition of the Gospel According to Luke*, 681.

For the word of God is living and active and sharper than any two-edged sword, and piercing as far as the division of soul and spirit, of both joints and marrow, and able to judge the thoughts and intentions of the heart (Hebrews 4:12, NASB).

When the Lord returns to judge the wicked servant, the instrument of that judgment will apparently be the Word of God. It is able to pierce to the heart of a man, to cut to the inner being, and to discern underlying motivations. As a result, all is revealed:

And there is no creature hidden from His sight, but all things are open and laid bare to the eyes of Him with whom we have to do (Hebrews 4:13).

At this moment the stern warning of our Lord will have pointed meaning:

There is nothing covered up that will not be revealed, and hidden that will not be known. Accordingly, whatever you have said in the dark shall be heard in the light, and what you have whispered in the inner rooms shall be proclaimed upon the housetops (Luke 12:2-3).

The Lord's point is not that our sins will be published to others but that all sins, even those covered up and in private in our secret rooms, will be fully revealed to the believer and his Lord and will be accounted for at the judgment day.

The servant in Matthew's account is not literally cut in pieces, but his secret motivations are exposed. His "work is burned up" (1 Corinthians 3:15), and he draws back "in shame at the Lord's coming" (1 John 2:28). To use Paul's term, he is "disqualified for the prize" (1 Corinthians 9:27), and according to John, he will forfeit what he has worked for and lose his full reward (2 John 8). We must remember that these are *parables* and full of metaphors which are not to be taken literally. Rather, they symbolically point to sober truths. In a similar way, Paul spoke of coming to discipline the carnal Corinthian believers "with a rod" (1 Corinthians 4:21). Like the statement about being cut to pieces at the future judgment, this does not speak of a literal rod but uses a metaphor for severe rebuke.

Instead of calling this evil servant "unfaithful" as Luke 12:46 does, in Matthew's version our Lord affirms that the unfaithful servant will be assigned a place with the "hypocrites" (Gr *hypokritēs*) (Matthew 24:51).

For some, this proves that the "unfaithful" in Luke 12:46 are in fact, unbelievers. According to Bock, "Efforts to argue that this person is 'saved, but disciplined' ignore the force of ὑποκριτής in Matthew's parallel, which, though distinct from Luke, is related to his account. It also ignores the picture of dismemberment. Both accounts picture total rejection."[2549]

Inexplicably, after arguing that the addressees in Luke 12 are regenerate leaders of the church, Bock has decided that instead they represent hypocrites whose commitment to Christ was not genuine.[2550] Bock reads his Experimental Predestinarian theology into the passage. Citing Luke 12:46 where this slave is "cut in pieces" and assigned a place with the "unbelievers" (Gr *apistos*), he concludes that the servant in view was not a Christian at all. He says that because "of the severe nature of the punishment, it (*apistos*) should be understood to mean 'unbelieving.'"[2551]

[2549] Bock, *Luke 9:51-24:53*, 1184. Bock, *Luke 1-9:50*, 1184.

[2550] Ibid., 1178.

[2551] Ibid., 1182.

However, apistos does not necessarily mean unbeliever. In Luke 12:46, because in context it appears as a contrast with pistos (faithful) in v. 42, it probably means "unfaithful."[2552] This translation is not uncommon.[2553] As is well known, the word "*apistos*" can be translated either "unbeliever" (KJV, NIV, NASV, NKJV) or "unfaithful" (RSV, ASV, ESV, ISV, NRSV, NET Bible, NLT, NAB) or "disobedient" (GNT). Why, one might ask, can't true believers who are saved as through fire, experience punishment at the Judgment Seat of Christ? It would seem that the passage can just as easily argue this point. Here is a servant of Christ, an apostle (Luke 12:22), who is warned about becoming indifferent to the Lord's return, and if he does, he will be punished for it.

Like Bock, those holding this view that Luke 12:46 refers to "unbelievers," point to Matthew 24:51 where the "unfaithful" are called "hypocrites." Luke calls them "unfaithful" and Matthew calls them "hypocrites." The word "hypocrisy" (Matthew 24:51) was used of a play actor.[2554] The wicked servant claims to be a servant of his master, but his hypocrisy is that he does not live like it, he is acting. Bock is correct that it is normally used of non-Christians,[2555] but it is also used by Christ of true Christians who judge others (their "brother"), while ignoring their own sin (Matthew 7:5). Barnabas and Peter were charged with hypocrisy by Paul (Galatians 2:13), and Peter speaks of "newborn babes" who are to put hypocrisy aside (1 Peter 2:1-2). The servant in Matthew 24:51 is the opposite of a "faithful and sensible" steward (v. 45). The opposite of "faithful and sensible" is "unfaithful," or, as Jesus puts it, he "*did not get ready or act in accord with his will*" (v. 47).

This man was not an unbeliever; he believed in his "master" and that his master was coming back. The fact that Luke's *apiston* is replaced by *hypokriton* (hypocrisy) in the parallel passage in Matthew suggests that *apiston* in Luke 12:46 should not be translated as "unbeliever" but as "unfaithful." His hypocrisy was not that he professed Christ outwardly but did not "truly" believe, but that even though he was assigned the role of a servant, he did not take care of the other servants and ended up serving only himself. The servant was not a non-Christian; he was an unfaithful Christian. It is for this that he will be judged and given a place with the other "unfaithful" believers.

But what is this "place" (Gr *meros*, Luke 12:46, Matthew 24:51) to which the unfaithful or hypocrites are assigned? Experimental Predestinarians commonly misunderstand the Partner view. Darrell Bock, for example says, "The Matthean figure also indicates total rejection, since it is often associated with being cast into outer darkness. Outer darkness does not mean being on the edge of the kingdom or on the edge of light, excluded only from participating in kingdom administration. It means totally outside."[2556] This is a partial misunderstanding. It is true that the Partner views the darkness as exclusion from the festivities of the Wedding Banquet in the New Jerusalem and from the Messianic Banquet in the millennium (Matthew 8:12; Luke 13:24-30). However, the "outer darkness" is not a

---

2552 According to Plummer, *A Critical and Exegetical Commentary on the Gospel according to St. Luke*, 333. See also A. T. Robertson, *Word Pictures in the Greek New Testament* (Nashville: Broadman, 1933), 2:181.

2553 VCED, 2:651; EDNT, 2:165; LexAL LXX , s.v "ἄπιστος"; ANLEX, 65; LEH LXX, s.v. "ἄπιστος".

2554 Ulrich Wilckens, "hypokrinomai," in TDNTA, 1235.

2555 Matthew 6:2, 5, 16.

2556 Roy B. Zuck, Darrell L. Bock, and Dallas Theological Seminary, *A Biblical Theology of the New Testament* (Chicago: Moody Press, 1994), 1183.

literal place on the "edge" of anything. This is a *story*. The metaphor refers to exclusion from fellowship and celebration and not from a physical location.

Bock continues, "The kingdom is light, so one cannot be in darkness and in the kingdom at the same time, much less in outer darkness!"[2557] However, as argued above, the Partners do not view this event as happening "in the kingdom" at all. It occurs in the New Jerusalem during the tribulation at the Judgment Seat of Christ. Furthermore, John tells us that it is possible for "brethren" to be in darkness (1 John 2:9-11). Partners think of the outer darkness in experiential rather than spatial terms. Light and darkness are metaphors for either the joy of the wedding festivities or the remorse of exclusion. One can imagine a place in the story in the New Jerusalem outside the banquet hall or on the hills of Jerusalem outside the Messianic Banquet. However, this is probably building too much on figurative language.

Using theological exegesis to support an illegitimate identity transfer,[2558] Stein opines on the fate of this unfaithful servant of the kingdom saying, "The parallel in Matthew 24:51 makes clear that the servant receives an eternal punishment because he goes with the hypocrites to the place 'where there will be weeping and gnashing of teeth.'"[2559] This statement assumes that because "weeping and gnashing of teeth" must refer to the experience of the unregenerate in one place, the unfaithful servant must therefore be in that place (the lake of fire) and be unregenerate. However, it is just as valid to say that, because this man is in fact regenerate, it is clear that the regenerate can experience weeping and gnashing of teeth at the Judgment Seat of Christ, thus negating a tenant of Westminster Calvinism, the inevitable perseverance of the saints in a life of good works to the final hour. This justified evil servant did not persevere. This passage supports the view that the doctrine of the saints' inevitable perseverance in holiness is fiction. This man is saved, but he did not persevere.

The parable would have no relevance to those who do not know Christ and who have not begun the process of serving Him. What is of concern is that the servant who begins his service will continue it until his Lord returns. Christians are capable of unfaithfulness and hypocrisy and can lead carnal lives which can be summed up as hypocritical. They will be in the kingdom but not at the wedding feast! The unfaithful servant will not be "at the table," though he is a servant and will be saved.

Wicked Christians?

A concern of Experimental Predestinarians is the fact that in the Partner view of these parables, a true believer can be designated as "wicked." The negative terminology that Jesus and the New Testament writers use to describe those whom the Partners believe are carnal Christians is quite severe. How could terms such as "wicked servant" (Gr *kokos*, "bad, evil") in Matthew 24:48 (ESV) and 25:26 (Gr *pornēos*, "wicked, evil, bad") be applied to those who are truly born again?

In the preceding chapters the Partner interpretation of a number of parables says

---

2557 Bock, *Luke 9:51-24:53*, 1183.

2558 That is, if the expression "wailing and gnashing of teeth" refers to the experience of the unbeliever in hell in two places (Matthew 13:42, 50), it must be a technical term for damnation everywhere else it is used. See refutation on pp. 792 ff.

2559 Robert H. Stein, *Luke*, The New American Commentary (Nashville: Broadman Press, 1992), 362.

that a true Christian might be "bound hand and foot" and cast into "outer darkness" (Matthew 22:13). Furthermore, this person might hear the fearful words, "*I do not know you*" (Matthew 25:12), or "*I do not know where you are from*" (Luke 13:27). In the parable discussed in this chapter, a true believer ignores the coming of his Master, is an unfaithful steward, gets drunk, and beats his fellow servants (Matthew 24:49). As a result, when the Master returns, the servant is "cut in pieces" and receives "many lashes" at the final judgment (Luke 12:41-48). In the parable of the talents, the unfaithful believer is called a "wicked, lazy servant" (Matthew 25:26). Yet elsewhere the "wicked" are the opposite of the "righteous," and therefore could be understood to be nonbelievers (Matthew 13:49). The majority of Bible scholars in the history of the church have taught that these phrases and experiences can refer only to the experience of non-Christians facing eternal damnation with the rest of unbelievers, that is, "hypocrites."

At least three assumptions underlie this concern. First, Experimental Predestinarians assume, due to their unbiblical doctrine of inevitable perseverance in holiness, that no true Christian could possibly have his service summed up as "wicked." Their logic goes like this:

1. True Christians always persevere in holiness to the final hour.
2. Those whom Christ describes as "wicked" or as "evil servant[s]" did not persevere in holiness.
3. Therefore, those described this way could not be true Christians.

Since (1) is considered "obvious" by Experimental Predestinarians, the conclusion (3) inevitably follows. But (1) is not true. As this book has shown, there are many in Scripture who did not persevere and yet were born again.[2560] There are those "in" the kingdom who not only disobey Christ's commands but teach others to do the same (Matthew 5:19). In the final summation of their lives, they could only be described as "wicked."

Second, Experimentalists assume that what qualifies a person for entrance into heaven is a life of works. Yet Scripture says that the only thing needed is faith alone. Apparently, it is difficult for many to accept the fact that God's grace accepts us unconditionally, without cost, as a free gift. Somehow, they think a moral life is necessary (not just obligatory), especially when one is trying to defend the Reformation against a charge of moral license!

But third, many say it seems "harsh" that Jesus would address one of His "brothers" and one of God's children in such negative terms. How can believers receive "many lashes," be assigned a place with hypocrites, be "cut in pieces," or be called lazy and wicked?

The Partners believe these are metaphors and do not reflect a literal reality. The literal meaning toward which the metaphor points is not being cut in pieces or being lashed with whips. The literal meaning behind this figure of speech is the expression of profound divine displeasure. These events occur *in the story*, and they symbolize spiritual realities.

The strong language is the language of story, designed to make a strong point. For example, consider the story of the prodigal son. We don't take the words of the father about rings, robes, and fatted calves to mean that we will receive rings, robes, etc. We understand them as his gracious welcome of all who come to Him (sinners or carnal Christians). In the same manner, the words of bound, cut, lashes, etc. are not to be understood literally. They

---

[2560] See Chapter 32.

are metaphors that depict the father's severe displeasure and warning regarding the time in which they must give an account.[2561]

What other term besides "wicked," "evil," or "lazy" would be appropriate for the person who sins continually to the point of physical death? The wilderness generation trusted in the Passover lamb and worshiped the Lord (Ex 12:27-28), believed in Him (Exodus 4:31; 14:31), were "devoted to him," and "followed him" (Jeremiah 2:1-3). Yet though they believed on Christ (1 Corinthians 10:3); they were called "wicked" by God (Numbers 14:27) and were judged in the wilderness (1 Corinthians 10:5). Carnal believers ***can*** be lazy and "neglect the so great salvation" (Hebrews 2:3). Born-again people are capable of murder and can live such a wretched life that they can be called "evildoers, thieves, and murderers" (1 Peter 4:15). Believers ***do*** sometimes mistreat their fellow servants. No doubt they do not think of it as "beating" them when they gossip behind their backs (Titus 2:3); slander their character, ignore them in time of need (James 2:15); show partiality (James 2:3); drag them into court (1 Corinthians 6:6, 7); "ruin" them by their example (1 Corinthians 8:11-12); exhibit jealousy and strife toward them (1 Corinthians 3:3); steal from them (Ephesians 4:28); jealously and competitively cause them distress (Philippians 1:17); act with contempt toward them (Romans 14:3-4); judge them and cause them to stumble (Romans 14:13); quarrel with them (1 Corinthians 1:11); sleep with one's mother-in-law (1 Corinthians 5:1); treat fellow Christians as "enemies" (Galatians 4:16); "complain" about one another (Colossians 3:12); have sexual intercourse with another believer's wife (1 Thessalonians 4:6,7); not provide for the needs of one's family (1 Timothy 5:8); betray and abandon a fellow believer because he is in trouble with anti-Christian authorities (2 Timothy 1:15); or upset the faith of fellow Christians (2 Timothy 2:17-18). Christians who do these things may not think they are "beating" or mistreating their "fellow" servants, but they are, and one day this will be revealed for what it really is, abuse that deserves rebuke! The metaphor of "many lashes" (Luke 12:47) and being "cut in pieces" is very appropriate.

If calling justified saints "wicked" seems extreme, one only has to turn to the Epistle to the Hebrews to see even worse language describing some believers. The writer of the epistle says, "*They are crucifying once again the Son of God to their own harm and holding him up to contempt* (Hebrews 6:6, ESV). Crucifying again the Son of God! Holding Him up to contempt! No wonder these regenerate saints[2562] harm themselves. Apart from any temporal consequences, they will be severely "harmed" when the Lord Jesus says to them at the Judgment Seat of Christ, "*I never knew you, depart from me, you who practice lawlessness*" (Matthew 7:21).

Because of the graciousness of our God, this description as wicked or evil does not follow them into eternity future. God will restore the carnal Christian to fellowship.[2563] Once the assessment is done, and the weeping is concluded, they are enfolded in grace into the heavenly Kingdom. They will not be hearing the words "wicked" for all eternity. But, as John tells us, there will be a period of "shame" (1 John 2:28) when they are saved "through fire" (1 Corinthians 3:15). The emotional pain of passing through the fire is only temporary; nevertheless, some of the results of that passing are eternal. While the subjective continuity

---

[2561] Suggested by Ken Mitchell, personal communication 24 August 2006.

[2562] For proof that those addressed in the Epistle to the Hebrews are regenerate saints see chapter 41 and especially pp. 641 ff.

[2563] For discussion of the duration of remorse experienced by the carnal Christian see pp. 326, 775 ff.

of shame will not follow them into the new heavens and the new earth, their loss of reward will.

There is a final and very important observation to be made about these terrible words. They clearly do not apply to the Christians who are striving (but, possibly, often failing) to live for Christ. These warnings are addressed to those believers who have fallen far; who have an "evil heart of unbelief" (Hebrews 3:12), and who have become hardened in sin (Hebrews 3:12). They are addressed to those who have "neglect[ed] the so great salvation" (Hebrews 2:3), not those who are concerned about it, but struggling to live Christ's way of life. They have either "thrown away" their confidence (trust in the person Christ) or are in danger of doing so (Hebrews 10:35).

Therefore, while the average Christian should not live in guilt, he should walk with a healthy fear of the Lord, a reverential awe, realizing that one day there will be an assessment of his life. These words strongly remind all believers that there is a final accounting; that we should all live our lives with the end of life in view. The fact that I am warned that I may swerve off the road and tumble down an embankment if I drive too fast, does not cause me to live in fear or guilt. But it does keep me from driving too fast.

Summary

The parable of the wicked servant is a pertinent warning to all who know Christ that the Judgment Seat of Christ involves more than mere "loss of reward." For the willfully indolent and carnal believer, there will a severe punishment, disinheritance, and rebuke from the Savior. Arminian interpreters might acknowledge that the servant began well, but he turned away from following his Master, became carnal, committed apostasy, and, in their assessment, as a result of apostasy, he lost his salvation.

Experimental Predestinarians say that this parable refers to two different servants, not one servant with two choices. With this approach, they maintain their doctrine that the wise servant is the "true" Christian and that the evil servant was never born again to begin with.

The Partner position is the simplest and most obvious. One servant has two paths of life open to him. If he chooses the path of disobedience (the broad way), he will be rebuked at the Judgment Seat of Christ, and with the other unfaithful believers he will experience profound regret because of his wasted life.

The timing of this event is clear. It cannot be the second coming because *that* event does not come on the world unexpectedly. In fact, anyone who knows the biblical prophecies about this period of time will be able to calculate precisely the time of the Lord's Second Advent. However, the pretribulation rapture occurs unexpectedly. "*The master of that slave will come on a day when he does not expect him and at an hour which he does not know*" (Matthew 24:50).

Because of his abusive treatment of his fellow servants, this slave can only be called an "evil slave." While this may seem harsh to assign this label to a believer, the rest of the Bible fully substantiates the fact the believers can and do act in evil and decadent ways, and some persist in this behavior to the point of physical death.

51
The Parable of the Ten Virgins

IN THE preceding chapter we began our discussion of the parables that Jesus tells at the conclusion of the Olivet Discourse. It must have been a shocking and mind-numbing experience for the disciples to hear from their Master that the temple would be torn down, there would be terrible tribulation in the future, and many believers would be persecuted and executed. Furthermore, they learned a number of details about events that would herald his *Parousia*, His return to earth. The sun would be darkened, the moon would cease to give light, and the powers of the heavens would be shaken (Matthew 24:29-31). They would then see the Son of Man coming on clouds of glory and hear a loud trumpet call. Over the centuries this chapter has unleashed a legion of date-setters and hundreds of speculative associations between events it describes and various historical circumstances.

While it is certainly true that prophecy should be diligently studied, and that we should do our best to discern the signs of the times, the major purpose of prophetic announcements is not to satisfy our curiosity about the future but to change our lives. When we hear these things, we are commanded to examine our lives and to see if we are living with the end in view. The wicked servant in the preceding parable was not living this way. He concluded that because of his master's delay, he could always fix things later and get around to serious discipleship whenever he wanted. The end result was that when the Master came, he was totally unprepared.

In the parable of the ten virgins (Matthew 25:1-13), we meet another example of a lack of preparedness in which five foolish virgins, like the wicked servant, were indifferent to the Lord's statement that they should live each day as if it might be "the day." Since no one knows when the Son of Man will come, we should always be prepared.

The parable raises several interpretive issues such as the relationship of the rapture and the marriage supper (Revelation 19:7-9) to the events described in the parable. Also, who are the virgins, and why is the bride not mentioned? What is the meaning of Christ's solemn statement to the foolish virgins, "*I do not know you*?" How are we to understand the application and warning in verse 13 in which the Lord tells His hearers, "*You do not know the day or the hour*"? If these events occur after the beginning of the tribulation, they certainly will know the day and the hour. It will occur exactly 2,520 days after the signing of the covenant between the Antichrist and Israel (Daniel 9:27) and 1,260 days after the abomination of desolation (Matthew 24:15).

In this chapter I will suggest that the call of the Bridegroom described in the parable refers to that aspect of the *Parousia* called the rapture. When the ten virgins go out to meet the bridegroom in the parable, this is to be understood theologically as the pretribulation rapture of the church. The shutting of the door and the frightening statement from the Lord, "I do not know you," refer to the negative assessment that unprepared (slothful, unfaithful) believers will experience at the Judgment Seat of Christ at the beginning of the tribulation.

The Wedding Banquet: Jewish Background

Because Jesus is appealing to an analogy of a wedding feast to illustrate an aspect of the kingdom, we must consider what was involved in a typical Jewish wedding. Under normal conditions, although there were exceptions, six activities were connected with a Jewish marriage: (1) the betrothal, (2) the transfer of the bride from her father's house to the bridegroom's house in a wedding procession, (3) the marriage ceremony, (4) the wedding supper, and (5) the wedding festivities celebration, and (6) the consummation.[2564]

The first event, the betrothal, was a legally binding transaction declaring the marriage covenant and specifying the terms agreed on by the contracting parties.[2565] The bridegroom traveled from his father's house to the home of the bride and negotiated a marriage covenant that was sealed by drinking a cup of wine. After that a benediction was pronounced. After the covenant was established, the groom left the bride's home and returned to his father's house. Although the bride and groom were legally married, they did not usually live together for a period of time. In fact, a delay of up to several years between the betrothal and the celebration of the marriage was common.[2566] At the time of Christ, that delay was normally one year.[2567] During this period they were considered married, and unfaithfulness was adultery. The bride was sanctified, that is, set apart for the bridegroom.

After this indeterminate period and after the various contractual obligations had been fulfilled, the bridegroom came, usually at night, accompanied by his friends to fetch the bride from her father's house and bring her back in a torch-lit procession to his own home where the marriage feast was held. The bride did not know the time of his coming even though she was expecting him to come. Therefore his arrival was preceded by a shout which warned the bride to be prepared for her bridegroom's arrival.[2568] The bride and groom were then accompanied by maidens who were involved in sword play and dancing. These are the ten virgins in the parable.

When a Jewish couple married, they did not go away for a honeymoon; they stayed at home. For a week they kept open house for the wedding celebrations.[2569] "The wedding

---

2564 R. K. Bower and G. L. Knapp, "Marriage," in *NISBE (1986)*, ed. G. W. Bromiley (Grand Rapids: William B. Eerdmans Publishing Co., 1986), 3:264; G. M. Mackie and W. Ewing, "Marriage," in *Dictionary of Christ and the Gospels*, ed. James Hastings (Edinburgh: T. & T. Clark, 1913), 2:137.

2565 Its central feature was the dowry (*mohar*), which was paid to the parents, not to the bride. It could take the form of service (Gen 29; 1 Sam 18:25). Eager, "Marriage," in *ISBE (1915)*, ed. James Orr (Albany, OR: Ages Software, George B.), s.v. "Marriage".

2566 Mackie and Ewing, "Marriage," 2:137.

2567 "Marriage," The Universal Jewish Encyclopedia, p. 172.

2568 James Neil, *Everyday Life in the Holy Land* (New York: Cassell and Company, 1913), 165.

2569 "The virgins will wait until a late hour of the night to accompany the bridal pair with lamps to the marriage house, where at a brightly illuminated table the seven-day feast will begin." E. Stauffer, "γαμέω, γάμος," TDNT, 1:654.

feast might last a day (Genesis 29:22), a week[2570] (Judges 14:12), or according to the Apocrypha even two weeks (Tob. 8:20; 10:7)."[2571] It was one of the happiest weeks in their lives. Only chosen friends were admitted to the festivities of that week. After the groom received his bride, the female attendants and the wedding party assembled at the home of the groom's father for the wedding feast (Gr *gamoi*), which lasted seven days.[2572] During this week of celebration the bride and groom were treated and addressed as prince and princess. At some time during these celebrations, probably at the beginning, although this is not certain, the marriage ceremony and the marriage supper (*deipnon tou gamou*) "the supper of the feast" was celebrated (Matthew 22:10; Revelation 19:9). A week of festivities followed and then the bride was conducted by her parents and/or by other members of the wedding party[2573] to the nuptial chamber (Judges 15:1), where, according to some accounts,[2574] she remained for seven days.[2575]

While many aspects of the customs and chronology of the parable fit well with what is known of Jewish wedding practices, one must remember this is a parable and the details cannot be pressed; only the main points are important.[2576] The above analysis assumes that the *gamoi* (Matthew 25:10) includes the entire wedding celebration including the general festivities, the marriage ceremony (the marriage of the Lamb) and the formal wedding supper (*deipnon tou gamou*, Revelation 19:7-9). The Marriage Banquet begins when the "door is shut."

The wedding supper (the actual meal) the following week of festivities are called the Wedding Feast of the Lamb (*gamos*, Revelation 19:9).[2577] This time period of seven days of the wedding celebration may be compared to the seven years in which the church celebrates with Christ in heaven while tribulation falls on the earth.

2570 "The ancient Jewish custom of extending the marriage over several days (a whole week in the case of a virgin), and also of celebrating far into the night, is reflected in the parable in Luke 12:36, where it may be well after midnight before the κύριος returns ἐκ τῶν γάμων," Ethelbert Staufer, "*gameō, gamos,*" in TDNT 1:648.

2571 Edwin Yamauchi, "Cultural Aspects of Marriage in the Ancient World," *BibSac* 135, no. 539 (July-September 1978): 247.

2572 "The Huppah," in *The Universal Jewish Encyclopedia*, ed. Isaac Landman (New York: Universal Jewish Encyclopedia Co., 1942). See Judges 14:8, 10, 12 and m. *Nega'im* 3:2 A.

2573 "Veiling of the Bride," The Universal Jewish Encyclopedia, 10,399, cited by Renald Showers, *Maranatha: Our Lord Come!* (Bellmawr, NJ: Friends of Israel Gospel Ministry, 1995), 165.

2574 In later years (the seventeenth century), the consummation of the marriage occurred at the beginning of the festivities, and the bride and groom were not involved in the festivities. Instead, they consummated their marriage while the guests celebrated outside the wedding chamber for seven days. "The Huppah," 373. See http://www.jewishencyclopedia.com/articles/7941-huppah. The bridal procession—a festal affair in which the whole town participated—culminated in the ushering into the *ḥuppah* of the bride and bridegroom. Outside the *ḥuppah* (in former times inside) the groomsmen and bridesmaids stood as guards awaiting the good tidings that the union had been happily consummated with reference to Deuteronomy 22:17 (see Yer. Ket. i. 25a; Tan., Ḳoraḥ, ed. Buber, p. 96; Pirḳe R. El. xii.), while the people indulged in dancing, singing, and especially in praises of the bride (cf. John 3:29; Matthew 25: 1-13). The bride had to remain in the *ḥuppah* for seven days, as long as the wedding festivities lasted (Judges 14:10, 12, 17); hence the name of these festivities, "the seven days of her" or "of the *ḥuppah*" (Pesiḳ. 149b).

2575 P. Trutza, "Marriage," in *The Zondervan Pictorial Encyclopedia of the Bible*, ed. Merrill C. Tenny (Grand Rapids: Zondervan Publishing Houise, 1975), s.v. "Marriage".

2576 For discussion of the present writer's approach to interpreting parables see pp. 780 ff.

2577 Ethelbert Stauffer, "*gamos*," in TDNT, 1:654.

Many of the feasts of Israel lasted seven days.[2578] Various events happened at different times during the feasts. In Israel's history various feasts could last for days. The feast of Unleavened Bread, for example, was crowned with a meal on the last day, the seventh day of the feast (Exodus 13:3-10). In apocryphal literature (4 Esdras 7:28-29) the seventh millennium (parallel to the seventh day of Creation) will see the kingdom established.[2579] In other words, the number seven often played a significant role.

The relevance of Jewish wedding practices to the interpretation of this parable probably cannot be pressed in detail. Notions of a literal marriage between Christ and the church and their subsequent retirement to the nuptial chamber are beyond the parabolic intent. The main idea is that there was a time of celebration lasting, perhaps, several days. Therefore I suggest that parallels with Christ's return should be based only upon specific references in the parable.

That said, the eschatological implications of the Jewish wedding celebration for the chronology of the parable of the Ten Virgins may suggest this sequence.

1. Christ comes to fetch His bride, the church, at the rapture (Matthew 25:6) and takes them to the mansions prepared for them in the New Jerusalem (John 14:1-3).
2. The door is shut and those unprepared are excluded from the wedding festivities and marriage ceremony. The Judgment Seat of Christ probably occurs at this time, and the result is that the door to the wedding banquet is shut. Unprepared believers are not permitted to enter (Matthew 25:10, 2 Corinthians 5:10).
3. The Marriage Banquet continues for seven years (Revelation 19:7-9). The foolish virgins, while in the New Jerusalem, are not involved. They are outside the banquet hall and experience profound regret. Matthew uses the metaphor "outer darkness" to describe this experience of regret caused by being excluded and disinherited.[2580]
4. At the end of the seven years, the Lord Jesus returns to earth and establishes his reign, the thousand year kingdom (Revelation 19:11-21).
5. The Messianic Banquet, that is, the celebration which occurs at the beginning of the millennium on earth begins. Faithful believers will recline at the table with the king (Matthew 8:11; Luke 13:29) and the unfaithful will not enjoy this privilege. This banquet differs from Christ's Marriage Banquet which he celebrates with the church in heaven during the tribulation and before his physical return to earth at the Second Coming.

The foolish are excluded from the week of festivities, the Marriage Banquet, by the Lord's sobering words, "*I do not know you*." It is possible that the parable intends an actual marriage ceremony. If it does, it would probably occur at the beginning of the feast. In either case, the unfaithful believers are excluded from the festivities. They are in the darkness outside the banquet hall. This is probably not a spatial reference but a metaphor for the experience of exclusion and regret. One might ask, "How is possible that some members of the bride do not participate in the actual marriage ceremony?" How can they be married to the King if they do not attend the ceremony? I answer, this is a parable and

[2578] The Feast of Dedication, mentioned in the New Testament in John 10:22, lasted eight days.

[2579] M. De Jonge, "*chriō*, et al." in TDNT, 9:511.

[2580] While one might infer that this is a spatial location, this speculation goes beyond the central intent of the parable.

to raise issues about these details is to over-interpret the details of the parable. The parable may not intend us to understand that there is a literal ceremony. Furthermore, one can easily speculate that the foolish virgins are invited into the actual marriage ceremony and do participate. But this is unimportant speculation that goes beyond the central point of the parable: celebration for those who are prepared and loss for those who are not..[2581]

While it is true that the bride is adorned with the righteous acts of the saints and the unfaithful believers are not, it does not logically follow that the unfaithful believer is not part of the bride. The bride in Revelation 19 is a figure of speech for the Church. It is a synecdoche, the part for the whole. Just as the sheep at the judgment of the sheep and goats includes faithful and unfaithful sheep, so the bride is composed of faithful and unfaithful believers. If I say, "The White House said ....," all would know that not everyone in the White House said it or believed it. The phrase "White House" is synecdoche of the part, the White House, for the whole, everyone in it. No one would conclude that those who did not say it are therefore not part of the White House. Similarly if a reporter says, "Congress concluded ...," no one would assume that those in Congress who did not vote for the bill are not really in Congress. This is a story, a metaphor, and there is no literal banquet, no literal table for millions of people, and no literal marriage ceremony.

The Time of the Wedding Feast (Matthew 25:1)

Jesus begins the parable saying, "*The kingdom of heaven shall be likened* [*homoioō*] *to ten virgins*." However, as discussed in previous chapters, the phrase "*shall be likened to*" is not used by Matthew to draw a precise equivalence of terms between "wedding feast" and "kingdom."[2582] Rather, the term is more general and is used to "illustrate an aspect of" the kingdom, and not the kingdom itself.[2583] Thus, entrance into the Marriage Banquet cannot automatically be equated with entrance into the kingdom. Indeed, to do so would mean, as

---

2581 For discussion of the interpretation of parables see pp. 780 ff.

2582 For example, when Jesus says, "The kingdom of heaven is like a man who sowed good seed" (Matthew 13:24), He does not mean the kingdom of heaven equals a sower, and when He says, "The kingdom of heaven is like a mustard seed" (Matthew 13:31), He is not saying that the kingdom of heaven equals a mustard seed. Rather, in both instances He is saying there is an aspect of, or truth about, the kingdom that can be compared to a mustard seed or a sower.

2583 Allan H. M'Neile, *The Gospel According to St. Matthew*, reprint ed. (London: Macmillan & Co., 1961), 196. Tasker agrees that it would be misleading to literally equate terms connected by this verb. Toussaint says, "It means there is a truth in the parable that is related to the kingdom." Toussaint, *Behold the King*, 181. Elsewhere Toussaint comments, "It should be noted that when the Lord says, 'The kingdom of heaven is like' or 'may be compared to,' He does not mean the kingdom is like a man, or a woman, or a seed, or leaven, etc. It means there is a truth in the parable that is related to the kingdom. A good illustration is the parable of the unforgiving slave in Matthew 18:23–34. The kingdom itself is not like any specific thing in the parable. The truth taught in the parable is obvious: heirs of the kingdom should be forgiving because they have been forgiven an impossible debt. So then, the clause 'the kingdom of heaven (or God) is like' means some truth tangential to the kingdom is found in the parable[s] in Matthew 13. The truths are ones that had not before been revealed." See Toussaint, "The Church and Israel," 63. Hagner agrees, "ὁμοιώθη here means not simply 'is like' but reflects the Aramaic formulaic *le*·, which means 'it is the case with ... as with.'" Hagner, *Matthew 1-13*, 728. "The kingdom of heaven," he says, "is likened not to the virgins, but to the story of what happens to them when the sudden arrival of the bridegroom occurs, some are ready and some are not." Peters captures the thought well, "The Kingdom of Heaven in its manner of introduction or realization will meet with such a reception, or bring forth such a result." Peters, *The Theocratic Kingdom of Our Lord Jesus, the Christ, as Covenanted in the Old Testament and Presented in the New Testament*, 3:306.

we shall see below, that entrance to the kingdom requires a lifetime of preparatory works[2584] and "the righteous acts of the saints" (Revelation 19:9), a point of view far removed from the freeness of the offer of salvation through faith alone and without cost (Revelation 21:7).

What aspect of the kingdom of heaven is in view? The thrust of the parable is about a judgment on the believer's life work, preparedness. Thus when Jesus says "*The kingdom of heaven shall be likened to*," He probably refers to the believer's responsibility for that aspect of the kingdom message which we have called, "the kingdom way of living." Christ's kingdom involves final accountability. The kingdom of heaven is like that. It is like believers being judged for how they have lived out its message.

When will the events in Matthew 25 occur? The parable opens with the words, "*Then the kingdom of heaven will be comparable to ten virgins*." To what does "*then*" refer? It is previously used of an unexpected coming when one is taken and one is left (vv. 40-41, "then"). This close proximity to a parallel usage of the words suggests that it refers to the same event,[2585] that aspect of the *Parousia* that is completely unexpected. I believe this best describes the pre-tribulation rapture of the church.[2586]

Some incorrectly argue, that this parable applies to events at the end of the tribulation at the second coming when, they say, the bridegroom "came" (Matthew 25:10).[2587] However, the coming of the Lord described in the parable occurs at a time when no one will know the day or the hour (Matthew 25:13). That is hardly the situation at the second coming of Christ. At the time believers will not only know the day and the hour, but they can calculate it. It will occur exactly 1,260 days (Revelation 12:4-6) after the abomination of desolation (Matthew 24:15)[2588] and 2,520 days after the Antichrist signs a treaty with Israel. This begins the last seven years of that era (Daniel 9:27).[2589]

If, for example, they witnessed the abomination of desolation occurring on Saturday, March 4, 2135 at 12:00 noon, they could easily calculate that the Son of Man will return in glory on Saturday, August 16, 2138 at 12:00 noon, 1,260 days later. If they saw the Antichrist make a covenant with Israel at 12:00 noon on Saturday April 23, 2140, they

---

[2584] Matthew 25:7-10. The oil in the parable represents a life of preparedness.

[2585] Keener notes also, "This parable most naturally focuses on the time of judgment as the preceding one (24:45-51)," which, of course, refers back to the time of that same unheralded event (24:40, 42, 50). Craig S. Keener, *Matthew* (Downers Grove, IL: InterVarsity Press, 1997), 595.

[2586] For full discussion establishing that the pre-tribulation rapture of the church, and not the second coming is the subject of Matthew 24:36-44, see John F. Hart, "Should Pretribulationists Reconsider the Rapture in Matthew 24:36-44? - Part 1 of 3," *JOTGES* 20, no. 39 (Autumn 2007): 47-70; John F. Hart, "Should Pretribulationists Reconsider the Rapture in Matthew 24:36-44? - Part 2 of 3," *JOTGES* 21, no. 40 (Spring 2008): 45-62; John F. Hart, "Should Pretribulationists Reconsider the Rapture in Matthew 24:36-44? - Part 3 of 3," *JOTGES* 21, no. 41 (Autumn 2008): 42-64.

[2587] Louis A. Barbieri, "Matthew," in *The Bible Knowledge Commentary: New Testament*, ed. John F. Walvoord and Roy Zuck (Colorado Springs: Cook, 2002), 2:79.

[2588] When Jesus connects the events of Matthew 24:15, Daniel's "Abomination of desolation" with the starting point of the Great Tribulation, we are alerted to the fact that He understands this to be the second half of the seven-year period, which precedes the end described by Daniel 9:27. In the midst of the week, the abomination of desolation occurs, and this one half of a week period is called a "time, times, and half a time," which John tells us is three-and-one-half years, forty-two months, or 1,260 days (cf. Revelation 12:14; 11:2-3; 13:5). Therefore, the alert believer during the tribulation era knows precisely the day and the hour of the Lord's return. It is exactly 1,260 days after the abomination of desolation.

[2589] This observation, of course, assumes a particular view of Daniel's seventieth week and is fully developed by Harold W. Hoehner, *Chronological Aspects of the Life of Christ* (Grand Rapids: Zondervan Publishing House, 1977), 115-40. See also Showers, *Maranatha: Our Lord Come!*, 41-71.

would know with certainty that the coming of the Son of Man would occur 2,520 days later on Saturday, March 18, 2147 at 12:00.[2590] They would know "the day and the hour."

The second coming described in Matthew 24:15 occurs in the midst of global catastrophe and signs in the heavens.[2591] It is clear from Matthew 25:13 that the coming of the Lord in the parable of the Ten Virgins comes unexpectedly[2592] and hence does not fit well with the second coming aspect of the *Parousia,* the Second Advent. But it does harmonize with the beginning of the *Parousia* at the rapture of the church which occurs at least seven years earlier.

Thus, at the outset we are told that at the time of an unexpected coming of Christ, at *that* time, the kingdom of heaven, or an aspect of it will be comparable to ten virgins going out to meet the bridegroom. Two different aspects of the same *Parousia* must be in view.

Who Are the Virgins? (25:2)

In the previous passage (Matthew 24:45-51) there was a single servant who was either faithful or wicked. Now the image shifts to a believer who is either wise or foolish. The vast majority of interpreters in the history of interpretation of this parable have understood the virgins as representative of the church,[2593] an equation suggested by 2

2590 Calendar calculators are easily available on the Internet, and supposedly many would flock to these programs when they saw those striking events. I just did! From the time I did a Google search for a program to the time I had installed it and made the calculation, about 90 seconds had elapsed. Cf. http://leithauserresearch.com/datecalc.html.

2591 When Jesus connects the events of Matthew 24:15, that is, Daniel's "abomination of desolation" with the starting point of the Great Tribulation, we are alerted to the fact that He understands this to be the second half of the seven-year period which precedes the end described by Daniel 9:27. In the midst of the week, the abomination of desolation occurs, and this one-half-of-a-week period is called a "time, times, and half a time," which John tells us is three-and-one-half years, forty-two months, or 1,260 days (cf. Revelation 12:4; 11:2-3; 13:5). Therefore, the alert believer during the tribulation era knows precisely the day and the hour of the Lord's return. It is exactly 1,260 days after the abomination of desolation.

2592 Joachim Jeremias, "νύμφη, νυμφίος," TDNT, 4:1103 notes: "The parable of the ten virgins is one of the group which deals with the sudden coming of the end. It belongs to the same series as the reference to the flood (Matthew 24:37–39; Luke 17:26 f.), the parable of the thief by night (Matthew 24:42–44; Luke 12:39 f.), that of the watchful servants (Mark 13:33–37), and that of the faithful and evil servants (Matthew 24:45–51; Luke 12:42–46). All these are parables of judgment. They warn the hearers to be ready for the unexpected coming of the end, which will bring judgment and separation. Just as the flood was a surprise, or the thief by night, or the return of the master of the house, or the call which wakened the sleeping virgins at midnight: 'The bridegroom cometh' (Matthew 25:6), so the final catastrophe will be a surprise when it comes on a race unprepared." The simile "like a thief" can suggest two things. When accompanied with the tag line "you do not know the day or the hour," the stress is not on the violence of the thief's coming, but upon its unexpectedness (Revelation 3:3; Mt. 24:43, 50). When a thief comes, the victim does not know the time of his arrival. The simile is used this way in Revelation 3:3. In some cases it may suggest the notion of coming with violence (Matthew 6:19; 1 Thessalonians 5:2-4, and Revelation 16:15). "But the entry of the thief is marked also by a violent element" (διορύσσω, Preisker, "κλέπτω, κλέπτης", TDNT, 3:755). This seems to be the connotation in Rev 16:15 where the Lord speaks of His violent irruption into history at the second coming by saying, "Behold, I am coming like a thief." He will come in judgment. The former instance (Revelation 3:3), describes how He will come on those in the inter-advent era, unexpectedly, with no prior notice, and with a violent beginning of the Day of the Lord. The latter reference (Revelation 16:15) occurs during the tribulation and concerns a coming that is decidedly not unexpected but is certainly violent.

2593 See for example, Lange, "The Gospel of Matthew," 8:439. Lange further insists that the "ten virgins signify not merely a part of the Church, but the whole of it." See also, E. Stauffer, "*gameō, gamos,*" in TDNT, 1:655. See also Hagner, *Matthew 14-28*, 729. He seems to say that the foolish virgins are lost.

Corinthians 11:2 (cf. Revelation 14:4). The virgins are not merely companions of the bride but represent the bride. We suggest that the virgins are all believers in the inter-advent age.[2594]

That both wise and foolish are regenerate is suggested by the purity of a virgin. Paul describes virgins as those "betrothed to Christ" (2 Corinthians 11:2). Therefore, there is no reason to doubt that both groups are regenerate. One cannot argue that the foolish virgins proved themselves to be unregenerate because they were denied entrance into the festivities, unless one assumes beforehand that a lack of perseverance is proof that one is unregenerate.

Oil in the Lamps (25:3-4)

The kind of lamp the virgins used is debated. Some view the lamp as a torch with cloth soaked in oil wrapped around the end of a stick. Others see the lamp as the so-called "Herodian lamp,"[2595] a small clay lamp. These lamps were accompanied by an additional vessel that contained oil to keep the lamp burning after the smaller amount of oil in the lamp itself was exhausted. These extra vessels are referred to in verse 4. The custom was for the lamp to be lit at dusk prior to the arrival of the bridegroom several hours later. There was, however, only enough oil in these lamps to burn for a few hours. At that time, after the lamps had begun to burn low, they needed to be replenished by the extra oil carried in the auxiliary vessels.[2596]

They all had lamps to guide them to the banquet hall. They were not indifferent to the coming of the Lord; all ten had gone out in faith to meet him. All ten of the virgins also had oil, but the foolish ones "took no [extra] oil with them." They apparently expected no delay.[2597]

This Herodian lamp was excavated from remains near Jerusalem. It may be of the same type used by the Ten Virgins.

The precise meaning of the oil is not specified. Many commentators say that it has no particular interpretive significance.[2598] Some suppose that it signifies good works.[2599] If the oil has any special significance, the point of the parable suggests it is the life which is

---

[2594] Who is the bride? There is confusion because the virgins and the bride are the same. The parable does not clarify this issue. That the bride is not mentioned in the parable is undoubtedly a detail unimportant to the story.

[2595] G. F. Hasel, "Lamp," in NISBE, 3:69.

[2596] Ralph Alexander, former Professor of Old Testament, Western Conservative Baptist Seminary, personal communication, 18 August 1989.

[2597] See M'Neile, *The Gospel According to St. Matthew*, 361. See also Richard Chenevix Trench, *Notes on the Miracles and the Parables of Our Lord*, complete original unabridged two volumes in one ed. (Westwood, NJ: Fleming H. Revell, 1953), 2:225.

[2598] See, for example, Hagner, *Matthew 14-28*, 728.

[2599] Ibid.

prepared to meet the master. The issue is preparedness. The wise virgins anticipate that the coming of the bridegroom might be delayed and therefore wanted to be prepared for whenever he might come. This is why they were wise (Gr *phronimos,* "sensible, thoughtful, prudent, wise").[2600]

They Slept (25:5)

The fact that the virgins nodded off and fell asleep probably has no significance since both the wise and the foolish slept. No fault is being assigned. It is an incidental detail of the parable. After all, it was approaching midnight.[2601]

Why the delay? There are many reasons. Jeremias suggested that the cultural background of this period of delay was the financial haggling that went on between the father of the bridegroom and the father of the bride.[2602] Elsewhere, we are told that God's delays are sometimes because of forbearance and grace (2 Peter 3:9). God desires to provide time and opportunity for all to come to acknowledge the need for repentance. There are many plans and purposes He chooses to accomplish in the current era. Though the delay is long, His *Parousia* is sure.

The End of the Story (25:6-13)

The coming of the bridegroom was heralded by a shout, "*Behold the bridegroom. Come out to meet him.*" When they heard this, the virgins arose, trimmed their lamps (i.e., "cleaned and oiled them so they would burn brightly"),[2603] and made their way to join the procession at some convenient point. Then they would travel with the lamps to the wedding festivities at the bridegroom's home.[2604] The foolish virgins, however, discovered that their oil had run out. They then asked the wise virgins for some of their extra oil, but they declined. Instead, the wise virgins counseled them to go and buy some for themselves.

The simple exchange between the wise and unwise virgins belies its importance, for it is at that moment that the foolish virgins recognized that they did not prepare adequately for meeting the bridegroom. The rest of the parable is a denouement, describing the consequences of their lack of preparedness.

When the foolish virgins did return with some oil, they found the door to the wedding feast shut, and they called out to the bridegroom to open the door. He answered, "*I don't know you.*" I suggest that this event corresponds with the negative assessment of an unprepared life at the Judgment Seat of Christ at the beginning of the tribulation. Matthew concludes with the exhortation to the readers to watch, be prepared (unlike the foolish virgins), for neither the day nor the hour of the Lord's coming is known.

As elsewhere in Scripture (e.g., 1 Thessalonians 5:1-11), disciples are exhorted to be alert, be prepared always for the Lord's coming. There are never any excuses. Disciples

---

[2600] BDAG, 1066.

[2601] Hagner, *Matthew 14-28*, 728.

[2602] Jeremias, *The Parables of Jesus*, 178.

[2603] Hagner, *Matthew 14-28*, 729.

[2604] Trench, *Notes on the Miracles and the Parables of Our Lord*, 2:248.

must persist in the things that lead to spiritual preparedness. Paul called it "finishing the course." This requires a lifetime of learning and growing; something that cannot be acquired at the last minute.

I Do Not Know You (25:12)

But if the five foolish virgins are truly regenerate, though unfaithful Christians, why does the Lord say to them, "*I do not know you*"? Surely, He would not say this to a true child of God. Or would He?

The words are so strong that some have maintained that the Lord rejects them as unbelievers, often pointing to Matthew 7:23. In the discussion above I argued that all of the virgins were believers. Someone might ask, however, "If the foolish virgins are truly regenerate, surely Jesus would not speak this way to a true child of God!"[2605] How can this view be maintained?

The use of the familiar Greek for "to know" (*oida*), as is well known, means to know by reflection; it is a mental process based on information.[2606] In classical Greek it meant to "*know, have knowledge of, be acquainted with.*"[2607]

Interestingly, *oida* sometimes means "respect" or "appreciate:"[2608] Bishop Ignatius (107 A.D.) equates "knowing" with honoring. "It is good," he says, "to acknowledge (*oida*) God and the bishop: he who honors (Gr *timaō*) the bishop is honored by God," (*Smyrnaens*, 9.1). Paul also uses *oida* in the sense of "to honor."

> *But we request of you brethren, that you* ***appreciate*** *[Gr oida], those who diligently labor among you, and have charge over you in the Lord and give you instruction (1 Thessalonians 5:12).*

The context seems to require the nuance "to respect." While the basic meaning of *oida* could fit here (i.e., "to acknowledge" or "to recognize"), the context seems to require the nuance "to respect." Paul wants the Thessalonians to recognize as their leaders precisely those people who functioned in such a way as to toil for them, to protect and care for them physically and materially, and to direct them ethically.[2609] Some translate the expression as "know in their true character"[2610] or "recognize them for what they are, and as entitled to respect because of their office."[2611] That the word can have the meaning "to respect" or "to honor" is confirmed by verse 13, where "it is clear that the two verbs 'to appreciate' and 'to esteem (very highly)' are used synonymously."[2612]

[2605] In Luke 13:27 the Lord says to the unsaved, "I do not know (Gr *oida*) where you are from." This is irrelevant to the usage in Matthew 25:12. Knowing where a man is from and knowing him in a saving sense are not equivalent.

[2606] Abbott-Smith, 92. LSJ cites examples where it means "to be kindly disposed toward," 483. These examples refer, of course, to classical usage and do not necessarily carry over into the New Testament.

[2607] LSJ, 483.

[2608] John Maldonatus, *A Commentary on the Gospels: St. Matthew's Gospel Chapter 25 to the End* (London: John Hodges, 1888), 311.

[2609] C. A. Wanamaker, *The Epistles to the Thessalonians: A Commentary on the Greek Text* (Grand Rapids: Wm. B. Eerdmans Publishing Co., 1990), 193.

[2610] George Milligan, *St. Paul's Epistles to the Thessalonians* (London: Macmillan, 1908), 71.

[2611] Vincent, *Word Studies in the New Testament*, 4:47.

[2612] William Hendriksen and Simon J. Kistemaker, *Exposition of 1 and 2 Thessalonians* (Grand Rapids: Baker Book House, 1953-2001), 134. The translation "respect" is quite common. For example, NCB has "appreciate,"

> *And that you **esteem them very highly** in love because of their work. Live in peace with one another (1 Thessalonians 5:13).*

The lexicon lists references in extrabiblical Greek where it means "to honor."[2613] This is the meaning in the parable. When the Lord says that He does not know them, He means that He does not appreciate, respect, or honor them; He does not "esteem them highly." It is obvious that He knows them (*oida*) by observation in that He has information about who they are. So to translate *oida* in the sense of "recognize" makes no sense here. He clearly recognizes them and knows who they are. This suggests that another usage of *oida*, "to honor, to esteem, or to respect," fits the context better. Some authorities, ancient and modern, agree that *oida* here refers to the fact that He does not approve of the foolish virgins.[2614]

They are not excluded from all blessings of the kingdom or even with mingling with the saved there. Olshausen is certainly correct: "It is clear that the words 'I know you not' (v. 12) cannot denote eternal condemnation; for, on the contrary, the foolish virgins are only excluded from the marriage festivities. They must be viewed as parallel with the persons described in 1 Corinthians 3:15, whose building is destroyed, but who are not thereby deprived of eternal happiness."[2615] They are excluded only from the joy of the wedding feast and from co-heirship with Christ. The door is shut to the joy of the feast, not to entrance into the kingdom. He will not "know" them in the sense that the Thessalonians knew and appreciated the faithful labor of the apostles in their midst.[2616] He will not say to them, *"Well done, good slave, because you have been faithful in a very little thing, you are to be in authority over ten cities"* (Luke 19:17).

We should also consider that the phrase "I do not know you" may reflect the Rabbinic ban formula discussed in chapter 22.[2617] If that is the case, then the foolish virgins are not permanently excluded from access to the Bridegroom. They do not miss the kingdom; they only miss the joy of the wedding festivities. Rewards, both negative and positive are eternal.

Why are the foolish virgins excluded from the Marriage Banquet? We are told that only those arrayed with the righteous acts of the saints will be admitted.(Matthew 22:11; cf. Revelation 19:6).[2618] They were not prepared as they stand at the Judgment Seat of Christ (2 Corinthians 5:10) at the time of the pre-tribulation rapture when they were excluded from the festivities. Unlike the wise virgins, they did not make preparations for the event.[2619]

---

and the NIV, NRSV, ESV, GNT, NAB have "respect."

2613 BAGD, 559. See also Thayer, *Thayer's Greek-English Lexicon of the Greek New Testament*, 174.

2614 For an example of an older commentator see Maldonatus, *A Commentary on the Gospels: St. Matthew's Gospel Chapter 25 to the End*, 305.

2615 Olshausen, *Biblical Commentary of the New Testament*, 2:226.

2616 George N. H. Peters, *The Theocratic Kingdom of Our Lord Jesus, the Christ, as Covenanted in the Old Testament and Presented in the New Testament*, 3:306. "The declaration 'I know you not' [is] expressive of exclusion to a position which the others because of their preparation and readiness, obtain. The foolish are only excluded from these marriage festivities, but will ultimately be saved."

2617 See discussion of Ban Formula in the Talmuds, on pp. 330 ff.

2618 It is also possible to understand the white linen (the righteous acts of the saints) not as the acts themselves. But in view of the fact that it is "given" (v. 8), we might say that "the fine linen is the reward for (or result of) the righteous deeds of the saints." See Beale, *The Book of Revelation: A Commentary on the Greek Text*, 936.

2619 The fact the foolish virgins did not prepare for the marriage does not suggest they are not part of the Bride. One cannot argue this way: Major Premise: the Bride is ready; Minor Premise: the foolish virgins are not

In Revelation 19:7, at the marriage of the Lamb, "*His bride has made herself ready*" (Gr *hetoimazō*). The concept of being "ready" (Gr *hetoimos*) is also clearly pictured in Matthew 25:10.[2620] Their failed attempt to rectify things at the last moment, by trying to buy what they did not produce during a lifetime, is intended to teach the futility of their situation. All meet the bridegroom, but only the wise enter the wedding feast. This exclusion is the pronouncement of loss which will occur at the Judgment Seat of Christ.[2621]

When does the Judgment Seat of Christ occur? In view of the fact that the foolish virgins are excluded from the wedding banquet, it is plausible to connect this negative assessment of their lives with their drawing back in shame at His coming (1 John 2:28); having all their works burned up (1 Corinthians 3:15); and being recompensed for the bad they have done (2 Corinthians 5:10-11). I find the placement of this event at the pre-tribulation rapture of the church quite satisfying.[2622] The foolish virgins endure, perhaps, seven years of remorse as they reflect on their wasted lives and see the joy of Christ's *Metochoi* inside the banquet hall in the New Jerusalem.

The parable of the virgins has nothing to do with Christians losing their salvation. It refers to the forfeiture of honor due only to faithful servants when the Lord returns. Those saved as through fire (1 Corinthians 3:15)[2623] and who may be ashamed at His coming (1 John 2:18) will be excluded from the joy of the feast. They are not excluded from the millennium but only from reigning with Christ there, a privilege limited to those who "overcome" (Revelation 2:26-27).

You Do Not Know the Day or the Hour (25:13)

Because believers in the future tribulation will know the day and the hour (they can calculate it: it will be exactly 1,260 days from the abomination of desolation and 2,520 days from the signing of the covenant between Israel and the Antichrist (Daniel 9:27), the

---

ready; Conclusion: therefore, they are not part of the Bride. This syllogism fails because it assumes its conclusion, that *every member of the Bride* is ready. As suggested previously, the Bride is a figure of speech called, synecdoche, that is the part for the whole. The fact that the Bride as a whole is ready does not logically require that each of its members are ready.

2620 The related words, *hetoimos* "ready" and *hetoimazō* "to make ready, to prepare," are found in these two passages.

2621 Why was the servant without the wedding garment in Matthew 22 permitted entrance to the wedding feast, but the foolish virgins found that the door was shut? It seems that both parables are teaching the same thing: the unfaithful Christian forfeits his inheritance in the kingdom. The distinction between the parables is accidental, and such details should not be pressed.

2622 There are passages which could be cited that suggest that this judgment occurs at the second coming. For example, Jesus says, "*For whoever is ashamed of me and my words, of him will the Son of Man be ashamed when he comes in his glory, and the glory of the Father and of the holy angels*" (Luke 9:26). Clearly Christ coming in "His Glory" occurs at the second coming (Matthew 24:30) and not at the rapture. However, all this proves is that there will be a judgment at the second coming as well as at the rapture. Jesus also says, "*For the Son of Man is going to come in the glory of his Father with his angels; and will then recompense every man according to his deeds*" (Matt 16:27). This certainly proves that there will be a judgment at the Second Coming but it does not say that this is the Judgment Seat of Christ. It is perfectly plausible to suggest this is a judgment of the Overcomers and those who did not overcome during the tribulation period. Perhaps, the Old Testament saints are judges and rewarded at this time as well. There are other times in which believers are judged. For example, we infer that there must a judgment on the works of the millennial believers at the resurrection which precedes the eternal state.

2623 For discussion of this passage, see pp. 769 ff.

coming of the Lord described in this parable certainly cannot refer to His second coming to earth. Rather, it is the sudden, unexpected, coming that occurs seven years earlier, the beginning of the *Parousia*, at the rapture of the church.

This is a central point of the parable. Just because there is a delay in the inter-advent era, and His return seems so distant and far off, we should not be lulled into slothfulness. We should be prepared each day! As we look into the azure sky and see that lovely cloud, we should daily ask ourselves, "Could that be the one?"

Marriage Banquet and Messianic Banquet (Revelation 19:6-9)

In the Old Testament (e.g Isaiah 25:6) the prophets spoke of a Messianic Banquet. This appears to be a metaphor for the time of celebration which occurs at the beginning of the millennium. It will be a period of richness, celebration, and joy. In a number of parables in the New Testament, Jesus refers to this celebration at the beginning of the kingdom of heaven, as a Messianic Banquet (Isaiah 25:6; Matthew 8:10-13; Mark 14:25; Luke 13:22-30; 14:16-24; 22:29-30).

In Revelation 19:7-9 and in two parables, Jesus refers to another banquet, the Marriage Banquet of the Lamb (Matthew 22:1-14; 25:1-13). This is distinguished from the Messianic Banquet in that it is uniquely related to the Messiah's marriage to His Bride, the church. The Messianic Banquet includes saints of all ages and has a special focus on the great ones of Israel's history, Abraham, Isaac, and Jacob (Luke 13:28). It is a metaphor for the celebration which occurs at the beginning of the millennium, or, possibly, a metaphor for the joy of reigning with Christ throughout the entire millennium. It celebrates the fulfillment of God's covenant promises to Israel and the inclusion of the church into those promises. The Marriage Banquet of the Lamb, however, is a special time for the saints of the church age and celebrates the marriage of the Lamb to His Bride, the church.

When interpreting parables, wise scholars follow two basic criteria: (1) discern the central points of the parable, and (2) give incidental details interpretive significance only if they in some way contribute to the central points.[2624] The major themes of the parable of the virgins are: the Lord will come unexpectedly; we must be prepared; there will be a judgment of the believer's works; and then the Lord will celebrate with those who are prepared. A particular chronology of these events is not as important as the ethical demands to which the parable calls us.[2625]

Nevertheless, it is helpful to see how easily the events of the parable can be harmonized with Revelation 19:7-9.

With stirring words, John announces that the marriage of the Lamb has come.

2624 Henry Virkler, *Hermeneutics: Principles and Processes of Biblical Interpretation* (Grand Rapids: Wm. B. Eerdmans Publishing Co., 1981), 172. See also Trench, *Notes on the Miracles and the Parables of Our Lord*, 2:31-48; Craig Blomberg, "Parables," in *The International Standard Bible Encyclopedia*, ed. G. W. Bromiley and Everett F. Harrison (Grand Rapids: William B. Eerdmans Publishing Co., 1986), 3:657. For the present writer's approach see discussion on pp. 780 ff.

2625 Like Luke 12:35-40, this is a parable whose primary intention is to teach readiness (note Luke 12:40!), not to give an exact chronology of end-time events. The point is that the Lord will come unexpectedly; we must be prepared; there will be a judgment on the believer's works; and then the Lord will celebrate with those who are prepared. Those saved as through fire (1 Corinthians 3:15) and who may be ashamed at this coming (1 John 2:18) will be excluded from the joy of the feast. They are not excluded from the millennium but only from reigning with Christ there, a privilege limited to those who "overcome" (Revelation 2:26-27).

Let us rejoice and be glad and give the glory to Him, for the marriage [Gr gamos] of the Lamb has come and His bride has made herself ready. And it was given to her to clothe herself in fine linen, bright and clean; for the fine linen is the righteous acts of the saints. And he said to me, "Write, 'Blessed are those who are invited to the marriage supper of the Lamb'" [Gr deipnon tou gamou]. And he said to me, "These are true words of God" (Revelation 19:7–9).

When did this event occur? To some extent the answer to the question depends on the meaning of the aorist verb "has come" (Gr *ēlthen,* aorist). This could be understood as an ingressive aorist. In that case one would understand that the Marriage Banquet is about to begin.[2626] Some view the aorist tense as a proleptic anticipation of the coming feast at the beginning of the millennium[2627] or in the eternal state after the millennium.[2628] Others understand the verb to be a culminative aorist, describing an event which has already occurred and reached its conclusion.[2629] Because the Marriage Banquet occurs at an unexpected time which cannot be calculated, it seems unlikely that this is an ingressive aorist referring to the second coming which does not come unexpectedly but at an arrival time that can be calculated. A culminative aorist fits the context well and another use of *ēlthen* in Revelation.[2630] In my view the marriage of the Lamb has already occurred in the banquet hall in the New Jerusalem. Now the Lord comes to earth at the Second Coming of Christ with His bride/wife (Rev 21:9). While some have plausibly argued that the New Jerusalem in 21:2 is the wife, it seems to me that John's point is that it is "like" (Gr ōs, "like, … a point of comparison," BDAG, 1104) a bride in the sense that it too has been "made ready" (John 14:3) He comes with His church to destroy His enemies and to celebrate the Messianic Banquet on earth with the faithful saints of all ages (Revelation 19:11-24, Isaiah 25:6).[2631]

Matthew refers to the fact that the wise virgins "*went with him into the wedding feast*."

And while they were going away to make the purchase, the bridegroom came, and those who were ready went in with him to the wedding feast and the door was shut (Matthew 25:10).

Jesus associates this entrance into the feast with an event which had no preceding signs at all. It was on this basis that we suggested that the wedding feast of the parable began in heaven during the tribulation period.[2632]

2626 Paul Tanner, for example, says, "More probably this is an *ingressive aorist,* and refers to what is soon to happen." See Paul Tanner, "The 'Marriage Supper of the Lamb' in Rev. 19:6-10: Implications for the Judgment Seat of Christ," *Trinity Journal* 26, no. 1 (2005): 50.

2627 Also Henry Alford, "Revelation," in *Alford's Greek Testament: An Exegetical and Critical Commentary* (Bellingham, WA: Logos Bible Software, 2010), 4:724.

2628 Mounce, *The Book of Revelation,* 347.

2629 Osborne, *Revelation,* 672. R. C. H. Lenski, *The Interpretation of St. John's Revelation* (Minneapolis: Augsburg, 1963), s.v. "Revelation 19:7".

2630 For example, after describing the outpouring of the six seals judgment of Revelation, we are told that the "the great day of his wrath has come" (Gr *ēlthen* Revelation 6:19). It is ridiculous to say that the great day of His wrath now begins (ingressive aorist). This day has been preceded by the opening of five seals which have unleashed the wrath of God from heaven including the destruction of a fourth of the earth's population (Rev. 6:7-8). Like Revelation 19:7, this is clearly a culminative aorist.

2631 For discussion of the time of the rapture in Revelation see William K. Harrison, "The Time of the Rapture as Indicated in Certain Scriptures Part IV: The Time of the Rapture in Revelation," *BibSac* 115, no. 459 (July 1958): 201-11.

2632 Stanton's conclusions are very satisfying. He says, "In context, the event is associated with heavenly worship,

Eschatological Implications

The meeting in Matthew 25:6 (when the ten virgins go out to meet the bridegroom) is parallel to the meeting between the Lord and His church at the rapture described in 1 Thessalonians 4:16-17.

> *For the Lord Himself will descend from heaven with a shout, with the voice of the archangel, and with the trumpet of God; and the dead in Christ shall rise first. Then we who are alive and remain shall be caught up together with them in the clouds to meet [apantēsis] the Lord in the air (NASB).*

Both passages use the same word for "meet" (*apantēsis*). At the rapture the church will "meet (*apantēsis*) the Lord in the air" (1 Thessalonians 4:17). In Matthew 25:6, the ten virgins go out to meet (*apantēsis*) the Bridegroom. This word is understood by some to be a technical term for a civic custom of antiquity whereby a public welcome was accorded by a city to important visitors.[2633] Similarly, when Christians ascend at the rapture, they will welcome Christ in the "air, acclaiming Him as *kurios* [Lord]."[2634] The use of *apantēsis* in Matthew 25:6 coupled with the imagery of a "shout"[2635] implies a parallelism of these two passages.[2636] All three occurrences of the noun in the New Testament refer to going out to meet an important personage.[2637]

We suggest that the meeting is that of the church, Christ's bride on earth, being transferred into the air to meet the Lord at the rapture and accompanying the risen dead in Christ and the bridegroom to the home of the bridegroom, the mansions prepared in the New Jerusalem. The ten virgins are the church, and John 14:3 is fulfilled.

The announcement of the approach of the bridegroom is the cry of the bridegroom in Matthew 25:6 heralding the rapture of the church. The parallels are impressive and suggest that Matthew 25:6 and 1 Thessalonians 4:17 refer to the same events, the shout of the bridegroom followed by the rapture of the church.

---

the presence of the twenty-four elders and the four living creatures, a voice 'out of the throne,' and the mighty voice of a heavenly multitude (Revelation 19:1-6). Without doubt, the whole wonderful scene takes place in heaven. The saints have all been raptured, but as yet the revelation has not taken place." Gerald B. Stanton, *Kept from the Hour: Biblical Evidence for the Pretribulational Return of Christ* (Miami Springs, FL: Schoettle Publishing Co., 1991), 261.

[2633] Erik Peterson, "*apantēsis*," TDNT, 1:380-381. "The use of *apantēsis* in 1 Thess 4:17 is noteworthy. The ancient expression for the civic welcome of an important visitor or the triumphal entry of a new ruler in the capital city and thus to his reign is applied to Christ." W. Mundle, "*katantaō*", in IDNTT, 1:325. See also Keener, *A Commentary on the Gospel of Matthew*, 597. See also MM, 53, "The word seems to have been a kind of technical term for the official welcome of a newly arrived dignitary – a usage accords excellently with the New Testament usage." Note, however, this technical use is disputed by M. Lattka, "*apantēsis*" in EDNT, 1:115.

[2634] Peterson, "*apantēsis*" in TDNT, 1:380.

[2635] *Kraugкē* in Matthew 25:6 and *keleusma* ("cry of command," in EDNT, 1:280) in 1 Thessalonians 4:16.

[2636] The noun *apantēsis* is used three times in the New Testament: twice of going out to meet the Lord at the *Parousia* (1 Thessalonians 4:17; Matthew 25:6) and once of believers going out to meet the Apostle Paul at the Market of Appius (Acts 28:15). We are assuming that the technical usage is probably employed in Matthew 25:6.

[2637] Matthew 25:6; Acts 28:15; 1 Thessalonians 4:17.

Summary

All attempts to work out a precise chronology of these events are open to challenge. We are attempting to build too much on too little information. Furthermore, the data

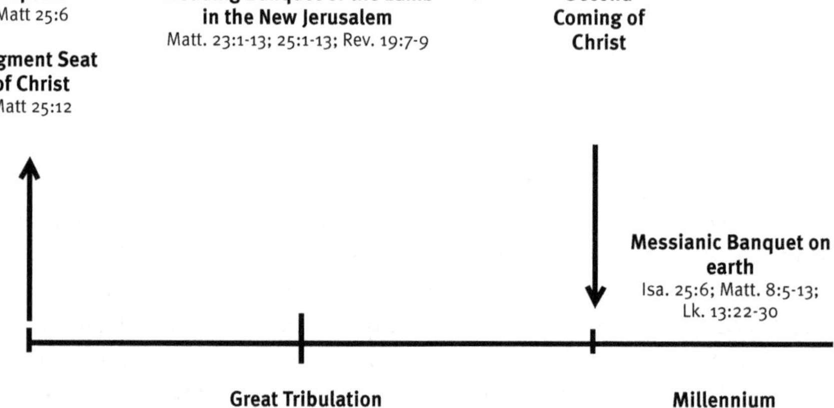

comes from figurative language and parables. Nevertheless, it is incumbent on the interpreter to suggest a plausible scenario. I offer the following chart in an attempt to clarify the chronology of events suggested in the above discussion.

The parable of the ten virgins presents the problem of unpreparedness. It occurs at the pre-tribulation rapture of the Church. At this time the Judgment Seat of Christ occurs and the five foolish virgins are excluded from the festivities. There will be "wailing and gnashing of teeth" as they remain in the darkness outside of the lighted wedding hall and reflect upon their wasted lives. The Marriage Banquet begins with the rapture and continues throughout the tribulation and ends just prior to the second coming.

The ten virgins in the parable refer specifically to the church saints but by application they represent believers of every era. Some will be prudent and anticipate a delay in the Lord's return and will be joyfully prepared when He arrives. Some will not. Others will be imprudent and will not prepare for His coming. They will receive a stern, "I do not know you" from Him, but this will not mean exile to eternal judgment. It will only express His disapproval, grief, and lack of respect for their wasted lives.

Excursus on Parallels with Jewish Wedding Practices

The following chart summarizes these correlations.[2638]

JEWISH MARRIAGE CUSTOM	CHRIST AND THE CHURCH
The Jewish bridegroom left his father's house and traveled to the home of his prospective bride and established a marriage covenant.	Jesus left His Father's house and traveled to earth and established the New Covenant by which the church was betrothed to Him.
The Jewish bridegroom paid a purchase price (actually "compensation") for the bride.	Jesus paid a purchase price by which He obtained the church (1 Corinthians 6:19-20).

[2638] These parallels are developed by Showers, *Maranatha: Our Lord Come!*, 166-69. See also Arnold G. Fruchtenbaum, *The Footsteps of the Messiah*, rev. ed. (Tustin, CA: Ariel Ministries, 2003), 587-90.

JEWISH MARRIAGE CUSTOM	CHRIST AND THE CHURCH
The Jewish bride was declared sanctified and set apart exclusively for her groom.	The church was sanctified and set apart exclusively for Christ (Ephesians 5:25-27; 1 Corinthians 1:2; 6:11; Hebrews 10:10; 13:12).
The Jewish bridegroom left his bride's home and returned to his father's house.	Jesus left earth, the home of His bride, at His ascension to His Father.
The Jewish bridegroom was separated from his bride for a period of time after he left her home.	Jesus has been separated from the church on earth for 2,000 years. This is the "delay of the Bridegroom" (Matthew 25:5).
The Jewish groom prepared a home in his father's house for his bride.	Jesus is preparing a dwelling place in His Father's home for the church (John 14:2).
The Jewish groom came to take his bride to live with him after a period of separation.	Jesus will come to fetch His bride to live with Him at the end of a period of separation (Matthew 25:6; 1 Thessalonians 4:17; John 14:3).
When the Jewish groom came to fetch his bride to live with him in his father's house, he came with a procession of male escorts.	When Jesus returns at the Rapture to fetch His bride, He will be accompanied by an angelic escort (1 Thessalonians 4:16-17) and a wedding procession (Matthew 25:1-7).
The Jewish bride did not know the time when the bridegroom would come for her.	The church does not know the "day or the hour" when Jesus will return to fetch her at the rapture (Matthew 25:13).
The Jewish bridegroom's arrival was heralded by a shout.	When Christ returns to fetch His bride there will be a shout (1 Thessalonians 4:17; Matthew 25:6).
The Jewish bride returned with the groom to the groom's father's house. This is the wedding procession involving the Ten Virgins in Matthew 25.	When Jesus comes for His church, He will take her to His Father's house (John 14:3; 1 Thessalonians 4:17).
Only invited guests and family and friends could attend the wedding feast.	While all are invited to the wedding feast, only those prepared with the righteous acts of the saints are chosen to participate (Matthew 22:14; 25:10; Revelation 19:7-9; Matthew 22:11).
The Jewish bride and groom celebrate in the groom's father's house for seven days or more.	The church celebrates in Jesus' Father's house , the New Jerusalem, for seven years while the tribulation rages on earth.

52

The Parables of the Talents and the Minas

AT THE conclusion of the Olivet Discourse, Jesus' purpose was to apply the prophetic teaching to the lives of believers in view of the fact that He could return at any moment and no one knows the day or hour. In the last chapter we showed that this aspect of His *Parousia* cannot refer to the second coming because for those living during the tribulation period the date, day, and hour can be precisely calculated. Furthermore, the Second Advent is not unexpected, it is preceded by worldwide signs, the Great Tribulation, and millions and millions will know full well that His coming is nigh.

In the parable of the Wicked Servant we met a servant who mistreated his fellow servants because he believed that the Lord's return was in the far distant future and he did not need to regulate his life in view of this distant event. The foolish virgins illustrated a lack of preparedness. They took no extra oil out to meet the Bridegroom at the pre-tribulation rapture.

In Matthew 25:24-30, we meet a third servant of the Lord, who like the carnal believers in the preceding parables, is likewise unwilling to invest his talents in the service of the Master.

The Parable of the Talents

> *For it is just like a man about to go on a journey, who called his own slaves, and entrusted his possessions to them. And to one he gave five talents, to another, two, and to another, one, each according to his own ability; and he went on his journey (Matthew 25:14–15).*

Of course in this parable, the man who went on a journey is the Lord Jesus Christ, and before His departure He entrusted His possessions to His servants (believers in the current era), to each according to his ability. The "talents" are metaphors for areas of responsibility. Some were given more, and some were given less.

The ascription *doulos*, "servant," refers to a slave "owned" by the master.[2639] While it is true that the metaphor for servant could possibly be simply a metaphor for anyone inferior to a superior, this particular servant was Christ's "own." When *idios* "one's own" is used, it often has emphasis.[2640] They are His "own" servants (Gr *idios*). It carries the sense of being

---

[2639] See discussion in any of the standard lexicons or Bible dictionaries, e.g., Karl Heinrich Rengsdorf, "*doûlos*," in TDNT, 2:270.

[2640] MM, 90.

peculiarly one's own. Like all believers in Christ, servants in the ancient world were either born into slavery or they were purchased, suggesting the spiritual analogies of regeneration and redemption. Furthermore, Jesus is entrusting His work to these servants. Would Jesus entrust kingdom work to nonbelievers who had merely professed faith? Jesus is referring to His own apostles, the Twelve.

The Lord continues,

> *Immediately the one who had received the five talents went and traded with them, and gained five more talents. In the same manner the one who had received the two talents gained two more. But he who received the one talent went away and dug in the ground, and hid his master's money. Now after a long time the master of those slaves came and settled accounts with them (Matthew 25:16–18).*

The "talents" refer to opportunities and, probably, abilities, to serve the master. Money is a good metaphor for the investment of one's life in service for Christ. Greater opportunity and ability means greater responsibility to utilize the gifts God has given. They are assets entrusted by the Master to the servants to invest on the Master's behalf. The parable is about what Christ's servants will make of the opportunities for service He has entrusted to them.

Two of the Lord's servants invested their lives well, but one of them did nothing with the opportunities the Lord had set before him. He buried them in the ground.

> *Now after a long time the master of those slaves came and settled accounts with them. And the one who had received the five talents came up and brought five more talents, saying, "Master, you entrusted five talents to me; see, I have gained five more talents." His master said to him, "Well done, good and faithful slave; you were faithful with a few things, I will put you in charge of many things, enter into the joy of your master" (Matthew 25:19–21).*

The first servant hears the wonderful words, "Well done!" The Master then turns to the second servant,

> *The one also who had received the two talents came up and said, "Master, you entrusted to me two talents; see, I have gained two more talents." His master said to him, "Well done, good and faithful slave; you were faithful with a few things, I will put you in charge of many things; enter into the joy of your master" (Matthew 25:22–23).*

Similarly, he too hears the Master say, "Well done." It is significant that each received the same commendation even though the first servant produced a five-talent return for his Master and the second servant produced a lesser two-talent return. Perhaps this is due to differing levels of ability. This is very instructive. Jesus does not judge us on how much we have produced for Him. Instead, He evaluates us on the basis of how much we make of the abilities we have and the opportunities He gave us with which to work. A janitor or a poor widow may not have the worldwide impact of a Billy Graham, but he or she may have the same reward, if he or she fully invests his or her life using what he or she has.

France summarizes, "The principle of different levels of responsibility depending on the slaves' individual ability hints at the parable's intended application. The kingdom of heaven is not a 'one-size-fits-all' economy … God's people are different, and he treats them differently; 'much will be expected of those to whom much has been given' (Luke 12:48). In the Lukan version of this parable the point is made by the different trading results of slaves who are given the same initial capital; here the principle of individuality is built into the initial distribution. It will be the slaves' responsibility not to look with envy at the different hand which has been dealt to their colleagues, but to make the most of what they have, and it will be important to note that the first two slaves will receive identical commendations in verses 21 and 23 even though the sums they have gained differ, since each has succeeded in proportion to his initial endowment."[2641]

> *And the one also who had received the one talent came up and said, "Master, I knew you to be a hard man, reaping where you did not sow, and gathering where you scattered no seed. And I was afraid, and went away and hid your talent in the ground; see, you have what is yours" (Matthew 25:24–25).*

What kind of excuse is this? The Lord rebukes him severely.

But his master answered and said to him, "You wicked, lazy slave, you knew that I reap where I did not sow, and gather where I scattered no seed. Then you ought to have put my money in the bank, and on my arrival I would have received my money back with interest" (Matthew 25:26–27).

The man who had the least ability and opportunity made the excuse. But what is emphasized is not his lack of giftedness but his laziness.

The exchange between this servant and his master raises a question, "Is this kind of excuse a common one given by Christians who do not take advantage of the abilities and opportunities for service Christ grants to them?" Who uses the excuse that because Jesus is a harsh master, it is better not to take any initiatives toward discipleship for fear of failure and His subsequent anger? No one I know. I asked a number of Christians the same questions and none of them knew anyone who used this excuse and could not imagine using it themselves.

If few can identify with this kind of excuse, what then is Jesus warning about in giving this parable?

Some suggest that a person who has few gifts or very small ones may be more hesitant to enter into service for Christ because he feels inadequate. He reasons that since he cannot make any difference, why should he try? Hagner opines, "Fear had motivated this servant, the fear of failure and losing the talent he had been given."[2642]

Another possibility is that personal self-interest may have been the issue. "He could not expect to get any significant personal benefit from whatever his trading might achieve, so why bother?"[2643] It is possible that some believers would take this attitude. They can see no laudable return in this life in exchange for the cost of discipleship, so they reason, "Why should I invest my life in the kind of service that is rewarded only in the distant future, the afterlife?"

Perhaps, as Craig Blomberg says, the servant had a view of God that "proliferated among ancient religions and unfortunately recurs far too often among Christians as

---

[2641] France, *The Gospel of Matthew*, 953-54.

[2642] Hagner, *Matthew 14-28*, 735.

[2643] France, *The Gospel of Matthew*.

well."[2644] Certainly, there are too many Christians who labor under the burden of viewing God as harsh, distant, and disapproving. "Fear of the master who is the judge does not free a person for forward-looking behavior; it leads instead to a defensive attitude that bears no fruit."[2645]

Perhaps the best explanation is that the excuse was insincere, and the slave was a hypocrite. Jesus says, in effect, "If you knew that I was harsh, if you really believed this, '*then you ought to have put my money in the bank*.'" The inference seems to be that the slave did not really believe this; it was a phony excuse. Indeed, the point of the parable is that all excuses for not utilizing one's God-given abilities and investing the Master's money (the opportunities for service He grants to us) are phony. There are no excuses!

Jesus clearly says that the servant's problem was not fear, it was sloth! He calls him a "wicked, lazy slave." Elsewhere in the Gospels, Jesus met believers who had various excuses for not committing to full discipleship (Matthew 8:21; Luke 9:59). For too many Christians, the reason for a lack of commitment is that it is simply too much trouble. They have a comfortable life and do not want it disturbed by self-sacrifice.

Possibly, Jesus has the sluggard from the book of Proverbs in mind. He will not begin to do anything. "*How long will you lie down, O sluggard? When will you arise from your sleep?*" (Proverbs 6:9). The wise man asks, "*How long?*" and "*When?*" The slothful Christian does not want to be definite on when he will decide to commit. Kidner says, "He does not commit himself to a refusal, but deceives himself by the smallness of his surrenders. So by inches and minutes, his opportunity slips away."[2646] Perhaps the third servant reasoned that he was making some sacrifice; he buried it and therefore received no personal benefit.

Not only does the lazy Christian not begin things; he also does not complete what he begins. "*A slothful man does not roast his prey, but the precious possession of a man is diligence*" (Proverbs 12:27). He kills the animal but never roasts it. But the real problem with the third servant is that he makes up phony excuses and will not face things. "*The sluggard says, 'There is a lion outside; I shall be slain in the streets!'*" (Proverbs 22:13). A lion outside? Now, there is an excuse! Like the third servant in the parable, the sluggard in Proverbs makes up one sham pretext for inaction after another. He rationalizes his laziness, "*I knew you to be a hard man, reaping where you did not sow,*" etc.

Such inaction will have serious consequences at the Judgment Seat of Christ.

> *Therefore take away the talent from him, and give it to the one who has the ten talents. For to everyone who has shall more be given, and he shall have an abundance; but from the one who does not have, even what he does have shall be taken away. And cast out the worthless slave into the outer darkness; in that place there shall be weeping and gnashing of teeth (Matthew 25:28–30).*

Because the lazy servant did not invest his life for the cause of Christ, what opportunities he had will be given to one who has demonstrated by a life of faithful service that he will utilize them to the maximum.

[2644] Blomberg, *Matthew*, 373.

[2645] Luz and Koester, *Matthew 21-28: A Commentary*, 257.

[2646] Kidner, *Proverbs: An Introduction and Commentary*, 42.

In earlier chapters we have demonstrated that "outer darkness" should be rendered "the darkness outside."[2647] As the wise virgins celebrate with the Lord in the banquet halls in the New Jerusalem, unfaithful servants, like the foolish virgins and the third servant, are led into the relative darkness outside the festivities. The darkness is a metaphor for exclusion. To wail and gnash one's teeth is not necessarily the experience of the unbeliever in the lake of fire as it is in Matthew 13:51. Here it is more likely a metaphor for the profound regret that the unfaithful Christians will experience when they face the final meaning of their wasted lives.

Matthew 25:30 is not referring to the Great White Throne where unbelievers are cast into the lake of fire (Revelation 20:11-15). Instead, this passage relates to the Judgment Seat of Christ where our Lord will assess the final meaning of our lives. Eduard Schweizer is certainly correct in his belief that the third servant is "saved 'as through fire'" as in 1 Corinthians 3:15.[2648]

The Parable of the Minas (Luke 19:12-27)

A similar parable with a slightly different emphasis also warns believers that they must not neglect the repeated calls to the highest level of discipleship. In the parable of the Minas (Luke 19:12-27) Jesus says,

> *A certain nobleman went to a distant country to receive a kingdom for himself, and then return. And he called ten of his slaves, and gave them ten minas, and said to them, "Do business with this until I come back" (Luke 19:12–13).*

In contrast to the parable of the Talents, in the parable of the Minas each servant received the same amount, ten minas. A mina was about three months' wages, so this would be about two-and-a-half years' salary.

Like the previous parable, the first two slaves were faithful. The first had doubled the original investment and returned an additional ten minas to the master. The master said to him, "*Well done, good slave, because you have been faithful in a very little thing, you are to be in authority over ten cities*" (Luke 19:17). The second servant was also rewarded but received only five cities. Neither did he receive the praise of "Well done!" So in contrast to the parable of the Talents, where each received different initial opportunities but the same reward, in this parable a different truth is taught. All three servants received the same initial opportunities, but they differed in their levels of effort and faithfulness, and the resulting reward was commensurate. Contrary to the teaching of some, there are degrees of reward and differences in the experience of eternal life among different Christians. The servant who returned five minas represents the believer who does not maximize his gifts but who does not bury them either.

[2647] See extensive discussion in chapters 22 and 49.

[2648] Eduard Schweizer, *The Good News According to Luke* (Atlanta: John Knox Press, 1984), 295. Hermann Olshausen also believes that the third servant is a believer but incorrectly assumes that these metaphors suggest exclusion from the millennium altogether. Olshausen, *Biblical Commentary of the New Testament*, 1:269. He notes that the fact that children of light are cast into "darkness" distinguishes this from the fate of the children of darkness who are cast into the everlasting fire. Ibid., 1:270.

What about the third servant? Like the third servant in the previous parable, he has an empty excuse.

> *And another came, saying, "Master, behold your mina, which I kept put away in a handkerchief; for I was afraid of you, because you are an exacting man; you take up what you did not lay down, and reap what you did not sow" (Luke 19:20–21).*

Can this servant possibly be a saved man? Yes! He is a servant like the other two, and the Master entrusted His wealth to him. Jesus would not entrust His wealth to a nonbeliever. The only reason for denying that this servant was saved (like the first two) is what happens to him at the judgment.

Danker says in regard to the third salve, "He is simply not entrusted with the program of the future. … Mediocre, middle-of-the-road, play-it-safe disciples will not be allowed to retard progress in the New Age yet to dawn. Paul holds out more explicit hope that such people will be saved in respect to their persons but will lose much opportunity that might have been theirs (see 1 Corinthians 3:15)."[2649] Olshausen agrees, saying that this servant is "an inactive member of the body of Christ the Church, who failed to perform his duty."[2650]

His punishment is severe. He loses opportunities for service in the future kingdom. There is a correlation between the capacities we develop now and our experience of life in the future kingdom.

> *And he said to the bystanders, "Take the mina away from him, and give it to the one who has the ten minas" (Luke 19:24-27).*

This third servant is specifically contrasted with nonbelievers in the next verse.

> *But these enemies of mine, who did not want me to reign over them, bring them here and slay them in my presence (Luke 19:27).*

Jesus says, regarding His enemies, "Slay them in my presence" (Luke 19:27). No doubt, this represents the destruction of Jerusalem in 70 A.D. The introduction of this fourth person, who is clearly unsaved, and who represents Jewish unbelief, confirms our interpretation of the parable of the talents as well. All three servants were believers; only the fourth kind of person, who is an unbeliever, is contrasted with the first three in both parables.

Summary

These two parables stress two different aspects of how the final significance of our lives will be assessed. In the first, we are told that we will be judged on the basis of how we have utilized the abilities and opportunities God gave us. A person with very few gifts may well have far greater reward than a person with many. The issue is what he has done with the gifts God gave him, not how much impact he has had for Christ.

But in the second parable, the Parable of the Minas, a different truth is emphasized.

[2649] Danker, *Jesus and the New Age: A Commentary on St. Luke's Gospel*, 309-10.

[2650] Olshausen, *Biblical Commentary of the New Testament*, 4:270.

The three servants in Luke 19:11-27 were each given the same amount, ten minas. But they did not receive the same commendation. One received ten cities, one received five, and one got nothing. All three started at the same place, but since all arrived at different destinations, all got different rewards. Here, the message is that those believers who are equally gifted, will be judged on their diligence to use the gifts they received. They will be expected to return a greater yield for the master and will be evaluated accordingly.

In the Parable of the Minas, we are introduced to the judgment on nonbelievers. for the first time. In the final Olivet parable in Matthew 25, the parable of the sheep and the goats, Jesus describes what happens seven years later, at the second coming when He comes in His glory to judge all the nations.

53

The Parable of the Sheep and the Goats

THROUGHOUT THE Olivet discourse (Matthew 24:1-25:46), the *Parousia* of the Son of Man has been the dominant theme. That theme now comes to its majestic climax in a grand vision of a judgment on all the nations, commonly called the Judgment of the Sheep and the Goats (Matthew 25:31-46). At this time, all humanity will be separated into two categories, sheep and goats, believers and unbelievers.

> *But when the Son of Man comes in His glory, and all the angels with Him, then He will sit on His glorious throne. All the nations will be gathered before Him; and He will separate them from one another, as the shepherd separates the sheep from the goats; and He will put the sheep on His right, and the goats on the left. Then the King will say to those on His right, "Come, you who are blessed of My Father, inherit the kingdom prepared for you from the foundation of the world" (Matthew 25:31–34).*

The context is obviously the second coming, "when the Son of man comes in His glory" and sits on His "glorious throne" (Matthew 25:31). It is the time when He establishes His kingdom, and there will be a "judgment of the nations" (v. 32). The result of this judgment will be either to "inherit the kingdom" (v. 34) and experience "eternal life" (v. 46), or to be cast into eternal fire (v. 41) and "eternal punishment" (v. 46).

The conditions for inheriting the kingdom are good works of charity to the hungry, the lonely, the prisoner, and those who were sick (Matthew 25:35-39). France says, "This passage has traditionally been an embarrassment, especially to Protestant readers, because it appears to say that one's final destiny—and nothing could be more final than 'eternal punishment' or 'eternal life' (v. 46)—depends upon acts of philanthropy, a most un-Pauline theology."[2651]

Some argue that this clearly teaches that final salvation is in part based on works. For example, Ron Sider says that Jesus "warned his followers in the strongest possible words that those who do not feed the hungry, clothe the naked and visit the prisoners will experience eternal damnation."[2652] Sider's book is a relevant challenge to all of us to remember the poor, but is this passage really teaching that those who do not perform acts of charity will go to the lake of fire? Does not Paul state that salvation is by faith alone apart from works?

2651 France, *The Gospel of Matthew*, 957.

2652 Ronald J. Sider, *Rich Christians in an Age of Hunger*, 2nd ed. (Downers Grove, IL: InterVarsity Press, 1984), 60.; cited by Kenneth R. Mitchell, *Justice and Generosity* (Baltimore: PublishAmerica, 2008), 253.

Catholic writers understandably find fodder for their doctrine of faith plus works in this parable. Catholic apologist Robert Sungenis, for example, says, "The Lord will reward the sheep specifically because they (1) fed the hungry, (2) gave drink to the thirsty, (3) invited the stranger, (4) clothed the naked, (5) took care of the sick, and (6) visited those in prison."[2653]

In response to this, some writers, such as Karl Pagenkemper, urge us to reject the tendency of some to start with Paul and John and interpret Matthew in that light, or with others to start with Matthew and interpret Paul and John in view of Matthew's theology. In other words, he says a holistic view that incorporates the viewpoints of both is necessary. By "holistic," Pagenkemper means the Reformed doctrine of perseverance. According to Pagenkemper, Matthew is not in disagreement with Paul; he is simply emphasizing what is necessary evidence of salvation, what comes after believing. Paul, on the other hand, while agreeing with Matthew, is emphasizing the starting point; but he never neglects the necessary works that must certainly follow. Sungenis, understandably, is not satisfied with this Protestant evasion of the obvious meaning of the text. He says, "Many a Protestant exegete would like to relegate this teaching to the category of mere metaphor, concluding that Jesus is not really talking about salvation by good works but only pointing out who among those who follow Christ really have true faith."[2654]

The starting point for discussion must be the meaning of "inherit" and what is inherited in Matthew 23:34.

What Is Inherited in Matthew 25:34?

The sheep are told to:

> ***Inherit the kingdom*** *prepared for you from the foundation of the world (Matthew 25:34).*

While this is often taken to mean final acceptance into the kingdom or personal salvation, this "kingdom" is not said to be the kingdom "*of heaven*" or the kingdom "*of God*." The word "kingdom" (Gr *basileia*) is used fifty-five times in Matthew. When it occurs with a genitival modifying phrase such as "of God" or "of heaven," we may understand it to refer to Christ's kingdom (either the millennium or the eternal state). However, in this instance there is no modifier or definite article ("the" kingdom) and we are to understand kingdom in its most basic sense, a "sphere of rule," "a reign," "the act of ruling," or "kingship."[2655] Instead of the kingdom prepared *for Christ*, this is a kingship prepared "*for you*"; they themselves "will become kings, sharing in the kingly authority of their Lord." [2656] This inheritance is a vassal (subordinate) kingship (five cities, ten cities, etc.)[2657] within the future kingdom of God. (Matthew 19:28 says it occurs in the "regeneration.")

[2653] Sungenis, *Not By Faith Alone*, 215.

[2654] Ibid., 215.

[2655] BDAG, 168.

[2656] R. T. France summarizes this nicely, "But this 'kingship' is not here said to be 'the kingdom of God/heaven.' Rather it is a kingship prepared 'for you:' they themselves will become kings, sharing in the kingly authority of their Lord. This is what Jesus has promised to the Twelve in 19:28, and the same idea is found in Luke 12:32 where the kingship is given to the 'little flock" of Jesus' disciples." France, *The Gospel of Matthew*, 963.

[2657] Luke 19:17-19.

Elsewhere, Christ promised these subordinate kingships within His kingdom to those who persevered with Him in His trials.

> *You are those who have stood by Me in My trials; and just as My Father has granted Me a kingdom, I grant you that you may eat and drink at My table in My kingdom, and you will sit on thrones judging the twelve tribes of Israel (Luke 22:28–30).*

The high honor of sitting on thrones with Messiah is granted on the basis of the works for a faithful life, standing by Him in His trials. The honor of judging the twelve tribes is equivalent to receiving a kingship (cf. Matthew 19:28). To inherit the kingdom is not exactly the same as final salvation, but France is correct that the "verb draws attention to a significant aspect of their salvation."[2658]

The kingdoms (vassal kingships) assigned to the disciples are within but not equal to Christ's kingdom. Paul said the same thing: "*and if children, heirs also, heirs of God, and fellow-heirs with Christ if indeed we suffer with Him in order that we may also be glorified with Him*" (Romans 8:17). We are fellow-heirs with Christ *if* we suffer with him.[2659] Some Christians will and some will not. Those who do will be awarded "kingships" (Luke 19:12-27) because of their perseverance. Furthermore, only those who have been granted these "kingships" will eat and drink at his table (v. 30). This refers to the celebratory Messianic Banquet which inaugurates the millennial kingdom. Elsewhere, the Lord said that only the great ones in Israel's history would enjoy this privilege (Luke 13:28).[2660] All believers will be "in" the kingdom, but only the faithful among His sheep will be "at the table."

France says it well, "Thus the 'righteous' [always ethically righteous in Matthew] will receive status as 'kings', faithfulness is rewarded with increased levels of authority."[2661] Those who inherit are *not*, he says, "The saved as a whole." Rather, "God has prepared this kingship for those who will prove worthy of it."[2662] In other words, the sheep at the judgment are a mixture of faithful and unfaithful believers. Recall the parable of the lost lamb; some do wander off, but they are all sheep.

A similar phrase, "receive a kingdom," was used by our Lord in the parable of the Minas regarding a landowner who went to a far country to "receive a kingdom" (Luke 19:12), that is, to receive a kingship. As Bock puts it, "This man needed to journey to a distant land to secure a vassal [one in a subservient or subordinate position] kingship."[2663] When he returned, "after receiving a kingship" (Luke 19:15), there was a distribution of rewards to his faithful servants, five cities, ten cities, etc. (Luke 19:17-26). This is similar to the special reward granted to the Twelve.

[2658] France, *Matthew*, 636.

[2659] See discussion of Romans 8:17 in Chapter 5.

[2660] For discussion of the Messianic Banquet, see pp. 333 ff., 825 ff.

[2661] France, *The Gospel of Matthew*, 963.

[2662] See ibid., 963. Of course, France, being an Experimental Predestinarian, defines worthy "on the basis of their response to the gospel and to the will of God." This is accurate but France is unclear here about the salvation of those who do respond to the gospel and are saved but who do not "do the will of God." According to Jesus, they too are in the kingdom (Matthew 5:19), but they will have no kingships there.

[2663] Zuck, Bock, and Seminary, *A Biblical Theology of the New Testament*, 1532.

The subject matter of Matthew 25:34 is authority over various cities, "kingships," not final entrance into the kingdom.[2664] What is inherited or received is not personal salvation or entrance into heaven. As Paul put it, "*If we are faithful, we will reign with him*" (2 Timothy 2:12). When the rich young ruler asked Jesus, "What shall I do to inherit eternal life?" (Luke 18:13), Jesus did not reply saying, "Whoever believes in Me will have everlasting life," as He said to the unregenerate Nicodemus. Instead, He said, "*You know the commandments.*" Entering eternal life by faith alone is one thing, but to inherit it requires the conditions of obedience to Torah. The former refers to regeneration; the latter refers to reward.

While Matthew 25:32 mentions only sheep as a general category of faithful disciples, Jesus says, in the parable of the Minas (Luke 19:11-27), that there are three categories of sheep or servants: those who receive a ten-city kingship, those who receive a five-city kingship, and those who do not receive any ruling authority with Him at all. In fact, what they have will be taken from them. They will be in the kingdom, but they will not inherit a kingship there.

Thus, when Jesus says to the sheep, "Come, possess the vassal kingships [subordinate spheres of authority] prepared for you," He is not simply granting them entrance; He is bestowing on them reward for their faithfulness to the demands of discipleship and ministry to the poor.

If inheriting the kingdom applies to salvation by works, as Ron Sider says, how does one harmonize that interpretation with the faith-alone means of eternal salvation in the rest of the New Testament? On Sider's view it would seem that we must obtain our final salvation by means of charity. Either that, or we must convince ourselves, *knowing* that we are saved, that this passage does not mean what it seems to mean; therefore, we cannot take the passage at face value, and we subconsciously minimize the importance of it.

On the other hand, if the phrase "inherit the kingdom" means possess a subordinate kingship within the kingdom of God, and relates to reward, the passage takes on new force in our personal lives; it relates our treatment of the poor to our standing at the Judgment Seat of Christ. But also we no longer need wrestle with the issue of eternal salvation. The issue we must face is that we will be held accountable for our ministry to the poor. Then, when we consider the rest of the New Testament, we find that it is not *just how we treat the poor* but showing the compassion and love of Christ in every relationship of life that is requisite. This is one of the primary areas of focus in the epistle of James. Showing favoritism or partiality is a sign of pride and certainly does not qualify as the kind of concern God has for those in need of support and comfort.

But, it may be asked, "Where are these divisions among the sheep alluded to in Matthew 25?" It seems that *all* the sheep inherit a vassal kingship, and *all* the sheep enter into eternal life, and, conversely, *all* the goats are condemned.

Do ALL Sheep Inherit?

These questions beg for an answer. Karl Pagenkemper objects to the interpretation above, saying, "In this context, the concept of 'inheritance' is clearly connected with *all*

[2664] It is clear that these kingships are allotted in the future kingdom and not in the church age as some maintain. See Peter K. Nelson, "Luke 22:29-30 and the Time Frame for Dining and Ruling," *Tyndale Bulletin* 44, no. 2 (November 1993).

those who are part of the kingdom, as is made clear by the fact that all those who are judged are divided into two groups who gain either eternal life or eternal separation. One might suggest that those who are inheriting the kingdom are a special class of people, but the identification of 'all nations' ***indicates that all people fall into either one group or the other.***"[2665]

Pagenkemper has put his finger on a possible objection to the Partner interpretation. It may appear that "all" implies there are only two categories of people, sheep or goats. Their outcome is either eternal life or damnation, and there is no further division, such as faithful vs. unfaithful sheep. Similarly, William Brown objects: "*All* the righteous 'inherit the kingdom' while *all* the wicked go into the 'everlasting fire.'"[2666] The argument is based on the fact that there are only two categories of people mentioned as being at this judgment, not three. We see only sheep and goats, Christians and non-Christians, and not two categories of Christians and one of unbelievers. "It is this presupposition [that there are only two kinds of sheep]," argues Brown, "that makes their [i.e., the Partners'] arguments for a merited inheritance inconclusive."[2667]

Well, if there are, in fact, two categories of sheep (the faithful and the unfaithful) at the judgment (and there are as the differing rewards prove—ten cities, five cities or zero), why are they not mentioned? There are two reasons. First, the unfaithful sheep are not mentioned because our Lord is speaking in broad terms, and the focus is on the reward to the faithful. As a group, the believers surviving the tribulation are viewed in terms of their expected and anticipated performance, which is faithfulness. That some were faithful and some were not in no way negates the general offer of the inheritance to the faithful sheep among them. All would understand that not all sheep have been faithful and that technically only the faithful sheep receive the inheritance. It seems to this writer that to argue otherwise is a wooden use of language that would prevent men from ever speaking in general terms or risk being misunderstood.

Earlier in the context, Jesus said that there are unfaithful Christians: the wicked, hypocritical servant (24:48), the foolish virgins (25:2), and the wicked servant (25:26). All three of these pictures of unfaithful Christians are sheep, saved people, as argued elsewhere.[2668]

Is this a case of special pleading? Is it not clear that the term "sheep" lacks any qualification and that there is no reference to faithful *and* unfaithful sheep? In reply we would say that there are many things about these sheep that are not mentioned but which are nevertheless taught elsewhere in Scripture. It is not mentioned that the sheep are distinguished elsewhere into various classes according to differing degrees of reward; nevertheless, they will be. Some will receive ten cities and some five. It is not mentioned that they will receive resurrection bodies at this time with varying degrees of glory, but they will.[2669] It is not mentioned that some will sit on thrones and some will not. It is not mentioned that some will be great in the kingdom and some will be least (Matthew 5:19).

[2665] Pagenkemper, "An Analysis of the Rejection Motif in the Synoptic Parables and Its Relationship to Pauline Soteriology", 315.

[2666] Brown, "The New Testament Concept of the Believer's Inheritance", 81. (italics added).

[2667] Ibid.

[2668] See above in chapters 50, 51, and 52.

[2669] 1 Corinthians 15:41-42.

Everything does not have to be said in every verse! If the distinctions among sheep are taught elsewhere and not contextually denied here (and they are not), there is no exegetical reason for denying these differences in this passage even if they are not specifically mentioned.

The second reason that two categories of sheep are not specifically mentioned is related to a very common form of figurative speech which Jesus utilizes here. Ken Mitchell has suggested that Jesus is actually referring to the entire group of sheep by means of synecdoche.[2670] Using synecdoche, a part of an idea or concept is put for the whole, or the whole is put for the part.[2671] For example, such a synecdoche occurred on the front page of the *Dallas Morning News* (Dec. 28, 1961) in a caption which stated: "Map locates key spot in new British moves to send arms to the Persian Gulf sheikdom of Kuwait." The word "arms" is synecdoche for an entire army that included tanks, ships, soldiers, uniforms, food, and lots of food, equipment, and planes. In 2 Chronicles 19:7, the word "chariots" is used by synecdoche for "chariots, horsemen, and riders"; "flesh and blood" in 1 Corinthians 15:50 is an idiomatic synecdoche for the body.[2672] When God says to Satan in Genesis 3:15, "*And I will put enmity between you and the woman, and between your seed and her seed,*" the word "seed" is the part, her immediate children, standing for the whole, the entire human race. In reality, this figurative way of speaking is so common that we all use it, often without even being aware that it is figurative. "He sold fifty head of cattle." (What did the rancher do with their bodies if only "heads" were sold?) The Psalms often use synecdoche. Many other illustrations could be cited.[2673] Mitchell suggests that the sheep in view here are the faithful sheep, but by synecdoche they are representative of all the sheep, the species for the genus.

That a part, the faithful, would be put for the whole (all the sheep), is characteristic of how the New Testament presents believers. Believers are those who are *characteristically* faithful and who do good works. The identity of a believer is *normally* one who does good works. Statements with this inference can be found all over the New Testament; faith will normally produce a life of works. Few would dispute this. Thus it would be

---

2670 Mitchell, *Justice and Generosity*, pp. 261-62.

2671 A synecdoche is "a figure of speech by which a part is put for the whole (as fifty sails for fifty ships), the whole for a part (as society for high society), the species for the genus (as cutthroat for assassin), the genus for the species (as a creature for a man), or the name of the material for the thing made (as boards for stage)" *Merriam-Webster's Collegiate Dictionary*, s.v. "synecdoche".

2672 This figure of speech is extremely common in Scripture. For example, "two eyes" (Matt 18:9; Mark 9:47), "two hands" (Matt 18:8; Mark 9:43), and "two feet" (Matt 18:8; Mark 9:45) are synecdoches for the whole body. "Jerusalem" in Luke 23:37, by synecdoche, refers to Israel's religious establishment, not the city in particular. "Psalms" in Luke 24:44 represents, by synecdoche, all parts of the Hebrew Bible other than the Pentateuch and the Prophets. "Your right hand" in Exodus 15:6 is synecdoche for God Himself.

2673 In Revelation 12:9 John uses the synecdoche of the whole for the part, the "world" for that part of the world which is deceived (the elect are not, according to Jesus, deceived). It is possible that Abraham's offering of Isaac in James 2:21 is synecdoche for all ten of his tests. When Paul speaks of the child-bearing of women in 1 Timothy 2:15, he is probably using synecdoche to refer to the general scope of activities for which women alone were uniquely designed by God. The lampstands in Revelation 1:19-20, mere temple furniture, refer by synecdoche to the temple which, in turn, represents faithful Israel. The request for "daily bread" in the Lord's Prayer (Matthew 6:11) is, by synecdoche, a reference to all the necessities for sustaining life. The baptism of John is an instance of synecdoche (Matthew 21:25) in which the reference is to John's prophetic ministry. "Whenever Moses is read" (2 Corinthians 3:15) means whenever the Old Testament is read; the word "Moses" stands for the Old Testament as a whole.

natural to present the sheep at the final judgment as a reference to the faithful sheep. Hence, Pagenkemper's point that there are only two categories mentioned and all must fit without further qualification into one of these two does not necessarily follow. All would understand that there are categories of sheep, degrees of glory, and that some sheep receive ten cities and some none. Unless Pagenkemper "knows" before he looks at this passage that all sheep are faithful and persevere in a life of works, his argument is not particularly convincing.[2674]

The Experimental Predestinarian idea that all sheep are faithful Christians, encounters serious problems. It violates a mountain of biblical testimony to the contrary, which demonstrates that many Christians are not faithful and are consequently warned about their sloth.[2675] In reality, not one of us has lived a life totally free of any unfaithfulness. James says that we all stumble in many ways! It also violates two thousand years of Christian experience. Pagenkemper himself admits, "There is also the possibility that believers might not be pleasing to God."[2676] So, contrary to all his claims otherwise, by his own admission there are at least two categories of sheep: those who are "pleasing to God," and those who are not. Pagenkemper believes that 1 Corinthians 3:15 teaches that all that is "worthless in the believer's life will be destroyed at the judgment." In reference to 1 Corinthians 3:1-3, he admits, "Although the Corinthians should have been more mature than they were, they continued to walk in such a manner as to reflect the lives of those who do not know Christ. They were not spiritual men."[2677] Thus, once again he admits there are two categories of believers, those who should be more mature than they are and those who are not mature.

He is therefore admitting what his interpretation of the parable of the Sheep and the Goats does not allow, that is, there are two categories of sheep,[2678] carnal and faithful. He says that the "lack of good works indicated to Paul that they [the carnal Corinthians] were not walking by faith, but were walking as 'mere men'."[2679] He says, "They were walking as unbelievers; he is not calling them unbelievers."[2680] Thus sheep can walk as "mere men." Where do these kinds of sheep fit into Pagenkemper's view of the sheep and goats judgment? It would seem that the category of sheep in that judgment must be expanded to include what the rest of the New Testament teaches and what Pagenkemper himself and some Experimental Predestinarians admit, namely, that there are those who have faithful to the end as well as those who have walked as "mere men."

The faithful sheep are now being rewarded with the inheritance. This is the fulfillment of the Lord's promise: "*But he who stands firm to the end will be saved*."[2681] They are those

[2674] Also, it is certain that the unsaved are punished for a lot more than failure to minister to the poor. Similarly, the saved are rewarded for a lot more than ministry to the poor. Possibly, charity to the poor is also used by synecdoche for either a faithful life in its totality or failure to show charity for the lack of it.

[2675] See extensive discussion in chapter 32.

[2676] Pagenkemper, "An Analysis of the Rejection Motif in the Synoptic Parables and Its Relationship to Pauline Soteriology", 361.

[2677] Ibid., 365.

[2678] Ibid., 365.

[2679] Ibid.

[2680] Ibid., 366.

[2681] Matthew 24:13. As will be discussed below, to be "saved" refers here to more than mere physical survival; it means to enter into the messianic blessing, the coming of the kingdom, and to rule there. It refers to the "fruition" of their salvation, the Davidic salvation, not the beginning of it. David exclaimed regarding this future event, "Will He not bring to fruition my salvation, and grant me my every desire?" (2 Samuel 23:5).

who persevered under persecution unto the end (Revelation 14:12). Jesus has already explained that Christians who annul the least of the commands and teach others to do the same will be *in the kingdom* but will be "called least" there (Matthew 5:19). On the other hand, "*whoever practices and teaches these commands will be called great in the kingdom of heaven.*" Being called "great" in the kingdom is to be one of the meek who "*will inherit the earth*" (Matthew 5:5). To those "*who are persecuted because of righteousness*" belongs "the kingdom of heaven" (Matthew 5:5). These are the faithful Christians to whom the Lord Jesus said: "*Rejoice and be glad, because great is your reward in heaven, for in the same way they persecuted the prophets which were before you*" (Matthew 5:12). These verses from the lips of our Lord in the same gospel make it clear that the sheep in Matthew 25:34 are the faithful sheep; otherwise, they would not have inherited the kingdom. The unfaithful are not mentioned because they are not relevant here, since they receive no reward. And because inheriting the kingdom is *conditioned* on faithful perseverance, it cannot be equated with justification, and theologically interpreted as continuation in holiness because a perfect perseverance and obedience would be necessary for that (Matthew 5:48). Peters explains:

> *The Savior, therefore, in accord with the general analogy of the Scripture on the subject, declares that when He comes with His saints in glory to set up His Kingdom, out of the nations those who exhibited* ***a living faith by active deeds of sympathy and assistance*** *shall—with those that preceded them...inherit (i.e., be kings in) a Kingdom. It is a direct lesson of encouragement to those who live during the period of Antichrist in the persecution of the Church, to exercise charity, for which* ***they shall be rewarded*** *[emphasis is his]. Hence it follows that the test presented is precisely the one needed to ascertain,* ***not who would be saved*** *(for that is not the train of thought, although connected with it),* ***but who would inherit a Kingdom or gain an actual, real rulership in it.***[2682]

The parable of the Sheep and the Goats is not a comprehensive statement of everything that takes place at the judgment. Jesus deliberately uses synecdoche to make His teaching more poignant. By using synecdoche the ministry to the poor is the issue; He is stressing the importance of it.

The Opposite of Condemnation Is Eternal Life

At the conclusion of the parable of the Sheep and the Goats, Jesus says that the sheep will go away to eternal life and the goats to eternal punishment.

> *These will go away into eternal punishment, but the righteous into eternal life (Matthew 25:46).*

Of course the sheep in this parable will go to heaven when they die, and "eternal life" in this context means "heaven when one dies." All sheep, faithful and unfaithful, "will go into eternal life." However, it means more than that. It refers to that dimension of the experience of heaven which can be enhanced by how our lives are conducted on earth. Jesus speaks not of mere entrance into eternal life but instead to that aspect of entrance that

[2682] Peters, *The Theocratic Kingdom of Our Lord Jesus, the Christ, as Covenanted in the Old Testament and Presented in the New Testament*, 3:376.

is conditioned on works. The apostle Peter taught us, "*For in this way the entrance into the eternal kingdom of our Lord and Savior Jesus Christ will be **abundantly supplied** to you*" (2 Peter 1:11). In what way? Peter says that it is by doing "these things." What things? Earlier he explained,

> *Now for this very reason also, applying all diligence, in your faith supply moral excellence, and in your moral excellence, knowledge; and in your knowledge, self-control, and in your self-control, perseverance, and in your perseverance, godliness; and in your godliness, brotherly kindness, and in your brotherly kindness, love (2 Peter 1:5–7).*

The *abundant* entrance into eternal life is conditioned on faith plus works, and not faith alone.

A common argument is that because the goats are sent to eternal punishment, the opposite, the destiny of the sheep, *must be* heaven. We agree. But it is also more than heaven; it is treasure there. Do we know that "eternal life" in this context refers to heaven, or could it refer both to heaven and to something in addition to heaven, a richer experience of eternity with God? Is it not obvious that eternal life is a parallel phrase for "inherit the kingdom" (Matthew 25:34), that is, "possess a subordinate (vassal) kingship?" This parallelism suggests that eternal life in this passage is not the only final destiny of the saints in heaven, but a richer experience of that destiny, additional authority over various cities, kingships.

We have discussed this concept before. The rich young ruler wanted to inherit eternal life. Jesus told him that in order to do that, he must obey the commandments and follow Him. The righteous sheep in this chapter, unlike the rich young ruler, did that. As a result, they obtain the promise Jesus made to those who give up all for Him.

> *And everyone who has left houses or brothers or sisters or father or mother or children or farms for My name's sake, shall receive many times as much, and shall inherit eternal life (Matthew 19:29).*

A parallel thought is found in Galatians 6:8, "For the one who sows to his own flesh will from the flesh reap corruption, but the one who sows to the Spirit will from the Spirit reap eternal life." There is no suggestion here that Paul is speaking of personal, eternal salvation. Mitchell explains, "He is writing to believers and instructing them on the consequences of the choices they make with their lives."[2683] They do not achieve eternal life by means of their works, "but rather they will experience to a greater degree the life of God now and in the future as well."[2684]

In 1 Timothy 6:18-19 the apostle says, " Instruct them to do good, to be rich in good works, to be generous and ready to share, storing up for themselves the treasure of a good foundation for the future, so that they may take hold of that which is life indeed." Taking hold of that which is "life indeed" is what the faithful sheep did. A difference exists between possessing eternal life in the sense of regeneration and "taking hold" of it. Those addressed

---

[2683] Mitchell, *Justice and Generosity*, 259.

[2684] Ibid., 259.

already possess eternal life, and they are now being exhorted to seize or grasp it.[2685] "The sheep in Matthew 25 are those who have taken hold of the eternal life they already have. Paul said, "Fight the good fight of faith; take hold [take hold of in order to make one's own][2686] of the eternal life to which you were called, and you made the good confession in the presence of many witnesses" (1 Timothy 6:12). No doubt, this is what Jesus referred to in John 12:25, "He who loves his life loses it, and he who hates his life in this world will keep it to life eternal."

In Matthew 25:46 eternal life is something earned by faith plus charitable deeds. As discussed previously,[2687] the phrase "eternal life" occurs 41 times in the New Testament, and in every place where it is presented as something to be acquired in the future, it is always conditioned on works. Conversely, whenever eternal life is described as personal salvation possessed or obtainable in the present, it is obtained by faith alone.[2688] Since that is so, it is wrong to think that because it is contrasted with eternal damnation it must mean eternity in heaven and nothing more. The most extreme contrast to the lake of fire is not heaven, but an inheritance in heaven, something in addition to the gift aspect of eternal life.

Summary

The parable of the Sheep and the Goats describes the final judgment at the end of the tribulation. Unlike the preceding judgments on the wicked servant, the foolish virgins, and the slothful servant in the previous parables, this judgment is a judgment on believers (sheep) and nonbelievers (goats).

We are explicitly told that the reason the sheep inherit kingships and go to eternal life is because of their works of charity toward the poor during the tribulation era. Experimental Predestinarians explain the works, not as conditions for salvation, but as characteristics of all who are "truly" saved. Catholics take the text at face value and argue that the text teaches salvation by works.

Both these viewpoints fail to satisfy for two fundamental reasons. First, the Bible everywhere contradicts this doctrine that believers will always finish well and complete their perseverance in good works to the final hour.[2689] Second, both viewpoints assume that "inherit a kingdom" and "eternal life" can refer only to personal salvation or final entrance into heaven or the millennium. Yet in many places in the New Testament, an inheritance is connected with reward (Colossians 3:24) and "treasure in heaven" (Matthew 19:21). It does not always refer to personal salvation.[2690]

While it is true that the text does not explicitly say that there are both faithful and unfaithful sheep standing before the King, we know from the rest of the New Testament that both will certainly be there. Some will be saved through fire. Furthermore, we know that the sheep in view are the faithful sheep because the text says so. Jesus explains that they will inherit because of their faithful lives. We know from other Scripture that not all

---

[2685] "*Epilambanomai*, seize, grasp," in EDNT, 2:30.

[2686] BDAG, 373.

[2687] See discussion in chapter 17.

[2688] John 3:15, 16, 36; 4:14; 5:24; 6:37, 40, 44, 54, 10:28; 17:2-3; Acts 14:28; Romans 5:21; 1 Timothy 1:16; 1 John 5:10.

[2689] See extensive scriptural documentation of this in chapter 32.

[2690] These points have been established in earlier chapters. See table of contents.

believers live faithful lives, and we know that no one obtains heaven because of a faithful life. That destination is secured by faith alone.

The next four chapters will deal with what for many will be the most controversial conclusion of this book, a conclusion arrived at after the author's five years of research and reflection. While the Bible definitely teaches eternal damnation in the lake of fire, it is extremely unlikely that *Gehenna*, or "hell," has anything to do with it.

54

Gehenna in the Old Testament and the Pseudepigrapha

CAN BELIEVERS be threatened with the fate of *Gehenna*? Surprisingly, the answer is yes (Matthew 5:22, 29; 18:8-9). But to what does *Gehenna* refer? Is this a reference to eternal damnation as is commonly believed? If so, why would Jesus threaten His believing followers with a destiny He knows would never happen to them?

The word *Gehenna* is often translated "hell" or "fiery hell." It occurs twelve times in the New Testament and eleven of those are in the Gospels. These occurrences in the Gospels may be divided into three groups. First, some are warnings to believing disciples concerning stumbling blocks (Matthew 18:8-9; Mark 9:43-48); second, some are warnings to believing disciples regarding their final destiny (Matthew 5:22, 29-30; 10:28; 18:8-9; Luke 12:4-5); and, third, others are warnings addressed to the Pharisees (Matthew 23:15; 33).[2691]

Jesus' disciples are warned that unless they deal radically with lust, they will be cast into *Gehenna* (Matthew 5:27-29). They are told that if they should call a "brother" a fool, they will be in danger of "hell fire." When Jesus sends them out on an evangelistic mission, He warns them that if they fail to persevere, they may face the danger of having their body and soul destroyed in "hell" (Gr *Gehenna*).

Such warnings raise issues regarding the doctrine of eternal life. One's initial impression might be that it is possible for believers to lose salvation and end up finally damned. We have shown in chapter 47 that this is impossible. These passages beg for careful consideration.

In the discussion that follows the writer proposes that *Gehenna* does not refer to final damnation. Instead, when applied to believers, it is a metaphor for a negative assessment of one's life. The phrase speaks of shame and disgrace. Due to failure and lack of perseverance in faith, at the Judgment Seat of Christ a believer's life can be assessed to be of no more value than a corpse tossed into a garbage dump (*Gehenna* was a burning garbage dump in the Valley of Hinnom outside the walls of Jerusalem).[2692]

In this chapter we will discuss the background of the concept of *Gehenna* as expressed in the Old Testament and in the pseudepigraphal literature of Second Temple Judaism. Much of the case for *Gehenna* referring to damnation in the afterlife is based on 15 references in the Pseudepigrapha with the assumption that the concepts found in this

---

[2691] See discussion in Hans Scharen, "Part 1: Gehenna in the Synoptics," *BibSac* 149, no. 195 (July 1992): 323-37; Tom Holland, *Contours of Pauline Theology* (Fearn, Scotland: Christian Focus Publications, 2004).

[2692] While the writer is satisfied with this view, it should be emphasized that one does not need to accept it to be consistent with the Partner paradigm.

literature were widespread in Palestine and informed the thinking of Jesus and the Gospel writers. As we will see, this conclusion is highly questionable.

Note how the Mishnah (circa AD 200) understands *Gehenna*:

In this regard did sages say, "So long as a man talks too much with a woman, (1) he brings trouble on himself, (2) wastes time better spent on studying Torah, and (3) ends up an heir of Gehenna."[2693]

R. Judah says in his name, "Most ass drivers are evil, most camel drivers are decent, most sailors are saintly, the best among physicians is going to Gehenna, and the best of butchers is a partner of Amalek."[2694]

And the judgment of the wicked in Gehenna is twelve months.[2695]

Do these references reflect the understanding of Jesus? We begin our discussion where Jesus would have begun, in the Old Testament.

Gehenna in the Old Testament

Gehenna in the Old and New Testament times referred to the Valley of Hinnom (Heb *gė hinnom*), just south of Jerusalem. The Old Testament has thirteen references to the Valley of Hinnom[2696] and none of them refer to hell. On five occasions it refers to a place where God's wrath is poured out in time as a judgment on the nation because they offered human sacrifices.[2697] This valley had been desecrated by the sacrifice of children to Molech (2 Kings 16:3; 23:10; Jeremiah 7:31; 32:35), so that, as an accursed place, it was used for the city garbage in the southeast corner of the Valley of Hinnom, where maggots gnawed and fires burned.[2698] Because of this, Jeremiah predicted that as a result of the Babylonian exile in 605 BC "the valley would be used as a mass grave for the corpses of the people of Judah killed by an invading army" (Jeremiah 7:30–34).[2699] Jeremiah further states that as a result of the Babylonian invasion of 605 BC, this valley would be known as a "valley of slaughter." *"Therefore, behold, days are coming," declares the* Lord*, "when it will no longer be called Topheth, or the valley of the son of Hinnom, but the valley of the Slaughter; for they will bury in Topheth because there is no other place"* (Jeremiah 7:32). He later adds that the whole valley will be full of "*the dead bodies and of the ashes*" (Jeremiah 31:40).[2700] It became a burial ground for corpses.[2701]

2693 Abot (3), m. Abot 1:5, Neusner, *The Mishnah: A New Translation*, 673. Citations from m. 'Abot are controversial. This section of the Mishnah probably dates from around AD 250. Its connection with the rest of the Mishnah has long been a subject of debate. Chapter 6 'Abot de Rabbi Nathan is of medieval origin. See Alexander, "Torah and Salvation in Tannaitic Literature," 1:274.

2694 m. Quiddushin 4:14L, Neusner, *The Mishnah: A New Translation*, 498.

2695 m. Eduyyot, 2:10F, ibid., 647.

2696 Joshua 15:8 (2x); 18:16 (2x); 2 Kings 23:10; 2 Chronicles 28:3; 33:6; Nehemiah 11:30; Jeremiah 7:31, 32; 19:2, 6; 32:35.

2697 2 Chronicles 33:6; Jeremiah 7:31-32; 19:6; 2 Kings 23:10; Jeremiah 19:6

2698 WPNT, s.v. "Mark 9:43." This was the southwest corner of Jeremiah's Jerusalem.

2699 "Hell," 376.

2700 The southeastern corner of the Hinnom valley by the Potsherd Gate (Dung Gate) was where dead bodies and ashes were thrown (cf. Jeremiah 7:30-34; 19:1-6).

2701 There seems to be some evidence that the southwest corner of the valley was also a burial location. Many tombs have been found there dating from as early at 400 BC to AD 70. Besides being a burial site it was also a place for cremation. See Barkay, "The Riches of Ketef Hinnom."

Because of this, Jeremiah said that God's judgment on the nation would occur there (Jeremiah 19:6). However, it should be noted that for Jeremiah, as the following verses make clear, the punishment of *Gehenna* was *not* eternal damnation, but *judgment on the nation in time* (Jeremiah 19:7-9).

The Valley of Hinnom (©LifeintheHolyLand.com)

According to Jeremiah, the Valley of Hinnom was located by the entrance of the potsherd gate (Jeremiah 19:2) near today's southeast corner of the city. This is considered by many to be the Dung Gate to which Nehemiah refers (Nehemiah 2:13; 3:13; 12:31).[2702] The Hebrew word *ʾašpōt* for "dung" used in Nehemiah 2:13 "can mean 'ash-heap' (Lamentations 4:5, NIV), 'refuse-heap, dung hill,' referring to human and animal excrement and other refuse connected with the sacrificial syste. The gate next to it would be in an area of easy access and would be expected to be on the side of the city less offensive, where the wind would blow the odors away (the south or east side).

The Hebrew lexicons translate the word for the dung gate as "refuse-heap, dung-hill"[2703] or as "heaps of garbage and manure."[2704] The most likely location for the Dung[2705] Gate is at the east end of the Hinnom Valley."[2706]

2702 Dale C. Liid, "Potsherd Gate," in *Anchor Yale Bible Dictionary*, ed. David Noel Freedman (New York: Doubleday, 1992), 5:427.

2703 BDB, 1046.

2704 HAL, 97.

2705 The Hebrew word for "dung" in "Dung Gate" refers to the practice that "Human dung was carried out of every city to a heap, also the general garbage dump (Luke 14:35), which in places long-inhabited became a high 'dunghill' (Hebrewʾ *ašpôṯ*). There it was periodically burned. Sitting among the ashes of the dunghill was a sign of degradation through grief, of poverty, and of disease (1 Samuel 2:8; Psalm 113:7; Lamentations 4:5; RSV "ash heap"; cf. Job 2:8; Isaiah 58:5; Jonah 3:6). The transformation of a house's site into a dunghill was a means of degrading the memory of executed persons (Ezra 6:11; perhaps Daniel 2:5; 3:29; cf. 2 Kings 10:27)."

2706 "Dung Gate" in Liid, "Potsherd Gate," 2:240. "A gate of Jerusalem leading to Topheth and the Potter's Field at the east end of the Valley of Hinnom, possibly the same as the Dung Gate." Smith, "Book of Life," 3:913.

According to most researchers, "In the 1st century AD the valley was used as a refuse dump for the city of Jerusalem."[2707] This is consistent with its use in Nehemiah's time and substantiates Rabbi Kimchi's assertion that "*Gehenna* was a despised place into which was thrown garbage and dead bodies and a fire was there perpetually to burn filth and bones. Therefore, parabolically, the judgment of the impious was called *Gehenna*."[2708] When the abominable child sacrifices and the last vestiges of idolatry were abolished after the exile, the Jews looked on Hinnom with horror, and it became a fitting place to dump garbage—in the spot where they once worshiped Molech.

People burned their offal there using sulfur, the flammable substance used today in matches and gunpowder. These fires were part of life for those who lived in Jerusalem in biblical times. The excavations cited in footnote 2709 below clearly establish that there was a garbage dump near the south-eastern side of the city of David.

Lloyd Bailey and others have rejected the association of *Gehenna* with city offal on the basis, they say, that it is grounded solely on the testimony of Rabbi Kimchi (twelfth century) in his commentary on Psalm 27. He asserts, "Kimchi's otherwise plausible suggestion, however, finds no support in literary sources or archaeological data from the inter-testamental or rabbinic periods. There is no evidence that the valley was, in fact, a garbage dump, and thus his explanation is insufficient."

That may be incorrect.[2709] Bailey is not taking into consideration that the Old Testament itself identifies the Valley of Hinnom as the refuse pile adjacent to the Dung Gate in Jeremiah's time and says there was burning there (2 Chronicles 28:3; 33:6;

[2707] Fyfe, *The Hereafter: Sheol, Hades and Hell, the World to Come, and the Scripture Doctrine of Retribution According to Law*, 126.

[2708] Rabbi David Kimchi's commentary on Psalm 27:13 (ca. AD 1200). Cited by ibid., 126.

[2709] Due to recent excavations since Bailey's widely cited 1986 article, we now know that there was a garbage dump on the south-eastern slope of the City of David in the Kidron Valley. Excavations have revealed bones of sheep, goats, donkeys and fish, ordinary household garbage, pottery shards, coins dated during the time of Pilate (26-36 AD), and urban rubbish collected from the city and dumped over the city limits where it reached a depth of 10 meters. See Guy Bar-Oz et al:, ""Holy Garbage": A Quantitative Study of the City-Dump of Early Roman Jerusalem," *Levant* 39 (2007): 1-2, 9. See also Ronny Reich and Eli Shukron, "The Jerusalem City-Dump in the Late Second Temple Period," *Zeitschrift des Deutschen Palätina-Verein* 119, no. 1 (2003): 12-118. For Bailey's article see Bailey, "The Topography of Gehenna," 189. For the "man on the street" in the 1st century, it was is likely that the Valley of Hinnom included the Kidron as one continuous valley because they both joined at the SE corner of the city. As Masterman has observed, "names are so frequently transferred from one locality to another in Palestine that no argument can be based on a name alone" (E.W.G. Masterman, "ZOHELETH, THE STONE OF," in *ISBE*, ed. James Orr (Albany, OR: Ages Software, 1915), s.v. "Zoheleth".) Some writers equate the two valleys. For example, Bruce Chilton says, "The term Gehenna refers in a literal sense to the Valley of Hinnom in the Kidron Valley, just across from the temple in Jerusalem." (See Bruce Chilton, "RABBINIC LITERATURE: TARGUMIM," in *Dictionary of New Testament background: a compendium of contemporary biblical scholarship.*, ed. S. E. Porter, & Evans, C. A. (Downers Grove, IL: InterVarsity Press, 2000), 907.) The majority of Bible dictionaries, journal articles, and commentaries this writer has consulted disagree with Bailey, however, and accept the traditional view that *Gehenna* was a garbage dump on the south east side of Jerusalem. See Walter C. Kaiser et al., *Hard Sayings of the Bible* (Downers Grove, IL: InterVarsity Press, 1997), 359.; Chad Brand, "Gehenna," in *Hollman Illustrated Bible Dictionary*, ed. Chad Brand, Charles Draper, and Archie England (Nashville: Holman Bible Publishers, 2003), 631. *Tyndale Bible Dictionary*, 2:717; Smith, "Book of Life." Hagner, *Matthew 14-28*, 117.; France, The Gospel of Matthew, 201. Barbieri, "Matthew," 13. Larry Crutchfield, "The Third Jewish Sect: The Essenes," *The Bible and the Space* 2, no. 4 (Autumn 1989): 112. Robert Peterson, "Does the Bible Teach Annihilationism?," *BibSac* 156, no. 621 (January 1999): 14. Carson says, "Late traditions suggest that in the first century it may still have been used as a rubbish pit, complete with smoldering fires," Carson, "Matthew," 149.)

Jeremiah 32:36), and that bodies were dumped there with the burned ashes (Heb *desn*, "fatty ashes of burnt wood mixed with fat on the altar[2710]) after the Babylonian invasion (Jeremiah 31:40). Archaeologists have not found these remains, but Jeremiah says they are there and they are probably buried under many layers since Jerusalem has been leveled eighteen times. Even if there was no extra-biblical evidence that the Valley of Hinnom was a burning garbage dump in the first century, there is no reason to doubt Kimhi's assertion. In fact, a garbage dump excavated in the Kidron Valley probably identifies it with Hinnom (see footnote 2706).

To argue that we cannot accept Kimchi's assertion because there is no archaeological evidence for a garbage dump in that area in the first century would require that we cannot accept Jeremiah's statements that there was a garbage dump in the seventh century BC; but there was, even if it has not yet been discovered. Since Jerusalem has been leveled 18 times already, it may be hard to find the original garbage dump that was probably localized and did not cover the whole valley. Time and again, biblical places have been written off as fictional on the grounds that archaeologists could find no evidence of their existence only to yield to later archaeological excavations that verified the biblical data.[2711]

Jeremiah says it was a dung heap, and this must have been the place where the Romans dumped thousands of Jewish bodies during the invasion of AD 70. Jesus also associated *Gehenna* with maggots in the future millennium by citing Isaiah's millennial prophecy which states that in Hinnom "their maggot does not die" (Mark 9:46). So *Gehenna* was a garbage dump before the time of Christ, and will also be one in the millennium (or at least the first part of it). Because the associations are so clear in the Bible and because the Valley of Hinnom is close to the refuse pile by the Dung gate and closely associated with garbage in the Kidron, there is no obvious reason to deny Kimchi's assertion that Jewish tradition associated Hinnom with a burning garbage pit in the first century. It is possible that Hinnom was the name of the continuous valley which included the Valley of Hinnom and today's Kidron.

In addition to being a metaphor for judgment, the Valley of Hinnom was also a metaphor for shame and disgrace. It was here that the high places of Topheth were built (Jeremiah 7:31). "Topheth" is probably derived from an original bi-radical verb for "to spit" (*tōph* mimicking the sound for spitting) which led to the thought of the object spit on and hence became a word for contempt.[2712] "The corpses, heaped up in the Valley of

---

2710 HAL, 234.

2711 For example, early in the twentieth century critics said there was no historical information to support the biblical descriptions of the culture during the patriarchal periods. Instead, what we read in the Bible was projections from eighth and ninth centuries BC back to when these narratives were composed. Then in 1925-1941 the Nuzi Tablets were discovered, which revealed that many of the cultural characteristics described in Genesis were in fact prevalent during the time in which Abraham lived. In the nineteenth century critics said that the Bible was in error because of its 40 references to the Hittites. There were no Hittites, they said. Then in 1906, Hugo Winckler went to the site known as Boghas-koi and excavated the capital of the Hittite Empire. Examples could be multiplied. See Joseph P. Free, *Archaeology and Bible History* (Wheaton, IL: Scripture Press, 1969). See also Merrill F. Unger, *Archaeology and the Old Testament* (Grand Rapids: Zondervan Publishing House, 1954).

2712 *Tophet* has an uncertain etymology. At least four possibilities have been proposed: (1) It is derived from *toph* or "drum" and has reference to the drums used to drown the screams of the children offered alive to Molech in the fires. (2) *Tōphe̱t* may be derived from *tophleh*, a word of Assyrio-Persian origin meaning contempt or place of burning. (3) If it is closely related to (2), then it means "the place of the god of fire," (HAL, 1781). Or (4) *tōpe̱t* may be formed from *tōph*, ***"act of spitting"*** (TWOT, 967) and mean properly a

Ben Hinnom, are denied the dignity of burial and become carrion for vultures and wild beasts"[2713] (Jeremiah 7:33). Jeremiah referred to this disgrace when he announced that Jehoiakim "*will be buried with a donkey's burial, dragged off and thrown beyond the gates of Jerusalem*" (Jeremiah 22:19). Motyer translates *top̄teh* in Isaiah 30:33 as "the disgraceful burning place."[2714] Association with garbage was a common representation of disgrace and shame in the Old Testament (e.g., Job 2:8; Lamentations 4:5).

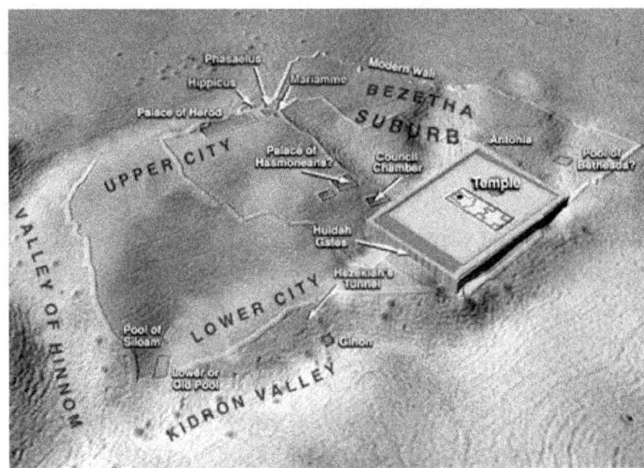

There is uncertainty about the location of this valley, but according to Meir it is at the southernmost lower end of the city,[2715] directly south of Mount Zion at the southeast corner of the city. Because of extensive construction through the ages, it is concealed from view today.[2716]

While it is true that the judgment involved is "fire," that in no way justifies the claim that the fire of damnation must be meant. Charles Bing has shown that in the Old Testament "the concept of eternal hellfire is difficult if not impossible to find."[2717] Bing cites Old Testament references where "fire" is used of divine discipline,[2718] and as a cleansing or purifying trial or judgment.[2719] The same usage is common in the New Testament, where it is used of the discipline that comes on carnal believers, who do not bear fruit and are as useless as vines that are burned (John 15:6);[2720] of the fire at the Judgment Seat of Christ in

spitting out, then came to refer to that before or on which one spits (as in Job 17:6), an object of deepest abhorrence. Keil and Delitzsch, *Commentary on the Old Testament*, 8:106. See 2 Kings 23:10; Jeremiah 7:31–32; 19:6, 11, 14. See also James Fyfe, *The Hereafter: Sheol, Hades and Hell, the World to Come, and the Scripture Doctrine of Retribution According to Law*, 131,32.

2713 McKane, Jeremiah, 179.

2714 J. A. Motyer, *The Prophecy of Isaiah: An Introduction & Commentary* (Downers Grove: InterVarsity Press, 1993), s.v. "Isa. 30:33".

2715 Ben-Dov Meir, *Historical Atlas of Jerusalem*, trans. David Louvish (New York: Continuum Publishing Group, Inc., 2002), 11.

2716 D. Thane Norris, "The Logos Delux Map Set" (Oak Harbor: Logo Research Systems, 1997), s.v. "Jerusalem at the Time of Christ".

2717 Bing, "Does Fire in Hebrews Refer to Hell?," 150.

2718 Leviticus 10:1-2; Numbers 11:1-3; 16:35; Psalms 78:21; 80:14-16; 89:46; Isaiah 42:25; Jeremiah 4:4; 11:16; 15:14; 17:4; Lamentations 2:3-4; 4:11; Amos 2:5.

2719 Psalm 66:10-12; Zechariah 13:9; Malachi 3:2-3.

2720 See full discussion of John 15 on pp. 611 ff.

which the believer's carnal, dead works are burned away (1 Corinthians 3:13); and of the fiery trials that come on believers (1 Peter 4:12).

The word *Gehenna* is the Greek transliteration of the Hebrew phrase *gėhinnom*, Valley of Hinnom. Even though most of the commentaries and lexicons translate *Gehenna* as "hell," this is an interpretation, not a translation. In popular consciousness today it is associated with endless material torment, a concept completely foreign to the word in the Old Testament. In the intertestamental literature damnation (not *Gehenna*) was a purifying punishment that was not endless.

It is probably not wise to render *Gehenna* by a word so full of superstitions derived from paintings in churches and Dante's *Inferno*. These fables about cauldrons of lead and brimstone, and cloven-footed demons who pursue the damned throughout all eternity are often falsely associated with biblical teaching in popular lore. The word "hell" is *never* used in Scripture in the manner in which it is often understood. When the translators of the NASB render all twelve instances of *Gehenna* by the word "hell," it is legitimate to ask if they may be doing a disservice to Bible readers. They should have rendered the word *Gehenna* by "Valley of Hinnom." The word *Gehenna* plainly does not mean "hell" as understood in today's popular culture nor, for that matter, in first century Palestine.

Gehenna in the Pseudepigrapha

The Second Temple built by Herod the Great stood on the same site as Solomon's magnificent edifice. The period known as the Second Temple period dates from the Babylonian invasion of 586 BC to the Bar-Kochba revolt in AD 135. During this time a sizable corpus of literature was produced: the Apocrypha, the Pseudepigrapha (Jewish literature between 200 BC and AD 200); the Dead Sea Scrolls; the writings of Philo of Alexandria (20 BC – AD 50), and the histories of Flavius Josephus (AD 37-100). Our attention in this section will focus primarily on the Pseudepigrapha (Philo[2721] and Josephus do not even mention *Gehenn*a).

Much of the argument for equating *Gehenna* with hell is derived from references in the Pseudepigrapha. Citing Jeremias, Kendall S. Harmon asserts, "The New Testament was written in an environment 'saturated' in the conceptions and imagery of the Apocalyptic writings."[2722] Although Jeremias is Harmon's source,[2723] Jeremias never cites the references to prove his thesis, and the ones he does cite *do not use the word Gehenna*. When Jeremias sees words like "abyss in the midst of the earth full of fire,"[2724] or a land in which is found an "accursed valley,"[2725] he assumes without discussion or proof that these citations refer to

---

[2721] Although, he does mention Tartarus three times and equates it with final damnation.

[2722] Kendall S. Harmon, "The Case against Conditionalism," in *Universalism and the Doctrine of Hell: Papers Presented at the Fourth Edinburgh Conference in Christian Dogmatics*, ed. Nigel M. De. S. Cameron (Grand Rapids: Baker Book House, 1992), 207.

[2723] TDNT 1:657.

[2724] 1 Enoch 90:1.

[2725] 1 Enoch 27:1.

Gehenna.[2726] "The deep valley burning with fire"[2727] is said to be *Gehenna* and so is "the chasm in the abyss of the Valley."[2728] However, even if it could be shown that this valley is *Gehenna*, because Paul told us to avoid Jewish myths (1 Timothy 1:4; 2 Timothy 4:4; Titus 1:4), Jesus certainly would not have equated Gehenna with hell based upon a pseudepigraphal myth. The word *Gehenna* is a transliteration into Greek of the Hebrew words for Valley of Hinnom (Heb *gė hinnom)* and is not found in the Hebrew Old Testament. But the Valley of Hinnom is the *Gehenna* to which Jesus refers (see discussion below).

In Enoch's vision of hell he sees a river of fire covering it. Sometimes there is freezing ice and "merciless angels, carrying instruments of atrocities torturing without pity."[2729] He tells his readers that those who are cast into the "Accursed Valley" [Gr *pharagx*, "a ravine," there is no specific mention of *Gehenna*], remain there forever (1 Enoch 27:1-2). At any rate, the valley Enoch saw was to the "west" amid "mountains of gold!" and is not said to be adjacent of Mount Zion where the Valley of Hinnom is located, southwest of the city of David (southeast of today's Jerusalem).[2730] Also, I am unaware of any "mountains of gold" in the vicinity of Jerusalem. Therefore, whatever he saw, it is certain that it was not final damnation (hell) in the Valley of Hinnom. Nor could this valley be equated with the Kidron Valley to the east of the city (Zechariah 14:4). which some writers equate with the Hinnom Valley (see footnote 2706).

The Vision of Ezra (4 Ezra) tells us that in hell angels throw fire in the faces of unbelievers and whip them with fiery scourges. This is the fate, he says, of those women who are not virgins and of wives who adorn themselves but not for their husbands.[2731] Is this what Jesus believed? According to another writer hell is a place where fiery axes revolve around the ears and the wicked hang by their eyelids while angels beat on them.[2732]

Were Jesus and those in Galilee saturated with these concepts and images, as Harmon and others maintain? Are these fantastical descriptions a basis for understanding the New Testament concept of *Gehenna*? These visions are clearly the product of mystical hallucinations, or, like those of Joseph Smith, deliberate fabrications designed to enhance the spiritual authority of the "prophet."

As Tom Holland has pointed out, these writings are called the "Pseudepigrapha" because "they were attributed to important historical Jewish figures who clearly did not compose them."[2733] The writers of many of these works falsely ascribe their works to biblical

---

[2726] Bauckham does the same thing: "In this second version of the tour, Enoch also sees the place of punishment for the wicked after the last judgment (located literally in the Valley of Hinnom: 26:3-27:4)." Bauckham, *The Fate of the Dead: Studies on the Jewish and Christian Apocalypses*, 53. Yet, Enoch does not mention "Hinnom" specifically. He does, however, connect a "cursed valley" with a ravine to the west of Jerusalem, which could not refer to the Valley of Hinnom which is to the south and east. Later Enoch tells us that the place for the judgment on the wicked is in the third heaven.

[2727] 1 Enoch 54:1.

[2728] 1 Enoch 56:3.

[2729] 2 Enoch 10:1-3.

[2730] 1 Enoch 26:4; 67:4.

[2731] The Vision of Ezra is actually a composite of Christian and Jewish documents dated between AD 350 and 600.

[2732] The Greek Apocalypse of Ezra (4:14-19; 22-24). Date AD 150 to 850, quoted by Ken Penner and Michael Heiser, *Old Testament Greek Pseudepigrapha with Morphology* (Bellingham, WA: Logos Research Systems, 2009). Penner says, "The work is considered an amalgam of Jewish and Christian sources put together by a Christian sometime after the 2nd century AD, but no later than the 9th century."

[2733] Holland, *Contours of Pauline Theology*, 55. Holland teaches New Testament and hermeneutics at the Evangelical Theological College of Wales.

Enoch, Baruch, Moses, and Ezra. Charles attempts to exonerate them from the charge of forgery by saying they were forced into it because of persecution.[2734]

Would Jesus endorse this fiction with His use of *Gehenna*? Holland maintains that the assumption that there is a correspondence between terms and themes of these writings and the New Testament must be questioned.[2735]

Commentators often read into these texts their own view of *Gehenna* derived from their Christian pre-understanding of the word, and then use these texts to interpret the meaning of *Gehenna in the* New Testament! The approach is circular. Scholars have read their own meaning into the term and then used that to show what the New Testament meant.[2736]

The list below tabulates the fifteen references commonly understood to refer to *Gehenna* in Second Temple literature.

1. *Then said I: "For what object is this blessed land, which is entirely filled with trees, and this **accursed valley** between?" Then Uriel, one of the holy angels who was with me, answered and said: "This **accursed valley** is for those who are accursed forever: here shall all [the accursed] be gathered together who utter with their lips against the Lord unseemly words and of His glory speak hard things" (1 Enoch 27:1-2).* [2737]

[2734] He says, "Some of its [Book of Enoch] authors—and there were many—belonged to the true succession of the prophets, and it was simply owing to the evil character of the period, in which their lot was cast, that these enthusiasts and mystics, exhibiting on occasions the inspiration of the O.T. prophets, were obliged to issue their works under the aegis of some ancient name. The Law which claimed to be the highest and final word from God could tolerate no fresh message from God, and so, when men were moved by the Spirit of God to make known their visions relating to the past, the present, and the future, and to proclaim the higher ethical truths they had won, they could not do so openly, but were forced to resort to pseudonymous publication." R. H. Charles, ed. *The Apocrypha and Pseudepigrapha of the Old Testament in English* (Oxford: Clarendon Press,1913), 2:163.

[2735] Holland, *Contours of Pauline Theology*, 60.

[2736] Ibid., 61. Many scholars are now questioning the extent to which the Pseudepigrapha is being used to understand the New Testament. Cf. Sandmel, "Parallelomania," 1-13. See also Philip S. Alexander, "Rabbinic Judaism and the New Testament," *Zeitschrift für die Neutestamentliches Wissenschaft* 74(1983): 1237-46. This kind of circular argumentation is found in the interpretation of the Pseudepigrapha itself. A good example of this is the treatment of *Gehenna* in Enoch, a book where the word *Gehenna* is not used. However, because interpreters "know" that the "accursed valley" (1 Enoch 27:1); the "deep valley" (1 Enoch 54:1-6), "ravine" (1 Enoch 10:13), "abyss" (1 Enoch 90:26-27), and the "fiery furnace" (1 Enoch 98:3) all refer to *Gehenna*, they cite these passages in 1 Enoch as if they are references to *Gehenna*. In fact, they have simply read their own interpretation into those phrases and then used those phrases to prove that *Gehenna* is found in these books. The "accursed valley" in 1 Enoch is located on earth and the concept of hell being located at the farthest extremities of earth, not in some location below the earth (see discussion in Bauckham, *The Fate of the Dead: Studies on the Jewish and Christian Apocalypses*, 84). It was not until the first and second centuries AD that the "cosmic secrets," supposedly seen by Enoch, were located above the earth instead of on the earth. Are we to assume that since Jesus used the word "*Gehenna*" that He believed the Enochian concepts of hell as a place on earth? This may be an illustration of Sandmel's warning: "Two passages [i.e., accursed valley in 1 Enoch and Hinnom in the Old Testament] may sound the same in splendid isolation from their context, but when seen in context, reflect difference rather than similarity." See Sandmel, "Parallelomania," 3.

[2737] Enoch was written over a period from the second century BC to the first century AD by many authors and speaks of "that accursed valley," but never uses the word *Gehenna*. See Charlesworth, ed. *The Old Testament Pseudepigrapha*, 1. First Enoch 27 comes from a section of Enoch dated prior to 171 BC. He speaks of a valley "filled with trees," hardly a description of hell in the Gospels. Enoch often speaks of judgment in the last day. However, it is a judgment in time involving temporal destruction, and those judged are "accursed forever" (1 Enoch 27:2). Furthermore, in some places Enoch makes it clear that the duration of the judgment is not endless, saying it lasts "till ten thousand years, the time entailed by their sins, are consummated" (1 Enoch 21:6). If this is the hell of traditional theology, then modifications need to be made. Furthermore, if one is to

2. *And I looked and turned to another part of the earth, and saw there a* ***deep valley***[2738] *with burning fire. And they brought the kings and the mighty, and began to cast them into this deep valley (1 Enoch 54:1).*
3. *But the sinners shall die with the sinners, and the apostate* ***go down***[2739] *with the apostate (1 Enoch 81:6).*
4. *Now they shall say unto themselves: "Our souls are full of unrighteous gain, but it does not prevent us from descending from the midst thereof into the burden of* ***Sheol****" (1 Enoch 63:6).*
5. *And I saw at that time how a* ***like abyss*** *was opened in the* ***midst of the earth****, full of fire, and they brought those blinded sheep, and they were all judged and found guilty and cast into this* ***fiery abyss****, and they burned; now this abyss was to the right of that house (1 Enoch 90:26).*[2740]
6. *And thou* ***shalt look*** *from on high and shalt see thy enemies in* ***Ge(henna)****, And thou shalt recognize them and rejoice, and thou shalt give thanks and confess thy Creator (Assumption of Moses 10:10).*
7. *And he answered me and said: When the Most High made the world, and Adam, and all that came of him, he first prepared* ***the Judgment****, and the things that pertain unto* ***the Judgment*** *(4 Ezra 7:70).*[2741]
8. *And then shall the pit of torment appear, and over against it the place of refreshment; the* ***furnace of Gehenna*** *shall be made manifest, and over against it the Paradise of delight (4 Ezra 7:8-9).*
9. *And the mouth of* ***Gehenna****, and the station of vengeance, and the place of faith, and the region of hope (2 Baruch 59:10).*[2742]
10. *There is the sentence of corruption, the way of fire, and the path which bringeth to* ***Gehenna*** *(2 Baruch 85:13).*[2743]

---

quote Enoch, then 1 Enoch 50:4 should be included, "At His judgment the unrepentant shall perish before Him." To "perish" in this passage refers to annihilation, and not endless torment. Lexicons often cite 1 Enoch 54:1-6 as proof that *Gehenna* refers to hell, but the word *Gehenna* is not used. Rather, it refers to a deep valley burning with fire. It is here that the notion that the fires of *Gehenna* are a "burning furnace" is mentioned. Later in the book we are told that in the last day, sinful shepherds are cast into the "fiery abyss," but there is no mention of *Gehenna* (90:25-27), and there is no indication of endless torment that is irreversible as in the concept of hell in traditional theology. Over 80 percent of the book of Enoch is a translation of a translation (Charles, *Commentary on the Pseudepigrapha of the Old Testament*, 2:163). We do not have the original. There is nothing in the references to judgment in Enoch that shows they do not mean "annihilation" and the words for "eternal" cannot be proven to mean "endless." But the whole discussion is irrelevant anyway because *Gehenna* is never mentioned by name in the book!

2738 The deep valley is supposedly *Gehenna*. However, this is only an assumption.

2739 Because the phrase "go down" is used, Charles says, with no proof, that this means "go down to *Gehenna*." Charles, *Commentary on the Pseudepigrapha of the Old Testament*, 2:163.

2740 Charles says the apostates are cast into *Gehenna*. However, the word is not used and at any rate the *Gehenna* of the New Testament is not in the "midst of the earth," that is, in Jerusalem. Ibid., 2:259.

2741 There is no reference to *Gehenna*. Because *Gehenna* was supposedly created before the creation of the world, and in this passage judgment was created before the creation of the world, therefore it is argued that "the Judgment" must equal *Gehenna*.

2742 The text only refers to "the Valley" and not *Gehenna*. If one knows before looking at this, that "valley" must mean Valley of Hinnom, then Charles's translation would be justified. Charles has a tendency to see *Gehenna* in every reference to pit, abyss, valley, accursed valley, or fire, or furnace of fire. After looking up all these references, the present writer sees no necessary connection. In this concept of *Gehenna*, the righteous rejoice as they watch the rest of the world writhe in torture. Is this the postmortem damnation of which Jesus spoke!?

2743 Yet this *Gehenna* leads to "destruction," annihilation, not eternal damnation (2 Baruch 85:15).

11. *They were a mighty army, of great form, but nevertheless they went under the dread house of Tartarus guarded by unbreakable bonds, to make retribution, to* ***Gehenna*** *of terrible, raging, undying fire (Sibylline Oracles 1:103).*
12. *Then in the dead of night they will be thrown under many infernal beasts in* ***Gehenna,*** *where there is immeasurable darkness (Sibylline Oracles 2:291-93).*
13. *As many as sinned by impiety, these will a mound of earth cover, and the broad* ***Tartarus*** *and repulsive recesses of* ***Gehenna.*** *But as many as are pious, they will live on earth again when God gives spirit and life and favor (Sibylline Oracles 4:186).*
14. *And after [one thousand] three hundred and thirty-two days the Lord will come with his angels and with the hosts of the saints from the seventh heaven, with the glory of the seventh heaven, and will drag Beliar, and his hosts, into* ***Gehenna*** *(Ascension of Isaiah 4:14).*
15. *He created the* ***abysses*** *and the darkness, eventide <and night>, and the light, dawn and day, which He hath prepared in the knowledge of his heart (Jubilees 2:2).*[2744]

These fifteen references in seven pseudepigraphal books supposedly establish that in the minds of Jesus' listeners, *Gehenna* referred to eternal torture in the afterlife. Yet, only the *Ascension of Isaiah, 4th Sibylline Oracles (AD 80 – 100), 2 Baruch,*[2745] *4 Ezra*, and the *Assumption of Moses* even use the word "*Gehenna*" and only one of them is possibly dated before the time of Christ (*The Assumption of Moses*[2746]). Some of the references do not reflect Second Temple Jewish thought but Christian redactions.[2747]

Certainly, there is some value in using the Pseudepigrapha for understanding some of the background of the New Testament era. However, those who believe that *Gehenna* refers to eternal damnation need to explain how these uninspired writers came to understand *Gehenna* as eternal torment in such a different sense from the Old Testament. They then must explain why the inspired New Testament writers would accept their viewpoint. "It is their business to show," Balfour correctly says, "that this gradual change in the meaning of *Gehenna* did not originate from the invention of men, but from the authority of God."[2748]

To demonstrate this supposed development is complicated by a number of factors that require that these texts be used with extreme caution. Regarding *Gehenna* the following summary points are relevant.

2744 Compiled about 100 BC this was originally written in Hebrew and translated into Greek. But this version was lost. We only have a corrupted Ethiopic translation. Furthermore, equating the *Gehenna* (2:2) with hell is a real stretch, considering that the author does not even use the word *Gehenna*! It speaks of the abyss and the darkness.

2745 Charles dates 2 Baruch in the latter half of the first century. Charles, ed. *The Apocrypha and Pseudepigrapha of the Old Testament in English*, 2:470.

2746 Emil Schürer has a good discussion of this work and dates it soon after the death of Herod. Emil Schürer, *A History of the Jewish People in the Time of Jesus Christ: First Division*, 2nd and rev. ed., 2 vols., vol. 1 (Edinburgh: T. & T. Clark, 1890), 5:78-79.

2747 I have been able to find one other pseudepigraphical reference to "the *Gehenna* of fire." This is in the Greek Apocalypse of Ezra 1:9. This can safely be removed from the discussion because it is generally understood as a Christian document and does not reflect normative Judaism of the first century. According to Penner, "The work is considered an amalgam of Jewish and Christian sources put together by a Christian sometime after the 2nd century A.D., but no later than the 9th century." "The Greek Apocalypse of Ezra," in Penner and Heiser, *Old Testament Greek Pseudepigrapha with Morphology*, s.v. "Introduction".

2748 Walter Balfour, *An Inquiry into the Scriptural Import of the Words Sheol, Hades, Tartarus, and Gehenna in the Common English Version* (Charlestown, MA: Geo. Davidson, http:\\www.books.google.com, 1824), 273.

1. *Gehenna* in the Old Testament referred to the Valley of Hinnom, which was used of the garbage dump near the southeast corner of Jerusalem where the Hinnom and Kidron Valleys merge,[2749] (southwest corner of the City of David in Jeremiah's time).
2. No Jewish sources prior to the time of Christ associate *Gehenna* with eternal damnation.[2750] References in the Talmuds appear hundreds of years later and are influenced by pseudepigraphal references and early Christian interpretations[2751] of the words.[2752] *Gehenna* and "hell" are only ambiguously cited in the Mishnah (AD 200),

[2749] "*Gehenna*" in Old Testament times referred to the Valley of Hinnom, just south of Jerusalem. This valley had been desecrated by the sacrifice of children to Molech (2 Kings 16:3; 23:10), so that, as an accursed place, it was used for the city garbage where maggots gnawed and fires burned. Because of this, Jeremiah said that God's judgment on the nation would occur there (e. g., Jeremiah 19:6). However, it should be noted that for Jeremiah, as the following verses make clear, the punishment of *Gehenna* was not eternal damnation, but judgment on the nation in time (Jeremiah 19:7-9). R. E. Davies, "Gehenna," in *Zondervan Pictorial Encyclopedia of the Bible*, ed. Merrill C. Tenney (Grand Rapids: Zondervan Publishing House, 1975), 2:671.

[2750] "There are no known Jewish uses of the term [*Gehenna*] that definitely pre-date the Gospel uses." Nolland, *Luke 9:21-18:34*, 678. Bailey concurs, "The earliest mention of the underworld under the name *Gehenna*, is found in the New Testament and in the early rabbinic literature." Bailey, "The Topography of Gehenna," 189. By "rabbinic literature" he refers to materials dated after AD 70.

[2751] Richard Bauckham points out that the notion that all Jewish influence on Christianity passed through the New Testament is misleading. The fact is "that the early Christians were reading the extra-canonical apocalypses during and after the New Testament period.... In fact, of course, almost all the pre-rabbinic Jewish literature which we know, apart from the Dead Sea Scrolls, we know only because Christians preserved it." Bauckham is referring to extra-canonical apocalypses. Bauckham, *The Fate of the Dead: Studies on the Jewish and Christian Apocalypses*, 82. The point is that the second-century Christians got their ideas not primarily from the New Testament but from these extra-canonical fantasies and preserved them. It is therefore questionable to read their views back into the New Testament. Bauckham says, "Christians read the extra-canonical Jewish apocalypses; they revised, adapted and interpolated them....It is only a small exaggeration to say that the apocalyptic tradition was a literary tradition which in passing from Judaism into Christianity by-passed the New Testament." Ibid., 82. Robert A. Kraft concurs, "A third problem area is the Hypotheses Regarding Origins and Transmission of Pseudepigrapha. If a manuscript has been preserved only by Christians, as is normally true for the Pseudepigrapha, how strong is the possibility that the writing actually was compiled in its preserved form(s) by a Christian? To what extent is it possible that some or all of the supposedly Jewish contents are actually Christian in origin? What are suitable criteria for distinguishing 'Jewish' from 'Christian' elements? Is it possible that Christians appropriated the document or some of its Jewish contents from Jews in the medieval/byzantine period? What do we know of Jewish-Christian contacts after 135 C.E.? What do we know of Christian writing and reading habits during the first millennium of Christian existence? What are acceptable criteria for the identification of 'glosses,' 'interpolations,' 'redactions' and 'recessions,' and how do these types of literary activity differ from each other? Who translated these materials from one language to another, for what reasons, and under what conditions?" See Robert A. Kraft, *The Pseudepigrapha in Early Christianity* (University of Pennsylvania, 1994).

[2752] Much is made of the fact that the Talmud has over 200 references to *Gehenna* that speak of hell in the afterlife. Two Talmuds (Palestinian and Babylonian) include the Mishnah and serve as commentaries on and expansions of the Mishnah. The Mishnah is a philosophical law code, produced in Roman-occupied Palestine around AD 200. The first Talmud was formed in this area around AD 400 and is called "the Talmud of the Land of Israel" or "the Jerusalem Talmud," and in Hebrew, "the *Yerushalmi*." This Talmud covers thirty-nine of the Mishnah's sixty-two tractates. The second Talmud was created in Babylonia (present-day Iraq) near Baghdad, around AD 600, and is called "the Talmud of Babylonia," and, in Hebrew, "the *Bavli*." However, it seems unlikely that a commentary, even though it is based on oral tradition compiled in Babylon in AD 400 to AD 600 based on the Mishnah (AD 200) would be a valid source of beliefs regarding *Gehenna* in AD 30. Furthermore, the Talmud derives its views of *Gehenna* from the Pseudepigrapha and not from the Old Testament. *Gehenna* is mentioned five times in the Mishnah but never clearly equated with eternal damnation, and yet the Talmud in AD 600 was a commentary on the Mishnah. Neither Philo nor the Septuagint ever mention *Gehenna*. See discussion in H. Gaster, "Gehenna" in George Arthur Buttrick, *The Interpreter's Dictionary of the Bible*, 4 vols. (New York: Abingdon Press, 1962), 2:363. Gaster says that the concept was influenced by Iranian ideas and is patterned on the Avestan doctrine of the

but the meaning is uncertain (see discussion below). The word *Gehenna* is not even mentioned in Philo (20 BC – AD 50) or Josephus (AD 37 – 100).[2753]

When lexicographers utilize these sources to define the meaning of *Gehenna* in the first century, they are sometimes guilty of semantic anachronism. While not all these references are anachronistic, still, as Bock expresses it, "Another example of this problem is when appeal is made to later Jewish or Greek materials to support a first-century meaning for a term that lacks attestation for that sense in earlier sources." [2754]

3. The idea that *Gehenna* refers to eternal damnation arose from fifteen allusions in the Pseudepigrapha[2755] found in seven books, only five of which even use the word:[2756]
   a. *4 Ezra*[2757] (AD 100-135)[2758]
   b. *2 Baruch*[2759] (second century AD)[2760]

---

ultimate judgment of the wicked in a stream of molten metal.

2753 This is in accord with this writer's concordance search, and in regard to Josephus and Philo it is confirmed by Joachim Jeremias, "*Gehenna*" in TDNT, 1:657. However, Philo does mention Tartarus three times, and Tartarus is linked to the *Gehenna* in the *Sibylline Oracles* 4:186. Additionally, 2 Peter 2:4 seems to equate Tartarus with eternal damnation. See "Rewards and Punishment" in Philo, "On the Life of Moses," 664.

2754 Darrell L. Bock, "New Testament Word Analysis," in *Introducing New Testament Interpretation: Guides to New Testament Exegesis*, ed. McKnight Scot (Grand Rapids: Baker Books, 1989), 110.

2755 1 Enoch 27:1-2; 54:1-6; 90:26-27; 4 Ezra 7:36; 2 Baruch 59:10, 85:13; Sibylline Oracles 1:103; 2:291-2; 4:186; Ascension of Isaiah 4:14, Jubilees 2:2, Assumption of Moses 10:10.

2756 In addition to a concordance search of all pseudepigraphical literature and Charles's commentary on it, this writer researched the references to *Gehenna* in The Anchor Bible Dictionary; BDAG, Jeremias; "*Gehenna*" in TDNT, 1:658, EDNT, 1:239; "Hell" in ISBE, 2:677; "*Gehenna*," IDB; vol. E-J, p. 363; and Davies and Allison, *A Critical and Exegetical Commentary on the Gospel According to Saint Matthew*, 1:514. All these writers cite essentially the same passages in the Pseudepigrapha. I have chosen these sources to represent my assessment of where the equivalence of *Gehenna* with "hell" was derived. A concordance search of *Gehenna* in the Pseudepigrapha yields references to this word in only five pseudepigraphal books. It is never mentioned by name in the Book of Enoch (200 BC – AD 200).

2757 Here, we learn of the "pit of torment" (2 Esdras 7:36 or 4 Ezra 7:36) and a "furnace of hell," supposedly referring to *Gehenna*. However, 2 Esdras, a product of rabbinic and diaspora Judaism was written after AD 120 and thus is an uncertain source for the views of Palestinian peasants or "ordinary Judaism" during the ministry of Christ (AD 29-33). However, it is believed that parts of it may date to the late 60s. This pit of torment is equated with *Gehenna*. The Latin Vulgate translation of 7:36, "*et clibanus Gehennae*" ("and oven of *Gehenna*") is of uncertain origin because we do not possess the Greek manuscripts on which it is based. This may well be an interpretation based on early Christian speculations. Furthermore, there is nothing in the passage that suggests that the torment is endless and irreversible like the traditional doctrine of hell. Indeed, elsewhere the author refers to the annihilation of the multitude of sinners, not endless torment ("Perish, then, the multitude which has been born in vain; but let my grape be preserved, and my plant, which with much labour I have perfected!" 4 Ezra 9:22). See Charles, ed. *The Apocrypha and Pseudepigrapha of the Old Testament in English*, 2:552.

2758 Ibid. Sanders argues that because of the fall of Jerusalem, *4 Ezra* is not a reliable source of pre-70 AD Judaism. He says, "It is if anything less representative of Judaism before 70 than Rabbinic literature. One must even doubt its usefulness of very much of Judaism after 70." Sanders, *Paul and Palestinian Judaism*, 427.

2759 The Second Syriac Apocalypse of Baruch (2 Baruch) refers, in two places, to *Gehenna* as, "There is the sentence of corruption, the way of fire, and the path which bringeth to *Gehenna*" (2 Baruch 59:10, 85:13)." The sentence of corruption refers to annihilation and that is what happens in *Gehenna*, whether in time or eternity. Furthermore, the version we have was translated from Syriac into Greek, and the Greek version is lost! Charlesworth, ed. *The Old Testament Pseudepigrapha*, 1:616. It was written sometime between AD 100 and 120, long after the time of Christ (ibid., 1:617). Is this a valid source of opinion regarding *Gehenna* in New Testament times? Since we have no access to the original and have no idea how much theological intrusion has occurred and since we do not even know the location in which it was originally written, caution must be employed.

2760 Penner and Heiser, *Old Testament Greek Pseudepigrapha with Morphology*, s.v. "Introduction".

c. The 4th book of the *Sibylline Oracles*[2761] (AD 80 – 100),[2762] an ecstatic fantasy[2763] of which Charles says that the bulk of them are, "*late and of comparatively little intrinsic worth.*[2764]
d. *Assumption of Moses* (AD 7 – 29?). The reference to a "Valley"[2765] contains the only possible reference to *Gehenna* before the time of Christ.
e. *Ascension of Isaiah* (AD 100)?[2766]

4. We have no idea how widely these pseudepigraphical concepts were known in first-century Palestine. Thus, one should be careful to assume without specific evidence that Jesus' audience or Jesus Himself would have (or would not have) associated *Gehenna* with eternal damnation. While Craig Blomberg certainly sees value in the use of these

---

2761 The 4th book of the Sibylline Oracles is considered to be of Jewish origin. Sibylline Oracles, 1:103 speaks of *Gehenna* as a terrible raging and undying fire and is equated with Tartarus (2:300). The phrase, εις γενναν μαλερου λαβρου πυρος ακαματοιο ("into *Gehenna* of fierce, mighty, unbending fire") is a different wording from what Jesus used when He said, "βληθηναι εις την γενναν του πυρος" ("cast into the *Gehenna* of fire," Matthew 18:9); Sibylline Oracles 2:291 refers to the judgment on sorcerers and sorceresses who in the dead of night "will be thrown under many terrible beasts in *Gehenna*, where there is immeasurable darkness." They will "gnash their teeth." Sibylline Oracles 4:186 refers to "Tartarus and the repulsive recesses of *Gehenna*."

2762 Charlesworth, ed. *The Old Testament Pseudepigrapha*, 1:382. See discussion in Collins, "Sibylline Oracles," 6:2.

2763 The "Sibyl" means "prophetess." She is always depicted as an aged woman uttering ecstatic prophecies. Oracles ascribed to a Sibyl come from Asia and the West. In Greek mythology she was granted by Apollo to live as many years as there are grains of sand, a favor that she declined (Charlesworth, 1:317). According to Jewish legends she was a daughter-in-law of Noah. There are collections of Sibylline oracles from many nations. A major characteristic is the doom pronounced on nations, a disaster from the wrath of the gods. The most famous Sibylline Oracles were the Roman. They were kept by 15 men and consulted in a time of crisis for the state. See Charlesworth, ed. *The Old Testament Pseudepigrapha*, 1:319. Half of the books were written in Egypt (3, 5, 11-14), others in Syria, and none show clear knowledge of the historical events they describe. It is in the second book that the equation of *Gehenna* with hell is found, a book that is Christian in origin. The fact that it incorporates phrases directly from Matthew 5:29 and 18, την γεενναν του πυρος, suggests that the Gospels do not necessarily reflect the viewpoint of the Oracles; rather, the Oracles may have taken phrases out of the Gospels and interpreted them in accord with Jewish pseudepigraphal literature in the second century AD. However, we do not have the originals of the Oracles. The current version is a redaction by an unknown author who could have been either Jewish or Gentile. There is no evidence that it was known in first-century Palestine. It was compiled in the fifth or sixth centuries (TDNT, 1:657), and it is uncertain when it was originally written, but it is evidently a compilation over many years. It was probably written in the Palestine, but even this is uncertain. Many feel Oracles 1 and 2 are a separate book written between 30 BC and AD 250. However, the obvious Christian redaction, references to Christ and the fall of Jerusalem (1:393-96), clearly put parts of these two books in the second century AD or later. Some scholars believe it was written in Egypt. Thus, we do not know who wrote it, when it was written (but probably after the time of Christ), and we are not even certain where it was written. Some of the Oracles contain Christian interpretations of later centuries. (See ibid., 333.) Yet this is the best evidence we have for the equation of *Gehenna* with hell in the Pseudepigrapha!

2764 Charles, ed. *The Apocrypha and Pseudepigrapha of the Old Testament in English*, 2:368. However, there is a reference in Sibylline Oracles 4:186 which seems to equate Tartarus with *Gehenna* in 2 Peter 2:4. Peter equates Tartarus with the place where the fallen angels were cast. This passage, however, does not predate the Gospel and at any rate we have no evidence that the Sibylline Oracles or an oral tradition on which they were based were known in Galilee at the time of Christ's ministry.

2765 Ibid., 2:407. Charles translated "valley" as *Gehenna* which, while plausible, could be a reference to another valley, the Valley of Jehoshaphat. See Assumption of Moses 10:10 in ibid., 2:421.

2766 The Martyrdom and Ascension of Isaiah is a Christian document. The first five chapters are called the Martyrdom of Isaiah and probably date to the end of the first century AD. See Charlesworth, ed. *The Old Testament Pseudepigrapha*, 143-54. The visions are ridiculous, and to associate them in any way with Jesus fifty years earlier is preposterous.

sources for understanding the New Testament, nevertheless, he issues this caveat: "The vast majority of Jews in Israel... did not concern themselves with the numerous oral traditions and additional legislation that had grown up around the Bible."[2767] Furthermore, are we to assume, Sandmel warns, that there was good communication between the caves on the West Bank of the Dead Sea and Galilee?[2768]

Even if one grants that the pseudepigraphal writings do reflect at least some first-century views, Holland asks, "How widely were the pseudepigraphal writings known? How far had their message penetrated wider Judaism? How can we know that an apparent reference, or even an echo from the Jewish Pseudepigrapha, could have been recognized by the readers of the New Testament? How do we decide each individual writer's knowledge of the Pseudepigrapha?"[2769] We have no evidence that any of these views were part of accepted teaching in the time of Christ.[2770]

5. The New Testament epistles were written to communities outside of Palestine, and this makes it even more unlikely that the theology of the Pseudepigrapha would have had much influence on word meanings or cultural practices reflected in the writings of Paul, Mark, Luke, or John. Recipients of these letters probably would have no access to the Pseudepigrapha.
6. It is unlikely that Jesus would derive His ideas on *Gehenna* from pseudepigraphal fantasies.[2771] It is much more likely that *Gehenna* meant for Him what it meant in the Old Testament, and this would have been the most probable understanding of the Palestinian audience He addressed.[2772] The descriptions of *Gehenna* in the Targums and Pseudepigrapha are so ridiculous that to connect Jesus in any way with these beliefs casts doubt not only on the inspiration of Scripture but also on the divinity of Christ as well.[2773] One is reminded of Schweitzer's comment on those who attempt to

---

[2767] Craig L. Blomberg, *Jesus and the Gospels: An Introduction and Survey* (Nashville, Tenn.: Broadman & Holman, 1997), 47.

[2768] Sandmel, "Parallelomania," 5.

[2769] Holland, *Contours of Pauline Theology*, 63.

[2770] David Instone-Brewer, personal communication, May 5, 2008.

[2771] James Orr's comment of Jesus' familiarity with and use of apocalyptic literature in general is relevant: "It is difficult to pronounce on the extent to which Jesus was acquainted with current apocalyptic beliefs, or allowed these to color the imagery of parts of His teachings. These beliefs certainly did not furnish the substance of His teaching, and it may be doubted whether they more than superficially affected even its form....What Jesus taught on these subjects sprang from His own Messianic consciousness, with the certainty He had of His triumph over death and His exaltation to the right hand of God. It was in Old Testament prophecy, not in late Jewish apocalypse, that His thoughts of the future triumph of His kingdom were grounded" [italics added]. James Orr, "Jesus Christ," in *The International Standard Bible Encyclopedia*, ed. James Orr (Grand Rapids: Wm. B. Eerdmans Publishing Co., 1915). It is reasonable to assume that His views of *Gehenna* were similarly grounded in His Old Testament.

[2772] In response, it might be argued that when Jesus was referring to *Gehenna*, He was in no way endorsing the pseudepigraphal fantasies. He could simply be using the language of the time. However, it is questionable whether the language of the time ever applied the word *Gehenna* to hell, that is, final condemnation. Furthermore, to use this language without comment does imply an endorsement when it is taken directly from the Old Testament (as Jesus did) and assumes a certain interpretation of the Old Testament that is flatly contradictory to the contexts in which it is used.

[2773] The Jewish Encyclopedia summarizes the range of rabbinic teaching on *Gehenna*. For example, its depth is infinite; it is located (according to one opinion) above the firmament, and yet, according to another, behind dark mountains; the whole world is a lid for *Gehenna*, and it is 1/60th the size of the Garden of Eden; the sun receives its fire from *Gehenna*; the fire of *Gehenna* is 60 times the heat of a

explain Paul's very Jewish thought on the basis of Hellenism. They are, he says, "like a man who should bring water from a long distance in leaky watering-cans in order to water a garden lying beside the stream."[2774] The "stream" of the Old Testament lies at-hand; there is no need to go cross-country to the Pseudepigrapha!

7. Jesus certainly would not have embraced or affirmed these pseudepigraphal fantasies, nor would the majority of Jews living in Palestine. While some Jewish cults (like Mormons today) were fascinated with these fabrications, as Blomberg (above) says, the common people did not concern themselves with them. Indeed, since the exile and the Maccabean revolt (165 BC), the tendency was not assimilation of Greek ideas but all-out rejection of them!
8. Furthermore, a point regarding *Gehenna* which has not been mentioned is that the Old Testament teaches that the final eschatological judgment occurs in the Valley of Jehoshaphat and not in the Valley of Hinnom. Thus, it really makes little difference what the Pseudepigrapha or the rabbis said. The Valley of Hinnom in the Old Testament is not the place of post-mortem condemnation. (See discussion in the next section).
9. The question of "excerpt vs. context"[2775] is not always well attended to. In other words, are the seeming parallels really parallels, or does the term *Gehenna* mean one thing in one context and another in another, and yet are they all accepted as saying the same thing? Frequently, it is best to press for the basic meaning of the word "parallel," two lines that never meet!
10. The references in the Talmuds (AD 400 – 600) record only the conclusions of the rabbis hundreds of years after the time of Christ and say little about the evolutionary development of the ideas that were believed at a certain time.[2776]
11. There is no orderly arrangement of these concepts that would allow us to see a logical, consistent development of the concept of *Gehenna*. Hans Scharen, who believes *Gehenna* refers to final damnation, nevertheless admits that the student of this literature "is confronted with a disarray of thought that is impulsive and often contradictory."[2777]
12. It is possible the interpreter has misunderstood the first century idea. John Piper notes, "It is remarkable how frequently there is the tacit assumption that we can be more confident about how we interpret secondary first-century sources than we are

wood fire; a fiery stream falls upon the head of the sinner in *Gehenna*; according to the Babylonian Talmud, those who have sinned but not led others to sin spend 12 months in *Gehenna*, and then their bodies are destroyed and their souls burned, and the wind strews the ashes under the feet of the pious; when Nebuchadnezzar descended to *Gehenna*, all its inhabitants were fearful that he had come to rule over them; one can escape *Gehenna* by philanthropy, fasting, visiting the sick, reading the *Shemah* and *Hallel*, and eating three meals on the Sabbath; those who commit adultery or who follow the advice of their wives will be cast into *Gehenna*. For these details see *The Jewish Encyclopedia* at http://www.jewish encyclopedia.com/view.jsp?artid=115&letter=G&search=*Gehenna*. Do we really believe that Jesus would have associated Himself with this? For a fuller discussion of all these Jewish speculations and fantasies about hell, see Fox, *Hell in Jewish Literature*.

2774 Quoted by Wright, *Jesus and the Victory of God*, 213.

2775 Sandmel's phrase. See discussion in Sandmel, "Parallelomania," 7 ff.

2776 For decades scholars have cited references to Strack-Billerbeck's *Kommentar zum Neuen Testament aus Talmud und Midrasch*, using these citations to construct a view of Jewish thinking in the first century. However, this source presented "isolated quotations without sufficient regard to context or time period." See Instone-Brewer, *TRENT*, xviii. This is not to say that it is impossible to construct Jewish viewpoints in the first century. The point is that the reported constructions to date are not conclusive.

2777 Scharen, "Part 1: Gehenna in the Synoptics," 325.

of how we interpret the New Testament writers themselves."[2778] In this chapter and the next, we will document how this may well be the case in regard to *Gehenna.* It should be obvious that we can have more confidence in our interpretations in the New Testament than we do of the much less studied Second Temple Literature. We have a much greater awareness of the context due to our knowledge of the Old Testament. Plus, we know that the New Testament is divinely inspired and that the Holy Spirit will illumine our minds to understand it. Piper continues, "Yet there seems to be an overweening confidence in the way some scholars bring their assured interpretation of extra-biblical texts to illumine their less sure reading of the biblical texts."[2779]

13. Related to no. 12 above, it is sometimes assumed that Judaism in the first-century was more-or-less monolithic. In fact, however, there was no "Judaism," but there were many "Judaisms." Thus, even if one branch did equate the Valley of Hinnom with damnation, this by no means indicates that this was the common view of *Gehenna* in the first century. John Piper is correct, "Whether a New Testament writer embraced the particular way of thinking that a scholar has found in the first century is not obvious from the mere existence of that way of thinking."[2780] Consider for example the rather loose definition of "evangelical" today and the many cults, such as the Mormons, who claim that identity. Just because a first-century extra-biblical document has a phrase or word which is found in the New Testament, one must be cautious about saying "this is how first-century Jews understood the world."
14. Finally, the New Testament expressly denounces the pseudepigraphal fantasies. It is likely that these "myths" (Gr *muthos*) were the subject of Paul's warnings to Timothy.

> *As I urged you upon my departure for Macedonia, remain on at Ephesus so that you may instruct certain men not to teach strange doctrines, nor to pay attention to myths and endless genealogies, which give rise to mere speculation rather than furthering the administration of God which is by faith (1 Timothy 1:3–4).*

These "myths" are Jewish myths (Titus 1:4) and refer directly to the fantasy stories found in the pseudepigraphal literature.[2781] The references to "genealogies" points to the speculative extra-biblical "biographies" of various Old Testament characters.[2782]

[2778] Piper, *Future of Justification*, 34.

[2779] Ibid., 35. Piper adds, "We all need to be reminded that the last two hundred years of biblical scholarship is the story not just of systematic categories obscuring the biblical tests [systematic theology], but even more dramatically, of a steady stream of *first-century ideas* sweeping scholarship and then evaporating in the light of stubborn clarity of the biblical texts," ibid. A good example of this is the ever-changing explanation of who Jesus "really was" in the so-called Jesus Quest. For a good survey see Ben Witherington III, *The Jesus Quest: The Third Search for the Jew of Nazareth* (Downers Grove, IL: InterVarsity Press, 1995).

[2780] Piper, *Future of Justification*, 36.

[2781] Regarding this point, Philip Towner says, "This usage especially opens up the possibility that Paul is identifying the practice among the false teachers of speculating on stories about the early biblical characters as well as actual genealogical lists such as occur there or in other more speculative non-canonical Jewish writings (e.g. Jubilees). Speculation fitting roughly into this category was known to have been practiced in Jewish communities, and the reference in 1:7 to the opponents' aspirations to be "teachers of the law" helps to locate the sources of this practice within the repository of Jewish literature (cf. Titus 1:14 and the reference to 'Jewish myths')." Towner, *The Letters to Timothy and Titus*, 110.

[2782] Philo seems to link the term "genealogies" to the myths surrounding the early chapters of Genesis regarding "the punishment of the wicked, and of the honors bestowed on the just." See "Life of Moses," 2.47 in Philo, "On the Life of Moses," 495.

These "strange doctrines" composed of "mere speculation" accurately describe the Pseudepigrapha, that is, a kind of Gnostic Judaism.[2783] They teach "false doctrine" (1 Timothy 1:3); they are "*godless and silly*" (1 Timothy 4:7) and are in contrast to "*the words of faith and sound doctrine*" (v. 6). They appeal to believers who want *"to have their ears tickled"* (2 Timothy 4:3-4) and who allow themselves to be deceived by false teachers; they are not conducive to being "*sound in the faith*" (Titus 1:14). Peter says that these myths are "cleverly *devised*" (2 Peter 1:16), that is, they are imaginative speculations with no historical basis. As Alfred Plummer says, the Judaizers were "adulterating the Gospel" with "worthless traditions and strained misinterpretations"[2784] (2 Corinthians 4:2). This preoccupation with myths, which supposedly led to deeper piety and profound insights into the background of various biblical characters, is rampant in today's fascination with the Gospel of Thomas, of Peter, and the inane stories about Jesus' childhood.

Whether or not these myths refer to the Pseudepigrapha directly is not the point. They clearly describe the character of these documents as anyone who has read them will testify. *Therefore, it is not likely that the inspired writers of Scripture would give them any heed and neither should we.* Because modern liberal scholars do not consider the New Testament documents to be unique, truthful revelations, they have been led astray drawing parallels between them and the New Testament, and interpreting the New Testament in light of this supposed background of pre-understanding of the New Testament writers. Unfortunately, many evangelical scholars have followed suit.[2785]

A good argument against points (4), (5) and (12) above would, of course, be that Jude 14 quotes 1 Enoch 1:9.[2786] Peter also alludes to a passage from a Pseudepigraphal book in 2 Peter. Furthermore, the evidence is strong that John was aware of the Assumption of Moses. Much of the figurative language of the book of Revelation can be seen in Assumption of Moses 10. Some scholars go so far as to say, "Without a knowledge of the Pseudepigrapha it would be impossible to understand our author [John]."[2787]

Are we to conclude that three inspired writers of the New Testament did give heed to these myths? No! If they endorsed it, then that particular saying was not a myth. That they accepted certain statements does not mean they accepted the theology of the book. Penner and Heiser speak to this issue, "Other such instances, like Paul's quotation of pagan Greek poets or lines from the Baal Cycle found in various Old Testament prophetic writings, do not mean that the quoted sources are canonical. If the material was quoted formulaically as Scripture is cited, that would be another matter."[2788] The fact that one

---

[2783] Büchsel, "*genealogia*," in TDNT 1:663.

[2784] Alfred Plummer, *The Second Epistle of Paul to the Corinthians*, Cambridge Greek Testament for Schools and Colleges (Cambridge: Cambidge University Press, 1903), 71.

[2785] This passage (1 Timothy 1:3-4) is also a warning to some Greek professors who instruct their students that unless they are familiar with the pseudepigraphal literature and the Mishnah, they are not qualified to interpret the New Testament. Bauckham says, "Firsthand work on Jewish material should now be virtually a prerequisite for competent historic research in New Testament Studies." Bauckham, *The Jewish World around the New Testament*.

[2786] However, this remains to be proved. Until it can be established that Jude is quoting Enoch, and not a commonly known oral tradition that is attributed to Enoch, one should not so readily assume that Jude knew of this document.

[2787] R. H. Charles, *A Critical and Exegetical Commentary on the Revelation of St. John*, International Critical Commentary (Edinburgh: T. & T. Clark, 1920), 1, lxv.

[2788] Penner and Heiser, *Old Testament Greek Pseudepigrapha with Morphology*, s.v. "Introduction: Relevance for

finds truthful statements in modern cult literature from the Mormons and the Jehovah's Witnesses does not mean that one accepts the books or the theology contained in those books. False cults (like the one represented by the book of Enoch) often quote valid biblical truth. Jude, apparently, considered this particular statement from the false cult to which Enoch belonged to be truthful.[2789]

However, this is not proof that Jude knew the book of Enoch, or that he believed *Gehenna* refers to the hades of the Gospels. He may have been aware of a tradition that was known by some in Palestine which was later included in the book of Enoch. Also, the word *Gehenna* is not found in Enoch anyway. But even if Jude was aware of Enoch, this in no way proves that believers in the first century were generally aware of the other inter-testamental literature or that the apostles considered them sources of valid revelatory information. Furthermore Gentile believers in Corinth, Ephesus, and Rome would hardly be acquainted with this material (although Jewish believers may have been familiar with it).[2790]

The Valley of Jehoshaphat: A Metaphor for Hell?

The Valley of Jehoshaphat on the Plain of Esdraelon would be a more likely metaphor for final damnation in the Pseudepigrapha than the Valley of Hinnom.

The Valley of Jehoshaphat/Megiddo

I will gather all the nations and bring them down to ***the valley of Jehoshaphat****. Then I will enter into judgment with them there on behalf of My people and My inheritance, Israel, whom they have scattered among the nations; and they have divided up My land (Joel 3:2).*

The location of this valley has not been ascertained with certainty. Duane Garrett suggests, "The word 'Jehoshaphat' means 'Yahweh judges' and is most often identified with the famous Valley of Jezreel extending from Mount Carmel past Megiddo and on to

---

Exegesis in Cannonical Material".

2789 For a thoughtful discussion on this difficulty see Kaiser et al., *Hard Sayings of the Bible*, 754-56.

2790 This was suggested by Tom Holland, personal communication, Aug 3, 2006.

Bet Shean and the Jordan River. This valley has seen many historical battles and is often identified as the site of the Battle of Armageddon in Revelation 16:16."[2791]

Joel continues:

> *Let the nations be roused; let them advance into* ***the Valley of Jehoshaphat****, for there I will sit to judge all the nations on every side. Swing the sickle, for the harvest is ripe. Come, trample the grapes, for the winepress is full and the vats overflow—so great is their wickedness! Multitudes, multitudes in* ***the valley of decision****! For the day of the Lord is near in the valley of decision. The sun and moon will be darkened, and the stars no longer shine (Joel 3:12-15, NIV).*

John used these terms to describe the final judgment in the Valley of Armageddon.[2792] The references to judging all the nations, the sickle and the harvest, the darkening of the sun and the moon, and the harvest of grapes are "so similar in Revelation 14:15 and Joel 3:13 that we can hardly take them as anything less than parallel. Moreover, in both Joel 3:13 and Revelation 14 the harvesting of wheat is followed by a harvest of grapes."[2793] This is where the final battle of human history occurs. "*And they gathered them together to the place which in Hebrew is called Har-Magedon*" (Revelation 16:16), a mountain rising above the plain of Megiddo, also known as the Valley of Jezreel or the Plain of Esdraelon. The Valley of Jehoshaphat is commonly associated with the Valley of Megiddo. This plain is about twenty miles south-southeast of Haifa, and the valley today is about twenty miles by fourteen.[2794]

It has been suggested by some that the Valley of Harmon-gog to which Ezekiel refers is in fact the Valley of Jezreel in the plain of Megiddo (Ezekiel 39:11).[2795]

Jesus uses similar imagery in reference to the Day of the Lord in Matthew 13:30, 39, 42, 49, 50; 24:7, 29-31, making us wonder if He had the Valley of Jehoshaphat in mind.

In accordance with the Old Testament the Valley of Hinnom would be a metaphor for a temporal judgment of shame and disgrace by being tossed in the fire (either before or after death). But the Valley of Jehoshaphat would be a better metaphor for eternal damnation, although it is not used that way in the New Testament. Based on the texts in Revelation cited above, the Valley of Jehoshaphat in Joel is the same as the Valley of

---

[2791] Duane A. Garrett, *Hosea and Joel*, New American Commentary (Nashville: Broadman Press, 1997), 378. Joel also calls it the "valley of decision" (Joel 3:14). It is not likely that this valley is equated with the Valley of Hinnom because the Valley of Jehoshaphat seems to be a broad plain. The Hebrew word translated "valley" is properly a "plain between two mountain ridges, or between a mountain and the water" (HAL 847). While it could refer to a narrow valley, it is normally a broad one, and at any rate a very broad one is necessary to accommodate all the nations that will be gathered at this judgment. Geoffrey W. Wood notes that "*ēmeq* suggests a broad valley." Geoffrey E. Wood, "Joel and Obadiah," in *The Jerome Biblical Commentary*, ed. Raymond Edward Brown, Joseph A. Fitzmyer, and Roland Edmund Murphy (Englewood Cliffs, NJ: Prentice-Hall, 1968).

[2792] For a full discussion of these parallels between the gathering of armies in the Valley of Jehoshaphat in Joel 3 and Har-Megiddon in Revelation 14:14-20 and 16 see Beale, *The Book of Revelation: A Commentary on the Greek Text*, 775.

[2793] Michael J. Svigel, "The Apocalypse of John and the Rapture: A Re-evaluation," *Trinity Journal* 22, no. 1 (Spring 2001): 49.

[2794] It is true that since the fourth century the Valley of Jehoshaphat has been linked with the Kidron Valley outside of Jerusalem, but there is no evidence for this association. See Brand, "Gehenna," 878.

[2795] Melvin Hunt, "Megiddo, Plain of," in *Yale Anchor Bible Dictionary*, ed. David Noel Freedman (New York: Doubleday, 1992), 4:679.

Armageddon. Perhaps this is the "Valley" referred to frequently in the Pseudepigrapha.[2796] If that is so, then the commonly assumed equation in the Pseudepigrapha of *Gehenna* as the final resting place of the damned, even if it was true, contradicts the Old Testament. Contrary to Pseudepigraphal fantasies, the Valley of Hinnom in the Old Testament is a place of temporal, not eternal, judgment. The Old Testament says that the place of eternal judgment is the Valley of Jehoshaphat. Thus, all grounds are removed for connecting the Valley of Hinnom with hell in the Gospels.[2797] It was not the Valley of Hinnom, but the Valley of Jehoshaphat that Joel associates with eschatological judgment.

A final minor point must be addressed. According to Zechariah 14:4, when the Lord returns, His feet will stand on the Mount of Olives which is east of Jerusalem. Although there is not enough scriptural detail to know with certainty, Paul Tanner suggests the following sequence of events.

1. Many nations and their armies converge on Israel.
2. The Antichrist and his main army (armies?) position themselves in Israel (Daniel 11:44-45).
3. A multi-nation assault is launched against Jerusalem (Zechariah 12).
4. Jerusalem is ravaged (Zechariah 14:1) and brought to the point of annihilation (some inhabitants are exiled while some remain).
5. Out of this desperate situation, many Jews (but not all of them in light of Zechariah 13) turn in faith to the Lord Jesus Christ (Zechariah 12:10; Hosea 3:5; Acts 3:19-21).
6. As a result of the Jewish "national repentance," Jesus returns in power and glory to the Mount of Olives (Zechariah 14:4; cf. Acts 1:11).
7. Jesus splits the Mount of Olives (Zechariah 14:4-5) and delivers those at Jerusalem who turned to Him (cf. Joel 2:32).
8. "The War of the Great Day of God, the Almighty" (Revelation 16:14).

Possibly, after delivering the Jews at Jerusalem, the Lord then encounters the armies

[2796] First Enoch 53:1-7 itself speaks of a valley in terms very similar to the description in Joel 3:2, 12 of the Valley of Jehoshaphat and equates it with eternal damnation. According to Mare, "In Jewish tradition, 1 Enoch 53:1 speaks of final judgment in a deep valley where all people come to be judged, a place which many equate with the Valley of Jehoshaphat." W. Harold Mare, "Jehoshaphat, Valley of," in *ABD*, ed. David Noel Freedman (New York: Doubleday, 1992), 3:667. Enoch states that the "kings and mighty of the earth" will be gathered for the final judgment in this valley (1 Enoch 53:5). The language is similar to that used by John in describing the destruction of these armies by the Lord Jesus in the valley of Megiddo, that is, Armageddon (Revelation 19:15-18). It is therefore unclear why the accursed valley in 1 Enoch 27:1 is linked by some to the Valley of Hinnom. Charles makes the connection (without proof), citing 1 Enoch 48:9, 54:1, 2, 62:12, 13, 90:26, 27, which never make the connection between the "accursed valley" and Hinnom. The only connection in these verses between the valley and Hinnom is the word "fire." See Charles, *Commentary on the Pseudepigrapha of the Old Testament*, 2:205, s.v. "1 Enoch 27:1".

[2797] While some identify the Valley of Jehoshaphat with the Kidron Valley, Wolff doubts this because "that valley, narrow as it is, is no 'plain' but rather a 'wadi.' Here [in Joel 3] the thought is of a spacious area, though framed by mountains, in which a giant assembly for judgment (vv. 2b, 12b) and a battle of nations (vv. 11, 14) can take place. The name, being symbolic, is completely determined by the significance of the place where Yahweh's act of 'judgment' will come to pass. The prophet knows the geographical location as little as he knows an exact date for the final conflict of Yahweh with the nations. The 'valley—plain of Jehoshaphat' is a cipher; the use of such was quite popular in the emerging apocalypticism." Hans Walter Wolff and S. Dean McBride, *A Commentary on the Books of the Prophets - Joel and Amos*, Hermenia - A Historical and Critical Commentary on the Bible (Philadelphia: Fortress Press, 1977), 76.

that are assembled at *Har-Magedon*. The conflict itself is described in Revelation 19:17-21. Notice verse 19 especially: "*And I saw the beast and the kings of the earth and their armies assembled to make war against Him who sat on the horse and against His army.*" So this does seem to be a "post-2nd coming" event. Joel 3:2 says, "I will gather all the nations and bring them down to the valley of Jehoshaphat. Then I will enter into judgment with them there." In view of the fact that it is unlikely that there will be two massive gatherings of nations for judgment, it is probable that Revelation 19:17-21 should be equated with Joel 3. It is a valley of judgment, and it is a "valley of decision" for the nations (Joel 3:14). The actual place is probably *Har-Magedon*.

If this scenario is correct, there would be no problem with the Lord Jesus returning to Jerusalem first, and then subsequently going to *Har-Magedon* to encounter the Antichrist and all the nations in league with him. The events of Joel 3 and Revelation 19 take place soon after the actual Second Advent to the Mount of Olives. This harmonizes nicely. It appears that when the Lord returns to the Mount of Olives, not every threat against His people has been obliterated. Otherwise, why create a valley of escape for the inhabitants of the city? There is more to do. He must go north and destroy the warring armies gathered against Him in the Valley of Jehoshaphat, the Valley of *Har-Magedon*.

The Valley of Hinnom, *Gehenna*, in the Old Testament, is associated with temporal judgments. It is therefore likely that it could have a temporal reference, that is, destruction of the city, or of a burning garbage dump and also be a metaphor for a supra-historical eschatological judgment. We will explore these options in detail in the next chapter.

Summary

According to the Old Testament, the Valley of Hinnom was a place of temporal judgment on the nation of Israel. In wartime, the bodies of the dead were buried here and for centuries the bodies of criminals were cast into *Gehenna* and burned. After the siege of Jerusalem in AD 70, the Romans heaped up and burned thousands of Jewish bodies in this putrid valley. Before the time of Jesus, we know that the people dumped their trash here, and the burning garbage continued day and night. The fire never went out. As it smoldered beneath the surface, it incinerated smelly garbage. New garbage was dumped on top of old: slimy vegetables, rotting fish, and decaying human refuse smelled up the entire area. Because rotting trash was there, maggots followed, eating the refuse. This was a fire that burned "forever," (i.e., a long time) and those maggots multiplied as they feasted on these rotting corpses for years; people held their noses as they dumped their trash in the ravine. When Jesus spoke of *Gehenna*, this is what His hearers thought of, not eternal damnation. But Jesus used it as a figure of speech for another kind of judgment after death: rebuke, salvation through fire (1 Corinthians 3:15), shame (1 John 2:28), reward for doing bad (2 Corinthians 5:10), and a negative assessment on one's life.

The argument that it became a metaphor for eternal damnation in the Pseudepigrapha is weak and circular and faces too many obstacles to be merely assumed or asserted. Furthermore, there is no evidence that these ideas were widespread around the Sea of Galilee. Indeed, it seems preposterous to believe that either Jesus or His apostles would have implicitly endorsed these pseudepigraphal fantasies, if they even knew about them. While unproven, it would make more sense to understand the Valley of

Jehoshaphat as the location of and metaphor for eternal damnation rather than the Valley of Hinnom.

If one is to assume that first-century Palestinian Jews were familiar with the pseudepigraphical literature or even the ideas that it contained (debatable points as will be shown in chapter 55), the references to *Gehenna* in that literature do not always speak of it as eternal damnation; it is normally used for temporal, temporary, and purifying judgments and never meant the condemnation was irreversible."[2798] Unlike the hell of the New Testament, none of these texts suggest that the duration of this judgment is endless.[2799] The common opinion was that *Gehenna* was a place of doom from which the vast majority escaped after a brief period. If one therefore bases his understanding of *Gehenna* on the Pseudepigrapha and other rabbinical writings, he must at least consider what else the term meant to the writers of these fantasies who used the phrase.

Because the words *Gehenna* and "hell" are freighted with fantastic associations in popular thinking today as well as in the Pseudepigrapha, in the discussion to follow, we will usually translate *Gehenna* as "Valley of Hinnom." This enables the reader to hear the expression as a first-century Palestinian was likely to have heard it.

It is probable that in the first centry, Hinnom and Kidron were viewed as one continuous valley and that the name "Hinnom" was sometimes applied to both areas. Long ago Fyfe argued, "the valley of Hinnom instead of being confined as it usually is in modern times, to the valley south of Jerusalem, includes, if it is not identical with, the glen of Kidron, east of the city (See James Fyfe, *The Hearafter: Sheol, Hades, Hell, the World to Come and the Scripture Doctrine of Retribution According to Law*, 126). Recent archaeological excavations in today's Valley of Kidron have uncovered a first century garbage pit and confirmed this identity. This pit is very similar to the garbage pit of Hinnom described by Jeremiah and suggests that the name "Hinnom" could have been applied to both. Thus, the place name "Hinnom" became a name for a burning garbage pit in "Hinnom-Kidron and suggests that the name "Hinnom" by polyonymia could have been applied to both or, possibly, that Hinnom (the part) is a synecdoche for the whole (Hinnom plus Kidron).

In the following chapters we will suggest that the New Testament references to the burning garbage dump southeast of the modern city of Jerusalem (southwest of the city in Jeremiah's time), do not refer to eternal damnation, but are metaphors for a (1) negative assessment of the believer's life at the Judgment Seat of Christ; (2) the coming national catastrophe of 70 AD; and (3) the corrupt sin nature of man. If the New Testament references to *Gehenna* do not refer to eternal damnation, how does this affect our understanding of its twelve usages in the New Testament? We will discuss these metaphors in chapter 56, but first we must detour to a discussion of *Gehenna* in the Rabbinic literature.

[2798] F. W. Farrar, *Mercy and Judgment: A Few Last Words on Christian Eschatology, with Reference to Dr. Pusey's "What Is of Faith?"* (New York: E. P. Dutton Co., 1881), 183.

[2799] For extensive documentation of this, see ibid., 182-200.

55

Gehenna in the Rabbinic Literature and Targums

IN THE preceding chapter we considered the Old Testament and Pseudepigraphal background for *Gehenna* and concluded that it did not ever refer to the hell described in the New Testament. In the Old Testament it was always connected with a temporal judgment. In the Pseudepigrapha it was a temporary and purifying judgment in the afterlife, and was pregnant with fantastic embellishments that could never be associated with Jesus.

But what about the later literature? Is it possible that the post-AD 70 rabbinic materials may represent an oral tradition that does in fact reflect a first-century worldview? Of course, the answer is a guarded "yes." In this chapter we will consider the possible contributions to first-century understanding of *Gehenna* suggested by the rabbinic literature.

Gehenna in the Rabbinic Literature

By rabbinic literature we refer to the Mishnah, Targums, the Tosephta, and the Talmuds. Because the Talmuds are quite late (AD 200–500), and the Tosephta is insignificant for New Testament interpretation,[2800] our attention here will focus on the Mishnah and the Targums (see the next section below).

In AD 70 the Romans invaded the city of Jerusalem and completely burned it to the ground. The central shrine of Judaism, the temple, which protected the city, was destroyed. All the gold was removed, melted, and used to ornament the walls of the Coliseum in Rome. Over 500,000 Jews were slaughtered, burned alive, or thrown over the walls into the valleys just below the city. Hundreds of thousands were sold as slaves. The Jewish faith verged on total extinction. According to tradition, R. Yohanan ben Zakkai, already in his 70s and close to death, was smuggled out of the city by two of his students.[2801] Yohanan approached the Emperor Vespasian, asking for permission to build an academy for the study of the Jewish faith in Yavneh (Jamnia), a city on the northern border of Palestine about 13 miles south of Jaffa and three miles from the sea.[2802]

[2800] An interesting reference in the Toseptha suggests that punishment in *Gehenna* is temporary, a kind of purgatory. Beth Shamai says: "There are three classes: one for life eternally, one for shame, and for abomination eternally. These are completely evil. The evenly balanced go down to *Gehenna* and squeal and rise again and are healed," Sanh 13:3 quoted in David Instone-Brewer, *Techniques and Assumptions in Jewish Exegesis before 70 CE* (Tübingen: J.C.B. Mohr (Paul Siebeck), 1992), 145.

[2801] Jack P. Lewis, "Jamnia (Jabneh), Council of," in *Yale Anchor Bible Dictionary*, ed. David Noel Freedman (New York: Doubleday, 1992), 3:635.

[2802] This story is probably not completely true. Alon has argued that the rabbi was forced by Titus (Vespasian) to go to Yavneh. He concludes that Yavneh was merely a Roman internment camp for refugees and Rabban Yohanan was a political prisoner and not much more than that. But that it became a center for post-AD 70

It was here, according to the Talmudic legend, that rabbinic Judaism was born (sometimes called Tannaitic Judaism). Now there was no sacrifice, temple, or a high priest. In fact, the priests were subject to the rabbis. The Jewish faith was being modified by the scholars at Yavneh. This break complicates the problem of assigning post-AD 70 concepts to the first-century Jewish worldview and theology. Yet these so-called Tannaitic (AD 70 – 200) writings are a major source for the speculative reconstruction of the beliefs regarding *Gehenna* and the kingdom of God supposedly held by first-century Palestinian peasants living around AD 30.[2803]

During the period from AD 70 to 200 the tenets of what we call rabbinic Judaism emerged and were "repeated," that is, passed on by the Tannaim ("repeaters"). We have no written records of Tannaitic Judaism.[2804] There may have been written sources, but these were always considered inferior to the oral sources, and the oral law, being considered inferior to Torah, was never written down.[2805] Eventually, these traditions were compiled into what are called the Mishnah[2806] around AD 200 and the Tosephta around AD 400.[2807] It is generally believed that the Tosephta is of much less importance.[2808]

Subsequent to the compilation of these Tannaitic materials and the Talmuds (c. AD 400-600), commentaries of various books of the Bible were collected. These are called Midrashim (plural of Midrash, commentary).[2809] The use of these materials to establish

---

Judaism cannot be denied. See Gedalyahu Alon, *Jews, Judaism and the Classical World*, trans. Israel Abrahams (Jerusalem: The Magnes Press, 1977), 269-313.

2803 Regarding the works of Josephus, Fraade asks, "To what extent are his schematic portrayals of Judaism's 3 or 4 'philosophies' or 'schools' (*hairēsis*), as he calls them, colored by his desire to present Judaism in philosophical terms attractive to a Hellenized audience?" (ibid, 3:1056). Josephus never mentions *Gehenna*, and his presentation of the afterlife is of little value in clarifying the views of first-century Judaism. See Farrar, *Mercy and Judgment*. According to Archbishop Ussher, "It is not to be disguised that having promised to derive his materials from the sacred records of the Hebrews, without diminution or addition, he has done this with little fidelity" (quoted in ibid., 195). The same problem is found in rabbinic texts of the third century. "The newly expanded and solidified class of sages sought to position themselves so as to transform Israel's practices, institutions, and self-understandings along rabbinic lines."

2804 After AD 70 rabbinic Judaism [Tannaitic Judaism] emerged. "Without the Temple and without a nation, the focus of piety became the individual, his table, his prayer, his study of the Torah, and particularly the study of the commandments. Through the work of the Tannaim ('repeaters') the oral law was maintained and further developed until it was edited and put into final form, in what is known as the Mishnah, by Judah the Patriarch, A.D. 200. Other Tannaitic materials (Baraitoth) were gathered into the Tosephta ('supplement'), and their work can also be seen in the Midrashim (commentaries on Scripture). Further custodians of rabbinic tradition, the Amoraim ('speakers') continued work that eventually came to fruition in the commentaries on the Mishnah, represented by the Babylonian and Palestinian Talmuds. And thus the course and tone of Judaism was set down to its present manifestations." See D. H. Hagner and George Ladd, "Judaism" in J. D. Douglas, *The New Bible Dictionary*, 3rd ed. (Downers Grove, IL.: InterVarsity Press, 1962), 624.

2805 Instone-Brewer, *TRENT*, 1:7.

2806 The Mishnah became the subject of study in the rabbinical schools both of Palestine and Babylonia, and the resulting commentary is called the Gemara. The Mishnah and the Gemara together from the Talmud, and there are thus two Talmuds, known respectively as the Jerusalem and the Babylonian. See Charles, *Commentary on the Pseudepigrapha of the Old Testament*, 2:687.

2807 Other writings are commonly associated with this literature such as the Baraotot of the Jerusalem and Babylonian Talmuds, the Mekhilta of Rabbi Ishmael (on Exodus), Sipra (on Leviticus), and Sipre (on Numbers and Deuteronomy).

2808 According to Instone-Brewer, the Tosephta is quoted in the Jerusalem Talmud but is not quoted in the Babylonian Talmud. Instone-Brewer, *TRENT*, 1:6.

2809 Ibid., 1:10.

anything regarding the beliefs of first-century Palestinian Judaism is highly questionable.[2810] These texts do not represent Jewish "orthodoxy" in the first few centuries. There were various "Judaisms" including that of the diaspora. Only centuries later did the Palestinian Rabbinate put its stamp on the "popular" Judaism of Palestine, the Judaism practiced by "ordinary" Jews.[2811] Alexander points out, "It would be wrong to assume that Tannaitic literature reflects the beliefs or practices of either of these non-rabbinic groups."[2812] Flusser agrees. "The latter-day Judaism as well as Christianity did not evolve from the religion of Israel in the Old Testament, but from the Jewish religiosity that flourished during the inter-testamental period. This type of religiosity is no longer identical with the creed reflected in the Old Testament."[2813] Yet the ordinary Jews were the target of much of Jesus' ministry. While Christianity certainly *did not evolve* from inter-testamental Judaism (it was *revealed* through Christ and His apostles), as David Flusser says, latter-day Judaism did.

As a result, the only record we have of *Gehenna* in this period is found in five questionable analogies from the Mishnah. Here they are.

> *The disciples of Balaam and the wicked inherit Gehenna and go down to the Pit of Destruction, as it is said, But you, O God, shall bring them down into the pit of destruction; bloodthirsty and deceitful men shall not live out half their days (m. Abot 5.19g).*[2814]

2810 Saldarini cites many problems. (1) There is no normative Judaism in this period. It was very complex and there was considerable conflict between the wealthy (who collected taxes for the Romans) and the majority. (2) At that point, Rabbinic Judaism was not even dominant and had not been articulated. (3) There is considerable evidence that these rabbinic sources retrojected their understanding of Jewish life and institutions onto Judaism as far back as Ezra in the fifth century. (4) "New Testament scholars who have used rabbinic literature have often succumbed to "parallelomania," the associative linking of similar words, phrases, patterns, thoughts, or themes, in order to claim the influence or dependence of one text or tradition on another. Many of the earlier studies using rabbinic sources were based on isolated and superficial similarities in very dissimilar texts. Their argument for a relationship between the New Testament and rabbinic literature was based on the assumptions that the later traditions in rabbinic literature were unchanged from the 1st century, and that the fabric of Judaism was uniform enough for literary and theological details to be related to one another as if deriving from one context." Anthony Saldarini, "Rabbinic Material and the New Testament," in *The Anchor Yale Bible Dictionary*, ed. David Noel Freedman (New York: Doubleday, 1992), 5:602-04. Bruce Chilton issues a similar warning. "First, the relatively late date of the literature must be taken into account, although the continuities between rabbinic Judaism and Pharisaism of the first century suggest some analogies between the Gospels and rabbinica. Second, a recognition of the social and religious transformations involved in the emergence of rabbinic Judaism must alert the reader to the possibility of anachronistic attributions or to the presentation of early teachers as spokesmen of later theologies." Bruce Chilton, "Rabbinic Traditions and Writings," in Bruce D. Chilton, "Targums," in *Dictionary of Jesus and the Gospels*, ed. Joel B. Green, Scot McKnight, and I. Howard Marshall (Downers Grove, IL: InterVarsity Press, 1992), 659.

2811 According to Penner and Heiser, "There can be no doubt after reading the Pseudepigrapha that Judaism during the relevant period was hardly monolithic. That is, the idea of a 'normative Judaism,' an idea once held widely, is rightly set aside in recognition that there was more than one form of Judaism during the time period from which the Pseudepigrapha derives." Penner and Heiser, *Old Testament Greek Pseudepigrapha with Morphology*, s.v. "Why Should We Read and Study the Pseudepigrapha?".

2812 Alexander, "Torah and Salvation in Tannaitic Literature," 262.

2813 David Flusser, "A New Sensitivity in Judaism and the Christian Message," *Harvard Theological Review* 61(1968): 109.

2814 Mishnah, Fourth Division, Pirkē Abot 5:19G, Neusner, *The Mishnah: A New Translation*, 688. See Pirkē Aboth, 5, 22 in Charles, ed. *The Apocrypha and Pseudepigrapha of the Old Testament in English*, 2:709. This is the only place in the Pseudepigrapha (per Charles) where the term "pit of destruction" is used. Therefore, there is insufficient evidence to clearly link it with eternal damnation in the Pseudepigrapha, especially when it seems to echo the idea of premature death in the Psalms.

In this passage the Mishnah equates the Valley of Hinnom with the Pit of Destruction in Psalm 55:23, a reference to physical destruction by premature death, not eternal damnation. It can easily be understood to mean that the bold-faced (shameless) man faces shame and a premature death. In fact, that is exactly what the verse says, they shall "***not live out half their days***" (m. Abot 5:19g).

If one chooses to see eternal damnation in this Mishnaic passage, the following train of logic must be presupposed:

1. Psalm 55:23 speaks of physical death of David's enemies.
2. The Mishnah changed the meaning from physical death to eternal damnation.
3. The word used for eternal damnation is *Gehenna.*
4. Therefore *Gehenna* in first-century Palestine meant eternal damnation.
5. Therefore even though His own Bible understood "pit of destruction," as temporal death, Jesus preferred the meaning of the Pseudepigrapha.

In a second citation we read,

He would say, "The shameless go to Gehenna, and the diffident [reserved, unassertive] to the garden of Eden."[2815]

A theme in the Targums is that *Gehenna* was created during the creation week and was the place of eternal damnation and the Garden of Eden was created for the just.[2816] This could therefore be the thought in the Mishnah, which refers to Psalm 55:24-25 above. However, there is nothing in the context of the Mishnah and more importantly in Psalm 55 that suggests that eternal damnation is in view.[2817]

In a third Mishnaic reference we read,

In this regard did sages say, "So long as a man talks too much with a woman, (1) he brings trouble on himself, (2) wastes time better spent on studying Torah, and (3) ends up an heir of Gehenna."[2818]

There is nothing in the context of this passage, indeed it seems ridiculous, to say that a man who talks too much to his wife faces eternal damnation. Rather he is less of a man, not a leader in his home; he should be ashamed, and his inheritance is garbage.

R. Judah says, "Most ass drivers are evil, most camel drivers are decent, most sailors are saintly, the best among physicians is going to Gehenna, and the best of butchers is a partner of Amalek."[2819]

2815 Pirkē Abot 5:20 B, Neusner, *The Mishnah: A New Translation*, 689.

2816 David J. Powys, *'Hell': A Hard Look at a Hard Question: The Fate of the Unrighteous in New Testament Thought* (Carlisle, PA: Paternoster Press, 1998), 177-79.

2817 This reference was added to the Mishnah by a later author who is unknown, Charles, *Commentary on the Pseudepigrapha of the Old Testament*, 2:709.

2818 Abot (3), m. Abot 1:5, Neusner, *The Mishnah: A New Translation*, 673. Citations from m. 'Abot are controversial. This section of the Mishnah probably dates from around AD 250. Its connection with the rest of the Mishnah has long been a subject of debate. Chapter 6 'Abot de Rabbi Nathan it is of medieval origin. See Alexander, "Torah and Salvation in Tannaitic Literature," 274.

2819 m. Quiddushin 4:14L, Neusner, *The Mishnah: A New Translation*, 498.

While this could be a joke about eternal damnation, there is nothing in the context that requires this. It can just as easily be saying that these poor souls deserve a shameful burial in the Valley of Hinnon.

Finally, in a fifth citation we read,

and the judgment of the wicked in Gehenna is twelve months.[2820]

It is not difficult to imagine that the judgment of *Gehenna* here does refer to what we would call "hell." However, if it does, it is the only clear reference to *Gehenna* as "hell" from AD 70 to 200. It may only represent the conclusions of the compiler of the Mishnah in AD 200, possibly derived from the Pseudepigrapha, more than 100 years after the time of Christ. It is also possible that 12 months of judgment are a metaphor for 12 months of sitting in a garbage heap in shame and disgrace (remember Job). Whatever *Gehenna* refers to here, it is unlikely that it is the same as the "hell" of the New Testament, which lasts considerably longer than 12 months.

The temporal nature of *Gehenna* in the rabbinic literature warrants further comment. Rabbinic Judaism, unlike the New Testament, had no concept of eternal, endless torment. For the Rabbis, *Gehenna* was of limited duration. David Powys, in his exhaustive study of *Gehenna* in the rabbinic literature, concluded, "It is therefore not certain that '*Gehenna*' when employed in the early rabbinical literature consistently or ordinarily denoted unending suffering."[2821] The Targum of Isaiah tells us that *Gehenna* lasts only until the righteous have seen enough torture. In the Babylonian Talmud we read, "The judgment of the ungodly is for ten months" (m. Adyoth, 2, 10),[2822] and Abhoda Zara says, "*Gehenna* is nothing but a day in which the impious shall be burned."[2823] Why do interpreters extract from the rabbinic materials the references to fire and brimstone and neglect those references which limit its duration and then carry this modified rabbinic view of *Gehenna* into the New Testament?[2824]

That's it! The entire evidence for the equation of *Gehenna* with hell in the Tannaitic literature is based on five references, of uncertain date, of questionable meaning and derivation, compiled about AD 200! For this reason, the whole program of using these Tannaitic materials to construct a view of pre-AD 70 Judaism's view of *Gehenna* should be hotly contested.[2825] Part of the problem is that we are unsure of the dating of some of these documents, which has been demonstrated to be highly questionable; it is reached on subjective grounds; and we are sometimes dealing with margins of error of 200 years.[2826] Evans notes, "The principle dangers of making use of rabbinic literature are anachronism

[2820] m. Edduyot 2:10F, ibid., 646.

[2821] Powys, *'Hell': A Hard Look at a Hard Question: The Fate of the Unrighteous in New Testament Thought*, 190.

[2822] F. W. Farrar, *Eternal Hope* (London: Macmillan and Co., 1878), 82.

[2823] Quoted in ibid., 82.

[2824] Of course these passages could be used to support one version of annihilationism, which says that unbelievers will experience punishment but will then be annihilated.

[2825] As early as 1930 Burton Scott Easton demonstrated the difficulty of using rabbinic sources as direct evidence for conditions at the time of Christ. He noted, "The Talmudists often have no hesitation in revising the past in any matter that does not seem right to the mind of a later age." See B. S. Easton, Christ in the Gospels, 1930 quoted in Perrin, *The Kingdom of God in the Teaching of Jesus*, 55.

[2826] Alexander, "Rabbinic Judaism and the New Testament," 240.

and misleading generalization."[2827] Citing Fitzmyer's criticism of this tendency to use the Mishnah and Talmuds to describe first-century Judaism, Douglas Moo says, "Fitzmyer offers a rather strong criticism of E. P. Sanders's work on *Paul and Palestinian Judaism.* He finds Sanders's two basic assumptions in his use of rabbinic materials to be unfounded and says that 'the whole question of the relevance of rabbinic material for the interpretation of Pauline writings needs serious, new assessment.'"[2828] Powys adds, "There is no sure ground in this field of inquiry."[2829]

In spite of this, scholars seem quite flexible in how they utilize Mishnaic literature to substantiate their interpretations of the New Testament. If the Mishnah supports their view, they will cite it as proof. However, if the Mishnah contradicts their position, they will point out that after all it was written long after the time of Christ, and we do not know for sure if what it says reflects Second Temple Judaism.[2830]

The attempts to derive the teachings of biblical Judaism (i.e., pre-AD 70) from the rabbinic literature are fraught with difficulties. After the fall of the temple in AD 70, rabbinic Judaism triumphed over the other "Judaisms" which had opposing views. These opposing parties were greater in number than the Rabbinics. It must be remembered that those who triumph are not known for preserving the viewpoints of their opponents. Tom Holland's analysis of this issue deserves our attention.

> *These opposing parties were far from being peripheral groups. They probably had greater numerical support than the Rabbinics themselves had. To say that the Rabbinic texts represent Judaism is not only presuming that they accurately and faithfully recorded the rabbinical oral tradition; it also ignores the facts of history. Triumphant parties, whether political or religious, do not promote or even preserve the teachings of those whom they have conquered. It is massive presumption to assume that pre-AD 70 Judaism is substantially mirrored in the Rabbinic texts. At most, these texts mirror a part of, and certainly not most of, Second Temple Judaism. In other words, it is always the triumphant who write the official account of history, and it is their account. As it would be foolish to say that Lutheranism represented pre-Reformation Christianity, so it would be well off the mark to claim that Rabbinic Judaism represented Second Temple Judaism.*[2831]

Alexander notes that it is unlikely that in the rabbinical sources, the quotations we have are from the rabbis to whom they are ascribed.[2832] "Time and again," he says, "we find

---

[2827] Craig A. Evans, *From Prophecy to Testament: The Function of the Old Testament in the New* (Peabody: Hendrickson Publishers, 2004), 18.

[2828] Douglas J. Moo, "Book Reviews. "Righteousness" in the New Testament: "Justification" in the United States Lutheran-Roman Catholic Dialogue. By John Reumann. With responses by Joseph A. Fitzmyer and Jerome D. Quinn. Philadelphia: Fortress/New York and Ramsey: Paulist, 1982, xvii - 278 pp.," *Journal of the Evangelical Theological Society* 27, no. 1 (March 1984): 103.

[2829] Powys, *'Hell': A Hard Look at a Hard Question: The Fate of the Unrighteous in New Testament Thought*, 433.

[2830] For example, in response to Lohse's article (Eduard Lohse, "sunedrion," in TDNT 7:868–70), who argues from the Mishnah that there were many violations of Jewish law in the trials of Christ, Bock correctly observes, "The uncertainty about these supposed violations rests partially on the question of whether these laws are as old as the early first century A.D., given that the Mishnah was composed over a century later." See Bock, Luke 9:51-24:53, 1792. Yet Bock often cites the Mishnah for clarification of certain New Testament passages. Cf. Ibid., 476, 479, 523, 542, 1115, 1218, 1258.

[2831] Holland, *Contours of Pauline Theology*, 202.

[2832] Ibid., 240.

them [New Testament scholars] quoting texts from the 3rd, 4th, or 5th centuries A.D., or even later, to illustrate Jewish teaching in the 1st century."[2833]

Steven Fraade concludes,

> *Most of what we think we know of the lives and teachings of the mishnaic sages known as the tanna'im (first 2 centuries AD) has been filtered through the works of the post-mishnaic amora'im (3rd through 4th centuries AD in Palestine). The same can be said for the other major rabbinic constructions of the third century, those being the earliest collections of rabbinic scriptural commentary or midrash (the Mekiltas, the Sifra, and the Sifres); while incorporating traditional raw materials with long prehistories, they configure them according to the pedagogical plans and purposes of those 3rd-century documents.*
> ***We therefore have virtually no internal or external direct witnesses to Judaism of Palestine between the year 90 C.E. and the early 3d century***[2834] *[emphasis added].*

If the evidence is so scanty and uncertain, why is it that the majority of biblical scholars have connected the Valley of Hinnom with eternal damnation? No doubt the fear of being accused of heresy has silenced the public comment of many. "After all, everyone "knows" that *Gehenna* means hell." "Are you questioning the doctrine of eternal damnation?" For the record, this writer is not. The question is, "Does the word '*Gehenna*' have any relevance to the biblical doctrine of hell?" It does not.

Probably the Latin Vulgate's use of the word has also been a factor. Also, Charles's influential *Commentary on the Pseudepigrapha of the Old Testament* has had enormous impact. Even though there are only five direct references to the word *Gehenna* in the Pseudepigrapha, every time Charles sees the word "abyss," or "pit," or "accursed valley" in his commentary, he will say, without proof, that this refers to *Gehenna* (his first assumption) and that *Gehenna* refers to eternal damnation (his second unproven assumption).[2835]

However, there is no doubt that the main source of the equation of *Gehenna* with eternal damnation derives from the fact that this equation was often held by the early church fathers and has been the most prominent view of interpreters who followed them. Yet, there is no unanimity among the Fathers on their view of the afterlife. Some believed in universalism;[2836] some believed that the duration of hell was limited.[2837] Apparently,

---

[2833] Ibid., 244. While much is often made of the "oral tradition" that lies behind these later writings, it is overlooked that AD 70 and the Bar Kochba rebellion (AD 135) created a radical discontinuity in the history of Judaism before and after AD 70. Thus the burden of proof is on those who assume continuity between supposed pre-AD 70 oral traditions and Jewish writings of later centuries.

[2834] Fraade, "Juda (Place) - Judaism," 3:1055. Ridderbos concurs, saying that because of the lack of consistency in eschatological outlook in this material, "it is very difficult to state accurately what the future outlook of the Jews was at the beginning of the Christian era." Ridderbos, *The Coming of the Kingdom*, 11.

[2835] Of course the New Testament has different words for hell and the writers of the Pseudepigrapha could also have had different words, *Gehenna* being only one of them. Instone-Brewer comments, "Arguably 'the chains' or 'Tartarus' is a separate location, but it refers to the same concepts without referring to '*Gehenna*' (e.g. Luke 13.28; Matthew 3.12; 8.12; 13.42, 50; 22.13; 24.51; 25.41, 46) and 'hades' is linked with these same concepts (Luke 6.23, 24; cf. Matthew 8.11-12)." David Instone-Brewer, personal communication, Oct 24, 2010. That said, there needs to be some connection between *Gehenna* and these other terms to establish an identity. Charles gives none.

[2836] Clement of Alexandria (c. AD 218) in Clement of Alexandria, Fragments, III, Comments on the 1 John, s.v. "1 John 2:2".

[2837] According to F. W. Farrar this was the view of Ambrose on Psalm 1.

fifteen hundred years later, Luther thought that nonbelievers could come to faith in the afterlife.[2838]

Like some of their other errors, such as justification by faith plus works, salvation by baptism, the impossibility of a second repentance, confusion about the deity of Christ and the Trinity, uncertainty about the extent of the canon, and denial of eternal security, this became something one does not have to think about. It was the basis for the Catholic ruminations about purgatory and was thus embedded in Christian theology ever since.

Gehenna in the Aramaic Targums

A second category of rabbinic literature is the Aramaic Targums. As spoken Hebrew declined after the Babylonian captivity, the dominant language in Palestine became Aramaic. It became necessary to provide an Aramaic translation of the Old Testament to be read in the synagogues. However, even though there was a long period of oral tradition, most of these Aramaic translations, called Targums, were compiled long after the New Testament era. Actually, they are paraphrases more than translations, a kind of "Living Bible" of the era.[2839] Their goal was to explain the reconstructed Judaism (post-AD 135) to the common people. With a possible exception of a few scraps found at Qumran, there were no written Targums available during the New Testament period.

While there may be elements in these documents that were contemporaneous with the New Testament, "such a case remains always to be made, and may not be assumed."[2840] Bruce Chilton says, "The myth of the Targums as the Bible of the people has been exploded."[2841] It has been suggested that it was upon these paraphrases the Jewish people relied for their understanding of the sacred text, and hence this affected their understanding of the Old Testament in the first century.[2842] Although a few of these paraphrases seem to be of first-century origin, most of them were compiled hundreds of years later, some in the fifth to ninth centuries AD.[2843] Nevertheless, there is almost a consensus among contemporary scholars that these documents contain much material that can illuminate the background and word meanings in the New Testament.[2844]

[2838] Martin Luther, for example, seems to have left the door open: "It would be quite a different question whether God can impart faith to some in the hour of death or after death so that these people could be saved through faith. Who would doubt God's ability to do that?" Martin Luther, "Letter to Hans von Rechenberg," in *Luther's Works*, ed. J. J. Pelikan, H. C. Oswald, and H. T. Lehmann (Philadelphia: Fortress Press, 1968), 43:53.

[2839] "They are interpretive translations, and these interpretations can vary from the paraphrase of a word to an extensive explanation of a word or a verse," A. du Toit, *The New Testament Milieu* (Halfway House, London: Orion Publishers, 1998), s. v. "Aramaic Translations".

[2840] Bruce Chilton, *Judaic Approaches to the Gospels* (Atlanta: Scholars Press, 1994), 311.

[2841] Ibid., 310.

[2842] Roger Le Deaut, "Targumic Literature and New Testament Interpretation," *Biblical Theological Bulletin* 4, no. 3 (October 1974): 244.

[2843] The Targums of Onkelos and Jonathan, which are often quoted, appear to be in the third century. Schürer, *A History of the Jewish People in the Time of Jesus Christ: First Division*, 1:155. The Targum of the Psalms is of very uncertain date. The best current guess is that it was composed from the fourth to the sixth century AD. See *The Targum of the Psalms*, trans. David M. Stec, vol. 16, The Aramaic Bible (Collegeville, MN: Liturgical Press, 2004), 2.

[2844] P. Nickels, *Targum and New Testament: A Bibliography Together with a New Testament Index* (Rome: Pontifical Biblical Institute, 1967).

The Targum of Job is dated between AD 476 and 942,[2845] and that of Proverbs is of unknown date, estimates range from the middle of the second century to the eighth or ninth centuries.[2846] "But care must also be taken lest the perspective of *later materials* be accepted uncritically as representative of an *earlier period*, thus resulting in anachronistic exegesos. There are clearly readings in the Targums which presuppose events long after the death of Jesus."[2847] The Aramaic of the Targums is not that of the first century. Furthermore, the Judaism of the first century is not monolithic. Therefore, it is impossible to say that a reading of one Targum represents "normative" pre-AD 70 Jewish beliefs. This fact plus the quality of the translations has given many scholars pause in how to use them in interpreting the New Testament.[2848]

If the interpretations found in the Targums represent Old Testament understanding that Jesus accepted, serious problems arise. This is especially true of the many Targumic references to *Gehenna*. For example, the Masoretic text of the Old Testament in Psalm 68:13 is rendered by the NASB, "When the Almighty scattered the kings there. It was snowing in Zalmon." From this Old Testament passage the Targum on the Psalms paraphrases, "When she scattered her hand over the sea in prayer, the Almighty humbled the kingdoms; and for her sake he purified *Gehenna* (to be) like the snow; he delivered her from the shadow of death" (Targum Psalm 68:15).[2849]

In Targum Psalm 37:20, we are told that the wicked will perish "and they shall be destroyed in the smoke of *Gehenna*." The Masoretic Text reads, "*But the wicked will perish; and the enemies of the Lord will be like the glory of the pastures, they vanish—like smoke they vanish away*" (Psalm 37:20). The Masoretic Text understands this as a temporal judgment, while the Targum (written 400 years after the time of Christ) mistranslates the psalm and uses it to show that *Gehenna* (which is not even mentioned in the Masoretic Text) is eternal. Many other illustrations of this kind of exaggerated exegesis could be cited.[2850]

2845 *The Targum of Job*, trans. Celine Mangan, vol. 15, The Aramaic Bible (Edinburgh: T. & T. Clark, 1991), 6-7.

2846 *The Targum of Proverbs*, trans. John F. Healey, vol. 15, The Aramaic Bible (Endinburgh: T. & T. Clark, 1991), 10.

2847 Chilton, "Targums," 802.

2848 For discussion of the many New Testament passages that might possibly be clarified by the Targumic literature, see Le Deaut, "Targumic Literature and New Testament Interpretation," 243-89.

2849 "Ps. 68:15,"*The Targum of the Psalms*, 130. This Targum refers to *Gehenna* 17 times. "It is mentioned in connection with fire and smoke (21:10; 37:20; 120:4; 140:11), darkness (88:13), and decay (49:15). It is a place of judgment (49:10, 11, 16; 50:21), but from which one can be delivered (69:16; 103:4); and God even purified *Gehenna* to be like the snow."

2850 Ibid., 219. Targum Psalms 120:4 states that the lying lips of the psalmist's enemies will be judged by "the broom tree that burns in *Gehenna* from below." Yet the Masoretic Text reads, "Sharp arrows of the warrior, with the burning coals of the broom tree" (Psalm 120:4). Again, this makes no mention of *Gehenna*. Which version of this would Jesus affirm, His Old Testament or some speculative oral tradition behind the later Targum? Targum Psalm 140:11 reads, "Let burning coals from heaven come upon them; and may he make them fall into the fire of *Gehenna* with the sparks of debris, so that they may not rise to everlasting life. The man who speaks slander cannot be established in the land of the living; for the man of violence, let evil hunt him down, let the angel of death strike him down into *Gehenna*." Yet the Masoretic Text reads, "May burning coals fall upon them; may they be cast into the fire, into deep pits from which they cannot rise. May a slanderer not be established in the earth; may evil hunt the violent man speedily" (Psalm 140:10-11). Again, there is no mention of *Gehenna*. The Targums have a tendency to exaggerate these judgments that do not even mention *Gehenna*. When these Aramaic translators see words like "deep pits" and "burning coals," they read *Gehenna* into this and then make a further assumption that *Gehenna* refers to hell. Targum Psalms 49:11 has David saying, "For the wise one shall see the wicked being judged in *Gehenna*." Yet the Masoretic Text

The Targum of Isaiah was compiled after AD 70, but no doubt it reflects rabbinic Judaism from the inter-testamental era and possibly first-century Palestine.[2851] It mentions *Gehenna* once.[2852] The Targum on Isaiah 66:24 reads,

> *And they shall go forth and look on the bodies of the sinful men who have rebelled against my Memra [word]; for their breaths will not die and their fire will not be quenched, and the wicked shall be judged in Gehenna until the righteousness will say concerning them, "we have seen enough."*[2853]

The Masoretic Text reads,

> *Then they will go forth and look on the corpses of the men who have transgressed against Me. For their worm will not die and their fire will not be quenched; and they will be an abhorrence to all mankind (Isaiah 66:24).*

Once again, one can see the Targumic exaggeration. The Old Testament simply says, "*They will be an abhorrence to all mankind.*" From this, the Targum discerns the meaning to be that they will be judged in *Gehenna* and will be released when the righteous have concluded they have seen enough torture. Can anyone seriously believe that this view of *Gehenna* influenced Jesus' views on the subject?

The Targum also mentions *Gehenna* in Isaiah 26:19. "For *Gehenna* has long been prepared in view of their sins; indeed, the eternal king has made it ready, deepening and widening its dwelling. Fire burns in it as an abundant wood, the Memra [word] of the Lord like a mighty stream of brimstone, it burns in it."[2854] In this passage *Gehenna* is a pit in the earth, and in 33:17 *Gehenna* is a "land" on earth. These conceptions have no parallel in the New Testament. The rebellious people face "retribution in *Gehenna* where the fire burns all the day."[2855]

---

reads, "For he sees that even wise men die; the stupid and the senseless alike perish and leave their wealth to others" (Psalm 49:10). The Targumic translation from Hebrew in the Aramaic is quite creative here. There is no mention of eternal damnation in the Masoretic Text. In fact, a few verses earlier in the Masoretic Text we read, "No man can by any means redeem his brother or give to God a ransom for him—For the redemption of his soul is costly, and he should cease trying forever—That he should live on eternally, that he should not undergo decay" (Psalm 49:7-9). Yet the Targum (which some suggest may reflect Jesus' understanding of *Gehenna*) translates, "A wicked man will surely not redeem his brother who has been taken captive, nor will he give to God his ransom which if he gave (it), would be as precious as the redemption of his own soul, and his misery and punishment would cease forever and he would yet live forever and not see the judgment of *Gehenna*" (Psalm 49:8-10). The Masoretic Text refers to the decay of the body in the tomb, and the Targum exaggerates this into eternal damnation of *Gehenna*. In the Masoretic Text of Psalm 69:15, the psalmist prays, "May the flood of water not overflow me nor the deep swallow me up, nor the pit shut its mouth on me." But in the Targum we read, "Let not a mighty king exile me, and let not a strong ruler swallow me up and let not *Gehenna* be opened up for her mouth to cover over me" (Psalm 69:15). The Masoretic Text understands the pit as the grave, and once again, the Targum exaggerates this to mean eternal damnation in *Gehenna* which is not mentioned in the Masoretic Text, ibid 102.

2851 Chilton says that the Isaiah Targum was composed between AD 70 and 135 and then completed sometime before AD 333. Chilton, *Judaic Approaches to the Gospels*, 250-51.

2852 *The Isaiah Targum*, vol. 11, The Aramaic Bible (Edinburgh: T. & T. Clark, 1987), xxiv-xxv. However, it was the product of many generations of work over a period of time. It cannot be said to represent a definite historical period (ibid., xxv.). Thus it is impossible to assign a particular passage to either pre- or post-AD 70 Judaism.

2853 "Isa. 66:24," ibid., 128.

2854 "Isa. 30:33," ibid., 61.

2855 "Isa. 65:5," ibid., 123.

Similar creative exegesis can be found in the Targum[2856] of Qohelet. In Qohelet 6:6 the Targum opines that if one does not occupy himself with the study of Torah "on the day of his death his soul goes down to *Gehenna*."[2857] The Masoretic Text reads, "Do not all go to the same place" (Ecclesiastes 6:6), that is, the grave.

As an illustration of the tenuous nature of Targumic associations with New Testament references to the Valley of Hinnom, consider this statement from Bruce Chilton: "In much the same way, Jesus in Mark 9:48 links a phrase from Isaiah 66:24 to the idea of punishment in *Gehenna*, a linkage also attested in the Targum."[2858] However, there is little in Isaiah 66:24 which requires that the clauses "*their worm will not die, nor will their fire be quenched*" refer to eternal damnation. In context they clearly refer to judgments of a temporal nature. Chilton's logic goes like this,

1. Targumic references to *Gehenna* are interpretations of many Old Testament passages which do not mention the word *Gehenna*.
2. Some of these references may reflect the beliefs of Jews in pre-AD 70 Palestine.
3. Jesus, a product of His age, would possibly accept these interpretations rather than those of His own Bible, the Old Testament.
4. Even though *Gehenna* is not mentioned in Isaiah 66:24 and even though the images refer to temporal judgments on dead bodies, it is interpreted as eternal damnation because that is how the Targums viewed it and hence were possibly a popular conception in first-century Palestine.
5. Thus *Gehenna* in the New Testament is most likely a reference to eternal damnation even though it is never used that way in the Bible Jesus used, that is, the Old Testament. Yet, his points (2) and certainly (3), (4), and (5) are questionable.

If we are to accept the variegated descriptions of *Gehenna* in the Targums, one would conclude it is on land and in a pit; it was or will be purified white as snow; it is a place of darkness, fire and brimstone; its duration is temporary until the righteous have seen enough torture; and it is a place where the bodies, not the immaterial souls, of the wicked will rot with worms and burn. Is it a valid procedure to pull out some aspects of the Targumic depictions such as fire, darkness, and burning, and ignore the others, and then use those aspects as illuminating details behind the New Testament references to the Valley of Hinnom?

Analysis of these documents and their possible relevance to the New Testament is a vast field of study. Only experts who have devoted years to the task are qualified to comment. This writer is certainly no expert and hence his observations should be read

[2856] *The Targum of Qohelet*, trans. Peter S. Knobel, vol. 15, The Aramaic Bible (Edinburgh: T. & T. Clark, 1991), 15. The Targum of Ecclesiastes (Qohelet) mentions *Gehenna* six times. Once again, the date of its compilation is uncertain, but it seems to have been translated sometime after the sixth century AD. There is little relationship between the Masoretic Text and the Targumic interpretation of it. In Ecclesiastes 9:14, for example, the "small city" of the Masoretic Text is spiritualized to become "the body of a man." Evil inclinations can enter this body and "capture him in the great snares of *Gehenna*." Thus this is a snare that occurs in this life and not in eternity. At any rate, what relevance does this have to the first-century understanding of *Gehenna*? None! The "large seigeworks" of the Masoretic Text are spiritualized to become "snares of *Gehenna*" in the Targums. "Qohelet 9:14," ibid., 46.

[2857] "Qohelet 6:6," ibid., 36.

[2858] Chilton, "Targums," 803.

in that light. But perhaps it is time to bring in outside accountants who are not members of the guild! It does appear, however, that a serious work on these documents from an evangelical perspective (such as Larry Helyer's work on the Second Temple literature)[2859] is needed. A perusal of the critical comments on these sources leaves the present writer with the impression that the habitual critical fascination with parallels is at work here. Only with difficulty can one discern a true parallel to some New Testament sayings in their writings. They may be utilized to help us understand possible Jewish interpretations of the Old Testament many centuries after the time of Christ. However, the relevance of those interpretations for understanding the New Testament is often oblique. For Jesus and His followers, the intended meaning of the Old Testament writers is more likely the basis of their understandings.

Summary

With eager anticipation that he is on the verge of some new discoveries in his area of biblical studies, Professor Jones sips his morning cup of coffee. As the caffeine begins to awaken his brain in the early morning hour, he opens again to the documents he discovered in the remains of an old church several months ago. The year is AD 4010. Scores of similar documents have been under careful scrutiny by New Testament scholars attempting to understand the general beliefs of Christians in the twentieth century. This newly discovered document refers to God as "Jehovah" and seems to have been written by someone whose last name begins with "arms," perhaps referring to a man who last name was Arms or, possibly, Armstrong.

What is particularly striking is that the view of *Gehenna* in this manuscript seems to correlate well with some other documents written by two men from England, Wenham and Stott. In all three sources *Gehenna* is viewed as annihilation, cessation of being, and the place of literal physical destruction. This seems to establish that there was a wide body of Christians in this era from vastly different geographical locales who understood the New Testament to teach that there is no eternal hell, rather, only nonexistence. No doubt, Professor Jones concluded, this sheds light on the frequent references to *Gehenna* found in much of the literature of this period.

With growing satisfaction over his find, he picks up his pen and begins to write an article for the *Biblical Studies Journal* entitled, "The View of Twentieth Century Christians on Post-Mortem Damnation: Recent Manuscript Evidence."

From the standpoint of those of us who live in the twentieth century, such an approach would appear ludicrous. This has a number of methodological errors.

First, Professor Jones assumed on the basis of a few documents that there was a common view of this subject shared by the majority of writers in the twentieth century. In fact, this was not a widespread view, and the document he found was from a non-Christian cult called the Jehovah's Witnesses. Their prolific tract distribution had resulted in a widespread dissemination of their views. He did not fully grasp that there were hundreds of Christian sects during this period, all disagreeing with one another on various issues.

2859 Larry R. Helyer, *Exploring Jewish Literature of the Second Temple Period: A Guide for New Testament Students* (Downers Grove, IL: InterVarsity Press, 2002).

Second, instead of interpreting many other writers of the era on the basis of the internal evidence of their own writings and how they understood the New Testament, he interpreted them from the standpoint of what he thought was a widely accepted view of the time.

This scenario represents the approach of many New Testament scholars over the past century with their fascination for all things pseudepigraphal. They often write as if there was a monolithic Judaism from 200 BC to AD 200, even though they know, or at the very least *should* know, this is not the case. Many Jewish sects were in existence, and to extract a viewpoint from a few of them and conclude this was a shared viewpoint is often very tenuous.

But even more serious is the second tendency illustrated in Professor Jones's approach. The Jehovah's Witnesses interpreted the New Testament references to "destruction" as annihilation of being. Since that was the "shared" view of the era, it is likely, Professor Jones's contemporaries argued, that this was the view of other twentieth century scholars as well. In a similar way many scholars assume that because Baruch, the Mishnah, or the *Sibylline Oracles* interpreted the Old Testament references to the pit and the Valley of Hinnom as references to postmortem torture, this may be the shared view of Jesus and His contemporaries. In the analogy with the Professor Jones scenario, it is more likely that the majority of the New Testament scholars of the twentieth century got their ideas of the meaning of "destruction" from the New Testament than from the writings of the Jehovah's Witnesses. In a similar way, it is more likely that Jesus would get this interpretation of Hinnom from the Old Testament and not from the speculative, fantastic references of the variegated Judaism of His era.

To put this in perspective, recall that there is no reference to *Gehenna* in any Jewish document predating the time of Christ (the *Assumption of Moses* is a possible exception). In the Mishnah, compiled in AD 200, there are five references, some of which are capable of being understood in different ways. Moving to the Talmuds in AD 400-600, one finds over 200 references to *Gehenna*, all referring to postmortem damnation. Does anyone see the development of an idea here? The fact that the rabbis in the Babylonian Talmud exaggerated the Old Testament references into preposterous legends of the intermediate state is hardly relevant to how Jesus would have approached the interpretation of the Old Testament!

In the final analysis it is only of mild interest what *Gehenna* means in the inter-testamental, Mishnaic, or Targumic literature. All that really matters is the meaning of the Valley of Hinnom in the Old Testament and the New. In the New Testament the Valley of Hinnom is mentioned twelve times.[2860] So we now turn our attention to the New Testament data.

[2860] Matthew 5:22, 29, 30; 10:28; 18:9; 23:15, 19; Mark 9:43, 45, 47; Luke 12:5; James 3:6.

56

Cast into *Gehenna*

THE CONCLUSIONS reached in the preceding chapters have enormous implications for our understanding of the *Gehenna* references in the New Testament. The Valley of Hinnom in the Old Testament never refers to hell. When one turns to extra-biblical materials, we found that there is no mention of it in any document predating the time of Christ in which *Gehenna* is equated with final damnation. Therefore the common assumption that Palestine was saturated with these fantasies at the time of Christ's ministry and that these fables informed His understanding and that of His hearers in regard to *Gehenna* is without basis.

Significantly, this fact eliminates a difficulty which has perplexed biblical scholars. In several places in the Gospels, believers (saved people) are told that if they want to avoid damnation, they must do good works, or at least, avoid doing "bad" ones. Since Jesus said that no believer will ever lose his eternal salvation,[2861] one must wonder, "What is the meaning of these warnings?" Would Jesus say in one place that believers can never lose their eternal salvation (John 6:39; 10:27-29) and in another warn them that they might? Would He teach them that escape from the lake of fire was by means of works instead of by faith alone as He taught elsewhere?

Consider Matthew 10:28 in this regard.

> *And do not fear those who kill the body, but are unable to kill the soul; but rather fear Him who is able to destroy both soul and body in hell (Matthew 10:28).*

The discourse containing this verse concludes with the words, "*When Jesus had finished giving his instructions* ***to his twelve disciples***" (Matthew 11:1). This phrase indicates that the discourse was directed toward those who were already saved. Yet, Matthew 10:28 seems to warn these regenerate people of the danger of eternal damnation. This conundrum emerges from the incorrect interpretation that *Gehenna* refers to the lake of fire.

This chapter will argue that being cast into Gehenna does not refer to final damnation. The normal meaning that would be understood by a first-generation Palestinian listener is that Jesus was speaking of a burning garbage dump in the Valley of Hinnom. However, Jesus used the word as a metaphor: (1) for a looming national catastrophe; (2) for a negative assessment of the believer's life; and (3) Jesus' brother, James, uses it as a metaphor for the corruption in the heart of man.

[2861] This was demonstrated in chapter 47 above.

The Judgment of *Gehenna*

The Greek word *Gehenna* occurs twelve times in the New Testament.[2862] However, several of them are in parallel passages.[2863] All but one occurs in the Gospels from the lips of Jesus. When all instances are considered, we see that Jesus used the word nine times as a warning to believers (Matthew 5:22, 29, 30; 10:28; 18:9; Mark 9:43, 45, 46; Luke 12:5), and James used it once (James 3:6). Otherwise, Jesus used the word two times in addressing the nonbelieving Pharisees (Matthew 23:15; 33). It is extremely doubtful that Jesus would have warned His believing disciples of a fate, namely, damnation, that He knew would never befall them.

Gehenna is never used by Paul, nor is it found in the Gospel of John or the book of Acts. It is used once in James 3:6 but found in no other New Testament epistle. While many commentaries teach that *Gehenna* refers to damnation, many scholars have raised doubts about this.

Regarding those who believe that *Gehenna* refers to an endless damnation in the afterlife, over one hundred years ago L. F. W. Andrews said,

> *[They] relied upon the supposed figurative meaning of this very word to prove their doctrine, yet they were compelled to acknowledge, that in its primary and outward import it had no other signification than the valley of Hinnom: and that it ever became an emblem of torment in a future world is mere conjecture, without a particle of proof to sustain the position.*
>
> *In its outward and primary sense [Gehenna] related to that dreadful doom of being burnt alive in the Valley of Hinnom.*[2864]

Although the vast majority of commentaries assume that *Gehenna* refers to eternal damnation, many in the evangelical community do not hold this view and agree with Andrews' opinion (above).[2865] Adam Clarke, for example, argues that the judgments of *Gehenna* in Matthew 5:22, 29, and 33 refer to being "burned alive."[2866] A. B. Bruce agrees, saying that being cast into *Gehenna* in Matthew 5:29 means that "he deserves to be burned alive in the Valley of Hinnom." He compares it with the temporal judgment that comes on those who hurt Christ's little ones (Matthew 18:6).[2867] A similar conclusion is echoed by W. F. Albright and C. S. Mann who say the one who is cast into *Gehenna* is one who "merits a fiery death."[2868] Dallas Willard argues that the reference is to being cast into a

---

[2862] Matthew 5:22, 29, 30; 10:28; 18:9; 23:15, 33; Mark 9:43, 45, 47; Luke 12:5; James 3:6.

[2863] Matthew 5:29, 30; 18:9; Mark 9:43, 45, 47. So also are Matthew 10:28 and Luke 12:5. Other instances are Matthew 5:22; 23:15, 33, and James 3:6.

[2864] L. F. W. Andrews, *The Two Opinions: Salvation or Damnation; Being an Inquiry into the Truth of Certain Theological Tennants Prevalent in the Year of Our Lord 1837* (Macon, GA: Self Published, 1837), 72. Available at http://www.books.google.com.

[2865] Anthony Thiselton seems hesitant to commit to this meaning and explores the idea that *Gehenna* is a temporary experience, perhaps leading to cessation of being. Anthony C. Thiselton, *Life after Death: A New Approach to the Last Things* (Grand Rapids, MI: Wm. B. Eerdmans Publishing Co., 2012), 151-59.

[2866] "It is very probable that our Lord means no more here than this—if a man charged another with apostasy from the Jewish religion, or rebellion against God, and cannot prove his charge, then he is exposed to that punishment (burning alive) which the other must have suffered, if the charge had been substantiated." Clarke, *Matthew*. Adam Clarke, A. (1999). Clarke's Commentary: Matthew, electronic ed. (Logos Library System; 1999), s.v. Matthew 5:22.

[2867] A. B. Bruce, "Matthew," in *The Expositor's Greek Testament*, ed. W. Robertson Nicoll (Grand Rapids: Wm. B. Eerdmans Publishing Co., 1967), 5:107.

[2868] W. F. Albright and C. S. Mann, *Matthew: A New Translation and Introduction*, Anchor Yale Bible Commentaries (New Haven, CT: Yale University Press, 1995), 60 ff.

"garbage dump."[2869] F. W. Farrar says that the primary significance is to an "earthly Jewish punishment," a disgraceful death by being burned alive and tossed into the garbage of the Valley of Hinnom.[2870] An older Jewish commentary by Rabbi Kimchi says that "Gehenna is a repugnant place, into which filth and cadavers are thrown, and in which fires perpetually burn in order to consume the filth and bones; on which account, by analogy, the judgement of the wicked is called 'Gehenna.'"[2871]

According to Farrar, the most severe sentence in this passage [Matthew 5:22], being cast into *Gehenna*, is the Jewish "sentence which ordered the body to be burnt and then flung forth and consumed in the Valley of Hinnom."[2872] Death by burning was a recognized punishment in the Law (Leviticus 20:14) and "had special horror to the Jewish mind, on the ground that they... attached intense importance to burial rites."[2873] In ancient Israel, burial was considered extremely important.[2874] Solomon says a stillborn child was better off than a man "*who has no burial*" (Heb *qĕbūrâ, "grave, burial"*)[2875] (Ecclesiastes 6:3). Johnson notes that "non-burial was a sign of particular opprobrium [something that brings disgrace], in Israel and throughout the ancient world. Even a criminal executed and hung on a tree was to be buried the same day (Deuteronomy 21:22)."[2876]

In Matthew 5:22 Jesus warns that if this kind of arrogance and disrespectful attitude toward others continues (calling one a fool), it can certainly result in a negative assessment of the believer's life. But since the addressees here are saved people, the disciples, there is no possibility that the outcome would be eternal damnation. Instead of viewing this as eternal damnation, Dallas Willard in his exposition of the Sermon on the Mount, *The Divine Conspiracy*, got it right when he observed that the judgment contemplated by this phrase was "consigning the offender to the smoldering garbage dump of human existence, *Gehenna*."[2877] Such a fate, either before or after death, is a metaphor for a shameful life.

If these writers are correct, the judgment of *Gehenna* has no immediate eschatological implications at all. Instead it is a temporal sentence of execution exercised by a Jewish court for various crimes against Yahweh. Specifically, it refers either to being cast into the fires of the Valley of Hinnom and being burned alive or having one's corpse cast there after death. The latter signifies an ignominious and shameful death. This explanation seems to work well for the two references applied to believers in Matthew 5:22 and 29, and, possibly, 18:8-9. However, it faces difficulties in Luke 12:54 where Jesus warns His believing disciples that they might face the judgment of *Gehenna* after physical death, that is, "after these things" (Gr *meta tauta*).

2869 Dallas Willard, *The Divine Conspiracy* (San Francisco: Harper, 1998), 154.

2870 Farrar, *Mercy and Judgment*, 375.

2871 David Kimchi and R.G. Finch, *The Longer Commentary of R. David Kimchi on the First Book of Psalms*, ed. W. O. E. Oesterley and G. H. Cox (S.P.C.K.), 107.

2872 Farrar, *Mercy and Judgment*, 449.

2873 Ibid., 450. "If a man fathers a hundred children and lives many years, however many they be, but his soul is not satisfied with good things and he does not even have a proper burial" (Ecclesiastes 6:3).

2874 Abraham, for example, was determined to own a family burial plot (Genesis 23). "Barzillai declines David's offer of hospitality and prefers to return home 'so that I may die in my own town, near the grace of my father and my mother'" (2 Samuel 19:37). See Johnston, *Shades of Sheol: Death and the Afterlife in the Old Testament*, 51.

2875 TWOT, 784.

2876 Johnston, *Shades of Sheol: Death and the Afterlife in the Old Testament*, 55.

2877 Willard, *The Divine Conspiracy*, 154.

Even granting that the judgment of the eternal fire of *Gehenna* refers to being burned alive or having one's corpse cast into the Valley of Hinnom, such a judgment upon a carnal believer obviously has implications for a negative assessment on one's life at the Judgment Seat of Christ.

Once we eliminate the fanciful idea that *Gehenna* refers to final damnation, we have a key to unlock the meaning of many perplexing passages in the New Testament that have often defied rational interpretation.

In the following discussion we will argue that the New Testament writers use this well-known refuse heap as a metaphor for three things: (1) the coming national catastrophe facing the nation; (2) a negative assessment of a carnal believer's life; and (3) the rotten sin-nature of man. Only point (1) links *Gehenna* with an earthly, temporal punishment.

Gehenna and the Judgment of AD 70 (Matthew 23:33)

Recently N. T. Wright has taken the view that *Gehenna* in Matthew 5 may possibly refer to the destruction of Jerusalem.[2878] In reference to the words of John the Baptist (Matthew 3:12; Luke 3:17) he says, "These warnings are to be taken in a thoroughly historical sense. Just as the wrath of YHWH within the Hebrew Scriptures consisted as often as not of military conquest and consequent social disaster,[2879] so we may assume that John's hearers would have heard, and John would have intended, a reference to a great national disaster."[2880] He continues, "The extent to which it [*Gehenna*] is used in the gospels metaphorically for an entirely non-physical place of torment, and the extent to which, in its metaphorical use, it retains the sense of a physical conflagration such as might accompany the destruction of Jerusalem by enemy forces, ought not to be decided in advance of a full study of Jesus' meaning."[2881]

That national disaster is probably what is referred to in Matthew 23:33, "*You serpents, you brood of vipers, how shall you escape the sentence of hell?*" (Gr πῶς φύγητε ἀπὸ τῆς κρίσεως τῆς γεέννης; "How would you escape the condemnation of the Valley of Hinnom?") (Matthew 23:33). The condemnation of the Valley of Hinnom is explained in verse 36, "*Truly I say to you, all these things shall come upon this generation.*" "These things" refers to the destruction of the temple and the invasion of Jerusalem by the Roman armies in AD 70. That is the "the sentence of *Gehenna*," of which Jesus speaks, the condemnation of the Valley of Hinnom.

This is validated by His closing comments,

> *O Jerusalem, Jerusalem, who kills the prophets and stones those who are sent to her! How often I wanted to gather your children together, the way a hen gathers her chicks under her wings, and you were unwilling. Behold, your house is being left to you desolate! For I say to*

[2878] Wright, *Jesus and the Victory of God*, 332-68. See also the discussion of this theme in Larry R. Helyer, "Luke and the Restoration of Israel," *Journal of the Evangelical Theological Society* 36, no. 3 (1993): 317-29.

[2879] For example, 2 Chronicles 36:16-21

[2880] Wright, *Jesus and the Victory of God*, 326.

[2881] Ibid., 445. Wright, of course, is a preterist, and his tentative view of *Gehenna* fits into that prophetic scheme which suggests that Jesus spoke of the judgment which came in AD 70. However, one does not have to accept his preterism to acknowledge that he may have a valid point in regard to the temporal nature of *Gehenna*.

you, from now on you shall not see Me until you say, "Blessed is He who comes in the name of the Lord!" (Matthew 23:37-39; cf. Luke 13:34-35)[2882]

In this same discourse, Jesus referred to the fact that when the Pharisees made a proselyte, they made him a "son of *Gehenna*" (Matthew 23:15). Those who heard this would most likely have understood something like "one worthy of the severest punishments." To be a "son of" anything, was to share something in common. In this case, it refers to the utter corruption and hypocrisy of the Pharisees as the preceding woes demonstrate.

Throughout His ministry, Jesus warned about the destruction of "this generation."[2883] Both Luke and Matthew quoted John the Baptist saying, "*The axe is already at the root of the tree and that every tree that does not produce good fruit will be cut down and thrown into the fire*" (Luke 3:9; Matthew 3:10).[2884]

When Jesus refers to the Valley of Hinnom in Matthew 23:33, He is invoking the imagery of Jeremiah 7:31-32, associating those fires with the Valley of Hinnom. He is more likely thinking in Old Testament terms than drawing imagery from Pseudepigraphal fantasies, which He would have rejected (just as Paul later advised Timothy to do in 1 Timothy 1:4). In Jeremiah, fire imagery is associated with Israel's judgment (Jeremiah 11:16; 15:14; 17:4, 27; 21:10, 12). Jeremiah prophesied that the Valley of Hinnom would become for the apostates "a valley of slaughter" (Jeremiah 7:32; 19:6).

Jesus may have had passages like the following in mind.

"So beware, the days are coming," declares the Lord, "when people will no longer call this place Topheth or the Valley of Ben Hinnom, but the Valley of Slaughter. In this place I will ruin the plans of Judah and Jerusalem. I will make them fall by the sword before their enemies, at the hands of those who seek their lives, and I will give their carcasses as food to the birds of the air and the beasts of the earth. I will devastate this city and make it an object of scorn; all who pass by will be appalled and will scoff because of all its wounds. I will make them eat the flesh of their sons and daughters, and they will eat one another's flesh during the stress of the siege imposed on them by the enemies who seek their lives" (Jeremiah 19:6-9, NIV).[2885]

2882 Cf. Luke 20:15-16.

2883 Matthew 23:32-36; 24:34; Luke 11:45-52; 13:1-5; 19:39-44; 21:8-24, etc.

2884 These warnings refer not to events surrounding the second coming or final damnation to hell, but to events that will come on the generation of Jesus' day, a generation that would be held liable for the murders of all the prophets (Luke 11:49–51). Elsewhere, noting the atrocity perpetrated by Pilate, Jesus tells His listeners that "unless you repent, you too will all perish" (Luke 13:1–5), another reference to a temporal perishing caused by the Roman legions.

2885 While Jesus is not saying the judgment is the fulfillment of that prophecy, He is using the imagery of temporal judgment in the Valley of Hinnom, which Jeremiah used, and applying it to a temporal judgment on the nation in the first century. What kind of temporal judgment? Probably, this means being burned alive like garbage in the Valley of Hinnon, the ultimate disgrace and negative assessment of a wasted life. Remember, this is figurative speech. He is using hyperbole, exaggeration to make a point. We should not picture Jesus advocating burning people alive as in the Inquisition of the 15th and 16th centuries. Jesus did not want His followers to literally "hate" their parents. When the Romans sacked Jerusalem, the devastation was bad, but not to the point that there were *literally* no stones on top of others. Anyone visiting Jerusalem today can see recently unearthed foundation stones from Herod's temple. These huge, white stones are still stacked several deep in some places. Hyperbole is a common way of speaking that any reasonable person would never use to discredit the truth or falsity of a statement.

The Valley of Hinnom in the Old Testament refers to a temporal judgment, as indicated in Jeremiah 17:4 (cf. 17:27; 25:9), where eternal fire refers to a terrible fire that lasts a long time and is a symbol of temporal judgment. One must remember that even though the fires in Hinnom in Jeremiah's prophecy (Jeremiah 17:4) ended with the Babylonian exile, they were still called a fire "*which will burn into eternity*" (Heb *ʿôlam* "eternity"). Yet, in the context this verse clearly means that it burns for a limited duration. In Jeremiah 21:12, it is an "unquenchable fire,"[2886] yet it refers to judgment in time.[2887] Obviously, this "everlasting devastation" Jeremiah mentions is a "terrible" devastation and not one that lasts forever. Jerusalem was restored again under Ezra and Nehemiah, and the city will be finally restored in the kingdom (Jeremiah 31:38-40).

Jesus repeats this warning to His generation in the parable of the fig tree, which states that the nation has only one more year to bring forth the fruits of repentance (Luke 13:6-9). At the time of the triumphal entry Jesus weeps over the city, saying,

> *If you had only known on this day, even you, the things that make for peace! But now they are hidden from your eyes. For the days will come upon you when your enemies will build an embankment against you and surround you and close in on you from every side. They will demolish you—you and your children within your walls—and they will not leave within you one stone on top of another, because you did not recognize the time of your visitation from God (Luke 19:42-44, NET).*

Jesus informs His disciples that this national catastrophe will occur within "this generation" (Matthew 24:34).[2888] We therefore conclude that in some passages *the Valley of Hinnom is a place of judgment in time. All these references speak of a temporal punishment on the nation and not the eternal damnation of unbelievers.*

According to Josephus, over one million Jews were killed by the Roman armies under Titus.[2889] There can be little doubt that some of these bodies were literally thrown into the valleys just below the city. The Romans set fire to parts of the city, and its walls were completely demolished.[2890] Equating *Gehenna*, that is, the burning garbage of the Valley of Hinnom, with the coming national catastrophe, N. T. Wright summarizes, "Faced with this prospect, it would be better to abandon that which is most cherished [i.e., one's "life"] rather than go straight ahead into the conflagration [with Rome]."[2891]

2886 LXX, οὐκ ἔσται ὁ σβέσων.

2887 Fire imagery relating to judgment of limited duration is frequently found in Jeremiah: in 22:6-9 Jerusalem and the cedars will be thrown into the fire; in 29:22-23 the king of Babylon roasted Zedekiah and Ahab in the fire; in 32:29 the Chaldeans will enter the city and set fire to it; and in 34:2-3 God says He is giving the city into the hand of the king of Babylon, and He will burn it with fire (cf. 38:17, 18, 23).

2888 The reference to "this generation" is controversial. This writer follows J. R. Edwards's suggestion that Mark 13 is arranged in an A B A B pattern, and it appears that Matthew 24 is arranged is a similar fashion. In a classical prophetic manner, Jesus alternates between events that will occur in "this generation," the end of the temple and fall of Jerusalem ("these things"), and those that will occur at the future Day of the Lord ("that day," "those days"). A = Mark 13:1-13; Matthew 24:1-14. B = Mark 13:14-27; Matthew 24:15-31. A^2 = Mark 13:28-31; Matthew 32-35, B^2 = Mark 13:32-37; Matthew 24:36-4. "That Day," is frequently associated with the Day of the Lord in the prophetic literature (Isaiah 4:2; 27:1; Ezekiel 39:11; Zeph 1:15, etc.). See J. R. Edwards, *The Gospel of Mark*, Pillar New Testament Commentary (Grand Rapids: Wm. B. Eerdmans Publishing Co., 2002), 385.

2889 Josephus, "The Wars of the Jews," 6.9.3.420. The stench was so horrible, Josephus says, that the soldiers immediately moved away from the heaps of bodies among which they were obliged to walk (6.9.4.428).

2890 Ibid. 6.9.4.434.

2891 Wright, *Jesus and the Victory of God*, 330.

Long ago Walter Balfour asked, "Is it rational to suppose that our Lord quoted texts from the Old Testament which speak altogether of temporal punishment, when he intended that what he said about *Gehenna* or hell should be understood of eternal punishment?"[2892]

How fitting of John and Jesus to announce the coming Roman invasion of AD 70 in terms of this Old Testament parallel. Like the siege by the Babylonians, the destruction of Jerusalem by the Romans also resulted in cannibalism, as predicted in Deuteronomy 28:53 (cf. Lamentations 4:10). Indeed, some commentators see the Babylonian invasion as a foreshadowing of the Roman invasion.[2893] The details of the destruction by Nebuchadnezzar are similar to those documented by Josephus in describing the destruction of Jerusalem in AD 70.

The Duration of *Gehenna*

If *Gehenna* in the Gospels sometimes relates an invasion by Rome; a negative consequence which may come on an unfaithful believer at the Judgment Seat of Christ; or the rottenness of our sin nature, one must ask, "Why is it called an 'eternal' (Gr *aiōnios,* Matthew 18:8) and 'unquenchable' fire?" The lexicon lists the first meaning of this word as "a long period of time"[2894] and for the noun, *aiōn,* a long period of time or an "age."[2895] The Roman invasion did not last forever, but the fires of *Gehenna* according to Matthew 5:22 "*will burn and not be quenched.*" In this terrible place "*their worm does not die*" (Mark 9:43).[2896]

John the Baptist uses it of the burning of chaff in the judgment on Jerusalem which links it with the wrath of AD 70 (Matthew 3:12). Yet, to argue that this fire lasts for all eternity presses the metaphor beyond its bounds and its clear usage in the Old Testament.[2897] Davies and Allison state that, "Unquenchable does not necessarily mean eternal."[2898] This fire only lasts until the threshing floor is "thoroughly cleared." The hyperbole does not suggest that chaff burns forever.[2899]

[2892] Balfour, *An Inquiry into the Scriptural Import of the Words Sheol, Hades, Tartarus, and Gehenna in the Common English Version*, 234. Balfour denies the existence of eternal damnation altogether, which I do not. I am only saying that *Gehenna* is not related to it.

[2893] "The Lord, because of their breach of covenant, used King Nebuchadnezzar's neo-Babylonian army to raze Jerusalem and its temple. They were reduced to a 'mound of ruins,' foreshadowing the Roman destruction of A.D. 70." See Kenneth L. Barker and D. Waylon Bailey, *Micah, Nahum, Habakkuk, Zephaniah*, New American commentary (Nashville: Broadman & Holman, 1999), p. 81.

[2894] BDAG, 37.

[2895] BDAG, 32.

[2896] Matthew 3:12; Mark 9:43; Luke 3:17.

[2897] Hendriksen, for example says, "So also the wicked, having been separated from the good, will be cast into hell, the place of unquenchable fire. Their punishment is unending. The point is not merely that there is always a fire burning in *Gehenna* but that the wicked are burned with unquenchable fire." Hendriksen and Kistemaker, *Exposition of the Gospel According to Matthew*, 201.

[2898] Davies and Allison, *A Critical and Exegetical Commentary on the Gospel According to Saint Matthew*, 319. As proof that unquenchable does not necessarily mean "eternal," these writers cite Isaiah 34:10; 66:24; Jeremiah 7:20; Mark 9:48; and Jude 7.

[2899] The early church fathers sometimes used the word "eternal" of temporal judgments. For example, Eusebius speaks of two martyrs, Julian and Cronion, who were beaten and finally burned in "unquenchable fire" which Schaff translated "burned in a fierce fire" (Gr *asbestō puri*); and that of two others, Epimachus and Alexander, who were similarly destroyed by "unquenchable fire." Does anyone believe that Eusebius referred to a miraculous fire that continued to burn for all eternity? Instead, it was a "terrible" fire. Eusebius, "Church History," in *The Nicene and Post-Nicene Fathers: Second Series*, ed. Philip Schaff (Oak Harbor, WA: Logos Research Systems, 1997), 41:15, p. 284. See also ibid., Letters, # 298, 8:307.

Rather, as in every instance of the word in the Old Testament, it refers to a "terrible" fire, or one that lasts a long time (Isaiah 32:14-16; 34:10; 66:24; Jeremiah 7:20), signifying there is no second chance and "the impossibility of averting the punishment of evil."[2900] "It is," says Farrar, "inexcusable to force and exaggerate the meaning of the word."[2901] He points out that this phrase from the Old Testament refers to the brief flame which burns up the gates of Jerusalem and the dry trees of the forest of the south.[2902] It is ambiguous at best to claim that the word "eternal" always means "forever" any more than that David's prayer for length of days lasting "forever and ever" meant that David believed he would never die (Psalm 21:4).[2903]

Examples could be multiplied. Deuteronomy 15:17 speaks of one having a "slave for life" (Gr *aiōn*)[2904] Obviously, *aiōn*, "age" (LXX) means "for the rest of your life," and not for eternity.[2905] The inheritance of Caleb was "forever" (Joshua 14:9).[2906] The Day of Atonement was to "*be a permanent* (Heb *ʿôlām*, LXX *aiōnios*) *statute to them throughout their generations*" (Leviticus 17:7),[2907] yet it ended at the Cross.

What about the "worm which does not die?" The image of the maggots devouring dead bodies in the grave is a frequent way in which the Old Testament describes the decay of the body in time, not eternity (Job 17:13-16; 24:19-20). This is a symbol for disgust and shame. Nothing is more repulsive or shameful than to end up with one's body being consumed by a teeming mass of maggots.[2908]

Consider Isaiah's pronouncement of temporal judgment in Isaiah 66:24.

> *Then they shall go forth and look on the corpses of the men who have transgressed against Me. For their worm shall not die, and their fire shall not be quenched; and they shall be an abhorrence to all mankind (NASB).*

Gehenna is also a place where "the worm [Gr *skōlēx, 'maggot,'*] does not die." Jesus cites this passage in Mark 9:48. It speaks of the decay of the body as maggots consume it

[2900] Morris, *The Gospel According to Matthew*, 62.

[2901] Farrar, *Mercy and Judgment*, 407.

[2902] Isaiah 1:28-31; Jeremiah 17:27; Ezekiel 20:47-48.

[2903] It is well known that "eternal" can mean "for a long time or until God decides to change the situation." See Isaiah 1:31; 34:10; 66:24; Jeremiah 4:4; 7:20, 17:27; 21:12; Ezekiel 20:47, 48.

[2904] Gr οἰκέτης εἰς τὸν αἰῶνα, a slave "forever."

[2905] Cf. Genesis 9:16 (*aiōnios*); 17:7; Ex. 31.16; Leviticus 24:8, all of which refer to covenants or celebrations that last as long as Israel or the earth exists, not endlessly into eternity.

[2906] LXX εἰς τὸν αἰῶνα, מֵעוֹלָם for eternity.

[2907] If *aiōnios* always means "without end" how it is that the "permanent" priesthood (Exodus 29:28; 30:21; Lev. 7:34 changed (Hebrews 7:10, 18-19, 23) and a once and for all sacrifice was made by our Lord (Hebrews 7:27)? If *aiōnios* always means "without end," how is it that the "permanent" (Gr *aiōnios*) Feast of Tabernacles (Leviticus 23:41) is no longer celebrated (Romans 10:4)? If *aiōnios* always means "without end," how is it that the Law ended with Christ (Romans 10:4) and a new and better covenant was established (Hebrews 8:7-8) and the Day of Atonment, including the entire "permanent" sacrificial system, became "obsolete" and disappeared (Hebrews 8:13)? If the Jews believed that *ʿôlām* and *aiōnios* always meant "without end," they would have urged this point as a complete refutation of Christianity. Similarily the feast of Passover was to be *aiōnios* (Ex 12:14).

[2908] "The word 'worm' occurs seven times in the Old Testament, always in contexts describing decay in food (Exodus 16:24) or in the body (Job 7:5; Isaiah 14:11). The root appears also in Job (17:14; 21:26; 24:20) and in a special metaphorical usage, 25:6." William White, "*rimm*," in TWOT, 850.

in time,[2909] not of tormenting of conscious persons.[2910] These literal maggots eating corpses clearly have a metaphorical meaning as well. Literal maggots would die and would be destroyed by the fire. These "worms" are also metaphors for shame. The passage could be translated, "Their *shame* does not die," that is, it is unending.[2911] This speaks of a judgment of unregenerate rebels who attack Israel. As our Lord hung on the cross, He exclaimed, "*But I am a worm and not a man, a reproach of men and despised by the people. All who see me sneer at me; they separate with the lip, they wag the head, saying*" (Psalm 22:6-7). Jesus declared that He had become a worm, that is, an object of shame.

As the millennial inhabitants of the city look over the walls and down into the Valley of Hinnom, they will see the corpses of these rebels, eaten by maggots and consumed with fire as part of the city's garbage.[2912] Throughout the kingdom era, this will serve as a constant reminder of the consequences of rebellion against God.[2913] This picture is more consistent

---

[2909] Louw-Nida, 2:224. The image of the worm devouring the dead bodies in the grave is a frequent way in which the Old Testament describes the decay of the body in time, not eternity (Job 17:14; 21:24, 26; 24:20). This word (Heb *rimmâ,* maggot) occurs seven times in the Old Testament, always in contexts describing decay (Exodus 16:24) in food or in the body (Job 7:5; Isaiah 14:11). See TWOT, 850. Isaiah, describing a scene in the millennium, says, "Then they shall go forth and look on the corpses of the men who have transgressed against Me. For their *worm shall not die*, and their *fire shall not be quenched*; and they shall be an abhorrence to all mankind." To say, "their worm shall not die" means that their shame is unending. The worm eating rotting flesh is a metaphor for shame and disgrace (cf. Psalm 22:6).

[2910] William Lane interprets the text through the eyes of the apocryphal book of Judith 16:17 (150 BC), a ludicrous fiction full of historical errors and psychological improbabilities (NISBE, 1:1165). "Woe to the nations that rise up against my race: The Lord Almighty will take vengeance of them in the day of judgment, to put fire and worms in their flesh; and they shall weep and feel their pain forever." Would Jesus have derived His views of the afterlife from such a fantastic source? See Lane, *Commentary on the Gospel of Mark*, 349.

[2911] Morgan argues that it should be translated "their torment" is unending. See this excellent article: Morgan, "The New Testament Use of Gehenna: Its Historical Background and Its Significance for the Doctrine of Eternal Punishment." Morgan differs from the view of this author. He takes the traditional view that *Gehenna* is a metaphor for eternal damnation.

[2912] "When they go out from the city, the pilgrims cannot avoid seeing the corpses of persons who were rebelling against God. Complete separation of servants and enemies allowed the restoration to be completed and the pilgrims to come for worship. But the memory of the bitter opposition cannot be forgotten. 'Their bodies have been thrown out on the city's dump....their bodies feed maggots (14:11; 15:8) and fire.' And they, too, have become a kind of permanent facet of the city, an abhorrence to all flesh who worship there, a reminder of the stubborn group in Israel who resisted God to the very end." John D. W. Watts, *Isaiah 34-66*, Word Biblical Commentary (Dallas: Word, 1998), 366.

[2913] Some have suggested that Isaiah 66:22 places this scene in the new heavens and the new earth, not in the millennium. "'For just as the new heavens and the new earth, which I make will endure before Me,' declares the LORD, 'So your offspring and your name will endure.'" The description of maggots and fire follows. This would be in conflict with Revelation 21:1, which says the new heavens and the new earth appear after the millennium and not before it or during it. However, the text does not say in Isaiah 66:22 that the new heavens and the new earth are established. It says the promises of God to Israel are as firm as the promise that the new heavens and new earth will endure forever. God's promises to the Jewish people are steadfast and as certain as the enduring reality of the new heavens and the new earth. The text says nothing about when the new heavens and the new earth are created. We wait until Revelation 21:1 for that information. Another passage thought to be in conflict with Revelation 21:1 and which suggests that the new heavens and the new earth encompass the millennium is Isaiah 65:17, "For behold, I create new heavens and a new earth; and the former things will not be remembered or come to mind." What follows is clearly a millennial scene and not the eternal state. The problem is only apparent as many translations recognize. The translation "I create" (NASB, KJV) leaves the time of this creation unspecified. Many other translations clarify a bit by translating, "I will create" (NIV, HCSB, NCV, LXX "there will be"). Others translate, "I am creating," describing the millennium as a phase of the process that will be consummated in the eternal state (NLT, CEV, GNT). It is best to translate it as "I am creating," thus eliminating any conflict with Revelation 21:1.

with Ezekiel 39:11-16, which refers to the seven-month burial of contaminating corpses after the victory over the enemies of God.

The argument above does not imply that "eternal" can never mean "endless." It clearly does in Matthew 25:41, 46.[2914] That there is an eternal lake of fire, that has no ending, is not denied (Matthew 25:46; Revelation 14:11; 20:10). What is denied is that *Gehenna* has anything to do with it.

How does one know when to understand "eternal" as "endless" and when to take it to mean "for a long time"? This depends on the words with which it is associated in each context. When "eternal" is used to describe the nature of God (Romans 16:26; Deuteronomy 33:27), we understand from that association that the intended meaning of "everlasting" (Heb *'ôlam*) is "without beginning or end." But when the word "eternal" is associated with something which is manifestly temporal, like the "eternal hills" (Habakkuk 3:6) and could not be endless, we understand "eternal" to mean "for a long time" or as a figure of speech for, in this case, "enduring."

Because "eternal fire" of *Gehenna* does not always mean "endless fire" there is no lexical objection to applying Jesus' warning to the nation regarding the coming Roman invasion of 70 AD. The city and the people were literally cast into the burning garbage dump of the Valley of Hinnom. [2915]

The threat to that generation was that they would be destroyed and cast into the Valley of Hinnom if the nation failed to implement the principles of the Sermon on the Mount and repent of their sins as John the Baptist and Jesus commanded (e.g., Mark 1:4). When Jesus repeatedly warned that the nation was hurtling toward a national catastrophe and evoked *Gehenna* from a context (Jeremiah 7) which warned Old Testament Israel of similar

---

[2914] There is no question that *aiōnios* can mean "endless," as in "these will go away into eternal punishment, but the righteous into eternal life" (Matthew 25:46). Because eternal life is endless and is parallel to and contrasted with eternal punishment, it is correctly argued that eternal punishment must mean endless punishment.

[2915] In a number of places in the Bible "eternal" is used of a period of both endless duration and limited duration in the same verse! "He stood and surveyed the earth; He looked and startled the nations. Yes, the perpetual mountains were shattered, the ancient hills collapsed. His ways are everlasting" (Habakkuk 3:6). "His ways," says the prophet, "are everlasting." (הֲלִיכוֹת עֹלָם לוֹ lit., "eternal doings are to him"). The LXX (3:7) renders it πορείας αἰωνίας αὐτοῦ, "his eternal ways." Yet the same phrases are used of the "perpetual mountains" (עֹלָם שַׁחוּגִבְעוֹת"eternal hills are bent over"). The LXX renders this ἐτάκησαν βουνοὶ αἰώνιοι "the eternal hills melt," that is, disappear, become liquid, or collapse. Obviously, the eternal hills are not endless even though they occur in the same verse as God's eternal works, which are. Or consider Romans 16:25-26, "Now to Him who is able to establish you according to my gospel and the preaching of Jesus Christ, according to the revelation of the mystery which has been kept secret for long [αἰώνιος] ages past, but now is manifested, and by the Scriptures of the prophets, according to the commandment of the eternal [*aiōnios*] God, has been made known to all the nations, leading to obedience of faith" (Romans 16:25-26). According to the logic of those who require that *aiōnios* always means "endless," this passage teaches that ages that are "past" are, in fact, "endless." That is an absurdity! The NASB correctly renders it "long ages past" not "eternal ages past." Finally, consider Jude 7, "just as Sodom and Gomorrah and the cities around them, since they in the same way as these indulged in gross immorality and went after strange flesh, are exhibited as an example in undergoing the punishment of eternal fire" (NASB). Jude tells us that the temporal burning from sulfur and volcanic coals that came on Sodom in time was an "eternal (*aiōnios*), fire" which means it was horrible and lasted a long time. There is no connection with hell here. Jude's point is that the still smoldering site of the cities of Sodom and Gomorrah is a warning of retribution. The reason it is "eternal" is that it still burns. "Whereas a testimony to its wickedness, there *yet remain[s] a smoking desert.* Plants bearing fruit that never ripens, and the tomb of a disbelieving soul, a standing pillar of salt" (Wisdom of Solomon 10:7). Philo similarly comments on the present existence of the "eternal" fire in his day, saying, "And even to this day there are seen in Syria monuments of the unprecedented destruction that fell upon them, in the ruins, and ashes, and sulphur, and smoke, and dusky flame which still is sent up from the ground as of a fire smoldering beneath." "On the Life of Moses" in Philo, "On the Life of Moses," Book 2, 56, p. 495. As is well known the word "eternal" (*aiōnios*) can mean either "a long period of time" or "a period of unending duration," BDAG 33. ἀis is set forth as "example" (Gr δεῖγμα, BDAG, 214) that God will judge in the future because He had done it in the past. "Look," a prophet could say, "the fires are still burning today."

national peril, He invested the term, for His Palestinian listeners, with profound temporal significance.

Gehenna and the Judgment Seat of Christ

The second way in which the metaphor of the Valley of Hinnom is used in the New Testament is related to believers.

THE CHARACTER OF THE *GEHENNA* JUDGMENT: TERRIBLE (MATTHEW 18:8-9)

Based on the Old Testament, Jesus and His contemporaries would not have understood *Gehenna* as a place of final damnation. This was a place of dead corpses (Jeremiah 31:40), slaughter, and garbage; it would have evoked thoughts of shame and disgrace. We believe that when Jesus applies the warnings regarding *Gehenna* to those who are justified, He speaks of a postmortem judgment with eternal consequences which befalls faithless, but eternally saved, believers (i.e., the Judgment Seat of Christ). We agree with Michael Eaton, author of the Tyndale commentary on Ecclesiastes, who suggests that *Gehenna* refers not to eternal damnation but to negative consequences that may come on unfaithful believers at the Judgment Seat of Christ.[2916] But, one might ask, why then is gehenna called an "eternal fire"?

In response we note that "fire" in Jesus' bible (the OT) never has the sense of lake of fire.[2917] Jesus uses it here as a metaphor for a future judgment on disciples' works (18:8). Regarding the word "eternal," we note that the adjective *aiōnios* can express quality. For example, "eternal life" can refer to a *quality* of life as well as its *duration* after death. Farrar says, "The epithet expresses the *character of the life, not its duration.*"[2918] The lexicon of Louw-Nida agrees, "In combination with ζωή there is evidently not only a temporal element, but also a qualitative distinction."[2919] Jesus' metaphorical reference to Hinnom as an "eternal" fire may describe the quality of the fire (it is a *future terrible judgment*). We use "eternal this way in English. For example, recently the Prime Minister of Japan expressed his "eternal condolences" for the atrocities committed by Japan against American POWs. He was expressing his **deeply sincere** condolences, not condolences that last into infinity.[2920]

That an eternal fire can mean an enduring fire that lasts a long time and not an eternal one is proven by Jude 7, "*Just as Sodom and Gomorrah and the cities around them, since they in the same way as these indulged in gross immorality and went after strange flesh, are exhibited as an example in undergoing the punishment of eternal fire*" (Jude 7). The volcanic ash which fell on Sodom and Gomorrah did not burn forever, but it was terrible! It was still visible and was a reminder of God's judgments in time.[2921]

2916 Eaton, *No Condemnation: A New Theology of Assurance*, 206-7.

2917 In the OT It always refers to a temporal judgment see discussion above, pp. 835 ff. The Gospels sometimes use "fire" of temporal judgment (Matthew 3:10, 12; Luke 17:29).

2918 F. W. Farrar, *Mercy and Judgment: A Few Last Words on Christian Eschatology, with Reference to Dr. Pusey's "What Is of Faith?"* (New York: E. P. Dutton Co., 1881), 395.

2919 LN, 1:641.

2920 Oren Dorell, "'Eternal Condolences': Japan's Abe stands by WWII Apollogies," *USA Today* April 30, 2015, 2A. A young unmarried man in his thirties is sometimes referred to as an "eternal bachelor," that is, a man seemingly committed to being single. The bible speaks of "everlasting joy" in Isaiah 35:10 meaning "exuberant" joy; and an "everlasting" covenant, meaning an "irrevocable" covenant in Jeremiah 27:5; and "eternal" power meaning "incredible" power (Romans 1:20), etc.

2921 When some commentators opine that this is "a warning picture of the fires of hell," they do so with no appeal to evidence in the text. The judgment of Sodom and Gomorrah was physical. According to Josephus "for the

THE TWO FIRES IN THE AGE TO COME

If the eschatological judgment of "*Gehenna* of fire" cannot refer to the eternal fire of the lake of fire, to what fire does it refer? We know from other scriptures that there are two fires which occur in the afterlife (1) "the eternal fire which has been prepared for the devil and his angels" (Matthew 25:41), that is, the lake of fire (Revelation 19:20; 20:14) and (2) the fire of the Judgment Seat of Christ (1 Corinthians 3:15).

That the same expression can have a different meaning when applied to different things should not surprise us. For example, consider Isaiah 63:12. In this verse Heb *olam* (Gr *eis ton aiōna,* LXX) is applied to God's everlasting name, but in Deuteronomy 15:15 the very same expressions are applied to the lifetime of a slave. Just because there is an eternal fire (*eis to pur to aiōnion*) prepared for the devil and his angels (the lake of fire, Matthew 25:41), that does not mean that it means the same thing when the same expression is applied to believers who could never experience the lake of fire (Matthew 18:8)?

The judgment of the eternal fire of *Gehenna* is best defined in a general sense as a *judgment which occurs in the future age*. But which judgment (fire) is in view depends upon the context. In Matthew 18:8, since it is a warning of a destiny which might befall believing disciples, it cannot refer to the lake of fire because that could never happen to them. Therefore we may safely assume that it refers to the fire of the Judgment Seat of Christ.

We are on familiar ground here. Paul spoke of being "saved through fire" (1 Corinthians 3:15) and Jesus said that the unfaithful branches would be cast into the fire and burned (John 15:6).[2922] In His Sermon on the Mount, Jesus said that those who do not enter the narrow gate and follow the narrow way will face "destruction" (Matthew 7:12-13). The anonymous writer of the homily to the Hebrews informs us that when the believer's life produces thorns and thistles, this produce "ends up being burned" (Hebrews 6:8). The apostle John warns his readers that they might face "shame" at the return of Christ (1 John 2:28) and loss of reward (2 John 8).

As argued elsewhere, the unfaithful virgins and other unfaithful believers will hear the terrifying words, "*I never knew you*" and "*depart from me*."[2923] They will then be sent to "the darkness outside" and excluded from the joy of Christ's *Metochoi* ("Partners") in the celebratory wedding activities that transpire in the New Jerusalem during the tribulation. When they realize the horror of their wasted lives, there will be "weeping and gnashing of teeth" (Matthew 25:24).

We therefore suggest that when the phrases "eternal fire" of *Gehenna (eis to pur to aiōnion,* Matthew 18:8) and the "fiery *Gehenna*" (*geenan tou puros*, v. 9) are metaphorically applied to genuine believers, they may be expressed this way:

> *Gehenna is a metaphor for the terrible rebuke Christ directs toward the unfaithful believer because of the shame and disgrace of his unfaithful and wasted life; a life which is of no more value than an unburied corpse cast into a burning refuse dump.*

---

impiety of its inhabitants it was burnt by lightning; in consequence of which there are still the remainders of that divine fire; and the traces [or shadows] of the five cities are still to be seen." "Wars of the Jews" in Josephus and Whiston, *The Works of Josephus: Complete and Unabridged*, 4:484. According to Philo, "even to this day there are seen in Syria monuments of the unprecedented destruction that fell upon them, in the ruins, and ashes, and sulphur, and smoke, and dusky flame which still is sent up from the ground as of a fire smoldering beneath." Philo, "On the Life of Moses," 495-96, vol. 2, v. 56.

[2922] For discussion of this verse see scripture index.

[2923] See discussion on pp. 320 ff.

When "eternal fire" (*eis to pur to aiōnion*) is metaphorically applied to nonbelievers (Matthew 25:41) it refers to the lake of fire.

Jesus appropriated the continuous fire of the Valley of Hinnom as a metaphor for an intense judgment which occurs in the future age. It is called an eternal fire (*eis to pur to aiōnion*) because it occurs during a period of exclusion from the Messianic banquet, and the intense, eternal consequences which befall a carnal believer because of a failed life.

How long will they weep? How long will they feel shame? While their disinheritance and loss of reward marks them throughout all eternity, because of the grace of God, the emotions of remorse will replaced by joy and gratitude.[2924] The Bema occurs in a moment of time, but the loss of opportunity to serve, the loss of honor, and the loss of enhanced intimacy with the King will endure forever.

To summarize, we believe that when Jesus speaks of "fiery *Gehenna*" (Matthew 18:9), we interpret this *literally* as the "burning garbage dump in the Valley of Hinnom." When He speaks of "fires that will burn and not be quenched" (Mark 9:43), alluding to the temporal burning of garbage in the Valley of Hinnom (Matthew 18:8), His hearers certainly would have thought of a fire that consumes refuse outside of Jerusalem[2925] which burns "24/7," that is, "all the time,"[2926] or is very intense. That said, the contexts of these warnings require us to believe that Jesus invests this maggot infested burning refuse heap with eschatological significance. It refers to an "eternal" fire which involves forfeiture of honor and greatness in the future kingdom of heaven (Matthew 18:3-4).

A LACK OF RECONCILIATION LEADS ONE TO *GEHENNA* (MATTHEW 5:22, 29)

> *But I say to you that everyone who is angry with his brother shall be guilty before the court; and whoever shall say to his brother, "Raca," shall be guilty before the supreme court; and whoever shall say, 'You fool,' shall be guilty enough to go into the fiery hell [Gehenna] (Matthew 5:21-22).*

There are a number of problems raised by this warning to the disciples. First of all, most would agree with Hans Scharen that "The main point relevant to determining the meaning of *Gehenna* in this text is the incongruity between the crimes listed and the severity of their respective punishments."[2927]

But there is an even greater problem. As argued above, if "fiery hell" refers to final damnation, there is no escape from the conclusion that Jesus is lying to His believing followers warning them of a judgment which could never happen to them.

How do the commentators address this problem? The short answer is, "They don't." When I checked thirty-two standard commentaries on a similar warning in Matthew 18:8-

---

[2924] For discussion of the duration of remorse see pp. 326, 775 ff.

[2925] Later rabbinical literature (after AD 400) associated *Gehenna* with damnation because this valley was a place where "carrion and other impurities were constantly being burned. It was therefore a place where the fire was never extinguished." See Fox, *Hell in Jewish Literature*, 7. Thus an "eternal fire" is one that burns "all the time."

[2926] Fire imagery is associated with Israel's judgment in time in Jeremiah (Jeremiah 11:16; 15:14; 17:4, 27; 21:10, 12). In 17:4 this is an "eternal fire," yet it means "for a long time." In 21:12 it is an "unquenchable fire," yet it refers to judgment in time; in Jeremiah 22:6-9 Jerusalem and the cedars will be thrown into the fire; in Jeremiah 29:22-23 the king of Babylon roasted Zedekiah and Ahab in the fire; in 32:29 the Chaldeans will enter the city and set fire to it; and in 34:2-3 God says He will give the city into the hand of the king of Babylon, and he will burn it with fire (cf. Jeremiah 38:17, 18, 23).

[2927] Hans Scharen, "Part 2: Gehenna in the Synoptics," *BibSac* 149, no. 196 (Oct 1992): 455.

9, only one of them indirectly alluded to the difficulty and the rest simply ignored it. It is this kind of lacuna which has given rise to the barb, "It is amazing how much light the Bible casts upon the commentaries." The busy pastor attempting to prepare a sermon on these verses will find little help.

For example, Hans Scharen tells us that "Jesus' main concern ... is not His listeners' consignment to *Gehenna*, but His urging and encouragement of people to take drastic steps to avoid at all costs such a dreaded destiny."[2928] Notice, he ambiguously refers to Jesus' audience as "His listeners," in order to leave open the possibility that some are not believers. Luz calls them "members of the church"[2929] and Turner says they are "member[s] of the community."[2930] Both of these labels obviously enable them to avoid the problem that true believers are being addressed.[2931]

Out of all the works consulted, only Craig Blomberg hints at a solution. He says those addressed are "professing believers" who "may well not be Jesus disciples at all and thus remain under the threat of damnation."[2932] He gives no proof and does not discuss how his view directly contradicts the explicit statement that the disciples, and not a mixed group, are being addressed (Matthew 18:1).

Some commentaries simply ignore the problem, leaving the student to wrestle with the theological implications with no help.[2933] Others dismiss the problem by saying the warning is a "paradoxical exaggeration by which Jesus' sayings often compel the reader's attention."[2934]

Another writer suggests that the warning is directed to those who are trusting in a Pharisaic works-righteousness, that is professing believers, and not those who possess the imputed righteousness of Christ.[2935] However, as argued elsewhere, the "surpassing righteousness" in the Sermon on the Mount is not the imputed righteousness of Christ but the kingdom way of living out the ethical precepts of the sermon. Furthermore, Jesus makes it emphatic in verse 20 that He is speaking specifically to His disciples with the emphatic "if you." Jesus is not addressing professing believers who are trusting in Pharisaic works-righteousness. He is addressing His disciples (Matthew 5:1-2).[2936]

A common interpretation is that all Christ means in His warning to someone who calls his brother a fool is that he "is guilty *enough* to go into the hell of fire."[2937] But the Greek text does not include the word "enough." It says he is guilty and he will go there! Furthermore, how can a believer be guilty enough to go to damnation when Christ has already paid the penalty for his guilt?

2928 Scharen, "Part 1: Gehenna in the Synoptics," 33..

2929 Luz, *Matthew: A Commentary*, 435.

2930 Turner, *Matthew*, 438.

2931 Similarily other commentators avoid the issue. Cf. Hagner, 523; Davies and Allison, 766; Keener, IVP; Allen, 195; Nolland; Expositor's Commentary on the Bible; Carson, 399; A, T. Robertson, *Word Pictures*; Mounce, 174; Alford; Matthew Henry; Wiersbe, etc.

2932 Blomberg, *Matthew*, 275.

2933 E.g., D. A. Carson, "Matthew," in *Expositor's Bible Commentary, Volume 8: Matthew, Mark, Luke*, ed. Frank E. Gabelein, et al. (Grand Rapids: Zondervan Publishing House, 1984), 149.

2934 France, *The Gospel of Matthew*, 202.

2935 Haller, "Matthew," 26.

2936 See discussion on pp. 271 ff.

2937 Morris, *The Gospel According to Matthew*, 115. BDAG explains that the Gr *enochos* as "brachylogy" means one is "guilty enough to go into the hell of fire" (p. 339).

What is Jesus saying here?

We may now apply the conclusions of the preceding discussion. We established that the eternal fire of *Gehenna* is a terrible judgment in the future age. We have argued that there are two kinds of judgment in the afterlife: (1) the eternal fire prepared for the devil and his angels (Matthew 25:41); and (2) the fire of the Judgment Seat of Christ (1 Corinthians 3:15). We discern which judgment is meant by noting to whom it is addressed. Since those addressed in Matthew 5:22, 29 and 30, are believers, we know that the Valley of Hinnom in those passages is not a metaphor for the eternal fire prepared for the angels. To adopt that conclusion leads to the moral impossibility that Christ is lying to His disciples about a fate He knows will never happen to them in order to motivate them to obey His teaching in the Sermon on the Mount. It also leads to the theological impossibility that the way one avoids damnation is to refrain from calling a fellow believer a fool. It is unbelief in Christ, not avoiding sin, that is the cause of damnation (John 3:18).

LUST AND STUMBLING BLOCKS LEAD TO *GEHENNA* (MATTHEW 5:29-30; 18:8-9)

> *And if your right eye makes you stumble, tear it out, and throw it from you; for it is better for you that one of the parts of your body perish than for your whole body to be thrown into the Valley of Hinnom. And if your right hand makes you stumble, cut it off, and throw it from you; for it is better for you that one of the parts of your body perish, than for your whole body to go into the Valley of Hinnom (Matthew 5:27-30; cf. Matthew 18:8-9).*

In Matthew 18:8-9 Jesus expands this warning beyond lust and adultery to stumbling blocks in general.

> *If your hand or your foot causes you to stumble, cut it off and throw it from you; it is better for you* ***to enter life*** *crippled or lame, than to have two hands or two feet and be cast into the eternal fire. If your eye causes you to stumble, pluck it out and throw it from you. It is better for you to enter life with one eye, than to have two eyes and be cast into the fiery hell (Matthew 18:8–9).*

Regarding Matthew 5:22 and 29, John Piper told his congregation, "Jesus treats anger the way he treats lust. If you don't fight lust, you don't go to heaven (Matthew 5:29). If you don't forgive others, you won't get to glory (Matthew 6:15)."[2938] Is David in hell? Solomon certainly did not fight lust, he gave in to it (1 Kings 11:1-11). Is everyone who failed to fight lust and gave in to it eternally damned? How about those who do not fight gossip, or who do not fight pride? Or, let's say they fight lust, gossip, and pride but fail repeatedly. How many failures constitute "not fighting"?

In spite of his vigorous denials, we believe that Piper cannot escape the charge that he is teaching salvation by one's own efforts, that is, works. Why? This battle to forgive and fight lust is our battle and involves efforts we must make. Piper, of course, will say that the Partners do not understand the relationship between God's commands and His mysterious working in our hearts to fulfill His commands. He will point out that the work is ultimately God's work, not ours, so we errantly accuse him of teaching salvation by works. We

---

[2938] John Piper, "Battling the Unbelief of Bitterness (1988, Sermon 658)," http://www.desiringgod.org/resourceLibrary..

do not. We understand his viewpoint; we simply do not agree with it. Piper knows the Reformed faith consistently teaches that sanctification is a synergistic affair involving the works of God and of man (see Philippians 2:12-14; 4:13). Therefore, if *Gehenna* refers to damnation, then works are necessary if the believer is to avoid this fate. Thus we are kept from damnation by means of something we must do (or, in this case, avoid doing) and not by faith alone" in Christ alone. However, if *Gehenna* refers to a negative assessment of a carnal Christian's life, there is no conflict with the doctrines of grace,

For three reasons it is doubtful that Jesus refers to being cast into the lake of fire because of adultery.

FIRST, THE PUNISHMENT EXCEEDS THE CRIME. The punishment for adultery in the Old Testament was not eternal damnation, but stoning (Leviticus 20:10; Deuteronomy 22:22), a temporal judgment. Guelich is correct to note that if *Gehenna* refers to eternal damnation, there is a "disproportionate relationship between the offense and the consequence."[2939]

SECOND, THEIR ARGUMENT IS BASED UPON THE INCORRECT PREMISE THAT TO ENTER INTO LIFE MEANS GO TO HEAVEN WHEN ONE DIES. If "enter life" and "enter the kingdom" mean "go to heaven when you die," then one could argue that the opposite, the "eternal fire" of *Gehenna*, means final consignment to the lake of fire. Hans Scharen says, "The New Testament views 'entrance into life' or the kingdom of God as entering 'the age to come' (*aiōn mellōn*), the new and everlasting creation representing the final order of things."[2940] However, as discussed elsewhere, the meaning of "eternal life" can be new life now as well as entrance into heaven when one dies.[2941] Jesus in this passage is speaking about entering into the kingdom way of living *now*; entering into life *now.*[2942] Discipleship ("entering into life") is costly.

Obviously, Jesus is not teaching that true believers can enter into eternal life (in the sense of going to heaven) with maimed resurrection bodies! This is a metaphor for radical discipleship. To enter the kingdom of God maimed is to enter the experience of kingdom life now by committing to the kingdom way of life taught in the Sermon on the Mount (Matthew 5:27-29). One lexicon translates, "It is better for you to come to experience (true) life with one hand than to keep two hands and end up in *Gehenna*."[2943]

[2939] Robert A. Guelich, *The Sermon on the Mount: a Foundation for Understanding* (Waco, TX: Word Books, 1982), 188. Experimental Predestinarian William Hendriksen is typical of those who view the punishment here as eternal damnation. He says, "Nothing, no matter how precious it may seem to us at the moment—think of the right eye or the right hand—should be allowed to doom our glorious destiny." Like many commentators he never explains the problem his interpretation creates. We are left to conclude that non-Christians can go to heaven only on the condition that they do not commit adultery (i.e., by works), or Christians must maintain their salvation by works, avoiding certain sins. Hendriksen and Kistemaker, *Exposition of the Gospel According to Matthew*, 303.

[2940] Scharen, "Part 2: Gehenna in the Synoptics," 336. It is possible that Scharen has confused extra-biblical Jewish references to entering into life in the "world to come" (e.g. b. Ber. 28b; Genesis Rab. 9.8 [on Genesis 1:31]; b. Abod. Zar. 18a) with the Sermon on the Mount's emphasis of entering into life now—a life of discipleship. The Talmudic references are hundreds of years after the time of Christ and are irrelevant for understanding first-century Judaism. Scharen, "Part 1: Gehenna in the Synoptics," 336.

[2941] See discussion in Chapter 17.

[2942] For fuller discussion of the phrase "enter into life see footnote 1195, and pp. 346 ff.

[2943] Louw-Nida, 1:807.

To experience the kingdom now and to have high honor in the kingdom may cost the believer everything (cutting off his hand, etc.). As pointed out earlier, entering the kingdom is a broad term encompassing entering into life and discipleship now, leading to greatness and an abundant future entrance into the restored Davidic theocracy.[2944] What is in view here, since this entry is predicated on works, is not initial, eternal salvation, but the growing experience of a rich life now, leading to greatness in the future reign. Such greatness only comes through living out the Sermon on the Mount, that is, by becoming the servant of all. Craig Evans is correct in saying, "The goal of self-discipline is to enter life." But Evans never explains how this is to be correlated with the New Testament teaching that salvation is by faith alone and costs nothing (Revelation 21:6; 22:17). If life means "the kingdom way of living" (i.e. "life indeed"), and "enter into life" means enter into that way of living, there is no difficulty in harmonizing this passage with the rest of the New Testament.

THIRD, THE PASSAGE IS ADDRESSED TO THE SAVED DISCIPLES. According to Craig Evans Jesus teaches here that, "One has a choice," of "going the way of the world and risking being cast into hell, or removing the cause of temptation and entering life."[2945] In Evans's view Jesus is warning saved people[2946] that they will go to hell if they cause little ones to stumble or if they give in to lust. In response one should note that according to Mark, Jesus is addressing His disciples (Mark 9:31; cf. Matthew 18:1), and He is warning His born-again brethren of a danger that faces them. This common Reformed solution fails because it requires that Jesus warns believers of a destiny which He knows in fact will never happen to them (John 6:39-40; 10:27-29).

Jesus says to them *"if **your** hand," "if **your** foot," "if **your** eye"* causes you to stumble. John Nolland notes that "A striking feature of 18:8–9 is the move to second person singular address. The materials in vv. 6–7 have been impersonally expressed in the third person singular, as also vv. 1–5 with the exception of v. 3, which uses second person plural forms."[2947] This suggests that He is speaking *particularly* to His believing disciples.

Is He warning His justified disciples that ***they*** will lose their justification and burn eternally in hell if they do not make these difficult choices (as Arminians maintain)? Or, is He telling them that if they do not make these choices, this will prove they are really not saved and are in fact unbelievers (as Experimental Predestinarians assert)?[2948] Arminians and Experimental Predestinarians are convinced of their view, but such a reading of the passage strains credulity. They are convinced of their interpretation because they "know" that the Valley of Hinnom refers to eternal torment in burning flames, and that "enter the kingdom" means to enter either the millennium or the eternal state as eternally saved people. As a result, they are forced either into a theological sophistry not mentioned in the text[2949] or else into teaching a doctrine of works for eternal salvation.

2944 See discussion on entering into greatness on pp. 271, 279.

2945 C. A. Evans, *Mark 8:27-16:20*, Word Biblical Commentary (Dallas: Word, 2002), 70-71.

2946 He would probably say that professing, not possessing, believers are in view, but he never explains.

2947 Nolland, *The Gospel of Matthew: A Commentary on the Greek Text*, 738.

2948 John Grassmick, "Mark," in *The Bible Knowledge Commentary: New Testament*, ed. John F. Walvoord and Roy Zuck (Colorado Springs: Cook, 1996), 147.

2949 That is, that the character of the saved rather than the conditions of avoiding damnation are in view.

Therefore, as we have repeated many times above, it is impossible that the warning concerns the lake a fire because (1) that is a destiny which will never befall them and (2) it involves Jesus in a falsehood.

Gehenna and the Heart of Man

The third way the New Testament uses the Valley of Hinnom is as a metaphor for something that sets on fire "the course of our life" and "defiles the entire body" (James 3:6). Dibelius states the common view, with no proof, that this statement refers to Satan.[2950] But, let us imagine a world in which when James and his readers hear a speaker mention, "the Valley of Hinnom" they would immediately think of a burning garbage dump outside the city of Jerusalem. In this world they had never heard of the association between the Valley of Hinnom and final damnation mentioned occasionally in Second Temple post-AD 70 literature. While this is not the world in which the majority of modern commentators live, I have shown in the preceding chapters that this was the world of first-century Palestine. To those listeners, the valley of Hinnom did not speak of postmortem confinement in the lake of fire. They saw fire, smelled stench, burning garbage, sewage, maggots, and corruption. Jesus did not live in the world of post-AD 70 rabbinic Judaism or of the early church.

What would the phrase "set on fire by the Valley of Hinnom" mean to them?[2951] According to Jesus, what was it that had the power to set on fire the course of one's life and defile the whole body? His answer is "the heart." When James says the tongue is set on fire by hell, it is absurd to say, as Calvin does, that it is set on fire by Satan. Why not go to the many references in the Old and New Testaments which teach that the source is evil inside?[2952]

Since we have explicit teaching from James' Half-Brother about this issue, we need not speculate what the early church or rabbinic Judaism say about the matter. Jesus said that adultery is committed in the "heart," and He asked, "*Why do you think evil in your hearts?*" (Matthew 9:40). More specifically, He taught, "*Out of the abundance of the heart the mouth speaks*" (Matthew 12:34). The source of life defilement is not Satan, it is "the heart," which is dominated by the corrupt sin-nature within. "*The good man out of his good treasure [the heart] brings forth what is good; and the evil man out of his evil treasure brings forth what is evil*" (Matthew 12:35). James and his readers would most likely have thought that the source of defilement was the corruption within. They would *not* have thought about remote and probably unfamiliar associations we do not see until a few post-AD 70 fantasies. None of the Second Temple literature or any Greek literature associates the Valley of Hinnom with

---

2950 Dibelius and Greeven, *James: A Commentary on the Epistle of James*, 198.

2951 Davids assures us that the Apocalypse of Abraham, chapters 14 and 31, "point to the existence of Azazel (Satan) in hell." Davids, *The Epistle of James: A Commentary on the Greek Text*, 143. The Apocalypse of Abraham was probably written in the latter half of the first century. However, it has been preserved only in the Old Church Slavonic translation (the language and script of the Slavs in the Balkans) from the ninth century. We have no certainty what the original text said. The text refers to Satan being commanded to go "into the inaccessible parts of the earth," and says of Satan, "be thou the burning coal of the Furnace of the earth" (Apocalypse of Abraham 14). The text never refers to the Valley of Hinnom or *Gehenna*. Davids just assumes that the reference is to *Gehenna*, probably because he "knows" that the traditional view equating *Gehenna* with an eternal furnace of fire is true. Instead, the Apocalypse refers to the fire of hades, not *Gehenna* in Apocalypse of Abraham 31, which is usually associated with sheol and the intermediate state, not the *Gehenna* of the New Testament. Yet, this one citation is the only evidence generally cited in the commentaries for equating *Gehenna* in James 3:6 with Satan.

2952 Proverbs 6:17; 10:20; 17:4; 18:21.

the person of Satan prior to AD 70. They would not turn to such fantasies anyway but would have more likely thought about what one of their own prophets taught them.

> *Wash your heart from evil, O Jerusalem, that you may be saved. How long will your wicked thoughts lodge within you? (Jeremiah 4:14)*
>
> *The heart is more deceitful than all else and is desperately sick; who can understand it? (Jeremiah 17:9)*

There are 601 references to the heart in the Old Testament. This massive testimony to the source of good and bad affecting the "course of our life" would surely overwhelm any remote association of Hinnom with Satan.

However, we need not speculate on the matter because James himself makes it clear that he does not believe Satan to be the source of fire that defiles the whole body. He explicitly says that the source is our own lust, "*But each one is tempted when he is carried away and enticed by his own lust. Then when lust has conceived, it gives birth to sin; and when sin is accomplished, it brings forth death*" (James 1:14–15). Clearly, the Valley of Hinnom in James 3:6 is a metaphor for man's "own lust." And what a fitting metaphor this is. The sin-nature is a rotten stench, full of maggots and city refuse. Neither Jesus nor the Bible ever bought into the devil-made-me-do-it excuse. That may work for Flip Wilson in his comedy routines, but the apostle James and his older Brother (Jesus) would reject it entirely. The sin nature, not Satan, lights the fire. Satan can pour gasoline on it, but we have no excuse that he causes it (that excuse didn't work for Eve either).

James is using the shock treatment to get his readers to realize that the sin-nature is not something that is rather tame; it must be aggressively dealt with. How shocking it would be to hear that the inner core of one's being is a rotten stench infested with maggots, dung, and garbage. One does not need to go to Satan to be shocked about what is within. By calling their inner life this kind of thing, James is dramatically getting their attention.

In summary we say that the fount of the tongue's sin is the lust (*epithumia*) of the individual, as shown in James 1:14. Thus *Gehenna* in James 3:6 is a metaphor for burning internal lusts and not Satan nor postmortem material torments!

Seasoned with Salt

In Mark's account of the warning about *Gehenna*, he explains that temptations of lust, anger, and broken relationships mentioned in the previous verses, are trials which can cause believers to lose their saltiness, if they do not resist them. He warns them that once their lives fail in this way, it is difficult to regain their testimony for Christ. This is another way of saying they face the danger of loss at the Judgment Seat of Christ, the eternal fire of *Gehenna*.

> *For everyone will be salted with fire. Salt is good; but if the salt becomes unsalty, with what will you make it salty again? Have salt in yourselves, and be at peace with one another (Mark 9:49-50).*

The key to understanding this difficult passage is its concluding application to the disciples beginning in verse 49 with the word "for."

The life of a disciple will be "salted with fire." Living in the world will require difficult decisions described with hyperboles as "plucking out one's eye," "cutting off one's hand," etc. Disciples will be purified by fiery trials (Proverbs 27:21; Isaiah 48:10; 1 Peter 1:7; 4:12; esp. Numbers 31:23).[2953] These trials will "purge out what is contrary to God's will and preserve what is consistent with it." If, however, the salt becomes un-salty, if the believer fails to preserve himself through the fiery trials, if he is preoccupied with status (v. 34) instead of being a servant of all (v. 35), he faces a more serious fire, the judgment and shame of a wasted life. Therefore, the disciples are exhorted to "have salt in yourselves." That is, let your lives be seasoned with salt.[2954] Be the kind of disciple who, when faced with difficult choices, makes the right choices and lives to be a servant of all no matter what the cost. Such persons allow the trials to purify themselves, that is, they are seasoned with salt. The issue is not the distinction between a believer and a nonbeliever (eleven of the Twelve were believers) but between being a disciple who follows Christ no matter how difficult the trial and one who does not. Specifically they are "*to be at peace with one another*." They are to forget about the question of who is the greatest (v. 33). In fact, to achieve greatness one must be "*last of all and servant of all*" (v. 35). This spirit of self-denial may be costly. Thus, the discourse reverts to where it began: Jesus modeled the very path to greatness; He now exhorts them to follow (v. 31). Their disputes regarding greatness endangered their chances for real greatness and for new life via the kingdom way of living.

So we see that Jesus begins and ends this pericope (Mark 9:30-50) with the subject of sacrifice. He tells them, "The Son of Man is to be delivered into the hands of men, and they will kill Him; and when He has been killed, He will rise three days later" (Mark 9:31). He then ends the pericope with the exhortation to be willing to do the same: "*have salt within yourselves*" (just as His life exhibited the preserving and flavoring qualities of salt). Like their Master, they are to have salt within themselves and to be harder on themselves (vv. 43-48) than they are on others (vv. 38-41) and not worry about greatness but instead to "be at peace with one another" (v. 50).

When Jesus says it is better to "enter the kingdom" maimed, He is referring to the self-sacrifice required to pursue the path of kingdom living now, the narrow gate and the narrow way, and as a result, obtain an abundant entrance into the kingdom in the future (Matthew 6:33; 2 Peter 1:11). Even though living this way is costly, involving radical decisions (cutting off one's hand), a refusal to follow Christ no matter how difficult the choice, may cost one everything. A wasted life is of no more value than that of a worm-infested corpse thrown on the garbage heap of the fires of Hinnom (1 Corinthians 3:15; 1 John 2:28).

Summary

The view presented in this chapter that *Gehenna* has nothing to do with final damnation is certainly a departure from the commentary tradition. However, as we have argued above, that tradition should be challenged for seven reasons. At this point in our discussion, let us review and summarize the argument.

1. There is no evidence for this identification in either the Old Testament or any extra-biblical literature prior to 30 AD. Therefore Jesus' listeners would never had made that association.

[2953] Clarke, *Adam Clarke's Commentary*, s. v. "Mark 9:49".

[2954] See Leviticus 2:13 and Ezekiel 43:24.

2. The Apostle Paul explicitly forbids his readers from paying attention to any Pseudepigraphal myths. Therefore neither Jesus nor the Apostles, even if they were aware of them, would ever use the Valley of Hinnom as a metaphor for hell even if there was an example of that equivalence in these fantasies.
3. A first century Jewish audience upon hearing Jesus refer to the Valley of Hinnom would immediately have thought of the burning garbage dump on the southeast side of the city in Jesus' time (southwest of the City of David in Jeremiah's time). That this was a metaphor for hell would never have occurred to them.
4. There is no compelling argument derived from any of the twelve New Testament references which *requires* interpreting Gehenna as hell.
5. It is theologically and morally impossible that Jesus' warnings to His disciples could be interpreted as hell. It is theologically impossible because such an interpretation would require that final entrance into heaven is, in part, at least, awarded on the basis of not committing such sins as anger and lust. In other words, Jesus would be teaching salvation by works.
6. It is morally impossible because if *Gehenna* refers to final damnation, they embroil Jesus in issuing warnings to His disciples regarding destinies He knows could never befall them. In effect, He is lying to His followers in order to secure obedience to His demands.
7. Finally, the explanations for these warnings offered by Experimental Predestinarians are, in this writer's opinion, unsatisfactory. There is good biblical evidence suggesting that the warnings regarding *Gehenna* do not refer to threats of postmortem consignment to eternal condemnation, but instead can easily be understood in three ways.

   First, it is a metaphor for a national catastrophe facing Israel if they do not repent as a nation and embrace Christ as their messiah.

   Second, it is a metaphor for the terrible rebuke Christ directs toward the unfaithful believer because of the shame and disgrace of his unfaithful and wasted life; a life that is of no more value than an unburied corpse cast into a burning refuse dump.

   Third, it is a metaphor for the rotten stench of our sin-nature.

   Seen in this light, the incredible dissonance between the crime of lust or calling someone a fool, and the punishment of eternal condemnation, admitted by many scholars, is removed.

In the next chapter we turn to one of the most perplexing passages about *Gehenna*, Matthew 10:28. Addressing His saved and justified disciples, Jesus warns them of the danger of being destroyed in *Gehenna*.

> *And do not fear those who kill the body, but are unable to kill the soul; but rather fear Him who is able to destroy both soul and body in the Valley of Hinnom (Matthew 10:28).*

He further exhorts them saying, "*But whoever shall deny Me before men, I will also deny him before My Father who is in heaven*" (Matthew 10:33). How is it possible that a saved person could ever be denied by Christ at the judgment?

57

Gehenna and Perseverance

IN THE preceding chapters, we considered the Old Testament and extra-biblical evidence for the traditional assertion that *Gehenna* refers to final damnation. To this writer and a growing number of others, this evidence is wanting. The Valley of Hinnom in the Old Testamement and the New never refers to hell. When one turns to extra-biblical materials, we found that there is no mention of it in any document predating the time of Christ in which Gehenna is equated with final damnation

As discussed in the last chapter, some passages in the New Testament seem to indicate that believers may be sent to *Gehenna,* and are warned that this may be the final outcome of their lives. The traditional answers are, of course, to be expected. Either those addressed are true believers and are being warned that they might lose their eternal salvation if they do not change their ways (Arminian), or they are merely professing believers who should reexamine their foundations to see if they are "truly" "in the faith," that is, justified (Experimental Predestinarian).[2955] Neonomian and Catholic writers believe that believers are being warned about the possibility of final damnation;[2956] and can secure their salvation only by faith plus works.[2957]

This discussion must now be applied to a particular warning regarding the Valley of Hinnom which is addressed to Christ's believing followers (Matthew 10:28). We will show that only by accepting the conclusions of the preceding chapters (1) that one can harmonize this warning with the teaching of the New Testament that salvation cannot be lost; (2) that justification comes by faith alone in Christ alone; and (3) that works or repentance (when defined as "turning" or obedience), or perseverance in holiness have nothing to do with the initial saving transaction or one's final arrival in heaven.

Failure to Persevere Leads to *Gehenna*

> *And you will be hated by all on account of My name, but it is the one who has endured to the end who will be saved (Matthew 10:22).*

[2955] Out of 32 commentaries I consulted, only one explicitly stated view. Craig Blomberg says, those addressed are "professing believers" who "may well not be Jesus disciples at all and thus remain under the threat of damnation," Blomberg, *Matthew*, 275. Blomberg gives no proof because there is none. He merely asserts it in order to fit the requirements of his Experimentalist theology.

[2956] Stanley, *Did Jesus Teach Salvation by Works*, 254.

[2957] Stanley says, "These passages patently teach salvation via endurance." Ibid., 248. Similarly, Schreiner and Caneday say, "Jesus' words indicate that perseverance to the end is the necessary condition. Perseverance is the means that God has appointed by which one can be saved." Schreiner and Caneday, *The Race Set Before Us*, 151-52.

And do not fear those who kill the body, but are unable to kill the soul; but rather fear Him who is able to destroy both soul and body in the Valley of Hinnom (Matthew 10:28).

Therefore everyone who confesses Me before men, I will also confess him before My Father who is in heaven. "But whoever denies Me before men, I will also deny him before My Father who is in heaven" (Matthew 10:32–33).

In Luke's account we read,

And I say to you, "My friends, do not be afraid of those who kill the body, and after that have no more that they can do. But I will warn you whom to fear: fear the One who after He has killed has authority to cast into the Valley of Hinnom; yes, I tell you, fear Him!" (Luke 12:4-5).

These three passages are related and will be considered together. Jesus is reminding His followers who are being sent out on a missionary journey that God cares for them and considers them of great value (Matthew 10:31-32). They should take comfort in that love when faced with tribulation. The danger is that because of persecution or the fear of physical death, they may fail to complete their task successfully. We will argue that the meaning of these passages is that it is much better to endure the pain of physical death now than to forfeit one's final significance at the Judgment Seat of Christ. The believer, in other words, when faced with the temptation to deny Christ under threat of persecution, must "fear" God.

But before we begin, let us assume for a moment that the Valley of Hinnom does in fact refer to eternal damnation. It would still not be necessary to draw the conclusions which the Neonomians, Arminians, and Experimental Predestinarians derive from the text. Note that the disciples are to fear "Him," "the One" who can send them to *Gehenna*. Does this imply a danger that God might send them to eternal damnation if they deny Him? Not necessarily. The following verses assure them that He will not do that.

Are not two sparrows sold for a penny? Yet not one of them will fall to the ground apart from the will of your Father. And even the very hairs of your head are all numbered. So don't be afraid; you are worth more than many sparrows (Matthew 10:29-31).

So the God who can destroy in final damnation is the same God who intently cares for them. It seems a bit incongruous that in verse 28 they are supposed to fear that God will send them to eternal damnation and then in verse 29 they are told, "*Don't be afraid*."

Ken Mitchell has suggested that "the reference to *Gehenna* is not a threat, but a comfort in His authority and power. Possibly it is a reference to His authority over the persecutors, asserting that they cannot eternally harm the believer. In other words we might paraphrase,

And do not fear those who kill the body, but are unable to kill the soul; but rather fear Him who is able to destroy both soul and body ***of those who persecute you*** *in the Valley of Hinnom.*

This is consistent with Psalm 73, where the psalmist finds his comfort in the judgment that will come on the wicked. "Their doom is sure."[2958] God is our Father. As "Father" He created us and incorporated us into His family. Of course He could remove one from the family; He has that kind of authority. But no father really keeps his child in this kind of fear.

[2958] Ken Mitchell, personal communication, August 5, 2005.

While this viewpoint is plausible and has appealed to many, for me it is not satisfying. The specific characteristic of God, which is to evoke the fear of the Lord, is His ability and authority to send one to *Gehenna*. I see no reason to select this particular characteristic of the divine being other than to warn those addressed that He might send them there. If the only thought is to "Fear Him," in some general sense, then why not refer to His omnipotence, His holiness, or many other attributes? I suspect that those holding this view are driven to it by their prior assumption that *Gehenna* must refer to final damnation.

If, on the other hand, the Valley of Hinnom does not refer to eternal damnation, but to some other consequence for unfaithfulness, the interpretation to follow explains the details of the passage quite well.

TO WHOM IS IT ADDRESSED?

Throughout Luke 12 Christ speaks about the danger of *Gehenna* with the believing disciples whom He addresses as His "friends" (Luke 12:4, "a bond of relationship or love,"[2959]) "His disciples" (v. 1), and His "little flock" (v. 32). These are the believing disciples who can be taught by the Holy Spirit what to say when they are brought before tribunals for testifying for Christ (v. 11).[2960] In Luke 12:33-34 He encourages believers to lay up treasure in heaven; in verse 35 He encourages them to be ready when He, the Son of Man, comes.

In Luke 12:42-48, in response to Peter's question as to whether Jesus is addressing the disciples or the crowds in general, Jesus gives the parable of the unjust steward, warning them that because they have been given much, much will be required. Darrell Bock is correct in stating, "God may require martyrdom *of his disciples*"[2961] [emphasis added]. But then Bock inconsistently links this judgment on God's believing disciples as being cast into the fire of hell![2962] Scharen does the same, "The sayings counsel believers to fear God because His power extends beyond death, enabling Him to inflict final, irrevocable punishment on man by condemning the whole person to *Gehenna*."[2963] Yet Scharen, like Bock, does not believe that such a fate can ever come on a believer. Nevertheless, Scharen suggests that God threatens believers with a fate he knows will never happen to them!

WHO CAN CAST INTO HELL?

Jesus warns that His disciples should fear "*the One who after He has killed has authority to cast into hell.*" This is most likely a direct warning to believers of what God might do and not just what He is capable of doing. The UBS Handbook suggests, "This relative clause may be easier to express as a separate sentence: '*But instead you should fear God. He is the one who can kill you and destroy your soul in hell.*'"[2964]

[2959] So Gustav Staehlin, "*philos* et. al.," in TDNT, 9:163.

[2960] These "disciples believed in Him" (John 2:11); their names are recorded in heaven (Luke 10:20), and they are therefore saved (John 3:16).

[2961] Bock, *Luke 9:51-24:53*, 1135.

[2962] Ibid., 1136. "In judgment from God [they will] be cast into fire."

[2963] Scharen, "Part 2: Gehenna in the Synoptics," 463.

[2964] Newman and Stine, *A Translator's Handbook on the Gospel of Matthew*, 307.

Many have argued that this refers to Satan.[2965] The command to fear *Gehenna,* it is said, cannot possibly be a command to fear God because the phrase means "to be afraid of." Also, Satan is the "soul-murderer," not God; the Bible never says that God destroys the soul. Most important to this view is the fact that this context is about God bringing encouragement to believers in the midst of persecution or the threat of martyrdom.

In response, it should be noted that nowhere in Scripture is such power (to send one to eternal damnation) attributed to Satan. After Satan kills the body, Jesus says, "*there is no more that [he] can do*" (Luke 12:4).[2966] The command to "fear Him" (v. 5) does not mean "be afraid of Him." Rather it points to the well-known phrase "the fear of the Lord."[2967] The change of construction from "be afraid" (Luke 12:4) to the command, "fear him" (v. 5) "would lead the mind on out of the terror before spoken of in v. 4, into that better kind of fear always indicated by that expression when applied to God, and so prepare the way for the next verse."[2968] This fear in v. 5 of Him who can cast the whole person into *Gehenna,* is not a cowering anxiety regarding one's eternal damnation; rather it is a wholesome "reverential awe." In the Bible it is a positive sense of reverence and submission emerging out of an understanding of who the Lord is and His steadfast love and grace for us. Jesus wants us to always live with a consciousness of His presence and be aware that He is not only with us and cares, but that He is aware of every word uttered and every decision made, and will one day hold us accountable.[2969]

To "fear Him" refers to fearing His authority or more specifically the kind of fear associated with the Judgment Seat of Christ.

> *For we must all appear before the Judgment Seat of Christ, that each one may be recompensed for his deeds in the body, according to what he has done, whether good or bad. Therefore knowing* ***the fear of the Lord,*** *we persuade men, but we are made manifest to God; and I hope that we are made manifest also in your consciences (2 Corinthians 5:10-11).*

Because we can experience recompense for good or bad works, we are to live in a healthy fear of God as we look toward His final assessment of our lives.[2970] Why then are we to fear God? We are to fear Him because He is the one who after death has authority to consign our "body and soul" to the Valley of Hinnom. This valley is obviously used as a metaphor for some kind of judgment after death. The question is, "What kind?"

Some argue that Matthew 10:28 has fear of damnation in view.[2971] They suggest that a contrast is being made between the danger of physical death (the killing of the body) and eternal death (the killing of the soul; eternal damnation). Physical death thus pales in comparison with the prospect of eternal punishment.[2972] Persecutors (or Satan?), it is

---

2965 J. J. Van Oosterzee, "Luke," in *A Commentary on the Holy Scriptures*, ed. John Peter Lange, et al. (Bellingham, WA: Logos Research Systems, 2008), 8:196.

2966 He does have the power over physical death (Hebrews 2:14).

2967 J. Reiling and J. L. Swellengrebel, *A Handbook on the Gospel of Luke*, UBS Handbook Series: Helps for Translators (New York: United Bible Societies, 1993), s.v. "Luke 12:5".

2968 Van Oosterzee, "Luke," 8:196. Cf. James 4:12.

2969 Bruce K. Waltke, "The Fear of the Lord: The Foundation for a Relationship with God," in *Alive to God*, ed. J. I. Packer and Loren Wilkinson (Downers Grove, IL: InterVarsity Press, 1992), 17-33.

2970 Suggested by Wendall Hollis, personal communication August 3, 2006.

2971 Stanley, *Did Jesus Teach Salvation by Works*, 244.

2972 Blomberg, *Matthew*, 177.

said, can only destroy the body, but we should fear God who can destroy the soul, that is, consign it to eternal damnation. The believer when threatened with the possibility of martyrdom is warned that denial of Christ (apostasy) will result in final consignment to the abyss.

According to Ralph Yarbrough, this fear of damnation is supposedly "a positive motivation to grasp the nettle of Christian service boldly even when it involves the likelihood of loss, pain, and earthly destruction. Temporary discomfort here and now is preferable to permanent calamity in the age to come."[2973]

Such an interpretation, though common,[2974] implicitly teaches that in order to motivate them to live faithfully God warns believers of a fate that He knows can never happen to them. In other words God lies to believers in order to secure their perseverance. John Calvin actually endorsed this kind of thinking in his discussion of Romans 11 when he said, even though "this cannot happen to the elect [i.e., loss of salvation], they have need of such warning, in order to subdue the pride of the flesh which needs to be terrified with the dread of perdition." [2975]

Would Christ warn His believing disciples of the possibility that they might go to the lake of fire if they do not live faithfully or stand up under threat of death? Certainly not! Experimental Predestinarian writer Darrell Bock ignores the problem. On the one hand he acknowledges that those addressed are believing disciples, but then he applies this passage to postmortem condemnation to hell, leaving his readers perplexed as to why Jesus would warn true believers of a fate He knows will never befall them.[2976]

This notion not only contradicts the note of encouragement in the context; it also violates His explicit teaching elsewhere. He has already told them that "*the one who comes to Me I will certainly not cast out*" and "*that of all that He has given Me I will lose nothing, but raise it up on the last day*"; and "*For this is the will of My Father, that everyone who beholds the Son and believes in Him, may have eternal life; and I Myself will raise him up on the last day*" (John 6:37-40). His disciples had indeed beheld the Son and believed in Him. I suspect that the reason so many commentators pass over the difficulty with no explanation is because they have no explanation. If *Gehenna* refers to final damnation, as they assume, there is simply no obvious solution.[2977]

If being cast into the Valley of Hinnom after death is not a metaphor for eternal damnation, then to what does it refer? To "kill the soul" and have both body and soul destroyed in hell cannot refer to eternal damnation, for then annihilationism would be taught.[2978] *Therefore, it must be a metaphor for some other kind of judgment after death.* We have already argued that a first-century Palestinian would not have understood this to be a reference to hell but to a literal casting of the body into the burning garbage in the

---

2973 Yarbrough, "Chapter 3: Jesus on Hell."

2974 Bock, *Luke 9:51-24:53*, 1136.

2975 Calvin, *Romans*, s.v. "Rom. 11:22".

2976 Bock, *Luke 9:51-24:53*, 1135-36. David Turner says, "if there were no hell to avoid, there would be one less reason to be faithful to Jesus and one more reason to deny him." Turner, *Matthew*, 279.

2977 For example, Joel Green passes over the difficulty without comment. Green, *The Gospel of Luke*, 481. Likewise, after noting that this is addressed to disciples and "friends," Nolland moves on and gives us no help. Nolland, *Luke 9:21-18:34*, 680.

2978 For a strong argument against annihilationism see Peterson, "Does the Bible Teach Annihilationism?," 13-27. For an argument in favor, see Farrar, *Mercy and Judgment*.

Valley of Hinnom, a shameful *physical* death. He would have understood it as a judgment in time, *and that is the way it was used in the Old Testament*. It is clear, however, that Jesus is investing it with a deeper meaning, a metaphor (technically a hypocatastasis)[2979] for postmortem judgment.

Did Jesus ever speak of other kinds of judgments? Yes, He did. As discussed in the last chapter, on many occasions He warned of the coming catastrophe of AD 70.[2980] He also frequently referred to rewards and the possible forfeiture of them.[2981] Jesus is ultimately the one who will judge us (John 5:22). He warned that a servant of Christ could actually be rebuked as an "evil slave" and be judged and experience profound regret at the Judgment Seat of Christ (Matthew 24:45-51). Other ill-prepared believers may hear the Lord saying to them, "I do not know you," that is, "I do not honor or respect you" (cf. Matthew 25:12).[2982] Still others will find that even what they have will be taken from them (Matthew 13:12). He also pointed out that the carnal believer may forfeit being entrusted with spiritual riches, rewards in the life to come (Luke 16:11). The believer who has become "saltless" is as useless as a pile of manure (Luke 14:35). These and other verses establish that Jesus taught the possibility of either positive or negative assessments of our lives could occur at the final judgment.

But can true believers experience shame at the Judgment Seat of Christ, as this interpretation suggests? Yes!

> *Now, little children, abide in Him, so that when He appears, we may have confidence and not* ***shrink away from Him in shame at His coming*** *(1 John 2:28).*

JUDGMENT ON THE BELIEVER'S LIFE

Besides the unlikelihood that being cast into the Valley of Hinnom refers to eternal damnation, there are two considerations that suggest that a judgment on the believer's life work is in view.

First is the word "destroy" in Matthew 10:28. The verb "to destroy" (Gr *apollumi*), while sometimes referring to damnation,[2983] is never used in Matthew's Gospel in this sense.[2984]

[2979] As a figure of speech, it differs from a metaphor because in a metaphor the two nouns are both named and given; while in a *hypocatastasis* only one is named and the other is implied, or, as it were, is *put down underneath* out of sight. Hence a hypocatastasis is an implied resemblance or representation, that is, an implied simile or metaphor. If *metaphor* is more forceful than *simile*, then *hypocatastasis* is more forceful than *metaphor*, and expresses as it were the superlative degree of resemblance. For example, one may say to another, "You are *like* a beast." This is a simile, tamely stating a fact. If, however, he said, "You *are* a beast" that would be metaphor. But, if he said simply, "Beast!" that would be a *hypocatastasis*, for the other part of the simile or metaphor ("you") would be implied rather than stated. This figure, therefore, is calculated to arouse the mind and attract and excite the attention to the greatest extent. E. W. Bullinger, *Figures of Speech Used in the Bible: Explained and Illustrated*, reprint ed. (Grand Rapids: Baker Book House, 1968), 744.

[2980] Matthew 3:7; 23:36; Luke 3:9; 13:1-5, 6-9; 21:20.

[2981] Cf. Matthew 6:6; 16:24-27; 20:8; 25:45-47; Mark 9:41; Luke 6:23, 25; 14:10-14; 19:11-27. For a motivating and excellent biblical development of these and other passages, see Bruce Wilkinson, *A Life God Rewards* (Portland, OR: Multnomah Press, 2002).

[2982] See elsewhere in this book, pp. 821 ff. and 320 ff.

[2983] Luke 19:12; John 3:16; 10:28; Romans 2:12; 1 Corinthians 1:19; 15:18; 2 Corinthians 2:15; 4:3; 2 Thessalonians 2:10.

[2984] Alan Stanley points out that the danger is that the body and soul might be "destroyed" (Gr *apollumi*) and that this refers to damnation. He then cites Matthew 8:25, where Peter, fearful of drowning, cries, "Save us, we

Normally, it is used of the destruction of a person or object in time (e.g., Matthew 2:13; 8:25; 9:17; 12:14; 22:7; 26:52).[2985] It refers to ruin or waste; and there is no notion of eternal damnation as part of the semantic value of the word.[2986] It can refer to a loss of reward (see *apollumi* in 2 John 8; Matthew 10:42).

Paul uses it, for example, of the total ruin that can come to the spiritual life of a weaker brother when he is emboldened to do things against his conscience by observing the example of a stronger Christian (1 Corinthians 8:11). Using a synonym for *apollumi*, Paul exhorts Titus to rebuke false teachers who are "ruining [Gr *anatrepō*] whole households" (Titus 1:11; cf. 2 Timothy 2:18). This verb can mean "to jeopardize someone's inner life, upset, ruin."[2987]

And, second, having one's life destroyed is sometimes used of a negative judgment on the significance of that person's life. The phrase "soul and body" (Luke 12:4), like "heaven and earth," is probably a merism, referring to the whole "person" and is not a comment on biblical psychology. Being cast into the Valley of Hinnom is equivalent to what Jesus spoke of often in other contexts when He referred to "losing one's life" by trying to "find it." The "destruction" of the soul and body in the Valley of Hinnom is a metaphor for the total loss of one's life work and reward (cf. 1 Corinthians 3:15). He is "ruined." His opportunities for service for Christ in the kingdom and capacity for enhanced intimacy with God are lost. *This is precisely the point that Jesus makes, in Matthew's version, a few verses later.*

> *He who has found his life [soul] shall lose it [Gr apollumi], and he who has lost his life for My sake shall find it (Matthew 10:39; cf. 16:25).*

If we understand *apollumi* in the sense of "to cause to lose, to lose," reward as it does in v. 42, (see BDAG, 116, 2), these two passages may be understood in this manner.

> *And do not fear those who kill the body, but are unable to kill the soul; but rather fear Him who is able **to cause the loss** [Gr apollumi] of all that you are [your soul and body] in the Valley of Hinnom (Matthew 10:28).*

> *He who has found his life **shall lose** [Gr apollumi] it, and he who has lost his life for My sake shall find it (Matthew 10:39).*

Understood in this way we see a parallel with 1 Corinthians 3:15.

> *If any man's work is burned up, he **shall suffer loss** [Gr zēmioō "to suffer loss, be punished"[2988]]; but he himself shall be saved, yet so as through fire (1 Corinthians 3:15).*

---

are perishing." Obviously, this has nothing to do with damnation, as Stanley implies. Stanley, *Did Jesus Teach Salvation by Works*, 148.

2985 In an instructive usage of "soul" in Luke 6:9, Jesus says, "*I ask you, is it lawful on the Sabbath to do good, or to do harm, to save a life, or to destroy it?*" (Luke 6:9; Gr ψυχὴν σῶσαι ἢ ἀπολέσαι) The opposite of saving a life ("soul") is not consigning it to hell, but harming it. In this case the harm done is physical death. The Greek idiom "to save a soul" does refer to salvation, salvation from some danger, but certainly not eternal salvation from hell. "Saving a life here is not a technical term for salvation, but simply refers to deliverance in a general sense, to the restoration and healing that give the man possession of full physical skills." Bock, *Luke 1-9:50*, 529.

2986 LN, s.v. "*apollumi*"; BDAG, 115.

2987 BDAG, 74.

2988 BDAG, 428.

As discussed elsewhere in this book,[2989] gaining or forfeiting one's soul in Matthew 10:39 refers not to gaining or forfeiting one's eternal destiny, but to the gaining or forfeiting of true life, final significance. *Hence when Jesus speaks of the soul being cast into Gehenna, and then defines the term Himself in the verses to follow by the phrase "losing one's life," we conclude that the metaphor is related not to eternal damnation but to the judgment on a believer's life work.* Instead of appealing to the Pseudepigrapha to understand the meaning of Gehenna, why not appeal to the Old Testament, and for the loss in *Gehenna*, consider v. 42, where *apollumi* refers to "loss of reward" (not damnation)? The infatuation of modern scholars for all things pseudepigraphal has sent them baying down fanciful trails in the hunt for false scents of extra-biblical writers while the correct object of the hunt, the immediate context and the Old Testament, lay squarely before them.

The persecutors may kill the body, but only God has power over the soul and thus the whole person, the summation of his life. Those who fail that judgment will suffer total disgrace in the afterlife, something like what the nation would experience in the destruction of AD 70.

The above interpretation obviously involves providing a nuance to the phrase "who is able to destroy your body and soul" to mean something like "is able to ruin" or "causes to lose [Gr *apollumi*] the final significance of your life." This in turn requires that the "body and soul" is a metaphor for one's total life, a plausible suggestion that fits this context well and makes good sense of Jesus' application in verse 39, "whoever finds his life will lose [Gr *apollumi*] it." The believer who fails to endure will lose his life, that is, lose the final meaning of his life. As we demonstrated in an earlier chapter, the meaning of this saying is as follows:

> *Whoever wishes to avoid the hardships and self-denial of wholehearted discipleship [save his life] will trifle his life away and lose its final significance [will lose it], but whoever denies himself and places the will of God first [whoever loses his life for my sake] will find a rich life now and abundant reward at the Judgment Seat of Christ [will save it].*[2990]

When Jesus commands us to fear the one who has power to cast us into the Valley of Hinnom, He means, "Fear the One who has the authority to punish you by issuing a negative assessment of your life."

IF YOU DENY ME

Jesus' warning to the apostles continues:

> *Therefore everyone who confesses Me before men, I will also confess him before My Father who is in heaven. But whoever shall deny Me before men, I will also deny him before My Father who is in heaven (Matthew 10:32-33).*

> *And I say to you, everyone who confesses Me before men, the Son of Man will confess him also before the angels of God; but he who denies Me before men will be denied before the angels of God (Luke 12:8-9).*

[2989] See elsewhere in this book 205 ff.

[2990] See discussion in chapter 15.

While it is common to assume that Christ's confession before the Father is a confession of the disciples' saved condition, John Hart has correctly observed, "What Christ actually confesses when He says, 'him I will also confess before My Father,' is not distinctly specified. From the text as it stands, it is just as likely that Christ will confess us to be faithful believers as it is that He will confess us to be eligible for heaven."[2991] To be denied by Christ is parallel to having the final significance of life counted as garbage in the Valley of Hinnom (v. 28).

The notion that being denied by Christ is a warning of eternal damnation is probably based on the assumption that Jesus would never "deny" a true believer, so this must refer to His rejection of false believers, hypocrites, who did not really believe in the first place. These hypocrites revealed their lack of faith by apostasy, final rejection of Christ, and hence Jesus rejects them. But if Christ's confession of a believer before the Father is that the believer's life has been faithful, then the opposite, the denial, would be a denial that he was faithful.

Suppose this startling premise that Christ would never "deny" a true believer is untrue. Suppose there is New Testament evidence that Jesus would in fact "deny" a true believer in some sense, and yet such a denial does not relate to damnation, but instead the loss of reward or loss of the right to possess or rule in the kingdom. One enmeshed in Experimentalist ways of thinking cannot imagine a negative occurring at the Judgment Seat of Christ because in that system all Christians obey. So how could there be any negative punishment? As shown elsewhere, there is considerable New Testament evidence to support the fact that carnal Christians will face negative judgment. And I will argue later that there is no theological difficulty with the notion of a punishment at the judgment seat even though Christ has already paid the penalty for our sins.[2992]

We propose that this denial by Christ does not refer to the rebuke of false Christians who have only professed faith and who have failed to persevere under trial. Instead, it refers to genuine Christians who failed, and as a result, they are denied the right to possess the earth with Him in the fulfillment of human destiny.

This is brought out in 2 Timothy 2:11-13.

> *It is a trustworthy statement: For if we died with Him, we shall also live with Him; if we endure, we shall also reign with Him; if we deny Him, He also will deny us; if we are faithless, He remains faithful; for He cannot deny Himself (2 Timothy 2:11–13).*

Notice the phrase, "*If we endure, we shall also reign with Him.*" This parallels what Jesus taught when He said, "*It is the one who has endured to the end who will be saved*" (Matthew 10:22). The two sayings equate being saved with reigning with Him.[2993] This is not a

[2991] Hart, "Why Confess Christ: The Use and Abuse of Romans 10:9-10," 7. Hart cites R. Larry Moyer, *Free and Clear: Understanding and Communicating God's Offer of Eternal Life* (Grand Rapids: Kregel Publications, 1997), 267, who suggests several possible ways in which the Son confesses us before the Father for future reward: (1) He may grant us honor in the kingdom (John 12:26); (2) He may grant us a position of service or responsibility in the kingdom (Luke 19:17, 19).

[2992] See discussion in Chapter 15.

[2993] Philip Towner notes that "At the end of the test is the reward ... The literal promise of 'ruling with the king' broadens out in the New Testament to the well-known theme of sharing in Christ's eschatological role of king and judge, the source of which was undoubtedly the Jesus-tradition (Matthew 19:28 '*I tell you the truth, at the*

salvation from physical death or a salvation from damnation. It is the joy of participating in the messianic salvation, the future reign of the servant kings!

The passage also speaks of the possibility that we may deny Him, and if we do, He will deny us. The "disowning of Christ" to which Paul refers is likely the forsaking mentioned throughout his letter. To forsake an apostle is to forsake Christ. He says all in Asia have "turned away from me" (2 Timothy 1:15) including Demas who loved this present world and deserted him (2 Timothy 4:10). In fact he said, "All deserted me" (4:16). Thus the denial in view is a denial of Christ by believers, and not by nonbelievers. Paul's missionary companions were those who abandoned him.

Unfortunately, commentators give little help as to what this denial means. Towner, for example, says, "The meaning is clear: disowning Christ, whether as desertion caused by fear of suffering for the faith or as apostasy, carries fearful eternal consequences." However, he never tells what he thinks these "eternal consequences" are.[2994] The connection with the preceding "if" clause, "we will reign with Him" suggests that Christ's denial is the denial of the right to reign with Him. But, He says that if we deny Him, even if "we are unfaithful" (v. 12), He will remain faithful to us. In other words, Christ is faithful to His promises of salvation to the point that He will save erring believers. But, even though that is true, there is a danger for the believer who lives unfaithfully.

This danger is expressed in various ways. Mark says, "If anyone is *ashamed* of me and my words in this adulterous and sinful generation, the Son of Man will be *ashamed* of him when he comes in his Father's glory with the holy angels" (Mark 8:38, NIV).[2995] Instead of the word "deny," Mark says Jesus "will be ashamed." That Jesus can be ashamed of true believers at the second coming certainly sounds less damning than "deny" and is in fact stated elsewhere. "And now, dear children, continue in him, so that when he appears we may be confident and *unashamed* before him at his coming" (1 John 2:28). Suppose, then, that "deny" is understood in the milder sense of "to be ashamed." In Luke 9:25-26, we learn that this shame is a consequence that falls on the believer who is unwilling to "lose his life."[2996] This language of "shame" evokes a central idea of being cast into the Valley of Hinnom.

To what then does the denial refer? Mark and Luke help us here by clarifying the setting in which this event occurs. It happens at the last judgment when the Son of Man "*comes in his Father's glory with the holy angels*" (Mark 8:38; Luke 12:8; Matthew 16:27). That the reference clearly evokes Daniel 7:23-27 is commonly accepted.[2997] There Daniel speaks of a time when the saints will receive (possess) a kingdom (Daniel 7:18, 22, 27). Consistent with Matthew 16:27, the context of the "denial" is the time in which the saints will "receive the kingdom" (i.e., receive royal authority there)[2998] and possess it. It is a time

---

renewal of all things, when the Son of Man sits on his glorious throne, you who have followed me will also sit on twelve thrones, judging the twelve tribes of Israel'; cf. Luke 22:30)." Towner, *The Letters to Timothy and Titus*, 512.

2994 Ibid.

2995 Also Luke 9:26.

2996 I have argued elsewhere that to "lose one's life" by attempting to "save" it refers to loss of life's true meaning and fulfillment, not damnation to hell. See chapters 15 and 16.

2997 France, *The Gospel of Matthew*, 405. Davies and Allison, *A Critical and Exegetical Commentary on the Gospel According to Saint Matthew*, 2:217.

2998 As demonstrated in an earlier chapter, the phrase "to receive the Kingdom" does not mean to "enter" the kingdom, but to receive royal authority there (Luke 19:12). Some saints will, and some will not. It depends on their faithfulness in this life.

of rewards. Not all saints receive this authority and hence possess the kingdom with Christ. This is clear from many Scriptures. All Christians are heirs of God, but only those who suffer with Him will be co-heirs with Him and rule in the kingdom.[2999] Those Christians who "overcome," and only those Christians, will be "given authority" over the nations (Revelation 2:26-27),[3000] and only faithful servants will receive the right to rule over cities (Luke 19:15-19).[3001]

We are therefore on firm ground when we understand that the denial by Christ refers to the denial of the right to share with Him in the fulfillment of human destiny. This fits the context perfectly. The apostles are being sent out on a mission and are warned that they will face much persecution. They are encouraged, on the one hand, that God is concerned about the details of their lives and, on the other hand, warned that if they turn back and fail to persevere, they will risk forfeiture of their great reward of judging over the twelve tribes of Israel (Matthew 19:28; Luke 22:30). They will be denied that wonderful privilege.

We have argued in the preceding paragraphs that the issue of being confessed by Christ or being saved in Matthew 10 relates not to damnation or entrance into heaven. Rather, the salvation in view is a prophet's reward. This understanding is confirmed by Christ's concluding encouragement.

> *He who receives a prophet in the name of a prophet shall receive a prophet's reward [Gr misthos]; and he who receives a righteous man in the name of a righteous man shall receive a righteous man's reward (Matthew 10:41).*

What is at stake for the disciples is reward or its loss. A reward in Matthew is not equal to heaven; it is something in heaven. The word *misthos* refers to payment for work done. The prophet's reward is not salvation; it is honor and opportunities for greater service (five cities, ten cities, etc.).[3002]

[2999] For example, Romans 8:17, "And if children, then heirs—heirs of God, and joint heirs with Christ, *if indeed we suffer with Him*, that we may also be glorified together" (NKJV). See Chapter 5, where it was argued that two heirships are in view. Jesus makes the same point in Luke 22:27-29 where He says that the disciples will receive kingships over the twelve tribes because they stayed with Him in His sufferings. We are all heirs of God by faith in Christ, but only those who persevere in suffering will reign with him. Also Paul wrote, "If we endure, we shall also reign with Him. If we deny Him, He also will deny us" (2 Timothy 2:12, NKJV). Those Christians who endure (Gr *hypomenō*) will reign with Him. Those who do not, will not reign. Yet, even though they will not reign, Christ will be faithful to save them into eternal life because He cannot deny Himself. The parallelism suggests that the "denial" is not final damnation to hell, but denial of the right to reign with Him. See pp. 635 ff. for discussion of this passage.

[3000] As demonstrated elsewhere, the "overcomer" of Revelation 2:26-27 is not the same as the one who "overcomes the world" in 1 John 5:4. See elsewhere in this book, pp. 30 and 674 ff.

[3001] For discussion of this parable see chapter 52. As shown there, the third servant is not assigned to hell but forfeits his right to rule in the coming kingdom.

[3002] Stanley cites Matthew 5:46b and 47b. He strangely argues that the phrase "what reward do you have" in verse 46 and "what surpassing thing do you do" in verse 47 equal each other. However, one is an adjective describing a noun and the other (reward) is a payment for work done. Of course doing something will result in the reward but to do something "surpassing" does not equal a reward. Stanley says that Matthew 5:20, which refers to the ways one cannot enter the kingdom with our "surpassing righteousness," shows that entering the kingdom is a reward. "Quite clearly then entering the kingdom and reward are in some sense synonymous since 'surpassing' and 'reward' are synonymous." Stanley, *Did Jesus Teach Salvation by Works*, 274. First, "surpassing" and "reward" are not synonymous. But second, Stanley misunderstands what it means to enter the kingdom. As shown in previous chapters, "entering the kingdom" does not mean, as he maintains, enter into final salvation. Rather, it means to enter into a kingdom way of living now which leads to greatness. This one fact invalidates the majority of Stanley's entire book.

There is little to justify the claim that *Gehenna* refers to eternal damnation.[3003] It is more probable that the judgment of the Valley of Hinnom is a warning about a negative assessment of a wasted life.

Protestant Purgatory?

Is this a "Protestant Purgatory?" No. There are fundamental differences between the Roman Catholic concept of purgatory and what is being suggested here. In the Catholic tradition, purgatory involves the following concepts:[3004]

1. A recent Catholic writer says, "Purgatory involves a period of cleansing after death which comes to an end when the person's guilt has been expiated."[3005] According to the Council of Trent, "If anyone shall say that after the reception of the grace of justification, to every penitent sinner the guilt is so remitted and the penalty of eternal punishment so blotted out that no penalty of temporal punishment remains to be discharged either in this world or in the world to come in purgatory before the entrance to the kingdom of heaven can be opened: let him be anathema."[3006]

We disagree. The negative assessment at the Judgment Seat of Christ has nothing to do with purification or expiation (atonement for sin) as it relates to one's eternal destiny. That has been accomplished completely by the finished work of Christ. Unlike the Catholic Purgatory, the judgment facing the carnal believer is not a punishment relating to one's eternal destiny (heaven or hell), rather it is a punishment for sins within the family, a punishment for a failed life. There is no necessity of satisfying the wrath of God for eternal life. Also, unlike the Catholic Purgatory, there is no indication in Scripture that the Judgment Seat of Christ (1 Corinthians 3:11-15; 2 Corinthians 5:10-11; Colossians 3:25; 2 John 8) is remedial. The bad works that are burned up relate to loss of rewards, not to cleansing.

2. Purgatory, according to Catholic theology, lasts for a long period of time, until the final judgment of heaven or hell is rendered. However, at the Judgment Seat of Christ there is no lengthy process of purgation, cleansing, or atonement. Regarding the duration of purgatory one Catholic apologist speculates that the conclusions derived from many revelations to saints through the ages are "unanimous: the shortest time in purgatory

[3003] Against the interpretation suggested in this chapter, Luke 12:10 could plausibly be cited. There the reference is clearly to nonbelievers and, it could be argued, parallels the judgments of being denied and of being cast into *Gehenna*. Granted that this is a difficulty, it is also possible that Jesus is including that judgment on the unbelievers as a comfort to His apostles who will face persecutions before the courts (Luke 12:11). Those who blaspheme the Holy Spirit (i.e., reject Christ and the kingdom offer as testified to by the miracles of the Holy Spirit) will one day be judged. God will take care of their persecutors. One day there will be a righting of all wrongs.

[3004] See Zachary J. Hayes, "The Purgatorial View," in *Four Views of Hell*, ed. William Crocket (Grand Rapids: Zondervan Publishing House, 1996), 91-131.

[3005] Catholic apologist John Salza says, "The word 'purgatory' comes from the Latin *purgare* which means to purge, purify, or make clean. The Church teaches that it is a place or condition of temporal punishment for departed souls who are destined for heaven but not completely purified from sin. Through this purgative process, spiritual contamination is removed and the soul is made wholly pleasing to God so it can live forever with Him in heaven." John Salza, *The Biblical Basis of Purgatory* (Charlotte, NC: Saint Benedict Press, LLC, 2009), 15-16.

[3006] Session 6, Decree Concerning Justification, Canon 30 (January 13, 1547).

seems to be an extraordinarily, excessively long time. Hence, like the pains of sense and loss, this pain of duration (length of time) is intensified beyond anything we have experienced in this life. In fact, it is because the sufferings of purgatory (sense and loss) are so incredibly intense that the soul perceives time as it does."[3007] While the Catholic Purgatory involves years of torment and physical pain, the Judgment Seat of Christ involves only emotions of profound regret and loss of honor, service, and intimacy in eternity future. There is no physical torture!

3. Purgatory includes the idea that the living can have beneficial influence on the state of the dead by means of their love and prayers. The Judgment Seat of Christ includes no such possibility.

Is there a Protestant Purgatory? I believe evangelicals should be open to thinking about this. Those inclined to interpret the meaning of *Gehenna* in the New Testament with reference to the Pseudepigrapha should be aware that whatever *Gehenna* meant in those writings, it was purgatorial.[3008] Of course, we cannot accept the Catholic understanding mentioned in the three points above, nor should we use the term "purgatory" which implies cleansing, purgation, and atonement. That said, this book does argue that there will be a time of grief. Clark Pinnock suggests that we consider ridding ourselves of our knee-jerk reaction to the idea and consider our purgatory, "not as a place of punishment or atonement (because of our view of the sufficient and finished work of Christ), but we can think of it as an opportunity for maturation and growth."[3009] We would add that it is initially a time of rebuke, regret, reflection, and repentance.

[3007] Salza, *The Biblical Basis of Purgatory*, 43-44.

[3008] If one were to look for any parallels in later Jewish literature referring to the meaning of *Gehenna*, it is likely that the notion of some regarding a temporary punishment in the afterlife would be the referent and not eternal damnation. While we have no idea whether these ideas were present in the first century, they do suggest something like a negative assessment and temporary rebuke by the Lord at the Judgment Seat of Christ. Later Judaism regarded *Gehenna* as the purgatory of faithless Jews, and the place of eternal perdition for the Gentiles. See "1 Enoch 27:1-2" in Charles, *Commentary on the Pseudepigrapha of the Old Testament*, 2:205. "It is significant that the oldest Rabbinic reference to *Gehenna* (T.Sanh., 13, 3 and par.) tells us that the disciples of Shammai, as distinct from those of Hillel, ascribe to *Gehenna* a purgatorial as well as a penal character." Joachim Jeremias, "*Gehenna*", TDNT, 1:658. By "purgatorial" these writers mean a temporary time of cleansing. Edersheim notes, "Only the perfectly just enter at once into paradise; all the rest pass through a period of purification and perfection, variously lasting, up to one year. But notorious breakers of the law, and especially apostates from the Jewish faith, and heretics, have no hope whatever, either here or hereafter! Such is the last word which the Synagogue has to say to mankind," Alfred Edersheim, *Sketches of Jewish social life in the days of Christ* (Grand Rapids: Wm. B. Eerdmans Publishing Co., 1974), 180. E. P. Sanders cites T. Sanhedrin 13:3 (Tosefta Sanhedrin, part of the Babylonian Talmud, ca. AD 600), "The School of Shammai say: There are three classes; one for 'everlasting life' and another for 'shame and everlasting contempt' (Daniel 12:2) (these are wholly wicked) [and a third class which is] evenly balanced. These go down to *Gehenna* where they scream and again come up and receive healing, as it is written: "And I will bring the third part through the fire, and will refine them as silver is refined, and will try them as gold is tried; and they will call on my name and I will be their God' (Zechariah 13:9). And of these last Hanna said: 'The Lord killeth and the Lord maketh alive, he bringeth down to Sheol and bringeth up' (1 Sam 2:6)." Sanders, *Paul and Palestinian Judaism*, 142. Apart from the indications of physical torment, one is reminded of 1 Corinthians 3:11-15.

[3009] Clark H. Pinnock, "Response to Zachary J. Hayes," in *Four Views on Hell*, ed. William Crocket and Stanley N. Gundry (Grand Rapids: Zondervan Publishing House, 1996), 130.

This raises a final question. "Rebuke" and "disinheritance" sound a lot like "punishment." But how can God punish a believer at the Judgment Seat of Christ if the punishment of all our sins, past and future, have already been paid for by Christ? Would not that mean the penalty is being born not only by our Substitute but also a second time by the believer? We will address this issue in detail in chapter 59.

Although I know of no Scripture that explicitly teaches this, I suggest that when the carnal believer is confronted with the wasted life he has lived, he will confess, repent, and be restored to fellowship with Christ just prior to the second coming (Revelation 7:17). There is no thousand years of grieving or an eternity of punishment. The diminished capacity to experience God in eternity future is a consequence of an unfaithful life. It is the outworking of a fundamental principle of God's governance of His universe. "*Do not be deceived, God is not mocked; for whatever a man sows, this he will also reap*" (Galatians 6:7). If one does not develop an enhanced capacity to experience God in this life, such an enhanced capacity will not be imparted to him in the resurrection.

Summary

Jesus promised "salvation" to those who endure to the end.

> *And you will be hated by all on account of My name, but it is the one who has endured to the end who will be saved (Matthew 10:22).*

They will face terrible persecution; they will be hated, but they will find the true meaning of their lives, "salvation," their final significance, and the Master's "well done" if they persevere.

However, if they do not endure, they will not be "saved"; they will lose the final significance of their lives. He warns them,

> *Fear Him who is able to cause the loss of your life's significance in the Valley of Hinnom (Matthew 10:28).*

Because of this danger they are to have a healthy and wholesome fear of God. He has the power and the authority to cause the loss ("to destroy") of all that they are (soul and body), and all their works will be burned up.

If by their lives they have denied Christ, they will hear these sobering words:

> *But whoever shall deny Me before men, I will also deny him before My Father who is in heaven (Matthew 10:33).*

They will lose everything. Their lives will truly be destroyed. They will be denied opportunities for service and will not be co-heirs with Him in the fulfillment of human destiny. In fact, they will lose even what they have.

> *I tell you, that to everyone who has shall more be given, but from the one who does not have, even what he does have shall be taken away (Luke 19:26).*

There are many reasons why a believer may fall out of the race and fail to persevere. A common one is that the sacrifices required for the life of discipleship do not seem to be worth losing the comforts and safety of an uncommitted life. As a result they seek "life" in what this world has to offer rather than the true life of final significance. Therefore expressing this loss once again in a final warning, our Lord says,

> *He who has found his life shall lose it, and he who has lost his life for My sake shall find it (Matthew 10:39).*

The warning about *Gehenna* is not about final damnation. It is about loss. Unlikely is the notion that Jesus would warn His friends, who had placed their trust in Him, that unless they stood up under persecution, He would judge them with eternal damnation. The Valley of Hinnom was known as a place of shame and disgrace in first-century Palestine. Jesus used the phrase as a metaphor for the shame of a failed life, a life that is ruined, totally destroyed, and experiencing a loss of its final significance at the Judgment Seat of Christ.

While He also applied this disgrace of *Gehenna* to the national catastrophe that will come on "this generation" (Matthew 10:36), in Matthew 10:28, He warned that what God would do to the nation, He would do to the failed disciple as well. Having one's life cast into the Valley of Hinnom is therefore best understood as a metaphor for a negative assessment on his life at the Judgment Seat of Christ.

58 Accursed

SEVERAL PASSAGES of the New Testament refer to individuals who may be accursed (Gr *anathema*). Paul almost wishes that he could be "accursed from Christ" for the sake of his nation.

> *For I could wish that I myself were accursed, separated from Christ for the sake of my brethren, my kinsmen according to the flesh (Romans 9:3, NASB).*

Elsewhere Paul warns,

> *If anyone has no love for the Lord, let him be accursed. Our Lord, come! (1 Corinthians 16:22, ESV).*

> *But even if we, or an angel from heaven, should preach to you a gospel contrary to what we have preached to you, he is to be accursed! (Galatians 1:8, NASB)*

Are these warnings addressed to true believers who are in danger of apostasy and final damnation? Or, are they addressed to those who have merely professed faith in Christ, but who have demonstrated by their character and behavior that their professions were not genuine and that they too are on the highway to final damnation unless they repent and examine their foundation?

Many commentators assign 1 Corinthians 16:22 and the word *anathema*, "accursed," to eschatological damnation.[3010] Many assume that those who do not "love the Lord" reveal by their behavior that they are not "real" Christians, are "under the wrath and curse of God [final damnation] (cf. John 3:36),"[3011] and do not "belong to the Lord."[3012] What does *anathema* mean?

Anathema in Greek Literature

The Greek word "*anathema*" ("something dedicated or consecrated to the deity")[3013] is found twelve times in the Septuagint[3014] and its verbal cognate *anathematizō* ("to curse, to

3010 For example, David E. Garland, *1 Corinthians* (Grand Rapids: Baker Academic, 2003).

3011 W. Harold Mare, "1 Corinthians," in *The Expositor's Bible Commentary* (Grand Rapids: Zondervan Publishing House, 1976), 297.

3012 Fee, *The First Epistle to the Corinthians*, 839.

3013 Johannes Behm, "ἀνάθεμα, ἀνάθημα, κατάθεμα" in TDNT 1:354.

3014 Leviticus 27:28; Numbers 21:3; Joshua 6:17; 7:12; Judges 1:17; 1 Chronicles 2:7; Zechariah 14:11.

invoke divine harm upon") fifteen times.[3015] In the New Testament, *anathematizō* occurs four times, and it never refers to damnation.[3016] For example, it refers to Peter laying a curse on himself and means to "curse and swear"[3017] (Mark 14:71). This should suggest caution in asserting that its nominal cognate, *anathema*, means damnation. Something that is *anathema* is something that has been dedicated to God in either a positive sense (e.g., an offering) or in a negative sense for physical and temporal destruction or exclusion from the believing community (e.g., Ezra 10:8).[3018] The related Hebrew word for *anathema*, *cherem* ("devoted thing") occurs twenty-nine times,[3019] and the verb *charem* ("to devote") is found fifty times.[3020] The predominant meaning of the Greek and Hebrew words is "devoted to destruction." These Greek words are never found in the Greek Pseudepigrapha or the Greek apostolic fathers. They appear four times in Josephus.[3021] None of these occurrences refer to eschatological rejection.

If there is no instance anywhere in Greek literature outside of the New Testament where *anathema* means "an eternal damnation" [such as, to the lake of fire], and no example in the LXX, why do so many commentators assume without any proof that "anathema" refers to final eschatological rejection? The lexical evidence suggests that it can mean either "devoted to physical destruction" or "excommunication," not "damnation." In fact, according to the *Oxford Dictionary*, this came to be the prominent meaning in Jewish literature in Second Temple Judaism: "after the Exile [*anathema*] was normally confined to exclusion from the community and loss of goods."[3022] The word is also found in later

---

3015 Numbers 8:14; 21:2-3; Deuteronomy 13:16; 20:17; Joshua 6:21; Judges 1:17; 21:11; 1 Kings 15:3; 2 Kings 19:11; 1 Chronicles 4:41; Ezra 10:8; Daniel 11:44.

3016 Mark 14:71; Acts 23:12; 14, 21.

3017 Louw-Nida, 1:441.

3018 Ezra says, "And that whoever would not come within three days, according to the counsel of the leaders and the elders, all his possessions should be forfeited and he himself **excluded** from the assembly of the exiles" (Ezra 10:8, NASB). The word translated "excluded" in Hebrew is *charem*. The Septuagint translates it *anathematizō*. This is the only instance in the LXX or the Hebrew text where these words clearly refer to "being excluded." However, that usage fits well in 1 Corinthians 16:22 and Galatians 1:8. But in Romans 9:3 that meaning does not fit well. Thus, to be devoted to destruction from Christ means "to be physically destroyed, if we are to be faithful to the usage of *anathema* elsewhere. If this is the meaning, then Paul is saying he would be willing to receive "from Christ" the sentence of physical death if this would result in the physical salvation of the nation from the coming national catastrophe predicted by John the Baptist and Jesus. H. Aust and D. Müller comment, "Ezra 10:8 distinguishes between a ban on all belongings and personal exclusion from the community. In the Old Testament ban and excommunication are always different measures. In excommunication those referred to are exiled from the community and so from the sphere of salvation, but they are not, as in the case of the banned, directly given over to God and destroyed. H. Aust & D. Müller "*anathema*," in NIDNTT, 1:414.

3019 For example, it is used in a negative sense in Leviticus 27:29; Deuteronomy 27:6; 1 Samuel 15:21; Isaiah 43:28, to mean "devoted to destruction." In a positive sense it is found it Leviticus 27:21, 28 ("devoted to the Lord").

3020 For example, Exodus 22:19; Leviticus 27:28, 29; Numbers 21:2, 3; Deuteronomy 2:34; 7:2; 13:6; 20:17; Joshua 10:28; 11:11; 12, 20, 21; 1 Samuel 15:3, 8, 9, 15, 18, 20; 1 Kings 9:21; 2 Kings 19:11; 1 Chronicles 4:41; 2 Chronicles 20:23; 32:14; Isaiah 34:2; 37:11; Jeremiah 25:9; 50:21, 26; 51:3; Daniel 11:44.

3021 Flavius Josephus, "Against Apion," in *The Works of Flavius Josephus: Complete and Unabridged*, ed. W. Whiston (Peabody, MA: Hendrickson Publishers, 1987), Book 1, 113. Idem, The Antiquities of the Jews, 17:162; and idem, The Wars of the Jews, 7:10. In Against Apion, *anathema* is best translated "donations of gold."

3022 F. L. Cross and E. A. Livingston, *The Oxford Dictionary of the Christian Church* (Oxford; New York: Oxford University Press, 2005), 58.

Judaism.[3023] The early church often cited Galatians 1:8 and 1 Corinthians 16:22 as a basis for excommunication, and in the opinion of some, this is Paul's meaning as well.[3024] Why not apply *that* meaning in these passages? Commenting on Galatians 1:8, Behm succinctly summarizes the answer, "We can hardly think of an act of Church discipline, since the apostle uses the phrase *apo tou Christou*, 'from Christ' (Romans 9:3) and also considers that an angel from heaven (Galatians 1:8) or even Jesus Himself (1 Corinthians 12:3) might be accursed."[3025] We will address the phrase "from Christ" below. But what kind of logic is this? The fact that a demon spirit might shout out "Jesus be accursed" is hardly evidence that *anathema* means damnation. As for Galatians 1:8, Behm takes a literal statement as a figurative hyperbole. In other words, because *anathema* "obviously" means damnation, this must be hyperbole! Burton is more cautious, noting, "Precisely what thought the expression ['accursed,' Gr *anathema*] represented in Paul's mind is difficult to determine, because it is impossible to know precisely how largely the hyperbole of impassioned feeling entered into the words."[3026]

Anathema in Romans 9:3

We are left, then, with Romans 9:3 and the qualifier "from Christ," as the only possible basis for equating *anathema* with damnation.

> *For I could wish that I myself were accursed, separated from Christ for the sake of my brethren, my kinsmen according to the flesh (Romans 9:3).*

Therefore, before considering the meaning of 1 Corinthians 16:22 and Galatians 1:8, it is imperative that we digress a bit and consider Romans 9:3.

Since "accursed" is said to be "accursed *from Christ*" in Romans 9:3, many assume that eschatological damnation is meant.[3027] However, in view of the usage of the word in the Septuagint and in the New Testament and the immediate context of Romans 9, such a view is far too hasty. And if the word does not mean final damnation in Romans 9:3, then it probably does not mean it in 1 Corinthians 16:22 and Galatians 1:8. Based on the lexical data, there are two other options for the meaning of *anathema* in Romans 9:3. Jewett (who believes this refers to damnation), acknowledges that it could refer to excommunication. "The function of this curse is to ban someone from a religious congregation."[3028] The other

[3023] Schrage "*aposunagōgos*", in TDNT, 7:849. The Talmud says that *cherem* referred not to damnation, but to an unlimited exclusion from the synagogue and avoidance of all contact. But "this excommunication ... could be lifted. As a domestic discipline excommunication was designed to amend, convert, or win back the person concerned, not to ban him permanently from the synagogue as in the case of apostates and heretics."

[3024] Cross and Livingston, *The Oxford Dictionary of the Christian Church*, 58. "Paul uses the word to denote separation from the Christian community inflicted for sins such as preaching a gospel other than his (Galatians 1:8 f.) or for not loving the Lord (1 Corinthians 16:22)."

[3025] Johannes Behm, "*anathema, anathēma, katathema*," TDNT, 1:354-55.

[3026] Ernest De Witt Burton, *A Critical and Exegetical Commentary on the Epistle to the Galatians* (Edinburgh: T. & T. Clark, 1964), 363.

[3027] For example Schreiner, *Romans*, 480. He says, "The term refers to eschatological judgment: one is cursed forever and separated from the presence of Christ."

[3028] R. Jewett, R. D. Kotansky, and E. J. Epp, *Romans: A Commentary*, Heremenia: A Critical and Historical Commentary on the Bible (Minneapolis: Fortress Press, 2006), 560. They said, "This formulation may reflect Paul's internalization of the anathemas expressed against himself in synagogue disputes in which he claims to

possibility, and the one suggested below, is that Paul *almost wishes* that Christ would take his *physical life* in order that the nation of Israel might be spared from the coming catastrophe.

Thus, we are left with the expression "from Christ" as the only indicator in all of biblical Greek literature that might possibly contextually invest the word *anathema* with the notion of damnation. But should not the use of *anathema* in the Septuagint and its Hebrew counterparts be the starting point of consideration for the meaning of "from Christ" in Romans 9:3? The usual practice is to assume (without proof) that "from Christ" means eternal separation from Him, and then interpret the meaning of *anathema* based on this. Once that is done, then that meaning of *anathema* is carried through the New Testament. However, only if "devoted to physical destruction" as the meaning of *anathema* cannot reasonably fit the Romans context, should other interpretations be considered. As we shall see, it fits the Romans context quite well.

What does it mean that one is *anathema* "from Christ"? A relevant question which most commentators do not address is "what is the meaning of the word *from*?" This Greek preposition, *apo*, can imply either separation or source.[3029] If it means "separation," then the text speaks of some kind of separation from Christ. That could refer to many things other than eternal damnation, such as separation from ministry for Him or from fellowship with Him.[3030] But if it refers to source (as it does in 1 Timothy 1:2; 2 Timothy 1:2; Titus 1:4), then the thought is receiving *from* Christ an *anathema* (which obviously includes the idea of separation).

The Greek preposition followed by "Christ" or "God," that is, "from Christ" is found elsewhere,

> *You have been* ***severed from Christ****, you who are seeking to be justified by law; you have fallen from grace (Galatians 5:4).*

Instead of "anathema from Christ," Paul here uses "severed" (Gr *katargeō*). One meaning of this word is "to be unproductive."[3031] The KJV renders the verse, "Christ is become of no effect to you," and the NIV has, "Alienated from Christ."[3032] The passage speaks of separation from fellowship and effective Christian living because of legalism. The believers have fallen from a grace way of life. Possibly, Paul thinks of severance from ministry and fellowship with Christ, or even physical death, in Romans 9:3.

To understand how Paul is using the phrase "*anathema* from Christ," the parallel with Moses' offer to have his name removed from the book that God had written is instructive.

---

have received the penalty of thirty-nine lashes on five separate occasions (2 Corinthians 11:24). The banning ἀπὸ τοῦ Χριστοῦ ("from the Christ") includes the article that makes clear that separation from the Messiah and his community are at stake."

3029 BDAG, 105, e.g., "from heaven" in Mark 8:11.

3030 The Galatians had fallen from the grace way of living and were "severed" from (*apo*) Christ (Galatians 5:4). The unfruitful branches in John 15 were cut off from fellowship with Him. (See discussion of this passage in chapter 39.)

3031 BDAG, 525.

3032 Because the notion of "alienation" or separation is found in the word anathema as well (Ezra 10:8), it is possible that 1 Corinthians 16:22 and Galatians 1:8 refer to separation from fellowship including exclusion from the Christian community.

Moses begged God, as Paul did, to take his own physical life as atonement for the sins of his people (Exodus 32:30-32).[3033]

> *On the next day Moses said to the people, "You yourselves have committed a great sin; and now I am going up to the Lord, perhaps I can make atonement for your sin." Then Moses returned to the Lord, and said, "Alas, this people has committed a great sin, and they have made a god of gold for themselves. "But now, if You will, forgive their sin—and if not, please blot me out from Your book which You have written!" The Lord said to Moses, "Whoever has sinned against Me, I will blot him out of My book. But go now, lead the people where I told you. Behold, My angel shall go before you; nevertheless in the day when I punish, I will punish them for their sin" (Exodus 32:30–34, NASB).*

To be removed from God's book meant to experience physical death, not eternal damnation.[3034] Some say this was the book of life in Revelation 20:15 and 21:27 that lists believers' names, but more likely it was the census of the people. It has nothing to do with eternal life as does the "book of life" in the New Testament. Durham explains, "Moses asks Yahweh to forgive Israel or to erase his own name from the book Yahweh has written, a reference apparently to a register of those loyal to Yahweh and thereby deserving his special blessing (cf. Psalm 69:28; Isaiah 4:3; Ezekiel 13:9)."[3035] "Moses' statement probably indicated he was willing to die a premature death (but not suffer eternal torment in hell)."[3036]

If, as many suggest,[3037] Moses' willingness to die for his people is behind Paul's emotional outburst, then Paul is saying he would be willing for Christ to take his physical life (receive an "*anathema* from Christ") as a substitute for some kind of judgment that he anticipates will fall on his people, the nation Israel.

Moses was offering to die physically as atonement for his people (Exodus 32:31) so that his people would not die nationally in a temporal judgment. This atonement did not convey personal salvation. Rather, it was for salvation from a national catastrophe that God threatened to bring on His people because they worshiped the golden calf. In the same way, Paul is offering himself as a substitute for his people so that his nation might not face the temporal consequences of their national rejection of their Messiah. Nations do not go to

---

3033 See Morris, *The Epistle to the Romans*, 560.

3034 "It is used of natural life, Psalm 69:28, where 'let them be blotted out of the book of the living' means 'let them die'. Cf. Exodus 32:32f., where Moses prays to be blotted out of God's book if Israel is to be destroyed." Mounce, *The Book of Revelation*, 96.

3035 John Durham, *Exodus*, Word Biblical Commentary (Dallas: Word, 2002), 3:432. Six references to the "book of life" in the Old Testament are in Exodus 32:32, 33; Psalm 69:28; Isaiah 4:3; Ezekiel 13:9; and Daniel 12:1. All of them refer to the register of the physically living. To be "blotted" out of this book is to die physically, not eternally. Kaiser says, "To be blotted out of the Book of Life is to be cut off from God's favor, to suffer an untimely death, as when Moses pleads that he be blotted out of God's book—that he might die, rather than that Israel should be destroyed (Exodus 32:32; Psalm 69:28)." See L. Kaiser, "Book of Life" in L. Kaiser, "Book of Life," in *The International Standard Bible Encyclopaedia* (Grand Rapids: Wm. B. Eerdmans Publishing Co., 1939), 1:503.

3036 Allen P. Ross, "Genesis," in *Bible Knowledge Commentary: The Old Testament*, ed. John F. Walvoord and Roy B. Zuck (Colorado Springs: Cook, 1996), 156.

3037 For example, L. L. Belleville, "Moses" in *Dictionary of Paul and His Letters*, ed. Gerald F Hawthorne, Ralph P. Martin, and Daniel G. Reid (Downers Grove, IL: InterVarsity Press, 1993), 620. "Moses' request to be blotted out of Yahweh's book for the sake of Israel (Exodus 32:30–35) is probably behind Paul's willingness to be cut off from Christ for the sake of his Jewish kinsmen (Romans 9:3)."

the lake of fire, individuals do. Like Moses, Paul is offering that he might die rather than Israel be destroyed.

What was the nature of this possible destruction of Israel? If Paul is saying that he is willing to experience an untimely physical death should God spare His people, then one must consider that he has in mind that they too would be spared from a comparable judgment, some kind of temporal national judgment, and not final damnation. Thomas Schreiner acknowledges that in verse 3 the fate is not specified.[3038] He then argues that the terms in the following context such as "called," "children of God," "election," and so forth, prove that personal salvation is in view.[3039] Thus, the fate from which Paul wants to deliver them and which is the source of his immense grief is, according to Schreiner, the fate that individual Jews might experience damnation. This is a common view.[3040] Then in a classical illustration of an illegitimate identity transfer, he asserts that since terms like "children of God" and "election" elsewhere in Paul's writings refer to individual salvation, they must also mean that here. However, in Romans 9, the nation, not individuals, is in view. The "children of God" and the "called" in this chapter are not born-again Christians, but "the children of Israel." This is a covenant and theocratic relationship and does not necessarily imply that these children of God who are the objects of "election" are saved people. The election in Romans 9 is national and not individual.

The context requires us to believe that a national salvation from some temporal catastrophe is in view. The very passage often quoted to prove individual salvation is Romans 9:12, "the elder shall sever the younger," a phrase taken from Genesis 25:23, which says, "*The Lord said to her, '**Two nations** are in your womb; and **two peoples** will be separated from your body; and one people shall be stronger than the other; and the older shall serve the younger.'*" Jacob and Esau represent **two nations** and not two individuals elected from eternity past to personal salvation. After the death of Jacob, the term "Jacob" always refers to the nation of Israel.

In verse 11 Paul says that God's election (of Jacob) stands not on the basis of works but because of God's calling. What is that purpose? Vance is correct in saying, "*The purpose of God according to election* (Romans 9:11) had nothing to do with individual salvation or reprobation at all. It concerned the Messianic line of Abraham-Isaac-Jacob-Jesus Christ."[3041]

What then was the kind of salvation that Paul wanted them to experience? His grief was that his generation of Israelites, "this generation" (Matthew 24:34), had forfeited their right to participate in that messianic salvation, to rule in or inherit the kingdom of heaven, promised in the Old Testament prophets.[3042] As a result, they faced the national catastrophe predicted by John the Baptist (Matthew 3:10) and Jesus (Luke 13:34; 21:23; 23:28), namely, the destruction of the city and the Temple by the Romans.[3043] So certain is this coming

[3038] Schreiner, *Romans*, 479.

[3039] Thomas R. Schreiner, "Corporate and Individual Election in Romans 9: A Response to Brian Abasciano," *JETS* 49, no. 2 (June 2006): 371, 74.

[3040] H. W. Kuhn, "*anathema*," in EDNT, 1:81. "In Rom 9:3 Paul expresses the impossible wish that for the sake of the salvation of his people he might take upon himself vicarious rejection: 'would that I myself were accursed and cut off from Christ,' i.e., so that he would be banned from association with Christ."

[3041] Vance, *The Other Side of Calvinism*, 322.

[3042] For full discussion of the meaning of "salvation" in Romans see pp. 165 ff.

[3043] The vessels of God prepared for destruction in Romans 9:22 refer collectively to the nation described as "this generation," an evil generation. It is pure blasphemy to suggest, as many Experimental Predestinarians do,

judgment that Paul can say that it "has come" on the nation (1 Thessalonians 2:16). In his comment on this passage Gordon D. Fee opines that "we are here dealing with a prophetic word on the part of the apostle. Thus, Paul is so certain of God's soon-coming judgment on his ancient people that he speaks of it—future though it still is—as an event that has already taken place."[3044] Jesus explicitly announced a curse on "this generation," and surely Paul has his Lord's prediction in mind in Romans 9-11. When the leaders screamed to Pilate, "We have no king but Caesar," they committed apostasy from Yahweh, their theocratic King. They preferred apostasy rather than accept Jesus as their rightful sovereign. On that morning the soul of the nation died, and 37 years later (within one generation) the body died as well.

Schreiner points to Romans 10:1 as his final proof that salvation refers to personal deliverance from final damnation. Paul says, "*Brethren, my heart's desire and my prayer to God for them is for their salvation*" (Romans 10:1). Schreiner is absolutely correct when he says, "We have compelling evidence that the issue in Paul's mind throughout Romans 9–11 is the messianic *salvation* of Israel."[3045] But one must ask, "Salvation of whom (individuals or the nation), and from what (a temporal catastrophe or eternal damnation)?" In an earlier chapter we demonstrated that national messianic salvation was in view.[3046]

Paul continues this theme of coming national judgment in Romans 11. There, Paul speaks of the nation being broken off from the wild olive tree. That tree is not a figure for personal salvation. It refers to the Abrahamic promises of a great name, land, and nation and that one day Israel will receive a kingdom. Again, national "cutting off" is in view. This is an *anathema* to which the nation was subject. As proof that a national rather than an individual focus is in view, Paul continues by saying that when the deliverer comes from Zion, "*all Israel will be saved*" (Romans 11:26) and He will "*take away their sins*," that is, restore them from exile.[3047] It was sin that sent them into exile, and removal of national sin will bring them back. Not every Jew will be saved personally from damnation, but Israel as a whole, the nation, will be saved in the sense of deliverance from surrounding

---

that these individuals who were predestined in eternity past will burn in the lake of fire forever. This doctrine of double-predestination, which Calvin called a "horrible" decree, is the secret teaching of Experimental Predestinarians that they never speak about, but their doctrine of individual, unconditional election to heaven or the lake of fire in Romans 9 requires it.

3044 Gordon D. Fee, *The First and Second Epistles to the Thessalonians*, New International Commentary on the New Testament (Grand Rapids: Wm. B. Eerdmans Publishing Co., 2009), 102.

3045 Schreiner, "Corporate and Individual Election in Romans 9: A Response to Brian Abasciano," 374.

3046 See chapter 13. Paul speaks of a salvation from a temporal catastrophe by the passages he quotes from the Old Testament using the word "save." Citing Isaiah 10:22-23, in Romans 9:27 Paul applies the principle of the salvation of a remnant from the Assyrian invasion in 722 BC to the needed salvation of a remnant in the first century. For Israel to be "saved" in this sense does not refer to personal salvation of individuals, but to deliverance from the coming catastrophe facing the nation because of their rejection of their Messiah. National salvation, not individual, is in view. Referring again to "salvation" in Romans 10, Paul cites Joel 2:32 in Romans 10:13, "*Everyone who calls upon the name of the Lord will be saved.*" Saved from what? In the Joel passage, salvation from surrounding enemies is the subject. If the nation of Israel would repent and embrace the "one whom they pierced," and "confess him as Lord," they would be saved from the coming Roman invasion, because everyone who calls on Christ for help in the midst of distress will receive it. For full discussion of this passage, see pp. 192 ff.

3047 See pp. 44 ff. above for discussion of the fact that the forgiveness of sins in view is national and does not refer to personal salvation but is instead a metonymy of cause where "forgiveness of sins" is put for "return from exile." See Bullinger, *Figures of Speech Used in the Bible: Explained and Illustrated*, 540 ff.

enemies, restoration from exile, and final enjoyment of the restored Davidic theocracy, that is, messianic salvation. [3048]

Thus when Paul says, "*I could wish myself accursed from Christ for my brethren, my countrymen,*" we paraphrase,

> *I almost wish that Christ would devote me to physical destruction on behalf of my nation so that they would not have to endure physical destruction of their city and its inhabitants.*

As Jesus put it, "*Greater love has no one than this, that one lay down his life for his friends*" (John 15:13, NASB). Is it not preposterous to believe that Paul would consider burning forever in the lake of fire in order that his kinsmen would not?

Anathema in 1 Corinthians 16:22

Understanding that *anathema* does not refer to damnation will certainly affect our understanding of the term in 1 Corinthians 16:22 and Galatians 1:18.[3049] We read in 1 Corinthians 16:22,

> *If anyone does not love the Lord, let him be accursed [Gr anathema]. Maranatha (1 Corinthians 16:22).*

What does it mean "to love the Lord"? Is this a description of *all* those who are truly born again? Or are those who do not love the Lord, Christians who are being disobedient

---

[3048] Schreiner errs when he says of corporate and individual election that "we cannot have the one without the other." Schreiner, "Corporate and Individual Election in Romans 9: A Response to Brian Abasciano," 376. Experimental Predestinarians contradict this assertion all the time. Israel as a nation was elect in the Old Testament, but this does not mean that every individual Jew was regenerate. True, God elected Israel as a group to be the people through whom He would implement His plan to restore righteousness to the earth, but He did not elect particular members of that group to personal salvation from eternity past and consign others to eternal damnation. Schreiner correctly understands the viewpoint represented here when he criticizes it by saying that "God's work is wrapped up in corporate election, and we access the benefits of corporate election by individually believing" (ibid., 377). Schreiner thinks this is inconsistent. But it is only inconsistent with his view of divine foreknowledge which many do not share, including this writer. Because God is outside of time and has the name "I AM," there is no past or future, only the eternal present. Anthony Badger summarizes one view of this perplexing problem. He says, "What God knows He determines, and what He determines He knows. This being so, those whom God eternally and unmistakably knows as believers He chooses. Consequently, those who believe are those who [sic] He chooses or elects. There need be no before or after, no logical or chronological progression in His eternal knowledge, no decision to elect based on anything except for the carrying out of His eternal decree, which decree was always in place." See Anthony Badger, "TULIP:A Free Grace Perspective Part 2: Unconditional Election," *JOTGETS* 16, no. 2 (Autumn 2003): 41. While this viewpoint also has problems, they are not as serious as the nonsensical assertion by Schreiner "that those who do not exercise faith [because they are non-elect] are responsible and should have done so." Thomas R. Schreiner, "Does Romans 9 Teach Individual Election unto Salvation? Some Exegetical and Theological Reflections," *JETS* 36, no. 1 (March 1993): 39. This violates the law of noncontradiction. Brian Abasciano, in his response to Schreiner, is closer to the truth regarding this difficult issue when he says, "Schreiner would like to relegate the relationship between divine sovereignty and human responsibility to the status of mystery. But I would argue that the theological/philosophical (as opposed to biblical) concept of mystery that Schreiner invokes should be reserved for realities in which we do not know how something works, but in which there is no logical contradiction." Brian Abasciano, "Corporate Election in Romans 9: A Reply to Thomas Schreiner," *JETS* 49, no. 2 (June 2006): 368. For further discussion of the question of unconditional/conditional election from the Partner viewpoint see Vance, *The Other Side of Calvinism*, 241-404.

[3049] For an excellent discussion of this warning see Krell, *Temporal Judgment and the Church: Paul's Remedial Agenda in 1 Corinthians*, 220.

to Him? Can Christians be disobedient and persist in disobedience over a period of time? If one's theology denies this possibility, then for that person the one who does not love the Lord is "obviously" a nonbeliever, and to pronounce *anathema* on him "obviously" means damnation.

But the love and hate language elsewhere is applied to Christians. Throughout 1 Corinthians, Paul writes to saints concerning their lack of proper love for the Lord. Rather than walking in obedience to Christ Jesus, they are acting like mere men. Jesus said,

> *If you keep My commandments, you will abide in My love; just as I have kept My Father's commandments, and abide in His love (John 15:10, NASB).*
>
> *You are My friends, if you do what I command you (John 15:14, NASB).*

The Corinthians were not obeying, so they did not abide in His love, and they were not His "friends." Gordon Fee assumes that those addressed are Paul's opponents.[3050] It seems obvious to him that anyone who does not obey what an apostle teaches could not be a believer and is a false teacher. However, we have shown elsewhere that this assumption is patently false and contradictory to biblical revelation.[3051] Keith Krell summarizes,

> *The difficulty with the false professors view is that the immediate context suggests that Paul aims his anathema at true believers. Paul would seem to need a clear identification if he is introducing a second audience (i.e., false professors) into the midst of an address to true believers. Since the context depicts Paul's intended audience as a believing community, it seems inconsistent to argue that 16:22 targets unbelievers in the midst of the church. While Paul appears to allow for the possibility that unbelievers may be present in the house churches of Corinth (cf. 14:24), they are not his intended recipients. Additionally, he does not seem to consider an unbeliever who enters the corporate gathering a part of the church. This argument can be further sustained by Paul's claim that he does not judge "outsiders" (5:12–13).*
>
> *In view of the lexical data, the word anathema, as it is used in postexilic Judaism and by the early church, never means damnation. Thus, there is little basis for reading that meaning into 1 Corinthians 16:22 and Galatians 1:8. We are left with two options, either turning a person over to physical death (e.g., 1 Corinthians 5:5, "the destruction of the flesh") or separating him from the body of believers. On many occasions, Paul called on believers to separate from the disobedient Christians in their midst. For example, he commands the Thessalonians not to associate with believers who refuse to work (2 Thessalonians 3:14-15); an incestuous believer is to be "put out of the church" (1 Corinthians 5:2); Christians are to "have nothing to do" with a divisive believer (Titus 3:10-11); they are to "keep away from" believers who cause divisions and who deceive others (Romans 16:17-18); and two believers who shipwrecked their faith, Hymenaeus and Alexander, were handed over to Satan so that they might be taught not to blaspheme (1 Timothy 1:20).*[3052]

Summary

In 1 Corinthians 16:22 and Galatians 1:8 Paul probably has in mind the blessings and curses set before the children of Israel as the background for this thought (Deuteronomy

---

3050 Fee, *The First Epistle to the Corinthians*, 838.

3051 See discussion of the carnal Christian in chapter 32.

3052 Krell, *Temporal Judgment and the Church: Paul's Remedial Agenda in 1 Corinthians*, s.v. chapter 7.

28–30). In these chapters they are being warned about curses that will fall on them if they are disobedient after they enter the Promised Land. All of these consequences refer to some kind of judgment in *time, not eternity*. Stuart summarizes,

> *Twenty-seven types of curses are found in these contexts, representing virtually all the miseries one could imagine occurring in the ancient world, but these may be summarized by six terms: defeat, disease, desolation, deprivation, deportation, and death. Such curses are warnings of what God will cause to happen to Israel if they disobey the covenant.*[3053]

Damnation is not on the list. There is no lexical support for the notion that *anathema* refers to eternal damnation. This understanding is derived from an ambiguous reference to *anathema* in Romans 9:3, which is most likely a reference to Paul's willingness to experience physical death, as Moses did, if his nation could be saved from a national catastrophe.

To be *anathema* in Galatians 1:8 and 1 Corinthians 16:22 means to be subjected to some kind of temporal judgment, including severance *from* fellowship with Christ, which also terminates that disobedient believer's involvement with his fellow Christians, as in Ezra 10:8.

[3053] Douglas Stuart, "Curse," in Gillman, "Demas," 1:1218. See also E. W. Smith, "Book of Life" in Smith, "Book of Life," 1:534.

59

Negative Judgment and the Believer

THE POSSIBILITY that some believers will not overcome and hence will have their names (reputations, Revelation 3:5) removed from the book of life raises a troubling question. How could it be that those who have been justified before God and have become His children would not partake of the tree of life and would not rule over the nations? How can carnal Christians whose sins have been paid for and whose trespasses are forgiven ever experience a negative judgment from God again? Could a just God be guilty of double jeopardy? Is this not a double payment required to pay for the same offense, once on Christ and then a second time on the believer?

In order to answer these questions, we must answer a prior question, "What was the intent and the extent of the atonement?" That is, was the atonement intended to pay for the sins of all men (believers and unbelievers) without exception? Or, was it limited particularly for the payment of those who believe, that is, in Reformed terminology, for the elect only.

Universal Payment for Sin

There are passages that teach that the atonement was intended to cover the sins of all men without exception. For example, Peter tells us that the unbelieving false prophets were "*bought*" (redeemed) by the death of Christ (2 Peter 2:1). John asserts that Christ was the propitiation not only for believers' sins, but also for the sins of the "***whole world***" (1 John 2:2). Paul agrees, saying that Christ "*gave himself as a ransom for **all***" (1 Timothy 2:4) and that He is the "*savior of **all men***, especially of believers" (2 Timothy 4:10). The writer of the Epistle to the Hebrews affirms that Christ tasted death, providing a substitutionary atonement "***for everyone***" (Hebrews 2:9). The favorite scripture verse for many believers asserts that "*God so loved **the world**, that he gave his only begotten son*" (John 3:16). Finally, we are told (2 Corinthians 5:19, ESV) that "*in Christ God was reconciling **the world** to himself, not counting their trespasses against them, and entrusting to us the message of reconciliation.*"

Men Are Still Judged

JUDGMENT ON THE NONBELIEVER

Even though Christ has paid the penalty for the sins for the world the Bible clearly states that the unbeliever is condemned, judged, and will be assigned to the lake of fire because of sin, and because he lacks eternal life. For example, Jesus says, "*Whoever believes and is baptized will be saved, but whoever does not believe will be condemned* [Gr *katarinō*]" (Mark 16:16, NIV). *Katarinō* means "to pronounce a sentence after determination of guilt."[3054] But if the satisfaction of Christ actually eliminated all barriers of sin, then why is a sentence pronounced based upon guilt? Has not all guilt been expiated?

The writer to the Hebrews agrees saying that God condemned [Gr *katarinō*] the world because of their utter corruption and because they would not listen to Noah (Hebrews 11:7). Why was the world punished either temporally or eternally if the propitiation of Christ actually removed sin as an issue for all men?

In addition, the cities of Sodom and Gomorrah were condemned [Gr *katarinō*] to destruction because of their ungodly behavior (2 Peter 2:6). How can their condemnation to the lake of fire as a judgment/penalty be applied when the propitiation, redemption, and reconciliation of Christ has removed sin as an obstacle between man and God?

Peter tells us, "*Then the Lord knows how to rescue the godly from temptation, and to keep the unrighteous under punishment* [Gr, *kolazō*] *for the day of judgment*" (2 Peter 2:9). The Greek for "punishment" is *kolazō*, and it means "penalize, punish."[3055] How can the unrighteous suffer a penalty if the penalty has already been paid? How can sin remain as a barrier between man and God?

In the Sermon on the Mount Jesus said, "*And do not judge and you will not be judged; and do not condemn, and you will not be condemned* [Gr *katadikazō*]; *pardon, and you will be pardoned*" (Luke 6:37). Apparently, believers can still be judged for the sin of judging or not forgiving others. The word "condemned" is *katadikazō*, which means to "condemn, find/pronounce guilty."[3056] "*Katadikazō* is always used in the NT in the sense of condemn, pass judgment against, find guilty."[3057] But if the propitiation was intended to remove guilt, why are men still guilty? If they have already been pardoned, why do they still need to be pardoned?

Jesus made it clear that He will judge [Gr *krinō*] men at the last day (John 12:48). But if all judgment has been poured out on Christ and God's justice is satisfied, how can men ever be judged for sin again? Paul makes it clear that unbelievers will not escape "the judgment [Gr *krima*] of God" (Romans 2:3). Also, we are told that those who do not have access to special revelation from God (Torah, the Bible) will perish without the special revelation (Romans 2:12).

If the atonement actually paid for the sins of men who have not believed, how does one explain passages like this: "*For we know Him who said, 'Vengeance is Mine, I will repay.' And again, 'The Lord will judge His people'*" (Hebrews 10:30). And in Revelation, "*They cried out with a loud voice, saying, 'How long, O Lord, holy and true, wilt Thou refrain from judging and avenging* [Gr *ekdikeō*] *our blood on those who dwell on the earth*?'" (Revelation 6:10). The word for avenging is *ekdikeō*, and it means "to inflict appropriate penalty for wrong done."[3058] But if sin is no longer a barrier, how can a penalty for sin be inflicted since the sin was actually paid for by the propitiatory sacrifice of Christ?

3054 BDAG, 519.

3055 BDAG, 554. Cf. Acts 4:21.

3056 BDAG, 516.

3057 NIDNTT, 2,370.

3058 BDAG, 300.

John says,

> *And I saw the dead, the great and the small, standing before the throne, and books were opened; and another book was opened, which is the book of life; and the dead were judged from the things which were written in the books, according to their deeds. And the sea gave up the dead which were in it, and death and Hades gave up the dead which were in them; and they were judged, every one of them according to their deeds (Revelation 20:12–13, NASB).*

The reason people will be judged at the Great White Throne judgment is because their names are not written in the book of life. Why are their names not written there? It is mere assertion to say that their names are not written there because they do not possess life. The rest of the New Testament makes it clear that the reason for exclusion is that they did not trust in the person of Christ for the payment for their sins (e.g., John 3:18), and thus they will be judged, says, John, "*according to their deeds,*" not their lack of life. They are condemned because of the absence of deeds adequate enough to place a claim on God for admittance into the new heaven and the new earth.

Is damnation a payment for the penalty of sin?[3059] Paul says that it *is* a penalty. "*And these will pay the penalty of eternal destruction, away from the presence of the Lord and from the glory of His power*" (2 Thessalonians 1:9). The word for "to pay" is *tinō* and for "penalty" is *dikē*. According to Danker, *tinō* means, "To experience retribution, pay, and undergo a penalty.[3060] They will pay the penalty of "eternal destruction," that is, the lake of fire. If the penalty was paid at the cross. why is it necessary for the penalty to be paid again?

Paul goes on to say that "retribution" will be dealt out to unbelievers because of their sins, that is, because they do not know God and do not obey the gospel of the Lord Jesus (2 Thessalonians 1:8). "*Dealing out retribution [Gr ekdikēsis] to those who do not know God and to those who do not obey the gospel of our Lord Jesus.*" *Ekdikēsis* means a "penalty inflicted upon wrongdoers, punishment."[3061] Jesus adds that unbelievers "*will go away into eternal punishment, but the righteous into eternal life*" (Matthew 25:46). The word for punishment is *kolasis* which means "transcendent retribution, punishment."[3062]

In view of these passages, why does Zane Hodges say the following?

> ***Question:*** *Then why does God send people to hell for not believing?*
> ***Answer:*** *He doesn't. The Bible nowhere says that.*[3063]

But the Bible *does* say that, it says it in John 3 and John 16.

> *He who believes in Him is not judged; he who does not believe has been judged [Gr krinō] already,* ***because he has not believed in the name of the only begotten Son of God*** *(John 3:18).*

3059 Zane Hodges says that unbelief is "not the reason they are condemned to hell." He explains, "A *cause* and a *reason* are not the same thing. Unbelief is the *cause* for the unsaved not having eternal life. Not having eternal life is the *reason* they are condemned to hell." Zane C. Hodges, "The Sin of Unbelief," *Grace Focus Newsletter* (November-December 2007). I am uncertain as to what he is saying. As far as I can tell, this is a distinction without a difference!

3060 BDAG, 1006.

3061 BDAG, 301.

3062 BDAG, 555.

3063 Hodges, "The Sin of Unbelief."

And He, when He comes, will convict the world concerning sin, and righteousness, and judgment [Gr krisis]; concerning sin, ***because they do not believe in Me****" (John 16:8–9).*

Temporal as well as eternal judgments are assigned to unbelievers and believers alike: "*But a certain terrifying expectation of judgment, and* THE FURY OF A FIRE WHICH WILL CONSUME THE ADVERSARIES" (Hebrews 10:27, NASB). The writer continues, "*And inasmuch as it is appointed for men to die once and after this comes judgment*" (Hebrews 9:27). The word for judgment, *krisis*, can refer to a "judgment that goes against a person, condemnation, and the sentence that follows."[3064] But if the judgment and sentence and condemnation have already been executed on Christ, how can anyone experience condemnation? If the legal process has already occurred, and judgment has already been executed at Calvary, how can anyone undergo this legal process and condemnation in the future?

JUDGMENT ON BELIEVERS

What about judgment on believers? Can they too experience judgment/punishment from God? On the one hand, the Scriptures affirm that the child of God, under grace, shall not come under judgment for sin (John 3:18; 5:24). Our sin (past, present, and future) has been borne by a perfect substitute, and we are therefore forever placed beyond condemnation (Colossians 2:10), accepted as perfect in Christ (1 Corinthians 1:30; Ephesians 1:6; Colossians 2:14; Hebrews 10:14), and loved as Christ is loved (John 17:23).

But, on the other hand, the Scriptures also affirm in many other passages that God *does* judge us when we become carnal, and He *does* remember our sin. First of all, it is clear that God will punish us temporally for sins we commit. Consider:

Unless I wash you, you have no part with me (John 13:8).

If we confess our sins, he is faithful and just and will forgive us our sins (1 John 1:9).

If the Christian does not confess, he is not forgiven. This certainly appears to be a penalty for willful sin.

If you obey my commands, you will remain in my love (John 15:10).

If the Christian refuses to obey, he will apparently no longer remain in Christ's love. This is true even though Paul has declared elsewhere that "*nothing shall be able to separate us from the love of God*" (Romans 8:39).

The Exodus generation is described as those who "*all ate the same spiritual food; and all drank the same spiritual drink, for they were drinking from a spiritual rock which followed them; and the rock was Christ*" (1 Corinthians 10:3-4). Considering the entire multitude as one group, Paul views them as saved people. "*Nevertheless, with most of them God was not well-pleased; for they were laid low in the wilderness.* ***Now these things happened as examples for us***" (1 Corinthians 10:1-6). Just as those ancient believers experienced punishment from God, so can we. What happened to them occurred "as examples for us." Paul tells the Corinthians that a believer will be recompensed (Gr *komizō*), for what "he has

[3064] BDAG, 569.

done, whether good or bad" (2 Corinthians 5:10-11), and John tells us that the disobedient Christian may lose his crown (Revelation 3:11). "*Judgment*" (Gr *krima*), said Peter, must "*begin with the household of God*" (1 Peter 4:7). These verses make it clear that God will judge believers.

Apparently, Christians, because of their sin, can "have no part" with Christ, can be unforgiven, and can be outside His love. Scores of other passages could be cited.[3065] We are also told that we will reap what we sow. We have been warned that there is no sacrificial protection from judgment in time (Hebrews 10:26) for willful sin. For the persistently carnal Christian, a dreadful experience awaits him at the last day. He will "*suffer loss*" of everything but will be saved as through fire (1 Corinthians 3:15).

Not only will Christians face temporal punishment from God as the above passages indicate, but they will also face eschatological punishment for willful and unrepentant failure.

It is clear that the consistently carnal Christian (which Experimentalists, of course, say does not exist) faces three negative consequences at the Judgment Seat of Christ. First, for some there will be a stinging rebuke. This is the meaning of the Lord's warning that some will be "cut in pieces" (Matthew 24:51) and of His stern denunciation, "You wicked, lazy, servant" (Matthew 25:26). Second, such unfaithful Christians face millennial disinheritance. When the Lord declares that He will "deny" those who are ashamed of Him and when Paul says, "If we deny Him, He will deny us," disinheritance is in view.[3066] A father may disinherit his son, but that son remains his son. To be disinherited is simply to forfeit our share in the future reign of the servant kings. And third, the carnal Christian faces exclusion from the joy of the wedding banquet, "Friend, how did you get in here without wedding clothes?" (Matthew 22:12).

These passages all teach that Christ *does* remember our sin and *does* take it into account. This raises a perplexing theological problem and a troubling practical problem. For many, these conflicting bits of data cloud their view of the love and unconditional acceptance of God. Instead of being perceived as a merciful and forgiving Father, He begins to appear more like a stern judge, and the biblical picture of His love retreats from view.

There are numerous biblical illustrations where God does punish justified saints. For example, note the judgment on Ananias and Sapphira; the sickness that came on drunk believers at the Lord's Table in 1 Corinthians 11:27-31; or the punishment David received for his adultery and murder. Peter writes that judgment must begin with the family of God (1 Peter 4:17), and the writer to the Hebrews says that the Lord will judge His people (Hebrews 10:30).

When Adam sinned, the penalty was physical and spiritual death (Romans 5:12-14) even though the Lamb of God died for his sin before the foundation of the world. The Lord

---

[3065] See also Romans 2:7; 1 Corinthians 11:29-32; Galatians 6:7-8; Revelation 3:16; Matthew 24:50-51; 22:13. In addition, Christ gave stern warning to the wicked servant that he would be cast into the place of weeping and gnashing of teeth. The foolish virgins are excluded from the wedding banquet, and the man without the proper attire for the banquet was cast into the darkness outside. The exegetical data in these passages argues well for the regenerate state of the individuals undergoing these punishments. We cannot say they are unregenerate just because our theological system teaches that these punishments could not come on the regenerate. That is the point in question.

[3066] See 2 John 8 and Hebrews 10:36 and the possibility of not entering into one's inheritance/rest. See volume 1, chapters 10 and 11.

made it clear that we cannot be counted as His friend unless we obey Him (John 15:14). Failure to respond to discipline can result in a believer being condemned with the world (1 Corinthians 11:32-33). These judgments can include sickness and death. It is difficult to remove the notion of judgment and penalty from the stern exhortation of the writer to the Hebrews, *"And he punishes everyone he accepts as a son"* (Hebrews 12:6). Hymenaeus and Alexander are punished and turned over to Satan (1 Timothy 1:20). Throughout the Old Testament there are numerous judgments that came upon the people of God. Moses warned of many curses that would come upon the disobedient (Deuteronomy 28:9-26). Saul was punished by God by being rejected as the king (1 Samuel 15:23). God punished Solomon by taking the kingdom from him and raising up many adversaries (1 Kings 11:11). King Uzziah was punished by God with leprosy (2 Chronicles 26:20). These inflictions are clearly penal in nature even though Christ is the propitiation for all sin and the justice of God was to be totally satisfied by that one sacrifice!

Scripture shows that any believer may experience a penal judgment either in time or eternity. The Bible does not teach that it is impossible for a believer to ever experience a penal judgment. The judgment of physical death is a penal judgment on sin (Romans 5:12-14).[3067] While Adam and Eve died spiritually the day they sinned, they began to die physically as well[3068] (Romans 8:20-22). Moo is correct, "'Death' refers clearly to physical death, but not to physical death alone; as in v. 12, spiritual death, condemnation, is also involved."[3069]

Although spiritual death certainly occurred the moment Adam sinned, Ryrie says, "Physical death is the particular penalty connected with imputed sin (Romans 5:13–14)."[3070] In Romans 6:9, Paul says that "*death is no longer master over Him,*" indicating that physical death is in view.

It appears that Paul does not necessarily connect physical death with personal sins. No man sinned "in the likeness of Adam's transgression" (v. 14) but in Adam "all sinned" (v. 12). This seems to be clarified by v. 18 where Paul says,

> *For if by the* ***transgression of the one****, death reigned through the one, much more those who receive the abundance of grace and of the gift of righteousness will reign in life through the One, Jesus Christ. So then as* ***through one transgression there resulted condemnation to all men****, even so through one act of righteousness there resulted justification of life to all men.* ***For as through the one man's disobedience the many were made sinners****, even so through the obedience of the One, the many will be made righteous (Romans 5:17–19).*

Somehow Paul views us as in Adam and the transgression of just one is our transgression as well. Similarly, he views believers as in Christ and having obeyed when He obeyed. It seems Paul is thinking in terms of the Semitic idea of corporate identity. Just

---

3067 See Murray, *Redemption—Accomplished and Applied*, 181-82. See also Shedd, *A Critical and Doctrinal Commentary on the Epistle of St. Paul to the Romans*, 122.

3068 Godet says, "*Death* cannot denote more here than the loss of life in the ordinary sense of the word. There is no reference either to spiritual death (sin, Gess), or to the sufferings and infirmities of life (Hodge), but simply to the fact that between Adam and Moses men *died* though there was no law." See Godet, *Commentary on Romans*, 359.

3069 Moo, "Romans," 333.

3070 Ryrie, *Basic Theology*, 260.

as Achan sinned and yet all Israel was held guilty (Joshua 7:1, 11), in a similar way Adam sinned and as a result all men are guilty and condemned in him. This perplexing problem is far beyond this book,[3071] but it appears that Adam was our Federal representative and that his sin was imputed to us.

If all believers are exempt from any kind of condemnation without exception, then why do all believers undergo the penal judgment of physical death (Romans 5:14-18)? Experimental Predestinarians, such as Berkhof, in defense of their doctrine of limited atonement, argue that because Christ is the propitiation for all sin, the experience of physical death cannot be penal in nature.[3072] What then is it? Nowhere does Scripture say, "The penal element is removed from death," and, specifically, Scripture does say that penal death is a judgment for sin.

> *Therefore, just as through one man sin entered into the world, and **death through sin,** and so **death spread to all men,** because all sinned—for until the Law sin was in the world, but sin is not imputed when there is no law. Nevertheless **death reigned from Adam until Moses,** even over those who had not sinned in the likeness of the offense of Adam, who is a type of Him who was to come (Romans 5:12–14, NASB95).*

If God can bring condemnation on believers in time, as these examples prove, there is no necessary reason to believe all punishments have been removed at the Judgment Seat of Christ. Indeed, there seem to be numerous Scriptures that indicate that this is the case.[3073] The condemnation, however, has nothing to do with the believer's eternal salvation. The atonement has forever settled that issue.

How are we to deal with these apparently contradictory strains of biblical teaching?[3074] Since Paul, who taught the forgiveness of sins, also anticipated that we would one day be judged according to our bad works as well as our good, the ideas cannot be incompatible. Kendall correctly insists, "We must deduce from this that there is no contradiction between Paul's doctrine of justification and his conception of the judgment of God; and that being declared righteous so as to escape the wrath of God (Romans 5:9; 1 Thessalonians 1:10) does not exempt us from rewards or punishment in the Last Day."[3075] Jesus said every idle word will be judged (Matthew 12:36). This is frightening, but we have been warned. This is why Paul could say, "*For if we would judge ourselves, we should not be judged*" (1 Corinthians

---

[3071] For some help see S. Lewis Johnson, "G. C. Berkouwer and the Doctrine of Original Sin," *BibSac* 132, no. 528 (October 1975): 316-26. Also see Hodge, *Systematic Theology*, 2:197-205.

[3072] Berkhof, *Systematic Theology*, 671.

[3073] The man in the parable of the Talents who buried his money will lose what he has and will be cast into the darkness outside. The foolish virgins will hear the terrifying words, "I do not know you." See the extensive discussion of these negative judgments in chapters 48-58.

[3074] Roman Catholics have used these two strains of biblical thought to seek to prove their doctrine of purgatory. They argue that Scriptures such as these establish that the death of Christ did not completely satisfy the justice of God. The believer must assist with this satisfaction in purgatory. For a good discussion, see Dabney, *Lectures in Systematic Theology*, 538-45. Purgatory must be rejected. The Scriptures teach that believers are made perfect at death (Ephesians 5:26-27; Jude 24-25), and there is therefore no room for a "purgatorial cleansing." Furthermore, salvation in Christ provides eternal, unconditional acceptance and immediate entrance to heaven at death. Therefore, whatever befalls the glorified saint at the judgment seat cannot exclude him from immediate entrance into heaven.

[3075] Kendall, *Once Saved, Always Saved*, 123.

11:31). If we repent now, we will not be judged for sin later.[3076] However, we will be judged for our works and experience reward or the loss. I am speculating here, but it seems to me that this means that a carnal Christian who has confessed and been forgiven in this life will not, for example, Be rebuked at the Judgment Seat of Christ. Only unconfessed sin will be judged. However, his reward may be small and his treasures in heaven few.

The difficulty is obvious. If Christ is truly the satisfaction for sin and has therefore satisfied the justice of God, why then do believers still have to satisfy that justice by undergoing more penalties? Historically, there have been four different explanations: universalism; limited atonement; the Dispensational solution; the Partner solution.

Answers to the Problem of Double Payment

UNIVERSALISM

Some say that since the penalty is already paid, the Bible teaches universalism. That is, everyone, including Hitler will eventually be saved.[3077] However, this is refuted by many passages (1 Thessalonians 1:10; Luke 16:26; Matthew 25:46). "Forever and ever" in Revelation 14:10-11 is unlimited (cf. Rev 1:6, 9, 10; 10:6; 22:5).

LIMITED ATONEMENT

The Reformed faith has usually advocated another alternative — limited atonement, or as they prefer, definite atonement or particular redemption. In other words, Christ died only for the elect.[3078] His death, they say, was never intended to satisfy the wrath of God on all men without exception.

In order to avoid the conclusion of universalism, they argue that "world" means "world of the elect" and "all" means "all kinds of men, both Jews, Gentiles, kings, and governors."[3079] Thus, there is no "double payment" because the intent of Christ's atonement was to pay for the sins of the elect only.

R. C. Sproul explains,

1. "Either the Atonement was intended for all or only for some (the elect).
2. If the Atonement was intended for all, then all will be saved (since God's sovereign intentions will come to pass).
3. If the Atonement was not intended for all, then it was intended only for some (the elect).
4. Therefore, either universalism is true or limited atonement is true."[3080]

3076 Martin Luther reportedly claimed he would have three surprises in heaven: that some would be there he did not expect to see, that some would be missing that he thought would be there, and that he himself was there. We should expect to see some saved by fire and some having an "abundant entrance" (2 Peter 1:11).

3077 For a popular and rather shallow exposition of universalism see Rob Bell, *Love Wins: A Book about Heaven, Hell, and The Fate of Every Person Who Ever Lived* (New York: Harper Collins, 2011). For a more serious and scholarly discussion see Gregory MacDonald, *The Evangelical Universalist* (Eugene, OR: Cascade Books, 2006). In response to universalism, one might note Christopher W. Morgan and Robert A. Peterson, *Hell under Fire* (Grand Rapids: Zondervan, 2004). Also see the popular responses to Bell by Francis Chan and Preston M. Sprinkle, *Erasing Hell* (Colorado Springs: David C. Cook, 2011); Mark Galli, *God Wins* (Carol Stream, IL: Tyndale House Publishers, 2011).

3078 For a defense of this viewpoint, see Gary D. Long, *Definite Atonement* (Phillipsburg, NJ: Presbyterian and Reformed Publishing Co., 1976).

3079 For capable exposition of this view, see ibid.

3080 R. C. Sproul, *Chosen By God* (Wheaton: Tyndale Publishers, 1997).

There is, of course, another option which we will discuss below.

Because of the clear fact that believers have had the penalty for their sin already paid, Experimental Predestinarians argue that any negatives accruing to the believer at the Judgment Seat of Christ **are not judicially punitive in nature.**[3081]

Experimentalists correctly maintain that one purpose in the judgment on the believer is disclosure. Every careless word will be revealed (Matthew 12:36). Hidden motives will be brought to light (Romans 2:16). When it is argued that the sins of believers will never be mentioned at the judgment, Experimental Predestinarians properly object that since this judgment concerns our deeds, words, and thoughts, surely the sins of believers will be revealed on that day. "But," Hoekema stresses, "and this is the important point, the sins and shortcomings of believers will be revealed as **forgiven sins**, whose guilt has been totally covered by the blood of Jesus Christ."[3082]

This solution is commonly found in Reformed[3083] and Lutheran[3084] theology texts and is certainly plausible. However, it rests on mere assertion that such judgments cannot be punitive, and it arbitrarily redefines judgment to mean "disclosure."

Starting from the premise that the death of Christ was designed by God to satisfy all the claims of justice against the believer's sin, Hoekema is led to deny that the Judgment Seat of Christ is truly a judgment. It is only a revelation of forgiven sins. It is difficult to see that in the texts in question. After all, the sins that have not been confessed are not forgiven according to 1 John 1:9. The above Scriptures seem to require a penal sense both in time and at the Judgment Seat of Christ. Why would unforgiven sins in time suddenly be forgiven at the Judgment Seat of Christ?

THE DISPENSATIONAL SOLUTION

Another view is common in dispensational circles.[3085] Lewis Sperry Chafer argued as follows:

> *At the Judgment Seat of Christ sin will not be the subject of consideration. At that time believers will be perfect, with no sin nature, and will never sin again in thought, word, or deed. Therefore, any concept of discipline because of previous sins is unnecessary and would be unfruitful. The question of righteousness before God was settled when they were justified by faith. The Judgment Seat of Christ deals with works, not with sin. Believers will be judged on whether their works were good (worth something) or whether they were bad (worthless), as stated in verse 10.*[3086]

[3081] Hoyt, "The Judgment Seat of Christ in Theological Perspective, Part 2: The Negative Aspects of the Christian's Judgment," 125.

[3082] Hoekema, *The Bible and the Future*, 529. See also Berkhof, *Systematic Theology*, 732.

[3083] For example, Dabney, *Lectures in Systematic Theology*, 543.

[3084] For example, "The appearance of the believers before God's judgment seat will therefore not have the nature of a condemnatory judgment since their sins are forgiven through faith in Christ (Matthew 25:34)." Mueller, *Christian Dogmatics*, 630.

[3085] When we refer to a "dispensational" solution to the problem, we do not intend to imply that there is anything intrinsic to dispensationalism that results in a certain solution. Rather, we are referring to the fact that the views described here have been common in dispensationalist circles. While the present writer is a classical dispensationalist in the Pentecost-Ryrie-Walvoord-McClain mold, he would prefer to believe that even though the kingdom has not been inaugurated (there is no "already but not yet"), some aspects of that future kingdom are being experienced now, for example, the New Covenant offer of forgiveness and the new ministries of the Holy Spirit.

[3086] Lewis Sperry Chafer, *Systematic Theology*, ed. John F. Walvoord, abridged ed., 2 vols. (Wheaton: Victor, 1988), 2:474.

Walvoord similarly affirms that the child of God under grace shall not come into judgment[3087] because the penalty for all sins (past, present, and future) has been paid by his Substitute. The believer is therefore beyond condemnation, perfect in Christ, and loved as Christ is loved. Walvoord says that when we stand at the Judgment Seat of Christ, the only issue is rewards that will be reckoned on the basis of merit. The believer's "good works are distinguished from his bad works, and on the basis of good works the believer is rewarded."[3088] This is not, Walvoord says, a matter of sin being judged, "because the believer is already justified." Furthermore, it is not a matter of sanctification such as is "experienced in present chastisement for failure to confess sin, because the believer is already perfect in the presence of God." He concludes that "the only remaining issue, then, is the quality of the believer's life and the works that God counts good in contrast with works that are worthless."[3089]

The Partner Solution

While there is much to commend the Reformed and Dispensational solutions, this writer prefers a fourth alternative. It might be labeled, "sufficient for all, efficient for those who believe."[3090] First advocated by Augustine, it is quite common among those who hold to unlimited atonement, that is, Christ died for all men without exception.[3091]

This view teaches that the death of Christ *provisionally* achieved a satisfaction for the sins of all men, and it becomes *actual* for the one who believes. The atonement is "sufficient for all," but "efficient" for those who believe on Christ alone for justification. [3092]

[3087] Lewis Sperry Chafer and John F. Walvoord, *Major Bible Themes: 52 Vital Doctrines of the Scripture Simplified and Explained* (Grand Rapids: Zondervan Publishing House, 1974), 283. Walvoord cites John 3:18; 5:24; 6:37; Romans 5:1; 8:1; and 1 Corinthians 11:32 as proof.

[3088] Ibid., 285

[3089] Ibid., 286. Pentecost also affirms, "To bring the believer into judgment concerning the sin question, whether his sins before his new birth, his sins since his new birth, or even sins unconfessed since the new birth, is to deny the efficacy of the death of Christ and nullify the promise of God that 'their sins and iniquities will I remember no more.'" Pentecost, *Things to Come: A Study in Biblical Eschatology*, 222.

[3090] For the sake of completeness, I will mention another option. There are some who agree that Christ's death was indeed universal and the sins of all men were paid for. Therefore, no unbeliever ever faces judgment again as far as his eternal destiny is concerned. Why then do unbelievers end up in the lake of fire? Those advocating this view say it is because two things are required to enter heaven: (1) an atonement erasing sin's penalty and (2) the impartation of eternal life. Since the atonement has already taken care of the first obstacle, the only thing keeping unbelievers out of heaven is that they do not have eternal life. They come to Christ believing in His promise to grant life, and they are justified. Why then do people go to eternity without God? Is that not a penalty? No! The answer according to Zane Hodges is, "Not having eternal life is the reason they are condemned to hell." See Zane C. Hodges, "The Sin of Unbelief," *Grace Focus Newsletter* (November-December 2007). A corollary to this way of thinking is that the content of saving faith does not include trusting Christ for forgiveness of sins or an admission of guilt because unbelievers are no longer guilty as far as eternal salvation. All they lack is life. Regarding the problem of believers facing judgment as a penalty for their sins, they say that Christ did not die for all our sins, only those related to our eternal damnation. Thus, God does execute the universal penalty of physical death in the present and also penalties on sinning Christians at the Judgment Seat of Christ. Because Christ did not pay for sins related to how they live, believers must pay the penalty themselves when they face final accountability for how they lived. Although some scholars I respect hold this view, and since the meaning of this viewpoint is unclear to me, and since there is little in writing to explore it thoroughly, we will not discuss further.

[3091] See the comment on this in chapter 3.

[3092] Ryrie, *Basic Theology*, 373.

In order to understand the various issues behind all the theories, one must first ask, "What was the intent of the atonement?"

THE INTENT OF THE ATONEMENT

The atonement of Christ is either a satisfaction for the sins of some men (limited atonement) or a satisfaction for the sins of all men without exception.[3093] It cannot be the former because the Scriptures say it was a satisfaction for the sins of the whole world (1 John 2:2). The atonement must, therefore, be a satisfaction for the sins of all men without exception. Thus we would agree with Ryrie who says, "The death of Christ pays for all the sins of all people. But not one individual has his own account settled until he believes. If he never believes, then even though the price has been fully paid, his sins will not be forgiven."[3094]

The texts mentioned above which speak of redemption, reconciliation, substitution, and propitiation indicate that the atonement was more than a provisional satisfaction; it was also an actual satisfaction. That seems to be the obvious intent of these passages as Experimental Predestinarians correctly point out.

That being so, we must then ask, "In what respect is it a satisfaction?" It is either a satisfaction for sin *in all respects* or a satisfaction for sin in *some limited respect*. It cannot be a satisfaction in all respects, because then all men would be saved—the viewpoint of the universalists. The Bible refutes this. The teaching that the intent was limited to the elect contradicts 1 John 2:2, Romans 5:18, 2 Corinthians 5:19, and 2 Peter 2:1. If the claims of justice have truly been satisfied in *all* respects, then surely no man should have to satisfy again those same claims himself by suffering the penalty of damnation. The fact is that people will go to the lake of fire (1 Thessalonians. 1:10-11; Revelation 14:10-11; 20:10; Luke 16:26; Matthew 25:46). Therefore, the atonement must be a satisfaction for sin in a special sense.

What then was the atonement intended to accomplish? The intent of the atonement is to satisfy the justice of God completely in a limited and specific sense. The intent of the atonement as Paul explained elsewhere was "*for the demonstration, I say, of His righteousness at the present time, so that He would be just and the justifier of* ***the one who has faith in Jesus***" (Romans 3:26). The atonement freed God so that He would be just when He justified those who believed. It did not obligate Him to provide a payment to anyone, but it made the payment available to "*the one who has faith in Jesus.*"

What kind of justice accepts a penalty for sin and then extends its benefits only far enough to grant acceptance before the judge to those who believe but not far enough to acquit the sin of those who do not? Can the benefits of a pardon be variously applied and extended at the discretion of the judge?

Our Heavenly Judge can extend the benefits of the atonement as far or near as He chooses. God is not obligated by the atonement to save anyone. He is freed by it to save whomever He pleases, and He pleases to confer the benefit of justification upon those who believe. The atonement of Christ actually satisfied the justice of God in the sense that it

---

3093 The case for unlimited atonement has been argued by Robert P. Lightner, *The Death Christ Died: A Case for Unlimited Atonement* (Des Plaines, IL: Regular Baptist Press, 1967).

3094 Ryrie, Basic Theology, 373.

removed any restraints on His love and justice. He is freed by the satisfaction of Christ to throw the bars of heaven open, but He is not obligated to extend the benefits of this atonement to all men apart from faith.

Reformed theologian Dabney takes virtually the same position when he explains why believers still pay the penalty of physical death. He argues that the satisfaction of Christ does not *obligate* God to cancel our *whole* indebtedness, precisely the view of this writer. Rather, His acceptance of Christ's death as a legal satisfaction "was, on His part, an act of pure grace; and therefore the acceptance acquits us just so far as, and no farther than God is pleased to allow it."[3095] The person who does not believe is condemned to final damnation because God did not extend the atonement to cover the sin of anyone who does not believe. When a person does believe, he is not only unconditionally accepted by the Father, but the benefits of the atonement are extended in his case to protect him from final damnation on the condition of faith in Jesus. This extension occurs through the free gift of justification, acquittal at the divine bar of justice.

Consider this illustration from the Exodus. What happened to the Israelite who refused to apply the blood of the Passover lamb to the doorpost of his houses? Were his sins paid for twice? According to Exodus when the lamb was slain, the sins were covered. Nevertheless, if the individual Israelite did not apply the blood to the doorpost, his sins were not covered and he died. This was not a second payment for sin because the first and sufficient payment was not applied for that particular house. Similarly, Christ who is "our Passover has been sacrificed" for us (1 Corinthians 5:7), but unless we appropriate what was provided it will never be applied.

God is not obligated by the atonement to save anyone. He is freed by it to save whomever He pleases, and He pleases to confer the benefit of justification on those who believe. He is also freed by the atonement to extend the benefits of that satisfaction as far as He chooses in the lives of those who are already saved, but He is not obligated to do so.

Ryrie gives this helpful illustration.

> *In one school where I have taught, the student aid was handled in this way. People made gifts to the student aid fund. Needy students applied for help from that fund. A committee decided who would receive aid and how much. But when the actual money was distributed, it was done by issuing a check to the student, who then was expected to endorse it back to the school, which would then place the credit on his account. The money was not moved directly from the aid fund to the individual student's account. The student had to receive it personally and place it on his account. Let us suppose you gave a gift to cover one student's tuition for one year. You could properly say that his tuition was fully paid. But until the selection is made by the committee, and until the student receives the gift and places it on his account, his tuition is not paid. If he fails to endorse the check, it will never be paid even though it has been paid!*[3096]

There is therefore no double condemnation (once on Christ and once on the sinner) when the unbeliever is condemned. The divine Judge never intended Christ's atonement to cover the sin of the person who will not believe. That person therefore dies in his sin.

[3095] Dabney, *Lectures in Systematic Theology*, 819.

[3096] Ryrie, *Basic Theology*, 373.

TWO KINDS OF RELATIONSHIP WITH GOD

The understanding of the intent of the atonement explained above clarifies how God can punish believers for sins when Christ is the satisfaction for sin. The answer is that the divine Judge extends the benefits of Christ's atonement to cover the sins of believers for sins within the family of God only if they repent and confess them. Christ's atonement only renders God free to accept unconditionally into His family those who believe. Like all children we enjoy two kinds of relationships with our Father. We are forever safe and secure in His family, but our fellowship with our Father can vary depending on our behavior. With God, our eternal relationship is secure and unchanging because it depends solely upon Him; it was secured by the atonement and granted to us freely and irrevocably through faith alone (John 6:39-40).[3097] But our temporal fellowship is variable because it depends cooperatively on us. We must confess our sins and walk daily in the light of His Word. Then, and only then, will He extend the benefits of the atonement to provide forgiveness within the family.

Imagine, for example, that you are a teacher in a classroom. Your son is one of the students in your English class. One day you catch him cheating on the final examination. Will he not pay penalties? Yes. Is he not still your son? Of course. Or, suppose you are the owner of a small business. Your son is employed at the cash register. One day you catch him stealing money from the cash register. The fact that he has stolen money in no way affects the fact that he is your son. It does, however, mean that even though he is your son, he will pay penalties for his crime.

True sons of God can likewise pay penalties. The intent of the atonement was obviously not to remove all penalties from the life of the Christian. The atonement was intended by God (1) to free Him so that He can confer unconditional acceptance on those who believe and (2) to extend the benefits of Christ's death to cover sins within the family for believers who repent and confess those sins.

Unconfessed sin in the life of one who is already justified relates not to forensic forgiveness but to familial forgiveness. Any sin is a barrier to fellowship but does not endanger our eternal relationship. "Daily forgiveness of those who are within the family of God is distinguished from the judicial and positional forgiveness which was applied forensically to all of a person's sins the moment he believed in the Lord Jesus Christ."[3098] Forensic forgiveness is the subject of Colossians 2:13, but familial forgiveness is in view in 1 John 1:9.

Thus when John 5:24 assures us that we will not come into judgment and yet 2 Corinthians 5:10 states that we do, the resolution is that John is referring to judgment with respect to one's eternal destiny and Paul is referring to wages for work. John speaks of forensic justification, and Paul refers to familial forgiveness. John speaks of our escape from retribution; Paul speaks of our rewards and punishments within the family of God. The satisfaction of Christ unconditionally and irrevocably covers the former but is only extended to cover the latter when the believer confesses and repents. We must confess sin daily in order to obtain the benefits of having the atonement extended to forgive sin within the family of God.

[3097] For proof of the doctrine of eternal security see volume 2, chapter 47.

[3098] Samuel L. Hoyt, "The Judgment Seat of Christ in Theological Perspective - Part 1: The Judgment Seat of Christ and Unconfessed Sins," *BibSac* 137, no. 545 (January-March 1980): 38.

Practical Concerns

But we may ask, "What is the purpose of such a negative judgment against the believer at the Judgment Seat of Christ?" Since the believer is redeemed, why must his sin be punished? The answer is that God only chooses to extend the benefits of the atonement to believers for family forgiveness on the conditions of confession and repentance. The atonement did pay the penalty for these kinds of sins, but, the penalty will not be applied to the carnal believer at the Judgment Seat of Christ because he did not meet the conditions for forgiveness within the family during his life on earth. To use Ryrie's illustration, the benefits of the atonement for the believer are not applied until he goes to the bank and cashes the check.

Throughout Scripture God gives warnings of negative consequences to motivate believers toward sanctification. Why must God punish a believer who sins? For two reasons: (1) He warned him, and He must honor His Word, and (2) justice requires that all sin (both eternal and familial) be punished. We reap what we sow. So God must punish the carnal Christian. Otherwise, He is not just and fair.

Will God judge us for sins we have confessed? The answer is no. However, the repentant Christian will face loss of reward. We must remember that Scripture speaks in a threefold sense of the judgment of believers.[3099] Sauer points out that we are judged as sinners, children, and servants. As sinners we were judged at the cross. There, the sentence of damnation was fully executed on our Substitute as far as our eternal destiny is concerned. Then as children we are judged in the present. It is a penalty (1 Corinthians 11:32), but its purpose is to advance our sanctification (Hebrews 12:10). Third, we are judged as servants in the future at the Judgment Seat of Christ. Here, some believers may "suffer damage."[3100]

A believer who sins an extended period of time and then confesses those sins cannot expect to receive the same reward as one who lives a godly life. While the sins are forgiven, the rewards that could have been obtained are lost (Luke 19:24).

> *Watch yourselves, that you do not lose what we have accomplished, but that you may receive a full reward (2 John 8).*

This answers a common question. Each of us is accumulating a storehouse of sins as we journey through life. We experience the consequences of these sins in broken relationships, discipline from God, and, for some, even death. We experience these consequences even when we repent and confess them and are restored to fellowship. Does negative judgment at the Judgment Seat of Christ then imply that we will be judged again and that we have negative rebuke to look forward to even if we have confessed? Absolutely not. We have been forgiven and cleansed. There is no punishment at the judgment seat once forgiveness has been granted and fellowship has been restored. At that point there is a judgment in the sense of an evaluation on the believer's works (not a punishment), but not his sin.

> *For his anger lasts only a moment, but his favor lasts a lifetime; weeping may remain for a night, but rejoicing comes in the morning (Psalm 30:5, NIV).*

3099 Eric Sauer, *From Eternity to Eternity* (Grand Rapids: Wm. B. Eerdmans Publishing Co., 1963), 79.

3100 Ibid.

Blessed is he whose transgressions are forgiven, whose sins are covered. Blessed is the man whose sin the Lord does not count against him and in whose spirit is no deceit (Psalm 32:1-2, NIV).

David believed that once he had confessed his sin for restoration of fellowship within the family, there was no more guilt for which he could be punished.

*Then I acknowledged my sin to you and did not cover up my iniquity. I said, "I will confess my transgressions to the Lord"—**and you forgave the guilt of my sin**. Selah (Psalm 32:5, NIV).*

If the guilt is forgiven and gone, we do not answer again for it with punishment at the Judgment Seat of Christ. We will lose what we have worked for, but we will be embraced and rewarded positively by the King. There will be no millennium of tears, rejection, disinheritance, or rebuke. Negative consequence only falls on the carnal Christian who refuses to repent and confess.

The Lord's attitude toward the Christian who continues to walk in the light is clear. In spite of our many failures, as long as we stay in the race, we will be crowned. He is our Shepherd "*who crowns you with lovingkindness and compassion*" (Psalm 103:4).

*He will not always strive with us, **Nor will He keep His anger forever**. He has not dealt with us according to our sins, Nor rewarded us according to our iniquities. For as high as the heavens are above the earth, So great is His lovingkindness toward those who fear Him. As far as the east is from the west, So far has He removed our transgressions from us (Psalm 103:8-12).*

He will not "keep His anger forever." In fact, we are told that He has compassion on us as a father has compassion on his son.

Just as a father has compassion on his children, so the Lord has compassion on those who fear Him. For He Himself knows our frame; He is mindful that we are but dust (Psalm 103:13-14).

How does He know our "frame"? He designed us the way we are (Psalm 139:13-16). He knows we are weak and made of dust. He designed us that way. He is therefore not angry with us when we fail as long as we remain in the race; He has compassion and understanding. We have a high priest who is one with us and who is not ashamed of us (Hebrews 2:11). He is our "brother," the Captain of our salvation, and is a merciful high priest.

Therefore, He had to be made like His brethren in all things, so that He might become a merciful and faithful high priest in things pertaining to God, to make propitiation for the sins of the people. For since He Himself was tempted in that which He has suffered, He is able to come to the aid of those who are tempted (Hebrews 2:17-18, NASB).

Therefore no Christian who is pursuing God need worry about the failures and confessed sins that occur in his life resulting in rebuke at the Judgment Seat of Christ. He should anticipate meeting a compassionate Father and a merciful high priest who understands the struggle, who Himself participated in it. The faithful believer should anticipate the Judgment Seat of Christ with joy, not fear. Only those who persist in carnality and who refuse to repent and confess need view the coming judgment with a sense of dread. However, even the Lord's displeasure with the carnal believer does not last. There is no millennium of tears and regret.

What about the believer who lives a carnal life for years and then on his deathbed sincerely decides to confess his sin? Will he be punished? The answer is no (1 John 1:9). There is no penal punishment, but there is loss of what he could have had. Once he confesses, he is forgiven, but he will still be held accountable as a servant. Indeed, when he wakes up in heaven, in the full power of his glorified body, no restraint from sin will be felt. Any failure in the past has already been forgiven and he will enter the kingdom in complete fellowship with the Savior. However, he will suffer loss at the Judgment Seat of Christ. Here, he is judged in the sense of losing intimacy, service, and honor. His reward will be minimal. His loss will be great.

We must remember that God knows everything in our hearts[3101] and always deals with fairness and respect to our deepest motivations.[3102] In addition, the parable of the Vineyard Workers should remind us that God does not dispense His blessing on the basis of legal merit. He can, and does, bring blessing and reward to those who have been in the battle for fewer years than others.

Summary

Four things may be said about the negative consequences that come on the believer at the Judgment Seat of Christ.

First, God's love and acceptance of the sinning Christian does not affect the Christian's eternal relationship to God and permanent membership in His family. We are forever perfectly accepted in Christ and perfectly loved.

Second, the negative consequences for believers at the Judgment Seat of Christ may be viewed as the final chastisement that the Lord has ordained for His people. The fact that some of the punishments are experienced in eternity rather than in time enhances their value for sanctifying us now. The anticipation of negative chastisements serves to keep us humble, to pursue faithful lives, and to live spiritually in the present. While they are a punishment for an unfaithful life, their main purpose is to effect sanctification now. When the believer repents (Philippians 2:10-11), the satisfaction of God's justice provided by the atonement is extended to cover all sin at the judgment seat.

Third, this view of the judgment seat should not lead to introspection. For most of us our inner life is confusing and full of mixed motives. How can we have any confidence to stand before Christ if we know that every word will be recalled and every deed evaluated? Many identify with the apostle Paul when he said, "*For I am conscious of nothing against myself, yet I am not by this acquitted; but the one who examines me is the Lord*" (1 Corinthians 4:4).

This being true, the expectation of being punished for our sin can be a frightening and disheartening prospect. How can we quiet the claims of conscience? The Christian who is walking in the light, even though he fails repeatedly, has no need for concern. While even persevering disciples will have regrets and loss at the judgment seat, their predominant sense will be that of joy and gratitude.

The apostle John says that a condemning heart can be silenced only by resting in the fact of God's omniscience: "*For if our heart condemns us, God is greater than our heart, and*

[3101] 1 John 3:20.

[3102] 1 Chronicles 29:17; 1 Samuel 16:7; Proverbs 16:2.

knows all things" (1 John 3:20, NKJV). Specifically, John counsels us to love other Christians. He says that if we are demonstrating practical love (v. 18), then we can know that we are practicing the truth (v. 19) even if we do not do it perfectly. Indeed, Peter has assured us that our love for one another will cover a multitude of sins (1 Peter 4:8). Surely God's love for us will do no less. With this we can face the future judgment with anticipation and joy.

At this point Experimental Predestinarians object that the Partner system of motivation leads to as much unhealthy introspection as theirs. However, unhealthy introspection is generally problematic only for unusually introspective people. No matter how the doctrine is presented, these sensitive souls will likely be troubled. However, it is astounding that Experimental Predestinarians can accuse the Partners of advocating a system of unhealthy introspection. The believer caught up in the doctrine of the Experimentalists is continually worried about his eternal damnation! Surely, this is a wretched perversion of the grace and assurance offered in Scripture. It is one thing to be introspective regarding our eternal salvation. It is entirely another to be introspective regarding our rewards or the loss thereof.

Fourth, God's motive in warning about these future punishments is merciful and loving. He desires that all His children enjoy the fullness of co-heirship with His Son in the final destiny of man. He knows more than anyone how grieved we will be to miss out on the reign of Christ's *Metochoi* ("partners") in the coming kingdom. He, more than anyone, wants us to have the richest possible experience of heaven. He is not to be viewed as angrily, sternly, rejecting His child as He casts the carnal believer to the darkness outside. Rather, Jesus weeps with pain that His children must be excluded from the joy of the great future. We are specifically told during our time on earth that *"the Lord disciplines those whom he loves"* (Hebrews 12:4).

Another illustration is found in Christ's grief over Jerusalem. As He approached the city at the beginning of the last week of His life, He wept in anticipation of the terrible judgment that would befall its people in AD 70: *"And when He approached, He saw the city and wept over it, saying, 'If you had known in this day, even you, the things which make for peace!... For the days shall come upon you when your enemies ... will surround you, and hem you in on every side'"* (Luke 19:41-43). *"How often I have longed to gather your children together, as a hen gathers her chicks under her wings, but you were not willing. Look, your house is left to you desolate"* (Matthew 23:37-38). We must never view God as cold and uncaring when He carries out these punishments. The Father's heart weeps with the full knowledge of what His child is about to undergo and to forfeit. Furthermore, we must remember that the duration of this punishment is momentary and the subsequent remorse does not last into eternity.[3103] When we arrive in eternity future, everyone's cup will be full, but the cups will be of different sizes.

[3103] For discussion of the duration of remorse see pp. 326, 775 ff.

60

Treasures in Heaven 1 — Greater Intimacy

THE GUARDIAN angel was troubled. His charge, an American military policeman stationed in West Berlin, was in imminent danger.

"Come quickly," he said to the archangel. "One of the heirs is unaware of what faces him."

A middle-aged man nervously approached Checkpoint Charlie, the border crossing between East and West Berlin, from the Western side. Apart from his darting eyes, he seemed no different from the thousands of others who had to brave this former relic of the cold war. As he fumbled for his papers, the American military policeman on duty that day became suspicious and took time for a more careful examination of the travel documents. Little did he know that the nervous man before him carried automatic weapons and was capable of inflicting instant death. He was a seasoned intelligence agent for the Soviet Committee for State Security, the KGB.

He carried a small microfilm canister of sensitive Western intelligence which could have dramatic impact on the outcome of the cold war.

As the delay lengthened, the man realized he must make a quick decision: Should he break and run? With intuition developed from years of experience, he knew the moment was critical and that the proper decision was obvious.

Suddenly and decisively he made his move. With a burst of energy he raced along the barbed wire and concrete barricade.

"Halt!" the American MP shouted.

Immediately the sirens came on, and the floodlights bathed the area. With years of espionage work hanging in the balance, he began to claw his way over the barricade.

"If you do not stop, we will open fire," said the voice booming out of the speaker system over the area.

Ignoring the final warning, the intelligence officer continued his desperate attempt to salvage his mission.

As he climbed over the wall, the Americans opened fire. Scores of machine gun bullets riddled the man's body, and he fell face downward on the ground.

The military policeman who had first talked to him ran to the agent and, putting a hand on his shoulder, rolled him over on his back. With his last dying words and with hatred in his eyes, the KGB operative looked at the American and said,

"I'm dying for communism. What are you living for?"[3104]

3104 This story is true. It was told to this writer in 1966 by a professional football player, a committed Christian, who was the MP at Checkpoint Charlie on that fateful day.

What is the final significance of human life? What are we living for? Or, better, what should we be living for?

Materialist scientist Carl Sagan begins his book on cosmic evolution with the confident words, "The Cosmos is all that is or ever will be."[3105] Throughout the book he spells cosmos with a capital "C." An aura of mystical wonder akin to what the religious man calls worship pervades his description of his Cosmos. He is so impressed with what is "out there" that at times he almost seems to ascribe the attributes of deity to the organized mass of atoms known as the universe. He has, in fact, given us a modern-day nature myth.[3106] Of its own accord these atoms came into existence out of nothing and subsequently organized themselves into the enormously complex universe which invokes Sagan's reverence.

But is this really all that will ever be? Some modern cosmologists seem to think so. As he concludes his scientific account of this modern nature myth, the big bang theory, Stephen Weinberg, former professor of physics at Harvard University, turns to the questions of final significance. His theory has led him to the depressing conclusion that the universe is without purpose or design. We are, he concludes, merely specks in an overwhelmingly hostile universe. He says, "The more the universe seems comprehensible, the more it also seems pointless."[3107]

What solace does he offer? What is the significance of man? What are we to do with the pointless situation his hostile cosmos has thrust on us? Listen:

> *The effort to understand the universe is one of the very few things that lifts human life a little above the level of farce, and gives it some of the grace of tragedy.*[3108]

One can sympathize with the pain Weinberg must feel at having to summarize the final significance of his life in such pointless terms. We can also appreciate his honesty. On materialist presuppositions not much more can be said.

The following chapters will discuss the biblical answer to Weinberg's dilemma. According to the Bible the universe is only temporarily hostile to man and was created to be ruled by him. The original Edenic commission, "rule and have dominion," has yet to be fulfilled. Our purpose in life is not found by making the best of a bad situation but by striving mightily to obtain the high honor of partnering with Christ in the final destiny of man. That destiny is called "the inheritance." This is the future reward the writers of Scripture everywhere exhort us to pursue:

> *Knowing that from the Lord you will receive the reward of the inheritance. It is the Lord Christ whom you serve (Colossians 3:24).*

Many writers have discerned various rewards the believer can obtain: crowns, co-rulership, participation in the heavenly priesthood, special honor, and others. The content of this heavenly inheritance is called "treasure in heaven" by Jesus. The believer's reward is

---

3105 Carl Sagan, *The Cosmos* (New York: Random House, 1980), 4.

3106 A "nature myth" is a pantheistic theory of matter found in ancient civilizations like Babylon, Egypt, Persia, and Canaan. In this view God pervades and lives in the stuff of which things are made, and hence the cosmos itself is God.

3107 Stephen Weinberg, *The First Three Minutes* (New York: Basic Books, 1977), 154.

3108 Ibid., 155.

mentioned more than thirty times in the New Testament. Paul equates these rewards with the idea of the inheritance, our eternal possessions granted to us as a result of a faithful life.

The idea of our future inheritance is a central theme of the Bible. As demonstrated elsewhere, all Christians are heirs of God but not all are co-heirs with Christ.[3109] All will have God as their inheritance, but not all will "receive an inheritance from the Lord as a reward." It is this latter inheritance which is the subject of this chapter.

What are the contents of this inheritance? While the Old Testament prefigured this inheritance, the New Testament writers enriched the concept immeasurably.

We Reap What We Sow

There is a correlation between our life now and our experience of eternal life in the new heavens and the new earth.

As He gazed on His disciples, instructing them about the kingdom way of life, the Lord Jesus said,

> *Give, and it will be given to you. Good measure, pressed down, shaken together, running over, will be put into your lap. For with the measure you use it will be measured back to you (Luke 6:38, ESV).*

According to Bock, "The measuring of the corn is a process which is carried out according to an established pattern. The seller crouches on the ground with the measure between his legs. First of all he fills the measure three-quarters full and gives it a good shake with a rotatory motion to make the grains settle down. Then he fills the measure to the top and gives it another shake. Next he presses the corn together strongly with both hands. Finally he heaps it into a cone, tapping it carefully to press the grains together; from time to time he bores a hole in the cone and pours a few more grains into it, until there is literally no more room for a single grain. In this way, the purchaser is guaranteed an absolutely full measure; it cannot hold more."[3110]

The passive verb ("will be measured back") expresses God's promise to reward the disciple's gracious actions toward others. There is a correspondence between the believer's life today and his experience of life in the future.

Scripture tells us that we will reap what we sow (Galatians 6:8). The apostle said that his determined purpose in life was to "know Him" and the power of His resurrection (Philippians 3:10). Knowing God is a dynamic process, like knowing one's wife, husband, or close friend. As that knowledge grows and becomes more intimate, the more diligently it is pursued. Some will pursue that knowledge more diligently than others and thus will have closer intimacy with God than others. That degree of intimacy will naturally carry over into eternity future. God allowed Job to face terrible trials. Whatever His reasons, it is clear, that for Job, the outcome was that he came to know God more intimately. He said *"I have heard of Thee by the hearing of the ear; but now my eye sees Thee"* (Job 42:5, NASB).

[3109] See vol. 1, chapters 3-5.

[3110] Bock, *Luke 1-9:50*, 607-8.

Treasures in Heaven

The broad term the New Testament uses for our reward in heaven is inheritance. This and the following two chapters discuss the content of this inheritance. Jesus referred to this as "treasures in heaven."

> *But lay up for yourselves* ***treasures in heaven****, where neither moth nor rust destroys, and where thieves do not break in or steal (Matthew 6:19–20, NASB).*

In His encounter with the rich young ruler,

> *Jesus felt a love for him, and said to him, "One thing you lack: go and sell all you possess, and give to the poor, and you shall have* ***treasure in heaven****; and come, follow Me" (Mark 10:21).*

Elsewhere He taught,

> *Sell your possessions and give to charity; make yourselves purses which do not wear out, an unfailing* ***treasure in heaven****, where no thief comes near, nor moth destroys (Luke 12:33, NASB).*

> *For where your treasure is,* ***there will your heart be also*** *(Luke 12:34, NASB).*

This verse has variously been interpreted as meaning (1) that if a believer places his treasure in the things of God, his heart will follow, or, (2) if his heart is set on God's values and priorities, he will put his treasure into those things.

The various aspects of these future treasures may be summarized as (a) enhanced intimacy with God, (b) honor and praise from Christ, and (c) expanded opportunities to serve Him and minister throughout all eternity. These may be diagramed as follows.

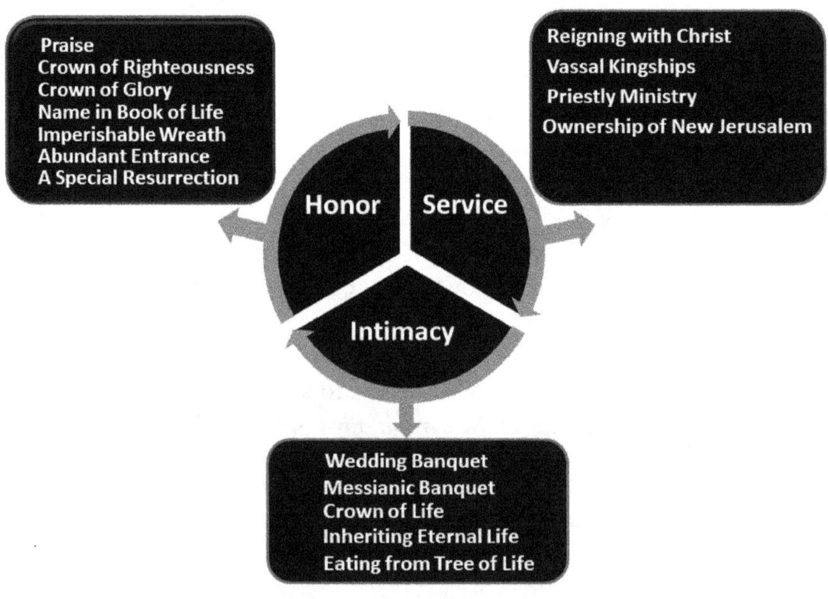

In the following pages, we will see that these rewards are only available to believers who overcome. Who are these overcomers? Because they figure so prominently in the treasures in heaven, one must identify them carefully. Experimental Predestinarians view the term "overcomer" as another word for all Christians. We responded to this Experimentalist viewpoint in Chapter 43. The Partners teach that the overcomers are the faithful Christians, Christ's *Metochoi* ("partners").

To those who are victorious in some specific test, the Lord promises a special prize. These prizes are aspects of the treasures in heaven promised by Jesus in the Gospels. The Partners believe that the challenges to the overcomers in Revelation are addressed to those who are already saved; they are exhortations to persevere in works in order to obtain a reward.

In the discussion below and the following two chapters, we will explore in more detail each of the treasures that compose intimacy, honor, and service. We begin with what is the most important treasure, enhanced intimacy with Christ. The New Testament uses four metaphors to describe this eschatological blessing: participation in the wedding banquet, eating from "the tree of life," receiving the "crown of life," and inheriting eternal life.

PARTICIPATION IN THE WEDDING BANQUET

We have discussed the marvelous celebratory Marriage Banquet celebrating the marriage between Christ and His church in the New Jerusalem during the tribulation.[3111] The Marriage Banquet is a time of special celebration for Christ and His faithful *Metochoi* from the Church era. During this time Christ will reward them for lives well-lived. This time of fellowship speaks of special intimacy with Christ that is illustrated by the wise virgins who prepared for and watched for His return (Matthew 25:1-13) and the believers who are dressed in the righteous acts of the saints (Matthew 22:11; Revelation 19:8).

We will not review those passages here but John adds additional information about this glorious feast. One of the prizes to the overcomer is "hidden" manna and a "new name" written on a "white stone."

> *He who has an ear, let him hear what the Spirit says to the churches. To him who overcomes, I will give some of the hidden manna. I will also give him a white stone with a new name written on it, known only to him who receives it (Revelation 2:17).*

We will discuss the meaning of "new name" and the "white stone" in the next chapter.[3112]

The meaning of the "hidden manna" promised to overcomers is not known. Elsewhere John connected *manna* with feasting on the Lord Jesus, the bread of life. He called Him the living bread that comes down from heaven (John 6:49-51). This writer is inclined to accept Walvoord's suggestion that "this seems to refer to the benefits of fellowship with Christ."[3113] I suggest that to feast on the manna from heaven in this eschatological context refers to the Wedding Feast of the Lamb of Revelation 19:9. Feasting is a common metaphor for fellowship. Thus to be given this "hidden manna"

[3111] It will be followed by the Messianic Banquet on earth that which inaugurates the millennial era.

[3112] See p. 967.

[3113] Walvoord, *The Revelation of Jesus Christ.*

may signify a time of special intimacy with Christ in the company of His *Metochoi*. Beale says, "The promise of 'hidden manna' is a metaphorical portrayal of end-time fellowship and identification with Christ, which will be consummated at the marriage supper of the Lamb."[3114] The danger of forfeiting the manna is the danger found in the parables of the Wedding Banquet, that is, exclusion from that time of intimacy with Christ and His *Metochoi*.

The intimacy with Christ enjoyed by those admitted to the marriage feast is wonderful to anticipate, and it gives overcomers high motivation to persevere in the midst of trials.

EATING FROM THE TREE OF LIFE

Another expression used to symbolize this enhanced intimacy with Christ is the promise that the overcomers will eat from the tree of life.

> *He who has an ear, let him hear what the Spirit says to the churches. To him who overcomes, I will give the right to eat from the tree of life, which is in the paradise of God (Revelation 2:7).*

Eating a meal is a common Semitic metaphor for close fellowship. The Partners view this promise as a promise of enhanced intimacy with the King for believers who remain faithful to Him.

We have discussed this passage in detail in vol. 2, chapter 43, and that discussion need not be repeated here.[3115] In that chapter we concluded that those who do not eat are not non-Christians but are regenerate people who have "lost their first love" (2:4); they must have loved Christ at one time. The danger is that they will lose their share in the tree of life as well. This tree is the inheritance of those "who wash their robes" and is reserved for those among the saved who have a right to the tree and to "enter by the gates" (Revelation 22:14).[3116] Entrance by the gates refers to entrance with special honor. All Christians enter the city, but only the overcomers, the victors, will enter by the gates.

The Lord, speaking of the church as a whole at Ephesus, says they will be removed (Revelation 2:5). The removal of the lampstand is not the loss of salvation of individual Christians. It is the removal of the corporate church as a light and witness. The church as a whole is the lampstand (Revelation 1:20). To lose that first love or lose one's share in the tree of life, however, refers to individual Christians who had a first love for Christ; thus they were regenerate. How could unregenerate professing Christians lose their share in the tree of life if they never had it to begin with?

THE CROWN OF LIFE

> *Be faithful until death, and I will give you* ***the crown of life*** *(Revelation 2:10).*

When Romania became a kingdom in 1881, King Charles realized that there was no crown for him to wear. He instructed his soldiers to go to the arsenal and secure some iron from a canon which had been captured from the enemy. They then melted it and fashioned

---

[3114] Beale, *The Book of Revelation: A Commentary on the Greek Text*, 252.

[3115] For fuller discussion of the "tree of life" and Revelation 22:14, see pp. 678 ff.

[3116] See pp. 681 ff.

it into an iron crown. His intent was that this crown would be a token of what he won on the field of battle. It had been bought and paid for with many Romanian lives.[3117]

The crown the believer obtains is the victor's crown (Gr *stephanos*). This crown was given for victory in the games, achievement in war, and places of honor at the feasts.[3118] "In the New Testament it is plain that the *stephanos* whereof St. Paul speaks is always the conqueror's and not the king's."[3119] This crown is not like the royal crown. It is a crown that is given on the basis of merit. It was woven of oak, ivy, spruce, myrtle, or olive. Jesus' crown, though made of thorns, depicted ultimate victory (Matthew 27:29). Five crowns are mentioned in the New Testament.[3120]

Jesus exhorts the church at Smyrna,

> *I know your tribulation and your poverty (but you are rich), and the blasphemy by those who say they are Jews and are not, but are a synagogue of Satan.*
>
> *Do not fear what you are about to suffer. Behold, the devil is about to cast some of you into prison, that you may be tested, and you will have tribulation ten days.*
>
> *Be faithful until death, and I will give you* ***the crown of life****.*
>
> *He who has an ear, let him hear what the Spirit says to the churches. He who overcomes* ***shall not be hurt by the second death*** *(Revelation 2:9-11).*

For some Christians the purpose of God includes severe testing, even martyrdom. This high honor will be duly compensated with a special distinction, namely, receiving the crown of life.

Throughout the centuries many Christians have been called on to give their lives for Christ. This honorable heritage was pioneered by Christ and His apostles. James was beheaded in Jerusalem in AD 44. Philip was cruelly scourged and afterward was crucified. Matthew was claimed by the sword in Parthea in AD 60. Mark was dragged through the streets of Alexandria by his feet and then burned to death the following day. Luke was hanged on an olive tree in Greece. James the Less was thrown from a pinnacle of the temple in Jerusalem and beaten to death down below. Matthias was stoned and beheaded. Andrew was crucified on a cross where he hung for three days and constantly told people around him of the love of Jesus Christ. Peter was scourged and crucified upside down. He chose this posture himself because he did not think he was worthy to suffer in the same manner as his Lord. Thomas was thrust through with a spear in India. Jude was crucified in AD 72. Bartholomew was beaten to death with clubs. John was condemned to a cauldron of boiling oil, though he escaped death and later died in exile on the island of Patmos. Barnabas was stoned to death by Jews in Salonica. Paul was beheaded in Rome by Nero.[3121]

What is the crown of life? It is not given as a result of regeneration, because regenerate life comes by means of faith alone apart from works and is not given for faithfulness under persecution. Since the crown of life is a reward given for an accomplishment subsequent to initial faith, it is probable that "life" refers to a higher quality of life in the kingdom. It

[3117] Sauer, *In the Arena of Faith: A Call to a Consecrated Life*, 66.

[3118] William E. Rafferty, "Crown," in *NISBE (1988)*, 1:831.

[3119] Trench, *Synonyms of the New Testament*, 78.

[3120] See Quick, "The Doctrine of Eternal Significance", 223-39. Also Sauer, *In the Arena of Faith: A Call to a Consecrated Life*, 59-67.

[3121] John Foxe, *Foxe's Christian Martyrs of the World* (Chicago: Moody Press, n.d.), 24-25.

would be the same as that aspect of eternal life that can be earned,[3122] the special richness of eternal life merited by faithful service on the field of battle. This is the victor's crown, awarded to the one who finishes well and as a result obtains an abundant entrance into the kingdom, of which Peter spoke (2 Peter 1:11).

John's readers are also reminded that even if they lose their physical lives, they will never lose eternal life. He reminds them, "*You will never be hurt by the second death.*" The word "never" is very emphatic in Greek, a double negative (*ou mē*, "definitely not"). This expression is common in categorical and emphatic denials.[3123]

What is the second death? It likely refers to the lake of fire (Revelation 20:14). Experimentalists like Thomas Schreiner say, "The call to conquer is necessary in order to escape eternal judgment in the lake of fire."[3124] We disagree. This is not a warning to those who do not overcome; it is a figure of speech encouraging those who do. God would not threaten true believers with a judgment He knows would never happen to them. Nor would He tell them that in order to secure final entrance into heaven, they must work and be successful. Though Schreiner strenuously denies he teaches a works salvation, he does.[3125] What then does John mean?

When John says they will never be hurt by the second death, he is using a figure of speech called litotes.[3126] Litotes is an "understatement in which an affirmative is expressed by the negative of the contrary."[3127] For example, when Luke says of the Ephesian elders that "they were not a little comforted" (Acts 20:22), he means they were greatly comforted by Paul's parting words.[3128] Or, when standing before Felix the governor, Paul says that he was from Tarsus, which is "no obscure city." He means it is a very important city.[3129] When we say, "Michael Jordan is not a bad basketball player," we mean he is an outstanding basketball player. So to say one will not be hurt by the second death is actually a way of expressing the positive idea that even if a person suffers physical death, *he will experience a rich eternity with God.* He is assured of an eternity with Christ. This is a great encouragement. Even though they can hurt the body, they can never take away eternal life with Christ.

There is a problem, however, with taking this promise as litotes. If it is true that one who overcomes is not hurt by the second death, then what happens if one does not overcome? Would it not follow that he *would be* hurt by the second death, that is, damned? If this is truly litotes, then the answer is, "No." If we say, "Michael Jordan is not a bad basketball player," we mean he is a very good basketball player. However, the reverse does not follow, "If you are not Michael Jordan, you are definitely **not** a good basketball player." A litotes cannot be read in reverse. Ed Ediger correctly observes, "Jesus does not

---

3122 See discussion in vol. 1, chapter 17.

3123 Louw-Nida, 1:664.

3124 Schreiner, *Run to Win the Prize*, 39.

3125 See extensive discussion of the warning passages in Chapters 33-38 above.

3126 Lloyd-Jones, *Romans Chapter 8:17-39: The Final Perseverance of the Saints*, 314 ff. Litotes is a figure of speech in which a positive statement is made by negating its opposite. Explanation and illustrations of litotes were given in chapter 20.

3127 *Merriam-Webster's Collegiate Dictionary*, s.v. "litotes".

3128 BDAG, 642.

3129 For full discussion of the figure of speech litotes, see Bullinger, *Figures of Speech Used in the Bible: Explained and Illustrated*, 155 ff.

say that a failure to 'overcome' will result in 'the second death.' Possible implications, particularly opposite ones, are not necessarily intended by the speaker. Negative implications are not always true."[3130]

For another example of the impossibility of reversing a litotes, note that Jesus used litotes when He said, "*The one who comes to me I will certainly not cast out*" (John 6:37). His meaning is something like, "I will embrace him fully." But one cannot reverse the statement and say, "The one who does not come to me, I will certainly cast out." The one who does not come to Christ cannot be cast out from a relationship with Christ because he never came into a relationship with Christ from which he could be cast out![3131] As Marty Cauley says, "An object has to be in a container before it can be cast out of the container."[3132] It is a litotes.

In regard to Revelation 2:11, Lang says, "It is not safe to reverse divine statements, as is done by inferring here that a believer who does not overcome *will* be hurt of the second death" (emphasis his).[3133] The passage is not addressed to nonbelievers, it is addressed to overcomers, that is, believers, and according to Jesus, believers will never experience the second death (John 6:39).

Not being hurt by the second death is a litotes for an abundant life with God in the future kingdom.[3134] *It is a promise and encouragement to believers.* Like similar promises to overcomers in Revelation,[3135] the believers are promised that if they overcome, they will experience a rich life with God and if they do not overcome they will not. Not being hurt by the second death is litotes for abundant life with God and is equivalent to ruling with Christ (Revelation 2:26), inheriting the kingdom (Revelation 21:7), obtaining an abundant entrance into the kingdom (2 Peter 1:11), or entering "by the gates" into the city (Revelation 22:14).

The overcomer, in addition to having the gracious certainty of heaven when he dies, will also be richly rewarded with an enriched experience of eternal life, the crown of life, for whatever sacrifices he is called upon to make in the present. In effect, John is saying,

> *Be faithful unto death, and I will reward you with a richer experience of eternal life. This is the abundant entrance into the kingdom of which Peter spoke (2 Peter 1:11). Always remember, the first death may hurt you, but only briefly, but the second death will not harm you at all, for you will spend eternity regally with Christ.*

INHERITING ETERNAL LIFE

A final aspect of intimacy with Christ is called inheriting eternal life. As discussed above, this refers to an enhanced experience of eternal life and not regeneration or final

---

3130 Edwin Aaron Ediger, *Faith in Jesus: What Does it Mean to Believe in Him?* (Boomington, IN: Westbow Press: A Division of Thomas Nelson, 2012), 393.

3131 If this reverse statement were true, it amounts to saying that (1) salvation is by works or (2) you could not be a Christian to begin with because all Christians overcome. We have shown in chapter 32 that (2) is impossible, and we know from the rest of Scripture that salvation is not by works.

3132 Cauley, *The Outer Darkness*, 485.

3133 G. H. Lang, *Revelation*, reprint ed. (Miami Springs, FL: Schoettle Publishing. Co., 1985), 96.

3134 For good discussion of litotes and its significance in the overcome passages in Revelation see Cauley, *The Outer Darkness*, 481-95.

3135 Revelation 2:7, 26; 3:5, 12, 21; 5:5; 12:11; 15:2; 21:7.

entrance into heaven.[3136] One day as Jesus journeyed south along a dusty Palestinian road, an enthusiastic young man ran to Him and said,

> *Good Teacher, what shall I do to inherit eternal life? (Mark 10:17, NASB).*

We have discussed this encounter in considerable detail in an earlier chapter and will not repeat it here.[3137] It is enough here to say that Jesus did not think the rich young ruler was asking how to get to heaven. We know that by how Jesus answers it. He says, "You know the commandments," and then He told him to sell all he has, give it to the poor, and "follow me." If Jesus thought the young man was asking about personal salvation, He would have responded as He did to the unsaved Nicodemus, *"For God so loved the world, that He gave His only begotten Son, that whoever believes in Him should not perish, but have eternal life"* (John 3:16, NASB).

As shown in chapter 22, this young man was not an unbeliever, He was a believer who wanted to know how to be "complete," that is, what the next step is. His desire was that he might not just have eternal life in the sense of personal salvation, but that he might also have it in the sense of a full experience of it. He wanted to inherit it, that is, possess it fully; he wanted special intimacy with Christ.

Summary

A correlation exists between the degree of intimacy we develop with Christ now and the degree of our intimacy with Him throughout eternity. Our intimacy with Him in the millennium and in the new heavens and the new earth is described in several ways. Those who are invited to participate in the joyful wedding festivities which fill the New Jerusalem during the tribulation period will rejoice in an intimate way with their king. The Partners of Christ will also "eat of the tree of life," enjoying a rich fellowship meal with their Lord. They will also receive the crown of life, marking their victory in trials and their enhanced enjoyment of eternal life. They will receive a white stone with their name on it, a ticket for entrance in the wedding festivities from which unfaithful believers will be excluded.

The overcomers of 1 John and Revelation are all believers, for all believers are overcomers in the sense that through faith in Christ they have overcome the world and are justified in Christ. However, there is more to overcoming the world than initial faith. Persistent faith and obedience to the final hour are required to become an overcomer withrespect to rewards and being one of the Metochoi.

The overcomer in Revelation is the victorious Christian who has finished well and who can look forward to greater intimacy, honor, and opportunities for serving Christ in the future era.

The next chapter discusses the honor and praise that faithful Christians will hear from Christ as He stands before him at the Judgment Seat of Christ.

[3136] See discussion in chapter 17.

[3137] See vol. 1, chapter 22.

61

Treasures in Heaven 2 — Eternal Honor

STEPHEN COVEY has written a book which is the result of years of research in the success literature of the past two centuries. In addition, his insights have been gleaned from his twenty years of experience worldwide as a management consultant to numerous corporations. He is a recognized expert on principles of personal and organizational leadership development. His experience and studies have led him to the discovery that there are common denominators among all highly effective people, what he calls "seven habits." The second habit is "Begin with the end in mind."[3138]

Imagine yourself driving to the funeral of a loved one. As you get out of the car and enter the funeral parlor, you see numerous flowers, friends, and relatives. Gentle music is playing in the background. The sense of sorrow and grief permeates the air, and there are many tears. As you walk down the aisle to the front of the church to look into the casket, you gasp with surprise. When you look into the casket, you see yourself. All these people are here to honor you! This is your funeral, three years from today. These gathered friends and relatives are here to express their love and appreciation.

Still stunned by what you see, you take your seat and wait for the services to begin. Glancing at the program, you note there are to be four speakers. The first is to be from your family both immediate and extended, representing children, brothers, and grandchildren, nephews, nieces, aunts, uncles, cousins, and grandparents. They have come from all over the country to be present at this event. The second speaker is your best friend. He is someone who can give a sense of who you are as a person. The third speaker is someone from your office. This person will, of course, have perspective on what kind of boss you were and what kind of employee you were. Finally, an elder from your church will be called on to share a few personal comments.

Now think about this scene! What would you like these speakers to say about you and your life? What kind of husband, father, employee, Christian would you like their words to reflect? What contributions and achievements would you like these people to remember? Look carefully at the people around you. What difference does it make to them that you lived or died? What impact have you had in their lives?

Now, Covey counsels, take a few moments and jot down the thoughts that come to your mind, the answers to these questions. If you thought deeply about this scene, you discovered something about yourself that you may not have known before. You discovered some of your deep, fundamental values. To "begin with the end in mind" is to begin today

---

[3138] Covey, *The Seven Habits of Highly Effective People*, 96.

with the image, picture, and paradigm of the end of your life as the frame of reference or the criterion by which everything else in your life is examined. By doing this, each part of your life can be examined in the context of the whole according to what you have concluded is most important to you. By keeping the end in mind, you can clearly evaluate whether on any given day you have violated your deepest values. You can determine whether that day, that week, that month has or has not contributed toward the vision you have of life as a whole.

The second aspect of these treasures in heaven is the honor we will receive from Christ if we have faithfully tried to live out His way of life. There are eight aspects to this eternal honor which we will discuss in this chapter: praise, the crown of glory, the crown of righteousness, a new name, a name recorded in the book of life, an imperishable wreath, an abundant entrance through the gates, and a special resurrection. First we consider praise from Christ.

Praise

It is self-evident that our motivation to accomplish a given task is directly related to how significant we feel the task is. When Paul said, "*Whatever you do, work at it with all your heart, as working for the Lord, not for men, since you know that you will receive an inheritance from the Lord as a reward*" (Colossians 3:23-24), he was appealing to this same motivational force. This verse reveals a central aspect of what makes us feel something is significant: a task will be viewed as significant if the people who matter to us value it as so. In this case since it is God who determines the ultimate significance of the work, it will be perceived as highly important: "*Always give yourselves fully to the work of the Lord, because you know that your labor in the Lord is not in vain*" (1 Corinthians 15:58).

But one more thing is needed for us to feel that our work is truly significant. There must be recognition and affirmation by someone else. Someone other than ourselves, someone who has expertise and authority to affirm that a particular task is valuable must give his affirmation. This recognition could be given with a plaque, a word of praise, a compliment, a promotion, or a dinner in the person's honor. "But in some way one must receive the proof from the people who matter that he has done well."[3139] The illustration of the imaginary funeral above illustrates the emotional impact of such praise. However, once we are gone, we will not hear it.

What is evident in the interpersonal relationships in this life can now be applied to our eternal relationship with God. He is the ultimate one who will evaluate our work, and who after we are gone will pronounce the desired words, "Well done." And He is the one who matters more than anyone. Our eternal security gives us freedom to pursue our significance. We do not have to worry about eternal separation from our Father, that is, loss of salvation. But even though we cannot lose our justification, the warnings in the Bible tell us we can forfeit the inheritance, we can lose our eternal significance. The Biblical promises that our lives can matter motivate us to make sacrifices, to take risks, to work hard, knowing that our work is not in vain in the Lord. God values whatever we do for Him. The warnings that we can lose rewards should inspire the fear of the Lord in our hearts and cause us to labor to avoid that terrible consequence.

[3139] Ibid., 13-14.

The other side of significance is final accountability. It is true that our lives can matter; they can make a difference. It is true that through service to Him we can attach eternal value to the life we have lived; however, some of us will pursue this goal more diligently than others. Some Christians, to their great shame and eternal loss, will not pursue this worthy goal at all. The differences will become evident when we stand before Him at the Judgment Seat of Christ.

Hearing the King's "Well done" is a powerful motivation. Who would not want to hear these words?

> *His master said to him, "Well done, good and faithful slave; you were faithful with a few things, I will put you in charge of many things, enter into the joy of your master" (Matthew 25:21, NASB).*

Crown of Glory

Christ will bestow special recognition on those who have labored faithfully to care for and disciple other Christians. It is significant that the crown of glory and the crown of righteousness have been designated as awards for those who have given their lives to evangelism and discipleship:

> *To the elders among you, I appeal as a fellow elder, a witness of Christ's sufferings and one who also will share in the glory to be revealed. Be shepherds of God's flock that is under your care, serving as overseers, not because you must, but because you are willing, as God wants you to be; not greedy for money, but eager to serve; not lording it over those entrusted to you, but being examples to the flock. And when the Chief Shepherd appears, you will receive the crown of glory that will never fade away (1 Peter 5:1-4).*

Here the faithful pastor and elder who work in the church are honored.

Crown of Righteousness

Paul's second epistle to Timothy exhorts him to evangelize. This epistle contains Paul's last words. He was beheaded by Nero shortly thereafter. Sensing that the end was near, he penned these moving phrases,

> *For I am already being poured out like a drink offering, and the time has come for my departure. I have fought the good fight, I have finished the race, I have kept the faith. Now there is in store for me the crown of righteousness which the Lord, the righteous Judge, will award to me on that day — and not only to me, but also to all who have longed for his appearing (2 Timothy 4:6-8).*

For those Christians who long for Christ's return, who live their lives in view of this event, there will be special honor. The crown may be symbolic of the righteous life lived. It is "like a soldier's medal for valor in the face of battle. The medal does not contain valor, but it does declare that its possessor is valorous."[3140] It is a crown of approval. Righteousness in this passage should be understood as "upright behavior."[3141] It is a crown of vindication, a

---

[3140] Quick, "The Doctrine of Eternal Significance", 227.

[3141] BDAG, 248.

crown which says "Paul, you have lived well." When it is bestowed, the Lord Jesus is saying, Paul was right, and Rome was wrong. As he wrote, Paul stood before an unrighteous judge receiving an unrighteous reward. But one day, he will stand before the only Judge that matters and that Judge will grant to him a righteous crown, a crown of vindication saying, "Paul, you were right, Rome was wrong! Thank you for serving Me."

A New Name

> *To him who overcomes, to him I will give some of the hidden manna, and I will give him a* ***white stone****, and a* ***new name*** *written on the stone which no one knows but he who receives it (Revelation 2:17).*

What is the "white stone" and the "new name"?

The white stone has been interpreted in various ways. Mounce's suggestion fits the context well. He says, "In the context of a messianic feast (the 'hidden manna') it seems best to take the white stone as a *tessera* [a small tile] that served as a token for admission to the banquet."[3142] These white stones served as admission tickets to the athletic games and to banquets.[3143] So to have one's name written on it identified the holder of the ticket.[3144]

Another possibility is suggested by Eric Sauer who relates this to a custom of the Greek athletic games.This is also mentioned by Osborne. A victor's prize at the games often included objects of value and gifts of gold. According to Plutarch, winners at the Isthmian games were given one hundred drachmas and at the Olympics, five hundred. The winner received a certificate of victory with a small tablet of white stone in which the name of the victor was inscribed by an expert carver.[3145]

The believer possessing this white stone with a name on it received from the heavenly judge is recognized as a victor in the battle and has a "ticket" to the Wedding Feast of the Lamb. Even though despised on earth, he will be honored in heaven. The sentence of rejection received from earthly judges (like Nero) will be reversed. Those hated and expelled here will be honored with heavenly riches and eternal glory.

The giving of a "new name" was a Jewish custom of assigning a name at a point in life which characterizes the person.[3146] In the early church James was called "camel knees" because of the calluses on his knees from so much kneeling while he was praying. Our Lord called Simon by a new name, Peter, which means "rock," signifying his future as the rock of stability in the church. Joseph, a Levite of Cyprian birth, was called "Barnabas," which means "son of encouragement." James and John were known as the "sons of thunder" and Saul of Tarsus preferred to be known as "Paul" ("little"), remembering that he was the least of the apostles and the greatest of sinners.

But perhaps the greatest illustration of the gift of the new name was the name given to a carpenter's son who grew up in a military camp town, Nazareth. Because He was obedient,

---

3142 Mounce, *The Book of Revelation*, 83.

3143 Osborne says, "It was common for members of a guild or victors at the games to use stones as a ticket for admission to feasts, and also for free food or entrance to the games." Osborne, *Revelation*, 149.

3144 It is unlikely that the name written on the "ticket" was God's or Christ's. Their names were not "hidden."

3145 Sauer, *In the Arena of Faith: A Call to a Consecrated Life*, 64-65.

3146 See Judges 6:31-32, where Gideon was renamed Jerub-Baal, which means "Let Baal contend with him" because he took a stand against Baal and cut down his altars.

even to the death of a cross, He was given a new name, "THE LORD JESUS CHRIST."[3147] Just as His new name was earned by faithful obedience, so it is with the many sons He is leading to glory.[3148]

Christ will give to each overcomer a new name, a name of honor. Yet this name is known to no one but Christ and the one to whom He gives it. Each believer has his own particular life message, his own particular history of struggle and demonstration of God's life in his. God is a God of the individual as well as of the church. The secrecy of the name implies a special relationship between Christ and each overcomer. It will be a name which in some way signifies an outstanding characteristic of that person's life. This of course challenges every believer to consider the question, "What will my name be?" And more importantly, "What would I like my name to be?"

Name Recorded in the Book of Life (Revelation 3:5)

As discussed elsewhere, the overcomer is promised that his name will not be blotted out of the book of life.[3149] This means either (1) that his eternal reputation is secure no matter what they do to his body under persecution, or (2) it is another example of litotes, emphatically reminding them of their eternal security even if they are physically killed:

> *He who overcomes will thus be clothed in white garments; and I will not erase his name from the book of life, and I will confess his name before My Father and before His angels (Revelation 3:5).*

This act of persevering is to be equated with being clothed in white garments. The "white robes are the righteousness of the saints, not the [imputed] righteousness of God."[3150]

To have one's name confessed before the Father is to have his service and worth praised.

Imperishable Wreath

The apostle Paul also spoke of receiving such honor and praise in terms of the athletic metaphor,

> *Do you not know that in a race all the runners run, but only one gets the prize? Run in such a way as to get the prize (1 Corinthians 9:24).*

To what then do the crown, the prize, and the race refer in 1 Corinthians 9:24-27? The "race" to which Paul refers is the competition at the Isthmian games held every three years in honor of Poseidon, the god of the sea.[3151] The site was a spruce grove dedicated to him on the Isthmus of Corinth.[3152] Vast crowds attended these ancient Greek games. The Olympiad hosted fifty thousand at the Coliseum in Rome. That of Saurus held eighty

---

[3147] Philippians 2:9.

[3148] Hebrews 2:10.

[3149] See vol. 2, chapter 43, pp. 685 ff.

[3150] G. Campbell Morgan, *A First Century Message to Twentieth Century Christians* (New York: Revell, 1902), 149.

[3151] Robertson and Plummer, *A Critical and Exegetical Commentary on the First Epistle of Paul to the Corinthians*, 194.

[3152] Sauer, *In the Arena of Faith: A Call to a Consecrated Life*, 36.

thousand persons. A total of over 270 Roman amphitheaters are known.[3153] The prize at Corinth was a spruce wreath, the tree sacred to Poseidon.[3154] To participate in the games one had to be a freeborn Greek.[3155]

This starting gate for the foot race in the Isthmian games dates about 700 BC. The grooves in the track were lines where string connecting to the starting gates was laid. They slid under small metal nails to release all the gates at precisely the same time.

Paul continues,

Everyone who competes in the games exercises self-control [Gr *egkrateuomai*] *in all things (1 Corinthians 9:24–27).*

Everyone who competes in the games exercises self-control. The NIV translates *egkrateuomai* with the phrase "goes into strict training." The word pictures strong self-discipline. It is an appropriate word to use for the demanding process of "getting in shape" to participate in the games. The athletes were selected by local elimination trials, after which they submitted to rigorous training for ten months under professional trainers. After their arrival for training they were examined by the officials, and they took an oath swearing to obey all the rules.[3156] If an athlete left the gymnasium once during the ten months of training, he was disqualified and could not participate in the games. His diet consisted of cheese, figs, and dried meats. No wine was allowed. If he was caught violating the diet, he was disqualified.

Every morning there were two trumpet calls. The first was the warning trumpet. When it blew, the athlete's personal trainer came and rubbed down the athlete with oil. The second trumpet was the signal to begin the daily workout in the exercise square called the "agony." As he exercised, there were "marshals" observing his effort. If he caught an athlete loafing just once during this entire ten months, he was disqualified. If an athlete missed

[3153] Ibid., 39.

[3154] Ibid., 48.

[3155] Will Durant, *The Life of Greece*, vol. 2, The Story of Civilization (New York: Simon and Schuster, 1966), 2:213.

[3156] Ibid.

one trumpet call the entire ten months, he was disqualified from the games. The athletes trained and competed naked,[3157] regardless of the weather or temperature.

Now why did they do all this? First, they did it to obtain a spruce wreath on their head! Each winner bound a woolen cloth about his head, and the judges placed the wreath/crown on it. Then a herald announced the name and the city of the winner, a custom continued in the Olympiads of our day. This wreath was the only prize given at the games, yet it was the most eagerly contested distinction in Greece.[3158]

However, there was more to it than that. After the victory celebration great honors were heaped on the athlete when he returned home.

These are the remains of an ancient "locker room" where the athletes at Pergamum trained in preparation for the games. Usually ten months were spent in training at this ancient gymnasium under very careful scrutiny of the referees.

A breach in the city wall was cut. This was to signify that the protection of the wall was no longer needed now that an athlete of this stature had returned home. The winner was then placed on a chariot and led through the city in a festive procession.[3159] Many cities voted substantial sums of money to the victors. Some made them generals, and the crowd idolized them so openly that the Greek philosophers complained. Poets were hired by the victor and his parents to pen odes to his greatness. These odes were sung by a chorus of boys in the procession that welcomed him home. Sculptors were paid to capture the athlete in his most athletic pose.[3160] Some cities fed the athlete's children and wife at public expense for the rest of their lives. The children were allowed to enter the best academy in the ancient world, paid by the city. The athlete was given a seat of honor on the city council and a box seat at the Isthmian games for the rest of his life.[3161] Last, but definitely not least, he was exempt from all income tax![3162]

3157 Ibid., 2:214.

3158 Ibid., 2:216.

3159 Sauer, *In the Arena of Faith: A Call to a Consecrated Life*, 59.

3160 Durant, *The Life of Greece*, 2:216.

3161 Sauer, *In the Arena of Faith: A Call to a Consecrated Life*, 59.

3162 Ibid.

They do it to get a crown that will not last; but we do it to get a crown that will last forever (1 Corinthians 9:25, NIV).

Paul says that Christians also will receive a reward if they, like the athletes, are willing to sacrifice and live the life of discipleship, a life that similarly requires strong self-discipline. It is like entering the city. It is this magnificent reward which is referred to as entering "through the gates into the city" in Revelation 22:14. To enter through the gates was to enter in the victory procession of the returning champion.

Paul continues:

Therefore I do not run like a man running aimlessly (1 Corinthians 9:26).

The stadium sprint was the most popular event at the games. This race course, supposedly the length of one footprint of Hercules, was 192 meters or one-seventh of a mile. Only free men (no slaves) could participate. An athlete trained for ten months in his hometown and for one month at Isthmia.

The race to which he probably refers was the most popular contest at the games, the stadium sprint, usually about two hundred meters.[3163] Another race was a four-hundred-meter run and another went for about four kilometers. We have no knowledge of the records, but one ancient Greek writer avows that the athletes jumped over fifteen meters. This only proves that one cannot believe everything he reads![3164]

For a runner to run "aimlessly" is to run without focusing on the goal. Paul says that our lives must always be "run" with a clear view of the final accounting we will all face. All decisions must be made in view of this coming event. A Christian who lacks this perspective or who ignores it is simply living life without purpose:

I do not fight like a man beating the air. No, I beat my body and make it my slave so that after I have preached to others, I myself will not be disqualified for the prize (1 Corinthians 9:26-27).

3163 Durant, *The Life of Greece*, 2:214.

3164 Ibid.

This victor's monument from the Isthmian games dates from the time of the apostle Paul. On it the names of the victors and their judges were inscribed.

Boxing was another popular sport at the games. The Greek boxers did not hit straight out from the shoulder as modern boxers do. They fought by swinging their arms in a kind of windmill fashion.[3165] Furthermore, the Romans introduced weighting the leather gloves with iron, lead, and metal studs. Terrible wounds were often inflicted. This naturally caused the boxers to adopt evasion as their chief strategy.[3166] The Christian life, however, must be lived aggressively, not avoiding danger but challenging it. Christians must not be beating the air, windmill fashion, but must use their fists in dead earnest, intending to make every blow count. In other words, the Christian is not to practice a life of evading his Christian responsibilities. He is to aggressively pursue them. He is to make every blow count for Christ. He is to live his life with purpose and intensity.

When Paul says, "I beat my body," he uses a Greek athletic term for what we would call a "knockout." The word, *hypōpiazō*, literally means "to give a black eye by hitting."[3167] This was the decisive blow which won the fight, the "first blow under the eye."[3168] He means that as Christians we must defeat our bodies. We must exercise strong discipline. The self, the "I," must be dealt a knockout blow. The self is our real enemy, and that is what he means by "body." The real opponent is the self with its longings for convenience, its desire to be spared at all costs, its wishes and longings.

Though Paul does not give this crown a name, it is a crown awarded to those who have fought the battle with the flesh and through self-discipline have emerged victorious. They have dealt the "I" a "knockout blow." It is a crown for those who have mastered the body.

How tragic it would be for one who has instructed others in the rules for obtaining the prize to find that, when the race was over, he should be disqualified for the prize for failing to keep the rules he himself taught.

It should be noted, in conclusion, that these crowns can be lost (Revelation 3:11; Matthew 25:29). We must be faithful to the end of life if we are to obtain these tokens of special honor.

[3165] G. F. Hasel, "Games," in *NISBE*, 2:397.

[3166] Ibid.

[3167] Robertson and Plummer, *A Critical and Exegetical Commentary on the Second Epistle of St. Paul to the Corinthians*, 196.

[3168] Sauer, *In the Arena of Faith: A Call to a Consecrated Life*, 53.

After a vigorous workout the athletes at the gymnasium at Pergamum would take their "showers" in these wash basins.

In the book of Revelation, the twenty-four elders are pictured as casting their crowns to the feet of the Lamb:

> *Whenever the living creatures give glory, honor and thanks to him who sits on the throne and who lives for ever and ever, the twenty-four elders fall down before him who sits on the throne, and worship him who lives for ever and ever. They lay their crowns before the throne (Revelation 4:9-10).*

This verse reveals that a major purpose of the crowns is to be tokens of worship. Like the twenty-four elders, rewarded believers also will lay at His feet the very honors He gave them. This process is not a one-time event but occurs "***whenever*** *the living creatures give glory, honor, and thanks to Him who sits on the throne*." Throughout eternity these tokens of honor will be laid at Christ's feet in acts of worship. Each time the rewarded believer approaches the throne, he will remove his crown, lay it at the feet of Jesus, and worship. A central motivation for obtaining these crowns is to be found in the desire to have these tokens of worship.

An Abundant Entrance "Through the Gates"

Another aspect of praise, that Christ will heap on the believer who has persevered faithfully to the end, is an entrance "through the gates," into the New Jerusalem. The apostle John spoke of those "who may enter by the gates into the city" (Revelation 22:14).

> *Blessed are those who wash their robes, so that they may have the right to the tree of life, and may enter by the gates into the city (Revelation 22:14).*

Some have argued that since only those who "wash their robes" can enter the city, and since entering the city will be a blessing conferred on all Christians, therefore all Christians are those who have washed their robes and are overcomers (22:14). However, John is placing the emphasis not on entering the city, but on entering "by the gates" into the city. All will enter the city, but only some will come in through the gates. In the Greek text this is emphatic and would be best rendered, "and may by the gates enter into the city. John is giving emphasis to the way of entrance, that is, by the gates, and not the fact of entrance.

John probably had in mind the victory arches that towered over the main thoroughfares entering into Rome. Through these gates the triumphant Roman generals and their soldiers would march. This is the Arch of Titus near the Forum in Rome. It was constructed after his victory over Jerusalem in AD 70. Engravings on it show Roman soldiers bringing back treasures from the temple in Jerusalem. Similarly, those Christians who remain faithful to their King will enter the city in victory and will be likewise honored.

Gates of ancient cities were for defense or honor or both. To be known "in the gates" was to sit among the "elders of the land" and have a position of high honor and authority (Proverbs 31:23, cf ISBE 2:408). Since defense is not a function of these "gates" into the heavenly city; they are to be regarded as places of honor and authority. The overcomer was promised "authority" over the nations (Revelation 2:26). John describes them elsewhere, as memorials to the twelve tribes of Israel (21:12, 14). We are reminded of the Roman victory arches which sat astride the main thoroughfares entering into Rome. There were thousands of entry ways into Rome, but Caesar entered by the gates, by the victory arch. Through these gates, according to John, "*the honor and glory of the nations*" will enter (Revelation 21:27). As Lange has suggested, to enter by the gates means to enter "as conquerors in triumphal procession."[3169]

We conclude that the expression "enter by the gates" is a functional equivalent for "enter with special honor." Some will enter the New Jerusalem with special honor, and some will not. This privilege goes to those who "wash their robes." This refers to confession of sin in the life of the believer and removal of all that is impure, such as sorcery, immorality, murder, idolatry, and lying (Revelation 22:15). The need to "wash" one's robes can be paralleled with the Lord's instruction concerning the need to wash the feet, that is, daily confession of sin (John 13:10).

[3169] John Peter Lange, "The Revelation of John," in *A Commentary on the Holy Scriptures*, ed. John Peter Lange, et al. (Bellingham, WA: Logos Bible Software, 2008), 12:446.

Perhaps the only thing that can properly be alleged against this interpretation is that those who partake of the tree of life are contrasted in the next verse with nonbelievers who are outside the city (Revelation 22:15). One could legitimately argue that the opposite of a non-Christian is any Christian, not just overcomers. However, that would depend on the intent of the contrast. Is it not evident that the intent of the contrast here is moral righteousness versus unrighteousness? When making contrasts, it is appropriate to point to the extremes and not items located on a continuum between the extremes. It would therefore be quite natural to contrast the nonbeliever with the victorious overcomer and not with, for example, the lukewarm Christians of Laodicea whom God will spew out of His mouth (Revelation 3:16). Carnal Christians would simply not supply the suitable contrast John has in mind.

John attaches different conditions to becoming regenerate and to becoming an overcomer. He tells us that "*the water of life is without cost*" (Revelation 22:17), and yet a few verses earlier he explained that becoming an overcomer, obtaining a reward, and securing the right to eat of the tree of life will cost everything (22:11). It depends on continuing to practice righteousness, remaining holy, and giving attention to our works (22:12). The very chapter under consideration then sets two categories of Christians before us.

It is possible for some Christians, like the Ephesian believers, to become so preoccupied with the Lord's work that they forget their devotional relationship to the Lord. They too can lose their first love (Revelation 2:4).

To "enter through the gates" was to enter in the victory procession of the returning champion.

A Special Resurrection

A final indication of the special honors the faithful will receive is a special class of resurrection.

> *That I may know Him and the power of His resurrection and the fellowship of His sufferings, being conformed to His death; in order that I may attain to the resurrection from the dead (Philippians 3:10–11, NASB).*

This passage will be discussed in detail in chapter 65. At this point we note that there is something uncertain about Paul's future. He was not sure he will attain to the "resurrection from the dead." How can this be? One possibility that we will present later is that because a special word for "resurrection" is used, perhaps Paul is speaking about a special category of resurrection. The fact that he equates it with the "prize" in Philippians 3:14 (Gr *brabeion*, an award in the athletic games) suggests that this resurrection is a prize, a special honor (See chapter 65).

Summary

The honors granted to the overcomer are indeed magnificent. Imagine receiving from the King a crown of glory for faithful discipline and caring for other Christians. How wonderful it will be to hear the praise, "Well done!" For those of us who are enduring insults, persecution, and being unjustly criticized, what an encouragement to know that one day, we will receive the crown of righteousness, the crown of vindication saying that the criticism was unfair and that God honors our silence and perseverance.

It is astounding to think that the Lord Jesus will record our names in a book of remembrance, recording there a list of faithful disciples, who manifested Christ's way of life to a needy world.

With other servant kings, Christ's *Metochoi* will receive the special honor of entrance through the gates of the New Jerusalem, a privilege for those who persevered in faith to the end of life.

These honors greatly exceed in motivational impact any impulse toward godliness provided in the Experimental Predestinarian system. Instead of threatening the lukewarm with the lake of fire, these biblical honors provide a more ennobling and enticing motivation for living life.

62

Treasures in Heaven 3 — Reigning and Serving

THE THIRD aspect of the inheritance is our opportunity to serve Him throughout all eternity. One day, as the Scriptures everywhere affirm, the struggle of fallen man will finally come to an end. This consummation will not be achieved by social engineering or by the successful implementation of any human ideology. Rather, it will be accomplished by a supernatural intervention of God in history, the second coming of Christ. Finally, history will achieve a worthy outcome—the kingdom of God. Page after page of Scripture speaks of this glorious future and the possibility that those who are Christ's servants now can be granted enhanced opportunities for ministry in the future reign of Christ's servant kings and achieve positions of honor in that future glory.

The Extent of the Kingdom

The divine drama of universal history has been played out on a stage called "earth." On earth the fall of man occurred. On earth Satan lived and ruled. On earth the Son of God came and answered the Satan's lie. Therefore, it is fitting that on earth the final resolution of universal history will occur.

However, there are intimations in Scripture that the future reign of the servant kings in the millennium will embrace the universe as well. And in the eternal state it will embrace the new heavens and the new earth. We are told, for example, that the saints will one day not only rule the world but will also rule over the angels:

> *Do you not know that the saints will judge the world?... Do you not know that we shall judge angels? (1 Corinthians 6:2)*

Since the domain of the angels extends far beyond terrestrial boundaries, we may assume that the kingdom of those who rule over them does so as well.

David reflected on the divine commission in Genesis to "rule and have dominion" saying,

> *What is man that You are mindful of him?*
>
> *You have made him a little lower than the angels and You have crowned him with glory and honor.*
>
> *You have made him to have dominion over the works of Your hands. You have put all things under his feet (Psalm 8:4-6, NKJV).*

While David specifies that the "all things" refers to things on earth, the writer to the Hebrews expands that concept when he says:

> *You have put all things in subjection under his feet.*
>
> *For in that He put all in subjection under him. He left nothing that is not put under him (Hebrews 2:8).*

It is clear that the reign of the Messiah extends to heaven and earth. Since the *Metochoi* (partners) are co-heirs with Him (Romans 8:17), their reign by virtue of association with Him will therefore extend to the cosmos itself:

> *At the name of Jesus every knee should bow, of those in heaven, and those on earth (Philippians 2:10, NKJV).*

> *Now when all things are made subject to Him, then the Son Himself will also be subject to Him who put all things under Him, that God may be all in all (1 Corinthians 15:28, NKJV).*

> *God ... in these last days ... has spoken to us by His Son whom He appointed heir of all things (Hebrews 1:1-2, NASB).*

> *The entire creation awaits the future reign of God's servant kings:*
>
> *Now if we are God's children, then we are heirs — heirs of God, and co-heirs with Christ if indeed we share in his sufferings in order that we may also share in his glory.*
>
> *I consider that our present sufferings are not worth comparing to the glory that will be revealed to us. The creation waits in eager expectation for the sons of God to be revealed.*
>
> *For the creation was subjected to frustration, not by its own choice, but by the will of the one who subjected it, in hope that the creation itself will be liberated from its bondage to decay and brought into the glorious freedom of the children of God (Romans 8:17-21).*

Obviously, this future kingdom embraces the entire created order. One day mankind will conquer the galaxies! While it is true that one purpose of the heavens was to "declare the glory of God," it seems that they were also created to be placed in subjection to man. Perhaps the future kingdom with its reign of universal righteousness and perfect government will result in a technological explosion as well as a spiritual one. Then and only then, in submission to the King, will man be able to achieve his fondest dreams, to rule and have dominion. The future kingdom will witness the greatest explosion of human creativity and useful work in the history of man. Man will finally be what God intended him to be.

When man first began to understand the enormity of the universe in the late eighteenth century, an intellectual revolution of the first order occurred. Prior to this new knowledge man always viewed himself as having a central role in the cosmos. This gave him a sense of identity and significance. But when scientists discovered that the observable universe was twenty-eight billion light years in diameter, a profound change occurred. How could man be considered significant anymore? To learn that he is located on the edge of a minor galaxy among billions of similar and larger galaxies caused modern man to lose his sense of significance. However, if his final significance is to rule this vast created order, then instead of demeaning man, these discoveries, when viewed through the biblical promise, magnify him. His importance is far greater than had been formerly supposed. Instead of merely being destined to rule a small planet, mankind has been chosen to rule something far greater, the vast cosmos itself. No challenge could be greater than to be placed over all the works of God's hands!

Reigning with Christ

This is the kingdom of the Son of God of which we are speaking. "He is the head over all rule and authority" (Colossians 2:10). Our future is closely linked with His. Those Christians who are faithful to Him now will reign with Him then.

> *Peter answered him, "We have left everything to follow you! What then will there be for us?" Jesus said to them, "I tell you the truth, at the renewal of all things, when the Son of Man sits on his glorious throne, you who have followed me will also sit on twelve thrones, judging the twelve tribes of Israel" (Matthew 19:27-28).*

> *You are those who have stood by me in my trials. And I confer on you a kingdom* [*basielia*, a "kingship," Majority text], *just as my Father conferred on me, so that you may eat and drink at my table in my kingdom and sit on thrones, judging the twelve tribes of Israel (Luke 22:28-30).*

The overcomer is one who does His will to the end, either by physical death (Revelation 12:11; 2:10) or until the rapture or second coming. As a reward, he is given a kingship within the kingdom of heaven:

> *To him who overcomes and does My will to the end, I will give authority over the nations — he will rule them with an iron scepter; he will dash them to pieces like pottery — just as I have received authority from My Father, I will also give him the morning star. He who has an ear, let him hear what the Spirit says to the churches (Revelation 2:26-29).*

Nowhere are we told in Revelation that all Christians will overcome and receive this reward. As quoted previously, "A command that everyone keeps is superfluous, and a reward that everyone receives for a virtue that everyone has is nonsense."[3170] The overcomer is the individual Christian who enjoys special benefits in eternity for refusing to give up his faith in spite of persecution, doubt, or difficulties during life on earth.

The meaning of the "morning star" is uncertain. The phrase may be taken from the Balaam prophecy regarding the morning star as a title of Christ (Numbers 24:17; Revelation 22:16). If that so, then this may be the promise that Christ allows the church to share in his messianic glory as the "morning star."

The overcomer will sit on the Father's throne:

> *To him who overcomes, I will give the right to sit with Me on My throne, just as I overcame and sat down with My Father on His throne. He who has an ear, let him hear what the Spirit says to the churches (Revelation 3:21).*

The reference is once again to joint participation with Messiah in the kingdom rule. John's intent is to address them not as "wheat and tares" (as Experimentalists maintain) but as regenerate Christians. He refers to them as "*those whom I love*" and says He will "*reprove and discipline*" (Revelation 3:19) them. This is proof of their regenerate state "*for what son is not disciplined by his father? If you are not disciplined then you are … not true sons*" (Hebrews 12:8).

Faithful believers will sit with Christ on His throne! Based upon Revelation 20:4-6, some have argued that all believers will sit on His throne; therefore, all believers are overcomers. The argument is circular. We know from Revelation 2:26 that an overcomer

[3170] Fuller, "I Will Not Erase His Name from the Book of Life (Revelation 3:5)," 299.

is defined as "*he who keeps my works until the end, and I will reward him with authority over the nations.*" Therefore, those who sit upon the throne with Christ are those believers, and only those believers, who keep His works to the end. We have proven elsewhere that according to the Scriptures, not all true believers keep His works until the end (chapter 32). Some do and some do not.

Vassal Kingships

As discussed in chapter 53, the faithful sheep who minister to the poor will receive special recognition. Jesus says to them, "*Come, you who are blessed of My Father, inherit the kingdom prepared for you from the foundation of the world*" (Matthew 25:34, NASB). This "kingdom" is "the" kingdom specifically prepared for the faithful sheep. It is not Christ's kingdom but is a subordinate "territory ruled by a king," a kingship in the kingdom of heaven. Jesus explained this in the Parable of the Minas, promising faithful servants five cities and ten cites (Luke 19:17-19).

It is likely that the references to cities and kingships should be understood as metaphors for opportunities for ministry and service rather than being mayors of cities.

Priestly Ministry

While the Jews were in exile under Persian rule in 520 BC, God raised up the prophet Zechariah. Through him some of the most amazing prophesies of Scripture were communicated to the nation. These prophesies announced the coming of the "Branch," the Messiah who will one day restore the Davidic theocracy (Zechariah 3:7-8). The high priest at that time, Joshua, was challenged to be faithful in his duties and was given this wonderful promise to motivate him.

> *Thus says the Lord of hosts, "If you will walk in My ways and if you will perform My service, then you will also govern My house and also have charge of My courts, and I will grant you free access among these who are standing here" (Zechariah 3:7).*

His reward in the future kingdom will be threefold. First, he will "govern My house." That is, he will be in charge of the worship carried out in the millennial temple of which Ezekiel spoke (Ezekiel 40-47). Second, he will have responsibility to "guard my courts." That is, he will protect the temple precincts from any negative influences that might seek to come in. And third, he will have "free access among those who are standing there." In other words, during the millennial reign Joshua will have special access to and intimacy with God. We do not know who will serve with Joshua to help him fulfill these responsibilities. The fact is that others will be involved, and they too would have to meet the requirement to "walk in his ways," if they are to serve with him.

The faithful overcomer will be a pillar in God's temple. This means he will have special responsibilities in the millennial temple. Jesus says to the church at Philadelphia,

> *I am coming soon. Hold on to what you have, so that no one will take your crown. Him who overcomes I will make a pillar in the temple of my God. Never again will he leave it. I will write on him the name of my God and the name of the city of my God, the new Jerusalem which is coming down out of heaven from my God; and I will also write on him my new name. He who has an ear, let him hear what the Spirit says to the churches (Revelation 3:11-13).*

The fact that Christ says, "Never again will he leave it," suggests to some that security is in view. Because the city of Philadelphia had been subject to earthquakes that caused its people to flee to the countryside and establish temporary dwellings, Mounce suggests that "the promise of permanence within the New Jerusalem would have a special meaning."[3171] For those holding this view, this "permanence" is heaven when one dies. One's theology will no doubt bias the interpretation.

Because works of perseverance are required in order to become a pillar in the temple and not to have one's crown taken, Experimental Predestinarians have a problem—works salvation. The Partner's theological bias and the indications in the immediate context suggest that final entrance into heaven is not in view at all. Instead, something in addition to heaven, reward, is the subject. Indeed, is that not what John says, "*Hold on to what you have, so that no one will take your crown*" (v. 11)? If the "crown" is salvation, then contrary to Experimentalist teaching, salvation can be lost if the person does not "hold fast." Mounce does not comment on this difficulty. Rosscup objects, saying, "Revelation 3:11 more probably refers to an unsaved persecutor who can 'take' the crown from a person who has only a professed relationship with Christ and his church."[3172] With respect to this good scholar, such a claim is clearly mere assertion in an effort to justify the Reformed doctrine of perseverance.

Thus, we prefer Kistemaker's suggestion which fits the context well. He says, "This means that the saints are honored within that heavenly temple, which in fact is nothing less than the very presence of God."[3173] The idea that having one's name written on a "pillar" signifies some kind of honor is well established. Wilkinson notes that "it is reasonable to believe that 'pillar in the temple' of Revelation 3:12 is intended to be understood symbolically in the context of the coronation allusions of this specific section."[3174] He points out that in this very context John focuses on David in verse 9 and on kingly rule in verses 11 and 21.

As is well known, pillars in the New Testament and in Jewish literature refer to prominent leaders in the community. For example, Paul referred to Peter and John as "pillars" (Galatians 2:9). In his comments on a series of articles by Daniel K. K. Wong based on his doctoral dissertation,[3175] Robert Wilkin correctly observes, that "since Wong has already determined that all believers are overcomers, he must reject any interpretation that requires the overcomers to be a faithful group of believers. Obviously the idea that some will have special prominence in the kingdom must thus be rejected. This leads to an interpretation that is hardly a 'reward.' All believers are eternally secure by the grace gift of God. Their works have absolutely no bearing on their security."[3176]

[3171] Mounce, *The Book of Revelation*, 104. Beale agrees, "Such a promise of permanently dwelling in God's temple would have been appreciated by the Philadelphians, since their city suffered from earthquakes more than any other of the cities addressed." Beale, *The Book of Revelation: A Commentary on the Greek Text*, 294.

[3172] Rosscup, "The Overcomers of the Apocalypse," 272.

[3173] Simon J. Kistemaker, "The Temple In The Apocalypse," *JETS* 43, no. 3 (September 2000): 444.

[3174] Richard H. Wilkinson, "The ΣΤΥΛΟΣ of Revelation 3:12 and Ancient Coronation Rites," *JBL* 107, no. 3 (September 1988): 500.

[3175] Daniel K. K. Wong, "The Pillar and the Throne in Revelation 3:12, 21," *BibSac* 156, no. 623 (July-September 1999): 297-307.

[3176] Robert N. Wilkin, "Periodical Reviews: 'The Pillar and the Throne in Revelation 3:12, 21,' Daniel K. K. Wong, *BibSac* (July-September 1999), 297–307," *JOTGES* 12, no. 2 (Autumn 1999): 106.

Some believers will be crowned as kings, and some will not. The next reference to the overcomer speaks of his right to sit with Christ on His throne. Jesus promised the faithful sheep that they would inherit a subordinate kingship (Matthew 25:34). Earlier, the overcomer was promised that if he keeps "My deeds to the end," he will be given authority over the nations (Revelation 2:26-27).

But there is more here than the reward of coronation as a king. The text specifically says that these pillars are pillars "in the temple." What do prominent persons do in the temple? They conduct worship. This passage speaks not only of the coronation to kingship but the installation of the faithful believers as priest-kings directing the worship of Christ in His heavenly temple.

Ownership of the New Jerusalem

The overcomer is promised meritorious ownership over the New Jerusalem, and that God will be proud to be known as his God.

> *He who overcomes will inherit all this, and I will be his God and he will be my son (Revelation 21:7).*

As discussed in chapter 20, the correct sense of "inherit" must be pressed here. An inheritance is not always something that comes by virtue of birth but in many passages is obtained by virtue of faithful perseverance, as chapters 4-11 have shown. Seen in this light, there is a difference between Christians who dwell in the New Jerusalem and those who inherit it, own it, that is, rule there.

In every reference to the overcomer in Revelation, he is one who is a victor in battle.[3177] The central theme of the entire book is to exhort the saints to persevere and to be victorious. If all saints persevere and are victorious, the exhortations and promises of rewards are pointless. An exhortation to do something everyone does anyway to obtain a reward that all will receive anyway is absurd.

Conditions for Greatness

While some have rejected the notion that there will be distinctions in eternity based upon faithfulness in this life, the Bible is clear that God judges every person according to their works. In the kingdom there will be those who are great and those who are least:

> *But many who are first will be last, and the last will be first (Matthew 19:30).*

> *Whoever therefore breaks one of the least of these commandments and teaches men so, shall be called least in the kingdom of heaven; but whoever does and teaches them, he shall be called great in the kingdom of heaven (Matthew 5:19, NKJV).*

There will be authority granted over varying numbers of cities (Luke 19:17-24). Some will have responsibility for many things, and others will have responsibility for nothing (Matthew 25:20-30). As discussed above, only the overcomers will achieve a share in the reign of Christ and have authority over the nations. Some will even have the high honor of sitting at Christ's right hand during the kingdom (Mark 10:35-40).

Jesus specified three basic conditions for positions of high honor in the kingdom.

[3177] See also Revelation 12:11; 13:7; 15:2; 17:14.

WE MUST BE FAITHFUL TO USE THE GIFTS WE HAVE BEEN GIVEN

In the Parable of the Minas (Luke 19:11-27) Jesus describes a nobleman who gave one mina to each of his ten servants and then departed. When he returned, the first servant had doubled the number of minas. The Lord makes this an illustration of the final judgment on believers and says:

> *Well done, good servant; because you were faithful in a very little, have authority over ten cities (Luke 19:17, NKJV).*

The second servant who was also given ten minas had earned less: five minas. He was honored with less:

> *And the second came saying, Master, your mina has earned five minas. Likewise he said to him, "You also be over five cities" (Luke 19:18-19, NKJV).*

Each had been given the same amount but one had produced more with what he had been given and was rewarded accordingly.

The last servant produced nothing and kept his minas hidden in a handkerchief. The Lord severely rebukes this lethargic Christian and takes the mina away from him and gives it to the servant who had been given ten cities. He summarizes:

> *He replied, "I tell you that to everyone who has, more will be given, but as for the one who has nothing, even what he has will be taken away" (Luke 19:26).*

More opportunities, gifts, money, and training a Christian receives will result in greater accountability at the judgment seat.

> *For everyone to whom much is given, from him much will be required, and to whom much has been committed, of him they will ask the more (Luke 12:48, NKJV).*

WE MUST BECOME SERVANTS NOW

The second condition for high honor is that we must strive to be servants of all. Jesus Himself modeled this when He took the form of a servant and became obedient to death. As a result God highly exalted Him (Philippians 2:5-11). Paul says, "Let this mind be in you."

> *The kings of the Gentiles exercise lordship over them, and those who exercise authority over them are called "benefactors."*
>
> *But not so among you; on the contrary, he who is greatest among you, let him be as the younger, and he who governs as he who serves.*
>
> *For who is greater, he who sits at the table, or he who serves? Is it not he who sits at the table? Yet I am among you as the One who serves (Luke 22:25-27, NKJV).*

> *Whoever wishes to become great among you shall be your servant. And whoever of you desires to be first shall be slave of all (Mark 10:43-44, NKJV).*

WE MUST FAITHFULLY PERSEVERE TO THE END

In passage after passage, the New Testament writers invest human suffering with high dignity. It is through suffering with Christ that we are trained and equipped to join the great company of the *Metochoi*. Consider:

Therefore, among God's churches we boast about your perseverance and faith in all the persecutions and trials you are enduring. All this is evidence that God's judgment is right, and as a result you will be counted worthy of the kingdom of God, for which you are suffering (2 Thessalonians 1:4-5).

An eternal honor is being achieved for those who persevere in suffering:

For our light and momentary troubles are achieving for us an eternal glory that far outweighs them all (2 Corinthians 4:17).

In order for us to experience great joy at the appearing of Christ, we must rejoice (i.e., respond in faith) to the sufferings we experience now:

Dear friends, do not be surprised at the painful trial you are suffering, as though something strange were happening to you. But rejoice that you participate in the sufferings of Christ, so that you may be overjoyed when his glory is revealed (1 Peter 4:12-13).

The Fulfillment of Human Destiny

A major purpose of the incarnation was, according to the writer of the Epistle to the Hebrews, the bringing of many sons to the place of honor, the final destiny of man, the predicted messianic salvation. This was achieved by the suffering of the Son and His many brothers.

God's intention was to place man over the works of His hands. This was called "salvation" by the Old Testament prophets:

Are not all angels ministering spirits sent to serve those who will inherit salvation? (Hebrews 1:14).

That this salvation to be inherited is not deliverance from final damnation is made clear when he says:

It is not to angels that he has subjected the world to come about which we are speaking (Hebrews 2:5).

The "salvation" to be inherited is not entrance into heaven but the subjection of the world to come. God has not yet fulfilled His intention. Out of the lesser He will bring the greater. Man will rule the angels! We see Jesus as a kind of promissory note:

In putting everything under him, God left nothing that is not subject to him. Yet at present we do not see everything subject to him. But we see Jesus, who was made a little lower than the angels, now crowned with glory and honor because he suffered death, so that by the grace of God he might taste death for everyone (Hebrews 2:8-9).

"We do not see everything subject to him." That statement is an apt summary of human history. How visibly true this is. Man attempts to exercise dominion, but he cannot do it. This desire was planted in man's heart in the Garden, and the vestige of it remains today. That is why men throughout history have dreamed of having dominion over the planet. That is why we cannot keep off the highest mountain. That is why we want to go to the stars.

Man consistently manifests this remarkable racial memory. Our problem is that the more we attempt to exercise dominion, the more frustrated we are because it is beyond our reach. We try to control the insects eating our crops, and it turns out that the pesticides contain poisons that harm us in various ways. We try to begin an energy conservation program, but private interest groups are treated unfairly. We attempt to distribute food to the poor, and it rots in shipyards. The history of man is one of continually precipitating a crisis by attempting to exercise dominion.

This applies not only on a universal scale but also to individuals. Who among us has achieved all our dreams? When we try to achieve gain from our labor, we are attempting to fulfill the God-given urge to have dominion. When a man attempts to lead his family, he is doing the same. Yet too often we never exercise the dominion. Our objectives are not accomplished. Our dreams are shattered. This is simply part of the human condition and will be until the kingdom.

We have only one hope today. We see one man who has forged the path. This Man, like us, had His dreams shattered. He suffered, and yet He presently exercises dominion. Furthermore, through His incarnation we have become united with Him so that, if we are faithful to Him, we can share in His ultimate victory.

It is God's purpose to bring many sons to glory:

> *In bringing many sons to glory, it was fitting that God, for whom and through whom everything exists, should make the author of their salvation perfect through suffering (Hebrews 2:10).*

The great theme of Christ's union with His many sons is close to our writer's heart. Here Christ is our "leader"; in other places He is called our sympathetic priest. We are told that He will give us help in time of need.

> *For we do not have a high priest who cannot sympathize with our weaknesses, but One who has been tempted in all things as we are, yet without sin. Therefore let us draw near with confidence to the throne of grace, so that we may receive mercy and find grace to help in time of need (Hebrews 4:15–16).*

We are to imagine Christ right next to us in our suffering. He has His left arm around our shoulder, and His right arm is lifted up to the Father. He says, "Father, I now bring My brother before You. He is in great suffering and needs Your help. For the sake of Your glory and because I have died for him, I ask that You would strengthen him in the inner man. Give him the courage to face his suffering and the power to endure it. Most of all, Father, let him know Your comfort."

The "glory" to which the many sons will be brought is evidently subjection of the world to come (Hebrews 2:5), the messianic salvation. They will be brought to this destiny, this high honor, by the "author" of their salvation. The Greek word *archēgos* means "leader, ruler, prince, founder, author, or originator," depending on the context. In the three other places in the New Testament where *archēgos* is used, Christ is called "the author of life" (Acts 3:15), "the Prince and Savior" (Acts 5:31), and "the author and perfecter of our faith" (Hebrews 12:2). In the ancient world he was the leader, the one at the front, the hero of the city, its defender.[3178] If we were to dramatize these ideas and pictures, words like "pioneer" or "captain" would be fitting.

In every respect Jesus is the one out front, our supreme leader and example in the life of faith. Whenever we experience difficulties, He knows what we are going through and is there to lead us through them victoriously. When we face temptation, He knows what that is like, and He is ready to strengthen us and leads us away from the temptation. Whatever our needs and weaknesses, He knows them and is able to help, to lead, and to win. As the Author of life, He gave us earthly and eternal life. As the Captain of life, He leads us now in and through life. And as the Prince of life, He is the one who will lead us into the final destiny of man—dominion over the creation.

He alone is qualified to achieve this for mankind. His commitment to us is total. He has died for us, and He lives for and in us.

His leadership includes suffering. For Christ to become a sympathetic priest, He must experience the suffering of those He has come to represent:

> *For this reason he had been made like his brothers in every way, in order that he might become a merciful and faithful high priest in the service of God. . . . Because he himself suffered when he was tempted, he is able to help those who are being tempted (Hebrews 2:17-18).*

Jesus gained honor and learned sympathy by the things that He suffered. His way is to be the way of the "many sons" He is leading to the same glory:

> *Therefore I will allot Him a portion with the great ... because He poured out Himself to death (Isaiah 53:12).*

> *And being found in appearance as a man, He humbled Himself by becoming obedient to the point of death, even death on a cross. Therefore also God highly exalted Him, and bestowed upon Him the name which is above every name (Philippians 2:8-9, NASB).*

> *But we see Jesus, who was made lower than the angels, now crowned with glory and honor because He suffered death, so that by the grace of God He might taste death for everyone (Hebrews 2:9).*

Two truths unite in the exaltation of God's King-Son. First, He had been appointed by God to be the heir of all things (Hebrews 1:1). But, second, it was necessary that Christ vindicate His appointment by showing Himself worthy of it through victorious suffering. "And it is upon precisely the same double condition that Christ's people will share with Him His honors."[3179]

> *And you are those who have stood by Me in My trials; and just as My Father has granted Me a kingdom, I grant you that you may eat and drink at My table in My kingdom, and you will sit on thrones judging the twelve tribes of Israel (Luke 22:28-30, NASB).*

Authority in the kingdom and the honor of sitting at the table at the Final Gathering and enjoying the royal feast are plainly promised as superior rewards for superior devotion. His way is to be our way.

[3178] Gerhard Delling, "archegos," in TDNT, 1:487.

[3179] Lang, *The Epistle to the Hebrews*, 63.

The goal of obtaining glory (i.e., "honor") in the future kingdom is a principal intent of the suffering we endure. God purposes to equip us for rulership in the great future by preparing through suffering a race of servant kings. God does not grant this honor to anyone except those who have suffered with Him. We must first learn obedience and service:

> *Although he was a son, he learned obedience from what he suffered and, once made perfect, he became the source of eternal salvation for all who obey him (Hebrews 5:8-9).*

Summary

The final significance of man is the fulfillment of God's commandment in the Garden of Eden, "let them rule."[3180] A fifth column had been placed in the Satan's world, and the man and his wife, even though they were less than the angels, were commanded to take back that which the Satan had stolen. They were to live in dependence and obedience, in contrast to the Satan's disobedience and unbelief. The lesser creature who lived by these principles would one day obtain a higher position than the greater creature aspired to, thus rebuking pride.

The arduous flow of history reveals the operation of these principles, and one day in the messianic partnership with the Second Man and the Last Adam, human destiny will finally be achieved, and God's grace will be gloriously manifested.

During the millennial phrase of man's rule, Jesus said that His servant kings would be awarded vassal kingships (five cities, ten cities, etc.). This is a metaphor for opportunities for ministry to Him and with Him. These opportunities for ministry include priestly direction of the worship of God, a special rule in the administration, and servant leadership over the New Jerusalem.

What are the requirements to share in this messianic partnership? In this chapter we mentioned three. First, according to the parable of the talents we must be faithful to utilize the gifts and opportunities to serve Him now. Secondly, Jesus stressed over and over again that the true mark of His *Metochoi* is a servant attitude, like that of the Servant King who emptied Himself and became a servant of those for whom He came to die. Finally, those awarded this incredible privilege of special opportunities to minister for Him throughout all eternity are characterized by perseverance in faith, no matter what the trial, to the end of life.

[3180] Genesis 1:26.

63

Rewards, Motivation, and Degrees of Glory

THE WRITER well remembers the time when as a new Christian he had just learned about the doctrine of eternal rewards. In youthful fervor I rushed to visit my pastor only to have my new enthusiasm crushed. "Do you mean to tell me," he replied, "that there will be distinctions in heaven? God does not show partiality!"

Of course, later I learned that there WILL be distinctions in heaven. God will judge each person according to his works. In the kingdom there will be those who are great and those who are least:

But many who are first will be last, and the last will be first (Matthew 19:30).

Whoever therefore breaks one of the least of these commandments and teaches men so, shall be called least in the kingdom of heaven; but whoever does and teaches them, he shall be called great in the kingdom of heaven (Matthew 5:19, NKJV).

The notion that the future kingdom is a kind of classless society where all are equal and rewarded equally has contributed in no small way to the laxness witnessed in the lives of many in the twentieth-century church. Many have subconsciously reasoned that, since all are equal, their lives have no eternal significance. In the final analysis their lives will be rewarded as much as those who labored more diligently.

Millard Erickson asks,

Will there be varying rewards in heaven? That there apparently will be degrees of reward is evident in, for example, the parable of the pounds (Luke. 19:11–27). Ten servants were each given one pound by their master. Eventually they returned differing amounts to him and were rewarded in proportion to their faithfulness.[3181]

However, Craig Blomberg and others have complained that the doctrine of differences in eternity future diminishes grace and has a devastating psychological effect on the mental health of sincere Christians. Furthermore, the doctrine in the way the Partners present it, he says, smacks of legalism.

He recounts a conversation with one of his students, in which the student commented that,

---

[3181] Erickson, *Christian Theology*, 1241.

> *In most of the conservative Christian circles of which he had been a part, the Christian life was like a free, trial membership to an elite country club: The first year is wonderful, but after that you pay through the nose.*[3182]

While the views of the future espoused by Blomberg are not widespread, a number of capable scholars hold to it. Therefore, these issues are addressed in this chapter.

Jesus certainly teaches that there are degrees of glory. In the parable of the Minas, He says some will receive ten cities, some five cities, and some none (Luke 19:27). Distinctions are found throughout the New Testament. At the Judgment Seat of Christ, we will receive rewards for both the good and the bad we have done (2 Corinthians 5:10-11). Some will receive rewards, and some will be saved only "through fire" (1 Corinthians 3:15). John urged his readers, "*Watch yourselves, that you do not lose what we have accomplished, but that you may receive a full reward*" (2 Jn. 8). *The word "full" surely signifies that there is a partial reward or even no reward.* In fact, one can "lose" his reward. Christ often spoke of the "least" and "greatest" in the kingdom (Matthew 5:19; 11:11; 18:1; 20:26-27; Luke 19:30).[3183]

Dennis Smith correctly observes, "Notice how the parable [of the Vineyard] functions to symbolize how rankings will be assigned in the kingdom by reference to a recognized custom in the culture. The custom is obviously well understood and taken for granted; otherwise the parable would not work."[3184] Similarly, Hoehner says, "If believers love their enemies, do good and lend goods or money expecting nothing in return, they will receive a 'great' reward (Luke 6:35)."[3185]

Some of the greatest saints in history have unashamedly embraced the notion of degrees of glory. For example, Augustine said,

> *The saints, like the stars in the sky, obtain in the kingdom different mansions of diverse degrees of brightness.*[3186]

And Martin Luther wrote,

> *And yet many* ***differences or degrees of glory will prevail among us*** *... each one in accord with the works which he has performed.*[3187]

Also Calvin wrote,

> *The doctrine of Scripture on the subject ought not to be made the ground of any controversy, and it is that as God, in the varied distribution of gifts to his saints in this world, gives them unequal degrees of light, so when he shall crown his gifts, their degrees of glory in heaven will also be unequal.*[3188]

3182 Blomberg, "Degrees of Reward in the Kingdom of Heaven?," 170.

3183 See Luke 17:7-11.

3184 Dennis E. Smith, "Table Fellowship as a Literary Motif in the Gospel of Luke," *JBL* 106, no. 4 (Dec 1987): 619. In this article Smith gives an interesting summary of the significance of table fellowship and the importance of rankings at the table in contemporary Greek and Jewish culture.

3185 Harold W. Hoehner, "Reward," in *New Dictionary of Biblical Theology*, ed. T. Desmond Alexander and Brian S. Rosner (Downers Grove, IL: Inter-Varsity Press, 2000).

3186 Augustine, "Tractates on John," 7:321.

3187 Luther, "1 Corinthians 7, 1 Corinthians 15, 1 Timothy," 28:184, s.v. "1 Corinthians 15:39-42".

3188 Calvin, "Institutes," iii, xxv,10.

Few doubt that there is variation in degrees of glory.[3189] How do rewards relate to spiritual motivation and a merit?

Objections to Rewards as Motivation for Christian Living

A disconnect seems to exist between the many passages that urge us to action, service, and perseverance on the basis of reward, and what actually motivates us. This may explain why teaching on the subject of rewards is so rarely heard in our churches. It is not perceived as highly relevant to daily life.

Why is this? We believe there are seven reasons.

First, it is seen as selfish to pursue a reward. Is not the Christian ethic one of lack of self-interest?

Second, any kind of final accountability based on our work done could possibly place many under a sense of legalism and a performance-based relationship with God. Works are necessary as a means of securing God's ultimate approval. Did not the Reformation free us from this perspective?

Third, perhaps the emphasis in our culture on the God of love and the seemingly unlimited opportunity for second chances runs counter to all notions of the ennobling and often cited "fear of the Lord" in the biblical documents (e.g., 2 Corinthians 5:10).

Fourth, a common folklore theological statement says, "God is not a respecter of persons." The ethic of equality of outcomes is a "given" in the minds of many. This is particularly evident in the political debates between liberals and conservatives where the former insist on equality of outcomes, not just the equality of opportunity. How, it is asked, could a loving God possibly differ from our assumed notions of equality?

Fifth, would not such an emphasis lead to competitiveness, jealousy, and an eternity of comparison and/or regret?

Sixth, possibly the plague of Neo-Platonism has affected the dialogue on this issue. This destructive doctrine instructs the faithful that the spiritual is "higher" and drives a wedge between the secular and the spiritual. Things associated with this world, such as reward for work done, are suspect because they are not part of the supposedly higher values of the spiritual realm. This can be seen in the monastic attempts at disinterestedness via asceticism, the rejection of the idea of a material millennial reign of Christ (amillennialism), and the tendency to view secular pursuits and culture to be either avoided or at least valued of lesser importance. Reward, some believe, is a bit too characteristic of the secular culture, so it could not be part of God's higher, more "spiritual" plan for our lives.

Seventh, if according to the Partner view, everyone's cup will be full in eternity, yet the cups will be of different sizes, what is the motivational benefit anyway? At the end of the day all are equally happy. With this observation Blomberg dismisses the subject of rewards because, he says, it fails at its core to motivate. No matter what one does, Blomberg incorrectly assumes, there will be no negative consequence.

One reason Blomberg and others feel this way is that they have misinterpreted the vast amount of Scripture that speaks of the potential of a negative consequence at the Judgment Seat of Christ. They are incorrect when they say that everyone will be equally happy. That

[3189] Jesus spoke of "reward" and "great reward" (Matthew 5:12; Luke 6:23), and He spoke of some receiving five cities and some ten (Luke 19:11-17).

will not even be true in eternity future, and at the Judgment Seat of Christ there will be moments of terrible grief, weeping, rebuke, and possible millennial disinheritance for carnal Christians. Paul makes it clear,

> *For we must all appear before the Judgment Seat of Christ, that each one may be recompensed for his deeds in the body, according to what he has done, whether good or bad. Therefore knowing the fear of the Lord, we persuade men (2 Corinthians 5:10-11).*

This subject has been fully discussed in the preceding chapters and need not be revisited here. But it does seem that Blomberg and those who share his viewpoint simply do not believe that anything "**bad**" will be dispensed at the Judgment Seat of Christ. For some reason, they stop reading at the end of 2 Corinthians 5:10 and never consider (at least in their writings) verse 11, *"knowing the fear of the Lord."* All will not be rosy and happy at the Judgment Seat of Christ.

Rewards and Merit: Protestant Dilemma in Regard to Rewards

This discussion introduces a very difficult problem in the New Testament. On the one hand, the ethics of the New Testament are dominated throughout with the idea of reward, of recompense for work done. Yet, on the other hand, our Lord clearly teaches in numerous places that we should pursue disinterestedness. The New Testament ideal is selflessness and serving others, that is, freedom from selfish motive or interests (1 Corinthians 13:5; Philippians 2:1-11).

> *And He summoned the crowd with His disciples, and said to them, "If anyone wishes to come after Me, he must deny himself, and take up his cross and follow Me. For whoever wishes to save his life will lose it, but whoever loses his life for My sake and the gospel's will save it. For what does it profit a man to gain the whole world, and forfeit his soul? (Mark 8:34–36)*

Are we not told, on the one hand, that we are to obey because of the mercies of God (Romans 12:1) and that "the love of Christ controls us" (2 Corinthians 5:14) rather than the love of rewards? Is not doing something for the purpose of obtaining a reward a far less worthy motive than doing it out of love and gratitude?

Yet, on the other hand, the reward motivation is clear. Each of the beatitudes comes with a promise. The poor in spirit are promised a reward, the kingdom of heaven. The pure in heart are promised that they will "see God." Those who endure persecution are promised that they will "receive" a kingship. Those persecuted are promised reward in heaven, and so forth.

Jesus promises that those who are in the last position now may be first in the kingdom. He stresses rewards emphatically when He says to His astonished disciples,

> *Truly I say to you, that you who have followed Me, in the regeneration when the Son of Man will sit on His glorious throne, you also shall sit upon twelve thrones, judging the twelve tribes of Israel. And everyone who has left houses or brothers or sisters or father or mother or children or farms for My name's sake, shall receive many times as much, and shall inherit eternal life. But many who are first will be last; and the last, first (Matthew 19:28-30).*

Even the most basic command of Christianity, to love others, is enhanced with the motivation of repayment at the resurrection of the righteous.

> *But when you give a reception, invite the poor, the crippled, the lame, the blind, and you will be blessed, since they do not have the means to repay you; for you will be repaid at the resurrection of the righteous (Luke 14:10-14).*

Humility itself is enjoined as the basis for reward,

> *But when you are invited, go and recline at the last place, so that when the one who has invited you comes, he may say to you, "Friend, move up higher"; then you will have honor in the sight of all who are at the table with you. For everyone who exalts himself shall be humbled, and he who humbles himself shall be exalted (Luke 14:10-11).*

The motivation for humility is that we will be exalted in the future and that we will have greater honor now!

Even forgiveness, a decided personal benefit, is conditioned on our forgiving others, *"For if you forgive men for their transgressions, your heavenly Father will also forgive you"* (Matthew 6:14). Why not forgive others with no notion of personal forgiveness? Shouldn't we forgive because it is the right thing to do and not because of some benefit that accrues to ourselves? Shouldn't we secretly strive for completely disinterested reasons?

According to Jesus, the answer is, "No." Rather, we are to practice our piety in secret so that our "*Father who sees what is done in secret will reward you*" (Matthew 6:4). If there was ever a system of ethics grounded on mercenary considerations and dominated by the motive of recompense, it is the system, critics argue, that is found in the Gospels. Whatever one might urge against those who obey with "selfish" hopes of reward, can, they say, be urged equally against the Gospel writers.

The problem cannot be ignored. The main thrust of Jesus' teaching is certainly that of asking people to forget themselves and focus their aspirations on God alone and on the needs of others, not on some personal benefit.

This difficulty cannot be resolved unless we first acknowledge that the manner in which Jesus presents reward is completely different from our common understanding of the term, and from that of His critics. We will address this problem in more detail in the next chapter.

"But what," we must ask, "do the Scriptures say?" In the following pages we will address this issue directly from two central passages, the parable of the Unworthy Servant (Luke 17:7-10) and the parable of the Laborers in the Vineyard (Matthew 20:1-16).

The Parable of the Unworthy Servant

Perseverance in holiness is not the necessary and inevitable result of justification. It is necessary for rewards in heaven but not for entrance into heaven itself. However, this is our "obligation" (Romans 8:12) and " duty":

> *Suppose one of you had a servant plowing or looking after the sheep. Would he say to the servant when he comes in from the field, "Come along now and sit down to eat"? Would he not rather say, "Prepare my supper, get yourself ready and wait on me while I eat and drink; after that you may eat and drink"? Would he thank the servant because he did what he was told to do? So you also, when you have done everything you were told to do, should say, "We are unworthy servants; we have only done our duty" (Luke 17:7-10).*

When we have done all we can do, when we have been faithful to the end, we still have only done what is required of all servants, namely, that they be faithful. *"Now it is required that those who have been given a trust must prove faithful"* (1 Corinthians 4:2). So the reward we receive is still a matter of grace. That God should reward us for our work is an obligation He assumed because of His grace. He did not have to enter into this arrangement. This is a further manifestation of His unmerited favor!

Consider this illustration. If a father gives a large sum of money as an inheritance, with no conditions attached, it is a free gift. If the son then proceeds to invest that money in charitable causes, that is honorable.

However, on reading the father's will, to the son's immense surprise he sees the words, "Son, if you will invest this money in giving to the poor, serving others, etc., I want you to know that I have laid aside additional wealth which the trustee of my estate is authorized to add to your inheritance. I have freely entered into this obligation to pay you this wage, but understand, the fact that I have chosen to place this obligation on myself is not based on anything other than my freely-given love."

Furthermore, for the son to invest that money and receive a return was simply a matter of duty, being responsible (as the parables teach). If the son invests, and receives a return, he has only done his duty. In a similar way, God has agreed to grant a reward as a merit, or better, an over-generous wage, but He had no obligation to do so. The fact that He has chosen to give us something we do not deserve in the first place, a reward for works, is still pure grace. In other words, the reward itself is merited and deserved; the decision to give reward is purely God's grace.

Thus, we can say that good works *do* obligate God to give us a reward in heaven. However, this is only because God has agreed to obligate Himself (Hebrews 6:16-18) in this arrangement.[3190]

We should not conclude from this, as Dabney does, that the believer's works are the result **only** of generosity and not merit. The believer's works, according to Dabney, "contribute nothing essential to earning the inheritance; in that point of view it is as wholly gratuitous to the believer as though he had been all the time asleep."[3191] He asserts that the merit that earned the reward was Christ's, but it is never clear how the passages describing the believer's meriting it himself are to be explained. *While it seems clear that there is no legal connection between work and reward, it is equally clear that, if there was no work at all, there would be no reward.* To say, as Dabney does, that a believer could sleep through life and do nothing is just as absurd as the other extreme, namely, that for everything he does, God is legally placed in the believer's debt.

The Parable of the Laborers in the Vineyard

Part of the problem the Reformers had in regard to the place of merit in eternal rewards is that they construed "merit" in the Catholic and legal sense—a precise, legal obligation. For every work done God was legally obligated to measure out some specified degree of reward. However, the Scriptures present the matter in a different light in the parable of the Vineyard Workers (Matthew 20:1-16).

3190 See discussion in the next chapter, pp. 1006 ff.

3191 Dabney, *Lectures in Systematic Theology*, 683.

At the outset, we must reject the unfortunate notion presented by Jeremias, Blomberg, and others that "in the parable of Jesus [as Jeremias says], the laborers who were engaged last show nothing to warrant a claim to a full day's wages ... in this apparently trivial detail," Jeremias says, "lies the difference between two worlds: the world of merit, and the world of grace; the law contrasted with the gospel."[3192] However, this parable is not about the "gospel." It is about being "hired," and being first or last in the kingdom, that is, status in the kingdom. It is about rewards, and rewards *do* involve merit, as established elsewhere.[3193] Once this is granted, Jeremias's argument flounders. That degrees of reward are an important aspect of this parable is evident by the closing phrase, *"the last will be first and the first last"* (Matthew 20:16). Earlier in Matthew Jesus spoke of the same concept, referring to those who would be "least" in contrast to those who would be "great" in the kingdom (Matthew 5:19). The difference, He said, was related to doing, and not only "grace."

Blomberg responds, "But it may also be a vivid equivalent to the more prosaic truth that all numerical positions are interchangeable."[3194] What "truth" is this? Apparently saying that all numerical positions are interchangeable results in the conclusion that all numerical positions are interchangeable! This is no answer at all. Why are all numerical positions interchangeable? Apparently, Blomberg has been "uncomfortable" with the rewards doctrine. He says, "In the twenty years of my adult Christian life I have grown progressively more uncomfortable with any formulation that differentiates among believers as regards our eternal rewards."[3195] He then cites the conversation with a student mentioned at the beginning of this chapter who was psychologically harmed by the doctrine of rewards.

Nevertheless, Blomberg has a point. It is possible for sincere believers to be emotionally troubled in their relationship with God if they misunderstand the *Fatherly context* of the call to rewards. Lacking that, there is a danger that the Partner view of rewards might degenerate into a performance-based relationship with God about which Blomberg is correctly concerned. We will discuss this issue later.[3196]

Blomberg's misunderstandings continue. Somewhere he picked up the idea that all who disagree with him teach that "surely people would live with some unending sense of regret and sadness if they realized that they had not attained to as high a level of enjoyment or privilege in heaven as they might have, had their lives on this earth proved more meritorious."[3197] While it is true that a few have held this idea,[3198] it is not held by the majority of those who hold to the various understandings of the Partner viewpoint. The present writer believes that the remorse is temporary.[3199] However, contrary to Blomberg's view, one should note that for some there will be a period of remorse and shame (1 John 2:28) at the Judgment Seat of Christ. Hoehner responds clearly,

> *Will difference in rewards distinguish people in heaven for eternity? Biblical references to heaven suggest that entering will be far more important than any variation of rewards. Though*

[3192] Jeremias, *The Parables of Jesus*, 139.

[3193] See pp. 583 ff.

[3194] Blomberg, "Degrees of Reward in the Kingdom of Heaven?," 161.

[3195] Ibid., 157.

[3196] See pp. 1006 ff. and 1040 ff.

[3197] Blomberg, "Degrees of Reward in the Kingdom of Heaven?," 162.

[3198] Cauley, *The Outer Darkness*, 519-64.

[3199] See pp. 326 and 775 ff. for discussion.

> *these may exist, those in heaven will be glorified, and their values will be completely different from earthly values. There will not be envy or jealousy, but rather praise. It will not be, "Why did you get more rewards than I?" but more likely "It is wonderful how you allowed the power of the Lord to work in you," or, "It is amazing what persecution you endured for the Lord." Finally, everyone in heaven will realize that rewards, like salvation, are of God's grace, and will give him praise accordingly.*[3200]

Matthew's account of the rich young ruler is followed immediately by the parable of the Laborers in the Vineyard (Matthew 20:1-16), the classic treatment of the subject of rewards in the New Testament.

To understand this parable it is important that the conclusions reached regarding the encounter with the rich young ruler be kept in mind.[3201] There, we learned that the rich young ruler was a believer who came to Jesus seeking counsel on how he could obtain higher status, reward, or "rich entrance" into the kingdom (cf. 2 Peter 1:11). He wanted to know what he must "do." He was seeking a legal arrangement in which so much work would result in so much reward, an inheritance in the kingdom. Jesus obliged him with a reminder to keep the Ten Commandments. When the man claimed he had done this, Jesus put His finger on the fact that the man really had not. Jesus told him to sell all he had and give it to the poor and then come and follow Him as His disciple. This would involve giving up all the earthly status that his culture ascribed to the rich and in which he himself trusted for a full and meaningful life. After the young ruler walked away, feeling sorrowful, Peter said, "*Lord we have done all that this man refused to do, what will we have*?" Instead of rebuking him, the Lord gloriously affirmed his theology by saying,

> *Truly I say to you, that you who have followed Me, in the regeneration when the Son of Man will sit on His glorious throne, you also shall sit upon twelve thrones, judging the twelve tribes of Israel. And everyone who has left houses or brothers or sisters or father or mother or children or farms for* ***My name's sake,*** *shall receive many times as much, and shall inherit eternal life.* ***But many who are first will be last; and the last, first*** *(Matthew 19:28-30).*

Luke and Mark clarify that Matthew's "many times as much" is to be expected "at this time" or "now in the present age." What is more, there is great reward in the age to come.

> *And He said to them, "Truly I say to you, there is no one who has left house or wife or brothers or parents or children, for the sake of the kingdom of God, who shall not receive* ***many times as much at this time*** *and* ***in the age to come****, eternal life" (Luke 18:29-30).*

> *Jesus said, "Truly I say to you, there is no one who has left house or brothers or sisters or mother or father or children or farms, for* ***My sake and for the gospel's sake,*** *but that he shall receive a hundred times as much* ***now in the present age****, houses and brothers and sisters and mothers and children and farms, along with persecutions; and* ***in the age to come****, eternal life" (Mark 10:28-30).*

The reward in this present age for all the relationships given up is new ties with fellow disciples (Mark 3:31-35). Leaving "house" and being rewarded with "houses" probably uses

---

[3200] Hoehner, "Reward."

[3201] See discussion in volume 1, chapter 24.

the Greek *oikia* in its common sense of "household" or "family" and is not referring to literal dwellings.[3202]

The opening word "for" in Matthew 20:1 alerts us to the fact that what follows is an elaboration in some way on the discussion of rewards that closed the preceding pericope in the account of the rich young ruler. The lynchpin of interpretation is the logion "the last shall be first and the first, last," which both introduces and concludes the parable (cf. Matthew 19:30; 20:16), though, in reverse order.

This parable is probably the most variously interpreted of all of Christ's parables. Any credible interpretation must satisfactorily answer three questions. First, how is this parable in harmony with the saying that introduces and concludes it?

But many who are first will be last; and the last, first (Matthew 19:30).

So the last shall be first, and the first last (Matthew 20:16).

The problem is that if all receive the same reward, a denarius, how is one last and another first? The parable is obviously intended to illustrate this principle of first and last in some way. The question is "How?"

Second, there is a moral difficulty. How can it be fair that the laborers who labored for only an hour received the same reward as those who labored faithfully in the hot sun all day? If this principle were applied to industry today, the results would be catastrophic! The owner seems to be overly generous on the one hand and grossly unfair on the other. Many have known capricious employers who unfairly reward some more than others. Can God be unfair like this?

Third, what is the parable's main point and application to us today?

Several different approaches have been taken. For some, the key to the parable is the fact that a denarius was given to all the workers, no matter how long they worked. This, they say, shows that there are no differences of reward in the kingdom of God; all are equal.[3203] Yet, however attractive this seems, it is flatly contradicted by the saying that introduces and concludes the parable. If all are rewarded equally, there would be no reversal; all would have the same rank in the kingdom.

Others have taken the approach that God does not regard the length of time in which men are engaged in His service; rather, He considers fidelity and strenuous exertion. However, while that is no doubt true, it is purely gratuitous to assume that the laborers who were hired first did not work as hard as those who were hired last. In fact, they claim they labored hard to the point of exhaustion[3204] and under the hot sun (v. 12).

Another approach is to assume that the point is that no matter when a person is called into the Lord's work, as a child, a young person, or an adult, he can receive the same reward as those who have worked diligently all their lives. Some were called to Christian service as teenagers, the present writer was called as a college student, and C. I. Scofield was called at age 36. However, while this may be true and is certainly a valid application of the parable, is this the main point?

3202 BDAG, 695. E.g. Mark 3:25 and 1 Corinthians 16:15.

3203 Blomberg, "Degrees of Reward in the Kingdom of Heaven?," 159-72.

3204 The text reads, "have borne the burden" (v. 12). Literally, this might be translated, "we bore up under very difficult circumstances, working to the point of exhaustion" (Gr τοῖς βαστάσασι τὸ βάρος).

We begin by assuming that the parable is closely connected with issues raised in the encounter with the rich young ruler and also the repetitive statements about the first and the last that bracket the parable. The opening word "for" points in the immediate context to the concluding summary of this encounter: *"But many who are first will be last; and the last, first"* (Matthew 19:30). The rich young ruler may be "first" in this world, but he will be "last" in the kingdom *because he shunned the call to discipleship*. Peter and the other disciples, however, although last in this world, will be first in the kingdom. It seems that this refutes the common interpretation that the parable of the Laborers in the Vineyard was intended to correct Peter's selfish question, "What shall we have?" His question is not selfish at all. It is perfectly appropriate and is a question Jesus Himself encouraged, based on this extensive teaching on rewards.

The introductory "for" does not point to that question, it points to the teaching about first and last in verse 30 which in turn points to the entire encounter with the rich young ruler. The Lord never rebukes Peter for asking this question. This parable, is not a comment on Peter's selfishness but on the whole notion of the great reversal and further clarification on how rewards are dispensed.

The parable describes a common scene in Palestine, the grape harvest. Often at harvest time extra workers were needed.

> *For the kingdom of heaven is like a landowner who went out early in the morning to hire laborers for his vineyard.* ***When he had agreed with the laborers for a denarius*** *for the day, he sent them into his vineyard (Matthew 20:1-2).*

A denarius was the normal wage for a day's work paid to harvesters. These laborers entered into the work on a different ground than those who followed. Like the rich young ruler who wanted to know what he must do to inherit eternal life, these laborers likewise hammered out an agreement with the owner of the land. Jesus points out that position in the kingdom cannot be formally arranged as in a legal labor contract, that is, so much work results in so much compensation. Other issues are involved such as the inward motivations and the attitudes of the workers. This wrong spirit eventually erupts into various other problems as noted in verses 11-12.

Apparently, however, as the day wore on and the hot sun ripened the fruit, it became evident to the owner of the vineyard that the harvest could not be completed without additional help. So he went into the marketplace to hire more workers at nine o'clock, noon, and three in the afternoon. The marketplace in a Palestinian village is similar to today's oriental bazaar.

> *And he went out about the third hour and saw others standing idle in the marketplace; and to those he said, "You also go into the vineyard, and* ***whatever is right*** *I will give you." And so they went. Again he went out about the sixth and the ninth hour, and did the same thing (Matthew 20:3-5).*

These workers in the parable entered the work under a different arrangement with the landowner than the workers in vv. 1-2. They trusted the landowner to do "*whatever is right*." Morris notes, "There is no specific offer of a job, nor is there any indication of haggling over terms or even of coming to an acceptable agreement (as in the case of the first workers)."[3205] This draws us into the story, making us wonder, "What is right?" This detail is surely important to the interpretation of the parable as their approach differs from those who were hired first, who had an agreement of so much work for so much wages.

As the day closed and still the work had not been completed, and the fruit was in danger of spoiling, the owner returns to the marketplace at the eleventh hour (five o'clock) to hire more workers. He finds a number of potential hires *standing around.*

> *And about the eleventh hour he went out and found others standing around; and he said to them, "Why have you been standing here idle all day long?" They said to him, "Because no one hired us." He said to them, "You go into the vineyard too" (Matthew 20:5-7).*

Apparently, they were not lazy, as some have suggested. The problem was that no one had hired them.

According to the Law, the workers were to be paid in the evening (Leviticus 19:13; Deuteronomy 24:15), and so when evening came (about the twelfth hour or six o'clock), the landowner ordered his foreman to summon the workers to pay them their due.

> *"Call the laborers and pay them their wages, beginning with the last group to the first." When those hired about the eleventh hour came, each one received a denarius (Matthew 20:8-9).*

However, surprisingly, he pays those whom he hired at five o'clock (the eleventh hour) first.

Normally, those hired first would be paid first. Those who worked for only one hour must have been surprised at getting a full day's wage. They had made no bargain with their employer and had been content to trust him to do what was right. The parable speaks of the compassion of the landowner.

No doubt this suggested to those who were hired first that since they had worked twelve hours and those hired last had worked only one, they would receive twelve denarii instead of the agreed-on one denarius.

> *When those hired first came, they thought that they would receive more; but each of them also received a denarius (Matthew 20:10).*

But to their chagrin, they received what those who had worked one hour received—one denarius!

"How unjust," they thought; and they began to grumble.

> *When they received it, they grumbled at the landowner, saying, "These last men have worked only one hour, and you have made them equal to us who have borne the burden and the scorching heat of the day (Matthew 20:11-12).*

Their gripe seems legitimate. They had labored to the point of exhaustion for twelve hours while the scorching heat of the burning east wind had blistered them all day (Isaiah 49:10; Ezekiel 19:12; Hosea 13:15; James 1:11). Yet, they received no more than those who worked for one hour in the cool evening breezes. The reader must ask himself, "Am I like these grumbling workers? If so, how?"

[3205] Morris, *The Gospel According to Matthew*, 500.

If rewards were a matter of strict legal recompense for each amount of work done, we would expect the landowner to say, "You are correct. I should pay you more." However, he says:

> *Friend, I am doing you no wrong; did you not agree with me for a denarius? Take what is yours and go, but I wish to give to this last man the same as to you. Is it not lawful for me to do what I wish with what is my own? Or is your eye envious because I am generous? (Matthew 20:13-15).*

"Look," he says, "I kept my bargain with you, the agreement *you* wanted, and I have a perfect right as the owner of the vineyard to be generous to others."

Therefore, there is not a precise correlation between work and reward as in a labor contract. The idea of legal merit is excluded; only mercy is emphasized. Moreover, the point of the parable is to demonstrate that it *is God's sovereign prerogative to do as He pleases with each of us.*

He says to those hired first, "Take what is yours and *go*" (Gr *hupagō*). We may detect here (as the accompanying rebuke regarding envy suggests) that "depart" is a better translation. The expression sometimes is a bit stronger than just "go."[3206]

We are now getting close to the central issue in the parable, the incorrect attitudes toward reward that characterized these envious workers. The parable highlights three: (1) a commercial approach to rewards, (2) their grumbling about the right of the owner to be overgenerous, and (3) envy, "*Is your eye envious because I am generous?*" They were infected with commercialism, grumbling, and envy!

To work for rewards with a sense of competition or with a desire to have higher status than others (envy) in the coming kingdom is ruled out. The kingdom of heaven is not like modern industry. Taking the lowest status and becoming the servant of all is what counts before the divine Landowner, as taught in the discussion that follows the parable (Matthew 20:25-28). Only those who do not envy others for their blessings will receive overgenerous wages. Only those who work, fully confident that the Lord will always do "what is right" (who do not have a commercial attitude), and who do not worry about the amount of reward they will receive (who do not grumble), will receive any reward.

In their approach to service for the landowner, those hired first apparently wanted a guarantee, an agreement worked out in advance; so much work resulting in so much payment (v. 2). However, the other laborers agreed to trust the landlord to pay them "whatever is right" (v. 4). These are diametrically opposite approaches to working for Christ and have led to dramatically different modes of service for Christ in the history of the church. This legalistic-commercial approach was eventually perverted into the practice of indulgences. A certain amount of money would result in a specific reduction in purgatory sentence.

The attitude of the first-hired laborers may remind us of the approach of the rich young ruler who also wanted to know what he must do to obtain an inheritance in the kingdom. Did a contractual, commercial approach to rewards lurk in the mind of the rich young ruler? It had developed in the minds of the apostles as well. Recall how they jostled about who would be the "greatest." To Peter's question, however, the Lord immediately gives an affirming answer with no implication of impropriety on Peter's part. The parable

---

[3206] This word is used, for example, of commanding demons to "depart" (Matthew 8:32).

of the Laborers in the Vineyard addresses the wrong attitude of the rich young ruler and the relationship between reward and work done. This teaches that the relationship is not one of contract, but of overgenerous wages, grace.

Jesus acknowledges that Peter and the other disciples have, in fact, done what is right and will obtain one-hundred-fold returns. A return of this magnitude is definitely a blue-chip investment, which is overly generous compared to the work done. Yet, since the rich young ruler wanted a contractual relationship, Jesus offered him one, *"You know the commandments,"* just as the landowner does in the parable of the Laborers. The apostles, on the other hand, apparently never approached the Lord with such a contract but had simply followed Him out of love and, like the other laborers in the vineyard, simply trusted the Lord to do "whatever is right" (v. 4).

In the denouement each receives a denarius. Too much attention has been focused on the denarius. The denarius is probably a mere artifact of the story to bring out the salient lessons. The denarius is not the final reward. If anything, it would parallel the reward given in the present age promised in response to Peter's question. The man hired last did in fact receive twelve times more than those hired first, for he worked only one hour. Rather, *the final reward is being either first or last.* That is the punch line of the parable.

So the last shall be first, and the first last (Matthew 20:16).

Who are the last and who are the first? The *"last who will be first"* refers to those who like the apostles have given up everything and adopted poverty to follow Christ. They are the "unworthy." Paul would later call them the "foolish" and among the "not many mighty" and the "not many wise" (1 Corinthians 1:26) and the "weak" and the "base things of the world" (1 Corinthians 1:27). The *"first who will be last,"* then, would be those who, like the rich young ruler, had greater opportunity and capacity but were unwilling to give up the status of the rich. Evidently, those hired first were similarly proud and envious. That spirit of envy had governed their labor and was revealed only at the end of the day.

In this statement, the reward of those hired first is clear; they will be last in the kingdom. It seems that they forfeited their reward, as this sobering statement declares. In fact, they are commanded to "depart" (*Take what is yours and **go***). They are being politely dismissed. Why? Because they had the wrong motives. They served only in order to obtain reward, not because of love for the job or the landowner. Also, they were full of envy. That is, they compared themselves with other laborers and were jealous of their honors. They were filled with an unloving and proud spirit. The other laborers, however, had served, trusting that the landowner would do what was right (Matthew 20:4). And he did. In this life they received a greater return (three-fold or twelve-fold) over those who had labored first, and they were also given higher status in the kingdom, first instead of last. These laborers illustrate that whatever decisions believers make now will be justly remunerated at the last day, but these laborers were not concerned about a precise correlation between their work and their wages.

The "reward" for these unworthy servants was not the denarius; it was being commanded to depart and to assume the lowest status in the kingdom. It was evident from their actions that they had labored with an eye toward wanting to achieve more honors than the other laborers and with an attitude that suggested that being rewarded was more important than the work itself.

In the Lord's work it is wrong to serve for rewards on a contractual basis, with the anticipation that so much work yields so much reward. Rather, we work because we love the King and trust Him to be fair and righteous. When we do, we will be astonished at His generosity, even if we started late in the day. There is nothing here about grace trumping justice. The King is both gracious and just. Rewards are not strictly tied to the amount of work done. The King will take every circumstance into consideration. But most of all we learn that He is generous. Just as He promised a one thousand percent return to the disciples, He granted the highest honor to the laborers who were hired last.

Summary

This chapter has addressed two central parables regarding the doctrine of eternal rewards. From the parable of the Unworthy Servant, we learn that when we have done all we can do, when we have been faithful to the end, we still have only done what is required of all servants, namely, that they be faithful. That being so, it is gracious of God to condescend to reward us at all.

In the second parable, the parable of the Laborers in the Vineyard, those hired first, unlike the rich young ruler, did agree to work for the Master. But like the rich young ruler, they failed to give up all for Him. They clung to their idea that they were owed a reward; they were envious, and they did not like the fact that the Master could be overgenerous to some. The rich young ruler would not give up his money; these workers would not give up their incorrect attitudes about reward, their envy, and their bitterness over the Master's grace. In the encounter with the rich young ruler we learn that we must give up all to be Jesus' disciples, and in the parable of the Laborers in the Vineyard we learn that we must also work for Him with proper attitudes toward our Lord and toward other laborers in the vineyard.

The Bible clearly teaches that there will be "degrees of glory." Differences will exist in eternity future. This raises questions about the apparent conflict between a reward motivation and the Christian ethic of disinterestedness. This issue is addressed in more detail in the next chapter.

64

Rewards and Merit

GEOFFREY CHAUCER (c. 1340–1400) was born to a well-to-do, middle-class family. Perhaps his best-known work is that enduring classic of English literature, *The Canterbury Tales.* Written in verse, this is a collection of twenty-four stories told by a group of travelers to amuse themselves during a pilgrimage from London to the shrine of Thomas à Becket at Canterbury. The vivid *Prologue* to *The Canterbury Tales* offers a memorable picture of contemporary life in its description of thirty-one pilgrims. Each tale is known by the name of the character who tells it, and one of the best known is the tale of the Pardoner.[3207]

As Chaucer paints him, he was a grotesque figure, riding bareback from village to village, with bulging, yellow hair flowing in the wind as he sang, "Come hither love, to me." His leather pouch was "brimful of pardon, come all hot from Rome." In his story we see Chaucer's most violent attack on the practice of indulgences in the medieval church. His backpack contained, he says, a pillowcase carrying Mary's veil and a shred of cloth from the very sail that Peter used before Jesus called him. He boasts that he can make more money in a day selling indulgences than a country parson can make in two months.

Furthermore, he loves explaining how he does it. First, he tells his listeners he is from Rome and shows them papal bulls certifying his indulgences. Then he displays other warrants signed by the bishop:

> *That none may be so bold, no priest nor clerk,*
> *To interfere with Jesus' holy work.*

And what was his "holy work"? This hawker of indulgences was determined to scam every Christian in England. What were "indulgences"? Basically, they were monies paid to the Church of Rome to help build St. Peter's Cathedral. This payment was supposedly able to reduce the purgatory sentences of those for whom the money was designated.

The Pardoner had about one hundred years to ply his trade before one of his descendants, a real pardoner, Johann Tetzel, approached Wittenberg, Germany, in 1517. When he put his ear to the graves in a local graveyard to listen to the cries of those in purgatory, and then exclaimed to horrified relatives, "*A coin in the coffer rings, and a soul from purgatory springs,*" he irritated the wrong monk, Martin Luther. Luther promptly responded with his 95 theses, and the Protestant Reformation was born.

3207 P. M. Bechtel, "Chaucer, Geoffrey," in *Who's Who in Church History*, ed. J. D. Douglas and Philip W. Comfort (Wheaton, IL: Tyndale House, 1992), 156, s.v. "1 Corinthians 15:39-42". See also Lance Wilcox, "Everyday Faith in the Middle Ages," *Christian History Magazine (No. 49)* 1996, s.v. "The Pardoner".

The tale of the Pardoner and the real life actions of John Tetzel lead us into the profound problem of the Middle Ages, the commercialization of the doctrine of rewards. By "commercialization," we mean so much work would result in so much reward. There was a legal, commercial relationship.

Spiritual Commercialism?

Emma Disley in an excellent article, "Degrees of Glory," warns of the dangers of what she calls "spiritual commercialism."

The theology of future reward and punishment represents a constant latent propensity of the Christian faith to lapse into formalism, or spiritual commercialism, or legalism, which, in themselves, strike at the very heart of Christian disinterestedness and self-forgetfulness.[3208]

REWARDS AND MERIT

As discussed in chapter 62, all of the Greek words for reward—*misthos* (1 Corinthians 3:14), *antapodidōmi* (Luke 14:14), *misthapodosia* (Hebrews 10:35), *stephanos* (1 Corinthians 9:25), *brabeion* (Philippians 3:14), *antapodosis* (Colossians 3:24), *and misthapodotēs* (Hebrews 11:6)—express the idea of something obtained by means of effort, remuneration for work done, wages, or payment.

How are rewards and merit related? Even though it is clear from the New Testament that rewards are in a sense "earned" or merited, in the final analysis they are the result of grace, not our work. This is true for four reasons.

First, God was not obligated to give any reward in return for any amount of work. The fact that He chose to obligate Himself in this way is an act of unmerited favor, pure grace. In view of man's depravity and the imperfection in any work one might do, God would be perfectly just never to give any reward at all. This was His choice. The obligation comes from Himself. The works do not obligate Him. *Rather, He has obligated Himself to reward the works.*

The psalmist makes this clear saying,

> *Once God has spoken; Twice I have heard this: That power belongs to God; and lovingkindness is Thine, O Lord, for Thou dost recompense a man according to his work (Psalm 62:11–12, NASB).*

Why does God reward our works? He does so, because in His "lovingkindness" (Heb *chesed*), He has obligated Himself to do so. His *chesed,* or love and mercy, is the basis of this obligation.[3209]

A. A. Hodge and Charles Hodge, commenting on the Westminster Confession, put it this way,

> *God's infinite superiority to us, his absolute proprietorship in us as our Maker, and sovereignty over us as our moral Governor, necessarily exclude the possibility of our actions deserving any*

[3208] Emma Disley, "Degrees of Glory: The Protestant Doctrine and the Concept of Rewards Hereafter," *JTS* 42, no. 1 (April 1991): 77-105.

[3209] See R. Laird Harris, "*chesed,*" in TWOT, 306 ff. Harris demonstrates that *chesed* is granted freely, without obligation, and is related to mercy and grace.

> *reward at his hand.* ***No action of ours can profit God or lay him under obligation to us****. All that is possible to us is already a debt we owe him as our Creator and Preserver. When we have done our utmost we are only unprofitable servants. Much less, then, can any possible obedience at one moment atone for any disobedience in another moment. (4) As already proved under chapter 13, on Sanctification, our works, which could merit nothing even if perfect, are in this life, because of remaining imperfections, most imperfect. They therefore, the best of them, need to be atoned for by the blood, and presented through the mediation of Christ, before they can find acceptance with the Father.*[3210]

While we would agree that no work of ours could place any obligation on God, God Himself could agree to accept an obligation to remunerate works. That He enters into obligatory relationships with His creatures is taught in many passages; they are called covenants and promises. Our good works deserve nothing from His hand, but in His grace He has chosen to grant reward to those works, all out of proportion to their value.

We are in full agreement with Charles Hodge when he says,

> *Protestants ... teach that God does reward his people for their works. Having graciously promised for Christ's sake to overlook the imperfection of their best services, they have the assurance founded on that promise that he who gives to a disciple even a cup of cold water in the name of a disciple, shall in no wise lose his reward. The Scriptures also teach that the happiness or blessedness of believers in a future life will be greater or less in proportion to their devotion to the service of Christ in this life. Those who love little, do little; and those who do little, enjoy less. What a man sows that shall he also reap. As the rewards of heaven are given on the ground of the merits of Christ, and as He has a right to do what He will with his own, there would be no injustice were the thief saved on the cross as highly exalted as the Apostle Paul. But the general drift of Scripture is in favour of the doctrine that a man shall reap what he sows; that God will reward every one according to, although not on account of his works.*[3211]

Second, the rewards God grants are so astonishingly out of proportion to any work we could ever do that we can only conclude they are the result of grace. It might be best to call them "overgenerous wages." If we do enough work to obtain a day's wage and yet He gives us a year's worth of remuneration, that is grace. While it is true we would not receive anything if we did not do that day's labor, the amount of remuneration so far outstrips the effort such that we can only exclaim, "Praise God for His matchless grace." We can in no sense say, "We earned it" or "We deserved it."

Third, whatever works we do would never have been done at all unless God had called us to salvation, motivated us to do them and then, by His strengthening help, enabled us to do them.

Fourth, the main point of the parable of the Laborers in the Vineyard seems to be, "Do not be among the first who became last." We must avoid the attitude of work for pay. We must approach our service for Christ not with an attitude that He owes us something because we have made a particular sacrifice, but rather with the attitude that we want to be faithful to Him and He will do what is right. We are to take encouragement from the fact that He remembers "every cup of water" and that if He chooses to honor our service, that act is only overgenerous wages. That, Jesus says, is what the kingdom of heaven is like.

3210 Hodge and Hodge, *The Confession of Faith: With Questions for Theological Students and Bible Classes.*

3211 Hodge, *Systematic Theology*, 3:244.

The parable of the Laborers in the Vineyard corrects this widespread error in thinking and tells us that we do not labor for the amount of reward. Rather, we labor out of love and trust the owner of the vineyard to do whatever is right. Legal reward is not our goal. It is very comforting and encouraging to know that He will remember every cup of water. We are not to focus on a tight legal relationship between work and reward. Instead, we are to rejoice in His amazing grace. Whatever we get will be so out of proportion to what we deserve that it can only be called grace, and not legal merit. Whatever He gives will be "right," and that is all that matters.

Of course we deserve nothing. "We have only done our duty." That God has agreed to reward us for our work is an act of grace. We are told that when a servant has done all he can do, he has *only* done his duty. For the owner of that slave to reward him for what he should do anyway is pure grace.

DISINTERESTED BENEVOLENCE

Because of the strong emphasis on rewards in the New Testament, Christianity has often been accused by philosophers as being self-seeking. Secular philosopher John Hospers argues that when believers justify being moral on the basis of a doctrine of eternal rewards and punishments, this is "simply an appeal to self-interest … [N]othing," he says, "could be a clearer appeal to naked and unbridled power than this."[3212]

We seem to have two conflicting modes of thought: "self-centeredness" and "God-centeredness." Did not Paul make it clear that "love seeks not its own" (1 Corinthians 13:5)? How then can seeking for rewards be consistent with biblical love? If it be argued, "Virtue is its own reward," this still does not justify exhorting disciples to pursue virtue because it brings personal happiness. Are the commands of the Gospels to be obeyed because of the personal benefit such obedience might bring? Is not this really veiled self-centeredness, rather than love or virtue?

This view of ethics is sometimes called "disinterested benevolence." This is the atheistic ethic in which good is done only for the sake of the good, with no consideration of reward for the doing of it.[3213] It is atheistic because atheists do not believe in an afterlife, eternal judgment, or any final accountability for one's life. Therefore, the only appeal they have for love is altruism.

By forgetting the possibility of reward, a man supposedly honors the ethical standard in its purity. The motivation for obedience is to be found only in the command itself. Only in this manner, maintains the atheist, can the selfishness of man be crushed and a pure altruism found. This motivation is "purely moral." The reason this is the "only" way this can be done is because there is no other; there is no final accountability. As history has shown, this ethic has been catastrophically unsuccessful in prompting human betterment. Witness, for example, the 85-year experiment in the Soviet Union.

There are many objections to this viewpoint. First, it is completely contrary to what we know about human nature based on empirical observation for thousands of years.

[3212] John Hospers, "Why Be Moral," in *Reading in Ethical Theory*, ed. John Hospers and Wilfrid Sellars (EnglewoodCliffs, NJ: Prentice Hall, 1970), 739. Cited by J. P. Moreland, "Ethical Egoism and Biblical Self-Interest," *WTJ* 59, no. 2 (Fall 1997): 255.

[3213] For a response to this atheistic ethic see G. C. Berkouwer, *Faith and Justification* (Grand Rapids: Wm. B. Eerdmans Publishing Co., 1954), 117.

There is no such thing as pure altruism. Man's depravity means that even in the best of men, a person's altruism always contains an element of improper motive. No one performs good acts entirely or even primarily out of perfect love for others or for God. There are always other motivations lurking in the background: the preference of one's own self-interest or of some other object less than God. Thus, even the good is tainted.

Second, the ethic of disinterested benevolence would impose on us an ethical motivation that is not only contrary to our nature but is also impossible to fulfill. For example, the "purely moral" would demand that childless couples adopt babies solely for the babies' sake. Such an approach is naïve and far removed from the realities of life. It would be ridiculous to demand that a man who marries a woman because he loves her must do it only for the good of the woman he loves with no personal motive to have his own needs met. Of course, to marry for the single purpose of having one's own needs met would be sin, but everyone marries with a mixture of motives, and they can be good and proper motives. In fact, God said it was not good for a man to be alone. So, it is "good" to marry in order to have our "alone" needs met.[3214]

Third, to pursue altruism, lack of self-interest, or self-sacrifice can be as calculated and ego-centered as a naked pursuit of reward. When one sets out to be selfless, he is immediately focused on some standard by which he can measure whether he is being truly altruistic, some code that will define the altruistic life. Thus, his mind is turned away from God and toward the code. This leads to endless self-examination and introspection, the error of legalism.

The history of the church is littered with the wrecks of such vain pursuits. From the self-flagellation of those seeking penance, to the scrupulous rules of behavior laid down by the monks involving poor diet, sackcloth for clothing, and hours of meditation every day, sincere believers have vainly attempted a life void of self-interest, all the while paradoxically focusing on themselves.

Fourth, J. P. Moreland explains, "We need to distinguish between self-benefit as a bi-product of an act vs. self-interest as the sole intent of an act. Scriptural passages that use self-interest may simply be pointing out that if you intentionally do the right thing, then a good bi-product of this will be rewards of various kinds."[3215] In other words, just because self-benefit serves as "a" motive for something, it does not follow that it is the reason that justifies the action in the first place. "The Bible may be citing self-interest as a motive for action and not as the reason for what makes the act our duty."[3216] It may be that Scripture cites rewards not as the fundamental reason for an action, but as a prudent or wise reason for action, and not the moral basis or only reason for it.

Fifth, as C. S. Lewis argued, there are different kinds of rewards, some are based on selfish motivations and some are not. Some are proper because they have a natural,

---

[3214] Along these lines Moreland says, "Genuine altruism requires that an altruistic act have, as its sole, or at least main intent, the benefit of the other. An act whose sole or ultimate intent is self-interest but which, nevertheless, does result in the benefit of others is not genuine altruism. If you found out that someone 'loved' you or acted 'altruistically' toward you solely or ultimately with the intent of benefiting himself, then you would not count that as genuine love or altruism even if the act happened to benefit you in some way." Moreland, "Ethical Egoism and Biblical Self-Interest," 263.

[3215] Ibid., 265.

[3216] Ibid., 266.

intrinsic connection with the things we do to earn them and because they are expressions of what God made us to be by nature. For example, one would be a mercenary if he married for money, because that is not the natural reward for love. A general who pursues victory only in order to obtain another star would be selfish. But victory is the consummation of the activity and intrinsically related to the activity itself. We will discuss this in more detail below.

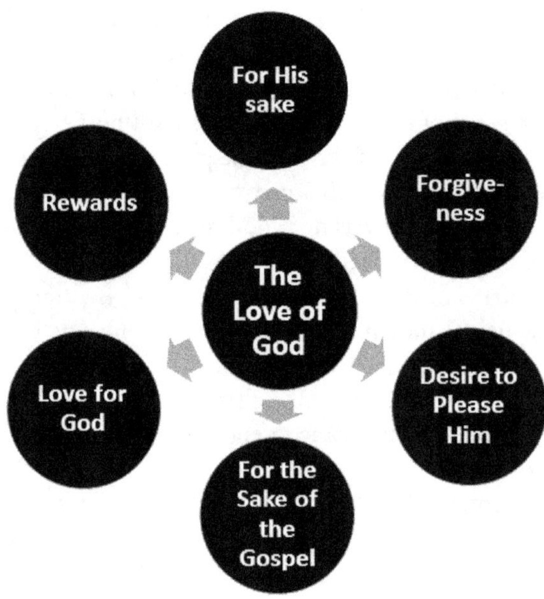

Rewards are one of seven major motivations for following Christ's way of life.

Rewards Are Only One of the Biblical Motivations

Some of the reaction to the Protestant doctrine of rewards may be blamed on the way in which the doctrine is sometimes presented by its adherents. It is a mistake to extract the reward motivation found in the Bible from other equally important or even more important motivations the biblical authors present. The chart above illustrates the context in which the doctrine of rewards should be placed.

GOD'S LOVE FOR US

There is no question that the central motivation for following Christ is God's love for us. Because this is so important, let us consider this amazing fact in some detail.

Millions of Christians in the United States wonder why they are not experiencing the fullness of resurrection life promised in the New Testament. John Maisel answers,

> *No doubt many factors are at work. But if I had to boil it down to one main issue, it would be this: You cannot experience the fullness of Christ's life unless and until you are gripped*

by the depth of Christ's love — His love for you. Not just knowing about His love. Not just talking about it. But personally ***experiencing*** *His love for you.*[3217]

Yes, rewards are an important and much neglected spiritual motivation, but God's love for us and our love for Him are the most important.

Paul states this in his prayer for us,

So that Christ may dwell in your hearts through faith; and that you, being rooted and grounded in love, may be able to comprehend with all the saints what is the breadth and length and height and depth, and to know the love of Christ which surpasses knowledge, that you may be filled up to all the fullness of God (Ephesians 3:17–19).

The heart of this prayer is not that we would love God, which is important, but that we would know God's love for us. This love "surpasses knowledge." That tells us that more than intellectual acknowledgment is meant. As Maisel explains, "To know Christ in the sense Paul is describing it means to be affected by that love at the core of who we are. We give in to it, we respond to it, we feel it thrilling our hearts, we trust it, we rest in it."[3218]

We love, because He first loved us (1 John 4:19).

We know love by this, that He laid down His life for us; and we ought to lay down our lives for the brethren (1 John 3:16).

Greater love has no one than this, that one lay down his life for his friends (John 15:13).

Only this kind of knowledge of His love can result in the "fullness of God," the profound motivation for discipleship which God desires of us.

Maisel summarizes,

The depth of our willingness to surrender to Jesus is directly related to the depth of our belief that God really loves us with a perfect love. Only as we trust His love will we surrender to His authority and experience a relationship with God that becomes real and satisfying.[3219]

OUR LOVE FOR GOD

All would agree that a second motivation for following Christ is our love for Him and our gratitude for what He has done for us.

For this is the love of God, that we keep His commandments; and His commandments are not burdensome (1 John 5:3).[3220]

If you love Me, you will keep My commandments (John 14:15).

[3217] John Maisel, *Radical Trust: The Two Most Important Things Jesus Wants You to Know* (Dallas: East-West Ministries International, 2012), 9-10. John's book is the most significant book on the spiritual life that I have ever read. You can order a copy from East-West Ministries at info@eastwest.org.

[3218] Ibid., 10.

[3219] Ibid., 12.

[3220] We understand the phrase "of God" to be an objective genitive meaning "love for God."

The Apostle Paul explains his central motivation this way:

For the love of Christ compels us, because we judge thus: that if One died for all, then all died (2 Corinthians 5:14).

The word "compel" (Gr *sunechō*) is quite strong. In this context it means "to provide an impulse, urge on, impel."[3221]

FOR HIS NAME'S SAKE

Third, Jesus says we should be motivated "for my name's sake" (Matthew 19:29). In other words, we serve for His sake and not for our own benefit. While that does not exclude the thought of our own recompense, it decidedly places it in perspective!

BECAUSE OF HIS FORGIVENESS

Fourth, from the incident with the woman who had led an immoral life and received forgiveness, it is clear that gratitude for forgiveness is a central motivation.

Therefore I say to you, her sins, which are many, are forgiven, for she loved much. But to whom little is forgiven, the same loves little (Luke 7:47, NKJV).

BECAUSE WE WANT TO PLEASE HIM

Many believers are motivated spiritually for a desire to please Christ, and rewards are not a central part of their thinking. This is biblical to the core.

Therefore also we have as our ambition, whether at home or absent, ***to be pleasing to Him*** *(2 Corinthians 5:9).*

No soldier in active service entangles himself in the affairs of everyday life, ***so that he may please the one who enlisted him as a soldier*** *(2 Timothy 2:4).*[3222]

FOR THE SAKE OF THE GOSPEL

Paul also says we should be motivated simply "for the sake of the gospel" (1 Corinthians 9:23).

The Protestant Doctrine of Rewards

As mentioned earlier, all the Greek words for reward express the idea of something obtained by means of effort, remuneration for work done, wages, or payment. This sense of merit and personal benefit has often been misunderstood. However, six important observations on this issue provide a biblically satisfying perspective.

(1) REWARDS ARE THE COMPLETION OF A LIFE WELL-LIVED

We must not be defensive when nonbelievers and some Christian writers, citing Immanuel Kant and the Stoics, falsely assume they are on a higher moral ground, rebuking

---

[3221] BDAG, 971. Luke 8:37, "gripped by" fear; 12:57, "distressed" until it is accomplished; Paul says he is "hard pressed" between alternatives, Philippians 1:27, etc.

[3222] See also Colossians 1:10; 1 Thessalonians 4:1; 1 John 3:22 and Hebrews 13:21.

Partners for their mercenary motives. While it is true that rewards could be pursued for selfish motives, this is not the way the New Testament presents them. There are different kinds of rewards. Unlike biblical rewards, some kinds of rewards bear no connection with the things one does to obtain them. These are selfish. For example, as C. S. Lewis points out, "Money is not the natural reward of love; that is why we call a man a mercenary if he marries a woman for the sake of her money."[3223] On the other hand, marriage is the proper reward granted to someone who loves a potential mate.

In a similar way, the general who fights for victory in order to obtain a higher rank is a mercenary. However, if he fights for victory because it is the proper reward for battle, he is not being selfish. We can see that biblical rewards are not added onto the activities of a faithful life but are, in fact, the consummation or completion of a life well-lived. Victory is the reward for battle, and marriage is the reward for love. So being honored by Christ and seeking that honor is no more mercenary than seeking marriage or victory. This is the intrinsic outcome and desired goal of the Christian life.

A reward is like the feeling one has when he completes a task after long effort (in this case a lifetime) and learns he has done well. Many have invested their lives in various projects, some requiring years to achieve and then experience the immense satisfaction and reward of achievement. Is that selfish? In the sphere of eternal life, Christians live well, aspiring to finish the "project" of a life well-lived, and they are motivated by that distant goal. As the Apostle put it,

> *For I am already being poured out as a drink offering, and the time of my departure has come. I have fought the good fight, I have finished the course, I have kept the faith; in the future there is laid up for me the crown of righteousness, which the Lord, the righteous Judge, will award to me on that day; and not only to me, but also to all who have loved His appearing (2 Timothy 4:6-8, NASB).*

Was Paul "selfish" because he lived to "Fight the good fight" and yet will receive a "crown of righteousness" as a result of it? His life purpose was to fight a good fight, finish his course, and keep the faith. When the end came, he could look back with an immense sense of satisfaction and say, "By the grace of God I have done it!" A crown of righteousness,[3224] that affirmation that he had invested his life well, was at the center of his daily motivation.

When a mother studies and counsels with other mothers regarding the skills of motherhood and then receives the rewarded satisfaction of knowing these new skills, no one accuses her of being a mercenary because she sought the reward of this sense of satisfaction.

When a missionary dreams of one day being able to converse with those around him in their language, he is not a mercenary as he seeks that reward thereby finding motivation in it for the drudgery of studying the verb system and memorizing word lists. Furthermore, as he progresses, he experiences the first glimmers of that future reward when he can say a few simple sentences. In a similar way, as the Christian practices faithfulness and experiences the sense of divine approval and inner satisfaction for having served his King,

---

[3223] C. S. Lewis, *The Weight of Glory* (New York: Simon and Shuster, 1975), 26.

[3224] This is not a crown "which is" righteousness, that is, the justification of Christ, but a "righteous crown" in contrast to the unrighteous crown he was receiving from Nero. One day, the righteous Judge, the only one who matters, will say that Paul invested life well and Paul will receive a "righteous crown."

the motivation derived from that experience creates an even stronger desire to experience it fully in the life to come. He more frequently begins to view each act as a foretaste of that great future. As the fleeting moments of this experience multiply, the desire for the reward to experience "Well done" increases until it becomes a life-consuming passion. The notion that this approach to life is mercenary is a ridiculous absurdity!

(2) REWARDS ARE OPPORTUNITIES FOR GREATER SERVICE (2 TIMOTHY 2:12; REVELATION 2:26)

Part of our difficulty is the way we view these rewards. In their most general sense they refer to the joy of participating with Christ in God's eternal purposes, the inheritance. This eternal purpose is a good and wonderful purpose: to extend the glory and blessing of God to all creation. Whatever it involves, those who know Christ as their King must strive to have a share in this. It is not a striving so much for personal benefit but persevering in good works so that we can achieve the goal of being His co-heirs in the future reign of the servant kings.[3225] Whatever our role in that great future is, it will be magnificent. Because we love Him, we want to earn the right to rule with Him and minister with Him. So it is our love for Him and the joy set before us that motivates. The desire for future reward, so that we may serve Christ more fully in the extension of His glory throughout the created order, far exceeds and replaces altruism as a motivation. As Paul put it, "*If we endure, we will also reign with Him*" (2 Timothy 2:12).

(3) REWARDS ARE ENCOURAGEMENT IN TRIALS (HEBREWS 10:32-36; MATTHEW 5:10-12)

The most characteristic context that mentions reward as a motivation is one reminding us that one day there will be a righting of all wrongs; one day God will let us know that he remembered every cup of water; one day our sufferings now will be gloriously reversed.

> *But remember the former days, when, after being enlightened, you endured a great conflict of sufferings, partly, by being made a public spectacle through reproaches and tribulations, and partly by becoming sharers with those who were so treated. For you showed sympathy to the prisoners, and accepted joyfully the seizure of your property,* ***knowing that you have for yourselves a better possession and an abiding one****. Therefore, do not throw away your confidence, which has* ***a great reward****. For you have need of endurance, so that when you have done the will of God,* ***you may receive what was promised*** *(Hebrews 10:32–36).*

> *Blessed are those who have been* ***persecuted for the sake of righteousness, for theirs is the kingdom of heaven.*** *Blessed are you when men cast insults at you, and persecute you, and say all kinds of evil against you falsely, on account of Me. Rejoice, and be glad, for* ***your reward in heaven is great****, for so they persecuted the prophets who were before you (Matthew 5:10–12).*

It is not selfish to endure because we know that the universe is moral, that one day our secret choices will be remembered and honored.

This theoretical discussion can be clarified with a simple illustration. Consider a young mother of four. Her husband is a brutal alcoholic. He has on occasion abused her and

---

[3225] Geisler, *Systematic Theology*, 4:310.

heaped enormous debts on the family. In addition to the pain he causes, he is unfaithful and lets her know it. Now the Bible tells her to love this man in spite of the pain and hurt. I am not saying she should not at some point decide to leave him, but before that decision, she chooses to love for Christ's sake. After all, He first loved us. But in addition, she looks to the future. She knows that her Master will be greatly pleased and that she will be honored then, if not now. Her confidence that the universe is moral, that justice will one day prevail, and that her sufferings now equip her to reign with her King provide a greatly enhanced motivation to persevere. Even if the "purely moral" see this as selfish, the One before whom we will render an account clearly does not. When He exhorted us to show hospitality to those who cannot pay, He did not appeal to duty as the motive. Rather, He said, "*Although they cannot repay you, you will be repaid at the resurrection of the righteous*" (Luke 14:14).

(4) REWARDS ARE PROMISED ONLY TO THOSE WHO LOVE FOR CHRIST'S SAKE

> *And Jesus said to them, "Truly I say to you, that you who have followed Me, in the regeneration when the Son of Man will sit on His glorious throne, you also shall sit upon twelve thrones, judging the twelve tribes of Israel. And everyone who has left houses or brothers or sisters or father or mother or children or farms for* ***My name's sake****, will receive many times as much, and will inherit eternal life. But many who are first will be last; and the last, first (Matthew 19:28-30).*

Elsewhere, Jesus says that we should become disciples "*for the sake of the kingdom of God*" (Luke 18:29-30) and "*for the gospel's sake*" (Mark 10:29).

Jesus promised reward ***only*** to those who had already promised to follow Him with motive other than the reward alone! For example, in the classic passage on rewards quoted above, Jesus makes it clear that the motive for the path of discipleship is first of all, "for my sake" (Matthew 19:29) and for the sake of the kingdom of God (Luke 18:29) or for "the gospel's sake" (Mark 10:29). In each case the prior motive is central. To seek reward only for the purpose of obtaining personal benefit in the next life would be to forfeit the very blessedness that was sought. In fact, the reward may also come to those who have no consciousness that they had done good at all. "*Lord, when did we see You hungry, and feed You, or thirsty, and give You drink?*" (Matthew 25:37).

(5) REWARDS ARE OVERGENEROUS WAGES

As explained in the parable of the Laborers in the Vineyard (Matthew 20:1-16), whatever reward we get is an "overgenerous" wage (see chapter 63).

(6) REWARDS PROVIDE US WITH TOKENS OF WORSHIP AND GRATEFULNESS

Several years ago, a dear friend of ours, Jean Baumgardner, wrote us a wonderful letter. Jean and John and their children lived in Los Alamos, New Mexico, where John worked as a scientist at the Los Alamos weapons lab. After twenty years of a very close marriage, they had just received devastating news—Jean had come down with terminal cancer and had only a few months to live. As she prepared herself to meet the Lord Jesus, amidst the grief, there was an increasing joy. She began to read the five hymns of praise sung by the saints, the twenty-four elders, and the angelic host in John's vision of the heavenly choirs in the book of Revelation.

The apostle John had been transported to the heavenly court and stood before the throne of God. From this throne came flashes of lightning and peals of thunder. Before the throne was a sea of glass, clear as crystal. This signaled that the sea (that is, the nations) was calm and not chaotic; all was under the sovereign control of the King.

In Revelation 4 and 5, John records five hymns. The first two are addressed to God, the next two to the Lamb, and the last to both. As we move from hymn to hymn, the choirs become larger and larger and build to a climax where every creature sings to God and the Lamb.

Jean began to memorize and sing these hymns to herself. As she anticipated her imminent death she wrote, "I am learning my lines."

The second hymn marks the praise of the twenty-four elders and the four living creatures. With enthusiastic praise they sing,

> *And the four living creatures, each one of them having six wings, are full of eyes around and within; and day and night they do not cease to say, "HOLY, HOLY, HOLY, is THE LORD GOD, THE ALMIGHTY, WHO WAS AND WHO IS AND WHO IS TO COME." And when the living creatures give glory and honor and thanks to Him who sits on the throne, to Him who lives forever and ever, the twenty-four elders will fall down before Him who sits on the throne, and will worship Him who lives forever and ever, and **will cast their crowns before the throne**, saying, "Worthy art Thou, our Lord and our God, to receive glory and honor and power; for Thou didst create all things, and because of Thy will they existed, and were created" (Revelation 4:8–11).*

Notice their posture—they fall down in submission to His majestic authority. They praise Him for His worthiness. He is worthy to receive such adulation because He has created everything that exists and by His will He allows all to continue to exist (cf. Job 38:4-7). His power and authority are absolute, His majesty beyond comprehension.

That being so, what do the elders do? They fall before Him and repeatedly cast their crowns at the foot of the throne. These crowns, as discussed in previous chapters, represent honor they have received from Christ. Yet now, in the face of His overwhelming glory, they relinquish all honor to Him. As Allen P. Ross says, "No one can acclaim God to be worthy of all glory, honor, and power and yet cling to one's bit of honor and power, no matter how well deserved it may be."[3226]

These crowns are not to be worn throughout eternity, thus drawing attention to us. Instead, they provide us with tokens of worship, symbols of relinquishment of all personal honor, which we can lay at His feet in gratitude, submission, and reverence.

Summary

The *biblical* doctrine of eternal rewards is a magnificent incitement to a faithful life. In our opinion, the church would benefit significantly in its task of motivating believers to fuller commitment if this great vision of serving with Him in the fulfillment of human destiny were more frequently held before our gaze.

There is no "spiritual commercialism" or selfishness involved in the pursuit of honor, opportunities for ministry, and the desire for maximum intimacy with Christ. These are

[3226] Ross, *Recalling the Hope of Glory*, 483.

noble and inspiring goals, fully approved by Christ and His apostles. They focus ultimately on Him, not ourselves.

To summarize, believers are to strive for reward (1) with a more fundamental heart motive that what we do is for Christ's sake and in response to Christ's love (2 Corinthians 5:14); (2) with a realization that, once we have done all we can do, we still have only done our duty (Luke 17:10); (3) with a heart's desire to "please the One who enlisted us as soldiers" (2 Timothy 2:4); (4) with a prior motive of serving Him for Christ's sake (Matthew 19:28-30); (5) with an understanding that there is no strict contractual correspondence between a certain amount of work resulting in a certain amount of reward, for whatever we get is overgenerous wages (Matthew 20:1-16); and (6) most importantly, with the realization that rewards enable us to obtain tokens of worship and gratitude that, like the twenty-four elders, we too can repeatedly lay at His feet (Revelation 4:10).

At the Judgment Seat of Christ, we will be summoned to the victor's platform to hear the words, "Well done." The believers who hear those words are Christ's *Metochoi*, His servant kings, who will one day serve with Him in the fulfillment of human destiny. As they rise to meet Him, they will participate in the "upward call" to a better kind of resurrection. In the next chapter we will discuss this glorious event.

65

The Upward Call

IT WAS AD 68, and he knew that the end had come. As he wasted away in a cold, unsanitary Roman prison, the apostle Paul reflected on his life, knowing that the final summons was near. He picked up his pen and wrote these memorable words.

> *For I am already being poured out as a drink offering, and the time of my departure has come. I have fought the good fight, I have finished the course, I have kept the faith; in the future there is laid up for me the crown of righteousness, which the Lord, the righteous Judge, will award to me on that day; and not only to me, but also to all who have loved His appearing (2 Timothy 4:6–8, NASB).*

Shortly after laying down his pen for the final time, the old warrior went to his death. He had been imprisoned with serious criminals in the Mammertine Prison, adjacent to the Roman Forum. It was an obnoxious dungeon, three meters underground and three meters by six meters long, reached only by a rope or ladder let through a hole in the floor above. Here, his body could only rest on rough stones. The air was foul and sanitation was nonexistent. It was cold and damp, and he was lonely.

In this squalid, wet, and isolated prison cell, the apostle Paul wrote, "I have fought the good fight, I have finished the course, I have kept the faith" (2 Timothy 4:7-8). Here in the Mammertine prison he spent his last days, triumphant in Christ. He was beheaded by Nero shortly after writing these words.

All his associates in Asia had deserted him. There were 26 exhortations in the epistle, and only one of them is repeated three times, "Come see me before winter." It is over. He has endured incredible hardship in the service of the gospel: he was beaten with rods, whipped, stoned, shipwrecked at sea for three days; he endured many all-night travels on cold dusty roads. Now this is what it has all come to, imprisonment and execution. Yet, he confidently asserts, "*I know whom I have believed and am persuaded that he is able to guard that which I have entrusted to him for that day.*" At the end he notes, "*I have fought a good fight, I have finished my course, I have kept the faith.*" The end had arrived. As the shadows lengthened, it appeared that his life work had come to nothing. Persecution was breaking out; the Christians were being imprisoned, and now their leader, unnoticed, deserted, and incarcerated in a lonely cell, was about to be beheaded. Yes, from a human perspective it was over for Paul. Rome had won!

According to Gaius, the Romans beheaded Paul with the sword. Eusebius places his death in 67; Jerome says 68. The persecutions of Nero began in 64. According to *The Acts of Paul*, he was sentenced to death for treason by the Roman senate. It occurred three miles from Rome near the Ostian Way in a little pinewood glade called The Three Fountains, which are said to have miraculously gushed forth from the blood of the apostolic martyr. They had marched him here the day before, and he spent the night in a tiny cell. If Luke was allowed to stay by his window or if Timothy and Mark had reached Rome in time, the sounds of the night vigil would not be those of weeping, but of singing. He himself said he was "sorrowful yet always rejoicing, and as dying and, behold, we live."

When the dawn came the soldiers took Paul to a pillar. The executioner stood ready, stark naked. The soldiers stripped Paul to the waist and tied him, kneeling upright, to the low pillar that left his neck free. He was beaten with rods as a prelude. Then, mercifully, the executioner's sword fell. A rich Roman lady named Lucina is said to have buried him on her land near the place of execution in a sand grave.

Here ends the final course of the greatest of the apostles and the greatest missionary in the history of the church. It was the heroic career of a warrior, who lived for serving his King and for winning others to obedient service for Him. He had labored more abundantly than them all, yet he sincerely believed himself to be "the least of the apostles." A few years earlier he had confessed, "I am the least of all the saints," and shortly before his death he wrote, "I am the chief of sinners." His humility grew as he learned more of God's grace and as he ripened for heaven.

Philip Schaff eulogizes the great apostle, saying, "Paul had passed through life as an insignificant player on Rome's pretentious stage. He died unnoticed by the mighty and wise of his age. Yet how infinitely more noble, beneficial and enduring was his life and work than the dazzling march of military conquerors like Alexander and Napoleon, who, prompted by ambition, absorbed millions of treasure and a myriad of lives only to die at last in a drunken fit at Babylon, or of a broken heart on the rocks of St. Helena. Their empires have long since crumbled to dust."[3227] Yet, that lonely old man had launched a movement that would change the course of history. Rome is no more!

Like the apostle Paul, one day all of us will receive a summons. We will be asked by the Lord Jesus to render an accounting for how we have invested our lives and opportunities.

[3227] Philip Schaff, *History of the Christian Church*, 8 vols. (Grand Rapids: Wm. B. Eerdmans Publishing Co., 1910), 1:331.

Those who have invested well will be honored; those who have not will suffer loss. In the New Testament this summons is variously described as a call to a better resurrection, the fullness of resurrection, or being counted worthy of the resurrection.

The Better Resurrection

> *Women received back their dead by resurrection; and others were tortured, not accepting their release, so that they might obtain a* ***better resurrection*** *(Hebrews 11:35).*

What is this "better" resurrection? Better than what? Most commentators see it as a contrast between the temporal resuscitation of verse 35a and the eschatological resurrection to eternal life. However, the requirement of enduring torture for obtaining this better resurrection is without parallel as a requirement for final entrance into heaven! Faithful saints were tortured and did not accept release "*in order that*" they might obtain this better resurrection.

The Greek for "to torture" is *tumpanizō*. It originally meant *to beat a drum.*[3228] Hence, *to beat, to cudgel.*[3229] In this form of torture, a person was stretched out on a rack, and then his taut stomach was beaten as one beats a drum until the muscle-walls collapsed and death occurred from internal injuries. From this practice the verb came to mean "to break on a wheel."[3230]

Yet, rather than recanting their faith (which would have secured their release), they remained faithful to God at the cost of their own lives. As a result, "in this resurrection to come, they were consoled in knowing that God would reward them for having suffered for their faith."[3231] The better experience refers to a better experience in their resurrection and rewards honoring their faithfulness. To believe that this better resurrection is simply a resurrection unto final salvation flies in the face of the entire New Testament witness that salvation is obtained by faith alone, plus nothing else. Enduring torture is not a condition for entrance into heaven when one dies. Furthermore, are we to believe that anyone who caves in under such torture is abandoned to the lake of fire?!

Instead, this better resurrection is the reward to the martyrs, the crown of life of which James speaks (James 1:12). This resurrection is "better" because it involves not just eschatological raising to life, but final reward and hearing the Master say, "Well done!" This is better because it involves a higher status and not because it is a final resurrection in contrast to a temporal resuscitation. In fact, the Greek for "better," *kreittōn*, can carry this sense of "pertaining to having a higher status in comparison to something else"[3232] or "being of high status, *more prominent, higher in rank*"[3233] (cf. Hebrews 1:4, 7:7).

This is the same resurrection the apostle Paul desired in Philippians 3:11.

3228 "torture" in Vine, 2:145.

3229 Vincent, Word Studies in the New Testament, 4:533.

3230 William L. Lane, *Hebrews 9-13*, Word Biblical Commentary (Dallas: Word, Inc., 2002), 238.

3231 Tanner, "Hebrews," 1085.

3232 Louw-Nida, 1:736.

3233 BDAG, 566.

The Fullness of Resurrection Life

In one of the most personal and motivating passages in the New Testament, the great apostle to the Gentiles lays bare his heart:

> *That I may know Him and the power of His resurrection and the fellowship of His sufferings, being conformed to His death; if perhaps I may attain to the resurrection from the dead (Philippians 3:10-11, author's translation).*

The overall thrust of Philippians 3:7-10 is that Paul's supreme goal in life is to know Christ more intimately, to know the power of Christ in his life, and to share in Christ's sufferings. He wants this so that "if perhaps" he might "attain" to the "resurrection" from the dead. At first glance, the text seems to say that Paul is striving to arrive at the inevitable, that is, entrance into heaven, when he dies. The apostle seems to say that he feels that there is something uncertain about his attaining to the resurrection.

COUNTING ALL THINGS LOSS

Paul begins with a decision he made at the time of his conversion on the Damascus Road, which was confirmed a few days later when he received his divine commission and was baptized (Acts 9:15-18).

> *But whatever things were gain to me, those things I have counted as loss for the sake of Christ (Philippians 3:7).*

Formerly, he had trusted in heritage, position, and education, as the means for living life under the Old Covenant and for obtaining justification. But there came a time when he realized that was nothing but loss, so he jettisoned all of it and trusted in Christ.[3234] A few days later he embraced his life mission and was baptized.

> *More than that, I count all things to be loss in view of the surpassing value of knowing Christ Jesus my Lord, for whom I have suffered the loss of all things, and count them but rubbish so that I may gain Christ (Philippians 3:8).*

From that dramatic point on the Damascus Road up to the present day, he says, "I count all things to be loss."[3235] This is something the rich young ruler refused to do.[3236] Paul continues to count any personal advantage or human achievement as "rubbish"[3237] in comparison with the value of knowing Christ.

Paul may have his Lord's teaching in mind.[3238]

> *For what will it profit a man if he gains the whole world and forfeits his soul? Or what will a man give in exchange for his soul? (Matthew 16:26).*

[3234] The phrase "I have counted as loss" is in the perfect tense in Gr and suggests a decisive event that occurred in past time but that has a present reality.

[3235] He switches to the Greek present tense to emphasize that the decision he made years ago still characterizes his attitude today.

[3236] See discussion elsewhere in this book in volume 1, chapter 24.

[3237] The Greek means "dung" or unspeakable filth, "human excrement." LSJ, 1616; BDAG, 932.

[3238] For discussion of the "salvation of a soul," see pp. 201 ff..

What does Paul mean in Philippians 3:8 by "knowing Christ Jesus"? This knowledge (Gr *ginōskō*) probably speaks of his current intimacy, not his initial reception of eternal life. He refers to the ongoing development of fellowship with Christ. This "Hebrew of the Hebrews" is no doubt thinking in Old Testament terms where "knowing" God meant experiencing close fellowship with Him.[3239]

When Paul speaks of "sharing in his sufferings," this recalls his exposition of this theme elsewhere where he said that the outcome of suffering with Christ is reward. Believers will be, he says, "*fellow heirs with Christ if indeed we suffer with Him so that we may also be glorified with Him*" (Romans 8:17). And to Timothy he said, "*If we endure, we will also reign with Him*" (2 Timothy 2:12). The inheritance/reward and reigning with Him are contingent on perseverance. Believers are therefore alerted at the outset that this passage is about rewards in heaven and not about entrance into heaven.

GAINING CHRIST

Paul wrote,

In order that I may gain Christ (Philippians 3:8).

He continues by saying that he has "suffered the loss of all things" and "counts them as rubbish" for two purposes: (1) that he might "gain Christ," and that (2) "he may be found in Him."

But what does it mean to "gain Christ," that is to "earn" (Gr *kerdainō*) Christ?[3240] This is not a word Paul would have used to describe gaining Christ in the sense of finding salvation. Since he already has gained Christ in a saving sense, most commentators understand this to mean that he desires to gain more of Christ, to experience Him more richly.[3241]

BEING FOUND IN HIM

And may be found in Him (Philippians 3:9).

Paul not only wanted to gain Christ; he also wanted to be "found in Him." Often, this word "being found" is used in the sense of "being seen, discovered, or proved to be."[3242] This is how it is used in Philippians 2:8, where Paul says that Christ "was found in human form." This means that any human observer would have looked at Christ and concluded He is a man. Similarly, Paul wants whoever looks at him to see a man in fellowship with Christ.[3243] He wants to "be found" living Christ's way of life, that is "in Him" or "in fellowship with Him."

3239 Cf. Hosea 6:6; 4:1, 6. Vriezen describes it as "living in a close relationship with something or somebody, such a relationship as to cause what may be called communion." T. C. Vriezen, *Outlines of Old Testament Theology*, 129.

3240 Louw-Nida, 1:578; BDAG, 541.

3241 Peter T. O'Brien, *The Epistle to the Philippians: A Commentary on the Greek Text*, The New International Greek Testament Commentary (Grand Rapids: Wm. B. Eerdmans Publishing Co., 1991), 391.

3242 Marvin R. Vincent, *A Critical and Exegetical Commentary on the Epistles to the Philippians and Philemon*, International Critical Commentary (Edinburgh: T. & T. Clark, 1897), 101. See Acts 5:39; Romans 7:10; 1 Corinthians 4:2; 2 Corinthians 11:12; Galatians 2:17.

3243 This is suggested by Alec Motyer, *The Message of Philippians* (Downers Grove, IL: InterVarsity Press, 1984), 164.

The thought is similar to 1 Corinthians 4:2-5. In verse 2, Paul speaks of his desire as a servant to "be *found* faithful,"[3244] using the same Greek word, and in the sense of "proven to be" or "shown to be." He wants to ensure that throughout his life and up to the final day when he meets his King at the Judgment Seat of Christ, he will be found to be in close communion with Christ[3245] and fully prepared to meet his King. Unlike the five foolish virgins[3246] (Matthew 25:1-13), he wants to be prepared. This supreme goal can be realized only "if he is continuously and progressively living in him [in close fellowship] during this mortal existence."[3247]

THE PERFECT RIGHTEOUSNESS

Not having a righteousness of my own derived from the Law, but that which is through faith in Christ, the righteousness which comes from God on the basis of faith (Philippians 3:9).

But all this effort to gain Christ and to be found in Him must be clarified. Paul knows that the ethical righteousness which was possible by keeping the Old Testament Law is no longer valid. He speaks of "not having a righteousness of my own derived from the law." The only kind of righteousness which could be derived from the law was ethical righteousness. It could not provide right standing before God, that is, forensic justification. As discussed previously, the purpose of the Law was a guide to ethical living. It was related to sanctification and not justification.[3248] Paul had abandoned the law way of life with its legalisms and externalisms. It did not work for him. He will stand on the basis of judicial righteousness imputed to him through faith in Christ.

All his efforts continually to count all things loss, striving to gain Christ, and to be found in intimate union with Him do not contribute in any way to any personal saving righteousness or ground for claiming an entrance into heaven. In this verse, Paul is reverting back to what he said in verse 7 when he spoke of having counted all things loss (perfect tense). That transfer of trust from his heritage to Christ, and that alone, is all that gives him a right to be at the Judgment Seat of Christ. At that moment, when he responded in faith, the righteousness of God was freely granted to him. That righteousness is the basis of his eternal security and confidence that he will never be cast out.

PAUL'S UNCERTAINTY

In order that I may attain to the resurrection (Gr *exanastasis*) *from the dead (Philippians 3:11).*

However, even though his eternal destiny is assured based on these certainties, beginning in verse 11, the passage strikes a note of uncertainty by opening with the Gr *ei pōs* which means "if perhaps, if somehow."[3249] Does this mean that he is uncertain ("if

---

3244 The Greek construction is ἵνα πιστός τις εὑρεθῇ (the verb is an aorist passive).

3245 To be "found" in Christ means to be executing the ministry Christ has given him (Colossians 4:17); to be hospitable (Philippians 2:29); to live in harmony (Philippians 4:2); to obey one's parents if you are a child (Ephesians 6:10); to find one's strength in Him (Ephesians 6:10).

3246 See chapter 51 above.

3247 O'Brien, *The Epistle to the Philippians: A Commentary on the Greek Text*, 392.

3248 See discussion in chapter 13.

3249 O'Brien, *The Epistle to the Philippians: A Commentary on the Greek Text*, 411. The phrase is incorrectly

perhaps") about whether or not he will arrive at the resurrection?[3250] If "the resurrection" refers to his final arrival in heaven, the impossible conclusion is that Paul is not sure he will be saved. If the latter translation ("if somehow") is correct, then he is uncertain about the *means of arrival*, that is, whether by life or death.[3251]

Vincent, who holds that Paul is uncertain about his arrival in heaven suggests,

> *On the human side, the attainment of the goal may be regarded as doubtful, or at least conditioned upon humble self-estimate, on the side of the working of divine grace it appears certain.*[3252]

However, Paul has asserted elsewhere that he has no doubt ("on the human side") about his own eternal destiny, and to cast doubt on that fact here contradicts the note of certainty in verse 9 and what he has said in Philippians 1:23, as well as his other statements which say that baptism into Christ is a foretaste of the final resurrection.[3253]

That view would also flatly contradict what Paul said in 2 Corinthians 4:14: "Because **we know** that the one who raised the Lord Jesus from the dead **will also raise us** with Jesus and present us with you in his presence."[3254]

Carson correctly asks, "Does not attaining to the resurrection depend on faith alone? Could the apostle be in doubt about his final salvation?"[3255] But Carson then brings his Reformed theology in and says, "Faith must endure to the end." However, nothing in the text suggests this.

---

translated in some translations as "in order that." Cf. BDAG, 278. It expresses uncertainty: *ei pōs* is found four times in the New Testament: Acts 27:12; Romans 1:10; 11:14; Philippians 3:11, and it occurs in the LXX in Jeremiah 28:8 (51:8 Eng and Heb).

3250 Johnson says, "There are several things which point definitely to doubt in the passage. In the first place, the usage of *ei pōs* elsewhere points to this. The two words are found in Acts 27:12, Romans 1:10; 11:14. In each of the occurrences doubt is expressed. In the second place, while the verb katantēsō here can be a future indicative, it probably is an aorist subjunctive." S. Lewis Johnson, "The Out-Resurrection from the Dead," *BibSac* 110, no. 438 (April-June 1953): 141.

3251 See Acts 27:12; Romans 1:10; 11:14; and Philippians 3:11. In the Romans passage it refers to uncertainty about the outcome, i.e., "if perhaps." In Acts it could be rendered "if somehow" to express uncertainty about the means of arrival, which would fit with the idea that Paul's uncertainty in Philippians 3:11 is uncertainty about the route to arrival to the resurrection (KJV, NASB). However, in this passage it can just as easily be translated "if perhaps" (New Century "They hoped"; TNIV [Acts 27:12], "hoping to reach", Darby, "if perhaps", ESV, "on the chance"; GNT, "if possible," Holman, "hoping somehow"; NAB, "in the hope of"). Judith M. Gundry Volf asserts, "That the other instances of *ei pōs* do not suggest that an element of doubt is inherent to the construction. Rather, it simply communicates hope or expectancy." Gundry Volf, *Paul and Perseverance*, 257. However, the other instances clearly do imply uncertainty. Volf gives no proof, only assertion. For example, Paul was definitely uncertain as to whether he would make it to Rome in Romans 1:10 (cf. 15:31). Volf then commits the illegitimate totality transfer and attempts to import the idea of God's enablement into the *ei pōs* construction, thus supposedly guaranteeing the certainty of the outcome. But God's enablement is purely a theological idea and is in no way inherent in the phrase. While it is true that Paul must consciously depend on God for the attainment of the goal of arrival at Rome, this in no way implies that he will successfully continue to depend. Thus, his arrival clearly has a degree of uncertainty! There is nothing in Romans 11:14 to remove the notion of uncertainty. The fact that Paul wants to move his countrymen to jealousy by God's enablement in no way implies that this will certainly happen or that he expects it to happen. Hope and desire are not the same as certainty. In fact, it did not happen, as the judgment of AD 70 proves.

3252 Vincent, *A Critical and Exegetical Commentary on the Epistles to the Philippians and Philemon*, 106.

3253 Romans 6:5; 2 Corinthians 4:14; Ephesians 2:6; Colossians 2:12.

3254 The resurrection is presented as the certain hope of the Christian elsewhere in the New Testament, cf. 1 Corinthians 15:20 and 2 Corinthians 5:1.

3255 Foulkes, "Philippians," s.v. "Philippians 3:8".

Experimental Predestinarian interpretation of this passage extracts a heavy toll on the emotional life of a believer. One of their commentators puts it this way:

> *He was willing to do anything, or suffer anything, that he might attain that resurrection [i.e. obtain final entrance into heaven]. The hope and prospect of it carried him with so much courage and constancy through all the difficulties he met with in his work. He speaks as if they were in danger of missing it, and coming short of it. A holy fear of coming short [i.e. going to hell] is an excellent means of perseverance.*[3256]

In this view the "resurrection" is to be worked for; Paul might not attain to it; and it refers to final salvation, and for a person to wonder whether he will go to the lake of fire is supposedly a "holy fear" that he might go to the lake of fire if he fails!

Others view the expression "if perhaps" as a statement of humility, without reflecting any doubt.[3257] However, the words *do* reflect real doubt *and* humility. The thought is perfectly parallel to 1 Corinthians 4:4-5.

> *For I am conscious of nothing against myself, yet I am not by this acquitted; but the one who examines me is the Lord. Therefore do not go on passing judgment before the time. . .*

The issue for Paul in 1 Corinthians 4 is not his eternal destiny. Instead, it is uncertainty regarding how the Lord will find him at the last day (cf. 4:2, "be found faithful" = "be found in him" in Philippians 3:9).

Perhaps the viewpoint most widely accepted by contemporary scholars is that the uncertainty refers not to the obtaining of the resurrection but to the "*way or route by which the apostle will reach it,*" such as martyrdom, some other kind of death, or the rapture (Philippians 1:20–26). "The resurrection is certain," O'Brien says, but "the intervening events are uncertain."[3258] Paul does not know whether he will attain to the resurrection by rapture while living, or by the resurrection at the last day. Thus, by "any means" refers to by life or death, perhaps, martyrdom.[3259]

This view is widely held and may be correct. However, this view labors under the burden of importing martyrdom, death, or rapture into the passage as the route of arrival, whereas the passage tells what the route is, namely, daily conformity to His death. In various ways he expounds this theme:

- counting all things as loss for Christ
- gaining more personal experience of Christ ("gain Christ")
- pursuing intimacy with Him ("be found in Him")
- enduring faithfully to the end of life ("I press on")
- increasing fellowship ("that I may know Him")

3256 Matthew Henry, "Matthew," in *Matthew Henry's Commentary on the Whole Bible* (Peabody, MA: Hendrickson Publishers, 1996), s.v. "Philippians 3:9".

3257 Foulkes, "Philippians," s.v. "Philippians 3:11". See also Hawthorne, *Philippians*, 200.

3258 Peter T. O'Brien, *The Epistle to the Philippians: A Commentary on the Greek Text* (Grand Rapids: Wm. B. Eerdmans Publishing Co., 1991), 412.

3259 S. Lewis Johnson believes that the out-resurrection is the rapture of the church and that Paul's only doubt is whether or not he will attain to it while he is still living or in the future resurrection. "His great hope is to be alive at the time of the resurrection and arise into the Lord's presence a complete victor over death." Johnson, "The Out-Resurrection from the Dead," 144.

- experiencing His power in the midst of suffering ("the power of His resurrection, and the fellowship of His sufferings")
- dying daily to the power of sin ("being conformed to His death"),
- striving for the reward ("I press toward the goal of the prize")

All these thoughts are obviously parallel. If one is to arrive at the resurrection, these thoughts explain one another and imply work done and persistent faith to the end of life. The route to the resurrection is by means of the items above, not by martyrdom or death.

Most interpreters correctly associate the phrase "if perhaps" with the preceding phrase "fellowship of his sufferings, being conformable to his death."[3260] The theme of fellowship with His sufferings is often linked in Scripture with reward (Romans 8:17; 2 Timothy 2:12). Being conformed to His death is usually thought to refer to sanctification, with the sequence of knowing, reckoning, and yielding in view, as stated in Romans 6. Thus, attaining to this kind of resurrection (Gr *exanastasis*) is achieved through the route of sanctification, not death.

To what, then, does this uncertainty refer? Paul makes his participation in the resurrection contingent on a process currently going on in his life on earth, namely, his being conformed to Christ's death, that is, sanctification. Some have suggested, based on the experiential emphasis of the preceding context, that this refers to "the present life of identification with Christ in His Resurrection,"[3261] in other words, "resurrection to a rich and enhanced experience of life now." The uncertainty then is not about arriving in heaven but about obtaining a rich walk with Christ now. S. Lewis Johnson responds, "This explanation cannot account for the change from *anastasis* (v. 10) [resurrection] to *exanastasis* (v. 11) [out resurrection]. The apostle must have had a purpose for this change. It is a wonderful fact that believers are identified with Christ in His resurrection; there is no uncertainty about this at all. This identification comes by grace at the point of regeneration."[3262]

THE FULLNESS OF RESURRECTION LIFE

> *In order that I may attain to* ***the resurrection*** **(Gr** ***exanastasis*****)** ***from the dead*** *(Philippians 3:11).*

The uncertainty to which Paul refers in Philippians 3:11 is whether or not he will attain to the resurrection (Gr *exanastasis*). He will explain in v. 14 that this resurrection is a prize to be obtained, a reward to be merited. But why would Paul use the word "resurrection" in the sense of a prize to be obtained, a reward to be merited? The answer may lie in the fact that Paul departs from the usual word for resurrection, *anastasis,* and uses a unique word, *exanastasis.* This is the only time this word for resurrection is used in the Greek Bibles (LXX and New Testament); it is never found in the Pseudepigrapha, and it occurs in Josephus only one time. This word for resurrection adds the prefix preposition *ek*, making it a compound word. Current scholarship is almost in unanimous agreement

---

3260 O'Brien, *The Epistle to the Philippians: A Commentary on the Greek Text*, 411. Vincent, *A Critical and Exegetical Commentary on the Epistles to the Philippians and Philemon*, 106.

3261 Vine, 87.

3262 Johnson, "The Out-Resurrection from the Dead," 142-43.

that the two words are virtually synonyms.[3263] However, O'Brien argues that "the presence of the preposition ἐκ, argues against such an equivalence."[3264] What is the distinction?

There is an obscure usage of *exanastasis* in the second century AD where it is translated "ornament" in the sense of enhancing the beauty of something.[3265] While it would be precarious to read that single instance into a first-century document, it does suggest that the word in the first century could mean something besides a general resurrection from the dead[3266] and might imply a more glorious resurrection adorned with honor and praise at the Judgment Seat of Christ (1 Corinthians 9:25).

Danker distinguishes this word, *exanastasis*, from the normal word, *anastasis*, by saying, "The compound in contrast to the simple ἀνάστασις that precedes connotes a coming to fullness of life."[3267] Rather than use the word "life," why not use Paul's word, "resurrection"? Kenneth Mitchell has suggested that it be translated "fullness of resurrection." He suggests this meaning based on the correct thesis that the prefix *ek* often intensifies the sense of the noun or verb to which it is prefixed.[3268] Because the kingdom age is sometimes referred to as "the resurrection" (e.g., Luke 20:33), it is possible that by "resurrection" Paul simply means the kingdom age and the *ek-resurrection* is the fullness of that experience. He wants a full experience of the kingdom. He not only wants to be in the kingdom; he also wants to "recline at the table" with Abraham, Isaac, Jacob, and all the prophets (Luke 13:29). He desires the maximum experience of resurrection at the Judgment Seat of Christ. Michael Eaton concurs with Mitchell, saying, "Philippians 3 is concerned not simply with justification but with ... reaching the *exanastasis, receiving the prize for one's labors.*"[3269]

In favor of this interpretation the following context associates this resurrection with obtaining the "prize" (Gr *brabeion*, v. 14) and declares that strenuous effort, not death or martyrdom, is necessary to obtain it. Therefore, this "full" resurrection is the reward of hearing the Master's "Well done!" The "out-resurrection" and the "prize" (v. 14) appear to be the same thing. The "fullness of resurrection" includes not only the notion of physical glorification but also the promise of the "prize" to those who are "found in Him." Kenneth Mitchell summarizes this nicely.[3270]

3263 Rather than accept that the word means something different than *anastasis*, Kremer lamely says, "Rather it [*exanastasis*] gives special emphasis to the reality of the resurrection as redemption from the realm of death (more likely as a defense against enthusiasts)." Kremer, EDNT, 1:90. This appears to explain the prefix *ek* by not explaining anything!

3264 Gary Strauss and Carol Memmott, "Wallace's death marks end of old-school era," *USA Today* April 4, 2012. O'Brien suggests the translation "out from among the dead ones." He denies that this resurrection is a reward. O'Brien, *The Epistle to the Philippians: A Commentary on the Greek Text*, 414.

3265 LSJ, 584.

3266 Evidently the word *anastasis* does not always refer to a physical resurrection either. See Luke 2:34.

3267 BDAG, 345. Michael agrees, "But as the two forms occur in such close propinquity it is probable that there is some significance in the change of word." See John Hugh Michael, *The Epistle of Paul to the Philippians*, The Moffatt New Testament commentary (Garden City, NY: Doubleday, Doran & Company, Inc., 1929), 154. Cited by Johnson, "The Out-Resurrection from the Dead," 142.

3268 For example, δέχομαι, "receive" and ἐκδέχομαι, "wait for," δίδωμι, "to give or donate," and ἐκδίδωμι, "to let out for hire, lease," διώκω, "to harass," and ἐκδιώκω, "to persecute," καθαίρω, "to clean," and ἐκκαθαίρω, "to clean out or cleanse," θαυμάζω, "to marvel," and ἐκθαυμάζω, "to wonder greatly."

3269 Eaton, *No Condemnation: A New Theology of Assurance*, 119.

3270 Dr. Kenneth Mitchell, Pastor, Westside Christian Family Chapel. Jacksonville, FL, personal communication, September 14, 2006.

The resurrection (Gr anastasis) is assured to all believers. What Paul is seeking and working for is the ekanastasis, the full resurrection. This is the prize/reward of the games that is awarded by the judge. It is his reward for faithful service. The reward is ekanastasis, not just resurrection, but "full resurrection," a fuller experience of resurrection life. This is the same as the "better resurrection" of Hebrews 11 and the abundant entrance of 2 Peter 1:11.[3271]

In the following verse Paul speaks of "obtaining" this resurrection.

Not that I have already obtained [Gr katalambanō] all this, or have already been made perfect, but I press on to take hold of that for which Jesus took hold of me (Philippians 3:12).

Obtained what? The reference is obviously to the resurrection mentioned in the preceding verse. It makes no sense to raise the issue of whether he has already obtained physical glorification (*anastasis*). Obviously, he has not. This suggests that he is not thinking of the resurrection in that sense; rather, he is thinking of it as the time when he may or may not be found faithful (1 Corinthians 4:2, or "found in fellowship with him," Philippians 3:9) at the Judgment Seat of Christ (Gr *exanastasis,* "out-resurrection"). Indeed, he clarifies his meaning with the very next phrase "have already been made perfect," or better, "have already arrived at the goal." What is that goal? "The fullness of resurrection life."

Christ has taken hold of the believers for a purpose, to attain to this resurrection/ reward. Athletic imagery of rewards in the games is evident. Paul pictures this goal as a prize to be won. The word *katalambanō*, "obtain," is found in 1 Corinthians 9:24, where it is used for the striving of the athlete to obtain the prize in the Isthmian games.[3272] What is this "prize"?

THE PRIZE

Brothers, I do not consider myself yet to have taken hold of it. But one thing I do: Forgetting what is behind and straining [Gr epekteinomai] toward what is ahead, I press on toward the goal to win the ***prize*** *[Gr brabeion] for which God has called me heavenward in Christ Jesus (Philippians 3:13-14).*

The use of the Gr word *brabeion* is significant. It signifies the victor's prize in an athletic contest, something earned.[3273] In secular Greek it was used "of the completion and crown of life's work."[3274] Paul says that he is "straining forward" toward the "goal" (Gr *skopos*). The word "goal" refers to the finish line in the race on which the athlete in the games fixes his gaze.[3275] Metaphorically here, it refers to the goal or marker that controls one's life. Paul's point is that his pressing on is not aimless, but purposeful. What is that goal? It is "*the prize of the upward call of God in Christ Jesus.*"

[3271] In view of the evidence cited above it is surprising that S. Lewis Johnson says of this interpretation, "There is nothing in its favor," Johnson, "The Out-Resurrection from the Dead," 143.

[3272] For discussion of the Hellenic games, see p. 969.

[3273] BAGD, 146. O'Brien, *The Epistle to the Philippians: A Commentary on the Greek Text*, 430.

[3274] Ethelbert Stauffer, "*brabeion,*" in TDNT, 1:368.

[3275] O'Brien, *The Epistle to the Philippians: A Commentary on the Greek Text*, 429.

The prize is a reward to be won. The *brabeion* ("prize") in verse 14 is a full or complete experience of the resurrection (the *exanastasis*).[3276] Because he is specifying a particular aspect or kind of resurrection in v. 11, Paul uses the word *exanastis* instead of *anastasis.*

The same word "prize" is used in 1 Corinthians 9:24, "*Do you not know that those who run in a race all run, but only one receives the prize?* [Gr *brabeion*]. Run in such a way that you may win." The similarity of the two contexts (1 Corinthians 9:24-27 and Philippians 3:14) suggests that similar ideas are in view. If so, then the prize in Philippians 3:14 is the reward received by the faithful believer when he finishes his race.

This prize cannot be heaven itself because Paul and his "brothers" have already been promised that they will finally enter heaven, and they have already passed into that life that is eternal (John 5:24). But here, we have Paul describing something for which there is a continued need to obtain. Heaven is not a prize for our effort but a gift in response to our faith.[3277] The goal Paul seeks to take hold of is obtained by "straining" (Gr *epekteinomai*), not by faith.[3278] This is a metaphor for the foot race,[3279] picturing the runner stretching forward with his chest or chin, straining with all his might toward the tape. One might think of the modern-day expression, "the home stretch." If the Experimental Predestinarians were correct, this would be a novel way of obtaining heaven!

Tertullian, however, did just that, and he linked the verse with a works salvation when he said the passage refers to "that judgment which we shall have to undergo as the recompense *of our deeds*."[3280] Nevertheless, though his soteriology was confused, he did recognize that the passage is about rewards for a faithful life. Clement of Rome understood the "prize of the upward call" as the "victor's crown."[3281] Athanasius understood this as a reward for martyrdom.[3282]

3276 I owe this suggestion to Dr. Kenneth R. Mitchell, Pastor, Westside Christian Family Chapel, Jacksonville, FL, personal communication, September 13, 2006.

3277 Experimental Predestinarian Ralph Martin attempts to explain away the predicament that his works salvation view imposes on the passages. He says, "The notion of merit is entirely excluded by the reminder that God's enabling call and persevering grace are required before the race can be completed." Ralph P. Martin, *Philippians* (London: Tyndale Press, 1959), 154. There is simply no logic to the statement that because God enables, there is no merit. A person must chose to accept that enablement and the Bible everywhere says he will merit reward, *misthos*, for doing so. The whole point of the context is that there is merit, a *brabeion*, a reward in the games.

3278 The verb literally means "to stretch out, strain" (BAGD, 284).

3279 VEDNTW, 2:604.

3280 Tertullian, "On the Resurrection of the Flesh," in *The Ante-Nicene Fathers Vol. III : Translations of the Writings of the Fathers Down to A.D. 325, Latin Christianity: Its Founder, Tertullian*, ed. Alexander Roberts, James Donaldson, and A. Cleveland Coxe (Oak Harbor, WA: Logos Research Systems, 1997), chapter 23, 155, p. 562.

3281 Clement, "The First Epistle of Clement to the Corinthians," in *The Ante-Nicene Fathers: Volume 1: The Apostolic Fathers with Justin Martyr and Irenaeus*, ed. J Roberts, J. Donaldson, and A. C. Coxe (Buffalo, NY: Christian Literature Company, 1885), chapter 5, 43-44. He says that this is the reward for striving for virginity!

3282 Athanasius says, "For thither, as He called the disciples to the upper chamber, so does the Word call us with them to the divine and incorruptible banquet; having suffered for us here, but there, preparing the heavenly tabernacles **for those who most readily hearken to the summons, and unceasingly, and [gazing] at the goal, pursue the prize of their high calling**; where for them who come to the banquet, and strive with those who hinder them, **there is laid up both a crown, and incorruptible joy**. For even though, humanly speaking, the labour of such a journey is great, yet the Saviour Himself has rendered even it light and kindly." See Athanasius, "Festal Letters," in *A Select Library of the Nicene and Post-Nicene Fathers of the Christian*

THE SUMMONS

I press on toward the goal for the prize of ***the upward call*** *of God in Christ Jesus (Philippians 3:14).*

What is the "upward call"? The precise content of the *brabeion* is said to be "*the upward call of God in Christ Jesus.*"

Chrysostom first suggested that the prize of the upward call refers to rewards, not salvation. He noted that the "prizes are not equal," and that "*the most honored of the wrestlers and charioteers are not crowned in the course below, but the king* ***calls them up*** *and crowns them there. Thus too is it here, in heaven thou receivest the prize.*"[3283] This prize is not heaven, but it is received there. Chrysostom views the "upward call" as the summons by the officials at the games to receive the victor's reward.

This is the judgment seat at Philippi. The arrow points to the victor's platform. When it became time to reward the athlete for his victory, the judges called him up to this platform to reward him. This is the "upward call" to which Paul refers in Philippians 3:14.

The phrase "upward call" is taken directly from the games. The phrase could be translated "the prize *that is* the upward call of God in Christ Jesus."[3284] If the athlete was victorious, he received an "upward call," from the king or presiding officials, a summons to the victory platform, to receive his prize from their hands. This is not a call to salvation, but to receive reward.[3285] This upward call is the out-resurrection. F. F. Bruce notes, "On

Church, Second Series, Volume 4: St. Athanasius: Select Works and Letters, ed. P. Schaff and H. Wace (Buffalo, NY: Christian Literature Company, 1982), Letter 28, p. 550.

3283 Chrysostom, Homilies on the Epistle of St. Paul to the Philippians, 12. This view is shared by Hawthorne, "In keeping with the vivid imagery drawn from the Greek games that pervades this section," he says that the "upward call" is "an allusion to the fact that the Olympian games, originally foot-races, were organized and presided over by the ἀγωνοθέτης, 'judge,' and highly respected officers called Ἑλλανοδίκαι, 'chief judges' [and] after each event they had a herald announce the name of the victor, his father's name and his country, and the athlete or charioteer would come and receive a palm branch at their hands." Hawthorne, *Philippians*, 210.

3284 In Wallace's categories the phrase "of the upward call of God" may be a genitive of apposition, clarifying that the upward call is a part or an aspect of the *brabeion* (Wallace, *Greek Grammar Beyond the Basics*, 95).

3285 In a glaring example of an illegitimate totality transfer, O'Brien says that the call "can be understood in its customary Pauline sense of the divine calling to salvation, particularly the initial summons. He rejects the view of F. F. Bruce and the view adopted above by saying, "This view assumes that Paul has continued the athletic imagery with his use of κλῆσις, that its meaning is to be determined from the wider games context

special occasions in Rome this call might come from the emperor himself; how proudly the successful athlete would obey the summons and step up to the imperial box to accept the award."[3286] Thus, the upward call is limited to those Christians who are to be rewarded.

Star Differs from Star in Glory

The interpretation suggested here says that the general resurrection to life consists of two parts: (a) the select resurrection of the faithful believers (*exanastasis*) as part of (b) the general resurrection to life of all (*anastasis*). As Paul put it elsewhere,

> *There is one glory of the sun, and another glory of the moon, and another glory of the stars; for star differs from star in glory.* ***So also is the resurrection*** (Gr *anastasis*) ***of the dead*** *(1 Corinthians 15:41-42).*

While the main thrust of this passage is clearly the contrast between the earthly and the heavenly bodies, it appears that Paul also alludes to the fact that there are various degrees of glory of the resurrection body: "*star differs from star in glory.*" Calvin overstates his case when he says that this "has nothing to do with Paul's object. For he is not arguing as to what difference of condition there will be among the saints after the resurrection, but in what respect our bodies at present differ from those that we will one day receive."[3287] The fact that differences in reward among saints are not part of Paul's *central thrust* may be true, but this does not negate the notion of degrees of glory among saints as well. We agree with Godet, who, while holding Calvin's view, nevertheless insists that "we need not deny the possibility of a purely secondary allusion, to the diversity which God may be pleased to make between the bodies of the risen."[3288]

Godet's view was common among the church fathers as well.[3289] Chrysostom, for example, commenting on this verse said, "*Although they be all in God's kingdom, all shall not enjoy the same reward.*"[3290] Luther agreed saying, there are "*various differences in yonder*

rather than customary Pauline usage." O'Brien, *The Epistle to the Philippians: A Commentary on the Greek Text*, 432. In other words, he is taking a nuance in another context, reading it into the word, and bringing it into Philippians 3, even though by his own admission Philippians 3 discusses the athletic games and not the Damascus Road!

[3286] F. F. Bruce, *Philippians*, A Good News Commentary (San Francisco: Harper & Row, 1983), 96.

[3287] Calvin, *1 Corinthians*, s.v. "1 Corinthians 15:41".

[3288] Godet, *Commentary on First Corinthians*, 838.

[3289] For example Hermas, "The Pastor of Hermas," in *The Anti-Nicene Fathers: Volume II: Fathers of the Second Century: Hermas, Tatian, Athenagoras, Theophilis, and Clement of Alexandria*, ed. A. Roberts, et al. (Buffalo, NY: Christian Literature Company, 1885), Book 3, similitudes 9, chapter 28, p. 52. John Chrysostom, "Homilies on Romans," in *Nicene and Post-Nicene Fathers, First Series*, ed. Philip Schaff (Oak Harbor: Logos Research Systems, 1997), 31. Augustine, "A Treatise on the Spirit and the Letter," in *A Select Library of the Nicene and Post-Nicene Fathers of the Christian Church, First Series, Volume V: Saint Augustin: Anti-Pelagian Writings*, ed. Philip Schaff (Buffalo, NY: Christian Literature Company, 1987), chapter 48, p. 103. Ambrose, "Selections from the Letters of Ambrose: Letter 22," in *A Select Library of the Nicene and Post-Nicene Fathers of the Christian Church, Second Series, Volume X: St. Ambrose: Select Works and Letters*, ed. Philip Schaff and H. Wace (Buffalo, NY: Christian Literature Company, 1986), 436. Tertullian says, "Then at last, having conclusively shown by his examples that the difference was one of glory, not of substance, he adds: 'So also is the resurrection of the dead.' How so? In no other way than as differing in glory only," Tertullian, "On the Resurrection of the Flesh," Chapter 52, p. 586.

[3290] Chrysostom, "Homilies on First Corinthians," Homily 41:41, p. 251.

life. Each body will have its own peculiar clarity; each member will have its own peculiar glory."[3291] Many modern interpreters have understood the phrase "star differs from star in glory," as differences in glory among resurrected saints. Robertson, for example, notes, "*It is legitimate to apply these differences in the heavenly bodies to possible differences in the glories of the risen saints, and it is not impossible that the Apostle had this thought in his mind.*"[3292]

Adam Clarke suggests that "the bodies of the dead, though all immortal, shall possess different degrees of *splendor* and *glory*, according to the state of holiness in which their respective souls were found."[3293] This suggests that all believers, faithful and unfaithful, will not stand alike after the resurrection. This is what Paul means when he says that he hopes to attain to a "full resurrection." He hopes to earn a place among that special class of resurrected saints who have been faithful to their Master to the final hour. He wants to be not just "in the kingdom" but "at the table."

Those who strive toward that goal will rule and have dominion (Hebrews 2:5-10). Paul says that he has made it his goal to take hold of the same thing. In other words, he wants to make it his purpose in life to achieve Christlikeness and as a result to share with Christ in that final victory, thus obtaining that special crown reserved for those who have loved "His appearing" (2 Timothy 4:8).

Counted Worthy of the Kingdom

All Christians will experience the resurrection, but only some will be worthy of it. To be worthy of the resurrection and to "attain to the fullness of resurrection" seem to be parallel concepts and explain one another.

This theme is expressed elsewhere by our Lord:

> *But those who are considered worthy to attain to that age and the resurrection from the dead, neither marry nor are given in marriage (Luke 20:35).*

Being considered worthy of the kingdom of God elsewhere refers not to initial justification but to a life of perseverance. Paul states that the goal of his life is that he himself and the other elect may "*obtain the salvation which is in Christ Jesus and with it eternal glory*" (2 Timothy 2:10). Since Paul and the elect are already saved in the sense of final

---

[3291] Luther, "1 Corinthians 7, 1 Corinthians 15, 1 Timothy," 28:183.

[3292] Robertson and Plummer, *A Critical and Exegetical Commentary on the First Epistle of Paul to the Corinthians*, 371.

[3293] Adam Clarke says, "The rabbis have some crude notions concerning different degrees of glory, which the righteous shall possess in the kingdom of heaven. They make out seven degrees: 'The first of which is possessed by צדיקים *tsaddi kim*, the just, who observe the covenant of the holy, blessed God, and subjugate all evil affections. The second is possessed by those who are ישרים *yesharim*, the upright; whose delight it is to walk in the ways of God and please him. The third is for תמימים *temimim*, the perfect: those who, with integrity, walk in the ways of God, and do not curiously pry into his dispensations. The fourth is for קדושים *kedoshim*, the holy ones; those who are the excellent of the earth, in whom is all God's delight. Ps 16:3. The fifth is for בעלי תשובה *baaley teshuvah*, the chief of the penitents; who have broken through the brazen doors, and returned to the Lord. The sixth is for תינוקות של בית רבן *tinukoth shel beith raban*, the scholars and tender ones; who have not transgressed. The seventh is for צידים [*sic*] *chasidim*, the godly: and this is the innermost of all the departments. These seven degrees require a comment by themselves. There is a saying among the rabbis very like that of the apostle in this and the preceding verse Siphri, in Yalcut Simeoni, page 2, fol. 10: 'The faces of the righteous shall be, in the world to come, like suns, moons, the heaven, stars, lightnings: and like the lilies and candlesticks of the temple.'" Clarke, "First Corinthians," s.v. "1 Corinthians 15:42".

deliverance from damnation, it is evident that he speaks of the future salvation "with eternal glory" (i.e., honor).[3294] He desires that he and his disciples will be counted worthy of the resurrection and obtain reward. This is verified by the following verses: "*If we endure, we will reign with him*" (2 Timothy 2:12). This worthiness is consistently based on works (cf. Luke 21:36 for a similar idea). In 2 Thessalonians 1:5, the believers who are already justified are "considered worthy" because of their perseverance in suffering.[3295] A few verses later, Paul prays that the Thessalonian believers would be "counted worthy" of their calling (v. 11). Some will be counted worthy and some will not, depending on whether they persevere. The same phrase, "found worthy," appears in Acts 5:41, "*So they went on their way from the presence of the Council, rejoicing that they had been* ***considered worthy*** *to suffer shame for His name.*" They are not considered worthy because they are justified but because they are persevering in suffering.

Luke 20:35 is problematic for all interpreters. Being counted worthy is always a product of human faithfulness, not divine justification. But if that meaning is used here, then final salvation is based on human works. Many Neonomians have no problem with this because they believe that salvation is conditioned on works, that is, conditioned on "non-meritorious" God-produced works. We believe this is a clever way of avoiding the charge of a works-salvation, and this has been answered elsewhere.[3296]

Since being "considered worthy" is elsewhere a result of faithful perseverance in the walk of faith, in the interest of consistency that should be the preferred interpretation here in Luke 20:35. Therefore, our Lord contrasts two extremes, "the sons of this age" and "the worthy," that is, between the unsaved reprobate and the faithful believers. If one should object that the opposite of the unsaved is all the saved, I respond that the extreme opposite of the unsaved are the faithful believers. By synecdoche (the part for the whole), the faithful stand for all believers, the part for the whole. Similarly the faithful sheep in Matthew 25 stand for all the sheep.[3297]

Jesus did not mention unfaithful believers in Luke 20:35 because they do not fit the normative expectation of diligent discipleship in the rest of His teaching. Those counted worthy of the resurrection are those who will experience the *exanastasis,* the fullness of resurrection and receive the *brabeion,* the prize, the better resurrection. They are those who will be found in close fellowship with Him and who have strained forward to obtain the prize of hearing the summons, "Well done!"[3298]

3294 "The fact that Paul includes himself—who is already saved—shows that he is thinking primarily of their eschatological salvation, the fullness of salvation that will be theirs at the consummation of God's kingdom." See Mounce, *Pastorals*, 514.

3295 Green curiously argues that believers are counted worthy of the kingdom of God because of their suffering. Green, *The Letters to the Thessalonians*, 285. It is not suffering that renders one worthy, but faithful perseverance through the suffering (2 Thessalonians 1:4). That is why Paul boasts about them and that is why they are "counted worthy."

3296 See volume 2, chapters 37-38.

3297 For discussion of this part of speech and examples of its use in other passages see pp. 844 ff.

3298 A plausible alternative interpretation suggests that the passive voice should be pressed, "are considered worthy," and Jesus refers to justification. Thus, like Abraham who was "reckoned righteous" (Genesis 15:6), they are considered worthy because of the imputed righteousness of Christ, and not based on their own efforts. Also, the fact that the worthy are not permitted to marry does not imply that believers who are not worthy are also not permitted to marry. Neither worthy nor unworthy believers will be permitted to marry. Only the worthy are under discussion in the parable.

Summary

Believers who have faithfully persevered will gain an honored status before the King, being "worthy of a better resurrection." Paul referred to this honor when he said that he hoped to obtain a "better resurrection." There was nothing uncertain about Paul's attaining to the resurrection of the body, and the context explains how this resurrection is to be obtained. It is not by life or death, but by means of faithfulness and sanctification. So this special word, *exanastasis*, might be translated "out-resurrection," which probably means a "fullness of resurrection," that is, a separate category of resurrection experience involving that class of committed disciples who have given their lives totally to Christ—Christ's *Metochoi*. There will then be degrees of glory as Paul taught in 1 Corinthians 15.

66

The Partners

IT WAS a most impressive gathering. Nothing had been spared to celebrate the victory of those in attendance. The King Himself had taken off His robes and was serving them (Luke 22:27). The roll call of those present consisted of those millions unknown to history but who were proven in battle. No conclave had ever been more magnificent, more rejoicing had never been witnessed. They gathered to remember and to give thanks. It was the "Final Gathering," the Messianic Banquet that inaugurates the millennial kingdom![3299]

The writer to the Hebrews designated those gathered as the "Partners," those who had been faithful to Christ to the final hour, the great company of the *Metochoi*. They are the "overcomers" of the book of Revelation. To this elite group, rewards were now being given, and they were being invited to share with their King in the future reign of the servant kings, to rule and have dominion over the created order.

This final chapter addresses some of the practical considerations raised by such a magnificent vision of the future. For sensitive readers there is likelihood that the possibilities of rebuke and exclusion from millennial joy are an occasion for unnecessary introspection and discouragement. What Christian has been as obedient as he should? What Christian has believed God as he should? The answer is "no one." Who then are the objects of the Lord's displeasure when He returns? We must remember that the parables of the Wise and Foolish Virgins, the Good and the Wicked Servant, and the Faithful and Unfaithful Believer are sharp contrasts. The warnings and parables do not deal with the daily lapses and failures to which all who know the Lord are subject. Instead, they deal with those who willfully persist in such unfaithfulness. Many in our day do not really want permanent solutions to their emotional stresses. Rather, they seek a temporary relief. These sober warnings are given to those who refuse to grow, who sin willfully, who spurn exhortation, and who dismiss their need to repent and change.

A number of years ago the writer lived in Philadelphia. Many who lived outside the city commuted to work by a network of trains. One morning a young family awoke late and rushed frantically so that the father might catch the 8:05 a.m. commuter train to the central city. As they dashed around the kitchen making breakfast, young Johnny, their five-year-old son, was continually underfoot and slowing the process down. Finally, the father put him out the front door and asked him if he would play in the front yard for a while. As Johnny walked down the front steps, his eye beheld a wonderful sight! It had

[3299] Isaiah 25:6; Matthew 8:10-13; Mark 14:25; Luke 13:22-30; 14:16-24; 22:29-30.

rained the night before, and there was a gigantic mud puddle in the middle of the front yard. He straightaway walked into it and gleefully began to roll in the mud.

About this time his father, hurriedly looking at his watch, burst out the front door on his way to the 8:05, it was now 8:00. He took one look at Johnny and in horror picked him up, brought him inside, and deposited him into his mother's care. Even later now, he rushed out the front door again and to save time, cut across the front yard. As he passed the beautiful mud puddle, he suddenly slipped and fell right into it. "Ugh," he moaned, "how disgusting." He immediately got up out of the mud and ran into the house for a change of clothes. Realizing that he had no time, he decided to go to work covered with mud anyway and brush it off when his suit dried. With that, he rushed off to his goal, the 8:05.

Now, there are a number of similarities and differences between Johnny and his dad. They both fell into the mud, it was the same mud, and they both got dirty. The difference, however, was that Johnny liked it in the mud and had no particular desire to get out. His dad, on the other hand, when he slipped, was disgusted and immediately got out. An even more significant difference, however, is that Johnny's father had a goal, the 8:05. He was going someplace. Johnny, however, had no goal; he just wanted to have fun in the mud.

This parable illustrates the two sides of the sharp contrast drawn by the warning passages and the parables in the New Testament. All Christians fall into the mud. Sometimes it is the same mud, the same sins into which non-Christians fall. The difference is that the *Metochoi* do not like it there and want to get out. Furthermore, they are on their way to a goal, to hear the Lord say, "Well done." To use the words of Paul, they "love His appearing."

Teddy Roosevelt once said, "It is not so important what a man is as what he is becoming, because he shall be what he is now becoming." Perhaps the Lord echoed a similar sentiment when He looked at unstable Simon and said, "You are Peter." Simon, the unstable, was to become Peter the rock!

We all bring a lot of negative emotional patterns into our Christian lives. This background includes genetic and environmental factors which, in part at least, determine what we are. It is therefore easier for some to live victoriously than others. It is clear, however, that the issue is not success but faithfulness!

> *Let a man regard us in this manner, as servants of Christ, and stewards of the mysteries of God. In this case, moreover, it is required of stewards that one be found faithful (1 Corinthians 4:1-2).*

Faithfulness means getting back up out of the mud, asking forgiveness, and persevering toward the goal. God is less concerned with our success than He is with our hearts. We have a human Priest in heaven to represent us. A man is at the throne of God today! He has been tempted in all ways just as we have, and therefore He understands our pain. He bids us to "*draw near with confidence to the throne of grace, that we may receive mercy and may find grace to help in time of need*" (Hebrews 4:16). No rejection is here, no lack of compassion, only sympathy and understanding.

Some of us come from broken homes, alcoholic homes, or some of us have certain genetic predispositions to stress, anxiety, and other emotional difficulties that often make trusting God more difficult than for others. While Scripture never allows us to use these things as an excuse for disobedience, our great High Priest knows about these things and takes them into account now and surely will at the final reckoning. At that time many who are first will be last, and the last will be first. Just because someone struggles with persistent failure now does not mean he forfeits his reward; in fact it means just the opposite. The fact that he stays in the struggle and returns to the battle is evident proof that he is one of the Partners. Remember, David committed adultery and murder, and yet at the end of his life God said of him that he was a "man after God's own heart." Success is not the only issue; faithful perseverance, even after failure, is!

What then is necessary to become one of Christ's *Metochoi*? In its most general statement the requirement is "*to hold fast the beginning of our assurance firm until the end*" (Hebrews 3:14). Those who have actively kept on believing and trusting God to the end of life are all included in this company. Is that all? Jerry Bridges was certainly correct when he wrote, "It often seems more difficult to trust God than to obey Him. The moral will of God given to us in the Bible is rational and reasonable. The circumstances in which we must trust God often appear irrational and inexplicable."[3300] The recipients of the Epistle to the Hebrews were not troubled with problems of disobedience so much as trust. It was the seeming distance of God in the midst of their troubles, His lack of apparent involvement in their difficulties, that caused them to doubt. For this reason the writer set before their vision the great heroes of faith in chapter 11, who "*died in faith, without receiving the promises*" (Hebrews 11:13). It is difficult to "trust God when it hurts." While ultimately the life of faith cannot be separated from the life of obedience, God seems to particularly exalt the person who persists in faith: "*And without faith it is impossible to please Him, for he who comes to God must believe that He is, and that He is a rewarder of those who seek Him*" (Hebrews 11:6). When the storm was over and the sea had been stilled, Jesus was still greatly troubled. He asked His disciples, "*How is it that you have no faith?*" The development of their faith was most important to Jesus.

Holding fast our confession does imply more than steadfast trust, but steadfast trust is of the greatest importance. It is of higher importance because it requires dependence, humility, and humble submission to the sovereignty of God. Having said that, however, the life of discipleship, practical obedience to His commands, is also necessary for those who would be numbered with the *Metochoi*. Here, the stern challenges of Jesus to be willing to leave father and mother, to sell all one has, to deny oneself, take up one's cross and follow Him all come to the forefront. These are not challenges to become Christians but are challenges to Christians to become "overcomers."

The Motivation of Joint Rulership

When Jesus offers the joy of reigning over "ten cities" or when Paul says, "If we endure, we will reign with Him" (2 Timothy 2:12), no doubt many readers will think to themselves (even if they do not say it out loud), "I am not particularly motivated by the thought of reigning with Christ or having rulership in the future world."

Several things may be said about this. Those who have not persevered in faith, who have denied their King now will have feelings of deep shame and regret because they took

[3300] Jerry Bridges, *Trusting God When It Hurts* (Colorado Springs: Nav Press, 1988), 17.

Him for granted and wasted their lives. The pain will be acute, and there will be weeping and gnashing of teeth.

However, for the majority of believers, this judgment will be a time of joy. Some may not find the motivation of rewards as significant in their walk with God as the other motivations discussed in chapter 64.[3301] That said, it seems to me, that all of us should consider this biblical emphasis to live with the end in view.

Furthermore, the notion of reigning with Christ, or ruling over cities, should not be trivialized as if it means various administrative positions in a kingdom or being a mayor of a city. The theme is much broader, and the vision more glorious. What is signified by these expressions is not so much administrative positions as the joy of participating with the Messiah in the final destiny of man, to serve Him and minister with Him in the millennium and the future world. We aspire to higher position because we can then be more effective in the service of our King. To have ten cities instead of five means that we will have greater opportunity to serve Him, to demonstrate our love and gratitude to Him, and to extend the knowledge of His love and goodness throughout the cosmos. To miss that is to miss much.

Also, it should be stressed that the motivation behind our perseverance in holiness is not just the crowns we receive but why we want these crowns. We do not want crowns so that in carnal hubris we can compare ours with others' throughout eternity! There will be no sin nature, no selfishness, no envy, and no pride there.

Like the twenty-four elders, the victorious *Metochoi* surrounding the heavenly throne will repeatedly throughout all eternity lay their crowns at His feet. He says they "will cast their crowns before the throne" (Revelation 4:10). The crowns are ours to use as tokens of worship and gratitude. This casting of the crowns at His feet is our way of saying, "Thank You, Lord Jesus, for dying for me." Each crown with which we are rewarded is a token of our gratitude for eternal salvation.

Performance and Unconditional Acceptance

Does this doctrine imply that God no longer accepts us unconditionally? Does this shift our attention from love and grace over to works? Does this mean that we must earn God's acceptance by performing correctly?

On the principles of the Experimental Predestinarians, the answer would seem to be "yes." Their emphasis on obtaining assurance by means of works and their method of motivating by warning that one may not be justified have often led to an unhealthy introspection. The Experimental Predestinarian can never assure anyone that he has God's acceptance because that assurance cannot come until one has persevered to the final hour.

The Partner, on the other hand, can be assured of God's unconditional acceptance. Furthermore, he can receive the warnings of the New Testament not as raising doubts about his acceptance with God but about his loss of reward. When he is warned, he falls back on the bedrock assurance of God's love and commitment to him, an assurance of which the Experimental Predestinarian can have only theoretical knowledge. Therefore, the warnings emerge from a sense of grace, not uncertainty.

When we become Christians, the Scriptures affirm that we enter into two different relationships with Christ. The first, Paul called being "in Christ." This relationship is eternal

[3301] For discussion of the biblical motivations for Christian living see pp. 1010 ff.

and unchanging. It depends on God alone and is received through faith on the basis of the justifying righteousness of Christ. We are born into His family and are the eternal objects of unconditional love.

The second relationship is often called "Christ in us," and it refers not to our eternal relationship but to our temporal fellowship. This relationship with Christ is changeable and depends on our responses in faith to His love and grace. Within this relationship God requires performance in order to secure His approval and His future inheritance. As any father would, He disciplines His children. We must not forget the fatherly context in which the rewards and the accountability for "good" and "bad" are set. An ideal earthly father loves us deeply, accepts us completely, and yet motivates us with various positive and negative incentives. If our son disobeys us, we still love him, and he will always be our son. But our fellowship is broken until he confesses. Similarly, our fellowship with God is hampered and His blessing is withdrawn from the believer who refuses to respond to His grace displayed in justification:

> *Unless I wash you, you have no part with me (John 13:8).*

> *I write to you dear children, because your sins have been forgiven ... Do not love the world or anything in the world. If anyone loves the world, the love of the Father is not in him (1 John 2:12, 15).*

> *If we confess our sins, he is faithful and just and will forgive us our sins (1 John 1:9).*

> *Your iniquities have separated you from your God; your sins have hidden his face from you (Isaiah 59:2).*

> *Husbands, in the same way be considerate as you live with your wives ... so that nothing will hinder your prayers (1 Peter 3:7).*

To deny this is simply to deny that God holds us accountable for our behavior. If the Reformation placed too much emphasis on the fear of God, it is possible that our generation, inspired by the benevolent God of liberal theology and the narcissistic nature of our culture, has placed too much emphasis on God's love. Or at least we have defined love in a way that excludes accountability.

If this book has placed what may seem to be too much emphasis on accountability, it is only because of the widespread contemporary neglect of this biblical theme. We must emphasize, however, that our central focus should always be where the God of grace wants it—on His love and unconditional acceptance. Paul appeals not to duty to inspire his readers but to God's mercy. He asks for a response based not on obligation but on heartfelt gratitude (Romans 12:1-2). Luther once said, "A law-driver insists with threats and penalties; a preacher of grace lures and incites with divine goodness and compassion shown to us; for he wants no unwilling works and reluctant services, he wants a joyful and delightful service to God."

In his farewell speech to the Ephesian elders, the apostle Paul declared, "*I commend you to God and to the word of His grace, which is able to build you up and give you an inheritance among all those who are sanctified*" (Acts 20:32). Grace builds and motivates. Let us think of His wonderful death for our sins and His love for us before we think of our accountability. Then, and only then, can the doctrine of final accountability be seen in its biblical context.

Finally, and most important, we must not forget that the requirement God places on us for obtaining reward in the Christian life is faithfulness and not success. Faithful is something we can all be, and that is all God demands.

In this case, moreover, it is required of stewards that one be found trustworthy (1 Corinthians 4:2).

To His good servants at the Judgment Seat of Christ He says,

Well done, good and faithful slave; you were faithful with a few things, I will put you in charge of many things; enter into the joy of your master (Matthew 25:23).

Furthermore, he did not judge them on the basis of whether they returned five or ten talents, for all received the same honor. He judged them on the basis of what they did with the responsibilities they were given. These perspectives should be sufficient to remove fears of a performance-based relationship with God.

The Purpose of the Messianic Kingdom

It is vitally important that the purpose and nature of this rulership be understood. Only then can our doctrine be properly defended from critics who degrade the glorious joint-heirship as too "carnal." Some prefer an indefinite and unexplained reign of the saints, either in heaven now or in the new heavens and new earth. To them it is material and carnal to talk of an earthly kingship. It is difficult to see how such a view could ever emerge from the plain intent of these wonderful predictions. To reign jointly with Christ is the most precious and glorious future that can be set before the mind of man.

What is the purpose of this great future? The design of this glorious reign of the *Metochoi* is to deliver the world from the results of sin and to fill it with blessing and glory! These *Metochoi* are ruling not for themselves but for others.

Part of our problem is that in the present world, rulership nearly always implies the appropriation of power because of selfish motives. This has the connotation of "lording over" others. Nevertheless, the King Himself has taught about another kind of rulership, servant-rulership. The *Metochoi* of Jesus are not above their Master. They too are servant-rulers.

The kings of the Gentiles lord it over them; and those who exercise authority over them call themselves Benefactors. But you are not to be like that. Instead, the greatest among you should be like the youngest, and the one who rules like the one who serves. For who is greater, the one who is at the table or the one who serves? Is it not the one who is at the table? But I am among you as one who serves (Luke 22:25-27).

How are such rulers developed? Only through undergoing the trials of sin and suffering can true compassion emerge. This is the theme of Hebrews 2 where our great High Priest is said to have learned obedience by the things He suffered, and He is leading many sons along a similar path to glory. Indeed, the kingdom has been postponed and delayed for several thousand years precisely for this purpose, to raise up a body of rulers who will sustain it with dignity, purity, compassion, and selflessness worthy of the Messiah,

Jesus. The reason the kingdom was not established under Moses or David or Jesus' first advent is surely to be explained by the apparent fact that man was not yet prepared for it. A period of time is necessary to prepare the future rulers. God knows the number of those who will share in the reign of David's greater Son, and until this number (known only to God) is completed, the kingdom itself will not be established.

If the *Metochoi* are to enjoy these unspeakable privileges, they must be trained in obedience, suffering, temptation, and trial just as their Captain was. They are so elevated simply because they have learned these lessons and have persevered in them to the end of life. The King has told them that in the kingdom those who are the greatest servants now will be the greatest rulers then! When they finally inherit this kingdom, the wisdom of the divine plan will be evident. Their constant contact with evil and trials now uniquely fits them for their role.

This will not only enhance their relationships to each other but will also bring them into sympathy with the nations of the earth. They will know and understand the struggle with sin that engages their subjects, the mortal inhabitants of the millennial earth. The experience gained now fits them to be wise, intelligent kings and sympathetic and loving priests. Their goal is not to exert authority but to serve those over whom they have been placed. They will model their Master's servant heart and will be greatly loved and respected by their subjects. They think only of the good they can do for others and the ways in which they can extend the glory and blessing of God to the created order. They will be universally honored for their love, graciousness, and friendship, as well as for their authority.

We may view the present world as the training ground for the aristocracy of the future kingdom, the ruling class of the world to come. A man may be in abject poverty now and completely ignored by the leaders of this world. He may be despised and without means to provide adequately for his family. Yet, that same person may now be a prince and will one day inherit his kingdom. Then he will obtain a position far higher and with more grandeur than that of any human ruler who ever lived. This truth is based on numerous promises in Scripture which God intends to fulfill!

Security and Significance

Few would disagree with the observation that two of the most important needs of man are for security and significance.[3302] The interplay of these emotions are obviously crucial in our motivations. Larry Crabb defines them this way:

> **SECURITY:** *A convinced awareness of being unconditionally and totally loved without needing to change in order to win love, loved by a love that is freely given, that cannot be earned and therefore cannot be lost.*
>
> **SIGNIFICANCE:** *A realization that I am engaged in a responsibility or job that is truly important, whose results will not evaporate with time, but will last through eternity, that fundamentally involves having a meaningful impact on another person, a job for which I am completely adequate.*[3303]

[3302] For the discussion following, the writer is indebted to Quick, "The Doctrine of Eternal Significance", 4-27.

[3303] Lawrence J. Crabb, *The Marriage Builder: A Blueprint for Couples and Counselors*, rev ed. (Grand Rapids: Zondervan Publishing House, 1982), 29.

It is vitally important for our mental wholeness that we feel both secure and significant with God. As this book has attempted to prove, contrary to the views of the Arminians and the Experimental Predestinarians, God does not threaten His children's security as a means of motivating them. Then again, God does deal seriously with His children in terms of their final significance.

Obviously, the most fundamental human need is for secure love. Children who lack this are often scarred for life. Marriages without it are often full of anguish. Intimacy in marriage requires it. If one spouse fails to meet the need of the other spouse for security, the likely result is divorce.

If this is true in all human relationships, how much more so is it in our relationship to God? And God has freely granted us this thing we need and desire most from Him, namely, primary security. Salvation is unconditional. The man who believes in Christ and has accepted His offer of forgiveness has:

1. No fear of loss of salvation (Romans 11:29; Ephesians 1:13).
2. No fear of eternal condemnation (John 5:24; Colossians 2:13-14).
3. No fear of divine rejection as His child (John 10:27-28; Romans 8:34-39).
4. Positive assurance (1 John 5:1, 10-12; Hebrews 11:2; John 6:39-40).

We can know we are God's children forever. We can know He loves and accepts us, no matter what. The result is that our primary security is established by God.[3304]

Yes, our eternal security depends on God, and that is why it is secure indeed. No matter what our sin, no matter how far we wander, no matter how fruitless our lives or difficult our struggle, God always remains committed to us.

God's acceptance and adoption gives us a basis for life. As an earthly parent always loves his child, so our heavenly parent remains committed to us. Like an earthly parent, however, our heavenly parent does not always approve of our actions, and He will hold us accountable for them. In some cases He will deal severely with our willful failures.

But we also have a need for significance. In order for us to be motivated in what we do, we need to feel that our task and our lives are significant and that there is a final accounting for what we do. Without that feeling, work is a burden, and our lives lack focus and meaning. That this is so can be seen in numerous life situations.

A housewife cares for her family, fixes meals, and stays up until 2:00 AM talking with her teenage children. She chooses to stay home and commit twenty years of her life to being a mother instead of having a career. If she does not see fruit from her labor, if she does not see her children turning out well, if she is not affirmed by them and by her husband, she will lose motivation. She perceives that what she is investing her life in is not significant.

A secretary in a large Christian missionary organization labors daily behind the scenes. Because she is there, the teachers and evangelists are able to minister more freely. Yet, if the organization fails to affirm the importance of her role, she loses the vision. She will no longer connect the computer on which she labors with conversions in the field. She will no longer feel her work is significant, and she will lose motivation.

A highly successful civil engineer has invested many years of his life in building buildings and bridges. One day he surveys what he has done and reasons, "All that I have built will perish. I want to build things that will last for eternity." He has concluded that his

---

[3304] Quick, "The Doctrine of Eternal Significance", 11.

work no longer has significance. He loses his motivation. His view, of course, is incorrect. What makes a task significant is the motive for doing it and the One for whom it is done. Nevertheless, in his motivational system, having concluded that his work is not significant, he leaves his job to become a foreign missionary.

A systems analyst has put together numerous computer systems for large corporations. One day he looks at what he has done and concludes there must be more to life than helping a business make more money. He no longer feels what he is doing is significant, and his motivation wanes.

Examples could be multiplied. Our motivation to accomplish a given task is directly related to how significant we feel the task is. When Paul said, "*Whatever you do, work at it with all your heart, as working for the Lord, not for men, since you know that you will receive an inheritance from the Lord as a reward*" (Colossians 3:23-24), he was appealing to this same motivational force. This verse reveals a central aspect of what makes us feel something is significant: *a task will be viewed as significant if the people who matter to us value it as such.* In this case since it is God who determines the ultimate significance of the work, it will be perceived as highly important: "*Always give yourselves fully to the work of the Lord, because you know that your labor in the Lord is not in vain*" (1 Corinthians 15:58).

For us to believe that our work is truly significant, there must be recognition and affirmation by someone else. Someone other than ourselves, someone who has expertise and authority to affirm that a particular task is valuable must give his affirmation. This recognition could be given with a plaque, a word of praise, a compliment, a promotion, or a dinner in the person's honor. "But in some way one must receive the proof from the people who matter that he has done well."[3305]

What is evident in our interpersonal relationships in this life can be applied to our eternal relationship with God. He is the ultimate one who will evaluate our work and will pronounce the desired, "Well done." And, He matters more than anyone. Our eternal security gives us freedom to pursue our significance. We do not have to worry about rejection or about loss of salvation. But even though we cannot lose our justification, the warnings in the Bible tell us we can forfeit our inheritance; we can lose our eternal significance. The promises that our life can matter motivate us to make sacrifices, to take risks, to work hard, knowing that our work is not in vain in the Lord. God values whatever we do for Him. The warnings that we can lose rewards inspire the fear of the Lord in our hearts and cause us to labor to avoid that terrible consequence. The other side of significance is final accountability.

We see then that there are two sides to the motivational influence. Positively, there is the legitimate desire for Christ's approval and for eternal significance. Negatively, there is a legitimate fear of Christ's displeasure and the loss of eternal significance.

Our lives can matter. They can make a difference. Through service to Him we can attach eternal value to the life we have lived. Some of us will pursue this goal more diligently than others. Some Christians, to their great shame and eternal loss, will not pursue this worthy goal at all. The differences will become evident when we stand before Him at the Judgment Seat of Christ.

Love could not grow between a father and son where the father, throughout the son's life, deals with his disobedience by (1) raising questions whether the young man was really his son (Experimental Predestinarian) or (2) threatening him with exclusion from the

---

[3305] Ibid., 13-14.

family (Arminian). However, love is possible in the midst of disobedience when the father affirms his love for his son and assures him he can never be put out of his family, but then disciplines him. In extreme situations he may warn him of possible disinheritance. "*The Lord disciplines those He loves and He punishes everyone He accepts as a son. . . . If you are not disciplined... then you are illegitimate children and not true sons*" (Hebrews 12:6-8, NIV).

"I've Never Heard This Before"

Recently I received a letter in which the following objections were made to the Partner viewpoint.

> *My plain reading of Scripture, personal study and experience, and "gut feelings" (I like to think of this as His Spirit witnessing with my spirit) do not lead me to your conclusions. Yes, I have been influenced by many teachers, pastors, theologians, and books throughout my life, almost all of whom would not land at your position.*
>
> *It seems to me the main body of present-day evangelical pastors, teachers, and theologians would place in question your position. Does that mean you are wrong and they are right? No, but it does raise significant doubt in my mind about your position.*
>
> *Are there significant writers throughout the history of the church that give your position prominent consideration?*

The person who wrote these words is a mature Christian for whom I have great respect. Some readers of this book may also have come across interpretations of various passages that are new to them. Like the person in the letter, they might be forgiven for asking, "If this is correct, why have I never heard this before?" The main reason, like my friend revealed in his note above, is that most tend to read books and articles consistent with their own particular viewpoints.

When fire begins to consume a house, it is time to evacuate! This writer believes that there is smoke rising in the house of Calvin; and so it is time to abandon the burning Experimental Predestinarian paradigm. However, to those steeped in Westminster Calvinism, the call to vacate is a false alarm. The only thing burning, they say, is a small brush fire on the edge of the evangelical community called "Free Grace." They ask, "How could there be any new paradigms for understanding historic Christianity?" To say there might be, they conclude, amounts to a naïve suggestion that something new may be developing in the hallowed halls of evangelical orthodoxy. Thus with a wave of the hand, the air is cleared and a notice is sent out that all that smoke was only a false alarm.

The advocates of Free Grace have lobbed a grenade into the hallowed halls of Westminster Calvinism. The viewpoint of those accepting the Partner position is a dramatic *if—then.* Haven't the Westminster Confession and its Puritan adherents properly defined Protestant orthodoxy for the past 450 years? Haven't they contributed enormously to the growth and apologetic defense of the "once for all delivered to the saints' faith"? Hasn't their viewpoint dominated the commentaries and theological works that have enriched the lives of many? Yes, yes, yes! This magnificent confession has set a standard for determining right from wrong, truth from heresy, and a benchmark for identifying which church one should attend. When these undeniable facts are set forth, it is no wonder that the smell of smoke is dismissed as a brushfire. *If* the Partner position is correct, *then* a central doctrine of Westminster Calvinism is simply wrong.

Experimental Predestinarians often claim that their interpretations are "mainstream" and reflect the consensus view of church history.[3306] The truth is that there has been considerable difference in the history of the church regarding the issues of lordship salvation and assurance. It is easy to demonstrate that Augustine, Calvin, Luther, and the Lutheran Confessions (e.g., the Formula of Concord) all held views of saving faith that differ radically from those of John MacArthur, Martyn Lloyd-Jones, John Piper, and R. C. Sproul.[3307]

But we must also remember that there is continual clarification in the development of Christian thought. It took four centuries to formalize the doctrine of the hypostatic union (the union of two natures in one person in Christ); it finally occurred at Chalcedon in 451. Another thousand years passed before the errors of Augustinian soteriology were finally refuted in the Protestant Reformation. Over one hundred years later the church's attention was directed to a more systematic and original study of the millennial issue. In the twentieth century the church's attention was directed to the questions of inerrancy and inspiration in a more focused way. This came as a result of a reaction to post-Enlightenment rationalism which forced a reexamination of this orthodox doctrine. An enormous amount of literature refined, clarified, and defended those themes. Those opposed would often use the same fallacious historical arguments that this was new and did not represent the beliefs of the church for centuries.

An issue for our time is a mediation soteriology between the extremes of Arminianism and Experimental Predestinarian theology. Once again a crisis in the church brought the issue to the forefront. As the culture of postmodernism and its denial of absolutes swept into the church like a tidal wave, the issue of the "carnal" Christian was thrust to the forefront. As a result, many Scriptures related to the issues of lordship salvation and perseverance in holiness were examined in more detail. Hundreds of theologians and exegetes are addressing themselves to the issues discussed in this book. While not all are coming to the same conclusions, there is a consensus building that the old paradigm must go if the health of the church is to be preserved. Lawrence Vance's outstanding work *The Other Side of Calvinism;*[3308] R. T. Kendall's published doctoral dissertation at Oxford University, *Calvin and English Calvinsim to 1943;*[3309] and Michael Eaton's seminal work, *No Condemnation: A New Theology of Assurance*[3310] are recent examples. Kendall was the pastor of Westminster Chapel in London, where Martyn Lloyd-Jones was pastor for many years. Many others could be cited. Scores of journal articles are being produced and new commentaries written, all reflecting variations of the Partner viewpoint. To this should be added the excellent books by Robert Wilkin, current president of the Grace Evangelical Theological Society, a strong advocate of the Partner position.[3311]

3306 For example, John MacArthur asserts that his views (on lordship salvation) "are exactly what the true church has always believed," MacArthur, *The Gospel According to Jesus*, 222 and pp. xiv, 21.

3307 See the excellent discussion of this issue by Thomas G. Lewellen, "Has Lordship Salvation Been Taught throughout Church History?," in *Vital Theological Issues: Examining Enduring Issues of Theology*, ed. Roy B. Zuck (Grand Rapids: Kregel Publications, 1994), 153-64.

3308 Vance, *The Other Side of Calvinism.*

3309 Kendall, *English Calvinism*. Kendall, *Once Saved, Always Saved.*

3310 Eaton, *No Condemnation: A New Theology of Assurance.*

3311 See Robert N. Wilkin, *Confident in Christ: Living by Faith Really Works* (Irving, TX: Grace Evangelical Society, 1999). Robert N. Wilkin, *Secure and Sure: Grasping the Promises of God* (Irving, TX: Grace Evangelical Theological Society, 2005).

The church is continually reflecting on and refining its understanding of God's written revelation. The minority viewpoint, like that of the Reformers, is not always wrong. If students of the Word are to be required to march lockstep with the current consensus, little room exists for creativity and imagination. If this kind of objection were allowed to stand, all fresh interpretive work would die on the vine. N. T. Wright asks, "Do we really want to tell our doctoral students (as Oscar Cullman was reportedly told as a postgraduate) that all problems are now solved and they had better study something else?"[3312] At the turn of the twentieth century, Lord Kelvin announced that all the fundamental questions of physics had now been answered. All that was now needed, he said, was more precise measurement of the data. Fortunately, Albert Einstein demurred, and a few years later revealed the theories of special and general relativity.

With the rapid spread of Christianity across the Roman world into different cultures, it is reasonable to think that many things in the New Testament were not obvious to the second-century church and beyond. Wright continues, "It is not only possible, but highly likely that things which were extremely clear to first century authors were rapidly forgotten in the very different and subsequent circumstances."[3313] We know, for example, that as early as the second century, salvation by grace alone through faith alone became a minority viewpoint, and works salvation came rapidly to the forefront. The point is that certain interpretations shaped by the experience of the later church became fixed paradigms through which the New Testament was viewed. A similar process took place subsequent to the Reformation in which the Westminster Confession became codified in one segment of evangelical orthodoxy for four hundred years. A paradigm had been established which led people to say, "This is a settled issue, something we no longer need to think about."

A common foible in biblical studies is the transformation of a hypothesis (such as the perseverance of the saints in holiness) into dogma. Clayton Sullivan, in his compelling critique of the "already-not-yet" hypothesis held by most contemporary biblical scholars, concludes that this transformation occurs "even though the evidence upon which a hypothesis is based, subsequently falls into disarray."[3314] The Experimentalist hypothesis is in disarray, and if the arguments presented in this book are correct, *it is not true*.[3315]

But, to answer the objection more directly, the writer would like to suggest that most of the readers have heard some aspects of the Partner view of New Testament soteriology. For example, for many years we have been told of the "loss" of rewards at the Judgment Seat of Christ (2 Corinthians 5:10), yet one rarely hears anything about what that loss entails. This book not only presents the positive rewards but attempts to help us understand the negative consequences that are usually ignored. Furthermore, virtually all evangelical believers accept as obvious that there is such a thing as a carnal Christian, even though Experimental Predestinarians vociferously deny it. What is new in the Partner paradigm is a systematic presentation of these truths dealing with the web of related Scriptures which it entails.

3312 N. T. Wright, "In Greatful Dialogue," in *Jesus and the Restoration of Israel: A Critical Assessmenet of N. T. Wright's Jesus and the Victory of God*, ed. Cary C. Newman (Downers Grove, IL: InterVarsity Press, 1999), 247.

3313 Ibid.

3314 Sullivan, *Rethinking Realized Eschatology*, 115.

3315 See extensive discussion of the biblical evidence for the permanently carnal Christian in volume 2, chapter 32.

What can one say to an objector who claims that his interpretations are in part based on the so-called "plain reading of Scripture, personal study and experience, and 'gut feelings' (I like to think of this as His Spirit witnessing with my spirit)"? What is the "plain reading" of Scripture? When a person believes his reading is the "plain reading," is it possible that he unintentionally refers to a view that is consistent with his prior theological bent? What is plain to him is not plain to all. Indeed, what is considered "plain" to those steeped in Westminster Calvinism would not even have occurred to a first-century reader. The issue then, is what would be plain to Peter, Paul, and Jesus? The only way that can be determined is by examining the words they used and the way they used them, not how the majority of pastors or theologians use them today. When one does that, it becomes evident that the gap between Reformation polemics and first-century usage is wide.

Furthermore, since both Partners and Experimental Predestinarians think the Spirit is speaking to them, to which one of them is the Holy Spirit speaking? The only way this issue can be adjudicated is not by "gut feelings" or majority vote; instead, we must heed the apostle's injunction, "*Be diligent to present yourself approved to God as a workman who does not need to be ashamed, accurately handling the word of truth*" (2 Timothy 2:15). In studying the Bible, believers need to be like the Bereans who "*were more noble-minded than those in Thessalonica, for they received the word with great eagerness, examining the Scriptures daily to see whether these things were so*" (Acts 17:11). They did not settle issues by "gut feelings" or majority vote but by careful study of the Scriptures themselves. We too must be diligent workmen.

In response to the assertion that the Partner view is not "mainstream," we respond that depends on which "stream" one considers to be "main." Those from an Experimental Predestinarian perspective view their writers and churches as "mainstream." Those from an Arminian perspective naturally see their views as "mainstream" and can point to a long history including John Wesley and many contemporary scholars. The fact of the matter is that the majority of the exegetical commentaries and systematic theologies were written by Experimental Predestinarian teachers and scholars. Thus, the influence of Westminster Calvinism has been broad.

"Mainstream" also depends on which country a person lives in. If, for example, one determines truth by which view is "main" in China, then over 60 million members of the Chinese house churches who are Arminian and forcefully reject the doctrine of eternal security, would be considered mainstream. The same situation prevails throughout most of the evangelical communities in Eastern Europe and the former Soviet Union.[3316] For one thousand years, the "mainstream" view of salvation was that it was obtained through the sacraments and works. This was the heritage of Augustine's confused soteriology which the Reformer's corrected.

Of course, not all within Experimental Predestinarian or Arminian circles agree with one another on every issue, even within their own tradition. Likewise, while not all those espousing the Partner viewpoints agree on the specific interpretation of various passages, the Partner view can hardly be rejected as out of the mainstream. Should Lewis Sperry Chafer, founder and president of Dallas Seminary, be counted as out of the "mainstream"? His *Systematic Theology* forcefully presents the non-lordship views of salvation maintained by the Partners. Professor Zane Hodges, former department chairman of the New Testament department at Dallas Seminary, has been very influential in presenting these views. Dr.

[3316] This writer has personal experience of these facts, having worked in Eastern Europe and China for 28 years.

Earl Radmacher, former president of Western Conservative Baptist Seminary in Portland, Oregon, is a strong advocate of the Partner viewpoint.[3317] To this we must add Dr. Charles Ryrie, who, while not holding all the viewpoints represented in this book, nevertheless is a strong advocate of the non-lordship viewpoint.[3318] Is Charles Stanley, twice-elected president of the Southern Baptist Convention and pastor of First Baptist Church of Atlanta, to be considered out of the mainstream? He holds many of the viewpoints represented by the Partner.[3319] Is Erwin Lutzer, pastor of Moody Memorial Church in Chicago, not a valid representative of a large contemporary evangelical viewpoint? He too holds the Partner view of eternal security.[3320] Likewise, Steven Lyon, editor-in-chief of Moody Publishers, advocates many of the Partner viewpoints. Bruce Wilkinson, former president of *Walk Through the Bible*, and Warren W. Wiersbe, formerly of *Back to the Bible Broadcast*, both share the basic viewpoints of the so-called "Free Grace" position. Paige Patterson, former president of the Southern Baptist Convention and professor of theology at Southwestern Baptist Theological Seminary has long been a strong advocate of "Free Grace." Is he not mainstream?[3321] Randall C. Gleason, chairman and professor of theological studies and director of ThM Studies at the International School of Theology—Asia, shares views similar to that of the Partner in his analysis of the warnings in Hebrews.[3322]

Roy Zuck, editor of the Dallas Theological Seminary's journal *Bibliotheca Sacra* for many years, held many of the distinctive viewpoints of the Free Grace soteriology. In addition, new journals are being published representing scholarly articles presenting aspects of the Partner viewpoint.[3323] Outstanding commentaries at both a popular and scholarly level have recently been published.[3324] Recently Keith Krell published his excellent doctor's dissertation from the University of Bristol and Trinity College entitled *Temporal Judgment and the Church* in which he convincingly establishes that the warning passages in 1 Corintians are all addressed to true believers and the outcome is divine judgment in time or loss at the Judgment Seat of Christ, precisely the Partner view.[3325] Marty Cauley's work on the *Darkness Outside*[3326] may be the most extensive and thorough discussion of this theme in the history of the Church. Ed Ediger's outstanding book, *Faith in Jesus: What it Means to Believe in Him*, represents a high caliber of gracious Christian scholarship.[3327]

3317 See Radmacher, *Salvation*. See also Derickson and Radmacher, *The Disciplemaker: What Matters Most to Jesus*.

3318 See Ryrie, *So Great Salvation: What It Means to Believe in Jesus Christ*.

3319 See Stanley, *Eternal Security: Can You Be Sure?*

3320 Erwin W. Lutzer, *Your Eternal Reward: Triumph and Tears at the Judgmenet Seat of Christ* (Chicago: Moody Press, 1998).

3321 Dr. Patterson is also one of the editors of the *Believer's Study Bible*..

3322 Randall Gleason, "A Moderate Reformed View," in *Four Views of the Warning Passages in Hebrews*, ed. Herbert W. Bateman (Grand Rapids: Kregel Publications, 2007), 336-77.

3323 For example, the *Journal of the Grace Evangelical Theological Society*, and the Chafer Theological Seminary Journal.

3324 For example, see Anderson, *Maximum Joy*. Hodges, *The Epistles of John: Walking in the Light of God's love: A Verse by Verse Commentary*. López, "Romans." Hodges, *The Epistle of James: Proven Character Through Testing: A Verse by Verse Commentary*. See also Hodges, "Hebrews."

3325 Krell, *Temporal Judgment and the Church: Paul's Remedial Agenda in 1 Corinthians*.

3326 Cauley, *The Outer Darkness*.

3327 Ediger, *Faith in Jesus: What Does it Mean to Believe in Him?*

To maintain that the Partner view is not mainstream or is held by a small minority is to adopt a myopic view of the matter, asserting that only those writers from one's own particular background and experience are to be considered the most reliable representatives of the evangelical faith.

To a large extent, this objection is flawed by its near phobia of anything that smacks of newness and freshness. Of course, we should be suspicious of newness and always be willing to test biblical interpretations by the wisdom of the centuries. But surely "the wisdom of the centuries" includes our own century.[3328] Experimental Predestinarians would do well to recall Matthew 13:52: *"And he said to them, 'Therefore every scribe who has been trained for the kingdom of heaven is like a householder who brings out of his treasure things new and old.'"* As Don Garlington noted, "I would say the appropriate response to matters 'new' and 'fresh' is not skepticism but the Berean spirit of searching the Scriptures to see if these things are so (Acts 17:11)."[3329] With this, Calvin would agree. When accused that the conclusions of the Reformation were a novelty, he replied,

> *First, in calling it new, they are exceedingly injurious to God, whose sacred word deserved not to be charged with novelty. That it long lay buried and unknown is the guilty consequence of man's impiety; but now when, by the kindness of God, it is restored to us, it ought to resume its antiquity just as the returning citizen resumes his rights.*[3330]

In the final analysis, however, we are back to the beginning of our discussion, the power of paradigms. The Experimental Predestinarian paradigm of perseverance has so dominated the thinking of many that it is difficult for them to take a fresh look at the Scriptures from a new perspective. One is reminded of the problem that confronted modern physics at the turn of the twentieth century. Convinced as they were that electromagnetic radiation needed a medium in which to propagate, even though thirteen experiments proved this elusive medium, "ether," did not exist, scientists doggedly maintained its existence anyway. When Einstein established that light consists of photons and is not totally explained by the wave theory, the need for a medium was eliminated and a revolution in physics ensued. As I have tried to show in the preceding pages, to continue to lean on the broken reed of Experimental Predestinarian readings of the New Testament can only continue to propagate profound errors in our basic understanding of the gospel, eternal security, assurance, and a host of related issues, including eternal rewards.

Do we detect here, in the words of Thomas Khun, "the faint smell of smoke"? The Experimental Predestinarian paradigm is clearly on fire. From personal experience this writer can testify that many believers, biblical scholars, and churches are abandoning it and turning to various aspects of the Partner paradigm. The smoke alluded to above is not from a brushfire on the edge of the desert; it is the burning of the house of Calvin. Do we sense in the reaction of those who tenaciously cling to this tired perspective, a heavy commitment to it, even though it has less explanatory power and indeed a much higher degree of combustibility than was formerly supposed? Throughout this book we have argued that Experimental Predestinarian exegesis is often characterized by *ad hoc* assumptions read into

3328 Don Garlington, "Review of John Piper, The Future of Justification: A Response to N. T. Wright," *Review of Biblical Literature* (May 23, 2008). http://www.bookreviews.org/bookdetail.asp?TitleId=63 78.

3329 Ibid.

3330 Calvin, "Institutes," vi. Of course, Calvin would not hold to many of the interpretations held by Partners.

passage after passage. These assumptions are required in order to sustain their theological system. When theological exegesis proceeds like this, the result is building castles in the air, and those adhering to the Partner paradigm, though they are a minority, need not feel like second-class citizens because they refuse to rent space in them.[3331]

New paradigms often suffer the charge of being novel and innovative. They are often superficially refuted with appeals to Scriptures, many taken out of context, and appeals to commentaries, church histories, and theological works on the bookshelf of the interlocutor. The cry of alarm is heard throughout the land. That does not make them wrong; it only reveals a selective reading to support a paradigm whose usefulness is past. The skeptic, fully committed to his views, will always find a way of doubting.

Final Accountability

In his book *The Closing of the American Mind*, Allan Bloom, professor of social thought at the University of Chicago, makes a disturbing observation of our university culture:

> *There is one thing a professor can be absolutely certain of: almost every student entering the university believes, or says he believes, that truth is relative. If this belief is put to the test, one can count on the student's reaction: they will be uncomprehending. That anyone should regard the proposition as not self-evident astonishes them, as though he were calling into question 2 + 2 = 4.*[3332]

These are things, says Bloom, which we no longer need to think about. For them the relativity of truth is a moral postulate. To deny it is to place ourselves in the same category as a man who believes in witches or believes that the earth is flat. The study of world history teaches us that there were mad men in past ages. There have always been men who were overly certain they were right, and such dogmatism has even led to war. The proposed answer is to eliminate the demon of absolutism and inculcate relativity in our academic curriculum. The virtue of our modern society is "openness."

While no one questions the necessity of generous attitudes in a pluralistic society, the way we have arrived at this condition has revealed that the price was too high, the removal of any sense of final accountability. Perhaps not coincidentally, the student's moral outrage against the evils of absolutism tended to correspond to their own desires to be free from all the restraints imposed by moral absolutes. At any rate, in our society today the removal of moral absolutes has brought with it the removal of any sense of final accountability for one's actions.

Even the absolute God of the Bible has seemingly acquired this virtue of openness. Many people think He understands our sin and will make exceptions. Surely, some say, an eternal damnation does not exist. While it has often been true that the church eventually adopts the evils of the society, the ease with which the modern church has accepted the values of the surrounding culture has surprised many. Only minor statistical differences now exist between the divorce rates among Christians and non-Christians. Premarital sexual activity among Christian young people has for many of them, like their non-

[3331] This phraseology is adapted from Wright, "In Greatful Dialogue," 247.

[3332] Allan David Bloom, *The Closing of the American Mind: How Higher Education Has Failed Democracy and Impoverished the Souls of Today's Students* (New York: Simon and Schuster, 1987), 25.

Christian counterparts, become a "non-issue." Marriage is no longer "till death do us part" but "till difficulties do us in!"

Why has the church, which is supposedly a bastion of absolutism in the surrounding sea of relativism, so easily accepted the values of the encircling culture? This is a question with which church and cultural historians will wrestle, but it is clear that a profound theological error is near the heart of the matter. The doctrines of Westminster Calvinism, while designed to promote a high degree of moral purity, have virtually robbed the church of any sense of final accountability.

This is true for three reasons. First, an emphasis on evidences of regeneration as the true test of salvation has led many who are not regenerate to look at some meager evidence that they are regenerate and conclude that they are saved when they are in truth on the highway to the lake of fire.

But second, and just as serious, the misguided emphasis on the practical syllogism has all but eliminated the central scriptural motivations for moving carnal Christians back to the path of growth to maturity. The Bible does not tell them that they may not be "truly" saved. Rather, it tells them that, if they are, they will miss out on the final destiny of man. It does matter to God when we live inconsistently with the faith we claim to possess. One day there will be a reckoning, and for some there will be weeping and shame. Because these negative consequences of a carnal life have rarely been defined and even rejected by Experimentalists, many Christians do not live with a healthy fear of God. They often take the grace of God for granted because Experimental Predestinarians have told them they will all be rewarded, only some not as much as others. No doubt, many settle back into a life of lukewarmness under such teaching.

Third, their system emasculates numerous warnings in Scripture of their force. The warnings, we are told, do not apply to true Christians but to professing Christians. Since the lukewarm Christian in the pew is already assured of his saved status on the basis of looking at some evidences of works in his life, he concludes that the warnings do not apply to him. There is no danger. He is also told that he cannot lose his salvation and will be rewarded anyway.[3333]

A combination of these three errors has so permeated our Christian culture that to raise the issue of disinheritance (which the Bible everywhere does!) draws gasps of surprise. Like the students in Bloom's university classroom, these are things that you do not need to talk about. As a result, this theology has contributed unintentionally to the very spiritual lethargy against which it constantly rails.

To counteract this, Experimental Predestinarians can only point professing Christians to the opposite extreme and raise questions about their justification. For example, Buswell insists:

> *So long as a professing Christian is in the state of carnality, no pastor, no Christian friend, has the slightest ground for holding that this carnal person has ever been regenerated. . . . It is*

[3333] John Hart is absolutely correct when he says, "The blame for this may well lie at the feet of the true-faith-versus-false-faith theology that has been made to override all other concerns in James 2 and the epistle as a whole. In my opinion, the primary purpose of the latter half of James 2 is to incite within the Christian reader the need to be active in doing more good works that meet practical needs. That kind of exhortation is radically lost if we force on the unit a false faith/true faith purview." Hart, "How to Energize Our Faith: Reconsidering the Meaning of James 2:14-26," 41.

the pastor's duty to counsel such a person, "You do not give evidence of being in a regenerate state."[3334]

But the Scriptures do not urge such people to examine the fruits of regeneration in their lives to ascertain whether they are Christians. They point them to the great future. Instead of threatening them with the fear of damnation, the Scriptures warn them of profound regret and millennial disinheritance in the future. The danger is missing the Master's "Well done!" This is a healthy and ennobling fear that inspires men to growth and discipleship. The continual challenge to reconsider whether one is saved can hardly compare with this for spiritual incitement. Indeed, it leads backward to introspection and legalism instead of forward to confidence and freedom in Christ. Love and grace have always been higher and more powerful motivators than fear of damnation, but the Experimental Predestinarian cannot offer these incentives because a carnal lifestyle suggests to him that the man in question has not experienced the love and grace of God at all. All that is left in his bag of motivational influences is to warn the man that he may not be saved and is in danger of perishing. Rarely do the Experimental Predestinarians attempt to motivate by means of appeal to the magnificent future.[3335] In fact, they often disparage it as "some millennial crown."[3336]

Numerous examples of the devastating effects of this theology can be culled from the everyday life of the church. Not long ago, a businessman related to this writer how he was leading a Bible study using a recent book written by a well-known Experimental Predestinarian Bible teacher. The thrust of this book was to challenge professing Christians that they cannot be sure of their salvation unless they live up to the demands of discipleship taught by Christ. When one man, who had faithfully attended for years, failed to continue, he was asked what was wrong. The man revealed that the book had a strong negative impact on his spiritual motivation because it seemed impossible to love or to be loved by a God who demanded such perfection in order to be accepted into His family. He had many business and personal trials in life at that time, and he could not find the comfort he needed from his relationship with God when he was continually exposed to such introspective perfectionism.

The Experimental Predestinarian has a genuine and biblical concern. He does not want the grace of God to be taken for granted. It therefore grieves him to contemplate that a permanently carnal Christian could ever be the object of God's saving grace. He is concerned that a man who embraces the Partner view of eternal security will reason this way: "I realize that my life of sin will exclude me from the future destiny of man, but I really don't care about that anyway. Even if I experience profound regret, it will only be temporary, and in the final analysis, in eternity future, I will have a full cup, even if it is not as large as others." This is the shibboleth of "cheap grace." However, all this Experimental Predestinarian hand-wringing about cheap grace is ridiculous. Grace is not only cheap, it is

---

[3334] J. Oliver Buswell, *A Systematic Theology of the Christian religion* (Grand Rapids: Zondervan Publishing House, 1962), 2:147.

[3335] In John MacArthur's Experimental Predestinarian book, in which he is attempting to motivate the church to godliness, he devotes only one line of text to the subject of rewards! The remaining 253 pages are devoted to proving that a man with insufficient evidences of regeneration is in fact not a Christian at all. MacArthur, *The Gospel According to Jesus*, 146.

[3336] Pink, *An Exposition of the Sermon on the Mount*, 361.

free; as the apostle John put it, "*I will give to the one who thirsts from the spring of the water of life* ***without cost***" (Revelation 21:6).

While the response above is possible, it is not typical. Usually, when Christians are challenged with the great future and reminded of the love of God, their hearts incline toward discipleship. Grace, love, and reward are normally powerful motivators. However, it is possible that some people will take the grace of God for granted. Indeed, who of us does not do this every day! It is possible that some will argue, "*Let us continue in sin that grace may abound*" (Romans 6:1). The apostle Paul was criticized for this very thing. Any doctrine of grace that cannot be so misunderstood is not a biblical doctrine of grace. Grace is, after all, unmerited favor. This is one of the most obvious objections to the Experimental Predestinarian view of eternal security and assurance. It is impossible that their view of perseverance (i.e., that it is inevitably and necessarily linked with justification) could ever result in the accusation, "*Let us continue in sin that grace may abound*." Their view, then, differs from the apostle Paul's. Westminster Calvinism could never be open to the charge of antinomianism because any antinomian is, by definition in their system, not a believer at all.

But the Bible is more realistic. Men like Saul, Solomon, and Alexander were all regenerate, but they did not persevere in either faith or well doing to the end of life. They presumed on the grace of God.

While it is true that Westminster Calvinism could never be accused of teaching antinomianism, it nevertheless indirectly promotes the very antinomianism it abhors. Experimental Predestinarians have seemingly removed future accountability from the life of the Christian. The Judgment Seat of Christ is like the Super Bowl, and salvation is a ticket. Moses and Paul will be seated on the fifty yard line. Even if we are in the last row of seats in the end zone, at least we are there. The difference between Moses and us will be irrelevant in the coming kingdom. Would it not follow that many who embrace this view of eternal security would begin to lapse into spiritual dullness? Without consequence and accountability people simply feel that the commands are negotiable.

The writer is aware that his Experimental Predestinarian friends will reply that, by exhorting their congregations to examine themselves to see if they are really saved, they have in fact introduced accountability. The fear that one is not really saved is supposedly a strong motivator to do good works. Apart from the fact that this approach is noticeably absent from the Scriptures, it does not work anyway. When confronted with such preaching, the average Christian does not reason, "My works are not good enough. Therefore, I am not saved, and I must make a new beginning." Rather, he assures himself, "I *know* I am saved. Therefore, my works *must* be good enough!" He intuitively senses the very thing the Experimental Predestinarian knows full well. It is impossible to define a certain level of works that are adequate to calm the claims of conscience and establish that one is saved. Therefore, such preaching is simply ignored, as it should be. Thus assured, he continues in his lethargy.

Granted, in the Partner view of eternal security, in eternity future the differences between Moses and us will not be an occasion of eternal regret, and we will know joy unspeakable. However, for the unfaithful believer, the future kingdom will be a time of profound temporary regret. The negative incentives of millennial disinheritance and missing the Master's "Well done!" will be deeply felt. The vast body of evangelical believers sitting under the Experimental Predestinarian system have concluded that, based on the fact they have believed and have glimmerings of life, they are born again. Simultaneously, they are taught that if they are born again, they cannot lose salvation. Furthermore, they are taught that the warnings, such as those in Hebrews 6, apply not to them but only to professing Christians. Having trusted in glimmerings of works in their lives, these Christians conclude they are saved and that they cannot lose salvation and that it will make no significant difference at the second coming anyway.

Furthermore, most of the Experimental Predestinarian objections to the Partner view of eternal security are focused too narrowly on the relative few who might take the grace of God for granted. They seem to reason that any system that allows a few to be saved who have presumed on grace could not be biblical. They are preoccupied with the few. The Partners are also concerned about those who abuse God's grace and mercy. However, they believe that this problem is caused, in part, by the fact the vast majority of Christians have lost their sense of accountability at the Judgment Seat of Christ. Why? It is because Experimental Predestinarians have assured them that because they are born again the warnings do not apply to them.

We believe the great neglect of Western Christianity is not that our pulpits have failed to warn people who claim the name of Christ that they are perishing. Our neglect is that we have not sufficiently explained the great future joy of sharing in the coming messianic partnership and the danger of forfeiting this inheritance. If such a vision were consistently held before our congregations, the love and fear of God would be greatly increased. Surely, many of those 50 million reported by the Gallup poll who claim to be born again would begin to act like it.

Conclusion

We now come to the end of the matter. The Lord promises to all who know Him they will enjoy unspeakable privilege in the final kingdom of David's Greater Son. That great future must constantly be set before the vision of all who name the Lord Jesus as their King. We should daily be evaluating our lives, our priorities, and our hearts in view of how we will feel about our decisions ten thousand years from now. Only those who live like this and who finish their course with the flag at full mast will share in the future reign of the servant kings.

Let us

> *lay aside every encumbrance, and the sin which so easily entangles us, and let us run with endurance the race that is set before us (Hebrews 12:1).*

After all, we

> *are Partners [Metochoi] of Christ, if we hold fast the beginning of our assurance firm until the end (Hebrews 3:14).*

The conclusion, when all has been heard, is: fear God and keep His commandments, because this applies to every person. For God will bring every act to judgment, everything which is hidden, whether it is good or evil (Ecclesiastes 12:13–14).

Epilogue

"NOW, I understand," said the archangel Michael, many years later as he reflected on the amazing grace revealed in the divine plan. "How appropriate, that the co-heirs should find their ultimate significance by following the same path as their Savior, and that the Savior Himself should enter their path as well."

"How typical of the Father," he thought, "that He would rebuke Satan's rebellion in a way that would cost Him the sacrifice of His beloved Son."

"How wise and how unexpected, that He would establish the inferior creatures as the aristocracy of the future kingdom."

The Lord of hosts had forever demonstrated the superiority of servanthood. The inferior creature, man, through the victory of *the Man,* had recovered through obedience and dependence what Satan had stolen in independence and unbelief. Truly, there was no place for pride in God's eternal purpose. God not only achieved this purpose but through the incarnation of His Son this became the principle illustration of a life of love and service necessary for its accomplishment:

> *Oh, the depth of the riches of the wisdom and knowledge of God! How unsearchable His judgments, and His paths beyond tracing out! Who has known the mind of the Lord? Or who has been His counselor? (Romans 11:33-34)*

The future reign of the servant kings is a central theme of the Bible. Everything relates in some way to the establishment of the kingdom of heaven. McClain has well said, "If there be a God in heaven, if the life which He created on the earth is worthwhile, and not something evil *per se*, then there ought to be in history some worthy consummation of its long and arduous course."[3337]

Without an earthly kingdom, history becomes a staircase, and nothing more, a stairway that goes nowhere. It is a loaded gun which, when the trigger is pulled, fires a blank cartridge. "Such a philosophy of history not only flies in the face of the clear statements of Scripture, but also runs contrary to the reason of man in his finest moments and aspiration."[3338] Yet this is exactly where many interpreters of the Bible have ended the story: centuries of misery and incomplete progress, and then a sudden catastrophic finish to the whole of it![3339]

[3337] Alva J. McClain, *The Greatness of the Kingdom* (Chicago: Moody Press, 1959), 530.

[3338] Alva J. McClain, "A Premillennial Philosophy of History," *BibSac* 113, no. 450 (1956).

[3339] McClain, *The Greatness of the Kingdom*, 531.

Alva J. McClain continues, "It is just here that we must part company with any theological school which dogmatically asserts that there will never be such a 'Golden Age' upon earth in history, which argues that for the present we must be satisfied with a mere pittance of progress in such matters, that the world which now is must continue with its terrible needs, its tragic handicaps, struggles and problems, to the very end. And then God will suddenly write a catastrophic finish to the whole of it, abolish human existence on its first and natural plane, and thrust us all, both saved and unsaved, out into the eternal state."[3340]

This incomplete philosophy of history will never satisfy the deepest longings of man. History finds its meaning and significance in the future reign of the servant kings. Within history, meaning and direction can be found. The fall of man and creation occurred within history, and it is essential that the redemption of man and creation occur within that process as well.

"What's wrong, Michael?" asked one of the other angels. The archangel seemed dejected.

"If only they would listen," he said.

"What do you mean?" the concerned angel replied.

"I have been thinking about the joy of the *Metochoi* at the Final Gathering. What an unspeakable privilege to be there and to be entrusted with the accomplishment of the Father's eternal purpose. Yet, some of those saved by the Son's sacrifice seem completely indifferent to eternal verities. They live as if the only reality is affluence and personal peace."

"Their ingratitude does become tiring," said Michael's colleague.

But then the archangel's face brightened when he remembered the millions who have persevered. Men and women to whom he had ministered, unknown to history, but who had proved faithful in the outworking of the eternal purpose. He warmly remembered the labors of the twelve apostles, the preaching of Whitefield and Wesley, the scholarly labors of John Calvin, the faithfulness of Adoniram Judson in Burma, of Hudson Taylor in China, and William Carey in India. He thought of the millions who have lived a life of discipleship in the workplace, of mothers in the home, of faithful pastors shepherding their flocks. He paused and thanked the Father for the privilege of encouraging such men and women in the accomplishment of their final destiny.

Then, servant that he was, Michael turned from his reflections and doubled his efforts to serve "*those who will inherit salvation*" (Hebrews 1:14).

3340 McClain, "A Premillennial Philosophy of History."

Scripture Index

Proverbs

Ecclesiastes

Isaiah

Jeremiah

Lamentations

Mark

Luke

John

Acts

Romans

1 Corinthians

2 Corinthians

Galatians

Ephesians

Philippians

Colossians

James

1 Peter

2 Peter

Author Index

Subject Index

T

Y

Z

Bibliography

Abasciano, Brian. "Corporate Election in Romans 9: A Reply to Thomas Schreiner." *JETS* 49, no. 2 (June 2006): 349-71.

Adams, Dwayne H. *The Sinner in Luke*. Eugene, OR: Pickwick Publications, 2008.

Albright, W. F., and C. S. Mann. *Matthew: A New Translation and Introduction*, Anchor Yale Bible Commentaries. New Haven, CT: Yale University Press, 1995.

Aldrich, Willard Maxwell. "Perseverance." *BibSac* 115, no. 457 (January - March 1958): 10-19.

Alexander, Archibald. *Thoughts on Religious Experience to which is added an appendix containing "Letters to the aged"*. Philadelphia: Presbyterian Board of Publication, 1844.

Alexander, Philip S. "Rabbinic Judaism and the New Testament." *Zeitschrift für die Neutestamentliches Wissenschaft* 74 (1983): 237-46.

Alexander, Philip S. "Torah and Salvation in Tannaitic Literature." In *Justification and Variegated Nomism: The Complexities of Second Temple Judaism*, edited by D. A. Carson, Peter Thomas O'Brien and Mark A. Seifrid. Grand Rapids: Baker Academic, 2001.

Alexander, Ralph. "Ezekiel." In *The Expositor's Bible Commentary: Isaiah, Jeremiah, Lamentations, Ezekiel*, edited by Frank E. Gaebelein. Grand Rapids: Zondervan Publishing House, 1986.

Alford, Henry. "2 Peter." In *The Greek Testament*. Chicago: Moody Press, 1966.

Alford, Henry. "Revelation." In *Alford's Greek Testament: An Exegetical and Critical Commentary*. Bellingham, WA: Logos Bible Software, 2010.

Alford, Henry. "Romans." In *Alford's Greek Testament: An Exegetcial and Critical Commentary*. Bellingham, WA: Logos Bible Software, 2010.

Alford, Henry, and Everett Falconer Harrison. "Matthew." In *The Greek Testament: with a Critically Revised Text, a Digest of Various Readings, Marginal References to Verbal and Idiomatic Usage, Prolegomena, and a Critical and Exegetical Commentary*. Chicago: Moody Press, 1958.

Allen, Willoughby C. *A Critical and Exegetical Commentary on the Gospel According to St. Matthew*, The International Critical Commentary. New York: C. Scribner's Sons, 1907.

Alon, Gedalyahu. *Jews, Judaism and the Classical World*. Translated by Israel Abrahams. Jerusalem: The Magnes Press, 1977.

Ambrose. "Selections from the Letters of Ambrose: Letter 22." In *A Select Library of the Nicene and Post-Nicene Fathers of the Christian Church, Second Series, Volume X: St. Ambrose: Select Works and Letters*, edited by Philip Schaff and H. Wace. Buffalo, NY: Christian Literature Company, 1986.

Anderson, Dave. "Repentance is for all Men." *Journal of the Grace Evangelical Theological Society* 11, no. 1 (Spring 98): 3-20.

Anderson, David R. *Free Grace Soteriology*. Lakeland, FL: Xulon Press, 2010.

Anderson, David R. *Maximum Joy: First John - Relationship or Fellowship*. Irving, TX: Grace Evangelical Society, 2005.

Anderson, David R. "The National Repentance of Israel." *JOTGES* 11, no. 2 (Autumn 1998): 18-37.

Andrews, L. F. W. *The Two Opinions: Salvation or Damnation; Being an Inquiry into the Truth of Certain Theological Tennants Prevalent in the Year of Our Lord 1837*. Macon, GA: Self Published 1837.

Aquinas, Saint Thomas, and John Henry Newman. *St. Matthew* Vol. 1, Catena Aurea: Commentary on the Four Gospels, Collected out of the Works of the Fathers. Oxford: John Henry Parker, 1874.

Arminius, Jacobus, James Nichols, William Nichols, and Carl Bangs. *The Works of James Arminius*. London, Reprint ed. 3 vols. Grand Rapids: Baker Book House, 1986.

Athanasius. "Festal Letters." In *A Select Library of the Nicene and Post-Nicene Fathers of the Christian Church, Second Series, Volume 4: St. Athanasius: Select Works and Letters*, edited by P. Schaff and H. Wace. Buffalo, NY: Christian Literature Company, 1982.

Attridge, Harold W., and Helmut Koester. *Hebrews: A Commentary on the Epistle to the Hebrews*, Hermeneia. Philadelphia: Fortress Press, 1989.

Augustine. *City of God*.

Augustine. "On the Predestination of the Saints." In *The Nicene and Post-Nicent Fathers of the Church - Anti pelagian Writings*, edited by Philip Schaff. Grand Rapids: Wm. B. Eerdmans Publishing Co., 1956.

Augustine. "Tractates on John." In *Nicene and Post-Nicene Fathers* edited by Philip Schaff. Oak Harbor, WA: Logos Research Systems, 1997.

Augustine. "A Treatise on Nature and Grace: Chapter 48 - How the Term 'All' Is to Be Understood." In *Nicene and Post Nicene Fathers First Series Volume V: Saint Agustin: Anti-Pelagian Writings*, edited by Philip Schaff. New York: Christian Literature Company, 1887.

Augustine. "A Treatise on the Spirit and the Letter." In *A Select Library of the Nicene and Post-Nicene Fathers of the Christian Church, First Series, Volume V: Saint Augustin: Anti-Pelagian Writings*, edited by Philip Schaff. Buffalo, NY: Christian Literature Company, 1987.

Aune, David E. *Revelation 1-5*, Word Biblical Commentary. Dallas, TX: Word Books, 1997.

Aune, David Edward. *Prophecy in early Christianity and the ancient Mediterranean world*. Grand Rapids: Wm. B. Eerdmans Publishing Co., 1983.

Badger, Anthony. "TULIP: A Free Grace Perspective Part 2: Unconditional Election." *JOTGETS* 16, no. 2 (Autumn 2003): 16-41.

Bailey, Kenneth E. *Poet and Peasant and through Peasant Eyes: A Literary-cultural Approach to the Parables in Luke*. Grand Rapids: Wm. B. Eerdmans Publishing Co., 1983.

Bailey, Kenneth E. "The Pursuing Father." *Christianity Today* (October 26, 1998): 34-40.

Bailey, Lloyd. "The Topography of Gehenna." *Biblical Archaeologist* 49 (September 1986).

Balfour, Walter. *An Inquiry into the Scriptural Import of the Words Sheol, Hades, Tartarus, and Gehenna in the Common English Version*. Charlestown, MA: Geo. Davidson, http:\\www.books.google.com, 1824.

Ball, W. E. *St. Paul and Roman Law and Other Studies on the Origin and Form of Doctrine*. Edinburgh: T&T Clark, 1901.

Barbieri, Louis. "Matthew." *In BKC: New Testament*, edited by John Walvord and Roy B. Zuck. Colorado Springs: Cook, 1996.

Barclay, William. *The Gospel of Matthew*. rev. ed. 2 vols. Philadelphia: Westminster Press, 1975.

Barkay, Gabriel. "The Riches of Ketef Hinnom." *Biblical Archaeological Review* 34, no. 4-5 (2005): 22-35, 122-26.

Barker, Kenneth L., and D. Waylon Bailey. *Micah, Nahum, Habakkuk, Zephaniah*, New American commentary. Nashville: Broadman & Holman, 1999.

Barnett, Paul. *The Second Epistle to the Corinthians*, The New International Commentary on the New Testament. Grand Rapids: Wm. B. Eerdmans Publishing Co., 1997.

Barnhouse, Donald G. *Messages to the Seven Churches*. Philadelphia: Eternity Book Service, 1953.

Barnhouse, Donald Grey. *God's Last Word: Revelation; an Expository commentary*. Grand Rapids: Zondervan Publishing House, 1971.

Barnhouse, Donald Grey. *The Invisible War*. Grand Rapids: Zondervan Publishing House, 1965.

Bar-Oz, Guy, Ram Bouchnik, Ehud Weiss, Lior Weissbrod, Daniella E. Bar-Yosef Mayer, and Ronny Reich. "Holy Garbage": A Quantitative Study of the City-Dump of Early Roman Jerusalem." *Levant* 39 (2007): 1-12.

Barr, James. *The Semantics of Biblical Languages*. London: Oxford University Press, 1961.

Barrett, C. K. *A Commentary on the Second Epistle to the Corinthians*. New York: Harper & Row, 1973.

Bass, Christopher D. *That You May Know: Assurance of Salvation in 1 John*. Edited by E. Ray Clendenen, NAC Studies in Bible & Theology. Nashville: B & H Publishing Group, 2008.

Bauckham, Richard. *The Fate of the Dead: Studies on the Jewish and Christian Apocalypses*, Supplements to Novum Testamentum. Boston: Brill, 1998.

Bauckham, Richard. *The Jewish World around the New Testament*. Tübingen: Mohr Siebeck, 2008.

Bauckham, Richard. *Jude, 2 Peter*, Word Biblical Themes. Dallas: Word Publishers, 1990.

Baxter, J. Sidlow. *Mark These Men: Practical Studies in Striking Aspects of Certain Bible Characters*. Grand Rapids: Zondervan Publishing House, 1960.

Baxter, Wayne. "The Narrative Setting of the Sermon on the Mount." *Trinity Journal* 25, no. 1 (Spring 2004): 27-37.

Beale, G. K. *The Book of Revelation: A Commentary on the Greek Text*. Grand Rapids: Wm. B. Eerdmans Publishing Co., 1999.

Beale, G. K., and D. A. Carson. *Commentary on the New Testament Use of the Old Testament* Grand Rapids: Baker Academic, 2007.

Bechtel, P. M. "Chaucer, Geoffrey." In *Who's Who in Church History*, edited by J. D. Douglas and Philip W. Comfort. Wheaton, IL: Tyndale House, 1992.

Beeke, Joel. "Personal Assurance of Faith and Chapter 18:2 of the Westminster Confession." *WSJ* 55, no. 1 (Spring 1993): 1-30.

Bell, M. Charles. *Calvin and the Scottish Theology: The Doctrine of Assurance*. Edinburgh: Handsel Press, 1985.

Bell, Rob. *Love Wins: A Book about Heaven, Hell, and The Fate of Every Person Who Ever Lived*. New York: Harper Collins, 2011.

Benedict, Richard R. "The Use of *Nikaō* in the Letters to the Seven Churches of Revelation." Th.M. thesis, Dallas Theological Seminary, 1966.

Berkhof, Louis. *Systematic Theology*. Grand Rapids: Wm. B. Eerdmans Publishing Co., 1996.

Berkouwer, G. C. *Faith and Justification*. Grand Rapids: Wm. B. Eerdmans Publishing Co., 1954.

Berkouwer, G. C. *Faith and Perseverance*. Grand Rapids: Wm. B. Eerdmans Publishing Co., 1958.

Bernard, J. H., and A. H. McNeile. *A critical and exegetical commentary on the Gospel according to St. John*. 2 vols. Edinburgh: T. & T. Clark, 1928.

Betz, Hans Dieter. *Galatians: A Commentary on Paul's Letter to the Churches in Galatia*, Hermenia. Philadelphia: Fortress Press, 1979.

Betz, Hans Dieter, and Adela Yarbro Collins. *The Sermon on the Mount: A Commentary on the Sermon on the Mount, Including the Sermon on the Plain (Matthew 5:3-7:27 and Luke 6:20-49)*, Hermeneia. Minneapolis: Fortress Press, 1995.

The Bible Knowledge Commentary: New Testament. Edited by John F. Walvoord and Roy B. Zuck. reprint, Colorado Springs: Cook, 1996 ed. Wheaton, IL: Victor Books, 1983.

The Bible Knowledge Commentary: Old Testament. Edited by John F. Walvoord and Roy B. Zuck. Reprint, Colorado Springs: Cook, 1986 ed. Wheaton, IL.: Victor Books, 1985.

Billheimer, Paul E. *Destined for the Throne*. rev. ed. Minneapolis: Bethany House, 1975.

Bing, Charles C. "Coming to Terms with Discipleship." *JOTGES* (Spring 1992): 35-49.
Bing, Charles C. "The Condition for Salvation in John's Gospel." *JOTGES* 9, no. 1 (Spring 1996): 24-36.
Bing, Charles C. "Does Fire in Hebrews Refer to Hell?" *BibSac* 167, no. 667 (July-September 2010): 342-57.
Bird, Michael F. "Incorporated Righteousness A Response To Recent Evangelical Discussion Concerning The Imputation Of Christ's Righteousness in Justification." *JETS* 47, no. 2 (June 2004): 253-75.
Blaising, Craig A., and Darrell L. Bock. *Progressive Dispensationalism*. Wheaton, IL: Bridgeport - Victor Books, 1993.
Blomberg, Craig. *Interpreting Parables*. Downers Grove, IL: InterVarsity Press, 1990.
Blomberg, Craig. "Parables." In *The International Standard Bible Encyclopedia*, edited by G. W. Bromiley and Everett F. Harrison. Grand Rapids: William B. Eerdmans Publishing Co., 1986.
Blomberg, Craig L. "Degrees of Reward in the Kingdom of Heaven?" *JETS* 35, no. 2 (1992): 159-72.
Blomberg, Craig L. *Jesus and the Gospels: An Introduction and Survey*. Nashville, Tenn.: Broadman & Holman, 1997.
Blomberg, Craig L. *Matthew*, New American Commentary. Nashville: Broadman and Holman Publishers, 2001.
Blomberg, Craig L. "When is a Parallel Really a Parallel? A Test Case: The Lucan Parables." *WTJ* 46, no. 1 (Spring 1984): 78-103.
Bloom, Allan David. *The Closing of the American Mind: How Higher Education Has Failed Democracy and Impoverished the Souls of Today's Students*. New York: Simon and Schuster, 1987.
Blum, Edward. "1 Peter." In *The Expositor's Bible Commentary*, edited by Frank E. Gaebelein. Grand Rapids: Zondervan Publishing House, 1976.
Blum, Edward A. "John." In *BKC: New Testament*, edited by John F. Walvoord and Roy Zuck. Colorado Springs: Cook, 2002.
Bock, Darrell L. "Current Messianic Activity and OT Davidic Promise: Dispensationalism, Hermeneutics, and NT Fulfillment." *TJ* 15, no. 1 (Spring 1994): 55-87.
Bock, Darrell L. *Luke*. 2 vols. Grand Rapids: Baker Books, 1994.
Bock, Darrell L. *Luke 1-9:50*, Baker Exegetical Commentary on the New Testament. Grand Rapids: Baker Book House, 1996.
Bock, Darrell L. *Luke 9:51-24:53*, Baker Exegetical Commentary on the New Testament. Grand Rapids: Baker Book House, 1996.
Bock, Darrell L. "New Testament Word Analysis." In *Introducing New Testament Interpretation: Guides to New Testament Exegesis*, edited by McKnight Scot, 96-114. Grand Rapids: Baker Books, 1989.
Bock, Darrell L. "A Review of *The Gospel According to Jesus*." *BibSac* 146, no. 581 (January-March 1989).
Boettner, Loraine. *The Reformed Doctrine of Predestination*. Pittsburgh: Presbyterian and Reformed Publishing Co., 1932.
Boice, James Montgomery. *The Sermon on the Mount*. Grand Rapids: Zondervan Publishing House, 1972.
Bonar, Horatius. *God's Way of Holiness*. Chicago: Moody, n.d.
The Book of Concord and the Confessions of the Evangelical Lutheran Church. Edited by T. G. Tappert. Philadelphia: Mühlenberg Press, 1959.
Borg, Marcus J. "Jesus (Person)." In *The Anchor Yale Bible Dictionary*, edited by David Noel Freedman, Gary A. Herion and David F. Graf. New York: Doubleday, 1996.
Bovon, François, and Helmut Koester. *Luke: A Commentary on the Gospel of Luke*. Minneapolis: Fortress Press, 2002.

Bower, R. K., and G. L. Knapp. "Marriage." In *NISBE (1986)*, edited by G. W. Bromiley. Grand Rapids: William B. Eerdmans Publishing Co., 1986.

Boyer, James L. "First Class Conditions: What Do They Mean?" *GTJ* 2, no. 73-114 (Spring 1981).

Brain, Karl. *The First Epistle General of John*. Edited by J. P. Lange, P. Schaff, K. Brain and J. I. Mombert. Electronic, Reprint ed, A Commentary on the Holy Scriptures: 1, 2, 3, John. Bellingham, WA: Logos Research Systems, 2008.

Brand, Chad. "Gehenna." In *Hollman Illustrated Bible Dictionary*, edited by Chad Brand, Charles Draper and Archie England. Nashville: Holman Bible Publishers, 2003.

Bridges, Jerry. *Trusting God When It Hurts*. Colorado Springs: Nav Press, 1988.

Briggs, Charles A., and Emilie Grace Briggs. *A Critical and Exegetical Commentary on the Book of Psalms*. 2 vols. Edinburgh: T. & T. Clark, 1906.

Brindle, Wayne A. "The Causes of the Divisions of Israel's Kingdom." *BibSac* 141, no. 563 (July-September 1984): 220-33.

Brooke, A. E. *Critical and Exegetical Commentary on the Johannine Epistles*. New York: Scribner's Sons, 1912.

Brown, David. "Matthew." In *Commentary Critical and Explanatory on the Whole Bible*, edited by Robert Jamieson, A. R. Fausset and David Brown. Oak Harbor, WA: Logos Research Systems, 1997.

Brown, Perry C. "What is the Meaning of 'Examine Yourselves' in 2 Cor. 13:5?" *BibSac* 154, no. 614 (April-June 1997): 174-88.

Brown, Raymond Edward. *The Epistles of John*. 1st ed. Garden City, NY: Doubleday, 1982.

Brown, William E. "The New Testament Concept of the Believer's Inheritance." ThD diss., Dallas Theological Seminary, 1984.

Bruce, A. B. "Matthew." In *The Expositor's Greek Testament*, edited by W. Robertson Nicoll. Grand Rapids: Wm. B. Eerdmans Publishing Co., 1967.

Bruce, F. F. *The Epistle to the Hebrews*. rev. ed, The New International Commentary on the New Testament. Grand Rapids: Wm. B. Eerdmans Publishing Co., 1990.

Bruce, F. F. *The Epistles to the Colossians, to Philemon, and to the Ephesians*. Grand Rapids: Wm. B. Eerdmans Publishing Co., 1984.

Bruce, F. F. *The Letter of Paul to the Romans: An Introduction and Commentary*. 2nd ed, Tyndale New Testament commentaries. Grand Rapids: Wm. B. Eerdmans Publishing Co., 1985.

Bruce, F. F. *Philippians*, A Good News Commentary. San Francisco: Harper & Row, 1983.

Bruce, F. F. *Romans: An Introduction and Commentary*, Tyndale New Testament commentaries. Downers Grove, IL: Intervarsity Press, 2008.

Bullinger, E. W. *Figures of Speech Used in the Bible: Explained and Illustrated*. Reprint ed. Grand Rapids: Baker Book House, 1968.

Bultmann, Rudolf K. *The Johannine Epistles: A Commentary on the Johanine Epistles*, Hermeneia. Philadelphia: Fortress Press, 1973.

Burton, Ernest De Witt. *A Critical and Exegetical Commentary on the Epistle to the Galatians*. Edinburgh: T. & T. Clark, 1964.

Bush, George. *Notes, Critical and Practical, on the Book of Numbers*. Minneapolis: Klock & Klock, 1981.

Buswell, J. Oliver. *A Systematic Theology of the Christian Religion*. Grand Rapids: Zondervan Publishing House, 1962.

Buttrick, George Arthur. *The Interpreter's Dictionary of the Bible*. 4 vols. New York: Abingdon Press, 1962.

Cadoux, Cecil John. *The Historic Mission of Jesus: A Constructive Re-examination of the Eschatological Teaching in the Synoptic Gospels*. New York: Harper, 1943.

Calvin, Jean, and John Kelman Sutherland Reid. *Concerning the Eternal Predestination of God.* Louisville, KY: Westminster John Knox Press, 1997.

Calvin, John. *1 Corinthians.* Electronic ed, Calvin's Commentaries. Albany, OR: Ages Software, 1998.

Calvin, John. *1 John.* Electronic ed, Calvin's Commentaries. Albany, OR: Ages Software, 1998.

Calvin, John. *2 Peter.* Electronic ed, Calvin's Commentaries. Albany, OR: Ages Software, 1998.

Calvin, John. *Acts of the Council of Trent: with the Antidote.*

Calvin, John. *Ephesians.* Electronic ed, Calvin's Commentaries. Albany, OR: Ages Software, 1998.

Calvin, John. *Galatians.* Electronic ed, Calvin's Commentaries. Albany, OR: Ages Software, 1998.

Calvin, John. *The Harmony of the Gospels: Calvin's Commentary on Matthew, Mark, and Luke*, Calvin's Commentaries. Albany, OR: Ages Software, 1998.

Calvin, John. *John.* Electronic ed, Calvin's Commentaries. Albany, OR: Ages Software., 1998.

Calvin, John. *Joshua.* Electronic ed, Calvin's Commentaries. Albany, OR: Ages Software, 1998.

Calvin, John. *Luke.* Electronic ed, Calvin's Commentaries. Albany, OR: Ages Software, 1998.

Calvin, John. "Prefatory Address to Francis, King of France." In *Institutes of the Christian Religion.* Grand Rapids: Wm. B. Eerdmans Publishing Co., 1964.

Calvin, John. *Romans*, Calvin's Commentaries. Albany, OR: Ages Software, 1998.

Calvin, John, and John Owen. *Commentary on the Epistle of Paul to the Romans*, Calvin's Commentaries. Bellingham, WA: Logos Bible Software, 2010.

Campbell, Barth Lynn. "Flesh and Spirit in 1 Cor 5:5: An Exercise in Rhetorical Criticism of the NT." *JETS* 36, no. 3 (1993): 331-42.

Campbell, W. S. "Olive Tree." In *Dictionary of Paul and His Letters*, edited by Gerald F Hawthorne, Ralph P. Martin and Daniel G. Reid. Downers Grove, IL: InterVarsity Press, 1993.

Canon and Decrees of the Council of Trent. Translated by H. J. Schroeder. Rockford, IL: Tan, 1978.

Caragounis, C. C. "Kingdom of God/Kingdom of Heaven." In *Dictionary of Jesus and the Gospels*, edited by Joel B. Green, Scot McKnight and I. Howard Marshall. Downers Grove, IL: InterVarsity Press, 1992.

Carroll, Lewis. *Through the Looking-glass.* New York: Duell, 1959.

Carson, D. A. *The Gospel According to John.* Downers Grove, IL: InterVarsity, 1991.

Carson, D. A. *Jesus' Sermon on the Mount and His Confrontation with the World.* Grand Rapids: Baker Book House, 1987.

Carson, D. A. "Matthew." In *The New Bible Commentary: 21st Century Edition*, edited by D. Guthrie and J. A. Motyer. Downers Grove, IL: InterVarsity Press, 1994.

Carson, D. A. "Matthew." *In The Expositor's Bible Commentary, Volume 8: Matthew, Mark, Luke.* Grand Rapids: Zondervan Publishing House, 1984.

Carson, D. A. *The Gospel According to John.* Downers Grove, IL: InterVarsity, 1991.

Carson, D. A. "Reflections on Christian Assurance." *WTJ* 54 (Spring 1992).

Cauley, Marty. *The Outer Darkness.* 2 vols. Sylva, NC: Misthological Press, 1231 Monteith Branch Road, 2012.

Chafer, Lewis Sperry. "The Doctrine of Sin: Part 5." *BibSac* 93, no. 369 (January-March 1936): 5-25.

Chafer, Lewis Sperry. "The Sins of Christians." *BibSac* 109, no. 433 (January-March 52).

Chafer, Lewis Sperry. *Systematic Theology.* Edited by John F. Walvoord, abridged ed. 2 vols. Wheaton: Victor, 1988.

Chafer, Lewis Sperry. *Systematic Theology.* Dallas: Dallas Seminary Press, 1947.

Chafer, Lewis Sperry, and John F. Walvoord. *Major Bible Themes: 52 Vital Doctrines of the Scripture Simplified and Explained.* Grand Rapids: Zondervan Publishing House, 1974.

Chan, Francis, and Preston M. Sprinkle. *Erasing Hell.* Colorado Springs: David C. Cook, 2011.

Charles, R. H., ed. *The Apocrypha and Pseudepigrapha of the Old Testament in English.* Oxford: Clarendon Press, 1913.

Charles, R. H. *A Critical and Exegetical Commentary on the Revelation of St. John*, International Critical Commentary. Edinburgh: T. & T. Clark, 1920.

Charles, Robert Henry. *Commentary on the Pseudepigrapha of the Old Testament*. 2 vols. Bellingham, WA: Logos Research Systems, 1913, 2004.

Charlesworth, James H., ed. *The Old Testament Pseudepigrapha*. 1st ed. Garden City, NY: Doubleday, 1983.

Chay, Fred. "A Textual and Theological Exposition of the Logion: The Salvation of the Soul." PhD diss., Trinity Theological Seminary, 2003.

Chay, Fred, and John P. Correia. *The Faith That Saves: The Nature of Faith in the New Testament*. Haysville, NC: Schoettle Publishing Co., 2008.

Chilton, Bruce. *Judaic Approaches to the Gospels*. Atlanta: Scholars Press, 1994.

Chilton, Bruce D. "Jesus and the Repentance of E. P. Sanders." *Tyndale Bulletin* 39, no. 1 (1988): 1-18.

Chilton, Bruce D. "Targums." In *Dictionary of Jesus and the Gospels*, edited by Joel B. Green, Scot McKnight and I. Howard Marshall, xxv, 933 p. Downers Grove, IL: InterVarsity Press, 1992.

Chilton, Bruce. "RABBINIC LITERATURE: TARGUMIM." In *Dictionary of New Testament background: a compendium of contemporary biblical scholarship.*, edited by S. E. Porter, & Evans, C. A. . Downers Grove, IL: InterVarsity Press, 2000.

Chisholm, Robert B. "Does God Change His Mind?" *BibSac* 152, no. 2 (October-December 1995).

Chrisope, Terry A. *Jesus is Lord: A Study in the Unity of Confessing Jesus as Lord and Saviour in the New Testament*. Welwyn, Hertfordshire, UK: Evangelical Press, 1982.

Chrysostom, John. "Homilies on First Corinthians." In *A Select Library of the Nicene and Post-Nicene Fathers of the Christian Church, First Series, Volume XII: Saint Chrysostom: Homilies on the Epistles of Paul to the Corinthians*, edited by Philip Schaff. Buffalo, NY: Christian Literature Company, 1989.

Chrysostom, John. "Homilies on Matthew." In *A Select Library of the Nicene and Post-Nicene Fathers of the Christian Church, First Series, Volume X*, edited by P. Schaff. New York: Christian Literature Company, 1988.

Chrysostom, John "Homilies on Romans." In *Nicene and Post-Nicene Fathers, First Series*, edited by Philip Schaff. Oak Harbor: Logos Research Systems, 1997.

Ciampa, R. E., and B. S. Rosner. *The First Letter to the Corinthians*, Pillar New Testament Commentary. Grand Rapids: Wm. B. Eerdmans Publishing Co., 2010.

Clark, Gordon Haddon. *What Is Saving Faith?* Jefferson, MD: Trinity Foundation, 2004.

Clarke, Adam. *Adam Clarke's Commentary*. Logos Library System Electronic ed. Albany, OR: Ages Software, 1999.

Clarke, Adam. "First Corinthians." In *Clarke's Commentaries*. Albany, OR: Ages Software, 1999.

Clarke, Adam. *Matthew*, Clarke's Commentary. Albany, OR: Ages Software, 1999.

Clarke, Adam. "Numbers." In *Adam Clarke's Commentary*. Albany, OR: Ages Software, 1999.

Clement. "The First Epistle of Clement to the Corinthians." In *The Ante-Nicene Fathers: Volume 1: The Apostolic Fathers with Justin Martyr and Irenaeus*, edited by J Roberts, J. Donaldson and A. C. Coxe. Buffalo, NY: Christian Literature Company, 1885.

Colijn, Brenda B. "The Three Tenses of Salvation in Paul's Letters." *Ashland Theological Journal* 22 (1990): 29-37.

Collins, John J. "Sibylline Oracles." In *Anchor Bible Dictionary*, edited by David Noel Freedman. New York: Doubleday, 1922.

Constable, Tom. *Tom Constable's Expository Notes on the Bible*. Garland, TX: Galaxie Software, 2003.

Conzelmann, Hans. *1 Corinthians: A Commentary on the First Epistle to the Corinthians*, Hermeneia. Philadelphia: Fortress Press, 1975.

Coppes, Leonard J. *Are Five Points Enough? The Ten Points of Calvinism*. Denver: the author, 1980.

Covey, Stephen R. *The Seven Habits of Highly Effective People*. New York: Schuster, 1989.
Crabb, Lawrence J. *The Marriage Builder: A Blueprint for Couples and Counselors*. rev ed. Grand Rapids: Zondervan Publishing House, 1982.
Craig, William Lane. "Lest Anyone Should Fall: A Middle Knowledge Perspective on Perseverance and Apostolic Warnings." *International Journal for Philosophy of Religion* 29, no. 2 (1991): 65-74.
Craigie, P. C. *Psalms 1-50*, Word Biblical Commentary. Dallas: Word, 2002.
Craigie, Peter C., Kelly Page H., and Joel F. Drinkard. *Jeremiah 1-26*, Word Biblical Commentary. Dallas: Word Books, 1991.
Cranfield, C. E. B. *A Critical and Exegetical Commentary on the Epistle to the Romans*. New York: T. & T. Clark International, 2004.
Craston, R. C. "Inheritance." In *Evangelical Dictionary of Theology*, 561. Grand Rapids: Baker Book House, 1984.
Cremer, Hermann. *Biblico-theologial Lexicon of New Testament Greek*. New York: T. & T. Clark, 1954.
Crenshaw, Curtis I. *Lordship Salvation: The Only Kind There Is - An Evaluation of Jody Dillow's The Reign of the Servant Kings and Other Antinomian Arguments*. Memphis: Footstool Publications, 1995.
Cross, F. L., and E. A. Livingston. *The Oxford Dictionary of the Christian Church*. Oxford; New York: Oxford University Press, 2005.
Crouch, Owen L. *Expository Preaching and Teaching: Hebrews*. Joplin, Mo.: College Press Pub. Co., 1983.
Crutchfield, Larry. "The Third Jewish Sect: The Essenes." *The Bible and the Space* 2, no. 4 (Autumn 1989): 104-13.
Culver, Robert D. "A Neglected Millennial Passage from Saint Paul." *BibSac* 113, no. 450 (April-June 1956): 141-52.
Cunningham, William. "Sec.IV: Justification by Faith." In *Historical Theology: A Review of the Principal Doctrinal Discussions in the Christian Church Since the Apostolic Age*. Edinburgh: T&T Clark, 1864.
Curtis, E. L., and A. A. Madson. *A Critical and Exegetical Commentary on the Books of Chronicles*, International Critical Commentary. New York: Scribner Sons, 1910.
Dabney, Robert L. *Lectures in Systematic Theology*. Reprint ed. Grand Rapids: Zondervan Publishing House, 1972.
Danker, Frederick W. *Jesus and the New Age: A Commentary on St. Luke's Gospel*. completely rev. and expanded. ed. Philadelphia: Fortress Press, 1988.
Davids, Peter H. *The Epistle of James: A Commentary on the Greek Text*. Grand Rapids: Wm. B. Eerdmans Publishing Co., 1982.
Davids, Peter H. *The First Epistle of Peter*, New International Commentary on the New Testament. Grand Rapids: Wm. B. Eerdmans Publishing Co., 1990.
Davidson, A. B. *The Epistle to the Hebrews*. Edinburgh: T. & T. Clark, 1959.
Davies, R. E. "Gehenna." In *Zondervan Pictorial Encyclopedia of the Bible*, edited by Merrill C. Tenney. Grand Rapids: Zondervan Publishing House, 1975.
Davies, W. D. *The Setting of the Sermon on the Mount*. Cambridge: University Press, 1964.
Davies, W. D., and Dale C. Allison. *A Critical and Exegetical Commentary on the Gospel According to Saint Matthew*. Edinburgh: T. & T. Clark, 1988.
Davison, James E. "Anomia and the Question of an Antinomian Polemic in Matthew." *JBL* 104, no. 4 (Dec. 1985): 617-36.
Deissman, G. Adolph. *Bible Studies*. Reprint, 1923 ed. Winona Lake: Alpha Publications, 1979.
Denny, James. "Paul's Epistle to the Romans." In *The Expositor's Greek Testament*, edited by W. Robertson Nicoll. Grand Rapids: Wm. B. Eerdmans Publishing Co.
Denzer, George A. "The Pastoral Letters." In *Jerome Biblical Commentary*, edited by Raymond E.

Brown, Joseph A. Fitzmeyer and Roland E. Murphy. Englewood Cliffs, NJ: Prentice Hall, 1968.

Derickson, Gary W. "Viticulture and John 15:1-6." *BibSac* 153, no. 609 (January-March 1996): 34-52.

Derickson, Gary W. "What is the Message of 1 John?" *BibSac* 150, no. 597 (January-March 1993): 88-105.

Derickson, Gary W., and Earl D. Radmacher. *The Disciplemaker: What Matters Most to Jesus*. Salem, OR: Charis, 2001.

Derrett, J. Duncan. "The Merits of the Narrow Gate." *JSNT* 15 (1982): 20-29.

Dibelius, Martin, and Heinrich Greeven. *James: A Commentary on the Epistle of James*. 11th rev. ed, Hermeneia. Philadelphia: Fortress Press, 1975.

Dictionary of Paul and His Letters. Edited by Gerald F Hawthorne, Ralph P. Martin and Daniel G. Reid. Downers Grove, IL: InterVarsity Press, 1993.

"Didache." In *The Apostolic Fathers: Greek Texts and English Translations of their Writings*, edited by Joseph Barber Lightfoot, J. R. Harmer and Michael W. Holmes. Grand Rapids: Baker Book House, 1992.

Dillard, Raymond B. "Reward and Punishment in Chronicles: The Theology of Immediate Retribution." *WSJ* 46, no. 1 (Spring 1984): 164-71.

Dillow, Joseph C. *The Reign of the Servant Kings: A Study of Eternal Security and the Final Significance of Man*. Miami Springs, FL: Schoettle Publishing Co., 1992.

Disley, Emma. "Degrees of Glory: The Protestant Doctrine and the Concept of Rewards Hereafter." *JTS* 42, no. 1 (April 1991): 77-105.

Dodds, Marcus. "The Epistle to the Hebrews." In *The Expositor's Greek Testament*, edited by W. Robertson Nicoll. Grand Rapids: Wm. B. Eerdmans Publishing Co., 1967.

Douglas, J. D. *The New Bible Dictionary*. 3rd ed. Downers Grove, IL.: InterVarsity Press, 1962.

du Toit, A. *The New Testament Milieu*. Halfway House, London: Orion Publishers, 1998.

"Dung." In *The Eerdmans Bible Dictionary*, edited by Allen C. Myers. Grand Rapids: Wm. B. Eerdmans Publishing Co., 1987.

Dunn, James D. G. *Romans 1-8*, Word Biblical Commentary. Dallas: Word, 2002.

Dunn, James D. G. *Romans 9-16*, The Word Biblical Commentary. Dallas: Word, 2002.

Durant, Will. *The Life of Greece*. Vol. 2, The Story of Civilization. New York: Simon and Schuster, 1966.

Durham, John. *Exodus*, Word Biblical Commentary. Dallas: Word, 2002.

Eadie, John. *A Commentary on the Greek Text of the Epistle of Paul to the Philippians*. Grand Rapids: Zondervan Publishing House, 1953.

Eager, George B. "Marriage." In *ISBE (1915)*, edited by James Orr. Albany, OR: Ages Software.

Eaton, Michael. *Living Under Grace*. Nashville: Word Publishing, 1994.

Eaton, Michael. *Return to Glory: Preaching Through Romans*. Carlisle, UK: Paternoster Press, 1999.

Eaton, Michael A. *No Condemnation: A New Theology of Assurance*. Downers Grove, IL: InterVarsity Press, 1995.

Eckert, P. *Steve Green's MIDI Hymnal: A Complete Toolkit for Personal Devotions and Corporate Worship*. Bellingham, WA: Logos Bible Software, 1998.

Edersheim, Alfred. *The Life and Times of Jesus the Messiah*. New American Edition ed. 2 vols. Grand Rapids: Wm. B. Eerdmans Publishing Co., 1962.

Edersheim, Alfred. *Sketches of Jewish Social Life in the Days of Christ*. Grand Rapids: Wm. B. Eerdmans Publishing Co., 1974.

Edgar, Thomas R. "The Meaning of 'Sleep' in 1 Thessalonians 5:10." *JETS* 22, no. 4 (December 1979): 344-49.

Edgar, Thomas R. "Robert H. Gundry and Revelation 3:10." *Grace Theological Journal* 3, no. 1 (Spring 1982): 19-42.

Ediger, Edwin Aaron. *Faith in Jesus: What Does it Mean to Believe in Him?* Boomington, IN: Westbow Press: A Division of Thomas Nelson, 2012.

Edwards, J. R. *The Gospel of Mark*, Pillar New Testament Commentary. Grand Rapids: Wm. B. Eerdmans Publishing Co., 2002.

Edwards, James R. *Romans*, New International Biblical Commentary. Peabody, MA: Hendrickson Publishers, 1992.

Ellingworth, Paul, and Howard A. Hatton. *A Handbook on Paul's First Letter to the Corinthians*, UBS Handbook Series. New York: United Bible Societies, 1995.

Erickson, Millard J. *Christian Theology*. Grand Rapids: Baker Book House, 1985.

Essel, W. W. "James - Literary Character - Diatribe Theory." In *NISBE*, edited by G. W. Bromiley. Grand Rapids: Wm. B. Eerdmans Publishing Co., 1988.

Eusebius. "Church History." In *The Nicene and Post-Nicene Fathers: Second Series*, edited by Philip Schaff. Oak Harbor, WA: Logos Research Systems, 1997.

Evans, C. A. *Mark 8:27-16:20*, Word Biblical Commentary. Dallas: Word, 2002.

Evans, Craig A. *From Prophecy to Testament: The Function of the Old Testament in the New*. Peabody: Hendrickson Publishers, 2004.

Fairbairn, Patrick. *Pastoral Epistles*. Reprint ed. Minneapolis: Klock & Klock, 1980.

Fairbairn, Patrick. *Typology of Scripture*. Reprint ed. Vol. 2. New York: Funk and Wagnalls, 1900.

Farrar, F. W. *The Epistle of Paul the Apostle to the Hebrews*, Cambridge Greek Testament for Schools and Colleges. Cambridge: Cambridge University Press, 1984.

Farrar, F. W. *Eternal Hope*. London: Macmillan and Co., 1878.

Farrar, F. W. *Mercy and Judgment: A Few Last Words on Christian Eschatology, with Reference to Dr. Pusey's "What Is of Faith?"*. New York: E. P. Dutton Co., 1881.

Fausset, A. R. "The First Epistle of Paul the Apostle to the Corinthians." In *Commentary Critical and Explanatory on the Whole Bible*, edited by Robert Jamieson, A. R. Fausset and David Brown. Oak Harbor: Logos Research Systems, 1997.

Fee, Gordon D. *The First and Second Epistles to the Thessalonians*, New International Commentary on the New Testament. Grand Rapids: Wm. B. Eerdmans Publishing Co., 2009.

Fee, Gordon D. *The First Epistle to the Corinthians*. Grand Rapids: Wm. B. Eerdmans Publishing Co., 1987.

Ferguson, Sinclair B. "The Assurance of Salvation." *The Banner of Truth*, no. 186 (March 1979).

Findlay, G. G. *St. Paul's First Epistle to the Corinthians*. Edited by W. Robertson Nicoll. Reprint ed, The Expositor's Greek Testament. Grand Rapids: Wm. B. Eerdmans Publishing Co., 1967.

Fitzmeyer, Joseph A. "First Peter." In *The Jerome Biblical Commentary*, edited by Raymond E. Brown, Roland E. Murphy and Joseph A. Fitzmeyer. Englewood Cliffs, NJ: Prentice-Hall, 1968.

Fitzmeyer, Joseph A. "Romans." In *The Jerome Biblical Commentary*, edited by Raymond E. Brown, Joseph Fitzmeyer and Roland E. Murphy. Englewood Cliffs, NJ: Prentice-Hall, 1968.

Flusser, David. "A New Sensitivity in Judaism and the Christian Message." *Harvard Theological Review* 61 (1968): 107-27.

Foakes-Jackson, F. J., Kirsopp Lake, Henry Joel Cadbury, and James Hardy Ropes. *The Beginnings of Christianity: The Acts of the Apostles*. 5 vols. Grand Rapids: Baker Book House, 1979.

Foulkes, Francis. "Philippians." In *The New Bible Dictionary: 21st Century Edition*, edited by D. A. Carson, R. T. France, J. A. Motyer and G. J. Wenham. Downers Grove, IL: InterVarsity Press, 1994.

Fox, Samuel J. *Hell in Jewish Literature*. Northbrook, IL: Whitehall Co., 1972.

Foxe, John. *Foxe's Christian Martyrs of the World*. Chicago: Moody Press, n.d.

Fraade, Steven D. "Juda (Place) - Judaism." In *The Yale Anchor Bible Dictionary*, edited by David Noel Freedman. New York: Doubleday, 1966.

Frame, James Everett. *A Critical and Exegetical Commentary on St. Paul's Epistles to the Thessalonians*. New York: Scribner's Sons, 1912.

France, R. T. *The Gospel of Mark: A Commentary on the Greek Text*. Grand Rapids: Wm. B. Eerdmans Publishing Co. , 2002.

France, R. T. *The Gospel of Matthew*, New International Critical Commentary. Grand Rapids: Wm. B. Eerdmans Publishing Co., 2007.

France, R. T. *Matthew*, Tyndale New Testament Commentaries. Grand Rapids: Wm. B. Eerdmans Publishing Co., 1985.

France, R. T. "Matthew." In *The New Bible Commentary*, edited by D. A. Carson. Downers Grove, IL: InterVarsity Press, 1994.

Free, Joseph P. *Archaeology and Bible History*. Wheaton, IL: Scripture Press, 1969.

Fruchtenbaum, Arnold G. *The Footsteps of the Messiah*. rev. ed. Tustin, CA: Ariel Ministries, 2003.

Fuller, J. William. "I Will Not Erase His Name from the Book of Life (Revelation 3:5)." *JETS* 26, no. 3 (1983): 297-306.

Fung, Ronald Y. K. *The Epistle to the Galatians*, The New International Commentary on the New Testament. Grand Rapids: Wm. B. Eerdmans Publishing Co., 1988.

Fyfe, James. *The Hereafter: Sheol, Hades and Hell, the World to Come, and the Scripture Doctrine of Retribution According to Law*. Edinburgh: T. & T. Clark, 1890.

Galli, Mark. *God Wins*. Carol Stream, IL: Tyndale House Publishers, 2011.

Gangle, Kenneth O. *2 Peter*. Edited by John F. Walvoord and Roy Zuck. Reprint ed, Bible Knowledge Commentary. Colorado Springs: Cook, 1996.

Garland, D. E. *2 Corinthians*, New American Commentary. Nashville: Broadman & Holman Publishers, 1999.

Garland, David E. *1 Corinthians*. Grand Rapids: Baker Academic, 2003.

Garlington, Don. *An Exposition of Galatians: A New Perspective/Reformational Reading*. 2nd ed. Eugene, OR: Wipf and Stock Publishers, 2004.

Garlington, Don. "Review of John Piper, The Future of Justification: A Response to N. T. Wright." *Review of Biblical Literature* (May 23, 2008).

Garrett, Duane A. *Hosea and Joel*, New American Commentary. Nashville: Broadman Press, 1997.

Geisler, Norman L. "Moderate Calvinism." In *Four Views on Eternal Security*, edited by J. Matthew Pinson. Grand Rapids: Zondervan Publishing House, 2002.

Geisler, Norman L. *Systematic Theology*. 4 vols. Minneapolis: Bethany House, 2002.

Geldenhuys, Norval. *The Gospel of Luke*, New International Commentary on the New Testament. Grand Rapids: Wm. B. Eerdmans Publishing Co., 1977.

George, Timothy. *Galatians*, The New American Commentary. Nashville: Broadman & Holman Publishers, 1994.

Gerstner, John. "Perseverance." In *Baker's Dictionary of Theology*, edited by Everett F. Harrison. Grand Rapids: Baker Book House, 1960.

Gerstner, John H. *Wrongly Dividing the Word of Truth: A Critique of Dispensationalism*. 1st ed. Brentwood, TN: Wolgemuth & Hyatt, 1991.

Gillman, Florence Morgan. "Demas." In *The Anchor Bible Dictionary*, edited by David Noel Freedman. New York: Doubleday Co., 1992.

Girdlestone, Robert Baker. *Synonyms of the Old Testament: Their Bearing on Christian Doctrine*. Grand Rapids: Wm. B. Eerdmans Publishing Co., 1948.

Gleason, Randall. "A Moderate Reformed View." In *Four Views of the Warning Passages in Hebrews*, edited by Herbert W. Bateman. Grand Rapids: Kregel Publications, 2007.

Godet, Frédéric Louis. *Commentary on First Corinthians*. Reprint ed. Grand Rapids: Kregel Publications, 1977.

Godet, Frédéric Louis. *Commentary on Romans*. Reprint ed. Grand Rapids: Kregel Publications, 1977.

Godet, Frédéric Louis, and A. Cousin. *Commentary on St. Paul's Epistle to the Romans*. 2 vols. Bellingham, WA: Logos, 2009.

Godfrey, W. R. "Law and Gospel." In *New Dictionary of Theology*, edited by Sinclair B. Ferguson and J. I. Packer. Downers Grove, IL: InterVarsity Press, 2000.
Gonzalez, Guillermo, and Jay W. Richards. *The Privileged Planet: How Our Place in the Cosmos Is Designed for Discovery*. Washington D.C.: Regnery, 2004.
González, Justo L. *From the Protestant Reformation to the Twentieth Century*. rev. ed. Vol. 3, A History of Christian Thought. Nashville: Abingdon Press, 1975.
Govett, Robert. *Govett on Revelation*. 2 vols. Miami Springs, FL: Schoettle Publishing, 1981.
Grassmick, John. "Mark." In *The Bible Knowledge Commentary: New Testament*, edited by John F. Walvoord and Roy Zuck. Colorado Springs: Cook, 1996.
Green, Gene L. *The Letters to the Thessalonians*, The Pillar New Testament Commentary. Grand Rapids: Wm. B. Eerdmans Publishing Co., 2002.
Green, Joel B. *The Gospel of Luke*, New International Commentary on the New Testment. Grand Rapids: Wm. B. Eerdmans Publishing Co., 1997.
Gregory, T. M. "Mourning." In *Zondervan Pictorial Encyclopedia of the Bible*, edited by Merrill C. Tenny. Grand Rapids: Zondervan Publishing House, 2009.
Griffith, Terry. "A Non-Polemical Reading of 1 John: Sin, Christology, and the Limits of Johannine Christianity." *Tyndale Bulletin* 49, no. 2 (1998): 252-76.
Grogan, Geoffrey W. "Isaiah." In *Expositor's Bible Commentary*, edited by Frank E. Gabelein. Grand Rapids: Zondervan, 1986.
Grudem, Wayne. *1 Peter*, Tyndale New Testament Commentaries. Grand Rapids: Wm. B. Eerdmans Publishing Co., 1988.
Guelich, Robert A. *Mark 1-8:26*, Word Biblical Commentary. Dallas: Word Books, 2002.
Guelich, Robert A. *The Sermon on the Mount: a Foundation for Understanding*. Waco, TX: Word Books, 1982.
Gundry, Robert. *The Church and the Tribulation*. Grand Rapids: Zondervan Publishing House, 1973.
Gundry Volf, Judith M. *Paul and Perseverance: Staying in and Falling Away*. Tübingen: J.C.B. Mohr [Paul Siebeck], 1990.
Hagner, Donald A. *Matthew 14-28*, Word Biblical Commentary. Dallas: Word Books, 2002.
Hagner, Donald. A. *Matthew 1-13*, Word Biblical Commentary. Dallas: Word, 2002.
Haldane, Robert. *Exposition of the Epistle to the Romans*. Marshallton, DL: The National Foundation for Christian Education, 1970.
Hall, Christopher. "Rejecting the Prodigal." *Christianity Today* (October 26, 1998): 73-76.
Haller, Hal M. "Matthew." In *The Grace New Testament Commentary*, edited by Robert N. Wilkin. Denton, TX: Grace Evangelical Society, 2010.
Hare, Douglas R. A. *Matthew*, Interpretation: A Bible Commentary for Teaching and Preaching. Louisville: John Knox Press, 1993.
Harmon, Kendall S. "The Case against Conditionalism." In *Universalism and the Doctrine of Hell: Papers Presented at the Fourth Edinburgh Conference in Christian Dogmatics*, edited by Nigel M. De. S. Cameron. Grand Rapids: Baker Book House, 1992.
Harris, Murray. "Review of A. M. Hunter, Probing the New Testament." *JETS* 15, no. 4 (Fall 1972): 246-47.
Harris, Murray J. *2 Corinthians*. Edited by Frank E. Gabelein, Everett F. Harrison, W. Harold Mare, Murray J. Harris and Jame M. Boice, The Expositor's Bible Commentary, Volume 10: Romans Through Galatians. Grand Rapids: Zondervan Publishing House, 1976.
Harris, Murray J. *Exegetical Guide to the Greek New Testament: Colossians and Philemon*. Grand Rapids: Wm. B. Eerdmans Publishing Co., 1991.
Harris, Murray J. "Prepositions and Theology in the Greek New Testament." In *NIDNTT*, edited by Colin Brown, 1171-214. Grand Rapids: Zondervan Publishing House, 1986.
Harrison, Everett F. "Romans." In *The Expositor's Bible Commentary*, edited by Frank E. Gaebelein

and Everett F. Harrison. Grand Rapids: Zondervan Publishing House, 1976.
Harrison, R. K. "Vine." In *NISBE*.
Harrison, R. K., and F. N. Hepper. "Vine, Vineyard." In *The New Bible Dictionary*, edited by D. R. W. Wood and I. H. Marshall. Downers Grove, IL: InterVarsity Press, 1996.
Harrison, William K. "The Time of the Rapture as Indicated in Certain Scriptures Part IV: The Time of the Rapture in Revelation." *BibSac* 115, no. 459 (July 1958): 201-11.
Hart, J. H. A. "The First Epistle General of Peter." In *The Expositor's Greek Testament*, edited by W. Robertson Nicoll. Grand Rapids: Wm. B. Eerdmans Publishing Co., 1967.
Hart, John F. "The Faith of Demons." *JOTGES* 8, no. 2 (1995): 40.
Hart, John F. "Should Pretribulationists Reconsider the Rapture in Matthew 24:36-44? - Part 1 of 3." *JOTGES* 20, no. 39 (Autumn 2007): 47-70.
Hart, John F. "Should Pretribulationists Reconsider the Rapture in Matthew 24:36-44? - Part 2 of 3." *JOTGES* 21, no. 40 (Spring 2008): 45-63.
Hart, John F. "Should Pretribulationists Reconsider the Rapture in Matthew 24:36-44? - Part 3 of 3." *JOTGES* 21, no. 41 (Autumn 2008): 43-64.
Hart, John F. "Why Confess Christ: The Use and Abuse of Romans 10:9-10." *JOTGES* 12, no. 2 (1999): 3-35.
Hart, John F. . "How to Energize Our Faith: Reconsidering the Meaning of James 2:14-26." *JOTGES* 12, no. 1 (Spring 1999): 37-66.
Hasel, G. F. "Games." In *NISBE*.
Hawley, John F., and Katherine A. Holcomb. *Foundations of Modern Cosmology*. 2nd. ed. Oxford: University Press, 2005.
Hawthorne, Gerald F. *Philippians*, Word Biblical Commentary. Waco, TX: Word Books, 1983.
Hayes, Zachary J. "The Purgatorial View." In *Four Views of Hell*, edited by William Crocket. Grand Rapids: Zondervan Publishing House, 1996.
Heide, Gale Z. "The Soteriology of James 2:14." *GTJ* 12, no. 1 (Spring 1991): 69-98.
"Hell." In *Dictionary of Biblical Imagery*, edited by Leland Ryken, Jim Wilhoit and Tremper Longman. Downers Grove, IL: InterVarsity Press, 2000.
Helm, Paul. "Article Review: Calvin, English Calvinism and the Logic of Doctrinal Development." *Scottish Journal of Theology* 34, no. 2 (1981).
Helyer, Larry R. *Exploring Jewish Literature of the Second Temple Period: A Guide for New Testament Students*. Downers Grove, IL: InterVarsity Press, 2002.
Helyer, Larry R. "Luke and the Restoration of Israel." *Journal of the Evangelical Theological Society* 36, no. 3 (1993): 317-29.
Hendriksen, William. *Exposition of the Gospel According to Luke*. Grand Rapids: Baker Book House, 1978.
Hendriksen, William, and Simon Kistemaker. *Exposition of Colossians and Philemon*. Grand Rapids: Baker Book House, 1964.
Hendriksen, William, and Simon Kistemaker. *Exposition of the Gospel According to Matthew*. Grand Rapids: Baker Book House, 2001.
Hendriksen, William, and Simon J. Kistemaker. *Exposition of 1 and 2 Thessalonians*. Grand Rapids: Baker Book House, 1953-2001.
Henry, Matthew. "Matthew." In *Matthew Henry's Commentary on the Whole Bible*. Peabody, MA: Hendrickson Publishers, 1996.
Hermas. "The Pastor of Hermas." In *The Anti-Nicene Fathers: Volume II: Fathers of the Second Century: Hermas, Tatian, Athenagoras, Theophilis, and Clement of Alexandria*, edited by A. Roberts, J. Donaldson, A. C. Coxe and H. Wace. Buffalo, NY: Christian Literature Company, 1885.
Hewitt, T., and John Owen. "Corruption." In *Dictionary of Biblical Imagery*, edited by Leland Ryken, Jim Wilhoit and Tremper Longman. Downers Grove, IL: InterVarsity Press, 2000.

Hill, David. "False Prophets and Charismatics: Structure and Interpretation in Matthew 7:15-23." *Biblia* 57 (1976): 327-48.

Hirsch, E. D. *Validity in Interpretation*. New Haven, CT: Yale University Press, 1967.

Hixson, J. B. *Getting the Gospel Wrong*. Longwood, FL: Xulon Press, 2008.

Hodge, Archibald Alexander. *A Commentary on the Confession of Faith: with Questions for Theological Students and Bible Classes*. Philadelphia: Presbyterian Board of Publication, 1992. Reprint, Reprint.

Hodge, Archibald Alexander, and Charles Hodge. *The Confession of Faith: With Questions for Theological Students and Bible Classes*. Simpsonville, SC: Christian Classics Foundation, 1992.

Hodge, Archibald Alexander, and Presbyterian Church in the U.S.A. Board of Publication. *A Commentary on the Confession of Faith: with Questions for Theological Students and Bible Classes*. Philadelphia: Presbyterian Board of Publication, 1926.

Hodge, Charles. *St. Paul's Epistle to the Romans*. Reprint ed. Grand Rapids: Wm. B. Eerdmans Publishing Co., 1950.

Hodge, Charles. *Systematic Theology*. 3 vols. Grand Rapids: Wm. B. Eerdmans Publishing Co., 1977.

Hodges, Zane C. *Absolutely Free! A Biblical Reply to Lordship Salvation*. Dallas: Redención Viva, 1989.

Hodges, Zane C. *The Epistle of James: Proven Character Through Testing: A Verse by Verse Commentary*. Irving, TX: Grace Evangelical Society, 1994.

Hodges, Zane C. *The Epistles of John: Walking in the Light of God's love: A Verse by Verse Commentary*. Irving, TX: Grace Evangelical Theological Society, 1999.

Hodges, Zane C. *Harmony with God: A Fresh Look at Repentance*. Dallas, TX: Redención Viva, 2001.

Hodges, Zane C. "Hebrews." In *BKC: New Testament*, edited by John F. Walvoord and Roy B. Zuck. Colorado Springs: Cook, 1996.

Hodges, Zane C. "Light from James 2 from Textual Criticism." *BibSac* 120, no. 480 (October-December 1963): 341-50.

Hodges, Zane C. "Problem Passages in the Gospel of John: Untrustworthy Believers." *BibSac* 135, no. 538 (April 1978): 139-53.

Hodges, Zane C. "Regeneration: A New Covenant Blessing." *JOTGES* 22, no. 42 (Spring 2009): 72-78.

Hodges, Zane C. *Romans: Deliverance from Wrath*. Ed. Robert N. Wilkin and John N. Niemelä. Corinth, TX: Grace Evangelical Theological Society, 2013.

Hodges, Zane C. "Romans 8: Who are the Heirs?" *Chafer Theological Journal* 9, no. 2 (Fall 2003): 2-17.

Hodges, Zane C. "The Sin of Unbelief." *Grace Focus Newsletter* (November-December 2007).

Hodges, Zane C. "A Voice from the Past: The Salvation of King Saul." *Grace in Focus*, November-December 2011.

Hoehner, Harold W. *Chronological Aspects of the Life of Christ*. Grand Rapids: Zondervan Publishing House, 1977.

Hoehner, Harold W. *Ephesians: An Exegetical Commentary*. Grand Rapids: Baker Academic, 2002.

Hoehner, Harold W. "Reward." In *New Dictionary of Biblical Theology*, edited by T. Desmond Alexander and Brian S. Rosner, xx, 866 p. Downers Grove, IL: Inter-Varsity Press, 2000.

Hoehner, Harold W. "Rewards." In *New Dictionary of Biblical Theology*, edited by T. D. Alexander and B. S. Rosner. Downers Grove, IL: InterVarsity Press, 2001.

Hoekema, Anthony A. *The Bible and the Future*. Grand Rapids: Wm. B. Eerdmans Publishing Co., 1979.

Hoeksema, Herman. *Reformed Dogmatics*. Grand Rapids: Reformed Free Publishing Association, 1966.

Hogg, C. F., and W. E. Vine. *The Epistle to the Thessalonians*. Grand Rapids: Kregel Publications, 1952.

Holland, Tom. *Contours of Pauline Theology*. Fearn, Scotland: Christian Focus Publications, 2004.

Hollis, Wendall. Personal Communication, Sept. 2011.

Holmes, Michael W. *The Apostolic Fathers: Greek texts and English translations*. Grand Rapids: Baker Book House, 1999.

Honeyman, A. M. "Merismus in Biblical Literature." *JBL* 71 (1952): 11-18.

Hospers, John. "Why Be Moral." In *Reading in Ethical Theory*, edited by John Hospers and Wilfrid Sellars. EnglewoodCliffs, NJ: Prentice Hall, 1970.

Howard, George E. "Christ The End of the Law: The Meaning of Romans 10:4 ff." *Journal of Biblical Literature* 88, no. 3 (September 1969): 331-37.

Howard, Tracy L. "The Meaning of `Sleep' in 1 Thessalonians 5:10 - A Reappraisal." *GTJ* 6, no. 2 (1985).

Howe, Fred. "God's Grace in Peter's Theology." *BibSac* 157, no. 628 (October-December 2000): 432-38.

Howe, Frederick R. "A Review of Birthright by David Needham." *BibSac* 141, no. 161 (January-March 1984): 67-78.

Hoyt, Samuel L. "The Judgment Seat of Christ in Theological Perspective - Part 1: The Judgment Seat of Christ and Unconfessed Sins." *BibSac* 137, no. 545 (January-March 1980): 32-39.

Hoyt, Samuel L. "The Judgment Seat of Christ in Theological Perspective, Part 2: The Negative Aspects of the Christian's Judgment." *BibSac* 137, no. 546 (April 1980): 124-31.

Hughes, Philip Edgcumbe. *A Commentary on the Epistle to the Hebrews*. Grand Rapids: Wm. B. Eerdmans Publishing Co., 1977.

Hunn, Debbie. "The Believers Jesus Doubted: John 2:23-25." *TJ* 25, no. 1 (Spring 2004): 15-24.

Hunt, Melvin. "Megiddo, Plain of." In *Yale Anchor Bible Dictionary*, edited by David Noel Freedman. New York: Doubleday, 1992.

"The Huppah." In *The Universal Jewish Encyclopedia*, edited by Isaac Landman. New York: Universal Jewish Encyclopedia Co., 1942.

Hurst, L. D. "Ethics of Jesus." In *Dictionary of Jesus and the Gospels*, edited by Joel B. Green, Scott McKnight and I. Howard Marshall. Downers Grove, IL: InterVarsity Press, 1992.

Inglis, James. "Simon Magus." *Waymarks in the Wilderness* 5 (Spring 1867): 35-50.

Instone-Brewer, David. *Techniques and Assumptions in Jewish Exegesis before 70 CE*. Tübingen: J.C.B. Mohr (Paul Siebeck), 1992.

Instone-Brewer, David. *Traditions of the Rabbis from the Era of the New Testament: Vol. 1, Prayer and Agriculture* Grand Rapids: Wm. B. Eerdmans Publishing Co., 2004.

Irenaeus. "Fragments from the Lost Writings of Irenaeus." In *The Ante-Nicene fathers. Translations of the Writings of the Fathers down to A.D. 325*, edited by Philip Schaff. Grand Rapids: Wm. B. Eerdmans Publishing Co., 1962.

The Isaiah Targum. Vol. 11, The Aramaic Bible. Edinburgh: T. & T. Clark, 1987.

Jamieson, Robert, A. R. Fausset, and David Brown. *A Bible Commentary: Critical, Practical and Explanatory*. Oak Harbor, WA: Logos Research Systems.

Jastrow, Marcus. *A Dictionary of the Targumi, the Talmud Babli and Yerushalmi, and the Midreashic Literature*. New York: Judaica, 1985.

Jeremias, Joachim. *New Testament Theology*. New York: Charles Scribner's Sons, 1971.

Jeremias, Joachim. *The Parables of Jesus*. 6th ed. London: SCM, 1963.

Jeremias, Joachim. *The Sermon on the Mount*. Philadelphia: Fortress Press, 1963.

Jewett, R., R. D. Kotansky, and E. J. Epp. *Romans: A Commentary*, Heremenia: A Critical and Historical Commentary on the Bible. Minneapolis: Fortress Press, 2006.

Jobes, Karen H. *Peter*, Baker Exegetical Commentary on the New Testament. Grand Rapids: Baker Academic, 2005.

Johnson, Gary L. W., and Guy P. Waters. *By Faith Alone: Answering Challenges to the Doctrine of Justification*. Philipsburg, NJ: R. & R. Publishing, 2006.

Johnson, H. Wayne. "The "Analogy of Faith" and Exegetical Methodology: A Preliminary Discussion on Relationships." *JETS* 31, no. 1 (1988): 69-80.

Johnson, S. Lewis. "Freedom in Christ versus Falling from Grace: An Exposition of Galatians 5:1-12." *Emmaus Journal* 15, no. 2 (Winter 2006): 25-36.

Johnson, S. Lewis. "G. C. Berkouwer and the Doctrine of Original Sin." *BibSac* 132, no. 528 (October 1975): 316-26.

Johnson, S. Lewis. "The Out-Resurrection from the Dead." *BibSac* 110, no. 438 (April-June1953): 139-46.

Johnson, S. Lewis. "Paul and the 'Israel of God': An Exegetical and Eschatological Case-Study." In *Essays in Honor of J. Dwight Pentecost*, edited by Stanley D. Toussaint and Charles H. Dyer. Chicago: Moody Press, 1968.

Johnston, Philip S. *Shades of Sheol: Death and the Afterlife in the Old Testament*. Downers Grove, IL: InterVarsity Press, 2002.

Josephus, F., and W. Whiston. *The Works of Josephus: Complete and Unabridged*. Peabody, MA: Hendrickson Publishers, 1987.

Josephus, Flavius. "Against Apion." In *The Works of Flavius Josephus: Complete and Unabridged*, edited by W. Whiston. Peabody, MA: Hendrickson Publishers, 1987.

Josephus, Flavius. "The Wars of the Jews." In *The Works of Josephus: Complete and Unabridged*, edited by W. Whiston. Peabody, MA: Hendrickson Publishers, 1987.

Käiseman, Ernst. *Commentary on Romans*. Grand Rapids: Wm. B. Eerdmans Publishing Co., 1980.

Kaiser, L. "Book of Life." In *The International Standard Bible Encyclopaedia*. Grand Rapids: Wm. B. Eerdmans Publishing Co., 1939.

Kaiser, Walter. "The Law as Guidance for the Promotion of Holiness." In *Five Views on Law and Gospel*, edited by Wayne G. Strickland. Grand Rapids: Zondervan Publishing House, 1996.

Kaiser, Walter. *Toward an Old Testament Theology*. Grand Rapids: Zondervan Publishing House, 1978.

Kaiser, Walter. *The Uses of the Old Testament in the New*. Chicago: Moody Press, 1985.

Kaiser, Walter C. "Leviticus 18:5 and Paul: Do This And You Will Live (Eternally?)." *JETS* 14, no. 1 (Winter 1971): 18-28.

Kaiser, Walter C., Peter H. Davids, F. F. Bruce, and Manfred T. Baruch. *Hard Sayings of the Bible*. Downers Grove, IL: InterVarsity Press, 1997.

Karlberg, Mark W. "The Search for an Evangelical Consensus on Paul and the Law." *JETS* 40, no. 4 (December 1997).

Keathly, Ken. "Does Anyone Really Know if They are Saved?" *JOTGES* 15, no. 1 (Spring 2002).

Keener, Craig S. *A Commentary on the Gospel of Matthew*. Grand Rapids: Wm. B. Eerdmans Publishing Co., 1999.

Keener, Craig S. *The IVP Background Commentary*. Downers Grove, IL: InterVarsity Press, 1993.

Keener, Craig S. *Matthew*. Downers Grove, IL: InterVarsity Press, 1997.

Keil, C. F., and F. Delitzsch. *Commentary on the Old Testament*. Reprint ed. Peabody, MA: Hendrickson Publishers, 2002.

Kelber, Werner H. "Oral Tradition, New Testament." In *Anchor Yale Bible Dictionary*, edited by David Noel Freedman, Gary A. Herion, David F. Graf, J. D. Pleins and A. B. Beck. New York: Doubleday, 1992.

Kendall, R. T. *Calvin and English Calvinism to 1649*. Oxford: Oxford University Press, 1979.

Kendall, R. T. *Once Saved, Always Saved*. Reprint, Waynesboro, GA: Authentic Media, 2005 ed. London: Hodder and Straughton, 1984.

Kickasola, Joseph. "Leviticus and Triune Communion." *Ashland Theological Journal* 10 (1977): 3-58.

Kidner, Derek. *Proverbs: An Introduction and Commentary*, Tyndale Old Testament Commentaries. Downers Grove, IL: Intervarsity Press, 1975.

Kimchi, David, and R.G. Finch. *The Longer Commentary of R. David Kimchi on the First Book of Psalms*. Edited by W. O .E. Oesterley and G H. Cox: S.P.C.K.

King, Guy H. *A Leader Led*. Edinburgh: Marshall, Morgan, & Scott, 1951.

Kirk, Kenneth E. *The Vision of God: The Christian Doctrine of the Summum Bonum*, The Bampton Lectures for 1928. New York: Longmans, Green and Co., 1928.

Kistemaker, Simon J. *Exposition of the First Epistle to the Corinthians*. Grand Rapids: Baker Book House, 1993.

Kistemaker, Simon J. "The Temple In The Apocalypse." *JETS* 43, no. 3 (September 2000): 433-41.

Kistemaker, Simon J., and William Hendriksen. *Exposition of the Second Epistle to the Corinthians*, New Testament Commentary. Grand Rapids: Baker, 2001.

Kittel, Gerhard. "Preface." In *Theological Dictionary of the New Testament*, edited by Gerhard Kittle. Grand Rapids: Wm. B. Eerdmans Pub. Co., 1964.

Kling, Christian Friedrich. *The First Epistle of Paul to the Corinthians*. Edited by J. P. Lange, Philip Schaff, Christian Friedrich Kling and Daniel W. Poor. 12 vols, A Commentary on the Holy Scriptures. Grand Rapids: Zondervan Publishing House, 1960.

Kraft, Robert A. *The Pseudepigrapha in Early Christianity*: University of Pennsylvania, 1994.

Kraus, Hans-Joachim. *Psalms 1-59: A Continental Commentary*. Minneapolis: Fortress Press, 1993.

Krauss, Lawrence M. *A Universe from Nothing: Why There Is Something Rather Than Nothing*. New York: Free Press, a Division of Simon & Schuster, 2012.

Krell, Keith R. *Temporal Judgment and the Church: Paul's Remedial Agenda in 1 Corinthians*. Dallas: Biblical Studies Press, L.L.C., 2011.

Kruse, Colin G. *The Letters of John*, The Pillar New Testament Commentary. Grand Rapids: Wm. B. Eerdmans Publishing Co., 2000.

Kruse, Colin G. "Sin and Perfection in 1 John." *Southern Baptist Theological Journal* 23, no. 1 (Fall 2005): 51-64.

Kubo, Sakae. "1 John 1:9: Absolute or Habitual." *Andrews University Seminary Studies* 7, no. 1 (January 1969): 47-56.

Kümmel, W. G. *Promise and Fulfillment*. London: SCM Press, 1957.

Ladd, George E. *Theology of the New Testament*. Grand Rapids: Wm. B. Eerdmans Publishing Co., 1974.

Lane, William. *Commentary on the Gospel of Mark*. Grand Rapids: Wm. B. Eerdmans Publishing Co., 1974.

Lane, William L. *Hebrews 9-13*, Word Biblical Commentary. Dallas: Word, Inc., 2002.

Laney, J. Carl. "Abiding Is Believing: The Analogy of the Vine in John 15:1-6." *BibSac* 146, no. 582 (January-March 1989): 55-66.

Lang, G. H. *Revelation*. Reprint ed. Miami Springs, FL: Schoettle Publishing. Co., 1985.

Lang, G. H. *The Epistle to the Hebrews*. Hayesville, NC: Schoettle Publishing Co., 1985.

Lang, G. H. *Firstborn Sons: Their Rights and Risks*. Reprint ed. Miami Springs, FL: Schoettle Publishing Co., 1984.

Lange, John Peter. "The Gospel of Matthew." In *Commentary on the Holy Scriptures, Critial, Doctrinal, and Hommelitical*, edited by John Peter Lange. Grand Rapids: Zondervan Publishing House, 1960.

Lange, John Peter. "The Revelation of John." In *A Commentary on the Holy Scriptures*, edited by John Peter Lange, Philip Schaff, Moore E., E. R. Craven and J. H.; Woods. Bellingham, WA: Logos Bible Software, 2008.

Larger Catechism of the Westminster Standards. Edited by M. H. Smith. Greenville, SC: Presbyterian Theological Seminary Press, 1996.

Le Deaut, Roger. "Targumic Literature and New Testament Interpretation." *Biblical Theological Bulletin* 4, no. 3 (October 1974): 243-89.

Lea, Thomas D., and Hayne P. Griffin. *1, 2 Timothy, Titus*, New American Commentary. Nashville: Broadman & Holman, 2001.

Leitch, A. H. "Adoption." In *The Zondervan Pictorial Encyclopedia of the Bible*, edited by Merrill C. Tenney. Grand Rapids: Zondervan Publishing House, 1975.

Lenski, R. C. H. *The Interpretation of I and II Corinthians*. Minneapolis: Augsburg Publishing Co., 1963.

Lenski, R. C. H. *The Interpretation of St. John's Revelation*. Minneapolis: Augsburg, 1963.

Lenski, R. C. H. *The Interpretation of St. Matthew's Gospel*. Reprint ed. Minneapolis: Augsburg Publishing Co., 1943.

Lenski, R. C. H. *The Interpretation of the Epistles of St. Peter, St. John, and St. Jude*. Minneapolis: Augsburg Publishing Co., 1966.

Lewellen, Thomas G. "Has Lordship Salvation Been Taught throughout Church History?" In *Vital Theological Issues: Examining Enduring Issues of Theology*, edited by Roy B. Zuck, 153-64. Grand Rapids: Kregel Publications, 1994.

Lewis, C. S. *The Weight of Glory*. New York: Simon and Shuster, 1975.

Lewis, Gordon, and Bruce Demarest. *Integrative Theology*. Grand Rapids, MI: Zondervan Publishing House, 1987.

Lewis, Jack P. "Jamnia (Jabneh), Council of." In *Yale Anchor Bible Dictionary*, edited by David Noel Freedman. New York: Doubleday, 1992.

The Lexicon Webster Dictionary: Enclyclopedic Edition. English-Language Institute of America, Inc., 1976.

Liddon, H. P. *Explanatory Analysis of St. Paul's Epistle to the Romans* Reprint ed. Minneapolis: James and Klock, 1977.

Lightner, Robert P. *The Death Christ Died: A Case for Unlimited Atonement*. Des Plaines, IL: Regular Baptist Press, 1967.

Liid, Dale C. "Potsherd Gate." In *Anchor Yale Bible Dictionary*, edited by David Noel Freedman. New York: Doubleday, 1992.

Lincoln, Andrew T. *Ephesians*. Dallas: Word Books, 1990.

Lindsay, F. Duane. "Leviticus." In *BKC*, edited by John F. Walvoord and Roy B. Zuck. Colorado Springs: Cook, 1996.

Litfin, A. Duane. "1 Timothy." In *BKC New Testament*, edited by John F. Walvoord and Roy B. Zuck. Colorado Sprngs: Cook, 1985.

Lloyd-Jones, Martyn. *Romans Chapter 8:17-39: The Final Perseverance of the Saints*. Grand Rapids: Zondervan Publishing House, 1976.

Lloyd-Jones, Martyn. *The Sons of God: Exposition of Romans 8:5-17*. Grand Rapids: Zondervan Publishing House, 1975.

Lloyd-Jones, Martyn. *Studies in the Sermon on the Mount*. Grand Rapids: Wm. B. Eerdmans Publishing Co., 1971.

Logan, Samuel T. "The Doctrine of Justification in the Theology of Jonathan Edwards." *WTJ* 46, no. 1 (Spring 1984).

Lohse, Eduard. *Colossians and Philemon A Commentary on the Epistles to the Colossians and to Philemon*, Hermeneia. Philadelphia: Fortress Press, 1971.

Long, Gary D. *Context! Evangelical Views of the Millennium Examined*. Charleston, SC: Sovereign Grace Ministries, 2002.

Long, Gary D. *Definite Atonement*. Phillipsburg, NJ: Presbyterian and Reformed Publishing Co., 1976.

Longenecker, Richard. *Paul, Apostle of Liberty*. New York: Harper and Row, 1964.

Longnecker, Richard N. *Galatians*, Word Biblical Commentary. Dallas: Word, 2002.

López, René A. "Does the Vice List in 1 Corinthians 6:9-10 Describe Believers or Unbelievers." *BibSac* 164, no. 653 (January-March 2007): 59-73.

López, René A. "Old Testament Salvation - From What?" *JOTGES* 16, no. 2 (Autumn 2003): 50-57.

López, René A. "The Pauline Vice List and Inheriting the Kingdom." PhD diss., Dallas Theological Seminary, 2010.

López, René A. "Romans." In *The Grace New Testament Commentary*, edited by Robert N. Wilkin. Denton, TX: Grace Evangelical Society, 2010.

Louw, J. P. and Nida, E. A., *Greek-English Lexicon of the New Testament : Based on Semantic Domains*, 2 ed., 2 vols. (New York: United Bible Societies, 1996).

Louw, J. P. *Semantics of New Testament Greek*. Philadelphia: Fortress Press, 1982.

Louw, J. P. "Verbal Aspect in the First Letter of John." *Neotestamentica* 9 (1975): 98-104.

Lovelace, Richard F. *Dynamics of Spiritual Life: An Evangelical Theology of Renewal*. Downers Grove, IL: InterVarsity Press, 1979.

Lowe, Chuck. "There Is No Condemnation (Rom. 8:1): But Why Not?" *JETS* 42, no. 2 (June 1999).

Lowery, David. "1 Corinthians." In *BKC: New Testament*, edited by John F. Walvoord and Roy B. Zuck. Colorado Springs: Cook, 1996.

Luomanen, Petri. *Entering the Kingdom of Heaven: A Study on the Structure of Matthew's View of Salvation*. Tübingen: Mohr Siebeck, 1998.

Lust, J., Erik Eynikel, K. Hauspie, and G. Chamberlain. *A Greek-English Lexicon of the Septuagint*. Stuttgart: Deutsche Bibelgesellschaft, 1992.

Luther, Martin. "1 Corinthians 7, 1 Corinthians 15, 1 Timothy." In *Luther's Works*, edited by J. J. Pelikan, H. C. Oswald and H. T. Lehman. Philadelphia: Fortress Press, 1973.

Luther, Martin. "Career of the Reformer IV." In *Luther's Works*, edited by H. C. Pelikan. Philadelphia: Fortresss Press, 1999.

Luther, Martin. *The Disputation Concerning Justification*. Edited by J. J. Pelikan, H. C. Oswald and H. T. Lehman, Luther's Works. Philadelphia: Fortress Press, 1999.

Luther, Martin. "Letter to Hans von Rechenberg." In *Luther's Works*, edited by J. J. Pelikan, H. C. Oswald and H. T. Lehmann. Philadelphia: Fortress Press, 1968.

Luther, Martin. *Luther's Works*. Edited by J. J. Pelikan, H. C Oswald and H. T. Lehmann. Philadelphia: Fortress Press, 1968.

Luther, Martin. "Preface to the New Testament." In *Word and Sacrament*, edited by Theodor Bachman. Philadelphia: Fortress Press, 1960.

Luther, Martin. "Table Talk: No. 3232c: Description of Luther's "Tower Experience" Between June 9 and July 21, 1532." In *Luther's Works*, edited by J. J. Pelikan, H. C. Oswald and H. T. Lehman. Philadelphia: Fortress Press, 1999.

Lutzer, Erwin W. *Your Eternal Reward: Triumph and Tears at the Judgmenet Seat of Christ*. Chicago: Moody Press, 1998.

Luz, Ulrich, and Helmut Koester. *Matthew 1-7: A Commentary*. rev ed, Hermeneia. Minneapolis: Fortress Press, 2007.

Luz, Ulrich, and Helmut Koester. *Matthew 21-28: A Commentary*, Hermeneia. Minneapolis: Augsburg Publishing Co., 1989.

Lybrand, Fred. *Back to Faith: Reclaiming Gospel Clarity in an Age of Incongruence*. Lakewood, FL: Xulon Press, 2009.

Lybrand, Fred. "Does Faith Gurantee Works? Rethinking the Cliché." DMin diss., Phoenix Theological Seminary, 2007.

M'Neile, Allan H. *The Gospel According to St. Matthew*. Reprint ed. London: Macmillan & Co., 1961.

Macalister, A. "Tear, Tears." In *International Standard Bible Encyclopedia, Revised*, edited by G. W. Bromiley. Grand Rapids: Wm. B. Eerdmans Publishing Co., 2002.

MacArthur, John. "Faith According to the Apostle James." *JETS* 33, no. 1 (March 1990): 13-34.

MacArthur, John. "Gehenna." In *Tyndale Bible Dictionary*, edited by Walter Elwell and Philip Wesley Comfort. Wheaton, IL: Tyndale House, 2001.

MacArthur, John. *The Gospel According to Jesus*. Grand Rapids: Zondervan Publishing House, 1988.

MacArthur, John. *Hard to Believe: The High Cost and Infinite Value of Following Jesus*. Nashville: Thomas Nelson, 2003.

MacArthur, John. *Hebrews*. Chicago: Moody Press, 1983.

MacDonald, Gregory. *The Evangelical Universalist*. Eugene, OR: Cascade Books, 2006.

Mackie, G. M., and W. Ewing. "Marriage." In *Dictionary of Christ and the Gospels*, edited by James Hastings. Edinburgh: T. & T. Clark, 1913.

Maisel, John. *Radical Trust: The Two Most Important Things Jesus Wants You to Know*. Dallas: East-West Ministries International, 2012.

Maldonatus, John. *A Commentary on the Gospels: St. Matthew's Gospel Chapter 25 to the End*. London: John Hodges, 1888.

Manson, T. W. *The Teaching of Jesus: Studies of its Form and Content*. 2nd ed. Cambridge: University Press, 1955.

Manson, T. W. *The Teaching of Jesus: Studies of its Form and Content*. Cambridge: University Press, 1963.

Mare, W. Harold. "1 Corinthians." In *The Expositor's Bible Commentary*. Grand Rapids: Zondervan Publishing House, 1976.

Mare, W. Harold. "Jehoshaphat, Valley of." In *ABD*, edited by David Noel Freedman. New York: Doubleday, 1992.

Marshall, I. Howard. *The Epistles of John*, New International Commentary on the New Testament. Grand Rapids: Wm. B. Eerdmans Publishing Co., 1978.

Marshall, I. Howard. *The Gospel of Luke: A Commentary on the Greek Text*. Grand Rapids: Wm. B. Eerdmans Publishing Co., 1978.

Marshall, I. Howard. *Kept by the Power of God: A Study of Perseverance and Falling Away*. 2nd ed. Minneapolis: Bethany Fellowship, 1974.

Marshall, I. Howard. "Who is a Hypocrite?" *BibSac* 159, no. 634 (April-June 2002): 131-50.

Marshall, John E. "Rabbi Duncan and the Problem of Assurance (I)." *Banner of Truth*, no. 201 (June 1980): 16-27.

Marshall, John E. "Rabbi Duncan and the Problem of Assurance (II)." *The Banner of Truth*, no. 202 (July 1980).

Martin, Brice L. *Christ and the Law in Paul*. Eugene, OR: Wipf and Stock Publishers, 1989.

Martin, John "Isaiah." In *BKC: Old Testament*, edited by John F. Walvoord and Roy B. Zuck. Colorado Springs: Cook, 1996.

Martin, Ralph P. *2 Corinthians*, Word Biblical Commentary. Dallas: Word, 1998.

Martin, Ralph P. *James*, Word Biblical Commentary. Dallas: Word, 2002.

Martin, Ralph P. *Philippians*. London: Tyndale Press, 1959.

Masterman, E. W. G. "Vine." In *ISBE*, edited by James Orr. Albany, OR: Ages Software, 1999.

Masterman, E.W.G. "ZOHELETH, THE STONE OF." In *ISBE*, edited by James Orr. Albany, OR: Ages Software, 1915.

Mathison, Keith. *Dispensationalism, Rightly Dividing the People of God?* Phillipsburg, NJ: Presbyterian and Reformed Publishing Co., 1995.

McClain, Alva J. *The Greatness of the Kingdom*. Chicago: Moody Press, 1959.

McClain, Alva J. "A Premillennial Philosophy of History." *BibSac* 113, no. 450 (1956).

McCoy, Brad. "Secure, Yet Scrutinized: 2 Tim 2:11-13." *JOTGETS* 1 (Autumn 1988): 21-33.

McIver, Robert K. "The Parable of the Weeds Among the Wheat (Matt 13:24-30, 36-43) and the Relationship Between the Kingdom and the Church as Portrayed in the Gospel of Matthew." *JBL* 114, no. 4 (1995): 643-59.

McKenzie, John L. "Matthew." In *The Jerome Biblical Commentary*, edited by Raymond E. Brown, Joseph A. Fitzmyer and Roland E. Murphy. Englewood Cliffs, NJ: Prentice-Hall, 1996.

Meier, John P. *Law and History in Matthew's Gospel: A Redactional Study of Mt. 5:17-48*. Rome: Biblical Institute Press, 1976.

Meir, Ben-Dov. *Historical Atlas of Jerusalem*. Translated by David Louvish. New York: Continuum Publishing Group, Inc., 2002.

Meisinger, George. "Salvation by Faith Alone Part 1 of 2." *Chafer Theological Journal* 5, no. 2 (April 1999): 2-27.

Melick, Richard R. *Philippians, Colossians, Philemon*, New American Commentary. Nashville: Broadman and Holman, 1991.

Merriam-Webster's Collegiate Dictionary. Springfield, MA: Merriam-Webster, Inc., 2003.

Meyer, Heinrich August. *A Critical and Exegetical Handbook to the Epistle to the Romans*. Winnona Lake, IN: Alpha Publications, 1979.

Michael, John Hugh. *The Epistle of Paul to the Philippians*, The Moffatt New Testament commentary. Garden City, NY: Doubleday, Doran & Company, Inc., 1929.

Michaels, J. Ramsey. *1 Peter*, Word Biblical Commentary. Dallas: Word, 2002.

Mickelsen, A. Berkley. *Interpreting the Bible*. Grand Rapids: Wm. B. Eerdmans Pub. Co., 1963.

Midrash Rabba. Translated by Rabbi L. Rabinowitz. Edited by Rabbi H. Freedman and Maurice Simon. 10 vols. Vol. 8. London: Soncino Press, 1939.

Miley, John. *Systematic Theology*. Originally published by Hunt & Eaton, 1893 ed. 2 vols. Peabody, MA: Hendrickson, 1989.

Milligan, George. *St. Paul's Epistles to the Thessalonians*. London: Macmillan, 1908.

Minear, Paul S. "Audience Criticism and Markan Ecclesiology." In *Neues Testament und Geschichte*, edited by Oscar Cullman and Bo Reicke. Tübingen: J. C. B. Mohn [Paul Siebeck], 1972.

Minor, Mitzi. "Luke 13:22-30 - The Wrong Question, The Right Door." *Review and Expositor* 91, no. 4 (Fall 1994): 546-56.

Mitchell, Kenneth R. *Justice and Generosity*. Baltimore: PublishAmerica, 2008.

Mohrlang, Roger. *Matthew and Paul: A Comparison of Ethical Perspectives*, Monograph series / Society for New Testament Studies. New York: Cambridge University Press, 1984.

Moll, Carl B. *Hebrews*. Edited by J. P. Lange. Reprint ed, *A Commentary on the Holy Scriptures*. Bellingham, WA: Logos Bible Software, 2008.

Montefiore, C. G. "Rabbinic Conceptions of Repentance." *Jewish Quarterly Review* 16, no. 2 (January 1904): 209-57.

Montefiore, Hugh. *A Commentary on the Epistle to the Hebrews*. Peabody, MA: Hendrickson Publishers, 1987.

Moo, Douglas J. "Book Reviews. "Righteousness" in the New Testament: "Justification" in the United States Lutheran-Roman Catholic Dialogue. By John Reumann. With responses by Joseph A. Fitzmyer and Jerome D. Quinn. Philadelphia: Fortress/New York and Ramsey: Paulist, 1982, xvii - 278 pp." *Journal of the Evangelical Theological Society* 27, no. 1 (March 1984).

Moo, Douglas J. *Colossians and Philemon*, The Pillar New Testament Commentary. Grand Rapids: Wm. B. Eerdmans Publishing Co., 2008.

Moo, Douglas J. *The Epistle to the Romans*, The New International Commentary on the New Testament. Grand Rapids: Wm. B. Eerdmans Publishing Co., 1996.

Moo, Douglas J. *The Letter of James*, The Pillar New Testament Commentary. Grand Rapids: Wm. B. Eerdmans Publishing Co., 2000.

Moo, Douglas J. "Romans." In *New Dictionary of Biblical Theology*, edited by T. D. Alexander and B. S. Rosner. Downers Grove, IL: Intervarsity Press, 2001.

Moreland, J. P. "Ethical Egoism and Biblical Self-Interest." *WTJ* 59, no. 2 (Fall 1997): 257-68.

Morey, Robert. *Death and the Afterlife*. Minneapolis: Bethany House, 1984.

Morgan, Christopher W., and Robert A. Peterson. *Hell under Fire*. Grand Rapids: Zondervan, 2004.

Morgan, G. Campbell. *A First Century Message to Twentieth Century Christians*. New York: Revell, 1902.

Morgan, Kenneth J. "The New Testament Use of Gehenna: Its Historical Background and Its Significance for the Doctrine of Eternal Punishment." (May 1975), http://rediscoveringthebible.com/Geenna.pdf.

Morris, Leon. *The Epistle to the Romans*, Pillar New Testament Commentary. Grand Rapids: Wm. B. Eerdmans Publishing Co., 1988.

Morris, Leon. *The First Epistle of Paul to the Corinthians: An Introduction and Commentary*, The Tyndale New Testament commentaries. Grand Rapids: Wm. B. Eerdmans Publishing Co., 1983.

Morris, Leon. *The Gospel According to Matthew*, The Pillar New Testament Commentary. Grand Rapids: Wm. B. Eerdmans Publishing Co., 1992.

Morris, Leon. *The Gospel of John*, The New International Commentary on the New Testament. Grand Rapids: Wm. B. Eerdmands Publishing Co., 1995.

Motyer, Alec. *The Message of Philippians*. Downers Grove, IL: InterVarsity Press, 1984.

Motyer, J. A. *The Prophecy of Isaiah: An Introduction & Commentary*. Downers Grove: InterVarsity Press, 1993.

Motyer, J. A. *The Prophecy of Isaiah: An Introduction and Commentary*. Downers Grove, IL: InterVarsity Press, 1993.

Moulton, James H., and Nigel Turner. *A Grammar of New Testament Greek, Volume 3: Syntax*. Reprint ed. Edinburgh: T. & T. Clark, 1963.

Moulton, James Hope. *Grammar of New Testament Greek: Prolegomena*. Reprint ed. 3 vols. Edinburgh: T. & T. Clark, 1963.

Mounce, R. H. *Romans*, The New American Commentary. Nashville: Broadman & Holman, 1995.

Mounce, Robert H. *The Book of Revelation*, The New International Commentary on the New Testament. Grand Rapids: Wm. B. Eerdmans Publishing Co., 1997.

Mounce, W. D. *Pastorals*, Word Biblical Commentary. Grand Rapids: Wm. B. Eerdmans Publishing Co., 2002.

Mueller, John T. *Christian Dogmatics*. St. Louis, MI: Concordia Publishing House, 1955.

Murphy, Roland Edmund. *Proverbs*, Word Biblical Commentary. Nashville: Thomas Nelson, 1998.

Murray, Iain H. "Will the Unholy Be Saved?" *The Banner of Truth* no. 246 (March 1984).

Murray, John. "Definite Sanctification." In *Collected Writings of John Murray*. Edinburgh: Banner of Truth Trust, 1977.

Murray, John. *The Epistle to the Romans*. Grand Rapids: Wm. B. Eerdmans Publishing Co., 1965.

Murray, John. *Redemption—Accomplished and Applied*. Grand Rapids: Wm. B. Eerdmans Pub. Co., 1955.

Nägelsbach, Carl Wilhelm Eduard. "The Prophet Isaiah." In *Lange's Commentary on the Holy Scriptures*. Grand Rapids: Zondervan Publishing House, n.d.

Nee, Watchman. *The Normal Christian Life*. Fort Washington, PA: Christian Literature Crusade, 1957.

Neff, Ken. *A Defense of Grace: An Examination of Saving Faith, Comparing Grace and Reformed Theology*. Available from prgneff@primeresearchgroup.com: Privately Published, 1996.

Neil, James. *Everyday Life in the Holy Land*. New York: Cassell and Company, 1913.

Nelson, Peter K. "Luke 22:29-30 and the Time Frame for Dining and Ruling." *Tyndale Bulletin* 44, no. 2 (November 1993): 350-61.

Neufeld, Edmund K. "The Gospel in the Gospels: Answering the Question 'What must I do to be saved?' From the Synoptics." *JETS* 51, no. 2 (June 2008): 267-96.

Neusner, Jacob. *The Mishnah: A New Translation*. New Haven, CT: Yale University Press, 1988.

The New American Bible Commentary: 21st Century Edition. Edited by D. A. Carson. 3rd ed. Downers Grove, IL: InterVarsity Press, 1994.

Newell, William R. *Romans: Verse by Verse*. Chicago: Moody Press, 1938.

Newman, Barclay Moon, and Philip C. Stine. *A Translator's Handbook on the Gospel of Matthew*. New York: United Bible Societies, 1992.

Nickels, P. *Targum and New Testament: A Bibliography Together with a New Testament Index*. Rome: Pontifical Biblical Institute, 1967.

Nicole, Roger. "Some Comments on Heb. 6:4-6 and the Doctrine of Perseverance of God with the Saints." In *Current Issues in Biblical and Patristic Interpretation*, edited by Gerald G. Hawthorne. Grand Rapids: Wm. B. Eerdmans Publishing Co., 1975.

Nicoll, W. Robertson. "Faith and Works in the Letter of James in Essays on the General Epistles of the New Testament." *Neotestamenticia* 9 (1975).

Niemelä, John. "Faith Without Works: A Definition 1." *Chafer Theological Seminary Journal* 6, no. 2 (April 2000): 2-19.

Niemelä, John. "For You Have Kept My Word." *Chafer Theological Journal* 6, no. 1 (January 2000): 12-38.

Niemelä, John. "If Anyone's Work is Burned: Scrutinizing Proof Texts." *Chafer Theological Journal* 8, no. 1 (2002): 22-42.

Niemelä, John. "James 2:24: Re-translation Required (Part 1 of 3)." *CTSJ* 7, no. 1 (January 2001): 2-15.

Nolland, John. *The Gospel of Matthew: A Commentary on the Greek Text*. Grand Rapids: Wm. B. Eerdmans Publishing Co., 2005.

Nolland, John. *Luke 9:21-18:34*, Word Biblical Commentary. Dallas: Word, 2002.

Norris, D. Thane. "The Logos Delux Map Set." Oak Harbor: Logo Research Systems, 1997.

O'Brien, Peter T. *The Epistle to the Philippians: A Commentary on the Greek Text*, The New International Greek Testament Commentary. Grand Rapids: Wm. B. Eerdmans Publishing Co., 1991.

O'Brien, Peter T. *The Epistle to the Philippians: A Commentary on the Greek Text*. Grand Rapids: Wm. B. Eerdmans Publishing Co., 1991.

O'Brien, Peter Thomas. *The Letter to the Ephesians*, The Pillar New Testament Commentary. Grand Rapids: Wm. B. Eerdmans Publishing Co., 1999.

Oberholtzer, Kem. "The Thorn Invested Ground in Hebrews 6:4-12." *BibSac* 145 (July-September 1988): 319-28.

Oberholtzer, Thomas Kem. "The Eschatalogical Salvation of Hebrews 1:5-2:5." *BibSac* 145 (January-March 1988): 83-97.

Olshausen, Hermann. *Biblical Commentary of the New Testament*. Translated by A. C. Kendrick. Reprint ed. Bowling Green, OH: Guardian of Truth Foundation, 2005.

Olshausen, Hermann. *Ephesians*. Translated by A. C. Kendrick. Reprint ed. 6 vols. Vol. 5. Bowling Green, KY.: Reprint by Guardian of Truth Foundation, 2005.

Orchard, Bernard. *A Catholic Commentary on Holy Scripture*. Nashville: Thomas Nelson, 1953.

Orr, James. "Jesus Christ." In *The International Standard Bible Encyclopedia*, edited by James Orr. Grand Rapids: Wm. B. Eerdmans Publishing Co., 1915.

Osbeck, K. W. *101 Hymn Stories*. Grand Rapids: Kregel Publications, 1982.

Osborne, Grant. *Revelation*, Baker Exegetical Commentary on the New Testament. Grand Rapids: Baker Academic, 2002.

Owen, John. *Hebrews*.

Packer, J. I., Merrill Chapin Tenny, and William White. *Illustrated Manners and Customs of the Bible*. Nashville: Thomas Nelson, 1997.

Pagenkemper, Karl. "An Analysis of the Rejection Motif in the Synoptic Parables and Its Relationship to Pauline Soteriology." PhD diss., Dallas Theological Seminary, 1990.

Pagenkemper, Karl. "Rejection Imagery in the Synoptic Parables." *BibSac* 153, no. 611 (July-September 1996): 308-31.

Pak, Joseph K. "A Study of Selected Passages on Distinguishing Marks of Genuine and False Believers." PhD diss., Dallas Theological Seminary, 2001.

Pass III, William N. W. "A Reexamination of Calvin's Approach to Romans 8:17." *BibSac* 170, no. 677: 69-81.

Pass III, William N. W. "A Reexamination of Calvin's Approach to Romans 8:17." *BibSac* 170, no. 677 (January-March 2013): 68-81.

Pearcey, Nancy, and Charles B. Thaxton. *The Soul of Science: Christian Faith and Natural Philosophy*. Wheaton, IL: Crossway Books, 1994.

Penner, Ken, and Michael Heiser. *Old Testament Greek Pseudepigrapha with Morphology*. Bellingham, WA: Logos Research Systems, 2009.

Pentecost, J. Dwight. "The Purpose of the Sermon on the Mount: Part 3." *BibSac* 115, no. 460 (October-December 1958): 313-19.

Pentecost, J. Dwight. *Things to Come: A Study in Biblical Eschatology*. Reprint ed. Grand Rapids: Zondervan Publishing House, 1964.

Perkins, William. *The Works of that Famous and Worthy Minister of Christ in the University of Cambridge*. 3 vols. Cambrdige: John Legatt, 1612.

Perrin, Norman. *The Kingdom of God in the Teaching of Jesus*. Philadelphia: Westminster Press, 1963.

Peters, George N. H. *The Theocratic Kingdom of Our Lord Jesus, the Christ, as Covenanted in the Old Testament and Presented in the New Testament*. Reprint ed. Grand Rapids: Kregel Publications, 1972.

Peters, George W. "The Meaning of Conversion." *BibSac* 120, no. 479 (July - September 1963): 234-42.

Peterson, Robert. "Does the Bible Teach Annihilationism?" *BibSac* 156, no. 621 (January 1999): 13-27.

Philo. "On the Life of Moses." In *The Works of Philo: Complete and Unabridged*, edited by C. D. Younge. Peabody, MA: Hendrickson Publishers, 1996.

Pink, Arthur. *The Doctrine of Sanctification*. Swengel, PA: Reiner Publications, 1975.

Pink, Arthur. *Eternal Security*. Grand Rapids: Baker Book House, 1974.

Pink, Arthur. *An Exposition of Hebrews*. Grand Rapids: Baker, 1968.

Pink, Arthur. *An Exposition of the Sermon on the Mount*. Grand Rapids: Baker Book House, 1974.

Pinnock, Clark H. "Response to Zachary J. Hayes." In *Four Views on Hell*, edited by William Crocket and Stanley N. Gundry. Grand Rapids: Zondervan Publishing House, 1996.

Piper, John. "Battling the Unbelief of Bitterness (1988, Sermon 658)." http://www.desiringgod.org/resourceLibrary.

Piper, John. *Beyond the Gold*: Desiring God Radio, May 14, 2006.

Piper, John. *The Future of Justification: A Response to N. T. Wright*. Wheaton, IL: Crossway Books, 2007.

Pliny. "The Culture of the Vine and the Various Shrubs which Support It." In *The Natural History*. Medford, MA: Taylor and Francis, 1855.

Plummer, Alfred. *A Critical and Exegetical Commentary on the Gospel according to St. Luke*. 5th. ed. Edinburgh: T. & T. Clark, 1922.

Plummer, Alfred. *The Second Epistle of Paul to the Corinthians*, Cambridge Greek Testament for Schools and Colleges. Cambridge: Cambidge University Press, 1903.

Pokorny, Ptr. *Colossians*. Peabody, MA: Hendriksen Publishers, 1991.

Pollock, John. *George Whitefield and the Great Awakening*. Garden City, NY: Doubleday, 1972.

Powys, David J. *'Hell': A Hard Look at a Hard Question: The Fate of the Unrighteous in New Testament Thought*. Carlisle, PA: Paternoster Press, 1998.

Poythress, Vern S. *Understanding Dispensationalists*. Grand Rapids: Zondervan Publishing House, 1987.

Quick, Ken. "The Doctrine of Eternal Significance." DMin diss., Dallas Theological Seminary, 1989.

Radmacher, Earl. *Salvation*. Dallas: Word Publishing, 2000.

Rafferty, William E. "Crown." In *NISBE (1988)*.

Rainbow, Paul A. *The Way of Salvation: The Role of Christian Obedience in Justification*. Waynesboro, GA: Paternoster, 2005.

Raisanen, H. *Paul and the Law*. Philadelphia: Fortress Press, 1986.

Ramm, Bernard. *Protestant Biblical Interpretation*. Boston: W. A. Wilde Co., 1956.

Ramsay, W. M. *The Letters from the Seven Churches of Asia*. London: Hodder and Stoughton, 1904.

Redpath, Alan. *Victorious Christian Living*. Old Tappan, NJ: Revell Co., 1955.

Reich, Ronny, and Eli Shukron. "The Jerusalem City-Dump in the Late Second Temple Period." *Zeitschrift des Deutschen Palätina-Verein* 119, no. 1 (2003): 12-18.

Reiling, J., and J. L. Swellengrebel. *A Handbook on the Gospel of Luke*, UBS Handbook Series: Helps for Translators. New York: United Bible Societies, 1993.

Ridderbos, Herman. *The Coming of the Kingdom*. Grand Rapids: Presbyterian and Reformed Publishing Co., 1962.

Ridderbos, Herman. *Matthew*. Translated by Ray Togtman, Bible Student's Commentary. Grand Rapids: Zondervan Publishing House, 1987.

Robbins, John W. "Justification and Judgment." *JOGES* 15, no. 1 (Spring 2002): 60-74.

Roberts, Maurice. "Final Perseverance." *Banner of Truth Trust*, no. 265 (October 1985).

Robertson, A. T. *A Grammar of the Greek New Testament in the Light of Historical Research*. Reprint ed. Bellingham, WA: Logos Bible Software, 2006.

Robertson, A. T. *Word Pictures in the Greek New Testament*. Nashville: Broadman, 1933.

Robertson, Archibald, and Alfred Plummer. *A Critical and Exegetical Commentary on the First Epistle of Paul to the Corinthians*, The International Criticial Commentry. New York: C. Scribner's Sons, 1911.

Robertson, Archibald, and Alfred Plummer. *A Critical and Exegetical Commentary on the Second Epistle of St. Paul to the Corinthians*, International Critical Commentary. Edinburgh: T. & T. Clark, 1915.

Robertson, O. Palmer. "Genesis 15:6: New covenant expositions of an old covenant text." *WTJ* 42, no. 2 (1980): 259-90.

Rooker, M. F. *Leviticus*, The New American Commentary. Nashville: Broadman and Holman, 2000.

Ropes, J. H. *A Critical and Exegetical Commentary on the Epistle of St. James*. New York: Scribner's Sons, 1916.

Ross, Allen P. "Genesis." In *Bible Knowledge Commentary: The Old Testament*, edited by John F. Walvoord and Roy B. Zuck. Colorado Springs: Cook, 1996.

Ross, Allen P. *Recalling the Hope of Glory*. Grand Rapids: Kregel Publications, 2006.

Rosscup, James E. "The Overcomers of the Apocalypse." *Grace Theological Journal* 3 (Fall 1982): 261-86.

Rutherford, John. "Gnosticism." In *ISBE (1915)*, edited by James Orr. Albany, OR: Ages Software, 1915.

Ryle, J. C. *Expository Thoughts on the Gospels*. Grand Rapids: Zondervan Publishing House, n.d.

Ryrie, Charles. *Basic Theology*. Chicago: Moody Press, 1999.

Ryrie, Charles. *The Ryrie Study Bible: New American Standard Translation*. Chicago: Moody Press, 1978.

Ryrie, Charles. *So Great Salvation: What It Means to Believe in Jesus Christ*. Wheaton, IL: Victor Books, 1989.

Ryrie, Charles. *What You Should Know about the Rapture*. Chicago: Moody Press, 1981.

Ryrie, Charles C. *The Basis of the Premillennial Faith*. New York: Loizeaux Brothers, 1953.

Sagan, Carl. *The Cosmos*. New York: Random House, 1980.

Saldarini, Anthony. "Rabbinic Material and the New Testament." In *The Anchor Yale Bible Dictionary*, edited by David Noel Freedman. New York: Doubleday, 1992.

Salza, John. *The Biblical Basis of Purgatory*. Charlotte, NC: Saint Benedict Press, LLC, 2009.

Sanday, William. *A Critical and Exegetical Commentary on the Epistle to the Romans*. 6th ed. Edinburgh: T. & T. Clark, 1975.

Sanday, William, and Arthur C. Headlam. *A Critical and Exegetical Commentary on the Epistle of the Romans*. New York: Scribner's Sons, 1897.

Sanders, E. P. *Jesus and Judaism*. Philadelphia: Fortress Press, 1985.

Sanders, E. P. *Paul and Palestinian Judaism*. Minneapolis: Fortress Press, 1977.

Sandmel, Samuel. "Parallelomania." *JBL* 81, no. 1 (1962): 1-13.

Sapaugh, Gregory P. "A Call to the Wedding Celebration: An Exposition of Matthew 22:1-14." *JOTGES* 5, no. 1 (Spring 1992): 10-34.

Saucy, Mark "The Kingdom-of-God Sayings in Matthew." *BibSac* 151, no. 602 (April 1994): 175-98.

Saucy, Robert L. *The Case for Progressive Dispensationalism: The Interface between Dispensational & Non-dispensational theology*. Grand Rapids: Zondervan Publishing House, 1993.

Sauer, Eric. *From Eternity to Eternity*. Grand Rapids: Wm. B. Eerdmans Publishing Co., 1963.

Sauer, Eric. *In the Arena of Faith: A Call to a Consecrated Life*. Grand Rapids: Wm. B. Eerdmans Publishing Co., 1956.

Sauer, R. C. "A Critical and Exegetical Examination of Hebrews 5:11-6:8." PhD diss., University of Manchester, 1981.

Schaff, Philip. "The Canons of the Synod of Dort." In *The Creeds of Christendom: The Evangelical Protestant Creed*. Grand Rapids: Baker, 1985.

Schaff, Philip. "The French Confession of Faith." In *The Creeds of Christendom: The Evangelical Protestant Creed*. Grand Rapids: Baker, 1985.

Schaff, Philip. "The Heidelberg Catechism." In *The Creeds of Christendom: The Evangelical Protestant Creed*. Grand Rapids: Baker, 1985.

Schaff, Philip. *History of the Christian Church*. 8 vols. Grand Rapids: Wm. B. Eerdmans Publishing Co., 1910.

Schaff, Philip. "Westminster Shorter Catechism." In *The Creeds of Christendom: With a History and Critical Notes*. Grand Rapids: Baker Book House, 1985.

Scharen, Hans. "Part 1: Gehenna in the Synoptics." *BibSac* 149, no. 195 (July 1992): 323-37.

Scharen, Hans. "Part 2: Gehenna in the Synoptics." *BibSac* 149, no. 196 (Oct 1992): 455-70.

Schmidt, Alvin J. *Under the Influence: How Christianity Transformed Civilization*. Grand Rapids: Zondervan Publishing House, 2001.

Schoenweiss, H. "Firm, Foundation, Certainty, Confirm." In *NIDNTT*, 1:168.

Schreiner, Thomas R. "Corporate and Individual Election in Romans 9: A Response to Brian Abasciano." *JETS* 49, no. 2 (June 2006): 373-85.

Schreiner, Thomas R. "Did Paul Believe in Justification by Works? Another Look at Romans 2." *Bullietin for Biblical Research* 3 (1993): 131-58.

Schreiner, Thomas R. "Does Romans 9 Teach Individual Election unto Salvation? Some Exegetical and Theological Reflections." *JETS* 36, no. 1 (March 1993): 23-40.

Schreiner, Thomas R. "Perseverance and Assurance: A Survey and a Proposal." *SBJT* 2 (1998): 32-64.

Schreiner, Thomas R. *Romans*. Grand Rapids: Baker Book House, 1998.

Schreiner, Thomas R. *Run to Win the Prize: Perseverance in the New Testament*. Wheaton, IL: Crossway Books, 2010.

Schreiner, Thomas R., and Ardel B. Caneday. *The Race Set Before Us: A Biblical Theology of Perseverance and Assurance*. Downers Grove, IL: InterVarsity Press, 2001.

Schürer, Emil. *A History of the Jewish People in the Time of Jesus Christ: First Division*. 2nd and rev. ed. 2 vols. Vol. 1. Edinburgh: T. & T. Clark, 1890.

Schweizer, Eduard. *The Good News According to Luke*. Atlanta: John Knox Press, 1984.

Schweizer, Eduard. *The Good News According to Matthew*. Atlanta: John Knox Press, 1975.

Sellers, C. Norman. *Election and Perseverance*. Miami Springs, FL: Schoettle Publishing Co., 1987.

Selwyn, Edward Gordon. *The First Epistle of Peter*. London: Macmillan & Co., 1947.

Shank, Robert. *Life in the Son: A Study of the Doctrine of Perseverance*. Springfield, MO: Westcott Publishers, 1961.

Shedd, William G. T. *Commentary on Romans*. Reprint ed. Grand Rapids: Zondervan Publishing House, 1967.

Shedd, William G. T. *A Critical and Doctrinal Commentary on the Epistle of St. Paul to the Romans*. Reprint ed. Grand Rapids: Zondervan Publishing House, 1967.

Shedd, William G. T. *Dogmatic Theology*. Classic Reprint ed. Minneapolis: Klock & Klock, 1979.

Shedd, William G. T., and Alan W. Gomes. *Dogmatic Theology*. 3 vols. in 1 ed. Phillipsburg, NJ: Presbyterian and Reformed Publishing Co., 2003.

Shepherd, Norman. "Justification by Faith Alone." *Reformation and Revival* 11, no. 2 (2002): 71-91.

Showers, Renald. *Maranatha: Our Lord Come!* Bellmawr, NJ: Friends of Israel Gospel Ministry, 1995.

Sider, Ronald J. *Rich Christians in an Age of Hunger*. 2nd ed. Downers Grove, IL: InterVarsity Press, 1984.

Smalley, S. S. *1, 2, 3 John*, Word Biblical Commentary. Dallas: Word Inc., 2002.

Smith, Charles R. "The Unfruitful Branches in John 15." *Grace Journal* 9, no. 2 (Spring 1968): 10-20.

Smith, Dennis E. "Table Fellowship as a Literary Motif in the Gospel of Luke." *JBL* 106, no. 4 (Dec 1987): 613-38.

Smith, E. W. "Book of Life." In *NISBE*, 1979.

Smith, J. B. *A Revelation of Jesus Christ*. Scottsdale, PA: Mennonite Publishing House, 1961.

Smith, J. M. P., W. H. Ward, and J. A. Bewer. *A Critical and Exegetical Commentary on Micah, Zephaniah, Nahum, Obadiah and Joel*. New York: Scribner's Sons, 1911.

Smith, Wilber M. *The Biblical Doctrine of Heaven*. Chicago: Moody Press, 1968.

Snodgrass, Klyne. *Stories with Intent: A Comprehensive Guide to the Parables of Jesus*. Grand Rapids: Wm. B. Eerdmans Publishing Co., 2008.

Spencer, Jeff. "The Destruction of Hell: Annihilationism Examined." *Christian Apologetics Journal* 1, no. 1 (Spring 1998): 1-20.

Sprinkle, Preston M. *Law and Life*, Wissenschaftliche Untersuchungen zum Neuen Testament - 2 Reihe. Tubingen: Mohr Siebeck, 2008.

Sprinkle, Preston M. "The Use of Genesis 42:18 (Not Leviticus 18:5) in Luke 10:28: Joseph and the Good Samaritan." *Bulletin for Biblical Research* 17, no. 2 (2007): n. pag.

Sproul, R. C. *Chosen By God*. Wheaton: Tyndale Publishers, 1997.

Sproul, R. C. *Grace Unknown: The Heart of Reformed Theology*. Grand Rapids: Baker Book House, 1997.

Sproul, R. C. *Pleasing God*. Wheaton, IL: Tyndale House, 1988.

Spurgeon, Charles. *The Psalms Vol. 1 and 2*. Wheaton, IL: Crossway Books, 1993.

Spurgeon, Charles. *The Treasury of David: In Three Volumes*. Grand Rapids: Zondervan Publishing House, 1966.

Spurgeon, Charles H. *Spurgeon's Sermons*. Albany, OR: Ages Software, 1998.

Stanley, Alan P. *Did Jesus Teach Salvation by Works? The Role of Works in Salvation in the Synoptic Gospels*. Eugene, OR: Pickwick Publishers, 2006.

Stanley, Alan P. "The Rich Young Ruler and Salvation." *BibSac* 649, no. 163 (January - March 2006): 46-62.

Stanley, Alan P. *Salvation Is More Complicated Than You Think*. Colorado Springs: Paternoster, 2007.

Stanley, Charles. *Eternal Security: Can You Be Sure?* Nashville: Oliver Nelson, 1990.

Stanton, Gerald B. *Kept from the Hour: Biblical Evidence for the Pretribulational Return of Christ.* Miami Springs, FL: Schoettle Publishing Co., 1991.

Steffen, Daniel S. "The Messianic Banquet And The Eschatology Of Matthew's Gospel." *Global Journal of Classical Theology* 5, no. 2 (January 2006).

Stegall, Thomas L. *The Gospel of the Christ: A Biblical Response to the Crossless Gospel Regarding the Contents of Saving Faith.* Milwaukee: Grace Gospel Press, 2009.

Stein, Robert H. *Luke*, The New American Commentary. Nashville: Broadman Press, 1992.

Stott, John R. *Men Made New*. Downers Grove, IL: InterVarsity Press, 1966.

Stowers, Stanley K. "Diatribe." In *Anchor Yale Bible Dictionary*, edited by David Noel Freedman, Gary A. Herion, David F. Graf, J. D. Pleins and A. B. Beck. New York: Doubleday, 1992.

Strachan, R. J. "The Second General Epistle of Peter." In *The Expositor's Greek Testament*, edited by W. Robertson Nicoll. New York: George H. Doran, 1967.

Strauss, Gary, and Carol Memmott. "Wallace's death marks end of old-school era." *USA Today*, April 4, 2012, 1A-2A.

Strong, Augustus Hopkins. *Systematic Theology*. Philadelphia: Judson Press, 1907.

Suetonius. "The Deified Agustus." In *The Lives of the Caesars*: Availabe at www.books.google.com.

Sullivan, Clayton. *Rethinking Realized Eschatology*. Macon, GA: Mercer University Press, 1988.

Sungenis, Robert A. *Not by Faith Alone: The Biblical Evidence for the Catholic Doctrine of Justification.* Goleta, CA: Queenship Publishing, 1997.

Svigel, Michael J. "The Apocalypse of John and the Rapture: A Re-evaluation." *Trinity Journal* 22, no. 1 (Spring 2001).

Swanson, James. *A Dictionary of Biblical Languages: Greek New Testament.* 2nd ed. Seattle: Logos Research Systems, 2001.

Swanson, James. *Dictionary of Biblical Languages: Hebrew Old Testament.* 2nd ed. Seattle: Logos Research Systems, 2001.

Talbert, Charles H. *Reading the Sermon on the Mount: Character Formation and Ethical Decision Making in Matthew 5-7*. Grand Rapids: Baker Academic, 2004.

Tanner, J. Paul. "The New Covenant and Paul's Quotations from Hosea." *BibSac* 162, no. 645 (January 2005): 95-110.

Tanner, Paul. "Hebrews." In *The Grace New Testament Commentary*. Denton, TX: Grace Evangelical Society, 2010.

Tanner, Paul. "The "Marriage Supper of the Lamb" in Rev. 19:6-10: Implications for the Judgment Seat of Christ." *Trinity Journal* 26, no. 1 (2005): 47-68.

The Targum of Job. Translated by Celine Mangan. Vol. 15, The Aramaic Bible. Edinburgh: T. & T. Clark, 1991.

The Targum of Proverbs. Translated by John F. Healey. Vol. 15, The Aramaic Bible. Edinburgh: T. & T. Clark, 1991.

The Targum of Qohelet. Translated by Peter S. Knobel. Vol. 15, The Aramaic Bible. Edinburgh: T. & T. Clark, 1991.

The Targum of the Psalms. Translated by David M. Stec. Vol. 16, The Aramaic Bible. Collegeville, MN: Liturgical Press, 2004.

Tate, M. E. *Vol. 20: Psalms 51-100: Word Biblical Commentary*. Dallas: Word, Inc., 1998.

Taylor, S. S. "Faith, Faithfulness." In *New Dictionary of Biblical Theology*, edited by T. D. Alexander and B. S. Rosner. Downers Grove, IL: InterVarsity, 2001.

"TDNT."

Tertullian. "On the Resurrection of the Flesh." In *The Ante-Nicene Fathers Vol. III: Translations of the Writings of the Fathers Down to A.D. 325, Latin Christianity: Its Founder, Tertullian*, edited by Alexander Roberts, James Donaldson and A. Cleveland Coxe. Oak Harbor, WA: Logos Research Systems, 1997.

Thayer, Joseph. *A Greek-English Lexicon of the New Testament*. New York: American Book Co., 1898.
Thayer, Joseph H. *Thayer's Greek-English Lexicon of the Greek New Testament*. Grand Rapids: Associate Publishers and Authors, 1889.
Thiessen, Henry Clarence, and Vernon D. Doerksen. *Lectures in Systematic Theology*. rev. ed. Grand Rapids: Wm. B. Eerdmans Publishing Co., 1979.
Thiselton, Anthony C. *The First Epistle to the Corinthians: A Commentary on the Greek Text*. Grand Rapids: Wm. B. Eerdmans Publishing Co., 2000.
Thiselton, Anthony C. *Life after Death: A New Approach to the Last Things*. Grand Rapids, MI: Wm. B. Eerdmans Publishing Co., 2012.
Thomas, Ian. *The Saving Life of Christ*. Grand Rapids: Zondervan Publishing House, 1955.
Thomas, Robert L. "The Rich Young Man in Matthew." *GTJ* 3, no. 2 (1982): 235-60.
Thrall, Margaret E. *A Critical Exegetical Commentary on the Second Epistle of the Corinthians*, International Critical Commentary. New York: T&T Clark, 2004.
Tosti, J. A. Tony. "Perseverance: The Other Side of the Coin." *The Banner of Truth Trust* 259 (1985).
Toussaint, Stanley D. *Behold the King*. Portland, OR: Multnomah Press, 1980.
Toussaint, Stanley D. "The Church and Israel." *Conservative Theological Journal* 2, no. 7 (Dec 1998): 350-74.
Toussaint, Stanley D. "The Spiritual Man." *BibSac* 125, no. 498 (April-June 1968): 139-46.
Toussaint, Stanley D., and Jay A. Quine. "No, Not Yet: The Contingency of God's Promised Kingdom." *BibSac* 164, no. 654 (April-June 2007): 131-47.
Towner, Philip H. *The Letters to Timothy and Titus*, New International Commentary on the New Testament. Grand Rapids: Wm. B. Eerdmans Publishing Co., 2006.
Townsend, Jeffery. "Is the Present Age the Millennium?" *Bib Sac* 140, no. 559 (July 1983): 206-21.
Trench, Richard Chenevix. *Notes on the Miracles and the Parables of Our Lord*. complete original unabridged two volumes in one ed. Westwood, NJ: Fleming H. Revell, 1953.
Trench, Richard Chenevix. *Synonyms of the New Testament*. Reprint ed. Grand Rapids: Wm. B. Eerdmans Publishing Co., 1953.
Trutza, P. "Marriage." In *The Zondervan Pictorial Encyclopedia of the Bible*, edited by Merrill C. Tenny. Grand Rapids: Zondervan Publishing Houise, 1975.
Turner, David L. *Matthew*, Baker Exegetical Commentary on the New Testament. Grand Rapids: Baker Academic, 2008.
Tuttle, Gary A. "The Sermon on the Mount: Its Wisdom Affinities and their Relation to its Structure." *JETS* 20, no. 3 (1977): 213-30.
Twelftree, G. H. "Scribes." In *Dictionary of Jesus and the Gospels*, edited by Joel B. Green, Scot McKnight and I. Howard Marshall. Downers Grove, IL: InterVarsity Press, 1992.
Tyndale Bible Dictionary. Edited by Walter A. Elwell and Philip Wesley, Tyndale Reference Library. Wheaton, IL: Tyndale House, 2001.
Unger, Merrill F. *Archaeology and the Old Testament*. Grand Rapids: Zondervan Publishing House, 1954.
Unger, Merrill F. *Unger's Bible Dictionary*. Chicago: Moody Press, 1961.
Van Oosterzee, J. J. "Luke." In *A Commentary on the Holy Scriptures*, edited by John Peter Lange, Philip Schaff, J. J. van Oosterzee and Charles C. Starbuck. Bellingham, WA: Logos Research Systems, 2008.
Vance, Lawrence M. *The Other Side of Calvinism*. rev. ed. Pensecola, FL: Vance Publications, 1991, 1999.
VanGemeren, Willem. *New International Dictionary of Old Testament Theology and Exegesis*. 5 vols. Grand Rapids: Zondervan Publishing House, 1997.
VanLandingham, Chris. *Judgment & Justification in Early Judaism and the Apostle Paul*. Peabody, MA: Hendrickson Publishers, 2006.

Vincent, Marvin R. *A Critical and Exegetical Commentary on the Epistles to the Philippians and Philemon*, International Critical Commentary. Edinburgh: T. & T. Clark, 1897.
Vincent, Marvin R. *Word Studies in the New Testament*. Grand Rapids: Wm. B. Eerdmans Publishing Co., 1946.
Vine, W. E., John R. Kohlenberger, and James A. Swanson. *The Expanded Vine's Expository Dictionary of New Testament Words*. Minneapolis: Bethany House, 1984.
Virkler, Henry. *Hermeneutics: Principles and Processes of Biblical Interpretation*. Grand Rapids: Wm. B. Eerdmans Publishing Co., 1981.
von Rad, Gerhard. *Old Testament Theology*. 2 vols. New York: Harper, 1962.
Vos, Gerhardus. *The Pauline Eschatology*. Grand Rapids: Wm. B. Eerdmans Publishing Co., 1972.
Wakefield, Andrew H. *Where to Live: The Hermeneutical Significance of Paul's Citations from Scripture in Galatians 3:1-14*. Atlanta: Society of Biblical Literature, 2003.
Wallace, Daniel. *Greek Grammar Beyond the Basics*. Grand Rapids: Zondervan Publishing House, 1996.
Wallis, Wilber B. "The Problem of an Intermediate Kingdom in 1 Corinthians 15:20-28." *JETS* 18, no. 4 (Fall 1975): 229-49.
Walls, Jerry L., and Joseph Dongell. *Why I am not a Calvinist*. Downers Grove, IL: InterVarsity Press, 2004.
Walters, G. "Sanctification, Sanctify." In *New Bible Dictionary*. Grand Rapids, MI: Wm. B. Eerdmans Publishing Co., 1962.
Waltke, Bruce K. *The Book of Proverbs*. 2 vols. Grand Rapids: Wm. B. Eerdmans Publishing Co., 2004.
Waltke, Bruce K. "The Fear of the Lord: The Foundation for a Relationship with God." In *Alive to God*, edited by J. I. Packer and Loren Wilkinson. Downers Grove, IL: InterVarsity Press, 1992.
Waltke, Bruce K. *Genesis: A Commentary*. Grand Rapids: Zondervan Publishing House, 2001.
Waltke, Bruce K., and Charles Yu. *An Old Testament Theology: An Exegetical, Canonical, and Thematic Approach*. 1st ed. Grand Rapids: Zondervan Publishing House, 2007.
Walvoord, John F. *The Millennial Kingdom*. Findlay, OH: Dunham Publishing Co., 1959.
Walvoord, John F. "Premillennialism and the Tribulation Part IV: Pretribulationism (continued)." *BibSac* 112, no. 446 (April 1955): 97-106.
Walvoord, John F. *The Prophecy Knowledge Handbook*. Dallas: Dallas Seminary Press, 1990.
Walvoord, John F. *The Revelation of Jesus Christ*. Chicago: Moody Press, 1966.
Wanamaker, C. A. *The Epistles to the Thessalonians: A Commentary on the Greek Text*. Grand Rapids: Wm. B. Eerdmans Publishing Co., 1990.
Warfield, Benjamin B. "Faith in Its Psychological Aspects." In *Biblical and Theological Studies*. Philadelphia: Presbyterian and Reformed Publishing Co., 1968.
Warfield, Benjamin B. "The Leading of the Spirit." In *Biblical and Theological Studies*. Phildelphia: Presbyterian and Reformed Publishing Co., 1968.
Watson, D. F. "People, Crowd." In *Dictionary of Jesus and the Gospels*, edited by Joel B. Green, Scott McKnight and I Howard Marshall. Downers Grove, IL: InterVarsity, 1992.
Watts, John D. W. *Isaiah 34-66*, Word Biblical Commentary. Dallas: Word, 2002.
Watts, John D. W. *Isaiah 34-66*, Word Biblical Commentary. Dallas: Word, 1998.
Weinberg, Stephen. *The First Three Minutes*. New York: Basic Books, 1977.
Wenham, Gordon J. *The Book of Leviticus*, New International Commentary on the Old Testament. Grand Rapids: Wm. B. Eerdmans Publishing Co., 1979.
Wenham, Gordon J. *Genesis 1-15*. Dallas: Word, 1987.
Wesley, John. *The Works of John Wesley: Addresses, Essays, and Letters*. Albany, OR: Ages Software, 2000.
Westcott, B. F. *Colossians: A Letter to Asia*. Reprint ed. Minneapolis: Klock & Clock, 1914.

Westcott, B. F. *The Epistle to the Hebrews*. Reprint ed. Grand Rapids: Wm. B. Eerdmans Publishing Co., 1965.

Westcott, B. F. *Saint Paul's Epistle to the Ephesians*. New York: Macmillan & Co., 1909.

Westcott, B. F. *Saint Paul's Epistle to the Ephesians: The Greek Text with Notes and Addenda*, Classic Commentaries on the Greek New Testament. New York: The MacMillian Company, 1909.

Westerholm, Stephen. *Israel's Law and the Church's Faith*. Grand Rapids: Wm. B. Eerdmans Publishing Co., 1988.

Westerholm, Stephen. *Understanding Matthew: The Early Christian Worldview of the First Gospel*. Grand Rapids: Baker Book House, 2006.

"Westminster Confession of Faith." *In The Creeds of Christendo*, edited by Philip Schaff. Grand Rapids, MI: Baker Book House.

Westminster Confession of Faith. Edited by Philip Schaff. Grand Rapids, MI: Baker Book House, 1985.

Weymouth, Richard F. *The New Testament in Modern Speech*. London: James Clark and Co., 1905.

White, R. E. O. "Salvation." In *Evangelical Dictionary of Theology*, edited by Walter Elwell. Grand Rapids: Baker Book House, 1984.

Wiersbe, Warren W. *The Bible Exposition Commentary*. Wheaton: Victor Books, 1996.

Wilcox, Lance. "Everyday Faith in the Middle Ages." *Christian History Magazine (No. 49)*, 1996.

Wilkin, Robert. "Another View of Faith and Works in James 2." *Journal of the Grace Evangelical Society* 15, no. 2 (Fall 2002): 3-22.

Wilkin, Robert. "Christians Who Lose Their Legacy: Gal 5:21." *JOTGES* 4, no. 2 (Autumn 91): 23-37.

Wilkin, Robert N. *Confident in Christ: Living by Faith Really Works*. Irving, TX: Grace Evangelical Society, 1999.

Wilkin, Robert N. "Does Your Mind Need Changing? Repentance Reconsidered." *JOTGES* 11, no. 1 (Spring 1998): 34-46.

Wilkin, Robert N. "Is Justification by Faith Alone." *JOGES* 9, no. 2 (Autumn 1996): 2-20.

Wilkin, Robert N. "Periodical Reviews: "The Pillar and the Throne in Revelation 3:12, 21, " Daniel K. K. Wong, BibSac (July-September 1999), 297–307." *JOTGES* 12, no. 2 (Autumn 1999): 105-08.

Wilkin, Robert N. *Secure and Sure: Grasping the Promises of God*. Irving, TX: Grace Evangelical Theological Society, 2005.

Wilkin, Robert N. "Striving for the Prize of Eternal Salvation: A Review of Schreiner and Caneday's *The Race Set Before Us*." *JOTGES* 15, no. 1 (Spring 2002).

Wilkinson, Bruce. *A Life God Rewards*. Portland, OR: Multnomah Press, 2002.

Wilkinson, Richard H. "The ΣΤΥΛΟΣ of Revelation 3:12 and Ancient Coronation Rites." *JBL* 107, no. 3 (September 1988): 498-501.

Willard, Dallas. *The Divine Conspiracy*. San Francisco: Harper, 1998.

Wilson, G. Todd. "Conditions for Entering the Kingdom." *Perspectives in Religious Studies* 5 (Spring 1978).

Windisch, Hans. *Der sinn der Bergpredigt, ein Beitrag zum geschichtlichen verständnis der Evangelien und zum Problem der Richtigen Exegese*. 2., stark umgearb., erweiterte und verbe aufl. ed. Leipzig: J. C. Hinrichs, 1937.

Winfrey, David G. "The Great Tribulation: Kept 'out of' or 'through'?" *GTJ* 3, no. 1 (1982): 3-18.

Witherington III, Ben. *The Jesus Quest: The Third Search for the Jew of Nazareth*. Downers Grove, IL: InterVarsity Press, 1995.

Witmer, John A. "Romans." In *BKC: New Testament*, edited by John F. Walvoord and Roy B. Zuck. Colorado Springs: Cook, 1996.

Wolff, Hans Walter, and S. Dean McBride. *A Commentary on the Books of the Prophets - Joel and Amos*, Hermenia - A Historical and Critical Commentary on the Bible. Philadelphia: Fortress Press, 1977.

Wong, Daniel K. K. "The Pillar and the Throne in Revelation 3:12, 21." *BibSac* 156, no. 623 (July-September 1999): 297-307.

Wood, Geoffrey E. "Joel and Obadiah." In *The Jerome Biblical Commentary*, edited by Raymond Edward Brown, Joseph A. Fitzmyer and Roland Edmund Murphy, 2 v. in 1. Englewood Cliffs, NJ: Prentice-Hall, 1968.

Wretlind, Dennis O. "The Last Trumpet: A Demarcation Event between the Present Temporal World and the Eternal World to Come." PhD diss., Dallas Theological Seminary, 1997.

Wright, N. T. "In Greatful Dialogue." In *Jesus and the Restoration of Israel: A Critical Assessmenet of N. T. Wright's Jesus and the Victory of God*, edited by Cary C. Newman. Downers Grove, IL: InterVarsity Press, 1999.

Wright, N. T. *Jesus and the Victory of God*. Minneapolis: Fortress Press, 1996.

Wright, N. T. *Justification: God's Plan and Paul's Vision*. Downers Grove, IL: InterVarsity, 2009.

Wright, N. T. *The New Testament and the People of God: Christian Origins and the Question of God*. Reprint, SPCK ed. London: Society for Promoting Christian Knowledge, 1992.

Wright, N. T. "Righteousness." In *New Dictionary of Theology*, edited by Sinclair B. Ferguson and J. I. Packer. Downers Grove, IL: InterVarsity Press, 2000.

Wuest, Kenneth. *Wuest's Word Studies from the Greek New Testament*. Grand Rapids: Wm. B. Eerdmans Publishing Co., 1984.

Yamauchi, Edwin. "Cultural Aspects of Marriage in the Ancient World." *BibSac* 135, no. 539 (July-September 1978).

Yarbrough, Robert W. "Chapter 3: Jesus on Hell." In *Hell under Fire: Modern Scholarship Reinvents Eternal Punishment*, edited by Christopher W. Peterson. Grand Rapids: Zondervan Publishing House, 2009.

Zodhiates, Spiros. *The Complete Word Study New Testament: King James Version*. Chattanooga: AMG Publishers, 1991.

Zodhiates, Spiros. *Hebrew-Greek Key Word Study Bible*. Chattanooga: AMG Publishers, 2008.

Zuck, Roy B. "Book Review of The Race Set Before Us: A Biblical Theology of Perseverance and Assurance by Thomas R. Schreiner and Ardel B. Caneday." *BibSac* 160, no. 638 (April-June 2003): 241-43.

Zuck, Roy B., Darrell L. Bock, and Dallas Theological Seminary. *A Biblical Theology of the New Testament*.

The Author

JODY (JOSEPH) Dillow came to Christ while majoring in Electrical Engineering at Oregon State University in 1963 and graduated in Science from the University of Oregon. Upon graduation he went to Dallas Theological Seminary where he majored in New Testament Greek and received his ThD in 1978 in Systematic Theology. While there he directed the Campus Crusade work at SMU and later at Cornell University in Ithaca, New York.

In 1977 he served briefly as a visiting professor in Systematic Theology at Trinity Evangelical Divinity School in Deerfield, IL.

In 1978, God led Jody and his wife, Linda, to Vienna, Austria where they were used of God to found and direct the ministry which is now known as BEE World (Biblical Education by Extension World). For 14 years they ministered behind the Iron Curtain and then in 1992 moved to Hong Kong to launch BEE in China, South Korea, and Vietnam. BEE's mission is to provide extension biblical training in closed countries to those who might not otherwise have access to it. In 1995 they returned to the United States where they are carrying on the same ministry.

BEE works in twenty countries including Nepal, India, Burma, Vietnam, China, Pakistan and the Middle East. For information about this ministry see www.beeworld.org.

Currently the ministry of BEE World is also offering its curriculum on the Internet in Chinese, Arabic, Vietnamese and several other languages (www.internetseminary.org). As of February 2013, over 5,000 students in 144 countries are taking on-line courses.

Dr. Dillow is the author of several books including *The Reign of the Servant Kings: A Study of Eternal Security and the Final Destiny of Man; The Waters Above: Earth's Pre-Flood Vapor Canopy, Speaking in Tongues, Solomon on Sex,* and with his wife, Linda, and Dr. Pete and Lorraine Pintus - *Intimacy Ignited.*

The Dillows live in Monument, Colorado. They have four grown children and ten grandchildren.

For additional information about the **Internet Biblical Seminary**, scan the QR code to the right
www.internetseminary.org

Biblical Education by Extension
BEE World
www.beeworld.org

Additional copies of *Final Destiny*
Grace Theology Press
www.gracetheology.org

CPSIA information can be obtained
at www.ICGtesting.com
Printed in the USA
LVHW061128080820
662079LV00066B/658